W9-CAI-158

STUDENT EDITION
OF
WEINSTEIN'S EVIDENCE MANUAL
7th Edition

A Guide to the Federal Rules of Evidence Based on Weinstein's Federal Evidence

JACK B. WEINSTEIN
Adjunct Professor
Columbia Law School
Judge United States District Court
Eastern District of New York

MARGARET A. BERGER
Professor and Associate Dean
Brooklyn Law School

2005

LexisNexis™

Library of Congress Cataloging-in-Publication Data

Weinstein, Jack B.
    Student edition ofWeinstein's evidence manual / Jack B. Weinstein. – 7thed.
    p. cm.
    Includes bibliographical references and index.
    ISBN 0-8205-6357-9 (hardbound)
    1. Evidence (Law)–United States. I. Berger, Margaret A. II. Title. III. Title:
Weinstein's Evidence manual.
    KF8935.W4 2005
    347.73'6–dc22

                                                                              2005009199

This publication is designed to provide accurate and authoritative information in regard to the subject matter covered. It is sold with the understanding that the publisher is not engaged in rendering legal, accounting, or other professional services. If legal advice or other expert assistance is required, the services of a competent professional should be sought.

LexisNexis and the Knowledge Burst logo are trademarks of Reed Elsevier Properties Inc, used under license. Matthew Bender is a registered trademark of Matthew Bender Properties Inc.

Copyright © 2005 Matthew Bender & Company, Inc., a member of the LexisNexis Group.
All Rights Reserved. Originally published in 1987.

No copyright is claimed in the text of statutes, regulations, and excerpts from court opinions quoted within this work. Permission to copy material exceeding fair use, 17 U.S.C. § 107, may be licensed for a fee of 10¢ per page per copy from the Copyright Clearance Center, 222 Rosewood Drive, Danvers, Mass. 01923, telephone (978) 750-8400.
of the LexisNexis Group.

Editorial Offices
744 Broad Street, Newark, NJ 07102 (973) 820-2000
201 Mission St., San Francisco, CA 94105-1831 (415) 908-3200
701 East Water Street, Charlottesville, VA 22902-7587 (804) 972-7600
www.lexis.com

Statement on Fair Use

LexisNexis Matthew Bender recognizes the balance that must be achieved between the operation of the fair use doctrine, whose basis is to avoid the rigid application of the copyright statute, and the protection of the creative rights and economic interests of authors, publishers and other copyright holders.

We are also aware of the countervailing forces that exist between the ever greater technological advances for making both print and electronic copies and the reduction in the value of copyrighted works that must result from a consistent and pervasive reliance on these new copying technologies. It is LexisNexis Matthew Bender's position that if the "progress of science and useful arts" is promoted by granting copyright protection to authors, such progress may well be impeded if copyright protection is diminished in the name of fair use. (See Nimmer on Copyright § 13.05[E][1].) This holds true whether the parameters of the fair use doctrine are considered in either the print or the electronic environment as it is the integrity of the copyright that is at issue, not the media under which the protected work may become available. Therefore, the fair use guidelines we propose apply equally to our print and electronic information, and apply, within §§ 107 and 108 of the Copyright Act, regardless of the professional status of the user.

Our draft guidelines would allow for the copying of limited materials, which would include synopses and tables of contents, primary source and government materials that may have a minimal amount of editorial enhancements, individual forms to aid in the drafting of applications and pleadings, and miscellaneous pages from any of our newsletters, treatises and practice guides. This copying would be permitted provided it is performed for internal use and solely for the purpose of facilitating individual research or for creating documents produced in the course of the user's professional practice, and the original from which the copy is made has been purchased or licensed as part of the user"s existing in-house collection.

LexisNexis Matthew Bender fully supports educational awareness programs designed to increase the public's recognition of its fair use rights. We also support the operation of collective licensing organizations with regard to our print and electronic information.

Table of Contents

A COMPLETE SYNOPSIS FOR EACH CHAPTER APPEARS AT
THE BEGINNING OF THE CHAPTER

Table of Contents

Table of Contents

Table of Contents

Table of Contents

FOREWORD

References to Treatise throughout this volume are to the multi-volume *Weinstein's Federal Evidence* treatise.

PREFACE

This volume comprehensively covers the Federal Rules of Evidence. It was designed for judges, lawyers and students who need a concise guide to the practical and theoretical information required in the court, office, and classroom.

It is assumed that any user will have access to our multi-volume *Weinstein's Federal Evidence* (Matthew Bender 2d ed.) for purposes of more detailed research and briefwriting. The multi-volume **Treatise** contains comprehensive legislative history, more extensive analysis, and many more citations to federal cases. Nevertheless, there are enough citations in this single volume to support daily practice and to provide a starting point for more intensive work.

The references to **"Treatise"** throughout this volume are to the multi-volume Treatise.

We have provided the exact language of each of the Rules so that quotations as well as paraphrasing for meaning are readily available to the advocate, judge or student. While the volume is comprehensive, every effort has been made to limit its size so that it can be conveniently carried home or to court and kept for ready reference at the desk.

Now that the Federal Rules have been in effect for more than two decades, some clear lines of interpretation have begun to emerge. We have summarized those areas and indicated places where further clarification is needed.

The authors gratefully acknowledge William J. Schneier's assistance in the preparation of this work while he was a student at Brooklyn Law School.

Jack B. Weinstein
Margaret A. Berger

Original Authors

Jack B. Weinstein

Margaret A. Berger
Contributing Authors

Brigid T. Brennan

Lynne Avakian Campbell

A. Richard Poehner

Publisher's Editorial Staff

Steve Revell, J.D.
Practice Area Director

Dana Vinicoff, J.D.
Practice Area Editor

Karin Newton
Index Manager

Bill Kinsey
Index Editor

Orlando Fernandez
Manager, Publishing Operations

Rebecca VanRheenen
Publishing Operations Associate

CHAPTER 1

Application of Rules and Construction

SYNOPSIS

§ 1.01 All Relevant Evidence Is Admissible With Certain Exceptions—Rule 402[1]

[1]—Purpose For Rule

Rule 402, a restatement of Thayer's classic formulation,[2] expresses the only universal rule of evidence:

Rule 402.   Relevant Evidence Generally Admissible; Irrelevant Evidence Inadmissible.

All relevant evidence is admissible, except as otherwise provided by the Constitution of the United States, by Act of Congress, by these rules, or by other rules prescribed by the Supreme Court pursuant to statutory authority. Evidence which is not relevant is not admissible.

[Adopted Jan. 2, 1975, effective July 1, 1975.]

The principal reason for admitting all relevant evidence is that, generally, the probability of ascertaining the truth about a given proposition increases as the amount of the trier's knowledge grows. Truth finding must be a central purpose. The enforcement of the substantive law is properly the primary aim of litigation. The substantive law can best be enforced if litigation results in accurate determinations of facts made material by the applicable rule of law.[3] The assumption that accurate fact finding is possible is fundamental to our judicial system.

Rule 402 also provides that irrelevant evidence is inadmissible.[4] The purpose of

---

[1] See discussion in **Treatise** in Ch. 402, *Relevant Evidence Generally Admissible; Irrelevant Evidence Inadmissible.*

[2] Thayer, A Preliminary Treatise on Evidence at Common Law 530 (1898) ("[T]he rules of evidence should be simplified; and should take on the general character of principles, to guide the sound judgment of the judge, rather than minute rules to bind it. The two leading principles should be brought into conspicuous relief, (1) that nothing is to be received which is not logically probative of some matter requiring to be proved; and (2) that everything which is thus probative should come in, unless a clear ground of policy or law excludes it.").

[3] *See, e.g.,* United States v. Cruz, 326 F.3d 392, 395 (3d Cir. 2003) (when defendant's primary defense to drug conspiracy charges was lack of personal participation in actions of charged conspiracy, trial court properly admitted his parole status to suggest that he delegated responsibility to his codefendants to protect himself from arrest for parole violation); Anderson v. WBMG-42, 253 F.3d 561, 564 (11th Cir. 2001) (evidence that similarly situated employees are disciplined more leniently is admissible to support disparate treatment claim when plaintiff has established that co-employees are in fact similarly situated).

[4] Fed. R. Evid. 402; *see, e.g.,* United States v. Blue Bird, 372 F.3d 989, 995 (8th Cir. 2004) (trial court erred in admitting evidence that alleged victim in sexual abuse case was virgin at time of incident because witness's sexual proclivities were not at issue and prosecution failed to suggest any legally relevant inference that trier of fact could draw from evidence).

this branch of the rule is to exclude any evidence that is not logically probative of some matter to be proved.[5]

Evidence that is otherwise relevant and admissible does not become irrelevant and inadmissible under Rule 402 merely because the party against whom it is offered stipulates to the consequential fact it is offered to prove.[6] The question of admissibility then becomes an issue for resolution through the means provided by the various rules that permit exclusion of relevant evidence, such as Rule 403.[7]

[2]—Policies Behind Exclusion of Relevant Evidence

[a]—Conflicting Goals of Litigation

Truth finding is not always the law's overriding aim, so many exclusionary rules apply to evidence that would otherwise be admissible under Rule 402. Trials in our judicial system are intended to do more than merely determine what happened. Goals in addition to truth finding that the rules of procedure and evidence seek to satisfy include: (1) terminating disputes, (2) economizing resources, (3) inspiring public confidence in the judicial system, (4) supporting independent social policies, (5) permitting ease in prediction and application of the rules, (6) adding to the efficiency of the entire legal system, and (7) tranquilizing disputants. Rule 402 makes no attempt to enumerate the underlying policies that dictate exclusion.

Any set of evidentiary or procedural rules is constantly obliged to strike a balance between these and other often competing goals.[8] Thus, while Rule 402 acknowl-

---

[5] *See, e.g.,* Morrison v. Int'l Programs Consortium, Inc., 253 F.3d 5, 9–10 (D.C. Cir. 2001) (because IRS assessment did not collaterally estop defendant from contending plaintiff was independent contractor rather than employee, it was not relevant to issue whether plaintiff was employee under FLSA and D.C. labor laws).

[6] *See, e.g.,* Old Chief v. United States, 519 U.S. 172, 179, 117 S. Ct. 644, 136 L. Ed. 2d 574 (1997) (relevance of evidence does not depend on whether fact evidence is offered to prove is in dispute); United States v. Hill, 249 F.3d 707, 710–713 (8th Cir. 2001).

[7] *See, e.g.,* Old Chief v. United States, 519 U.S. 172, 192–193, 117 S. Ct. 644, 136 L. Ed. 2d 574 (1997) (when defendant offered to stipulate to his status as felon in prosecution for possession of firearm by felon, and government proposed to prove his status by introducing record of his conviction of felonious assault, both stipulation and record of conviction were equally probative, but record was much more prejudicial than stipulation, and Rule 403 required exclusion of record of conviction in light of defendant's offer to stipulate).

[8] *See, e.g.,* Belk v. Charlotte-Mecklenberg Bd of Educ., 269 F.3d 305, 335 (4th Cir. 2001) (en banc; relevant evidence, although prima facie admissible under Rule 402, is properly excluded when its probative value "is substantially outweighed by considerations of the needless presentation of cumulative evidence"); Wheeling Pittsburgh Steel Corp. v. Beelman River Terminals, Inc., 254 F.3d 706, 718 (8th Cir. 2001) (letter containing many references to defendant's liability insurance was prejudicial but was nevertheless erroneously excluded under Rule 403 because it was relevant concerning whether defendant took reasonable precautions to protect products in its warehouse from flood water damage).

edges that relevant evidence is prima facie admissible,[8.1] it also recognizes that other evidentiary rules,[9] procedural rules, Acts of Congress,[10] or the Constitution may require the exclusion of evidence that meets the relevance test of Rule 401.

The constitutional principles and provisions in statutes and Federal Rules that cause exclusion of otherwise relevant evidence can be grouped into two classes that have very different objectives. One class, that Wigmore termed "auxiliary rules of probative force,"[11] excludes certain types of evidence, although relevant, because admission would hamper rather than advance the search for truth.[12] The second class of rules limits admissibility to implement an extrinsic policy that the law considers more important than ascertaining the truth in a particular law suit.[13]

[b]—Auxiliary Exclusionary Rules of Probative Force

A lawsuit involves numerous propositions that cannot be viewed or proved in isolation. A line of proof directed to one proposition may cause confusion or prejudice concerning another. A certain type of proof may be inherently lacking in trustworthiness so that its admission would interfere with ascertaining the truth.

Many of the provisions in the Federal Rules of Evidence are designed to increase the likelihood of accurate determinations. Rule 403 restricts admissibility when the danger of confusion or prejudice is so great that the truth probably would be obscured. See discussion in Chapter 6. The succeeding rules in Article IV of the Rules rest, at least in part, on the same notion. See discussion in Chapter 7. Rules governing authentication (Article IX of the Rules, discussed in Chapter 8), best evidence (Article X of the Rules, discussed in Chapter 9), and many of the provisions relating to witnesses (see Chapters 10, 12, and 13) are all grounded in the desire to protect the trier of fact from evidence that may not be worthy of belief.

[8.1] *See, e.g.,* United States v. Cruz-Garcia, 344 F.3d 951, 954 (9th Cir. 2003) (federal evidence rules "start from the proposition that 'all relevant evidence is admissible.' ").

[9] *See, e.g.,* Old Chief v. United States, 519 U.S. 172, 192, 117 S. Ct. 644, 136 L. Ed. 2d 574 (1997) (Rule 403 barred, in prosecution for possession of firearm by felon, introduction of documentary record of defendant's prior conviction, although relevant to prove status element of offense, because defendant offered to stipulate to felon status); United States v. Cabrera, 222 F.3d 590, 596 (9th Cir. 2000) (trial court erred in admitting police officer's many unnecessary references to national origin of drug dealers whom he was investigating, which was same as that of defendants, because testimony was irrelevant under Rule 402 and prejudicial under Rule 403).

[10] *See, e.g.,* Huber v. United States, 838 F.2d 398, 403 (9th Cir. 1988) (in action asserting that negligence of Coast Guard contributed to drowning of crewmen after yacht sank, Coast Guard investigating officers' conclusions and recommendations in investigative reports were inadmissible in evidence as party admissions because federal regulations promulgated pursuant to Congressional authorization prohibit such use).

[11] 8 Wigmore, Evidence, § 2175 (McNaughton rev. 1961).

[12] *See* [b], *below.*

[13] *See* [c], *below.*

The hearsay rule also finds its main justification in truth finding (see discussion in Chapters 14–17).

This policy is also served by other enactments. Basic to the discovery practice of the Federal Rules of Civil and Criminal Procedure is the underlying assumption that the possibility of ascertaining the truth is enhanced by having witnesses testify orally in open court. Consequently, despite relevancy, depositions of witnesses may not be admitted at trial as substantive evidence unless certain conditions regarding deponents' unavailability are met.[14]

Constitutional doctrine may also further the reliability of evidence. The Supreme Court is viewing reliability as the main concern of the Confrontation Clause, and other constitutional requirements, such as restrictions on the use of eyewitness testimony, also further the trustworthiness objective. See discussion in Chapter 14.

[c]—Exclusionary Rules of Extrinsic Policy

The privilege rules in Article V are the most obvious example of evidentiary rules designed to further some policy other than ascertaining the truth. See Chapter 18. Rules 404 through 412 all rest at least in part on the notion that certain evidence may be excluded because of goals other than truth finding. See Chapter 7. Even the hearsay rule serves more than a trustworthiness of evidence rationale. Although its main justification lies in truth finding, some of its vitality is due to its psychic value to litigants, who feel that those giving evidence against them should do so publicly and face to face.

The Advisory Committee's notes to Rule 402 list a number of Congressional enactments that restrict the admissibility of evidence through the formulation of a privilege or of a prohibition against disclosure.[15] Procedural rules, such as Rule 37(b)(2)(B) of the Federal Rules of Civil Procedure, that impose sanctions may also have the effect of restricting the use of evidence in order to discourage behavior destructive to the judicial process. Constitutional exclusionary rules, though less favored by the Supreme Court than in the past, also operate to exclude relevant evidence in order to further important societal policies such as the deterrence of unlawful police conduct.

---

[14] Fed. R. Civ. P. 32(a); Fed. R. Crim. P. 15. Depositions of adverse parties are admissible for any purpose on the same rationale as are other admissions. *See* 7 MOORE'S FEDERAL PRACTICE, Ch. 32, *Use of Depositions in Court Proceedings* (Matthew Bender 3d ed.); 25 MOORE'S FEDERAL PRACTICE, Ch. 615, *Depositions* (Matthew Bender 3d ed.). See Rule 801(d)(2), which is discussed in Chapter 15.

[15] *See* **Treatise,** Ch. 402, *Relevant Evidence Generally Admissible; Irrelevant Evidence Inadmissible,* § 402App.01[2].

§ 1.02   Purpose and Construction—Rule 102[1]

[1]—Flexibility is Basic Principle in Construing Evidence Rules

Under Rule 102, flexibility is the basic principle underlying the guidelines for construing and interpreting the Federal Rules of Evidence. Rule 102 necessarily promotes flexibility in the construction of the other rules by establishing sometimes conflicting goals that application of the evidence rules as a whole should achieve. The rule provides:

Rule 102.   Purpose and Construction.

These rules shall be construed to secure fairness in administration, elimination of unjustifiable expense and delay, and promotion of growth and development of the law of evidence to the end that the truth may be ascertained and proceedings justly determined.

[Adopted Jan. 2, 1975, effective July 1, 1975.]

Frequently promoting the truth-finding function of a trial will at least apparently be at odds with minimizing expense and delay in the proceedings. Thus, Rule 102 implicitly instructs the courts to eschew technical rules and mechanical analysis of admissibility questions, and to exercise their discretion to facilitate truth finding by the trier of fact and justice dispensing by the judicial system.

Flexibility in the judicial assessment of evidence is a theme that is repeated throughout the evidence rules, many of which at least implicitly require the trial judge to exercise discretion, in light of the facts of the particular case, in making rulings admitting or excluding evidence.[2] For example, Rule 403 explicitly allows the trial court to exclude relevant evidence if its probative value is substantially outweighed by its potential for causing unfair prejudice, confusion, or delay.[3] In making that determination, the trial court must, of necessity, assess the probative value of the proffered evidence in the context of all the other evidence in the record as well as information the finder of fact will never see or hear. The balancing process demands that the trial court exercise a reasoned discretion, in light of the peculiar facts of the case, directed towards realizing the stated goals of Rule 102.

Similarly, the rules governing the trial court's control over the conduct of the trial require the trial judge to take into account the facts of the particular case in ruling on questions such as: (1) the order of interrogating witnesses and of pre-

---

[1] See discussion in **Treatise** in Ch. 102, *Purpose and Construction*.
[2] *See, e.g.,* United States v. Meserve, 271 F.3d 314, 319 (1sth Cir. 2001) ("Generally, questions of admissibility of evidence that do not raise issues of law are reviewed for abuse of discretion.").
[3] *See* Ch. 6 for complete discussion of Rule 403.

sentation of evidence,[4] (2) the admissibility of evidence for limited purposes,[5] (3) the admissibility of the remainder of writings or recorded statements when the proponent offers only parts of them,[6] and (4) the advisability of the court's calling its own witnesses or of the court's interrogating witnesses called by the parties.[7] The trial court's legitimate exercise of its powers under those rules depends largely on its assessment of the fairness of ruling one way or the other in light of the facts as the parties have developed them, which is merely another way of saying that those rules confer reasoned discretion on the trial court to be flexible in its rulings so as to facilitate achieving the goals of Rule 102.[8]

The rules relating to expert testimony, hearsay, and privilege, as Congress adopted them, extensively revised the common-law evidence rules to make them more flexible in their application. Rule 702 eliminates common-law restrictions on the use of expert testimony in favor of a "helpfulness" test that recognizes the need for case-by-case analysis.[9] Even the hearsay rule, which was traditionally mechanical and technical under the common law, was infused with flexibility by the definition of certain out-of-court declarations offered for the truth of their content as not hearsay,[10] the emphasis in the hearsay exceptions on the trustworthiness of the proffered evidence,[11] and the addition of what has become a single residual exception.[12] Congress's action in rejecting the detailed rules on privilege drafted by the Advisory Committee rejected the establishment of a closed system with absolute rules in favor of a case-by-case approach that evaluates existing and proposed new privileges "in the light of reason and experience."[13] In fact, the courts regularly recognize the goals of Rule 102 in their construction of other federal evidence rules.[14]

[2]—Conflicting Goals of Rule 102 Require Flexibility

The trial courts need considerable leeway in interpreting the evidence rules because Rule 102 directs them to pursue sometimes conflicting goals. Absent

---

[4] Fed. R. Evid. 611.

[5] Fed. R. Evid. 105.

[6] Fed. R. Evid. 106.

[7] Fed. R. Evid. 614.

[8] *See* Ch.2 for discussion of trial court's authority to control proceedings before it.

[9] Fed. R. Evid. 702; *see* Ch. 13.

[10] Fed. R. Evid. 801(d); *see* Ch. 15.

[11] Fed. R. Evid. 803; Fed. R. Evid. 804; *see* Chs 16, 17.

[12] Fed. R. Evid. 807; *see* Ch. 14.

[13] Fed. R. Evid 501; *see* Ch. 18.

[14] *See, e.g.,* United States v. Munoz, 16 F.3d 1116, 1122 (11th Cir. 1994) (trial court properly facilitated goal of Rule 102 of providing speedy, inexpensive, and fair trial by admitting bank deposit slips and check application form from Panamanian bank under residual hearsay exception (now Fed. R. Evid. 807)).

flexibility at the trial court level in the application of the rules of evidence, the trial courts would experience significant difficulty in reconciling the elimination of unjustifiable expense and delay with the ascertainment of truth, and the appellate courts would expend unnecessarily large amounts of time in reviewing admissibility determinations.

Rule 102's mandate that the courts construe the evidence rules to promote the ascertainment of the truth and the just determination of the proceedings has its counterpart in Rule 1 of the Federal Rules of Civil Procedure. That rule requires the courts to construe the civil rules to "secure the just, speedy, and inexpensive determination of every action."[15] Taken together, the two rules allow trial courts considerable flexibility in arriving at just solutions to situations in which the pursuit of truth might otherwise be achieved only by a sacrifice of considerable fairness in the proceedings, if each rule were followed blindly. It may happen, for example, that an expert witness who has stated conclusions in a written report during discovery may change those conclusions or the reasoning behind them because of statements of opposing experts in subsequently disclosed reports and in their depositions. If the expert's revised supporting basis, although revealed in a timely fashion, is not made known to the opposition until after the trial has begun, Rule 102's goal of the pursuit of truth strongly supports permitting the expert to testify to the revisions in his or her thinking. On the other hand, allowing the testimony without further discovery would run counter to the civil rules' goal of promoting discovery from testifying experts and put the opponent at a severe disadvantage in preparing cross-examination or in obtaining rebuttal reports and testimony from its experts. The trial court can use the flexibility granted by Civil Procedure Rule 1 to permit the opponent to depose the expert again.[16]

[3]—Flexibility Principle Permits Recognition of Differences in Types of Cases

Rule 102 also recognizes that trial judges may be justified in some situations in employing procedures that will lead to a cheap and swift approximation of the truth, even though there may be an increased risk of error.[17] On the other hand, it does not give trial judges carte blanche to ignore the minimal constraints individual rules

---

[15] Fed. R. Civ. P. 1.

[16] *See, e.g.,* Blue Cross & Blue Shield of N.J., Inc. v. Philip Morris, Inc., 199 F.R.D. 484, 485–487 (E.D.N.Y. 2001) (Weinstein, J.).

[17] *See, e.g.,* Salas v. Wang, 846 F.2d 897, 904 (3d Cir. 1988) (under Rule 102's goal of providing expeditious and efficient proceedings, trial court did not abuse its discretion in permitting expert witness to testify to aggregated damages suffered by brain damaged child after having testified to elements of projected damages and to description of present value calculation).

impose on proffered evidence simply because they view it to be trustworthy.[18] Nor does it permit trial courts to ignore provisions contained in individual rules that were designed to curtail evasions of specific prerequisites to admissibility established by other rules.[19]

In the implementation of the goals of Rule 102 it is necessary to recognize very real distinctions in practice between bench and jury trials, between criminal and civil cases, and among civil and criminal cases asserting claims of varying degrees of legal and factual complexity. The fulfilment of the goals of Rule 102 does not require the same level of formalities in a bench-tried federal tort claim involving minor property damage caused by a post office truck as is necessary for the achievement of those goals in a major organized crime prosecution before a jury.

The emphasis in Rule 102 on the ascertainment of truth and justly determined proceedings authorizes trial judges in appropriate circumstances to modify the law of evidence, to reject precedent, and even, in some circumstances, to ignore requirements of other rules of evidence for the admissibility of evidence.[20] In fact, Rule 102 may operate as an escape route from evidentiary rules that have their foundation outside the Federal Rules of Evidence and that have become burdensome or inapposite with the passage of time.[21]

---

[18] *See, e.g.,* United States v. Pelullo, 964 F.2d 193, 203–204 (3d Cir. 1992) (trial court erred in admitting important bank records containing hearsay statements and summaries based on them with no foundational evidence even though appellate court agreed with trial court that they were trustworthy; "the goals underlying the Federal Rules of Evidence would not be furthered" by admitting the documents, since to do so "would necessarily eviscerate the requirements of [the] Rules," even though the rules "are to be liberally construed in favor of admissibility").

[19] *See, e.g.,* United States v. Horn, 185 F. Supp. 2d 530, 560–561 (D. Md. 2002) (in DUI/DWI prosecution, arresting officer may testify as lay witness about observations of defendant, including defendant's performance of standard field sobriety tests, and to lay opinion, if qualified to do so under Rule 701, that defendant was intoxicated, but absent proof that field sobriety tests are reliable in accordance with Rule 702, cannot evade Rule 701's stricture against lay opinion testimony based on scientific, technical, or other specialized knowledge by cloaking those tests in aura of scientific validity by using terms such as "test" and "standardized clues" in describing tests or "passed" or "failed" in describing defendant's performance). *See also* § 10.02 for discussion of lay opinion testimony.

[20] *See, e.g.,* United States v. Sutton, 801 F.2d 1346, 1368–1369 (D.C. Cir. 1986) (when rule of completeness, Fed. R. Evid. 106, requires admission of evidence that, when considered with portion of document already admitted into evidence, still presents distorted picture, Rule 102's requirement that evidence rules be construed to secure fairness permits admission of additional evidence to remove distortions, even though additional evidence would otherwise be inadmissible under other federal evidence rules).

[21] *See, e.g.,* Herbert v. Wal-Mart Stores, Inc., 911 F.2d 1044, 1048–1049 (5th Cir. 1990) (trial court properly refused, under Rule 102, to instruct jury that it could draw adverse inference from defendant's failure to call witness purportedly under its control based on so-called "uncalled witness rule"; uncalled witness was available to both parties and rule is anachronistic and should be abolished because it "has no place in federal trials conducted under the Federal Rules of Evidence,"

§ 1.03   Applicability of the Federal Rules of Evidence—Rules 101 and 1101[1]

[1]—Evidence Rules Are Broadly Applicable

The Federal Rules of Evidence are not "Rules" in the sense of having been adopted through the rule making power provided for by the Rules Enabling Act.[2] Although the Federal Rules of Evidence originally were intended to become effective as a result of promulgation by the Supreme Court, they ultimately were enacted by Congress as a statute.[3] They are, consequently, immune from attack on the ground that they deal with substantive issues beyond the scope of rule-making. The language of the rules generally receives great deference because the rules represent a positive legislative enactment.[4]

Rule 101 provides that the Federal Rules of Evidence apply in the courts of the United States and before United States bankruptcy judges and United States magistrate judges, except for those situations specifically enumerated in Rule 1101. The text of Rule 101 is as follows:

Rule 101.   Scope.

These rules govern proceedings in the courts of the United States and before the United States bankruptcy judges and United States magistrate judges, to the extent and with the exceptions stated in Rule 1101.

[Adopted Jan. 2, 1975, effective July 1, 1975; amended Mar. 2, 1987, effective Oct. 1, 1987; amended Apr. 25, 1988, effective Nov. 1, 1988; amended Apr. 22, 1993, effective Dec. 1, 1993.]

Rule 101 is not totally self-contained. It specifically refers to Rule 1101 for details concerning the courts and specific types of proceedings in and to which the rules apply, wholly or in part.

Rule 1101(a) identifies very broadly the courts in which the Federal Rules of

---

since, under federal rules, witnesses are not "controlled" by any party).

[1]   *See* discussion in **Treatise** at §§ 101.02, 1101.02.

[2]   28 U.S.C. § 2071 *et seq.*

[3]   *See* discussion of legislative history of Federal Rules of Evidence in Preface of **Treatise**.

[4]   *See, e.g.,* In re Oil Spill by the Amoco Cadiz, 954 F.2d 1279, 1304–1305 (7th Cir. 1992) ("The Federal Rules of Evidence are statutes, and district judges may not disregard statutes no matter how inconvenient or cumbersome they believe the rules to be"); Fox v. United States, 934 F. Supp. 1133, 1136–1138 (N.D. Cal. 1996) (Coast Guard regulation purportedly limiting effect of accident investigative report on issues other than determination of fault did not supersede Federal Rules of Evidence relating to admissibility of government documents under exceptions to hearsay rule and relevance, because mere agency regulations cannot override Federal Rules of Evidence, which are statutes enacted by Congress).

Evidence are applicable.[5] Rule 1101(b) specifies, again very broadly, the types of actions and proceedings in which the Federal Rules of Evidence are applicable.[6] Rule 1101(c) makes the rule respecting privileges applicable at all stages of all actions, proceedings, and cases, without regard to whether the other rules of evidence are applicable.[7] It recognizes that confidentiality, once breached, cannot be restored, and that an evidentiary privilege is effective only if it bars all disclosure at all times.[8] Rule 1101(d) lists situations in which the rules of evidence do not apply, but specifically provides that the rule respecting privileges continues to apply in those situations.[9] Rule 1101(e) lists certain proceedings to which the rules of evidence are applicable, but only to the extent that (1) Congress has not provided for the handling of evidentiary matters in the statutes governing those proceedings, or (2) the Supreme Court, pursuant to statutory authority, has not provided for the handling of evidentiary matters in other rules it has prescribed specifically for those proceedings.[10]

Rule 1101 provides as follows:

Rule 1101.   Applicability of Rules.

(a)

Courts and judges.—

These rules apply to the United States district courts, the District Court of Guam, the District Court of the Virgin Islands, the District Court for the Northern Mariana Islands, the United States courts of appeals, the United States Claims Court, and to United States bankruptcy judges and United States magistrate judges, in the actions, cases, and proceedings and to the extent hereinafter set forth. The terms "judge" and "court" in these rules include United States bankruptcy judges and United States magistrate judges.

(b)

Proceedings generally.—

These rules apply generally to civil actions and proceedings, including admiralty and maritime cases, to criminal cases and proceedings, to contempt proceedings except those in which the court may act summarily, and to proceedings and cases under title 11, United States Code.

---

[5]   Fed. R. Evid. 1101(a).

[6]   Fed. R. Evid. 1101(b); **Treatise,** Ch. 1101, *Applicability of Rules,* § 1101.02[1].

[7]   Fed. R. Evid. 1101(c).

[8]   *See, e.g.,* In re Malfitano, 633 F.2d 276, 277 (3d Cir. 1980).

[9]   Fed. R. Evid 1101(d); *see, e.g.,* United States v. Matthews, 178 F.3d 295, 303 (5th Cir. 1999) (federal evidence rules are inapplicable in sentencing proceedings); United States v. Monsanto, 924 F.2d 1186, 1198 (2d Cir. 1991) (rules of evidence inapplicable in pretrial adversarial hearing on probable cause as to defendant's commission of narcotics offense and forfeitability of assets).

[10]   Fed. R. Evid. 1101(e); **Treatise,** Ch. 1101, *Applicability of Rules,* § 1101.03[10].

(c)

Rule of privilege.

The rule with respect to privileges applies at all stages of all actions, cases, and proceedings.

(d)

Rules inapplicable.—

The rules (other than with respect to privileges) do not apply in the following situations:

(1)

Preliminary questions of fact.—

The determination of questions of fact preliminary to admissibility of evidence when the issue is to be determined by the court under rule 104.

(2)

Grand jury.—

Proceedings before grand juries.

(3)

Miscellaneous proceedings.—

Proceedings for extradition or rendition; preliminary examinations in criminal cases; sentencing, or granting or revoking probation; issuance of warrants for arrest, criminal summonses, and search warrants; and proceedings with respect to release on bail or otherwise.

(e)

Rules applicable in part.—

In the following proceedings these rules apply to the extent that matters of evidence are not provided for in the statutes which govern procedure therein or in other rules prescribed by the Supreme Court pursuant to statutory authority: the trial of misdemeanors and other petty offenses before United States magistrate judges; review of agency actions when the facts are subject to trial de novo under section 706(2)(F) of title 5, United States Code; review of orders of the Secretary of Agriculture under section 2 of the Act entitled "An Act to authorize association of producers of agricultural products" approved February 18, 1922 (7 U.S.C. 292), and under sections 6 and 7(c) of the Perishable Agricultural Commodities Act, 1930 (7 U.S.C. 499f, 499g(c)); naturalization and revocation of naturalization under sections 310–318 of the Immigration and Nationality Act (8 U.S.C. 1421–1429); prize proceedings in admiralty under sections 7651–7681 of title 10, United States Code; review of orders of the Secretary of the Interior under section 2 of the Act entitled "An Act authorizing associations of producers of aquatic products" approved June 25, 1934 (15 U.S.C. 522); review of orders of petroleum control boards under section 5 of the Act entitled "An Act to regulate interstate and foreign commerce in petroleum and its products by prohibiting the shipment in such commerce of petroleum and its products produced in violation of State law, and for other purposes," approved February 22, 1935 (15 U.S.C. 715d); actions for fines, penalties, or forfeitures under part V of title IV of the Tariff Act of 1930 (19 U.S.C. 1581–1624), or under the Anti-Smuggling Act (19 U.S.C. 1701–1711); criminal libel for condemnation, exclusion of imports, or other proceedings under the Federal Food, Drug, and Cosmetic Act (21 U.S.C. 301–392); disputes between seamen under sections 4079, 4080, and 4081 of the Revised Statutes (22 U.S.C. 256–258); habeas corpus under sections 2241–2254 of title 28, United States Code; motions to vacate, set aside or correct sentence under section 2255 of title 28, United States Code; actions for penalties for refusal to transport destitute seamen under section 4578 of the Revised Statutes (46 U.S.C. 679); actions against the United States under the Act entitled "An Act authorizing suits against the United States in admiralty for damage caused by and salvage service rendered to public vessels belonging to the United States, and for other purposes," approved March 3, 1925 (46 U.S.C. 781–790), as implemented by section 7730 of title 10, United States Code.

[*Adopted Jan. 2, 1975, effective July 1, 1975; amended Dec. 12, 1975; Nov. 6, 1978, effective Oct. 1, 1979; Apr. 2, 1982, effective Oct. 1, 1982; Mar. 2, 1987, effective Oct. 1, 1987; Apr. 25, 1988, effective Nov. 1, 1988; Apr. 22, 1993, effective Dec. 1, 1993.*]

The broad generality of Rule 101, however, coupled with the very narrow and specific exceptions carved out by Rule 1101, makes it clear that the Federal Rules of Evidence control the admissibility of evidence in the vast majority of proceedings that are brought in federal courts.

[2]—Federal Question Cases

The Federal Rules of Evidence are clearly applicable in trials of cases in which subject matter jurisdiction is founded on the laws of the United States.[11] They are applicable to trials of both civil and criminal cases.[12]

[3]—Diversity Cases and Pendent State Law Claims

The Federal Rules of Evidence are also applicable in trials of cases in which subject matter jurisdiction is dependent upon diversity of citizenship of the parties

---

[11] *See, e.g.,* Park v. City of Chi., 297 F.3d 606, 611–612 (7th Cir. 2002) (Federal Rules of Evidence govern admissibility of evidence in federal courts when claims are governed by federal law).

[12] *See, e.g.,* United States v. North, 910 F.2d 843, 907 (D.C. Cir. 1990) (under Rule 101, Federal Rules of Evidence govern both civil and criminal proceedings in federal courts).

and in federal question cases including pendent claims asserted under state law.[13] If the federal rule is sufficiently broad to cover the issue of admissibility before the court, it controls the trial court's decision on that issue.[14]

If, however, the state law is not purely procedural, but has a substantive impact, it can affect the admissibility issue. Thus, for example, the collateral source rule is generally construed both as an evidentiary rule and as a rule of substantive law that affects the determination of the amount of a proper damage award in a tort case. The federal courts in diversity cases are bound to apply the law of the state under which the claim arises, including its collateral source rule, in the determination of the plaintiff's damages.[15] They are not required, however, to apply the evidentiary aspect of the collateral source rule, since the relevance rules of the Federal Rules of Evidence, specifically Rule 403, are sufficiently broad and flexible to provide the district court with the tools necessary to decide admissibility questions.[16] On the other hand, if the admissibility aspect of the state rule is inextricably intertwined with the substantive goal it attempts to achieve, the admissibility question is governed by the state rule of law, even though a federal evidentiary rule might provide a different result than would the state rule.[17]

Widespread adoption of the Federal Rules of Evidence by the states has minimized some of the problems of diverse federal and state rules.[18]

---

[13] *See, e.g.,* Legg v. Chopra, 286 F.3d 286, 289 (6th Cir. 2002) (Federal Rules of Evidence, rather than state evidentiary laws, apply in federal diversity proceedings).

[14] *See, e.g.,* Fitzgerald v. Expressway Sewerage Constr., Inc., 177 F.3d 71, 73–74 (1st Cir. 1999) (federal evidence rules govern in diversity cases, even though state law provides rule of decision; if federal evidentiary rule is sufficiently broad to control particular issue, trial court must apply it).

[15] *See, e.g.,* Fitzgerald v. Expressway Sewerage Constr., Inc., 177 F.3d 71, 73 (1st Cir. 1999); 17A MOORE'S FEDERAL PRACTICE, Ch. 124, *The Erie Doctrine and Applicable Law* (Matthew Bender 3d ed.).

[16] *See, e.g.,* Fitzgerald v. Expressway Sewerage Constr., Inc., 177 F.3d 71, 73–74 (1st Cir. 1999); *see also* In re Air Crash Disaster Near Chicago, Ill., 701 F.2d 1189, 1211 (7th Cir. 1983) (in diversity case, although state law provides rule of decision regarding measure of damages, trial court should apply federal evidentiary rules in determining admissibility of proffered evidence, and should make relevance determination in light of state substantive law of damages); *see* Ch.6 for complete discussion of exclusion of relevant evidence on grounds of prejudice, confusion, or waste of time.

[17] *See, e.g.,* Daigle v. Maine Med. Ctr., 14 F.3d 684, 688 (1st Cir. 1994) (state statute requiring pre-litigation screening of medical malpractice claims, allowing panel's findings into evidence despite their hearsay nature, and precluding impeachment of those findings was binding on federal trial court trying state malpractice claim, even though Rule 806 would otherwise entitle opponent to impeach hearsay declarant's credibility).

[18] *See* WEINSTEIN'S FEDERAL EVIDENCE, *Table of State and Military Adaptations of Federal Rules of Evidence* (Matthew Bender 2d ed.).

[4]—Incorporation of State Law in Federal Rules of Evidence

Congress specifically provided that state law would govern certain aspects of federal evidentiary law. Thus, the effect of civil presumptions,[19] questions of privilege,[20] and the competence of witnesses when state law "supplies the rule of decision"[21] are all controlled by state law. Moreover, the authenticity of some documentary evidence is determined in accordance with state law: Rule 903 provides that a writing need not be authenticated by testimony of a subscribing witness unless such testimony "is required by the law of the jurisdiction whose laws govern the validity of the writing" and Rule 902(9) permits self-authentication of commercial papers, signatures on those papers and documents relating to them in accordance with the "general commercial law," which generally means the Uniform Commercial Code.[22]

Some of the rules concerning privileges that the Supreme Court proposed and Congress eliminated when it enacted the Federal Rules of Evidence also incorporate state law. For example, Standard 502, which is the rule the Supreme Court proposed as Rule 502, accords a privilege to reports required by law if the law that requires the reports also grants them a privilege.[23] Those seemingly disavowed rules are of significance because the courts frequently refer to them and find them persuasive in their development of the federal common law of evidence respecting privileges.[24]

[5]—Proceedings in Which Federal Rules of Evidence Are Inapplicable

Under Rule 101, the Federal Rules of Evidence are applicable only in proceedings "in the courts of the United States and before the United States bankruptcy judges and United States magistrate judges."[25] They are, therefore, generally not applicable in administrative hearings.[26] Nor are they applicable in specific pro-

---

[19] *See* Fed. R. Evid. 302, discussed in Ch. 5.

[20] *See* Fed. R. Evid. 501, discussed in Ch. 18.

[21] *See* Fed. R. Evid. 601, discussed in Ch. 10.

[22] *See* Fed. R. Evid 903; Fed. R. Evid. 902(9), discussed in Ch. 8.

[23] *See* **Treatise,** Ch. 502, *Required Reports Privileged by Statute (Supreme Court Standard 502).*

[24] *See, e.g.,* United States v. McPartlin, 595 F.2d 1321, 1337 (7th Cir. 1979) (proposed evidence rules, as "recommendations of the Advisory Committee, approved by the Supreme Court, are a useful guide to the federal courts in their development of a common law of evidence").

[25] Fed. R. Evid. 101; *see, e.g.,* Williams v. Price, 343 F.3d 223, 230 n.3 (3d Cir. 2003) (federal evidence rules do not control proceedings in state courts, even those subject to review in federal courts in habeas corpus proceedings).

[26] *See, e.g.,* American Coal Co. v. Benefits Review Board, 738 F.2d 387, 391 (10th Cir. 1984) (Rule 301 did not prevent administrative law judge from shifting burdens of proof in proceeding for award of benefits under Black Lung Benefits Act, because Rule 301 and other federal evidence rules are not applicable in administrative proceedings).

ceedings in United States courts or before United States bankruptcy or magistrate judges when Congress has statutorily provided that they will not be applicable.[27]

Rule 1101(d) also lists certain specific types of proceedings to which the Federal Rules of Evidence, other than the rule relating to privileges, are inapplicable:[28]

- Proceedings relating to the determination of preliminary questions of fact respecting the admissibility of proffered evidence when the issue is to be determined by the court under Rule 104.

- Proceedings before grand juries.

- Proceedings for extradition or rendition.

- Preliminary examinations in criminal cases.

- Criminal sentencing proceedings.[29]

- Proceedings for granting or revoking probation.[30]

- Proceedings for the issuance of arrest warrants, criminal summonses, or search warrants.

- Proceedings respecting release on bail or otherwise.

Although the Federal Rules of Evidence, strictly speaking, do not apply in the situations listed in Rule 1101(d) (with the exception of the rule respecting privileges), in proceedings not within the scope of Rules 101 and 1101, or in tribunals other than those listed in Rule 1101(a), they nevertheless often offer useful guidance in determining the probative value of evidence even in those situations, proceedings, and tribunals to which they are not applicable.[31]

---

[27] *See, e.g.,* United States v. Monsanto, 924 F.2d 1186, 1195–1196 (2d Cir. 1991) (trial court is not bound by Federal Rules of Evidence in constitutionally required hearing to dissolve seizure order issued under Comprehensive Forfeiture Act of 1984, because governing statute provided for hearing before issuance of seizure orders and for exemption from Federal Rules of Evidence at such hearing).

[28] Fed. R. Evid. 1101(d).

[29] *See, e.g.,* United States v. Hopkins, 310 F.3d 145, 154 (4th Cir. 2002) (Federal Rules of Evidence do not apply to federal sentencing proceedings; trial court properly considered sentencing provisions from D.C. Criminal Code to determine applicability of recidivist statute).

[30] *See, e.g.,* United States v. Frazier, 26 F.3d 110, 113 (11th Cir. 1994) (courts should treat revocation hearings in same manner whether they relate to probation, parole, or supervised release; under Rule 1101, Federal Rules of Evidence do not apply to any such revocation proceedings).

[31] *See, e.g.,* Calhoun v. Bailar, 626 F.2d 145, 149 (9th Cir. 1980) (standards of Rule 803(24) (now Rule 807) may be helpful in determining whether hearsay declarations have sufficient probative value to constitute substantial evidence in an administrative proceeding).

§ 1.04   Amendments to Federal Rules of Evidence—Rule 1102

Rule 1102 sets forth the procedure for amending the Federal Rules of Evidence by referencing the statutory authority for doing so. Rule 1102 provides:

> **Rule 1102.   Amendments.**
>
> Amendments to the Federal Rules of Evidence may be made as provided in section 2072 of title 28 of the United States Code.

The United States Code gives the Supreme Court the power to prescribe rules of evidence.[1] Section 2074 of Title 28 of the Code provides that a proposed evidence rule amendment must be submitted to Congress, after which Congress has seven months in which to nullify or defer the effective date of any proposed amendment. The Supreme Court must transmit any proposed amendment to Congress by May 1 of the year in which it is to become effective. If it has done so, the amendment will take effect "no earlier than" the following December 1 unless Congress provides otherwise.[2] Section 2073 establishes the procedures for consideration of proposed rules by committee.[3]

Section 2074 requires Congressional approval of any rule or amendment "creating, abolishing or modifying an evidentiary privilege."[4] Also, section 2072 states that rules prescribed by the Supreme Court "shall not abridge, enlarge or modify any substantive right."[5] These provisions reflect Congress's intent to retain its control over matters of substantive law.

§ 1.05   Title—Rule 1103

Rule 1103 provides the rules with the name "the Federal Rules of Evidence." Rule 1103 states:

> **Rule 1103.   Title.**
>
> These rules may be known and cited as the Federal Rules of Evidence.

---

[1] 28 U.S.C. § 2072.
[2] 28 U.S.C. § 2074.
[3] 28 U.S.C. § 2073.
[4] 28 U.S.C. § 2074.
[5] 28 U.S.C. § 2072.

CHAPTER 2

Control by Trial Court Generally*

---

* Chapter revised in 1993 by ROBERT L. ROSSI, member of the Massachusetts bar.

§ 2.01 Overview of Trial Judge's Control

The trial judge is granted great discretion under the Federal Rules.[1] In this chapter specific reference is made to the judicial power to control the mode and order of interrogating witnesses (Rule 611), limited review of error in rulings on evidence (Rule 103), the authority to instruct on limited admissibility (Rule 105), application of the fairness concept in related writings (Rule 106), the right of the judge to call and interrogate witnesses (Rule 614), and the judge's power to sum up and comment (Standard 107). Other indicia of judicial discretion are found in Rule 102, on construction of the Rules (Chapter 1), Rule 104, on the authority to answer preliminary questions as a predicate for admissibility (Chapter 3), Rule 201, on discretionary power to take judicial notice under some circumstances (Chapter 4), Rule 403, on the power to weigh probative force against prejudice and other negative factors (Chapter 6), Rule 404, on the admissibility of character evidence (Chapter 7), Rules 608 and 609, on discretionary limits on the use of character and conviction evidence to impeach (Chapter 12), Rules 702–706, on the control of experts (Chapter 13), Rule 807, on the power to expand use of hearsay (Chapter 14), and in various other places discussed throughout the text.

To prevent abuse of these powers, the trial court must remain cognizant of its limited role. Under the adversary judicial system, primary decisions on tactics and style within very wide limits are assigned to the lawyers. In general, the best run trials have the smallest amount of colloquy and interjections by the judge.

Nevertheless, the judge should, whenever a question arises, explain clearly what factors were taken into account in the exercise of discretion. Rulings in advance should be encouraged to avoid surprises at trial; surprises lead to pressured and sometimes unwise spur-of-the-moment decisions. The lawyer must consider the applicability of the Rules before trial in order to request in limine rulings.

Wasteful side bars and continuances should be avoided. Explanations to the jury should be designed to inform, on the assumption that the jurors will do a more intelligent job if they understand the proceedings; the more information jurors have, the more likely they are to arrive at a sound and dispassionate estimate of the truth. This assumption underlies the tendency under the Federal Rules to admit rather than to exclude evidence whenever possible.

§ 2.02 Interrogation and Presentation of Witnesses—Rule 611

[1]—Text of Rule

Rule 611 is central to the scheme of the Federal Rules of Evidence. Subdivision (a) is the source of the trial court's power over the order and mode of the

---

[1] *See* **Treatise** at Preface and Ch. 102, *Purpose and Construction.*

presentation of evidence and the interrogation of witnesses. Subdivisions (b) and (c) set forth basic principles governing the examination of witnesses. The rule provides:

Rule 611. Mode and Order of Interrogation and Presentation.

(a) Control by court. The court shall exercise reasonable control over the mode and order of interrogating witnesses and presenting evidence so as to (1) make the interrogation and presentation effective for the ascertainment of the truth, (2) avoid needless consumption of time, and (3) protect witnesses from harassment or undue embarrassment.

(b) Scope of cross-examination. Cross-examination should be limited to the subject matter of the direct examination and matters affecting the credibility of the witness. The court may, in the exercise of discretion, permit inquiry into additional matters as if on direct examination.

(c) Leading questions. Leading questions should not be used on the direct examination of a witness except as may be necessary to develop the witness' testimony. Ordinarily leading questions should be permitted on cross-examination. When a party calls a hostile witness, an adverse party, or a witness identified with an adverse party, interrogation may be by leading questions.

[Adopted Jan. 2, 1975, effective July 1, 1975; amended Mar. 2, 1987, effective Oct. 1, 1987.]

---

[2]—Control by Court[1]

Rule 611(a) states a number of principles echoed elsewhere in the rules, particularly in Rules 102 and 403. The rule affirms the trial court's power to control the course of a trial so as to ascertain the truth, avoid needless consumption of time, and protect witnesses from harassment or undue embarrassment.

In the usual case, the order and mode of the presentation of evidence and interrogation of witnesses are determined by legal conventions and the parties' choice of trial tactics. The court steps in only when: (1) the parties ask for a ruling, (2) when it wishes to clarify matters,[2] or (3) when something out of the ordinary occurs that warrants intervention.[3] The court should defer to the parties' prefer-

---

[1] See discussion in **Treatise** at § 611.02.

[2] See, e.g., United States v. Simpson, 337 F.3d 905, 907 (7th Cir. 2003) (trial court did not abuse its discretion by interrupting trial proceedings to clarify ambiguous testimony).

[3] See, e.g., M.T. Bonk Co. v. Milton Bradley Co., 945 F.2d 1404, 1409 (7th Cir. 1991) (no abuse of discretion in terminating witness examination at end of period estimated by counsel, after prior examination had greatly exceeded counsel's time estimate; remark by judge that counsel's

ences respecting the mode of questioning and order of proof, so long as they promote the efficient ascertainment of the truth. Even if the court is trying to save time, which is one of the objectives of Rule 611(a), it must bear in mind that counsel are far more familiar with the case, so that a seemingly trivial ruling may impede rather than expedite the search for truth.[4]

Once the trial court exercises its power, its decision is virtually immune to attack, and will be overturned only in the rare case when the appellate court finds a clear abuse of discretion that seriously damaged a party's right to a fair trial.[5]

Subdivision (a) authorizes departures from the usual order of proof and innovations in the presentation of evidence. A trial court's decision to permit or deny a requested departure or innovation is entitled to great deference.[6] Some of the more frequently occurring examples of a court's power to depart from the normal order of proof are the following:

- Allowing the reopening of a case after a party has rested.[7]

- Allowing a witness to be recalled.[8]

- Allowing witnesses to testify out of order.[9]

---

extended examination was adversely affecting her client's case was also not improper, and indicated "a legitimate concern for the manner and mode of the presentation of evidence").

[4] See Civil Trial Practice Standard 12(a) (A.B.A. 1998) (limits on trial presentation should be imposed only after court has analyzed case, asked parties about adopting voluntary self-imposed limits, and given parties opportunity to be heard about amount of time, number of witnesses, and exhibits).

[5] See, e.g., Manley v. AmBase Corp., 337 F.3d 237, 246–248 (2d Cir. 2003) (trial court did not abuse its discretion in excluding portions of witness's discovery deposition when elderly witness had been subsequently deposed as substitute for appearing at trial, because party had not addressed those matters in trial deposition; even if trial court did abuse its discretion, error would not be reversible because relevant facts had been presented to jury via other exhibits).

[6] See Fed. R. Evid. 611(a); see also Civil Trial Practice Standard 14 (A.B.A. 1998) (in "cases of appropriate complexity, the court should exercise its discretion to alter the traditional order of trial where that will enhance jury comprehension and recollection or facilitate the effective presentation of evidence and argument, without unfair advantage to either side"); United States v. Holly, 167 F.3d 393, 395 (7th Cir. 1999) (since defense had announced its intent to present prior inconsistent statements of government witnesses, government was properly allowed to present in its case-in-chief evidence that defendant had intimidated witnesses into making those statements).

[7] See, e.g., Perry v. Dearing (In re Perry), 345 F.3d 303, 309–310 (5th Cir. 2003) (trial court has wide discretion to allow party to reopen, or to do so on its own motion).

[8] See, e.g., United States v. Brown, 954 F.2d 1563, 1572 (11th Cir. 1992) (no abuse of discretion in allowing government to recall witness; district court made reasoned determination that witness's further testimony was material to jury's ascertainment of truth, and gave defendant adequate opportunity to cross-examine after recall).

[9] See, e.g., Lis v. Robert Packer Hosp., 579 F.2d 819, 823 (3d Cir. 1978) (not error for court to allow defense to qualify plaintiff's witness, a physician, as its witness at conclusion of

- Admitting or excluding rebuttal or surrebuttal testimony.[10]

- Permitting witnesses to testify in installments.[11]

- Allowing witnesses to testify in a narrative.[12]

- Allowing jurors to question witnesses.[13]

- Permitting the parties to read the contents of documents admitted into evidence to the jury or preventing them from doing so.[14]

- Allowing witnesses to use charts as pedagogical devices.[15]

- Requiring party to delay "cross-examination" of its own employee, who had been called as a witness by its opponent, until the party's own case in chief.[15.1]

- Allowing parties to use non-expert witnesses to summarize complex documentary and testimonial evidence.[15.2]

cross-examination; court has discretion to accommodate expert witnesses' schedules even though calling defense witness during plaintiff's case-in-chief may disrupt planned presentation).

[10] *See, e.g.,* United States v. O'Brien, 119 F.3d 523, 531 (7th Cir. 1997) (no abuse of discretion in barring further testimony by defendant on same issue, because her surrebuttal testimony would be cumulative).

[11] *See, e.g.,* United States v. DeLuna, 763 F.2d 897, 911–912 (8th Cir. 1985) (no abuse of discretion when defendants had ample opportunity to cross-examine witnesses after each installment).

[12] *See, e.g.,* United States v. Young, 745 F.2d 733, 761 (2d Cir. 1984) (qualified expert properly permitted to give narrative testimony and opinions while videotape played for jury).

[13] *See, e.g.,* United States v. Hernandez, 176 F.3d 719, 723 (3d Cir. 1999) (juror questioning of witness in criminal trial is permissible "so long as it is done in a manner that insures the fairness of the proceedings, the primacy of the court's stewardship, and the rights of the accused").

[14] *See, e.g.,* United States v. Moskowitz, 215 F.3d 265, 270 (2d Cir. 2000) (district courts have discretion under Rule 611(a) to limit manner in which evidence is presented to jury, including preventing parties from reading contents of documents already in evidence to jury).

[15] *See, e.g.,* United States v. Taylor, 210 F.3d 311, 314 (5th Cir. 2000) (in conspiracy case, government's intermittent use throughout trial of chart that was not in evidence as device to assist jurors to distinguish between alleged conspirators, many of whom had same name, was within trial court's discretion under Rule 611(a), especially when jury was instructed at outset that chart indicated only what government believed facts to be, and it was jury's function to determine whether it was accurate); *see also* Ch. 9 concerning charts that are admitted into evidence in lieu of voluminous underlying data.

[15.1] Argentine v. USW, 287 F.3d 476, 486 (6th Cir. 2002) (Rule 611(a) gives trial judge discretion concerning order in which witnesses are called).

[15.2] *See, e.g.,* United States v. Sabino, 274 F.3d 1053, 1066–1068 (6th Cir. 2001) (IRS employee was properly allowed to summarize and analyze facts in evidence from documents and other witnesses indicating willful tax evasion, since accompanied by limiting instruction informing jury that summary itself did not constitute evidence).

- Allowing plaintiffs in mass tort cases to use sampling and statistical techniques to prove causation and damages rather than requiring proof that each victim suffered injury as the result of the defendant's actions.[15.3]

- Allowing parties to call the adverse party's expert witness during their case in chief and to examine him or her as a hostile witness when his or her adversity becomes apparent.[15.4]

This list is in no way exhaustive. The court has the power under Rule 611(a) to experiment with more radical variations on traditional practice.[16]

Rule 611(a)'s authorization of the court's intervention in the presentation of evidence for the purpose of enhancing its effectiveness in the ascertainment of the truth sometimes provides the trial court with discretion to admit into the record evidence that would otherwise be inadmissible.[16.1] It also sometimes serves as the source of the trial court's discretion in excluding what would otherwise be admissible evidence.[16.2]

Problems relating to the harassment or embarrassment of witnesses usually arise in the context of the permissible scope of cross-examination. The exact point at which the court must step in to prevent abuse is impossible to formulate since it depends on the specific circumstances of the case, the personalities of the parties, witnesses, and counsel, and the situation at the time the court is asked to intervene. A witness may be intimidated by the manner as well as the questions of the cross-examiner. Indeed, if the witness is easily intimidated, the process of cross-examination itself mat be quite uncomfortable. On the other hand, even fighting words may be unobjectionable if they are said with a smile. Appellate courts are

---

[15.3] *See, e.g.,* Blue Cross & Blue Shield of N.J., Inc. v. Philip Morris, Inc., 178 F. Supp. 2d 198, 247–262 (E.D.N.Y. 2001) (Weinstein, J.) (Rule 611 permits use of statistical techniques in mass tort cases to avoid otherwise crippling discovery and evidentiary costs).

[15.4] *See, e.g.,* National RR Passenger Corp. v. Certain Temporary Easements Above the RR Right of Way in Providence, RI, 357 F.3d 36, 42 (1st Cir. 2004).

[16] *See, e.g.,* Wilson v. Daimler Chrysler Corp., 236 F.3d 827, 828–829 (7th Cir. 2001) (trial court did not abuse its discretion under Rule 611(a) by granting defendant summary judgment after holding bench trial on causation and finding that plaintiff did not prove that her schizophrenia was caused by sexual harassment, assuming arguendo that harassment had occurred).

[16.1] *See, e.g.,* United States v. Marshall, 307 F.3d 1267, 1269 (10th Cir. 2002) (when defendant belabored arresting officer with absence of particular action from officer's incident report and prosecution offered officer's arrest affidavit as prior consistent statement, court did not abuse its discretion under Rule 611(a) in admitting both affidavit and incident report, which was not otherwise admissible, to clarify officer's testimony about entries in both documents).

[16.2] *See, e.g.,* Toth v. Grand Trunk R.R., 306 F.3d 335, 350 (6th Cir. 2002) (trial court did not abuse its discretion under Rule 611(a) in refusing to take judicial notice of federal regulations, although proper subject for judicial notice, based on grounds of improper foundation and being beyond scope of rebuttal).

reluctant to disturb a trial judge's decision restricting cross-examination since the cold record will not adequately reflect the actual situation in the courtroom. An appellate court will, however, review a judgment carefully if the trial court's efforts to protect a witness from embarrassment by imposing limitations on cross-examination may have affected the outcome of the trial.[17]

[3]—Cross-Examination

[a]—Scope[1]

Rule 611(b) accords with the majority position in the United States by restricting cross-examination to the subject matter of the direct examination and matters affecting the witness's credibility.[2] The rule permits trial courts, in the exercise of their discretion, to permit a cross-examiner to inquire into matters that were not raised in the direct examination, but the cross-examiner must proceed as if asking questions on direct examination.[3]

Trial courts have considerable discretion respecting the determination of the appropriate scope of cross-examination.[4] Their exercise of discretion must, however, be consonant with the rule's objective of promoting the orderly presentation of evidence without restricting relevant inquiry.[5] Moreover, when the trial court

---

[17] *See, e.g.,* United States v. Santos, 201 F.3d 953, 964 (7th Cir. 2000) (trial court abused its discretion under Rule 611(a)(3) by barring cross-examination designed to elicit witness's grudge against defendant for firing witness's lesbian lover, causing break-up of their relationship; although homosexuality is stigmatized by many Americans, this limitation was unnecessary, since witness was openly lesbian and a lesbian activist).

[1] *See* discussion in **Treatise** at § 611.03. The **Treatise** discusses in some detail the minority, English rule, which permits wide-open cross-examination. Rule 611(b) had been drafted as a rule of wide-open cross-examination, but Congress rejected this change. *See* discussion of Congressional Action on Rule 611 in **Treatise** at § 611App.01[2].

[2] United States v. Harris, 185 F.3d 999, 1008 (9th Cir. 1999) (even if government's cross-examination exceeded scope of direct examination, cross-examination on credibility "is often on topics outside the scope of the direct examination, but that is not a reason to exclude inquiry into the [matter].").

[3] Fed. R. Evid. 611(b).

[4] *See, e.g.,* United States v. McLaughlin, 957 F.2d 12, 17–18 (1st Cir. 1992) (no abuse of discretion in prohibiting cross-examination of government agents as to certain matters beyond scope of direct examination that were not related to credibility, since defendant could have called agents as defense witnesses); *see also* Taskett v. Dentlinger, 344 F.3d 1337, 1342 (Fed. Cir. 2003) (under Fed. R. Evid. 611(b), party was properly permitted to ask questions on redirect examination that arguably exceeded scope of cross-examination, because questions were necessary to clarify facts "that were not made sufficiently clear by either cross examination or direct examination").

[5] *See, e.g.,* Elcock v. KMart Corp., 233 F.3d 734, 751–754 (3d Cir. 2000) (trial court did not abuse its discretion under Rule 611 in excluding amount embezzled by expert witness being impeached with embezzlement conviction, even though appellate court would have admitted amount as bearing on witness's credibility).

exercises its discretion to control the scope of cross-examination to protect witnesses from harassment or undue embarrassment, it must do so within the confines of Rule 403.[5.1] Similarly, when the court exercises its discretion to permit the cross-examiner to inquire about matters that were not the subject of the direct examination, it must do so in a fashion that excludes unfairly prejudicial evidence.[5.2]

The trial court also has the power, pursuant to Rule 403, to limit cross-examination that would create prejudice or confusion, or that would be cumulative, even though it satisfies the test of Rule 611(b).[6]

In criminal cases, the court's right to curtail cross-examination is circumscribed by the defendant's Sixth Amendment right of confrontation.[7] The constitutional right to confront adverse witnesses, however, does not negate a district court's discretion to determine the relevance of a particular area of inquiry and the extent of cross-examination to be permitted on the topic.[8] Nevertheless, the court's discretion may be somewhat narrower when the right to confront adverse witnesses is at issue. Defendants must be permitted sufficient cross-examination to develop enough information so the jury can make an adequate assessment of the witness's

---

[5.1] Fed. R. Evid 403; *see, e.g.,* Fraser v. Major League Soccer, L.L.C., 284 F.3d 47, 66 (1st Cir. 2002) (trial court has authority to block impeachment questions that would damage witness's reputations, invade their privacy, or assault their personalities only when evidence's probative value is substantially outweighed by danger of undue prejudice).

[5.2] *See, e.g.,* United States v. Crenshaw, 359 F.3d 977, 1002 (8th Cir. 2004) (trial court abused its discretion in permitting government, under Rule 611, to cross-examine alibi witness concerning defendant's prior criminal convictions when witness did not act as character witness for defendant).

[6] *See, e.g.,* United States v. Spivey, 841 F.2d 799, 803 (7th Cir. 1988) (proper for trial court to limit cross-examination by one defendant when co-defendant had conducted extensive cross-examination on same issue).

[7] *See, e.g.,* United States v. Callahan, 551 F.2d 733, 737 (6th Cir. 1977) (when "court's restriction prevented defense counsel from cross-examining government's chief witness as to his reliability and veracity of his testimony on a required element of the charged offense, the defendant has been denied his Sixth Amendment right of confrontation").

[8] *See, e.g.,* United States v. Green, 305 F.3d 422, 428–429 (6th Cir. 2002) (trial court did not infringe defendant's rights under Confrontation Clause by precluding cross-examination of lawyer when questions went beyond scope of direct examination and of limited waiver of attorney-client privilege that permitted lawyer to give direct testimony).

credibility.[9] Any constitutional error in restricting cross-examination, however, is subject to harmless error analysis.[10]

[b]—Impact of Privilege Against Self-Incrimination[11]

Rule 611(b) is silent about the extent to which the privilege against self-incrimination limits the permissible scope of cross-examination. The question should be resolved by constitutional principles rather than evidentiary concerns about order of proof. The problem arises in civil as well as in criminal cases, and in the case of ordinary witnesses as well as party witnesses, but it is most difficult to solve when the accused takes the stand in a criminal case.

Courts generally assume that the scope of the privilege against self incrimination is determined by the scope of cross-examination permitted by the restrictive approach of Rule 611(b).[12] Consequently, they hold that a defendant taking the stand on his or her own behalf must answer all questions on cross-examination that are "reasonably related" to the subject of the direct examination and to credibility.[13]

Other restrictions may apply to a criminal defendant who chooses not to testify. For example, a criminal defendant who elects not to take the stand cannot claim on appeal that the district court erred in denying the defendant's motion in limine to restrict cross-examination.[14]

A party in a civil action who testifies voluntarily is in a position analogous to

---

[9] *See, e.g.,* United States v. Kone, 307 F.3d 430, (6th Cir. 2002) (trial court cannot limit criminal defendant's cross-examination of government witness designed to show witness is biased because he or she testified under promise or expectation of immunity); United States v. Lankford, 955 F.2d 1545, 1549 (11th Cir. 1992) (reversible error to have prevented defendant from cross-examining witness concerning his sons' drug arrests when such exclusion improperly limited defendant's sixth amendment right to cross-examine for possible bias or motive for testifying).

[10] *See, e.g.,* United States v. Turner, 198 F.3d 425, 430 (4th Cir. 1999) (although trial court erred in limiting cross-examination of witness regarding motive, error was harmless in light of other, overwhelming, evidence against defendant).

[11] *See* discussion in **Treatise** at § 611.04[1].

[12] *See, e.g.,* United States v. Ellis, 951 F.2d 580, 584 (4th Cir. 1991) ("A defendant who testifies waives his Fifth Amendment privilege in all areas subject to proper cross-examination").

[13] *See, e.g.,* United States v. Raper, 676 F.2d 841, 846 (D.C. Cir. 1982) ("any question which would have elicited testimony that was reasonably related to the inferences that might reasonably be drawn from his direct testimony would have been permissible"); United States v. Beechum, 582 F.2d 898, 907–909 (5th Cir. 1978) (en banc) (defendant's denial of unlawful intent on direct waived his privilege against self-incrimination at least to extent of cross-examination relevant to issues raised by his testimony; he could therefore be cross-examined about other crimes evidence that was admissible pursuant to Rule 404(b) as negativing innocent intent).

[14] Luce v. United States, 469 U.S. 38, 40, 105 S. Ct. 460, 462 83 L. Ed. 2d 443 (1984).

that of an accused who voluntarily takes the stand in a criminal case.[15] The civil party waives the privilege, at least as to matters relevant to direct examination, and risks sanctions for a refusal to testify. Moreover, unlike the situation in a criminal case, even the proper exercise of the privilege by a civil party may warrant the jury's drawing an adverse inference against that party.[16]

The position of the non-party witness is somewhat different. If subpoenaed, a non-party has no right to refuse to testify without being subject to contempt. Consequently, a non-party witness generally does not waive the privilege against self-incrimination by merely taking the stand. Such a witness has the right to claim the privilege if the answers sought may tend to be incriminating.

If on cross-examination a witness successfully claims the privilege against self-incrimination and does not answer proper questions fully, the court must strike the direct testimony if the witness's exercise of the privilege has deprived the cross-examiner of the ability to test the truth of the witness's direct testimony.[17] In certain cases of extreme prejudice, however, merely striking the direct testimony is an insufficient remedy and a mistrial may be necessary.[18] Courts may deny a motion to strike if they properly find that the direct testimony involved "collateral" matters.[19] They may also do so if the unanswered questions constitute an insignificant portion of the cross-examination.[20]

In criminal cases the government may grant a witness use immunity to obtain testimony. The courts have not recognized a defendant's right to demand that defense witnesses receive use immunity, at least so long as the government is not using its grant such immunity selectively and unfairly.[21]

---

[15] *See, e.g.,* Brown v. United States, 356 U.S. 148, 154–155 78 S. Ct. 622, 626 2 L. Ed. 2d 589 (1958).

[16] *See, e.g.,* Baxter v. Palmigiano, 425 U.S. 308, 316, 96 S. Ct. 1551, 1557 47 L. Ed. 2d 810 (1976).

[17] *See, e.g.,* Fountain v. United States, 384 F.2d 624, 628 (5th Cir. 1967).

[18] *See, e.g.,* Toolate v. Borg, 828 F.2d 571, 572 (9th Cir. 1987) (trial court struck testifying co-defendant's testimony when defendant was prevented from cross-examining him, but should have granted mistrial; error was harmless).

[19] *See, e.g.,* United States v. Yip, 930 F.2d 142, 147 (2d Cir. 1991) (subject of unanswered questions concerned a matter not raised on direct and was thus a collateral matter bearing solely on witness's credibility).

[20] *See, e.g.,* United States v. Seifert, 648 F.2d 557, 561 (9th Cir. 1980) (only one question was unanswered over course of lengthy cross-examination).

[21] *See, e.g.,* United States v. Mahney, 949 F.2d 1397, 1401 (6th Cir. 1991) (majority of circuits have rejected theory that trial court may grant immunity for defense witnesses, but government's selective grants of immunity could violate due process).

[4]—Leading Questions[1]

Rule 611(c) codifies the traditional practice concerning leading questions. It acknowledges that: (1) they are generally undesirable on direct examination,[1.1] (2) they are usually permissible on cross-examination, and (3) there are exceptions to both of those rules.[1.2]

Although it is not explicit on this point, the rule implies what has in fact long been the case, that the matter falls within the trial court's discretion.[2] Reversals on the basis of the trial court's refusal to require counsel to comply with Rule 611(c) are exceedingly rare.[3] Such error probably occurs most frequently in criminal cases, when a prosecutor, in the guise of asking leading questions, brings prohibited material to the attention of the jury.[4]

Rule 611(c) does not specify what makes a question "leading." The term is, however, well recognized in case law as a question that "so suggests to the witness the specific tenor of the reply desired by counsel that such a reply is likely to be given irrespective of an actual memory."[5] The tenor of the desired reply can be suggested in a number of ways, as, for example, by the form of the question, by emphasis on certain words, by the tone or nonverbal conduct of the examiner, or by the inclusion of facts still in controversy or as to which no evidence has been produced. Because of these myriad ways in which a suggestion can be conveyed, only the judge actually presiding at the trial is in a position to assess fully the impact of the question on the witness and the effect of any impropriety on the conduct of the litigation. The trial judge also has full discretion to decide whether the questioner may rephrase a question after an objection has been sustained on the ground

---

[1] *See* discussion in **Treatise** at § 611.06.

[1.1] *See, e.g.,* United States v. Grassrope, 342 F.3d 866, 869 (8th Cir. 2003) (whether counsel may use leading questions is within trial court's discretion; leading questions are frequently necessary to develop direct testimony of sexual assault victims, particularly children).

[1.2] *See, e.g.,* United States v. Smith, 378 F.3d 754, 756 (8th Cir. 2004) ("Generally, leading questions are best reserved for cross examination. However, leading questions may properly be used on direct examination with certain witnesses—such as an adverse party or a potentially hostile witness.").

[2] *See, e.g.,* United States v. Nambo-Barajas, 338 F.3d 956, 959–960 (8th Cir. 2003) (trial court did not abuse its discretion in permitting prosecution to develop testimony of witnesses with mental disabilities through leading questions).

[3] *See, e.g.,* Sanders v. New York City Human Resources Admin., 361 F.3d 749, 757 (2d Cir. 2004) (Rule 611's preference for non-leading questions on direct examination is purely precatory; trial court has very large amount of discretion in overseeing examination of witnesses).

[4] *See, e.g.,* United States v. Meeker, 558 F.2d 387, 389 (7th Cir. 1977) (permitting leading questions was improper when they implied prior misconduct and suggested that defendant had engaged in conduct for which he was not on trial, and thereby violated Rule 404(b)).

[5] United States v. Durham, 319 F.2d 590, 592 (4th Cir. 1963).

that it was leading.[6]

Rule 611(c) acknowledges that leading questions may be necessary to develop the testimony of a particular witness. Among the situations in which the court is most likely to permit leading questions are the following:

- A witness with less than a normal adult's mental capacity.[7]

- A witness who has difficulty testifying.[8]

- A witness who becomes evasive and unresponsive at a critical point in the testimony.[8.1]

- A witness whose memory is exhausted.[9]

- Testimony related to undisputed matters.[10]

If the witness is hostile to the examiner, there is no reason to prohibit leading questions since there is no danger of false suggestion. Accordingly, Rule 611(c) provides that interrogation may be by leading questions when a party calls a hostile witness, an adverse party, or a witness identified with an adverse party.[11] To show that the witness is hostile, the examiner will have to demonstrate the requisite degree of hostility, bias, or reluctance to the court's satisfaction.[12] As to an adverse party or a witness identified with an adverse party, leading questions are permitted once the examiner has made a sufficient showing of the witness's status.[13]

The second sentence of subdivision (c) states the traditional view that leading

---

[6] *See, e.g.,* United States v. Noone, 913 F.2d 20, 37 (1st Cir. 1990) (no abuse of discretion in allowing prosecutor to rephrase leading question and continue with examination).

[7] *See, e.g.,* United States v. Archdale, 229 F.3d 861, 865–866 (9th Cir. 2000) (direct examination of child witness is recognized exception to rule against leading questions).

[8] *See, e.g.,* United States v. Grassrope, 342 F.3d 866, 869 (8th Cir. 2003) (information concerning details of sexual assaults must often be elicited from victims of those crimes through leading questions).

[8.1] *See, e.g.,* United States v. Mora-Higuera, 269 F.3d 905, 912 (8th Cir. 2001) (no plain error in allowing leading questions when prosecution witness "became evasive and unclear" about types of drugs involved in conspiracy for which defendant was on trial).

[9] *See, e.g.,* Beckel v. Wal-Mart Assocs, Inc., 301 F.3d 621, 624 (7th Cir. 2002) (leading questions are appropriate on direct examination if witness has exhausted his or her memory).

[10] *See, e.g.,* United States v. Schepp, 746 F.2d 406, 410 (8th Cir. 1984) (leading questions were proper respecting preliminary and collateral matters to expedite the trial).

[11] Fed. R. Evid. 611(c).

[12] *See, e.g.,* United States v. Carboni, 204 F.3d 39, 44–45 (2d Cir. 2000) (trial court had discretion under to allow prosecution to use leading questions on direct examination of witness who continually evaded non-leading questions).

[13] *See, e.g.,* United States v. Hicks, 748 F.2d 854, 859 (4th Cir. 1984) (not abuse of discretion to allow prosecution to ask leading questions of defendant's girlfriend who was called as a government witness, since she was identified with adverse party).

questions may usually be asked on cross-examination as a matter of right, but that the right is not absolute. When the witness is biased in favor of the cross-examiner, the same danger of leading questions arises as on direct and the court may, in its discretion, prohibit their use.[14] The Advisory Committee noted two circumstances in which the prohibition may be applied: (1) when a party is "cross-examined by his counsel after having been called by his opponent," and (2) when an "insured defendant proves to be friendly to the plaintiff."[15]

§ 2.03 Rulings on Evidence—Rule 103

[1]—Preservation of Error in Admissibility Rulings[1]

Rule 103 establishes two major ground rules in connection with appellate review of trial court rulings on the admissibility of evidence: (1) the initiative for raising and preserving error in the admission or exclusion of evidence lies with the litigants at the trial court level, and (2) the appellate court reviewing the trial court's evidentiary rulings is not to reverse the lower court's decision on purely technical grounds, but to rectify only errors that affect substantial rights of the parties.

Appellate courts generally review a trial court's determination concerning evidence admissibility questions for abuse of discretion when the claim of error is properly preserved.[1.1] The Eighth Circuit, however, has noted that, while it is appropriate for an appellate court to accord deference to a trial court's evidentiary determinations when they involve a balancing of factors, in other circumstances the trial court's interpretation and application of the Rules of Evidence are matters of law, and should be reviewed de novo.[1.2]

To preserve error properly when the trial court's ruling admits evidence, the complaining party must be able to show the appellate court that its timely objection to the evidence or motion to strike it appears of record and that the objection or motion to strike states the specific ground of objection if the specific ground for objection is not otherwise apparent.[1.3] If the trial court's ruling excludes evidence,

---

[14] *See, e.g.,* Ardoin v. J. Ray McDermott & Co., 684 F.2d 335, 336 (5th Cir. 1982) (trial court has power to require party cross-examining friendly witness to employ non-leading questions; per se rule that employer cross-examining its own employees must use non-leading questions is inappropriate).

[15] Fed. R. Evid. 611(c) Advisory Committee's Note (1972) (reproduced verbatim in **Treatise** at § 611.App.01[2]).

[1] *See* discussion in **Treatise** at § 103.02–103.22.

[1.1] *See, e.g.,* United States v. Trujillo, 376 F.3d 593, 605 (6th Cir. 2004) (determinations under Fed. R. Evid. 404(b); United States v. Tse, 375 F.3d 148, 155 (1st Cir. 2004).

[1.2] United States v. Blue Bird, 372 F.3d 989, 991 (8th Cir. 2004).

[1.3] *See, e.g.,* United States v. Mitchell, 365 F.3d 215, 257 (3d Cir. 2004) (defendant's failure to include hearsay as ground for objection resulted in his failure to preserve that ground for appeal).

the complaining party must be able to show the appellate court that it made the substance of the evidence known to the trial court through an offer of proof on the record or that it was otherwise apparent from the context in which the evidence was offered.

Rule 103 governs civil and criminal cases, and jury as well as non-jury trials. In criminal cases, because of constitutional guarantees, certain errors in the admission or exclusion of evidence may at times, though rarely, be raised by collateral attack when similar errors would not be subject to collateral attack in civil cases.[2] Rule 103 is applicable both when an appellate court reviews a decision of an inferior court and when a trial court rules on a motion for a new trial.[3]

The rule provides:

Rule 103.   Rulings on Evidence.

(a) Effect of erroneous ruling.—Error may not be predicated upon a ruling which admits or excludes evidence unless a substantial right of the party is affected, and

(1) Objection.—In case the ruling is one admitting evidence, a timely objection or motion to strike appears of record, stating the specific ground of objection, if the specific ground was not apparent from the context; or

(2) Offer of proof.—In case the ruling is one excluding evidence, the substance of the evidence was made known to the court by offer or was apparent from the context within which questions were asked.

Once the court makes a definitive ruling on the record admitting or excluding evidence, either at or before trial, a party need not renew an objection or offer of proof to preserve a clam of error for appeal.

(b) Record of offer and ruling.—The court may add any other or further statement which shows the character of the evidence, the form in which it was offered, the objection made, and the ruling thereon. It may direct the making of an offer in question and answer form.

(c) Hearing of jury.—In jury cases, proceedings shall be conducted, to the extent practicable, so as to prevent inadmissible evidence from being suggested to the jury by any means, such as making statements or offers of proof or asking questions in the hearing of the jury.

---

[2] *See, e.g.,* Kimmelman v. Morrison, 477 U.S. 365, 371–380 106 S. Ct. 2574, 91 L. Ed. 2d 305 (1986).

[3] *See, e.g.,* Badami v. Flood, 214 F.3d 994, 998 (8th Cir. 2000) (when proffering party does not make offer of proof, trial court's error in excluding evidence is not proper ground for granting new trial).

> (d) Plain error.—Nothing in this rule precludes taking notice of plain errors affecting substantial rights although they were not brought to the attention of the court.
>
> *[Adopted Jan. 2, 1975, effective July 1, 1975; amended Apr. 17, 2000, effective Dec. 1, 2000.]*

Subdivisions (a)(1) and (a)(2) of Rule 103 specify in some detail the information that the parties must include in their objections to a trial court's evidentiary rulings. However, the rule is silent as to the factors a court must consider in determining whether substantial rights have been affected. This silence suggests that the determination is to be made in light of the record in the case as a whole, and indicates that the court must proceed on a case-by-case basis rather than apply a mechanical rule.

Prior to the 2000 amendment to Rule 103, in some circuits it was necessary for parties to make their objections or offers of proof at the trial; pretrial rulings, no matter how definitive, were not sufficient to preserve error. The 2000 amendments eliminated the necessity for renewed objections or offers of proof when the trial court rules definitively on the record, either before or at trial, that proffered evidence is admissible or inadmissible.[4]

Although plain error is the only class of error explicitly mentioned in Rule 103, the rule deals with three categories of error well recognized in statutory law and judicial opinion. "Harmless error" is error raised in the trial court that does not affect substantial rights. "Prejudicial" or "reversible" error is error raised in the trial court that does affect substantial rights. "Plain error" is error not raised in the trial court, but nevertheless considered by a reviewing court, that affects substantial rights. The distinction between harmless and reversible error thus turns on whether the error affected substantial rights, and the distinction between harmless and plain error turns on whether the circumstances under which the particular error in the case at hand was committed excuse the party's failure to bring it properly to the trial court's attention.

[2]—Objections to Admission of Evidence[1]

[a]—Timely Objection or Motion to Strike Must Appear on Record With Ground for Objection

Rule 103(a)(1) provides that error in the admission of evidence cannot be predicated on a ruling admitting evidence unless "a timely objection or motion to strike appears of record stating the specific ground of objection." As a result, if the

[4] *See* [4], *below.*
[1] *See* discussion in **Treatise** at §§ 103.10–103.14.

appellant did not make a timely and specific objection or motion to strike at trial, there can generally be no claim of error in the court's ruling admitting the evidence.[2] Alternatively, if the trial court ruled definitively on the record during pretrial proceedings that proffered evidence was admissible over a properly tendered objection, the objecting party's claim of error is preserved for appeal, even in the absence of an objection when the evidence is tendered at trial.[3]

Calling the trial court's attention to its error provides the court an opportunity to correct the error, which might obviate the need for further proceedings.[4] In addition, a properly phrased objection may provide both the court and the opposing party with the opportunity to correct deficiencies in foundational evidence.[5]

[b]—Failure to Make Timely Objection or Motion to Strike Constitutes Waiver

By failing to object to evidence at trial, a party waives the right to raise admissibility issues on appeal.[6] Preservation of error in the admission of evidence requires only a timely objection or a timely motion to strike, not both and objection and a motion to strike.[6.1] Rule 103 eliminates the necessity for the opponent to object when the evidence is offered at trial if the trial court has made a definitive pretrial ruling on the record that the evidence is admissible.[6.2] However, an

---

[2] *See, e.g.,* United States v. Duffaut, 314 F.3d 203, 209 (5th Cir. 2002) (complaining party waives right to abuse of discretion review of trial court's decision admitting testimony by not renewing objection at trial when trial court did not rule on pretrial objections; appellate court reviews admission of evidence under such circumstances for plain error only).

[3] Fed. R. Evid. 103.

[4] *See, e.g.,* United States v. Del Rosario, 388 F.3d 1, 10 (1st Cir. 2004).

[5] *See, e.g.,* Brookover v. Mary Hitchcock Memorial Hosp., 893 F.2d 411, 413–415 (1st Cir. 1990) (if defendant had made timely and explicit objection, stating that out-of-court statement was not admissible as admission by party-opponent because of lack of foundation under Rule 801(d)(2)(D), proponent might have presented personnel records to establish employment); United States v. Kragness, 830 F.2d 842, 868 (8th Cir. 1987) (objection that government was asking "loaded question" was insufficient to raise issue that testimony was without foundation; had opponent made such an objection, voir dire examination of witness might have established proper foundation).

[6] Bowman, v. Corrections Corp. of Am., 350 F.3d 537, 548 (6th Cir. 2003) (plaintiff's failure to object to witness's habit testimony waived plaintiff's right to complain about its admission on appeal); *see also* Densberger v. United Techs. Corp., 283 F.3d 110, 119 n.10 (2d Cir. 2002) (when plaintiff's expert testified without objection that prudent manufacturer would know what tests to run on its products, defendant forfeited objection).

[6.1] *See, e.g.,* United States v. Meserve, 271 F.3d 314, 325 (1st Cir. 2001) ("Because Rule 103 is written in the disjunctive, the right to review may be preserved either by objecting or by moving to strike and offering specific grounds in support of that motion").

[6.2] Fed. R. Evid. 103(a); *see, e.g.,* Zachar v. Lee, 363 F.3d 70, 75 (1st Cir.2004) (plaintiff's inartful objection at trial to admission of appraisal report did not waive error by failing to point to specific portions of report that were not admissible, because trial court's pretrial ruling denying

opponent's complete failure to assert an objection in the lower court waives that party's right to assert that the admission of the evidence was erroneous unless the error was plain and adversely affected the opponent's substantial rights.[7]

Thus, the decision whether to object should not be taken lightly. Although Rule 103(d) permits appellate courts to relieve a party of the consequences of a failure to object in the case of "plain error" that affects substantial rights, appellate courts often discern strategic patterns that underlie a decision not to object to evidence that might have appeared to have had a beneficial potential when it was offered but that, in retrospect, appears to have been harmful. They are extremely reluctant to consider errors in the admission of evidence when they suspect that the failure to object was attributable to legitimate trial tactics that failed to achieve the desired result.[8]

Counsel can also waive the right to assert on appeal an error in the admission of evidence by deliberately eliciting[9] or relying on it,[10] or by inadvertently eliciting it and failing immediately to move to strike it.[11] A party does not, however, invite error by merely cross-examining a witness who has already testified to objectionable evidence in an attempt to lessen its impact.[11.1] Waiver resulting from a failure to object or to move to strike evidence in a timely fashion has been found even

plaintiff's motion in limine explored all grounds for excluding report).

[7] *See, e.g.,* United States v. Diaz, 300 F.3d 66, 74–76 (1st Cir. 2002) (party's failure to object to expert testimony on reliability grounds waives right to complain about admission of testimony, absent plain error affecting party's substantial rights).

[8] *See, e.g.,* Polack v. Commissioner, 366 F.3d 608, 612 (8th Cir. 2004) (in offer of proof, proponent must "express precisely the substance of the excluded evidence" to inform both trial and appellate courts why exclusion of evidence was prejudicial error); United States v. Coonan, 938 F.2d 1553, 1561 (2d Cir. 1991) (in racketeering prosecution, defendant's failure to object to evidence of criminal activity by other enterprise members that occurred before defendant joined enterprise waived any error in admission of that evidence; defendant appeared to welcome that evidence at trial and was now "attempting to evade the consequences of an unsuccessful tactical decision").

[9] *See, e.g.,* Ohler v. United States, 529 U.S. 753, 755, 120 S. Ct. 1851, 1855, 146 L. Ed. 2d 826 (2000) (defendant who preemptively introduced prior conviction, after court granted prosecution's motion in limine to admit it, was barred from challenging its admission on appeal); Price v. Kramer, 200 F.3d 1237, 1250 (9th Cir. 2000) (parties "may not seek reversal on the basis of their own evidentiary errors").

[10] *See, e.g.,* United States v. Huerta-Orosco, 340 F.3d 601, 604 (8th Cir. 2003) (defendant waived his objection to evidence of his immigration status when he relied on it during direct examination).

[11] *See, e.g.,* United States v. Cabrera, 201 F.3d 1243, 1248–1249 (9th Cir. 2000) (when witness on cross-examination gives answer that contains objectionable material that might be characterized as unresponsive, counsel must move to strike objectionable matter immediately to preserve error; "error that is caused by the actions of the complaining party will cause reversal only in the most exceptional situation [when] reversal is necessary to preserve the integrity of the judicial process or to prevent a miscarriage of justice.").

[11.1] Elsayed v. California State Univ., Hayward, 299 F.3d 1053, 1063 n.6 (9th Cir. 2002).

when the alleged error involved a defendant's constitutional rights.[12]

[c]—Timing of Objection or Motion to Strike

An objection or motion to strike must be timely.[13] An objection or motion to strike is "timely" if it is made as soon as the opponent knows, or should know, that the objection is applicable.[14]

Some objections may have to be raised even before trial, such as motions for the suppression of evidence obtained through an illegal search or seizure[15] or as the result of a tainted out-of-court identification,[16] and objections relating to depositions,[17] In criminal cases, there should be a pretrial hearing at which the trial court can hear and determine any motions to suppress.

Some evidentiary issues are factually complex and their resolution will necessarily be quite time consuming. These issues should usually be determined in pretrial in limine hearings, to comply with Rule 103(c)'s provision that inadmissible evidence should not be suggested to the jury and to avoid wasting the jury's time with a lengthy recess. Many courts have held that, for example, reliability issues concerning proffered expert testimony should ordinarily be the subject of pretrial in limine hearings.[18]

---

[12] *See, e.g.,* Shaw v. United States, 403 F.2d 528, 530 (8th Cir. 1968) ("[B]arring plain error, we will not notice errors raised for the first time in the appellate court, including errors involving a defendant's constitutional right").

[13] *See, e.g.,* United States v. Meserve, 271 F.3d 314, 325 (1st Cir. 2001) (to preserve evidentiary issue for review, objection of party opposing admission must be timely); Christopher v. Cutter Labs, 53 F.3d 1184, 1192 (11th Cir. 1995) (timely objection necessary to preserve issue for appeal).

[14] *See* United States v. Carson, 52 F.3d 1173, 1187 (2d Cir. 1995) (objection is timely if it is brought to attention of court and opposing party at earliest possible time to alert court concerning proper course of action and to enable counsel to take proper corrective measures); United States v. Moore, 923 F.2d 910, 915 (1st Cir. 1991) (general motion to strike evidence at close of case not sufficient when no objection or motion to strike made at time evidence was offered).

[15] Fed. R. Crim. P. 12(b), Fed. R. Crim. P. 12(f); *see* 24 MOORE'S FEDERAL PRACTICE, Ch. 612, *Pleadings and Motions Before Trial; Defenses and Objections* (Matthew Bender 3d ed.).

[16] *See* United States v. Wade, 388 U.S. 218, 87 S. Ct. 1926, 18 L. Ed. 2d 1149 (1967).

[17] *See* Fed. R. Civ. P. 32(b); 7 MOORE'S FEDERAL PRACTICE, Ch. 32, *Use of Depositions in Court Procedures* (Matthew Bender 3d ed.).

[18] *See, e.g.,* Pride v. BIC Corp., 218 F.3d 566, 578 (6th Cir. 2000) (trial court properly excluded expert testimony after pretrial evidentiary hearing); Goebel v. Denver & Rio Grande Western R.R., 215 F.3d 1083, 1087 (10th Cir. 2000) ("[t]he most common method for fulfilling this function [of gatekeeper for expert testimony] is a *Daubert* hearing"); Padillas v. Stork-Gamco, Inc., 186 F.3d 412, 417–418 (3d Cir. 1999) (Third Circuit has strong preference for pretrial hearings respecting reliability of expert testimony, even if neither party requests one, whenever bases for proposed expert witness's opinion "are insufficiently explained and the reasons and foundations for them inadequately and perhaps confusingly explicated."); United States v. Sinskey, 119 F.3d 712, 717

The 2000 amendment to Rule 103 makes it clear that an objecting party can rely on a trial court's definitive ruling on the record at a pretrial in limine hearing to preserve error.[19]

The requirement of a timely objection means that counsel cannot gamble on letting inadmissible evidence in as long as it is favorable, and beginning to object only when the evidence becomes unfavorable. For instance, if a witness gives testimony that is inadmissible under the hearsay rule, opposing counsel cannot remain silent while the witness gives helpful testimony, and then object on the basis of hearsay once the witness gives damaging testimony.[20] Such silence is apt to be interpreted as a waiver of any objection.[21]

Speed and alertness of counsel are essential. Once the answer to an improper question has been given, the court is likely to rule that the objection came too late.[22] In appropriate circumstances, however, a later objection may be considered sufficiently timely to preserve the issue for appeal. Thus, a later objection adequately preserves the admissibility question for appeal when:

- The objecting party had previously made the same objection to numerous similar questions.[23]

- The questioning party was attempting to elicit inadmissible evidence through a non-responsive answer to a facially unobjectionable question.[24]

- The objecting party could not have been aware of the ground for the objection until after the witness gave the inadmissible evidence.[25]

(8th Cir. 1997) (trial court properly admitted expert testimony it found reliable during pretrial evidentiary hearing).

[19] *See* [4], *below.*

[20] *See, e.g.,* United States Aviation Underwriters, Inc. v. Olympia Wings, Inc., 896 F.2d 949, 956 (5th Cir. 1990); Willco Kuwait (Trading) S.A.K. v. De Savary, 843 F.2d 618, 624 (1st Cir. 1988).

[21] *See* [b], *above.*

[22] *See, e.g.,* Hutchinson v. Groskin, 927 F.2d 722, 725 (2d Cir. 1991) (general principle is that objection should be made after question has been asked but before answer has been given).

[23] *See, e.g.,* Hutchinson v. Groskin, 927 F.2d 722, 725 (2d Cir. 1991) (objection to hearsay testimony of expert was timely although made after witness answered; same objection had previously been made and overruled and trial court was familiar with its basis).

[24] *See, e.g.,* United States v. Pallais, 921 F.2d 684, 688–689 (7th Cir. 1990) (objection to government witness's hearsay testimony was sufficient to preserve issue for appeal when it was made before witness completed his answer or gave part of answer that was damaging to defendant; question literally called only for yes or no answer, neither of which would have been hearsay, and prosecutor obviously wanted witness to give hearsay evidence in response to question).

[25] *See, e.g.,* United States v. Meserve, 271 F.3d 314, 324–325 (1st Cir. 2001) (defendant's objection on ground that impeachment by evidence of 20-year-old conviction for disorderly conduct

[d]—Form of Objection or Motion to Strike

Rule 103(a)(1) requires that an objection or motion to strike state "the specific ground of objection." The timeliness requirement, however, frequently requires counsel to state the objection before the jury hears the objectionable evidence.[26] Counsel are afforded some leeway because trial courts recognize that the short period of time between when a question is asked and when it is answered may not be sufficient time for a thorough analysis of the errors that admission of the answer might entail.

General objections, such as "I object" or "incompetent, irrelevant and immaterial" will not usually satisfy the specificity requirement unless the ground for exclusion is obvious to the court and to opposing counsel,[27] or unless the basis for the objection is that the evidence is not relevant under Rule 401.

Under Rule 103(a), the objecting party must state all grounds for objection other than lack of relevance with specificity. If the trial court overrules a general objection and the objecting party should have made a specific objection, the objecting party is precluded from asserting the proper objection on appeal.[28] A specific objection made on the wrong grounds and overruled similarly precludes a party from raising a specific objection on other, tenable grounds on appeal.[29] An improper specific objection made when the objectionable question was asked should not, however, preclude preservation of error by a subsequent motion to strike the answer on a different ground made while the witness is still on the stand, since the policy of encouraging the elimination of error in the trial court is forwarded by permitting a motion to strike while the witness is still testifying.

If the trial court errs in overruling a specific objection and admits the proffered

---

was improper under Rule 609, made as soon as defendant learned of nature of conviction, was not untimely).

[26] See [c], above.

[27] See, e.g., United States v. Diaz, 300 F.3d 66, 75–76 (1st Cir. 2002) (defendant's objection to expert testimony, referring only to *Daubert* re competency to render the opinion in question failed to specify flaws with witness's methodology and application of that methodology to facts of case, especially since defendant's pretrial objection was limited to witness's qualifications); United States v. Haywood, 280 F.3d 715, 725 (6th Cir. 2002) (when defendant objected to other acts evidence on grounds of relevance and prejudice and government argued evidence was admissible under Rule 404(b), basis for defendant's objection was evident from context and Rule 404(b) objection was preserved for appeal).

[28] See, e.g., Bandera v. City of Quincy, 344 F.3d 47, 54 (1st Cir. 2003) (defendant's general objections without grounds, intermingled with objections on grounds of relevance and "time frame," did not preserve error in admission of lay opinion testimony).

[29] See, e.g., Diefenbach v. Sheridan Transp., Inc., 229 F.3d 27, 29 (1st Cir. 2000) (objection to expert witness's qualifications does not preserve objection that witness's opinion lacks reliability under *Daubert v. Merrell Dow Pharms, Inc.*, 509 U.S. 579, 591, 113 S. Ct. 2786, 125 L. Ed. 2d 469 (1993)); Shaw v. AAA Eng'g & Drafting, Inc., 213 F.3d 519, 537 (10th Cir. 2000).

evidence, the appellate court may permit the proponent of the evidence to advance a theory of admissibility that was never argued at trial, and on which the trial court never ruled.[30]

In all cases, objecting counsel should be prepared to explain to the court—if the court requests an explanation or obviously does not see the point—precisely how the admission of the evidence in question would transgress a rule of evidence. The explanation should be brief and to the point. Often it is sufficient to cite a Rule of Evidence by number.

[3]—Objections to Exclusion of Evidence[1]

[a]—Offer of Proof is Generally Necessary

Rule 103(a)(2) provides that error may not be predicated on a ruling excluding evidence unless the judge was informed of the substance of the evidence by an offer of proof, or could ascertain the substance from the context of the questions asked. As the Fifth Circuit has bluntly put it, "this circuit will not even consider the propriety of the decision to exclude the evidence at issue, if no offer of proof was made at trial."[2]

Rule 103 makes a pretrial offer of proof effective to preserve error in the exclusion of evidence without a renewal during the trial, so long as the trial court's ruling was definitive and on the record.[3] No offer of proof is necessary, either before the trial or when the evidence is offered, if the court has been apprised of the substance of the evidence and the basis on which it is admissible.[4]

The failure to make an offer of proof may be excused when it would be futile and would only result in an unseemly argument with the court, e.g., when the trial

---

[30] *See, e.g.,* United States v. Paradies, 98 F.3d 1266, 1290 (11th Cir. 1996) (no error in admitting evidence, even if reason for admission given by trial court is invalid, if evidence was properly admissible on other grounds); United States v. Williams, 837 F.2d 1009, 1012–1013 (11th Cir. 1988) (citing **Treatise,** when evidence was erroneously admitted pursuant to business records exception, proponent could rely on another hearsay exception admission theory on appeal; grounds for admissibility relied on at trial and on appeal serve same purpose, to permit introduction of evidence of out-of-court statements to prove the truth of the matter asserted; court distinguished such situations and those based "on a theory wholly unrelated to the ground advanced at trial").

[1] *See* discussion in **Treatise** at §§ 103.20–103.22.

[2] United States v. Winkle, 587 F.2d 705, 710 (5th Cir. 1979); *see also* Badami v. Flood, 214 F.3d 994, 998 (8th Cir. 2000) (party offering evidence must make offer of proof on record to preserve error in trial court's exclusion of evidence).

[3] Fed. R. Evid. 103(a); *see, e.g.,* United States v. McDermott, 245 F.3d 133, 140 n.3 (2d Cir. 2001).

[4] *See, e.g.,* Searles v. Van Bebber, 251 F.3d 869, 977 n.4 (10th Cir. 2001) (when record of parties' arguments shows substance of proffered evidence was conveyed to court, no further offer of proof is necessary).

judge prevents a formal offer.[5] Prompt filing of a written proffer may be helpful if the trial judge is uncooperative.

[b]—Offer Must Reveal Substance of Evidence and Ground for Admission

There are four traditional ways to make an offer of proof: (1) examining the witness on the record in the absence of the jury; (2) counsel's oral statement about the proposed testimony (which is the least favored approach); (3) counsel's written statement describing the proposed testimony in detail; and (4) the witness's signed, written statement describing the proposed testimony.[6]

However, a "formal proffer" need not always be made.[7] The proponent of the excluded evidence only has to have made known the substance of the proffered evidence and the grounds for its admissibility in sufficient detail to permit the trial court to determine whether the evidence would be admissible, and to permit the appellate court to assess the impact of the ruling in the process of determining whether the exclusion of the evidence constituted reversible error.[8]

When the record discloses sufficient information to permit both the trial and appellate courts to fulfill each of those respective functions, no further offer of proof is necessary.[9] Moreover, the party complaining about the exclusion of the evidence need not be the party who made the offer of proof. One party can take advantage on appeal of another party's effective offer of proof.[10]

---

[5] *See, e.g.,* Moss v. Ole South Real Estate, Inc., 933 F.2d 1300, 1310–1311, n.10 (5th Cir. 1991) (plaintiffs' failure to make offer of proof concerning witness's testimony would not preclude review of trial court's exclusion of testimony when trial judge refused to hear proffer).

[6] United States v. Adams, 271 F.3d 1236, 1241–1242 (10th Cir. 2001).

[7] *See, e.g.,* Okai v. Verfuth, 275 F.3d 606, 611–612 (7th Cir. 2001) ("Although a party need not make a formal offer of proof, he must at a minimum make known to the trial judge the substance of the evidence he hopes to present."); Tiller v. Baghdady, 244 F.3d 9, 13 n.3 (1st Cir. 2001) (proponent's offer of proof need not be in writing to preserve error in exclusion of evidence).

[8] *See, e.g.,* Polack v. Commissioner, 366 F.3d 608, 612 (8th Cir. 2004) (in offer of proof, proponent must "express precisely the substance of the excluded evidence" to inform both trial and appellate courts why exclusion of evidence was prejudicial error); United States v. Thompson, 279 F.3d 1043, 1047 (D.C. Cir. 2002) (when defendant offered evidence of out-of-court statements and court sustained hearsay objection, defendant's failure to inform court that statements were offered for non-hearsay purpose of showing declarant's state of mind resulted in appellate court's review of exclusion of evidence only for plain error).

[9] *See, e.g.,* Okai v. Verfuth, 275 F.3d 606, 611–612 (7th Cir. 2001) ("Although a party need not make a formal offer of proof, he must at a minimum make known to the trial judge the substance of the evidence he hopes to present"); Searles v. Van Bebber, 251 F.3d 869, 977 n.4 (10th Cir. 2001) (when record of parties' arguments shows substance of proffered evidence was conveyed to court, no further offer of proof is necessary).

[10] *See, e.g.,* United States v. Davis, 261 F.3d 1, 40–41 (1st Cir. 2001) (defendant who did not offer excluded evidence may take advantage of co-defendant's effective offer of proof on appeal;

In making an offer of proof, counsel must specify the evidence in question.[11] The proffering party must also articulate in his or her offer of proof every discrete ground on which the evidence is admissible.[12] On the other hand, when the trial court rules that specific evidence a party has offered as relevant to issues of liability is not admissible for any purpose, it is not necessary for that party to reoffer the same evidence respecting a subsidiary issue, such as whether there should be an award of punitive damages and, if so, how much they should be, to preserve the issue of admissibility for those purposes.[13]

[c]—Offer Must Be on Record

For error to be preserved, the proffering party's disclosure of the necessary information to the trial court and the trial court's ruling excluding the evidence must appear of record.[14] Moreover, the absence of an adequate record will make reversal for plain error extremely unlikely.[15]

Many problems are avoided if the trial court informs the parties of the ground on which it is sustaining a general objection, or on which of several urged specific grounds it is sustaining a specific objection. If the trial judge does not do so, the burden is on the proponent to request such a ruling. In addition, if the trial court has been unclear in explaining the ground for its decision to admit or exclude evidence, the appellate court can sometimes avoid a reversal and the resulting new trial by remanding to the district court for a hearing on the admissibility of the

---

Rule 103(a)(2) only requires that trial court be aware of nature of evidence and purpose of offer, not that appellant be party that made trial court aware of those matters).

[11] *See, e.g.,* United States v. Rettenberger, 344 F.3d 702, 706 (7th Cir. 2003) (trial court properly precluded defendant from presenting expert testimony not disclosed in discovery when, among other things, lack of disclosure kept trial court from knowing substance of expert's proposed testimony).

[12] *See, e.g.,* Reese v. Mercury Marine Div. of Brunswick Corp., 793 F.2d 1416, 1420–1421 (5th Cir. 1986) (it is proponent's duty to articulate clearly every ground for which proffered evidence is admissible; in wrongful death action, offer of proof arguing evidence was relevant to issue of causation was insufficient to preserve error in excluding evidence on ground it was relevant to theory of liability for failure to warn).

[13] *See, e.g.,* EEOC v. Ind. Bell Tel. Co., 256 F.3d 516, 526–527 (7th Cir. 2001) (en banc).

[14] *See, e.g.,* Macsenti v. Becker, 237 F.3d 1223, 1241 (10th Cir. 2001) (when record does not contain proffer or reveal what arguments were made to trial court, appellate court cannot say trial court's rulings were not within its discretion and, therefore, cannot hold evidentiary ruling not harmless).

[15] *See, e.g.,* Tompkin v. Philip Morris USA, Inc., 362 F.3d 882, 900 n.16 (6th Cir. 2004) (when plaintiff failed to offer portions of deposition transcripts, she waived her right to appeal trial court's alleged exclusion of those transcript portions).

evidence.[16]

[4]—Pretrial Rulings Admitting and Excluding Evidence[1]

Before Rule 103 was amended in 2000, many appellate courts held that objections presented and overruled in an in limine pretrial hearing must be renewed at trial to preserve error.[2] Other courts held that a ruling on a pretrial motion in limine that overruled an objection to evidence was sufficient to preserve error if:

- The trial court's unfavorable ruling was neither "conditional" nor "qualified."[3]

- The issue was thoroughly presented during the consideration of the pretrial motion, the issue was one that can appropriately be decided prior to trial, and the trial court's ruling was definitive.[4]

The courts of appeals were only slightly less insistent that the proffering party renew an offer of proof at trial after the trial court entered an in limine order excluding the evidence.[5] The focus in cases involving pretrial rulings excluding evidence was on the issue of the adequacy of the information in the record concerning the purpose of the offer and the reasons argued for the admissibility of

---

[16] See, e.g., United States v. Downing, 753 F.2d 1224, 1226 (3d Cir. 1985) (remanded to trial court for determination of admissibility of expert testimony concerning reliability of eye witness testimony).

[1] See discussion in **Treatise** at §§ 103.30, 103.31.

[2] See, e.g., United States v. McNeil, 184 F.3d 770 776–777 (8th Cir. 1999) (after trial court overrules motion in limine to exclude evidence, party's failure to object at trial when evidence is offered waives any error in its admission); McEwen v. City of Norman, 926 F.2d 1539, 1543–1545 (10th Cir. 1991) (objection to expert's testimony not preserved for appeal when raised in pretrial motion in limine but not at trial when expert's testimony was offered); Wilson v. Waggener, 837 F.2d 220, 222 (5th Cir. 1988) ("[a] party whose motion in limine is overruled must renew his objection when the evidence is about to be introduced at trial").

[3] See, e.g., United States v. Brawner, 173 F.3d 966, 970 (6th Cir. 1999) (unless district court's ruling on motion in limine is conditional or qualified, there is no need to register contemporaneous objection when evidence is offered at trial to preserve objection for appeal); Scott v. Ross, 140 F.3d 1275, 1285 (9th Cir. 1998) (when substance of objection was thoroughly explored during pretrial hearing and trial court's ruling was definitive, there is no need for contemporaneous objection at trial to preserve error for appellate review).

[4] See, e.g., National Envtl. Serv. Co. v. Ronan Eng'g Co., 256 F.3d 995, 1001–1002 (10th Cir. 2001) (three-part test applicable and satisfied).

[5] Compare United States v. Winkle, 587 F.2d 705, 710 (5th Cir. 1979) ("this circuit will not even consider the propriety of the decision to exclude the evidence at issue, if no offer of proof was made at trial") with McQuaig v. McCoy, 806 F.2d 1298, 1301–1302 (5th Cir. 1987) (when party seeking to introduce evidence concerning internal affairs investigation described evidence in detail during pretrial conference and argued why it should be admitted and later filed investigation report as part of record, functions of Rule 103(a)(2) were satisfied and admissibility issue was properly preserved for appeal despite party's failure to make offer of proof at trial).

the evidence under the Federal Rules of Evidence.[6] On the other hand, the focus in cases involving pretrial rulings admitting evidence over objection was on the timeliness of the objection, with a predisposition favoring requiring objections contemporaneous with the offer of the evidence at the trial.[7]

The 2000 amendment to Rule 103 eliminates the necessity for renewing an objection to the admission or exclusion of evidence when the trial court has made a definitive ruling on the record during a pretrial proceeding.[7.1] To preserve the error for appeal, the trial court's ruling must be both definitive and on the record.[7.2] Thus, it will continue to be necessary to raise an objection or make an offer during the trial when:

- The trial court fails or refuses to rule definitively on the motion in limine.[8]

- The trial court's pretrial ruling definitively admits the evidence, but leaves open issues as to how the evidence will be used at trial.[9]

- The trial court or opposing counsel violates the pretrial ruling.[10]

- The objection raised in the pretrial motion was less specific than necessary to assure thorough presentation of the issues to the trial court.[11]

- The trial court overrules a pretrial objection on one or more stated grounds, but opponent of evidence fails to make objection on other ground.[11.1]

---

[6] See [3], above.

[7] See [2], above.

[7.1] Fed. R. Evid. 103(a); see, e.g., United States v. McDermott, 245 F.3d 133, 140 n.3 (2d Cir. 2001).

[7.2] Fed. R. Evid. 103(a); see, e.g., Udemba v. Nicoli, 237 F.3d 8, 16 (1st Cir. 2001) (when trial court declined to rule on objection in limine but indicated likelihood that evidence would be admitted and opponent failed to object when evidence was offered, appellate review was limited to plain errors).

[8] See, e.g., C.P. Interests, Inc. v. California Pools, Inc., 238 F.3d 690, 701 (5th Cir. 2001) (when trial court reserves judgment on in limine motion with admonition that movant should object at trial each time evidence subject to objection raised in in limine motion is offered, movant's failure to raise objections at trial results in appellate court's review only for plain error).

[9] See, e.g., Wilson v. Williams, 182 F.3d 562, 567–568 (7th Cir. 1999) (en banc) (definitive pretrial ruling preserves admissibility issues for appeal without objection at trial, but does not preserve issues concerning use of evidence at trial).

[10] See, e.g., Collins v. Wayne Corp., 621 F.2d 777, 785–786 (5th Cir. 1980) (failure to object when trial court admits evidence in violation of its own in limine order waives error).

[11] See, e.g., Peteet v. Dow Chem. Co., 868 F.2d 1428, 1432 (5th Cir. 1989) (defendant who contended in motion in limine that expert testimony was inadmissible because witness's causation theory was "specious" failed to preserve error by failing to raise issue when evidence was offered at trial).

[11.1] See, e.g., United States v. Varela-Rivera, 279 F.3d 1174, 1178 n.3 (9th Cir. 2002) (defendant's objections at in limine hearing to drug-dealer profile testimony as irrelevant and

A pretrial objection does not have to reflect precisely the evidence that is ultimately admitted at trial to preserve the objection for review. All that is necessary is that the objection fairly meet the proffer made at the in limine hearing and the trial judge make a definitive ruling on the record in light of the proffer and the stated objections.[11.2] An unsuccessful pretrial offer of proof, on the other hand, must set forth accurately and precisely what the evidence will show to preserve error in the exclusion of evidence.[11.3]

A trial court's pretrial ruling that evidence is admissible is sufficiently "definitive" if its only condition is that the proponent's foundational evidence be the same as was offered at the in limine hearing.[11.4] Nevertheless, the retrospective nature of the appellate court's determination whether the trial court's pretrial ruling was "definitive" strongly suggests the wisdom of renewing any objection to evidence initially made in an unsuccessful in limine motion when the evidence is offered at trial. Failure to do so may result in a holding that the objection was not preserved for appeal.[12] Similarly, offers of proof during the trial concerning any evidence ruled inadmissible during a pretrial in limine hearing are wise.

Moreover, the trial court may always change its mind if additional facts relevant to the admissibility issues are brought to its attention after its decision on the in limine motion.[13] An offer of proof or a contemporaneous objection would, of course, be necessary under such circumstances.[14]

------

prejudicial preserved any error on those grounds, but failure to object on Rule 704(b) grounds before or during trial limited appellate court to plain error review on that ground).

[11.2] *See, e.g.,* United States v. Varela-Rivera, 279 F.3d 1174, 1176–1178 (9th Cir. 2002) (when government failed to state clearly at pretrial hearings nature of expert testimony it would offer at trial, defendant's objection was sufficient when it fairly met the proffer and stated defendant's ground for exclusion, appellate court was able to review admission of evidence for abuse of discretion); *see also* [2], *above.*

[11.3] *See, e.g.,* United States v. Adams, 271 F.3d 1236, 1241–1243 (10th Cir. 2001) (most efficacious method of making offer of proof is presentation of actual proposed testimony through questions and answers, least effective method is through representations of counsel; however proffer is made, it must include substance and significance of evidence, what evidence demonstrates, and why evidence is admissible to preserve abuse of discretion review); *see also* [3], *above.*

[11.4] *See, e.g.,* United States v. Gajo, 290 F.3d 922, 927 (7th Cir. 2002).

[12] *See, e.g.,* United States v. Birbal, 62 F.3d 456, 465 (2d Cir. 1995) (denial of motion in limine relieved moving party of obligation to object to general admissibility of evidence at time it was offered, but did not relieve party of obligation to object during trial to offer of specific inflammatory statements).

[13] United States v. Yannott, 42 F.3d 999, 1007 (6th Cir. 1994) ("the district court may change its ruling on a motion in limine where sufficient facts have developed to warrant the change").

[14] *See, e.g.,* United States v. Harrison, 296 F.3d 994, 1002–1003 (10th Cir. 2002) (after pretrial ruling that was definitive on some matters and conditional on another, it was duty of opponent to object at trial based on new evidence or lack of evidence concerning the conditional issue; thus, that issues was not available on appeal).

[5]—Procedures for Making Evidentiary Decisions

Rule 103(b) permits the trial court to add to the record, beyond what the parties provide in their presentations concerning the admissibility of evidence, "any other or further statement which shows the character of the evidence, the form in which it was offered, the objection made, and the ruling thereon." For example, the court may choose to provide additional reasoning in support of its ruling beyond its reaction to the specific arguments the parties made and the facts they presented. It also permits the court to require the proffering party to make its offer of proof in question and answer form.[1] These provisions confer broad discretion on the trial court in the determination of the format the parties should follow in presenting evidentiary questions.[2]

Rule 103(c) requires the trial court to conduct its proceedings in such a manner as to minimize the potential that the jury will hear inadmissible evidence during offers of potentially objectionable evidence or during offers of proof. It also provides that arguments as to the admissibility of evidence should be conducted out of the jury's presence, or at least under circumstances such that the jury will not hear the argument. The trial court's decision, however, as to how to proceed with evidentiary questions is by and large discretionary.[3]

The preference expressed in Rule 103(c), however, for conducting evidentiary proceedings outside the jury's presence, coupled with the authority to make definitive pretrial rulings recognized in the 2000 amendment to Rule 103, suggests that complex evidentiary issues should be addressed in a pretrial setting. In fact, some courts of appeals have strongly suggested that in some circumstances such hearings are required concerning expert testimony.[4] Other courts have merely upheld the trial court's refusal to revisit the question after exhaustive pretrial hearings that resulted in definitive rulings, thereby permitting the trial court to require the parties to come to the pretrial hearing with all of their ammunition at

---

[1] Fed. R. Evid 103(b).

[2] *See, e.g.,* United States v. Adams, 271 F.3d 1236, 1241 (10th Cir. 2001).

[3] *See, e.g.,* United States v. Galin, 222 F.3d 1123, 1126–1127 (9th Cir. 2000) (trial court has discretion, under Rule 103(c), to require all arguments concerning admissibility of evidence to occur at side bar, out of hearing of jury); United States v. Adames, 56 F.3d 737, 744 (7th Cir. 1995) (it is within court's discretion to select procedure used to keep inadmissible evidence from jury; therefore, numerous hearings interrupting defense cross-examination did not violate defendant's right to confront witnesses).

[4] *See, e.g.,* Goebel v. Denver & Rio Grande Western R.R., 215 F.3d 1083, 1087 (10th Cir. 2000) ("[t]he most common method for fulfilling this function [of gatekeeper] is a *Daubert* [pretrial] hearing"); Padillas v. Stork-Gamco, Inc., 186 F.3d 412, 417–418 (3d Cir. 1999) (Third Circuit has strong preference for pretrial hearings respecting reliability of expert testimony, even if neither party requests one, whenever bases for proposed expert witness's opinion "are insufficiently explained and the reasons and foundations for them inadequately and perhaps confusingly explicated.").

the ready.[5] Still other courts have upheld the trial court's discretion in deciding the admissibility of the evidence during the trial, so long as they took precautions to prevent the exposure of the jury to potentially inadmissible evidence.[6]

[6]—Harmless Error[1]

[a]—Harmless Error Rule

Rule 103(a) provides that an error by the trial court admitting or excluding evidence may be the basis for a reversal on appeal only if the error affected "a substantial right of a party." Error that does not affect substantial rights is commonly termed "harmless error,"[2] and the rule that harmless error is not a basis for reversal is known as the "harmless error rule." Generally, an evidentiary error affects a party's "substantial right" only if there is a substantial likelihood that the error affected the outcome of the case.[2.1]

The type of case in which the trial court made the alleged error may affect the appellate court's determination of whether error was harmless. The appellate court may reach different conclusions in a criminal case than in a civil case presenting essentially the same facts, and can be expected to scrutinize the record more harshly in a death penalty case than in a criminal case involving only a short term of imprisonment.[3]

The appellate courts rarely address directly in their harmless error analyses the question whether the affected right was "substantial." Whether the affected right

---

[5] *See, e.g.,* Pride v. BIC Corp., 218 F.3d 566, 578 (6th Cir. 2000) (trial court properly excluded expert testimony after pretrial evidentiary hearing); United States v. Sinskey, 119 F.3d 712, 717 (8th Cir. 1997) (trial court properly admitted expert testimony it found reliable during pretrial evidentiary hearing).

[6] *See, e.g.,* United States v. Hicks, 103 F.3d 837, 844–847 (9th Cir. 1996) (trial court properly admitted expert testimony it found reliable after evidentiary hearing conducted during trial); Cummins v. Lyle Indus., Inc., 93 F.3d 362, 365–370 (7th Cir. 1996) (trial court properly excluded expert testimony it found unreliable after evidentiary hearing conducted during trial).

[1] *See* discussion in **Treatise** at § 103.41.

[2] *See, e.g.,* United States v. Frazier, No. 01-14680, 2004 U.S. App. LEXIS 21503, at *56 n.21 (11th Cir. Oct. 15, 2004) (when evidentiary error does not affect substantial interest of adversely affected party, it is harmless and courts must disregard it); Manley v. AmBase Corp., 337 F.3d 237, 251–252 (2d Cir. 2003) (although deputy clerk's communication to deliberating juror was improper, it was harmless error, because it simply encouraged her to participate fully in deliberative process and not assume that her views could not influence her fellow jurors).

[2.1] *See, e.g.,* Tesser v. Board of Educ., 370 F.3d 314, 319 (2d Cir. 2004).

[3] *See, e.g.,* Kotteakos v. United States, 328 U.S. 750, 762, 66 S. Ct. 1239, 1246, 90 L. Ed. 1557 (1946) ("Necessarily the character of the proceeding, what is at stake upon its outcome, and the relation of the error asserted to casting the balance for decision on the case as a whole, are material factors in judgment. The statute in terms makes no distinction between civil and criminal cases. But this does not mean that the same criteria shall always be applied regardless of this difference.").

is grounded in a provision of the Constitution is, of course, of importance in determining its substantiality. In cases not involving constitutional rights (constitutionally protected rights are discussed in [8], *below*), the "right" allegedly affected by an evidentiary error is not generally even specifically identified. Implicit in those cases, however, is the assumption that the harmless error rule protects the right of every party to a lawsuit to receive a determination from the finder of fact that is supported by substantial admissible evidence.

Some courts hold that the alleged evidentiary error is harmless when the other evidence supporting the finder of fact's conclusion is strong or "overwhelming," without considering independently the probability that the alleged error affected the trier of fact's conclusion.[4] Other courts are not content with a determination whether the properly admitted evidence is independently sufficient to support the conclusion of the finder of fact, but analyze further to determine whether it is probable that the error had a substantial influence on the finder of fact in its deliberations.[5] The differences between the approaches used by appellate courts in applying the harmless error rule, however, may be more apparent than real. It often appears that the court concluded that the evidentiary error had no substantial impact on the fact finder's conclusion precisely because the erroneously excluded or admitted evidence was cumulative or the other evidence supporting the outcome was "overwhelming."[6]

For those appellate courts that appear to apply a harmless error analysis incorporating the question whether the error had an impact on the trier of fact's deliberations, there is no definitive standard of probability that they can use in that

---

[4] *See, e.g.,* United States v. Turner, 285 F.3d 909, 913–914 (10th Cir. 2002) (trial court's error in denying preadmission determination of reliability of proffered expert testimony, if any, was harmless, since other evidence of defendant's guilt that was sufficiently strong to support inference that, if expert evidence was improperly admitted, it did not affect fact finder's decision); United States v. Shea, 211 F.3d 658, 666 (1st Cir. 2000) (admission of apparently irrelevant evidence, while perhaps erroneous, was harmless in light of other substantial properly admitted incriminating evidence amply supporting jury's verdict).

[5] *See, e.g.,* Renda v. King, 347 F.3d 550, 556 (3d Cir. 2003) (reviewing court should affirm trial court despite error if reviewing court believes "that it is *highly probable* that the error did not contribute to the judgment"); Costantino v. Herzog, 203 F.3d 164, 173–174 (2d Cir. 2000) ("substantial right" is affected by evidentiary error only if it is likely "that in some material respect the factfinder's judgment was swayed by the error").

[6] *See, e.g.,* Walker v. Horn, 385 F.3d 321, 336 (3d Cir. 2004) (when evidence that was allegedly erroneously admitted was cumulative of other properly admitted evidence of same facts and there was additional evidence tending to prove facts for which evidence was admitted, there was little chance that evidence affected outcome of trial and its admission, if error, was harmless); Slayton v. Ohio Dep't of Youth Servs, 206 F.3d 669, 676 (6th Cir. 2000) (even if lay opinion testimony concerning meaning of term "sexual harassment" was erroneously admitted, error was harmless in light of brevity of testimony and amount of other evidence properly introduced to show that employer permitted plaintiff's supervisor to create hostile work environment).

analysis. The Third Circuit has suggested three possible tests for analyzing whether error is harmless: "(a) that it is more probable than not that the error did not affect the judgment, (b) that it is highly probable that the error did not contribute to the judgment, or (c) that it is almost certain that the error did not taint the judgment."[7]

The "more-probable-than-not" standard may in fact be the one that all of the appellate courts most often apply, but it is difficult to discern from the cases whether the articulation of a particular standard really matters. The appellate court is likely to affirm, regardless of the standard applied, when, after assessing the factors discussed in [b], *below,* it has no serious doubt about either the fairness of the trial or the outcome of the case.[8]

[b]—Factors in Determining Effect of Error

Any assessment of the impact of an evidentiary error on the finder of fact invariably entails an analysis of the circumstances peculiar to the individual case.[9] Thus, the following factors have been persuasive in the determination whether evidentiary error was harmless:

- The number of errors in relation to the length of the trial.[10]

- The closeness of the factual disputes.[11]

- The cumulative nature of the evidence improperly admitted or excluded in light of other evidence that was properly admitted.[12]

---

[7] Government of Virgin Islands v. Toto, 529 F.2d 278, 284 (3d Cir. 1976) (the three options were put forth by Chief Justice Traynor of California in The Riddle of Harmless Error (1970)).

[8] *See, e.g.,* Kotteakos v. United States, 328 U.S. 750, 765, 66 S. Ct. 1239, 1248, 90 L. Ed. 1557 (1946) ("But if one cannot say, with fair assurance, after pondering all that happened without stripping the erroneous action from the whole, that the judgment was not substantially swayed by the error, it is impossible to conclude that substantial rights were not affected"); Beck v. Haik, 377 F.3d 624, 634–635 (6th Cir. 2004) (*Kotteakos* standard is followed by most circuits in both civil and criminal cases).

[9] *See, e.g.,* United States v. Sarracino, 340 F.3d 1148, 1171 (10th Cir. 2003) (harmless error review entails review of entire record of trial).

[10] *See, e.g.,* Rabon v. Automatic Fasteners, Inc., 672 F.2d 1231, 1239 (5th Cir. 1982) (error in admitting evidence was harmless when evidence subject to objection was "a mere shred of the totality of the evidence").

[11] *See, e.g.,* Jordan v. Medley, 711 F.2d 211, 219 (D.C. Cir. 1983) (improper admission of testimony was not harmless when it went directly to central issue of case and evidence on that issue was closely balanced).

[12] *See, e.g.,* United States v. Perrotta, 289 F.3d 155, 165 (1st Cir. 2002) (admission of guns, brass knuckles, billy club, and fake bomb seized at time of defendant's arrest, if erroneous, was harmless, because jury already knew about those weapons from testimony of witnesses to which defendant did not object).

- The centrality of the issue to which the evidence is directed.[13]

- The prejudicial impact of the evidentiary ruling.[14]

- The cumulative effect of several errors.[14.1]

- The trial court's instructions with regard to the evidence.[15]

- Whether the adversely affected party was able to present the substance of its claim or defense despite the exclusion of admissible evidence.[16]

- Counsels' reliance on improperly admitted evidence or on the lack of improperly excluded evidence in their arguments.[17]

- Whether the complaining party solicited the improperly admitted evidence as part of an apparently unsuccessful trial strategy.[18]

The appellate courts also can be expected to find that the alleged error did not adversely affect a substantial right more frequently when the case was tried to the

---

[13] *See, e.g.,* Weyers v. Lear Operations Corp., 359 F.3d 1049, 1054–1056 (8th Cir. 2004) (trial court's exclusion of written record of plaintiff's description of early days in employment that was at variance with plaintiff's trial testimony describing early days as being filled with constant instances of intense age-related discrimination was not harmless, as nature and intensity of discriminatory incidents went to heart of plaintiff's age-discrimination claim).

[14] *See, e.g.,* Molnar v. Booth, 229 F.3d 593, 603–604 (7th Cir. 2000) (even if admission of evidence was error, it was harmless because it was not shocking and parties had ample opportunity to argue impact of evidence to jury); Fireman's Fund Ins. v. Alaskan Pride Partnership, 106 F.3d 1465, 1467 (9th Cir. 1997) (even if trial court's evidentiary ruling was abuse of discretion, reversal is warranted only if error was prejudicial); Bonilla v. Yamaha Motors Corp., 955 F.2d 150, 153-154 (1st Cir. 1992) (error in admitting evidence of plaintiff's prior speeding offenses was not harmless when evidence was "substantively important, inflammatory, and highly prejudicial"). *See also* discussion of exclusion of relevant evidence in § 6.02.

[14.1] *See, e.g.,* United States v. Meserve, 271 F.3d 314, 332–333 (1st Cir. 2001) (although minor individual errors may become reversible in the aggregate, errors in this case were independent of each other, and appellate court was convinced that trial was nonetheless fair).

[15] *See, e.g.,* Densberger v. United Techs. Corp., 283 F.3d 110, 119 (2d Cir. 2002) (any error in admitting testimony that may have involved conclusion of law was harmless in view of court's instruction to jury that it was to take its legal instruction from court and to disregard any contrary legal opinion in arguments of counsel or testimony of witnesses).

[16] *See, e.g.,* Mason v. Southern Ill. Univ. at Carbondale, 233 F.3d 1036, 1047–1048 (7th Cir. 2000) (erroneous exclusion of evidence is harmless when plaintiff was able to prove through other evidence all facts that excluded evidence would have tended to prove).

[17] *See, e.g.,* United States v. Ruffin, 575 F.2d 346, 360 (2d Cir. 1978) (substance of erroneously admitted testimony "must have been in the forefront of the jurors' minds when they retired to deliberate," because of "the extent to which the prosecutor dwelt [on it] both in his opening summation and his rebuttal"; erroneous admission of evidence was, therefore, not harmless).

[18] *See, e.g.,* United States v. Vaccaro, 816 F.2d 443, 453 (9th Cir. 1987) (admission of otherwise inadmissible testimony from defendant's co-conspirator was harmless error when defense elicited testimony on cross-examination for impeachment).

court than in a jury trial, because the trial court can be presumed to have ignored inadmissible evidence in arriving at its findings.[19]

[c]—Differing Treatment of Civil and Criminal Cases

There is disagreement as to whether the civil standard should differ from the standard applied in criminal cases involving non-constitutional error.[20] Some courts have applied the "highly probable" standard for non-constitutional error in criminal cases,[21] while others have opted for the "more-probable-than-not" standard.[22] Still other courts apply the same standard to both types of cases, but recognize that the differing burdens of proof may lead to differing results.[22.1]

The allocation of the burden of proof respecting whether an evidentiary error affected a substantial right depends on whether the case is civil or criminal. In a civil case, the burden of showing that the error caused prejudice is on the party asserting the error.[23] In a criminal case, the burden of proving that the error is harmless is on the government.[24]

---

[19] *See, e.g.,* United States v. Menk, 406 F.2d 124, 127 (7th Cir. 1968) ("a trained, experienced Federal District Court judge, as distinguished from a jury, must be presumed to have exercised the proper discretion in distinguishing between the improper and the proper evidence introduced at trial, and to have based his decision only on the latter, in the absence of a clear showing to the contrary by appellant.").

[20] *Compare* Haddad v. Lockheed California Corp, 720 F.2d 1454, 1459 (9th Cir. 1983) (harmless error standard in civil cases should reflect lesser burden of proof; to find error harmless in civil cases, appellate courts "need only find that the jury's verdict is more probably than not untainted by the error") *with* McQueeney v. Wilmington Trust Co., 779 F.2d 916, 927 (3d Cir. 1985) (standard of review in civil cases should be same as in criminal cases; error is not harmless unless it is "highly probable" that it did not affect a party's substantial rights).

[21] *See, e.g.,* United States v. Vigneau, 187 F.3d 82, 86 (1st Cir. 1999) (erroneous admission of business records was not harmless; conviction would have been upheld if it was "highly probable" that result would not have been different if disputed evidence had not been admitted); United States v. Werme, 939 F.2d 108, 113–116 (3d Cir. 1991).

[22] *See, e.g.,* United States v. Echavarria-Olarte, 904 F.2d 1391, 1398 (9th Cir. 1990); United States v. Neuroth, 809 F.2d 339, 342 (6th Cir. 1987); United States v. Lewis, 671 F.2d 1025, 1028 (7th Cir. 1982).

[22.1] *See, e.g.,* Beck v. Haik, 377 F.3d 624, 636 n.3 (6th Cir. 2004) (appellate court's "fair assurance" that error did not affect outcome may depend on burden of proof applicable to particular case under review).

[23] *See, e.g.,* Kona Tech. Corp. v. Southern Pac. Transp. Co., 225 F.3d 595, 601 (5th Cir. 2000) ("The burden of showing substantial prejudice lies with the party asserting error"); Qualley v. Clo-Tex Int'l, Inc., 212 F.3d 1123, 1127–1128 (8th Cir. 2000) ("the burden of showing prejudice rests on the party asserting it").

[24] *See, e.g.,* United States v. Velarde, 214 F.3d 1204, 1211 (10th Cir. 2000) ("The government bears the burden of proving that an error is harmless").

[7]—Plain Error[1]

[a]—Definition and Reviewability

Rule 103(d) states that an appellate court is not precluded from noticing plain error affecting substantial rights even though the error was not brought to the attention of the trial court or when the objecting party objected at trial on one specific ground and attempts to assert another specific ground on appeal.[2]

A number of courts have tried to define *plain error* with particularity. An erroneous ruling is "plain" if:

- The error that is obvious, and substantial, and "seriously affects the fairness, integrity, or public reputation of judicial proceedings."[3]

- There is (1) an error; (2) that is clear and obvious under current law; (3) that affects the defendant's substantial rights; and (4) that would seriously affect the fairness, integrity, or public reputation of judicial proceedings if left uncorrected.[4]

- The error is "so clear-cut, so obvious, a competent district judge should be able to avoid it without benefit of objection."[5]

In spite of these valiant attempts, the most that can be said is that there is some point beyond which a reviewing court will not tolerate the error below even though counsel did not adequately raise and preserve it at trial.[6] It almost goes without saying that relief from an error that was not called to the trial court's attention is very difficult, indeed, to come by.[7]

The language of Rule 103(d) makes it clear that the appellate court has discretion

---

[1] *See* discussion in **Treatise** at § 103.42.

[2] Fed. R. Evid. 103(d); United States v. Mitchell, 365 F.3d 215, 257 (3d Cir. 2004) (defendant's failure to include hearsay as ground for objection in trial court results in plain error review of trial court's allegedly erroneous admission of hearsay evidence); Conwood Co., L.P. v. U.S. Tobacco Co., 290 F.3d 768, 792 n.7 (6th Cir. 2002) (when party fails to preserve evidentiary error at trial, appellate court still reviews for plain error).

[3] Reddin v. Robinson Prop. Group, 239 F.3d 756, 760 (5th Cir. 2001).

[4] United States v. Lemmerer, 277 F.3d 579, 591 (1st Cir. 2002).

[5] United States v. Turman, 122 F.3d 1167, 1170 (9th Cir. 1997).

[6] *See, e.g.,* Sousa v. INS, 226 F.3d 28, 31 (1st Cir. 2000) ("Although the [plain error] test is a stringent one, it leaves open the opportunity for a reviewing court to avoid a miscarriage of justice in extreme cases"; citation omitted).

[7] *See, e.g.,* Employers Reinsurance Corp. v. Mid-Continent Cas. Co., 358 F.3d 757, 770 (10th Cir. 2004) ("Establishing entitlement to plain-error relief is an extraordinary, nearly insurmountable burden").

whether to review an asserted plain error that was not preserved at trial.[8] For example, the court has discretion to overlook errors that did not seriously affect the fairness, integrity, or public reputation of judicial proceedings,[9] and errors that do not rise to the level of plain error.[10] Some rights, primarily constitutional rights, however, are so substantial that an evidentiary ruling depriving a litigant of one of those rights must be reviewed under the plain error doctrine.[11]

Appellate courts often say that a party's failure to object to the trial court's order admitting or excluding evidence waives any error.[12] Appellate courts, however, always have discretion to review a trial court's evidentiary rulings for plain error.[13]

[b]—Effect of Plain Error Review

The plain error rule mitigates the harsh results that may flow from counsels' failures and omissions or unsuccessful trial strategies. However, appellate courts do not use their powers under the plain error rule to relieve parties of the effects

---

[8] Fed. R. Evid. 103(d) ("Nothing in this rule precludes taking notice of plain errors . . ."); *see, e.g.,* United States v. Polishan, 336 F.3d 234, 241 n.6 (3d Cir. 2003) (when reviewing trial court's admission of evidence for plain error, appellate court may, but need not, order correction of error that is both obvious and prejudicial; appellate court reverses only when trial court's error "seriously affects the fairness, integrity, or public reputation of judicial proceedings").

[9] *See, e.g.,* Bristol v. Bd. of County Comm'rs of Clear Creek, 281 F.3d 1148, 1167 n.8 (10th Cir. 2002) (when error clearly does not seriously affect fairness, integrity, or public reputation of judicial proceedings and party whom it adversely affected failed to preserve error below, appellate court has discretion not to review it for plain error).

[10] Fed. R. Evid. 103(d) (courts may take notice of plan errors if they affect "substantial rights"); *see, e.g.,* United States v. Thompson, 279 F.3d 1043, 1048 (D.C. Cir. 2002) (when adversely affected party fails to preserve error below, appellate court has discretion to review for plain error but only if (1) there is error, (2) that is plain, (3) that affects substantial rights and (4) that seriously affects fairness, integrity, or public reputation of judicial proceedings).

[11] *See, e.g.,* United States v. Ordonez, 737 F.2d 793, 799 (9th Cir. 1983) ("we are required to review plain errors affecting substantial rights although they were not brought to the attention of the trial court. . . . We are satisfied that a contention that the government failed to comply with the Confrontation Clause involves substantial rights which must be reviewed even in the absence of a timely objection").

[12] *See, e.g.,* C.P. Interests, Inc. v. California Pools, Inc., 238 F.3d 690, 695 (5th Cir. 2001) (defendant's failure to object to questions eliciting objectionable testimony results in failure to preserve admissibility of testimony for appeal); FDIC v. Schuchmann, 235 F.3d 1217, 1230 (10th Cir. 2000) (plaintiff's failure to object to ruling excluding evidence renders appellate court unable to review ruling).

[13] *See, e.g.,* DiCarlo v. Keller Ladders, Inc., 211 F.3d 465, 467 (8th Cir. 2000) (evidentiary errors plaintiff failed to object to at trial were reviewable under deferential plain-error standard); United States v. Cisneros, 203 F.3d 333, 346–347 (5th Cir. 2000) (defendant's failure to raise timely objection to admission of evidence results in review for plain error).

of their counsel's failures to protect the record.[14] They do so primarily to protect the fairness, integrity, and public reputation of the judicial system.[15] They exercise their powers only in the most egregious of circumstances.[16]

The plain error rule is applicable in civil cases.[17] Nevertheless, appellate courts subject the record in serious criminal cases to a more searching scrutiny.[18] Children, pro se litigants, criminal defendants represented by court-appointed counsel, and others who need the assistance of a court may be more likely than other litigants to be the beneficiaries of the plain error rule.[19] Moreover, the courts tend to relax the stringent requirements of the plain error rule when the error allegedly denied a right guaranteed by the Constitution.[20]

These general observations aside, the appellate courts proceed in their application of the plain error rule by examining the facts of the particular case, the gravity of the offense, the probable effects of the error, and the other factors they generally consider in their application of the harmless error rule.[21]

An appellate court may, at times, be willing to rectify the lower court's error in

---

[14] *See, e.g.,* United States v. Thompson, 279 F.3d 1043, 1046–1049 (D.C. Cir. 2002) (no plain error in refusal to admit testimony relevant to mens rea defense when counsel failed to make proper offer of proof but exclusion of testimony did not gravely hamper proponent's presentation of defense); Buchanna v. Diehl Mach., Inc., 98 F.3d 366, 372 (8th Cir. 1996) (plain error is an error that "almost surely affects the outcome of the case").

[15] *See, e.g.,* United States v. Meserve, 271 F.3d 314, 321–322 (1st Cir. 2001) (although unpreserved erroneous evidentiary ruling affected party's substantial interest, it is not basis for reversal unless it "seriously affected the fairness, integrity or public reputation of [the] judicial proceeding.").

[16] *See, e.g.,* Phillips v. Hillcrest Med. Ctr., 244 F.3d 790, 802 (10th Cir. 2001) (party challenging evidentiary ruling on plain error basis has "an extraordinary, nearly insurmountable burden").

[17] *See, e.g.,* Beachy v. Boise Cascade Corp., 191 F.3d 1010, 1016 (9th Cir. 1999) (because plaintiff failed to make hearsay objection to documents at trial, appellate court applies "the plain error standard, under which we consider whether the asserted error was highly prejudicial and affected [plaintiff's] substantial rights").

[18] *See, e.g.,* Johnson v. Ashby, 808 F.2d 676, 679 n.3 (8th Cir. 1987) ("The use of the plain-error exception to the normal rules of appellate procedure must be confined to the most compelling cases, especially in civil, as opposed to criminal, litigation").

[19] *See, e.g.,* Government of Canal Zone v. P (Pinto), 590 F.2d 1344, 1353 (5th Cir. 1979) ("We are especially sensitive in criminal cases . . . in which the defendants were represented by a series of court-appointed attorneys"; admission of evidence in violation of hearsay rule was plain error).

[20] *See, e.g.,* United States v. Chavez, 229 F.3d 946, 951 (10th Cir. 2000) (rigidity of plain error rule is relaxed somewhat when potential constitutional error is involved).

[21] *See, e.g.,* United States v. Perez-Ruiz, 353 F.3d 1, 13–14 (1st Cir. 2003) (trial court's erroneous admission of bolstering testimony was not plain error because matters covered by testimony that was bolstered were also covered by other testimony, prosecution did not rely on bolstering testimony in closing argument, and prosecution reminded jury in its closing argument that it was jury's responsibility to ascertain credibility of witnesses); *see also* [6], *above.*

ignoring a decisive issue of substantive law, even though counsel failed to bring it to the trial court's attention, particularly if counsel may have overlooked it because it is subtle or new.[22] An appellate court will be particularly reluctant, however, to find plain error if the failure to object to the admission or exclusion of evidence appears to have been part of a deliberate trial strategy.[23]

[8]—Constitutional Error[1]

Not all constitutional errors require an automatic reversal of the verdict below.[2] Over the years, the Supreme Court has gradually expanded the category of constitutional errors that are subject to harmless error analysis, and has changed the contours of the harmless constitutional error test.

The Court has held that per se reversal is justified only for those constitutional errors that "necessarily render a trial fundamentally unfair," and gave the following examples of errors in criminal trials that require reversal of a judgment of conviction:[3]

- The trial court's direction of a verdict of guilty.

- The denial of a defendant's right to be represented by counsel.

- The admission into evidence of a coerced confession.

- The conduct of the trial by a biased judge.

A criminal trial is fundamentally unfair when it "cannot reliably serve its function as a vehicle for determination of guilt or innocence." Those errors that interfere with fundamental fairness are, however, "the exception and not the rule." If the defendant "had counsel and was tried by an impartial adjudicator, there is a strong presumption that any other errors that may have occurred are subject to harmless error analysis."[4] Pursuant to this approach, the Supreme Court has found that a wide variety of constitutional errors may be harmless. For example, the Court has held

---

[22] *See, e.g.,* United States v. Moore, 571 F.2d 76, 88–89 (2d Cir. 1978) (defendant's conviction was based on presumption that trial court applied during trial; appellate court found application of presumption to be constitutional plain error).

[23] *See, e.g.,* United States v. McGill, 952 F.2d 16, 18–19 (1st Cir. 1991) (no plain error in admitting film into evidence when admission of entire film was pursuant to stipulation; "where a party has stipulated to the admission of particular evidence, courts have been especially slow to find plain error when the party belatedly decides that the stipulation was improvident"); United States v. Wynn, 845 F.2d 1439, 1443 (7th Cir. 1988) (no plain error in allowing testimony when defense counsel's decision not to object "was part of a deliberate trial strategy"); *see also* [2][b], *above.*

[1] *See* discussion in **Treatise** at § 103.43.

[2] Chapman v. California, 386 U.S. 18, 22, 87 S. Ct. 824, 827, 17 L. Ed. 2d 705 (1967).

[3] Rose v. Clark, 478 U.S. 570, 578, 106 S. Ct. 3101, 3106, 92 L. Ed. 2d 460, 471 (1986).

[4] Rose v. Clark, 478 U.S. 570, 577–580, 106 S. Ct. 3101, 92 L. Ed. 2d 460 (1986).

that it is possible for the following errors depriving criminal defendants of their constitutional rights to be harmless:

- Giving the jury in a murder case an instruction concerning the presumption of malice in homicide cases that has the effect of shifting the burden of proof respecting intent to the defendant.[5]

- Prohibiting all cross-examination concerning a prosecution witness's bias in violation of Confrontation Clause.[6]

- Denial of a criminal defendant's right to be present at trial.[7]

- Improper comment on the defendant's silence at trial.[8]

- Admission of identification evidence obtained in violation of the defendant's right to counsel.[9]

- Admission of a confession obtained in violation of the defendant's right to counsel.[10]

- Admission of evidence obtained in a search that violated the Fourth Amendment.[11]

- Admission of a non-testifying co-defendant's statement.[12]

Before a federal constitutional error can be held harmless, "the court must be able to declare a belief that it was harmless beyond a reasonable doubt."[13] That statement appeared to require the appellate courts to focus on the possible impact on the minds of the jurors of the erroneously admitted or excluded evidence, without considering the untainted evidence. Subsequent Supreme Court cases, however, suggest that when the untainted evidence of guilt is "overwhelming," no further inquiry into the effect of the error is necessary.[14] Thus, as long as the reviewing court is persuaded that "the record developed at trial establishes guilt beyond a reasonable doubt,"[15] it is commanded to affirm the judgment regardless

---

[5] Rose v. Clark, 478 U.S. 570, 575, 106 S. Ct. 3101, 3104 92 L. Ed. 2d 460 (1986).
[6] Delaware v. Van Arsdall, 475 U.S. 673, 674, 106 S. Ct. 1431, 1432 89 L. Ed. 2d 674 (1986).
[7] Rushen v. Spain, 464 U.S. 114, 121 104 S. Ct. 453, 457, 78 L. Ed. 2d 267 (1983) (per curiam).
[8] United States v. Hasting, 461 U.S. 499, 512, 103 S. Ct. 1974, 1982, 76 L. Ed. 2d 96 (1983).
[9] Moore v. Illinois, 434 U.S. 220, 232, 98 S. Ct. 458, 54 L. Ed. 2d 424 (1977).
[10] Milton v. Wainwright, 407 U.S. 371, 372, 92 S. Ct. 2174, 2175, 33 L. Ed. 2d 1 (1972).
[11] Chambers v. Maroney, 399 U.S. 42, 53, 90 S. Ct. 1975, 26 L. Ed. 2d 419 (1970).
[12] Harrington v. California, 395 U.S. 250, 253 89 S. Ct. 1726, 1728 23 L. Ed. 2d 284 (1969).
[13] Chapman v. California, 386 U.S. 18, 24, 87 S. Ct. 824, 827, 17 L. Ed. 2d 705 (1967).
[14] See, e.g., Milton v. Wainwright, 407 U.S. 371, 377, 92 S. Ct. 2174, 33 L. Ed. 2d 1 (1972) ("we do not close our eyes to the reality of overwhelming evidence of guilt fairly established"); see also United States v. Williams, 181 F.3d 945, 952–953 (8th Cir. 1999) (constitutional error was harmless because other evidence of defendant's guilt was "overwhelming").
[15] Rose v. Clark, 478 U.S. 570, 583, 106 S. Ct. 3101, 92 L. Ed. 2d 460 (1986).

of constitutional or other errors below.

In making the determination of harmlessness, the court should apply the same factors that determine the harm caused by non-constitutional errors. The Supreme Court has defined the task of the appellate court as follows:[16]

> The correct inquiry is whether, assuming that the damaging potential of the cross-examination were fully realized, a reviewing court might nonetheless say that the error was harmless beyond a reasonable doubt. Whether such an error is harmless in a particular case depends upon a host of factors, all readily accessible to reviewing courts. These factors include the importance of the witness's testimony in the prosecution's case, whether the testimony was cumulative, the presence or absence of evidence corroborating or contradicting the testimony of the witness on material points, the extent of cross-examination otherwise permitted, and, of course, the overall strength of the prosecution's case.

This approach suggests that some members of the Supreme Court are prepared to rule that there is no higher standard for constitutional error than for any other kind of error, unless the error is of that rare variety that renders a trial fundamentally unfair, in which case it would be reversible error without regard to whether the particular error concerned a right that the Constitution protects. However, most judges will continue to be more sensitive to constitutional errors.

§ 2.04 Limited Admissibility—Rule 105

[1]—Scope and Theory[1]

When the court admits evidence that is admissible under the evidence rules against one party but not against another, or that is admissible for one purpose but not for another, Rule 105 requires the court to grant a request for a limiting instruction to the jury that appropriately restricts its use of the evidence. The rule provides:

Rule 105. Limited Admissibility.

When evidence which is admissible as to one party or for one purpose but not admissible as to another party or for another purpose is admitted, the court, upon request, shall restrict the evidence to its proper scope and instruct the jury accordingly.

[Adopted Jan. 2, 1975, effective July 1, 1975.]

---

[16] Delaware v. Van Arsdall, 475 U.S. 673, 684, 106 S. Ct. 1431, 1438, 89 L. Ed. 2d 674 (1986); *see* [6][b], *above.*

[1] *See* discussion in **Treatise** at § 105.02.

For example, if a declarant's out-of-court statement is admitted to show why a party took certain actions, but not for the truth of the statement, on request the court should instruct the jury that it may consider the statement only as an explanation for the party's action, and not for the truth of its contents.[2] The courts generally assume that the jury understands and follows the court's limiting instruction when it is clear.[3]

Limiting instructions are generally not required in a jury trial unless they are requested.[4] Moreover, the request for a limiting instruction should be specific in stating the grounds for limiting the evidence.[5] If the party adversely affected by the admission of evidence with limited admissibility fails to request a limiting instruction, the appellate courts will seldom find reversible error.[6]

However, the absence of a request for an instruction will not prevent an appellate court from holding that the failure of the trial judge to give a limiting instruction was plain error when a party's substantial right was adversely affected.[7]

The jury may be instructed as the evidence is admitted, or as part of the general charge, or at both times.[8] There are sound reasons for giving limiting instructions as the evidence is received and again along with the rest of the jury charge. The impact of evidence in a case tends to be cumulative, each segment building on the evidence that preceded it. The jury will probably get a clearer picture of import of each piece of evidence if the court spells out the restrictions on its use as it is presented. It is unrealistic to expect jurors to suppress their impressions of the facts until after all the evidence has been admitted. It is also unrealistic to expect jurors in a lengthy trial to remember precisely at the conclusion of the trial instructions they received days or weeks before. Repetition at the end of the trial of limiting instructions given previously, when the evidence was received, if accompanied by

---

[2] *See, e.g.,* Rinehimer v. Cemcolift, Inc., 292 F.3d 375, 382–383 (3d Cir. 2002) (testimony that company doctor told company that plaintiff had respiratory problems and could not wear respirator was properly admitted for non-hearsay purpose of explaining why defendant did not permit plaintiff to return to work at former position, and trial court properly instructed jury it could use testimony only as explanation for defendant's refusal to permit plaintiff to resume former position).

[3] *See, e.g.,* Rinehimer v. Cemcolift, Inc., 292 F.3d 375, 383 (3d Cir. 2002).

[4] *See* Fed. R. Evid. 105 ("court, 'upon request' shall restrict the evidence").

[5] *See* Fed. R. Evid. 103(a).

[6] *See, e.g.,* Ansell v. Green Acres Contracting Co., 347 F.3d 515 (3d Cir. 2003) (plaintiff waived error in trial court's failure to give limiting instruction respecting jury's use of evidence of prior acts by failing to request instruction).

[7] Fed. R. Evid. 103(d); *see, e.g.,* United States v. Sauza-Martinez, 217 F.3d 754, 758–761 (9th Cir. 2000) (trial court committed plain error in failing to give limiting instruction immediately on admission of damaging testimony that was inadmissible against one defendant, even in absence of request); *see also* § 2.03[7] for complete discussion of plain error.

[8] *See, e.g.,* United States v. Chance, 306 F.3d 356, 387–388 (6th Cir. 2002) (trial court has discretion as to when to give limiting instruction).

a summary of the evidence, may help to clear up doubts and refresh the jury's memory.

[2]—Applying Rule 105[1]

[a]—Civil Cases

In civil cases, the extensive pretrial disclosure and discovery procedures available under the Federal Rules of Civil Procedure will usually reveal the potential for prejudice resulting from evidence with limited admissibility that another party will offer at trial. The opponent should bring the issue to the court's attention before the trial so that adequate measures can be taken. Counsel has the opportunity to advise the court of the problem before the trial begins at the Rule 16 pretrial conference,[2] by a motion in limine (see § 2.03[5]), or by a motion to sever or to bifurcate the issues.[3]

Rule 105 contemplates that parties will avoid prejudice through the court's limiting instruction.[4] It is the responsibility of the adversely affected party to request a limiting instruction.[5] Although it is generally sufficient to instruct the jury that they may use the evidence only for the purposes for which it was admitted, at times it may be necessary to instruct the jury concerning prohibited uses.[6]

If the adversely affected party requests a limiting instruction, the trial court does not have discretion to refuse.[7] Nevertheless, the trial court's erroneous refusal of

---

[1]   *See* discussion in **Treatise** at §§ 105.03–105.07.

[2]   Fed. R. Civ. P. 16; *see* 3 MOORE'S FEDERAL PRACTICE, Ch. 16, *Pretrial Conferences; Scheduling; Management* (Matthew Bender 3d ed.).

[3]   Fed. R. Civ. P. 20; Fed. R. Civ. P. 42; *see* 4 MOORE'S FEDERAL PRACTICE, Ch. 20, *Permissive Joinder of Parties* (Matthew Bender 3d ed.); 8 MOORE'S FEDERAL PRACTICE, Ch. 42, *Consolidation; Separate Trials* (Matthew Bender 3d ed.).

[4]   *See, e.g.,* United States v. Takahashi, 205 F.3d 1161, 1164–1165 (9th Cir. 2000) (trial court did not abuse its discretion in admitting evidence that defendant and witness were members of gang that required oaths of total loyalty to show bias when court took appropriate steps to minimize undue prejudice by giving limiting instruction and precluding government from introducing potentially inflammatory photographs of defendant's tattoos as evidence of his gang membership).

[5]   *See, e.g.,* Ansell v. Green Acres Contracting Co., 347 F.3d 515, 526 (3d Cir. 2003) Fruge v. Penrod Drilling Co., 918 F.2d 1163, 1168–1169 (5th Cir. 1990) (burden was on opponent to request limiting instruction; in absence of request and objection to court's failure to give limiting instruction, issue was waived).

[6]   *See, e.g.,* Sprynczynatyk v. General Motors Corp., 771 F.2d 1112, 1118 (8th Cir. 1985) (instructing jury on permissible use of videotapes while failing to warn of prohibited use as defendant requested was reversible error; rejection of defendant's requested limiting instruction in jury's presence improperly led jury to think proffered instruction was wrong).

[7]   *See, e.g.,* United States v. Prawl, 168 F.3d 622, 626–627 (2d Cir. 1999) (district court committed reversible error by refusing request to instruct jurors not to consider testifying codefendant's guilty plea as evidence of defendant's guilt).

a properly requested limiting instruction may constitute harmless error.[8]

[b]—Criminal Cases

[i]—Limiting Instructions in Criminal Cases

[A]— Same General Approach as in Civil Cases

Rule 105 does not distinguish between civil and criminal cases. Thus, in criminal cases, as in civil cases, if evidence of limited admissibility is admitted, the adversely affected party generally must request a limiting instruction to preserve error.[9] The trial court must give a limiting instruction in a criminal case if it is requested to do so.[10]

It is also fully within the court's power to instruct the jury without a request from counsel. However, that power should be exercised with caution, because counsel may have concluded that a limiting instruction will actually call the juror's attention to the prohibited inference.[11]

The trial court's failure to give a limiting instruction in a criminal case, absent a request to do so, is reversible error only if the lack of an instruction results in a miscarriage of justice.[12] Moreover, even if a limiting instruction is requested and erroneously refused, the appellate court may find the error to be harmless.[13]

---

[8] *See, e.g.,* Frederick v. Kirby Tankships, Inc., 205 F.3d 1277, 1285 (11th Cir. 2000) (in suit for unseaworthiness of vessel resulting in plaintiff's injury, evidence of defendant's termination of plaintiff's employment was properly admissible concerning plaintiff's motive to sue, but not for propriety of termination; trial court erred in refusing to give limiting instruction, but error was harmless because plaintiff failed to show resultant prejudice); *see also* § 2.03[6] for discussion of harmless error.

[9] *See, e.g.,* United States v. Sarracino, 340 F.3d 1148, 1166–1167 (10th Cir. 2003) (in murder prosecution, trial court properly admitted codefendant's statement to investigator, even though it contained statement that defendant "lost it" during beating of decedent; in absence of request, trial court did not commit plain error by not giving limiting instruction requiring jury to consider statement only against declarant).

[10] *See, e.g.,* United States v. Higgins, 282 F.3d 1261, 1274 (10th Cir. 2002) (admissibility of other acts evidence is dependent on trial court's giving limiting instruction if requested to do so).

[11] *See, e.g.,* United States v. Lewis, 693 F.2d 189, 197 (D.C. Cir. 1982) (although trial court commits reversible error by failing to give cautionary instruction after admission of highly prejudicial evidence, even in absence of request, court must give counsel opportunity to waive instruction).

[12] *See, e.g.,* United States v. Tracy, 12 F.3d 1186, 1195 (2d Cir. 1993) (when defendant fails to request limiting instruction, trial court's failure to instruct is a ground for reversal only when it constitutes error that is "egregious and obvious" and reversal is "necessary to redress a miscarriage of justice").

[13] *See, e.g.,* United States v. Werme, 939 F.2d 108, 113–116 (3d Cir. 1991) (error, but harmless, to have refused to give jury limiting instruction against using co-conspirators' guilty pleas as substantive evidence of defendant's guilt; evidence against defendant was overwhelming).

The trial court need not necessarily give a limiting instruction at the time the evidence with limited admissibility is admitted, although it is better practice to do so.[13.1] The trial court's failure to give the instruction contemporaneously with the admission of the evidence is an abuse of discretion only if the jury's inappropriate consideration of the evidence would be highly prejudicial, or the trial is of such length as to render ineffective a limiting instruction given at the end of the trial along with the general charge.[14] The presumption that juries understand and follow clear limiting instructions is as applicable to criminal cases as it is to civil cases.[15]

The trial court's limiting instruction also does not necessarily have to describe to the jury specifically the use that it cannot make of the evidence that is admissible only for limited purposes. It is sufficient if the instruction substantially reduced the risk of prejudice from inappropriate use.[16]

[B]— Evidence Admissible For One Purpose But Not Another

Rule 105 is frequently applicable in criminal cases because certain evidence rules, such as Rule 404 limiting the purposes for which other crimes and bad acts are admissible, apply primarily to criminal cases.[17]

Evidence of other crimes or wrongs committed by the defendant offers particularly difficult problems. In the first place, it is not always easy to determine whether the proffered evidence relates to the crime with which the defendant is charged or to a wholly separate act.[18] Admissible evidence relating to the crime with which the defendant is charged is admissible for all purposes, and the defendant is not entitled to a limiting instruction under Rule 105.[19]

Secondly, if the evidence is of a wholly separate act, it may not be admitted to show that the defendant had a greater propensity to commit the charged crime, but it may be used to show other relevant matters, such as intent, motive, or similarity of plan, to impeach the credibility of the defendant's character witness, or to rebut

---

[13.1] *See, e.g.,* United States v. Chance, 306 F.3d 356, 388 (6th Cir. 2002) (trial court has discretion to give limiting instruction contemporaneously with admission of evidence or within final charge).

[14] *See, e.g.,* United States v. Peterson, 244 F.3d 385, 394 (5th Cir. 2001).

[15] *See, e.g.,* United States v. Universal Rehabilitation Servs. (PA), 205 F.3d 657, 668 n.14 (3d Cir. 2000) ("jury is expected to follow instructions in limiting this evidence to its proper function," quoting *Spencer v. Texas,* 385 U.S. 554, 562–563, 17 L. Ed. 2d 606, 87 S. Ct. 648 (1967)).

[16] *See, e.g.,* United States v. Peterson, 244 F.3d 385, 395 (5th Cir. 2001).

[17] *See* §§ 7.01[5], 7.07[5], 7.09, 7.10[3].

[18] *See, e.g.,* United States v. Bowie, 232 F.3d 923, 927 (D.C. Cir. 2000) (distinguishing between "intrinsic" and "extrinsic" evidence for purposes of distinguishing between evidence of charged crime and evidence of other acts has proved difficult); *see also* § 7.01[5][b][vi].

[19] *See, e.g.,* United States v. Bowie, 232 F.3d 923, 928 (D.C. Cir. 2000) (effect of determination that proffered evidence relates to crime charged is to eliminate defendant's right, on request, to limiting instruction under Rule 105).

an entrapment defense.[19.1] Thus, the jury may not consider evidence of an act that is wholly separate from the charged crime as proof of the defendant's character for the purpose of inferring that the defendant acted consistently with that character in committing the crime charged. In such cases, the defendant, on request, is entitled to a limiting instruction under Rule 105.[19.2]

The efficacy of limiting instructions in restricting the jury's consideration of evidence of other crimes for proper purposes is questionable in many cases.[19.3] The balancing of probative value against prejudicial effect that Rule 403 requires may disclose that cautionary instructions will not adequately protect the defendant from prejudice and that evidence of other crimes will have to be excluded.[19.4]

[C]— Evidence Admissible Against One Party But Not Another

In joint trials of criminal defendants, it is often the case that evidence of what one defendant said or did is admissible against all of the defendants. In a conspiracy trial, for example, extrajudicial statements, normally admissible only against the declarant, may be admissible against all the coconspirators if the statement was made during and in furtherance of the conspiracy and, if they are admissible against the other conspirators, they are admissible for all purposes.[19.5] Similarly, evidence of acts in furtherance of the conspiracy committed by one conspirator are admissible against other members of the conspiracy unless the other members had withdrawn from the conspiracy prior to the commission of the acts. In such circumstances, the defendant who did not make the out-of-court statement or commit the act is not entitled to a limiting instruction under Rule 105.[19.6]

[19.1] Fed. R. Evid. 404(b).

[19.2] *See, e.g.,* United States v. Bowie, 232 F.3d 923, 928 (D.C. Cir. 2000) (effect of determination that proffered evidence relates to crime charged is to eliminate defendant's right, on request, to limiting instruction under Rule 105).

[19.3] *See, e.g.,* United States v. Crowder, 87 F.3d 1405, 1422 (D.C. Cir. 1996) (Rogers, C.J., concurring) ("limiting instruction [concerning other crimes evidence], while not perfect, is the only way to protect the rights of the accused while giving effect to the intent of Congress").

[19.4] *See, e.g.,* Awkard v. United States, 352 F.2d 641, 645–646 (D.C. Cir. 1965) (cross-examination of character witnesses that intimated past crimes similar to crime charged is extremely damaging to defendant, and cautionary instructions do not give accused adequate protection, since they cannot prevent jury from considering prior actions in deciding whether appellant has committed crime charged); *cf.* Huddleston v. United States, 485 U.S. 681, 688, 108 S. Ct. 1496, 1500, 99 L. Ed. 2d 771 (1988) (protection against unfair prejudice from admission of evidence of other crimes or wrongs emanates in part from trial court's balancing of prejudice against probative value under Rule 403 and from limiting instruction that trial court must give upon request pursuant to Rule 105).

[19.5] *See* § 15.02[6] for complete discussion of admissibility of out-of-court statements by coconspirators.

[19.6] *See, e.g.,* United States v. Lipford, 203 F.3d 259, 269 (4th Cir. 2000) (when one member of drug trafficking conspiracy shot police officer, evidence of shooting was admissible for all purposes against other members of conspiracy, since there was no evidence that conspiracy had

Even when a conspiracy is charged, however, not all the evidence presented in a joint trial will be admissible against all of the defendants. Such evidence includes extrajudicial statements made outside the framework of the conspiracy, evidence used to impeach one of the defendants who testifies, evidence of one defendant's participation in other similar crimes, or evidence seized in violation of one defendant's Fourth Amendment rights.[19.7]

In addition, defendants may be properly joined even though not all are charged with the same crimes, and in such a situation there is likely to be evidence admissible against some defendants but not against others. The "spillover" effect of such evidence will generally not require separate trials, since a jury is generally considered capable of properly compartmentalizing the evidence as to each defendant.[19.8] Nevertheless, in circumstances of potential spillover with extremely prejudicial results from evidence that would not be admissible against a defendant in severed trials, limiting instructions will be insufficient to offset the prejudice and separate trials will necessary.[19.9]

Situations may arise in which evidence that is admissible against one party but not another is so important and the possibility of prejudice to the party against whom the evidence is inadmissible is so great that exclusion is not a viable option and a limiting instruction will not provide adequate protection. In such cases, a severance pursuant to Rule 14 of the Federal Rules of Criminal Procedure is the only practical alternative even though repetitive trials are burdensome.[19.10] A trial court has a great deal of discretion, however, in determining whether to order separate trials due to prejudice created by joinder, and reversal of a denial of a motion to sever is rare.[19.11]

---

terminated or that other members had withdrawn before shooting; other conspirators were not entitled to limiting instruction).

[19.7] *See, e.g.,* United States v. Sarracino, 340 F.3d 1148, 1166 (10th Cir. 2003) (out-of-court statements made by one defendant not in furtherance of conspiracy were admissible against declarant but not against other defendants).

[19.8] *See, e.g.,* United States v. Bernard, 299 F.3d 467, 475–476 (5th Cir. 2002) (trial court's careful limiting instructions sufficiently protected joint defendants from adverse consequences of joint trial; appellate court must assume that jury heard, understood, and followed district court's instructions).

[19.9] *See, e.g.,* United States v. Davidson, 936 F.2d 856, 861 (6th Cir. 1991) (reversible error in failing to sever; defendant "suffered substantial prejudice from the spillover effect of the proof of the unrelated tax charges against his absent co-defendant"); *but see* United States v. Cox, 934 F.2d 1114, 1119 (10th Cir. 1991) (trial court did not err in refusing to grant separate trials even though defendant might have been prejudiced by lengthy testimony about co-defendant's marijuana smuggling activities).

[19.10] Fed. R. Crim. P. 14.

[19.11] *See, e.g.,* United States v. Cox, 934 F.2d 1114, 1119 (10th Cir. 1991) (trial court did not err in refusing to grant separate trials even though defendant might have been prejudiced by lengthy

The admission of hearsay evidence that is inadmissible against one defendant may implicate that defendant's rights under the Confrontation Clause of the Constitution (*see* [ii], *below*).

[ii]—Confrontation and Limiting Instructions: The *Bruton* Problem

The admission of hearsay evidence that may be used against only one of the defendants also has a constitutional dimension. In 1968, in *Bruton v. United States*,[20] the Supreme Court held that a limiting instruction did not sufficiently protect the defendant from the prejudice that resulted when a confession by his co-defendant implicating the defendant was admitted. The Court found that there was too great a risk "that the jury, despite instructions to the contrary, looked to the incriminating extrajudicial statements in determining petitioner's guilt. . . ."[21] In the immediate aftermath of *Bruton*, many courts reacted by routinely granting severances if the government intended to introduce admissions of a co-defendant inculpating a defendant.

However, the impact of *Bruton* has been blunted by a number of developments. In the first place, the Supreme Court has held that not every violation of *Bruton* constitutes reversible error.[22] With the expansion of the harmless error doctrine discussed above, more cases can be expected to fall into this category.[23] Second, the Supreme Court has held that the confession of a nontestifying co-defendant may be admitted into evidence when the confession was effectively redacted to omit all references to the defendant and defendant's existence, and the jury was instructed not to use the confession against the defendant.[24] A redaction is not effective to bypass the *Bruton* rule, however, if the deletions are obvious. When the defendant's

---

testimony about co-defendant's marijuana smuggling activities); *see also* 23 MOORE'S FEDERAL PRACTICE, Ch. 614, *Relief From Prejudicial Joinder* (Matthew Bender 3d ed.).

[20] Bruton v. United States, 391 U.S. 123, 134, 88 S. Ct. 1620, 20 L. Ed. 2d 476 (1968).

[21] Bruton v. United States, 391 U.S. 123, 126, 88 S. Ct. 1620, 20 L. Ed. 2d 476 (1968); *see also* United States v. Ramirez-Perez, 166 F.3d 1106, 1109–1111 (11th Cir. 1999) (admission of nontestifying co-defendant's inculpatory statement constituted reversible error, because it eliminated all innocent explanations for defendant's possession of gun).

[22] Schneble v. Florida, 405 U.S. 427, 432, 92 S. Ct. 1056, 31 L. Ed. 2d 340 (1972).

[23] *See, e.g.,* United States v. Lage, 183 F.3d 374, 386 (5th Cir. 1999) (in light of other evidence admitted at trial, district court did not err in admitting co-defendant's statements implicating defendant); United States v. Nutall, 180 F.3d 182, 188 (5th Cir. 1999) (admission of nontestifying cofedendant's confession that referred to defendant's home address was harmless error in light of defendant's own confession and evidence of his sudden wealth).

[24] Richardson v. Marsh, 481 U.S. 200, 211, 107 S. Ct. 1702, 1709, 95 L. Ed. 2d 176 (1987) (no violation of *Bruton* that confession became incriminating when linked to defendant through defendant's own testimony); *see* United States v. Edwards, 159 F.3d 1117, 1124–1126 (8th Cir. 1998) (admission of nontestifying co-defendants' statements was upheld because statements had been redacted and witnesses instructed to omit names of co-defendants when testifying about one defendant's admissions).

name is simply replaced with a blank space, the word "deleted," a symbol, or some "other similarly obvious indications of alteration," the confession is so accusatory in nature that it must be excluded.[25] Finally, although the Supreme Court held in 1987 that *Bruton* still applies even when the defendant's own confession, which corroborates that of a co-defendant, is introduced against the defendant,[26] the Court also acknowledged that there are times when a nontestifying co-defendant's statement may be directly admissible against the defendant.[27]

The hearsay exceptions for statements by co-conspirators and declarations against penal interest will often operate to authorize evidentiary use against a defendant of a statement made by a co-defendant. In the case of the co-conspirators exception, the Supreme Court has held that a statement that satisfies Rule 801(d)(2)(E) automatically satisfies the confrontation clause.[28] Prosecutors may have somewhat more difficulty in establishing that a declaration against penal interest can pass constitutional muster. But even when the declaration was made in custody by an accomplice, a situation characterized by the Supreme Court as "presumptively unreliable," the Court has conceded "that the presumption may be rebutted" if sufficient "indicia of reliability" are present.[29] A confession by a co-defendant inculpating the defendant, which was not made in a custodial setting, is obviously more likely to be directly admissible against the defendant.[30] Regardless of how the co-defendant's statement satisfies the hearsay rule, *Bruton* will not be implicated because the *Bruton* rule applies only when the co-defendant's statements are inadmissible because of evidentiary constraints.

---

[25] Gray v. Maryland, 523 U.S. 185, 118 S. Ct. 1151, 1157, 140 L. Ed. 2d 294, 298 (1998) (confessions from which a name has obviously been deleted are similar enough to unredacted confession to warrant the same legal results).

[26] Cruz v. New York, 481 U.S. 186, 191, 107 S. Ct. 1714, 95 L. Ed. 2d 162 (1987) (Court rejected view that *Bruton* does not apply to interlocking confessions; consequently the co-defendant's confession must be excluded or separate trials must be held); *see also* Howard v. Moore, 131 F.3d 399, 415–417 (4th Cir. 1997) (portions of defendant's confessions were properly excluded from evidence under *Bruton* rule and were not exculpatory).

[27] 481 U.S. *at* 193.

[28] Bourjaily v. United States, 483 U.S. 171, 183–184, 107 S. Ct. 2775, 97 L. Ed. 2d 144 (1987). *See* discussion in Chapters 14 and 15.

[29] Lee v. Illinois, 476 U.S. 530, 543, 106 S. Ct. 2056, 90 L. Ed. 2d 514 (1986).

[30] *See* discussion in Chapter 17.

§ 2.05 Remainder of or Related Writings or Recorded Statements—Rule 106[1]

[1]—Rule 106 is Partial Codification of Common-Law Rule of Completeness

Rule 106 gives the party against whom all or part of a writing or recorded statement is offered the right to require the contemporaneous introduction of any other part of that writing or statement or any other writing or recorded statement that ought, in fairness, to be considered with it.[2] The Rule provides as follows:

Rule 106. Remainder of or Related Writings or Recorded Statements.

When a writing or recorded statement or part thereof is introduced by a party, an adverse party may require the introduction at that time of any other part or any other writing or recorded statement which ought in fairness to be considered contemporaneously with it.

[Adopted Jan. 2, 1975, effective July 1, 1975; amended Mar. 2, 1987, effective Oct. 1, 1987.]

Although this power is not explicit in Rule 106, the trial court also has discretion to exclude evidence altogether when the offering party is not willing to provide additional material required under the rule.[3] If for some reason, such as the invocation of a privilege, evidence necessary to correct a misleading impression is not admissible, the misleading evidence may also have to be excluded.[4]

Rule 106 applies only to a writing or recorded statement, and thus does not cover oral statements.[5] Rule 106 is, thus, essentially a partial codification of the common-law rule of completeness.[6]

The trial court, however, may have power under Rule 611(a) to require the

---

[1] *See* discussion in **Treatise** at Ch. 106, *Remainder of or Related Writing or Recorded Statements.*

[2] Fed. R. Evid. 106.

[3] *See, e.g.,* United States v. Millan, 230 F.3d 431, 435 (1st Cir. 2000) (trial court did not abuse its discretion in excluding excerpt of document when excerpt was misleading and proffering party declined to offer document in its entirety).

[4] *See, e.g.,* United States v. LeFevour, 798 F.2d 977, 981 (7th Cir. 1986).

[5] *See, e.g.,* United States v. Ortega, 203 F.3d 675, 682 (9th Cir. 2000) (Rule 106 applies only to written and recorded statements; it does not apply to officer's testimony about unrecorded oral confession); United States v. Harvey, 959 F.2d 1371, 1376 (7th Cir. 1992) (trial court did not err in refusing to allow cross examination of government agent as to defendant's additional oral statements; Rule 106 applies only to written and recorded materials).

[6] *See, e.g.,* Blue Cross & Blue Shield of N.J., Inc. v. Philip Morris, Inc., 199 F.R.D. 487, 489 (E.D.N.Y. 2001) (Weinstein, J.; Rule 106 is modified expression of "rule of completeness").

contemporaneous introduction of the balance of oral statements.[7] Moreover, Rule 32(a)(4) of the Federal Rules of Civil Procedure, which governs the use of transcripts of depositions at trial in civil cases, has its own partial codification of the rule of completeness that operates similarly to Rule 106.[8]

Rule 106 is designed to avoid two dangers: "The first is the misleading impression created by taking a statement out of context, and the second is the inadequacy of repair work when delayed to a point later in trial."[9] Because both the misleading impression and the inadequacy of delayed repair work prejudice the party against whom the incomplete evidence is offered, only that party has standing to require the admission of additional evidence under Rule 106.[10]

Rule 106 provides for additional evidence only when required for fairness. It does not require the automatic introduction of the remainder of a document just because the opponent so demands.[11] Indeed, at times, honoring such a request would lead to unfairness, especially when the additional material is neither explanatory of, nor relevant to, the excerpts that are offered.[12]

Rule 106 applies not only to the remainder of a particular writing or recording but also to related writings or recordings. There may be instances, for example, when a document creates a misleading impression that can be eliminated only by consideration of other documents, such as exhibits to the document or related correspondence. Rule 106 permits the contemporaneous introduction of such additional documents or recordings in those instances.

---

[7] Fed. R. Evid. 611(a); *see* § 2.02 for full discussion of trial court's power to control order of proof.

[8] Fed. R. Civ. P. 32(a)(4); *see* 7 MOORE'S FEDERAL PRACTICE, Ch. 32, *Use of Depositions in Court Proceedings* (Matthew Bender 3d ed.).

[9] *See* Original Advisory Committee's Note (reproduced verbatim at **Treatise,** § 106App.01[2]); *see also* United States v. Denton, 246 F.3d 784, 788–789 (6th Cir. 2001) (when defense counsel impeached witness by having her read portions of her statements to police, with result that statements appeared to be inconsistent, trial court did not abuse its discretion by permitting government to rehabilitate witness by having her read statements in their entirety on redirect examination).

[10] *See, e.g.,* Echo Acceptance Corp. v. Household Retail Servs., 267 F.3d 1068, 1089–1090 (10th Cir. 2001) (party cannot introduce otherwise inadmissible evidence under Rule 106 on coattails of its own or stipulated exhibits; if evidence of offering party might damage offering party because it is misleading, he or she can avoid problem by not offering it).

[11] *See, e.g.,* United States v. Walker, 272 F.3d 407, 417 (7th Cir. 2001) (Rule 106 requires introduction of portions of document to explain or qualify portions already introduced; when additional portions do not fill that objective, trial court does not err in excluding them).

[12] *See, e.g.,* United States v. Ramos-Caraballo, 375 F.3d 797, 803 (8th Cir. 2004) (defendant's impeachment of officer with portions of his suppression hearing testimony, grand jury testimony, and police report did not warrant admission of entirety of transcripts of his testimony and of police report).

However, Rule 106 does not supersede the authenticity rules.[13] Thus, it does not require the court to admit additional portions of a document unless either the party proffering the additional portions authenticates them or the court can ascertain that they come from the same document.[14]

There is a split of authority about whether Rule 106 allows for the admission of evidence that is otherwise inadmissible. Most courts hold that is does not, but only regulates the order of proof.[15] However, some courts have upheld its use to introduce otherwise excludable evidence.[16]

[2]—Scope of Trial Court's Discretion

Rule 106 does not set a hard and fast rule about when additional materials should be introduced. It grants the trial court the power to determine whether "fairness" requires the introduction of additional information to qualify or explain the originally offered information or to place it into context.[17]

It is an abuse of discretion for the trial court to refuse to require admission of additional information that is necessary to explain the original material or to put it into context.[18] This is not to say, however, that the trial court lacks discretion in determining how the parties may use their trial time in exposing the jury to the additional material.[19]

---

[13] Fed. R. Evid. 901; Fed. R. Evid. 902.

[14] *See, e.g.,* Orr v. Bank of Am., NT & SA, 285 F.3d 764, 776 n.16 (9th Cir. 2002) (when unauthenticated portions "readily indicate" that they are from authenticated document).

[15] *See, e.g.,* United States v. Guevara, 277 F.3d 111, 127 (2d Cir. 2001) (Rule 106 does not make otherwise inadmissible hearsay admissible).

[16] *See, e.g.,* United States v. LeFevour, 798 F.2d 977, 980–982 (7th Cir. 1986) (otherwise inadmissible evidence that is necessary to correct misleading impression is "admissible for this limited purpose by force of Rule 106," or original evidence must also be excluded).

[17] *See, e.g.,* United States v. Bollin, 264 F.3d 391, 414 (4th Cir. 2001) (purpose of Rule 106 is "to prevent a party from misleading the jury by allowing into the record relevant portions of the excluded testimony which clarify or explain the part already received").

[18] *See, e.g.,* Beech Aircraft Corp. v. Rainey, 488 U.S. 153, 170–172, 109 S. Ct. 439, 102 L. Ed. 2d 445 (1988) ("[c]learly the concerns underlying Rule 106 are relevant here," but, under general rules of relevance, "when one party had made use of a portion of a document, such that misunderstanding or distortion can be averted only through presentation of another portion, the material required for completeness is ipso facto relevant and therefore admissible under Rules 401 and 402.").

[19] *See, e.g.,* United States v. Webber, 255 F.3d 523, 525 (8th Cir. 2001) (trial court did not abuse its "substantial discretion" to control manner in which parties presented surveillance tapes to jury when (1) both tapes and transcripts were admitted into evidence, (2) government was allowed to play individual tapes out of sequence during its case-in-chief, (3) court advised jury that tapes would be available for playing during its deliberations, and (4) defense was allowed to play all tapes in order during its case, or to urge jury to do so during its deliberations; defense had ample opportunity to use tapes in presenting its theory that defendant was merely "puffing" and telling

It is also an abuse of discretion for the trial court to require the introduction of additional material if the additional material does not put into context or clarify the portion of the evidence originally offered.[20]

A party seeking to introduce additional documentary information under Rule 106 should offer it when the other party offers the incomplete excerpt.[21] Nevertheless, the trial court's broad discretion to control the orderly presentation of evidence during a trial[22] may empower the court to delay presentation of the additional materials to a later time, to facilitate the orderly and coherent presentation of evidence.[23]

§ 2.06   Calling and Interrogation of Witnesses by Court—Rule 614[1]

Rule 614 is in accord with usual practice and the common-law tradition in recognizing the trial court's right to call and question witnesses. The source of this right lies in the nature of the judicial function: A trial is a search for the truth and the court is more than a mere umpire of the proceedings.[2] It is a right that is not unlimited; excessive intervention by the court interferes with the jury's right to decide facts, is at odds with the adversary system, and deprives parties of their right to an impartial arbiter.[2.1] The Rule provides as follows:

Rule 614.   Calling and Interrogation of Witnesses by Court.

(a) Calling by court. The court may, on its own motion or at the suggestion of a party, call witnesses, and all parties are entitled to cross-examine witnesses thus called.

---

stories in his dealings with law enforcement agents).

[20] *See, e.g.,* United States v. Moussaoui, 382 F.3d 453, 481 (4th Cir. 2004) (Rule 106's purpose is to shield party from improper adverse inferences; it allows only explanation or rebuttal of evidence already received).

[21] *See, e.g,.* Jamison v. Collins, 291 F.3d 380, 387 (6th Cir. 2002) (party seeking to have document introduced for sake of completeness must request that additional document be admitted at time of introduction of allegedly incomplete document).

[22] *See* Fed. R. Evid. 611; United States v. King, 351 F.3d 859, 866 (8th Cir. 2003) ("district court has broad discretion to conduct the trial in an orderly and efficient manner, and to choose among reasonable evidentiary alternatives to satisfy the rule of completeness reflected in Rule 106"); § 2.02.

[23] *See, e.g.,* Phoenix Assocs. III v. Stone, 60 F.3d 95, 103 (2d Cir. 1995) ("While the wording of Rule 106 appears to require the adverse party to proffer the associated document or portion contemporaneously with the introduction of the primary document, we have not applied this requirement rigidly").

[1] *See* discussion in **Treatise** at Ch. 14, *Calling and Interrogation of Witness by Court.*

[2] *See, e.g.,* United States v. Adedoyin, 369 F.3d 337, 342 (3d Cir. 2004).

[2.1] *See, e.g.,* Rivera-Torres v. Velez, 341 F.3d 86, 100 (1st Cir. 2003) (trial court's right to question witnesses is limited by requirement that court maintain its image of impartiality).

(b) Interrogation by court. The court may interrogate witnesses, whether called by itself or by a party.

(c) Objections. Objections to the calling of witnesses by the court or to interrogation by it may be made at the time or at the next available opportunity when the jury is not present.

By providing that the trial court "may" call witnesses, Rule 614(a) recognizes that calling witnesses is a matter of judicial discretion rather than duty,[3] and that a court's failure to call a witness on its own, or at the suggestion of a party, is not a ground for reversal.[4] Ordinarily, the court's exercise of its right will not lead to a reversal either, unless the appellate court concludes that the trial court's action interfered with the fairness of the trial.[5] Rule 614(a) provides that all parties are entitled to cross-examine a witness called by the court.

Although Rule 614(b) acknowledges the court's power to interrogate all witnesses,[6] it is often suggested that this right be exercised sparingly.[7] The court may ask questions of a witness to clarify testimony for the jury,[8] to correct misstatements, or to fully develop the relevant facts and assist the jury in giving meaning to such facts by organizing them in a coherent manner.[9] However, the court must at all times retain its role of impartial arbiter.[10] Although it has a duty to assist the

---

[3] See, e.g., United States v. Alfaro, 336 F.3d 876, 882 (9th Cir. 2003) (trial court did not abuse its discretion in calling and interrogating witnesses at defendant's sentencing hearing).

[4] See, e.g., United States v. Cochran, 955 F.2d 1116, 1122 (7th Cir. 1992) (trial did not err in refusing to call two confidential informants as court's witnesses; court noted that it was unable to find a single example of a reversal because of a trial court's decision not to call a witness).

[5] See, e.g., Gaydar v. Sociedad Instituto Gineco-Quirurgico y Planificacion Familiar, 345 F.3d 15, 22–23 (1st Cir. 2003) (trial judge's questioning of defendant's medical doctor fact witness, even when some questions called for expression of expert opinion, was not error when witness's expert testimony was minimal and corroborative of testimony given by expert witnesses called by both parties).

[6] See, e.g., United States v. Green, 293 F.3d 886, 892–893 (5th Cir. 2002).

[7] See Civil Trial Practice Standard 10 (Comment, n.4) (A.B.A. 1998) ("Although the court has the power to call witnesses under Fed. R. Evid. 614(a) and analogous state provisions, this power is rarely exercised, probably because the court has no opportunity to prepare a witness to testify and may, by calling an unprepared witness, inject evidence into a case that might damage a party unfairly"). The Civil Trial Standards are reprinted in an appendix to Imwinkelried & Schlueter, FEDERAL EVIDENCE TACTICS (Matthew Bender 1999).

[8] See, e.g., United States v. Davis, 285 F.3d 378, 381 (5th Cir. 2002) ("A trial judge's questioning of witnesses is permissible if aimed at clarifying the evidence or managing the trial.").

[9] See, e.g., Stevenson v. D.C. Metro. Police Dep't., 248 F.3d 1187, 1190 (D.C. Cir. 2001) (trial courts may question witnesses "repeatedly and aggressively" to clear up confusion and manage trials or where testimony is inarticulately or reluctantly given).

[10] See, e.g., United States v. Villarini, 238 F.3d 530, 536 (4th Cir. 2001) (although trial court has discretion to interrogate witnesses, it should not give appearance of partiality or undermine legitimate efforts of any party to present its case); see also Civil Trial Practice Standard 10(c)

jurors in eliciting the truth, it also has an obligation to ensure that they reach their own conclusions.

In a criminal case, in particular, the right to a fair trial may be jeopardized by overzealous questioning by the trial court.[11] In an extreme case, the appellate court will reverse if it finds that the judge acted as an advocate or invaded the province of the jury.[12] Reversals are rare, however. It is the impact of the questioning on the rights of the litigants, and not the sheer volume of the court's questions, that is decisive.[13]

Unless counsel are particularly obtuse, it should usually be enough for the court to suggest a line of questioning to counsel.[14] Particularly when expert testimony or technical terminology is involved, the court may suggest to counsel that the witness be asked to clarify testimony or define terms so that the lay jurors can follow.

As when the trial judge has applied Rule 103 or Standard 107, the appellate court

---

(A.B.A. 1998) ("Except in unusual circumstances, the court should not seek to impeach or rehabilitate a witness, nor seek to emphasize or de-emphasize the importance of any witness or testimony"). The Civil Trial Standards are reprinted in an appendix to Imwinkelried & Schlueter, FEDERAL EVIDENCE TACTICS (Matthew Bender 1999).

[11] *See, e.g.,* United States v. Green, 293 F.3d 886, 892–893 (5th Cir. 2002) (when interrogating witnesses pursuant to Rule 614, trial court must be careful not to express bias and to avoid confusing roles of judge and prosecutor); United States v. Beaty, 722 F.2d 1090, 1095-1096 (3d Cir. 1983) (trial judge's lengthy and "overzealous" questioning of three defense witnesses, including key alibi witness whose credibility was blatantly attacked, was reversible error).

[12] United States v. Tilghman, 134 F.3d 414, 416 (D.C. Cir. 1998) (trial judge's aggressive and overly pointed questioning of defendant affected defendant's substantial rights and constituted abuse of discretion); United States v. Saenz, 134 F.3d 697, 701–702 (5th Cir. 1998) (trial judge's intervention, which was both quantitatively and qualitatively substantial, denied defendant a fair trial).

[13] United States v. Martin, 189 F.3d 547, 553 (7th Cir. 1999) (in reviewing challenges to judge's questions to witness, appellate court makes two inquiries: first, whether, by its conduct, trial court conveyed to jury bias regarding defendant's honesty or guilt; and, second, whether complaining party can show serious prejudice resulting from court's comments or questions); *see, e.g.,* United States v. Lankford, 196 F.3d 563, 572–573 (5th Cir. 1999) (trial judge's frequent comments and questions did not stray from neutrality); United States v. Deters, 184 F.3d 1253, 1256–1257 (10th Cir. 1999) (judicial remarks during course of trial that are critical or disapproving of, or even hostile to, counsel, parties, or their cases, ordinarily do not support bias or partiality challenge).

[14] *See* Holland v. Commissioner, 835 F.2d 675, 676 (6th Cir. 1987) (trial judge's suggestion that the government procure a handwriting expert was "somewhat unusual," but was in substantial compliance with Rule 614); *see also* Civil Trial Practice Standard 10(a) (A.B.A. 1998) (court should not question witness about subjects not raised unless court has provided opportunity to explain omission; if court believes questioning is necessary, court should afford parties opportunity to develop subject on further examination of witness). The Civil Trial Standards are reprinted in an appendix to Imwinkelried & Schlueter, FEDERAL EVIDENCE TACTICS (Matthew Bender 1999).

will consider the trial judge's actions under Rule 614 in the context of the case. Factors a reviewing court may consider are: the extent to which the witnesses' testimony needed clarification; whether the witnesses were unusually hesitant and in need of assurance; the trial court's use of leading questions; the degree to which the court interfered with cross-examination, and whether the court's interruptions favored one side exclusively; whether the court instructed the jury to arrive at its own conclusions;[15] whether the parties were adequately represented;[16] the objections made to the court's questioning; and the complexity of the facts and the trial judge's familiarity with them.[17]

Subdivision (c) of Rule 614 is designed to accommodate the aims of Rule 605 (automatic objection when the judge is called as a witness) and Rule 103 (parties have the responsibility for making timely objections). It seeks to protect the attorney against the possible embarrassment attendant upon making objections in the presence of the jury, but insists on counsel's responsibility to object at a time when corrective measures can still be taken.[18] Since counsel need not object until the next opportunity when the jury is absent, counsel do not forfeit their rights by failing to object when the judge asks the first question. Rather, they have a limited opportunity[19] to assess the judge's attitude towards the particular witness before deciding whether an objection is required to protect their client's rights.

---

[15] *See* Civil Trial Practice Standard 10(d) (A.B.A. 1998) ("The court should instruct the jury that questions from the court, like questions from the lawyers, are not evidence; that questions by the court should not be given special weight or emphasis; and that the fact that the court asks a questions does not reflect a view on the merits of the case or of the credibility of any witness"). The Civil Trial Standards are reprinted in an appendix to Imwinkelried & Schlueter, FEDERAL EVIDENCE TACTICS (Matthew Bender 1999).

[16] *See* Civil Trial Practice Standard 10 (Comment) (A.B.A. 1998) ("In dealing with inexperienced counsel, particularly those with little or no trial experience, the court from time to time may interject questions without consulting counsel to save time"). The Civil Trial Standards are reprinted in an appendix to Imwinkelried & Schlueter, FEDERAL EVIDENCE TACTICS (Matthew Bender 1999).

[17] *See* cases cited in **Treatise** at § 614.04[2], [4][b].

[18] *See, e.g.,* United States v. Godwin, 272 F.3d 659, 671–674 (4th Cir. 2001) (when party fails to object to trial judge's interrogation of witness, appellate court can reverse only if defendant shows trial court abused its discretion, error was clear and obvious, and error actually changed trial's outcome).

[19] *See* United States v. Billups, 692 F.2d 320, 327 (4th Cir. 1982) (defense waived objection when it did not object to judge's interrogation of defendant until after testimony concluded; defendant could have objected at end of first day of testimony or at beginning of proceedings on next day when jury was absent).

§ 2.07   Summing Up and Comment by Judge—Standard 107[1]

[1]—Status of Standard

Supreme Court Standards are not part of the Federal Rules of Evidence. The Supreme Court originally proposed the Standards as Rules, but they were stricken by Congress before enactment of the Rules.[1] Standard 107 addresses the power of the trial court to summarize and comment on the evidence, provided any such comment informs the jurors that they have the ultimate responsibility for resolving issues of fact. The text is consistent with long-standing federal practice; it was not enacted by Congress, however, because of opposition by attorneys trained in states where the trial judge does not have these powers.[2] In striking the provision, Congress did not intend to affect federal practice. Consequently, the proposed rule should be viewed as a standard to be consulted as a useful restatement of existing law.

The standard provides:

Supreme Court Standard 107.   Summing Up and Comment by Judge.

After the close of the evidence and arguments of counsel, the judge may fairly and impartially sum up the evidence and comment to the jury upon the weight of the evidence and the credibility of the witnesses, if he also instructs the jury that they are to determine for themselves the weight of the evidence and the credit to be given to the witnesses and that they are not bound by the judge's summation or comment.

---

[2]—Summing Up

Federal common law authorizes the judge to summarize the evidence in the case for the benefit of the jury after the close of arguments by counsel. By retaining this traditional power, the federal judicial system preserves one of the most effective tools the court has at its disposal to assist the jury in arriving at a just verdict.[1] A

---

[1]   *See* discussion in **Treatise** at Ch. 107, *Summing Up and Comment by Judge (Sup. Ct. Standard 107).*

[1]   *See* discussion in **Treatise** at § 107.02.

[2]   *See* Congressional Action on Standard 107 in **Treatise** at § 107 App.01[3].

[1]   Nudd v. Burrows, 91 U.S. 426, 439 23 L. Ed. 286, 289 (1875) ("[I]t is the right and duty of the court to aid them [the jury], by recalling the testimony to their recollection; by collating its details; by suggesting grounds of preference where there is contradiction; by directing their attention to the most important facts, . . . by resolving the evidence, however complicated, into its simplest elements, and by showing the bearing of its several parts and their combined effect, stripped of every consideration which might otherwise mislead or confuse them. How this duty shall be performed depends in every case upon the discretion of the judge. There is none more important resting upon those who preside at jury trials. Constituted as juries are, it is frequently impossible for them to

statement by the court of its recollection of the evidence immediately following the summations of counsel can do much to place counsel's unavoidably partisan restatements in proper perspective.

The distinction between the court's power to summarize and its right to comment on the evidence should not be over-emphasized; some courts, in fact, use the terms interchangeably. To the extent that a summary given by the court falls short of a recitation of the entire transcript, the very process of choosing which testimony to review and which to leave out is in itself a comment on the evidence and the court must remind the jurors that if their recollection of the evidence is different from that of the court, then they should reach a verdict based upon the evidence as they remember it.

Although the court has broad discretion on when and how[2] to summarize, it is improper for the court to assume the existence of facts at issue by characterizing the evidence "as facts rather than as testimony"[3] to be considered by the jury in deciding the facts. In a criminal case where the facts are not in dispute, the court may not presume that the defendant committed the acts charged with the requisite criminal intent by failing to charge the jury that it must find intent.[4] Nor is it proper without the accused's consent for the court to characterize as "uncontroverted" or "undisputed" any fact that the prosecution must establish as true in order for the defendant to be found guilty.

When summarizing the case for the jury, the court must be careful to review only the evidence actually presented to the jury. Thus, it is error for the court, without the consent of the parties, to inform the jury of facts brought to the court's attention during hearings or colloquies conducted outside the jury's presence, or upon a hypothetical or conjectural state of facts not established by the evidence.

The court's summary of the evidence must be accurate. Although misstatements of facts of a minor nature will rarely be grounds for reversible error, serious distortion of the evidence or the theories proffered to explain it can constitute the basis for a reversal if it deprived the party of having the evidence impartially considered by the jury.

If a party requests the court to charge on a particular theory, the theory must be put before the jury, along with a statement of the evidence that supports it if the

---

discharge their function wisely and well without this aid. In such cases, chance, mistake, or caprice, may determine the result.").

   [2] *See* discussion of different ways in which the court can summarize the evidence in **Treatise** at §§ 107.10–107.13.

   [3] Hardy v. United States, 335 F.2d 288, 290 (D.C. Cir. 1964), *rev'd on other grounds,* 375 U.S. 277 (1964).

   [4] *See* discussion of presumptions in criminal cases in Chapter 5.

court desires,[5] as long as the theory is valid and is supported by evidence sufficient to go to the jury,[6] even if the court considers the evidence weak or improbable. It is not for the court to decide whether the evidence is worthy of belief; that is a question only the jury can resolve. It is reversible error "to submit the evidence and theory of one party prominently and fully . . . and not call attention to the main points of the opposite party's case."[7]

Regardless of the instructions offered by the parties, the court has an independent duty to charge the jury correctly on the law. Although numerous cases state that a court is relieved of its obligation to charge on a particular theory when a party does not appropriately request it, a reversal on the basis of plain error may occur if the reviewing court believes that substantial rights were ignored. As in the case of erroneous rulings on evidence governed by Rule 103, the appellate court's determination will hinge on the particular facts presented. It will consider factors such as the party's failure to object, the type of case—criminal or civil, complicated or simple—the length of the trial, the nature of the trial judge's summary and instructions, and the context in which they were given, in determining whether the trial court properly exercised its discretion in reviewing the evidence.

In the vast majority of cases there are no inflexible rules dictating the requisite method of summation. It is preferable for the court to keep an open mind as to which method should be used in a particular case or in a portion of the case. When appropriate, the court should not hesitate to adopt the form of evidentiary review best suited to meet the exigencies of the case before it. Some elements of the charge may require a detailed marshaling of the facts implicated by the charge, and for other portions a brief summary will suffice.

The jury should get the impression that the court is presenting its own—rather than a party's—summary and charge. Nevertheless, the jury will sometimes be

---

[5] *See* United States v. Fowler, 932 F.2d 306, 316 (4th Cir. 1991) (no error in refusing to give defendant's requested instruction setting forth facts supporting his theory of defense; court must instruct jury on law pertaining to theory of defense, but "it is not obligated to summarize the defendant's evidence").

[6] United States v. Shenker, 933 F.2d 61, 65 (1st Cir. 1991) (no error in denying requested instruction on theory of defense that was "impermissibly broad"); United States v. Evans, 924 F.2d 714, 718 (7th Cir. 1991) (no error in refusing to give instruction on entrapment, since the evidence was insufficient to raise a jury question on this theory of defense).

[7] Pullman v. Hall, 46 F.2d 399, 404 (4th Cir. 1931). *See* Bentley v. Stromberg-Carlson Corp., 638 F.2d 9, 10 (2d Cir. 1981) (reversible error for trial judge to stress defendant's contentions at great length by "an almost verbatim reading of [its] trial brief," and to make no reference to plaintiff's evidence). *See also* United States v. Blakeney, 942 F.2d 1001, 1012–1013 (6th Cir. 1991), *cert. denied,* 502 U.S. 1008 (1991), 502 U.S. 1035 (1992) (charge did not usurp jury's role or shift burden of proof; court summarized government's theory and defense theory and the respective supporting facts).

made aware of the source of an instruction or partial summary because it hears the court adopt the suggestion of counsel. Even when the objection is made at side bar after the main charge and the court turns to the jury and makes a further statement, it will be apparent that the addition favors a particular side and was made at the request of the side it favors. For this reason, among others, it is preferable to go over a full draft of the charge before it is delivered and make any changes after discussion with counsel. In reading the charge, the court may depart slightly from non-critical language to keep up the jurors' and its own interest. Communication to the jurors is more desirable than pandering to the appellate court.

Many errors can be avoided if counsel submit their requests for instructions and confer with the court well in advance of summation, when there is still time to clear up misunderstandings and to ensure that the instructions will accurately reflect the theories asserted by both sides. If a conference is impractical or disagreement persists, counsel must protect their clients by objecting at the time the instructions are delivered so that the court has a final opportunity to correct its remarks, and the objectors are assured of a record on which to appeal.

[3]—Comments on the Evidence

The power of a trial court to comment on the evidence, is broad.[1] Generally, no error results if the court confines its remarks to the evidence in the case, specifically instructs the jury that the opinions expressed are those of the court and are not binding, and informs the jurors that they have the ultimate responsibility for resolving issues of fact.[2] With the exception of certain situations,[3] the decision whether or not to comment on the evidence under the circumstances of a particular case lies almost entirely within the discretion of the trial court. A failure to comment on the evidence, as opposed to reviewing the evidence and stating the applicable law, does not constitute error.[4] Although the court has the option of indicating its own opinions on the evidence, it rarely does so explicitly.

---

[1] *See* discussion in **Treatise** at §§ 107.20–107.26.

[2] *See, e.g.,* United States v. Ray, 250 F.3d 596, 601–602 (8th Cir. 2001) (trial court may comment on evidence to assist jury's understanding so long as it makes it clear that jurors must make all factual determinations themselves); United States v. Sanchez-Lopez, 879 F.2d 541, 553 (9th Cir. 1989) (trial judge's comments to defendants' witness during cross-examination permissible; court instructed jury that its comments were merely expressions of opinion of the facts and the jury was free to disregard them).

[3] Limitations on the judge's power to comment are imposed by rule, case law and statute in some circumstances. *See, e.g.,* discussion of Standard 513 (prohibiting comment on assertion of a testimonial privilege) in Chapter 18; Griffin v. California, 380 U.S. 609, 615 85 S. Ct. 1229, 1233 14 L. Ed. 2d 106, *reh'g denied,* 381 U.S. 957 (1965) (comments on defendant's invocation of privilege against self-incrimination violated fifth amendment).

[4] *See, e.g.,* United States v. McClatchy, 249 F.3d 348, 357 (5th Cir. 2001) (trial court did not abuse its discretion in refusing proposed instructions because they sought comment on evidence);

In practice, the primary significance of the court's power to comment is that it enables an appellate court to uphold a jury verdict when the trial court did not intend to express an opinion on the evidence but where the record shows that the jurors could have inferred that it did from the wording of the charge or other remarks. If the trial court is so carried away in its remarks as to lose its sense of propriety and impartiality, the reviewing court may find that the parties have been deprived of their right to a fair and impartial trial.[5]

There is almost never any justification for informing the jurors which witnesses the trial court thinks are telling the truth.[6] Advising the jury about the factors to consider in evaluating a witness' credibility may be considerably more helpful. Jurors are, for instance, generally unaware of all the factors that should be taken into consideration in evaluating the testimony of an accomplice or an informer; a court may wish to caution the jury to treat such evidence with suspicion and caution.[7] In the case of witnesses who have no clearly defined biases, the better practice is simply to advise the jury with respect to the general factors used in evaluating the credibility of any witness and the freedom to reject part or all of a witness' testimony.[8]

Emergency One, Inc. v. American FireEagle, Ltd., 228 F.3d 531, 539 (4th Cir. 2000) (trial courts are not required to comment on evidence).

[5] *See, e.g.,* United States v. Hickman, 592 F.2d 931, 936 (6th Cir. 1979) ("When one combines the limitation on cross-examination, the anti-defendant tone of the judge's interruptions, the wholesale taking over of cross-examination of defense witnesses by the trial judge; one is left with the strong impression that these two defendants did not receive the fair and impartial trial which the Sixth Amendment to the Constitution guarantees them."); United States v. Yates, 553 F.2d 518, 521 (6th Cir. 1977) (court's comment that defendant had clearly admitted participation in robbery adversely affected substantial right of defendant to have defense fairly heard and guilt determined by jury). *See* discussion in **Treatise** of standards of review employed by the appellate courts in determining whether the trial judge's comments amounted to reversible error in **Treatise** at §§ 107.20–107.26.

[6] *See, e.g.,* United States v. Anton, 597 F.2d 371, 372 (3d Cir. 1979) (trial court's statement that he regarded defendant as "devoid of credibility" deprived defendant of right to have credibility determined by jury; reversible error when combined with favorable comments on testimony of 13 Roman Catholic priests who testified for prosecution).

[7] *See, e.g.,* United States v. Anguilo, 897 F.2d 1169, 1208 (1st Cir. 1990) (trial court instructed jury that the testimony of an informer who gives evidence for pay or other personal gain must be examined or weighed with care); United States v. Gleason, 616 F.2d 2, 15 (2d Cir. 1979), *cert. denied,* 444 U.S. 931, 1082 (1980) (court has duty to give balanced instructions; where it points out that certain witnesses' testimony is suspect, such as that of accomplices or co-conspirators, those who have made plea bargains or are awaiting sentence, those granted immunity, and defendants, "it must also direct the jury's attention to the fact that it may well find these witnesses to be truthful, in whole or in part").

[8] *See, e.g.,* United States v. Thompson, 944 F.2d 1331, 1344–1345 (7th Cir. 1991), *cert. denied,* 502 U.S. 1097 (1992) (no error to refuse to instruct jury that witness's testimony had been impeached; court properly instructed jury that it did not have to accept "as gospel" the testimony of

It is rarely, if ever, appropriate for a federal judge to exercise the prerogative to express views on the ultimate issues of a trial—guilt and liability. In civil cases, the power is superfluous. The court should direct a verdict if its opinion is based upon the conclusion that no other finding could be made by a reasonable juror. In a criminal case, the court must direct a verdict of acquittal if it believes that the evidence produced by the government, with all the inferences viewed in its favor, would not support a verdict of guilty beyond a reasonable doubt. If the court thinks that a verdict of acquittal is not indicated, the court is of most help to the jury when it confines its remarks to the considerations that the jury should take into account in order to reach a just verdict.[9]

The power of a trial judge to comment on the weight and sufficiency of the evidence is one of the tools for exercising substantial control over the admission and presentation of evidence. Together with Rule 105 (authorizing limiting instructions), Rule 403 (permitting the exclusion of relevant but unduly prejudicial evidence), Rule 611 (allowing the court to regulate the mode and order of the presentation of the evidence) and Rule 614 (allowing a judge both to call and to question witnesses), it allows the trial court to structure the reception of evidence in a manner which effectively promotes the search for truth while avoiding needless waste of time and unfairness to either party.

Allowing the court to give the jury the benefit of its experience by explaining and analyzing the evidence provides additional advantages. The power to comment on the probative value of the proof offered by the parties, coupled with the option of giving the jury an instruction limiting the application of the evidence to its proper scope, has an inevitably liberalizing impact upon the standards governing the admissibility of evidence. If the trial court had no power to control the effect of an offer of evidence once it was admitted, the tendency would be to admit less.

However, there are few occasions when the court should reveal its own conclusions on the weight of the evidence. When the court does comment, it should

the prosecution witnesses and that it was up to them to resolve any inconsistencies in the testimony); United States v. Dove, 916 F.2d 41, 42 (2d Cir. 1990) (failure to give balanced instruction on witnesses' identification was reversible error; court should have advised jurors that they were free to consider and weigh the effect of the witnesses' failure to identify the defendant in open court); United States v. Love, 767 F.2d 1052, 1064–1065 (4th Cir. 1985), *cert. denied,* 474 U.S. 1081 (1986) (court instructed jury as to factors it may consider in evaluating opinion of voice identification expert).

[9] *See, e.g.,* United States v. Chanthadara, 230 F.3d 1237, 1249–1252 (10th Cir. 2000) (jury's exposure, during penalty phase of trial, to magazine article in which trial judge was quoted as characterizing defendant's defense as "smoke screen" was sufficiently prejudicial, in light of paucity of evidence respecting aggravating factors, to warrant reversal of jury-imposed death sentence, even though trial court immediately gave jury effective instructions that it was sole judge of credibility of defendant's defenses).

be careful to explain the reasoning behind its conclusions so that the jury will be given a clear basis in the evidence upon which it can accept or reject the court's opinion. In such instances, the adequacy of the court's reminder to the jury that the remarks are not binding also becomes important.

Comments by the court can clear up ambiguities in the testimony, and indicate to the jury which inferences may rationally be drawn from the evidence before it. The court's comments should be guided by the same general principles of relevancy and prejudice that govern the introduction of evidence-in-chief. The court is expected to be more circumspect, less emotional, and more rational in its analysis than attorneys for the parties. Comments of an ad hominem nature are not within the scope of the power to comment on the weight and sufficiency of the evidence.

The federal trial court is not required to refrain from remarking on the evidence until after counsel have finished their closing arguments. It is fully consistent with the rationale underlying Standard 107 for the trial court to clarify the purpose for which evidence is being offered, to explain the evidentiary law underlying the court's ruling, or to offer any other advice that will enable the jury to better understand the evidence being presented or its significance.[10] In fact, this will generally be the better practice during a protracted trial, since the jury may have a difficult time relating instructions which they receive at the end of the trial to evidence which they heard earlier in the course of the trial.

---

[10]   *Cf.* United States v. Jarrett, 956 F.2d 864, 866 (8th Cir. 1992) (no error in trial court's comments during cross-examination by defendant; witness was becoming confused and trial court was merely attempting to clarify prior exchange between the witness and defense counsel); United States v. Bourgeois, 950 F.2d 980, 985 (5th Cir. 1992) (judge's comment to the jurors during witness's testimony properly provided them with enough information to understand the witness's testimony while preventing disclosure of prejudicial evidence).

CHAPTER 3

*Power of Court in Relation to Jury**

---

* Chapter revised in 1993 by SANDRA D. KATZ, member of the New York Bar.

§ 3.01   Preliminary Questions in General—Rule 104

[1]—Scope and Text of Rule[1]

The admissibility of proffered evidence frequently depends on resolution of a multitude of difficult preliminary questions of fact. Rule 104 partially resolves the dilemma by stating in subdivision (b) that the jury determines preliminary questions on which the *relevance* of evidence depends, but that the court, pursuant to subdivision (a), makes other determinations such as the "qualification of a person to be a witness, the existence of a privilege, or the admissibility of evidence." The allocation of functions between judge and jury rests on the notion that only a judge can appropriately apply technical, evidentiary rules grounded in policy concerns. Lay persons are ill-equipped to engage in the necessary legal reasoning or to evaluate certain kinds of evidence, and will be less likely to disregard evidence that should not have been admitted once it comes to their attention.

Subdivision (e) provides that the admissibility of evidence relevant to weight or credibility—an issue that clearly must be resolved by the fact-finder—is unaffected by Rule 104. The last sentence of subdivision (a) and subdivisions (c) and (d) of Rule 104 govern some of the procedures at preliminary hearings.

The Rule provides as follows:

Rule 104.   Preliminary Questions.

(a) Questions of admissibility generally. Preliminary questions concerning the qualification of a person to be a witness, the existence of a privilege, or the admissibility of evidence shall be determined by the court, subject to the provisions of subdivision (b). In making its determination it is not bound by the rules of evidence except those with respect to privileges.

(b) Relevancy conditioned on fact. When the relevancy of evidence depends upon the fulfillment of a condition of fact, the court shall admit it upon, or subject to, the introduction of evidence sufficient to support a finding of the fulfillment of the condition.

(c) Hearing of jury. Hearings on the admissibility of confessions shall in all cases be conducted out of the hearing of the jury. Hearings on other preliminary matters shall be so conducted when the interests of justice require, or when an accused is a witness and so requests.

(d) Testimony by accused. The accused does not, by testifying upon a preliminary matter, become subject to cross-examination as to other issues in the case.

---

[1] *See* discussion in **Treatise** at § 104.02.

> (e) Weight and credibility. This rule does not limit the right of a party to introduce before the jury evidence relevant to weight or credibility.

[2]—Questions of Fact Allocated to the Court[2]

[a]—Determination of Preliminary Questions

Instead of setting forth a formula for allocating functions between judge and jury, Rule 104(a) specifies two instances of preliminary fact-finding that must be left to the court—the qualifications of a witness and the existence of a privilege. It goes on to state that the judge decides all preliminary questions concerning the admissibility of evidence except for those in which the relevancy of the evidence is conditioned on a fact.[3] It is the jury's responsibility to make the final decision concerning the existence of conditional facts on which admissibility depends.[3.1]

The combination of subdivisions (a) and (b) requires the court to determine those preliminary questions of fact that hinge on the application of technical or exclusionary evidentiary rules. Rule 104(a) is silent about the applicable standard of proof. The Supreme Court has held, in *Bourjaily v. United States*,[4] that the courts must use a preponderance of the evidence standard in determining pursuant to Rule 104(a) whether the conditions for admitting a co-conspirator's statement have been satisfied.[5] In a later decision, the Court extended the preponderance standard to all issues determined under Rule 104(a).[6]

---

[2] *See* discussion in **Treatise** at §§ 104.10–104.17.

[3] *See* Rule 104(a), (b); *see also* Blake v. Pellegrino, 329 F.3d 43, 47–48 (1st Cir. 2003) (trial court erred in excluding evidence because of doubts concerning its persuasiveness; under Rule 104, trial court decides questions concerning foundational facts relating to admissibility, jury decides questions concerning persuasiveness of evidence).

[3.1] *See, e.g.,* United States v. Ansaldi, 372 F.3d 118, 130–131 (2d Cir. 2004) (when there was evidence in record that would support jury determination that defendant saw FDA "Talk Paper" before he sold drug, trial court properly admitted "Talk Paper" because it was conditionally relevant as evidence of defendant's state of mind at time of sale); United States v. Balthazard, 360 F.3d 309, 313 (1st Cir. 2004) (when relevance of proffered evidence is dependent on jury's determination that prerequisite fact existed, offering party need only introduce sufficient evidence to permit reasonable jury to find prerequisite fact by a preponderance of the evidence to establish relevance of proffered evidence); *see* [3], *below*.

[4] Bourjaily v. United States, 483 U.S. 171, 175, 107 S. Ct. 2775, 2779, 97 L. Ed. 2d 144 (1987); *see also* United States v. Freeman, 208 F.3d 332, 342–343 (1st Cir. 2000) (trial court could properly exclude statement of defendant's alleged coconspirator on preponderance of evidence "while, at the same time, concluding that the evidence, viewed in the light most favorable to the government, would permit a rational juror to find the defendant guilty beyond a reasonable doubt").

[5] *See* Fed. R. Evid. 801(d)(2)(E) 1997 Committee Note ("[a]ccording to *Bourjaily*, Rule 104(a) requires these preliminary questions to be established by a preponderance of the evidence"); *see also* Ch. 15.

[6] Daubert v. Merrell Dow Pharms., Inc., 509 U.S. 579, 591 n.10, 113 S. Ct. 2786, 125 L. Ed. 2d 469 (1993) (preliminary questions concerning admissibility of evidence "should be established

When the relevance of proffered evidence depends on a condition of fact, however, Rule 104 does not require the trial court to make a preliminary determination of the fact based on a preponderance of the evidence. Under Rule 104(b), the court should only consider whether the jury could reasonably find the fact based on all the evidence of record. If so, the court conditionally admits the evidence and the final determination of the preliminary fact is reserved for the jury.[7]

[b]—Qualification of Witness

The trial court's responsibility under Rule 104(a) to determine preliminary questions concerning the qualification of witnesses is largely vitiated by Rule 601, which makes all witnesses competent except when state law supplies the rule of decision and declares a witness incompetent. The rules in Article VI of the Federal Rules rely on the jury's capacity to evaluate the relative credibility of witnesses. They discard insanity, infancy, interest in the proceedings, and religious belief as absolute grounds of incompetence and retain only the requirement that the witness have personal knowledge of the matter to which the testimony relates.[8] Only if no reasonable person could give any credence to the witness, so that the probative weight of the testimony is at or close to zero, can the testimony be excluded. For example, the testimony of a witness who did not physically see what the testimony describes may be excludable on hearsay or opinion grounds, or under Rule 602 on the basis of lacking personal knowledge.

The trial court does, however, retain its power under Rule 104(a) to decide preliminary questions regarding the qualifications of expert witnesses and the reliability of their proposed testimony under Rule 702.[9] The nature of expert

---

by a preponderance of proof"); *see, e.g.,* United States v. Cherry, 217 F.3d 811, 815 (10th Cir. 2000) (trial court properly used preponderance of evidence standard in determining whether defendant wrongfully procured unavailability of witness and, therefore, forfeited objection to hearsay under Rule 804(b)(6)).

[7] Fed. R. Evid. 104(b) (court "shall admit" on "evidence sufficient to support a finding of the fulfillment of the condition"); *see* Huddleston v. United States, 485 U.S. 681, 690, 108 S. Ct. 1496, 99 L. Ed. 2d 771 (1988) (question whether defendant committed prior act is preliminary conditional question for admissibility of prior acts evidence under Rule 404(b)); Johnson v. Elk Lake Sch. Dist., 283 F.3d 138, 154–155 (3d Cir. 2002) (whether prior act was "offense of sexual assault" under Rule 413(d) is preliminary conditional question for its admissibility under Rule 415 and is to be determined by jury on preponderance of evidence if trial judge preliminarily determines, under Rule 104(b), that jury could reasonably make that determination); *see also* [3] *below.*

[8] *See* Rule 602, discussed in Chapter 10.

[9] Daubert v. Merrell Dow Pharms., Inc., 509 U.S. 579, 592, 597, 113 S. Ct. 2786, 125 L. Ed. 2d 469 (1993) (trial court must evaluate qualifications of proposed expert witnesses and must determine whether proposed testimony will assist trier of fact to understand or determine fact in issue); *see also* Gruca v. Alpha Therapeutic Corp., 51 F.3d 638, 643 (7th Cir. 1995) (district court erred in admitting expert testimony without first determining whether testimony was admissible under Rule 702); *see* Ch. 13.

testimony creates a danger that a jury will be unable to evaluate expert conclusions and opinions critically, without exercising the normal scrutiny that can be applied to lay testimony. This danger makes it imperative that expert opinion testimony be admitted only after the trial court has determined that the witness is properly qualified to give it and that the proffered testimony is reliable in an evidentiary sense.[10] This same danger leads to the trial court's obligation to make a determination under Rule 104(a) whether the facts or data on which proffered expert testimony is based, if they are not themselves admissible, are of a type reasonably relied on by experts in the field in forming their opinions or drawing their conclusions.[11]

The trial court also retains its authority under Rule 104(a) to decide preliminary questions regarding the qualifications of lay witnesses to give opinion testimony under Rule 701.[12]

[c]—Privileges

Numerous preliminary factual questions may have to be decided in ruling on the validity of a claim of privilege. For instance, a claim of attorney-client privilege may require resolution of such issues as whether the requisite relationship existed between the lawyer and the client, the communication in question was intended to be confidential, a waiver occurred, or an exception applied. All of these preliminary questions should be decided by the trial court pursuant to Rule 104(a).[13] Any other rule that allows privileged material to be divulged to the jury before the court rules on the existence of the privilege undermines the policies that led to the creation of the privilege in question. Irreparable damage to a confidential relationship may be sustained at the moment of disclosure regardless of whether the evidence is ultimately used by the trier of fact in reaching its verdict.

[d]—Hearsay

Rules 801, 803, and 804 require resolution of many preliminary issues of fact before it can be determined whether a proffered statement is excluded by the

---

[10] *See, e.g.,* Daubert v. Merrell Dow Pharms., Inc., 509 U.S. 579, 595, 113 S. Ct. 2786, 125 L. Ed. 2d 469 (1993) (capacity of expert evidence to be both powerful and quite misleading suggests that trial judges should exercise more control over experts than over other witnesses when implementing Fed. R. Evid. 403).

[11] *See* Fed. R. Evid. 703; In re "Agent Orange" Prod. Liab. Litig., 611 F. Supp. 1223, 1245 (E.D.N.Y. 1985), *aff'd,* 818 F.2d 187 (2d Cir. 1987); *see also* Ch. 13.

[12] *See, e.g.,* United States v. Rea, 958 F.2d 1206, 1216–1217 (2d Cir. 1992) (when lay opinion testimony is offered, trial court determines, under Rule 104(a), whether opinion is based on witness's personal knowledge and will be helpful to jury).

[13] *See, e.g.,* Cavallaro v. United States, 153 F. Supp. 2d 52, 56 (D. Mass. 2001) (applicability of attorney-client privilege to communications between client and accountant is preliminary question for court's determination under Rule 104(a)).

hearsay rule. Although Rule 104 is silent about the proper allocation of responsibility for this fact-finding as between court and jury, decisions under the Federal
Rules clearly indicate that it is the court pursuant to subdivision (a), rather than
the jury pursuant to subdivision (b), that must make these determinations.[14] Some
of the bases for admitting out-of-court statements require evidence of preliminary
facts that may be extremely prejudicial to the party against whom the statement
is offered. The appellate courts generally require in those circumstances that the
trial courts hold an evidentiary hearing outside the presence of the jury and that
the proffering party prove the preliminary facts by a preponderance of the evidence.[15]

Allocating to the court responsibility for preliminary questions about the applicability of the hearsay rule makes sense in terms of the principle underlying Rule
104(a)—that jurors should not have the responsibility of applying evidentiary rules
of a technical and exclusionary nature with a great potential for prejudice. Jurors
will not appreciate the relevant policy concerns underlying these rules, will not
assess the value of the evidence accurately, and will be unable to disregard the
improperly admitted evidence in reaching their conclusions.

The courts' treatment of the allocation issue can be seen most clearly with respect
to co-conspirators' statements governed by Rule 801(d)(2)(E).[16] The Supreme
Court has held that the court, rather than the jury, must find whether the requirements that allow co-conspirators' statements to be admitted have been satisfied.[17]
To ask the jurors to consider highly prejudicial statements of co-conspirators only
if they first find the existence of the conspiracy and defendant's participation in it,
is to present them with too tricky a task. When the conspiracy itself is charged, it
creates the absurdity of asking the jury in effect to decide the issue of guilt before
it may consider evidence that is probative of guilt. Although the court will be
deciding a preliminary fact that coincides with an ultimate fact in the case, the
parties are not deprived of a jury trial on the issue, since the judge and jury need
not agree on the resolution. Giving these preliminary questions to the jury would
violate the spirit of Rule 104, which calls for preliminary determinations by the

---

[14] *See, e.g.,* United States v. Harrison, 296 F.3d 994, 1001 (10th Cir. 2002) (trial court must
determine whether party adopted declarant's out-of-court statement for purposes of Rule
801(d)(2)(B)); Qualley v. Clo-Tex Int'l, Inc., 212 F.3d 1123, 1130 (8th Cir. 2000) (trial court, not
jury, must determine whether statements of alleged coconspirator are admissible under Rule
801(d)(2)(E)).

[15] *See, e.g.,* United States v. Dhinsa, 243 F.3d 635, 653–654 (2d Cir. 2001) (when government
seeks to introduce out-of-court statement of murder victim against alleged murderer under Rule
804(b)(6), trial court must hold evidentiary hearing out of jury's presence and government must
prove foundational facts by preponderance of evidence).

[16] *See* discussion of Rule 801(d)(2)(E) in Chapter 15, *Hearsay Exclusions.*

[17] Bourjaily v. United States, 483 U.S. 171, 175, 107 S. Ct. 2775, 97 L. Ed. 2d 144 (1987).

judge in all cases involving a high potential for prejudice. *See* Chs 15–17 for full discussion of preliminary issues applicable to the admissibility of out-of-court statements.

[e]—Coerced Confessions, Illegal Searches, and Improper Trial Procedures

On an evidentiary level, the exclusionary rules pose the same issues as the hearsay rule discussed above—the inability of the jury to comprehend the governing policies, to assess the reliability of the evidence, or to avoid being prejudiced by evidence that should have been excluded. Rule 104(a), therefore, governs the admissibility of this type of evidence.[17.1] In addition, constitutional requirements demand the same result.

[3]—Questions of Fact Allocated to the Jury[18]

Rule 104(b) creates a significant category of preliminary questions that are ultimately decided by the jury.

When a party offers evidence that is relevant only if the proffering party establishes a preliminary fact, the trial judge must determine whether the record would support a conclusion by a reasonable jury that the preliminary fact was established.[19]

If the trial judge's conclusion is in the affirmative, the jury must then determine whether the preliminary fact has been established. It may consider the evidence only if it concludes that the relevance has been established.[20] If the trial judge concludes that the record would not support a conclusion by a reasonable jury that

---

[17.1] *See, e.g.,* United States v. Del Rosario, No. 02-2377, 2004 U.S. App. LEXIS 22634, at *23 n.5 (1st Cir. Nov. 1, 2004) (trial court determines admissibility of evidence at suppression hearings, during which proscriptions against hearsay are not applicable).

[18] *See* discussion in **Treatise** at § 104.30.

[19] *See, e.g.,* Huddleston v. United States, 485 U.S. 681, 690, 108 S. Ct. 1496, 99 L. Ed. 2d 771 (1988) (whether defendant committed prior act is preliminary conditional question for admissibility of prior acts evidence under Rule 404(b); trial court need not determine that issue on preponderance of evidence, but should only consider whether jury could reasonably so find based on all evidence of record and, if so, conditionally admit the evidence); Johnson v. Elk Lake Sch. Dist., 283 F.3d 138, 154–155 (3d Cir. 2002) (whether prior act was "offense of sexual assault" under Rule 413(d) is preliminary conditional question for admissibility under Rule 415 and is to be determined by jury on preponderance of evidence if trial judge preliminarily determines, under Rule 104(b), that jury could reasonably make that determination).

[20] *See, e.g.,* Koster v. TWA, Inc., 181 F.3d 24, 33 (1st Cir. 1999) (court did not abuse its discretion in admitting provision from personnel manual; although there was some question whether manual applied to plaintiff, there was sufficient evidence of its applicability to support affirmative jury conclusion); MDU Resources Group v. W.R. Grace & Co., 14 F.3d 1274, 1281 (8th Cir. 1994) (trial court should have admitted article on danger of asbestos because plaintiff provided sufficient

the preliminary fact has been established, both the question concerning the preliminary fact and the evidence that was conditionally admitted are withdrawn from the jury's consideration.[21]

It is generally not necessary that the evidence of the preliminary fact be in the record when the conditionally admissible evidence is offered. The court may admit evidence on condition that the proffering party later provide evidence of the preliminary fact and "connect it up" with the evidence.[22]

The rationale behind giving such questions to the jury is that, since no protective evidentiary policy is at stake, "the jury is just as capable as the judge of making the determination. The only real discriminations required of the jurors in this process are evaluations of probative force such as they customarily make. Consequently, following the judge's instructions to disregard the primary evidence if they find against the preliminary fact does not call for the intellectual control required when they are told to ignore matters that should have been excluded under the rules discussed in connection with subdivision (a). In effect Rule 104(b) is an application of the order of proof rule, Rule 611(a).

Rule 104(b) must be read in conjunction with Rules 901(a) and 1008, which are discussed below.

[4]—Procedural Aspects of Preliminary Fact Determinations[23]

[a]—Applicability of Evidentiary Rules

The last sentence of Rule 104(a) states that, when a court is determining a preliminary question of fact pursuant to Rule 104(a), it need not apply any of the evidentiary rules except those with respect to privileges.[24] Because of their ex-

---

evidence to support jury finding defendant received article before installing asbestos in plaintiff's building).

[21] *See, e.g.,* United States v. Oliver, 278 F.3d 1035, 1042 (10th Cir. 2001) (when trial court admitted letter concerning defendant's DUI conviction on condition that government prove conviction was result of defendant's driving under influence of alcohol and subsequent information revealed defendant had been under influence of methamphetamine, letter was withdrawn and was never published to jury).

[22] *See* Fed. R. Evid. 104(b) ("court shall admit it upon, or subject to, the introduction of evidence"); *see also* United States v. Causor-Serrato, 234 F.3d 384, 389 (8th Cir. 2000) (district court conditionally admitted coconspirator statements and made final ruling on their admissibility at close of evidence); United States v. Santiago, 199 F. Supp. 2d 101, 105 (S.D.N.Y. 2002) (under Rule 104(b), court could admit coconspirator's statements subject to subsequent "connecting up" with evidence defendant was member of conspiracy).

[23] *See* discussion in **Treatise** at §§ 104.10, 104.40. Issues that arise at preliminary hearings in criminal cases are discussed in § 104.40.

[24] *See, e.g.,* United States v. Harrison, 296 F.3d 994, 1001 (10th Cir. 2002) (trial court is not bound by rules of evidence when it determines admissibility of proffered evidence).

perience and legal training, trial judges can be relied upon to properly evaluate the evidence and to put out of mind that which should be excluded. Thus, the judge will generally be fully cognizant of the inherent weakness of evidence by affidavit or hearsay and will take such weakness into account when evaluating its weight on the preliminary question.[25] Similarly, a trial judge generally is not bound by Rule 201 when taking judicial notice in connection with determinations of preliminary fact.[26]

Privilege rules are treated differently because any substantial breach of confidentiality threatens serious damage to the relationship protected by the privilege. Note, however, that in United States v. Zolin,[27] the Supreme Court held that Rule 104(a) does not bar a court from examining material as to which a claim of attorney-client privilege has been asserted to determine whether the crime-fraud exception applies.[28] "The Rule does not provide by its terms that all materials as to which a 'claim of privilege' is made must be excluded from consideration."[29]

[b]—Presence of Jury at Preliminary Hearings

Except for two specified instances, Rule 104(c) vests broad discretion in the trial court to decide whether preliminary hearings should be conducted outside the presence of the jury.[30] This flexibility comports with the fundamental concern of this rule for the protection of the parties. The primary consideration of the court in deciding whether to remove the jury is the potential for prejudice inherent in the evidence that the parties will produce on the preliminary question.[31] A court will, therefore, frequently exercise its prerogative to exclude the jury when, for instance, it has to rule on the admissibility of highly incriminating evidence proffered under

---

[25] See Bourjaily v. United States, 483 U.S. 171, 178, 107 S. Ct. 2775, 97 L. Ed. 2d 144 (1987) (trial court may rely on the very hearsay statements at issue in determining whether statements satisfy hearsay rule); see also United States v. $ 557, 933.89, More or less, in United States Funds, 287 F.3d 66, 84 (2d Cir. 2002) (trial court may properly rely on hearsay in ruling on suppression motion).
[26] See, e.g., Invest Almaz v. Temple-Inland Forest Prods. Corp., 243 F.3d 57, 69 (1st Cir. 2001).
[27] United States v. Zolin, 491 U.S. 554, 565, 109 S. Ct. 2619, 105 L. Ed. 2d 469 (1989).
[28] The Court stressed that in camera review should be granted only if the party opposing the privilege makes an adequate threshold showing.
[29] 491 U.S. at 566, 109 S. Ct. at 2628, 105 L. Ed. 2d at 487.
[30] See, e.g., United States v. White, 116 F.3d 903, 914–915 (D.C. Cir. 1997) (since courts have discretion under Rule 104(c) to admit co-conspirator statements "subject to connection" by later evidence, trial court had discretion to tentatively admit hearsay statements of deceased witness on a finding, itself based on hearsay, that the witness was murdered by the defendant, before jury heard admissible evidence of the murder; citing **Treatise** and collecting cases).
[31] See also Fed. R. Evid. 103(c) (hearings concerning admissibility of evidence be conducted so as to "prevent inadmissible evidence from being suggested to the jury").

an exception to the hearsay rule.[32]

In deciding to exercise its discretion under this subdivision, the court must, however, always be cognizant of the possible adverse effect on the jury's attitude toward the court and the parties if it is repeatedly excluded from what are apparently important decisions. The goal of this rule is protection of the interests of the parties and the possibility of an alienated jury must be weighed heavily against the potential harm involved in letting them hear the evidence on the preliminary question. In many instances the trial will move more swiftly and the intelligent jury will be less likely to fall into error if there are not constant interruptions for side-bar and other discussions outside the presence of the jury.

On the other hand, a pretrial in limine hearing, which would occur before a jury is impaneled, is probably appropriate when the admissibility issues are complex, such as when the court must determine the reliability of proffered expert testimony.[33] Many appellate courts strongly suggest the advisability of making those determinations in in limine hearings.[34] Generally, however, the trial court has broad discretion to determine the method by which it will make its admissibility determination, and is not required to hold a pretrial in limine hearing.[34.1]

---

[32] *See, e.g.,* United States v. Dhinsa, 243 F.3d 635, 653–654 (2d Cir. 2001) (prior to finding that criminal defendant waived his confrontation rights with respect to actual or potential witness's out-of-court statement admitted pursuant to Rule 804(b)(6), trial court must hold evidentiary hearing outside jury's presence in which government has burden of proving by preponderance of the evidence that (1) the defendant (or party against whom the out-of-court statement is offered) was involved in, or responsible for, procuring declarant's unavailability and (2) defendant (or party against whom out-of-court statement is offered) acted with intent of procuring declarant's unavailability).

[33] *See, e.g.,* Daubert v. Merrell Dow Pharms., Inc., 509 U.S. 579, 597, 113 S. Ct. 2786, 125 L. Ed. 2d 469 (1993) (trial court has obligation to determine reliability of proffered expert testimony before admitting it into evidence).

[34] *See, e.g.,* Pride v. BIC Corp., 218 F.3d 566, 578 (6th Cir. 2000) (trial court properly excluded expert testimony after pretrial evidentiary hearing); Goebel v. Denver & Rio Grande Western R.R., 215 F.3d 1083, 1087 (10th Cir. 2000) ("[t]he most common method for fulfilling this function [of gatekeeper for expert testimony] is a *Daubert* hearing"); Padillas v. Stork-Gamco, Inc., 186 F.3d 412, 417–418 (3d Cir. 1999) (Third Circuit has strong preference for pretrial hearings respecting reliability of expert testimony, even if neither party requests one, whenever bases for proposed expert witness's opinion "are insufficiently explained and the reasons and foundations for them inadequately and perhaps confusingly explicated."); United States v. Sinskey, 119 F.3d 712, 717 (8th Cir. 1997) (trial court properly admitted expert testimony it found reliable during pretrial evidentiary hearing); In re Paoli R.R. Yard PCB Litig., 916 F.2d 829, 859 (3d Cir. 1990) (in limine hearing is most efficient vehicle for trial courts to make pretrial admissibility decisions respecting proffered expert testimony).

[34.1] *See, e.g.,* Hangarter v. Provident Life & Accident Ins. Co., 373 F.3d 998, 1018 (9th Cir. 2004) (when trial court's probing of basis for expert witness's opinions expressed during testimony was sufficient to fulfill its gate-keeper function, it did not abuse its discretion by not holding formal *Daubert* hearing).

Other appellate courts, however, have upheld the trial court's discretion in deciding to hold evidentiary hearings on the reliability of expert testimony during the trial, so long as they took the necessary precautions to prevent the exposure of the jury to potentially inadmissible evidence.[35]

The court has no discretion when determining the admissibility of confessions or admissions of a defendant. The jury may not be present if there is a preliminary hearing on such a matter.[36] As a matter of sound practice, "in the interests of justice," hearings on the admissibility of illegally obtained evidence or the admissibility of eyewitness identification should also be conducted outside the presence of the jury because of the high likelihood of prejudice. Even if the evidence turns out to be admissible the jury may get the impression that the defendant falsely accused the law enforcement authorities of illegal activities to keep the jurors from learning the truth.

Rule 104(c) also requires the court to exclude the jury from a hearing on a preliminary matter when the accused is a witness, and so requests. Without this option, the defendant might not be in a position to testify freely on preliminary matters, and would be unable to take advantage of the protections afforded by Rule 104(d).

[c]—Testimony of Accused at Preliminary Hearing

Under Rule 104(d), an accused who testifies upon a preliminary matter is not subject to cross-examination as to other issues in the case. The government may cross-examine only on issues relevant to suppression of the evidence and credibility. The accused does not, therefore, completely waive the right to claim the privilege against self-incrimination when taking the stand on the preliminary question.[37] Additionally, a defendant does not waive the fifth amendment privilege not to testify at trial by testifying at a preliminary hearing.[38]

---

[35] *See, e.g.,* United States v. Hicks, 103 F.3d 837, 844–847 (9th Cir. 1996) (trial court properly admitted expert testimony it found reliable after evidentiary hearing conducted during trial); Cummins v. Lyle Indus., Inc., 93 F.3d 362, 365–370 (7th Cir. 1996) (trial court properly excluded expert testimony it found unreliable after evidentiary hearing conducted during trial).

[36] Rule 104(c). *See* Gilbert v. California, 388 U.S. 263, 272–273, 87 S. Ct. 1951, 18 L. Ed. 2d 1178 (1967) (hearings on confessions must occur outside of jury's hearing).

[37] United States v. Gomez-Diaz, 712 F.2d 949, 951–952 (5th Cir. 1983) (defendant could not limit his testimony at suppression hearing to answering a single question bearing on consent; Rule 104(d) permits full cross-examination on the "preliminary matter").

[38] United States v. Smith, 940 F.2d 710, 713 (1st Cir. 1991).

§ 3.02   Preliminary   Questions   of   Authentication   and Identification—Rule 901(a)[1]

Rule 901(a) treats preliminary questions of authenticity of writings and of identification as specialized applications of Rule 104(b).

Rule 901.   Requirement of Authentication or Identification.

(a) General provision. The requirement of authentication or identification as a condition precedent to admissibility is satisfied by evidence sufficient to support a finding that the matter in question is what its proponent claims.

The condition of fact that must be fulfilled by every offer of real proof is that the evidence is what its proponent claims.[2] The standard of admissibility is identical to that required under Rule 104(b) relating to matters of conditional relevance generally—would a finding of fulfillment of the condition be supported by the evidence?[3] Since the court must decide whether a reasonable juror might find for the proponent, the court should base its decision on the same evidence the jury will have before it—admissible evidence only. Once a prima facie showing of authenticity or identity is made, the evidence must be admitted.[4]

The trier may ultimately disbelieve the proponent's proof and entirely disregard or substantially discount the persuasive impact of the real proof. The opposing party may introduce evidence disputing genuineness and argue the point to the jury. Rule 901(a) recognizes that because the question for the jury is one of credibility and probative force, the jury is as competent as the court in deciding if the proffered evidence is what it purports to be.

---

[1] *See* discussion in **Treatise** at § 901.02.

[2] *See, e.g.,* Love v. National Med. Enters, 230 F.3d 765, 775 (5th Cir. 2000) ("The requirement of authentication or identification as a condition precedent to admissibility is satisfied by evidence sufficient to support a finding that the matter in question is what its proponent claims."); United States v. Tank, 200 F.3d 627, 629 (9th Cir. 2000) (citing **Treatise,** under Rule 901(a), proponent needs only make prima facie showing of authenticity, so that reasonable juror could find in favor of authenticity or identification).

[3] *See, e.g.,* L.A. News Serv. v. CBS Broad., Inc., 305 F.3d 924, 936 (9th Cir. 2002) (authentication does not require conclusive demonstration that article is genuine). Chapter 8 for discussion of different methods of authentication.

[4] *See, e.g.,* Smith v. City of Chicago, 242 F.3d 737, 742 (7th Cir. 2001) (once foundation for authenticity is laid, opponent of admission has burden to rebut).

§ 3.03 Preliminary Questions Concerning the Contents of Writings, Recordings and Photographs—Rule 1008[1]

[1]—Fact-Finding Functions of Court and Jury

Rule 1008 is a specialized application of the approach to preliminary questions adopted in Rule 104. It recognizes that those preliminary issues that involve only questions of probative force are for the jury, while issues that turn on the satisfaction of technical legal standards such as the best evidence rule are for the court. The rule provides as follows:

Rule 1008. Functions of Court and Jury.

When the admissibility of other evidence of contents of writings, recordings, or photographs under these rules depends upon the fulfillment of a condition of fact, the question whether the condition has been fulfilled is ordinarily for the court to determine in accordance with the provisions of Rule 104. However, when an issue is raised (a) whether the asserted writing ever existed, or (b) whether another writing, recording, or photograph produced at the trial is the original, or (c) whether other evidence of contents correctly reflects the contents, the issue is for the trier of fact to determine as in the case of other issues of fact.

The theory of Rule 1008 becomes easier to grasp when it is considered in relation to Rules 104(b), 401, 402, 602, and 901(a). All are consistent in providing that even when the jury is deciding an issue, the court must first determine if a reasonable juror could be persuaded. In this respect the court has a limited fact-finding function with respect to all evidence.

However, when the court is actually determining the existence of a fact necessary to satisfy a condition of the best evidence rule, before allowing evidence to be admitted—as in deciding if an adequate search for a "lost" document was made—it is actually deciding the fact and must be persuaded. Even in such circumstances, if it admits the evidence and finds that the document was lost, the same issue may be posed to the jury as one of credibility, probative force, and spoliation. It is apparent, therefore, that the judge and jury functions are often closely intertwined whether the judge or the jury is to make a determination under Rule 1008.

When the jury must make a factual determination, the court must decide if enough evidence has been introduced "to support a finding."[2] In making this

---

[1] *See* discussion in **Treatise** at §§ 1008.02–1008.05.
[2] *See* Rule 104(b), discussed in § 3.01[3].

determination the court does not decide credibility but leaves the matter to the jury so that a prima facie case suffices.[3]

When the court makes the preliminary factual determination in deciding if the best evidence rule is satisfied, it decides credibility and probative force, so a prima facie case may not suffice. In this latter circumstance the court must be satisfied that it is more probable than not that the fact exists. The burden of "more probable than not" with respect to preliminary matters is generally applicable in both civil and criminal cases. As a practical matter, the court, much like a jury, will act according to the general principle that "where the missing original writings in dispute are the very foundation of the claim, . . . more strictness in proof is required than where the writings are only involved collaterally."[4]

[2]—Questions for the Court

Administration of exclusionary rules established to vindicate some public policy—here, encouraging of the use of original writings at trial—is appropriately lodged in the trial court. Accordingly, it is the judge who decides whether the conditions of fact that allow secondary evidence to be introduced have been fulfilled according to the requirements of Rule 1002.[5] Giving the jury the burden of deciding whether certain documents should be admitted because it has been established that a search has been "diligent" or an original destroyed in "bad faith" would confuse and distract. The trial court also decides all hearsay, privilege, or constitutional challenges to the receipt of writings.

[3]—Questions for the Jury

The second sentence of Rule 1008 allocates the burden of resolving preliminary questions of conditional relevance of writings to the trier of fact. Such objections to admissibility of other evidence are based neither on technical exclusionary rules arising from the best evidence rule nor on the general incompetence of the evidence, but rather upon the lack of probative force of the secondary evidence—an issue for the jury. The three instances enumerated are not all-inclusive; they are the issues that will most frequently arise that must receive the treatment specified in Rule 1008 and Rule 104(b).

---

[3] *See* Fox v. Peck Iron and Metal Co., 25 B.R. 674, 679–680 (Bankr. S.D. Cal. 1982) (in a jury trial, the judge determines whether there is prima facie evidence to show that a document is what it is purported to be, and the jury then makes its own determination as to authenticity and weight; in a nonjury trial, the judge makes both determinations; court cited Rule 1008).

[4] Sylvania Elec. Prods., Inc. v. Flanagan, 352 F.2d 1005, 1008 (1st Cir. 1965).

[5] *See, e.g.,* Burt Rigid Box, Inc. v. Travelers Prop. Cas. Corp., 302 F.3d 83, 92 (2d Cir. 2002) (whether insured's search for copy of insurance policy was sufficiently diligent to permit admission of secondary evidence of policy was properly for court rather than for jury).

CHAPTER 4

Judicial Notice

SYNOPSIS

§ 4.01   Scope of Rule 201[1]

Rule 201—the only one of the Rules of Evidence to deal with judicial notice—was deliberately drafted to cover only a small fraction of material usually subsumed under the concept of "judicial notice." It covers only judicial notice of "adjudicative facts," the facts pertinent to the particular case. It does not address judicial notice of "legislative facts," those facts that "have relevance to legal reasoning and the law-making process."[2] The rule provides:

Rule 201.   Judicial Notice of Adjudicative Facts.

(a)
Scope of rule. This rule governs only judicial notice of adjudicative facts.

(b)
Kinds of facts. A judicially noticed fact must be one not subject to reasonable dispute in that it is either (1) generally known within the territorial jurisdiction of the trial court or (2) capable of accurate and ready determination by resort to sources whose accuracy cannot reasonably be questioned.

(c)
When discretionary. A court may take judicial notice, whether requested or not.

(d)
When mandatory. A court shall take judicial notice if requested by a party and supplied with the necessary information.

(e)
Opportunity to be heard. A party is entitled upon timely request to an opportunity to be heard as to the propriety of taking judicial notice and the tenor of the matter noticed. In the absence of prior notification, the request may be made after judicial notice has been taken.

(f)
Time of taking notice. Judicial notice may be taken at any stage of the proceeding.

---

[1] *See* **Treatise** at § 201.02.

[2] Fed. R. Evid. 201 Advisory Committee's Note (1972) (reproduced verbatim in **Treatise** at § 201App.01[2]); *see, e.g.,* Toth v. Grand Trunk RR, 306 F.3d 335, 349 (6th Cir. 2002) (judicial notice applies only to "adjudicative facts" of particular case, not "legislative facts" relevant to "formulation of a legal principle or ruling by a judge . . . or in the enactment of a legislative body"; whether fact is adjudicative or legislative depends on intended use of fact; "[a] legal rule may be a proper fact for judicial notice if it is offered to establish the factual context of the case, as opposed to stating the governing law").

> (g)
>
> Instructing jury. In a civil action or proceeding, the court shall instruct the jury to accept as conclusive any fact judicially noticed. In a criminal case, the court shall instruct the jury that it may, but is not required to, accept as conclusive any fact judicially noticed.
>
> [*Adopted Jan. 2, 1975, effective July 1, 1975*]

The Advisory Committee sought to limit the rule to that aspect of judicial notice intrinsic to the law of evidence by using the word "adjudicative" in the title of the rule. The Committee used the term in the sense proposed by Professor Kenneth Culp Davis, the originator of the terminology. Professor Davis wrote:[3]

adjudicative facts are those to which the law is applied in the process of adjudication. They are the facts that normally go to a jury in a jury case. They relate to the parties, their activities, their properties, their business.

In the body of the rule, subdivision (a) states that "[t]his rule governs only judicial notice of adjudicative facts." Facts from which the nonexistence of facts in issue can be inferred should also be subject to Rule 201. The test is really one of relevancy: might a reasonable trier find that the fact being judicially noticed tends to make the existence of any material fact more or less probable?

Excluded as inappropriate subjects for formalized treatment in the Rules of Evidence are: the general knowledge and reasoning ability a judge employs in fulfilling each task;[4] the materials a judge uses in finding, interpreting or reviewing the substantive law;[5] the extra-record information a judge utilizes in formulating evidential hypotheses by which the admissibility and sufficiency of evidence are determined; and the non-evidence data a judge consults when ascertaining "political facts," or in carrying out a number of functions specifically excepted in Rule 1101.[6]

---

[3] Davis, "Judicial Notice," 55 Colum. L. Rev. 945, 952 (1955).

[4] *See, e.g.,* United States v. Amado-Nunez, 357 F.3d 119, 121–122 (1st Cir. 2004) (Rule 201 not applicable to "vast array of 'background' facts commonly considered by judges and juries in deciding cases," such as fact that customs searches at airports are conducted on passengers arriving from foreign ports, not those arriving from domestic locations).

[5] *See, e.g.,* Toth v. Grand Trunk RR, 306 F.3d 335, 349 (6th Cir. 2002) (judicial notice under Rule 201 is not appropriate means to establish legal principles governing case); *but see, e.g.,* Gonzales v. City of Castle Rock, 307 F.3d 1258, 1266 n.2 (10th Cir. 2002) (appellate court may properly take judicial notice, under Rule 201, of applicable state statutes and their legislative history); Demos v. City of Indianapolis, 302 F.3d 698, 706 (7th Cir. 2002) (trial court may properly take judicial notice, under Rule 201, of applicable state statutes).

[6] For an analysis of the doctrine of judicial notice in its larger sense, *see* **Treatise** at §§ 201.03, 201.50–201.52.

§ 4.02   Facts Subject to Notice

Rule 201(b) imposes no artificial limits on the range of facts which may be judicially noticed. The broad scope of possible notice varies with the facts and issues in each case and the evolving state of knowledge.[1] The only implacable restriction on a court's authority to take judicial notice is that the adjudicative fact in question be one that is not reasonably subject to dispute.[2]

The obvious cost of establishing adjudicative facts in an adversary proceeding—in terms of time, energy and money—justifies dispensing with formal proof when a matter is not really disputable. Since there is no real issue of fact, the right to trial by jury is not infringed; nor is the Sixth Amendment right to confront witnesses abridged.[3] When facts do not possess this requisite degree of certainty, our traditional procedure has been to require proof within the framework of the adversary system.[4]

Because the Advisory Committee omitted "propositions of generalized knowledge" as one of the types of fact subject to judicial notice, treatises—such as medical treatises—or statements in treatises cannot be admitted to prove the truth of the matter stated except as provided in Rule 803(18),[5] unless the fact satisfies one of the two tests specified in Rule 201. A generally known or verifiable fact will not be excluded because it appears in a treatise, but specialized opinion requires proof by an expert.

Rule 201(b) contains two different tests for determining whether a proposition of fact has attained a high enough degree of certainty so that it would be consonant with fair procedure to dispense with proof. The first, traditional test, is whether the

---

[1] *See***Treatise** at §§ 201.10–201.13.

[2] Fed. R. Evid. 201 Advisory Committee's Note (1972) (reproduced verbatim in **Treatise,** Ch. 201, *Judicial Notice of Adjudicative Facts,* § 201App.01[2]) ("With respect to judicial notice of adjudicative facts, the tradition has been one of caution in requiring that the matter be beyond reasonable controversy. This tradition of circumspection appears to be soundly based, and no reason to depart from it is apparent"); United States v. Mitchell, 365 F.3d 215, 252 (3d Cir. 2004) (factual issue that was subject of five-day *Daubert* hearing, was clearly subject to reasonable dispute and therefore not proper subject for judicial notice).

[3] United States v. Mentz, 840 F.2d 315, 321–323 (6th Cir. 1988) (for criminal defendants, however, the court must tread very carefully in considering requests for judicial notice, particularly as to facts constituting elements of the government's burden of proof; moreover, the cautionary instruction of Rule 201(g) must be given in all criminal cases where the court proposes to take judicial notice).

[4] *See* United States v. Hoyts Cinemas Corp., 380 F.3d 558, 570–571 (1st Cir. 2004) (judicial notice is used with some stringency because it is a departure from traditional methods of proof).

[5] See Chapter 16, *Hearsay Exceptions—Availability of Declarant Immaterial,* for a discussion of how learned treatises can be admitted into evidence in conjunction with the testimony of an expert witness.

fact is "generally known" within the community.[6] The second, more modern, test is whether the fact is "capable of accurate and ready determination" by reference to authoritative sources.[7] When neither test is satisfied, judicial notice of adjudicative facts will not be taken.[8] Facts which are known to the judge, but are not generally known or verifiable, do not satisfy the Rule.[9]

In practice, the extent to which a court will be willing to take judicial notice will depend on the type of case, and the practicalities of every-day trials. Lawyers and judges accept differences between civil and criminal trials, between bench and jury trials, between hearings and trials where standards of probative force are high and there is time for a full trial, and hearings on such matters as preliminary injunctions when short cuts are desirable to accommodate the system's need for speed. Much more formality is required in jury trials—particularly in criminal trials—than in bench trials. In the latter case, adjournments, continuances and conferences can be used to allow the court to instruct itself from outside sources, and rules such as those limiting access to treatises have little applicability. What is vital, however, even in a bench trial, is that the parties be made aware of what information the judge is using and that they be given time to submit other information to meet what they consider to be unreliable data.[10] In point of fact most courts are not inclined to go

---

[6] *See* Carey v. Populaton Services International, 431 U.S. 678, 697, 97 S. Ct. 2010, 52 L. Ed. 2d 675 (1977) (in suit challenging state law restricting access of contraceptives to minors, Court took judicial notice that "with or without access to contraceptives, the incidence of sexual activity among minors is high, and the consequences of such activity are frequently devastating"); H20 Houseboat Vacations Inc. v. Hernandez, 103 F.3d 914, 917 (9th Cir. 1996) (judicial notice taken of fact that, to be injurious, carbon monoxide emissions must be contained within an enclosed space); Ritter v. Hughes Aircraft Co., 58 F.3d 454, 458 (9th Cir. 1995) (judicial notice of widespread layoffs at defendant company).

[7] Fed. R. Evid. 201(b)(2); *see, e.g.,* Massachusetts v. Westcott, 431 U.S. 322, 323, 97 S. Ct. 1755, 52 L. Ed. 2d 349 (1977) (quoting Rule 201(b) in taking notice of Coast Guard records); City of Philadelphia v. Fleming Cos., 264 F.3d 1245, 1251 n.4 (10th Cir. 2001) (trial court could properly take judicial notice of date of amendments to complaint in related litigation); United States v. Coutchavlis, 260 F.3d 1149, 1152–1153 (9th Cir. 2001) (trial court can properly take judicial notice of map to determine location where event at issue in litigation occurred).

[8] *See, e.g.,* Lee v. County of Los Angeles, 250 F.3d 668, 689–690 (9th Cir. 2001) (trial court erred in taking judicial notice of facts recited in record of extradition hearing that occurred in another court, since they were disputed by allegations in plaintiff's complaint); Oran v. Stafford, 226 F.3d 275, 288 (3d Cir. 2000) (court could properly take judicial notice of information concerning individual defendants' compensation levels and direct stockholdings in defendant corporation that was contained in corporation's public disclosure documents on file with SEC, so long as documents were properly authenticated).

[9] *See, e.g.,* LaSalle Nat'l Bank v. First Conn. Holding Group, L.L.C. XXIII, 287 F.3d 279, 289–290 (3d Cir. 2002) (contents of trial judge's private conversation with her law clerk were not proper subject of judicial notice).

[10] *See, e.g.,* United States v. Ritchie, 342 F.3d 903, 909 (9th Cir. 2003) (if contents of documents attached to affidavit were proper subject of judicial notice, opponent would have to

outside the record. When the importance of the case and their disquietude with the lawyer's presentation induces them to look at standard works, they should not be discouraged from doing so by a too narrow view of the power granted under Rule 201.

Judges should not confuse lack of information with indisputability. Unless convinced that the matter satisfies the tests of subdivision (b), the judge should seek the parties' assistance in deciding whether the matter is indisputable. If still unconvinced, the court should require proof by expert and other testimony in the usual manner, even though it considers the existence of the fact to be more probable than not.[11]

In applying Rule 201, the courts have not rigorously distinguished between the rule's two bases for determining whether the proposed fact is reasonably subject to dispute.[12]

§ 4.03 Discretionary and Mandatory Notice

Rule 201(c) and (d) provide that a court must take judicial notice only when a party so requests and furnishes it with the necessary information. The court may, however, in its discretion take notice regardless of request.[1]

The grant of discretionary authority does not mean, as it does in other situations, that the trial judge's determination is virtually insulated from appellate review. An appellate court is often in as good a position as the trial court to ascertain the degree of probability of a judicially noticeable fact. There is no need for the appellate court to defer to the trial judge's feel for the case.[2] Accordingly, subdivision (b) must be read in conjunction with subdivision (f) authorizing judicial notice "at any stage of the proceedings." If the trial judge failed to notice a fact which the appellate court

---

receive opportunity to show that judicial notice was improper).

[11] Oneida Indian Nation of New York v. State, 691 F.2d 1070 (2nd Cir. 1982); *see also* United States v. Martinez, 3 F.3d 1191, 1197 (8th Cir. 1993) (under *Daubert* and the Second Circuit's earlier decision in United States v. Jakobetz, 955 F.2d 786, 799–800 (2d Cir. 1992) district courts could take judicial notice of "the reliability of the general theory and techniques of DNA profiling. If new techniques are offered, however, the district court must hold an *in limine* hearing" under *Daubert*).

[12] *See* **Treatise,** Ch. 201, *Judicial Notice of Adjudicative Facts,* for complete discussion of specific instances in which courts have properly or improperly taken judicial notice of adjudicative facts and comprehensive survey of sources that have been held to be appropriate for ascertainment of indisputable facts.

[1] *See* **Treatise** at § 201.30.

[2] *But see* Johnson v. Chater, 108 F.3d 942, 946 (8th Cir. 1997) (on appellate review of administra tive decision, trial court had discretion to decline to take judicial notice of weight of gallon of gasoline, since issue should have been raised during administrative proceedings, in which appellant and administrative law judge assumed a different weight, and since taking notice would undermine administrative law judge's role as factfinder).

feels was a proper subject for judicial notice, the appellate court may notice the fact despite the grant of discretionary authority.[3]

Neither the mandatory phraseology of Rule 201(d) nor the authority of the appellate court to take judicial notice authorizes use of judicial notice to correct counsel's errors in failing to introduce evidence during the trial.[4] Moreover, the fact that judicial notice is mandatory on proper request does not mean that the courts must always take notice of indisputable adjudicative facts. For example, if the fact proposed for judicial notice would be barred by other rules of evidence, the court need not take notice of it.[5]

Appellate courts have adequate power in the reverse situation where they disagree with the trial judge's recognition of a fact. The reviewing court may reverse if it finds that the fact was neither "generally known" nor "verifiable."[6]

There are no limitations on methods of providing the court with information enabling it to decide whether it will take judicial notice. Nor are formal requirements specified for the request to notice. If not made on the record at trial it is best to provide it in writing so that a copy can be served apprising adverse parties, thereby enabling them to make arrangements to be heard pursuant to subdivision (e).

§ 4.04   Opportunity to Be Heard

Rule 201(e) provides that upon timely request a party will be given the opportunity to be heard on the propriety of taking judicial notice and the tenor of the matter to be noticed.[1] If the party was not notified before notice was taken, the party

---

[3] *See, e.g.,* Transmission Agency of N. Cal. v. Sierra Pac. Power Co., 287 F.3d 771, 776 n.3 (9th Cir. 2002) (when regulatory agency issued opinion in ongoing proceeding involving same issues as were involved in case pending on appeal in federal court, appellate court could take judicial notice of agency opinion).

[4] *See, e.g.,* United States v. Campbell, 351 F.2d 336, 341 (2d Cir. 1965) (court refused to take notice of Canadian law urged as applicable for first time on appeal); Johnson v. Goldstein, 864 F. Supp. 490, 494–495 (E.D. Pa. 1994), *aff'd,* 66 F.3d 331 (3d Cir. 1995) (trial court's refusal to take judicial notice of recorded deed did not injure defendant's presentation of its case, because defendant could have offered deed into evidence, but chose not to).

[5] *See, e.g.,* Toth v. Grand Trunk RR, 306 F.3d 335, 350 (6th Cir. 2002) (although administrative regulations codified in CFR are appropriate for judicial notice, court had discretion to bar them on grounds of improper foundation and scope of rebuttal).

[6] *See, e.g.,* LaSalle Nat'l Bank v. First Conn. Holding Group, L.L.C. XXIII, 287 F.3d 279, 291–292 (3d Cir. 2002) (because trial court's order imposing sanctions could not be divorced from fact of which trial court improperly took judicial notice, record did not support sanctions order and reversal was necessary).

[1] *See* **Treatise** at § 201.31.

must be given an opportunity to object afterwards.[2]

It is the burden of the party opposing the judicial notice to request a hearing on the matter.[3] In the absence of a request for a hearing, a party who was notified of the court's intent to take judicial notice fails to preserve the issue of the propriety of the notice for appeal.[4] Rule 201(e) does not specify any formal requirements for the hearing which would, of course, be conducted outside the hearing of the jury, and would generally resemble a hearing on preliminary questions of admissibility pursuant to Rule 104.

When taking notice is requested pursuant to subdivision (d), all parties are aware that judicial notice is a possibility and can prepare to request a hearing. Where the judge takes judicial notice without request, there is an obligation on the court to notify the parties where it would not be clear to them that judicial notice was being taken.[5]

There are undoubtedly situations in which a failure to notify would conflict with constitutional guarantees of a fair trial. While in a civil case, notice of a completely indisputable fact without affording the adverse parties an opportunity to be heard would not violate the right to trial by jury, procedural fairness includes the right to notification and an opportunity to be heard.[6] To date, the question of notification in civil cases has been raised primarily in the context of administrative law. There is no reason to set the standards for bench trials any lower than those for administrative hearings.[7]

When the fact in question is debatable, judicial notice without notification may

---

[2] Fed. R. Evid. 201(e); see, e.g., Rose v. Hartford Underwriters Ins. Co., 203 F.3d 417, 420–421 (6th Cir. 2000) (if trial court took judicial notice of plaintiff's arson indictment in connection with suit on fire insurance, it erred reversibly, because trial court did not give notice it was taking judicial notice and thereby deprived plaintiff of right to be heard under Rule 201(e)).

[3] See, e.g., In re Calder, 907 F.2d 953, 954 (10th Cir. 1990) (burden rests with opposing party to request hearing to challenge propriety of taking notice).

[4] See, e.g., Norman v. Housing Authority of Montgomery, 836 F.2d 1292, 1304 (11th Cir. 1988) (fact that court took judicial notice that rate for bookkeepers in area was $35 per hour could not be grounds for appeal absent request under Fed. R. Evid. 201(e) for hearing).

[5] See, e.g., Rose v. Hartford Underwriters Ins. Co., 203 F.3d 417, 421 (6th Cir. 2000) (if trial court took judicial notice of plaintiff's arson indictment in connection with suit on fire insurance, it erred reversibly, because trial court did not give notice it was taking judicial notice and thereby deprived plaintiff of right to be heard under Rule 201(e)).

[6] See, e.g., De la Llana-Castellon v. Immigration & Nat. Serv., 16 F.3d 1093, 1096 (10th Cir. 1994) (Board of Immigration Appeals denied petitioners due process by taking administrative notice of elections in Nicaragua without notice and opportunity to be heard; BIA's discretion in taking administrative notice under Fed. R. Evid. 201(b) depends on particular case before it, and petitioners' case warranted that they be given advance notice and opportunity to be heard).

[7] See, e.g., Ohio Bell Tel. Co. v. Public Util. Comm'n, 301 U.S. 292, 302, 57 S. Ct. 724, 729, 81 L. Ed. 1093 (1937) ("[w]hen price lists or trade journals or even government reports are put in

deprive the adversely affected party of the right to trial by jury as well, since the party will miss an opportunity to request a hearing at which rebutting information may be introduced, and subdivision (g) commands the judge to instruct a civil jury to accept as conclusive any facts judicially noticed. Similarly, if the person against whom the proposed judicially noticed fact is offered does not have access to the source, he or she is effectively denied a hearing on the propriety of taking judicial notice because he or she cannot review or take any position on the matter.[7.1]

In criminal cases, Rule 201(g) acknowledges that the scope of judicial notice is circumscribed by the constitutional protections afforded an accused.[8]

§ 4.05 Taking Notice at Any Stage of the Proceedings

Rule 201(f) provides that a court may take judicial notice at any stage of the proceedings.[1] A judge may therefore dispense with formal proof of adjudicative facts at any time during the course of a litigation, however, the court must abide by the requirements of Rule 201 when doing so.[1.1]

The failure or refusal of a court to take judicial notice at one stage of the proceedings does not preclude notice at a later stage. Although subdivision (f) does not specifically so state, judicial notice is permissible on appeal even if it had not been urged below, despite the usual rule limiting appeals to points raised at trial.[2] Thus, an appellate court may remedy a trial court's erroneous dismissal of an action for lack of subject matter jurisdiction by taking judicial notice of the facts necessary to support the determination that the plaintiff's principal place of business was in

---

evidence upon a trial, the party against whom they are offered may see the evidence or hear it and parry its effect.").

[7.1] *See, e.g.,* Fenner v. Suthers, 194 F. Supp. 2d 1146, 1149 (D. Colo. 2002) (defendant's request that trial court take notice of facts posted on world wide web denied in part because plaintiff, pro se inmate in state correctional institution, had no access to internet and therefore effectively could not be heard on matter).

[8] *See* **Treatise** at § 201App.01[2] for verbatim reproduction of Fed. R. Evid. 201(g) Advisory Committee's Note (1969) and pertinent portion of House Committee's Report respecting its substitution of Rule 201(g) from 1969 Advisory Committee's version of Rule 201 for Supreme Court's 1972 recommended version.

[1] *See* **Treatise** at § 201.32.

[1.1] *See, e.g.,* Banco Santander de Puerto Rico v. Lopez-Stubbe (In re Colonial Mortgage Bankers Corp.), 324 F.3d 12, 15–16 (1st Cir. 2003) (trial court may properly take judicial notice on motion to dismiss for failure to state a claim); Ochana v. Flores, 199 F. Supp. 2d 817, 831 (N.D. Ill. 2002) (trial court can properly take judicial notice at summary judgment stage of pretrial proceedings).

[2] *See, e.g.,* Wells v. City & County of Denver, 257 F.3d 1132, 1151 (10th Cir. 2001) (court of appeals took judicial notice of current events to determine whether defendants were engaging in selective enforcement of their policy against unattended display on government property).

a state other than the forum state, so that its citizenship was diverse from that of the defendant.[2.1]

The right of the appellate court to take judicial notice, however, is not a remedy for a party's failure to introduce readily available evidence of crucial facts at trial.[3] Moreover, considerations of fairness that sometimes rise to constitutional dimensions may prevent an appellate court from taking judicial notice of an adjudicative fact.[4]

Furthermore, in criminal cases, the power to take judicial notice at the appellate level may, at times, come into conflict with the policy expressed in subdivision (g) that gives the jury in a criminal trial the right to disregard a judicially noted fact. In such cases, the power of the appellate court to take judicial notice gives way to the jury's right to make its own determinations of fact.[5]

An appellate court contemplating original judicial notice should notify the parties of its intent to take judicial notice so that the propriety of taking notice and the tenor of the matter to be noticed can be argued. The point obviously may be decisive of the appeal or the court would not be considering it.[6] Even when the fact appears indisputable, it may be fairer to allow the adversely affected party to challenge its relevancy or raise the possibility of remanding for further proof. If oral argument has already been completed, the court should at least afford the parties an opportunity to submit supplemental briefs.

[2.1] *See, e.g.,* Capitol Indem. Corp. v. Russellville Steel Co., 367 F.3d 831, 836–837 (8th Cir. 2004) (appellate court may take judicial notice that insurance companies do not operate solely through efforts of independent agents, and infer that those other personnel have their offices in other states on basis of evidence of record that insurer does business in forum state only through independent agents, even though plaintiff did not request trial court to notice such facts).

[3] *See, e.g.,* McGinest v. GTE Serv. Corp., 360 F.3d 1103, 1123 n. 18 (9th Cir. 2004) (appellate court may properly refuse to take judicial notice of fact that plaintiff easily could have presented to trial court through evidence, but failed to do so).

[4] *See, e.g.,* Colonial Leasing Co. v. Logistics Control Group Int'l, 762 F.2d 454, 459–461 (5th Cir. 1985) ("Taking judicial notice after trial could implicate due process considerations"; e.g., it would be improper to notice important facts on appeal after defendant properly relied on plaintiff's failure to establish a prima facie case by declining to produce its own evidence).

[5] *See, e.g.,* United States v. Jones, 580 F.2d 219, 224 (6th Cir. 1978) (in wiretapping prosecution, government failed to prove that telephone company was a common carrier and trial court entered judgment of acquittal; appellate court affirmed acquittal and concluded it could not take judicial notice of fact, even though it was indisputable, because it would contravene right of juries in criminal cases to decide whether to accept judicially noticed facts).

[6] *See, e.g.,* Opoka v. I.N.S., 94 F.3d 392, 394–395 (7th Cir. 1996) (appellate courts must take judicial notice of relevant decisions of courts and administrative agencies, whether made before or after the decision under review; determinations to be judicially noticed include proceedings in other courts if those proceedings have a direct relation to the matters at issue).

§ 4.06　Effect of Taking Notice in Civil Cases[1]

[1]—Non-Jury Cases

If the court took judicial notice without having previously notified the parties that it would do so, procedural fairness requires, and Rule 201(e) provides, that the parties have an opportunity to object to the taking of notice.[1.1] In a bench trial, granting a hearing after notice was taken would do no harm because the objections and the evidence would be heard by the same trier. The trial court should include all facts that it has judicially noticed in its findings of fact. See Rule 52 of the Federal Rules of Civil Procedure.[2]

[2]—Jury Cases

Rule 201(g) provides that, after the judge has decided to take judicial notice of a fact in a civil case, the judge must instruct the jury to accept that fact as conclusive. As a result, the opposing party may not introduce evidence contravening the judicially noticed adjudicative fact.[1] See § 4.07 concerning the appropriate instruction in criminal actions.

If the judge declared the fact indisputable after a hearing pursuant to Rule 201(e), permitting the jury to hear further proof would defeat the principal reason for taking judicial notice. As the Reporter of the New Jersey Supreme Court Committee on Evidence stated:

> In light of the thoroughness with which a judge should consider the taking of judicial matter in the first place, it would be a waste of time to receive evidence on the matter again; moreover, to submit an indisputable fact . . . to a jury would permit the possibility of irrational results which the judicial notice rules are designed to prevent.[2]

---

[1]　*See* **Treatise** at § 201.33.

[1.1]　*See, e.g.,* Rose v. Hartford Underwriters Ins. Co., 203 F.3d 417, 420 (6th Cir. 2000) (if trial court took judicial notice of plaintiff's arson indictment in connection with suit on fire insurance, it erred reversibly, because trial court did not give notice it was taking judicial notice and thereby deprived plaintiff of right to be heard under Rule 201(e)); *cf.* Siderius v. M.V. Amilla, 880 F.2d 662, 666–667 (2d Cir. 1989) (court distinguished between those situations "when a court takes judicial notice of facts extraneous to a record, and when it takes notice of facts that are integrally related to the record"; here, the parties to this maritime suit had incorporated the "Interclub Agreement" by reference in their Charter Party; this agreement was therefore not extraneous to the record but a part of it; a post-trial hearing on whether the agreement should be noticed was not required).

[2]　Fed. R. Civ. P. 52; *see* 9 Moore's Federal Practice, Ch. 52, *Findings by Court; Judgment on Partial Findings* (Matthew Bender 3d ed. 1997).

[1]　*See* Fed. R. Evid. 201(g) Advisory Committee's Note (1972) (reproduced verbatim in **Treatise** at § 201App.02[2]).

[2]　Report of the New Jersey Supreme Court Committee on Evidence 37–38 (1963).

Furthermore, allowing the jury to hear evidence would destroy some of the flexibility inherent in judicial notice procedure. A jury may hear only admissible evidence, while one of the principal advantages of judicial notice is that the rules of evidence do not apply and the parties may introduce any pertinent material. It would be impossible for the jury to weigh the probative force of the evidence admitted against that considered by the judge and not admitted. Finally, the Advisory Committee felt that importing the consequences of presumptions into the law of judicial notice would affect "the substantive law to an extent and in ways largely unforeseeable." Consequently, subdivision (g) provides that the jury may not pass upon a fact once it is judicially noticed but must accept it as true for the basis of its deliberations in civil cases.

When no hearing was held because the court did not indicate that it was planning to take judicial notice, the aggrieved party's remedy is to ask for a hearing if the case is still pending, or petition for a rehearing. The party would argue that information could have been presented indicating that the fact was not a proper subject for judicial notice. This offer of proof must be made to the judge, outside the presence of the jury. (See Rule 103(c).) Even after a hearing has taken place on the issue, if a party is able to produce new information throwing doubt on the judge's determination, the matter of taking judicial notice should be reopened. Since the hearings and proffers take place outside the jury's presence, they can be worked into odd moments of the trial day without any loss of time.

§ 4.07   Instructions to Jury in Criminal Case[1]

Rule 201(g) provides that a judge must instruct a jury in a criminal case that it may, but need not, accept as conclusive any adjudicative fact in a case.[2] In a criminal case, therefore, the court's function of judicially noting facts against the defendant should be no greater than general power to comment on the evidence. See discussion in Chapter 2, *Control by Trial Court Generally*. There is some authority, however, that whether a particular location comes within the territorial jurisdiction of the United States constitutes a legislative issue not governed by Rule

---

[1]   *See* **Treatise** at § 201.34.

[2]   Fed. R. Evid. 201(g); *see* United States v. Bello, 194 F.3d 18, 24 (1st Cir. 1999) (trial court properly instructed jury that, although court took judicial notice that prison where offense occurred was within territorial U.S. jurisdiction, jury was not required to agree with court; location of offense within U.S. jurisdiction was adjudicative fact subject to judicial notice); United States v. Deckard, 816 F.2d 426, 428 (8th Cir. 1987) (in prosecution for interception of telephone communications, the trial judge properly took judicial notice that interstate communications are transported over Southwestern Bell telephone lines, including telephone lines to victim's residence, where judge instructed jury, as required by Rule 201, that it could, but was not required to, accept as conclusory any fact judicially noticed).

201.³

This approach to judicial notice is analogous to the operation of presumptions in criminal cases, which leaves juries free not to find the presumed fact even though the basic fact is established beyond a reasonable doubt. The unique treatment afforded criminal cases is probably compelled by constitutional guarantees expressed in the axiom "that a verdict cannot be directed against the accused . . . with the corollary that the judge has no authority to direct the jury to find against the accused as to any element of the crime."⁴

The Advisory Committee did not intend Rule 201 to apply to the utilization of general knowledge and reasoning abilities which are part of every normal person's mental equipment. In its Notes to an earlier draft of subdivision (g) (which was ultimately enacted), the Committee stated that "[w]hile matters falling within the common fund of information supposed to be possessed by jurors need not be proved, these are not, properly speaking, adjudicative facts but an aspect of legal reasoning."⁵ The Committee cites *State v. Dunn* ⁶ for this statement, a case in which the trial judge was held to have properly instructed that a club 22 inches long, 2½ inches wide and ¾ inch thick used to beat the victim was a "deadly weapon and

---

³ *See* United States v. Hernandez-Fundora, 58 F.3d 802, 812 (2d Cir. 1995), *cert. denied,* 515 U.S. 1127 (1995) (trial court properly instructed jury that prison where offense allegedly occurred was within territorial U.S. jurisdiction; jury was left to determine whether offense occurred there); *see also* United States v. Marks, 209 F.3d 577, 583 (6th Cir. 2000), *cert. denied,* 531 U.S. 882 (2000) (venue was established by evidence that crimes took place in Jefferson County, since statute defined judicial district as including that county; even if venue was in issue and court erred by failing to give Rule 201(g) instruction, error was clearly harmless, because issue was not one about which jurors could rationally disagree).

⁴ Advisory Committee's Notes to subdivisions (b) and (c) of Rule 301. *See, e.g.,* United States v. Herrera-Ochoa, 245 F.3d 495, 501 (5th Cir. 2001) (neither trial nor appellate court can properly take judicial notice of defendant's location at time of indictment for being in United States illegally after deportation because such judicial notice would improperly infringe on defendant's right to have each element of case against him proved beyond reasonable doubt); United States v. Southard, 700 F.2d 1, 26 (1st Cir. 1983) (court held that although court could take judicial notice of the minimum driving time between New Haven and Rhode Island, the defendant's actual knowledge could not be determined solely from this judicially-noticed fact: "When the knowledge to be proved is an element of the crime it cannot be assumed, even though such assumption is reasonable. It is the personal knowledge of the defendant that must be proved."). See discussion in **Treatise** at Ch. 303, *Presumptions in Criminal Cases (Sup. Ct. Standard 303).*

⁵ *Cf.* United States v. Gould, 536 F.2d 216, 221 (8th Cir. 1976) (court did not err in instructing jury that if it found confiscated substances to be cocaine hydrochloride then the applicable law classified the substance as a Schedule II Controlled Substance; this was legislative rather than adjudicative fact and consequently Rule 201(g) is inapplicable); Smith v. United States, 431 U.S. 291, 307 (1977) (in obscenity cases in addition to jurors' knowledge of community standards, state statute was part of evidence of that standard).

⁶ State v. Dunn, 221 Mo. 530, 120 S.W. 1179 (1909).

that the defendant therefore must be assumed to have known the consequences of such use."[7]

It is error for the court to fail to instruct the jury that it may disregard a judicially noticed adjudicative fact.[8] When the trial court fails to inform the jurors that they are free to ignore the judicially noted fact, however, the principles of harmless error may apply and prevent a reversal of a conviction.[9]

---

[7] *Id.* 120 S.W. at 1182. That part of the *Dunn* instruction which directs the jury to presume the defendant's intent to kill is in conflict with *Sandstrom v. Montana,* 442 U.S. 510, 524, 99 S. Ct. 2450, 61 L. Ed. 2d 39 (1979), in which the Supreme Court held unconstitutional an instruction that "the law presumes a person intends the ordinary consequences of his voluntary acts." The Court held that the instruction may have been interpreted as shifting the burden of persuasion, and therefore would have violated the Fourteenth Amendment's requirement that the state prove every element of a criminal offense beyond a reasonable doubt. *See* Chapter 5, *Presumptions,* and, for a discussion of the constitutional issues involved in presumptions in criminal cases, *see* **Treatise** at §§ 303.04–303.06.

[8] *See, e.g.,* United States v. Mentz, 840 F.2d 315, 322–323 (6th Cir. 1988) (trial court committed reversible error in instructing jury that banks robbed by defendant were insured by FDIC, even though this fact was easily and conclusively provable); United States v. Jones, 580 F.2d 219, 224 (6th Cir. 1978) (government's failure to prove essential fact that tapped telephone in question was furnished by "common carrier" could not be cured by appellate court's taking judicial notice, since criminal jury must have opportunity to disregard judicially noticed facts).

[9] *See* Fed. R. Evid. 103; *see, e.g.,* United States v. Marks, 209 F.3d 577, 583–584 (6th Cir. 2000), *cert. denied,* 531 U.S. 882 (2000) (since jurors could not rationally disagree with judicially noticed fact that Louisville, Kentucky, is within Western District of Kentucky; failure to instruct jury of its freedom to reject fact was "clearly harmless error beyond a reasonable doubt"); United States v. Berrojo, 628 F.2d 368, 370 (5th Cir. 1980) (in prosecution for possession of substance identified as cocaine when government failed to show that cocaine was listed on Schedule II, fact that trial court, after motion for acquittal, took judicial notice and, without objection, charged jury that cocaine is controlled substance without giving Rule 201(g) charge was not plain error); *see* § 2.03[6].

CHAPTER 5

Presumptions[*]

---

[*] Chapter revised in 1995 by SANDRA D. KATZ, member of the New York Bar.

§ 5.01 Overview of Presumptions

As indicated below, Congress decided to give presumptions the least weight possible. In civil cases, the burden of going forward will merely shift. In criminal cases, Congress left case law with a negligible effect on federal criminal cases where the burden of proof beyond a reasonable doubt on all material elements of the crime lies with the government.

Presumptions, despite their theoretically minimal impact, still enthrall the bench and bar. In the face of codification they still create difficulties in application. Their very ambiguity makes them attractive to legislatures, since they provide room for compromise with each lawmaking side gaining a sense that the rule will favor its view of which way the substantive law should lean.

For the judge and lawyer, a fundamental rule is: "never mention the word presumption to a jury." The rules of presumption are for the court: they tell the judge which side has, and has not met, the burden of going forward and which side has the burden of persuasion. All the jury has to know—if the matter gets to that point—is who has the burden of persuasion. If the court wishes to alert the jury to a legislative finding on weight of evidence, it should do so in terms of allowable inferences rather than of presumptions.

As indicated below, presumptions have no evidentiary weight. They represent purely procedural rules.

Rules 301 and 302 are the only rules on presumptions that emerged from Congress. In civil cases, Congress recognized that Rule 301 does not apply when state law governs the rule of decision in the case (see Rule 302), or Congress has created a different kind of presumption. Proposed Rule 303, which had been promulgated by the Supreme Court, was omitted. Thus, there is no Federal Rule of Evidence governing presumptions in criminal cases. The discussion below concerns the present status in the federal courts of presumptions in criminal cases, and the extent to which proposed Rule 303 can be relied upon as a Standard.

§ 5.02 Presumptions in General in Civil Cases—Rule 301

[1]—Definition and Procedure[1]

Rule 301 adopts one uniform rule for all presumptions in civil actions and proceedings,[2] except those governed by state law (see Rule 302), or those for which

---

[1] *See* **Treatise** at § 301App.100 for discussion of different varieties of presumptions, reasons for the creation of presumptions, and policies underlying choice of a particular definition of a presumption.

[2] See discussion in **Treatise** at §§ 301.02–301.05.

Congress provides otherwise.[3] The Rule provides as follows:

Rule 301. Presumptions in General in Civil Actions and Proceedings.

In all civil actions and proceedings not otherwise provided for by Act of Congress or by these rules, a presumption imposes on the party against whom it is directed the burden of going forward with the evidence to rebut or meet the presumption, but does not shift to such party the burden of proof in the sense of the risk of nonpersuasion, which remains throughout the trial upon the party on whom it was originally cast.

[*Adopted Jan. 2, 1975, effective July 1, 1975.*]

The term "presumption" is used to describe a procedural rule that requires the existence of fact B (presumed fact) to be assumed when fact A (basic fact) is established unless and until a certain specified condition is fulfilled.[4] An inference is not a presumption. In the case of an inference, the existence of B may be deduced from A by the ordinary rules of reasoning and logic; in the case of a presumption, the existence of B must initially be assumed because of a rule of procedural law. Rule 301 treats presumptions in the same way that statutes treat certain types of foundational evidence when they state that evidence of a specific fact is "prima facie" evidence of another fact.[4.1]

A so-called irrebuttable presumption does not satisfy the definition of a presumption because fact B must be assumed conclusively rather than conditionally. Fact B becomes another way of stating fact A if the presumption is irrebuttable. An irrebuttable presumption is a rule of substantive law when B is a material proposition.

Under Rule 301, presumptions, unless otherwise specified by statute or rule,

---

[3] For a discussion of some of the statutes created by Congress that establish presumptions, see **Treatise** at § 301.20–301.30.

[4] Morgan, Basic Problems of Evidence 32 (1962) ("Thayer, Wigmore, the American Law Institute, and commentators generally have argued and many courts have agreed, that the term 'presumption' should be used only to mean that when A is established in an action, the existence of B must be assumed unless and until a specified condition is fulfilled").

[4.1] *See, e.g.,* Texas Dep't of Community Affairs v. Burdine, 450 U.S. 248, 253, 101 S. Ct. 1089, 67 L. Ed. 2d 207 (1981) (if plaintiff presents sufficient evidence to make out prima facie case of employment discrimination, burden shifts to employer to produce evidence of legitimate, non-discriminatory reason for adverse action taken against plaintiff; burden is one of production only, not of persuasion); Am. Online, Inc. v. AT&T Corp., 243 F.3d 812, 818 (4th Cir. 2001) (certificate of trademark registration, like Rule 301 presumption, does not "disappear" in face of opposing evidence; both certificate of registration and Rule 301 presumption permit jury to find fact they suggest, even in face of opposing evidence).

operate only to shift the burden of producing evidence;[5] they are intended to have no effect on the burden of persuasion.[6] The drafters of Rule 301 intended that a presumption arising under the rule not disappear, regardless of the quality or quantity of evidence introduced by the opposing party and without regard to whether the party in whose favor it operated introduces additional evidence of the existence of the presumed fact.[7] Even if the adverse party introduces evidence sufficient to raise a genuine issue concerning the existence of the presumed fact, the presumption still permits the finder of fact to infer the existence of the presumed fact from mere proof of the basic fact.[8] Several courts have used language suggesting that, contrary to the position of the Advisory Committee,[9] Rule 301 adopts the "bursting bubble" theory of presumptions.[9.1] In fact, however, those courts are simply using imprecise language to express the generally recognized effect of a rebutted presumption, which permits the jury to infer the formerly presumed fact from the proof of the foundational facts in the record in spite of rebuttal evidence that is also in the record.[9.2]

---

[5] Williams v. First Govt. Mort'g. & Investors Corp., 225 F.3d 738, 751 (D.C. Cir. 2000) (Rule 301 presumption imposes burden of going forward with evidence to rebut or meet presumption, but does not shift burden of proof); Igloo Prods Corp. v. Brantex, Inc., 202 F.3d 814, 819 (5th Cir. 2000) (even if trademark infringement defendant were entitled to presumption of secondary meaning, burden of persuasion would not shift to plaintiff, only burden of going forward with evidence shifts under Rule 301; defendant would still have burden of persuasion).

[6] Official Comm. of Asbestos Claimants, v. G-I Holdings, Inc. (In re: G-I Holdings, Inc.), 385 F.3d 313, 318 (3d Cir. 2004) (presumptions under Rule 301 affect only party's burden of going forward with evidence; they do not affect burden of persuasion).

[7] Original Advisory Committee's Note to Fed. R. Evid. 301 ("bursting bubble" theory accords presumptions too "slight and evanescent" an effect; note is reprinted in **Treatise** at § 301App.01[2]); *see also* Fed. R. Evid. 301 House Report (1975) (reprinted in pertinent part in **Treatise** at § 301App.01[3]); Fed. R. Evid. 301 Senate Report (1975) (reprinted in pertinent part in **Treatise** at § 301App.01[3]).

[8] Fed. R. Evid. 301 Conference Action and Report (1975) (on admission of evidence contradicting presumed fact, court may not instruct jury that it may presume existence of presumed fact from proof of basic facts, but may instruct jury that it may infer existence of presumed fact from proof of basic facts; reprinted in pertinent part in **Treatise** at § 301App.01[3]); *see, e.g.,* St. Mary's Honor Ctr v. Hicks, 509 U.S. 502, 511, 113 S. Ct. 2742, 125 L. Ed. 2d 407 (1993) (trier of fact's rejection of rebutting evidence permits, but does not require, inference in accordance with presumption).

[9] Fed. R. Evid. 301 Advisory Committee's Note (1972) (reproduced verbatim at § 301.4[1[[b]) ("bursting bubble" theory accords presumptions too "slight and evanescent" an effect).

[9.1] *See, e.g.,* Retail Servs, Inc. v. Freebies Publishing, Inc., 364 F.3d 535, 543 (4th Cir. 2004) ("If sufficient evidence of genericness is produced to rebut the presumption, the presumption is 'neutralized' and essentially drops from the case); Nunley v. City of Los Angeles, 52 F.3d 792, 796 (9th Cir. 1995) ("bursting bubble" theory of presumptions is applicable to presumption that party received notice upon proof of mailing of appropriate papers).

[9.2] *See, e.g.,* Retail Servs, Inc. v. Freebies Publishing, Inc., 364 F.3d 535, 543 (4th Cir. 2004) (when presumption is rebutted, "the *evidence* giving rise to the presumption remains" in the case and

The courts have sometimes refused or failed to apply Rule 301 when a well-established court-created presumption shifts the burden of persuasion. Those instances are, by and large, limited to circumstances under which the court-created presumption is sufficiently venerable that it has, for all intents and purposes, become a part of the substantive law applicable to the particular case. For example, the presumption that damage caused by a drifting vessel was the result of negligence shifts to the vessel's owner the burden of proving that it was not negligent in allowing the vessel to drift.[10] A similar long-recognized court-created presumption is applied to the government's assessment of taxes due; the assessment is presumed correct, and the taxpayer has the burden of proving the assessment is erroneous.[11] Similarly, in patent infringement suits, the owner of issued patents is entitled to a presumption of validity that shifts the burden of persuasion to the party claiming invalidity.[12]

Rule 301 does not specify how much contrary evidence must be introduced by the opponent for the presumption to be rebutted. The appropriate burden on the opponent is to produce enough evidence so that a reasonable juror could be convinced that the contrary of the presumed fact is true.[13]

---

finder of fact may rely on it as basis for reasonable inferences (emphasis in original)); Nunley v. City of Los Angeles, 52 F.3d 792, 796 (9th Cir. 1995) ("Even after the 'bubble' of presumption has 'burst,' the factual question of receipt remains and may be decided in favor of receipt by a fact finder who may choose to draw inferences of receipt from the evidence of mailing, in spite of contrary evidence.").

[10] *See, e.g.,* Hood v. Knappton Corp., 986 F.2d 329, 331 (9th Cir. 1993) (admiralty rule imposing liability for damages caused if vessel drifts into collision, unless owner shows collision was not avoidable by any human skill or precaution, is necessarily intertwined with substantive principle of admiralty law it supports, and was unaffected by adoption of Fed. R. Evid. 301); James v. River Parishes Co., 686 F.2d 1129, 1133 (5th Cir. 1982) (presumption that damage caused by drifting vessel was the result of negligence shifted to defendant, custodian of drifting vessel, burden of disproving fault by preponderance of the evidence; presumption is matter of substantive law, and is, therefore, not governed by Rule 301).

[11] *See, e.g.,* Welch v. Helvering, 290 U.S. 111, 115, 54 S. Ct. 8, 78 L. Ed. 212 (1933).

[12] *See, e.g.,* Amgen, Inc. v. Hoechst Marion Roessel, 126 F. Supp. 2d 69, 136–137 (D. Mass. 2001) (burden of proving invalidity of patent is on party contesting validity; moreover, evidentiary standard is heightened from preponderance of evidence to clear and convincing evidence).

[13] *See , e.g.,* Rice v. Office of Servicemembers' Group Life Ins. Co., 260 F.3d 1240, 1249 (10th Cir. 2001) (trial court properly instructed jury that proof by preponderance of evidence was sufficient to overcome presumption); A.C. Aukerman Co. v. R.L. Chaides Constr. Co., 960 F.2d 1020, 1038 (Fed. Cir. 1992) ("[b]y raising a genuine issue respecting either factual element of a laches defense, the presumption of laches is overcome"); Clay v. Traders Bank, 708 F.2d 1347, 1351 (8th Cir. 1983) (presumption of insolvency 90 days prior to filing of bankruptcy petition requires party against whom presumption exists to come forward with "only some evidence of solvency"; "substantial evidence" was not the test to be applied).

[2]—Application of Rule 301[1]

Despite the fact that Rule 301 dictates one uniform rule for the incidents discussed above unless "otherwise provided for" by Congress, cases decided since the adoption of the Rule indicate that there is still a considerable lack of uniformity. First, the cases reveal that the courts are not always in agreement as to whether Congress exercised its prerogative to adopt a different type of presumption when creating a statutory presumption;[2] such statutory presumptions may not only shift burdens of persuasion but change the weight of the burden.[3] Second, some cases dealing with presumptions do not base their holdings on Rule 301. Even when the results are consistent with the Rule, it is impossible to tell whether the court was aware that Rule 301 controls.[4] Finally, although Rule 301 purports to apply "in all civil actions and proceedings," a number of courts have improperly bypassed Rule 301, finding that it applies to "procedural" presumptions but not to "substantive" ones.[5]

A careful practitioner must therefore check all cases construing the presumption in question regardless of whether the presumption is statutory or judicially created. Of course, counsel also needs to be aware of the operation of Rule 301 so that

---

[1] *See* **Treatise** at § 301.02[4] for discussion of conflicting presumptions.

[2] *Compare* Presbyterian-St. Luke's Medical Ctr. v. NLRB, 653 F.2d 450, 453 (10th Cir. 1981), *cert. denied*, 459 U.S. 1025 (1982) (Rule 301 is applicable to presumption, adopted under National Labor Relations Act, that a single facility bargaining unit was appropriate) *with* Big Y Foods, Inc. v. NLRB, 651 F.2d 40, 45 (1st Cir. 1981) (Rule 301 not applicable to presumption that meat department bargaining unit was appropriate in multi-department retail food store, because presumption is "substantive," rather than procedural).

[3] *See, e.g.*, United States v. Banco Cafetero Panama, 797 F.2d 1154, 1160 (2d Cir. 1986) (in forfeiture of narcotics proceeds, government need only show more than a suspicion that property was drug related, not prima facie proof; under congressional scheme, claimant must show proceeds of bank account not traceable to drug transactions).

[4] *See, e.g.*, Texas Dept. of Community Affairs v. Burdine, 450 U.S. 248, 254, 101 S. Ct. 1089, 1094 67 L. Ed. 2d 207 (1981) (establishment of prima facie case of unlawful discrimination pursuant to Title VII creates a presumption that shifts burden of production to defendant; Court noted in footnote 8 that the function of the presumption was a traditional one, citing Rule 301). *Cf.* Wards Cove Packing Co. v. Atonio, 490 U.S. 642, 659–660, 109 S. Ct. 2115, 2126, 104 L. Ed. 2d 733, 753 (1989) (in a 5-4 decision in which the Court held that the burden of persuasion remains with the plaintiff in a disparate impact Title VII case, the majority stated that "This rule conforms with the usual method for allocating persuasion and production burdens in the federal courts, see Fed. Rule Evid. 301").

[5] *See, e.g.*, James v. River Parishes Co., 686 F.2d 1129, 1133 (5th Cir. 1982) (holding that custodian of drifting vessel bears risk of non-persuasion that vessel was not cast adrift through negligence and that this is matter of substantive law to which Rule 301 does not apply; dissent argued that Rule 301 applies to all civil proceedings and that prior decisions were overturned by enactment of Rule 301); Bunge Corp. v. M/V Furness Bridge, 558 F.2d 790, 794 (5th Cir. 1977), *cert. denied*, 435 U.S. 924 (1978).

appropriate requests or objections can be made to the court.[6]

§ 5.03 Presumptions Governed by State Law—Rule 302

[1]—Scope and Text of Rule

Rule 302 recognizes that the rationale of the *Erie* decision[1] requires the effect of some presumptions in civil actions to be governed by state law. Before promulgation of the Federal Rules of Evidence, the Supreme Court had held in a number of cases that rules governing burdens of proof are substantive for *Erie* purposes.[2] Presumptions in which the presumed fact is a material proposition involve substantive law. The wording of the Rule is designed to restrict the applicability of state law to the area actually encompassed by the *Erie* decision. The Rule provides as follows:

Rule 302. Applicability of State Law in Civil Actions and Proceedings.

In civil actions and proceedings, the effect of a presumption respecting a fact that is an element of a claim or defense as to which State law supplies the rule of decision is determined in accordance with State law.

---

[2]—State Law Supplies Rule of Decision[1]

Rule 302 applies only when "state law supplies the rule of decision." This phrase was deliberately chosen as more accurately descriptive of the requirements of *Erie* than the commonly used term "diversity cases." *Erie* does not apply to a federal claim or issue even if jurisdiction is based on diversity, but does govern a non-federal claim or issue even in non-diversity cases.[2]

---

[6] *See, e.g.,* Sharp v. Coopers & Lybrand, 649 F.2d 175, 186, 189 n.2 (3d Cir. 1981), *cert. denied,* 455 U.S. 938 (1982) (court upheld presumption that cast burden of production and persuasion on defendant; on appeal, defendants argued that trial court had erred in creating presumption, but did not argue that if presumption was proper, shifting burden of persuasion to defendants was improper under Rule 301; appellate court noted requirement of Rule 301, but refused to consider issue since defendant had not objected to instruction).

[1] Erie v. Tompkins, 304 U.S. 64, 71–77, 58 S. Ct. 817, 82 L. Ed. 1188 (1938).

[2] Dick v. New York Life Ins. Co., 359 U.S. 437, 446, 79 S. Ct. 921, 927 3 L. Ed. 2d 935 (1959) ("Under the *Erie* rule presumptions (and their effects) and burden of proof are 'substantive' "); Palmer v. Hoffman, 318 U.S. 109, 117, 63 S. Ct. 477, 480 87 L. Ed. 645 (1943) (federal courts in diversity cases must apply state law on burden of proof as to contributory negligence); Cities Service Oil Co. v. Dunlap, 308 U.S. 208, 212, 60 S. Ct. 201, 84 L. Ed. 196 (1939). A rule allocating the burden of proof has an effect equivalent to a presumption that shifts the burden of proof. *See* **Treatise** at § 301.02.

[1] *See* **Treatise** at § 302.02.

[2] *See, e.g.,* Maternally Yours, Inc. v. Your Maternity Shop, Inc., 234 F.2d 538, 541 (2d Cir. 1956); Federal Sav. & Loan Ins. Corp. v. Musacchio, 695 F. Supp. 1053, 1065 (N.D. Cal. 1988) (in an action for fraud, negligence and breach of a supervisory agreement, defendant moved to dismiss

When state law provides the rule of decision on the effect of a presumption because the presumed fact is an element of a claim or defense, a federal court pursuant to Rule 302 must determine what the state court would have done and act accordingly. This may be exceedingly difficult.[3] Although theoretically adhering to one particular view of presumptions, the state court may actually be applying a number of different theories and requiring a different measure of proof depending on the particular type of presumption involved.[4] Since identical situations rarely recur, the court may have difficulty in ascertaining which presumption is to apply to the particular facts at hand, or what the state court would have done in a case of first impression, or what to do with conflicting presumptions. The problem is compounded when the parties are relying on causes of action based upon both federal and state substantive law. To avoid confusing the jury, and as a matter of practical judicial administration, some discretion should be used to ignore state presumptions that are not clearly substantive.

[3]—Element of Claim or Defense[1]

Some presumptions do not express a state's substantive policy; they are referred to as tactical. One instance is establishing the receipt of a mailed letter. These presumptions are designed to operate tactically as rules of convenience, regardless of whether they favor plaintiff or defendant, and regardless of the nature of the case in which they are invoked. *Erie* does not require state law to be applied in such situations because the presumption operates as a minor rule of procedure, rather than as a rule of substantive law. Rule 302 embodies the substantive-procedural dichotomy by limiting the applicability of state law to situations where the presumption operates upon "a fact which is an element of a claim or defense"—that is to say, when the presumed fact is a material fact.[2]

---

allegation he was "negligent per se" in not complying with certain statutes and regulations because the plaintiff was not a member of the class intended to be protected by the statute; California law was applicable under provisions of Rule 302; because evidence of the class the statute was intended to protect was ambivalent, court chose to accept applicability of state-law rebuttable presumption that person who violated statute or regulation failed to exercise due care). *See* 17 MOORE'S FEDERAL PRACTICE, Ch. 124, *The Erie Doctrine and Applicable Law* (Matthew Bender 3d ed. 1997).

[3] *See, e.g.,* Melville v. American Home Assurance Co., 443 F. Supp. 1064, 1068 (E.D. Pa. 1977), *rev'd,* 584 F.2d 1306 (3d Cir. 1978) (whether to apply New York, Delaware or Pennsylvania presumption against suicide in case with multi-state contacts).

[4] *See, e.g.,* the type of problem that may arise in applying presumptions in the Uniform Commercial Code discussed in **Treatise** at § 302.05[3].

[1] *See* **Treatise** at § 302.02.

[2] *See, e.g.,* National Indus., Inc., v. Republic Nat'l Life Ins. Co., 677 F.2d 1258, 1266 (9th Cir. 1982) (presumption that property acquired during marriage is community property is substantive and state law applies); Melville v. American Home Assurance Co., 584 F.2d 1306, 1308 (3d Cir. 1978) (presumption against suicide affects substantive claim or defense and is substantive in nature, therefore under Fed. R. Evid. 302 state law must be applied).

There may, nevertheless, be instances when the distinction between rules of substantive policy and procedural convenience remains blurred, even after a court has analyzed the reasons giving rise to the presumption.[3] In case of doubt, the policy embodied in Rule 302 suggests the application of federal rather than state law, since the drafters of the Rule deliberately chose to interpret the *Erie* doctrine as narrowly as possible.

§ 5.04 Presumptions in Criminal Cases—Standard 303

[1]—In General[1]

In criminal cases, theories must yield to constitutional considerations when a presumption is directed against an accused.[1.1] Although in a civil case, a presumption operates as a rule of procedure that requires a "presumed" fact to be found once the "basic" fact is established, in a criminal case, a presumption has a much more limited effect. Although Standard 303 was not adopted by Congress, it is useful to look at this more limited effect. Under Standard 303, once the "basic" fact is established, an inference may, rather than must, be drawn that the "presumed" fact also exists. The procedural device created in Standard 303 does not meet the usual criteria of a presumption. Even if the defendant offers no evidence contrary to the presumed fact, the court may refuse to submit the case to the jury, or if it does, the jury may refuse to convict.

Standard 303 was designed to instruct federal judges in the use of federal statutes in federal criminal cases. They should follow the Standard. In construing state statutes applied by state judges, more tolerance in accepting conduct not appropriate for federal judges is allowed.

Standard 303 provides:

Supreme Court Standard 303. Presumptions In Criminal Cases.

(a)

SCOPE. Except as otherwise provided by Act of Congress, in criminal cases, presumptions against an accused, recognized at common law or created by statute, including statutory provisions that certain facts are prima facie evidence of other facts or of guilt, are governed by this rule.

---

[3] *See, e.g.,* Maryland Casualty Co. v. Williams, 377 F.2d 389, 393 n.1 (5th Cir. 1967) (state may characterize presumption as "procedural" for choice of law purposes even though it may be "substantive" for *Erie* purposes).

[1] *See* **Treatise** at § 303.04.

[1.1] Presumptions against the government should be governed by Rule 301 practice since the constitutional limitations that underlie the adoption of Standard 303 apply only in the case of an accused.

(b)

SUBMISSION TO JURY. The judge is not authorized to direct the jury to find a presumed fact against the accused. When the presumed fact establishes guilt or is an element of the offense or negatives a defense, the judge may submit the question of guilt or of the existence of the presumed fact to the jury, if, but only if, a reasonable juror on the evidence as a whole, including the evidence of the basic facts, could find guilt or the presumed fact beyond a reasonable doubt. When the presumed fact has a lesser effect, its existence may be submitted to the jury if the basic facts are supported by substantial evidence, or are otherwise established, unless the evidence as a whole negatives the existence of the presumed fact.

(c)

INSTRUCTING THE JURY. Whenever the existence of a presumed fact against the accused is submitted to the jury, the judge shall give an instruction that the law declares that the jury may regard the basic facts as sufficient evidence of the presumed fact but does not require it to do so. In addition, if the presumed fact establishes guilt or is an element of the offense or negatives a defense, the judge shall instruct the jury that its existence must, on all the evidence, be proved beyond a reasonable doubt.

The existence of a presumption may still affect the outcome of a criminal case in two ways. In a borderline case, a trial court may be influenced by the legislative judgment of Congress to submit a basic fact to a jury that it would not have submitted as merely circumstantial evidence of the presumed fact.[2] The appellate court may, of course, reverse on the ground that the jury could not have found the presumed fact from the basic fact beyond a reasonable doubt (a requirement discussed below), but it too may defer to the Congressional finding. Insofar as the trial court refers to the presumption (using the word "inference") in instructing the jury, the jury may be influenced by hearing that the court (expressing Congressional will) considers proof of the basic fact sufficient evidence to convict of the charged crime. Though both of these effects are difficult to evaluate, since their impact is subjective and psychological, the existence of a statutory presumption probably does enhance the value of a basic fact for the prosecution beyond its purely inferential significance.

The constitutional limitations on the impact of presumptions in criminal cases have been spelled out by the Supreme Court in a number of cases, some of which were decided after Standard 303 was drafted by the Advisory Committee.[3] The

---

[2] *See, e.g.,* Maryland Casualty Co. v. Williams, 377 F.2d 389, 393 n.1 (5th Cir. 1967) (state may characterize presumption as "procedural" for choice of law purposes even though it may be "substantive" for *Erie* purposes).

[3] See **Treatise** at § 303.05, 303.06, 303.08.

Court has exercised control over the operation of presumptions in criminal cases by means of the "rational connection" test, restrictions on shifting the burden of proof to an accused, and requirements for instructing the jury. These mechanisms are discussed below.

The Supreme Court's decisions reveal the sensitivity of the drafters of Standard 303 to those issues that have emerged as constitutionally significant. With one possible caveat discussed below—the burden required for proof of the basic fact— Standard 303 satisfies constitutional requirements, and should be followed by the lower federal courts until advised to the contrary by Congress or the Supreme Court.

[2]—Scope of Standard 303; Tactical Presumptions[1]

Standard 303 accords identical treatment to statutory and nonstatutory presumptions, and recognizes a variety of statutory patterns as establishing presumptions. A typical provision, which the Advisory Committee had in mind as within the scope of the Standard, is one that provides that proof of a specific fact (such as possession or presence) is sufficient to authorize conviction.[2] Standard 303 also embraced provisions that add the qualification "unless the defendant explains the possession [or presence] to the satisfaction of the jury," and provisions that make possession evidence of a particular element of a crime. The Standard is expressly applicable when a statute provides "that certain facts are prima facie evidence of other facts or of guilt."

Subdivisions (b) and (c) accord different treatment to those presumptions upon which the prosecution relies as establishing guilt or negating a defense, and those presumptions that are merely tactical in nature. Non-tactical presumptions may not be submitted to the jury unless a reasonable jury could find the presumed fact (through normal inferential analysis) from the basic fact beyond a reasonable doubt (subdivision b), and the jury must be so instructed (subdivision c).

Standard 303 is silent as to any requisite connection between the basic fact and the presumed proposition of fact when the presumption is merely tactical in nature (as, for example, a presumption that a letter mailed by one codefendant was received by another to show knowledge of an event). The court still must be satisfied that there is "substantial" evidence of the basic proposition of facts, or that they "are otherwise established," and that the evidence as a whole does not "negative the existence of the presumed fact." Furthermore, even in the case of a

---

[1] *See* **Treatise** at § 303.03.

[2] *See, e.g.,* United States v. Gainey, 380 U.S. 63, 65, 85 S. Ct. 754, 13 L. Ed. 2d 658 (1965) ("The legislative record shows that Congress enacted these provisions because of the 'practical impossibility of proving actual participation in the illegal activities except by inference drawn from [the defendant's] presence when the illegal acts were committed").

tactical presumption, the court must instruct the jury that it may, but need not, regard the basic facts as sufficient evidence of the presumed fact.

[3]—The Rational Connection Test[1]

[a]—The Supreme Court's Position

In a series of decisions predating the promulgation of Standard 303, the Supreme Court had held that there must be a "rational connection" between the basic fact and the presumed fact in order for a presumption to pass constitutional muster.[2] Rational connection, according to the Court, meant that there had to be a connection between the basic fact and the presumed fact "in common experience."[3] It was not, however, clear from the Court's opinions whether the presumed proposition of fact must be inferable from the basic proposition of fact beyond a reasonable doubt, or whether the constitutional standard is met if the basic fact is more likely than not to support an inference of the truth of the presumed proposition.

In 1979, the Supreme Court returned to this issue in County Court of Ulster County v. Allen,[4] and muddied the waters. It avoided addressing the problem by treating the presumption as an inference that was not subject to the rules of presumptions. Inference type presumptions were called "permissible presumptions" and what Standard 303 refers to as presumptions were called "mandatory presumptions."

Allen was a case that challenged the constitutionality of a New York statute providing that, with certain exceptions, the presence of a firearm in an automobile is presumptive evidence of its illegal possession by all the occupants of the vehicle.

---

[1] *See* **Treatise** at §§ 303.05, 303App.101.

[2] *See, e.g,* Barnes v. United States, 412 U.S. 837, 841, 93 S. Ct. 2357, 37 L. Ed. 2d 380 (1973); Turner v. United States, 396 U.S. 398, 409, 90 S. Ct. 642, 24 L. Ed. 2d 610 (1970); Leary v. United States, 395 U.S. 6, 36, 89 S. Ct. 1532, 23 L. Ed. 2d 57 (1969); United States v. Romano, 382 U.S. 136, 139, 86 S. Ct. 279, 15 L. Ed. 2d 210 (1965); United States v. Gainey, 380 U.S. 63, 64, 85 S. Ct. 754, 13 L. Ed. 2d 658 (1965); Tot v. United States, 319 U.S. 463, 468, 63 S. Ct. 1241, 87 L. Ed. 1519 (1943).

[3] Tot v. United States, 319 U.S. 463, 468, 63 S. Ct. 1241, 87 L. Ed. 1519 (1943). *See, e.g.,* United States v. Romano, 382 U.S. 136, 141, 144, 86 S. Ct. 279, 15 L. Ed. 2d 210 (1965) (Court struck down statute that provided that presence at an illegal still is sufficient to authorize conviction for possession of still; Court had previously, in United States v. Gainey, 380 U.S. 63, 69, 85 S. Ct. 754, 13 L. Ed. 2d 658 (1965), approved statute that provided that same basic fact of presence was sufficient to authorize conviction for carrying on the business of distilling without giving bond; Court explained that "anyone present at the site is very probably connected with the illegal enterprise [b]ut presence tells us nothing about what the defendant's specific function was [and] its connection with possession is too tenuous to permit a reasonable inference of guilt. . . .").

[4] County Court of Ulster County v. Allen, 442 U.S. 140, 99 S. Ct. 2213, 60 L. Ed. 2d 777 (1979).

The evidence against defendants was strong and supported a verdict with or without the statutory presumption on normal inferential grounds. Four persons, three adult males and a sixteen-year-old girl, had been convicted of possession of two loaded firearms. The guns, protruding from the girl's handbag, were said to be in plain view when a police officer stopped the car in which the four were riding for speeding. Counsel for all four defendants objected to the introduction of the handguns into evidence on the ground that the state had not adequately demonstrated a connection between the defendants and the guns. The state trial court overruled the objection and the defendants were convicted. The case reached the Supreme Court after a writ of habeas corpus had been granted on the ground that the statute was unconstitutional.

In upholding the constitutionality of the statute, a plurality of the Court distinguished between "permissive" and "mandatory" presumptions, and held that only mandatory presumptions have to meet a reasonable doubt standard. The opinion for the Court set forth the following definitions:

> [T]he entirely permissive inference or presumption . . . allows—but does not require—the trier of fact to infer the elemental fact from proof by the prosecutor of the basic one and . . . places no burden of any kind on the defendant. . . . A mandatory presumption . . . tells the trier that he or they must find the elemental fact upon proof of the basic fact, at least until the defendant has come forward with some evidence to rebut the presumed connection between the two facts.[5]

The plurality in *Allen* also stated that the classification of a presumption as permissive or mandatory depends upon the instructions the court gives to the jury. After looking at these instructions, the plurality concluded that the New York statutory presumption at issue in *Allen* "gave rise to a permissible inference available only in certain circumstances, rather than a mandatory conclusion of possession . . . ."[6] When the prosecution utilizes a mandatory presumption, it may not rest its case entirely on the presumption "unless the fact proved is sufficient to support the inference of guilt beyond a reasonable doubt."[7] When, however, as

---

[5] 442 U.S. at 157. This analysis of the effect of a "mandatory presumption" seems incorrect insofar as federal prosecutions are involved, since the court is never authorized to direct the jury to find for the prosecution on a material proposition. Perhaps the Court was thinking of a form of affirmative defense or treatment by some states of insanity. It is also incorrect since the rules of presumption are designed to control judges, not juries.

[6] *Id.* at 161.

[7] *Id.* at 167. *See, e.g.,* Schwendeman v. Wallenstein, 971 F.2d 313, 316 (9th Cir. 1992), *cert. denied,* 506 US. 1052 (1993) (The Ninth Circuit reversed the district court's denial of defendant's habeas corpus petition. Defendant was convicted in state court of vehicular assault. At trial, the jury was instructed that they could infer that defendant had driven in a reckless manner, an essential

in *Allen*, the prosecution relies on a permissive presumption—i.e., inference—the presumed fact need only be more likely than not to flow from the basic fact, "[a]s long as it is clear that the presumption is not the sole and sufficient basis for a finding of guilt."[8] The beyond a reasonable doubt standard is apparently applicable when the prosecution relies solely on a presumption.

To determine whether the permissive presumption in question satisfies the 'more likely than not' standard, the court must look to the evidence presented in the case before it, rather than to the general experience of the community or the validity of the legislative findings.[9] A review of the evidence persuaded the Court that in this case the presumption (or, under our analysis, inference) of possession was "entirely rational."[10]

[b]—The 303 Standard

Standard 303 more than satisfies the rational connection test because it employs a "beyond the reasonable doubt" standard for all presumptions, other than those that are merely tactical, instead of the lesser "more likely than not" standard authorized by *Allen* for permissive presumptions.

[4]—Instructing the Jury[1]

[a]—The Supreme Court's Position

The Supreme Court's opinion in the *Allen* case, discussed above, has made the judge's instructions to the jury a crucial component of the constitutionality of presumptions. The Court perceived a significant distinction between what the Court termed mandatory and permissive presumptions, and rested the determination of which category a presumption falls into almost entirely on the formulation of the jury instructions.[2]

In cases decided subsequent to *Allen*, the Court has continued to stress the

---

element of the charge, solely from evidence that he was speeding. The appellate court held that this instruction was constitutionally defective because it did not meet the Supreme Court's standard for a permissive inference jury instruction set forth in Ulster County v. Allen, as the court could "not say with substantial assurance that the inferred fact of reckless driving more likely than not flowed from the proved fact of excessive speed." The error was not harmless since the instruction may have "materially affect[ed] the verdict.").

[8] 442 U.S. at 167.

[9] *Id.* at 162–63. As applied to the *Allen* case, the Court noted such factors as the girl's age, the size of the handbag and guns, the driver's easy access to the guns, and the presence of older men who were not hitchhikers or other casual passengers.

[10] *Id.* at 163.

[1] *See* **Treatise** at §§ 303.08, 303.10[4].

[2] The Court stated: "In deciding what type of inference or presumption is involved in a case, the jury instructions will generally be controlling, although their interpretation may require recourse to

importance of instructions to the jury. In Sandstrom v. Montana,[3] the Court insisted on "careful attention to the words actually spoken to the jury,"[4] and in Francis v. Franklin,[5] the Court found the crucial question to be "what a reasonable juror could have understood the charge as meaning."[6] It is not, however, entirely clear from looking at the instructions that were given in the cases decided by the Supreme Court precisely which words need to be used by the charging judge to ensure that the jury understands that it need not find the presumed fact.[7] What seems clear is that a federal judge (and a well-advised state judge) should not use the word "presumption" in charging the jury. It should also instruct the jury that the burden

---

the statute involved." County Court of Ulster County v. Allen, 442 U.S. 140, 157 n.16, 99 S. Ct. 2213, 60 L. Ed. 2d 777 (1979).

[3] Sandstrom v. Montana, 442 U.S. 510, 99 S. Ct. 2450, 61 L. Ed. 2d 39 (1979).

[4] 442 U.S. at 514.

[5] Francis v. Franklin, 471 U.S. 307, 105 S. Ct. 1965, 85 L. Ed. 2d 344 (1985).

[6] 471 U.S. at 315–316. See also Moss v. Lockhart, 971 F.2d 77, 79-80 (8th Cir. 1992) (The Eighth Circuit held that a jury instruction concerning the statutory affirmative defense did not impermissibly shift the burden of proof by requiring defendant to prove an element of the state's felony-murder case. The instruction on the murder charge stated that the prosecution had the burden of proving that defendant was involved in the robbery when the murder occurred. The instruction on the affirmative defense stated that defendant could be acquitted if he proved that he was not the only participant, and that he did not commit or instigate the murder.).

[7] Some of the instructions in the Allen case itself could have been understood to mean that the jury must find possession unless the defendant comes forward with some rebuttal evidence—the definition of a mandatory rather than a permissive presumption. See, e.g., County Court of Ulster County v. Allen, 442 U.S. 140, 161 n.20, 99 S. Ct. 2213, 60 L. Ed. 2d 777 (1979) ("In other words, those presumptions or this latter presumption upon proof of the presence of the machine gun and the hand weapons, you may infer and draw a conclusion that such prohibited weapon was possessed by each of the defendants who occupied the automobile at the time when such instruments were found. The presumption or presumptions is effective only so long as there is no substantial evidence contradicting the conclusion flowing from the presumption, and the presumption is said to disappear when such contradictory evidence is adduced."). Although the Court has indicated that the jury charge has to be taken as a whole in determining what a reasonable juror would have understood, there has been considerable disagreement among the Justices in determining the impact of any particular jury charge. See, e.g., Francis v. Franklin, 471 U.S. 307, 312 105 S. Ct. 1965, 85 L. Ed. 2d 344 (1985) (5–4 decision); compare Cunningham v. Zant, 928 F.2d 1006, 1014–15 n. 11 (11th Cir. 1991) (in a murder trial, the judge's charge to the jury that the law presumes that a person of sound mind intends the consequences of his acts, but that this presumption may be rebutted, was a violation of Sandstrom, as the court provided no instruction on how the presumption could be rebutted; the error was harmless, however, because the evidence overwhelmingly established the intent to kill) with United States v. Graham, 858 F.2d 986, 992 (5th Cir. 1988), cert. denied, 489 U.S. 1020 (1989) (jury instruction did not impermissibly shift burden of proof onissue of intent; the instruction stated in part, "It is reasonable to infer that a person ordinarily intends the natural and probable consequences of his or her knowing act. The jury may draw the inference that the accused intended all the consequences which one standing in like circumstances and possessing like knowledge should reasonably have expected to result from any intentional act or conscious omission"; the court held that this instruction properly stated a permissive inference).

is on the prosecution to prove each element of the crime by proof beyond a reasonable doubt.[8]

[b]—The 303 Standard

Subdivision (c) of Standard 303 requires a federal judge to instruct the jury that it may decline to regard the basic facts as sufficient evidence of the presumed fact. The judge is also required to instruct the jury that, except in the case of a purely tactical presumption, it must make its own finding that the presumed fact exists beyond a reasonable doubt. These instructions satisfy the constitutional concerns expressed in *Allen* in all cases in which the particular facts compel the conclusion that the prosecution was not relying solely on the presumption. This will usually be the case since the presumed fact is very likely to have some probability relationship to the basic facts; that is often why the presumption was created in the first place.

If, however, after looking at all of the facts, it appears that the prosecution relied solely upon the permissive presumption, according to *Allen*, the basic facts have to give rise to the presumed fact beyond a reasonable doubt. In that situation, Standard 303 may perhaps not afford sufficient constitutional protection because it does not require an instruction to the jury directing it to find the basic facts beyond a reasonable doubt. Such an instruction should be given in federal prosecutions.[9]

[5]—Shifting Burdens of Proof[1]

Considerable uncertainty existed prior to the promulgation of Standard 303 as to whether a presumption in a criminal case could constitutionally fulfill its usual civil case function of shifting either the burden of production or the burden of persuasion to the party against whom the presumption operates when the party is the accused. Traditionally, the law had recognized that not every element that might conceivably affect the outcome of a case rests initially with the prosecution. Affirmative defenses existed that required the defendant, rather than the prosecution, to produce evidence on particular issues, or even to persuade the jury with respect to them. A presumption has identical procedural consequences, although

---

[8] The Court had indicated in a footnote in United States v. Gainey, 380 U.S. 63, 70–71, n.7, 85 S. Ct. 754, 13 L. Ed. 2d 658 (1965), that "the better practice would be to instruct the jurors that they may draw the inference unless the evidence in the case provides a satisfactory explanation for the defendant's presence at the still, omitting any explicit reference to the statute itself in the charge." In County Court of Ulster County v. Allen, 442 U.S. 140, 145 99 S. Ct. 2213, 60 L. Ed. 2d 777 (1979), the trial court had informed the jurors that a presumption exists in the New York Penal Law.

[9] Hawaii and Oregon, which adopted rules governing criminal presumptions after the Supreme Court's decisions in *Allen* and *Sandstrom*, require the basic facts to be proved beyond a reasonable doubt. *See* Hawaii Evidence Rule 306; Oregon Evidence Rule 309.

[1] *See* **Treatise** at § 303.06.

not until the basic fact is established. Nevertheless, language in the Supreme Court's 1965 opinion in *United States v. Gainey* ² suggested that presumptions shifting the burden of disproof to the accused might be unconstitutional. The Court was silent as to the theoretical analogy between presumptions and affirmative defenses.

Cases decided by the Supreme Court since the promulgation of Standard 303 have not clarified the relationship between presumptions and affirmative defenses. In a series of cases dealing with a state's allocation of a burden of persuasion to the defendant via an affirmative defense, the Court declined to hold that affirmative defenses may never be shifted to a defendant. Instead, the Court adopted a formalistic test that disposed of the cases before it, but established no standard by which to test the constitutionality of affirmative defenses.

In Mullaney v. Wilbur,³ the Court reversed a Maine murder conviction. The jury had been instructed that were it to find the homicide both intentional and unlawful, then malice aforethought, essential to a finding of murder as opposed to manslaughter, was be conclusively implied unless the accused proved by a fair preponderance of the evidence that he acted in the heat of passion. Noting that Maine imposed very different penalties for murder and manslaughter, the Court explained that it could not "dra [w] this distinction, while refusing to require the prosecution to establish beyond a reasonable doubt the fact upon which it turns."⁴ Two years later, in *Patterson v. New York*,⁵ the Court upheld a New York statute that defined second degree murder as an intentional killing, and allowed the defendant to reduce the homicide to the less culpable crime of manslaughter if he proved by a preponderance of the evidence that he had acted under "extreme emotional disturbance." The majority explained that unlike the Maine statute, the New York provision does not require the prosecution to prove malice aforethought: New York's affirmative defense "does not serve to negative any acts of the crime which the State is to prove in order to convict for murder. It constitutes a separate issue on which the defendant is required to carry the burden of persuasion."⁶ The *Patterson* opinion ruled out interpreting *Mullaney* to mean that the prosecution has the burden of proving every fact that bears on culpability.

---

² United States v. Gainey, 380 U.S. 63, 68, 85 S. Ct. 754, 13 L. Ed. 2d 658 (1965) (existence of basic fact does not require court to submit case to jury, or jury to convict).

³ Mullaney v. Wilbur, 421 U.S. 684, 95 S. Ct. 1881, 44 L. Ed. 2d 508 (1975).

⁴ 421 U.S. at 698. The Court explained that "Maine denigrates the interests found critical in Winship." In In re Winship, 397 U.S. 358, 364, 90 S. Ct. 1068, 1073, 25 L. Ed. 2d 368, 375 (1970), the Court had stated that "the Due Process Clause protects the accused against conviction except upon proof beyond a reasonable doubt of every fact necessary to constitute the crime with which he is charged."

⁵ Patterson v. New York, 432 U.S. 197, 97 S. Ct. 2319, 53 L. Ed. 2d 281 (1977).

⁶ *Id.* at 432 U.S. at 207.

At this time, therefore, it appears that a state generally will be able to require a defendant to prove some factor bearing on guilt, provided the definition of the crime does not require the prosecution to prove the nonexistence of that factor.[6.1] To be sure, the *Patterson* majority conceded that there is some constitutional limit beyond which a legislature may not go in shifting affirmative defenses to a defendant, regardless of how it goes about defining crimes. But it failed to indicate how those limits may be found. Allocating the affirmative defense of insanity to the defendant has been upheld as constitutional.[7] The Court has also held, in *Martin v. Ohio*,[8] that the burden of proving self-defense may be placed on a defendant in a homicide case that does not require the prosecution to prove unlawfulness.[9]

Although the *Mullaney-Patterson* line of cases allows the burden of proof to be placed on the defendant under the circumstances indicated above, the Supreme Court's decisions on presumptions would bar allocating a functionally identical burden to the defendant by means of a presumption. Suppose, for instance, that a statute defines first-degree robbery as a robbery committed with what appears to be a firearm, and permits defendant to prove as an affirmative defense by a preponderance of the evidence that the firearm was not loaded, thereby reducing the crime to second-degree robbery. The constitutionality of such a statute was upheld by the Second Circuit in Farrell v. Czarnetzky,[10] as not violating *Mullaney*

[6.1] *See, e.g.,* United States v. Talbott, 78 F.3d 1183, 1186–1187 (7th Cir. 1996) (although Congress or a state legislature may enact laws giving criminal defendants the burden of proving affirmative defenses, absent such a statute, the burden of proof remains on the government to negate beyond a reasonable doubt any affirmative defense properly raised by the defendant); *see also* United States v. Juan, 59 F. Supp. 2d 210, 219–220 (D. Mass. 1999) (in context of sentencing guidelines, government bears burden of proving aggravating circumstances, while defendant bears burden of proving mitigating circumstances; citing *Treatise*).

[7] In Rivera v. Delaware, 429 U.S. 877, 877, 97 S. Ct. 226, 50 L. Ed. 2d 160 (1976), the Supreme Court dismissed, for want of a substantial federal question, an appeal challenging the placement of the burden of insanity on defendant. An earlier decision of the Court had upheld an Oregon statute requiring defendant to prove insanity beyond a reasonable doubt. Leland v. Oregon, 343 U.S. 790, 72 S. Ct. 1002, 96 L. Ed. 1302 (1952). *See* United States v. Byrd, discussing the Insanity Defense Reform Act, n.12 *infra.*

[8] Martin v. Ohio, 480 U.S. 228, 230 107 S. Ct. 1098, 94 L. Ed. 2d 267 (1987).

[9] *See, e.g.,* Hooper v. Perini, 641 F.2d 445, 446 (6th Cir.), *cert. denied,* 454 U.S. 817 (1981); *but see* Humanik v. Beyer, 871 F.2d 432, 433 (3d Cir.), *cert. denied,* 493 U.S. 812 (1989) (appellate court reversed the district court's denial of a convicted murderer's petition for *habeas corpus,* finding that the New Jersey trial court's application of the state "diminished capacity" statute unconstitutionally placed on the defendant the burden of proving by a preponderance of the evidence that he suffered from a mental disease or defect, which negated the existence of an intent to kill, an element of the crime charged; the appellate court held that there was "more than a reasonable likelihood" that the jurors understood the instruction to shift to defendant the government's burden to prove, beyond a reasonable doubt, defendant's intent to kill).

[10] Farrell v. Czarnetzky, 566 F.2d 381, 382 (2d Cir. 1977), *cert. denied,* 434 U.S. 1077 (1978). *See also* Jones v. Dugger, 928 F.2d 1020, 1029 (11th Cir. 1991), *cert. denied,* 502 U.S. 875 (1991)

or *Patterson*.

Suppose, however, that the legislature had instead chosen to define first-degree robbery as a robbery committed with a loaded weapon, and had further provided that when what appears to be a firearm is displayed in the course of committing a robbery, it will be presumed to be loaded unless the contrary is shown. Such a statute would suffer from a double infirmity. It would be invalidated under the burden of proof line of cases because it shifts to the defendant the proof of a factor—the gun was not loaded—the non-existence of which the prosecution is required to prove as an element of the crime.[11] It might also be invalidated under the Court's presumption line of cases, because for a mandatory presumption to be constitutional, the presumed fact—the gun was loaded—must flow from the basic fact—the gun was displayed during a robbery—beyond a reasonable doubt.[12] Whether any such inference could be drawn beyond a reasonable doubt is questionable, considering the number of robberies committed with what turn out to be

---

(in the penalty phase of a capital crime trial, the court may shift to the defendant the burden of establishing by a preponderance of the evidence the existence of mitigating circumstances; citing Walton v. Arizona, 497 U.S. 639, 110 S.Ct. 3047, 111 L.Ed.2d 511 (1990)).

[11] *See* Sandstrom v. Montana, 442 U.S. 510, 524, 99 S. Ct. 2450, 61 L. Ed. 2d 39 (1979) (presumption unconstitutional that relieves prosecution from proving intent). *But cf.* Rose v. Clark, 478 U.S. 570, 582, 106 S. Ct. 3101, 92 L. Ed. 2d 460 (1986) (a *Sandstrom* error may be harmless).

[12] *See* discussion of *Allen* case in [3][a], *above*. *But see* Smart v. Leeke, 856 F.2d 609, 611 (4th Cir. 1988) (panel opinion upheld district court's grant of habeas relief, finding that because the crime of murder in South Carolina included the element of malice, and lack of self-defense was one aspect of malice, the jury instruction improperly placed the burden of persuasion upon defendant who had put self-defense in issue; once evidence of self-defense was presented, the failure to prove malice beyond a reasonable doubt was "fatal from the prosecution's point of view"), *rev'd en banc*, 873 F.2d 1558 (4th Cir.), *cert. denied*, 493 U.S. 867 (1989) (*en banc* court of appeals reversed panel opinion, finding no significant difference between Ohio and South Carolina murder law); *Martin v. Ohio* was therefore controlling); Woods v. Butler, 847 F.2d 1163–1166 (5th Cir. 1988), *cert. denied*, 488 U.S. 970 (1988) (appeals court affirmed district court's denial of habeas relief for defendant convicted in state court of possession of a controlled substance; the statute under which defendant was convicted had two elements: possession of the substance and absence of a prescription for it; defendant argued that the burden of proof for the prescription element was impermissibly shifted to him because it placed the burden of proving the existence of a prescription on the accused; appeals court held that the issue whether defendant had a valid prescription was a defense to the crime of possession, not an element of the crime, and that a state could place the burden of going forward, and burden of persuasion, on a defendant who asserted an affirmative defense; citing Patterson v. New York); United States v. Byrd, 834 F.2d 145, 147 (8th Cir. 1987) (defendant appealed his conviction for robbery, arguing that the Insanity Defense Reform Act, 18 U.S.C. 17(b), which provides tha "[t]he defendant has the burden of proving the defense of insanity by clear and convincing evidence," was unconstitutional because by shifting to him the burden of proving insanity, it effectively shifted the burden of proving willfulness, an element of the crime of robbery; appeals court, affirming the conviction, noted that defendant's reliance on Mullaney v. Wilbur was misplaced because the crime of robbery does not include sanity among its elements, and willfulness and the legal concept of insanity are not coterminous).

water pistols, cap guns and starter pistols, as well as authentic, but unloaded, guns. Of course, in the affirmative defense case, the legislature has chosen to penalize using a firearm that appears to be loaded, whereas in the presumption case, first-degree robbery has been defined as using a gun that is loaded. Functionally, however, the result in both cases would be the same. The jury would find the defendant guilty of first-degree robbery if it believed that he committed the robbery, unless he came forward with a satisfactory explanation about the gun not being loaded.

Constitutional distinctions should not be based on technicalities in draftsmanship that do not affect the merits. Yet *Patterson* has the advantage of requiring the legislature to directly confront the political and policy problems of what the definition of the crime and defenses should be. There is a difference between "appears to be loaded" and "is loaded." Guns of the latter type can kill, while guns of the former type merely intimidate.

CHAPTER 6

*Relevancy Generally**

SYNOPSIS

---

* Chapter revised in 1993 by SANDRA D. KATZ, member of the New York Bar.

§ 6.01   Definition of Relevant Evidence—Rule 401

[1]—Nature of Concept[1]

The concept of relevancy is basic to the law of evidence; it is the cornerstone on which any rational system of evidence rests. Without regard to any other rules or considerations, an item of evidence cannot be admitted unless it meets the test of relevancy. Rule 401 is, therefore, the foundation on which the Federal Rules of Evidence rest. The Rule provides:

Rule 401.   Definition of "Relevant Evidence."

"Relevant evidence" means evidence having any tendency to make the existence of any fact that is of consequence to the determination of the action more probable or less probable than it would be without the evidence.

[Adopted Jan. 2, 1975, effective July 1, 1975.]

The nature of the concept of relevancy is such as to elude exact definition. "Relevancy," as the Advisory Committee notes, "is not an inherent characteristic of any item of evidence but exists only as a relationship between an item of evidence and a matter properly provable in the case."[2] According to Rule 401, relevancy is a relationship between a proffered item of evidence and a "fact that is of consequence to the determination of the action." Although some situations discussed below recur with sufficient frequency to permit formulation of particular rules of relationship, most cases do not fall into any set pattern and must be considered on an ad hoc basis. Rule 401 was designed as a general guide for handling such cases. Rules 404 through 412 provide more particular guidance as to relevancy with respect to recurrent fact patterns which also entail considerations of substantive policy.[3]

---

[1] *See* **Treatise** at § 401.02.

[2] Original Advisory Committee's Note to Fed. R. Evid. 401 (reprinted in **Treatise** at § 401App.01[2]); *see, e.g.,* United States v. Vallejo, 237 F.3d 1008, 1015 (9th Cir. 2001), *modified on other grounds,* 246 F.3d 115 (9th Cir. 2001) (quoting **Treatise,** "Relevance is not inherent in any item of evidence but exists only as a relation between an item of evidence and a matter properly provable in the case"); *see also* United States v. Russo, 104 F.3d 431, 433 (D.C. Cir. 1997) (first step in determining relevancy is to identify the matter properly provable; some matters "are properly provable only because the opposing party has made them such").

[3] *See* Ch. 7; *see also* Ch 3 for discussion of situations in which the relevance of evidence depends on the existence of preliminary fact, and thus presents issues of the relationship between judge and jury.

[2]—Consequential or Material Fact[4]

The Rules themselves are not consistent in their use of terminology. This is particularly true of what we refer to in this volume as a material proposition of fact.[5] This is the ultimate proposition of fact being proved that is required by the rule of substantive law to make out a prima facie case.[6] In Rule 401 it is referred to as a "fact that is of consequence to the determination of the action," and in Rule 405(b) as "an essential element of a charge, claim, or defense." In the **Treatise** it is referred to from time to time as a "consequential fact" or "material fact." Whether or not a proposition of fact is material—*i.e.,* of consequence—is determined not by the rules of evidence but by substantive law. In a diversity case, this means that the federal court will have to look to applicable state law because of the *Erie* doctrine.[7]

Although an understanding of the concept that what is consequential or material controls what is provable in a case is crucial for analytical purposes, the idea is implied in the definition of relevancy.[8] It need not, therefore, be the basis of a separate objection when evidence fails to relate to a consequential fact. This is so because the definition of relevancy posits that one term of the relationship is, as Rule 401 indicates, a "fact of consequence to the determination of the action." If an item of evidence tends only to prove a fact not of consequence to the determination of the action, it is, according to the terminology of the Federal Rules,

---

[4] *See* **Treatise** at § 401.04[3].

[5] This choice of terminology follows the approach of Professor Jerome Michael. For the most systematic discussion, *see* Michael and Adler, The Nature of Judicial Proof (1931); Michael and Adler, *The Trial of An Issue of Fact* (1934) (*reprinted in* 34 Colum. L. Rev. 1224, 1252 (1934)); Michael, *The Basic Rules of Pleading,* 5 Record of the Ass'n of the Bar of the City of New York 175 (1950).

[6] *See, e.g.,* Old Chief v. United States, 519 U.S. 172, 178–179, 117 S. Ct. 644, 136 L. Ed. 2d 574 (1997) (demonstration of prior conviction "was a step on one evidentiary route to the ultimate fact," because it placed defendant within class of offenders for whom firearms possession was outlawed); United States v. Yockel, 320 F.3d 818, 826 (8th Cir. 2003) (trial court properly excluded evidence of defendant's lack of intent to intimidate teller during bank robbery; evidence was irrelevant because bank robbery is not a crime involving specific intent and evidence of intent does not tend to prove consequential fact).

[7] *See, e.g.,* Girden v. Sandals Int'l, 262 F.3d 195, 203–204 (2d Cir. 2001) (citing **Treatise,** unwanted kissing constituted sexual assault under New York law and was, therefore, of consequence to determination of plaintiff's claim for tortious injury). *See also* **Treatise** at § 1101.04.

[8] *See, e.g.,* Lyons v. England, 307 F.3d 1092, 1110 (9th Cir. 2002) (in context of racial disparate treatment in employment claim, to be relevant, background evidence of employer's time-barred actions must indicate it is more or less probable that employer intentionally discriminated against employee because of his or her race); United States v. Russo, 104 F.3d 431, 434 (D.C. Cir. 1997) ("An item sought to be introduced may have little probative value or it may have a great deal. But as Rule 401 defines it, the item is either relevant or not; there is no in-between").

irrelevant.[9]

[3]—Credibility; Evidential Hypothesis[10]

Evidence that does not relate to any proposition of substantive law that must be proved may be admitted to help the trier of fact evaluate the credibility of witnesses.[11] Similarly, evidence unrelated to a material proposition of fact may be admissible to assist the trier of fact in evaluating the credibility of a claim or defense.[12] Evidence may also be relevant for the sole purpose of assisting the trier of fact in evaluating the credibility of other admissible evidence.[13] Such evidence is relevant not because it tends directly to prove or disprove any material fact, but because it will aid the court or jury in evaluating the probative value of other evidence offered to prove or disprove the existence of a material fact.

Evidence may also be relevant to assist the jury in evaluating the validity of an evidentiary hypothesis. An evidentiary hypothesis is a framework for reasoning proposed by one party that would, if the jury finds it to be valid, permit the jury to infer a material fact from circumstantial or otherwise only tangentially related evidence. Thus, in an action alleging age discrimination, other incidents of alleged

---

[9] *See, e.g.,* United States v. Wagner, 382 F.3d 598, 616 (6th Cir. 2004) (defendant's expert audiology testimony indicating his inability to hear and understand proceedings at bankruptcy court hearing was irrelevant because it could not have had an impact on issues of his filing fraudulent SBA mortgage and note before hearing occurred or explain his changing locks on building subject to mortgage after hearing occurred).

[10] *See* **Treatise** at § 401.04[4].

[11] *See, e.g.,* United States v. Abel, 469 U.S. 45, 48–49, 105 S. Ct. 465, 83 L. Ed. 2d 450 (1984) (trial court properly permitted prosecution to rebut defense witness's testimony with evidence that defendant and witness were both members of secret prison organization with creed that required members to lie, cheat, steal, and kill to protect other members; evidence was relevant to witness's credibility); United States v. Taylor, 239 F.3d 994, 997 (9th Cir. 2001) (after defendant attacked credibility of witness, a prostitute, with her prior inconsistent testimony, trial court properly admitted expert testimony concerning relationship between pimp and prostitute to explain those inconsistencies; expert testimony was relevant to witness's credibility).

[12] *See, e.g.,* Barnes v. Owens-Corning Fiberglas Corp., 201 F.3d 819, 829 (6th Cir. 2000) (district court properly allowed one defendant to read to jury portions of plaintiffs' complaint specifically naming other defendants, but not defendant, as having supplied products that caused decedent's injuries; evidence was relevant to issue of causation and to credibility of plaintiffs' claim against proffering defendant).

[13] *See, e.g.,* Crane v. Kentucky, 476 U.S. 683, 688, 106 S. Ct. 2142, 90 L. Ed. 2d 636 (1986) (criminal defendant was entitled to adduce evidence concerning manner in which his confession was obtained, as relevant to reliability and credibility of confession, even though trial court had decided before trial that confession was voluntary); Tiller v. Baghdady, 244 F.3d 9, 14 (1st Cir. 2001) (evidence of deposit made to defendant's bank account, in same amount as was realized from sales of stock owned by two of defendant's sisters and made only days before defendant purchased land, was relevant in that it might cause jury to question defendant's testimony he did not use those sales proceeds to purchase land).

age discrimination on the part of the employer were admissible. Such evidence, while anecdotal, may indicate the presence of a discriminatory atmosphere, and show the employer's state of mind, adding "color" to the factual background of the plaintiff's termination.[14] Similarly, a California driver's license in a defendant's brother's name, showing an address in Garden Grove, California, was relevant in a drug prosecution involving shipment by mail of methamphetamine when the address on the driver's license was the same as the return address on the shipment package, because it would support an inference by the jury that the recipient of the package would know from the return address and the coded words and numbers on the package what the package contained and who shipped it.[15] The information supporting the inference—that, for example, racially biased supervisors are more likely to be motivated by racial animus in their treatment of a member of the race against which they are biased than by job related performance—is normally supplied by the trier of fact's own general knowledge of life.

[4]—"Relevant" Evidence Alters Probabilities[16]

To be relevant, evidence must not only relate in some way to a consequential fact that substantive law requires a party to prove. It must also have some tendency to make the existence of the consequential fact "more probable or less probable than it would be without the evidence."[17] Any proffered evidence that appears to

---

[14] *See, e.g.,* Cummings v. Std. Register Co., 265 F.3d 56, 63 (1st Cir. 2001).

[15] *See, e.g.,* United States v. Nguyen, 284 F.3d 1086, 1089 (9th Cir. 2002).

[16] *See* **Treatise** at § 401.04.

[17] Fed. R. Evid. 401; *see, e.g.,* Ueland v. United States, 291 F.3d 993, 997–998 (7th Cir. 2002) (questions designed to elicit information that plaintiff experienced lower back pain before accident were relevant because they tended to undermine plaintiff's contention that automobile accident was cause of plaintiff's pain); Pipitone v. Biomatrix, Inc., 288 F.3d 239, 245 (5th Cir. 2002) (expert testimony on causation that is equivocal does not have a tendency to make existence of any fact more or less probable and is, therefore, not relevant); United States v. Parker, 262 F.3d 415, 418–420 (4th Cir. 2001) (trial court did not err in excluding evidence concerning law enforcement officers' actions against defendant's grandmother at time of defendant's arrest and confession, offered to prove defendant's confession was involuntary, because defendant was unaware of those actions when she made her confession, so actions could not have affected her mental state or induced her confession).

alter the likelihood of a consequential fact is relevant,[18] although it may be excluded because of other considerations.[19]

The Advisory Committee rejected a standard requiring more than an apparent altering of the probabilities as "unworkable and unrealistic." Requiring anything more would confuse relevance as a prerequisite to admissibility with the standard for determining the sufficiency of the evidence to create a triable issue of fact.[20] Thus, the relevance standard for admissibility is whether reasonable persons might believe the probability of the existence of the consequential fact to be different if they knew of the proffered evidence.[21]

[5]—Relevancy Determinations[22]

[a]—Definition of "Relevance" Implies Liberal Admissibility

Rule 401 defines "relevant evidence" in the widest possible terms. Evidence is relevant if it has *any tendency* to prove or disprove the existence of a consequential fact.[23] Rule 401's definition, therefore, implies a liberal standard of admissibility.[24]

The relevance of proffered evidence is largely determined on a case-by-case basis, considering the nature of the evidence, the consequential fact at issue, and the context in which the evidence is offered. For example, trial courts have properly found proffered evidence to be relevant in the following circumstances:

---

[18] *See, e.g.,* United States v. Hodges, 315 F.3d 794, 800 (7th Cir. 2003) (in prosecution for possessing stolen property, evidence of defendant's affiliation with street gang was relevant because it made it more likely that he had connections that made it easy for him to fence stolen property and that he possessed stolen guns for that purpose); Rutherford v. Harris County, 197 F.3d 173, 186 (5th Cir. 1999) (evidence that plaintiff's superior made sexual advances to her was relevant to plaintiff's gender discrimination claim because it showed that her superior began criticizing her work only after she rebuffed his advances, thereby increasing probability that those criticisms were grounded in his sexually based discriminatory intent).

[19] *See, e.g.,* § 6.02 concerning exclusion of relevant evidence because of prejudice, confusion, or waste of time.

[20] Original Advisory Committee's Note to Fed R. Evid. 401 (reprinted in **Treatise** at § 401App.01[2]); *see, e.g.,* C.P. Interests, Inc. v. California Pools, Inc., 238 F.3d 690, 701 (5th Cir. 2001) (contention that certain evidence was irrelevant because witness did not know of any relationship between two business entities confused sufficiency of evidence issues with less stringent relevance admissibility issues).

[21] *See, e.g.,* United States v. Boulware, 384 F.3d 794, 805 n.3 (9th Cir. 2004) (evidence need not prove consequential fact to be relevant; it only needs to make it more probable or improbable).

[22] *See* **Treatise** at §§ 401.03–401.07.

[23] Fed. R. Evid. 401 (emphasis added).

[24] Ferrara & DiMercurio v. St. Paul Mercury Ins. Co., 240 F.3d 1, 6 (1st Cir. 2001); *see also* Belk v. Charlotte-Mecklenburg Bd of Educ., 269 F.3d 305, 383 (4th Cir. 2001) (en banc; relevance typically is rather low barrier to admissibility).

- Child pornography found in the defendant's apartment was relevant because it made less probable his claim that he had ordered the child pornography at issue by mistake.[25]

- Evidence that the defendant had a marijuana cigarette in his pocket at the time of his arrest was relevant because it made it slightly more probable that he, rather than someone else, had placed marijuana in an unlocked suitcase that was also in his possession at the time of his arrest.[26]

- Testimony concerning an attempt by the defendant to launder money was relevant because it made it more probable that he was involved in a conspiracy to import and distribute illegal drugs.[27]

- Evidence of favorable treatment of a protected class is relevant to the issue of discriminatory intent in age discrimination case.[28]

- Opinion testimony from an insurance underwriter that the insured's claim was legitimate was relevant because it made it more likely that the insurer's denial of the claim was too hasty and the result of insufficient investigation.[29]

On the other hand, evidence should be excluded as irrelevant if the proponent cannot explain how it affects the degree of probability of a consequential fact.[30]

The liberality with which the courts interpret relevance for admissibility purposes means that any evidence that might affect the finder of fact's judgment concerning the existence of a consequential fact is potentially relevant. Thus, evidence concerning the credibility of a witness is relevant because it might affect the finder of fact's determination of the weight to attach to the witness's testimony regarding matters of significance to the determination of the action.[31] Background evidence may be relevant, although it might not relate to a consequential fact, so long as it is of some assistance to the trier of fact in assessing the probative value

---

[25] United States v. Dornhofer, 859 F.2d 1195, 1199 (4th Cir. 1988).

[26] United States v. Williams, 957 F.2d 1238, 1243–1244 (5th Cir. 1992).

[27] United States v. Smith, 995 F.2d 662, 673 (7th Cir. 1993).

[28] Ansell v. Green Acres Contracting Co., 347 F.3d 515, 525 (3d Cir. 2003) (if favorable treatment occurred after unfavorable incident at issue in lawsuit, its relevance will decrease with increase in length of time period between two incidents, so the connection may become too attenuated to be relevant; such determination must be made on case by case basis).

[29] Fireman's Fund Ins. v. Alaskan Pride Partnership, 106 F.3d 1465, 1467–1468 (9th Cir. 1997).

[30] *See, e.g.,* Achille Bayart & CIE v. Crowe, 238 F.3d 44, 49 (1st Cir. 2001) (single reference in memorandum to potential refinancing, without description of collateral to be offered as security, could not support jury inference that there was equity in corporation's assets beyond amount necessary to satisfy secured creditors, and memorandum was therefore irrelevant to issue whether transfer of all of corporation's assets to secured creditors was fraudulent transfer).

[31] *See* [3], *above.*

of other evidence offered to affect the probability of the existence of a consequential fact.[32]

Moreover, any "flaws" in proffered evidence generally go to its weight, not to its relevance or admissibility.[32.1] If the proffered evidence, alone or in conjunction with other evidence, makes the existence of any fact that is of consequence to the determination of the action more probable or less probable, then it is relevant, and thus admissible despite its flaws.[33] Similarly, if proffered evidence has any tendency to make a consequential fact less probable, it is relevant.[34] Evidence so flawed that it is only tenuously relevant, however, may be excluded as not relevant or too remote.[35]

[b]—Trial Court's Relevancy Determination is Discretionary

Because the relevance of evidence is so dependent upon the specific circumstances of the case appearing at the time the court's admissibility determination was made, that determination is highly discretionary.[36] The appellate court has only a cold record to review and cannot properly assess the demeanor of the witnesses. These disadvantages lead the appellate courts to defer to the trial court's judgment

---

[32] *See, e.g.,* United States v. Pena-Gutierrez, 222 F.3d 1080, 1090 (9th Cir. 2000) (diagram of car in which defendant attempted to smuggle illegal alien into United States, suggesting extreme uncomfortability of alien hidden in compartment for spare tire, was properly admitted as background, even though condition of alien was not relevant to issues at trial); *but see* United States v. Rovetuso, 768 F.2d 809, 815–816 (7th Cir. 1985) (cross-examination concerning witness's distant background, including means of support as teenager and activities as Panamanian security agent, was irrelevant).

[32.1] *See, e.g.,* United States v. Henderson, 337 F.3d 914, 918–919 (7th Cir. 2003) (after defense evidence showing that informant had motive to frame defendant, government could introduce evidence of informant's participation in other operations to bolster his credibility; potential flaws in rehabilitation evidence go to its weight rather than to its admissibility).

[33] *See, e.g.,* Adams v. Ameritech Servs., Inc., 231 F.3d 414, 425 (7th Cir. 2000) (expert statistical analysis of impact of reduction in force termination decisions on differing age groups would have aided jury in determining whether age factored into termination decisions, and expert witness's failure to complete regression analysis that would have made analysis more accurate did not justify trial court's exclusion of testimony).

[34] *See, e.g.,* United States v. Rhodes, 229 F.3d 659, 661 (7th Cir. 2000) ("Evidence relevant to undercut a charge is no less relevant [than evidence] to bolster it; the standard under Rule 401 is symmetric.").

[35] *See, e.g.,* Brown v. Sierra Nevada Mem. Miners Hosp., 849 F.2d 1186, 1191–1192 (9th Cir. 1988) (testimony about general personal perceptions was too tenuously relevant to have probative value on issue of racial discrimination).

[36] *See, e.g.,* Achille Bayart & Cie v. Crowe, 238 F.3d 44, 48 (1st Cir. 2001) (appellate court accords trial court wide latitude in evidentiary rulings; reversal will occur rarely and only in extraordinary circumstances); United States v. Taylor, 106 F.3d 801, 803 (8th Cir. 1997) (trial court's rulings on objections based on lack of relevance are reviewed only for abuse of discretion).

respecting most admissibility decisions, especially those concerned with the relevance of proffered evidence.[37]

The abuse of discretion standard of review does not, of course, mean that the trial court's relevance determinations are immune from appellate review. Trial courts can err in assessing the potential impact of proffered evidence.[38]

When relevancy was an issue at trial, appellate review generally requires that the trial court make a record of the factors it considered in arriving at its determination.[39] In some instances the trial court's failure to make a record of its decision-making process might result in a remand for that purpose[40] or outright reversal.[41]

[6]—Recurring Problems[42]

[a]—Categories of Facts That Recur

Certain categories of facts appear on a recurring basis in the case law to prove the same or similar issues. The Federal Rules of Evidence single out a number of areas for specific evidentiary treatment in Rules 404 through 412.[43] Other instances of recurring problems of relevancy are discussed below, as well as a few categories which are of interest because they indicate the interrelationship between relevancy

---

[37] *See, e.g.,* Diamond v. Howd, 288 F.3d 932, 934 (6th Cir. 2002) (appellate court reviews trial court's decisions concerning admissibility of evidence under abuse of discretion standard); Ferrara & DiMercurio v. St. Paul Mercury Ins. Co., 240 F.3d 1, 6 (1st Cir. 2001) (because of trial court's superior vantage point for determining relevance of proffered evidence, appellate court accords it broad discretion in making those decisions).

[38] *See, e.g.,* Gibson v. Mayor & Council of Wilmington, 355 F.3d 215, 232 (3d Cir. 2004) ("while Rule 401 gives judges great freedom to admit evidence, it diminishes substantially their authority to exclude evidence as irrelevant"). United States v. Pineda-Torres, 287 F.3d 860, 863–864 (9th Cir. 2002) (in prosecution for simple marijuana possession based on crossing border with marijuana hidden in car defendant was driving, expert evidence of structure of drug trafficking organizations was not relevant under Rule 401 because it did not tend to prove defendant's knowledge of presence of marijuana in car).

[39] *See, e.g.,* In re Paoli R.R. Yard PCB Litig., 113 F.3d 444, 453 (3d Cir. 1997) (district court's ruling on evidentiary matters is accorded particular deference, and, provided that court explained its ruling or reasons for its ruling are otherwise apparent from record, ruling may not be reversed unless determination is arbitrary and irrational).

[40] *See, e.g.,* In re Paoli R.R. Yard PCB Litig., 916 F.2d 829, 835, 858, 859 (3d Cir. 1990) (in determining whether to admit expert testimony, trial court is required to develop factual record and articulate reasons for rulings on reliability issues; "[w]e cannot affirm what we cannot review;" case remanded for hearing on record).

[41] *See, e.g.,* Equal Employment Opp. Comm. v. Manville Sales Corp., 27 F.3d 1089, 1093–1095 (5th Cir. 1994) (trial court's judgment in favor of employer in age discrimination case reversed because appellate court could find no defensible reason for trial court's exclusion of supervisor's disparaging remarks about employee's age).

[42] *See* **Treatise** at § 401.08.

[43] *See* Chapter 7, *Special Rules of Relevancy.*

disputes and the development of the substantive law.

[b]—Similar Incidents or Accidents

Evidence of prior or subsequent similar accidents is frequently offered by plaintiffs in personal injury actions as relevant to a variety of issues,[44] such as, to show notice to the defendant,[45] the magnitude of the danger involved, the defendant's ability to correct a known defect, the lack of safety for intended uses, strength of a product, the standard of care, and causation.[46]

Courts frequently state without qualification that the relevancy of such accidents depends on whether the conditions operating to produce the prior failures were substantially similar to the occurrence in question[47] and whether there was a close proximity in time of the accidents to each other. The requisite similarity and proximity will vary depending on what the other accident is intended to prove. If dangerousness is the issue, a high degree of similarity will be essential.[48] On the other hand, if the accident is offered to prove notice, a lack of exact similarity of conditions will not cause exclusion provided the accident was of a kind which should have served to warn the defendant.[49] Of course, a greater degree of similarity and proximity will usually enhance the probative value of the evidence. The

---

[44] For a discussion of the similarity required when evidence of other accidents is used to impeach an expert, *see* Wheeler v. John Deere Co., 862 F.2d 1404, 1415 (10th Cir. 1988), in which the court held that the trial court had erred in allowing an expert to be cross-examined about accidents not previously found to be similar because this in effect shifted the burden to defendant to prove dissimilarity on redirect.

[45] Koloda v. General Motors Parts Div., General Motors Corp., 716 F.2d 373, 375 (6th Cir. 1983); Stoler v. Penn Cent. Transp. Co., 583 F.2d 896, 898 (6th Cir. 1978).

[46] *See, e.g.,* Smith v. Ingersoll-Rand Co., 214 F.3d 1235, 1248–1249 (10th Cir. 2000) (evidence of other accidents involving defendant's milling machinery was relevant to plaintiff's theory of causation and admissible as proof of design defect and to show notice).

[47] Black v. M&W Gear Co., 269 F.3d 1220, 1227 (10th Cir. 2001) ("Before evidence of other accidents is admissible for any purpose, however, the party seeking its admission must show the circumstances surrounding the other accidents were substantially similar to the accident that is the subject of the litigation before the court").

[48] *See, e.g.,* Jodoin v. Toyota Motor Corp., 284 F.3d 272, 278–279 (1st Cir. 2002) (when expert witness attempts to demonstrate manufacturing defect by use of accident reconstruction with another vehicle, proffering party must show "substantial similarity in circumstances" between reconstruction and original accident); Lovett v. Union Pacific R.R. Co., 201 F.3d 1074, 1080–1081 (8th Cir. 2000) (since similar-incident evidence risks raising extraneous controversial issues and may be more prejudicial than probative, facts and circumstances of other incidents must be "substantially similar" to present case, which they were not here).

[49] *See, e.g.,* Jackson v. Firestone Tire & Rubber Co., 788 F.2d 1070, 1082–1083 (5th Cir. 1986) (in action against manufacturer of wheel rims, evidence of other accidents involving the same rims was admissible; "[f]or purposes of proving other accidents in order to show defendants' awareness of a dangerous condition, the rule requiring substantial similarity of those accidents to the accident at issue should be relaxed"; citing **Treatise**).

court may also take into account the danger that the jury will be confused by the prior accidents.[50]

In criminal cases, prior bad acts that are similar in kind (e.g., all drug-related) and not remote in time from the crime charged are relevant under Rule 401.[51] Admission of the evidence, however, will depend on whether it satisfies the requirements of Rules 403 and 404.[52]

[c]—Possession of Weapons or Other Paraphernalia Used in Committing Crimes

Evidence, such as that offered by ballistics experts, which links the defendant to the weapon actually used in committing a crime, is obviously relevant;[53] so is evidence that the defendant possessed weapons or other paraphernalia that may have been used in committing a crime.[54] In some cases, the courts have held that evidence of the possession of weapons or paraphernalia not used in the crime charged may also be relevant because it shows the opportunity to commit the crime or an awareness that the crime involves highly dangerous activity and may require the use of weapons.[55] Such evidence should be excluded if the crime charged is not of such a nature as to suggest a clear possibility of the need for dangerous

---

[50] See, e.g., Rye v. Black & Decker Mfg. Co., 889 F.2d 100, 103 (6th Cir. 1989) (it was not clear from complaints in earlier cases what actual cause of plaintiffs' injuries was).

[51] See, e.g., United States v. Fortson, 194 F.3d 730, 735 (6th Cir. 1999) (in drug prosecution, co-defendant's prior unrelated arrest in possession of cloned cell phones was relevant and independently admissible under Fed. R. Evid. 401 to show his prior "possession of materials commonly used in drug trafficking to avoid police detection of telephone calls"); United States v. Tomberlin, 130 F.3d 1318, 1321 (8th Cir. 1997) (prior convictions were admissible to prove knowledge and intent when defendant asserted defense of mere presence in drug prosecution).

[52] See discussion in Ch. 7.

[53] See, e.g., United States v. Peltier, 585 F.2d 314, 325 (8th Cir. 1978) (government introduced firearms used by defendants in shoot-out).

[54] See, e.g., United States v. Rhodes, 229 F.3d 659, 660 (7th Cir. 2000) (defendant's gun ownership was relevant to support inference defendant was drug dealer, because drug dealers use guns; fact that gun was pellet gun did not defeat relevance, since guns can be used to intimidate as well as to kill); United States v. Yazzie, 59 F.3d 807, 810–811 (9th Cir. 1995) (lewd magazines and a penis enlargement pump were relevant in sex abuse case as demonstrative evidence of how the abuse occurred and to corroborate the victim's description of abuse).

[55] See, e.g., Stevenson v. D.C. Metro. Police Dep't, 248 F.3d 1187, 1190–1191 (D.C. Cir. 2001) (in Section 1983 action alleging use of excessive force in effecting arrest, weapon in possession of plaintiff's companion at time of their arrest was relevant to show that plaintiff was intent on avoiding arrest at all costs and in doing so placed arresting officers at risk); United States v. Mosby, 101 F.3d 1278, 1282–1283 (8th Cir. 1996) (evidence that defendant charged with being felon in possession of ammunition had crossbow at time of his arrest was admissible to establish immediate context of crime charged, including his subsequent flight from a detective and his alleged assault on the detective with the crossbow).

weapons because the evidence then has low probative value coupled with a high potential for prejudice.[56]

[d]—Consciousness of Guilt

Under the rubric of consciousness of guilt, evidence of a party's behavior is often offered which, through a series of inferences, is deemed relevant to show that the party committed the charged crime or act. Courts admit on a consciousness-of-guilt theory evidence of such behavior as flight,[57] attempted suicide,[58] furtive conduct,[59] false exculpatory statements,[60] threats directed at witnesses,[61] spoliation of evidence or failure to produce witnesses who could exculpate the defendant,[62] the refusal of a person suspected of driving while intoxicated to submit to a blood-alcohol test,[63] or the use of false passports and identities.[64]

The probative value of this type of evidence may become seriously attenuated in a case where it is not clear that the defendant's behavior was prompted by a consciousness of guilt, or where another reason exists, other than the charged crime, which would adequately explain the defendant's behavior.[66] The same objection

---

[56] United States v. Ferreira, 821 F.2d 1, 6 (1st Cir. 1987) (guns seized from defendant at the time of his arrest were not relevant in a prosecution for unarmed bank robbery; reviews cases). *See also* discussion of Rule 403 in § 6.02.

[57] *See, e.g.,* United States v. Otero-Mendez, 273 F.3d 46, 53 (1st Cir. 2001) (evidence of defendant's flight from Puerto Rico to Connecticut in disguise and under false identity shortly after attempted car jacking was relevant to his consciousness of guilt).

[58] *Cf.* Tug Raven v. Trexler, 419 F.2d 536, 543 (4th Cir. 1969) (after tug disaster, suicide of supervisor eight days after he testified in Coast Guard proceeding was "circumstantial proof of a guilty conscience").

[59] *See, e.g.,* United States v. Lupino, 301 F.3d 642, 645–646 (8th Cir. 2002) (evidence that defendant was in hiding at time of arrest tended to show consciousness of guilt).

[60] *See, e.g.,* United States v. Green, 680 F.2d 520, 523–524 (7th Cir. 1982) (defendant's inconsistent exculpatory statements); United States v. Ingram, 600 F.2d 260, 262 (10th Cir. 1979) (statement by defendant that he had left Fort Carlson four hours after robbery took place was clearly intended to be exculpatory and thereby rendered admissible government's evidence that he had in fact left Fort Carlson six days before robbery).

[61] *See, e.g.,* United States v. Ramirez-Lopez, 315 F.3d 1143, 1154 (9th Cir. 2003).

[62] *See, e.g.,* United States v. Copeland, 321 F.3d 582, 597–598 (6th Cir. 2003) (spoliation evidence is generally admissible to show consciousness of guilt).

[63] South Dakota v. Neville, 459 U.S. 553, 561, 103 S. Ct. 916, 74 L. Ed. 2d 748 (1983) ("similar to other circumstantial evidence of consciousness of guilt").

[64] *See, e.g.,* United States v. Otero-Mendez, 273 F.3d 46, 53 (1st Cir. 2001) (evidence of defendant's use of false identity while fleeing from Puerto Rico to Connecticut shortly after attempted car jacking was relevant to his consciousness of guilt).

[66] *See, e.g.,* United States v. Copeland, 321 F.3d 582, 598 (6th Cir. 2003) (evidence that defendants discussed inducing somebody to "get" prosecutor assigned to their case had only marginal relevance, in that discussions may have been occasioned by circumstances other than consciousness of guilt).

could be raised to the admission of many other items of circumstantial evidence which nevertheless satisfy the minimal relevancy test of Rule 401.

[e]—Evidence of Indebtedness or a Sudden Acquisition of Large Amounts of Cash

In prosecutions for crimes whose purpose is pecuniary gain, evidence of sudden acquisition of large amounts of cash has frequently been held highly relevant.[67] Similarly, evidence of substantial indebtedness may be relevant to prove the motive for committing such crimes.[68] At times, of course, evidence that a defendant was owed money may be relevant as exculpatory evidence.[69]

[f]—Future Earnings, Inflation and Future Taxes

It is well settled that estimates of future earnings are relevant to the issue of damages in wrongful death and personal injury actions.[70] More controversial is the issue of whether evidence of future inflation[71] may be admitted as part of the proof of future earnings and future tax liability.[72]

[g]—Governmental, Professional and Industry Codes and Standards; Custom and Practice

Governmental, professional and industry codes, regulations and standards are often admitted in federal criminal cases as relevant to proving knowledge, intent

---

[67] *See, e.g.,* United States v. Taylor, 239 F.3d 994, 997 (9th Cir. 2001) (evidence of extraordinary expenditures paid through money orders and cash from unexplained sources supported inference that funds for expenditures came from illegal activity).

[68] *See, e.g.,* Ferrara & DiMercurio v. St. Paul Mercury Ins. Co., 240 F.3d 1, 6 (1st Cir. 2001) (evidence of substantial debt is relevant to motive to burn insured boat).

[69] United States v. Carriger, 592 F.2d 312, 315 (6th Cir. 1979) (in net worth income tax evasion prosecution, it was error to have excluded evidence of notes evidencing indebtedness by defendant's brother since they tended to make more probable defendant's claim that some of his expenditures came from a nontaxable source—the repayment of a pre-existing debt).

[70] *See, e.g.,* Chesapeake & Ohio R.R. Co. v. Kelly, 241 U.S. 485, 488 36 S. Ct. 630, 60 L. Ed. 1117 (1916).

[71] *See, e.g.,* Norfolk and Western Railway Co. v. Liepelt, 444 U.S. 490, 494, 100 S. Ct. 755, 62 L. Ed. 2d 689 (1980); Culver v. Slater Boat Co., 688 F.2d 280, 299 (5th Cir. 1982) (reviews arguments for and against consideration of inflation); Doca v. Marina Mercante Nicaraguense, S.A., 634 F.2d 30, 34–35 (2d Cir. 1980).

[72] Norfolk and Western Railway Co. v. Liepelt, 444 U.S. 490, 494, 100 S. Ct. 755, 62 L. Ed. 2d 689 (1980) (where impact of future taxes would be minimal, evidence might be excludable on Rule 403 grounds).

or lawful duty,[73] and in federal tort actions as relevant evidence of the appropriate standard of care.[74]

Evidence of post-event customs and practices may shed light on customs and practices that were in effect before the event giving rise to the lawsuit.[75]

[h]—Comparable Sales to Show Value of Real Property

The issue of the value of real property arises most often in federal court in condemnation cases, although it may also arise in other contexts, such as misuse of property.[76] The courts have held that the market value of real property may be proven with evidence of sales (or comparable transactions) of similarly situated property. To be relevant, such evidence must be of reasonably recent sales of property substantially comparable to the property in issue.

[i]—Profile Evidence

One issue that arises in a number of contexts is the relevance of testimony by an expert witness that a person involved in a lawsuit fits a scientifically defined "profile," and thus is a member of a class with certain characteristics. For example, evidence that a child suffered from "battered child syndrome" has been held relevant to prove that the parent lied when stating that the child's injuries were the result of an accident.[77] Similarly, evidence concerning the phenomenon of "battered woman syndrome" has been held relevant in cases in which a woman is claiming self-defense with respect to the killing of her abusive male companion.[78] Courts have also accepted as relevant evidence concerning profiles of pimps and

---

[73] *See, e.g.,* United States v. Kelly, 888 F.2d 732, 744 (11th Cir. 1989) (it was reversible error for the trial judge to have excluded defendant-attorney's testimony regarding his understanding of his professional obligations and how that understanding affected his conduct; it was relevant in evaluating defendant's criminal intent).

[74] *See, e.g.,* Brown v. Cedar Rapids Iowa City R. Co., 650 F.2d 159, 163 (8th Cir. 1981) (Safety Codes promulgated by governmental authority); In re Air Crash Disaster, 635 F.2d 67, 77 (2d Cir. 1980) (noncompliance with Federal Air Regulations).

[75] Bordanaro v. McLeod, 871 F.2d 1151, 1166–1167 (1st Cir. 1989) (plaintiffs beaten by police brought civil rights action; court properly admitted post-event evidence of lack of proper internal investigation of attack and failure to discipline officers involved as shedding light on custom and practice before attack).

[76] *See, e.g.,* United States v. 179.26 Acres of Land in Douglas County, Kansas, 644 F.2d 367, 371 (10th Cir. 1981); United States v. 429.59 Acres of Land, 612 F.2d 459, 462 (9th Cir. 1980) (condemnation proceeding).

[77] *See, e.g.,* Estelle v. McGuire, 502 U.S. 62, 69–70, 112 S. Ct. 475, 116 L. Ed. 2d 385 (1991); United States v. Bowers, 660 F.2d 527, 529 (5th Cir. 1981).

[78] *See, e.g.,* Ibn-Tamas v. United States, 407 A.2d 626, 634 (D.C. App. 1979) (applying District of Columbia equivalent to Rule 401; battered woman syndrome testimony improperly excluded, as it would have been relevant to defendant's claim she acted in self-defense in killing her companion).

prostitutes,[79] and alcoholics.[80]

Parties offering profile evidence concerning post-traumatic stress syndrome and compulsive gambling disorder as explanations for criminal behavior have been less successful.[81] Profile evidence respecting the way drug couriers appear and act is inherently prejudicial and is not admissible as evidence of guilt,[82] but may be relevant to rebut a claim of innocence[83] or for background information.[84]

§ 6.02 Exclusion on Grounds of Prejudice, Confusion, or Waste of Time—Rule 403

[1]—Trial Court Has Discretion to Exclude Relevant Evidence

Rule 403 is the major rule that explicitly recognizes the large discretionary role of the judge in controlling the introduction of evidence.[1] It allows the trial court to exclude relevant evidence if its probative value is substantially outweighed by the danger of unfair prejudice, confusion of the issues, or misleading the jury, or by considerations of undue delay, waste of time, or needless presentation of

---

[79] *See, e.g.,* United States v. Taylor, 239 F.3d 994, 997 (9th Cir. 2001) (after defendant attacked credibility of witness, a prostitute, with her prior inconsistent testimony, trial court properly admitted expert testimony concerning relationship between pimp and prostitute to explain those inconsistencies; expert testimony was relevant to witness's credibility).

[80] *See, e.g.,* United States v. Kills Ree, 691 F.2d 412, 414 (8th Cir. 1982) (doctor's testimony that defendant had experienced symptoms of alcohol withdrawal 4 days after automobile accident and that such symptoms occur when heavy drinkers suddenly stop drinking was relevant to corroborate witness's testimony that defendant had been drinking on night of accident).

[81] *See, e.g.,* United States v. Torniero, 735 F.2d 725, 730–731 (2d Cir. 1984) (in prosecution for interstate transportation of stolen jewelry, evidence of defendant's compulsive gambling disorder offered in support of insanity defense was properly excluded as irrelevant); United States v. Krutschewski, 509 F. Supp. 1186, 1190 (D. Mass. 1981) (evidence of post-traumatic stress syndrome excluded because defendant failed to show it was relevant to insanity defense); *but see* United States v. Burgess, 691 F.2d 1146, 1151–1153 (4th Cir. 1982) (evidence of defendant's post traumatic stress syndrome properly admitted respecting defendant's defense of insanity).

[82] *See, e.g.,* United States v. Williams, 957 F.2d 1238, 1241–1242 (5th Cir. 1992) (trial court erred in admitting testimony of DEA officer that defendant's actions and appearance fit profile of drug courier as evidence of guilt).

[83] *See, e.g.,* United States v. Murillo, 255 F.3d 1169, 1177–1178 (9th Cir. 2001) (drug courier profile evidence limited to testimony that drug trafficking organizations do not entrust large quantities of illegal drugs to unknowing couriers was properly admitted to counter defendant's assertion he was unaware of presence of drugs); United States v. Lim, 984 F.2d 331, 335 (9th Cir. 1993); *but see* United States v. Vallejo, 237 F.3d 1008, 1016 (9th Cir. 2001) (expert testimony about modus operandi of drug trafficking organizations was not relevant to explain fact that officers did not try to lift fingerprints from area in car where drugs were found, since defense did not assert lack of fingerprint evidence to show that he did not know of presence of drugs).

[84] *See, e.g.,* United States v. Hernandez-Cuartas, 717 F.2d 552, 554–555 (11th Cir. 1983).

[1] *See* **Treatise** at §§ 403.02, 403.03.

cumulative evidence.[2]

When presented with a Rule 403 objection, the trial court must perform the balancing that Rule 403 requires.[3] The balancing process itself, however, is subject to review for abuse of discretion.[4] The trial court's discretion, however, should be exercised with recognition that the remedy of exclusion is extraordinary and to be invoked sparingly. The trial court should strik the balance in favor of admission in most cases.[4.1]

The Rule applies to all forms of evidence: direct and circumstantial, testimonial, hearsay, documentary, real proof, and demonstration. The one instance in which Rule 403 does not accord discretion to a court is in ruling on the admissibility of convictions pursuant to Rule 609(a)(2).[5] The balancing approach of Rule 403 should be utilized in deciding on the admissibility of other types of evidence offered for impeachment. The Rule provides as follows:

Rule 403.   Exclusion of Relevant Evidence on Grounds of Prejudice, Confusion, or Waste of Time.

Although relevant, evidence may be excluded if its probative value is substantially outweighed by the danger of unfair prejudice, confusion of the issues, or misleading the jury, or by considerations of undue delay, waste of time, or needless presentation of cumulative evidence.

[*Adopted Jan. 2, 1975, effective July 1, 1975.*]

Rule 403 recognizes that passing the minimum relevancy test of Rule 401 does not guarantee admissibility—the question remains whether the value of the evidence in contributing to a rational solution is outweighed by attendant costs. The court must consider whether the search for truth will be helped or hindered by the interjection of distracting, confusing or emotionally charged evidence.

In making this determination, the court must assess the probative value of the proffered item as well as the harmful consequences specified in Rule 403 that might flow from its admission.[6] The countervailing factors to admissibility specified in

---

[2]   Fed. R. Evid 403; *see, e.g.,* United States v. Howell, 285 F.3d 1263, 1266 (10th Cir. 2002).

[3]   *See, e.g.,* Blind-Doan v. Sanders, 291 F.3d 1079, 1083 (9th Cir. 2002) (trial court erred in not performing Rule 403 balancing before excluding evidence of defendant's other misconduct).

[4]   *See, e.g.,* United States v. Cassell, 292 F.3d 788, 795–796 (D.C. Cir. 2002) (trial court is in best position to perform Rule 403's balancing, and its decision to admit or exclude evidence is reviewable only for "grave abuse" of its discretion).

[4.1]   *See, e.g.,* United States v, Dodds, 347 F.3d 893, 897 (11th Cir. 2003).

[5]   *See* Chapter 12, *Credibility.*

[6]   *See* United States v. Foster, 376 F.3d 577, 592 (6th Cir. 2004) ("this court takes a maximal view of the probative effect of the evidence and a minimal view of its unfairly prejudicial effect, and

the Rule—prejudice, confusion of issues, danger of misleading the jury, and considerations of delay, waste of time or needless presentation of cumulative evidence—predate enactment of the Rule.

Surprise is not specified as a separate ground for exclusion, and a continuance will often be more appropriate than exclusion. Opposing counsel in civil cases should only rarely be surprised by an offer of evidence, in view of the extensive opportunities available for learning of the existence of an opponent's evidence through pretrial discovery and the automatic disclosure requirements of Federal Rule of Civil Procedure 26.[7] When opposing counsel is taken by surprise, however, Rule 403 requires the court to assess whether a continuance can adequately protect against unfair prejudice or confusion. If the proffered evidence has limited probative value, the delay ensuing from a continuance may justify exclusion. In this sense, surprise may still prove a factor in determining admissibility. When the opponent's surprise is the result of the proffering party's failure to comply with a pretrial disclosure order, with the disclosure requirements of Civil Procedure Rule 26, or with legitimate discovery requests, exclusion of relevant evidence is proper on grounds independent of Rule 403.[8]

Unlike some of the subsequent rules in Article IV, Rule 403 sets no absolute standard, but rather is designed as a guide for handling situations for which no specific rules have been formulated. Consequently, as the cases decided since the enactment of the Federal Rules consistently acknowledge, the trial court has considerable discretion in making its determination under Rule 403.[9] The appellate court will not reverse simply because it would have weighed highly subjective factors differently.[10] Reversals are likely to occur only when the trial court did not

---

will hold that the district court erred only if the latter outweighs the former"; quoting United States v. Sassanelli, 118 F.3d 495, 498 (6th Cir. 1997)).

[7] *See* Fed. R. Civ. P. 26–37; 6 Moore's Federal Practice, Chs 26–29 (Matthew Bender 3d ed.); 7 Moore's Federal Practice, Chs 30–37 (Matthew Bender 3d ed.).

[8] *See* 6 Moore's Federal Practice, Ch. 26, *General Provisions Concerning Discovery; Duty of Disclosure* (Matthew Bender 3d ed.); 7 Moore's Federal Practice, Ch 37, *Failure to Make Disclosure or Cooperate in Discovery; Sanctions* (Matthew Bender 3d ed.).

[9] *See, e.g.,* United States v. Smith, 292 F.3d 90, 97–98 (1st Cir. 2002) ("Only rarely—and in extraordinarily compelling circumstances—will we, from the vista of a cold appellate record, reverse a district court's on-the-spot judgment concerning the relative weighing of probative value and unfair effect").

[10] *See, e.g.,* United States v. Adams, 375 F.3d 108, 113 (1st Cir. 2004) (appellate court has advantages of ample time to reflect and of ability to review all trial testimony; on that basis appellate court may reach conclusion contrary to that of trial judge concerning extent of prejudicial effect of proffered evidence; when trial judge's call is merely debatable, and was not egregiously erroneous, appellate court should allow trial court's decision to stand); United States v. Vega, 285 F.3d 256, 263 (3d Cir. 2002) ("if judicial self-restraint is ever desirable, it is when a Rule 403 analysis of a trial court is reviewed by an appellate tribunal.").

engage in the balancing process the Rule mandates or when it is impossible to determine from the record whether it did so.[11] Some circuits will even undertake the balancing process themselves when it appears that the trial court has failed to do so.[11.1]

The court has sufficient flexibility pursuant to Rule 403 to admit part of a line of proof while excluding the more prejudicial details.[11.2] A conditional ruling that admits some proof provided other evidence is excluded is another valid approach. If there is doubt about the existence of unfair prejudice, confusion of issues, misleading, undue delay, or waste of time, it is generally better practice to admit the evidence and take necessary precautions by way of contemporaneous instructions to the jury followed by additional admonitions in the charge.[12]

Motions in limine to exclude evidence on the basis of Rule 403 are being increasingly utilized by the courts.[13] Only if the court's ruling on an in limine motion is definitive and on the record is the objection preserved for appeal without being renewed at trial.[14] It is not necessary, however, that the trial court hold a hearing on the record when performing the balancing that Rule 403 requires, or even that it recite the balancing analysis. It is sufficient if the appellate court is able to discern from the record that the balancing took place.[15]

---

[11] *See, e.g.,* United States v. Verduzco, 373 F.3d 1022, 1029 n.2 (9th Cir. 2004) (when it appears from record as a whole that trial court adequately weighed probative value and prejudicial effect of proffered evidence before admitting it, trial court has performed task required by Rule 403); United States v. Buffalo, 358 F.3d 519, 527 (8th Cir. 2004) (trial court's rejection of defendant's proffered impeachment of his own witness without balancing probative value against prejudicial effect, as Rule 403 requires, was reversible error).

[11.1] *See, e.g.,* Ansell v. Green Acres Contracting Co., 347 F.3d 515, 525 (3d Cir. 2003).

[11.2] Gomez v. Rodriguez, 344 F.3d 103, 115 (1st Cir. 2003) (trial court may not exclude under Rule 403 entirety of witness's testimony merely because some of it may be excludable; Rule requires statement-by-statement balancing of probative value against factors permitting exclusion of relevant evidence).

[12] *See, e.g.,* United States v. Smith, 292 F.3d 90, 97–98 (1st Cir. 2002) (trial court properly minimized prejudice of Rule 404(b) evidence by giving jury limiting instruction when evidence was admitted and again in general charge).

[13] *See, e.g.,* United States v. LaFlam, 369 F.3d 153, 156–157 (2d Cir. 2004) (trial court properly denied defendant's in limine motion to exclude, on ground of prejudice, evidence of his drug use); United States v. Bennett, 368 F.3d 1343, 1349–1350 (11th Cir. 2004) (trial court properly denied defendant's in limine motion to exclude, on ground of undue prejudice, evidence of his prior possession of hand gun).

[14] Fed. R. Evid. 103(a); *see, e.g.,* United States v. Gajo, 290 F.3d 922, 927 (7th Cir. 2002) (because trial court's in limine ruling that evidence was admissible after Rule 403 balancing was definitive in sense that it depended only on government's foundational evidence at trial being same as presented at hearing, defendant preserved question of admissibility for appeal); *see also* § 2.03[2][c].

[15] *See, e.g.,* Blind-Doan v. Sanders, 291 F.3d 1079, 1083 (9th Cir. 2002).

[2]—Probative Value Is Substantially Outweighed by Detrimental Effects

Rule 403 requires the trial judge to balance the probative value of proffered evidence against the detrimental effects of admitting the evidence.[16] Such a balancing exercise requires the trial court to make a preliminary assessment of the probative value of the proffered evidence. Judges may differ in their assessment of probative value because, like jurors, they may disagree with respect to the evidentiary hypothesis and, consequently, the significance of the evidence to the case.[17]

A trial court may not, however, exclude evidence under Rule 403 on the ground that, in the court's view, the evidence is not persuasive.[17.1] Moreover, the trial court should conduct the balancing by according the proffered evidence the maximum reasonable probative value and assessing the minimum reasonable detrimental results from its admission.[18] This bias in favor of admitting relevant evidence results from the general thrust of the Federal Rules in favor of admissibility.[19]

When the probative value of the proffered evidence is minimal, however, and it clearly has a substantial prejudicial effect, the trial court should not admit it.[19.1] On the other hand, when the evidence is clearly relevant to a crucial issue in the case, the prejudicial effect of putting it before the jury would have to be substantial, indeed, to warrant its exclusion under Rule 403.[19.2]

---

[16] Fed. R. Evid. 403; *see, e.g.,* Blind-Doan v. Sanders, 291 F.3d 1079, 1083 (9th Cir. 2002) (trial court erred in not performing Rule 403 balancing before excluding evidence of defendant's other misconduct).

[17] *See, e.g.,* Chrysler Int'l Corp. v. Chemaly, 280 F.3d 1358, 1364 (11th Cir. 2002) (even though other courts might have decided issue differently, trial court did not abuse its discretion in excluding evidence as unduly prejudicial).

[17.1] *See, e.g.,* Blake v. Pellegrino, 329 F.3d 43, 47–48 (1st Cir. 2003) (trial court erred in excluding death certificate in jury trial believing it to be incorrect; it is jury's role to determine the persuasiveness of relevant evidence).

[18] *See, e.g.,* Deters v. Equifax Credit Information Services, 202 F.3d 1262, 1273–1274 (10th Cir. 2000) (in weighing admissibility under Rule 403, trial court should "give the evidence its maximum reasonable probative force and its minimum reasonable prejudicial value").

[19] *See, e.g.,* United States v. Grant, 256 F.3d 1146, 1155 (11th Cir. 2001) (Rule 403 carries strong presumption in favor of admissibility; its major function "is limited to excluding matter of scant or cumulative probative force, dragged in by the heels for the sake of its prejudicial effect").

[19.1] *See, e.g.,* United States v. Mayes, 370 F.3d 703, 708–709 (7th Cir. 2004) (evidence that witness received anonymous threat was clearly prejudicial to defendant and had little probative value, in that witness's demeanor on witness stand could easily have been explained without evidence; trial court erred in admitting evidence of threat).

[19.2] *See, e.g.,* United States v. Wilson, 355 F.3d 358, 360–361 (5th Cir. 2003) (evidence of defendant's physical abuse of his female coconspirators was not excludable under Rule 403, even though its admission clearly entailed risk of defendant's conviction for acts other than charged

Particular difficulties arise when the proffered evidence connects a party with a highly charged public issue.[20] Despite undoubted resulting prejudice, however, the probative value of the proffered evidence may compel its admission.[21] In other instances, the probative value may be so low as to warrant exclusion when prejudicial factors are present.[22]

Special rules govern the application of Rule 403 when evidence of prior sexual assaults or child molestations is made admissible by Rule 413, Rule 414, or Rule 415. In such cases, the trial court is required to apply Rule 403 balancing before admitting evidence of the prior sexual misconduct.[23] However, since these rules are intended to supersede the restrictive aspects of Rule 404 in sex abuse cases,[24] the presumption is in favor of admission. The Rule 403 analysis should not be applied so as to inhibit the intended effect of Rules 413-415.[25] *See* §§ 7.09 and 7.10 for a discussion of the relationship between Rule 403 and Rules 412–415.

---

crime, because of its relevance to crucial issue in case of females acting pursuant to defendant's instructions because of their fear of him).

[20] *See, e.g.,* Anderson v. Malloy, 700 F.2d 1208, 1211 (8th Cir. 1983) (in action concerning rape at motel, even though "general thrust of the Federal Rules of Evidence may be read to favor admission," trial court did not abuse its discretion in excluding testimony of woman who had been raped at defendant's motel five months prior to instant rape as too prejudicial and not sufficiently probative of motel owner's awareness of risk).

[21] *See, e.g.,* United States v. Arthur Andersen, LLP, 374 F.3d 281, 290–291 (5th Cir. 2004) (information concerning government's complaints against defendant arising from recent restatements of earnings of two of defendant's largest clients was highly probative in case stemming from defendant's action in shredding documents prior to receipt of SEC subpoena and, even though information was prejudicial, it was properly admitted in view of defendant's defense that it did not expect its audit papers to be at issue in SEC investigation of Enron's collapse).

[22] *See, e.g.,* United States v. Cabrera, 222 F.3d 590, 595–596 (9th Cir. 2000) (in drug prosecution, investigating officer's repeated racially inflammatory references to defendants' Cuban origin and his generalizations about Las Vegas' Cuban community and Cuban drug dealers were unfairly prejudicial, and their admission was plain error).

[23] *See, e.g.,* Johnson v. Elk Lake Sch. Dist., 283 F.3d 138, 144 (3d Cir. 2002) (even though Rules 413–415 establish preference for admission of prior acts of sexual misconduct in cases charging another act of sexual misconduct, this preference does not apply unless proof of prior act is specific and unequivocal and prior acts are similar in kind to charged act; trial court retains significant authority to exclude evidence of prior sexual acts under Rule 403).

[24] *See* § 7.01.

[25] *See, e.g.,* United States v. Drewry, 365 F.3d 957, 959 (1st Cir. 2004) (although trial courts must perform Rule 403 balancing of evidence of prior child molestation when it is offered in case charging defendant with child molestation, Rule 414 requires that such evidence be admitted liberally).

[3]—Exclusion of Relevant Evidence on Grounds of Undue Prejudice[26]

[a]—Prejudice Warranting Exclusion

In the absence of redeeming probative value, exclusion of evidence because of its capacity for prejudice has long been the practice. Of course, the evidence must be *unfairly* prejudicial, not merely prejudicial, to be excludable under Rule 403. Evidence that is relevant will, of necessity, be prejudicial; else it would not be relevant.[27] The prejudice contemplated by Rule 403 involves some adverse effect beyond tending to prove the fact or issue that justifies admission of the evidence.[28] Additionally, if the prejudice flows from the likelihood that the jury will misuse the evidence, the trial court may effectively minimize the prejudicial effect of admitting the evidence by giving the jury a limiting instruction.[28.1]

The Committee Notes explain that "unfair prejudice" means an "undue tendency to suggest decision on an improper basis, commonly, though not necessarily, an emotional one."[29] Evidence that appeals to the jury's sympathies,[30] arouses its sense of horror,[31] provokes its instinct to punish,[32] appeals to class, racial, religious,

---

[26] *See* **Treatise** at § 403.04.

[27] *See, e.g.,* United States v. Suggs, 374 F.3d 508, 516 (7th Cir. 2004).

[28] *See, e.g.,* United States v. Fleming, 215 F.3d 930, 937 (9th Cir. 2000) (trial court did not err, in prosecution for attempting to influence federal judge in allowing judge and his wife to testify concerning their reactions; judge's "prestige, dignity, and authority" and his wife's "vulnerability" did not make evidence unduly prejudicial); United States v. Garza, 118 F.3d 278, 285 (5th Cir. 1997) ("Danger of prejudice is always present; consequently, exclusion of extrinsic evidence based on its prejudicial effect should occur only sparingly").

[28.1] *See, e.g.,* United States v. Foster, 376 F.3d 577, 592 (6th Cir. 2004) ("A crucial assumption underlying the system [of trial by jury] is that juries will follow the instructions given them by the trial judge," *quoting Parker v. Randolph*, 442 U.S. 62, 73, 99 S. Ct. 2132, 60 L. Ed. 2d 713 (1979)).

[29] *See* **Treatise** at § 403App.01[2]. *See, e.g.,* United States v. Perrotta, 289 F.3d 155, 166 (1st Cir. 2002) (because nothing indicated that admission of guns, fake bomb, brass knuckles, and billy club invited jury to decide case on emotional grounds, trial court did not err in admitting them after Rule 403 balancing, even though they had only minimal probative value as corroboration for oral testimony about their presence at time of defendant's arrest).

[30] *See, e.g.,* United States v. George, 266 F.3d 52, 63 (2d Cir. 2001) (in prosecution for making false representations in passport application, trial court did not abuse its discretion in excluding videotape of defendant's wedding that was offered only to show defendant's slow and unresponsive behavior as demonstrative of cognitive problems on ground it might engender inappropriate sympathy from jury for defendant who was prevented from traveling to Japan to be with his wife by lack of passport).

[31] *See, e.g.,* United States v. Ward, 207 F.3d 1222, 1237 (10th Cir. 2000) (in prosecution of physician for euthanizing patient with potassium chloride, trial court erred in not excluding, as unduly prejudicial, testimony of government experts that potassium chloride is used to execute criminals and euthanize animals, because such testimony left impression that potassium chloride has no valid medicinal purposes).

or ethnic prejudices,[33] or triggers other mainsprings of human action[34] may cause a jury to base its decision on something other than the established propositions in the case.[35]

For example, evidence may be excluded as unduly prejudicial under Rule 403 when its sole probative value is to show a criminal defendant's propensity to commit the crime charged in the indictment.[35.1]

In addition, an appellate court may conclude that "unfair prejudice" occurred because an insufficient effort was made below to avoid the dangers of prejudice,[36] or because the theory on which the evidence was offered was designed to elicit a response from the jurors not justified by the evidence.[37]

---

[32] *See, e.g.,* United States v. Blue Bird, 372 F.3d 989, 995 (8th Cir. 2004) (trial court erred in admitting evidence that alleged victim in sexual abuse case was virgin at time of incident because prosecution failed to suggest any legally relevant inference that trier of fact could draw from the evidence).

[33] *See, e.g.,* United States v. Jackson-Randolph, 282 F.3d 369, 376–378 (6th Cir. 2002) (to avoid exclusion under Rule 403 because of improper appeal to class prejudice, evidence of defendant's lavish life style must be accompanied by other evidence bolstering its probative value).

[34] *See, e.g.,* Doe by and Through Rudy-Glanzer v. Glanzer, 232 F.3d 1258, 1266 (9th Cir. 2000) (trial court properly excluded evidence that defendant invoked Fifth Amendment privilege in response to deposition question whether he took penile plethysmograph test, because evidence would have been unduly prejudicial, in that (1) jury could properly infer from defendant's silence only that he had taken test, not that test results were unfavorable, and (2) test results would not have been admissible regardless what they indicated, because such tests are scientifically unreliable).

[35] *See* Old Chief v. United States, 519 U.S. 172, 117 S. Ct. 644, 136 L. Ed. 2d 574, 588 (1997) ("Such improper grounds include . . . generalizing a defendant's earlier bad act into bad character and taking that as raising the odds that he did the later bad act now charged (or, worse, as calling for preventive conviction even if he should happen to be innocent momentarily)"); citing **Treatise**; Mason v. Southern Ill. Univ. at Carbondale, 233 F.3d 1036, 1044 (7th Cir. 2000) (in racial harassment case alleging hostile work environment based on behavior of plaintiff's supervisor, trial court did not abuse its discretion in excluding as unduly prejudicial testimony concerning behavior of other co-workers not tied to supervisor).

[35.1] *See, e.g.,* United States v. Thomas, 321 F.3d 627, 630–633 (7th Cir. 2003) (in prosecution for unlawful firearm possession, trial court abused its discretion under Rule 403 when it admitted photograph of defendant's tattoo of two crossed pistols, because it had no probative value other than to show defendant's propensity to possess guns).

[36] *See, e.g.,* United States v. Carrasco, 257 F.3d 1045, 1049 (9th Cir. 2001) (trial court properly mitigated prejudicial effect of admitting evidence of drug paraphernalia and weapons seized from car recently driven by defendant by instructing jury it could consider evidence only in its determination whether defendant knowingly possessed paraphernalia and weapons as charged in indictment).

[37] *See, e.g.,* United States v. Pineda-Torres, 287 F.3d 860, 863–864 (9th Cir. 2002) (expert evidence of structure of drug smuggling operation should have been excluded as unduly prejudicial when government offered no evidence that defendant was part of drug smuggling operation, because evidence unfairly suggested defendant was member of drug smuggling operation and therefore knew that drugs were in car he was driving); United States v. Zaccaria, 240 F.3d 75, 79 (1st Cir. 2001)

However, if the party against whom proffered evidence is offered will suffer the prejudice in any event, because other admitted evidence of the same consequential fact is equally prejudicial, the proffered evidence is not excludable under Rule 403.[38] Similarly, if the person against whom the prejudicial evidence was offered opened the door to its admission, it generally is not excludable under Rule 403.[39] Moreover, that proffered evidence may be offensive to some members of the jury is not a ground for holding it unduly prejudicial for purposes of Rule 403.[39.1]

[b]—Stipulations to Avoid Prejudicial Effect

Courts are generally receptive to stipulations that will avoid some prejudicial aspects of evidence. Indeed, the Supreme Court, in *Old Chief v. United States,* has held that the trial court may abuse its discretion by refusing a defendant's offer to stipulate to a prior conviction that was relevant only to establish the defendant's status as a felon in a prosecution for unlawful possession of a firearm. In this case, the prior-conviction record presented a substantial risk of unfair prejudice that was not outweighed by any cognizable difference between the evidentiary significance of the stipulation and the legitimately probative component of the official record. In such a case, under Rule 403, the risk of unfair prejudice outweighs the probative value of the official record.[40] With its holding in *Old Chief,* the Court rejected the view of the Ninth Circuit, and other federal circuits, that regardless of the defendant's offer to stipulate to prior-felon status, the government is entitled to prove a prior felony offense through introduction of probative evidence.[41] The Court

---

(in absence of showing of exceptional circumstances, trial court properly rejected on ground of undue prejudice defendant's attempt to impeach government witness by showing he remained silent in response to government interrogation; "silence per se has little or no value for impeachment purposes, . . . and . . . evidence of the invocation of the right to remain silent is inherently prejudicial").

[38] *See, e.g.,* Diamond v. Howd, 288 F.3d 932, 935 (6th Cir. 2002) (in action for false arrest, trial court did not err in admitting tape recording of 911 call that included plaintiff's hysterical conversation with dispatcher because it was no more prejudicial than arresting officer's oral description of her drunken behavior).

[39] *See, e.g.,* United States v. Senffner, 280 F.3d 755, 763 (7th Cir. 2002) (party cannot introduce evidence that appears favorable and then complain, after circumstances are fully developed, that evidence necessary for further development was prejudicial).

[39.1] *See, e.g.,* United States v. Dhingra, No. 03-10001, 2004 U.S. App. LEXIS 15288, at *22–*23 (9th Cir. June 8, 2004), *as amended July 23, 2004.*

[40] Old Chief v. United States, 519 U.S. 172, 117 S. Ct. 644, 136 L. Ed. 2d 574, 584–585 (1997) (name and nature of prior offense raised risk of tainted verdict; noting that "Rule 403 prejudice may occur, for example, when evidence of convictions for prior, unrelated crimes may lead a juror to think that since the defendant already has a criminal record, an erroneous conviction would not be quite as serious as would otherwise be the case"); *see also* § 7.01[7][b].

[41] Old Chief v. United States, 519 U.S. 172, 117 S. Ct. 644, 136 L. Ed. 2d 574, 586 (1997) (rejecting the Ninth Circuit's claim that a stipulation is not proof, and, thus, has no place in the Rule 403 balancing process; citing United States v. Breitkreutz, 8 F.3d 688, 690 (9th Cir. 1993)).

noted that "this will be the general rule when proof of convict status is at issue, just as the prosecutor's choice will generally survive a Rule 403 analysis when a defendant seeks to force the substitution of an admission for evidence creating a coherent narrative of his thoughts and actions in perpetrating the offense for which he is being tried."[42]

Thus, admission of evidence may be proper despite the willingness of the opponent to stipulate to the proposition for which the prior conviction is offered when the issue is something other than a defendant's status as a convict.[43]

[4]—Exclusion of Relevant Evidence: Confusion of Issues, Misleading Jury[44]

Rule 403 recognizes that evidence may be excluded if it might confuse the issues or mislead the jury. As with prejudice, each case of possible confusion, or misleading the jury, turns on the facts in the particular case. It is impossible to state that any particular factors will dictate exclusion.[44.1]

Courts are reluctant to admit evidence that is seemingly plausible, persuasive, conclusive and significant if detailed rebuttal evidence or complicated judicial instructions would be required to demonstrate that the evidence actually has little probative value.[45] On the other hand, courts are reluctant to exclude highly relevant

---

[42] Old Chief v. United States, 519 U.S. 172, 117 S. Ct. 644, 136 L. Ed. 2d 574, 594–595 (1997) ("Proving status without telling exactly why that status was imposed leaves no gap in the story of a defendant's subsequent criminality, and its demonstration by stipulation or admission neither displaces a chapter from a continuous sequence of conventional evidence nor comes across as an officious substitution, to confuse or offend or provoke reproach").

[43] See, e.g., United States v. Bunnell, 280 F.3d 46, 49 (1st Cir. 2002) (defendant's stipulation he possessed weapon did not render weapon inadmissible under Rule 403 because government had to prove weapon had traveled in interstate commerce, and government's expert permissibly used weapon to illustrate his testimony on that point); United States v. Becht, 267 F.3d 767, 770–773 (8th Cir. 2001) (stipulation that computer images were child pornography did not preclude, under Rule 403, admission of images themselves; government needed as well to prove defendant's knowledge, and images were relevant and not unduly prejudicial for that purpose).

[44] See **Treatise** at § 403.05.

[44.1] See, e.g., Manuel v. City of Chicago, 335 F.3d 592, 597 (7th Cir. 2003) (trial court has discretion to exclude evidence under Rule 403 even though opponent has opened the door to its admission; "district court is required to weigh the need for and value of curative admissibility of previously inadmissible evidence (including whether a limiting instruction to the jury would obviate the need for any curative admissibility) against the potential for undue delay, confusion, and prejudice").

[45] See, e.g., United States v. Lawes, 292 F.3d 123, 131–132 (2d Cir. 2002) (affirming exclusion of police officer's citation by review board for excessive force in making unrelated arrest, even though based on board's disbelief of officer's testimony, because it would have had little probative value in showing officer's motivation to lie concerning defendant's weapon possession at time of defendant's arrest and would likely have distracted jury from consequential issues); Mason v.

evidence that is not extremely prejudicial, particularly when objections may be pointed out in cross-examination and argued to the jury.[46]

Courts also hesitate to admit evidence that has an aura of scientific infallibility,[47] particularly if the jury may use the evidence for purposes other than that for which it is introduced. On the other hand, some courts have been satisfied with a trial court's refusal to exclude expert testimony under Rule 403 on concluding that the testimony meets Rule 702's requirements for relevance, reliability, and helpfulness.[48] However, if a qualified expert witness strays beyond his or her expertise during his or her testimony, the admission of the unsupported evidence may violate the strictures of Rule 403.[48.1]

Courts are careful to scrutinize evidence of statistical probabilities; statistics can easily become, in the words of one court, "an item of prejudicial overweight."[49] They may suggest to the jury that the probability that the ultimate fact to be proved is true can be equated with the statistical probability offered in evidence.[50] How-

---

Southern Ill. Univ. at Carbondale, 233 F.3d 1036, 1044 (7th Cir. 2000) (in case alleging racial discrimination resulting from supervisor's creation of hostile work environment, evidence of harassment by co-workers was properly excluded because it could have confused jury in absence of evidence implicating supervisor).

[46] United States v. Doyon, 194 F.3d 207, 213 (1st Cir. 1999) (court properly admitted taped conversations even though tape recorder omitted first few seconds of each conversation; recordings had probative value that was not substantially outweighed by any tendency to mislead because of the omissions; recorded portions contained straightforward admissions and there was no suggestion that these admissions were qualified by anything said in omitted portions; citing **Treatise**); Jackson v. Quanex Corp., 191 F.3d 647, 662–663 (6th Cir. 1999) (trial court committed reversible error when it excluded as irrelevant or cumulative overwhelming evidence that plaintiff proffered documenting her employer's racially discriminatory conduct toward other African-American employees).

[47] See, e.g., Tidemann v. Nadler Golf Car Sales, Inc., 224 F.3d 719, 723 (7th Cir. 2000) (probative value of expert witness's testimony that defective set screw permitted excessive movement of shift lever was very low, in view of lapse of more than two years between accident and expert's examination of vehicle; trial court did not abuse discretion in excluding testimony on ground that it could confuse or mislead jury).

[48] See, e.g., United States v. Perez, 280 F.3d 318, 342 (3d Cir. 2002) (because expert's testimony that drug dealers use digital pagers to transmit coded messages and that police can simultaneously tap cellular phones and keep those using them under surveillance was relevant and helpful under Rule 702, trial court did not abuse its discretion in refusing to exclude it under Rule 403).

[48.1] See, e.g., United States v. Cruz, 363 F.3d 187, 194 (2d Cir. 2004).

[49] See, e.g., Kovacevich v. Kent State Univ., 224 F.3d 806, 831–832 (6th Cir. 2000) (in case alleging disparate treatment of female professors in university's wage and tenure decisions, statistical studies describing trends on university-wide basis were not admissible; studies must be restricted to particular department in question).

[50] See, e.g., People Who Care v. Rockford Bd. of Educ., 111 F.3d 528, 537 (7th Cir. 1997) (statistical study that used participation in school free lunch program as definition of poverty was inadmissible in desegregation case); United States v. Massey, 594 F.2d 676, 677 (8th Cir. 1979)

ever, when there is an adequate foundation for the statistical probabilities, and they are properly used and explained, their probative value will usually outweigh their tendency to confuse and mislead, thereby warranting their admission into evidence.[51] The confusion the courts fear with respect to scientific and statistical evidence can often be avoided if time is allowed for explanatory testimony.

Similarly, the courts have been skeptical of accident reconstruction evidence. Unless the proffering party shows that the circumstances of the reconstruction are "substantially similar" to the accident or incident that is at the heart of the case, the evidence's probative value is outweighed by the likelihood it will confuse the issue or mislead the jury, and it is properly excluded under Rule 403.[52]

In many cases involving confusion or misleading evidence, the courts exclude evidence because an inordinate amount of time would be consumed in clarifying the situation.[53]

[5]—Special Problems Related to Real Proof[54]

Real proof, otherwise known as real evidence or demonstrative evidence, refers to evidence that is directly cognizable by the senses of the trier of fact. Photographs, tape recordings, guns, and clothing are some of the categories of real proof most commonly encountered. Real proof may have such a powerful and unwarranted impact upon the trier that special care must be taken in considering its admissibility in connection with Rule 403.

Before an object can be admitted, it must be authenticated or identified as being that which its proponent claims it to be.[55] This requirement is an aspect of relevancy, since the object obviously is not relevant if it has no connection with that which is being proved. The process of identification is twofold: the object must be related to an issue in the case, and the condition of the object must be shown to be substantially the same as when the event in question took place, since if significant physical changes have occurred, the object, in the form it would be

---

(reversal where prosecutor on closing argument suggested that statistical odds showed a better than 99.44 percent chance of defendant's guilt).
[51] *See, e.g.,* Hemmings v. Tidyman's, Inc., 285 F.3d 1174, 1184–1187 (9th Cir. 2002).
[52] *See, e.g.,* Jodoin v. Toyota Motor Corp., 284 F.3d 272, 278 (1st Cir. 2002).
[53] *See, e.g.,* McEuin v. Crown Equip. Corp., 328 F.3d 1028, 1033–1034 (9th Cir. 2003) (trial court did not abuse its discretion in excluding evidence of military specifications for forklifts when specifications were not binding on defendant and because their introduction might have resulted in jury confusion and waste of time); Duran v. City of Maywood, 221 F.3d 1127, 1132 (9th Cir. 2000) (in civil rights action concerning shooting by police officer, trial court properly excluded evidence of subsequent shooting by same officer on ground it had marginal probative value and would have materially increased length and complexity of trial). *See* **Treatise** at §§ 403.05, 403.06.
[54] *See* **Treatise** at § 403.07.
[55] *See* discussion of Rule 901 in Chapter 8.

shown to the trier, may no longer be relevant. Courts sometimes view the latter requirement not as an aspect of relevancy, but as an instance of refusing to admit relevant evidence because of the danger that the jury might be confused by the change in condition.[56] The problem is particularly acute in the case of posed photographs, or experiments, because the trier may fail to keep in mind the hearsay and opinion elements that went into the artificially created event.

The usual objection raised to the admissibility of real proof is, however, not confusion, but the danger of unfair prejudice. The impact produced by the object itself is often so much greater than that produced by testimony about the object, that it is feared that jurors will overestimate its probative value.[57] There is a general mental tendency, when an object is produced as proving something, to assume, on sight of the object, all else that is implied in the case about it. In addition, there is the risk that if the object exhibited has gruesome or repulsive characteristics, the jury may be so emotionally aroused as to fail to assess the probative value of the other evidence in the case accurately.

This objection to the overpowering effect of real proof is often raised when a witness seeks to display physical injuries to the jury. Simple black and white pictures are usually the most neutral way to get this information to the jury. Color pictures or slides may be useful, as may movies or videotapes, but staged "Day in the Life" films are sometimes too prejudicial and often contain elements of hidden hearsay and opinion evidence.[58]

However, evidence may not be excluded merely because it is unpleasant. "[A] court cannot arrange for lively music to keep the jury cheerful while the state's case in a murder trial is being presented, and grewsome [sic] evidence cannot be suppressed merely because it may strongly tend to agitate the jury's feelings."[59] The possibility of prejudice is in itself insignificant; it is the danger of prejudice substantially outweighing the probative value of the proffered evidence that is

---

[56] *See, e.g.,* United States v. Dombrowski, 877 F.2d 520, 524–525 (7th Cir. 1989) (photo taken from across the street from the actual site of the alleged incident).

[57] *See, e.g.,* United States v. Perrotta, 289 F.3d 155, 166 (1st Cir. 2002) (introduction of weapons frequently follows testimony concerning them, even though jury has no determination concerning their physical characteristics to make; they corroborate testimony, and that added increment of probative value is appropriate unless it is substantially outweighed by danger of unfair prejudice).

[58] *See* Bannister v. Town of Noble, 812 F.2d 1265, 1270 (10th Cir. 1987) (review of dangers; court concluded there was no abuse of discretion in admitting "Day in the Life" film).

[59] State v. Moore, 80 Kan. 232, 236, 102 P. 475, 477 (1909) (bloodstained jacket of deceased admitted into evidence); *see, e.g.,* United States v. Myers, 280 F.3d 407, 414 (4th Cir. 2002) (trial court did not err in admitting murder scene evidence depicting blood and otherwise indicating violence even though defendant was not charged with committing murder, when murder was act "intrinsic" to charged crimes).

determinative. Otherwise, the more gruesome the crime or the greater the injuries, the more difficult it would become for the prosecutor or plaintiff to prove its case.

Objections are frequently raised to the admission of photographs—particularly color photographs—because disturbing objects or events may be represented, which could not otherwise be viewed by the jury. With proper instruction, the danger of jurors overvaluing such proof is slight. Jurors, exposed as they are to television, films, and magazines, are fairly sophisticated. If a fair audio or visual presentation would assist the jury, the court should not discourage its use.

When the probative value of evidence outweighs the danger of undue prejudice, the federal courts have admitted photographs and films or tapes or scale models of such unsavory objects and events as murder victims and scenes,[60] rape victims,[61] accident victims,[62] assault victims,[63] child pornography,[64] and the actual commission of a crime.[65] Demonstrations have also been permitted.[66] As in other instances when the admissibility of evidence is challenged on Rule 403 grounds, counsel and the trial court must carefully analyze and evaluate the probative value of the proffered evidence and balance it against the factors specified in Rule 403.

[6]—Exclusion of Evidence: Waste of Time[67]

Rule 403 provides that relevant evidence may be excluded if its probative value is substantially outweighed by considerations of undue delay, waste of time, or needless presentation of cumulative evidence.

Exclusion is generally appropriate if the evidence excluded merely repeats what

---

[60]   *See, e.g.,* United States v. Velazquez, 246 F.3d 204, 211 (2d Cir. 2001) (trial court did not abuse its discretion in admitting graphic autopsy photos of victim of homicide to evidence "cruel and unusual punishment" victim had suffered and to underscore defendant's moral blame attaching to his decision to cover up his crime); United States v. Salerno, 108 F.3d 730, 740 (7th Cir. 1997) (scale model of murder scene admissible).

[61]   United States v. One Feather, 702 F.2d 736, 739 (8th Cir. 1983).

[62]   Walker v. Norris, 917 F.2d 1449, 1453 (6th Cir. 1990).

[63]   *See, e.g.,* United States v. Lopez, 271 F.3d 472, 482 (3d Cir. 2001) (photographs of assault victim's mutilated hand, taken prior to restorative surgery, were relevant and not unduly prejudicial).

[64]   *See, e.g.,* United States v. Becht, 267 F.3d 767, 770–773 (8th Cir. 2001).

[65]   *See, e.g.,* Deters v. Equifax Credit Information Services, 202 F.3d 1262, 1274 (10th Cir. 2000) (videotape of perpetrator describing sexual harassment was relevant and not unfairly prejudicial); United States v. Wilson, 116 F.3d 1066, 1082 (5th Cir. 1997) (admission of videotape of gang members made by gang members for gang members was not abuse of discretion in drug trafficking conspiracy).

[66]   *See, e.g.,* Jones v. Ralls, 187 F.3d 848, 853 (8th Cir. 1999) (trial court properly allowed police officer to demonstrate the wristlock hold he had used on plaintiff); United States v. Jones, 124 F.3d 781, 786–787 (6th Cir. 1997) (videotaped explosion of a replica of bomb found on defendant's premises was not unduly prejudicial).

[67]   *See* **Treatise** at § 403.06.

has already been admitted.[68] In the case of cumulative evidence, the trial court must have wide discretion to exclude if it is to conduct a trial efficiently.[69]

Under this provision, the trial court may appropriately exclude evidence that, if admitted, would result in a lengthy exploration of issues that are only peripherally related to the parties' dispute. For example, the fact that issues have not been explored during discovery or in pretrial proceedings suggests that they are peripheral.[70] Similarly, if evidence has only tenuous relevance at best and would seriously extend the trial and unnecessarily confuse the jury, it may be excluded under Rule 403, even in a criminal case.[71]

On the other hand, Rule 403 does not mean that a court may exclude evidence that will prolong a trial regardless of its probative value; the exclusion of crucial evidence may amount to an abuse of discretion.[72]

---

[68] *See, e.g.,* Robert S. v. Stetson Sch., Inc., 256 F.3d 159, 169–170 (3d Cir. 2001) (trial court did not abuse its discretion in limiting expert testimony to prevent duplication of testimony already before jury from two similarly qualified expert witnesses); United States v. Adams, 914 F.2d 1404, 1408 (10th Cir. 1990).

[69] *See, e.g.,* Chadwell v. Koch Ref. Co., 251 F.3d 727, 732–733 (8th Cir. 2001) (no abuse of discretion in trial court's exclusion, as cumulative under Rule 403, of meeting notes reflecting comments of witness when witness testified at trial to same matters for which notes were offered).

[70] *See, e.g.,* Anderson v. WBMG-42, 253 F.3d 561, 567 (11th Cir. 2001) (trial court has discretion to exclude peripheral evidence that would require considerable trial time; "There is no abuse of discretion where a trial court prevents counsel from embarking on a lengthy examination of matters which have not been developed during discovery").

[71] *See, e.g.,* United States v. Sprong, 287 F.3d 663, 665 (7th Cir. 2002) (trial court properly excluded under Rule 403 testimony about dangers to world peace created by Trident submarine, international law relating to nuclear weapons, and history of civil disobedience in prosecution for destroying government property resulting in disruption of communications with submerged Trident submarines).

[72] *See, e.g.,* United States v. Barile, 286 F.3d 749, 756 (4th Cir. 2002) (prior inconsistent statements of witness were far too probative, even when introduced for impeachment, to be excluded under Rule 403).

CHAPTER 7

*Special Rules of Relevancy**

SYNOPSIS

---

* Chapter revised in 1992, and §§ 7.04–7.10 revised in 1995, by SANDRA D. KATZ, member of the New York Bar.

§ 7.01   Character and Criminal Conduct to Prove Conduct—Rule 404

[1]—Text and Scope of Rule[1]

The Federal Rules of Evidence do not define *character evidence. Character* is a general description of a person's disposition or of a personality trait such as honesty, temperance, or peacefulness. *Character* is not synonymous with *habit;* the admissibility of evidence of a person's habits is treated in Federal Rule of Evidence 406. Habits are more specific than character traits.[2]

Character is also distinct from reputation. Character is what a person is, while reputation is what other people think a person is. Thus, evidence of a person's reputation is one way to prove the person's character. Methods of proving character are generally governed by Federal Rule of Evidence 405.[3]

Rule 404 reads as follows:

Rule 404.   Character Evidence Not Admissible To Prove Conduct; Exceptions; Other Crimes.

(a) Character evidence generally.—Evidence of a person's character or a trait of character is not admissible for the purpose of proving action in conformity therewith on a particular occasion, except:

(1) Character of accused.—Evidence of a pertinent trait of character offered by an accused, or by the prosecution to rebut the same, or if evidence of a trait of character of the alleged victim of the crime is offered by an accused and admitted under Rule 404(a)(2), evidence of the same trait of character of the accused offered by the prosecution;

(2) Character of alleged victim.—Evidence of a pertinent trait of character of the alleged victim of the crime offered by an accused, or by the prosecution to rebut the same, or evidence of a character trait of peacefulness of the alleged victim offered by the prosecution in a homicide case to rebut evidence that the alleged victim was the first aggressor;

(3) Character of witness.—Evidence of the character of a witness, as provided in rules 607, 608, and 609.

(b) Other crimes, wrongs, or acts. Evidence of other crimes, wrongs, or acts is not admissible to prove the character of a person in order to show action in conformity therewith. It may, however, be admissible for other purposes, such as proof of motive, opportunity, intent, preparation, plan, knowledge,

---

[1]   *See* **Treatise** at § 404.02.
[2]   *See* § 7.03.
[3]   *See* § 7.02.

identity, or absence of mistake or accident, provided that upon request by the accused, the prosecution in a criminal case shall provide reasonable notice in advance of trial, or during trial if the court excuses pretrial notice on good cause shown, of the general nature of any such evidence it intends to introduce at trial.

[*Adopted Jan. 2, 1975, effective July 1, 1975; amended Mar. 2, 1987, effective Oct. 1, 1987; amended Apr. 30, 1991, effective Dec. 1, 1991; amended Apr. 17, 2000, effective Dec. 1, 2000.*]

[2]—General Inadmissibility of Character Evidence to Prove Conduct

Rule 404 is the basic rule governing the admissibility of character evidence to prove circumstantially that a person acted in accordance with that character. With limited exceptions, it precludes the use of character evidence for that purpose.[4] It also precludes the use of evidence of other acts of a person to prove that the person acted in accordance with those other acts.[5] It does not bar proof of a person's other acts when they are offered to prove matters other than the person's character and consequent conduct. In particular, other acts may be offered to prove elements of the party's case, such as identity, intent, and the like, or to prove foundational facts, such as opportunity or motive, from which those elements can be inferred.[6]

Rule 404 does not deal with the admissibility of character evidence when the substantive law makes character an element of a crime, a claim for relief, or a defense. The Advisory Committee characterized the substantive law in such situations as putting "character in issue." It gave as an illustration of such a situation an action for negligently entrusting a motor vehicle to an incompetent driver.[7] Similarly, if an accused in a criminal case raises the defense of entrapment, arguing that the crime would not have been committed but for the solicitation of the police, the accused's character and prior conduct become directly relevant in determining whether he or she was predisposed to commit the offense.[8] There are numerous other situations in which the substantive law puts a party's "character in issue" and thereby makes evidence of the party's character directly relevant; Rule 404 is not applicable to the evidentiary questions those situations present. If character evi-

---

[4]   Fed. R. Evid. 404(a); *see* [3], *below.*

[5]   Fed. R. Evid. 404(b); *see* [5], *below.*

[6]   Fed. R. Evid. 404(b); *see* [5], *below.*

[7]   *See* Original Advisory Committee's Note to Fed. R. Evid. 404 (reprinted in **Treatise** at § 404App.01[2]).

[8]   *See, e.g.,* Sorrells v. United States, 287 U.S. 435, 451, 53 S. Ct. 210, 77 L. Ed. 413 (1932); United States v. Coleman, 284 F.3d 892, 894 (8th Cir. 2002) ("Because Coleman claimed a defense of entrapment, evidence of prior bad acts was admissible to show Coleman's predisposition to the bad acts").

dence is admissible in such cases, Rule 405 sets forth the appropriate methods of proof.[9]

The use of character evidence addressed, and largely forbidden, by Rule 404 is as circumstantial proof of conduct.[10] The Advisory Committee gave as examples of the circumstantial use of character evidence proof of the defendant's violent disposition to support the inference that the defendant was the aggressor in an affray and evidence of honesty in disproof of a charge of theft. As the Advisory Committee noted, Rule 404 continues the proscription against the circumstantial use of character evidence in such ways that other jurisdictions and the common law had observed for a long time.[11]

Rules 413, 414, and 415 make evidence of prior sexual assaults and child molestation admissible for any purpose in criminal and civil cases involving those types of acts.[12] Rule 404's limitations and proscriptions on the use of character evidence, therefore, do not apply in those types of cases.[13]

[3]—Admissible Character Evidence to Prove Conduct

[a]—Exceptions Listed in Rule 404(a)

Rule 404(a) specifies seven exclusive situations in which evidence of a person's character is admissible as circumstantial proof that the person acted in accordance with that character trait:[14]

- The accused may offer evidence of his or her own pertinent character trait in defense against the crimes charged.[15]

- The prosecution may offer evidence of a pertinent character trait of the accused to rebut defense evidence about the accused's own character.[16]

- The accused may offer evidence of a pertinent character trait of the alleged victim of the charged crime in defense against the crime charged or in support of a defense.[17]

---

[9] *See* § 7.02.

[10] *See, e.g.,* United States v. Tan, 254 F.3d 1204, 1208 (10th Cir. 2001) (Rule 404(b) bars other acts evidence offered to prove criminal propensity).

[11] Original Advisory Committee's Note to Fed. R. Evid. 404 (reprinted in **Treatise** at § 404App.01[2]).

[12] Fed. R. Evid 413; Fed. R. Evid. 414; Fed. R. Evid. 415; *see* § 7.10.

[13] *See, e.g.,* United States v. Tyndall, 263 F.3d 848, 850 (8th Cir. 2001) (Congress, by enacting Rule 413, exempted sexual assault cases from Rule 404(b)).

[14] Fed. R. Evid. 404(a).

[15] *See* [b], *below.*

[16] *See* [b], *below.*

[17] *See* [c], *below.*

- If the accused has presented evidence about a character trait of the alleged victim of the crime, the prosecution may offer rebuttal evidence about the character of the alleged victim.[18]

- If the accused has presented evidence of a pertinent character trait of the alleged victim of the crime, the prosecution may offer evidence of the same character trait in the accused.[19]

- If the accused in a homicide case has presented evidence that the alleged victim was the first aggressor in the altercation, the prosecution may offer evidence of the alleged victim's peaceable character.[20]

- When Rule 607, 608, or 609 permits, character evidence may be used to impeach a witness.[21]

[b]—Evidence of Character of the Accused[22]

[i]—Introduction by Prosecution

Rule 404(a) restates the common-law rule that bars the prosecution from using evidence of the accused's character to prove that he or she committed the crimes charged, with a few exceptions.[23] The purpose of the proscription against the prosecution's use of character evidence in its case-in-chief is to protect the defendant from being convicted for "being bad."[24]

The prosecution may introduce evidence concerning the accused's character in the following circumstances: (1) as rebuttal after the accused has called character witnesses to testify about his or her good character,[25] (2) to respond to a character-based defense (such as entrapment), or (3) to rebut defense evidence concerning the character of the victim of the crime (*see* [ii], *below*).

Unless the defendant has opened the character issue in one of these ways, however, the prosecution may not present character evidence to show the defen-

---

[18]   *See* [c], *below*.
[19]   *See* [b], *below*.
[20]   *See* [c], *below*.
[21]   *See* [d], *below*; Ch. 12.
[22]   *See* **Treatise** at § 404.11.
[23]   Fed. R. Evid. 404(a)(1) (accused may introduce evidence of good character as defense); *see* [ii], *below*.
[24]   *See, e.g.,* United States v. Taylor, 284 F.3d 95, 101 (1st Cir. 2002).
[25]   Fed. R. Evid. 404(a)(1); *see, e.g.,* United States v. Bonner, 302 F.3d 776, 781–782 (7th Cir. 2002) (when defendant introduced evidence of his good character, and counsel "harped" on defendant's good character throughout trial, including in opening statement, defendant "opened the door" to prosecution's introduction of evidence of his bad character).

dant's propensity to commit the charged offense.[26] The defense may convert a prosecution witness into a character witness, however, if it elicits testimony about the defendant's reputation on cross-examination of the witness or otherwise opens the door during cross-examination.[27]

The accused may open the door to character evidence by raising certain defenses. For example, if the accused raises the defense of entrapment, arguing that he or she would not have committed the crime but for the solicitation of the police, evidence of the accused's character and prior conduct are admissible to show whether he or she was predisposed to commit the offense.[28] In entrapment cases, court have allowed evidence of defendant's general character and of prior criminal convictions.[29] Testimony is also allowed relating to prior or subsequent criminal activity of which the accused was not convicted.[30]

The accused may present evidence about the victim's character as a defensive matter.[31] If the accused does so, the door is open for the prosecution to present evidence of the same trait of character in the accused.[32] In a homicide or assault case, for example, an accused might offer evidence of the victim's character trait of violence or aggression to support a claim of self-defense, to show that the victim had a propensity for violence and thus is more likely to have been using unlawful force at the time of the crime.[33] When the accused presents such evidence, Rule 404(a)(1) allows the prosecution to rebut that claim with evidence showing the defendant's own propensity for violence or aggression.

---

[26] Fed. R. Evid. 404(a)(1); *see, e.g.,* United States v. Gilliland, 586 F.2d 1384, 1390–1391 (10th Cir. 1978) (reversible error for trial court to allow cross-examination of defendant's eyewitness about defendant's prior convictions, since defendant had not opened the issue of his character).

[27] *See, e.g.,* United States v. Vasquez, 267 F.3d 79, 85–86 (2d Cir. 2001) (when defendant, during cross-examination of prosecution witness, raised questions concerning witness's use of weapon against defendant, questioning "opened the door" to redirect examination concerning defendant's violent character).

[28] *See, e.g.,* Sorrells v. United States, 287 U.S. 435, 451, 53 S. Ct. 210, 77 L. Ed. 413 (1932); United States v. Coleman, 284 F.3d 892, 894 (8th Cir. 2002) ("Because Coleman claimed a defense of entrapment, evidence of prior bad acts was admissible to show Coleman's predisposition to the bad acts").

[29] *See, e.g.,* United States v. Kurkowski, 281 F.3d 699, 702 (8th Cir. 2002) (trial court did not err in admitting police officer's testimony that unidentified informant had reported defendant had engaged in drug sales preceding charged transaction because it was relevant to defendant's predisposition to engage in drug sales and to his entrapment defense).

[30] *See* discussion in **Treatise** at § 404.12.

[31] Fed. R. Evid. 404(a)(2); *see* [c], *below.*

[32] Fed. R. Evid. 404(a)(1).

[33] *See, e.g.,* Fortini v. Murphy, 257 F.3d 39, 48 (1st Cir. 2001) (trial court erred in excluding defendant's proffered self-defense evidence of homicide victim's violent confrontation with other persons shortly before he was killed in confrontation with defendant).

Taking the stand, alone, does not expose the defendant's character to attack,[34] except to the extent that evidence of bad character may be used to attack the defendant's credibility as a witness.[35] The defendant's own testimony may, however, open the defendant to a character attack if he or she says something that might suggest good character rendering him or her incapable of committing the charged offense.[36]

The appropriate methods of proving character are covered by Rule 405.[37] The appropriate methods of attacking and rehabilitating the credibility of a witness with character evidence are covered in Rules 608 and 609.[38]

[ii]—Introduction by Accused

The accused has an absolute right to introduce evidence concerning his or her own good character to suggest that such a person would not commit the charged offense. While it is necessary that the character evidence relate to the character of the accused and to a consequential matter at issue in the case,[39] a criminal case, the limitation that the evidence relate to a consequential and controverted issue is of very little effect. For example, an accused's character trait of law-abidingness is pertinent to almost all criminal offenses.[39.1] The Advisory Committee recognized that there was little in the way of logic to support the retention of a criminal defendant's common-law right to defend with circumstantial character evidence, but noted that the rule permitting such a defense was "so deeply rooted in our jurisprudence as to assume almost constitutional proportions."[40]

An accused's right to introduce character evidence is limited to evidence of the accused's own character. It does not apply to evidence of a co-defendant's character or to the character of an unindicted coconspirator.[40.1]

---

[34] *See, e.g.,* United States v. Wilson, 244 F.3d 1208, 1217–1218 (10th Cir. 2001) (trial court erroneously permitted prosecution to cross-examine defendant concerning his prior drug arrests; defendant's testimony that he never used, sold, or bought crack cocaine did not concern a trait of character and prior acts were inadmissible under Rule 404(b)).

[35] *See* § 12.03.

[36] *See, e.g.,* United States v. Bruguier, 161 F.3d 1145, 1148–1149 (8th Cir. 1998) (no error in admission of evidence that defendant had previously mistreated his children, since defendant had put his character in issue by introducing evidence that he was good father).

[37] *See* § 7.02.

[38] *See* §§ 12.03, 12.04.

[39] *See, e.g.,* United States v. Han, 230 F.3d 560, 564 (2d Cir. 2000) (only requirement for admissibility of evidence of accused's character when offered by accused is that it relate in some way to element at issue in case).

[39.1] *See, e.g.,* In re: Sealed Case, 352 F.3d 409, 412 (D.C. Cir. 2003).

[40] Fed. R. Evid. 404 Advisory Committee's Note (1972) (reproduced verbatim in **Treatise** at § 404App.01[2]).

[40.1] *See, e.g.,* United States v. Wright, 363 F.3d 237, 247 & n.3 (3d Cir. 2004).

Character evidence is particularly relevant when the accused asserts an entrapment defense, since the defense puts at issue the accused's predisposition to commit the charged offense.[41]

The trial court, in its discretion, may limit the scope of the proof, as by limiting the number of witnesses. The trial court can also require an orderly presentation of evidence by controlling the order of proof.[42]

The appropriate methods of proving character are covered by Rule 405.[43] The appropriate methods of attacking and rehabilitating the credibility of a witness with character evidence are covered in Rules 608 and 609.[44]

[c]—Evidence of Character of Alleged Victim[45]

Rule 404(a) permits the accused in a criminal trial to introduce evidence of a pertinent character trait of the alleged victim of the charged crime as circumstantial evidence that the victim acted, in accordance with that character trait, in a way that obviates or mitigates the accused's guilt.[46] The Advisory Committee suggested that a victim's character traits may be relevant to a claim of self defense to a charge of homicide.[47] The Committee also suggested that a victim's character traits may be relevant to a claim of consent to a charge of rape,[48] but Rule 412, which was enacted in 1978, limits the circumstances under which character evidence of a victim of an alleged sexual assault is admissible.[49]

If the accused offers evidence of the alleged victim's character, it must be in the form of opinion or reputation testimony; it may not be in the form of evidence concerning other acts.[49.1] When the accused offers evidence of the alleged victim's

---

[41]   *See, e.g.,* United States v. Thomas, 134 F.3d 975, 978–980 (9th Cir. 1998) (when predisposition to commit offense is at issue, defendant may introduce evidence of past good acts).

[42]   Fed. R. Evid. 611; *see* § 2.02.

[43]   *See* § 7.02.

[44]   *See* §§ 12.03, 12.04.

[45]   *See* **Treatise** at § 404.11[3].

[46]   Fed. R. Evid. 404(a)(2).

[47]   Original Advisory Committee's Note to Fed. R. Evid. 404 (reprinted in **Treatise** at § 404App.01[2]); *see, e.g.,* United States v. Emeron Taken Alive, 262 F.3d 711, 714–715 (8th Cir. 2001) (trial court erred in excluding defendant's evidence of arresting officer's character for violence in support of his self-defense claim in response to charges of resisting arrest and assaulting arresting officer).

[48]   Original Advisory Committee's Note to Fed. R. Evid. 404 (reprinted in **Treatise** at § 404App.01[2]).

[49]   Fed. R. Evid. 412; *see* § 7.09.

[49.1]   Fed. R. Evid. 405 *see, e.g.,* United States v. Geston, 299 F.3d 1130, 1138 (9th Cir. 2002) (trial court did not abuse its discretion in excluding proffered evidence of prior incidents of alleged victim's violence under Rule 404(a)(2), because "only reputation or opinion evidence is proper to show that the victim of an assault had a propensity towards violence").

character, then the prosecution is entitled not only to offer rebutting evidence about the victim's character,[50] but also to introduce evidence that the accused has the same character trait.[51]

When the accused offers evidence of a homicide victim's violent character, but does not show that the accused was aware of that character trait at the time of the incident resulting in the victim's death, the accused is offering the evidence as circumstantial proof of the alleged victim's violent behavior at the time of the incident in question, and the offer falls squarely within Rule 404(a)(2).[52] On the other hand, if there is evidence that the accused was aware of the alleged victim's violent nature at the time of the incident in question, evidence of the alleged victim's violent character is admissible in support of the accused's claim of self-defense, but not solely under Rule 404(a)(2). Under those circumstances, the evidence of the alleged victim's violent character is admissible independently of Rule 404(a)(2) because it is relevant to the accused's apprehension of imminent danger and the reasonableness of his or her defensive measures.[53]

The prosecutor in a homicide case may also offer evidence of the victim's character for peacefulness to rebut defense evidence that the victim was the first aggressor.[54]

[d]—Evidence of Character of Witness

Rule 404(a)(3) permits the parties to introduce evidence of the character of witnesses as permitted under Rules 607, 608, and 609, which govern impeachment of witnesses.[55] The term "witness," as used in Rule 404(a)(3) refers to a person who actually gives testimony at trial, and does not include a person who has extensive involvement in or knowledge of the events at issue but who does not give testimony.[55.1]

[4]—Character Evidence in Civil Cases[56]

Rule 404 applies to both civil and criminal cases, although it is obviously of far greater significance in criminal cases. It adopts the orthodox position of rejecting

---

[50] Fed. R. Evid. 404(a)(2).

[51] Fed. R. Evid. 404(a)(1); *see* [b], *above.*

[52] *See, e.g.,* United States v. Smith, 230 F.3d 300, 306–307 (7th Cir. 2000) (evidence of violent character of alleged victim clearly falls within Rule 404(a)(2) even if there is no evidence accused was aware of alleged victim's character trait at time of incident in question).

[53] *See, e.g.,* United States v. Saenz, 179 F.3d 686, 688–689 (9th Cir. 1999) (defendant claiming self-defense may introduce evidence that he knew of victim's prior acts of violence to show defendant's state of mind).

[54] Fed. R. Evid. 404(a)(2).

[55] Fed. R. Evid. 404(a)(3); *see* Ch. 12.

[55.1] *See, e.g.,* United States v. Stephens, 365 F.3d 967, 975 (11th Cir. 2004).

[56] *See* **Treatise** at §§ 404.02[2], 404.10, 404.22[6][b].

character evidence in civil actions offered to prove that a person acted in conformity with a particular character trait.[57] It does not prohibit the introduction of character evidence in a civil case when character is in issue or the evidence is being offered to reflect upon a witness's credibility.[58]

The language of the two exceptions in Rule 404(a) that permit use of character evidence to prove conduct conformity with that character trait suggest those two exceptions are not applicable in civil cases. Both subdivisions (1) and (2) use the terms "accused" and "prosecution," which relate to criminal cases, to identify the parties who are permitted to offer evidence concerning character traits of the "accused" and of the "victim." Moreover, the Advisory Committee Note suggests the inapplicability of those exceptions to civil cases.[59]

Nevertheless, the courts in interpreting Rule 404(a) do not always bar the use of character evidence as proof of action in conformity with a character trait in civil cases, particularly in cases in which the plaintiff's claim is based on conduct that is essentially criminal in nature. The courts may admit such evidence in civil cases because Rule 404 does not state explicitly that the two exceptions permitting affirmative or rebuttal use of such evidence are limited in their application to criminal cases, or because of their reluctance to apply a blanket rule of exclusion instead of balancing probative worth against possible prejudice.[60] Similarly, courts have admitted evidence of other acts under a Rule 404(b) analysis in civil cases charging discriminatory conduct.[61]

---

[57] *See, e.g.,* Gray v. Genlyte Group, Inc., 289 F.3d 128, 140–141 (1st Cir. 2002) (trial court properly excluded evidence that would primarily have shown defendant's employee's propensity for violent and sexually offensive conduct, which is forbidden by Rule 404(a)).

[58] *See, e.g.,* Paine v. City of Lompoc, 160 F.3d 562, 566 (9th Cir. 1998) (although evidence of plaintiff's violent behavior did create some risk of unfair prejudice, incident was relevant to damages and to witness's credibility).

[59] *See* Original Advisory Committee's Note to Fed. R. Evid. 404 (reprinted in **Treatise** at § 404App.01[2]).

[60] *See, e.g.,* Crumpton v. Confederation Life Ins. Co., 672 F.2d 1248, 1253–1254 (5th Cir. 1982) ("when evidence would be admissible under Rule 404(a) in a criminal case, we think it should also be admissible in a civil suit where the focus is on essentially criminal aspects, and the evidence is relevant, probative, and not unduly prejudicial").

[61] *See, e.g.,* Griffin v. City of Opa-Locka, 261 F.3d 1295, 1307–1312 (11th Cir. 2001) (evidence of sexual harassing actions and statements other than those directed at plaintiff admitted to show hostile working atmosphere and municipal custom and policy tolerating sexual harassment).

[5]—Evidence of Other Crimes, Wrongs, or Acts[62]

[a]—Relevant Other Acts are Generally Admissible[63]

[i]—Admissible Unless Offered Solely to Prove Propensity

That a defendant in a criminal case committed another crime may be relevant to a wide variety of consequential facts and material propositions. Rule 404(b) forbids the use of evidence of other crimes only when it is offered for the sole purpose of suggesting that the defendant has a character defect that led the defendant to commit the crime with which he or she is charged.[64] However, evidence that is not barred by Rule 404(b) may still be inadmissible under other Rules.[65]

Moreover, Rules 413, 414, and 415 make evidence of prior sexual assaults and child molestation admissible for any purpose, including proof of propensity, in criminal and civil cases involving those types of acts.[65.1] Rule 404(b)'s limitations and proscriptions on the use of evidence of other crimes, wrongs, or acts, therefore, do not apply in those types of cases.[65.2]

The question when Rule 404(b) permits admission of evidence of a particular criminal act is difficult to answer. The answer varies from case to case and from circuit to circuit.[66] Each circuit has articulated a set of rules that it applies to determine whether evidence of prior bad acts is admissible under Rule 404(b).[67] In general, however, evidence is admissible under Rule 404(b) if it relates to an issue other than the defendant's character and its probative value is not substantially

---

[62] *See* **Treatise** at §§ 404.20–404.23.

[63] *See* **Treatise** at §§ 404.21[2], 404.22[1][b].

[64] United States v. Moore, 375 F.3d 259, 263–264 (3d Cir. 2004) (evidence of defendant's violent acts directed toward step-daughter because of her refusal to sell drugs for him was not relevant to any issue of consequence other than defendant's propensity for violence in prosecution for committing arson and was inadmissible even in light of lack of objection); United States v. Tan, 254 F.3d 1204, 1208 (10th Cir. 2001) (Rule 404(b) is "inclusive," "admitting all evidence of other crimes or acts except that which tends to prove *only* criminal disposition").

[65] *See, e.g.,* United States v. Bowie, 232 F.3d 923, 930 (D.C. Cir. 2000) (evidence offered for proper purpose under Rule 404(b) remains subject to "general strictures limiting admissibility such as Rules 402 and 403").

[65.1] Fed. R. Evid. 413; Fed. R. Evid. 414; Fed. R. Evid. 415; see § 7.10.

[65.2] *See, e.g.,* United States v. Blue Bird, 372 F.3d 989, 992 (8th Cir. 2004) (Rule 413 supersedes Rule 404's prohibition against character evidence, allowing testimony of prior bad acts in sexual assault cases, provided it is relevant).

[66] *See, e.g.,* United States v. Murray, 103 F.3d 310, 316 (3d Cir. 1997) ("the line between what is permitted and what is prohibited under Rule 404(b) is sometimes somewhat subtle").

[67] *See* **Treatise** at §§ 404.20–404.23.

outweighed by undue prejudice.[68]

Occasionally, a criminal defendant may attempt to introduce evidence of other crimes, wrongs, or acts of another person, such as a witness for the prosecution. When the evidence is probative of a consequential fact other than propensity, Rule 404(b) does not require the exclusion of the evidence.[68.1]

Some circuits require trial courts, when they admit evidence of other acts, to give the jury a limiting instruction, even though the party against whom it is offered did not request one.[69] Because other acts evidence is not admissible to show a party's propensity to engage in wrongful conduct, the trial court must, in any event, give a limiting instruction if the party against whom the evidence is offered so requests.[70]

[ii]—Admissibility Not Limited to Crimes Occurring Before Charged Acts

Rule 404(b) is not limited in its applicability to evidence of other crimes. It uses the language "other crimes, wrongs, or acts" to suggest the impropriety of using evidence of anything a party has done other than acts alleged in the pending action, as circumstantial evidence that he or she has a propensity to commit acts of the type alleged.[71] Its use of that language also suggests the propriety of using such evidence as circumstantial proof of any fact to which it might be relevant other than propensity.

Rule 404(b) is also not limited in its applicability to acts that occurred prior to the act at issue in the case. Evidence of acts that occurred after the act at issue is admissible as circumstantial proof of any fact to which it might be relevant other than the actor's propensity to commit the act in question.[72]

---

[68]   Fed. R. Evid. 403, 404(b); United States v. Saucedo-Munoz, 307 F.3d 344, 350 (5th Cir. 2002); United States v. Escobar-de Jesus, 187 F.3d 148, 169 (1st Cir. 1999); *see* [b][i], [vii], *below.*

[68.1]   *See, e.g.,* United States v. Stephens, 365 F.3d 967, 974–975 (11th Cir. 2004) (defendant's evidence that prosecution witness had been drug dealer on prior occasions was probative to suggest that witness could have obtained drugs he claimed he obtained from defendant from another source, and was admissible under Rule 404(b)).

[69]   *See, e.g.,* United States v. Saucedo-Munoz, 307 F.3d 344, 350 (5th Cir. 2002) (evidence of defendant's conviction of similar crime is more probative than prejudicial, and any prejudicial effect may be minimized by proper jury instruction); United States v. Everett, 270 F.3d 986, 991–992 (6th Cir. 2001) (when trial court admits other acts evidence, it must instruct jury concerning fact it is introduced to prove, explain its materiality, and instruct jury not to draw inference forbidden by Rule 404(b)).

[70]   Fed. R. Evid. 105; *see* § 2.04.

[71]   *See, e.g.,* Okai v. Verfuth, 275 F.3d 606, 609–613 (7th Cir. 2001) (trial court properly excluded evidence of defendant prison guard's suspension when plaintiff failed to show it was admissible for proper purpose under Rule 404(b)); *see* [iii], *below.*

[72]   *See, e.g.,* United States v. Anifowoshe, 307 F.3d 643, 646-647 (7th Cir. 2002) (Rule 404(b) does not distinguish between prior and subsequent acts, although chronological relationship may

Rule 404(b) is equally applicable to civil and criminal cases. For example, it does not bar evidence of other good acts when it is relevant to a consequential fact other than propensity.[72.1]

[iii]—Rule 404's List of Other Purposes is Not Exhaustive

Rule 404(b) sets out examples of appropriate matters that a party may properly attempt to prove circumstantially through proof of other crimes, wrongs, or acts. The listed examples are "motive, opportunity, intent, preparation, plan, knowledge, identity, and absence of mistake or accident."[73] Some of these matters are consequential facts that a party must prove to make out a prima facie case, such as intent and identity. It also includes some matters that become consequential facts only to rebut particular defenses, such as absence of mistake or accident. Other matters, such as motive and opportunity, may support an inference of a consequential fact necessary either to make out a prima facie case or to rebut defensive evidence.

Rule 404(b)'s list is not exhaustive.[73.1] Thus, evidence of other crimes, wrongs, or acts can appropriately be offered as proof, circumstantial or direct, of matters such as the following:

- Credibility.[74]

- Jurisdictional facts.[75]

- Corroboration of other properly admitted evidence.[76]

---

affect admissibility determination); United States v. Mack, 258 F.3d 548, 553–554 (6th Cir. 2001) (evidence of uncharged bank robbery committed after last of charged bank robberies was admissible under Rule 404(b) to prove defendant's identity as perpetrator of charged robberies).

[72.1] *See, e.g.,* Ansell v. Green Acres Contracting Co., 347 F.3d 515, 520–525 (3d Cir. 2003) (in age discrimination in employment case, defendant's supervisor-employee's acts respecting favorable job actions toward employee who was same age as plaintiff were relevant to show supervisor-employee did not take unfavorable job actions toward plaintiff because of intent to discriminate against plaintiff because of his age).

[73] Fed. R. Evid. 404(b).

[73.1] *See, e.g.,* United States v. Cruz-Garcia, 344 F.3d 951, 955 (9th Cir. 2003) (witness's prior conviction for distributing heroin was admissible under Rule 404(b) because his propensity was not at issue (he had already pleaded guilty) and only inference jury could draw from evidence was that he had ability to distribute heroin on his own).

[74] *See, e.g.,* United States v. Boone, 279 F.3d 163, 175 (3d Cir. 2002) (evidence that character witness and defendant were involved in uncharged drug transactions was admissible under Rule 404(b) to show witness's potential bias in favor of defendant).

[75] *See, e.g.,* Sanabria v. United States, 437 U.S. 54, 69, 98 S. Ct. 2170, 57 L. Ed. 2d 43 (1978).

[76] *See, e.g.,* United States v. Bowie, 232 F.3d 923, 932 (D.C. Cir. 2000) (prior acts evidence was properly admitted because it increased probability that defendant's confession was true).

- Facts tending to refute an affirmative defense.[75.1]

- Context for other properly admitted evidence.[77]

- The existence of a criminal enterprise in racketeering prosecutions.[77.1]

[b]—Preliminary Considerations

[i]—Proper Theory of Relevance[78]

Evidence of other crimes, wrongs, or acts is admissible under Rule 404(b) only if the proponent convinces the trial court that it is relevant to an issue in the case other than the actor's propensity to commit the act that is at issue in the case.[79]

When the evidence of a defendant's other acts is offered to impeach a witness with evidence of a prior inconsistent statement, Rule 613(b) governs the admissibility of the evidence, and Rule 404(b) is not involved at all.[79.1]

Although the relevance of proffered evidence of other crimes, wrongs, or acts, whether they occurred before or after the act in issue, may appear obvious, proffering counsel must be prepared with a detailed analysis of the relevance of

---

[75.1] *See, e.g.,* United States v. Verduzco, 373 F.3d 1022, 1026–1029 (9th Cir. 2004) (defendant's other activities in smuggling drugs tended to show lack of duress and were admissible other acts evidence to rebut affirmative defense of duress).

[77] *See, e.g.,* United States v. Butch, 256 F.3d 171, 175–177 (3d Cir. 2001) (trial court properly admitted, under Rule 404(b), testimony of coconspirator regarding uncharged drug theft transactions to provide necessary background information, to show ongoing relationship between defendant and testifying coconspirator, and to help jury in understanding coconspirator's role in scheme).

[77.1] *See, e.g.,* United States v. Baez, 349 F.3d 90 (2d Cir. 2003).

[78] *See* **Treatise** at §§ 404.21[2], 404.22[1].

[79] *See, e.g.,* United States v. Tse, 375 F.3d 148, 156 (1st Cir. 2004) (when defendant contended he was with specific person on date of alleged drug sale, but did not sell drugs to that person, prosecution was entitled to introduce evidence of subsequent drug transaction between defendant and that person to prove nature of relationship between them); United States v. Walker, 272 F.3d 407, 416–417 (7th Cir. 2001) (evidence of defendant's drug activities on date of charged bank robbery was properly admitted under Rule 404(b) on cross-examination of defendant's alibi witness to rebut alibi).

[79.1] *See, e.g.,* United States v. Foster, 376 F.3d 577 591–592 (6th Cir. 2004).

the evidence.[80] The proffer is not sufficient if it merely recites the list of issues contained in Rule 404(b).[81]

It is, of course, necessary that the proponent tie the evidence of other crimes, wrongs, or acts to the person against whom the evidence is to be offered; otherwise the evidence is not relevant.[82] The proponent's showing is sufficient if the jury may properly find, on a preponderance of the evidence, that the person against whom the evidence is offered committed the other act.[82.1]

[ii]—Effect of Offer to Stipulate[83]

It is sometimes argued that bad acts become irrelevant if the defendant is willing to stipulate to the issue on which they are being offered. For example, if the defendant offers a stipulation that if the prosecution proves that defendant committed the charged criminal act the defendant will not contest intent, the trial court must determine whether to admit extrinsic evidence offered on that issue. However, the Supreme Court has held that. generally speaking, the prosecution is entitled to prove its case by evidence of its own choice when the issue is an element of the charged offense, and that it need not accept a stipulation in lieu of such proof.[84]

Correspondingly, most circuits hold that a criminal defendant cannot require the prosecution to accept a stipulation that would prevent it from introducing other acts evidence to prove an element of the crime such as intent or knowledge.[85] Moreover, an offer of a stipulation is doubly doomed to failure in those circuits if it is

---

[80] *See, e.g.,* United States v. Youts, 229 F.3d 1312, 1317 (10th Cir. 2000) (proffering party must precisely articulate evidentiary hypothesis by which fact of consequence may be inferred from other acts evidence); United States v. Murray, 103 F.3d 310, 316 (3d Cir. 1997) ("it is advisable for a trial judge to insist that a party offering Rule 404(b) evidence place on the record a clear explanation of the chain of inferences leading from the evidence in question to a fact 'that is of consequence to the determination of the action' ").

[81] *See, e.g.,* United States v. Lopez, 340 F.3d 169, 173 (3d Cir. 2003) ("Unless the reason is apparent from the record, a mere list of the purposes found in rule 404(b) is insufficient"; citations and quotation marks omitted).

[82] *See, e.g.,* United States v. Sumlin, 271 F.3d 274, 279 (D.C. Cir. 2001) (record must contain evidence defendant committed "other act" for it to be admissible under Rule 404(b)).

[82.1] *See, e.g.,* United States v. DeCicco, 370 F.3d 206, 212 (1st Cir. 2004).

[83] *See,* **Treatise** at § 404.23[2].

[84] Old Chief v. United States, 519 U.S. 172, 189, 117 S. Ct. 644, 136 L. Ed. 2d 574 (1997) (prosecution entitled to prove its case by evidence of its choice "free from any defendant's option to stipulate the evidence away").

[85] *See, e.g.,* United States v. Frazier, 280 F.3d 835, 846–847 (8th Cir. 2002) (evidence of defendant's prior conviction for drug offense was admissible in prosecution for possession with intent to distribute as proof of intent and knowledge, in spite of defendant's offer to stipulate to conviction).

ambiguous or tentative.[86] Nevertheless, the trial court should consider an offer to stipulate as one of the factors in balancing the probative value of proposed other acts evidence against its probable prejudicial effect, as required by Rule 403.[87]

Other circuits have stated that a defendant may bar bad acts evidence by offering to stipulate to the element of the charged crime for which the evidence is to be offered, but generally have failed to find that the proffered stipulation was sufficiently explicit to require exclusion of the other acts evidence.[88]

There is, however, one instance in which a criminal defendant's offer of an unequivocal stipulation absolutely prevents the prosecution from introducing other acts evidence to prove an element of a charged crime. When the issue is the defendant's status as a felon, as, for example, in a prosecution that charges the defendant, as a convicted felon, with illegally possessing a firearm, the court and the prosecution must accept an offered stipulation to prevent the defendant from suffering unfair prejudice resulting from the admission of the full record of the prior felony conviction.[89]

[iii]—Proponent's Burden of Proof

Similar act evidence "is relevant only if the jury can reasonably conclude that the act occurred and that the defendant was the actor." In determining whether other acts evidence is relevant, the trial court "simply examines all the evidence in the case and decides whether the jury could reasonably find the conditional fact by a preponderance of the evidence."[90] Defendants are protected against unfair preju-

---

[86] *See, e.g.,* United States v. Davis, 181 F.3d 147, 150–151 (D.C. Cir. 1999) (court's failure to weigh defendant's proposed stipulation in Rule 403 balancing was not abuse of discretion, since stipulation was ambiguous, conditional, and tentative, and could not have substituted for proof of knowledge and intent).

[87] *See, e.g.,* United States v. Crowder, 141 F.3d 1202, 1209–1210 (D.C. Cir. 1998) (offers to stipulate must be evaluated under Rule 403 to determine if exclusion of evidence is warranted by its potential for unfair prejudice); *see* Ch. 6.

[88] *See, e.g.,* United States v. Lowe, 145 F.3d 45, 51 (1st Cir. 1998) (defendant must express clear and unequivocal offer to stipulate that covers necessary substantive ground to remove issues from case); United States v. Tokars, 95 F.3d 1520, 1537 (11th Cir. 1996) (other crimes evidence was admissible because defendants did not affirmatively take issue of intent out of contention by stipulating that they possessed requisite intent).

[89] Old Chief v. United States, 519 U.S. 172, 174, 190–191, 117 S. Ct. 644, 136 L. Ed. 2d 574 (1997) (the "most the jury needs to know is that the conviction admitted by the defendant falls within the class of crimes that Congress thought should bar a convict from possessing a gun, and this point may be made readily in a defendant's admission and underscored in the court's jury instructions").

[90] Huddleston v. United States, 485 U.S. 681, 689–690, 108 S. Ct. 1496, 99 L. Ed. 2d 771 (1988); *see, e.g.,* United States v. Bowe, 221 F.3d 1183, 1191 (11th Cir. 2000) (prosecution's burden of proof respecting extrinsic acts under Rule 404(b) is subject to preponderance of evidence standard; uncorroborated word of accomplice is sufficient).

dice not by a higher standard of proof but by the requirement of a proper purpose for the evidence under Rule 404(b), the relevance requirement of Rule 402, and the balancing of probative value against prejudicial effect required by Rule 403.[91]

[iv]—Admissibility of Prosecutions Resulting in Acquittals or Dismissals

In the *Dowling* case, the Supreme Court concluded "that neither the Double Jeopardy nor the Due Process clause barred" the use of evidence of another crime of which the defendant had been acquitted as evidence of other crimes, wrongs, or acts.[92] Similarly, it is not necessary that the actor was ever charged with a crime for evidence of other crimes, wrongs, or acts to be admissible.[93]

The failure of the government to prove criminal charges beyond a reasonable doubt in a prior prosecution does not necessarily mean that the acts cannot be proved by a preponderance of the evidence.[94] Indeed, the language of Rule 404(b), referring to other "wrongs" and other "acts," rather than simply to other "crimes," suggests the propriety of this result.[95] There must, however, be sufficient evidence in the record to permit the jury to conclude the defendant committed the "other act."[96]

On the other hand, evidence of a charge against a defendant of which the defendant was acquitted is, upon a proper objection, subject to a Rule 403 balancing analysis and may be excluded if its probative value is outweighed by undue prejudice.[97]

---

[91] Huddleston v. United States, 485 U.S. 681, 691, 108 S. Ct. 1496, 99 L. Ed. 2d 771 (1988); *see* Chs 3, 6.

[92] Dowling v. United States, 493 U.S. 342, 344, 110 S. Ct. 668, 107 L. Ed. 2d 708 (1990) (evidence relating to charge of which defendant was acquitted is not so inherently unreliable as to raise due process concerns).

[93] *See, e.g.,* United States v. Fowler, 735 F.2d 823, 830 (5th Cir. 1984) (Rule 404 refers to evidence that reflects adversely on defendant's character regardless whether there has been a conviction or indictment).

[94] *See, e.g.,* Dowling v. United States, 493 U.S. 342, 344, 110 S. Ct. 668, 107 L. Ed. 2d 708 (1990); *see also* United States v. Jones, 266 F.3d 804, 814 (8th Cir. 2001) (trial court properly admitted evidence of defendant's prior narcotics transaction under Rule 404(b), even though he was acquitted of charges arising out of that transaction in state court); *see* [iii], *above.*

[95] *See, e.g.,* United States v. Vega, 188 F.3d 1150, 1154–1155 (9th Cir. 1999) (evidence of defendant's prior legal border crossings and bank deposits was subject to Rule 404(b) even though there was nothing intrinsically improper about them).

[96] *See, e.g.,* United States v. Sumlin, 271 F.3d 274, 279 (D.C. Cir. 2001).

[97] *See* Ch. 6.

[v]—Timing of Evidence of Other Crimes, Wrongs, or Acts[98]

Evidence of other crimes, wrongs, or acts is generally admissible in criminal cases to prove a wide variety of issues.[99] Many times, the prosecution plans to use such evidence to counter an affirmative defense or to solidify its evidentiary position respecting an element of the charged offense that the defense has indicated will be a major point of contention. The question then arises whether the prosecution can use evidence of other crimes, wrongs, or acts for those purposes during its case-in-chief.

Most Circuits prefer that the trial court and prosecution defer the introduction of evidence of other crimes, wrongs, or acts until it is clear that the specific issue for which it is to be offered will be sincerely contested and that the sensitive evidence will be needed.[100] Nevertheless, when it is clear from the outset that the defense will contest a specific issue, it may be appropriate for the prosecution to present other acts evidence concerning that issue during its case-in-chief.[101]

[vi]—Other Acts Intrinsic to Crime Charged[102]

Rule 404(b) applies to evidence of "other" crimes, wrongs, or acts. It does no apply to proof of acts that are part and parcel of the charged misconduct.[102.1] Sometimes it is difficult to draw a line between the crime charged and other wrongful acts to which it is closely related in terms of time, subject matter, or content.[103] Indeed, it may be quite impossible to prove the case without revealing evidence of other crimes.[104]

---

[98] *See* **Treatise** at § 404.23[3].

[99] *See* [a], *above.*

[100] *See, e.g.,* United States v. Olsen, 589 F.2d 351, 352 (8th Cir. 1978) (admission of evidence of other crimes should perhaps have been deferred until after defendant had testified to his purported lack of knowledge during defense's case-in-chief).

[101] *See, e.g.,* United States v. Houle, 237 F.3d 71, 77 n.2 (1st Cir. 2001) (defendant placed his intent to provide security for illegal activity at issue in trial with opening statement assertion that cocaine transaction for which he agreed to provide security was "written, produced, and directed by the United States Government").

[102] *See* **Treatise** at § 404.20[2].

[102.1] *See, e.g.,* Elliot v. Turner Constr. Co., 381 F.3d 995, 1004 (10th Cir. 2004) (evidence of defendant's unpreparedness to install bridge was directly related to plaintiff's claim that defendant had negligently installed bridge, resulting in his injuries, and was, therefore, not subject to Rule 404(b)).

[103] *See, e.g.,* United States v. McGauley, 279 F.3d 62, 72–73 (1st Cir. 2002) (when indictment charged defendant with engaging in scheme to defraud and alleged three specific instances of her fraudulent receipt of funds from victims of that scheme, evidence of 217 payments from other victims of same scheme was not evidence of "other acts" under Rule 404, but was part and parcel of charged scheme).

[104] *See, e.g.,* United States v. Taylor, 284 F.3d 95, 103–104 (1st Cir. 2002) (informant's testimony concerning defendant's display of and reference to gun during drug transaction that was

The courts employ two concepts for analyzing whether the so-called "other acts" are, in fact, separate from the charged crime and, therefore, subject to Rule 404. The first is the "inextricably entwined" doctrine, under which the uncharged bad acts, if they arise from the same transaction as the charged activity, are not "other" acts and evidence concerning them is not subject to any of the restrictions of Rule 404(b).[105]

The second is the "extrinsic evidence" doctrine. Under that doctrine, if the "other act" is so closely related in time and subject matter to the charged act as to be part and parcel of the charged act, it is not extrinsic to the charged act and evidence concerning it is, therefore, not governed by Rule 404(b).[106]

The two doctrines are so closely related that they may be the same.[107]

The courts are not, however, in agreement concerning the scope of the doctrine. Thus, some courts apply the doctrine quite broadly, so that, when evidence of uncharged acts will illuminate the chronology of events leading to the acts charged in an indictment, or will inform the jury concerning the circumstances surrounding the commission of the charged crime, the uncharged acts are held not to be "other acts" subject to Rule 404's proscriptions and limitations.[108] Other courts have applied the doctrine more restrictively,[109] and have criticized the broader approach

---

subject of indictment did not concern an "other act" subject to Rule 404(b)); United States v. Carboni, 204 F.3d 39, 46 (2d Cir. 2000) (other acts occurring at same time as charged conduct were properly admitted as part of defendant's "continued effort" to commit crime charged).

[105]   *See, e.g.,* United States v. Peters, 283 F.3d 300, 313 (5th Cir. 2002) (evidence that defendant purchased cocaine in uncharged transaction was admissible under Rule 404(b) because transaction occurred in same time frame as charged conspiracy to distribute cocaine and was, therefore, "inextricably intertwined" with evidence used to prove charged conspiracy).

[106]   *See, e.g.,* United States v. Alexander, 331 F.3d 116, 126–127 (D.C. Cir. 2003) (evidence of witness's 911 call, in which he said defendant "had a gun on" the witness, was intrinsic evidence of defendant's commission of crime of being felon in possession of gun and not subject to Rule 404(b)).

[107]   *See, e.g.,* United States v. Walters, No. 02-50874, 2003 U.S. App. LEXIS 23061, at *14 n.4 (5th Cir. Nov. 12, 2003) ("Evidence qualifies as intrinsic when it is 'inextricably intertwined' with evidence of the crime charged, is a 'necessary preliminary' to the crime charged, or both acts are part of a 'single criminal episode.' ").

[108]   *See, e.g.,* United States v. Senffner, 280 F.3d 755, 764–766 (7th Cir. 2002) (defendant's misappropriation of funds, false statements to federal officials, and perjured testimony were either initial acts in charged criminal enterprise or acts undertaken to conceal charged criminal acts; thus, all were "inextricably intertwined" with charged acts and were not "other acts" for Rule 404 purposes).

[109]   *See, e.g.,* United States v. Rock, 282 F.3d 548, 551 (8th Cir. 2002) (defendant's uncharged burglary, in which he obtained weapons whose possession was basis of charged offense, was admissible under Rule 404(b) because it was directly probative of charge that defendant possessed weapons).

on the ground that it emasculates Rule 404(b).[110]

[vii]—Balance of Probative Value Against Prejudicial Effect[111]

Even if the court finds that proffered evidence of other crimes is relevant to prove something other than the defendant's propensity to commit the charged crime, admission of the evidence does not follow as a matter of course. Because of its extremely persuasive nature and its tendency to paint criminal defendants as "bad" people in need of punishment, evidence of other crimes, wrongs, or acts has the potential for also being extremely prejudicial.[112] It is, therefore, almost always necessary for trial courts considering the admissibility of other crimes evidence to balance its probative value against its prejudicial effect.[113]

In determining the probative value of proffered other crimes evidence, the courts consider such factors as the following:

- The similarity between the charged and uncharged acts.[114]

- The reliability of the evidence being proffered.[115]

- The remoteness of the other acts, in terms of time and subject matter.[116]

---

[110] *See, e.g.,* United States v. Bowie, 232 F.3d 923, 928 (D.C. Cir. 2000) ("The 'complete the story' definition of 'inextricably intertwined' threatens to override Rule 404(b)").

[111] *See* **Treatise** at § 404.21.

[112] *See, e.g.,* United States v. Boone, 279 F.3d 163, 176, n.7 (3d Cir. 2002) (other acts evidence is dangerous because, although prosecutors will not admit it, it generally is offered, in part, to impugn defendant's character, as well as to prove a legitimate consequential fact).

[113] *See, e.g.,* United States v. Hassanzadeh, 271 F.3d 574, 678 (4th Cir. 2001) (evidence of other acts is admissible under Rule 404(b) only if its prejudicial effect, "in the sense that it tends to subordinate reason to emotion in the factfinding process," does not outweigh its probative value).

[114] *See, e.g.,* United States v. Anifowoshe, 307 F.3d 643, 646, 647 (7th Cir. 2002) (when other acts are strikingly similar to charged acts, similarity increases probative value of evidence and decreases risk of unfair prejudice; here, evidence of nearly identical fraudulent scheme was properly admitted to prove identity); United States v. Franklin, 250 F.3d 653, 659–660 (8th Cir. 2001) (charged and uncharged acts need not be identical; evidence of defendant's prior arrest inside known drug house, in proximity to cocaine base, plates, and razor blades was properly admitted under Rule 404(b) in prosecution for possession of cocaine with intent to distribute following defendant's arrest outside known drug house, in possession of cocaine base, cocaine powder, heroin, and several forms of drug paraphernalia).

[115] *See, e.g.,* United States v. Peterson, 808 F.2d 969, 975 (2d Cir. 1987) (in prosecution for knowingly possessing check stolen from mail, trial court improperly admitted evidence of another check allegedly forged by defendant when there were no facts to show similarity between two incidents, there was no evidence that other check was stolen, and there was no proof that defendant's possession or endorsement of other check was unauthorized); United States v. Melia, 691 F.2d 672, 676–677 (4th Cir. 1982) (vagueness of description of other acts diminished their probative value).

[116] *See, e.g.,* United States v. Franklin, 250 F.3d 653, 659 (8th Cir. 2001) (length of time between charged incident and other act affect relevance of evidence of other act; trial court did not abuse its discretion in admitting evidence of defendant's conviction following arrest for possession

- The theory of admissibility and the nature of the consequential fact that the other acts evidence is proffered to prove.[117]

- The proponent's need for the evidence.[118] In this context, the incremental value of other crimes evidence depends on the amount of other, less sensitive evidence that is available to prove the consequential fact the other crimes evidence is offered to prove.[119]

- Whether the proponent introduced other evidence to prove the fact the "other acts" evidence was offered to prove, thus lessening the prejudicial effect of the other acts evidence.[119.1]

- The factual detail incorporated in the proponent's offer of proof.[119.2]

In general, the greater the similarity between the other acts and the charged acts, the more probative and less prejudicial is the evidence of the other acts. In almost all instances, if the other acts are very similar to the charged act, any prejudice the

---

of cocaine base in 1992 in prosecution for possessing cocaine with intent to distribute in 1997).

[117] *See, e.g.,* United States v. Mack, 258 F.3d 548, 555 (6th Cir. 2001) (evidence of high-speed police chase following uncharged bank robbery was not sufficiently probative to be admissible under Rule 404(b) as proof of identity of perpetrator of charged robberies after which there was no high-speed police chase); United States v. Harrod, 856 F.2d 996, 1002 (7th Cir. 1988) (whether prior act is close enough in time to be relevant depends on theory of admissibility; when acts were so similar to charged acts that they showed pre-existing scheme as well as knowledge and intent, acts occurring in 1981 and 1984 were not too remote).

[118] *See, e.g.,* United States v. Haywood, 280 F.3d 715, 723–724 (6th Cir. 2002) (trial court erred in admitting evidence of defendant's possession of personal use amount of cocaine as evidence of intent in prosecution for possession with intent to distribute when prosecution had substantial direct evidence of defendant's intent); United States v. Sriyuth, 98 F.3d 739, 745–746 (3d Cir. 1996) (in balancing probative value against danger of unfair prejudice, court must assess prosecution's need for challenged evidence and balance need against risk that information will influence jury to convict on improper grounds).

[119] *See, e.g.,* United States v. Delgado, 56 F.3d 1357, 1366 (11th Cir. 1996) (defendant's subsequent drug conviction was properly admissible to show intent in charged drug conspiracy; "[t]he greater the government's need for evidence of intent, the more likely that the probative value will outweigh any possible prejudice"); Morgan v. Foretich, 846 F.2d 941, 945–946 (4th Cir. 1988) (in civil suit concerning alleged sexual abuse of child, error for trial court to have excluded evidence that child's half-sister had also been sexually abused; need for other act evidence was "compelling" because "there are seldom any eyewitnesses").

[119.1] *See, e.g.,* United States v. Peters, 283 F.3d 300, 312 (5th Cir. 2002) (prejudicial effect of evidence of defendant's operation of crack house 10 years prior to charged acts did not outweigh high probative value of evidence in light of other evidence defendant was involved in charged conspiracy and was supplier of crack cocaine).

[119.2] *See, e.g.,* Manuel v. City of Chicago, 335 F.3d 592, 596–597 (7th Cir. 2003) ("evidence" of other acts of employment discrimination, consisting of witness's opinion that supervisor was "racist," based on supervisor's treatment of employees, was of limited probative value without factual details of allegedly discriminatory actions).

opponent suffers as the result of introduction of evidence of those other acts may be so minimized by an appropriate limiting instruction that admission will not be an abuse of discretion under Rule 404(b).[119.3]

Evidence of other acts may be relevant to prove a consequential fact for which the use of such evidence is appropriate under Rule 404(b), but not have significant probative value to balance against its prejudicial effect. Moreover, the proponent's use of the evidence in the trial may indicate that the trial court should not have accorded it substantial probative value in the balancing process.[119.4]

If the government has a strong case, the other crimes evidence will add little.[120] On the other hand, if the government's case depends on the credibility of an eminently impeachable witness, other crimes evidence that tends to corroborate that witness's testimony can be of vital importance, indeed.[121]

The potential for unfair prejudice that the evidence will cause the defendant must be determined and weighed against the evidence's probative value.[122] The prejudice that is to be weighed against the probative value of the other crimes evidence, of course, is not the prejudice that results from the admission of any telling piece of evidence; it is prejudice resulting from the tendency of the evidence to suggest the propriety of finding the defendant guilty not for committing the charged acts, but because he or she is a bad person and deserves to be punished.[123] Moreover, to require the exclusion of the proffered other crimes evidence under Rule 403, the

---

[119.3] *See, e.g.,* United States v. Saucedo-Munoz, 307 F.3d 344, 350 (5th Cir. 2002) ("evidence of a . . . conviction for a similar crime is more probative than prejudicial and . . . any prejudicial effect may be minimized by a proper jury instruction").

[119.4] *See, e.g.,* United States v. Crenshaw, 359 F.3d 977, 1001–1002 (8th Cir. 2004) (evidence of defendant's prior conviction was relevant to prove intent, but it did not have significant probative value for that purpose, in view of trial court's failure to charge jury it could use it to support inference of intent and government's failure to mention prior act as evidence of intent; evidence should have been excluded because of its limited probative value and large prejudicial effect).

[120] *See, e.g.,* Old Chief v. United States, 519 U.S. 172, 184, 117 S. Ct. 644, 136 L. Ed. 2d 574 (1997) (evidence setting out details of defendant's prior felony conviction was not properly admissible under Rule 404(b) in view of defendant's willingness to stipulate to status as felon in connection with charge of possession of firearm by felon); United States v. Soundingsides, 820 F.2d 1232, 1237 (10th Cir. 1987) (incremental probative value was inconsequential when compared with prejudicial effect).

[121] *See, e.g.,* United States v. Vest, 842 F.2d 1319, 1327 (1st Cir. 1988) (there was strong need for other crimes evidence that corroborated testimony of witness in case that centered to large degree on credibility of that witness; "[n]ecessity can be an important element of Rule 403 balancing").

[122] *See, e.g.,* United States v. Jenkins, 345 F.3d 928, 938–939 (6th Cir. 2003) (weak probative value of evidence that defendant used crack cocaine to show her knowledge that distributable amounts of cocaine were in packages mailed to her was outweighed by prejudice inherent in such evidence).

[123] *See, e.g.,* United States v. Roberts, 88 F.3d 872, 880 (10th Cir. 1996) (evidence is unfairly prejudicial if it makes conviction more likely because it provokes emotional response or otherwise

unfair prejudice attaching to the evidence must "substantially" outweigh its probative value.[124]

In a joint trial against multiple defendants, some of whom were not involved in the other acts, the court must consider not only the prejudice to the defendants involved in those acts but also the spill-over prejudice the other co-defendants might suffer.[125]

The trial judge has wide discretion to determine whether the probative value of Rule 404(b) evidence is outweighed by its prejudicial character.[126] Thus, the parties must be prepared to convince the trial judge of the soundness of their position at the time the evidence is offered. More important than lists of similar cases is a detailed analysis of the facts to show why the proof of other crimes is needed or why its use may be prejudicial, and perhaps how some compromise or limitation may protect both parties. Holding arguments back for the appeal is dangerous and unsound, since the appellate court may make its decision solely on the basis of the situation as it was presented to the trial judge.[127] Furthermore, the harmless error rule will apply.[128]

The proponent of Rule 404(b) evidence should bear the burden of showing that

---

tends to affect adversely jury's attitude toward defendant apart from its judgment as to guilt of crime charged); *see also* § 6.02.

[124] Fed. R. Evid. 403; *see, e.g.,* United States v. Grimmond, 137 F.3d 823, 833 (4th Cir. 1998) (unfair prejudice must "substantially" outweigh proffered evidence's probative value to merit exclusion).

[125] *See, e.g.,* United States v. Betts, 16 F.3d 748, 758 (7th Cir. 1994) (although error was harmless, admission of evidence of marijuana and other items found in home of two defendants nearly two years after charged conspiracy ended was improper under Rule 404(b) because evidence was not probative as to defendants' state of mind at time of charged event, but only proved propensity; trial court properly instructed jury that evidence was not admitted against remaining defendant); United States v. Dworken, 855 F.2d 12, 28–29 (1st Cir. 1988) (no error when trial court emphasized in instructions to jury that each defendant was to be accorded distinct, individualized treatment, and jury's verdict showed it followed instructions by discriminating among defendants and charges).

[126] *See, e.g.,* United States v. Williams, 308 F.3d 833, 837 (8th Cir. 2002) (trial court's ruling admitting Rule 404(b) evidence will be reversed only when it clearly had no bearing on disputed issues and was introduced solely to prove defendant's propensity to commit criminal acts).

[127] *See, e.g.,* United States v. Zelinka, 862 F.2d 92, 98–99 (6th Cir. 1988) (admission of evidence that defendant possessed cocaine and plastic bags seventeen months after conspiracy charged to distribute cocaine had ended was reversible error; government had failed to articulate to trial court any theory of admissibility and appellate court refused to consider government's justification for admissibility on appeal).

[128] *See, e.g.,* United States v. Murphy, 241 F.3d 447, 452 (6th Cir. 2001) (trial court's apparent failure to determine whether probative value of evidence outweighed its prejudicial effect might have been error, but, if so, error was harmless in light of overwhelming evidence of defendant's guilt); United States v. Roberts, 887 F.2d 534, 536 (5th Cir. 1989); *see also* § 2.03.

the probative value of the evidence is not outweighed by the risk of prejudice.[129]

The same considerations apply in civil cases; the unfairly prejudicial effect of the evidence must not substantially outweigh its probative value.[130]

[viii]—Requirement of Notice[131]

Rule 404(b) requires the prosecution to give "reasonable" notice of its intent to use evidence of other crimes, wrongs, or acts "upon request by the accused."[132] In the absence of a clear request for notice under Rule 404, the prosecution has no obligation to provide the defense with any advance information concerning its intentions.[133]

The Rule does not specify what constitutes "reasonable" notice, but does state that notice should be given "in advance of trial" unless "the court excuses pretrial notice on good cause shown," in which case notice can be provided during trial. The Rule is similarly silent as to what constitutes "good cause," and what form the notice should take. It is within the court's discretion to decide whether notice was sufficiently timely and complete.[134]

---

[129]   *See, e.g.,* United States v. Harvey, 845 F.2d 760, 763 (8th Cir. 1988) (in reversing conviction in tax conspiracy prosecution, court noted that prosecutors' zeal had outrun their discretion; trial court had erroneously admitted testimony about unrelated drug activities and related monetary gains in 1960s and 1970s and had not given any limiting instruction); United States v. Biswell, 700 F.2d 1310, 1317 (10th Cir. 1983) (burden is on government to show relevance of other crimes evidence to consequential issues).

[130]   *See, e.g.,* Chrysler Int'l Corp. v. Chemaly, 280 F.3d 1358, 1363–1364 (11th Cir. 2002) (trial court did not abuse its discretion in excluding evidence of defendant's fraudulent alteration of bills of lading in case alleging fraudulent diversion of funds from company defendant controlled, because there was no similarity between those acts); Mathis v. Phillips Chevrolet, Inc., 269 F.3d 771, 775–777 (7th Cir. 2001) (trial court properly excluded under Rule 404(b) evidence of plaintiff's other discrimination suits against other car dealers because its prejudicial effect outweighed its probative value in showing a plan to harass local car dealers); United Fire & Cas. Co. v. Historic Preservation Trust, 265 F.3d 722, 728–729 (8th Cir. 2001) (witness's refusal to take polygraph was inadmissible under Rule 404(b) when offered to prove reasonableness of insurance company's refusal to honor insured's claim; polygraph evidence is very low in probative value because of unreliability of test, and potential for prejudice is high).

[131]   *See* **Treatise** at § 404.23[1].

[132]   Fed. R. Evid. 404(b).

[133]   *See, e.g.,* United States v. Tuesta-Toro, 29 F.3d 771, 774 (1st Cir. 1994) (defendant's broadly worded pretrial motion for discovery of all statements referring to defendant was insufficient to put prosecution on notice that defense was requesting pretrial notification of prosecution's intent to use Rule 404(b) evidence).

[134]   *See* Fed. R. Evid. 404 1991 Committee Note (reprinted in **Treatise** at § 404App.01[2]); *see also* United States v. Green, 275 F.3d 694, 701 (8th Cir. 2001) (trial court's determination that prosecution's notice of its intent to use Rule 404(b) evidence is reasonable is reviewed for abuse of discretion).

After a sufficient request for notice from the defense, notice is required whether the prosecution intends to use the other crimes evidence as part of its case-in-chief, for impeachment, or for rebuttal. If the prosecution fails to give notice after a proper request, the evidence is inadmissible.[135]

[c]—"Other" Acts in Furtherance of Conspiracy

Acts in furtherance of an illegal conspiracy that occur during the time the conspiracy is operative are not other crimes at all; they are part of the conspiracy itself.[136] Thus, although certain specific acts are charged in a conspiracy indictment, other acts performed in furtherance of the conspiracy that are not charged in the indictment are not "other acts" for purposes of Rule 404(b).[137]

Courts sometimes admit evidence of other crimes extraneous to the charged conspiracy as relevant to the existence of the conspiracy without any meaningful analysis of how the evidence relates to any consequential fact. The evidence of extraneous acts, therefore, appears to have no impact other than proof of the defendant's propensity to engage in crime, which would violate Rule 404(b).[138]

On the other hand, the defendant's involvement in other conspiracies with a similar objective is properly and frequently admitted under Rule 404(b) to show knowledge, intent, or absence of mistake concerning the charged conspiracy.[139] The temporal proximity of the extraneous conspiracy appears to play a significant role in determining its admissibility if the extraneous conspiracy occurred after the conspiracy alleged in the indictment,[140] but its role is less significant if the

---

[135] *See* Fed. R. Evid. 404 1991 Committee Note (reprinted in **Treatise** at § 404App.01[2]; notice requirement is condition precedent to admissibility of Rule 404(b) evidence, so evidence is inadmissible if court decides that notice requirement has not been met); *see, e.g.,* United States v. Carrasco, 381 F.3d 1237, 1241 (11th Cir. 2004).

[136] *See, e.g.,* United States v. Maynie, 257 F.3d 908, 915–916 (8th Cir. 2001) (coconspirator's acts that furthered conspiracy constitute substantive evidence of the conspiracy and is not governed by Rule 404(b)).

[137] *See, e.g.,* United States v. Lanas, 324 F.3d 894, 900–901 (7th Cir. 2003) (mailings other than those charged in indictment for conspiracy to commit mail fraud were not "other acts" for purposes of Rule 404(b), because they were made pursuant to conspiracy charged in indictment).

[138] *See, e.g.,* United States v. Reddix, 106 F.3d 236, 238 (8th Cir. 1997) (testimony of witness who was robbed of drugs and speculated that appellant had something to do with those drugs was properly admitted as relevant to establish appellant's knowledge of and participation in ongoing conspiracy to distribute crack cocaine).

[139] *See, e.g.,* United States v. Alarcon, 261 F.3d 416, 424 (5th Cir. 2001) (by pleading not guilty to counts of indictment charging defendant with conspiring to possess with intent to distribute and possession with intent to distribute, defendant put his motive, intent, knowledge, and absence of mistake at issue, so evidence of prior conviction for conspiracy to possess with intent to distribute was properly admitted under Rule 404(b)).

[140] *See, e.g.,* United States v. Betts, 16 F.3d 748, 758 (7th Cir. 1994) (although error was harmless, admission of evidence of marijuana and other items found in home of two defendants

extraneous conspiracy occurred before the charged conspiracy.[141]

In cases involving conspiracies to distribute drugs, the circuits are divided in their treatment of defendants' prior convictions for possession of drugs for their personal use. Some courts have concluded that evidence of prior personal use is relevant to prove knowledge or intent in a subsequent prosecution for distribution of narcotics.[142] Other courts, however, have concluded that possession of drugs for personal use is inadmissible to establish the intent to distribute narcotics.[143]

[d]—Consequential Facts Provable by Other Crimes Evidence

[i]—Intent[144]

Evidence of other crimes, wrongs, or acts is admissible only if it is offered to prove a fact that is of consequence to the determination of the action.[145] Thus, if specific intent is an element of the crime charged, the prosecution may offer relevant other crimes evidence to prove that fact, if it is needed and not unduly prejudicial.[146]

If specific intent is not an element of the crime charged, however, when the prosecution offers other crimes evidence to prove the defendant's intent, the court must determine whether intent is at issue. If the requisite general intent can be inferred from the evidence tending to show commission of the charged act, the defendant's intent may not be genuinely contested and, therefore, evidence of other crimes, wrongs, or acts may not be admissible to prove that intent.[147] On the other

---

nearly two years after charged conspiracy ended was improper under Rule 404(b) because evidence was not probative as to defendants' state of mind at time of charged event, but only proved propensity).

[141] *See, e.g.,* United States v. Broussard, 80 F.3d 1025, 1040 (5th Cir. 1996) (trial court acted within discretion in admitting 10-year-old prior conviction for marijuana distribution in current prosecution for cocaine distribution; remoteness in time may weaken probative value of extrinsic acts evidence but does not bar its use).

[142] *See, e.g.,* United States v. Arias, 252 F.3d 973, 977–978 (8th Cir. 2001) (prior conviction for possession of personal use amount of methamphetamine was admissible under Rule 404(b) to show defendant's knowledge of purpose of conspiracy).

[143] *See, e.g.,* United States v. Haywood, 280 F.3d 715, 721 (6th Cir. 2002) (defendant's possession of small quantity of cocaine for personal use on one occasion sheds no light on whether he intended to distribute crack cocaine in his possession on another occasion); *see also* **Treatise** at § 404.22[1].

[144] *See* **Treatise** at § 404.22[1].

[145] Fed. R. Evid. 404(b); *see* [a], *above.*

[146] *See, e.g.,* United States v. Green, 258 F.3d 683, 694 (7th Cir. 2001) (when defendant is charged with specific intent crime, such as conspiracy to distribute cocaine, evidence of defendant's prior drug transactions may be admissible under Rule 404(b) to show knowledge and intent).

[147] *See, e.g.,* United States v. Linares, 367 F.3d 941, 948 (D.C. Cir. 2004) (when government's proof of possession effectively precludes jury from concluding that defendant possessed firearm but did not intend to possess it, other acts evidence of similar possession is not admissible).

hand, if it is clear from the outset that the defense will meaningfully contest the issue of intent, the issue is consequential and suitable evidence of other crimes may be admitted.[148]

The defense's assertion of defenses such as the following puts the defendant's intent sufficiently in issue to warrant admission of evidence of other crimes:

- Intoxication.[149]

- Lack of consent.[150]

- Duress.[151]

- Entrapment.[152]

- Lack of participation in the charged conspiracy.[153]

Showing that intent is a consequential fact at issue is only the first step to the admission of evidence of other crimes, wrongs, or acts. The proffering party must also persuade the court that the particular evidence offered is relevant to the issue of intent.[153.1] Other acts are not relevant to the issue of the intent to commit the particular charged act unless they are similar to the charged act. If the other acts are too dissimilar from the charged act, they merely show an intent to commit illegal

---

[148] *See, e.g.,* United States v. Houle, 237 F.3d 71, 77 n.2 (1st Cir. 2001) (defendant placed his intent at issue with assertions in opening statement, which opened door to prosecution's use of other crimes evidence to prove intent).

[149] *See, e.g.,* United States v. Haukaas, 172 F.3d 542, 544 (8th Cir. 1999) (since defendant placed element of intent into issue by contending that he was intoxicated at time of stabbing, court did not err in admitting other acts evidence to establish that he acted with requisite intent).

[150] *See, e.g.,* United States v. Holman, 680 F.2d 1340, 1349 (11th Cir. 1982) (in prosecution for conspiring to distribute illegal drugs, one defendant's claim that he had allowed son to use his boat to smuggle drugs only because of threats on son's life provided proper basis for admission of evidence of that defendant's past smuggling activities).

[151] *See, e.g.,* United States v. Verduzco, 373 F.3d 1022, 1026–1029 (9th Cir. 2004) (defendant's activities in smuggling drugs tended to show lack of duress and were admissible other acts evidence to rebut affirmative defense of duress).

[152] *See, e.g.,* United States v. Coleman, 284 F.3d 892, 894 (8th Cir. 2002) (defendant's assertion of entrapment defense makes evidence of prior bad acts admissible to show defendant's propensity to commit bad acts).

[153] *See, e.g.,* United States v. Booker, 334 F.3d 406, 412 (5th Cir. 2003) (evidence of defendant's subsequent possession of large quantity of marijuana countered defense that defendant's only interest in codefendant concerned a painting job, not charged conspiracy to distribute cocaine).

[153.1] *See, e.g.,* United States v. Plancarte-Alvarez, 366 F.3d 1058, 1062 (9th Cir. 2004) (when incident of marijuana smuggling preceded charged marijuana smuggling incident by only nine days, and involved same drug being smuggled over same border by same type of vehicle, prior incident was sufficiently similar and close in time to be probative of knowledge, absence of mistake, and intent in connection with later incident).

or dishonest acts, and evidence of them is inadmissible propensity evidence.[153.2]

The courts have articulated a number of evidentiary hypotheses that support the use of other crimes evidence as a basis for inferring intent. Since criminal intent is a state of mind inconsistent with inadvertence or accident, evidence of another crime will be admitted when it tends to undermine the defendant's innocent explanation for the act.[154] Even if the defendant did not possess criminal intent on committing an unlawful act for the first time, it may be inferred that the defendant, in the course of committing the same type of act a number of times, must have arrived at a mental state inconsistent with innocence by the time he or she committed the charged act.[155]

There is substantial overlap between intent and knowledge, and the courts often lump them together in their analyses.[155.1] In many instances the defense disputes both intent and knowledge, so that they are both consequential facts. The prosecution must then introduce evidence to prove both matters, and they are often proved by the same evidence.[156]

The courts often stress the need for similarity between the charged acts and the other crimes, wrongs, or acts used to prove intent.[157] The degree of similarity required, however, will depend on the evidentiary hypothesis the prosecution employs to justify the use of the other crimes evidence.[158] The trial judge has

---

[153.2] See, e.g., United States v. Queen, 132 F.3d 991, 996 (4th Cir. 1997) ("The similarity of the acts is what distinguishes evidence 'introduced to show a particular intent' from evidence 'introduced only to show a much more generalized intent,' such as the intent to commit illegal or dishonest acts. The former may be admissible, while the latter is not.").

[154] See, e.g., United States v. Gold Unlimited, Inc., 177 F.3d 472, 487 (6th Cir. 1999) (evidence showing that six states had notified defendants they were operating illegal pyramid schemes was admissible to disprove defendants' claim that they believed their operation was legitimate).

[155] See, e.g., United States v. Tan, 254 F.3d 1204, 1209–1212 (10th Cir. 2001) (because intent is at issue in prosecution for second-degree murder, defendant's seven prior drunk driving convictions were admissible under Rule 404(b) when victim's deaths resulted from defendant's reckless driving while intoxicated).

[155.1] See, e.g., United States v. Linares, 367 F.3d 941, 948 (D.C. Cir. 2004) (when "intent" proponent seeks to prove general intent, rather than specific intent, there is substantial overlap between "intent" and "knowledge").

[156] See, e.g., United States v. Houle, 237 F.3d 71, 78 (1st Cir. 2001) (evidence that, only four days after agreeing to provide security for charged criminal transaction, defendant agreed to provide security for another criminal transaction was relevant to issues of knowledge and intent); see also [ii], below.

[157] See, e.g., United States v. Wash, 231 F.3d 366, 369 (7th Cir. 2000) (prior bad acts involving distribution amounts of cocaine were admissible to prove intent in prosecution for possession of cocaine with intent to distribute because of similarity between charged acts and other acts evidence).

[158] See, e.g., United States v. Ruiz, 178 F.3d 877, 880–881 (7th Cir. 1999) (if acts are similar in nature to those of charged crime, even substantial gap in time may not destroy relevance of acts to determination of defendant's intent in committing charged crime).

considerable leeway in determining the sufficiency of the similarity between the charged acts and the proffered other crimes evidence, both in making the initial determination under Rule 404(b) that the evidence is relevant to a consequential fact other than propensity, and subsequently in assessing probative value in applying the balancing test of Rule 403.

[ii]—Knowledge[159]

The defendant's knowledge is in issue when it is an element of the charged crime.[160] In prosecutions for crimes such as the following, the prosecution must prove the defendant's knowledge as part of its case, and it may do so with other crimes evidence:

- The knowing possession of a controlled substance.[161]

- The knowing possession of stolen property.[162]

- The knowing possession of a firearm.[163]

- The knowing importation of obscene matter.[164]

The defendant's knowledge is also in issue when the defendant claims that he or she was unaware that a criminal act was being committed.[165] The evidentiary

---

[159] *See* **Treatise** at § 404.22[2].

[160] *See, e.g.,* United States v. Copeland, 321 F.3d 582, 596 (6th Cir. 2003) (defendant's prior arrests for possession of narcotics during course of charged conspiracy were properly admitted in prosecution for conspiracy to distribute narcotics because issue whether defendant knowingly and voluntarily entered into conspiracy is always an element of conspiracy charge and prior arrests were probative of defendant's knowledge); United States v. Hassanzadeh, 271 F.3d 574, 578 (4th Cir. 2001) (trial court properly admitted evidence of defendant's prior conviction for smuggling under Rule 404(b) in prosecution for smuggling because knowledge is always an element of smuggling).

[161] *See, e.g.,* United States v. Hodge, 354 F.3d 305, 312 (4th Cir. 2004) (in prosecution for possession with intent to distribute narcotics, evidence of defendant's earlier drug transactions was properly admitted to show defendant's knowledge of drug trade).

[162] *See, e.g.,* United States v. Hardy, 289 F.3d 608, 612–613 (9th Cir. 2002) (in prosecution for possession of stolen property, testimony of federal agent that defendant told her of his involvement in illicit real estate scheme was probative of defendant's knowledge that goods that were at issue were stolen).

[163] *See, e.g.,* United States v. Carrasco, 257 F.3d 1045, 1048–1049 (9th Cir. 2001) (evidence that defendant possessed scale with narcotics residue and empty baggies commonly used in narcotics trade was admissible under Rule 404(b) as circumstantial evidence that defendant knowingly possessed the firearm also found at time of his arrest).

[164] *See, e.g.,* United States v. Garot, 801 F.2d 1241, 1246–1247 (10th Cir. 1986) (obscene matter found in defendant's bedroom, even though it was not illegal for defendant to possess it, "was vital evidence on the essential element of defendant's knowledge that the package he received through the mail contained obscene materials.").

[165] *See, e.g.,* United States v. Rush, 240 F.3d 729, 730–731 (8th Cir. 2001) (per curiam) (prior conviction of methamphetamine possession was properly admitted to refute defense of lack of

hypothesis in such cases is the likelihood that, even if the defendant's earlier actions were innocent, repeated instances of the same wrongful behavior would result in the defendant acquiring the state of knowledge necessary to make the charged conduct criminal.[166]

The defendant's knowledge may be in issue when the crime he or she is charged with having committed involves the use of knowledge or expertise that is not available to the average person with the level of the defendant's education and experience. In such cases, other acts evidence is admissible to show that the defendant, in fact, had the requisite knowledge to have committed the charged offense.[166.1]

Even though knowledge may be an element of a crime, however, there are circumstances when evidence of other acts is not admissible to prove that element. For example, when the government's proof of possession, in a prosecution for being a felon in possession of a firearm, includes eyewitness testimony that the defendant received the weapon from another person, that the defendant later fired the weapon several times, and that he later threw it out of the window of a moving car, the evidence effectively precludes an acquittal on the ground that the government failed to prove the knowledge element of the charged crime. In those circumstances, other acts evidence of the defendant's prior possession of a gun is not admissible to prove knowledge because it is not necessary.[166.2]

[iii]—Motive[167]

Evidence of other crimes may be admissible to prove motive if a person's motive is a fact of consequence in the case.[168] Since a criminal defendant's motive is

---

knowledge that others were manufacturing methamphetamine in defendant's garage).

[166] *See, e.g.,* United States v. Martinez, 182 F.3d 1107, 1111–1112 (9th Cir. 1999) (no error to admit prior acts evidence that made "existence of defendant's knowledge more probable than it would be without the evidence"); Orjias v. Stevenson, 31 F.3d 995, 1001 (10th Cir. 1994) (evidence of defendant's prior air quality violations was admissible to show defendant's knowledge of pollution problems).

[166.1] *See, e.g.,* United States v. Walters, 351 F.3d 159, 166 (5th Cir. 2003) (portions of defendant's copy of "The Anarchist's Cookbook" were properly admitted under Rule 404(b) to show defendant's knowledge of bomb manufacturing, because they contained instructions for making bomb consisting of tamped black powder with "booby-trap" triggering mechanism, all of which were characteristic of bomb that defendant was accused of having made and exploded on a federal reservation).

[166.2] *See, e.g.,* United States v. Linares, 367 F.3d 941, 946–947 (D.C. Cir. 2004).

[167] *See* **Treatise** at § 404.22[3].

[168] Fed. R. Evid. 404(b); *see, e.g.,* Suggs v. Stanley, 324 F.3d 672, 682 (8th Cir. 2003) (trial court properly admitted under Rule 404(b) evidence of defendants' desire for property of their deceased mother as tending to show their hostility toward plaintiff, who had obtained some of that property, and thus their malicious motive in making false report to police that plaintiff had obtained

almost never an element of the crime charged, the evidentiary hypothesis behind the use of other crimes evidence as circumstantial proof of motive involves two sequential inferences: (1) to infer from the other crimes evidence that the defendant was motivated to accomplish a specified goal,[168.1] and (2) then to infer that the defendant's desire to accomplish that goal led him or her to commit the acts charged.[168.2] The prosecution must provide evidentiary support for both of these inferences for other crimes evidence to be admissible as proof of motive.[169]

Evidence of other crimes has been admitted to show the defendant's motive in circumstances such as the following:

- The defendant needed money and the charged crime involved illegal acquisition of money.[170]

- The defendant regularly sold controlled substances and the charged crime was conspiracy to import large quantities of controlled substances.[171]

- The defendant needed illegal drugs for personal use and the charged crime involved theft of money or drugs.[172]

---

it by burglary; evidence of malice was necessary to overcome qualified privilege in defamation case for reports to police and for recovery of punitive damages).

[168.1] *See, e.g.,* Hitt v. Connell, 301 F.3d 240, 249–250 (5th Cir. 2002) (trial court properly admitted, under Rule 404(b), evidence of defendant's firing of other officers involved in union activities to show defendant's motivation for firing plaintiff, who was also involved in union activities).

[168.2] *See, e.g.,* United States v. Yousef, 327 F.3d 56, 121–122 (2d Cir. 2003) (defendant's letter containing threats of bombings abroad, and against American nuclear installations, was properly admitted under Rule 404(b) in prosecution growing out of 1993 bombing of World Trade Center because it established motive of retaliating against United States for its support of Israel).

[169] *See, e.g.,* United States v. Claxton, 276 F.3d 420, 422–423 (8th Cir. 2002) (in prosecution for being felon in possession of weapon, trial court properly admitted evidence of defendant's involvement in drug transactions as evidence of his desire to protect himself, which, in turn, permitted inference that he possessed weapons found at location of his arrest).

[170] *See, e.g.,* United States v. Shriver, 842 F.2d 968, 974 (7th Cir. 1988) (citing **Treatise,** evidence of defendant's need to save his failing business proved motivation to commit crime for economic gain with which defendant was charged).

[171] *See, e.g.,* Theobald v. United States, 371 F.2d 769, 770–771 (9th Cir. 1967) (testimony relating to witness's purchase of marijuana from defendant was properly admitted in prosecution for conspiracy to import marijuana: "This evidence was offered to show motive—that appellant had reason to import a substantial quantity of marijuana because he was engaged in the sale of marijuana").

[172] *See, e.g.,* United States v. Turner, 104 F.3d 217, 222 (8th Cir. 1997) (witness's testimony that defendant had previously dealt in large amounts of cocaine base was properly admissible to prove defendant's intent, motive, and knowledge in prosecution for distributing and conspiring to distribute cocaine base); United States v. Cunningham, 103 F.3d 553, 556–557 (7th Cir. 1996) (evidence of defendant's addiction to Demerol properly admitted as evidence of motive to steal it).

- The defendant was hostile toward another person and that person was the victim of the violent crime with which the defendant was charged.[173]

- The defendant had committed, but had not yet been prosecuted for, a previous crime and the crime charged involved violence or threatened violence against persons investigating that previous crime.[174]

- The defendant had committed, but had not yet been prosecuted for, a previous crime and the and the incident at issue involved the defendant's attempts to escape responsibility for that previous crime.[175]

- The defendant had committed a previous crime against another person and the charged crime involved violence or threatened violence against that person.[176]

[iv]—Identity[177]

Evidence of other crimes is admissible as proof of identity either (1) when the evidence proves indirectly that the defendant is the person who committed the charged act, or (2) when the evidence relates directly to identity.[178] When evidence of other acts is used to prove identity indirectly, it does so through the similarities in the ways in which the charged act and the other acts were committed. The evidentiary hypothesis behind such use of other acts evidence is that the other acts and the charged act were probably committed by the same person because they exhibit extensive or peculiar similarities.[179] A defendant seeking to prove mistaken

---

[173] *See, e.g.,* United States v. Russell, 971 F.2d 1098, 1106 (4th Cir. 1992) (evidence that defendant was dishonorably discharged from Marines, had extramarital affairs and had been violent to his wife was properly admitted to show motive in prosecution charging defendant with his wife's murder).

[174] *See, e.g.,* United States v. Gilbert, 181 F.3d 152, 161 (1st Cir. 1999) (evidence that nurse was being investigated for unexplained deaths was admissible as proof of motive in prosecution against nurse for making bomb threat against persons involved in investigation).

[175] *See, e.g.,* United States v. Young, 248 F.3d 260, 271–272 (4th Cir. 2001) (evidence of defendant's prior assault on prospective witness against him was properly admitted because it indicated his motive to intimidate witnesses and thereby attempt to avoid responsibility for criminal activity).

[176] *See, e.g.,* United States v. Bufalino, 683 F.2d 639, 647 (2d Cir. 1982) (tape recording of extortion attempt was properly admitted as evidence of motive in prosecution stemming from attempt to kill person to whom threat was made).

[177] *See* **Treatise** at § 404.22[4], [5][c].

[178] *See* Fed. R. Evid. 404(b); *see, e.g.,* United States v. Joseph, 310 F.3d 975, 978 (7th Cir. 2002) (trial court properly permitted prosecution to introduce evidence of defendant's uncharged act of stealing letter addressed to another person to link defendant with other person's name, which he used as an alias in charged scheme to defraud).

[179] *See, e.g.,* United States v. Mack, 258 F.3d 548. 553–554 (6th Cir. 2001) (in light of distinctive similarities between six of ten charged bank robberies and single uncharged bank robbery

identity may take advantage of this evidentiary hypothesis to show that other crimes similar in detail to the crime charged were committed at or about the same time by some other person in support of that defense.[180]

When evidence of other acts is used to prove identity directly it does so, by and large, in combination with other evidence concerning the charged act. For example, the fact that a defendant being tried for murder possessed a certain machine gun when arrested was properly admissible as direct evidence of his identity as the murderer, since the same model of machine gun and the murder weapon had been stolen from their owner the day before the murder, at a time and place to which one of the defendants had access.[181] Similarly, a photograph of the defendant masturbating that had been seized from the defendant's home was admissible as direct identification evidence in a prosecution for public indecency in front of a minor when the defendant was identified as the person depicted in the photograph and the photograph showed a person whose manner of dress and deportment were similar to those of the person who committed the charged act.[182] Other real and testimonial evidence relating to acts other than the crime charged is used in a wide variety of circumstances to identify the defendant as the person who committed the charged crime.[183]

If there is no issue as to defendant's identity because defendant admits committing the act, then other crimes evidence should not be admissible on this theory.[184]

[v]—Plan or Design[185]

[A]— Same or Common Plan

Evidence of other crimes, wrongs, or acts is frequently admitted under Rule 404(b) as background to place the charged act in context, or because it is impossible to prove the charged act without revealing the other act. The rationale for doing

---

defendant admitted having committed, uncharged robbery was admissible under Rule 404(b) to prove defendant's identity as perpetrator of charged robberies).

[180] *See, e.g.,* United States v. Lucas, 357 F.3d 599, 605 (6th Cir. 2004) (other acts evidence offered by a defendant to prove that another person committed the charged crime is called "reverse 404(b) evidence").

[181] United States v. Bonds, 12 F.3d 540, 572 (6th Cir. 1993).

[182] United States v. Todd, 964 F.2d 925, 930–934 (9th Cir. 1992).

[183] *See* **Treatise** at § 404.22[4].

[184] *See, e.g.,* United States v. DeVaughn, 601 F.2d 42, 47 (2d Cir. 1979) (in prosecution for possession with intent to distribute and distribution of heroin, when government claimed that defendant had received quinine in exchange for heroin, it was error to have introduced evidence of defendant's subsequent possession of quinine as relevant to identity since defendant had offered to concede that he had received quinine).

[185] *See* **Treatise** at § 404.22[5].

so is the conclusion that the other crime and the charged crime were committed pursuant to the same or a common, connected, or inseparable plan, scheme, or transaction.[186] Similarly, some courts hold that uncharged acts that are "inextricably intertwined" with the charged acts are "not extrinsic" to the charged acts, and evidence of them is admissible without reference to Rule 404(b).[187] Other courts hold that other crimes that are, effectively, part and parcel of the charged crime, are admissible as "intrinsic evidence," the admissibility of which is not governed by Rule 404(b).[188]

Under either approach, it is generally necessary for the proponent to introduce evidence linking the two acts together through a common goal that the defendant hoped to achieve with the commission of each act, either separately or in combination.[189] The linkage, however, need not be compelling for the other acts evidence to be admissible under Rule 404(b).[189.1]

[B]— Continuing Plan, Scheme, or Conspiracy

Rule 404(b) permits the introduction of evidence of other acts to show that the charged act was part of an ongoing scheme or plan.[190] The cases permitting other

---

[186] *See, e.g.,* United States v. Baptiste, 264 F.3d 578, 590 (5th Cir. 2001) (uncharged murders and attempted murders were admissible in face of Rule 404(b) challenge because it was impossible to "divorce the . . . murders and attempted murders" from charge of use of firearms during and in relation to drug trafficking).

[187] *See, e.g.,* United States v. Baptiste, 264 F.3d 578, 590 (5th Cir. 2001) (evidence of uncharged murders and attempted murders was "inextricably intertwined" with, and therefore not extrinsic to, charged use of firearms during and in relation to drug trafficking and was not excludable under Rule 404(b)); *see* [b][vi], *above.*

[188] *See, e.g.,* United States v. Lipford, 203 F.3d 259, 268 (4th Cir. 2000) (shooting at officers to protect defendants' supply of drugs was an intrinsic act, inextricably intertwined with charged drug conspiracy, so Rule 404(b) was not applicable to evidence concerning shooting); United States v. Loayza, 107 F.3d 257, 264 (4th Cir. 1997) (evidence of uncharged conduct is not considered other crimes evidence if it arose out of the same series of transactions); *see also* [b][vi], *above.*

[189] *See, e.g.,* United States v. Lattner, 385 F.3d 947, 957–958 (6th Cir. 2004 (proof that defendant used brand name of "world domanation" (sic) in connection with heroin seized when he was arrested for other acts pf possession with intent to distribute coupled with proof that ink pad with "world domination" on stamp was seized when he was arrested for charged acts of possession with intent to distribute was sufficient to show same or common plan).

[189.1] *See, e.g.,* United States v. Kravchuk, 335 F.3d 1147, 1156 (10th Cir. 2003) (when both prior acts and charged crimes involved burglary of ATM machines committed by same participants and prior acts occurred only seven months before charged acts, evidence of prior acts was properly admitted under Rule 404(b) to show defendant had developed plan and stable team of participants to burglarize ATM machines).

[190] Fed. R. Evid. 404(b); *see, e.g.,* United States v. Escobar-de Jesus, 187 F.3d 148, 169 (1st Cir. 1999) (evidence of uncharged 1988 heroin transaction was admissible to show how relationship of trust had developed between defendant and cooperating codefendant, which explained why codefendant agreed to finance defendant's cocaine trafficking charged in present case).

crimes evidence to show a continuing plan reveal a wide continuum of relationships between the other crimes and the charged acts.[191]

[C]— Unique Plan, Scheme, or Pattern

The details of an other crime and the charged act may show so much similarity and individuality as to create an inference that the same person committed both of them. If, for example, the perpetrators of the other crime and the charged act dressed and acted similarly during the commission of both acts and used the same or similar weapons, there is good reason to believe the perpetrators of both acts are the same persons.[192]

Mere proof that the defendant previously committed the same type of crime as that with which he or she is now charged is not sufficient to justify the introduction of the other crimes evidence under Rule 404(b).[193] Defendants cannot be identified as the perpetrators of charged acts simply because they have at other times committed the same commonplace variety of criminal act. Any probative value of such evidence relies on the forbidden inference of propensity. The proof must show more. The similarities must be "striking" and amount to a modus operandi that can legitimately be attributed to a single perpetrator.[194]

§ 7.02   Methods of Proving Character—Rule 405

[1]—Text and Scope of Rule[1]

Rule 405 provides for three different ways of proving character: (1) by testimony as to reputation, (2) by testimony in the form of opinion or (3) by evidence of

---

[191] *See e.g.,* United States v. Smith, 282 F.3d 758, 768 (9th Cir. 2002) (defendant's prior drug dealings with alleged coconspirator were admissible under Rule 404(b) to show why coconspirator would trust defendant to participate in charged conspiracy dealing different drug); United States v. Ramirez, 176 F.3d 1179, 1181–1183 (9th Cir. 1999) (evidence of defendant's prior border crossing was properly admissible as circumstantial evidence of ongoing conspiracy between defendant and another to import narcotics).

[192] *See, e.g.,* United States v. Mack, 258 F.3d 548, 553–554 (6th Cir. 2001) (when all robberies occurred in same neighborhood and involved small banks, perpetrator was always described as young, athletic black male around six feet tall wearing bulky clothing, and perpetrator used similar commands and always collected money himself, there was sufficient similarity to warrant admission of evidence of uncharged robbery defendant admitted committing to prove defendant committed charged robberies).

[193] *See, e.g.,* United States v. Mathis, 264 F.3d 321, 329 n.2 (3d Cir. 2001) (when evidence of other acts shows differing means of execution and limited similarities do not distinguish them from similar crimes committed by others, evidence is not admissible under Rule 404(b) to prove modus operandi).

[194] *See, e.g.,* United States v. Vaughn, 267 F.3d 653, 659 (7th Cir. 2001) (modus operandi evidence must demonstrate singularly strong resemblance to crime charged to warrant inference that defendant committed other crime or was part of conspiracy to commit crimes charged).

[1] *See* **Treatise** at § 405.02.

specific instances of conduct. Which method may be used depends on the status of character in the case.

The Rule reads as follows:

Rule 405.   Methods of Proving Character.

(a)
Reputation or opinion. In all cases in which evidence of character or a trait of character of a person is admissible, proof may be made by testimony as to reputation or by testimony in the form of an opinion. On cross-examination, inquiry is allowable into relevant specific instances of conduct.

(b)
Specific instances of conduct. In cases in which character or a trait of character of a person is an essential element of a charge, claim, or defense, proof may also be made of specific instances of that person's conduct.

[Adopted Jan. 2, 1975, effective July 1, 1975; amended Mar. 2, 1987, effective Oct. 1, 1987.]

When character is a material consequential fact that must be proved,[2] permitting the introduction of all relevant evidence is most likely to yield the truth about a crucial issue. Consequently, evidence of specific instances is allowed, in addition to proof by reputation or opinion.[3]

Rule 405 does not, however, allow evidence of specific instances of conduct to be admitted to prove character in those instances in which Rule 404(a) authorizes the circumstantial use of character as a basis for inferring that the person in question acted in conformity with his or her character. Consequently, an accused, seeking to prove his or her good character pursuant to Rule 404(a)(1), may only offer reputation or opinion evidence, and the same limitation applies to proof of the character of a victim pursuant to Rule 404(a)(2).[4] Rules 608 and 609, rather than

---

[2] *See* § 7.01[2]. This concept is referred to in Rule 405(b) as circumstances in which "character or a trait of character of a person is an essential element of a charge, claim, or defense."

[3] Rule 405(b).

[4] *See, e.g.,* United States v. Smith, 230 F.3d 300, 308 (7th Cir. 2000) (in connection with claim of self defense, trial court properly admitted evidence of alleged victim's reputation for aggressiveness and violent character while excluding misdemeanor convictions for domestic battery; convictions could have been admissible if defendant knew about them at time of altercation, because they could have impacted his decision to defend himself); United States v. Waloke, 962 F.2d 824, 830 (8th Cir. 1992) (in assault prosecution with claim of self-defense, trial court properly permitted defendant to offer evidence of victim's reputation for violence after drinking, while excluding evidence of victim's specific violent acts; although proffered evidence was admissible under Rule 405(b), it was properly excluded as unfairly prejudicial, confusing, and misleading, and because admission of evidence would have resulted in numerous collateral minitrials in which government

Rule 405, govern the proof of character when used for impeachment.[5] See Chapter 12.

Rule 405 prohibits evidence of specific instances in these circumstances for practical reasons. The jury may give this evidence too much weight, or an accused may be put to the difficult task of preparing to refute numerous charges covering potentially the entire period of his life. Moreover, it is likely to lead to claims of surprise and confusion. Disputes about whether the conduct took place, and what the surrounding mitigating circumstances were, may take a great deal of time.

Rule 405 departs from customary practice in allowing proof of character by opinion testimony as well as by the traditional method of testimony as to reputation, both in cases where character is an essential element and where it is being used circumstantially as a basis for inferring that a given act was committed.

When character evidence is offered solely to attack or support the credibility of a witness, including a party, Rules 608 and 609 govern.[6]

[2]—Methods of Proving Character; Reputation[7]

When defendants elect to call character witnesses to testify to their good reputation, the testimony must relate to their reputation in the community in which they reside, although particularly in urban communities where a next-door neighbor may be a stranger, defendants' reputation in non-residential business or professional groups with which they associate is acceptable. The witness must be able to demonstrate familiarity with the defendant's reputation, and competence to speak for the relevant community.[8] The testimony must relate to a time contemporaneous

---

and defendant would have characterized each incident differently).

[5] *See* United States v. Wilson, 244 F.3d 1208, 1217–1218 (10th Cir. 2001) (cross-examination questions about defendant's prior arrests were improper impeachment in drug prosecution, since arrests are not admissible under Rule 609; questions were also not authorized by Rules 404(a)(1) and 405(a); Rule 405(b) is limited to cases in which a character trait is an essential element, and no character trait is essential in drug prosecutions; even if prosecution were entitled to rebut defense evidence of not using drugs under Rule 404(a)(1), specific acts would be improper character evidence).

[6] *See* United States v. Danehy, 680 F.2d 1311, 1314 (11th Cir. 1982); *see also* **Treatise** Ch. 608, *Evidence of Character and Conduct of Witness,* Ch. 609, *Impeachment by Evidence of Conviction of Crime.*

[7] *See* **Treatise** at § 405.03.

[8] *See, e.g.,* United States v. Wellons, 32 F.3d 117, 120 n.3 (4th Cir. 1994) (cross-examination of defense witness regarding defendant's prior rape arrest, assault charges and positive drug test proper); United States v. Perry, 643 F.2d 38, 52 (2d Cir. 1981) (the court excluded a private investigator's proffered testimony about conversations he had with persons in defendant's community since a character witness must be able to demonstrate his own familiarity with defendant's reputation). *See also* Chapter 12, *Credibility.*

with the acts charged[9] and to character traits relevant to the offense in question.[10] It is admitted despite the hearsay rule, which would ordinarily bar evidence of opinions expressed outside the courtroom, and not subject to cross-examination, primarily because reputation evidence is a convenient way of obtaining the views of a large number of people. Even in big cities, television has not completely displaced gossip, and reputation does exist as a major factor in people's lives.

Once the defendant has opened the door to consideration of his or her character by calling character witnesses under Rule 404(a)(1)[11] the prosecution may both cross-examine the defendant's witnesses and call its own witnesses in rebuttal. Rebuttal witnesses may testify only to reputation and to opinion. Testimony pertaining to specific acts by the defendant is not allowed. When cross-examining the defendant's character witnesses, however, the prosecution may ask them whether they have heard about or know about specific acts of misconduct committed by the defendant that are incompatible with the good character traits they testified to on direct.[12] Since the cross-examination is designed to test the wit-

---

[9] United States v. Lewis, 482 F.2d 632, 641 (D.C. Cir. 1973) ("Since proof of a reputation at a given time may tend to indicate what the reputation at a later time is, his or her character witnesses might have been allowed to testify as to a reputation existent during a period prior to and not remote from the offense date. On the other hand, since the community's view of the accused's character could well be affected by the gossip which frequently follows on the heels of a criminal charge, his reputation in the community after the charge became publicized might not be a trustworthy index to his actual character. For this reason, the courts have generally held that a reputation subsequent to publication of the charge on trial is not admissible in evidence") (footnotes omitted).

[10] See, e.g., United States v. Hassouneh, 199 F.3d 175, 182 (4th Cir. 2000) (since defendant claimed to have identified his package as a bomb in jest and government had to prove that defendant acted with evil purpose or motive, trial court abused its discretion in excluding as irrelevant defendant's proffered evidence of his reputation for jocularity); United States v. Angelini, 678 F.2d 380, 381–382 (1st Cir. 1982) (in a narcotics prosecution, it was reversible error to have excluded evidence of defendant's "law abidingness"; federal rule was intended to restate the common law and there is no indication of a general common law rule against the admissibility of such evidence as compared to evidence of good character generally which is excluded because it does not qualify as relating to a specific trait; however, evidence of truthfulness was properly excluded as not pertinent to the trait charged).

[11] United States v. Holt, 170 F.3d 698, 701 (7th Cir. 1999) (by calling lay witnesses to testify about his law-abiding reputation, defendant opened door for prosecution to question defendant's character); United States v. Gilliland, 586 F.2d 1384, 1389 (10th Cir. 1978) (if defendant does not use witness as a character witness, "government may not turn him into a character witness by asking him what kind of man defendant was, and then use those questions to bootstrap into the case evidence of defendant's prior convictions which it was prohibited from using in its case-in-chief.").

[12] See **Treatise** at § 405.03[2][d] for extensive discussion of the leading case of Michelson v. United States, 335 U.S. 469, 69 S. Ct. 213, 93 L. Ed. 2d 168 (1948), and subsequent cases. See also United States v. Holt, 170 F.3d 698, 700–701 (7th Cir. 1999) (after defense witnesses testified about defendant's reputation as "honest and law-abiding individual," government was properly allowed to ask if they had heard allegations that defendant was behind on child support payments and that he had engaged in sexual harassment at his workplace; "questions were relevant to determine the extent

nesses's knowledge and standards, inquiries into defendant's prior arrests and rumors are permitted. Exposing the character witnesses to a searching cross-examination is the price the defendant pays for being allowed to open up the subject of character which otherwise would have been closed for the defendant's benefit.[13]

There are some restrictions on the cross-examination. The prosecution must have a good-faith basis for asking about the specific acts allegedly committed by the defendant.[14] Some courts prohibit the prosecutor from asking character witnesses whether their favorable opinions of the defendant's reputation would change if they assumed the charges were true.[15] Rule 405 is subject to Rule 403 so that the trial court, in its discretion, may limit cross-examination when prejudice substantially outweighs probative value.[16] When requested, the court should give an instruction advising the jury of the limited purpose for which the evidence of misconduct is admitted.[17]

[3]—Method of Proving Character; Opinion[18]

When character is being used circumstantially, Rule 405 permits proof by opinion evidence.[19] This broadening of the common-law rule was intended to encourage testimony illuminating the defendant's unique characteristics in place of empty formulae equally applicable to all. Jurors may possibly be less over-whelmed by inquiries as to the defendant's misdeeds elicited on cross-examination of the character witness if the testimony on direct is more personal.[20] It may be improper to cross-examine opinion character witnesses using hypotheticals that assume the defendant is guilty of the charged crime.[21]

Opinion evidence may be offered either through lay or expert witnesses. The lay

---

of the witness' familiarity with Holt's reputation and character").

[13] *See* **Treatise** at § 405.03[2]; *see also* United States v. Weston, 279 F.3d 163, 174–175 (3d Cir. 2002) (trial court properly allowed prosecution to cross-examine defense character witnesses about concerning defendant's past drug trafficking activities).

[14] *See, e.g.,* United States v. Reese, 568 F.2d 1246, 1249 (6th Cir. 1977) (trial judge should hold voir dire examination to determine whether there were rumors about defendant buying stolen goods before allowing cross-examination).

[15] *See, e.g.,* United States v. Oshatz, 912 F.2d 534, 539 (2d Cir. 1990) (prosecution barred from asking lay character witnesses guilt-assuming hypotheticals; error here was harmless).

[16] *See* discussion in **Treatise** at § 405.03[2][e].

[17] *See* instruction from the Federal Judicial Center reprinted in **Treatise** at § 405.05[2][c].

[18] *See* **Treatise** at § 405.04.

[19] For discussion of change from the common-law rule limiting proof to reputation only, *see* Congressional Action on Rule 405, **Treatise** at § 405App.01[3].

[20] United States v. Manos, 848 F.2d 1427, 1431 (7th Cir. 1988) (both opinion and reputation witnesses are subject to cross-examination regarding specific instances of conduct).

[21] United States v. White, 887 F.2d 267, 274 (D.C. Cir. 1989) (here, it was not an abuse of discretion; opinion reviews cases).

category usually consists of persons who enjoy close, personal relationships with the defendant. The trial court will have to exercise firm control over the proceedings to insure that the witness does not relate the particular incidents on which the opinion of defendant is based—for proof of character by specific acts is still prohibited. And as with all testimony, probative value must be weighed against the countervailing factors to admissibility specified in Rule 403.

Expert testimony by a psychiatrist or psychologist that the defendant does not fit the character profile of the perpetrator of the charged acts is more questionable. Although Rule 405 poses no obstacles to the admission of testimony by experts as to the defendant's character, the defendant wishing to present such evidence faces numerous hurdles. In the first place, the evidence must meet the general relevancy test of Rule 401. Courts may be more likely to admit evidence that the defendant is sexually normal and is unlikely to have committed a crime of sexual perversion or that abusive behavior is not compatible with defendant's background than that the defendant is well-adjusted and could not have passed a bad check. The court's decision will depend on judicial evaluation of the dependability of psychiatric and other expert opinion as to the trait in question;[22] expert evidence and writings should be made available to the court to permit an informed ruling on this point.[23] The liberality of the expert evidence rules tends to encourage this type of testimony.

The expert seeking to express an opinion about the defendant's character has to be appropriately qualified pursuant to Rules 702 and 703, and the proffered testimony must meet the test of Rule 403. Opponents of psychiatric testimony have expressed concern that if the prosecution offers rebutting evidence, the resulting battle of the experts will bewilder the jury. Rebuttal testimony that causes the jury to infer that the defendant has committed similar deviant acts in the past (although testimony as to specified acts is not permitted) may seriously prejudice the defendant. An even greater risk of prejudice arises on cross-examination of the defendant's witnesses. If the witness is asked whether he was aware of particular misdeeds of the defendant so that the jury may consider his familiarity with the defendant in evaluating weight and credibility, the resulting prejudice may require

---

[22] *See, e.g.,* United States v. MacDonald, 688 F.2d 224, 227 (4th Cir. 1982) (in murder prosecution of defendant for killing his wife and children, court rejected testimony of defense psychiatrist that defendant did not possess the personality type to commit charged acts; testimony would lead to battle of experts); United States v. Staggs, 553 F.2d 1073, 1075 (7th Cir. 1977) (assault; error to exclude psychologist's testimony that defendant would be more likely to hurt himself than others).

[23] *See* United States v. Roberts, 887 F.2d 534, 536 (5th Cir. 1989) (the trial court erred in excluding a psychologist's testimony that defendant's "naive and autocratic" personality traits were consistent with defendant's reverse-sting claim that he was on a mission to ferret out drug dealers; here, harmless error).

the judge to exclude the evidence pursuant to Rule 403.[24] Once this expert testimony is admitted, however, there is an almost certain need for some specificity under Rule 703, which allows the expert to state the basis of the opinion; this should be permitted.

[4]—Methods of Proving Character; Specific Acts[25]

The limitations of Rule 405 do not apply when evidence of misconduct is offered not as circumstantial evidence of other misconduct but as evidence of some other fact in issue. See Rules 404(a) and 405(b). Accordingly, proof of specific acts committed by either the accused or the victim, or by a party in a civil action, may be introduced to evidence intent, knowledge, plan or some fact other than character pursuant to Rule 404(b).

As noted above, character witnesses for the defendant may be asked on cross-examination whether they had heard of specific acts committed by the defendant, because the inquiry is not directed toward proving the defendant's conduct but toward evaluating the witness's credibility. Moreover, when a defendant testifies to his or her own general good character or presents character witnesses to provide such evidence, the prosecution may rebut that evidence with evidence of the defendant's other acts that tend to show the defendant's general bad character.[25.1] The prosecution may not, however, ask a character witness hypothetical questions that assume the defendant's guilt of the very act with which he or she is charged.[25.2]

Evidence of specific acts is permissible to prove character pursuant to Rule 405(b) in cases in which the person's character is an essential element of a charge, claim or defense.[26] For example, when criminal defendants assert the defense of entrapment, their predisposition to commit the charged crime, and thus their character, is an essential element of the defense. To be relevant to the defendant's predisposition to commit the charged crime, however, the "other act" must be

---

[24] See **Treatise** at § 405.04[2][f] for discussion of the constitutional implications arising from expert character testimony.

[25] See **Treatise** at § 405.05.

[25.1] See, e.g., United States v. Mendoza-Prado, 314 F.3d 1099, 1105 (9th Cir. 2002) (in narcotics prosecution, defendant's evidence that he worked hard to support his family was properly countered by evidence that he stole money, harassed American tourists while a Mexican police officer, and assisted another person in escaping from prison).

[25.2] See, e.g., United States v. Shwayder, 312 F.3d 1109, 1120–1121 (9th Cir. 2002) (guilt-assuming hypothetical questions of character witness undercut presumption of innocence and therefore deprived defendant of due process of law).

[26] See, e.g., Schafer v. Time, Inc., 142 F.3d 1361, 1372 (11th Cir. 1998) (since plaintiff's character was at issue in defamation case, Rule 405(b) permitted admission of evidence about specific instances of plaintiff's conduct as it related to his character).

similar to the charged act.[27]

The victim's character is usually not an essential element of a defendant's claim of self-defense. Thus, a victim's specific acts are generally not admissible to prove that the victim was the first aggressor. If, however, the defendant knew about these prior acts at the time of the charged altercation, they might be admissible as contributing to the defendant's decision to act in self-defense.[28]

§ 7.03 Habit and Routine Practice to Prove an Event—Rule 406

[1]—Text and Scope of Rule[1]

Rule 406 allows evidence of "habit" and "routine practice," but nowhere defines these terms.[2] The Rule reads as follows:

Rule 406.   Habit; Routine Practice.

Evidence of the habit of a person or of the routine practice of an organization, whether corroborated or not and regardless of the presence of eyewitnesses, is relevant to prove that the conduct of the person or organization on a particular occasion was in conformity with the habit or routine practice.

[Adopted Jan. 2, 1975, effective July 1, 1975.]

Rule 406 and the Advisory Committee's Note make it clear that "habit" evidence concerns individuals and "routine practice" evidence concerns organizations.[3]

The principal question in connection with evidence of habit or routine practice is not the probative value of a habit or practice, but whether the evidence offered to prove habit or practice is sufficient to demonstrate an actual habitual or routine practice.[4] Moreover, habit evidence only helps prove that the person or organization acted in accordance with the habit or routine practice on the occasion in

---

[27] *See, e.g.,* United States v. Mendoza-Prado, 314 F.3d 1099, 1104 (9th Cir. 2002) (when defendant in drug prosecution claimed entrapment, his theft of money, harassment of tourists while a Mexican police officer, and role in assisting a prison escape were not admissible to show defendant's propensity to commit narcotics defenses).

[28] United States v. Smith, 230 F.3d 300, 307 (7th Cir. 2000) (because defendant did not know about alleged victim's prior convictions at time of altercation, they could not have been factors in defendant's decision-making process; thus, they were properly excluded by trial court).

[1] *See* **Treatise** at § 406.02.

[2] *See* **Treatise** at § 406 App.01[2] for a discussion of antecedents and legislative history.

[3] Fed. R. Evid. 406 Advisory Committee's Note (1972) (reproduced verbatim in **Treatise** at § 406App.01[2]).

[4] Fed. R. Evid 406 Advisory Committee Note (1972) (reproduced verbatim in **Treatise** at § 406App.01[2]).

question; it does not necessarily show the actions of others.[5]

To rise to the level of habit, a person's reactions to similar situations must be similar, frequent, and automatic.[5.1] The same rule applies to routine practices of an organization: the practice is not routine unless members of the organization react to similar situations in a similar way and the reaction is frequent and automatic.[6]

Thus, evidence of past actions does not show a habit when it merely demonstrates that a person acted in a particular way a few times in the past.[7] On the other hand, testimony that an individual regularly engages in particular conduct may be sufficient to show a habit.[8] Similarly, evidence that members of an organization acted in a particular way in the past must also show sufficient frequency and regularity to constitute a routine practice by the organization.[9]

The extent to which a specific reaction to a given situation is automatic, rather than voluntary, is also important to the determination whether evidence is sufficient to show an individual's habit.[10] Similarly, when the question is whether evidence

---

[5] *See, e.g.,* Griffin v. Acacia Life Ins. Co., 151 F. Supp. 2d 78, 80–81 (D.D.C. 2001) (law office's practice of entering filing deadlines on calendar would support inference that lawyer believed filing deadline was on date indicated on calendar, but was questionable evidence that client told lawyer she received right to sue letter 90 days before indicated date, and was no evidence that client actually received letter at that time).

[5.1] *See, e.g.,* Bowman v. Corrections Corp. of Am., 350 F.3d 537, 549 (6th Cir. 2003) ("before a court may admit evidence of habit, the offering party must establish the degree of specificity and frequency of uniform response that ensures more than a mere 'tendency' to act in a given manner, but rather, conduct that is 'semi-automatic' in nature").

[6] *See* Fed. R. Evid 406 Advisory Committee Note (1972) (reproduced verbatim in **Treatise** at § 406App.01[2]); Bell v. Consolidated Rail Corp., 299 F. Supp. 2d 795, 801 (N.D. Ohio 2004) (statements that "it was not uncommon [or] unusual" for defrosters in locomotives to be non-functioning were insufficient to show that defendant routinely provided its trainmen with locomotives with inoperable defrosters).

[7] *See, e.g.,* Camfield v. City of Okla. City, 248 F.3d 1214, 1232–1233 (10th Cir. 2001) (trial court did not err in excluding proffered habit evidence showing, at best, that individual had acted in specific way six times).

[8] *See, e.g.,* United States v. Ware, 282 F.3d 902, 906–907 (6th Cir. 2002) (insurance agent's testimony that he routinely interviews applicants for insurance and observes them sign application was sufficient to prove his habit of doing so and to permit inferences by jury that he followed his routine procedure in connection with defendant's application and that defendant signed application).

[9] *Compare, e.g.,* Becker v. ARCO Chem. Co., 207 F.3d 176, 203 (3d Cir. 2000) (trial court committed reversible error in admitting, as evidence of routine practice, testimony that on one occasion employer had fabricated reasons to justify employee's termination) *with, e.g.,* United States v. Santa, 180 F.3d 20, 29 (2d Cir. 1999) (evidence of police department's practice of dealing with misdirected vacatur requests supported finding that department had handled request in issue according to its practice).

[10] *See, e.g.,* Diehl v. Blaw-Knox, Inc., 360 F.3d 426, 433 n.5 (3d Cir. 2004) (remedial measure taken by person charged with liability before injury that is basis of liability claim is not subsequent measure evidence that is barred by Rule 407).

shows an organization's routine practice, evidence that the organization had a rule or policy prescribing the actions its members should take in response to a given situation is significant.[11]

Evidence of habit must also demonstrate that both the individual's response and the situations to which the individual habitually responds are specific.[12]

Adequacy of sampling and uniformity of response are also key factors in assessing proffered evidence of habit or routine practice.[13] There are no precise standards for the number of times a specific response has to occur in reaction to a particular situation, but the evidence must support a conclusion that the person's conduct is a consistent and reflexive manner of responding to a particular stimulus.[14]

As is the case with other questions of relevance, admissibility of habit or routine practice evidence depends in large part on the trial judge's evaluation of the particular facts of the case. Consequently, appellate courts will accord great deference to the trial court's discretionary judgment.[15]

[2]—Habit and Routine Practice in Business and Organizations[16]

Courts are inclined to leniency in admitting evidence of business custom.[17]

This leniency results from the difference between business organizations and individuals. Both the very existence and the profitability of most business organizations depend on their employees' performance of routine tasks in the same way every time. This motivation to perform routine tasks in a routine fashion provides reliability and trustworthiness for evidence of their routine practices.

An objection to evidence of business practices should be made on the basis of sufficiency of the proof, not admissibility, except when low probative value ac-

---

[11] *See, e.g.,* United States v. Newman, 982 F.2d 665, 669 (1st Cir. 1992).

[12] *See, e.g.,* Diehl v. Blaw-Knox, Inc, 360 F.3d 426, 430 (3d Cir. 2004).

[13] *See, e.g.,* United States v. Newman, 982 F.2d 665, 669 (1st Cir. 1992) (trial court did not err in excluding testimony that witness had observed 75-100 instances of prisoners being handcuffed to cell bars and had never seen any cuffed to first bar, because of likelihood of large number of unobserved instances, so that sampling and uniformity of response were inadequate).

[14] *See, e.g.,* Babcock v. General Motors Corp., 299 F.3d 60, 66 (1st Cir. 2002) (testimony of three witnesses who had often ridden in automobiles with decedent driver that he always fastened his seat belt was sufficient evidence of habit to warrant submission to jury of question whether decedent had his seat belt buckled at time of fatal accident).

[15] *See, e.g.,* Loughan v. Firestone Tire & Rubber Co., 749 F.2d 1519, 1524 (11th Cir. 1985).

[16] *See* **Treatise** at § 406.03.

[17] Vining v. Enterprise Financial Group, Inc., 148 F.3d 1206, 1218 (10th Cir. 1998) (report about insurer's business practices was relevant to conduct at issue under Rule 406 because it showed that insurer engaged in "pervasive, consistent pattern of abusive rescissions").

companied by the danger of resulting prejudice, confusion, or waste of time mandates exclusion pursuant to Rule 403.[18] The broad definition of a business in Rule 803(6) applies in defining a business custom.

Courts have been divided as to the quantum of proof necessary for a proper foundation for the inference that the custom was followed. Generally, if a jury might be persuaded that the custom was followed, evidence of it ought to be admitted.[19]

Some cases have admitted evidence of business transactions between one of the parties and a third-party as tending to prove that the same bargain or proposal was made in the litigated situation.[20] Such evidence should not be admitted as showing a routine practice when similarities are weak and comparisons strained.[21] Subsidiary evidence of parallelism must be strong and convincing when dealing with third-party situations, and the court will be less likely to admit than when dealing with transactions between the same parties.[22]

[3]—Habit and Routine Practice in Negligence Cases[23]

Evidence of habit or custom is offered in a variety of situations in negligence cases and may involve the an individual's habits or the routine practice of an organization.[24] For example, a defendant may wish to introduce such evidence to

---

[18] *See, e.g.,* Utility Control Corp. v. Prince William Constr. Co., 558 F.2d 716, 721 (4th Cir. 1977) (alternatively holding that habit evidence should have been excluded pursuant to Rule 403).

[19] *See, e.g.,* Bouchat v. Baltimore Ravens, Inc., 241 F.3d 350, 354 (4th Cir. 2000) (testimony that it was routine for organization to forward incoming faxes addressed to individual to that person's other office was sufficient to establish routine practice and to warrant jury's inference that fax at issue in instant litigation was forwarded in accordance with that practice).

[20] *See, e.g.,* Rosenburg v. Lincoln Am. Life Ins. Co., 883 F.2d 1328, 1336 (7th Cir. 1989) (testimony relating to the routine practice of an insurance company's agents in giving oral assurances that coverage was effective immediately despite written conditions to the contrary).

[21] Simplex, Inc. v. Diversified Energy Sys., Inc., 847 F.2d 1290, 1293–1294 (7th Cir. 1988) (it was not error to exclude evidence of plaintiff's late and inadequate performance of other contracts; behavior does not approach the "level of specificity necessary to be considered semi-automatic conduct" and, in addition, defendant failed to allege adequately the frequency of the alleged conduct).

[22] *See* Seven Provinces Ins. Co. Ltd. v. Commerce & Indus. Ins. Co., 65 F.R.D. 674, 689 (W.D. Mo. 1975) (evidence of payments by other reinsurer offered by plaintiff to establish custom and usage with respect to duration of provisional binders rejected because it would have led to litigation of collateral issues).

[23] *See* **Treatise** at § 406.04.

[24] The Advisory Committee's endorsement of McCormick's distinction between habit and character indicates that evidence of prudence or carefulness, or, conversely, recklessness or carelessness, should not be admitted unless these traits manifest themselves in some specific response to a regularly repeated situation. The result as to admissibility may, therefore, under Rule 406, be somewhat more stringent than in jurisdictions adhering to rules where courts tend not to be

prove that the plaintiff was contributorily negligent because he was intoxicated,[25] that a claimed dangerous condition could not have existed,[26] or could not have been known[27] or that there was informed consent.[28] The plaintiff may wish to introduce such evidence to prove that the defendant had a duty to warn of impending danger,[29] or that he or she had a right to rely on the defendant's previous warnings,[30] and that, consequently, the plaintiff was not guilty of contributory negligence. Or the plaintiff may resort to custom in order to identify the defendant as the wrongdoer.[31]

Evidence of habit or custom is frequently introduced in negligence cases in order to establish a standard of conduct or care. This usage is not governed by Rule 406 since the evidence is not being introduced to prove that a person acted in conformity with the habit. Admissibility would be pursuant to the general relevancy Rules 401 to 403.[32]

---

as strict in their definition of habit. If, however, the admission of what theoretically is character rather than habit evidence is due to a state's substantive policy favoring recovery by plaintiffs in wrongful death actions where no witnesses are present, but plaintiff has the burden of proving freedom from contributory negligence, the thrust of the Erie decision argues for admission despite Rule 406. See **Treatise** at § 1101.04[2].

[25] *See* Loughan v. Firestone Tire & Rubber Co., 749 F.2d 1519, 1523 (11th Cir. 1985) (trial court properly admitted evidence from plaintiff, his employer, and his supervisor to establish plaintiff's drinking habit).

[26] *See, e.g.,* Hambrice v. F.W. Woolworth Co., 290 F.2d 557, 558 (5th Cir. 1961) (defendant's employee permitted to testify as to his "habit" of sweeping the floor every morning).

[27] *See, e.g.,* Eaton v. Bass, 214 F.2d 896, 899 (6th Cir. 1954) (testimony as to the custom of the company to check every unit before it was sent on the road was sufficient to take the question of negligence to the jury, even though defendant's witness "had no records or personal knowledge about the check which was given the particular truck involved in the accident.").

[28] Salis v. United States, 522 F. Supp. 989, 995 n.4 (M.D. Va. 1981) (treating physician who could not remember why he selected particular course of conduct could testify about his normal practice).

[29] *See, e.g.,* Stratton v. Southern Ry., 190 F.2d 917, 918–919 (4th Cir. 1951) (because defendant-railroad would have had duty to warn people crossing between cars if it had notice of the practice, plaintiff should have been allowed to introduce evidence of the practice).

[30] *See, e.g.,* Kozman v. Trans World Airlines, 236 F.2d 527, 531–532 (2d Cir. 1956) (action against airline by window cleaner who was injured when TWA revved up plane engines without warning so that air blast and sound waves knocked down plaintiff and ladder on which he was working; "error" to exclude evidence of a custom or habit on the part of TWA's employees to warn the window washers at the hangar of the proposed operation).

[31] *See, e.g.,* Mahoney v. New York Cent. R.R., 234 F.2d 923, 924–925 (2d Cir. 1956) (railroad employee injured by piece of wire protruding from gondola car; claim against Universal Pipe based on its alleged negligence in unloading the car without removing the wire; the car had been picked up from Universal a few hours prior to the accident; plaintiff should have been allowed to show that there was a general custom of securing the type of shipment Universal had just unloaded by means of wires attached to sides of gondola).

[32] *See* Chapter 6.

[4]—Methods of Proof[33]

Rule 406 provides for the admission of habit evidence despite the existence of eyewitnesses to the event.[34]

The Rule also specifically provides that evidence of routine practices may be admitted "whether corroborated or not." The effect of this language is that evidence of one witness or admitted document evidencing the custom will suffice as evidence of the custom.[35] Proof of custom may, therefore, be used even when the person who engaged in the routine practices is unavailable to testify. Even if the person is available, another witness may testify to the custom, although probative force will usually be enhanced by having the person testify as to his or her own custom. Thus, for example, a proponent need not offer the testimony of the actual clerk who mailed an item in order to establish that it was in fact mailed.[36] Similarly, in a denaturalization case[37] in which the government sought to divest the defendant of his citizenship on the ground that he had concealed his criminal record, a former INS employee was permitted to testify that the checkmarks and initials on the defendant's application indicated that the actual examiners asked the defendant questions relating to arrests and received the same answers that the defendant had given in writing.

§ 7.04 Subsequent Repairs—Rule 407

[1]—Text and Theory of Rule[1]

Rule 407 codifies the almost uniform practice of American courts of excluding evidence of subsequent remedial measures as an admission of fault.

Rule 407. Subsequent Remedial Measures.

---

[33] *See* **Treatise** at § 404.06.

[34] For a discussion of Rule 406's rejection of the eyewitness rule, *see* **Treatise** at § 406.05.

[35] *See, e.g.,* United States v. Ware, 282 F.3d 902, 906–907 (6th Cir. 2002) (insurance agent's testimony that he routinely interviews applicants for insurance and observes them sign application was sufficient to prove his habit of doing so and to permit inferences by jury that he followed his routine procedure in connection with defendant's application and that defendant signed application).

[36] *See, e.g.,* Envirex, Inc. v. Ecological Recovery Assocs., Inc., 454 F. Supp. 1329, 1333 (M.D. Pa. 1978), *aff'd mem.,* 601 F.2d 574 (3d Cir. 1979) (in a dispute over whether a complete contract was sent to defendant, an officer of the plaintiff-corporation was permitted to testify that as part of its routine business practice plaintiff would have sent a complete proposal).

[37] United States v. Oddo, 314 F.2d 115, 117 (2d Cir. 1963). *See also* United States v. Quezada, 754 F.2d 1190, 1195–1196 (5th Cir. 1985) (in addition to admitting physical evidence that defendant had been served with a warrant of deportation, INS agent was permitted to testify about "normal procedures followed in executing a warrant . . . [, even though] he had never personally observed the execution of a warrant").

[1] *See* **Treatise** at §§ 407.02, 407.03.

When, after an injury or harm allegedly caused by an event, measures are taken that, if taken previously, would have made the injury or harm less likely to occur, evidence of the subsequent measures is not admissible to prove negligence, culpable conduct, a defect in a product, a defect in a product's design, or a need for a warning or instruction. This rule does not require the exclusion of evidence of subsequent measures when offered for another purpose, such as proving ownership, control, or feasibility of precautionary measures, if controverted, or impeachment.

[*Adopted Jan. 2, 1975, effective July 1, 1975; amended Apr. 11, 1997, effective Dec 1, 1997.*]

The Advisory Committee gave two reasons in support of Rule 407. The first, an evidentiary rationale, rests on the ground that post-accident remedial measures are not an admission of fault, because they are as consistent with mere accident as they are with the fault of the party effecting the remedial measures. The second reason is grounded in the public policy of not discouraging people from taking steps in furtherance of increased safety.[2]

The public policy support for the exclusion of evidence of subsequent remedial measures may lead to the applicability of state, rather than federal, evidentiary rules respecting matters as to which state law provides the rule of decision. Thus, if state law controls the determination of a products liability suit and provides that evidence of subsequent remedial measures is admissible on the issue of strict liability, the state evidentiary rule is applicable, rather than Rule 407's exclusionary rule.[3]

The Rule is intended to apply to any post-accident[4] change, repair or precaution[5] when it is offered as evidence of another party's liability for damages.[5.1] Rule 407

---

[2] Fed. R. Evid. 407 Advisory Committee's Note (1972) (reproduced verbatim in **Treatise** at § 407App.01[2]).

[3] *See, e.g.*, Moe v. Avions Marcel Dassault-Breguet Aviation, 727 F.2d 917, 932 (10th Cir. 1984) ("the purpose of Rule 407 is not to seek the truth or to expedite trial proceedings; rather, in our view, it is one designed to promote state policy in a substantive law area"); Garcia v. Fleetwood Enters., 200 F. Supp. 2d 1302, 1305 (D.N.M. 2002) (New Mexico law concerning admissibility of evidence of subsequent remedial measures governs in products liability suit).

[4] J.B. Hunt Transp., Inc. v. General Motors Corp., 243 F.3d 441, 445 (8th Cir. 2001) (Rule 407 precludes admission of evidence of defendant's post-accident design change to prove fault).

[5] *See, e.g.*, Reddin v. Robinson Prop. Group, 239 F.3d 756, 759 (5th Cir. 2001) (evidence that after accident defendant's employees taped off site of plaintiff's fall was properly excluded under Rule 407, even though it was offered to impeach evidence that defendant's employees examined accident site and found no defect that could have caused accident).

[5.1] *See, e.g.*, HDM Flugservice GmbH v. Parker Hannifin Corp., 332 F.3d 1025, 1034 (6th Cir. 2003) (trial court properly excluded, under Rule 407, evidence that defendant, after plaintiff's accident, issued warning to users of its helicopter landing gear to use inspection method not mentioned in defendant's maintenance manual); Hickman v. Gem Ins. Co., 299 F.3d 1208, 1214

is broad enough to cover such diverse situations as the discharge of the employee responsible for the accident,[6] a change in company operating procedures or rules,[7] or the removal of a hazardous condition from the premises where the accident took place.[8]

Post-event tests or reports relating to the incident in question are generally held to be outside the scope of Rule 407, however, on the basis that they are conducted or prepared for the purpose of investigating the cause of the accident. They can rarely be characterized as "measures" that, if conducted previously, would have reduced the likelihood of an accident.[9]

The Advisory Committee has noted that the words "an injury or harm allegedly caused by" were added to the 1997 amendment to clarify that the Rule applies only to changes made after the occurrence that produced the damages giving rise to the action. Evidence of measures taken by the defendant prior to the event causing injury or harm do not fall within the exclusionary scope of Rule 407 even if they occurred after the manufacture or design of the product.[10] This rejects the minority view that applied Rule 407 to exclude evidence of pre-accident conduct to further the Rule's policy of encouraging safety precautions.[11]

Moreover, Rule 407 does not require the exclusion of subsequent remedial measures taken by a nondefendant. The policy behind Rule 407 of encouraging safety precautions is not furthered by excluding measures taken by persons not party to the suit. The logic behind this exception is that a nondefendant will not be inhibited from taking remedial measures if the measures are used against a defendant.[12] However, if Rule 407 is inapplicable, courts still have discretion to

---

(10th Cir. 2002) (trial court properly excluded, on basis of Rule 407, evidence that, after filing of instant action claiming that limiting reimbursement of hospital charges was abuse of fiduciary's discretion, defendant eliminated its limitation for such charges).

[6] *Cf.* Elliot v. Webb, 98 F.R.D. 293, 298 (D. Idaho 1983) (records and transcripts of disciplinary and reinstatement hearings fall within the Rule because they appeared to be essentially remedial in nature).

[7] Mills v. Beech Aircraft Corp., 886 F.2d 758, 762 (5th Cir. 1989) (revised shop manual).

[8] O'Dell v. Hercules, Inc., 904 F.2d 1194, 1205 (8th Cir. 1990) (plaintiffs sued the manufacturer of Agent Orange, alleging exposure to dioxin; the trial court correctly required that plaintiffs redact references to voluntary remediation in a study from the Centers for Disease Control).

[9] *See* McFarlane v. Caterpillar, Inc., 974 F.2d 176, 181–182 (D.C. Cir. 1992) (report on condition of hydraulic system before accident was not remedial measure).

[10] *See, e.g.,* Bogosian v. Mercedes-Benz of North America, Inc., 104 F.3d 472, 481 (1st Cir. 1997) (Rule 407 "does not apply where, as here, the modification took place before the accident that precipitated the suit").

[11] *See* Kelly v. Crown Equip. Co., 970 F.2d 1273, 1276–1277 (3d Cir. 1992) (excluding evidence or pre-accident conduct in failure-to-warn case under Rule 407).

[12] *See* TLT-Babcock, Inc. v. Emerson Elec. Co., 33 F.3d 397, 400 (4th Cir. 1994) (repairs performed by someone other than defendant admissible).

exclude evidence of actions by nonefendants pursuant to the general relevancy requirements of Rules 401, 402, and 403.[13]

Additionally, some courts do not apply Rule 407 to remedial measures taken pursuant to a governmental mandate.[14] This exception recognizes that the rule's policy goal of encouraging remediation does not apply when remedial action is mandated by a superior governmental authority.

[2]—Products Liability[15]

Rule 407 was amended in 1997 to provide that evidence of post-accident remedial measures is inadmissible in strict liability cases to prove a defect in a product, a defect in a product's design, or a need for a warning or instruction. This provision follows the practice in virtually all of the federal courts, in which Rule 407 has been applied to bar evidence of subsequent repairs in product liability actions.[16] Even the two circuits that held that Rule 407 does not bar evidence of subsequent remedial measures in strict liability cases seemed poised to reexamine their position.[17] The amendment also follows the practice in prescription drug warning cases, in which courts have held that Rule 407 applies to bar evidence of subsequently changed warnings when the actions are premised on a failure-to-warn theory, because of the close similarity between negligence and whether a warning is adequate.[18]

Of course, the exceptions specified in Rule 407 that allow evidence of subsequent measures to be admitted for other purposes also apply in products liability actions,

---

[13] *See, e.g.,* Keller v. United States, 38 F.3d 16, 31 (1st Cir. 1994) (excluding evidence of repair by nondefendant was not reversible error since evidence of remedial measures is only marginally relevant); *but see* Polec v. Northwest Airlines, Inc., 86 F.3d 498, 529–530 (6th Cir. 1996) (distinguishing cases admitting measures taken by nondefendants on ground that they involve nonparties, and plaintiff might be improperly motivated by desire to create helpful evidence); Mehojah v. Drummond, 56 F.3d 1213, 1215 (10th Cir. 1995) (distinguishing cases admitting measures taken by third parties on ground that they did not involve potential defendants).

[14] *See, e.g.,* O'Dell v. Hercules, Inc., 904 F.2d 1194, 1203–1205 (8th Cir. 1990) (but not applying exception to voluntary remediation).

[15] *See* **Treatise** at § 407.08.

[16] *See, e.g.,* Wood v. Morbark Industries, Inc., 70 F.3d 1201, 1206–1207 (11th Cir. 1995) (applying Rule 407 to unreasonably dangerous design of wood chipper is proper balance).

[17] *See* Burke v. Deere & Co., 6 F.3d 497, 506 (8th Cir. 1993) (noting that perhaps the issue should be revisited *en banc*); Huffman v. Caterpillar Tractor Co., 908 F.2d 1470, 1481–1482 (10th Cir. 1990) (court acknowledged that most circuits disagree with minority approach to applicability of Rule 407 in strict liability actions, but concluded that this was not proper case to reconsider its opinion).

[18] *See, e.g.,* Stahl v. Novartis Pharms. Corp., 283 F.3d 254, 271 n.10 (5th Cir. 2002) (post-1997 version of prescription drug package insert containing warning of potential liver damage resulting from use of pharmaceutical cannot be used as evidence that pre-1997 instructions not containing that warning were inadequate).

pursuant to the second sentence of the Rule,[19] as do the general standards of relevancy and prejudice under Rules 401 and 403.[20]

[3]—Recall Letters

Rule 407 was amended in 1997 to clarify that the Rule applies to letters sent by automobile manufacturers to car owners notifying them of possible defects. Less clear, however, is the way in which the mandatory nature of such letters might affect their admissibility. A court has noted that because manufacturers are required by federal law to send out recall notices, it is "unreasonable to assume that the manufacturers will risk wholesale violation of the National Traffic and Motor Vehicle Safety Act and liability for subsequent injuries caused by defects known by them to exist in order to avoid the possible use of recall evidence as an admission against them."[21] Moreover, an exception to Rule 407 has been recognized for "evidence of remedial action mandated by superior governmental authority because the policy goal of encouraging remediation would not necessarily be furthered by exclusion of such evidence."[22] Courts faced with the recall letter issue have not reached consistent results.[23]

[4]—Exceptions[24]

[a]—Proving Other Material Facts

Rule 407 precludes the use of evidence of subsequent remedial measures only when offered to prove negligence or other culpable conduct. The second sentence

---

[19] *See, e.g.,* Wood v. Morbark Industries, Inc., 70 F.3d 1201, 1206–1207 (11th Cir. 1995) (exceptions under Rule provide adequate balance to prevent defendants from taking unfair advantage of Rule).

[20] *See, e.g.,* Middleton v. Harris Press and Shear, Inc., 796 F.2d 747, 751–752 (5th Cir. 1986) (court has discretion to exclude evidence not barred by Rule 407 under Rule 403); *see also* Chapter 6.

[21] Farner v. Paccar, Inc., 562 F.2d 518, 527 (8th Cir. 1977).

[22] O'Dell v. Hercules, Inc., 904 F.2d 1194, 1203–1205 (8th Cir. 1990) (but not applying exception to *voluntary* remediation).

[23] *Compare* Rozier v. Ford Motor Co., 573 F.2d 1332, 1343 (5th Cir. 1978) (document prepared by defendant in anticipation of a revised safety standard to be required by National Highway Traffic Safety Administration did not meet exclusion rationale of Rule 407) *with* Chase v. General Motors Corp., 856 F.2d 17, 21–22 (4th Cir. 1988) (evidence of actual recall of plaintiffs' vehicle after date of accident must be excluded as a subsequent remedial measure in a products liability case which the circuit holds is barred by Rule 407) *and* Vockie v. General Motors Corp., 66 F.R.D. 57, 61 (E.D. Pa.), aff'd mem., 523 F.2d 1052 (3d Cir. 1975) (automobile manufacturer's recall letter excluded in trial charging manufacturer with negligent design: "If such statements are admissible on a wholesale basis, manufacturers will be reluctant to come forth and make a full unqualified disclosure of any potential safety hazards which they discover"; court also noted that "[s]uch evidence has minimal probative value to the existence of a defect in a particular vehicle.").

[24] *See* **Treatise** at § 407.04.

of the Rule explicitly recognizes that such evidence may be admissible to prove other material facts in issue.[25]

In applying the exceptions, particularly in the case of feasibility and impeachment, care should be taken that a mechanical reliance on the permissible uses specified in Rule 407 does not subvert the policy goals the Rule is designed to promote. Prejudice and waste of time remain for consideration under Rule 403.

[b]—Control or Ownership

Evidence of subsequent remedial measures is admissible to prove control or ownership of the place or object causing the injury. In addition, a photograph, taken the day after an accident, may be admitted if it serves to acquaint the jury with the scene, and no more neutral pictures are available, even though it indicates that repairs were made.[26] This situation presents a typical Rule 403 problem requiring the exercise of discretion and an instruction to the jury.

[c]—Feasibility

Rule 407 explicitly permits evidence of subsequent remedial measures to be used to show the feasibility of precautionary measures when the issue is controverted.[27] This exception is troublesome because the feasibility of a precaution may bear on whether it was negligent not have taken the precaution; thus, negligence and feasibility are often not distinct issues.[28] There is no difficulty when the defendant opens up the issue by claiming either that all possible care was being exercised at the time of the accident or that further precautionary measures were not practicable or feasible.[29] By raising the issue of feasibility, the defendant in effect has waived the protection of Rule 407, for it would be unfair not to allow the plaintiff to meet

---

[25] Rimkus v. Northwest Colo. Ski Corp., 706 F.2d 1060, 1065–1066 (10th Cir. 1983) (evidence of defendant's subsequent remedial measures admissible to rebut contributory negligence defense and to refute testimony); Wetherill v. University of Chicago, 565 F. Supp. 1553, 1559 (N.D. Ill. 1983) (subsequent released publications containing warnings admissible to prove causation).

[26] See, e.g., Jaeger v. Henningson, Durham & Richardson, Inc., 714 F.2d 773, 776 (8th Cir. 1983) (district court did not err in admitting photographs that were offered to show what the original specifications required).

[27] See Reese v. Mercury Marine Div. of Brunswick Corp., 793 F.2d 1416, 1429 (5th Cir. 1986) (manufacturer's subsequent warnings were admissible to rebut defendant's claim that only the retailer could properly instruct the ultimate consumer).

[28] See, e.g., Rimkus v. Northwest Colo. Ski Corp., 706 F.2d 1060, 1064 (10th Cir. 1983) (no abuse of discretion to admit evidence of defendant's subsequent remedial measures when jury was instructed that evidence was admissible as to feasibility and not to be considered as bearing on defendant's negligence).

[29] Anderson v. Malloy, 700 F.2d 1208, 1213 (8th Cir. 1983) (defendants controverted feasibility when they testified that peepholes and chains would not be useful but would provide false sense of security, because "[w]hether something is feasible relates not only to actual possibility of

the issue by showing the defendant's conflicting conduct—the subsequent remedial measures.[30] When the defendant has not raised the issue, however, the trial court should consider whether the offer of evidence is not designed merely to permit the jury improperly to infer negligence and whether the standards of Rule 403 are met.[31] Moreover, it is error to admit evidence of post-accident remedial measures as proof of feasibility when the party against whom the evidence is offered has stipulated to feasibility.[32]

[d]—Proof of Conditions

Another situation permitting a justifiable use of evidence of repairs involves a defendant's attempt to use proof of conditions at the time of the trial to prove the non-existence of a dangerous condition. It is obvious that plaintiff should, in rebuttal, be able to show that conditions have changed in material respects since the accident's occurrence.[33] If the jury has been apprised of the conditions of the place or object at the time of the trial, then the plaintiff may need to show post-accident changes. But even in such clear situations, counsel can eliminate much of the potential prejudice by introducing the evidence in such a way as to emphasize the original conditions and not the subsequent remedial measures.

---

operation, and its cost and convenience, but also to its ultimate utility and success in its intended performance").

[30] Donahue v. Phillips Petroleum Co., 866 F.2d 1008, 1011 (8th Cir. 1989) (since defendant claimed that it was not feasible to provide warnings, it was not error to admit a brochure containing a warning, even though the circuit would ordinarily exclude subsequent remedial measures in a failure to warn case involving an unavoidably dangerous drug).

[31] See, e.g., Probus v. K-Mart, Inc., 794 F.2d 1207, 1210 (7th Cir. 1986) (in a products liability action against the seller and manufacturer of a ladder, defendants' testimony that material used was appropriate did not open the door to proof that defendants subsequently used different material; defendants did not claim that material was either the best material available or that use of another material would not have been feasible).

[32] See, e.g., J.B. Hunt Transp., Inc., v. General Motors Corp., 243 F.3d 441, 445 (8th Cir. 2001) (trial court properly excluded evidence of defendant's post-accident remedial measures after defendant stipulated that stiffer seats were feasible).

[33] Kenny v. Southeastern Pa. Transp. Auth., 581 F.2d 351, 356 (3d Cir. 1978) (because it countered defendant's inference that light was adequate, evidence that several light bulbs were replaced soon after rape attack and new fluorescent fixture was installed was properly admitted). See also Pitasi v. Stratton Corp., 968 F.2d 1558, 1560–1561 (2d Cir. 1992) (in a negligence action against a ski resort following a ski accident, the trial court erred in refusing to permit plaintiff to introduce evidence of defendant's subsequent remedial actions regarding the closed trail in order to rebut testimony of defendant's employees concerning procedures used to close the trail in prior years; in the present case, plaintiff sought to impeach defendant's witnesses and to rebut its defense that plaintiff was contributorily negligent because the condition was so obvious and apparent that warning signs or ropes were unnecessary; citing **Treatise**).

[e]—Proof of Duty

The Advisory Committee's Note includes among the purposes for which exclusion is not required, "existence of duty."[34] The difference between "duty" and "negligence" is at best unclear, and attempts to distinguish the elements for purposes of evidentiary rulings in a jury trial seem futile in most cases. In many instances, the existence of a duty is dependent on whether the defendant had notice of a condition or circumstance that required remedial measures. For example, if an employer is charged with having negligently failed to correct a racially hostile atmosphere in the workplace, the plaintiff must show that the employer had notice of the atmosphere and failed to take corrective action within a reasonable time of its receipt of the notice. If there is evidence that the employer took remedial action after the plaintiff brought the offensive conditions to its attention, the plaintiff will need to show that those actions were too little and too late. Similarly, an employer may wish to defend against the imposition of respondeat superior liability for racially hostile working conditions by introducing evidence that it took remedial actions as soon as it reasonably could do so after learning of those conditions, albeit some time after it learned of the plaintiff's complaint. Evidence of post-incident remedial actions is freely admissible in those situations.[35]

[f]—Impeachment

The second sentence of Rule 407 explicitly recognizes that evidence of subsequent remedial measures may be used for impeachment.[36] The enactment of Rule 407, with its explicit recognition of the "exception" for impeachment, should not affect the court's traditional reluctance to permit cross-examination that reflects on the witness only by means of a prohibited inference of negligence from the subsequent remedial measures.[37] Moreover, evidence of subsequent remedial mea-

---

[34] *See* **Treatise** at § 407App.01[2].

[35] *See, e.g.,* Swinton v. Potomac Corp., 270 F.3d 794, 811–816 (9th Cir. 2001) ("In the employment discrimination context . . . post-occurrence remediation is part and parcel of the legal framework. Under the negligence standard, the plaintiff must prove that the employer failed to take reasonably prompt corrective action once it learns of the harassment. And, in the vicarious liability context, the *Ellerth/Faragher* defense encourages employers to introduce such evidence as a defense to liability").

[36] *See, e.g.,* Trytko v. Hubbell, Inc., 28 F.3d 715, 724–725 (7th Cir. 1994) (trial court properly admitted evidence of reminders company sent to employees concerning impending expiration of stock options over objection that they were subsequent remedial measures; evidence was proper impeachment of company's witness who testified that language of stock options respecting deadlines for exercising them was simple and straightforward).

[37] *See, e.g.,* Reddin v. Robinson Prop. Group, 239 F.3d 756, 759 (5th Cir. 2001) (evidence that after accident defendant's employees taped off site of plaintiff's fall was properly excluded under Rule 407, even though it was offered to impeach evidence that defendant's employees examined accident site and found no defect that could have caused accident).

sures is not admissible for impeachment when there is adequate other evidence available to the proponent for that purpose.[38]

[g]—Mitigation of Punitive Damages

Evidence of subsequent remedial measures is sometimes admissible to mitigate a potential punitive damages award. For example, defendants in products liability and employment discrimination suits frequently offer evidence that they remedied the circumstances giving rise to the plaintiff's injuries or damages as quickly as practicable after learning about them. The admissibility of such evidence for that purpose is discretionary with the trial court, and may depend on whether the implementation of the remedial measures appears to indicate the defendant's genuine interest in fulfilling its legal and moral obligations or its financial interest in avoiding a large punitive damages award.[39]

§ 7.05   Compromise Offers—Rule 408

[1]—Definition, Rationale, and Scope[1]

[a]—Text and Scope of Rule

Rule 408 codifies and extends the federal courts' long-standing practice of excluding evidence of proposed or accepted compromises when it is offered to prove the validity or invalidity of a claim or amount of damage. The Rule is as follows:

Rule 408.   Compromise and Offers To Compromise.

Evidence of (1) furnishing or offering or promising to furnish, or (2) accepting or offering or promising to accept, a valuable consideration in compromising or attempting to compromise a claim which was disputed as to either validity or amount, is not admissible to prove liability for or invalidity of the claim or its amount. Evidence of conduct or statements made in compromise negotiations is likewise not admissible. This rule does not require the exclusion of any evidence otherwise discoverable merely because

---

[38] *See, e.g.,* Stecyk v. Bell Helicopter Textron, Inc., 295 F.3d 408, 416 (3d Cir. 2002) (when plaintiff had adequate grounds for cross-examining defendant's witnesses without using post-accident changes, trial court properly precluded plaintiff from using evidence of post-accident changes for impeachment).

[39] *See, e.g.,* Swinton v. Potomac Corp., 270 F.3d 794, 811–816 (9th Cir. 2001) (in employment racial discrimination case, trial court's exclusion of employer's subsequent remedial measure was proper when evidence revealed that anti-harassment training was not conducted until seven months after plaintiff quit his job, five months after he filed his unemployment claim alleging racial harassment, and two months after he filed suit).

[1] *See* **Treatise** at §§ 408.02–408.07.

it is presented in the course of compromise negotiations. This rule also does not require exclusion when the evidence is offered for another purpose, such as proving bias or prejudice of a witness, negativing a contention of undue delay, or proving an effort to obstruct a criminal investigation or prosecution.

[*Adopted Jan. 2, 1975, effective July 1, 1975.*]

The Rule extends the exclusionary treatment to cover "evidence of conduct and statements made in compromise negotiations." Rule 408 reflects the judgment that free and frank settlement negotiations should be fostered.[2] Evidence of an offer to compromise is also excluded because it is of such low probative value. A settlement offer may be motivated by a desire to "buy peace" rather than by an acknowledgment of the merits of a claim.

The Rule applies to a number of different situations: (1) offers to compromise disputes; (2) completed compromises; and (3) conduct occurring and statements made during settlement negotiations.

Several Circuits have held that Rule 408 does not render compromises or offers to compromise civil disputes inadmissible in subsequent criminal prosecutions. These decisions are based largely on the Rule's use of the terms "claim" and "amount," terms that seem peculiarly applicable to civil rather than criminal litigation.[3] Other Circuits hold that Rule 408 applies in criminal proceedings just as forcefully as in civil proceedings for the following reasons: (1) the Federal Rules of Evidence apply generally to both civil and criminal proceedings; (2) nothing in Rule 408 explicitly states that it is inapplicable to criminal proceedings; (3) the final sentence of Rule 408 is arguably unnecessary if the Rule does not apply to criminal proceedings at all; and (4) the potential prejudicial effect of the admission of evidence of a settlement can be more devastating to a criminal defendant than to a civil litigant.[3.1]

---

[2] *See* Fiberglass Insulators, Inc. v. Dupuy, 856 F.2d 652, 654 (4th Cir. 1988) (citing **Treatise**); Reichenbach v. Smith, 528 F.2d 1072, 1074 (5th Cir. 1976); Bottaro v. Hatton Assocs., 96 F.R.D. 158, 160 (E.D.N.Y. 1982); Young v. Verson Allsteel Press Co., 539 F. Supp. 193, 196 (E.D. Pa. 1982).

[3] *See, e.g.,* United States v. Logan, 250 F.3d 350, 367 (6th Cir. 2001) (Rule 408 is inapplicable to criminal prosecutions); Manko v. United States, 87 F.3d 50, 54 (2d Cir. 1996) (Rule 408's use of words such as "validity" and "claim" establish that drafters intended it to apply solely in civil contexts; furthermore, purpose of Rule 408, which is to encourage settlement of civil cases, does not apply to criminal prosecutions); United States v. Prewitt, 34 F.3d 436, 439 (7th Cir. 1994) (plain language of Rule 408 reflects that it applies only to civil cases, "specifically the language concerning validity and amount of a claim").

[3.1] *See* United States v. Bailey, 327 F.3d 1131, 1146 (10th Cir. 2003) (citing other cases).

[b]—Offers to Compromise Disputes

Evidence of offers to compromise is excluded only if there is a dispute about either the validity or the amount of the claim.[4] The Advisory Committee Note also states that "the effort . . . to induce a creditor to settle an admittedly due amount for a lesser sum" would not further the underlying policy of the Rule and is therefore not protected. Yet a careful distinction must be made between a frank disclosure during the course of negotiations—such as "All right, I was negligent. Let's talk about damages" (inadmissible)—and the less frequent situation when both the validity of the claim and the amount of damages are admitted—"Of course, I owe you the money, but unless you're willing to settle for less, you'll have to sue me for it" (admissible). Likewise, an admission of liability made during negotiations concening the time of payment and involving neither the validity nor amount of the claim is not within the Rule's exclusionary protection.[5]

When interpreting Rule 408 to determine whether a statement was an offer to compromise, the court should construe the term "valuable consideration" broadly. For example, an apology or some private or public acknowledgment of a new policy is often the basis for bringing parties together, particularly when there is a continuing relationship. In the context of this rule, such a statement may be a valuable consideration. On the other hand, an offer to provide a party something to which he or she was already entitled does not offer anything of value in return for the settlement of the extant dispute, and is, therefore, not an offer to compromise for purposes of Rule 408.[6]

It is clear that Rule 408 includes offers both by the person against whom the claim is asserted and by the person asserting the claim. If either person makes an offer of compromise to a person other than the other potential litigant, the offer should be protected by exclusionary treatment.

---

[4] *See* Affiliated Mfrs., Inc. v. Aluminum Co. of America, 56 F.3d 521, 529 (3d Cir. 1995) (district court was within its discretion in determining that Rule applies where parties were in dispute regardless of whether there was threat of pending litigation, and parties' discussions and internal memoranda regarding negotiations were correctly excluded as evidence of compromise; citing **Treatise**).

[5] *See, e.g.,* S.A. Healey Co. v. Milwaukee Metropolitan Sewerage, 50 F.3d 476, 480 (7th Cir. 1995) (statement by defendant's engineer that plaintiff's claim "probably has merit" was admissible because no dispute existed until defendant rejected plaintiff's claim; citing **Treatise**).

[6] *See, e.g.,* Coleman v. Quaker Oats Co., 232 F.3d 1271, 1290–1291 (9th Cir. 2000) (exception to Rule 408's exclusionary rule for offers to compromise disputes that offer only severance packages to which other party was already entitled does not apply to offers that were not made simultaneously with party's termination; exclusionary rule applies if offer was made after termination and offer includes benefits to which party was not otherwise entitled).

[c]—Completed Compromises

Rule 408 extends the exclusionary treatment not only to offers of compromise, but also to completed compromises when offered against a compromiser.[7] A party cannot introduce evidence of an adversary's completed compromises with third persons if the agreement arose out of the transaction being litigated.[8]

[d]—Conduct Occurring During Settlement Discussions

Rule 408 also explicitly excludes evidence of all conduct occurring and statements made during settlement negotiations.[9] The exclusion applies, however, only when the evidence is offered to prove a party's liability or the amount of damages owed. The rule does not exclude such evidence when offered for other purposes.[9.1]

The rule eliminates the common-law requirement that admissions of fact are not protected unless stated hypothetically "for the sake of discussion only" or "without prejudice." Deciding whether or not there were compromise negotiations is a question for the court pursuant to Rule 104(a) and not for the jury. When making this determination, the trial judge should bear in mind that the principal purpose of the expanded exclusionary rule is to insure freedom of communication with respect to compromise negotiations. Since the Rule interferes with the admissibility of relevant evidence, some courts have, in spite of the Rule's policy, limited its exclusionary effect by holding that the statement in question was not an explicit offer of compromise or was not made within the context of express negotiations.[10]

---

[7] *See* Belton v. Fibreboard Corp., 724 F.2d 500, 504–505 (5th Cir. 1984) (court's instructions directing jury to consider amount of settlement in determining damage award violated Rule 408and constituted reversible error).

[8] *See* Quad Graphics v. Fass, 724 F.2d 1230, 1234–1235 (7th Cir. 1983) (evidence of settlement agreement between plaintiff and third person inadmissible to show invalidity of plaintiff's claim).

[9] Russell v. PPG Indus., Inc., 953 F.2d 326, 333-334 (7th Cir. 1992) (information from summary trial was inadmissible under Rule 408 as evidence of attempt to settle; if such evidence were admitted, summary trial's "utility as a settlement device would be significantly undermined."); Ramada Dev. Co. v. Rauch, 644 F.2d 1097, 1106 (5th Cir. 1981) (trial court did not err in excluding architect's report that functioned as a basis for settlement negotiations); Saf-Gard Prods., Inc. v. Service Parts, Inc., 491 F. Supp. 996, 1008 (D. Ariz. 1980) (licensing agreements entered into in compromise of infringement claims could not be admitted as measure of patent owner's damages).

[9.1] *See, e.g.,* Basha v. Mitsubishi Motor Credit of Am., Inc., 336 F.3d 451, 454 n.4 (5th Cir. 2003) (letter from counsel for settling defendants sent to plaintiff at conclusion of settlement discussions was not barred by Rule 408 when offered to interpret settlement agreement rather than to establish liability or amount of damages).

[10] *See* Mendelovitz v. Adolph Coors Co., 693 F.2d 570, 580 (5th Cir. 1982) (letter admissible because litigation was in progress; letter not part of settlement negotiation and did not offer to compromise or settle any claim in instant action); Big O Tire Dealers v. Goodyear Tire & Rubber Co., 561 F.2d 1365, 1373 (10th Cir. 1977) (district court's ruling that discussions between plaintiff and defendant were business communications and not offers to compromise was sustainable because "discussions had not crystallized to the point of threatened litigation").

Rule 408 is not, as its last sentence points out, intended to cover efforts to "buy off" the prosecution or a prosecuting witness. But a distinction must be made between illicit offers and legitimate "plea bargaining" protected under Rule 410. If a transaction gives rise to both civil and criminal remedies, it is unclear whether a good-faith offer to compromise the civil claim will be protected in both proceedings.[11]

The Rules should not be construed to render inadmissible otherwise discoverable evidence solely because it was presented during the settlement negotiations. The policy of allowing open and free negotiations between parties by excluding conduct or statements made during the course of these discussions is not intended to conflict with the liberal rules of discovery embodied in the Federal Rules of Civil Procedure.[12]

Rule 408 should be applied even though a state has an evidentiary rule that may embody a substantive policy favoring the disclosure of all relevant evidence, since the promotion of compromises is essential to the integrity of the federal court system.[13]

[e]—Use of Offers and Agreements of Compromise for Other Purposes[14]

The last sentence of Rule 408 contains two limitations on the general exclusionary treatment for evidence of offers or agreements of compromise. First, such

---

[11] *See, e.g.,* United States v. Gonzales, 748 F.2d 74, 78 (2d Cir. 1984) (statements made in the course of settlement negotiations are admissible to establish that one committed a crime because they are not offered to prove the validity or amount of a claim and their exclusion would not encourage the settlement of claims). The matter may become particularly important in a RICO or mail fraud case. A compromise of the civil claim should not be used in the criminal case. As to the converse problems, *cf.* Rule 803(22).

[12] Center for Auto Safety v. Department of Justice, 576 F. Supp. 739, 749 (D.D.C. 1983) (documents were not protected by "settlement negotiation" privilege because Rule 408 limits admissibility of evidence of settlement negotiations at trial, but does not affect its disclosure for other purposes); Manufacturing Sys., Inc. of Milwaukee v. Computer Tech., 99 F.R.D. 335, 336 (E.D. Wis. 1983) (fact that information might be inadmissible at trial under Rule 408 was not necessarily a bar to discovery; there need only be reasonable likelihood that information sought would lead to discovery of admissible evidence). *But cf.* Bottaro v. Hatton Assocs., 96 F.R.D. 158, 160 (E.D.N.Y. 1982) (discovery into terms of settlement agreement between plaintiff and one codefendant inadmissible in absence of "particularized showing of a likelihood that admissible evidence will be generated"); Ramada Dev. Co. v. Rauch, 644 F.2d 1097, 1107 (5th Cir. 1981) (documents that would not have existed but for negotiations are not discoverable because in this circumstance the negotiations are not being used as a device to thwart discovery).

[13] *Cf.* Morris v. LTV Corp., 725 F.2d 1024, 1030–1031 (5th Cir. 1984) (although controlling Mexican law provided that offers to compromise are binding admissions of liability, trial court did not err in concluding that evidentiary questions are procedural in nature and governed by law of forum).

[14] *See* **Treatise** at § 408.08.

evidence may be used to prove a material fact other than validity or invalidity of the claim or its amount.[15] Accordingly, evidence of offers or agreements of compromise have been admitted to prevent abuse of the general exclusionary rule and its policy of promoting compromises.[16] The existence of negotiations for compromise is admitted to demonstrate the existence of other parties that may have been responsible for the plaintiff's injury,[17] or to demonstrate the extent of a party's liability,[18] or to establish that a party was not successful for purposes of awarding attorney's fees,[19] or to show that the real party in interest had already settled with the defendant all claims outstanding from the transaction.[20] It would also be permissible to show that a party had relevant knowledge,[21] or that a party acted in bad faith,[22] or to rebut a claim that the behavior in question was a mistake or accident,[23] or that the amount in controversy exceeds the jurisdictional minimum

---

[15] *See, e.g.,* United States v. Technic Servs., Inc., 314 F.3d 1031, 1045 (9th Cir. 2002) ("The use of the phrase 'such as' [in Rule 408] implies that the ensuing list is not exhaustive, but is only illustrative").

[16] *See, e.g.,* United States v. Technic Servs., Inc., 314 F.3d 1031, 1045 (9th Cir. 2002) (Rule 408's exclusionary rule is inapplicable when statements made during settlement discussions are used to prove obstruction of EPA investigation); *see also* Starter Corp. v. Converse, Inc., 170 F.3d 286, 293–294 (2d Cir. 1999) (trial court did not abuse discretion in admitting evidence of settlement agreement in support of one party's argument that other was estopped by the agreement from using a disputed trademark).

[17] Belton v. Fibreboard Corp., 724 F.2d 500, 504–505 (5th Cir. 1984) (in a products liability action, evidence of settlements between plaintiff and fifteen other named defendants admitted to prove plaintiffs had been exposed to products of other defendants).

[18] Carney v. American University, 151 F.3d 1090, 1095–1096 (D.C. Cir. 1998) (settlement correspondence concerning plaintiff's racial discrimination claim was admissible to establish an independent violation, i.e., retaliation re severance pay based on plaintiff's decision to sue about earlier discrimination).

[19] B & B Inv. Club v. Kleinert's Inc., 472 F. Supp. 787, 791 (E.D. Pa. 1979).

[20] Coakley & Williams Constr., Inc. v. Structural Concrete Equip., Inc., 973 F.2d 349, 353–354 (4th Cir. 1992) (trial court properly considered prior settlement agreement between parties to pending suit arising out of same dispute to determine, for summary judgment purposes, that settlement was intended by all parties to resolve dispute entirely).

[21] Breuer Elec. Mfg. Co. v. Toronado Sys. of Am., Inc., 687 F.2d 182, 185 (7th Cir. 1982) (settlement evidence properly presented on motion to set aside entry of default judgment to rebut defendants' assertions that they were not aware of issues in suit prior to filing of action).

[22] *See, e.g.,* Athey v. Farmers Ins. Exch., 234 F.3d 357, 361 (8th Cir. 2000) (under controlling South Dakota law, insurance company's attempt to condition settlement of breach of contract claim on release of bad faith claim is evidence of bad faith; such evidence is admissible under Rule 408 even though offer containing conditional settlement of breach of contract claim was made during settlement discussions); Urico v. Parnell Oil Co., 708 F.2d 852, 854–855 (1st Cir. 1983) (testimony that detailed settlement negotiations between parties was not inadmissible, as it was offered to show defendant unreasonably prevented plaintiffs from mitigating their damages in an effort to reach an advantageous settlement).

[23] Bradbury v. Phillips Petroleum Co., 815 F.2d 1356, 1363 (10th Cir. 1987) (suit for trespass, outrageous conduct, and assault arising from defendant's hiring of drilling company, which

amount required to bring suit in federal court.[24] In addition, if the settlement negotiations and terms explain and are a part of another dispute, they must often be admitted if the trier is to understand the case.[25]

The second general exception to Rule 408's exclusionary rule is proof of a witness's bias or prejudice. Need for the evidence is most common when a witness has compromised his or her claims against a litigant in the suit being tried.[26] Rule 408 has determined, in effect, that the need to evaluate a witness's credibility normally outweighs the policy of encouraging compromises.[27] Yet the trial judge should guard against needless inquiry and concern over credibility factors, which could well result in unnecessarily undercutting the basic exclusionary rule.[28] The danger that the evidence will be used substantively as an admission is especially great when the witness sought to be impeached is one of the litigants in the suit being tried.

Despite the exceptions to Rule 408, care should be taken that an indiscriminate and mechanistic application does not result in undermining the Rule's public policy objective. The almost unavoidable impact of disclosure about compromises is that the jury will consider the evidence as a concession of liability. The problem is

---

erroneously drilled on one plaintiff's land and whose employees assaulted other plaintiff; trial court properly admitted evidence of seven similar incidents in which defendant compensated the landowners since they "bore on the central question of whether the driller engaged in reckless behavior or whether it was a mistake or accident").

[24] See, e.g., Cohn v. Petsmart, Inc., 281 F.3d 837, 840 n.3 (9th Cir. 2002) (plaintiff's lawyer's demand letter estimating value of plaintiff's trademark at $100,000 was admissible to prove that amount in controversy exceeded $75,000 in opposition to motion to remand removed suit to state court; evidence was not offered to prove amount of defendant's liability, but merely to show plaintiff's assessment of value of trademark).

[25] United States v. Wilford, 710 F.2d 439, 450–451 (8th Cir. 1983) (not error to admit evidence of settlement agreement between union and N.L.R.B. that union would cease its disputed activities and refund fees paid by non-union drivers when settlement was offered to show circumstances surrounding refunds); MCI Communications v. American Tel. & Tel. Co., 708 F.2d 1081, 1152 (7th Cir. 1983) (the trial court did not err in admitting testimony set forth in a prior agreement since evidence explained another dispute, assisted factfinder in understanding the case, demonstrated technical feasibility, and proper limiting instructions were given at time evidence was introduced).

[26] See County of Hennepin v. AFG Indus., Inc., 726 F.2d 149, 152–153 (8th Cir. 1984) (evidence of settlement between plaintiff and cross-defendant's insurer was held properly admitted against plaintiff to impeach testimony of plaintiff's witnesses).

[27] John McShain, Inc. v. Cessna Aircraft Co., 563 F.2d 632, 635 (3d Cir. 1977) (court properly admitted evidence that a sister corporation of witness's employer had been released from liability by plaintiff in exchange for witness's testifying for plaintiff).

[28] See, e.g., Goodyear Tire & Rubber Co. v. Chiles Power Supply, Inc., 332 F.3d 976, 982–983 (6th Cir. 2003) (appellant's proposed use of statements made in settlement discussions to impeach manufacturer's representatives if they testified that product failures resulted from customers' misuse would be attempt to use those statements to prove that products were defective, a use that Rule 408 prohibits).

similar to that of proof of other crimes, subsequent remedial measures, and liability insurance. The trial judge should weigh the need for such evidence against the potentiality of discouraging future settlement negotiations and apply Rule 403 [29] to exclude when the balance so dictates. Even if such evidence is admitted pursuant to an exception, an opponent can still argue to the jury that the admission has little probative force because of the accompanying circumstances.

[2]—Curing Error[30]

Rule 408's exclusionary treatment is broad. It covers all conduct occurring and statements made during compromise negotiations. It is therefore unlikely that every erroneous admission of evidence will be prejudicial. Automatic declarations of mistrial are not required. Rather, the trial judge should determine whether, after an adequate instruction, such a fixed impression of a concession of liability has been made on the minds of the jury as to probably influence its verdict.[31]

§ 7.06 Payment of Medical and Other Expenses—Rule 409[1]

Rule 409 excludes evidence of furnishing or offering or promising to pay medical, hospital or similar expenses occasioned by an injury.

Rule 409.   Payment of Medical and Similar Expenses.

Evidence of furnishing or offering or promising to pay medical, hospital, or similar expenses occasioned by an injury is not admissible to prove liability for the injury.

[Adopted Jan. 2, 1975, effective July 1, 1975.]

---

[29] Ramada Dev. Co. v. Rauch, 644 F.2d 1097, 1107 (5th Cir. 1981) (trial court had not abused discretion in excluding report since exception "was not intended to completely undercut the policy behind the rule," and "notice could be effectively provided by means less in conflict with the policy behind Rule 408"); John McShain, Inc. v. Cessna Aircraft Co., 563 F.2d 632, 635 (3d Cir. 1977) ("A sensitive analysis of the need for the evidence as proof on a contested factual issue, of the prejudice which may eventuate from admission, and of the public policies involved is in order before passing on such an objection.").

[30] *See* **Treatise** at § 408.10.

[31] *Compare* Almonte v. National Union Fire Ins. Co., 705 F.2d 566, 569 (1st Cir. 1983) (judgment for plaintiff reversed because trial court failed to give instruction to counteract prejudice created by receipt of evidence which would otherwise have been excluded because, inter alia, it partially concerned settlement negotiations) *and* Hawthorne v. Eckerson Co., 77 F.2d 844, 847 (2d Cir. 1935) (in case in which verdict was similar to amount of compromise with another accident victim, court concluded that evidence of compromise was improperly admitted to show agency) *with* Meyer v. Capital Transit Co., 32 A.2d 392, 393–394 (D.C. Mun. App. 1943) (inference from counsel's argument that client always settled with reasonable claimants to show unreasonableness of suit; careful instruction removed any prejudice).

[1] *See* **Treatise** at §§ 409.02–409.03.

The ground for exclusion relied upon by the drafters is the social policy of encouraging assistance to the injured party by removing the risk that such action will be used in a subsequent trial as an admission. Rule 409 excludes all such offers or payments to prove liability, even if the only motivation was the desire to mitigate the damages for which the aider might be subsequently held legally liable.

If the state rule is different, the court may consider the *Erie* problem. Since it is unlikely that the state rule on this matter is of great significance, uniformity needs will almost always result in application of the federal rule even when state substantive law is applied.[2]

Exclusion is required by the terms of Rule 409 only when the evidence is offered to prove liability. When the evidence is offered to prove another material proposition,[3] such as control or the status of the alleged tort-feasor,[4] the court may consider the underlying policy and exclude pursuant to Rule 403 if there is little probative force in the line of proof.

A troublesome question arises when an express admission of liability is coupled with an offer of assistance. Although Rule 409 excludes all such offers or tenders of assistance, the express admissions are generally admissible. If the admission can be disclosed without mentioning the furnishing, offering or promise to pay medical expenses, then it should be admitted.[5] Non-severable admissions—such as "Don't worry about it; since it's my fault, I'll pay your bills"—should generally be excluded, unless the circumstances are so compelling as to prevail over the Rule's general social policy.

§ 7.07   Plea Bargaining—Rule 410

[1]—Text and Scope of Rule

Rule 410 excludes evidence of withdrawn guilty pleas, nolo contendere pleas, and statements made in the course of federal or state plea proceedings. In addition, statements made in the course of plea discussions with the prosecutor are excluded.

---

    [2]   *See* 17 MOORE'S FEDERAL PRACTICE, Ch. 124, *The Erie Doctrine and Applicable Law* (Matthew Bender 3d ed. 1997).

    [3]   Employers Mut. Casualty Co. v. Mosqueda, 317 F.2d 609, 613 (5th Cir. 1963) (insurance company's payment of attorney fees for negligent driver admissible on issue whether driver had permission to drive insured's truck); Hartford Accident & Indem. Co. v. Sanford, 344 F. Supp. 969, 972 (W.D. Okla. 1972) (insurance company payment of medical expenses admissible on the issue of estoppel in an action by the company against the insured).

    [4]   Savoie v. Otto Candies, Inc., 692 F.2d 363, 370 (5th Cir. 1982) (in Jones Act action, evidence that employer made "maintenance payments" to plaintiff admissible to show plaintiff's status as a seaman).

    [5]   Sims v. Sowle, 238 Or. 329, 335, 395 P.2d 133, 135 (1964) (statements defendant made when he returned to apologize two days after paying plaintiff's medical expenses are admissible).

The evidence excluded by the rule may not be admitted against the defendant who made the plea or statement either for substantive or impeachment use in any civil or criminal proceeding.

Rule 410. Inadmissibility of Pleas, Plea Discussions, and Related Statements.

Except as otherwise provided in this rule, evidence of the following is not, in any civil or criminal proceeding, admissible against the defendant who made the plea or was a participant in the plea discussions:

(1)
a plea of guilty which was later withdrawn;

(2)
a plea of nolo contendere;

(3)
any statement made in the course of any proceedings under Rule 11 of the Federal Rules of Criminal Procedure or comparable state procedure regarding either of the foregoing pleas; or

(4)
any statement made in the course of plea discussions with an attorney for the prosecuting authority which do not result in a plea of guilty or which result in a plea of guilty later withdrawn.

However, such a statement is admissible (i) in any proceeding wherein another statement made in the course of the same plea or plea discussions has been introduced and the statement ought in fairness be considered contemporaneously with it, or (ii) in a criminal proceeding for perjury or false statement if the statement was made by the defendant under oath, on the record and in the presence of counsel.

[*Adopted Jan. 2, 1975, effective July 1, 1975; amended Dec. 12, 1975, effective Dec. 12, 1975; amended Apr. 30, 1979, effective Dec. 1, 1980.*]

The Rule does not exclude evidence of witnesses' withdrawn pleas or plea bargaining statements. Such evidence may be admitted to impeach the witness.[1] Nor does the Rule cover the admissibility of pleas of guilty or of nolo contendere

---

[1] *See* United States v. Maldonado, 38 F.3d 936, 936, 942 (7th Cir. 1994) (defendant was convicted of various cocaine charges; the trial court admitted, for impeachment purposes, statements defendant had made during a plea bargain proffer; the court of appeals affirmed, holding that the settled law of the Seventh Circuit is that defendant may sign a waiver making statements made during plea negotiations admissible for impeachment purposes; here, both defendant and defense counsel had signed a proper waiver; the appellate court cited United States v. Goodapple, 958 F.2d

against an alleged co-offender.[2] Even though a plea or statement is excluded by the rule, evidence of the underlying acts is admissible pursuant to other rules, such as Rule 404(b) [3] and Rule 609.[4] Rule 11(f) of the Federal Rules of Criminal Procedure provides that the "admissibility or inadmissibility of a plea, a plea discussion, and any related statement is governed by Federal Rule of Evidence 410."[5]

Although the justification for excluding each category of evidence varies, a common policy thread runs throughout: the promotion of plea bargaining and the avoidance of undue prejudice to the defendant. Rule 410 creates, in effect, a privilege of the defendant. Nolo contendere pleas, for example, are made inadmissible to encourage plea bargaining and because they are not factual admissions to the underlying crime.[6]

A defendant may proffer evidence of offers to plead or pleas that might be excluded were a prosecutor to offer them. Generally, the court should give a defendant considerable leeway in introducing such evidence. There are two clear exceptions to this rule of leniency in applying Rule 410. First, the defendant should not be permitted to prove a withdrawn plea or an offer to plead in order to show that a government attorney had doubts about his guilt.[7] The prosecutor's view of the defendant's guilt or innocence is irrelevant. Second, when there are joint trials, the introduction of such evidence by one defendant may prejudice a co-defendant.

1402, 1409 (7th Cir. 1992) as controlling, and declined to follow the Ninth Circuit's ruling to the contrary).

[2] The admissibility of such evidence is discussed in the **Treatise** at § 410.08. For a discussion of the use of criminal pleas which have not been withdrawn, in other causes of action, *see* **Treatise** at § 410.07.

[3] United States v. Wyatt, 762 F.2d 908, 912 (11th Cir. 1985) ("admissibility of the underlying facts is unaffected by the nolo plea").

[4] *See* § 12.04.

[5] Fed. R. Crim. P. 11(f); *see* 24 MOORE'S FEDERAL PRACTICE, Ch. 611, *Pleas* (Matthew Bender 3d ed. 1997).

[6] *See* Rose v. Uniroyal Goodrich Tire Co., 219 F.3d 1216, 1219–1221 (10th Cir. 2000) (defendant fired plaintiff after he pleaded nolo contendere to marijuana possession; in plaintiff's suit for wrongful discharge, Rule 410 did not prevent defendant from introducing the plea to show its reason for discharging plaintiff, since the plea was not being used "against the defendant" within the meaning of Rule 410).

[7] *See* United States v. Verdoorn, 528 F.2d 103, 107 (8th Cir. 1976) (trial court excluded evidence of plea bargaining which according to defendants would "disclose the lengths to which the government went in attempting to obtain vital testimony"; court relied on former Fed. R. Crim. P. 11(e)(6)); United States v. Collins, 395 F. Supp. 629, 633 (M.D. Pa. 1975).

[2]—Evidence of Pleas Excluded[8]

Rule 410 excludes evidence of withdrawn pleas, rejected pleas, and pleas of nolo contendere. Evidence of any withdrawn plea is excluded in any proceeding regardless of the pleader's knowledge and willingness.[9] Exclusion is required because permitting use of the withdrawn plea would make the trial meaningless. It is unlikely that the jury would use the plea merely as evidence of conduct inconsistent with the defendant's claim of innocence.[10] Withdrawn pleas are also excluded because flexibility, in making and withdrawing them without prejudice, is necessary to encourage negotiations between defense and prosecution counsel. A constitutional basis for exclusion has been suggested by a few courts.[11]

Evidence of rejected pleas is also inadmissible against the defendant. Exclusion effectuates the policy of promoting "plea bargaining" by protecting defendants against the use of unaccepted offers at subsequent trials.

As in the case of withdrawn pleas, the impact on the jury of the seeming admission of guilt cannot normally be overcome by an admonition. A defendant might well be forced to take the stand to explain the offer or to leave the evidence unrebutted, thereby creating a constitutional issue.

If information about a withdrawn or a rejected plea is disclosed, a mistrial may have to be declared. Certainly, if the prosecution or court deliberately reveals the existence of such pleas, the prejudice would seem to be incurable. The defendant, in view of the clarity of Rule 410, is in effect deliberately being tried by means declared to be unfair.

Counsel and the trial court can, without much effort, avoid the disclosure of the withdrawn or rejected plea or the plea of nolo contendere. Unlike matters of widespread knowledge—such as the existence of liability insurance—the probability of an inadvertent or unintentional disclosure by an unsuspecting witness of pleas barred by Rule 410 is not significant. Nevertheless, automatic retrials should not be granted if in fact it is perfectly clear that disclosure was inadvertent and reference to the plea did not affect the verdicts.

---

[8] *See* **Treatise** at §§ 410.02, 410.09[1].

[9] United States v. Lawson, 683 F.2d 688, 692 (2d Cir. 1982) (statement may not be used for impeachment).

[10] Bruton v. United States, 391 U.S. 123, 135, 88 S. Ct. 1620, 20 L. Ed. 2d 476 (1968) ("[T]here are some contexts in which the risk that the jury will not, or cannot, follow instructions is so great, and the consequences of failure so vital to the defendant, that the practical and human limitations of the jury system cannot be ignored.").

[11] *See, e.g.,* Wood v. United States, 128 F.2d 265, 278 (D.C. Cir. 1942) (admission of the withdrawn plea would be a form of self-incrimination since the court had compelled a plea).

[3]—Statement Made in Connection with Plea Bargaining[12]

Rule 410 expressly makes inadmissible statements made in the course of any proceedings under (1) Rule 11 of the Federal Rules of Criminal Procedure,[13] (2) state plea proceedings, and (3) plea discussions with an attorney for the prosecuting authority. Such statements are excluded to ensure that plea discussions are immunized sufficiently to promote the practice of plea bargaining.[14]

A number of grey areas remain for treatment on a case-by-case basis. It is not always clear whether the statements were made in the course of plea bargaining, which is a pre-requisite if the Rule is to apply.[15] A clear record obviously best enables the court to characterize accurately the nature of the discussions between the defendant and the prosecution. The careful United States Attorney will make it clear on a recording of the conversation and a form signed by the defendant that the statements were not made in connection with any plea negotiations or because of any promise of a plea or leniency.[16] In addition, the prosecutor should urge the defendant to obtain an attorney before speaking. If defense counsel is present and plea bargaining is taking place, counsel should make a written record as soon as possible, by exchange of letters or by stipulation, that any statements made by the client are in the course of plea negotiations pursuant to Criminal Rule 11(f) and Rule 410. Once the defendant accepts the plea offer, further statements are not covered by the Rule.[17]

Rule 410 applies to statements made in the course of "plea discussions with an attorney for the prosecuting authority which do not result in a plea of guilty or which result in a plea of guilty later withdrawn."[18] This is true whether the statement is made by the defendant or an attorney of the defendant who has been authorized

---

[12] *See* **Treatise** at §§ 410.09–410.11.

[13] Rule 11 governs procedures for pleas in the federal courts and establishes requirements designed to enhance the visibility and fairness of plea discussions. Fed. R. Crim. P. 11; *see* 24 MOORE'S FEDERAL PRACTICE, Ch. 611, *Pleas* (Matthew Bender 3d ed. 1997).

[14] *See, e.g.,* United States v. Young, 223 F.3d 905, 907 (8th Cir. 2000) (trial court did not abuse its discretion in concluding that affidavit defendant executed in exchange for government's agreement to permit him to remain free on bond was made in course of plea negotiations and thus inadmissible under Rule 410); United States v. Sayakhom, 186 F.3d 928, 935–936 (9th Cir. 1999) (statements made during plea discussions were not admissible to prove notice).

[15] *See, e.g.,* United States v. Lewis, 117 F.3d 980, 984 (7th Cir. 1997) (Rule 410 exclusion does not extend to statements made to law enforcement officers).

[16] United States v. Cunningham, 723 F.2d 217, 227–228 (2d Cir. 1983) (stipulation made by defendant at outset of interview that anything said could later be used against him made it clear that the interview was not a plea bargaining session).

[17] United States v. Knight, 867 F.2d 1285, 1288 (11th Cir. 1989).

[18] Fed. R. Evid. 410(4); *see* Fed. R. Crim. P. 11(f) ("admissibility or inadmissibility of a plea, a plea discussion, and any related statement is governed by Federal Rule of Evidence 410").

to speak on the defendant's behalf.[19] The rule applies whether the statement is made to a government attorney or to an individual whom a government attorney has authorized to negotiate the plea.[20] Moreover, "plea discussions" may include statements made in an effort to initiate plea bargaining.[21]

Some statements may be protected from disclosure even though they were not made to a prosecuting attorney. The government should not be permitted to by-pass Rule 410 by authorizing law enforcement officials to conduct plea negotiations.[22] Furthermore, there may be instances in which law enforcement officials misrepresent their authority and induce a defendant to make inculpatory statements while under the mistaken impression that he or she is engaging in plea bargaining. Such cases are governed not by Rule 410 but by the body of law dealing with the voluntariness of statements made while in police custody[23] and prohibitions against trickery by the police. However, Rule 410 does not protect statements that the defendant made to law enforcement officers under circumstances creating no rational basis for believing the conversation to be plea negotiations or for believing the officers to be authorized to engage in plea negotiations on behalf of the prosecuting authority.[24]

Once there has been an indictment or information filed, there is a strong inference that admissions were made in the course of plea negotiations. Prior to this event, a contrary inference would be reasonable and sound. Admissions in open court prior to trial at arraignment or pretrials will almost always be protected by Rule 410.

Rule 410(4)'s exclusion of statements made to a prosecuting attorney during plea negotiations that are not successful does not apply to statements made by the defendant to prosecutors in foreign countries. Such an exclusionary rule would be contrary to the explicit language of Rule 410(3), which applies only to plea proceedings under Rule 11 of the Federal Rules of Criminal Procedure or under

---

[19] United States v. Bridges, 46 F. Supp. 2d 462, 466–467 (E.D. Va. 1999).

[20] United States v. Porter, 821 F.2d 968, 976 (4th Cir. 1987).

[21] United States v. Bridges, 46 F. Supp. 2d 462, 466–467 (E.D. Va. 1999).

[22] See Rachlin v. United States, 723 F.2d 1373, 1376 (8th Cir. 1983); United States v. Bridges, 46 F. Supp. 2d 462, 466–467 (E.D. Va. 1999) (whether discussions between accused and law enforcement agent are protected plea negotiations is determined by "specific facts and circumstances surrounding the interchange at issue"; rule applies only if defendant has reasonable subjective belief that he or she is negotiating a plea).

[23] See Rachlin v. United States, 723 F.2d 1373, 1377–1378 (8th Cir. 1983); United States v. Gazzara, 587 F. Supp. 311, 327 (S.D.N.Y 1984).

[24] See, e.g., United States v. Mangine, 302 F.3d 819, 822 (8th Cir. 2002) (defendant's statements to officer were admissible in absence of allegation or evidence that officer represented he was prosecuting attorney or had authority to engage in plea discussions, when conversation between defendant and officer had no attributes of plea negotiations).

any comparable state procedure. Rule 11 does not apply to statements made in comparable proceedings to foreign prosecutors, thus, they are admissible. Because of the admissibility of foreign allocutions under Rule 410(3), it makes no sense to read Rule 410(4) as having any greater scope. Thus, statements made to representatives of the prosecuting authority in a foreign country are fully admissible in United States courts, even though the negotiations for the plea were not successful.[24.1]

[4]—Attacks on Credibility

The evidence excluded by Rule 410 may not be used in impeaching the defendant. Such use would usually compel defendant to remain off the witness stand. The remedy for brazen lying is prosecution for interfering with governmental activities or perjury.[25]

[5]—Exceptions[26]

Statements made by a defendant in connection with a plea or an offer to plead may be used in a criminal proceeding for perjury or false statement if the defendant made the statements under oath,[27] on the record, and in the presence of counsel.[28] They should be usable in a prosecution for obstruction of justice when the defendant has deliberately lied to a government agent.

If a defendant introduces statements made during plea discussions, then other relevant statements made in the same plea discussions are admissible under the rule of completeness.[29] Caution by defense counsel is called for. In addition, plea statements made pursuant to an agreement with the prosecutor may be admitted if the defendant withdraws from or violates the agreement.[30]

[24.1] *See, e.g.,* United States v. Orlandez-Gamboa, 320 F.3d 328, 331–332 (2d Cir. 2003).

[25] United States v. Udeagu, 110 F.R.D. 172, 175 (E.D.N.Y. 1986).

[26] *See* **Treatise** at §§ 410.05–410.11.

[27] *Cf.* United States v. Abrahams, 604 F.2d 386, 394 (5th Cir. 1979) (statement made before a magistrate could not be used against defendant in a perjury proceeding because defendant was never placed under oath).

[28] Fed. R. Crim. P. 17.1 provides: "No admissions made by the defendant or the defendant's attorney at the conference shall be used against the defendant unless the admissions are reduced to writing and signed by the defendant and the defendant's attorney." *See* 25 MOORE'S FEDERAL PRACTICE, Ch. 617.1, *Pretrial Conference* (Matthew Bender 3d ed. 1997).

[29] United States v. Williams, 295 F.3d 817, 819–820 (8th Cir. 2002) (when defendant testified he had entered plea agreement only because prosecutor promised him short sentence and had asked him to lie about his participation in charged drug conspiracy, prosecution could properly use, in accordance with waiver agreement, statements made during plea discussions and stipulation of facts to support guilty plea for impeachment).

[30] United States v. Stirling, 571 F.2d 708. 731–732, 736–737 (2d Cir. 1978) (defendant's plea statements made before grand jury could be used against him after he withdrew from written

Statements made in connection with a plea or offer to plead may also be admitted against a defendant if he or she knowingly and voluntarily agreed to waive the privileges conferred by Rule 410.[31] Although such waivers commonly allow the use of plea statements only to impeach the defendant's inconsistent testimony[32] or to rebut defense evidence,[33] some courts have held that a waiver allowing use of plea statements for all purposes will be enforced if it is knowing and voluntary.[34]

The plea and surrounding circumstances can be used in deciding the sentence

---

agreement with prosecution to plead guilty and testify for prosecution; defendant's failure to abide by his agreement "justly exposed him to prosecutorial use of his Grand Jury Testimony"); *see, e.g.,* United States v. Davis, 617 F.2d 677, 686 (D.C. Cir. 1979) (although plea agreement expressly gave prosecution right to use defendant's grand jury plea testimony if defendant breached agreement, express reservation of right is not needed for use of defendant's plea statement if defendant subsequently breaches plea agreement; allowing defendant to withdraw plea agreement and associated statements would not serve Rule 410's purpose). *See also* United States v. Perry, 643 F.2d 38, 52 (2d Cir. 1981) (statements made by defendant after violating his plea agreement properly admitted); United States v. Arroyo-Angulo, 580 F.2d 1137, 1149 (2d Cir. 1978) (court noted as alternative ground for not extending Rule 410 to statements in question that "[i]n view of Arroyo's blatant breach of the cooperation arrangement with the Government, to prohibit the introduction of his admissions would make a mockery of the investigation processes employed to secure evidence of serious crimes.").

[31] United States v. Mezzanatto, 513 U.S. 196, 200–204, 115 S. Ct. 797, 130 L. Ed. 2d 697 (1995) (although Rule 410 is silent about waiver, there is general presumption that legal rights generally, and evidentiary provisions specifically, are subject to waiver by voluntary agreement of parties); United States v. Swick, 262 F.3d 684, 686 (8th Cir. 2001) ("Absent some affirmative indication that the agreement was entered into unknowingly or involuntarily, an agreement to waive the exclusionary provisions of the plea-statement Rules is valid and enforceable").

[32] *See, e.g.,* United States v. Mezzanatto, 513 U.S. 196, 200–204, 115 S. Ct. 797, 130 L. Ed. 2d 697 (1995) (agreement that statements would be admissible for impeachment would be enforced); United States v. Maldonado, 38 F.3d 936, 942 (7th Cir. 1994) (settled law of Seventh Circuit is that defendant may sign waiver making statements made during plea negotiations admissible for impeachment purposes).

[33] *See, e.g.,* United States v. Rebbe, 314 F.3d 402, 406–408 (9th Cir. 2002) (pre-negotiation waiver agreement, made in writing in presence of defendant's counsel and signed by both defendant and his counsel, provides sufficient authority for prosecution to use statements defendant made during plea negotiations when defendant cross-examined witnesses and submitted evidence at trial that was inconsistent with statements); United States v. Krilich, 159 F.3d 1020, 1024–1025 (7th Cir. 1998) (defendant waived Rule 410's protections if he testified contrary to plea offer or "otherwise present[ed] a position inconsistent with the proffer"; since he presented an inconsistent position on cross-examination of prosecution witnesses, his conditional waiver became effective and plea statements were properly admitted in rebuttal).

[34] *See, e.g.,* United States v. Swick, 262 F.3d 684, 686 (8th Cir. 2001) ("Absent some affirmative indication that the agreement was entered into unknowingly or involuntarily, an agreement to waive the exclusionary provisions of the plea-statement Rules is valid and enforceable"); United States v. Burch, 156 F.3d 1315, 1320 (D.C. Cir. 1998) (an agreement including waiver of all rights under Rule 410 allows prosecution to use plea statements in its case in chief, "absent some affirmative indication that the agreement was entered into unknowingly or involuntarily").

in the case in which it is entered. It should also be usable in other criminal cases in deciding whether a nolo contendere plea should be accepted. A judge or administrative agency should be entitled to use the plea in determining a penalty either in a civil or criminal action.[35]

Courts still have to determine whether statements induced in ways that avoid the operation of Rule 410 should be immunized. For example, a court may have to determine whether statements made to a United States Attorney by a suspect after he is advised of his rights under *Miranda* and also advised that he is a target of an investigation are protected by Rule 410, when the United States Attorney has stated, "If you cooperate fully and tell us who else is involved, I will tell the court about your cooperation and forget about the gun count; otherwise you'll face 25 years." The rule of admissibility prevails unless there is a special reason to exclude, such as a *Miranda* violation or unacceptable trickery.

Rule 410 also does not require exclusion of evidence of a party's conviction on the basis of a nolo contendere plea, as distinguished from evidence of the plea, itself.[36] The courts adopting this narrow interpretation of the scope of Rule 410's exclusionary rule emphasize the Rule's focus on the impropriety of using nolo contendere pleas as admissions.[37] They also rely heavily on the difference between using the plea for the purpose of proving the defendant's guilt of the facts that underlie the conviction, a prohibited use, and using the conviction that resulted from the plea's acceptance by the court to prove the mere fact that the defendant has suffered a conviction.[38]

[6]—Waiver of Accused's Right to Exclude Plea Agreement Evidence

An accused can waive his or her protection against the use of statements made during plea discussions. When defendants agree, before the beginning of the plea discussions, that what they say during those discussions can be used as impeachment if they subsequently testify at the trial inconsistently with information given

---

[35] United States v. Schipani, 315 F. Supp. 253, 254 (E.D.N.Y.), *aff'd*, 435 F.2d 26 (2d Cir. 1970) (use of illegally obtained evidence for sentence).

[36] *See, e.g.,* Olsen v. Correiro, 189 F.3d 52, 58 (1st Cir. 1999) ("The evidentiary rules that exclude evidence of nolo pleas do not directly apply to the convictions and sentences that result from such pleas").

[37] *See, e.g.,* Brewer v. City of Napa, 210 F.3d 1093, 1096 (9th Cir. 2000) ("Rule 410 by its terms prohibits only evidence of pleas (including no contest pleas), insofar as pleas constitute statements or admissions").

[38] *See, e.g.,* United States v. Adedoyin, 369 F.3d 337, 344 (3d Cir. 2004) (defendant's earlier conviction based on his nolo plea was admissible in case in which it was not pertinent whether he was guilty of charges in earlier case, but question was whether, after his conviction, he had wilfully made false and misleading representation that he had not been convicted of crime).

during the discussions, the waiver is valid.[39] A waiver permitting the prosecution to use statements made during plea discussions in response to arguments that the defense might make at trial and evidence from witnesses other than the defendant that are inconsistent with those statements is also valid.[40]

A waiver of the defendant's rights to exclude evidence of plea agreements and of statements made during the course of plea discussions is valid only if the defendant agreed to the waiver knowingly and voluntarily. A defendant knowingly waives those rights if he or she, at the time the agreement was made, had a full awareness of both the nature of the right he or she was abandoning and the consequences of the decision to abandon it. The waiver is voluntary if it is the product of a free and deliberate choice, rather than of intimidation, coercion, or deception.[41]

Some courts hold that the scope of such a waiver may extend to the prosecution's use of plea agreement statements during its rebuttal case when the accused at trial develops evidence inconsistent with information contained in those statements through the presentation of other witnesses or through cross-examination of the prosecution's witnesses.[42] Others go even further and hold that the accused may agree, even at the outset of the plea discussions, that the prosecution may use what he or she says during those discussions in its case in chief, and is not restricted to using it solely for impeachment.[43]

Moreover, if the accused fails to object to the prosecution's use of Rule 410 evidence in any fashion, the failure constitutes a waiver of his or her rights under the Rule.[44]

There are, however, constitutional considerations that come into play when a waiver is interpreted that broadly. The prosecution would then be effectively

---

[39] United States v. Mezzanatto, 513 U.S. 196, 210, 115 S. Ct. 797, 130 L. Ed. 2d 697 (1995).

[40] *See, e.g.,* United States v. Velez, 354 F.3d 190, 195–196 (2d Cir. 2004).

[41] *See, e.g.,* United States v. Velez, 354 F.3d 190, 196 (2d Cir. 2004).

[42] *See, e.g.,* United States v. Rebbe, 314 F.3d 402, 406–408 (9th Cir. 2002) (pre-negotiation waiver agreement, made in writing in presence of defendant's counsel and signed by both defendant and his counsel, provided sufficient authority for prosecution to use statements defendant made during plea negotiations when defendant cross-examined witnesses and submitted evidence at trial that was inconsistent with statements).

[43] *See, e.g.,* United States v. Young, 223 F.3d 905, 909–911 (8th Cir. 2000) (defendant may waive, in plea agreement, right to prevent government from using during its case in chief information provided during plea discussions, and government need not explicitly inform defendant of nature of those rights for waiver to be voluntary and knowing); United States v. Burch, 156 F.3d 1315, 1319–1322 (D.C. Cir. 1998) (agreement including waiver of all rights under Rule 410 allows prosecution to use plea statements in its case in chief, "absent some affirmative indication that the agreement was entered into unknowingly or involuntarily").

[44] *See, e.g.,* United States v. Manzella, 782 F.2d 533, 546–547 (5th Cir. 1986).

permitted to use the plea bargain statements whenever the accused presents any evidence or makes any argument that does anything other than question the veracity or competence of the prosecution's witnesses or asserts the prosecution's failure to carry its burden of proving guilt beyond a reasonable doubt. In such a case, the broad waiver provision may amount to an unenforceable waiver of the rights under the Sixth Amendment to present a defense and to the assistance of counsel.[45]

§ 7.08   Liability Insurance—Rule 411

[1]—Text and Scope of Rule[1]

Rule 411 specifically excludes evidence not only of the existence but also of the nonexistence of insurance against liability on the issue of defendant's negligence or other wrongful conduct. The Rule provides as follows:

Rule 411.   Liability Insurance.

Evidence that a person was or was not insured against liability is not admissible upon the issue whether the person acted negligently or otherwise wrongfully. This rule does not require the exclusion of evidence of insurance against liability when offered for another purpose, such as proof of agency, ownership, or control, or bias or prejudice of a witness.

[Adopted Jan. 2, 1975, effective July 1, 1975; amended Mar. 2, 1987, effective Oct. 1, 1987.]

Such evidence is excluded in the first instance because it is irrelevant. In the average automobile case, the evidential hypothesis would be: "an insured person is more apt to be careless or reckless or to do an intentional harm than an uninsured person, because someone else will pay for any damages caused by his activity." The probative force of this line of proof is almost nil; no normal person operates a car more carelessly because he is insured. On the contrary, in a state where insurance is not required, carrying insurance shows a thoughtfulness warranting application of the hypothesis: "an insured person is more responsible than an uninsured person, and more responsible people are more apt to drive cars carefully." Even if the hypothesis of carefulness had any substantial probative force, it is likely that this line of proof would prove prejudicial because a juror might think, "After all, some rich insurance company will pay, so we might as well decide for

---

[45] *See, e.g.,* United States v. Duffy, 133 F. Supp. 2d 213, 214–218 (E.D.N.Y. 2001), *disapproved by* United States v. Velez, 354 F.3d 190, 195 (2d Cir. 2004) (section of proffer agreement waiving right to exclude statements made if accused presents any evidence or makes any arguments inconsistent with statements stricken because it amounts to effective waiver of Sixth Amendment rights to present defense and to assistance of counsel).

[1] *See* **Treatise** at §§ 411.02, 411.03, 411.05.

this plaintiff without respect to the law and facts." Taking into account the low probative force and the possibility of prejudice, evidence of insurance in an automobile liability case would probably be excluded under Rules 401 and 403, even without Rule 411.

Seen wholly from the standpoint of relevancy, the whole issue seems somewhat artificial, particularly in those states where automobile insurance is required, because jurors probably assume that most defendants are either insured or judgment proof. The same assumption is probably made with respect to other types of liability insurance.

Rule 411, in addition to excluding evidence of low probative force, also seeks to implement a general public policy favoring insurance. Both insurers and insured are, in effect, encouraged to enter into contracts of insurance with the implied promise that they will not, as a result of their forethought, have what they believe to be the somewhat harmful inference of carelessness used against them.

Although the Rule might be literally interpreted as not covering evidence of the existence or non-existence of the *plaintiff's* liability insurance, such a position would be without merit. Evidence of insurance would be relevant and prejudicial as indicative of fault on the plaintiff's part. Such evidence would further be prejudicial because it suggests that the plaintiff either may be seeking a double recovery or that the real party in interest is the subrogated insurer.

Rule 411, however, is not applicable to direct actions against the insurer. In such cases, it is not possible to keep the jury unaware of the insurance. It is, of course, appropriate for the court to attempt to minimize the possibilities of prejudice by appropriate instructions.[2]

---

[2] While there is discretion to deny impleader under Rule 14 of the Federal Rules of Civil Procedure or to grant separate trials under Civil Rule 42(b) because of prejudice if the jury learns that the defendant is insured, Rule 411 ordinarily does not inhibit courts from exercising their discretion to resolve an entire dispute in one litigation whenever possible. *See, e.g.,* Baker v. Moons, 51 F.R.D. 507, 510 (W.D. Ky. 1971) (impleader permitted); Crockett v. Baysen, 26 F.R.D. 148, 150 (D.C. Minn. 1960) (motion for separate trials denied); Schevling v. Johnson, 122 F. Supp. 87, 89 (D. Conn. 1953) (impleader permitted), *aff'd on opinion below,* 213 F.2d 959 (2d Cir. 1954). *But see* Arnold v. Eastern Air Lines, Inc., 712 F.2d 899, 906 (4th Cir. 1983), *cert. denied,* 464 U.S. 1040 (1984) (consolidation reversible error when it resulted in counsel's revelation to the jury of existence of insurance coverage, and compensatory damages awarded were extremely disproportionate to the average recovery of similarly situated plaintiffs).

Even if an insured co-defendant voluntarily discloses the presence of insurance, the uninsured co-defendant will generally not be permitted to show lack of insurance despite the possibility that the jury will assume all the defendants have insurance. City of Villa Rica v. Couch, 281 F.2d 284, 291–292 (5th Cir. 1960); Jenkins v. Nicholson, 162 F. Supp. 167, 170 (E.D. Pa. 1958). On request, appropriate instructions should be given.

[2]—Exceptions[3]

[a]—When Evidence Is Admissible

Evidence of defendant's insurance against liability is relevant and therefore admissible if its existence tends to prove some material issue and it does not require use of the forbidden hypothesis that "an insured person tends to be more careless (or more careful) than one who is uninsured."[4] Rule 411 sets forth the most common situations in which such evidence has generally been deemed admissible (*see* [b], [c], *below*). These explicit exceptions are not inclusive but are only illustrative.[5]

Although Rule 411 allows the introduction of evidence revealing that there is insurance coverage when it is relevant to issues other than liability, evidence of the limits of liability coverage is not admissible for any purpose. Moreover, curative instructions are not sufficient to remedy the error in admitting such evidence.[5.1]

Evidence that the defendant has insurance to cover the type of liability alleged by the plaintiff may be admissible in spite of Rule 411's exclusionary rule when the defendant has given the jury the impression that it lacks the resources to satisfy a judgment.[5.2] It may also be admissible when the party asserts that it acted in the way it did for economic reasons, rather than for an unlawful discriminatory motive or because it was negligent.[5.3]

---

[3] *See* **Treatise** at § 411.04.

[4] *See, e.g.,* Conde v. Starlight I, Inc., 103 F.3d 210, 214 (1st Cir. 1997) (although barring use of insurance to prove negligence, Rule 411 permits mention of insurance coverage to show possible bias or prejudice of a witness, so witness's status as insurance adjuster was relevant to his credibility as translator of plaintiff's statement).

[5] B. H. Morton v. Zidell Explorations, Inc., 695 F.2d 347, 351 (9th Cir. 1982), *cert. denied,* 460 U.S. 1039 (1983) (evidence that plaintiff secured liability insurance, effective day after contract signed, admitted to show that plaintiffs knew that agreement was binding); Varlack v. SWC Caribbean, Inc., 550 F.2d 171, 176 (3d Cir. 1977) (in support of argument that amendment adding party should relate back, evidence that proposed defendant provided insurance carrier with information and that carrier was real party in interest admitted); Posttape Assocs. v. Eastman Kodak Co., 537 F.2d 751, 758 (3d Cir. 1976) (evidence of indemnification insurance admitted to show party knew it was the custom of trade to limit damages to replacement costs).

[5.1] *See, e.g.,* Reed v. General Motors Corp., 773 F.2d 660, 663–664 (5th Cir. 1985).

[5.2] *See, e.g.,* DSC Communications Corp. v. Next Level Communications, Inc, 929 F. Supp. 239, 248 (E.D. Tex. 1996) (defense counsel opened door to admissibility of evidence regarding indemnification agreement when he implied case was matter of "life and death" to defendants).

[5.3] *See, e.g.,* Weiss v. La Suisse, Societe D'Assurances Sur La Vie, 293 F. Supp. 2d 397, 413–414 (S.D.N.Y. 2003) (defendant's defense that it limited its underwriting of insurance to plaintiffs was result of economic conditions rather than its intent to discriminate against Jews might open the door to evidence that it had reinsured part of the risk it had undertaken); Bernier v. Board of County Road Comm'rs, 581 F. Supp. 71, 78 (W.D. Mich.1983) (defendant's contention that it did not mark intersection where plaintiff's automobile accident occurred because it had limited funds and needed to allocate them to roadways most in need of repair might open door to evidence that

[b]—Control, Agency or the Like

Evidence concerning insurance against liability is admissible in vicarious liability cases when the issue of agency is contested. If the principal carries liability insurance covering the person alleged to be a agent or employee, this fact is strong evidence of the relationship. Evidence of insurance is also admissible to prove that defendant had control over certain property, or that defendant was the owner of the instrumentality causing the accident.[6]

If the evidence of insurance is admitted, the insured should be given a full opportunity to introduce evidence showing why, in the special circumstances of the case, insurance does not indicate control, agency or the like.

Evidence of the nonexistence of liability insurance would normally be less probative of the negative of issues, such as control or agency, than insurance is probative of the issue. Evidence of noninsurance should, therefore, not normally be admissible, since the possible prejudice outweighs any probative force. However, if insurance by the person claimed to be in control is an invariable practice, lack of insurance may be evidence of the person's belief that he or she was not in control.[7]

[c]—Credibility

Evidence disclosing the existence of defendant's liability insurance is admissible for purposes of impeachment.[8] Thus, should an attempt be made to impeach a witness by use of a written statement, plaintiff should be permitted to show that the person procuring the statement was an employee or a representative of a defendant's insurance company if that fact bears on trustworthiness.[9] Yet this rule is not without its limits; if the court has good reason to believe that the insurance

---

it had liability insurance covering its potential exposure to plaintiff).

[6] Hunziker v. Scheidemantle, 543 F.2d 489, 495 n.10 (3d Cir. 1976) (trial court should consider, outside the jury's hearing, whether insurance contract was evidence of agency relationship in order to determine whether exclusion would be more prejudicial to the plaintiff than its admission would be to the defendant).

[7] See § 7.03.

[8] See, e.g., Charter v. Chleborad, 551 F.2d 246, 249 (8th Cir. 1977) (reversible error for court to restrict impeachment of defendant's witness who was employed by insurance carrier representing defendant).

[9] Conde v. Starlight I, Inc., 103 F.3d 210, 214 (1st Cir. 1997) (Rule 411 permits mention of insurance coverage to show possible bias or prejudice of a witness, so witness's status as insurance adjuster was relevant to his credibility as translator of plaintiff's statement); Complete Auto Transit, Inc. v. Wayne Broyles Eng'g Corp., 351 F.2d 478, 481–482 (5th Cir. 1965); Zanetti Bus Lines, Inc. v. Hurd, 320 F.2d 123, 129 (10th Cir. 1963); Mideastern Contracting Corp. v. O'Toole, 55 F.2d 909, 912 (2d Cir. 1932). See also Granberry v. O'Barr, 866 F.2d 112, 114 (5th Cir. 1988) (an eyewitness to an accident who was an employee of an insurer under the same umbrella as defendant's liability carrier made statements immediately after the accident wholly consistent with his trial testimony).

question has almost no bearing on credibility but that it will be used prejudicially, it should exercise its power to exclude.[10] For example, when the witness admits both the authenticity and correctness of the written statement, it has been held that it is proper to refuse disclosure.[11] If the evidence of insurance is disclosed, courts should, if requested, specifically charge the jury that this information can be used only on the issue of credibility and not in determining defendant's liability or in fixing the measure of damages.

[3]—Application[12]

The standard of admissibility established by Rule 411 for evidence of liability insurance is not the same as that for pre-trial discovery. Discovery is permitted whenever the existence of insurance would tend to prove a material proposition of fact in the case. In addition, Rule 26(b)(2) of the Federal Rules of Civil Procedure permits widespread discovery of insurance.[13]

Nor is Rule 411 intended to cover the troublesome question of the propriety of questioning prospective jurors as to possible interest in connection with any insurance carrier, since the issue does not involve a rule of evidence. But the extensive practice of permitting such examinations on voir dire undermines the Rule's efficacy by reminding prospective jurors of the probable existence of insurance.

Federal courts have sought to "strike a balance between the probability of danger to plaintiffs that someone sympathetic to insurance companies may remain on the jury and the danger to defendant that the jury may award damages without fault if aware that there is insurance coverage to pay the verdict."[14] The general practice is that the panel may be questioned with respect to any interest or connection with any insurance company interested in the litigation, although the company is not a party.[15] If, however, the defendant does not possess insurance against liability,

---

[10] Brown v. Walter, 62 F.2d 798, 799 (2d Cir. 1933) (L. Hand, J.); Meek v. Miller, 38 F. Supp. 10, 12 (M.D. Pa. 1941); Coble v. Phillips Petroleum Co., 30 F. Supp. 39, 40 (N.D. Tex. 1939).

[11] Brown v. Edwards, 258 F. Supp. 696, 699 (E.D. Pa. 1966) (applying Pennsylvania law).

[12] See **Treatise** at §§ 411.05–411.06.

[13] Fed. R. Civ. P. 26(b)(2); *see* 6 MOORE's FEDERAL PRACTICE, Ch. 26, *General Provisions Governing Discovery; Duty of Disclosure* (Matthew Bender 3d ed. 1997).

[14] Langley v. Turner's Express, Inc., 375 F.2d 296, 297 (4th Cir. 1967) (examination not permitted, relying in part on state law).

[15] While some courts require plaintiffs to exhibit good faith in making the inquiry, e.g., Hinkle v. Hampton, 388 F.2d 141, 144 (10th Cir. 1968); Socony Mobil Oil Co. v. Taylor, 388 F.2d 586, 589 (5th Cir. 1967); Langley v. Turner's Express Inc., 375 F.2d 296, 297 (4th Cir. 1967), the Third Circuit, in Kiernan v. Van Schaik, 347 F.2d 775, 782 (3d Cir. 1965), held that plaintiffs in accident cases may make reasonable inquiries as a matter of right.

some courts refuse to permit questioning.[16] Others have suggested that questioning will be permitted, but the defendant will have the right to show absence of insurance coverage in order to counteract prejudice.[17] When the judge conducts the voir dire—the usual federal practice—a routine low key question on the subject, buried among many other queries, reduces the significance of the issue and its possible prejudice to the vanishing point.

The insurance rule sometimes does present difficult tactical and ethical problems for the practitioner. If a statement contains both an objectionable reference to insurance and admissible evidence and redaction may lead to misinterpretation, the whole statement will be admitted despite the resulting prejudice.[18] The general principle of Rule 403 provides the court with ample discretion to weigh prejudice against probative force.[19] Counsel for an insured party must be wary of unnecessary participation by insurance investigators in presenting the case, since opposing counsel may expose the insurance carrier's role by means of cross-examination. Thus, counsel must sometimes choose between using a party's written statement in impeaching his credibility and allowing the testimony to go uncontradicted. Using the statement for the purpose of refreshing memory without actually introducing it can sometimes suffice to bring the witness around without disclosing the presence of the insurer. A not uncommon situation is a non-responsive or inadvertent reference to insurance by a witness in response to a proper question. Such references will be stricken on request. They will not require a mistrial in the absence of any indication of bad faith on the part of the witness or of the examining counsel.[20]

---

[16] Hinkle v. Hampton, 388 F.2d 141, 143–144 (10th Cir. 1968); Socony Mobil Oil Co. v. Taylor, 388 F.2d 586, 588–589 (5th Cir. 1967) (relying in part on Texas law).

[17] Eppinger & Russell Co. v. Sheely, 24 F.2d 153, 155 (5th Cir. 1928) (dictum); Socony Mobil Oil Co. v. Taylor, 388 F.2d 586, 588 (5th Cir. 1967).

[18] *See* discussion of Rule 106 and the rule of completeness in Chapter 2.

[19] An admission of a party bearing on the issue of negligence or damages is normally highly probative so that the statement is admissible even if it contains a nonseverable reference to his insurance. Garee v. McDonell, 116 F.2d 78, 80 (7th Cir. 1940), *cert. denied,* 313 U.S. 561 (1941). But if the witness's testimony is clear without revealing the existence of insurance, or if the reference to insurance can be easily deleted from documentary evidence, disclosure is unnecessary and should be avoided. Jamison v. A. M. Byers Co., 330 F.2d 657, 661 (3d Cir. 1964) (failure to delete insurance provisions of a contract required new trial).

[20] *Compare* Cotter v. McKinney, 309 F.2d 447, 450–451 (7th Cir. 1962) (relying on strict Illinois rule to grant mistrial) *and* F.W. Woolworth Co. v. Davis, 41 F.2d 342, 345–346 (10th Cir. 1930) (court expressed disapproval of volunteered testimony suggesting presence of defendant's insurance, but reversed on other grounds) *with* Marks v. Mobil Oil Corp., 562 F. Supp. 759, 768–769 (E.D. Pa. 1983), *aff'd,* 727 F.2d 1100 (3rd Cir. 1984) (inadvertent mention by witness of contact with an insurance company agent in a context that did not affect the substantive rights of the parties was insufficient to support a mistrial).

In the absence of unusual circumstances,[21] the prejudicial effect of an improper disclosure of insurance can be sufficiently reduced to avoid a mistrial by striking, and admonishing the jury to disregard the information.[22] A related problem—the jurors' discovery of the existence of insurance from sources outside the courtroom—also should be handled by admonition rather than a new trial. In the event of improper disclosure, counsel should note the objection and request the attorney to desist at a sidebar conference. By making the objection outside the jury's presence, counsel avoids waiving the right to object to subsequent remarks about a client's insurance, avoids making the remark more prominent in the jury's mind, and preserves the record.

§ 7.09 Sex Offense Victim's Past Behavior—Rule 412[1]

Rule 412 makes inadmissible, except in specified instances, the past sexual behavior[2] of a victim of sexual abuse. Unlike Rule 404, which only makes evidence of one's character inadmissible if offered to prove that one acted in conformity with character, Rule 412 excludes evidence of sexual behavior regardless of the evidentiary hypothesis that is proffered.[3] The Rule provides as follows:

Rule 412.   Sex Offense Cases; Relevance of Alleged Victim's Past Sexual Behavior or Alleged Sexual Predisposition.

(a) Evidence Generally Inadmissible.—The following evidence is not ad-

---

[21]   Cotter v. McKinney, 309 F.2d 447, 450 (7th Cir. 1962) (improper argument by counsel; relying on strong Illinois policy); Transit Casualty Co. v. Transamerica Ins. Co., 387 F.2d 1011, 1013–1014 (8th Cir. 1967) (jury verdict indicated influence by improper references to reinsurance); Indamer Corp. v. Crandon, 217 F.2d 391, 394–395 (5th Cir. 1954) (in light of disproportionate damage award, new trial on damages ordered because of inadequate admonition).

[22]   Crusan v. Ackmann, 342 F.2d 611, 613 (7th Cir. 1965).

[1]   See **Treatise** §§ 412.02–412.05.

[2]   Cf. Government of Virgin Islands v. Scuito, 623 F.2d 869, 875 (3rd Cir. 1980) (holding that trial judge did not abuse discretion in holding that spirit of Rule 412 required him to deny motion by defendant seeking psychiatric examination of rape complainant).

[3]   United States v. Withorn, 204 F.3d 790, 795 (8th Cir. 2000) (absent an applicable exception, Rule 412 specifically bars admission of evidence of past sexual behavior of an alleged rape victim); United States v. Azure, 845 F.2d 1503, 1506 (8th Cir. 1988) (in a child sex abuse prosecution, proffered testimony by witness who claimed to have had sexual relations with the victim was properly excluded; defense claimed that the evidence should have been admitted for impeachment purposes since the victim had denied any contact with witness, and to demonstrate her capability to fabricate); United States v. Cardinal, 782 F.2d 34, 36 (6th Cir. 1986) (evidence that complainant had previously charged the defendant and her stepfather with sexual assault, but later withdrew the charge, was properly excluded even though this proof was offered for the purpose of impeaching the complainant's character for truthfulness). Not all courts recognize this distinction. See Doe v. United States, 666 F.2d 43, 48 (4th Cir. 1981) (reputation evidence admissible when offered solely to show defendant's state of mind).

missible in any civil or criminal proceeding involving alleged sexual misconduct except as provided in subdivisions (b) and (c):

(1) Evidence offered to prove that any alleged victim engaged in other sexual behavior.

(2) Evidence offered to prove any alleged victim's sexual predisposition.

(b) Exceptions.

(1) In a criminal case, the following evidence is admissible, if otherwise admissible under these rules:

(A) evidence of specific instances of sexual behavior by the alleged victim offered to prove that a person other than the accused was the source of semen, injury or other physical evidence;

(B) evidence of specific instances of sexual behavior by the alleged victim with respect to the person accused of the sexual misconduct offered by the accused to prove consent or by the prosecution; and

(C) evidence the exclusion of which would violate the constitutional rights of the defendant.

(2) In a civil case, evidence offered to prove the sexual behavior or sexual predisposition of any alleged victim is admissible if it is otherwise admissible under these rules and its probative value substantially outweighs the danger of harm to any victim and of unfair prejudice to any party. Evidence of an alleged victim's reputation is admissible only if it has been placed in controversy by the alleged victim.

(c) Procedure to Determine Admissibility.

(1) A party intending to offer evidence under subdivision (b) must—

(A) file a written motion at least 14 days before trial specifically describing the evidence and stating the purpose for which it is offered unless the court, for good cause requires a different time for filing or permits filing during trial; and

(B) serve the motion on all parties and notify the alleged victim or, when appropriate, the alleged victim's guardian or representative.

(2) Before admitting evidence under this rule the court must conduct a hearing in camera and afford the victim and parties a right to attend and be heard. The motion, related papers, and the record of the hearing must be sealed and remain under seal unless the court orders otherwise.

[Adopted Oct. 28, 1978, effective Nov. 28, 1978; amended Nov. 18, 1988; Apr. 29, 1994, effective Dec. 1, 1994; Sept. 13, 1994, effective Dec. 1, 1994.]

As the legislative history indicates, the rationale is to prevent the victim, rather than the defendant, from being put on trial.[4] The low incidence of reports of rape was believed to stem from the victim's reluctance to be cross-examined about her sexual past as was permitted under the common-law approach.[5]

The Advisory Committee provided a broad interpretation of the term "evidence of sexual behavior." It includes evidence of any physical sexual conduct and evidence that might imply sexual conduct, such as evidence of the use of contraceptives, of the birth of an out-of-wedlock child, or of the presence of venereal disease. It also extends to evidence of mental activities, such as evidence of sexual fantasies or dreams. Evidence of "predisposition" includes a victim's "mode of dress, speech, or life-style."[6]

The term "evidence of sexual behavior" also includes evidence of chaste behavior, and, therefore, includes evidence that the victim was a virgin at the time of the incident.[6.1] It does not, however, include conduct that is merely indicative of one person's interest in another.[6.2]

Rule 412 recognizes that evidence of the victim's past sexual behavior or predisposition is ordinarily of no probative value on the issue of whether a sexual assault occurred. Congress acknowledged, however, that under some circumstances a victim's sexual behavior may be relevant. Three situations are specified in Rule 412(b) that authorize the criminal defendant to proffer evidence of the victim's sexual behavior: (1) if the defendant is trying to show that someone else

---

[4] *See, e.g.,* B.K.B. v. Maui Police Dep't, 276 F.3d 1091, 1104 (9th Cir. 2002) (purpose of Rule 412 is "to safeguard the alleged victim against the invasion of privacy, potential embarrassment and sexual stereotyping that is associated with public disclosure of intimate sexual details and the infusion of sexual innuendo into the factfinding process").

[5] Rule 412 was amended effective December 1, 1994 "to diminish some of the confusion engendered by the original rule and to expand the protection afforded alleged victims of sexual misconduct." Advisory Committee Note to 1994 amendment. The Committee Note adds that the term "alleged victim" is used "because there will frequently be a factual dispute as to whether sexual misconduct occurred." *See* **Treatise** §§ 412App.03, 412App.100 concerning development of the 1994 amendments.

[6] Fed. R. Evid. 412 Advisory Committee's Note (1994) (reproduced verbatim at § 412.4); *see, e.g.,* United States v. Withorn, 204 F.3d 790, 794 (8th Cir. 2000) (Rule 412(a)(1) barred evidence that alleged victim had made prior accusations of sexual assault against another man); Socks-Brunot v. Hirschvogel, Inc., 184 F.R.D. 113, 120–124 (S.D. Ohio 1999) (Rule 412(b) applies in sexual harassment case to evidence that plaintiff spoke to her co-employees about personal, sexual matters).

[6.1] *See, e.g.,* United States v. Blue Bird, 372 F.3d 989, 995 (8th Cir. 2004).

[6.2] *See, e.g.,* Leidel v. Ameripride Servs, Inc., 291 F. Supp. 2d 1241, 1246 (D. Kan. 2003) (co-worker's testimony that she caught plaintiff looking at her in manner that suggested to her that he might ask her out fell far short of being descriptive evidence of his sexual behavior, sexual history, or sexual predisposition that Rule 412 precludes).

was the source of the semen or injury to the victim;[7] (2) if defendant is claiming consent and wishes to show that the victim had previously engaged in sexual behavior with the defendant; and (3) if the Constitution would so require.[8]

Rule 412's exclusionary rule is equally applicable to the person accused of the sexual misconduct and to the other parties. Thus, in criminal cases, if the defendant is forbidden to play on the jury's prejudices by introducing evidence of the alleged victim's past promiscuity, the government is also forbidden to play on the jury's prejudices by introducing evidence of the alleged victim's lack of sexual experience at the time of the incident.[8.1]

In civil cases, the trial court must assess the proffered evidence to determine whether its probative value outweighs the danger of harm or prejudice to a victim or party. In a decision in which the Eleventh Circuit assumed, without deciding, that Rule 412 applied to cases involving the wrongful transmission of sexually transmitted diseases, the court examined the plaintiff's argument that her sexual history and her employment as a nude dancer should have been excluded under Rule 412 as unfairly prejudicial. However, a central issue of the case was whether the plaintiff contracted herpes from the defendant, and thus the court found evidence of her prior sexual relationships and types of protection used during sexual intercourse to be highly relevant to defendant's liability. In addition, the court found that, despite the potentially prejudicial nature of the evidence, plaintiff's continued employment as a nude dancer was probative as to damages for emotional distress, as it suggested an absence of change in her body image following her herpes infection.[9]

Rule 412(c) requires a defendant to make a written motion at least fourteen days in advance of trial of an intention to offer evidence pursuant to the exceptions in subdivision (b), describing the evidence and the purpose for which it was offered. All parties must be served, and the victim must be notified. The motion, all related papers, and the record of the court's in camera hearing must be sealed and remain

---

[7] United States v. Torres, 937 F.2d 1469, 1474 (9th Cir. 1991) (court properly rejected the argument that evidence of incident occurring months after charged act was admissible under Rule 412 to show source of semen on victim's underpants; evidence irrelevant because garment had been in police custody since date of crime).

[8] *See, e.g.,* Lajoie v. Thompson, 201 F.3d 1166, 1175 (9th Cir. 2000) (ruling of state court that excluded evidence of victim's prior sexual assault by another person violated defendant's Sixth Amendment rights). When evidence of prior behavior is offered pursuant to Rule 412(b)(1) because it is constitutionally required, difficult problems of relevancy frequently arise. *See* **Treatise** at § 412.03[4].

[8.1] *See, e.g.,* United States v. Blue Bird, 372 F.3d 989, 995 (8th Cir. 2004).

[9] Judd v. Rodman, 105 F.3d 1339, 1339–1343 (11th Cir. 1997) (noting that the applicability of Rule 412 to cases involving sexually transmitted diseases has not yet been determined by any court); *see* discussion of relationship between Rule 412(b)(2) and Rule 403 in **Treatise** at § 412.04.

under seal unless the court rules otherwise.[10] A motion made during trial may be permitted by the court if there is "good cause."[11]

Before admitting evidence under Rule 412, the court must conduct a hearing in chambers and afford all parties a right to be heard.[12]

Even if the proffered evidence is found to be relevant to the issues specified in subdivision (b),[13] the subdivision further provides that its probative value must substantially outweigh its prejudicial effect, which is a stricter test than that imposed by Rule 403.[14] When the issue is the alleged victim's sexual conduct in public, however, there is no prejudice associated with the disclosure of that conduct in a litigation setting, because the victim, by acting in public, abrogated any intention to hide the conduct from others.[15]

§ 7.10 Evidence of Prior Acts in Sexual Assault and Child Molestation Cases—Rules 413, 414, and 415[1]

[1]—Criminal Prosecutions—Rules 413 and 414

Rules 413 and 414 apply to criminal proceedings in federal courts begun on or after July 9, 1995.[2] The rules attempt to deal with some of the problems involved in sex crimes prosecutions by greatly liberalizing admission of evidence of a

---

[10] Fed. R. Evid. 412(c)(2); *see, e.g.,* S.M. v. J.K., 262 F.3d 914, 919 (9th Cir. 2001) (trial court properly excluded evidence that was subject of defendant's Rule 412 motion as sanction for defendant's failure to file motion under seal).

[11] According to the Committee Note accompanying the 1994 amendment, in deciding whether to permit late filing, a court may consider the factors enumerated in the pre-amendment version of the Rule: whether the evidence is newly discovered and could not have been obtained earlier, or whether the issue to which the evidence relates is newly arisen.

[12] Records of such a hearing, as well as the motion papers, must remain sealed "unless the court orders otherwise." Rule 412(c)(2).

[13] *See, e.g.,* United States v. Azure, 845 F.2d 1503, 1505–1506 (8th Cir. 1988) (evidence of victim's past sexual conduct was properly excluded as irrelevant to show source of injury because it described conduct that would not have caused injury at issue, time of conduct was not clear, and witness had motive to fabricate testimony).

[14] *See, e.g.,* B.K.B. v. Maui Police Dep't, 276 F.3d 1091, 1104 (9th Cir. 2002).

[15] *See, e.g.,* Beard v. Southern Flying J, Inc., 266 F.3d 792, 801–802 (8th Cir. 2001) (even if Rule 412 is applicable to lawsuit alleging sexual harassment in employment, evidence of female employee's prior sexual misconduct in her workplace was not prejudicial because it was "non-intimate sexual behavior in a public place that she clearly had no intention to hide from others").

[1] *See* **Treatise** at Chapters 413, 414, and 415.

[2] Rules apply in trials commenced on or after effective date of the amendments to the Federal Rules of Evidence contained in the Violent Crime Control and Law Enforcement Act of 1994, Pub. L. 103–322; *see* clarifying amendment in Pub. L. 104–208, § 120.

defendant's similar offenses.[3]

Rule 413 states that evidence of a defendant's past commission of sexual offenses is admissible in criminal cases involving a sexual assault, and that the evidence may be considered for its bearing on any matter to which it is relevant. The rule requires the prosecution to notify the defense of the substance of the evidence at least 15 days prior to trial, although later notification may be permitted "for good cause."[4]

Rule 413 provides as follows:

Rule 413.　Evidence of Similar Crimes in Sexual Assault Cases.

(a) In a criminal case in which the defendant is accused of an offense of sexual assault, evidence of the defendant's commission of another offense or offenses of sexual assault is admissible, and may be considered for its bearing on any matter to which it is relevant.

(b) In a case in which the Government intends to offer evidence under this rule, the attorney for the Government shall disclose the evidence to the defendant, including statements of witnesses or a summary of the substance of any testimony that is expected to be offered, at least fifteen days before the scheduled date of trial or at such later time as the court may allow for good cause.

(c) This rule shall not be construed to limit the admission or consideration of evidence under any other rule.

(d) For purposes of this rule and Rule 415, "offense of sexual assault" means a crime under Federal law or the law of a State (as defined in section 513 of title 18, United States Code) that involved—

(1) any conduct proscribed by chapter 109A of title 18, United States Code;

---

[3] *See, e.g.,* United States v. Withorn, 204 F.3d 790, 794–795 (8th Cir. 2000) (because of parallels between charged assault and defendant's prior sexual assault against another girl, that other girl's testimony was probative evidence showing defendant's "propensity toward the type of behavior" charged; further, evidence did not present danger of unfair prejudice beyond that presented by all propensity evidence allowed by Rules 413 and 414); United States v. Castillo, 140 F.3d 874, 879 (10th Cir. 1998) ("In the cases in which this rule [414] applies, it replaces the restrictive Rule 404(b), which prevents parties from proving their cases through "character" or "propensity" evidence"); United States v. Enjady, 134 F.3d 1427, 1429 (10th Cir. 1998), *cert. denied,* 525 U.S. 887 (1998) ("In passing Rule 413 Congress believed it necessary to lower the obstacles to admission of propensity evidence in a defined class of cases").

[4] "Good cause" presumably might include whether the evidence is newly discovered and could not have been obtained earlier, or whether the issue to which the evidence relates is newly arisen, which are among the factors a court may consider in admitting evidence of a sexual assault victim's sexual history under Rule 412(b). *See* § 7.09.

(2) contact, without consent, between any part of the defendant's body or an object and the genitals or anus of another person;

(3) contact, without consent, between the genitals or anus of the defendant and any part of another person's body;

(4) deriving sexual pleasure or gratification from the infliction of death, bodily injury, or physical pain on another person; or

(5) an attempt or conspiracy to engage in conduct described in paragraph (1)–(4).

[Enacted Sept. 13, 1994, effective July 9, 1995.]

Rule 414 makes similar changes in the prosecution of child molestation cases, by allowing admission of evidence of other acts of molestation by the defendant.[5] The Rule mandates notice to the defense of intent to use such evidence at least 15 days prior to trial. As in Rule 413, later notice may be permitted for "good cause." "Child" is defined by the Rule as a person below the age of 14, and "child molestation" is defined as a crime involving sexual contact with a child, or an attempt or conspiracy to have such contact.

Rule 414 provides as follows:

Rule 414.　Evidence of Similar Crimes in Child Molestation Cases.

(a) In a criminal case in which the defendant is accused of an offense of child molestation, evidence of the defendant's commission of another offense or offenses of child molestation is admissible, and may be considered for its bearing on any matter to which it is relevant.

(b) In a case in which the Government intends to offer evidence under this rule, the attorney for the Government shall disclose the evidence to the defendant, including statements of witnesses or a summary of the substance of any testimony that is expected to be offered, at least fifteen days before the scheduled date of trial or at such later time as the court may allow for good cause.

(c) This rule shall not be construed to limit the admission or consideration of evidence under any other rule.

(d) For purposes of this rule and Rule 415, "child" means a person below the age of fourteen, and "offense of child molestation" means a crime under

---

[5] *See, e.g.,* United States v. Castillo, 140 F.3d 874, 879 (10th Cir. 1998) ("This rule allows the prosecution to use evidence of a defendant's prior acts for the purpose of demonstrating to the jury that the defendant had a disposition of character, or propensity, to commit child molestation").

Federal law or the law of a State (as defined in section 513 of title 18, United States Code) that involved—

(1) any conduct proscribed by chapter 109A of title 18, United States Code, that was committed in relation to a child;

(2) any conduct proscribed by chapter 110 of title 18, United States Code:

(3) contact between any part of the defendant's body or an object and the genitals of the body of a child;

(4) contact between the genitals or anus of the defendant and any part of the body of a child;

(5) deriving sexual pleasure or gratification from the infliction of death, bodily injury, or physical pain on a child; or

(6) an attempt or conspiracy to engage in conduct described in paragraphs (1)–(5).

[Enacted Sept. 13, 1994, effective July 9, 1995.]

[2]—Civil Actions—Rule 415

Rule 415 admits evidence of a defendant's past similar acts in civil cases involving a sexual assault or child molestation offense for its bearing on any matter to which it is relevant.[6] As in Rules 413 and 414, Rule 415 requires the party offering such evidence to notify the party against whom it is offered at least 15 days before trial, although the court may allow later notice for good cause.

Rule 415 provides as follows:

Rule 415.　Evidence of Similar Acts in Civil Cases Concerning Sexual Assault or Child Molestation.

(a) In a civil case in which a claim for damages or other relief is predicated on a party's alleged commission of conduct constituting an offense of sexual assault or child molestation, evidence of that party's commission of another offense or offenses of sexual assault or child molestation is admissible and may be considered as provided in Rule 413 and Rule 414 of these rules.

(b) A party who intends to offer evidence under this Rule shall disclose the evidence to the party against whom it will be offered, including statements

---

[6] *See* Cleveland v. KFC Nat. Management Co., 948 F. Supp 62, 65 (N.D. Ga. 1996) ("under Rule 415, evidence of past misconduct that supports plaintiff's story should be admitted"); *see also* **Treatise** at Chapter 415, *Evidence of Similar Acts in Civil Cases Concerning Sexual Assault or Child Molestation.*

of witnesses or a summary of the substance of any testimony that is expected to be offered, at least fifteen days before the scheduled date of trial or at such later time as the court may allow for good cause.

(c) This rule shall not be construed to limit the admission or consideration of evidence under any other rule.

[*Enacted Sept. 13, 1994, effective July 9, 1995.*]

[3]—Application of Rules 413–415

[a]—Rules Affect Admissibility of Past Similar Acts in Sexual Assault Cases

Rules 413–415 have been the subject of much debate, because they allow introduction of prior sexual assaults or child molestations as evidence of propensity for sexual violence.[7] The Rules do not specify any particular form of other acts evidence, and thus courts have permitted the introduction not only of prior convictions for sexual assault or child molestation, but also evidence of uncharged sexual assaultive or molestative conduct.[8] The burden of proof for admission is not heavy; the trial court need only determine that a reasonable jury could determine by a preponderance of the evidence that the other act came within the rule's definition of an "offense of sexual assault" or "an offense of child molestation" and that the defendant committed it for the evidence of the other act to be admissible.[9] In addition, the language of the Rules does not address the time limit between the charged offense and the prior offense. However, courts have noted that the legislative history indicates that "there is no time limit beyond which sex offenses by a defendant are inadmissible."[10]

Offenses of "sexual assault" and "child molestation" are defined to include

---

[7] *See* United States v. Enjady, 134 F.3d 1427, 1429–1435 (10th Cir. 1998), *cert. denied,* 525 U.S. 887 (1998) (in passing Rule 413, Congress specifically intended to lower the obstacles to admission of propensity evidence in sexual abuse cases); *see also,* Liebman, *Proposed Evidence Rules 413 to 415—Some Problems and Recommendations,* 20 U. of Dayton L. Rev. 753 (1995); Duane, *The New Federal Rules of Evidence on Prior Acts of Accused Sex Offenders: A Poorly Drafted Version of a Very Bad Idea,* 157 F.R.D. 95, 106 (1994).

[8] *See, e.g.,* Blind-Doan v. Sanders, 291 F.3d 1079, 1082–1083 (9th Cir. 2002) (proffered testimony that police officer offered to release her from custody if she had sex with him came within definition of "offense of sexual assault" in Rule 413; its exclusion without clear record showing court's analysis under Rules 403 and 415 was error).

[9] *See, e.g.,* Johnson v. Elk Lake Sch. Dist., 283 F.3d 138, 151–155 (3d Cir. 2002).

[10] *See, e.g.,* United States v. Gabe, 237 F.3d 954, 959–960 (8th Cir. 2001) (testimony about prior act that occurred 20 years before charged act was admissible under Rule 414 even though victim was only seven years old at time of her attack, because prior act was substantially similar to charged act and victim was able to testify to details of attack).

attempts or conspiracies to engage in conduct that is defined to constitute those offenses.[10.1] To qualify as an attempt to commit an offense of sexual assault, the evidence must show that the defendant intended to commit an offense of sexual assault and took some substantial step toward its commission.[10.2] Evidence of activity that does not include a "substantial step" toward the commission of a sexual assault, therefore, is not evidence of an attempt to commit the offense of sexual assault, and is not admissible under Rules 413, 414, or 415.[10.3]

Rules 413, 414, and 415 do not apply solely to acts committed before the charged act. They also permit the introduction of evidence of other offenses of sexual assault that the defendant committed after the charged offense.[10.4]

[b]—Relationship of Rules 413–415 to Other Evidence Rules

Although the language "is admissible" in Rules 413–415 could be read as requiring the admission of all sexual assault evidence in all circumstances, without regard to Rule 403, courts have interpreted the legislative history of the Rules to indicate that the district court must apply Rule 403 balancing.[11]

The Tenth Circuit has determined that Rule 413 would violate the Due Process clause without the safeguard of the balancing required by Rule 403.[12] With the protection of Rule 403 balancing, however, Rule 413 is constitutional.[13] Similarly,

---

[10.1] Fed. R. Evid. 413(d)(5); Fed. R. Evid. 414(d)(6).

[10.2] *See, e.g.,* United States v. Hayward, 359 F.3d 631, 640 (3d Cir. 2004) (defendant must have taken substantial step toward having oral sex with minor to have attempted to violate provisions of 18 U.S.C. § 2243(a) (contained in Chapter 109A)).

[10.3] *See, e.g.,* United States v. Blue Bird, 372 F.3d 989, 993 (8th Cir. 2004) (evidence of defendant's mere solicitation of some kind of sexual contact, coupled with his withdrawal when alleged victim indicated she was not interested, was not admissible under Rule 413 because it did not include evidence of substantial step toward engaging in sexual contact, so it is not evidence of attempted commission of offense of sexual assault).

[10.4] *See, e.g.,* United States v. Sioux, 362 F.3d 1241, 1245–1247 (9th Cir. 2004) (interpreting Rule 413).

[11] *See, e.g.,* Doe by and Through Rudy-Glanzer v. Glanzer, 232 F.3d 1258, 1269 (9th Cir. 2000) ("We find the reasoning adopted by the Tenth and Eighth Circuits regarding the subservience of Fed. R. Evid. 415 (and its companion rules) to Fed. R. Evid. 403 is persuasive and we adopt it as a rule of law for this circuit"); United States v. Guardia, 135 F.3d 1326, 1328–1332 (10th Cir. 1998) (trial court had discretion to exclude prior acts of sexual abuse offered under Rule 413 against physician accused of sexual abuse during course of gynecological examinations, on basis that they would unduly confuse the issues).

[12] United States v. Enjady, 134 F.3d 1427, 1429–1435 (10th Cir. 1998), *cert. denied,* 525 U.S. 887 (1998).

[13] United States v. Mound, 149 F.3d 799, 800–802 (8th Cir. 1998) (Rule 413 does not violate Due Process Clause because authorized evidence is not so "extremely unfair that its admission violates fundamental conceptions of justice"; Rule survives Equal Protection analysis because it does not burden a fundamental right, sex offense defendants are not suspect class, and legislative

Rule 414 does not violate the Due Process clause, because Rule 414 evidence is not admissible unless it surmounts the hurdles of Rules 402 and 403.[14] On the other hand, Rules 413 and 414 are rules of general admissibility, and trial courts must admit evidence of other acts of child molestation liberally.[14.1]

In this context, the Tenth Circuit has set forth four factors the trial court must consider in its Rule 403 balancing in a sexual assault case. First, the court must consider how clearly the prior act has been proved. In this regard, the similar acts must be established by a preponderance of the evidence to ensure that the jury does not hear evidence of similar acts that likely did not occur. Second, the trial court must determine how probative the other acts evidence is of the material fact that it is being offered to prove. Third, the trial court must consider how seriously the parties are disputing that material fact. Finally, the court must determine whether the government can prove the same point by using any less prejudicial evidence. In applying these factors, the court should consider (1) how likely it is that the evidence will contribute to an improperly-based jury verdict, (2) the extent to which the evidence will distract the jury from the central issues of the trial, and (3) how time consuming it will be to prove the prior conduct.[15]

Rules 413, 414, and 415 also state that they shall not be construed to limit the admission or consideration of evidence under any other rule.[16] Thus, the rules were not intended to bar or limit any evidence of past conduct that might be admissible under other evidence rules. For example, evidence of other crimes or misconduct might be admissible under Rule 404(b) to prove some matter other than character.[17]

---

classification bears rational relation to a legitimate end); United States v. Enjady, 134 F.3d 1427, 1429–1435 (10th Cir. 1998), *cert. denied,* 525 U.S. 887 (1998) (subject to Rule 403 protections, Rule 413 does not violate Due Process Clause).

[14] *See, e.g.,* United States v. LeMay, 260 F.3d 1018, 1027 (9th Cir. 2001) (if prior acts of child molestation were properly admitted under Rules 403 and 414, "there can have been no as-applied constitutional violation"); United States v. Gabe, 237 F.3d 954, 959 (8th Cir. 2001) (trial court properly applied Rule 403 to proffered Rule 414 evidence and held that probative value of proffered evidence was not substantially outweighed by its prejudicial effect on defendant); United States v. Castillo, 140 F.3d 874, 879–883 (10th Cir. 1998) (existence of Rule 402 and 403 procedural protections is most significant factor favoring Rule 414's constitutionality).

[14.1] *See, e.g.,* United States v. Drewry, 365 F.3d 957, 959 (10th Cir. 2004).

[15] United States v. Enjady, 134 F.3d 1427, 1429–1435 (10th Cir. 1998), *cert. denied,* 525 U.S. 887 (1998) (Rule 403 imposes essential safeguard on admission of other crimes evidence in sexual abuse cases).

[16] Fed. R. Evid. 413(c), 414(c), 415(c).

[17] *See, e.g.,* United States v. Meacham, 115 F.3d 1488, 1492, 1495 (10th Cir. 1997) (no abuse of discretion in admitting testimony about prior molestation to prove plan, preparation, and intent under Rule 404(b)).

CHAPTER 8

*Authentication and Identification**

SYNOPSIS

---

* Chapter revised in 1991 by WALTER BARTHOLD, of counsel to Ferber Greilsheimer Chan & Essner, New York, New York.

§ 8.01　Requirement of Authentication or Identification—Rule 901

[1]—Approach and Text of Rule 901[1]

Rule 901(a) provides that the evidentiary requirement of authentication or identification is satisfied by evidence sufficient to support a finding that the proffered evidence is what it purports to be.[2] Proof of authenticity entails a showing of how the proffered exhibit is related to the factual issue at hand.

As a prerequisite to admissibility, the proffering party must identify the exhibit in such a fashion as to indicate the information it contains or otherwise reveals is relevant to the pertinent factual issues.[3] Thus, a document may contain information that is apparently of significance to an issue the trier of fact has to decide, but it remains inadmissible unless the proffering party shows that the document is somehow related to the dispute before the court, as, for example, by showing that it is a business record containing pertinent information the proffering party generated in connection with the transaction that is at the heart of the dispute between the parties.[4] The burden of authenticating exhibits, however, is not difficult to satisfy.[4.1]

Rule 901(a) provides:

Rule 901.　Requirement of Authentication or Identification.

(a) General provision. The requirement of authentication or identification as a condition precedent to admissibility is satisfied by evidence sufficient to support a finding that the matter in question is what its proponent claims.

(b) Illustrations. By way of illustration only, and not by way of limitation, the following are examples of authentication or identification conforming with the requirements of this rule:

(1) Testimony of witness with knowledge. Testimony that a matter is what it is claimed to be.

---

[1]　*See* **Treatise** at § 901.02.

[2]　Fed. R. Evid. 901(a).

[3]　*See, e.g.,* Cooper v. Eagle River Mem. Hosp., Inc., 270 F.3d 456, 463–464 (7th Cir. 2001) (pathology slide was properly authenticated as containing specimen of plaintiff's placenta when reference number of slide matched specimen number in plaintiff's pathology report).

[4]　*See, e.g.,* Research Sys. Corp. v. IPSOS Publicite, 276 F.3d 914, 923 (7th Cir. 2002) (when document was offered to show it was in specific person's files and was available to that person at critical times and evidence was sufficient to support jury's conclusion those facts were true, it was not necessary for proponent to prove additional facts, such as identity of document's author, to gain admission).

[4.1]　*See, e.g.,* United States v. Tin Yat Chin, 371 F.3d 31, 37 (2d Cir. 2004) ("Rule 901 does not erect a particularly high hurdle").

(2) Nonexpert opinion on handwriting. Nonexpert opinion as to the genuinesss of handwriting, based upon familiarity not acquired for purposes of the litigation.

(3) Comparison by trier or expert witness. Comparison by the trier of fact or by expert witnesses with specimens which have been authenticated.

(4) Distinctive characteristics and the like. Appearance, contents, substance, internal patterns, or other distinctive characteristics, taken in conjunction with circumstances.

(5) Voice identification. Identification of a voice, whether heard firsthand or through mechanical or electronic transmission or recording, by opinion based upon hearing the voice at any time under circumstances connecting it with the alleged speaker.

(6) Telephone conversations. Telephone conversations, by evidence that a call was made to the number assigned at the time by the telephone company to a particular person or business, if (A) in the case of a person, circumstances, including self-identification, show the person answering to be the one called, or (B) in the case of a business, the call was made to a place of business and the conversation related to business reasonably transacted over the telephone.

(7) Public records or reports. Evidence that a writing authorized by law to be recorded or filed and in fact recorded or filed in a public office, or a purported public record, report, statement, or data compilation, in any form, is from the public office where items of this nature are kept.

(8) Ancient documents or data compilations. Evidence that a document or data compilation, in any form, (A) is in such condition as to create no suspicion concerning its authenticity, (B) was in a place where it, if authentic, would likely be, and (C) has been in existence 20 years or more at the time it is offered.

(9) Process or system. Evidence describing a process or system used to produce a result and showing that the process or system produces an accurate result.

(10) Methods provided by statute or rule. Any method of authentication or identification provided by Act of Congress or by other rules prescribed by the Supreme Court pursuant to statutory authority.

[Adopted Jan. 2, 1975, effective July 1, 1975.]

The proponent of an exhibit has the burden of introducing evidence sufficient to show that the exhibit is what the proponent claims it to be.[5] This burden is inherent in Rule 402's requirement that the courts permit the fact finder to consider only relevant evidence.[6] Once the proponent has made the requisite showing, the trial court should admit the exhibit, assuming it meets the other prerequisites to admissibility, such as relevance and avoidance of the hearsay rule, in spite of any demonstration the opponent may make that the authenticity of the exhibit is defective.[7]

The trial court's admission of the exhibit means only that the fact finder may consider the exhibit during its deliberations. The fact finder remains free to disregard the exhibit if it chooses to do so in light of the defects the opponent may illuminate during cross-examination of the sponsoring witness or through the presentation of direct evidence.[8]

Because authentication rulings are necessarily fact specific, the court reviews such rulings only for mistake of law or abuse of discretion.[9]

Rule 903 [10] adds an additional requirement to establishing authenticity in instances involving documents that under state law require the testimony of an attesting witness. The Rule provides as follows:

Rule 903.　Subscribing Witness' Testimony Unnecessary.

The testimony of a subscribing witness is not necessary to authenticate a writing unless required by the laws of the jurisdiction whose laws govern the validity of the writing.

Only when the validity of the document is in issue need the state's law on

---

[5]　Fed. R. Evid. 901(a).

[6]　*See, e.g.,* United States v. Meienberg, 263 F.3d 1177, 1181 (10th Cir. 2001) (documentary evidence is viewed as irrelevant in absence of proponent's introduction of foundation evidence demonstrating that evidence is what its proponent claims); United States v. Branch, 970 F.2d 1368, 1370 (4th Cir. 1992) (authentication is special aspect of relevance, since evidence cannot have tendency to make existence of disputed fact more or less likely if it is not what proponent claims it to be).

[7]　*See, e.g.,* United States v. Patterson, 277 F.3d 709, 713 (4th Cir. 2002) (proffering party needs only to introduce sufficient evidence to provide jury with basis to resolve authenticity question in his or her favor).

[8]　*See, e.g.,* Orr v. Bank of Am., NT & SA, 285 F.3d 764, 773 n. 6 (9th Cir. 2002) (trial judge's function is to determine whether proponent has presented prima facie evidence of genuineness; if so, evidence is admitted, and trier of fact makes its own determination of evidence's authenticity and weight).

[9]　*See, e.g.,* United States v. Meienberg, 263 F.3d 1177, 1180–1181 (10th Cir. 2001) (trial court's authentication decisions are reviewed for abuse of discretion, that is, they are reversed only when trial court's decision was "arbitrary, capricious, whimsical, or unreasonable").

[10]　*See* **Treatise** at § 903.02.

execution be followed. Thus, for example, if the issue is whether a will is valid and state law requires proof by subscribing witnesses, then the state's law should be followed. But if the will is to be admitted to prove a statement made in it as an admission, to show its contents for other purposes, or to show delivery, then the attesting witness is not required and authenticity can be demonstrated under Rules 901 and 902 rather than under the state statute.

[2]—Methods of Proof

Rule 901(b) provides 10 examples of methods that are acceptable means of providing proof of authenticity or identification of proffered exhibits. They are primarily applicable to documentary proof, are solely illustrations of proper methods of authentication, and in no way limit the means available to a proponent of adducing proof of authenticity or identification.[1] Thus, the general provision of Rule 901(a) controls the issue of proof of authenticity, and proponents may use any or all of the illustrations listed in Rule 901(b), or any combination of them, or any other proof that may be available to them to carry their burden of showing that the proffered exhibit is what they claim it to be.[2]

Exhibits may be authenticated by the testimony of witnesses with knowledge that they are what the proffering party claims them to be.[3] In keeping with the liberal bent of the Federal Rules of Evidence in favor of the admissibility of any evidence that might assist the trier of fact in the performance of its duties, and in recognition of the light burden the proponent of an exhibit has to carry in authenticating it, the "knowledge" requirement of Rule 901(b)(1) is liberally construed.[4]

The chain of custody method of authenticating a proffered exhibit is not mentioned in Rule 901(b)'s list of illustrative examples of proper methods of authentication. It is typically used in criminal cases with respect to evidence that was seized at the time of an arrest or during a search by law enforcement officers. It is also frequently used in connection with the introduction of tape recordings of conversations. The purpose of requiring the proponent to show the chain of custody

---

[1] Fed. R. Evid. 901(b) Advisory Committee's Note (1972) at **Treatise,** § 901App.01[2].

[2] *See, e.g.,* United States v. Tropeano, 252 F.3d 653, 661 (2d Cir. 2001) (Rule 901(b)'s list of methods of authentication is non-exclusive list of illustrative examples; other methods may suffice).

[3] Fed. R. Evid. 901(b)(1); *see, e.g.,* United States v. Mills, 194 F.3d 1108, 1111–1112 (10th Cir. 1999) (when proffered evidence has distinctive characteristics that make it unique, readily identifiable, and relatively resistant to change, its foundation for admission under Rule 901 may be established by testimony that evidence is what proponent claims it to be); *see also* **Treatise** at § 901.03.

[4] *See, e.g.,* Research Sys. Corp. v. IPSOS Publicite, 276 F.3d 914, 924 (7th Cir. 2002) (witness's position as executive in charge of marketing and sale of a product used to test advertising gave him personal knowledge to testify as lay witness that particular exhibit constituted part of a report created by using that product).

of a proffered exhibit is to provide assurances that the exhibit, at the time it is offered into evidence, is in substantially the same condition as it was in when it was seized or made.[5] The proffering party is not required to make a perfect showing of the chain of custody to gain admission of the exhibit; the existence of insubstantial, weak, or missing links in the chain go to the weight the exhibit is to be accorded by the trier of fact, not to its admissibility.[6]

Expert testimony is often useful in authenticating exhibits, and, in some instances, is necessary.[7]

In addition to identifying exhibits on the basis of personal knowledge, lay witnesses can identify them on the basis of their opinions. Rule 901(b) gives two examples of acceptable means of authentication utilizing lay opinion, identification of handwriting,[8] and voice identification.[9] They are both dependent on the lay witness's establishing familiarity with the handwriting or voice in question that was gained through observation.[9.1]

The illustrative example of Rule 901(b)(3) permits expert witnesses and the trier of fact to authenticate exhibits by comparing them with specimens that have already been authenticated.[10] When authentication of an exhibit is accomplished through a simple comparison with a specimen, the specimen, itself, must be proved to be authentic, regardless whether the comparison is made by a lay or an expert witness.[11] If the proponent of the exhibit fails to present a prima facie case for the authenticity of the specimen, even the most careful comparison between the proffered exhibit and the specimen will not suffice to authenticate the proffered exhibit.[12]

---

[5] *See, e.g.,* United States v. Gelzer, 50 F.3d 1133, 1140 (2d Cir. 1994) (principal function of chain of custody authentication is to provide assurances original item was not exchanged for another or otherwise tampered with).

[6] *See, e.g.,* Cooper v. Eagle River Mem. Hosp., Inc., 270 F.3d 456, 463 (7th Cir. 2001).

[7] *See, e.g.,* Tyson v. Keane, 159 F.3d 732, 757 (2d Cir. 1998) ("a jury cannot discern whether a fingerprint from the scene matches defendant's prints without expert assistance").

[8] Fed. R. Evid. 901(b)(2).

[9] Fed. R. Evid. 901(b)(5).

[9.1] *See, e.g.,* United States v. Mansoori, 304 F.3d 635, 665 (7th Cir. 2002) (witness who observed defendants in one court appearance gained sufficient familiarity with their voices to identify them as participants in recorded conversations studied by witness).

[10] Fed. R. Evid. 901(b)(3); *see, e.g.,* Stokes v. United States, 157 U.S. 187, 194–195, 15 S. Ct. 617, 39 L. Ed. 667 (1895) (when writing is determined or admitted to be in handwriting of person or subscribed to by person is in evidence for some other purpose in case, signature or writing on admitted exhibit can be used as comparison sample for authenticating another proffered exhibit); United States v. Keene, 341 F.3d 78, 84 (1st Cir. 2003) (trial court properly permitted jury to make comparison between authenticated handwriting samples of defendant and questioned document).

[11] Fed. R. Evid. 901(b)(3).

[12] *See, e.g.,* United States v. Wagner, 475 F.2d 121, 123 (10th Cir. 1973).

Proponents of exhibits may also prove their authenticity with circumstantial evidence. Indeed, Rule 901(b)(4) specifically permits proponents to prove the authenticity of any type of exhibit with evidence of its "appearance, contents, substance, internal patterns, or other distinctive characteristics, taken in conjunction with circumstances."[13] The proof of authenticity may consist entirely of circumstantial evidence; no direct evidence is required.[14]

[3]—Authentication of Particular Types of Evidence

[a]—Writings

Rule 901(b)(2) permits a lay witness to identify handwriting based on his or her familiarity with another person's handwriting, so long as the familiarity was not acquired for the purpose of the litigation.[1] The effect of a lay witness's opinion testimony identifying the handwriting on a handwritten document, or the signature on a document produced by a means other than handwriting, is to authenticate the document, either as having been prepared by the alleged author, or as having been adopted by the person whose signature appears on it.[2] Evidence of the lay witness's familiarity with the alleged author's handwriting must indicate that the witness's prior exposure to the alleged author's handwriting reasonably supports his or her conclusion concerning the identity of the author of the proffered exhibit.[3] Moreover, a witness's opinion testimony identifying handwriting must pass muster under Rule 701 as well as under Rule 901(b)(2).[3.1]

Rule 901(b)(3) clearly contemplates a role for expert witnesses in offering opinion testimony as to the authenticity of exhibits, including writings, by comparison with authenticated specimens.[4] In particular, many courts have recognized handwriting analysis as a field of expertise yielding admissible expert opinion to

---

[13]   Fed. R. Evid. 901(b)(4).

[14]   *See, e.g.,* United States v. Smith, 223 F.3d 554, 570 (7th Cir. 2000) (list describing hierarchical structure of organization that could only have been prepared by member of organization was properly authenticated by information it contained, as well as by its location when it was found during search; it was not necessary that proponent identify specific person who created it).

[1]   Fed. R. Evid. 901(b)(2); *see, e.g.,* United States v. Scott, 270 F.3d 30 (1st Cir. 2001); *see also* **Treatise**, at § 901.04.

[2]   *See, e.g.,* United States v. Scott, 270 F.3d 30, 49–50 (1st Cir. 2001) (lay testimony of law enforcement officer who had become familiar with defendant's handwriting during several previous criminal investigations was sufficient to authenticate handwriting on documents already in evidence as defendant's).

[3]   *See, e.g.,* United States v. Scott, 270 F.3d 30 (1st Cir. 2001) (IRS agent's testimony that he had seen defendant's handwriting on numerous documents during investigation extending over several years was sufficient to permit agent to authenticate handwriting).

[3.1]   *See, e.g.,* Hall v. United Ins. Co. of Am., 367 F.3d 1255, 1259 (11th Cir. 2004) (testimony must be rationally based on witness's perception).

[4]   Fed. R. Evid. 901(b)(3); *see* **Treatise** at §§ 901.04, 901.05.

assist the fact finder in comparing handwriting on proffered documents with samples of handwriting from other documents whose authenticity is not controverted or from handwriting exemplars.[5] Other types of experts, in addition to handwriting analysts, can provide opinion testimony useful to the finder of fact in determining the authenticity of written exhibits, assuming the testimony meets the requirements of Rule 702 and Rule 703. They should also be able to provide acceptable authentication evidence under the general authenticity rule, Rule 901(a), and as a witness with knowledge under the first illustrative example of acceptable authentication, Rule 901(b)(1), neither of which, on their faces, are restricted to lay testimony.[6]

Expert testimony is not necessary, however, to authenticate handwriting by the method of comparing the handwriting on a proffered exhibit with the handwriting on an admittedly authentic exemplar. The trier of fact may also perform that task.[7]

The contents or subject matter of written exhibits can contain circumstantial authenticating evidence indicating the identity of their authors. For example, if a writing contains entries relating to information known only to a few people, it is reasonable to assume one of them wrote it.[8]

Certain physical attributes of a written exhibit can also serve to authenticate it. Thus, a written document's post mark, return address, letterhead, or format may, individually, in combination with one another, or in conjunction with other authenticating factors, identify it with one or more of the parties to the law suit or with a fact at issue.[9]

Extrinsic evidence of circumstances preceding, surrounding, or following the

---

[5] *See, e.g.*, United States v. Mooney, 315 F.3d 54, 62–63 (1st Cir. 2002) (trial court properly admitted qualified and reliable expert testimony that questioned documents were written by defendant, based on comparison of questioned documents with exemplars of defendant's handwriting).

[6] *See, e.g.*, United States v. Chang, 207 F.3d 1169, 1173 (9th Cir. 2000) (government expert witness properly testified to opinion that certificate of obligation purportedly issued by Japanese government was counterfeit based on his knowledge of printing and manufacturing).

[7] Fed. R. Evid. 901(b)(3); *see, e.g.*, Traction Wholesale Ctr. Co. v. National Labor Rel. Bd., 216 F.3d 92, 104 (D.C. Cir. 2000) (trier of fact could properly use as specimens documents in employer's files that were signed by employee and on which employer relied in hiring employee).

[8] *See, e.g.*, United States v. Jones, 107 F.3d 1147, 1149–1150 (6th Cir. 1997) (writing may be authenticated by evidence that it deals with matter sufficiently obscure or peculiarly within knowledge of persons corresponding that contents of writing were not matter of common knowledge).

[9] *See, e.g.*, United States v. McMahon, 938 F.2d 1501, 1508–1509 (1st Cir. 1991) (unsigned handwritten note defendant passed to another person was authenticated as having been written by defendant, in part, by author's use of personal pronoun "I" twice in requests for help, suggesting in absence of signature that passer of note was its author).

creation of a written exhibit may authenticate it. If the parties to a business transaction follow a course of dealing consistent with information transmitted in correspondence between the parties, that course of dealing may authenticate the correspondence.[10] Similarly, when a written exhibit contains information that correlates closely to other admitted evidence, that correlation may authenticate the written document.[11] Moreover, correspondence that, on its face, appears to be responsive to other correspondence already in evidence carries strong indicia of reliability and is, therefore, taken as authentic.[12]

[b]—Audio and Video Recordings

Two Circuits have expressed particular concern with the potential for undetectable alterations of magnetic tapes recording conversations. Those concerns lead the Eighth and Third Circuits to adopt a formalized approach to authentication of audio tapes, requiring proof of the following facts in the authentication process:[13]

- The recording device was capable of recording the conversation;
- The operator was competent to operate the device;
- The recording was authentic and correct;
- No changes, additions, or deletions were made in the recording;
- The recording was preserved;
- The speakers are identified; and
- The elicited conversation was made without inducement.

Other Circuits have reasoned that the potential for undetectably altering magnetic media should not lead to a substantially different standard for the trial court's threshold determination of authentication. They have held that tape recorded conversations are appropriately authenticated when the proponent shows the fol-

---

[10] See, e.g., United States v. Hoag, 823 F.2d 1123, 1126–1127 (7th Cir. 1987) (letters were properly authenticated when all were written on real estate company's letterhead and referred to specific real estate transactions that occurred on or about each letter's date).

[11] See, e.g., United States v. Holmquist, 36 F.3d 154, 167 (1st Cir. 1994) (photocopy of check in amount of $2,500 dated December 20, 1988, and payable to defendant was authenticated by evidence of invoice in defendant's handwriting showing credit in favor of maker of check in amount of $2,500, also dated December 28, 1988).

[12] See, e.g., Winel v. United States, 365 F.2d 646, 648 (8th Cir. 1966) (principal situation in which letter can be authenticated by circumstantial evidence is when it was sent in reply to previous communication).

[13] United States v. McMillan, 508 F.2d 101, 104 (8th Cir. 1974); United States v. Starks, 515 F.2d 112, 121 (3d Cir. 1975).

lowing facts:[14]

- The operator's competence;

- The fidelity of the recording equipment;

- The absence of material alterations; and

- The identification of relevant sounds or voices.

The courts applying the more relaxed standard have not been rigorous in the enforcement of even those limited requirements. They recognize that the objective of authentication is to provide reasonable assurances that the taped conversation accurately portrays what each party to the conversation actually said, and uphold the trial court's exercise of its discretion in admitting recordings whenever the proponent's evidence gives those assurances, even though the proponent's proof may not address particular prerequisites to authentication as set forth in their precedents.[15]

Proof of authenticity of magnetic media can almost always be accomplished by evidence of a proper chain of custody (*see* [2], *above,* for discussion of authentication by chain of custody evidence).[16] Gaps in the chain usually go to the weight to be accorded the evidence, not to its admissibility.[17] Moreover, in the absence of substantial evidence of alteration while the tape recording was in government custody, the government is usually entitled to a presumption of regularity in its treatment of the evidence.[18]

Proof of authenticity of magnetic media can also almost always be accomplished through testimony from a participant in the events recorded, or from an eyewitness who observed those events, that the tape accurately recorded the events in question.[19]

---

[14] *See, e.g.,* Stringel v. Methodist Hosp., 89 F.3d 415, 419 (7th Cir. 1996); United States v. Biggins, 551, F.2d 64, 67 (5th Cir. 1977).

[15] *See, e.g.,* United States v. Westmoreland, 312 F.3d 302, 310–311 (7th Cir. 2002) (trial court properly admitted tape recordings of defendant's conversations based on testimony of police officer who overheard conversations while they were being recorded and testified to their accuracy).

[16] *See, e.g.,* Smith v. City of Chicago, 242 F.3d 737, 741 (7th Cir. 2001) (proponent can authenticate tape recording in one of two ways: (1) chain of custody, or (2) foundation testimony of accuracy and trustworthiness from eyewitness).

[17] *See, e.g.,* United States v. Mills, 194 F.3d 1108, 1111 (10th Cir. 1999) (except for obvious deletion, which was adequately explained by testimony, video tape was "readily identifiable" and chain of custody evidence was adequate to authenticate it, despite gaps in chain of custody evidence, which went to weight to be given to tape, not to its admissibility).

[18] *See, e.g.,* United States v. Rengifo, 789 F.2d 975, 978 (1st Cir. 1986).

[19] *See, e.g.,* United States v. Tropeano, 252 F.3d 653, 661 (2d Cir. 2001) (tape recorded conversations were properly authenticated by testimony of participants); Stringel v. Methodist Hosp., 89 F.3d 415, 420 (7th Cir. 1996).

Partial unintelligibility does not render tape recordings inadmissible unless the unintelligible portions are so substantial as to render the recording as a whole untrustworthy.[20] The trial court has discretion to permit the proffering party to provide the finder of fact with written transcripts of the tape recording to assist it in interpreting portions of the recording that are difficult to understand.[21] The proponent may also introduce an enhanced copy of a tape recording that has unintelligible portions, so long as the enhancement process does not alter the substance of the conversation that was recorded.[22]

A duplicate tape recording is authenticated by proof it is a true and correct copy of a duly authenticated original tape recording or in the same manner as the authenticity of the original is proved.[23] If there is a serious question as to the authenticity of the underlying original tape recording, however, the proponent must prove that the original is what the proponent claims it to be and that the duplicate is merely a copy.[24]

The rules for authenticating audio recordings in each Circuit are also generally applicable to video recordings.[25]

[c]—Voice Identification[26]

A lay witness may testify to his or her opinion concerning the identity of a person speaking on a particular occasion when the opinion is based on the witness's having heard that person's voice on at least one other occasion under circumstances connecting the voice with the person the witness identifies as having spoken on the

---

[20] *See, e.g.,* United States v. Solis Jordan, 223 F.3d 676, 688 (7th Cir. 2000).

[21] *See, e.g.,* United States v. Young, 105 F.3d 1, 10 (1st Cir. 1997) (written transcripts of tape recordings may be used to assist jury in interpreting tapes with low intelligibility if proper safeguards are employed).

[22] *See, e.g.,* United States v. Thompson, 130 F.3d 676, 683–684 (5th Cir. 1997) (copy of tape recording that enhances its intelligibility through use of audio filters to lessen effect of background noises without adding to or detracting from substance of conversation is admissible within discretion of trial court).

[23] *See, e.g.,* United States v. Rivera, 153 F.3d 809, 812–813 (7th Cir. 1998).

[24] *See, e.g.,* Smith v. City of Chicago, 242 F.3d 737, 741 (7th Cir. 2001).

[25] *See, e.g.,* United States v. Roach, 28 F.3d 729, 733 (8th Cir. 1994) (authentication of video tape was proper under *McMillan* (United States v. McMillan, 508 F.2d 101, 104 (8th Cir. 1974) standards, which are applicable to audio tapes, even though trial court did not specifically address several of the factors those standards establish for the authentication of audio tapes; evidence of record adequately established that some of those factors were adequately met, and opponent did not raise others).

[26] *See* **Treatise** at § 901.07.

particular occasion.[27] Such aural voice identification is not a proper subject of expert opinion testimony.[28]

Substantial familiarity with the voice to be identified will qualify a lay witness to give opinion identification testimony under either Rule 701 or Rule 901(b)(5).[29] The lay witness's familiarity with the identified speaker's voice, however, may be minimal and still suffice for identification under Rule 901(b)(5).[30]

[d]—Telephone Calls[31]

A telephone conversation with a specific person may be authenticated by evidence that the call was made to the number assigned at that time by the telephone company to that person, coupled with circumstances, such as self-identification, showing that the person who answered the telephone was the person called.[32] Generally, self-identification by the person who was called at a telephone number where that individual would be expected to be is sufficient to authenticate the call, when there is no probable motive for fraud.[33]

Self-identification by the person who places a call on the telephone, however, is not sufficient evidence of the authenticity of the conversation; additional evidence of identity is required.[34] The additional evidence to identify the person who placed the call need not fall in any set pattern, and can be purely circumstantial.[35]

Events prior or subsequent to a telephone conversation may sufficiently authen-

---

[27]   Fed. R. Evid. 901(b)(5).
[28]   Fed. R. Evid. 901(b)(5) Advisory Committee's Note (1972) (*see* **Treatise** at § 901App.01[2]).
[29]   *See, e.g.,* United States v. Briscoe, 896 F.2d 1476, 1490 (7th Cir. 1990) (witness who had spoken with certain defendants on at least 150 separate occasions prior to date tape recordings were made was qualified to identify their voices on tapes).
[30]   *See, e.g.,* United States v. Mansoori, 304 F.3d 635, 665 (7th Cir. 2002) ((Rule 901(b)(5) permits lay witnesses to identify voice of participant in tape recorded conversation based on one instance in which witness observed participant speaking during court proceeding).
[31]   *See* **Treatise** at § 901.08.
[32]   Fed. R. Evid. 901(b)(6).
[33]   *See, e.g.,* O'Neal v. Morgan, 637 F.2d 846, 850 (2d Cir. 1980) (self-identification of person called is not sufficient alone, but may be when joined by "some additional evidence," such as that person called was located where he or she reasonably was expected to be).
[34]   Fed. R. Evid. 901(b)(6) Advisory Committee's Note (1972) (*see* **Treatise** at § 901App.01[2]) (cases are in agreement that mere assertion of identity by person speaking on telephone is insufficient, by itself, to authenticate communication).
[35]   *See, e.g.,* United States v. Gurmeet Singh Dhinsa, 243 F.3d 635, 658 (2d Cir. 2001) (evidence sufficiently authenticated caller's identity as defendant's when caller identified himself as defendant and there was need for caller to let recipient of call know who he really was to receive benefit of threat made during telephone conversation).

ticate the call, with or without any further identification of the speakers.[36]

Telephone calls made to a business may be authenticated by evidence that the call was made to a place of business and that the conversation "related to business reasonably transacted over the telephone."[37] Listing a business telephone number in a directory or any other form of advertising that gives a business telephone number is assumed to be an invitation to the public to transact business with the company by calling that number without further identification.[38] A business owner should know that the public will act on that assumption. Thus, all that is necessary to gain admission of the content of the conversation is for the proponent to show that the call was placed to the place of business and that someone at that place answered, purporting to act for the business establishment.[39]

[e]—Computer Data

Computerized business records are admissible into evidence under essentially the same conditions as apply to the admission of non-computerized records of a regularly conducted activity under Rule 803(6). No additional authenticating evidence is required just because the records are in computerized form.[40] That the computer, itself, may have generated the data its data base contains is not a ground for denying authenticity, or even admissibility, to the record.[41]

The sponsoring witness needs only to meet the requirements of Rule 803(6) to authenticate the computerized business records and to qualify them for admission into evidence (see Ch. 16). It is not necessary that the sponsoring witness:

- be a computer programmer.[42]

---

[36] *See, e.g.,* United States v. Leon, 679 F.2d 534, 539 (5th Cir. 1982) (tapes of telephone call between witness and person she did not know were properly admitted when caller gave description of himself, arranged meeting with witness, told witness he had picture of her, and subsequently witness met man who fit description at arranged meeting place and he showed her picture of herself).

[37] Fed. R. Evid. 901(b)(6)(B).

[38] Fed. R. Evid. 901(b)(6) Advisory Committee's Note (1972) (*see* **Treatise** at § 901App.01[2]).

[39] *See, e.g.,* United States v. Portsmouth Paving Corp., 694 F.2d 312, 322 (4th Cir. 1982) (witness's testimony that he called defendant's business office supports inference that person who answered telephone was defendant's agent).

[40] *See, e.g.,* United States v. Jackson, 208 F.3d 633, 638 (7th Cir. 2000).

[41] *See, e.g.,* United States v. Meienberg, 263 F.3d 1177, 1181 (10th Cir. 2001) ("Any question as to the accuracy of the printouts, whether resulting from incorrect data entry or the operation of the computer program, as with inaccuracies in any other type of business records, would have affected only the weight of the printouts, not their admissibility").

[42] *See, e.g.,* United States v. Salgado, 250 F.3d 438, 453 (6th Cir. 2001) (sponsoring witness need not be person who programmed computer).

- be able to testify as to how the computer was tested for programming errors.[43]

- be the person who actually entered the data or prepared the record.[44]

- offer evidence the computer was mechanically accurate in producing reliable or accurate results beyond what is necessary to support a conclusion that the proffered information, itself, is reliable.[45]

When computerized records are prepared for purposes of litigation, they do not have the requisite reliability to qualify for admissibility as business records, the trustworthiness of which is dependent upon the business's reliance upon them in conducting their business, rather than in preparing for litigation (see **Treatise**, Ch 803 for discussion of bases for trustworthiness of records of regularly conducted activity). This does not mean, however, that printouts prepared specifically for litigation from databases that were compiled in the ordinary course of business are not identifiable and admissible as business records. To the contrary, they are fully as identifiable and admissible as are printouts that were, themselves, prepared in the ordinary course of business. The important issue is whether the database, not the printout that is prepared from the database, was compiled in the ordinary course of business.[46]

[f]—E-Mail and Chat Room Conversations

E-mail messages can generally be authenticated by the same types of circumstantial evidence as are effective to authenticate any other correspondence. *See* [2] *above,* for discussion of authentication in general by circumstantial evidence; [3][a], *above,* for discussion of circumstantial proof of authenticity of writings. Thus e-mail messages were properly authenticated as having been sent by the defendant by evidence that:[47]

- They bore the defendant's e-mail address;

- The e-mail address they bore was the same as the e-mail address on a message sent to the defendant that the defendant admitted having received;

---

[43] *See, e.g.,* United States v. Weinstock, 153 F.3d 272, 276 (6th Cir. 1998) (witness sponsoring computer generated business records need not know personally how company conducted safety checks for errors in database).

[44] *See, e.g.,* United States v. Hutson, 821 F.2d 1015, 1020 (5th Cir. 1987).

[45] *See, e.g.,* United States v. Salgado, 250 F.3d 438, 453 (6th Cir. 2001) (party offering computerized business records need not present evidence as to mechanical accuracy of computer when evidence indicates computer was sufficiently accurate that company relied on it in conducting its business).

[46] *See, e.g.,* United States v. Meienberg, 263 F.3d 1177, 1181 (10th Cir. 2001) (testimony of witness from office of state agency that computer printout reflected agency's record of approval numbers it issued to defendant's gun shop in connection with background checks it performed regarding his potential customers was sufficient to authenticate printout).

[47] United States v. Siddiqui, 235 F.3d 1318, 1322 (11th Cir. 2000).

- When a recipient of one of the messages in question sent a reply message using his e-mail client program's reply function, his e-mail client program automatically sent the reply message to the defendant's e-mail address;

- The content of the messages indicated the sender's knowledge of facts known peculiarly to the defendant;

- The e-mail messages referred to the sender by the defendant's nickname; and

- The defendant subsequently, during telephone conversations, made the same requests of the recipients of the e-mail messages as the sender had made in the e-mail messages.

The requirements for authenticating a chat room conversation are no different than the requirements for authenticating any other evidence. It is necessary that the proponent introduce evidence sufficient to sustain a finding that the proffered evidence is what the proponent says it is, along with evidence to connect the chat room conversation with the person against whom it is offered.[48]

The connection between a party and a chat room conversation can be shown by extrinsic circumstantial evidence.[49]

[g]—Translations

The 2000 amendments to Rule 701 appear to limit quite severely the circumstances under which lay witnesses can provide evidence by translating foreign languages into English.[50] Knowledge of a foreign language is certainly "specialized knowledge" within the terms of that Rule, and testimony translating a foreign language into English seems appropriately relegated, in most instances, to the realm

---

[48] *See, e.g.,* United States v. Tank, 200 F.3d 627, 630, 631 (9th Cir. 2000) (when assessing adequacy of authentication of chat room conversation print out, appellate court reviews trial court's finding of authenticity for abuse of discretion, foundational requirement is satisfied by evidence sufficient to sustain finding print out is what proponent says it is, proponent is required only to make prima facie showing, and proponent must establish connection between proffered evidence and party against whom it is offered).

[49] *See, e.g.,* United States v. Simpson, 152 F.3d 1241, 1250 (10th Cir. 1998) (chat room conversation authenticated by testimony from another participant that person participating in conversation gave testifying witness defendant's name as his own, along with defendant's correct street and e-mail addresses, coupled with evidence that subsequent e-mail exchanges between defendant and witness indicated use of e-mail address belonging to defendant and that documents seized from defendant's home contained testifying witness's screen name, along with his street address, e-mail address, and telephone number, all of which testifying witness had given to defendant during chat room conversation at issue).

[50] Fed. R. Evid. 701 (contains new language limiting lay witness opinion testimony to circumstances in which it is not "based on scientific, technical, or other specialized knowledge within the scope of Rule 702"); *see* Ch. 10.

of expert testimony.[51]

There are, however, instances in which it may be appropriate for the court to accept as accurate and authentic translations from a foreign language into English, or into another foreign language, by a lay witness. In some instances, the translation is done in an out-of-court setting and the results of the translation are what are reported to the court. In those circumstances, it may be appropriate for the court to admit evidence of the translation as accurate when it has been authenticated by circumstantial evidence.[52]

Some courts require the proponent of English language transcripts of tape recorded conversations conducted in a foreign language to present an expert witness to authenticate the translation transcripts, and others merely permit them to do so, making use of the techniques employed when there is a dispute for any reason concerning the accuracy of transcripts of recorded conversations to resolve disputes concerning the accuracy of translations.[53]

The fluency of any translator, expert or lay, is always subject to attack, either through cross-examination or presentation of rebuttal evidence.[54]

[h]—Public Records or Reports[55]

Rule 901(b)(7) permits authentication of certain documents by evidence that they are authorized by law to be recorded or filed in a public office and that they are in fact so recorded and filed. The proponent of recorded and filed documents may prove their authenticity by proving that the appropriate public office has custody of them, without further proof.[56] It is necessary, however, to show that the document was actually recorded and is kept in the public office's files of recorded

---

[51] *See, e.g.,* Mawby v. United States, 999 F.2d 1252, 1254 n. 1 (8th Cir. 1993) (expert witness is one who is knowledgeable in specialized area).

[52] *See, e.g.,* United States v. Nazemian, 948 F.2d 522, 527–528 (9th Cir. 1991) (although proponent presented no evidence of interpreter's formal qualifications, when one party to conversation concerning proposed transaction in illegal drugs spoke Farsi and other party spoke French, and each party's portion of conversation was translated for the other party by interpreter, accuracy of translation was shown by evidence that interpreter was motivated to perform translation accurately, and that actions of participants in conversation subsequent to conversation were consistent with interpreter's translations of what was said during conversation, and by defendant's failure to point out specific inaccuracies in reported translation).

[53] *See, e.g.,* United States v. Sutherland, 656 F.2d 1181, 1201–1202 (5th Cir. 1981).

[54] *See, e.g.,* Security Farms v. International Bhd. of Teamsters, 124 F.3d 999, 1010 (9th Cir. 1997) (trial court properly concluded employees' affidavits were not properly authenticated because they were in language in which employees were not fluent and affidavits had, in all likelihood, not been translated for employees before they executed them).

[55] *See* **Treatise** at § 901.09.

[56] Fed. R. Evid. 901(b)(7) Advisory Committee's Note (1972) (*see* **Treatise** at § 901App.01[2]).

documents, rather than in working files in that office.[57]

Rule 44 of the Federal Rules of Civil Procedure provides specific means of proving that a document has been recorded and filed in an appropriately authorized public office.[58] Rule 44's certification process, however, is not the only means available to proponents of recorded documents to authenticate them; any other means reasonably calculated to show that the document was duly filed and recorded is appropriate.[59]

Rule 901(b)(7) also permits authentication of documents that purport to be public records, reports, statements, or data compilations, without regard to their form, by evidence that they come from the public office where items of that nature are kept. The proponent of the evidence need only show that the office from which the records were taken is the legal custodian of the records.

Legal custodianship can be shown in the following ways:

- A certificate of authenticity from the public office.[60]

- The testimony of a person of the office authorized to attest to custodianship.[61]

- The testimony of a witness with knowledge that the evidence is in fact from a public office authorized to keep such a record.[62]

---

[57] *See, e.g.,* Amoco Prod. Co. v. United States, 619 F.2d 1383, 1391 n.7 (10th Cir. 1980) (mere proof that copy of deed was deposited in government agency's working file is not, by itself sufficient to authenticate deed, even though copy apparently bore stamps indicating recordation and filing).

[58] Fed. R. Civ. P. 44(a)(1) ("An official record . . . may be evidenced by an official publication thereof or by a copy attested by the officer having the legal custody of the record, or by the officer's deputy, and accompanied by a certificate that such officer has the custody.").

[59] *See, e.g.,* United States v. Hernandez-Herrera, 952 F.2d 342, 343 (10th Cir. 1991) (public records can be authenticated by any probative evidence that proves them to be what proponent claims them to be).

[60] *See, e.g.,* United States v. Layne, 973 F.2d 1417, 1422 (8th Cir. 1992) (court records were appropriately authenticated as public records under Rule 901(b)(7) by certification from clerk of court in which they were filed).

[61] *See, e.g.,* United States v. Jimenez Lopez, 873 F.2d 769, 772 (5th Cir. 1989) (prior judgment of conviction for illegal entry into U.S. was properly authenticated by border patrol agent).

[62] *See, e.g.,* United States v. Hernandez-Herrera, 952 F.2d 342, 343–344 (10th Cir. 1991) (testimony of Immigration and Naturalization Service agent concerning circumstances under which agency collected information and completed official forms, concerning information gathering and recording procedures of agency, and concerning how specific forms relating to defendant were retrieved from agency files was sufficient to authenticate forms relating to defendant under Rule 901(b)(7), even though authenticating witness played no role in compiling information concerning defendant and had not seen forms before he had them retrieved from agency office in which he had never worked).

[i]—Ancient Documents or Data Compilations[63]

Under Rule 901(b)(8), ancient documents and data compilations may be authenticated by a three-part foundation:[64]

- The document must appear to be in a form that does not create suspicion of alteration, incompleteness, or lack of genuineness.

- Evidence must be presented that the document was found in a location where one would expect an authentic item of the document's purported nature and vintage to be found.

- The document must be at least 20 years old at the time that it is offered as an exhibit.

The authentication requirements for ancient documents are precisely the same as the requirements for proving they are excepted from the hearsay rule. A document authenticated as an ancient document under Rule 901(b)(8) is, therefore, also automatically excepted from the hearsay rule as an ancient document.[65]

The suspicion of alteration, incompleteness, or lack of genuineness that properly bars authentication to a purportedly ancient document relates to whether the document is what it purports to be, not to the veracity of the contents. Any question about the credibility of the document's contents goes to weight, not to admissibility.[66]

While other elements of authentication as an ancient document, such as the document's age and non-suspicious condition, may be established by evidence appearing on the its face, the proponent of the document must introduce affirmative evidence to establish that the document was found in a reasonably expected place.[67]

The propriety of the location in which the document was found is largely dependent upon the nature of the document itself. Some examples of the locations

---

[63] *See* **Treatise** at § 901.10.

[64] Fed. R. Evid. 901(b)(8).

[65] *See, e.g.,* Threadgill v. Armstrong World Indus. Inc., 928 F.2d 1366, 1375–1376 (3d Cir. 1991) (internal corporate documents concerning health risks of working with asbestos authenticated as ancient documents are also excepted from hearsay rule).

[66] *See, e.g.,* Kalamazoo River Study Group v. Menasha Corp., 228 F.3d 648, 661 (6th Cir. 2000) (although Rule 901(b)(8) requires proffered ancient document to be free of suspicion, that suspicion does not go to document's content, but rather to whether document is what it purports to be; questions as to documents' content and completeness bear upon weight to be accorded to evidence and do not affect threshold question of authenticity).

[67] *See, e.g.,* Kalamazoo River Study Group. v. Menasha Corp., 228 F.3d 648, 661–662 (6th Cir. 2000) (when sponsoring witness was unable to identify report's author or to say why it was found in company's files, he was unable to authenticate it as ancient document under Rule 901(8)).

where documents were found that supported their qualification as ancient documents are:

- A deed in the custody of the grantee or heirs.[68]

- Maps or records found in the possession of a university library or municipal historical society.[69]

- A document or data compilation found in the possession of the office or person likely to have charge of such material.[70]

The age of a document or data compilation for purposes of authentication under Rule 901(b)(8) is to be determined from the date of the document's first existence until it is offered in evidence.

The contents of a document or data compilation may indicate that the material has been in existence for at least 20 years.[71] The document may refer to a state of affairs that has ceased to exist for 20 years or it may include references to the activities of persons who have been dead for 20 years or more. The person who notarized a document may have ceased to be a notary more than 20 years before the proffer of the notarized document, or the secretary or other person who recorded the document may have ceased to hold office more than 20 years before the document was offered into evidence. Similarly, the person operating the computer or filing system at the time the data compilation was entered may have relinquished his or her position 20 years or more before the offer of the data compilation into evidence.

[j]—Processes or Systems Producing Accurate Results[72]

The result of a process or system may be authenticated by evidence describing the process or system used to produce the result and showing that the process or system produces an accurate result.[73] The accuracy of the system or process may be shown by the testimony of lay witnesses concerning the installation, activation, and maintenance of the system.[74] It may also be shown by expert testimony.

---

[68] Fulkerson v. Holmes, 117 U.S. 389, 391, 6 S. Ct. 780, 29 L. Ed. 915 (1886).

[69] Burns v. United States, 160 F. 631, 633 (2d Cir. 1908) (maps in possession of Buffalo Historical Society were in proper location for ancient documents).

[70] Smyth v. New Orleans Canal & Banking Co., 93 F. 899, 912–914 (5th Cir. 1899) (records of land grant proceedings appropriately found in office of United States Surveyor General).

[71] See, e.g., Fulmer v. Connors, 665 F. Supp. 1472, 1490 (N.D. Ala. 1987) (payroll book of defunct coal company offered to prove coal miner's earnings during 1941 was admissible as an ancient document).

[72] See **Treatise** at § 901.11.

[73] Fed. R. Evid. 901(b)(9).

[74] See, e.g., United States v. Rembert, 863 F.2d 1023, 1026–1228 (D.C. Cir. 1988) (photographs taken by closed-circuit video surveillance camera at bank teller machine were

Computer output may be authenticated under Rule 901(b)(9).[75] Business and official governmental records generated by a computer can be authenticated by the testimony of a witness with knowledge of the facts necessary to qualify those records for their respective exceptions to the hearsay rule.[76]

When authentication is not accomplished through qualification of the computer generated information for a hearsay exception, and the proponent relies on the provisions of Rule 901(b)(9), it is common for the proponent to provide evidence of the input procedures and their accuracy, and that the computer was regularly tested for programming errors.[77]

Samples and other forms of scientific surveys have become increasingly important as certain types of litigation have become increasingly complex. In some cases, sampling techniques may provide the only practicable means to collect and present highly relevant data. For example, if a claim is made under the Lanham Act[78] that the defendant's use of a particular trademark infringes the plaintiff's registered trademark because of the similarity between the two marks, so that there is a likelihood the public is confused into believing that the defendant's product is, in fact, manufactured by the plaintiff, survey evidence is almost a necessity.[79]

It is the proffering party's burden to show that the samples were selected in a scientifically acceptable manner and that the conclusions are statistically acceptable.[80] The admissibility of survey or sampling results depends upon two factors:

---

authenticated by testimony of bank supervisor describing how the system worked).

[75] Advisory Committee's Note (1972) at **Treatise** § 901App.01[2].

[76] Fed. R. Evid. 803(6) (records of regularly conducted activity); Fed. R. Evid. 803(8) (public records and reports); Fed. R. Evid. 803(9) (records of vital statistics); *see* Ch. 16 for discussion of requisite qualifications of sponsoring witness for computerized business records; *see* **Treatise,** Ch. 803.

[77] *See, e.g.,* United States v. Weatherspoon, 581 F.2d 595, 598 (7th Cir. 1978) (printouts, which were compilation of information from enrollment certification forms submitted by defendant, were properly authenticated by testimony of Veterans Administration supervisory employee, who was familiar with preparation of printouts, showing "(1) what the input procedures were, (2) that the input procedures and printouts were accurate within two percent, (3) that the computer was tested for internal programming errors on a monthly basis, and (4) that the printouts were made, maintained, and relied on by the VA in the ordinary course of its business activities. Moreover, all the enrollment certificate forms submitted by . . . [defendant], which formed the data base fed into the computer, were made available to defense counsel for inspection.").

[78] 15 U.S.C. § 1051 et seq.

[79] *See, e.g.,* Sterling Drug, Inc., v. Bayer, A.G., 14 F.3d 733, 741 (2d Cir. 1994) (actual confusion of public is strong evidence of likelihood of confusion, which is touchstone for infringement cases).

[80] *See, e.g.,* Starter Corp. v. Converse, Inc., 170 F.3d 286, 296–297 (2d Cir. 1999) (survey not relevant, as it was little more than memory test, testing ability of participants to remember names of shoes they had just been shown).

necessity and trustworthiness.[81] "Necessity" does not equate to the total unavailability of firsthand evidence; great practical inconvenience, the need for extended trial time, or the expense of more conventional methods of proof will suffice to permit the use of survey evidence.[82] The trial court can refuse to admit the results of a survey if it concludes they are untrustworthy, either because of the survey's design or the unreliability of the method of analysis applied to its raw data.[83]

[4]—Methods Provided by Statute or Rule[1]

The authentication requirement of Rule 901 is satisfied by any method of authentication or identification provided for by an Act of Congress.[2] Congress has provided abbreviated procedures for authenticating statutes adopted by state and territorial legislatures,[3] records and judicial proceedings of state and territorial courts,[4] and non-judicial books and records kept in any public office of any state, territory, or possession of the United States.[5] Many, if not all, of the documents that are the subjects of those statutes are self authenticating under Rule 902.[6] These generally applicable statutes were adopted pursuant to Congress's power to enforce and implement the Full Faith and Credit Clause of the Constitution[7] and are, by their terms, applicable in all courts in the United States and its territories and possessions, not just the federal courts.

Congress has established authentication procedures in legislation implementing treaties with other countries when those treaties contemplate the involvement of the courts in accomplishing the treaties' purposes. For example, extradition treaties with various countries provide that each of the signing parties will extradite fugitives from justice to the other signing parties upon request. Those treaties contemplate that the recipient of a request for extradition will conduct a judicial or administrative hearing to establish the necessary foundational facts before the extradition becomes mandatory. At that hearing, the representative of the request-

---

[81] *See, e.g.*, Schering Corp. v. Pfizer, Inc., 189 F.3d 218, 238 (2d Cir. 1999) (remanding for determination whether surveys asking physicians to relate their memories and impressions of statements made by competitor's pharmaceutical representatives about competitor's antihistamine met these two criteria).

[82] *See, e.g.*, United States v. Aluminum Co. of America, 35 F. Supp. 820, 823–824 (S.D.N.Y. 1940).

[83] *See, e.g.*, Toys "R" Us, Inc. v. Canarsie Kiddie Shop, Inc., 559 F. Supp. 1189, 1201–1202 (E.D.N.Y. 1983).

[1] *See* **Treatise** at § 901.12.

[2] Fed. R. Evid. 901(b)(10).

[3] 28 U.S.C. 1738.

[4] 28 U.S.C. 1738.

[5] 28 U.S.C. 1739.

[6] *See* § 8.02.

[7] U.S. Const., Art. IV § 1.

ing government may produce evidence that the person to be extradited has properly been charged with a crime. That evidence is automatically authenticated for purposes of introducing it into evidence in courts of the United States if the principal diplomatic or consular officer of the United States in the foreign country requesting extradition has certified in writing that the evidence has been authenticated in such a manner as to entitle it to be received in evidence in the tribunals of the requesting foreign country.[8] Similarly, Congress has provided in the International Child Abduction Remedies Act[9] that no authentication is required for the presentation in court of applications, petitions, documents, or information relating to a proceeding determining the custody of a child conducted in a foreign country that is a signing party to the Hague Convention on the Civil Aspects of International Child Abduction as part of its implementation of that treaty and in accordance with its terms.

Congress has also adopted statutory provisions relating to the authentication of documents that concern issues arising in international commerce or other private activities in or with foreign countries. United States diplomatic and consular officers serving in foreign countries are the primary source of authenticating evidence for non-governmental documents generated in those countries and offered into evidence in federal courts.[10] United States consular officers in foreign countries can also authenticate numerous other papers, including assignments of copyright in a foreign country,[11] bills of health for vessels entering the United States from foreign ports,[12] certificates of transportation of destitute seamen,[13] and any oath, affirmation, affidavit, deposition, or notarial act made before them.[14]

Congress has also adopted statutes dealing with certain domestically generated documents. For example, trademark acknowledgments and verifications made in the United States can be authenticated by proof they were made before any person in the United States authorized by law to administer oaths.[15] Similarly, court reporters can authenticate handwritten or transcribed records of testimony and other court proceedings, as well as electronic sound recordings of those proceedings, by their certification.[16]

Rule 901's authentication requirement is also satisfied by any method of authentication or identification provided for by a rule prescribed by the Supreme

---

[8]   18 U.S.C. § 3190.
[9]   42 U.S.C. § 11601(a)(4).
[10] 15 U.S.C. § 1061.
[11] 17 U.S.C. § 204(b).
[12] 42 U.S.C. § 269(b).
[13] 46 U.S.C. § 1101(a).
[14] 22 U.S.C. § 4221.
[15] 15 U.S.C. § 1061.
[16] 28 U.S.C. § 753(b).

Court pursuant to statutory authority, such as the Rules of Civil or Criminal Procedure.[17] The Federal Rules of Civil and Criminal Procedure provide for methods of identification and authentication of specific evidence that may make resort to Rule 901 unnecessary. For instance, Civil Rule 44(a) prescribes methods for authenticating official records of domestic and foreign governmental agencies.[18]

§ 8.02   Self-Authenication—Rule 902

[1]—Text and Theory of Rule[1]

Rule 902 makes self-authenticating certain classes of writings when various considerations make it unreasonable to require further authentication.

The Rule provides as follows:

Rule 902.   Self-Authentication.

Extrinsic evidence of authenticity as a condition precedent to admissibility is not required with respect to the following:

(1)
Domestic public documents under seal. A document bearing a seal purporting to be that of the United States, or of any State, district, Commonwealth, territory, or insular possession thereof, or the Panama Canal Zone, or the Trust Territory of the Pacific Islands, or of a political subdivision, department, officer, or agency thereof, and a signature purporting to be an attestation or execution.

(2)
Domestic public documents not under seal. A document purporting to bear the signature in the official capacity of an officer or employee of any entity included in paragraph (1) hereof, having no seal, if a public officer having a seal and having official duties in the district or political subdivision of the officer or employee certifies under seal that the signer has the official capacity and that the signature is genuine.

(3)
Foreign public documents. A document purporting to be executed or attested in an official capacity by a person authorized by the laws of a foreign country to make the execution or attestation, and accompanied by a final certification as to the genuineness of the signature and official

---

[17]   Fed. R. Evid. 901(b)(10).
[18]   Fed. R. Civ. P. 44(a).
[1]   *See* **Treatise** at § 902.02.

position (A) of the executing or attesting person, or (B) of any foreign official whose certificate of genuineness of signature and official position relates to the execution or attestation or is in a chain of certificates of genuineness of signature and official position relating to the execution or attestation. A final certification may be made by a secretary of an embassy or legation, consul general, consul, vice consul, or consular agent of the United States, or a diplomatic or consular official of the foreign country assigned or accredited to the United States. If reasonable opportunity has been given to all parties to investigate the authenticity and accuracy of official documents, the court may, for good cause shown, order that they be treated as presumptively authentic without final certification or permit them to be evidenced by an attested summary with or without final certification.

(4)
Certified copies of public records. A copy of an official record or report or entry therein, or of a document authorized by law to be recorded or filed and actually recorded or filed in a public office, including data compilations in any form, certified as correct by the custodian or other person authorized to make the certification, by certificate complying with paragraph (1), (2), or (3) of this rule or complying with any Act of Congress or rule prescribed by the Supreme Court pursuant to statutory authority.

(5)
Official publications. Books, pamphlets, or other publications purporting to be issued by public authority.

(6)
Newspapers and periodicals. Printed materials purporting to be newspapers or periodicals.

(7)
Trade inscriptions and the like. Inscriptions, signs, tags, or labels purporting to have been affixed in the course of business and indicating ownership, control, or origin.

(8)
Acknowledged documents. Documents accompanied by a certificate of acknowledgment executed in the manner provided by law by a notary public or other officer authorized by law to take acknowledgments.

(9)
Commercial paper and related documents. Commercial paper, signatures thereon, and documents relating thereto to the extent provided by general commercial law.

(10)

Presumptions under Acts of Congress. Any signature, document, or other matter declared by Act of Congress to be presumptively or prima facie genuine or authentic.

(11)

Certified domestic records of regularly conducted activity. The original or a duplicate of a domestic record of regularly conducted activity that would be admissible under Rule 803(6) if accompanied by a written declaration of its custodian or other qualified person, in a manner complying with any Act of Congress or rule prescribed by the Supreme Court pursuant to statutory authority, certifying that the record—

(A)

was made at or near the time of the occurrence of the matters set forth by, or from information transmitted by, a person with knowledge of those matters;

(B)

was kept in the course of the regularly conducted activity; and

(C)

was made by the regularly conducted activity as a regular practice.

A party intending to offer a record into evidence under this paragraph must provide written notice of that intention to all adverse parties, and must make the record and declaration available for inspection sufficiently in advance of their offer into evidence to provide an adverse party with a fair opportunity to challenge them.

(12)

Certified foreign records of regularly conducted activity. In a civil case, the original or a duplicate of a foreign record of regularly conducted activity that would be admissible under Rule 803(6) if accompanied by a written declaration by its custodian or other qualified person certifying that the record—

(A)

was made at or near the occurrence of the matters set forth by, or from information transmitted by, a person with knowledge of those matters;

(B)

was kept in the course of the regularly conducted activity; and

(C)

was made by the regularly conducted activity as a regular practice.

The declaration must be signed in a manner that, if falsely made, would subject the maker to criminal penalty under the laws of the country where the declaration is signed. A party intending to offer a record into evidence under this paragraph must provide written notice of that intention to all adverse parties, and must make the record and declaration available for inspection sufficiently in advance of their offer into evidence to provide an adverse party with a fair opportunity to challenge them.

[*Adopted Jan. 2, 1975, effective July 1, 1975; amended Mar. 2, 1987, effective Oct. 1, 1987; Apr. 25, 1988, effective Nov. 1, 1988; Apr. 17, 2000, effective Dec. 1, 2000.*]

These classes of documents are made self-authenticating because the slight obstacle to fraud presented by authentication requirements is outweighed by the time and expense of proving authenticity. In addition, in some cases, the facts that would provide further evidence of authenticity are within the knowledge of the opponent of the evidence, making it even more unfair to require the proponent to present this evidence.

The trial judge should, therefore, not use discretion to exclude documents coming within Rule 902's classifications. The opponents of the evidence are in no way precluded from contesting authenticity, and evidence may be presented to the jury to be considered in deciding how much weight to give the document. They are only precluded from disputing admissibility on the ground of authentication.[2]

[2]—Domestic Public Documents Under Seal—Rule 902(1)[1]

Rule 902(1) provides that domestic public documents under seal are self-authenticating. The rule's application to public documents and the requirement of a political entity, subdivision, department, officer or agency precludes the use of private signets. The rule places no cut-off point on the scale of public authority below which the court will refuse to recognize the genuineness of the seal of an official without further authentication, whether the seal be that of an executing officer on the original documents, or the seal of a custodian on a certificate authenticating copies of public documents.[2] Since the rule requires, in addition to

---

[2] *See* United States v. Giacalone, 408 F. Supp. 251, 253 (E.D. Mich. 1975), *rev'd on other grounds,* 541 F.2d 508 (6th Cir. 1976) (defendant moved to dismiss indictment on ground that special United States Attorney had no authority to conduct grand jury proceedings; certified copy of oath of office established authority where defendant "neither contradicted nor challenged the authenticity of this document").

[1] *See* **Treatise** at § 902.03.

[2] *See, e.g.,* United States v. Bisbee, 245 F.3d 1001, 1006 (8th Cir. 2001) ("A document bearing a seal purporting to be that of the United States and a signature purporting to be an attestation requires no extrinsic evidence of authenticity as a condition precedent to admission."); United States

the seal, only a "signature purporting to be an attestation or execution," the signer need not actually have been authorized to make the attestation or to execute the document.[3]

[3]—Domestic Public Documents Not Under Seal—Rule 902(2)[1]

A document signed by an official without a seal is self-authenticating if the seal of another official is affixed.[2] The authenticating official must have "official duties" in the district or public subdivision of the officer whose signature is certified.[3] Rule 902(2) applies only to officials "having no seal" but the officer using a seal to authenticate another officer's signature will by inference also be certifying that there is no seal in the other's possession which the other officer could have used. The certifying official will by inference also be certifying that the executing officer signed in an official capacity.[4] See Rule 902(1).

Without a seal, a public record is not self-authenticating.[5]

---

v. Mackenzie, 601 F.2d 221 (5th Cir. 1979) (order of Texas Board of Medical Examiners cancelling license to practice medicine); United States v. Moore, 555 F.2d 658 (8th Cir. 1977) (certificate of United States Postal Service); United States v. Trotter, 538 F.2d 217 (8th Cir. 1976) (copy of motor vehicle registration).

[3] *See* United States v. Mateo-Mendez, 215 F.3d 1039, 1044 (9th Cir. 2000), *cert. denied,* 531 U.S. 983 (2000) (Rule 902(2) expressly requires signer of document not under seal to have acted in official capacity; thus, omission of that requirement in Rule 902(1) means that 902(1) does not require proof that signer of documents under seal was acting in official capacity, i.e., was legally authorized to do so).

[1] *See* **Treatise** at § 902.04.

[2] United States v. Wilson, 732 F.2d 404, 413 (5th Cir. 1984) (affidavit of Executive Director of the CIA self-authenticating because it was executed by the third highest official in the CIA whose duties include overall management, and it was attested to by General Counsel of CIA who is custodian of seal of CIA); Hunt v. Liberty Lobby, 720 F.2d 631, 651 (11th Cir. 1983), *further proceedings,* (affidavits of CIA officials, with certificates bearing CIA official seal and certificate of CIA's general counsel certifying that each affiant occupied position stated in his affidavit were self-authenticating).

Rule 901(a) permits courts to assume genuineness of a signature alone, without the necessity of further authentication. There is also no reason why a state statute adopting blanket presumptions of genuineness for official signatures as well as for official seals should not be followed.

[3] This requirement means only that there be some minimum connection between the two officers so as to enable one to have enough knowledge of the other officer to say that the signature is genuine. There need be no preliminary showing of this fact, since the seal raises the inference that the officer has the capacity to certify that officer's signature. *See* Rule 901(a).

[4] *See* United States v. Combs, 762 F.2d 1343, 1348 (9th Cir. 1985), citing United States v. Beason, 690 F.2d 439, 444 (5th Cir. 1982) (certification of custodial authority is not required).

[5] Nolin v. Douglas County, 903 F.2d 1546, 1552 (11th Cir. 1990).

[4]—Foreign Public Documents—Rule 902(3)[1]

Originals as well as copies of foreign public documents are presumed authentic if attested to by authorized foreign or American officials.[2] The authenticating official should certify to either (1) the genuineness of the signature of the executing official; or (2) the genuineness of the signature of the last officer in a chain of authenticating certificates.[3]

Rule 902(3) sets out two requirements for the self authentication of foreign public documents. First, there must be proof the document is what it purports to be. That burden of proof is satisfied under the Rule if (1) the document was executed by a proper public official in his or her official capacity or (2) the genuineness of the document is attested to by a proper public official in his or her official capacity. Second, there must be an indication the official vouching for the document is who he or she purports to be. That burden of proof is satisfied when (1) a second official of the foreign government certifies the signature and position of the person executing or attesting to the document or (2) one of the group of foreign officials specified in the Rule issues a "final certification" attesting to the genuineness of the signature and to the title of the person signing or attesting to the document.[3.1] Thus, nothing in Rule 902(3) requires that the documents themselves be signed or

---

[1] *See* **Treatise** at § 902.05.

[2] *See, e.g.,* United States v. Pluta, 176 F.3d 43, 49–50 (2d Cir. 1999), *cert. denied,* — U.S. —, 120 S. Ct. 248 (1999) (Polish passports did not meet requirements of Rule 902(3) for self-authentication); United States v. Doyle, 130 F.3d 523, 545 (2d Cir. 1997) (certification of Maltese officials was adequate to show that documents were records of Customs Department, thus documents were properly authenticated); United States v. Herrera-Britto, 739 F.2d 551, 552 (11th Cir. 1984) (certified document, signed and attested to by officials of Honduras, which stated that no registration for vessel was found in a search of vessel registration records, self-authenticating); United States v. Koziy, 728 F.2d 1314, 1322 (11th Cir. 1984) (documents used by Ukrainian Police bearing defendant's signature were self-authenticated under Rule 902(3) since Russian official authorized to authenticate such documents attested to documents at issue here; district court did not abuse discretion in admitting documents); United States v. Montemayor, 712 F.2d 104, 109 (5th Cir. 1983) (Mexican official records of birth were admissible when they were properly authenticated by certification of American consular officials); United States v. Regner, 677 F.2d 754, 758–759 (9th Cir. 1982) (court admitted certified records of state-run Hungarian taxicab company).

The formulation for the authentication of foreign public documents is adapted from Rule 44(a) of the Federal Rules of Civil Procedure. Fed. R. Civ. P. 44(a).

[3] *See, e.g.,* United States v. Squillacote, 221 F.3d 542, 562 (4th Cir. 2000) (foreign public documents are self-authenticating if either official executing document certifies its genuineness or if another official of same government attests that document is true and genuine; document itself need not be signed or contain attestation); United States v. Howard-Arias, 679 F.2d 363, 366 (4th Cir. 1982) (statement by affiant that he is official designated by Colombian law to certify that vessel on which marijuana was seized was not of Colombian registry was not required where official's signature was attested to as genuine by series of Colombian officials and certified by American consul).

[3.1] United States v. Squillacote, 221 F.3d 542, 561 (4th Cir. 2000).

contain an attestation. Foreign documents may be authenticated either by a certification from the official executing the document or by an official attesting to the document. So long as a proper official attests that the proffered document is true and genuine, it is self-authenticating even if unsigned.[3.2]

Rule 902(2) explicitly gives the trial judge discretion to forego final certification or to admit instead attested summaries with or without final certification. This final provision is a narrow exception to the hearsay and best evidence rules.

Where the parties have had an opportunity to check on the authenticity of the document, exclusion for lack of a final certificate is seldom justified.[4] Certainly it should be too late to raise the issue for the first time on appeal.[5]

Documents originating with a foreign government may be admissible by a route other than Rule 902 when, for example, they are offered other than as official records.[6]

[5]—Treaty May Make Compliance With Rule 902(3) Unnecessary[1]

Compliance with Rule 902(3) is no longer necessary in many instances because of the Convention Abolishing the Requirement of Legalization for Foreign Public

---

[3.2]   United States v. Squillacote, 221 F.3d 542, 562 (4th Cir. 2000).

[4]   *See, e.g.,* Raphaely Int'l, Inc. v. Waterman S.S. Corp., 972 F.2d 498, 502 (2d Cir. 1992), *cert. denied,* 507 U.S. 916 (1993) (district court did not err in admitting certificates of inspection issued by Gezira Trade & Services, Ltd. (Gezira) in compliance with Sudanese law; Gezira, having been nationalized by Sudanese government, was government entity engaged in inspection work that was required by Sudanese law, and certificates issued by it were accordingly foreign public documents for purposes of Rule 902(3); since no final certification accompanied documents, they could be treated as presumptively authentic if parties had reasonable opportunity to investigate authenticity of documents and there was showing of good cause; here, defendant's delay in challenging certificates and its failure to adduce at trial any evidence casting doubt on certificates' authenticity was sufficient to provide district court with basis for finding "good cause" so as to satisfy second condition); Black Sea & Baltic General v. S.S. Hellenic Destiny, 575 F. Supp. 685, 691–92 (S.D.N.Y. 1983) (magistrate correct in concluding that Saudi customs certificates were admissible as presumptively authentic, even absent a final certification; defendant did not produce any evidence casting doubt upon their authenticity, and there was independent deposition testimony supporting authenticity).

[5]   United States v. Rodriguez Serrate, 534 F.2d 7 (1st Cir. 1976) (counsel given extra day to examine documents and raised no objection directed to the absence of good cause); United States v. Padeco-Lovio, 463 F.2d 232 (9th Cir. 1972) (defense counsel was aware of copy government intended to use without a final certificate and made no objection).

[6]   United States v. Pluta, 176 F.3d 43, 49–50 (2d Cir. 1999), *cert. denied,* — U.S. —, 120 S. Ct. 248 (1999) (Polish passports did not meet requirements of Fed. R. Evid. 902(3), but were authenticated under Fed. R. Evid. 901 by INS inspector who was familiar with immigration law and procedures (citing **Treatise**)); Henein v. Saudi Arabian Parsons Ltd., 818 F.2d 1508, 1512 (9th Cir. 1987), *cert. denied,* 484 U.S. 1009 (1988).

[1]   *See* **Treatise** at § 902.05[4].

Documents.[2] Under the Convention, each country designates those public officials, by their titles, who may affix a form of certification known as the "apostille." The certificate simply states that the document was signed by an individual in an official capacity and that the seal or stamp is genuine. Public documents from countries which are parties to the Convention[3] are recognized in the courts here so long as the apostille is affixed.

Four categories of documents are deemed to be public documents: first, documents emanating from a judicial or other tribunal, including documents from a public prosecutor, clerk of court, or process server; second, administrative documents; third, notarial acts; and fourth, private documents that bear official certifications, such as a certificate of registration or an official authentication of a signature.

The treaty specifically excludes two categories of documents: (a) documents executed by diplomatic or consular officers, and (b) administrative documents dealing directly with commercial or customs operations.

[6]—Certified Copies of Public Records—Rule 902(4)[1]

Rule 902(4) provides that certified copies of public records are self-authenticating.[2] The Rule is to be used in conjunction with Rule 902(1), (2) or (3). Copies are certified by a certificate complying with those subdivisions, to which reference should be made for the manner in which certificates must be executed.

Rule 902(4) requires no additional certification to the fact of custody or to the custodian's authority.[3] The purported custodian's signature under a statement that he or she has custody of the original and that the copy is correct, whether or not accompanied by a seal, suffices to assure the accuracy of the copy as a substitute

---

[2] The relevant portions of the text of the Convention and a form of an Apostille can be found in **Treatise** at §§ 902App.04, 902.05[4].

[3] A list of countries that have signed or ratified the convention appears in Treaties in Force, Department of State Publication 9433 (1990) at 337. They are as follows: Antigua & Barbuda, Argentina, Austria, The Bahamas, Belgium, Botswana, Brunei, Cyprus, Fiji, Finland, France, Germany, Greece, Hungary, Israel, Italy, Japan, Lesotho, Liechtenstein, Luxembourg, Malawi, Malta, Mauritius, Netherlands, Norway, Portugal, Seychelles, Spain, Suriname, Swaziland, Switzerland, Tonga, Turkey, United Kingdom, United States, Yugoslavia.

[1] See **Treatise** at § 902.06.

[2] See, e.g., United States v. Torres, 733 F.2d 449, 455 n.5 (7th Cir. 1984) (certificate of enrollment prepared by Menominee enrollment clerk and certified by her at trial to be an accurate representation of the information contained in the original tribal roll was admissible under Rule 902(4) as a certified copy of an original public record).

[3] United States v. Beason, 690 F.2d 439, 444 (5th Cir. 1982), cert. denied, 459 U.S. 1177 (1983) (certificate by custodian of National Firearms Registration and Transfer Record that no registration in defendant's name existed sufficed without requiring certificate from Secretary of Treasury that custodian had been given custody).

for the original. The authenticity of the original is guaranteed by a certificate complying with Rule 902(1), (2), or (3).

The rule is silent as to what the custodian's certificate should contain. Any reasonable statement implying custody and correctness should suffice. For records kept within the boundaries of the United States, Rule 902 requires that the copy be a literal copy and not a summary. If a literal copy is not obtainable, Rule 1004, 1005 or 1006 may permit use of summaries. Rule 1005, for example has an escape clause when certified copies "cannot be obtained by the exercise of reasonable diligence." Copies of foreign official documents are explicitly permitted to be in summary form. See discussion of Foreign Public Documents, [4], *above.*

Rule 902(4) also provides that any form of certification may be used for copies of public records that comply with an Act of Congress or rule adopted by the Supreme Court.[4]

[7]—Official Publications—Rule 902(5)[1]

Publications that purport to be printed by public authority are admissible without further proof of authenticity. In point of fact, any reputable private printer's version should be accepted, since typically it is such versions upon which the bench and bar rely. *Cf.* Rules 803(17), 902(6). Almost never is there an error of critical importance in these conveniently obtainable volumes. Although most frequently applied to statutes, the same rule also applies to officially printed volumes of court decisions and miscellaneous public documents.[2]

Rule 902(5) is silent on what level of government must authorize the publication. The levels of government included here should be construed to be as broad as those outlined in Rule 902(1). Judicial notice provides ample authority for recognizing such publications.

[8]—Newspapers and Periodicals—Rule 902(6)[1]

Rule 902(6) eases, with respect to newspapers and periodicals, the common-law requirements of authentication for non-official publications. In the case of newspapers and periodicals, there is good reason not to require any more evidence of authenticity than that in the purported publication itself. The realities of newspaper publishing make forgery highly unlikely. This is as true of publications of general circulation as it is of specialized journals with a limited readership. For example,

---

[4] These provisions are listed and discussed in **Treatise** at § 902.06.

[1] *See* **Treatise** at § 902.07.

[2] California Ass'n of Bioanalysts v. Rank, 577 F. Supp. 1342, 1355 n.23 (C.D. Cal. 1983) (report of USDHHS, which bore facsimile of official seal of that agency on its cover page, was self-authenticating under Rule 902(5)).

[1] *See* **Treatise** at § 902.08.

the pink sheets showing over the counter prices are relied upon by a small group but the chance of forgery is remote.

The problem of authentication of these publications arises most often in libel actions. Since the defendant in a libel case is in a particularly good position to prove the forgery by producing a genuine copy of the publication and would know facts that would prove or disprove genuineness, it is not unreasonable to shift the burden to the defense to prove any forgeries.

[9]—Trade Inscriptions and the Like—Rule 902(7)[1]

Trade inscriptions affixed "in the course of business" are admissible without further proof of authentication.[2] This provision is based both on the overwhelming reliability of trade and brand names and on the fact that many trademarks and brand names are registered under federal or state laws that forbid others from using them. A number of cases have held that labels indicating foreign origin are prima facie evidence that the goods so labeled are in fact of foreign origin.[3]

This provision can be used to authenticate machinery, cans of food or clothing to which labels have been attached. Similarly, identifying materials contained within a product may constitute circumstantial evidence of the origin of the product.[4]

[10]—Acknowledged Documents—Rule 902(8)[1]

Rule 902(8) extends prima facie authenticity to all documents accompanied by a certificate of acknowledgment under the seal of a notary public or other authorized officer. The basis for this extension is the theory that if the notary is permitted to authenticate documents of title, which are documents of great legal effect, there is

---

[1] *See* **Treatise** at § 902.09.

[2] Fed. R. Evid. 902(2); *see, e.g.,* Los Angeles News Serv., Inc. v. CBS Broadcasting, Inc., 305 F.3d 924, 936 (9th Cir. 2002) (slate at beginning of videotape was self-authenticating under Rule 902(7) because it showed origin of videotape).

[3] 19 U.S.C. § 1615(2) ("Marks, labels, brands, or stamps, indicative of foreign origin, upon or accompanying mechandise [sic] or containers or merchandise, shall be prima facie evidence of the foreign origin of such merchandise."). *See, e.g.,* United States v. Alvarez, 972 F.2d 1000, 1004 (9th Cir. 1992) (per curiam) (trial court did not err in admitting firearm into evidence and permitting government to argue that inscription "Garnika, Spain" indicated where gun was manufactured, and was not inadmissible hearsay; because an inscription placed on a firearm by manufacturer is a mechanical trace, and not a statement for purposes of Rule 801(c); further, the Federal Rules do not require extrinsic evidence of authenticity for inscriptions, tags, signs, or labels that indicate workmanship, control, or origin, citing Rule 902(7)).

[4] *See, e.g.,* L.A. News Serv. v. CBS Broad., Inc., 305 F.3d 924, 936 (9th Cir. 2002) ("slate" at beginning of video tape containing news footage was circumstantial evidence of identity of producer of tape and consequently it authenticated tape under Rule 902(7)).

[1] *See* **Treatise** at § 902.10.

no reason for not allowing other writings to be proved in the same way.

Rule 902(8) states that the seal on the certificate of acknowledgment may, in addition to the seal of the notary, be that of some "other officer authorized by law to take acknowledgments." The rule itself does not authorize any particular officer to take an acknowledgment. It speaks only to those already authorized to do so. Thus, whether a particular officer will be able to take an acknowledgment under 902(8) will depend on whether he or she is authorized to take an acknowledgment under state or federal law. In the absence of contrary evidence, there is no reason for not presuming that the officer whose seal is affixed to the certificate of acknowledgment is authorized by law. This presumption is based on the theory that evidence to the contrary would be easily obtainable by the party opposing admission of the document.

[11]—Effect of Uniform Commercial Code—Rule 902(9)[1]

Documents covered by Sections 3-307, 3-510, 8-105(2) and 1-202 of the Uniform Commercial Code are treated as self-authenticating under paragraph 9 of Rule 902.[2] Other documents offered in connection with a suit governed by the Commercial Code's substantive provisions may or may not be self-authenticating depending upon whether they fall within Rule 901 or 902.

[12]—Presumption Under Acts of Congress—Rule 902(10)[1]

Paragraph (10) indicates that any mode of self-authentication provided for in an Act of Congress[2] may continue to be employed concomitantly with the procedures specified in Rule 902. The applicable acts often deal with best evidence aspects as well, allowing the prima facie authentic copies to be used instead of the original documents. See discussion of Rule 1002 in Chapter 9. In addition, statutory authentication rules often operate as exceptions to the hearsay rule.

[13]—Certified Domestic Business Records—Rule 902(11)[1]

Certified domestic business records are made self-authenticating by Rule 902(11).[2] Certified domestic business records are admissible under the hearsay

---

[1] *See* **Treatise** at § 902.11.

[2] *See* United States v. Hawkins, 905 F.2d 1489, 1493 (11th Cir. 1990) (returned checks held self-authenticating); In re Richter & Phillips Jewelers & Dist., Inc., 31 B.R. 512 (S.D. Ohio 1983) (original check was admissible without extrinsic evidence of authenticity); United States v. Carriger, 592 F.2d 312, 316–317 (6th Cir. 1979) (mere production of promissory note is prima facie evidence of its validity).

[1] *See* **Treatise** at § 902.12.

[2] The relevant statutes are discussed in the **Treatise** at § 902.12.

[1] *See Treatise* at § 902.13[1].

[2] Fed. R. Evid. 902(11) (effective December 1, 2000).

exception provided by Rule 803(6) without the live testimony of a custodian witness. The foundation that would have been established by a witness is presented instead by the declaration certifying that the record complies with the requirements of the exception.[3] Rule 902(11) is applicable to both civil and criminal cases.

Domestic records of a regularly conducted activity are self-authenticating if accompanied by a declaration executed by the custodian of the records or another qualified person[3.1] certifying that the record:[4]

- was made at or near the time of the occurrence of the matters set forth in the record by a person with knowledge of those matters or from information provided by a person with knowledge of those matters;

- was kept in the course of the regularly conducted activity; and

- was made by the regularly conducted activity as a regular practice.

A declaration that satisfies the requirements of 28 U.S.C. § 1746 would suffice for the purposes of Rule 902(11), as would any other comparable certification under oath.[5]

The party intending to offer self-authenticating domestic records of a regularly conducted activity must provide all adverse parties with advance notice of its intention to do so. The offering party must also make the supporting declaration and the records it supports available to all adverse parties for their inspection sufficiently in advance of their offer into evidence to permit the adverse party a fair opportunity to challenge their admissibility into evidence.[6]

[14]—Certified Foreign Business Records—Rule 902(12)[1]

Certified foreign business records are made self-authenticating by Rule 902(12).[2] Certified foreign business records are admissible under the hearsay exception provided by Rule 803(6) without the live testimony of a custodian witness. The foundation that would have been established by a witness is presented instead by the declaration certifying that the record complies with the requirements of the exception.[3] Rule 902(12) applies only to civil cases, because there is already a

---

[3] *See* Fed. R. Evid. 803(6); *see also* § 16.07[2].

[3.1] *See, e.g.,* United States v. Lauersen, 343 F.3d 604, 616 (2d Cir. 2003) (quoting **Treatise;** "witness need only have enough familiarity with the record-keeping system of the business in question to explain how the record came into existence in the ordinary course of business").

[4] Fed. R. Evid. 902(11).

[5] Committee Note to Rule 902, 2000 Amendment; *see* 28 U.S.C. § 1746.

[6] Fed. R. Evid. 902(11).

[1] *See Treatise* at § 902.13[2].

[2] Fed. R. Evid. 902(12) (effective December 1, 2000).

[3] *See* Fed. R. Evid. 803(6); *see also* § 16.07[2].

similar procedure in place for avoiding foundation witnesses for foreign records of regularly conducted activities.[4]

Foreign records of a regularly conducted activity are self-authenticating if accompanied by a declaration executed by the custodian of the records or another qualified person certifying that the record:[5]

- was made at or near the time of the occurrence of the matters set forth in the record by a person with knowledge of those matters or from information provided by a person with knowledge of those matters;

- was kept in the course of the regularly conducted activity; and

- was made by the regularly conducted activity as a regular practice.

The declaration must be signed in a manner that would subject the maker to criminal penalties under the laws of the country in which it was signed if the declaration is falsely made.[6]

The party intending to offer self-authenticating foreign records of a regularly conducted activity must provide all adverse parties with advance notice of its intention to do so. The offering party must also make the supporting declaration and the records it supports available to all adverse parties for their inspection sufficiently in advance of their offer to permit the adverse party a fair opportunity to challenge their admissibility into evidence.[7]

---

[4] *See* 18 U.S.C. § 3505.
[5] Fed. R. Evid. 902(12).
[6] Fed. R. Evid. 902(12).
[7] Fed. R. Evid. 902(12).

CHAPTER 9

*Best Evidence Rule**

---

  * Chapter revised in 1991 by RANDALL K. ANDERSON, member of the New York and District of Columbia Bars.

§ 9.01   Requirement of Original—Rules 1001 and 1002

[1]—Overview of Best Evidence Rule[1]

Rule 1002 adopts and somewhat expands in scope the so-called "best evidence" rule. There is no general rule that proof of a fact will be excluded unless its proponent furnishes the best evidence.[2] Rule 1002 only requires production of an "original" if a proponent is seeking to prove the content of a "writing," "recording," or "photograph." These terms are defined in Rules 1001(1), (2) and (3) which are discussed below.

The requirement of the rule is expressly dispensed with if other rules in Article X of the Federal Rules or Acts of Congress so provide.[3] These exceptions have proven to be sufficiently comprehensive to allow the admission of many writings, recordings, and photographs that were not originals.[4]

Rule 1002 states:

Rule 1002.   Requirement of Original.

To prove the content of a writing, recording, or photograph, the original writing, recording, or photograph is required, except as otherwise provided in these rules or by Act of Congress.

The function of the best evidence rule is to ensure that the trier of fact is presented with the most accurate evidence practicable in those situations where informed legal judgment has concluded that precision is essential.[5] There are many built in exceptions to the rule because the need for the rule is often obviated by the existence of modern techniques of reproduction and broad discovery rules that make it unlikely that a party would produce a fraudulent copy.

By giving accurate counterparts the status of duplicates (Rule 1001(4)) which can ordinarily be admitted to the same extent as originals (Rule 1003), the Federal Rules of Evidence recognize that a narrow concept of an original is usually not required as a protective device when modern technology is involved, but that

---

[1]   *See* **Treatise** at §§ 1002.02–1002.04.

[2]   Significantly, neither the article in which it appears nor the rule or its caption refer to "best evidence." This omission was deliberate on the part of the Advisory Committee which hoped thereby to hasten "the demise of a term regarded as misleadingly broad in its scope."

[3]   The relevant statutes are discussed in the **Treatise** at § 1002.04[4].

[4]   *See* §§ 9.02–9.05.

[5]   *See, e.g.*, United States v. Frigerio-Migiano, 254 F.3d 30, 35 n.4 (1st Cir. 2001) ("Normally, to prove the contents of a writing, the original writing is required in preference to testimony about its content."); United States v. Humphrey, 104 F.3d 65, 70 (5th Cir. 1997) (evidence about prior successful action for commissions was properly excluded because testimony of lawyer was not best evidence of judgment).

respect for the goal of precision is still necessary when dealing with documents, photographs and recordings.

Rule 1005 acknowledges that public writings by their very nature call for specialized treatment. Rule 1006 allows a departure from the general rule in the case of voluminous material which cannot conveniently be produced in court. Rule 1007 dispenses with application of the rule if the adverse party made an admission of the contents in writing or in the course of testifying. Rule 1002 itself acknowledges that the requirement of the original may be dispensed with in other situations provided for in statutes or other federal rules. Rule 1004(1) to (3) codifies situations in which the original cannot be produced but its production is nevertheless excused. Rule 1004(4) excuses production without inquiring whether the original is available when the "writing, recording or photograph is not closely related to a controlling issue." Overtechnical application of the rule is also avoided by the federal courts' insistence on applying waiver if an objection on the basis of the rule had not been properly raised at trial, and on finding that errors in admission were harmless unless a substantial possibility existed that the contents of the improperly admitted document were inaccurate and might therefore have affected the result.

When there is any doubt about whether the rule is applicable, secondary evidence should be admitted, leaving it to the jury to determine probative force discounted by the failure to produce an original. Reversals for admission will be rare to the vanishing point since almost never is there real prejudice that the opponent cannot overcome. Wrongful exclusion can, however, have more serious consequences and reversals for this kind of error are to be expected.

[2]—Application of Best Evidence Rule[1]

Rule 1002 is in accord with the traditional view in providing that an original is required when the object is "to prove the content of a writing, recording or photograph." When the content is involved, however, is not always easy to discern.

The best evidence rule has been interpreted as not applying when a witness refreshes his or her memory with a document,[2] when an expert resorts to material

---

[1] *See* **Treatise** at § 1002.05.

[2] While it makes no difference whether refreshment was with a copy or original, the opponent may be entitled to see the document actually used by the witness. Where there is a claim that the document may have been shown in copy form to mislead the witness, the court should insist on production of the original for comparison purposes.

as a basis for an opinion,[3] or when a witness testifies that examined books or records do not contain a particular entry.[4]

Some transactions, such as wills, contracts and deeds,[5] as a matter of substantive law take the form of a writing and any attempt to prove their happening necessarily involves the content of the writing and brings the best evidence rule into play.[5.1] But if an event does not take the form of a writing,[6] recording,[7] or photograph and is only incidentally memorialized, the rule does not apply and the witness may testify to the underlying event.

Accordingly, where the issue is what was said at a former time, the best evidence rule does not apply, so that any witness who heard may testify to the words even though they were transcribed or recorded.

The best evidence rule is triggered, even though an event is only incidentally memorialized, if a proponent chooses to prove the event by the content of the recordings.

It can be difficult to distinguish between when a writing is being used to prove content and when it is being used to prove something else which does not fall within

---

[3] *See, e.g.,* United States v. Ratliff, 623 F.2d 1293, 1296–1297 (8th Cir. 1980). See discussion under Rule 703.

[4] *See, e.g.,* United States v. Madera, 574 F.2d 1320, 1323 n.3 (5th Cir. 1978) (original document need not be produced when witness testifies that it does not contain a reference to a designated matter, but court notes that although the document is not the best evidence in the evidentiary sense it may actually be better evidence because jury can check for itself).

[5] *But see* United States v. Hernandez-Fundora, 58 F.3d 802 (2d Cir. 1995) (FBI agent could testify as to federal jurisdiction of prison without providing deed).

[5.1] *See, e.g.,* Dugan, v. R.J. Corman R.R. Co., 344 F.3d 662, 669 (7th Cir. 2003) (provisions of trust agreement allegedly requiring defendant to make contributions to union's retirement benefit plan could not be shown by affidavit quoting only portions of agreement; best evidence rule required that entire trust agreement be offered into evidence).

[6] *See, e.g.,* C.P. Interests, Inc. v. California Pools, Inc., 238 F.3d 690, 699 (5th Cir. 2001) (trial court did not commit plain error in permitting witnesses to give testimony about transfer of rights to use tradename, since defendant failed to prove that transfer was made pursuant to written document); United States v. Mayans, 17 F.3d 1174 (9th Cir. 1994) (error for district court to preclude cross-examination of co-defendants as to their understanding of their plea agreements by finding that the plea agreement itself was the best evidence); R & R Associates, Inc. v. Visual Scene, Inc., 726 F.2d 36, 38 (1st Cir. 1984) (in contract action, trial court properly permitted witness to testify even though written contract existed, where witness was in no way attempting to prove the contents of the writing but rather was attempting to prove cost to plaintiff to procure goods).

[7] *See, e.g.,* United States v. Fagan, 821 F.2d 1002, 1008 n.1 (5th Cir. 1987) (prosecution sought to prove content of conversation, not tape recording; "best evidence" rule does not preclude proving conversation by testimony of witness even though tape recording of conversation existed); United States v. Rose, 590 F.2d 232, 237 (7th Cir. 1978) (where government sought to prove contents of conversation, not contents of tape recording, best evidence rule is inapplicable).

the ambit of the best evidence rule.[8] Such problems should be settled at a pretrial conference. If opponents raise any questions about a recording, the original should be made available to them, so that they can test it or explain it away. Apart from best evidence rules, fairness requires that opponents see the key materials that will be used against them.

[3]—Writings, Recordings, and Photographs Defined—Rule 1001(1)–(2)[1]

Paragraph (1) of Rule 1001 contains the definitions of "writings" and "recordings," while "photographs" are covered in paragraph (2).

Rule 1001(1) states:

Rule 1001. Definitions.

For purposes of this article the following definitions are applicable:

(1)
Writings and recordings. "Writings" and "recordings" consist of letters, words, or numbers, or their equivalent, set down by handwriting, typewriting, printing, photostating, photographing, magnetic impulse, mechanical or electronic recording, or other form of data compilation.

The rule as adopted is broad enough to encompass any future medium that uses symbols as the equivalent of words. Symbols that do not have a verbal connotation have generally not been considered subject to the rule. It does seem desirable, however, to extend the rule to drawings whose exact form and content are critical.[2]

The extent to which the requirement of an original should be applied to chattels that have something written or marked on them is not free from doubt. Clearly, uninscribed chattels are not subject to the rule; there is no general rule of best evidence requiring the production of objects. However, numerous objects bear some kind of number or inscription. Money, badges, flags, and tombstones certainly fall within this category. Should one require production of the original inscribed

---

[8] *See* Allstate Ins. Co. v. Swann, 27 F.3d 1539 (11th Cir. 1994) (Rule 1002 requires production of an original only when the proponent seeks to prove the content of a writing; it does not require production of the document anytime facts within the document are testified to by a witness). *Cf.* Time Share Vacation Club v. Atlantic Resorts, Ltd., 735 F.2d 61, 64, 65 (3d Cir. 1984) (plaintiff corporation appealed dismissal of its breach of contract action for lack of in personam jurisdiction; since plaintiff had burden of proving defendant's minimum contacts with the forum for the purpose of establishing jurisdiction and was relying solely on contract with defendant towards that end, plaintiff had burden of producing a copy of the entire contract or proffering an explanation for its absence; citing Rules 1002, 1003, 1004).

[1] *See* **Treatise** at § 1001(1) §§ 1001.02–1001.07.

[2] Seiler v. Lucasfilm, Ltd., 808 F.2d 1316, 1318–1319 (9th Cir. 1986) (drawings).

chattel in court? While few courts have considered the question, most modern courts would probably agree that no hard and fast rule applies.[3] Rather most courts would probably apply a balancing test in which the ease of producing the chattel and the need for producing it are considered. A photograph of an inscribed object that cannot be conveniently brought into court should suffice.

Rule 1001(2) recognizes that there are instances when photographs of non-writing or non-documentary materials should be subject to the application of the best evidence rule because the contents of the photograph—*i.e.,* the photograph itself—will be sought to be proved. The rule states:

Rule 1001(2). Definitions.

For purposes of this article the following definitions are applicable:

. . .

(2)
Photographs. "Photographs" include still photographs, X-ray films, video tapes, and motion pictures.

The best evidence rule will usually apply when photographs, videotapes, or motion pictures are utilized in cases involving such matters as infringement of copyright, defamation and libel, pornography and the invasion of privacy. In such cases, the rationale of the best evidence rule warrants specifically including photographs within the rule even though it is unlikely that, in the absence of the requirement, a witness will attempt to testify about a film or photograph without actually producing the disputed item itself.

While in many instances photographs are used to illustrate and explain what a witness testifies about from independent observation, there are situations where a photograph, videotape, or motion picture will have independent probative value. It will be the best evidence of things that the witness has not described or mentioned.[4] Because the photograph continues to speak for itself and may have details not testified to by a witness, it is important to examine it carefully before it is introduced. If it is to be used for a limited purpose only, this fact should be made known to the jury at the time of introduction.

---

[3] *See, e.g.,* Driggers v. United States, 384 F.2d 158, 159 (5th Cir. 1967) (government witnesses were allowed to testify that there were no stamps on jugs instead of producing jugs); Chandler v. United States, 318 F.2d 356, 357 (10th Cir. 1963) (witness who testified about half-gallon glass jars "was describing a physical thing in testifying as to the absence of revenue stamps on such containers").

[4] *See, e.g.,* Bunting v. Sea Ray, Inc., 99 F.3d 887, 891 (8th Cir. 1996) (trial court properly admitted videotape that showed heavy exhaust fumes being emitted by engine similar to one whose carbon monoxide emissions were alleged to have caused death).

The ability of a photograph to speak for itself is of growing importance since automatic camera equipment is now used for such purposes as check cashing and in taking pictures of bank robbers. In such instances the photographs have been described as " 'mute', 'silent,' or 'dumb' independent photographic witnesses." Evidence of the way the camera was arranged and worked is sufficient to identify the picture even if it was taken as a result of a trip wire or photoelectric cell having snapped the shutter with no one present to observe the event other than the person pictured. Similarily, infra-red or light sensitive film or telescopic lenses may reveal matters that cannot be described by an observer.

The best evidence rule will not bar photographs of nondocumentary objects on the theory that the subject of the picture would be the best evidence. Such items of real evidence are not included in the definitions of Rule 1001, so that the best evidence rule does not apply to them. Their characteristics can be shown by testimony or photographs or both. As a matter of trial tactics to maximize probative force, it is often desirable to show the object by views, by bringing it to court, or by the use of models and diagrams, but this is a matter of choice, not compulsion.[5]

Under normal circumstances, the negative of a photograph and any print made from it are treated interchangeably as originals.[6] See Rule 1001(3), discussed in [4], *below*. A negative film may show more gradations of tone than any ordinary paper print. Hence some delicate tonal differences readily observable on the negative may not be detectable on a paper print when the print is viewed by ordinary reflected light as is ordinarily the case. For all practical purposes, a print is usually good enough from the tonal gradation standpoint and, of course, jurors ordinarily can understand positives better than negatives. There may be rare instances, however, especially in scientific fields such as fingerprints, firearms identification, and documents photography, when a print cannot be made that will show essential details. In these instances, if the reversal of light and shade does not matter, the negative should be produced.

Properly verified enlargements enhance the value of an exhibit, because many details which are not readily discernible in a small print are made obvious by enlargement. So long as cutting and rearranging do not distort or mislead, use of enlargements of specific areas should be permitted.[7]

The best evidence rule needs to be applied with flexibility to X-rays. Since it is

---

[5] *See, e.g,* Harvey by Harvey v. General Motors Corp., 873 F.2d 1343, 1355–1357 (10th Cir. 1989) (film illustrating vehicle dynamics and effects on occupants admissible to aid jury in understanding expert testimony).

[6] *See, e.g,* United States v. Levine, 546 F.2d 658, 668 (5th Cir. 1977) (authenticated work print and release prints of pornographic films were considered originals).

[7] *See* Pritchard v. Downie, 326 F.2d 323, 326 (8th Cir. 1964) (films of police action against civil rights marchers entered by defendant police were admissible despite editing).

the contents of the X-ray that are in dispute, i.e., what the X-ray purports to represent, and no one can directly see the internal structure the X-ray portrays, the best evidence rule is obviously theoretically applicable.[8] But an X-ray photograph alone is often relatively meaningless to the layperson without secondary evidence in the form of expert testimony to interpret and clarify the nebulous image. More modern equipment showing internal arrangements by sound, radar, or electro-magnetic processes should be treated in the same liberal way as X-rays.

Usually, for tactical reasons as well as because the Rules require it, the X-ray should be in court. At times when evidence other than X-rays is presented to aid the court in understanding the contents of the X-ray and no prejudice is shown, the X-ray itself will not be required.

Since Rule 705 allows an expert to give an opinion without first disclosing the data upon which he or she relies, when the opposing party has had an opportunity to examine the X-rays outside of court, such as through the discovery process, the court should allow the expert to testify without requiring production of the X-rays, unless prejudice can be shown.

Although an X-ray means little to an average jury when it is produced in court, the opposing party is entitled to see and examine it for cross-examination purposes. Discovery will normally have made the X-ray available to both parties and their expert witnesses who are able to interpret and explain the X-ray.

The best evidence rule is not inflexible as applied to X-rays or equivalent material.

[4]—Original Defined (Rule 1001(3))[1]

An "original" in the technical sense used in this rule may be quite different from an "original" in lay terms. The "original" is the document whose contents are to be proved. Its jural significance makes it the original whether it was written before or after another, was copied from another, or was itself used to copy from.[2]

Rule 1001(3) defines an original as follows:

Rule 1001(3). Definitions.

---

[8] *See* Gay v. United States, 118 F.2d 160, 162 (7th Cir. 1941) ("Complaint is also made of the admission of the testimony of Dr. Lyon's interpretation of an X-ray of plaintiff's chest without producing the X-ray plate. The testimony was not the best evidence and was erroneously admitted").

[1] *See* **Treatise** at § 1001.08.

[2] *See, e.g.,* United States v. Angle, 230 F.3d 113, 120 (4th Cir. 2000) (photocopies of marked bills used in sting operation with handwritten entry of date of photocopying were "originals" because officer who performed photocopying and entered dates intended those documents to record date on which photocopying was done and sting operation occurred).

(3)

Original. An "original" of a writing or recording is the writing or recording itself or any counterpart intended to have the same effect by a person executing or issuing it. An "original" of a photograph includes the negative or any print therefrom. If data are stored in a computer or similar device, any printout or other output readable by sight, shown to reflect the data accurately, is an "original."

The question of what is an original is essentially one of relevancy. If we ask, "what is the document being offered to prove?" the identity of the original often becomes apparent. If it is the terms of a contract, then the signed agreement is the contract containing its terms. If we are trying to show delivery of goods, the original is the signed receipt. If we are trying to show shipment of goods, the original may be the shipping clerk's tally sheet. If we are trying to show an offer, the original may be the signed letter received. If we are trying to show authority to make the offer, the original may be a carbon copy of the agent's letter in the principal's file.

Often the intent of the parties in creating the document controls, particularly in contract actions. When the party or parties to a writing intend that a specific duplicate or copy shall serve as the original, either instead of the chronological original or as an additional original, their intentions govern. Thus, when the writing constituting a bilateral transaction is executed by the parties in several counterparts, each of these parts is "the" writing, because each counterpart was intended to be legally effective, hence of equal standing and an original. Any question of preferring one over the other in evidence is thus foreclosed. Similarly, mere simultaneous production of two counterparts does not make each an "equivalent" original if only one of them is recognized by the parties through their acts and intentions as an original.[3]

When several counterparts are created but only one is signed, it is the original. Where a document is executed in duplicate but each party signs a different counterpart, then each counterpart is the original as to the party who signed it. The signature gives the document jural significance.

Depending upon the issue, a document may be both a copy and an original in the same case. To show an offer, the original signed copy of a letter is the original. To show that someone knew of the offer, a carbon copy in his file would be the original. The carbon would, however, be a copy when seeking to show what was received by the offeree, and the signed letter a copy to show what was in the file.

---

[3] *See* United States v. Taylor, 648 F.2d 565, 568 n.3 (9th Cir. 1981) (court noted, without deciding, that in context of letter telecopied from San Diego to Houston, either telecopied letter or photocopy of letter may have been original depending on which document a Texas bank relied on; citing **Treatise**).

Mere referral by the parties to a document as a "copy" is not decisive; they may have been using the term in its lay sense. Common usage will often label original telegrams, autographs and writings as "copies" even in situations where there is no copy. Substantive law indicates which of several documents will be relevant and therefore the original.

At times practical need controls what can be denominated an original. For example, the first permanent business records rather than the preliminary and temporary slips, tags, and invoices are originals. They must however, have been made in the regular course of business and must be fairly contemporaneous with the items entered. Many persons may be required to produce such an entry and the rationale of practicality and accuracy is identical to that supporting Rule 803(6). This position is recognized by state and federal business entry statutes that allow the first permanent entries to be recognized as originals.

A related situation controlled by practicalities rather than theory is where a counterpart other than the chronological original is accepted as a best evidence original because it is the first comprehensible document. Examples of this are prints made from a negative. While the negative is the chronological original, all but the best trained photographers cannot accurately visualize the scene photographed. Therefore any print made from the negative is recognized as an original for it is the first to be produced in a medium readily understood by the average person.[4] This is also true of computer printouts because the underlying permanent sources of information cannot be readily understood. The printout represents the first readable counterpart of this information and therefore is the original.[5]

[5]—Original Recordings[1]

The original of a recording is the recording itself. Concerning documentary evidence, the term original is defined by the circumstances of the case. However, Rule 1001(4) provides that the original recording is always the original while a rerecording is a duplicate. The only exception to this position is when a specific rerecording is at issue, then it is the original to be produced for the court. This distinction is treated with great flexibility by the courts, since all parties concur in the need for enhancement, redaction and the like in presenting recordings in court.

---

[4] *See, e.g.,* Lucas v. City of Charlotte, N.C., 14 F. Supp. 163, 167 (D.N.C. 1936), *aff'd,* 86 F.2d 394 (4th Cir. 1936) ("take what is popularly called a picture, but in fact it is what photographers call a 'negative' which is the outline of the subject on glass, and without which no complete photograph could be made").

[5] *Cf.* United States v. Foley, 598 F.2d 1323, 1338 (4th Cir. 1979), *cert. denied,* 444 U.S. 1043 (1980) (under Rule 1001(4), computer printouts are duplicates of diskettes).

[1] *See* **Treatise** at § 1001.10.

§ 9.02   Accurate Duplicates Admissible—Rule 1003

[1]—Scope and Text of Rule[1]

Rule 1003 sets out guidelines for admitting a duplicate as if it were an original. The rule states:

Rule 1003.   Admissibility of Duplicates.

A duplicate is admissible to the same extent as an original unless (1) a genuine question is raised as to the authenticity of the original or (2) in the circumstances it would be unfair to admit the duplicate in lieu of the original.

The rule recognizes that, because of the accuracy of modern techniques of reproduction, duplicates and originals should, for evidentiary purposes, normally be treated interchangeably. An original will be insisted upon only when a substantial question is raised as to the authenticity of either the original or the duplicate,[1.1] or when it is unfair under the circumstances to admit the duplicate in place of the original.[2]

[2]—Duplicate Defined—Rule 1001(4)[1]

[a]—Scope and Text of Rule

Rule 1001(4) defines the term duplicate. It states:

Rule 1001(4).   Definitions.

_____

[1]   *See* **Treatise** at § 1003.02.

[1.1]   *See, e.g.,* Opals on Ice Lingerie, Designs by Bernadette, Inc. v. Bodylines, Inc., 320 F.3d 362, 371 (2d Cir. 2003) (when defendant raised genuine issue as to authenticity of original document, trial court did not abuse its discretion in excluding plaintiff's proffered copy); United States v. Westmoreland, 312 F.3d 302, 311 (7th Cir. 2002) (when defendant offered no reason to question authenticity of original, trial court properly admitted "first generation" copies of tape-recorded conversations).

[2]   *See, e.g.,* Lozano v. Ashcroft, 258 F.3d 1160, 1166 (10th Cir. 2001) (when key information contained in photocopy is illegible, there is genuine question about authenticity of original, and photocopy is inadmissible under Rule 1003); United States v. Angle, 230 F.3d 113, 120–121 (4th Cir. 2000) (when defendant raised no question concerning authenticity of original or of prejudice resulting from trial court's use of duplicates of currency used in drug related sting operation, trial court did not abuse its discretion in admitting duplicates); United States v. Haddock, 12 F.3d 950, 958 (10th Cir. 1993) (trial court properly refused to admit defendant's photocopies as duplicates of bank documents because prosecution raised genuine question as to existence and authenticity of alleged originals).

[1]   *See* **Treatise** at § 1001.09.

> (4)
>
> Duplicate. A "duplicate" is a counterpart produced by the same impression as the original, or from the same matrix, or by means of photography, including enlargements and miniatures, or by mechanical or electronic re-recording, or by chemical reproduction, or by other equivalent techniques which accurately reproduces the original.

What was originally a "duplicate" can become, for evidentiary purposes, an "original," if a party used it as such in the course of its activities leading up to the suit in which the document is offered into evidence.[2]

The definition requires only that the reproduction measure up to a standard of accuracy, "designed to insure an accurate reproduction of the original."[3] It is designed to save the time and expense previously wasted in producing the original when an equally reliable counterpart was at hand. The rule still properly excludes from the definition of duplicate manually produced copies which are subject to human error in the process of reproduction. A duplicate of an original writing, recording, photograph, or computer printout is admissible regardless of the status of the original when the requirements of Rule 1001(4) and 1003 are satisfied.[4]

[b]—Writings[5]

The definition of duplicate includes carbon, microfilmed,[6] and Xerographic copies of writings as well as copies produced by other reliable techniques for reproducing originals,[7] such as holography and electronic image storage. Reproduction of the original in color or exact size is ordinarily not called for and enlargements of microfilm should be considered as equal to the microfilm itself.

---

[2] See, e.g., United States v. Angle, 230 F.3d 113, 120 (4th Cir. 2000) (prior to beginning narcotics sting operation, officer made xerographic copies of cash to be used by undercover operative in sting operation, noted date of reproduction on each copy, and provided copies to officers conducting operation; photocopy with date was "original" of document officer used to convey information concerning serial numbers of cash used in sting operation to other officers involved in operation, and were properly admitted as such).

[3] United States v. Perry, 925 F.2d 1077, 1082 (8th Cir. 1991) (photographic image made from videotape recording is a duplicate under Rule 1001(4) because it is "a counterpart produced by the same impression as the original").

[4] United States v. Gerhart, 538 F.2d 807, 810 n.4 (8th Cir. 1976) (photocopy could have been admitted as a "duplicate" under Rule 1003 instead of secondary evidence under Rule 1004 where the original was lost).

[5] See Treatise at § 1001.09.

[6] United States v. Carroll, 860 F.2d 500, 507–508 (1st Cir. 1988) (where originals of checks were either lost or destroyed, but not by proponent, microfilm prints of checks were admissible).

[7] See United States v. Stockton, 968 F.2d 715, 719 (8th Cir. 1992) (photographs of papers found in government search, although not originals, were admissible under Rule 1003 as duplicates, since defendant did not challenge their authenticity).

All that is usually required where no objection is offered by the opposing party is that testimony be offered that the copy is an accurate reproduction of its counterpart.

To admit carbon copies, the parties need not have signed the carbon or have shown a specific intention to treat it as part of the writing itself. Simultaneous production by the same impression as the original is all that is required.[8] Exact duplicates of books, printed notices and the like should be considered originals under Rule 1001(3). They are to be distinguished from printed copies of contracts where only the signed copies are originals. Changes on printed form leases, for example, are common. But some contracts of adhesion, such as bills of lading, are not commonly changed and any printed form should prove general terms as an original. The printed and unsigned copies, if they are shown to be identical to the executed copies, would be duplicates under Rule 1001(4).

[c]—Recordings[9]

Re-recordings should be accepted as duplicates when shown to have been made by a technique designed to ensure an accurate reproduction of the original.[10] In order to insure an accurate re-recording of the recorded conversation, it sometimes becomes necessary to edit tapes in order to delete irrelevant material and to suppress noise. When such editing or noise suppressing is done by experts or under the court's supervision, the re-recordings will be admitted into evidence,[11] but when parties other than the court selectively edit the tapes, the condensed version will sometimes be disallowed because of the risk of fraud or misleading.

Typewritten transcripts of recordings are often introduced to aid the jury in understanding and following the recorded conversations. Sometimes they are placed in evidence in conjunction with, or in place of, recordings. When this is done, a proper foundation must be laid by testimony that the transcript was

---

[8] *See* CTS Corp. v. Piher Int'l Corp., 527 F.2d 95, 104 n.29 (7th Cir. 1975) ("Although there is no direct testimony describing the document as a 'carbon copy', in the absence of any evidence to the contrary, we draw this inference from the copy of the document which was offered for examination in light of the testimony of the witnesses").

[9] *See* **Treatise** at §§ 1001.09[4], [8]; 1001.10.

[10] United States v. Carrasco, 887 F.2d 794, 802–803 (7th Cir. 1989) (accuracy of duplicate tape may be established through recollection of eyewitness to the event recorded); United States v. Balzano, 687 F.2d 6, 7–8 (1st Cir. 1982) (accuracy of tape established by testimony concerning method used for replication).

[11] United States v. DiMatteo, 716 F.2d 1361, 1368 (11th Cir. 1983), *vacated and remanded on other grounds,* 469 U.S. 1101 (1985) (where informant had tape-recorded his conversations with a conspirator and then forwarded tapes to DEA which in turn made copies of tapes, court held there was no error in admission of tapes; government properly established that introduced tapes were duplicates of originals by introduction of informant's testimony that duplicates were "exact recordings of conversations that were on the original tapes").

compared with the original recording and found to be a true copy.[12] The transcript is not, however, a duplicate original because it was not made by mechanical or electronic means assuring identity, but rather was copied by a person. Moreover, since the recording will reflect tones, inflections and pauses, it should be produced to be played if the opponent or the court wishes. If a jury wishes to see the transcript during deliberations, unless all parties consent, the recording must be played for them in court while they examine the transcript.

As a matter of sound practice, the original recording should be kept even after it is copied electronically or transcribed into written form. Even if the copy is admitted—as it generally should be—there will be some doubt in the trier's mind as to its completeness. An astute opponent can properly argue on the ground of spoliation that it should not be weighed against his client. Wire tapping and bugging statutes must be complied with in their details as to sealing of originals within specified periods and the like. This is a substantive rather than an evidentiary requirement.

[d]—Computer Records[13]

While Rule 1001(3) defines printouts as originals, such computer records should be considered duplicates if they are offered in evidence in place of underlying documents such as purchase orders, sales slips, invoices and notes. Thus, a record of a single sale by a department store would come under 1001(4), but an analysis of all sales for a period would be an original creation of the computer and would thus be classified under 1001(3). In practice it makes little difference whether a printout is characterized as coming within 1001(3) or 1001(4).

There is a technical problem in admitting computer records as duplicates because some of the copying of the source data into computer inputs is accomplished not, in the words of Rule 1001(4), by "electronic re-recording," but by people. This problem is overcome by use of Rule 803(6), which is discussed in Chapter 16.

[3]—Grounds for Excluding Duplicates[1]

[a]—Persuasive Reasons Required

When the opposing party concedes the duplicate's accuracy or does not object pursuant to Rule 1003, or fails to raise a genuine issue of authenticity,[2] the duplicate

---

[12] United States v. Slade, 627 F.2d 293, 302–303 (D.C. Cir. 1980) (discussion of appropriate procedures for use of transcripts not introduced into evidence).
[13] See **Treatise** at § 1001.11.
[1] See **Treatise** at §§ 1003.02, 1003.05.
[2] United States v. Chang An-Lo, 851 F.2d 547, 557 (2d Cir. 1988) (copies of telephone logs from hotel in Rio de Janiero were properly admitted because defendant raised no genuine issue of

must be admitted unless the court has strong reason to believe that the parties are conspiring to commit a fraud on the court. Even when accuracy is not conceded, the court should require persuasive reasons for rejecting duplicates, which should be routinely accepted as a convenience to the court and the parties.[3] A specific objection indicating why the original is needed should be required.[4]

Rule 1003 expressly provides two grounds for objection. It states that a duplicate can be excluded if the authenticity of the original is in doubt or if the admission of the duplicate would be unfair.

[b]—Question as to Authenticity of Original[5]

Duplicates can be excluded if there is a genuine question about the authenticity of the original. There are situations in which problems of authenticity will arise with respect to the original or the duplicate, despite the fact that Rule 1001(4) (see [2], above) requires that a duplicate be produced by a technique designed to insure an accurate reproduction of the original. One common situation is where an original and a duplicate are prepared but subsequently one is corrected or altered while such changes are omitted from the other counterpart, possibly out of forgetfulness or carelessness.[6] The duplicate must have been made after the original took on its final form: extensive conforming by hand makes it the equivalent of a hand drawn copy. Where there is a dispute about whether the parties authorized changes in a document and when it was changed, both the claimed unaltered version and the corrected

---

authenticity); United States v. Hausmann, 711 F.2d 615, 618 (5th Cir. 1983) (per curiam) (court affirmed conviction for making false statements to a United States agency holding that duplicates of falsified receipts were admissible since defendant did not raise a genuine issue as to their authenticity or show any unfairness resulting from their admission and the agency director testified that original receipts are normally copied and returned to the owner); United States v. Wilson, 690 F.2d 1267, 1276 n.2 (9th Cir. 1982) (photocopy of two false pieces of identification admissible as duplicate of originals; no objection at trial); United States v. Barnes, 443 F. Supp. 137, 139 n.2 (S.D.N.Y. 1977) (no reason not to admit state court hearing records where no issue had been raised as to their authenticity). Cf. Fidelity Philadelphia Trust Co. v. Pioche Mines Consol., Inc., 587 F.2d 27, 29 (9th Cir. 1978) (fact that records were lost is no excuse for lack of prosecution since Rules 1003 and 1004 allow copies to be used and copies were available).

　　³　United States v. Georgalis, 631 F.2d 1199, 1205 (5th Cir. 1980) (that government had exclusive possession of duplicates for five years raises no issue).

　　⁴　United States v. Benedict, 647 F.2d 928, 932–933 (9th Cir. 1981) (duplicate of false passport properly admitted since there was testimony that original had been lost in the State Department; since there was no credible showing of prejudice to defendant, unnecessary to decide whether loss of passport constituted negligence attributable to prosecution).

　　⁵　See **Treatise** at § 1003.03.

　　⁶　See, e.g., Lozano v. Ashcroft, 258 F.3d 1160, 1166 (10th Cir. 2001) (when key information contained in photocopy is illegible, there is genuine question about authenticity of original, and photocopy is inadmissible under Rule 1003).

counterpart should be admitted.[7]

Questions as to the authenticity of the original also arise where the circumstances surrounding the execution of the writing present a substantial possibility of fraud and where the party offering the duplicate has intentionally destroyed the original. In the latter case, courts look to see what intention the party had in destroying the original. When it is done by accident, mistake or in the regular course of business or for any nonfraudulent purpose, the duplicate is admissible.[8] When fraud is raised as an issue, the court may exclude the duplicate or any secondary evidence.

Under Rule 1003, the mere supposition that the original may have been altered should not prevent introduction of the duplicate without some indication that the original was altered. There must be a "genuine" dispute about the authenticity of the original.[9]

[c]—Circumstances of Unfairness[10]

Exclusion of the duplicate is also justified if it would be unfair to admit the duplicate in lieu of the original.[11] When deciding whether to exclude duplicates on unfairness grounds, the court should bear in mind the purpose of the rule. Rule 1003 was designed to make evidence easier to admit by taking advantage of modern accurate means of reproduction.[12]

Unfairness will sometimes arise even when accuracy of the contents of the writing would readily be conceded, as where something of substantial value may be gained by inspecting the original. The duplicate may, for example, fail to represent the entire writing and the undisclosed portion of the writing might either

---

[7] Amoco Prod. Co. v. United States, 619 F.2d 1383, 1391 (10th Cir. 1980) (in action to quiet title where there was dispute as to whether recorded deed accurately reflected original deed, trial court did not err in holding that what purported to be a conformed copy of the original deed could not be used to prove the contents of the original deed because the critical part of the conformed copy (the mineral reservation clause) was not completely reproduced).

[8] See, e.g., United States v. Balzano, 687 F.2d 6, 7–8 (1st Cir. 1982) (per curiam) (duplicate tape admitted where original was by necessity erased in process of transferring it to second cassette and appellant submitted no evidence suggesting lack of good faith).

[9] See, e.g., United States v. Westmoreland, 312 F.3d 302, 311 (7th Cir. 2002) (when defendant offered no reason to question authenticity of original, trial court properly admitted "first generation" copies of tape recorded conversations).

[10] See **Treatise** at § 1003.04.

[11] See Lozano v. Ashcroft, 258 F.3d 1160, 1165–1166 (10th Cir. 2001) (photocopy of EEOC decision letter was improperly admitted into evidence when most critical portion, time-date receipt stamp, was partially illegible).

[12] United States v. Enstam, 622 F.2d 857, 866 (5th Cir. 1980) (Xerox copy of corporate letterhead properly admitted as duplicate where it was properly identified as copy of original; court termed as "spurious" questions defendants raised as to authenticity: that there was no explanation for disappearance of original and that copy did not show original's colorings).

qualify the duplicated portion (*see* Rule 1006) or disclose additional relevant information, or there may be doubt about whether the original was executed. Or the original may be a pasted-together version that gives an entirely different impression than a smooth Xerox copy; interlineations in different color inks or pencils may be more readily seen in the original.[13] Determining authenticity of the signature may require production of the original where the signature on the original writing or type or ink color may have to be analyzed. The duplicate itself may be so mutilated, interlined, erased, unintelligible or illegible that fairness requires the original. In short, the category of unfairness encompasses any set of circumstances which enables the opposing party to show that there is a substantial likelihood of prejudice if the duplicate is admitted rather than requiring the original to be produced.

§ 9.03   When Is an Original Not Required—Rule 1004

[1]—Scope and Text of Rule[1]

Rule 1004 is primarily a restatement of the common-law rule excusing production of the original in four specified circumstances. Production of the original is excused in these instances because the best evidence rule is one of preference, not absolute exclusion, that gives way when efficiency and the need for relevant evidence become paramount. The rule states:

Rule 1004.   Admissibility of Other Evidence of Contents.

The original is not required, and other evidence of the contents of a writing, recording or photograph is admissible if—

(1) Originals lost or destroyed. All originals are lost or have been destroyed, unless the proponent lost or destroyed them in bad faith; or

(2) Original not obtainable. No originals can be obtained by any available judicial process or procedure; or

(3) Original in possession of opponent. At a time when an original was under the control of the party against whom offered, that party was put on

---

[13]   Greater Kansas City Laborers Pen. Fund v. Thummel, 738 F.2d 926, 928 (8th Cir. 1984) (court of of appeals upheld the trial court's decision admitting carbon copy of the contract as an original, even though at the signature line of the carbon someone had written defendant's name over the very dim carbon signature, stating that the fact that the signature was obscured would go to the weight not the admissibility of the document); Federal Deposit Ins. Corp. v. Rodenberg, 571 F. Supp. 455, 457–458 (D. Md. 1983) (in suit by assignee of promissory notes against personal guarantor of the notes, court held photocopies of relevant documents to be admissible despite the fact that minor portions were deleted in photocopying; relevant terms of promissory note and guaranty were clear and subject to only one reasonable interpretation).

[1]   *See* **Treatise** at § 1004.02.

notice, by the pleadings or otherwise, that the contents would be a subject of proof at the hearing, and that party does not produce the original at the hearing; or

(4) Collateral matters. The writing, recording, or photograph is not closely related to a controlling issue.

If production is excused because one of the four conditions enumerated in Rule 1004 is satisfied, secondary evidence of the contents is admissible.[1.1] Rule 1004 recognizes no degrees of secondary evidence. In other words, once the conditions of Rule 1004 are met, the party seeking to prove the contents of a writing, photograph or recording may do so by any kind of secondary evidence ranging from photographs and handwritten copies to oral testimony of a witness whose credibility is suspect. Of course, the opponent may attack the sufficiency of the secondary evidence including the credibility of the witness. This attack, however, goes not to admissibility but to the weight of the evidence and is a matter for the trier of fact to resolve.

While a rule establishing a hierarchy of secondary evidence may appear a natural complement of a "best evidence" rule, such a requirement was rejected because it is difficult to apply, and tactical factors ensure that the parties produce the best available evidence. Parties are naturally motivated to produce the best available evidence for fear of inferences the triers of fact might draw from their failure to do so; under the Federal Rules, the trial judge has significant latitude to comment on the evidence (Standard 107)[2] and to amplify the questioning of witnesses (Rule 614),[3] and discovery and pretrial procedures enable the opponent to discover what type of secondary evidence the proponent has in his possession. In the case of public records where the utmost accuracy is required and the originals cannot be produced without disruptive effects on public business, Rule 1005 sets forth special requirements for secondary evidence. See § 9.04.

[1.1] *See, e.g.,* United States v. Bennett, 363 F.3d 947, 954 (9th Cir. 2004) (to prove content of "writing" or "recording" by evidence other than original or duplicate, proponent must show that original was lost, destroyed, or otherwise unobtainable).

[2] Quercia v. United States, 289 U.S. 466, 470 (1933) ("The privilege of the judge to comment on the facts has its inherent limitations. . . . In commenting upon testimony he may not assume the role of a witness. He may analyze and dissect the evidence, but he may not either distort it or add to it. . . . [a]n expression of opinion upon the evidence 'should be so given as not to mislead, and especially that it should not be one sided.' "); *see* **Treatise** at Ch. 107, *Summing Up and Comment by Judge (Sup. Ct. Standard 107).*

[3] *See* Chapter 2.

[2]—Original Lost or Destroyed—Rule 1004(1)[1]

Rule 1004(1) follows long-recognized state and federal practice by providing that the non-fraudulent loss or destruction of an "original" creates a basis for the admission of secondary evidence.[2] The secondary evidence must be trustworthy to serve as an adequate substitute for the original of a destroyed or misplaced document.[3] By limiting the exclusion of secondary evidence to cases involving bad faith, the rule rejects the notion that any intentional destruction by the proponent bars the admissibility of secondary evidence.[4]

The Rule excludes secondary evidence when the loss of the original can be attributed to the proponent's bad faith. There is then too great a risk that any secondary evidence that the proponent might offer would be false or misleading. A proponent offering secondary evidence to prove the content of a lost or destroyed original has the burden of proving absence of bad faith. To satisfy this burden, the proponent must account for the loss or destruction of the absent document. Direct evidence of the destruction of the original will usually not be available except in those cases in which the proponent was responsible. A diligent search is required if the destruction of the document is in doubt.[5]

While some courts have attempted to lay down strict rules as to what constitutes a diligent search, the better reasoned decisions have recognized that the sufficiency

---

[1] *See* **Treatise** at §§ 1004.10–1004.13.

[2] *See, e.g.,* Paul Revere Variable Annuity Ins. Co. v. Zang, 248 F.3d 1, 9–10 (1st Cir. 2001) (in action to enforce arbitration, trial court properly admitted secondary evidence to prove defendant-employee had agreed to arbitration when plaintiff-employer had misplaced agreement containing arbitration clause, defendant made no claim misplacement of agreement was in bad faith, and there was no dispute defendant was registered with NASD, and registration necessarily entailed defendant's agreement to arbitration); Beggerly v. United States, 114 F.3d 484, 487–488 (5th Cir. 1997) (district court erred in not recognizing certified translation as best evidence of missing original Spanish land grant).

[3] *See, e.g.,* United States v. Wells, 262 F.3d 455, 460–461 (5th Cir. 2001) (oral testimony concerning contents of lost business record is not trustworthy).

[4] *See, e.g.,* Malkin v. United States, 243 F.3d 120, 123 (2d Cir. 2001) (in absence of evidence that loss of Internal Revenue Service form was anything other than inadvertent, it was not abuse of trial court's discretion to permit proof of defendant's having executed form through secondary evidence); United States v. Dudley, 941 F.2d 260, 264 (4th Cir. 1991) (report prepared by staff member of the Federal Reserve Bank showing that many of the bills found on defendant had not been released into circulation on the date on which defendant said she received them admissible even though the records upon which the report was based were destroyed by the Bank pursuant to its regular practice to destroy old records).

[5] *See, e.g.,* Los Angeles News Serv., Inc. v. CBS Broadcasting, Inc., 305 F.3d 924, 936 (9th Cir. 2002) (trial court properly precluded plaintiff from proving content of label indicating source of video tape through testimony when plaintiff offered no explanation why it could not offer original or copy through ordinary third-party discovery).

of a search depends upon the circumstances.[5.1] Loss of a deed may require turning the house upside down while loss of an easily replaced doctor's bill requires only turning a desk drawer over. The courts consider the following factors: (1) any circumstances suggesting fraud on the proponent's part; (2) the importance of the document and; (3) the age of the instrument. In addition, courts should consider the character of the document in question. It may be such that an inference of loss or destruction is so highly likely that a search will be excused or the degree of diligence required greatly minimized.[6] Good faith destruction may also be assumed when the proponent can demonstrate that the original was destroyed pursuant to a routine business practice.

In addition to accounting for the absence of the original, the proponent must authenticate the absent document. Before proof of contents can be admitted, the court should be satisfied that a reasonable juror could find the existence and due execution of the original in the same manner as if the original were produced. See discussion of authentication requirements in Chapter 8.

[3]—Original Not Obtainable—Rule 1004(2)[1]

Rule 1004(2) is in accord with prevailing practice in excusing production of the original if it cannot "be obtained by an available judicial process or procedure."[2] The rationale is obvious: if the original cannot be obtained by either party or court, it is as inaccessible as though it had been lost or destroyed. The need for relevant evidence takes precedence over the dangers of inaccuracy and fraud—issues left to the trier in assessing probative force—and allows the admission of secondary evidence.

While the rule is written in absolute terms, the courts are afforded a good deal of discretion to use common sense. *See, e.g.,* Rule 102. For example, it would be ludicrous to force a litigant to expend thousands of dollars to obtain a document from abroad when only $10,000 or so is at stake. The phrase "to the extent practicable and reasonable" should be read into the rule. In most instances the court can exercise its good offices at the pretrial conference to avoid making the litigation prohibitively expensive. This is a particularly important matter when a defendant in a criminal case finds it difficult to obtain an original.

[5.1] *See, e.g.,* Burt Rigid Box, Inc. v. Travelers Prop. Cas. Corp., 302 F.3d 83, 91–93 (2d Cir. 2002) (trial court did not abuse its discretion in finding plaintiff had made diligent search to locate original of insurance policy and properly admitted secondary evidence of its existence).

[6] United States v. Carroll, 860 F.2d 500, 507–508 (1st Cir. 1988) (where originals of checks were either lost or destroyed but not by proponent, microfilm prints of checks were admissible).

[1] *See* **Treatise** at §§ 1004.20–1004.21.

[2] United States v. Benedict, 647 F.2d 928, 933 (9th Cir. 1981) (testimony by DEA agents as to business records in Thailand).

The main difficulty with this exception to the best evidence requirement is determining the extent of the showing that must be made to demonstrate that resort to judicial process is ineffective. If the original is in the possession of the party against whom it is offered, the proponent need only show notice pursuant to Rule 1004(3) (*see* [4], *below*) rather than resort to process. If the original is within the possession of a third party within the jurisdiction of the court, service of a subpoena duces tecum would itself constitute a sufficient showing.[3] If the original is possessed by a person who is in the United States but outside of the court's jurisdiction, proof of service of an order to produce the original at a deposition should suffice to fulfill the condition of Rule 1004(2).

When the person who has possession of the document is outside the United States, the proponent must convince the court that no available practicable judicial process or procedure will bring forth the original. Procedures do exist for the production of documents in foreign countries. Does this mean that parties must invoke these procedures to prove compliance with Rule 1004(2) even if they know that such efforts will be fruitless because the particular country in which the item is sought will not cooperate? Certainly, if the fact of non-cooperation is so well known that a court would take judicial notice of it, no further showing should be required. Otherwise, the court might wish to insist upon a letter from the State Department or possibly a representation of counsel that efforts to secure cooperation with the judicial machinery of the United States are unavailing in the country involved.[4]

In criminal cases, because of the narrow scope of discovery, much less of a showing will ordinarily have to be made to convince the court that material outside the subpoena jurisdiction of the court cannot be obtained.

Privileged material is not subject to discovery[5] and will not be produced subject to subpoena. Thus, a claim of privilege is sufficient to excuse production of the original.

[4]—Original in Possession of Opponent—Rule 1004(3)[1]

Production of an original is excused if a party in possession of the item fails to produce it upon demand. The sufficiency of the proof of possession is a preliminary

---

[3] United States v. Taylor, 648 F.2d 565, 570 (9th Cir. 1981) (trial court did not err in admitting photocopy of crucial letter where government represented that subpoenas requesting the original letter had been served on the parties and the original was not produced, and defendant's counsel failed to object to admission of copy).

[4] *But cf.* United States v. Ratliff, 623 F.2d 1293, 1296–1297 (8th Cir. 1980) (trial court assumed it had no subpoena power over documents in Germany; in absence of demonstration, appellate court did not find court's finding to be clearly erroneous).

[5] Fed. R. Civ. P. 26(b)(1); *see* 6 MOORE'S FEDERAL PRACTICE, Ch. 26, *General Provisions Governing Discovery; Duty of Disclosure* (Matthew Bender 3d ed. 1997).

[1] *See* **Treatise** at §§ 1004.30–1004.32.

question for the judge to be determined pursuant to Rule 1008, which is discussed in Chapter 3. Notice implies a mere request without compulsive force. If the proponent actually requires the original, the appropriate remedy is resort to discovery procedures or a subpoena duces tecum. The purpose of Rule 1004(3) is to excuse production of the original, not to compel it.

Rule 1004(3), apart from stating that notice may be given by the pleadings, is silent as to other methods of notification. Notice by the pleadings is given by implication, when it is clear from the pleadings the contents of a document are essential to proof of the case.

Rule 1004(3) does not provide for any exceptions under which notice is unnecessary before secondary evidence of the original in the opponent's control may be used. Thus, although there have been some traditional exceptions dispensing with the need for notice when the opponent has fraudulently suppressed the original or the original is itself a notice, the proper course under Rule 1004(3) is to notify the opponent in any case.

Notification is also required by Rule 1004(3) when the original sought is in the hands of the accused in a criminal prosecution. Ordinarily notice should be given before trial, and specific notice may be excused if defendant is put on notice by the indictment that the contents of a particular document will be a subject of proof. Certainly, notice may not be given in the presence of the jury as this would amount to a derogation of the accused's privilege against self-incrimination. The requirement of Rule 1004(3) is merely intended to give defendant the opportunity to produce the original before secondary evidence can be used.

[5]—Collateral Matters—Rule 1004(4)[1]

Rule 1004(4) recognizes the exception commonly found in American jurisdictions for so-called collateral matters. This provision—which eliminates the need for an original when the document is only tangentially related to the material issues in the case—promotes efficiency and gives the trial judge discretion to apply the best evidence rule flexibly rather than over-technically. Although the term "collateral" is elusive and vague and few cases discuss the exception, Rule 1004(4) is useful as another vehicle for the exercise of common sense since it recognizes that the cost of producing an original may greatly outweigh the importance of the document and the financial capacity of the litigant.

---

[1] *See* **Treatise** at §§ 1004.40–1004.42.

§ 9.04 Public Records Exceptions—Rule 1005[1]

Rule 1005 creates a limited exception to the best evidence rule.

Rule 1005. Public Records.

The contents of an official record, or of a document authorized to be recorded or filed and actually recorded or filed, including data compilations in any form, if otherwise admissible, may be proved by copy, certified as correct in accordance with rule 902 or testified to be correct by a witness who has compared it with the original. If a copy which complies with the foregoing cannot be obtained by the exercise of reasonable diligence, then other evidence of the contents may be given.

Rule 1005 is concerned with copies of two kinds of public records: (1) official records—normally records produced by a government employee—and (2) documents authorized to be recorded or filed—normally those produced by private persons.

The Rule departs from Article X's rejection of the concept of degrees of secondary evidence and establishes a hierarchy of secondary methods for proving the content of public records. A copy can be used to prove the terms of the original if it is (1) certified in accordance with Rule 902(4), or (2) a witness attests that he or she has favorably compared the copy to the original.[2] Other secondary evidence is admissible to prove the terms of a public record only if a preferred copy "cannot be obtained by the exercise of reasonable diligence." Before other secondary evidence can be admitted the terms of Rule 1002 must be satisfied. Thus only if both the original and a Rule 1005 copy are unavailable may other evidence be used. Rule 1005 also does not specify what constitutes "other" evidence. Beyond the certified and compared copies which are mentioned in Rule 1005, the remaining general types of secondary evidence are: duplicates, copies which are uncertified or uncompared, oral testimony with memory refreshed by a previously written memorandum, and unrefreshed oral testimony.

Rule 1005 is designed to prevent the loss of and damage to public records and to permit public business to be conducted with a minimum of inconvenience to those who use records. Requiring the original to be provided would deprive the public of the record while it was in court. Compared or certified copies are preferred because they are easily obtained and the persuasive nature of public records makes some degree of protection against fraud desirable.

---

[1] *See* **Treatise** at §§ 1005.02–1005.06.
[2] United States v. Rodriguez, 524 F.2d 485, 488 n.6 (5th Cir. 1975) (agent testified that he made Xerox copy of vehicle certificate of title; although he was not specifically asked whether it was a "correct" copy, failure to indicate otherwise was sufficient to satisfy Rule 1005).

The preference for compared or certified copies results in the preemption of Rule 1003, which in the non-public record context allows copies that were produced by a method insuring accuracy to be used to the same extent as originals. Yet some flexibility in being sensible about proof of public documents is permitted by Rule 1002 despite the apparent rigidity of Rule 1005. There is no inconsistency between Rule 1005, on the one hand, and Rules 1001, 1002, 1004, 1006, 1007 and 1008 on the other. Under any of these rules a copy of an original not on file is admissible even though there may also be a copy on file as a public record.

For example, deeds are often recorded and a photostat is kept in the public file. The original is returned to the owner. The contents of the original in the hands of the owner may be proved in any way permitted by Article X. Alternatively, Rule 1005 can be used to prove the contents of the deed even if the original is still extant. If, however, what is sought to be proved is the contents of the deed actually on file, then Rule 1005 must be followed because the original, for this purpose, will be considered the document on file. If there is a question about whether the deed on file was the one actually recorded, then the original in the hands of the owner—or a duplicate or copy when authorized by the rules—as well as the authenticated copy of the public record may be required.[3] In cases of serious dispute, the court is justified in ordering the file of the public office produced in court, taking care to minimize inconvenience by returning the records as soon as possible.

These terms ought to be given the broadest possible interpretation for purposes of Rule 1005.[4] If not, the governmental agency will be disrupted by the necessity of bringing its original records to court instead of furnishing a certified copy. It is, after all, not the accuracy of the copy that is really being contested in most instances but the admissibility of contents. The main issue as to admissibility normally involves hearsay or relevancy rather than best evidence issues where public records are involved.

---

[3] Amoco Prod. Co. v. United States, 619 F.2d 1383, 1390 (10th Cir. 1980) (in action to quiet title where there was dispute as to whether recorded deed accurately reflected original deed apparently no longer in existence, error for trial court to apply Rule 1005 to exclude all other evidence of the contents of the deed; original deed is not a public record and Rule 1004 rather than Rule 1005 applies to it).

[4] United States v. Tombrello, 666 F.2d 485, 491–492 (11th Cir. 1982) (certified exemplified copies of docket entries from state court were admissible pursuant to Rule 1005); Seese v. Volkswagenwerk A.G., 648 F.2d 833, 845 (3d Cir. 1981) (computer printouts of fatal accidents maintained by National Highway Traffic and Safety Administration admissible as public records).

§ 9.05   Summaries—Rule 1006

[1]—Scope and Text of Rule[1]

Rule 1006 provides that the contents of voluminous writings, recordings, or photographs may be proven by secondary evidence in the form of charts, summaries, or calculations.

Rule 1006.   Summaries.

The contents of voluminous writings, recordings, or photographs which cannot conveniently be examined in court may be presented in the form of a chart, summary, or calculation. The originals, or duplicates, shall be made available for examination or copying, or both, by other parties at [a] reasonable time and place. The court may order that they be produced in court.

Rule 1006 is premised on the theory that charts,[2] summaries, or calculations are not only a convenient means of proving the contents of voluminous materials, but sometimes the only practicable method of doing so.[3] Rule 1006 may not apply solely to written summaries. At least one court has cited it as authorizing testimony that summarizes and condenses voluminous writings reviewed by the witness.[4] Rule 611 is the usual authority for allowing the use of a chart or testimony that summarizes other testimony or exhibits that have been admitted into evidence.[4.1]

Many courts hold that materials admitted pursuant to Rule 1006 constitute the evidence of the contents of the writings or recordings sought to be proved. Under

---

[1]   *See* **Treatise** at §§ 1006.02–1006.04.

[2]   *See, e.g.,* United States v. Weaver, 281 F.3d 228, 232 (D.C. Cir. 2002) (summary of payroll records was, itself, evidence, admitted in lieu of payroll records).

[3]   United States v. Francis, 131 F.3d 1452, 1457–1458 (11th Cir. 1997) (district court did not abuse its discretion in admitting summaries of voluminous wire-tapped conversations in lieu of actual recordings).

[4]   *See, e.g.,* United States v. Caballero, 277 F.3d 1235, 1247 (10th Cir. 2002) (witness's testimony summarizing voluminous business records was "clearly permitted by" Rule 1006); *but cf.* United States v. Fullwood, 342 F.3d 409, 413–414 (5th Cir. 2003) (although Rule 1006 may allow summary witnesses to summarize voluminous records, "rebuttal testimony by an advocate summarizing and organizing the case for the jury constitutes a very different phenomenon, not justified by the Federal Rules of Evidence or our precedent").

[4.1]   *See, e.g.,* United States v. Taylor, 210 F.3d 311, 315 (5th Cir. 2000) (use of charts as "pedagogical devices intended to present the government's version of the case is within the bounds of the trial court's discretion to control the presentation of evidence under Rule 611(a)"); United States v. Possick, 849 F.2d 332, 339 (8th Cir. 1988) (citing **Treatise;** use of organizational charts as demonstrative devices to aid jury's comprehension is within court's discretion under Rule 611(a)); *see* United States v. Fullwood, 342 F.3d 409, 413–414 (5th Cir. 2003) (Rule 1006 does not authorize testimony summarizing live testimony presented in court; although summary witnesses "may be appropriate for summarizing voluminous records, as contemplated by Rule 1006").

this line of authority, whether or not the originals are introduced at the trial, the summaries may be relied on as evidence in chief.[5] However, other courts hold that a summary is not itself evidence, but only an aid to understanding the underlying evidence (*see* [4][b], *below* (summaries used as pedagogical devices)).[6]

Because demonstrative evidence such as charts and other summaries can be quite potent, the proponent should have the opportunity to view each item of demonstrative evidence and raise any objections before it is shown to the jury.[7]

The rule differs conceptually from other aspects of the best evidence rule in that charts, summaries, or calculations are introduced under Rule 1006 as other evidence of materials available to all parties rather than as other evidence of materials which are lost, destroyed, or otherwise unavailable. The jury need not see the originals, but they must be made available to the other parties.[8] Instances where summaries may be used without reliance on Rule 1006 are discussed below.

Rule 1006 requires that the original or duplicate writings, recordings, or photographs be made available for examination or copying by other parties at a reasonable time and place.[8.1] This provision acts as a condition precedent which must be fulfilled before a summary, chart, or calculation may be admitted as evidence. Rule 1006 does not give the judge discretionary power to waive this condition.[9] Implicit in this requirement is the opposing party's right to adequate

---

[5] *See, e.g.,* United States v. Williams, 264 F.3d 561, 575 (5th Cir. 2001) (summary chart that meets Rule 1006's requirements is itself evidence and no instruction that it is mere jury aid is needed).

[6] United States v. Bray, 139 F.3d 1104, 1111–1112 (6th Cir. 1998) (summaries used as pedagogical devices are properly considered under Rule 611(a) if they are used to summarize admitted evidence and they reflect inferences and conclusions drawn from that evidence by their proponent; such summaries are not admitted into evidence, and limiting instruction is proper); *see* **Treatise** at § 1006.04; *see also* [4][b], *below.*

[7] *See, e.g.,* United States v. Richardson, 233 F.3d 1285, 1293 (11th Cir. 2000) (trial court is charged with responsibility to permit use of charts with grave caution, lest accused is "unjustly convicted in a trial by charts"); *see* Civil Trial Practice Standard 15(a) (A.B.A. 1998) (responsibility of court to provide opponents with opportunity to preview demonstrative evidence).

[8] *See* Zayre Corp. v. S.M. & R. Co., 882 F.2d 1145, 1148–1149 (7th Cir. 1989) (offer to make originals available for review at stores around country may have been inadequate but, absent objection, was adequate compliance with Rule 1006).

[8.1] *See, e.g.,* United States v. Modena, 302 F.3d 626, 633 (6th Cir. 2002) (proponent of Rule 1006 summary must tell opponent when and where underlying documents will be available for inspection, and cannot condition availability of documents on opponent's making materials available for proponent's inspection).

[9] *See* Amarel v. Connell, 102 F.3d 1494, 1517 (9th Cir. 1997) (district court ignored requirement "embodied in the mandatory language of Federal Rule of Evidence 1006 . . . that a party must make available to the opposing party the materials that have gone into preparing the summary exhibit"); Air Safety v. Roman Catholic Archbishop of Boston, 94 F.3d 1, 8 (1st Cir. 1996) (failure to request or obtain documents during discovery does not negate party's "absolute right to

time for the examination of the underlying documents in order to prepare a defense or challenge the accuracy of the summary. The problem of surprise should be minimized by the appropriate use of discovery procedures and pretrial hearings.

The final sentence of Rule 1006 gives the judge discretion to compel the production in court of the original or duplicate materials on which the chart, summary, or calculation is based.[10] For example, the originals may be needed when an opponent wishes to establish inaccuracies in the summary or to challenge the authenticity, accuracy or admissibility of the originals.

[2]—Admissibility of Summaries[11]

Before the charts, summaries, or calculations may be submitted to the jury pursuant to Rule 1006, the court must find that there is a sufficient factual basis for admitting them and that possible prejudice or confusion does not outweigh their usefulness in clarifying the evidence.[12] See discussion of Rules 401 and 403 in Chapter 6.

Charts, summaries, or calculations are inadmissible, if, for any reason, the materials on which they are based are inadmissible.[13] Consequently, unless the parties are willing to stipulate to the admissibility of the underlying documents, the party offering the exhibit must lay a foundation enabling the court to determine that the original or duplicate materials on which the exhibit is based are admissible. A chart, summary, or calculation is inadmissible if it is based on inadmissible hearsay,[14] on privileged matter, or on materials made inadmissible by the con-stitutional protection against self-incrimination. Nor will the summary satisfy Rule

---

subsequent production of material under Rule 1006, should that material become incorporated into a chart, summary or calculation").

[10] *See* United States v. Smyth, 556 F.2d 1179, 1184 n.11 (5th Cir. 1977) (implicit in Rule 1006 is the notion that the trial judge may choose to admit the underlying documents in evidence).

[11] *See* **Treatise** at §§ 1006.06–1006.07.

[12] *See, e.g.,* United States v. Leon-Reyes, 177 F.3d 816, 819–820 (9th Cir. 1999) (summaries of oral testimony are normally prepared by interested party and may be inaccurate or biased; in perjury prosecution based on defendant's testimony in earlier trial, summaries of others' testimony in that trial were properly admitted, since trial court reviewed summaries before trial and removed irrelevant and unduly prejudicial material).

[13] *See, e.g.,* PEAT, Inc. v. Vanguard Research, Inc., 378 F.3d 1154, 1159–1160 (11th Cir. 2004) (charts and summaries are admissible under Rule 1006 only when based on materials that are themselves admissible evidence; citing **Treatise**).

[14] Paddack v. Dave Christensen, Inc., 745 F.2d 1254, 1259–1260 (9th Cir. 1984) (summary not admissible where it was impossible to separate the admissible and inadmissible hearsay on which it was based); United States v. Goss, 650 F.2d 1336, 1344 n.5 (5th Cir. 1981) (Rule 1006 does not authorize the admission of summaries of the testimony of out-of-court witnesses; error to allow agent to testify as a "summary witness" that checks were mailed based on his interviews with witnesses).

1006 if it contains information not present in, or computed from, the original or duplicate materials on which it is based. This latter situation may arise if the preparer of the summary incorporates information drawn from his personal knowledge of the organization whose books he is summarizing, or statements made to him by knowledgeable persons to whom he has spoken in the process of preparing the exhibit.[15] Almost never will an exhibit prepared by an expert be excluded, since the expert will testify that the basis complies with Rule 703. See discussion in Chapter 13.

Some courts permit the introduction into evidence under Rule 1006 of summary charts that both summarize the contents of documents admitted or admissible into evidence and incorporate assumptions that the documents do not necessarily support. In those cases, the assumptions must be supported in the record, either by the testimony of witnesses or by the contents of other admitted trial exhibits, and the trial court must instruct the jury that it has the final decision as to the weight to be accorded to the summary charts.[16]

[3]—Preparation and Authentication of Summaries[17]

Rule 1006 does not require that charts, summaries, or calculations be prepared by persons with special expertise, although practical considerations may dictate the necessity of having technicians prepare the exhibits. Nor does Rule 1006 expressly require that summaries, charts, or calculations be authenticated on the witness stand by the person responsible for their preparation. As a practical matter it would be very difficult to authenticate any exhibit being offered pursuant to Rule 1006, or to establish its accuracy, without calling as a witness the person who supervised its preparation.[18] Courts have facilitated the authentication process by allowing

---

[15] *Cf.* United States v. Jennings, 724 F.2d 436, 441–442 (5th Cir. 1984) (although conclusions in summary charts were based on assumptions by government, no error in admitting charts where assumptions were explored in cross-examination and jury was instructed to give charts their appropriate weight; court noted that the nexus between the summary and the supporting evidence was "close to being as attenuated as should be allowed . . . and that . . . the trial court's ruling approached the limits of its discretion.").

[16] *See, e.g.,* United States v. Richardson, 233 F.3d 1285, 1293–1294 (11th Cir. 2000); United States v. Stoecker, 215 F.3d 788, 791 (7th Cir. 2000) (trial court did not err in admitting under Rule 1006 summary charts that summarized both documents in evidence and testimony of witnesses); United States v. Taylor, 210 F.3d 311, 315–316 (5th Cir. 2000) (charts based on documents and testimony are admissible under Rule 1006, so long as they do not depend on assumptions that are unsupported or contradicted by record evidence).

[17] *See* **Treatise** at § 1006.05.

[18] Vasey v. Martin Marietta Corp., 29 F.3d 1460, 1468–1469 (10th Cir. 1994) (trial court acted within discretion in excluding summary of documents purporting to show that age discrimination since, at trial, plaintiff's counsel was unable to explain meaning of one category in summary); United States v. Scales, 594 F.2d 558, 563 (6th Cir. 1979) (person who supervised compilation of summary was the proper person to attest to authenticity and accuracy of chart).

supervisory personnel to attest to the authenticity and accuracy of charts, summaries, or calculations in situations where many individuals, computers or other machines are used in the production of the exhibit.

A chart, summary, or calculation offered as evidence in civil cases without the testimony of the person responsible for its preparation should not be objectionable as violating the hearsay rule. Availability of the original or duplicate material on which the exhibit was based should adequately substitute for the absence of the person responsible for the exhibit's preparation. Failure by such person to testify where the chart, summary, or calculation is offered as evidence against a criminal defendant would raise the question of whether the defendant's constitutional right to confrontation is violated. As a tactical matter, it is almost inconceivable that a prosecutor would not use a witness to explain a chart unless the defendant stipulated to its admission in evidence.

[4]—Summaries Used Without Reliance on Rule 1006[19]

[a]—Summaries as Evidence

The provisions and considerations of Rule 1006 are inapplicable to charts, summaries, and calculations admitted as evidence under Rule 1001(3), 1004, and 1005. When the summary is printed by a computer and reflects data in the computer, the printout may be the original itself. Provided the requirements of Rule 1004 are fulfilled, charts, summaries, or calculations are admissible as other evidence of the contents of unavailable originals. Charts, summaries, and calculations are additionally admissible to prove the contents of public records, provided the requirements of Rule 1005 are satisfied.

A more complicated situation exists when some portion of the original or duplicate materials on which a chart, summary, or calculation is based is produced, but the balance of the materials is unavailable. The chart, summary, or calculation may then be admissible as other evidence of the contents of the unavailable original or duplicate materials under Rules 1004 and 1005, and also admissible as a summary of available materials under Rule 1006. All of the provisions and considerations of Rule 1006 are applicable to those elements of the chart, summary, or calculation which are based on unavailable original or duplicate materials, and which serve as other evidence of their contents under Rule 1004 and 1005.

[b]—Summaries as Pedagogical Devices

Care must be taken to distinguish between summaries or charts that constitute independent evidence pursuant to Rule 1006 (*see* [3], *above*) and summaries, charts, or other aids used as pedagogical devices to summarize or organize tes-

---

[19] *See* **Treatise** at § 1006.08.

timony or documents that have themselves been admitted in evidence.[20]

Courts allow summaries of admitted evidence as an aid to the fact-finder in cases involving complicated or voluminous evidence.[21] Such summaries need not be impartial. They may focus on evidence favorable to the proffering party, so long as the witness does not present the summary as being based on all of the evidence.[22]

Although pedagogical summary charts probably should not be admitted into evidence and should not be available to the jury during its deliberations,[23] some courts admit them into evidence, so long as any assumptions they are based on are fairly supported by record evidence and the court gives the jury appropriate cautionary instructions.[24] If the court admits them into evidence, limiting instructions should make it clear that they, unlike Rule 1006 summaries, are not evidence, but are only the proponent's organization of the evidence presented.[25] They should be shown to opposing counsel and approved by the court or by stipulation before they are unveiled before the jury and should not be allowed into the jury room

---

[20] *See* United States v. Bray, 139 F.3d 1104, 1109–1112 (6th Cir. 1998) (distinguishing between (1) Rule 1006 summaries ("primary-evidence summaries"); (2) "pedagogical-device summaries"; and (3) "secondary-evidence summaries," which are a hybrid of the first two types, being summaries of admitted evidence that are also admitted into evidence because the trial court finds that they "so accurately and reliably summarize comjplex or difficult evidence . . . as to materially assist the jurors").

[21] *See, e.g.,* United States v. Bray, 139 F.3d 1104, 1111–1112 (6th Cir. 1998) (pedagogical summaries are based on admitted evidence and are not themselves admitted into evidence; court's authority for their use stems from Rule 611(a) rather than Rule 1006); United States v. Gardner, 611 F.2d 770, 776 (9th Cir. 1980) (tax evasion case; court rejects defendant's claim that use of chart summarizing his assets, liabilities and expenditures was unduly prejudicial; chart was "summary of facts and calculations which were in evidence . . . the use of the chart contributed to the clarity of the presentation to the jury, avoided needless consumption of time and was a reasonable method of presenting the evidence"; no error to ultimately admit chart as evidence pursuant to Rule 1006).

[22] *See, e.g.,* United States v. Bishop, 264 F.3d 535, 547 (5th Cir. 2001) (summary evidence must be based on admitted evidence and should be accompanied by cautionary jury instruction); United States v. Bray, 139 F.3d 1104, 1111–1112 (6th Cir. 1998) (pedagogical summaries "may reflect to some extent, through captions or other organizational devices or descriptions, the inferences and conclusions drawn from the underlying evidence by the summary's proponent").

[23] *See, e.g.,* United States v. Buck, 324 F.3d 786, 791 (5th Cir. 2003) (pedagogical charts are not themselves evidence; they should not be admitted and should not be available to jury during its deliberations; court should instruct jury that they are not evidence and that it may consider them only as an aid in evaluating admitted evidence).

[24] *See, e.g.,* United States v. Richardson, 233 F.3d 1285, 1293–1294 (11th Cir. 2000).

[25] *See, e.g.,* United States v. Bishop, 264 F.3d 535, 547 (5th Cir. 2001) (summary pedagogical charts in particular are admissible when "(1) they are based on competent evidence already before the jury, (2) the primary evidence used to construct the charts is available to the other side for comparison so that the correctness of the summary may be tested, (3) the chart preparer is available for cross-examination, and (4) the jury is properly instructed concerning use of the charts").

without the consent of all parties since they are more akin to argument than evidence.[26]

Usually these pedagogical devices are introduced through an expert, such as an accountant or FBI agent. When used by an expert in explaining his or her opinion, they should be considered part of the expert's testimony pursuant to Rules 702 and 703, and they may then be exhibited to the jury if the relevant testimony is read to the jury during its deliberations. Sometimes they are used in summations even when not referred to earlier by a witness.

§ 9.06   Proof of Contents Through Testimonial or Written Admissions of Adverse Party—Rule 1007[1]

Rule 1007 permits a party to prove the contents of an original by introducing evidence of an adverse party's testimony, deposition, or written admission, including answers to interrogatories and requests to admit. An adverse party's oral admission cannot be used pursuant to this Rule.

Rule 1007.   Testimony or Written Admission of Party.

Contents of writings, recordings, or photographs may be proved by the testimony or deposition of the party against whom offered or by that party's written admission, without accounting for the nonproduction of the original.

Rule 1007 operates as an exception to Rule 1002 because it does not require a showing that the original material is lost, destroyed, or otherwise unavailable. When original materials are lost, destroyed, or unavailable, or constitute nonproducible public records, a party may offer an adverse party's admissions of contents—even if oral and not made in a deposition or testimony—as other evidence of contents under Rule 1004 or Rule 1005. In such a case, the provisions and considerations of Rule 1007 are inapplicable. The distinction between use of an adverse party's admissions as proof of contents under Rule 1007 and Rules 1004 and 1005 is important because an adverse party's oral extrajudicial admissions are acceptable evidence of contents when offered in place of absent original materials under Rules 1004 and 1005.

Rule 1007 is a rule of convenience that permits a party to use an adversary's admissions to prove contents of a writing, recording, or photograph in lieu of the more time-consuming process of introducing and authenticating the original ma-

---

[26]   *See, e.g.,* United States v. Taylor, 210 F.3d 311, 315 (5th Cir. 2000) (pedagogical devices are not admitted into evidence and they do not go into the jury room during jury deliberations).

[1]   *See* **Treatise** at §§ 1007.02–1007.07.

terial.[2] Admissions by an adverse party are considered acceptable proof of contents because it is assumed that such admissions—usually, but not always against interest—will be accurate and honest.[3] The purpose of the restriction in Rule 1007 limiting admissibility of an adverse party's oral admissions to those delivered as "testimony" is to protect the party against being misquoted or quoted out of context. Since a party's admission is assumed to be true, it is not necessary to require that the "testimony" be delivered under oath in order to prove contents. A guarantee of the accuracy of the report of what was admitted would exist where the statement is part of a transcript made at an official, but non-judicial hearing, such as one conducted by a legislative committee. It would also include grand jury testimony which is transcribed. Similarly, the term "written admission" as used in Rule 1007 should be interpreted to include any statement, including one made in a private conversation, that can be guaranteed to be accurately and completely recorded. A statement by an adverse party which is captured verbatim by a tape recorder or other recording process and which is introduced unedited should also suffice to satisfy the "writing" requirement of Rule 1007.

Use of an adverse party's admissions to prove contents should not be confused with use of an adverse party's admission to directly establish a fact also evidenced by a writing, recording, or photograph. In the latter situation, both admissions by the adverse party and documentary material are primary evidence. When a criminal defendant admits the commission of a crime and subsequently confesses in writing to the act, the oral admission and written confession are both primary evidence that the defendant committed the act. Or, when a defendant to a charge of negligence admits negligence and also fills out an accident report containing statements that establish the negligence, both items are primary evidence of negligence. Where, however, the defendant fills out an accident report and subsequently admits the genuineness of the report and states what its contents are, his or her admissions as to the contents are only other evidence of the report's contents, so that Rule 1007 applies. In situations where an adverse party's admission is introduced as other evidence of contents, the provisions and considerations of Rules 1002 and 1007 apply. Use of admissions as evidence-in-chief is governed by Rule 801(d)(2).

Since the theory behind the rule rests on the reliability of admissions (see discussion of the hearsay rule in Chapter 15), admissions given in a representative

---

[2] *See, e.g.,* B.D. Click, Co., Inc. v. United States, 614 F.2d 748, 754, 756 (Fed. Cir. 1980) (although not in record, release signed by plaintiff was "overwhelmingly" proved under Rule 1007 by plaintiff's written admissions in several documents filed with administrative agency in proceeding appealed from).

[3] *See, e.g.,* Metropolitan Life Ins. Co. v. Hogan, 63 F.2d 654, 656 (7th Cir. 1933) (appellant's agent's oral admissions of contents of a notice of death and proof of loss was admissible under "the rule generally adopted . . . that oral admissions to the contents of a written instrument are competent evidence of its contents").

capacity should qualify to the same extent as provided in Rule 801(d)(2).

CHAPTER 10

Witnesses Generally

SYNOPSIS

§ 10.01 General Rules of Competency—Rule 601

[1]—Scope and Text of Rule[1]

Under Rule 601, two standards of competency apply in federal courts. In civil cases where state law furnishes the rule of decision, state restrictions on competency govern. In criminal and civil cases when state law does not furnish the rule of decision, all persons—other than the presiding judge (Rule 605, *see* Chapter 11), or a member of the jury hearing the case (Rule 606, *see* Chapter 11)—are competent to testify as ordinary witnesses unless they have no personal knowledge of the events to which they seek to testify (Rule 602, *see* § 10.03), or refuse to declare that they will testify truthfully (Rule 603, *see* § 10.04). The rule states:

Rule 601. General Rule of Competency.

Every person is competent to be a witness except as otherwise provided in these rules. However, in civil actions and proceedings, with respect to an element of a claim or defense as to which State law supplies the rule of decision, the competency of a witness shall be determined in accordance with State law.

Under the Federal Rules, except when state law furnishes the rule of decision, most grounds for automatically disqualifying a witness have been converted into grounds for impeaching a witness.[2] Conviction of crime as a ground for impeaching a witness is treated in Rule 609, which is discussed in Chapter 12. Evidence of bias, lack of mental capacity, and infancy is not afforded special treatment in the rules but is highly relevant and will be admissible as bearing on credibility.[3] Rule 610 assures that evidence of religious belief may not be used to impeach (*see* Chapter 12).

A preliminary examination pursuant to Rule 104(a) for the purpose of deter-

---

[1] *See* **Treatise** at §§ 601.02–601.03.

[2] *See, e.g.,* United States v. Bell, 367 F.3d 452, 464 (5th Cir. 2004) (Rule 601 does not permit trial court to declare deaf and mute witness incompetent so long as witness can communicate by means of gestures, signs, and grunts that are understood by family members, friends, and close acquaintances). United States v. Davis, 261 F.3d 1, 38–39 (1st Cir. 2001) (one party's payments to lay witness for his time in preparing for and giving testimony did not render witness incompetent; evidence of payments went to witness's credibility, not to admissibility of his testimony).

[3] United States v. Abel, 469 U.S. 45, 31, 105 S. Ct. 465, 83 L. Ed. 2d 450 (1984) ("it is permissible to impeach a witness by showing his bias under the Federal Rules of Evidence just as it was permissible to do so before their adoption"); Andrews v. Neer, 253 F.3d 1052, 1062–1063 (8th Cir. 2001) (witness's status as involuntarily committed schizophrenic at time of testimony did not disqualify him from testifying; mental illness is ground for impeachment, so long as trial court is properly satisfied witness has ability to testify truthfully).

mining competency is usually not required.[4] This does not mean, however, that the trial judge no longer has any power to keep a witness from testifying.[5] A trial judge still has broad discretion to control the course of a trial (Rule 611, *see* Chapter 2) and to rule on relevancy (Rules 401 and 403, *see* Chapter 6). The trial judge may exclude all or part of the witness's testimony on the ground that no one could reasonably believe the witness could have observed, remembered, communicated or told the truth with respect to the event in question,[6] or on Rule 403 grounds that prejudice is greater than the probative force of the testimony. The judge may use the voir dire to make this determination. Particularly difficult problems may arise when the witness was or is taking psychotropic medication,[7] is an infant, is brain injured, is an interested attorney, or has had memory affected through hypnotism. [*see* [2], [3], *below*].

The Supreme Court, in *Rock v. Arkansas*,[8] held in a 5–4 decision that a criminal defendant could not be precluded from testifying in her own behalf on the basis of a per se rule excluding a defendant's hypnotically refreshed testimony. "A State's legitimate interest in barring unreliable evidence does not extend to per se exclusions that may be reliable in an individual case."[9] The Court suggested that a state "would be well within its powers if it developed guidelines to aid trial courts in the evaluation of posthypnosis testimony,"[10] and that in a given case hypnotically refreshed testimony might be excludable as too unreliable. The majority opinion contemplates a case by case analysis of the proffered testimony. The opinion does not purport to deal with non-party witnesses.[11]

---

[4] *See, e.g.,* United States v. Raineri, 91 F.R.D. 159 (W.D. Wis. 1980), *aff'd,* 670 F.2d 702 (7th Cir. 1982).

[5] Taylor v. Illinois, 484 U.S. 400, 415, 108 S. Ct. 646, 98 L. Ed. 2d 798 (1988) (preclusion may be appropriate when a criminal defendant fails to comply with a request to identify witnesses in advance of trial if "omission was willful and motivated by a desire to obtain a tactical advantage").

[6] *See, e.g.,* SEC v. Downe, 969 F. Supp. 149, 158 n.6 (S.D.N.Y. 1997) (witness's competence to testify depends on witness's capacity to observe, remember, communicate, and to understand nature of oath and duty it imposes to tell truth; determination of competence is for judge and issue of credibility is for jury), *aff'd,* 151 F.3d 42 (2d Cir. 1998).

[7] *See, e.g.,* United States v. Blankenship, 923 F.2d 1110 (5th Cir. 1991) (a key government witness was competent to testify even though she admitted that she had committed felonies, was currently incarcerated, had occasional hallucinations caused by drug use, and used drugs during the events about which she was testifying; these matters affected credibility, not competency).

[8] Rock v. Arkansas, 483 U.S. 44, 107 S. Ct. 2704, 97 L. Ed.2d 37 (1987).

[9] 483 U.S. at 61, 107 S. Ct. at 2714, 97 L. Ed.2d at 52.

[10] 483 U.S. at 61.

[11] Beck v. Norris, 801 F.2d 242 (6th Cir. 1986) (hypnotically refreshed recollection used to obtain composite sketch of defendant and trial testimony respecting sketch did not infringe defendant's right to confront witnesses in view of precautions taken to avoid giving witness suggestions while in hypnotic state and videotape of witness before and during hypnosis).

[2]—Children; Brain-Injured Persons[12]

The testimony of a plaintiff who suffered brain damage in the accident being sued on and who is one of only two eyewitnesses may be essential; the testimony of a congenitally brain-damaged child who was one of a number of uninvolved witnesses to an accident may be prejudicial, confusing, and probably cumulative and a waste of time if all or some of the other witnesses are in court. Certainly the court has power under Rule 611 to hear the plaintiff and to postpone hearing the child until the other witnesses have testified so that it can better assess whether the testimony is needed (*see* Chapter 2, *Control by Trial Court Generally*). If the child is the only witness, the need for his or her testimony would obviously be much greater. Its high probative value would, in fact, under the rules as written, probably compel admission, subject to challenge by cross-examination and impeachment. The court may instruct the jury to treat such evidence with care (Standard 107) and it may refuse to consider the testimony in deciding whether a prima facie case has been established.

Despite the strong pressure of the rules to admit the testimony of any child who might conceivably testify truthfully about an event, the careful attorney for the proponent will bear in mind that federal judges have exercised—albeit frugally—their power to exclude testimony of very young children. Sometimes the child's age at the time of the event or testimony, or the period between the event and the testimony, is such as to make it almost certain the child is echoing what the child's elders have said about the event. Even if the child can fairly accurately relate what happened shortly after the event, when the case comes to trial a year or more later it is almost hopeless to expect a clear recollection. The child's statement immediately after the event may be reported under one of the exceptions to the hearsay rule.[13] In addition, a promptly taken deposition may be useful. The testimony of child witnesses is increasingly held reliable, especially when precautions are taken against suggestibility.[14]

[3]—Attorneys[15]

Although the modern trend has been to regard attorneys with a pecuniary interest in the subject of the litigation as competent to testify,[16] federal judges have felt

---

[12] *See* **Treatise** at § 601.04[1], [2].

[13] *See, e.g.,* Rules 803(1), (2), (4), 807.

[14] *See, e.g.,* United States v. Snyder, 189 F.3d 640, 645–646 (7th Cir. 1999) (trial court did not abuse its discretion when it refused to order child to undergo psychological examination for competency); United States v. Allen J., 127 F.3d 1292, 1295–1296 (10th Cir. 1997) (inconsistencies in child victim's testimony in sex abuse case raised questions of credibility, not competency).

[15] *See* **Treatise** at § 601.04[3].

[16] United States v. West, 680 F.2d 652, 654–655 (9th Cir. 1982) (Assistant U.S. Attorney seated in spectator section properly allowed to testify about alleged signalling between defendant

empowered to prevent an attorney from doing so on ethical grounds.[17] One technique—that of conditioning the attorney's testimony on withdrawal from the case[18] —presumably rests on the court's inherent control over attorneys or on the court's power to control a trial, which is expressed in Rule 611.[19]

The federal courts have also recognized that forcing or permitting an attorney to withdraw may have serious repercussions on the trial in progress.[20] Even when substitution occurs before the trial starts, adjournments and delays often result. In some cases it has been suggested that the problem can be solved by not permitting the attorney to testify unless a clear need for the testimony is shown.[21]

A pre-trial conference before a criminal or civil trial provides a useful means of resolving the problem of foreseeable instances when attorneys may be needed as witnesses. Often the matter can be resolved by stipulations or by calling other witnesses with knowledge of the events. In addition, at trial an offer of proof[22] will often show that the evidence is excludable under Rule 403. In a bench trial, a more relaxed attitude is often warranted. Often, the parties will permit the court to take the attorney's statement without oath or cross-examination.[23]

---

and witness; only other alternate witness was F.B.I. agent seated at counsel's table whose testimony would have presented essentially the same risks).

[17] *See* ABA Code of Professional Responsibility DR–5–101, 5–102(1); ABA Canons of Professional Ethics No. 19; ABA Code of Professional Responsibility EC 5–9 ("If a lawyer is both counsel and witness, he becomes more easily impeachable for interest and thus becomes a less effective witness. Conversely, the opposing counsel may be handicapped in challenging the credibility of the lawyer when the lawyer also appears as an advocate in the case. An advocate who becomes a witness is in the unseemly and ineffective position of arguing his own credibility. The rules of an advocate and of a witness are inconsistent; the function of an advocate is to advance or argue the cause of another, while that of a witness is to state facts objectively.").

[18] *See, e.g.,* United States v. Clancy, 276 F.2d 617, 636 (7th Cir. 1960), *rev'd on other grounds,* 365 U.S. 312 (1961).

[19] *See* Travelers Ins. Co. v. Dykes, 395 F.2d 747, 749 (5th Cir. 1968) (court refused to permit defendant's co-counsel to testify in an attempt to impeach one of plaintiff's witnesses; appellate court affirmed noting that "Much considered and wise discretion must be accorded to a district judge as he deals with the infinite variables of evidence"; testimony was offered to impeach one of plaintiff's witnesses; no discussion in opinion of importance of witness or of testimony); *see* Chapter 2.

[20] *See, e.g.,* United States v. Brown, 417 F.2d 1068 (5th Cir. 1969) (attorney who wanted to contradict witness he had interviewed was neither permitted to testify while representing defendant nor allowed to withdraw; court notes that withdrawal at that stage of trial would have resulted in mistrial. A change in counsel after trial has commenced rests in the court's discretion).

[21] United States v. Bates, 600 F.2d 505 (5th Cir. 1979) (court was well within its discretion in not allowing defense counsel to take stand when cross-examination was used to present the same story the attorney would have told).

[22] *See* Rule 103(a)(2), which is discussed in Chapter 2.

[23] Bickford v. John E. Mitchell Co., 595 F.2d 540 (10th Cir. 1979) (not error to allow attorney to testify in light of the facts that 1) he had not previously participated in trial; 2) he withdrew from

[4]—Application of State Law Required[24]

In civil cases where state law furnishes the rule of decision, the "competency of the witness [is] determined in accordance with State law."[25] This provision was added to Rule 601 primarily to ensure that Dead Man's Acts would be given effect in cases governed by state law.[26] Dead Man's Acts generally prohibit the party-witness and sometimes other interested persons from testifying to conversations, transactions, or other dealings with a decedent or incompetent when the decedent's estate or the incompetent's representative is an adverse party.[27] A state's Dead Man's Act is applicable in an action in which the rule of decision is provided by state law even if it is not an "act" at all, but is included in the state's rules of evidence.[28]

The language of Rule 601 requiring the application of state competence law is sufficiently broad, however, to require the determination of a witness's competence to testify under state standards whenever state law supplies the rule of decision, not only when Dead Man's Acts are applicable to proffered testimony.[29] Nevertheless, when a federal statute provides substantive law the court will apply, or when state law supplies interstitial rules for the application of federal law, federal competence law is applicable.[30] Indeed, in cases arising under federal law, when the courts face an objection to expert testimony on competence grounds under Rule 601, they perform precisely the same analysis of the witness's competence to testify as they do in determining his or her qualification "by knowledge, skill, experience, training, or education" to testify under Rule 702.[31]

---

case before testifying; 3) trial to court and not to jury).

[24] *See* **Treatise** at § 604.05.

[25] Fed. R. Evid. 601; *see, e.g.,* Legg v. Chopra, 286 F.3d 286, 290 (6th Cir. 2002) (in diversity medical malpractice action, competence of expert witness is determined under state law, while witness's qualifications are determined under Rule 702).

[26] *See, e.g.,* Fed. R. Evid. 601 Advisory Committee's Note (1972) (reproduced verbatim in **Treatise** at § 601App.01[2]).

[27] *See, e.g.,* Paul v. Gomez, 118 F. Supp. 2d 694, 694 (W.D. Va. 2000) (applies Virginia Dead Man's Statute to permit testimony).

[28] *See, e.g.,* Electronic Planroom, Inc. v. McGraw-Hill Cos., & Estate of Devon Shire, 135 F. Supp. 2d 805, 815 n.11 (E.D. Mich. 2001).

[29] *See, e.g.,* Legg v. Chopra, 286 F.3d 286, 290-292 (6th Cir. 2002) (state statute providing that only licensed medical doctors from same or neighboring state may testify about standard of care in medical malpractice cases determines competence to testify, a substantive issue, and applies under Rule 601; *but see* Peck v. Tegtmeyer, 834 F. Supp. 903, 910 (W.D. Va. 1992), *aff'd* 4 F.3d 985, 985 (4th Cir. 1993) (unpublished) (Rule 601 is primarily concerned with dead man statutes; determining admissibility of proffered expert testimony exclusively under Rule 702).

[30] *See, e.g.,* Andrews v. Neer, 253 F.3d 1052, 1062 (8th Cir. 2001).

[31] *Compare* United States v. Lopez-Lopez, 282 F.3d 1, 15 (1st Cir. 2002) (customs agent was competent under Rule 601 to testify to modus operandi of drug smugglers because of his education as electrical engineer, experiences as electronics technician in Air Force and as customs agent in

When the Dead Man's Act permits both the interested party's testimony and the decedent's hearsay to be introduced, the effect in civil state-rule-of-decision cases should be to permit hearsay to be introduced which is not admissible under Article VIII of the Federal Rules. In non-state-rule-of-decision cases, testimony rendered competent by Rule 601 will still have to clear the hearsay hurdle. Unlike some state statutes that have specific provisions making statements by a decedent an exception to the hearsay rule, the Federal Rules of Evidence do not cover this situation expressly. The categories in Rules 803 and 804, however, are sufficiently broad to permit a witness, in most instances, to testify to conversations or transactions with a person now dead.

When state law does furnish the rule of decision, Rule 601 does not specifically direct itself to the question of which State's competency rule is to apply. No problem is presented if the case is brought to the federal court of State X and all the operative facts occurred in X. But consider the situation in which an action is brought in X to recover for a wrongful death that occurred in Y. Obviously, state rather than federal law will furnish the rule of decision, and, according to *Klaxon Company v. Stentor Electric Manufacturing Company*,[32] the federal court should look to the conflict-of-laws rule of X to determine whether X will apply the law of X or the law of Y in regard to wrongful death.[33]

§ 10.02   Opinion Testimony by Lay Witnesses—Rule 701

[1]—Rationale and Text of Rule[1]

Rule 701 is a rule of discretion. It replaces the orthodox rule excluding opinion evidence with a rule that requires the trial judge on the basis of the posture of the particular case to decide whether concreteness of detail in reported observations, abstraction, or a combination of both will be most effective in enabling the jury to ascertain the truth and reach a just result. The rule provides as follows:

Rule 701.   Opinion Testimony by Lay Witnesses.

  If the witness is not testifying as an expert, the witness' testimony in the form of opinions or inferences is limited to those opinions or inferences which

---

interdicting drug smuggling and infiltrating drug smuggling operations, and qualification as FCC licensed radio operator) *with* United States v. Plunk, 153 F.3d 1011, 1017 (9th Cir. 1998) (law enforcement officer was qualified under Rule 702 to testify as expert to jargon of narcotics trade on basis of training as police officer and experience in investigating narcotics violations); *see also* § 13.02[3].

[32]   Klaxon Co. v. Stentor Elec. Mfg. Co., 313 U.S. 487, 61 S. Ct. 1020, 85 L. Ed. 1477 (1941).

[33]   *See, e.g.,* Maltas v. Maltas, 197 F. Supp. 2d 409, 425 (D. Md. 2002) (in determining which of two potentially applicable Dead Man's Acts to apply, if any, federal court should determine what state courts of forum state would do in same circumstances).

[1]   *See* **Treatise** at § 701.02.

are (a) rationally based on the perception of the witness, (b) helpful to a clear understanding of the witness' testimony or the determination of a fact in issue, and (c) not based on scientific, technical, or other specialized knowledge within the scope of Rule 702.

[Adopted Jan. 2, 1975, effective July 1, 1975; last amended Dec. 1, 2000.]

Like the hearsay and authentication rules, the lay opinion rule is at heart a form of best evidence rule. The orthodox opinion rule,[2] rejected by the drafters of Rule 701, sought to ensure reliability by insisting that witnesses state facts rather than opinions. Although the supposed distinction between facts and opinions was impossible to apply, the rule had a core of sense. It recognized that more concrete descriptions are preferable because they are more reliable and because it is the trier's duty to draw inferences from observed data reported to it. The possibility of error probably increases with each level of abstraction by the witness. Requiring specificity exposes flaws in the witness' memory—instead of spouting forth generalities the witness is forced to give a detailed story that can be tested by cross-examination. Misconceptions can be exposed much more readily by examining the raw data on which the witness grounded his or her conclusion than by challenging the conclusion itself.

Contrary to the orthodox rule, Rule 701 assumes that the witness will give testimony by stating observations in as raw a form as practicable, but permits resort to inferences and opinions when this form of testimony will be helpful. Rule 701 is in accord with modern trends in conditionally favoring opinions provided two requirements are satisfied: the opinion or inference (1) must be rationally based on the witness's own perception and (2) must be helpful to the trier of fact in the form used.[3]

---

[2] *See* discussion of the history of the opinion rule in **Treatise** at § 701App.100.

[3] *See, e.g.*, United States v. Tocco, 200 F.3d 401, 418–419 (6th Cir. 2000) (despite "significant risk" of jury confusion, law enforcement officers are not entirely prohibited from testifying as both fact and expert witnesses); Staley v. Bridgestone/Firestone, Inc., 106 F.3d 1504, 1513 (10th Cir. 1997) (not abuse of discretion for court to admit testimony of game wardens, who had discovered body, concerning what deceased might have been doing at time he was killed); Fireman's Fund Ins. v. Alaskan Pride Partnership, 106 F.3d 1465, 1468 (9th Cir. 1997) (testimony of underwriter that claim was legitimate loss and that he was upset about denial of coverage was not improper lay opinion); Gross v. Burggraf Const. Co., 53 F.3d 1531, 1544 (10th Cir. 1995) (lay opinion concerning supervisor's preferences on women was inadmissible in gender discrimination action because opinion was not based on witness's personal knowledge of any statement made by supervisor); Williams Enters. v. Sherman R. Smoot Co., 938 F.2d 230, 233–234 (D.C. Cir. 1991) (insurance broker permitted to testify as to reason for increase in plaintiff's premiums; broker's opinion was based on facts, such as the account history, of which he had personal knowledge, and information was helpful to trier of fact); United States v. Juvenile Male, 864 F.2d 641, 647 (9th Cir. 1988) (victim could testify as to assailant's intent).

Through this formulation, Rule 701 seeks to balance the need for relevant evidence against the danger of admitting unreliable testimony. It recognizes that necessity and expedience may dictate receiving opinion evidence, but that a factual account insofar as feasible may further the values of the adversary system.

[2]—Prerequisites to Admissibility[4]

[a]—Opinion Must be Rationally Based on Witness's Own Perception

To comply with the first requirement of Rule 701, that the opinion be rationally based on the witness's own perception, the testimony must initially meet the personal knowledge requirement of Rule 602.[5] Lay opinion or inference testimony that is based on inferences or speculation is not based on the witness's personal perception, and is not admissible under Rule 701.[6]

The lay opinion or inference testimony must also be rationally connected to those personal perceptions.[7] The rational connection prerequisite means that the opinion or inference must be one that a normal person would form on the basis of the observed facts.[8] If the opinion or inference is based on speculation, it is proper for the trial court to exclude it as not rationally based on the witness's personal perceptions.[9]

Similarly, if the witness's observations could lead to several inferences, all of

---

[4] *See* **Treatise** at §§ 701.03–701.08.

[5] *See, e.g.,* Bandera v. City of Quincy, 344 F.3d 47, 54 (1st Cir. 2003) (lay witness's testimony concerning emotional effect on plaintiff of sexual harassment in her employment was clearly inappropriate lay opinion testimony and should have been excluded under Rule 701); United States v. Holmes, 229 F.3d 782, 788 (9th Cir. 2000) (six meetings with defendant, each lasting at least a half hour, provided witness with sufficient personal knowledge of defendant's appearance to permit her to provide lay opinion testimony identifying him as person pictured in surveillance photographs taken during bank robbery).

[6] *See, e.g.,* United States v. Scott, 270 F.3d 30 (1st Cir. 2001) (lay opinion testimony authenticating handwriting under Rule 901(b)(2) must be based on sufficient familiarity to satisfy personal perception requirement of Rule 901, which requires that witness have reasonable pre-litigation exposure to handwriting); Keller v. United States, 38 F.3d 16, 30–31 (1st Cir. 1994) (lay witness's testimony that plaintiff must have hit his head on railing prior to fall was inadmissible when it was not based on personal perception; witness neither saw plaintiff hit his head nor heard any noise associated with such an incident).

[7] Fed. R. Evid 701; *see, e.g.,* United States v. Bowe, 221 F.3d 1183, 1192–1193 (11th Cir. 2000) ("Non-expert witnesses may offer their opinions if they are rationally based on the witnesses' own perception and if they either help clarify the witnesses' other testimony or determine a fact in issue.").

[8] *See, e.g.,* Lubbock Feed Lots, Inc. v. Iowa Beef Processors, Inc., 630 F.2d 250, 263 (5th Cir. 1980).

[9] *See, e.g.,* Hester v. BIC Corp., 225 F.3d 178, 182 (2d Cir. 2000) (trial court erroneously permitted plaintiff's co-employees to testify to opinion that plaintiff's supervisor's neglect of plaintiff "must have been because of her race").

which are equally likely, it is appropriate for the trial court to exclude lay opinion or inference testimony relating only one of the possible inferences because of a lack of a reasonable connection between the facts observed and the conclusion drawn.[10] On the other hand, if the lay witness's opinion is based on extensive observations over a lengthy period of time, and is predicated upon concrete facts within the witness's own observation and recollection, it is an abuse of the trial court's discretion to exclude the opinion testimony.[11]

[b]—Opinion Must be Helpful

The witness may testify to the opinion or inference rather than the underlying observations only if they would be "helpful to a clear understanding of the testimony or the determination of a fact in issue."[12] Common situations in which lay opinion or inference testimony has been held useful include the following:

- The lay witness is in a better position than the trier of fact to form the opinion or to draw the inference.[13]

- A bald rendition of the facts is insufficient to convey a complete understanding of them to the jury.[14]

---

[10] *See, e.g.,* United States v. Glenn, 312 F.3d 58, 67 (2d Cir. 2002) (witness's lay opinion that defendant was carrying hand gun on day of murder, based on witness's having seen, from distance of "five or six houses away" bulge under defendant's jacket that was about two inches wide and four inches long when defendant raised his hands above his head for about five seconds, was not reasonably connected to facts witness observed).

[11] *See, e.g.,* Gossett v. Oklahoma ex rel. Bd. of Regents for Langston Univ., 245 F.3d 1172, 1179–1180 (10th Cir. 2001) (witness's position as instructor at nursing school and on Admissions Committee provided her with opportunity to observe firsthand for several years school's policies and practices with respect to its treatment of male students, and supported her lay opinion that school's negative actions against male student were result of gender-based discrimination).

[12] Fed. R. Evid. 701; *see, e.g.,* United States v. Gaines, 170 F.3d 72, 77 (1st Cir. 1999) (drug dealer witness was able, on basis of his first-hand perception, to explain particular references upon which he rendered opinion); United States v. Sheffey, 57 F.3d 1419, 1428–1429 (6th Cir. 1995) (witnesses who observed defendant driving prior to car accident could testify that, in their opinion, defendant was driving recklessly and in extreme disregard for human life).

[13] *See, e.g.,* United States v. Vega-Figueroa, 234 F.3d 744, 755 (1st Cir. 2000) (lay witness's opinion as to why her sister was killed was admissible in drug conspiracy prosecution, because testimony was well founded on personal knowledge and helped jury to understand motive behind the murder and how that act furthered interests of conspiracy).

[14] *See, e.g.,* United States v. Bogan, 267 F.3d 614, 619–620 (7th Cir. 2001) (lay witness's opinion testimony that defendants were "trying to kill" person they assaulted was properly admitted because witness was able to view assault adequately, opinion was rationally based on those observations, and opinion was helpful to jury); Government of Virgin Islands v. Knight, 989 F.2d 619, 629-630 (3rd Cir. 1993) (trial court erred in excluding eyewitness's lay opinion that shooting was accidental because testimony would have been helpful to jury in "relating facts with greater

- The opinion or inference will enhance the jury's understanding of the underlying facts.[15]

- The witness has specialized information the trier of fact does not have.[16]

It should be noted, however, that the precedential value of cases admitting lay opinion testimony that is based wholly or in part on specialized knowledge is now open to serious question, in view of the 2000 amendment to Rule 701 requiring that lay testimony not be based on "scientific, technical, or other specialized knowledge within the scope of Rule 702."[17]

Common situations in which lay opinion or inference testimony has been held not to be useful include the following:

- The evidence is clear and the trier of fact is perfectly capable of perceiving, understanding, and interpreting it.[18]

- The testimony relates to an issue, such as credibility of witnesses, that is usually reserved exclusively to the trier of fact for decision.[19]

- The testimony merely tells the trier of fact how to decide the case.[20]

---

clarity," since it is difficult to articulate all factors that would lead to conclusion that person did not intend to fire gun).

[15] *See, e.g.,* United States v. Vineyard, 266 F.3d 320, 331–332 (4th Cir. 2001) (lay opinion testimony that part of extraordinarily large severance payment constituted "hush money" was helpful to jury); Cawing v. Illinois Cent. Gulf R.R., 618 F.2d 332, 337 (5th Cir. 1980) (when condition of railroad crossing was at issue, trial court erred by excluding opinion testimony of lay witnesses about crossing because photographs of crossing had been admitted; non-conflicting evidence that enhanced and explained photographic evidence satisfied Rule 701).

[16] *See, e.g.,* United States v. Wash, 231 F.3d 366, 371–372 (7th Cir. 2000) (lay opinion testimony from dealer in crack cocaine identifying substance as crack cocaine was properly admissible); United States v. Flores, 63 F.3d 1342, 1359–1360 (5th Cir. 1995) (in narcotics case, coconspirator's testimony, based on his experience with defendants and drug trafficking, as to "secret meanings" in taped conversations, helped jury).

[17] *See, e.g.,* United States v. Peoples, 250 F.3d 630, 641 (8th Cir. 2001) ("Lay opinion testimony is admissible only to help the jury or the court to understand the facts about which the witness is testifying and not to provide specialized explanations or interpretations that an untrained layman could not make if perceiving the same acts or events"; 2000 amendment to Rule 701 emphasizes distinction between lay and expert opinion testimony; "[what is essentially expert testimony . . . may not be admitted under the guise of lay opinions").

[18] *See, e.g.,* United States v. Hence, 222 F.3d 633, 640 (9th Cir. 2000) ("If the jury already has all the information upon which the [lay] witness's opinion is based, the opinion is not admissible"; lay opinion on issue of defendant's knowledge was inadmissible).

[19] *See, e.g.,* United States v. Forrester, 60 F.3d 52, 63 (2d Cir. 1995) (witness may not give lay opinion testimony concerning credibility of another witness).

[20] *See, e.g.,* United States v. Garcia, 291 F.3d 127, 140–141 (2d Cir. 2002) (lay opinion testimony that ascribes to apparently coherent conversation meanings at variance with ordinary usage of terms used, when introduced without foundation evidence that participants were actually

- The testimony is mere speculation.[21]

- The testimony is an opinion or inference of law.[22]

The Advisory Committee recognized that there were circumstances in which even the most eloquent of witnesses has difficulty in expressing himself or herself in language other than that of opinion or inference.[23] Advisory Committee's Note (1972) (see **Treatise** § 701App.01[2]). That type of opinion or inference testimony is merely a shorthand rendition of the witness's observations, and is fully permissible under Rule 701.[24]

[c]—Opinion Must Not be Based on Scientific, Technical, or Other Specialized Knowledge

Rule 701(c), provides that lay witnesses not testifying as experts may not give opinions that are "based on scientific, technical, or other specialized knowledge within the scope of Rule 702."[25] Before the rule change, some courts had admitted lay opinion evidence of a technical nature on a showing that the testimony was based on sufficient experience or knowledge to make it reliable and helpful to the jury.[26] Now under Rule 701(c), a witness must testify as an expert if the opinions at issue are "based on scientific, technical, or other specialized knowledge within the scope of Rule 702."

A lay witness's specialized observations of the specific matters at issue in the case may impart to the witness a unique opportunity to formulate an opinion, for example, as to the meaning of jargon used in the narcotics trade, and thereby provide the witness with the means to express a lay opinion as to such matters even

---

speaking in code, does no more than tell jury how to decide matter reserved for its determination and is not useful under Rule 701).

[21] See, e.g., United States v. Santos, 201 F.3d 953, 962 (7th Cir. 2000) (opinion testimony that manager had ordered subordinate to terminate contractors who did not make campaign contributions was not based on personal observations); United States v. Gibson, 636 F.2d 761, 764 (D.C. Cir. 1980) (trial court properly excluded as mere speculation lay opinion testimony, based on observations conducted with unaided vision, that defendant could not have been seen in car from second story window even if watcher had aid of binoculars).

[22] See, e.g., United States v. Parris, 243 F.3d 286, 288–289 (6th Cir. 2001) (lay opinion testimony to legal conclusion is inadmissible; here, lay testimony that witnesses quit defendant's tax avoidance scheme because they thought it was "illegal" was properly admitted; benefits of scheme were so outrageous that its characterization as "illegal" was fair, if a bit casual).

[23] Fed. R. Evid. 701.

[24] See, e.g., Bandera v. City of Quincy, 344 F.3d 47, 54 (1st Cir. 2003) (Rule 701 permits only limited range of opinion testimony, such as "an estimate of car speed or whether a defendant was intoxicated").

[25] Fed. R. Evid. 701(c).

[26] See, e.g., Davoll v. Webb, 194 F.3d 1116, 1138–1139 (10th Cir. 1999) (treating physician properly testified as lay witness when describing patient's condition and treatment).

after the 2000 amendment to Rule 701.[27] For example, a witness who employs only processes used by ordinary persons for forming opinions or drawing inferences may testify to those opinions or inferences as a lay witness even though in the opinion-forming or inference-drawing process they have used particularized knowledge or information they gained in their everyday experience that other persons do not possess.[27.1] Such a circumstance is to be distinguished from the use of specialized experience in other matters as the bases for the formulation of an opinion, in which case the witness would have to qualify and be identified in pretrial proceedings as an expert.[28]

The Committee Note to the amendment adding Rule 701(c) states that the intent of the amendment is to prevent the "reliability requirements set forth in Rule 702" from being "evaded through the simple expedient of proffering an expert in lay witness clothing." The amendment is also intended to prevent parties from using Rule 701 to "evade the expert witness disclosure requirements" in Civil Rule 26 and Criminal Rule 16.[29]

§ 10.03   Lack of Personal Knowledge—Rule 602[1]

Rule 602 provides that a witness may testify only about matters of which he or she has first-hand knowledge.[2] A witness can acquire personal knowledge by

---

[27] *See, e.g.,* United States v. Miranda, 248 F.3d 434, 441 (5th Cir. 2001) (investigating officer's "extensive participation in the investigation of this conspiracy, including surveillance, undercover purchases of drugs, debriefings of cooperating witnesses familiar with the drug negotiations of the defendants, and the monitoring and translating of intercepted telephone conversations, allowed him to form opinions concerning the meaning of certain code words used in this drug ring based on his personal perceptions").

[27.1] *See, e.g.,* Texas A&M Research Found. v. Magna Transp., Inc., 338 F.3d 394, 402–403 (5th Cir. 2003) (witnesses involved in particular business may testify to lay opinions and inferences concerning their business affairs); Tampa Bay Shipbuilding & Repair Co. v. Cedar Shipping Co., 320 F.3d 1213, 1223 (11th Cir. 2003) (corporation's officer or employee may testify to industry practices and pricing without qualifying as expert); United States v. Espino, 317 F.3d 788, 796–798 (8th Cir. 2003) (witnesses experienced in purchasing methamphetamine may testify to their lay opinion concerning weight of drug they bought when opinion was based on their visual observation of drug when they purchased it).

[28] *See, e.g.,* Certain Underwriters at Lloyd's v. Sinkovich, 232 F.3d 200, 203–204 (4th Cir. 2000) (trial court erred in admitting lay opinion testimony from witness, not qualified or identified as expert witness, concerning assignment of responsibility for accident when witness did not personally observe accident, relied on testimony of other witnesses for basis of his opinion, and testified on the basis of knowledge available only to experienced seamen or to marine engineers).

[29] Committee's Note (2000) at **Treatise** § 701App.03[2]; *see, e.g.,* United States v. Martinez-Figueroa, 363 F.3d 679, 682 (8th Cir. 2004).

[1] *See* **Treatise** at §§ 602.02–602.04.

[2] Fed. R. Evid. 602; *see, e.g.,* Carmen v. San Francisco Unified Sch. Dist., 237 F.3d 1026, 1029 (9th Cir. 2001) (in suit alleging retaliatory refusal to hire, plaintiff failed to show basis in personal knowledge for her belief that she was denied employment because she had filed suit for racial

perceiving events though any one or more of the physical senses.[2.1] Witnesses may also testify about inferences and opinions that are based on personal observations and experience.[3]

Rule 602. Lack of Personal Knowledge.

A witness may not testify to a matter unless evidence is introduced sufficient to support a finding that the witness has personal knowledge of the matter. Evidence to prove personal knowledge may, but need not, consist of the witness' own testimony. This rule is subject to the provisions of rule 703, relating to opinion testimony by expert witnesses.

Rule 602 permits evidence of the requisite personal knowledge to be provided either through the testimony of the witness or through extrinsic testimony.[4] Expert witnesses are expressly exempted from the personal knowledge requirement of the rule.[5]

Rule 602 is subject to the hearsay rule.[6] A witness testifying to what he or she heard may do so unless what the witness heard is excluded under the hearsay rules of Article VIII.[7] The testimony may even contain hearsay within hearsay.[8] There is no inconsistency between Rule 602 and the hearsay rules since the "matter" the witness is testifying to is what was heard rather than the event described by the hearsay declarant.[8.1] "But a witness cannot offer the contents of a hearsay statement

---

discrimination; plaintiff's failure to cite statements by official that would have supported her belief made her evidence insufficient to withstand motion for summary judgment).

[2.1] *See, e.g.,* United States v. Santana, 342 F.3d 60, 68–69 (1st Cir. 2003) (trial court properly permitted lay witness to testify that contents of package were marijuana when he smelled it and was familiar with smell of marijuana through his work).

[3] *See, e.g.,* Sheek v. Asia Badger, Inc., 235 F.3d 687, 695 (1st Cir. 2000) (witness's conclusion that defendant performed design work and took steps to rectify design defect was based on his participation in construction project; it was inference based on personal observations and admissible under Rule 602).

[4] *See, e.g.,* Diamond Offshore Co. v. A & B Builders, Inc., 302 F.3d 531, 544 n.13 (5th Cir. 2002) (recitations in affidavit that witness had access to pertinent corporate documents relating to matters covered in testimony and that matters covered in testimony were based on his personal knowledge were sufficient to establish personal knowledge requirement of Rule 602).

[5] Fed. R. Evid 602; *see* Fed. R. Evid. 703; *see* § 13.03.

[6] *See, e.g.,* Combs v. Wilkinson, 315 F.3d 548, 555–556 (6th Cir. 2002) (investigative reports are admissible under exception to hearsay rule because they provide information concerning statements made to investigators by persons with personal knowledge of events they witnessed).

[7] *See, e.g.,* Elizarraras v. Bank of El Paso, 631 F.2d 366 (5th Cir. 1980) (reversible error to admit plaintiff's testimony when he had no personal knowledge and hearsay rule barred his relating what he had been told).

[8] *See* Rule 805, which is discussed in Chapter 14.

[8.1] *See, e.g.,* Norita v. Northern Mariana Islands, 331 F.3d 690, 697–698 (9th Cir. 2003) (summary judgment affidavits were insufficient to raise genuine issue of material fact without stating

as *his* personal knowledge."[9]

The personal knowledge requirement is also satisfied when non-expert witnesses summarize evidence previously admitted at trial. One court has admitted such testimony pursuant to a broad interpretation of Rule 1006, the rule providing for the admission into evidence of summaries of data which are too voluminous to be conveniently examined in court.[10] Admission may also be based on the well-established tradition of admitting summaries of evidence previously put before the jury. The admission of summary testimony is akin to the admission of pedagogical devices which are not evidence, but only the proponent's organization of the evidence admitted.[11] Courts admitting summary testimony should take care that no inadmissible hearsay is admitted along with the summarizing testimony.

Rule 602 has a two-fold significance: (1) it empowers judges to reject inherently incredible testimonial evidence; and (2) its personal knowledge requirement is incorporated into Rule 701, the opinion rule governing testimony by lay witnesses.[12] Under Rule 602, the judge has the power to reject the evidence if it could not reasonably be believed—*i.e.,* if as a matter of law no trier of fact could find that the witness actually perceived the matter testified to.[13]

The judge must admit the testimony even though the witness is not positive about what was perceived, provided the witness had an opportunity to observe and obtained some impressions from those observations.[14] In addition, the judge should admit the testimony if the jury could find that the witness perceived the event being testified to, since credibility is a matter for the jury.[15]

---

how affiants gained information they recited, because trial court could not determine whether they were made on personal knowledge or whether information they contained was subject to hearsay objection).

[9] Kaczmarek v. Allied Chem. Corp., 836 F.2d 1055, 1060-61 (7th Cir. 1987).

[10] United States v. Lemire, 720 F.2d 1327, 1347 (D.C. Cir. 1983).

[11] *See* Rule 1006, which is discussed in Chapter 9.

[12] *See, e.g.,* United States v. Garcia, 291 F.3d 127, 141 (2d Cir. 2002) (rational basis requirement of Rule 701 is same as personal knowledge requirement of Rule 602).

[13] United States v. Garcia, 291 F.3d 127, 141 (2d Cir. 2002) (proponent of evidence must lay foundation showing its admissibility, including witness's personal knowledge).

[14] Ward v. First Fed. Sav. Bank, 173 F.3d 611, 617–618 (7th Cir. 1999) (summary judgment affidavit stating that employee was "aware" of bank president's discriminatory acts did not specify source of awareness, and thus failed to establish his personal knowledge; it was properly disregarded by trial court); United States v. Sinclair, 109 F.3d 1527, 1536 (10th Cir. 1997) (evidence is inadmissible only if trial court finds, in proper exercise of its discretion, that witness could not have actually perceived or observed subject of testimony; citing **Treatise**).

[15] *See, e.g.,* United States v. Lake, 150 F.3d 269, 273 (3d Cir. 1998) (police officer who was lifelong resident of island had sufficient basis to testify about whether any motor vehicle manufacturing facilities were located there); United States v. Owens-El, 889 F.2d 913, 915–916 (9th Cir. 1989) (the trial court properly determined that the evidence was sufficient to support a finding

The requirement of personal knowledge may arise in two ways in conjunction with the lay opinion rule. The witness is required, first, to have made observations supporting the opinion and second, to have reported the observations by giving as much of the raw data as is practicable. In instances when a lay witness may appropriately render an opinion, the personal knowledge question is limited to whether the witness had the opportunity to observe the facts on which the opinion is based. Courts applying the personal knowledge requirement should require the witness to state the underlying observations, if they can be stated without difficulty. But when the witness encounters difficulty in disentangling the individual elements of the observation from the impression as a whole, the courts should not insist on the impossible chore of delineating the boundary line between personal knowledge and opinion.[16]

§ 10.04   Oath or Affirmation—Rule 603[1]

Rule 603 provides that prospective witnesses may not testify until they have declared that they will testify truthfully.[2]

Rule 603.   Oath or Affirmation.

Before testifying, every witness shall be required to declare that the witness will testify truthfully, by oath or affirmation administered in a form calculated to awaken the witness' conscience and impress the witness' mind with the duty to do so.

Because the purpose of the oath is to impress upon the witness the solemnity of the occasion, no reference to religious belief is required. Rule 603 does not operate as a rule of competency authorizing a judge to reject testimony on the grounds that the witness is incapable of telling the truth. However, such testimony should be excluded on the ground that it has no probative value.

Rule 603 requires that the oath or affirmation "be administered in a form

---

by a reasonable juror that the victim had personally perceived defendant to be his attacker; quoting **Treatise**).

[16] *See, e.g.,* United States v. Santana, 342 F.3d 60, 68–69 (1st Cir. 2003) (when witness's job exposed him to marijuana, he could testify from his personal knowledge that he smelled marijuana when he searched defendant's home).

[1] *See* **Treatise** at §§ 603.02–603.05.

[2] Fed. R. Evid. 603; *see* United States v. Ward, 973 F.2d 730, 731–734 (9th Cir. 1992) (the trial court committed reversible error in refusing to permit defendant to take an alternate oath; there is no fixed form of the oath); Ferguson v. Commissioner, 921 F.2d 588, 590–591 (5th Cir. 1991) (Tax Court judge abused his discretion in excluding the taxpayer's testimony and rejecting her alternative declaration to testify truthfully); United States v. Fowler, 605 F.2d 181, 185 (5th Cir. 1979) (court properly refused to allow defendant to testify after he refused either to swear or affirm to tell the truth).

calculated to awaken the witness's conscience and impress the witness' mind with the duty" to testify truthfully. The clerk who administers the oath should take the task seriously. While the oath is taken, the judge should put aside all other work and face the witness in a way that makes it clear the court expects the witness to tell the truth.

The judge may question the witness to determine whether he or she wishes to take the oath or affirmation and to ensure that the witness is impressed with the duty to testify truthfully. The judge must be careful to conduct this questioning outside the hearing of the jury when a possibility exists that some of the prospective witness' answers with respect to a belief in God or objections to an oath might lead to prejudice in the eyes of the jury.[3]

§ 10.05   Writing Used to Refresh Memory—Rule 612

[1]—Doctrine of Refreshed Memory; Scope and Rationale of Rule 612[1]

Rule 612 covers only a small portion of the law relating to the refreshing of recollections. A brief survey of some of the features of reviving memory is useful in understanding the rationale of the Rule and its scope even though these aspects will continue to be governed by case law.

Described below are the problems that generally arise from refreshment by the proponent of the witness, which is to be distinguished from the hostile kinds of "refreshment" by an opponent. Hostile "refreshment" is actually impeachment with an implied inconsistency—*e.g.,* "Now that you have examined the document and refreshed your recollection, is it not true that you were mistaken when you said. . ."

1. No means of arousing recollection may be used until the witness has satisfied the trial judge that he or she lacks effective present recollection.[2] Of course in a properly prepared case, counsel will have interviewed the witness prior to calling him or her to the stand. Sound preparation requires counsel to try to obtain as spontaneous a statement as possible from the witness in the course of preparing

---

[3] United States v. Rabb, 394 F.2d 230, 231 (3d Cir. 1968) ("Where the defendant is a follower of a minority religion which is unpopular with many persons in the community, it is better practice to permit him to affirm and have any questions on the subject of his religion asked out of the presence of the jury"); *see, e.g.,* United States v. Zizzo, 120 F.3d 1338, 1347–1348 (7th Cir. 1997) (single remark on cross-examination of 80-year old government witness that oath to testify truthfully meant nothing to him did not render him an unsworn witness, requiring exclusion of his entire three days' worth of testimony).

[1] *See* **Treatise** at § 612.02.

[2] *See, e.g.,* United States v. Balthazard, 360 F.3d 309, 318 (1st Cir. 2004) ("It is hornbook law that a party may not use a document to refresh a witness's recollection unless the witness exhibits a failure of memory"; citing **Treatise**).

for trial so that counsel can ascertain the facts as they are, rather than as the client would like them to be. But during the course of discussion it normally will be necessary, whether or not there is loss of memory, to ask the prospective witness leading questions and to show him or her documents or other objects. Consequently, it may often be impossible for the witness, let alone the judge, to differentiate between actual recollections independent of any memory juggling and recollections which owe their existence to pre-trial discussions with counsel and others. Although the trial judge "should in the first instance satisfy himself as to whether the witness testifies upon a record or upon his own recollection,"[3] the cases indicate that judges are likely to honor claims of loss of memory without extensive examination when considerable time has elapsed between the event and trial, or numerous details are involved,[4] or the witness is of a class that frequently testifies in like situations.[5]

2. Anything may be used to revive a memory—"a song, a scent, a photograph, and allusion, even a past statement known to be false."[6] Thus, a "writing" in Rule 612 includes sound recordings and pictures of all kinds.[7] It does not matter whether a statement was written by the witness, was made contemporaneously with the event itself, is a copy rather than an original, or was obtained in violation of a constitutional or procedural rule. Indeed, even inadmissible evidence may be used to refresh a witness's recollection.[7.1]

3. The witness's recollection must be revived after consulting the particular writing or object offered as a stimulus so that the testimony relates to a present recollection. If the witness's recollection is not revived, a memorandum may be read into evidence and admitted if it meets the test of recorded recollection set forth in Rule 803(5).[8] Obviously, however, particularly in light of pre- trial preparation, "the categories, present recollection revived and past recollection recorded are

---

[3] United States v. Riccardi, 174 F.2d 883, 889 (3d Cir. 1949).

[4] Bankers Trust Co. v. Publicker Indus., 641 F.2d 1361, 1363 (2d Cir. 1981) ("There is no required, ritualistic formula for finding exhaustion of memory"; no error in trial court's having permitted witness to use prepared chronology while testifying when events had occurred two years ago and there was no impermissible suggestiveness; comparison of chronology with testimony clearly demonstrated that witness was not reading a script).

[5] *See, e.g.,* Goings v. United States, 377 F.2d 753, 761, n.11 (8th Cir. 1967) ("Generally, doctors, engineers, accountants and other lay witnesses testifying should be allowed continuously to refer to data on their reports, etc.").

[6] United States v. Rappy, 157 F.2d 964, 967 (2d Cir. 1947); *see also* United States v. Muhammad, 120 F.3d 688, 699 (7th Cir. 1997) (Rule 612 permitted government witness to refresh her memory with summary of interview with defendant prepared by other agent who interviewed defendant with her).

[7] *Compare* Rule 1001, which is discussed in Chapter 9.

[7.1] *See, e.g.,* Fraser, v. Goodale, 342 F.3d 1032, 1037 (9th Cir. 2003).

[8] *See* discussion in Chapter 16.

clearest in their extremes but they are, in practice, converging rather than parallel lines; the difference is frequently one of degree."[9]

Two safeguards have been adopted by the courts to temper the possibility of the witness putting before the court inaccurate, though perhaps unconscious, inventions that purport to be present recollection. The first, which remains a matter of case law, is that the trial court has considerable discretion at various points to reject the testimony. As already noted, it can hold that the witness is not lacking in memory, or that the writing did not refresh the witness's memory, or the court can find as in the case of leading questions[10] that the danger of unfair suggestion outweighs any value the writings may have for refreshing the witness's recollection.[11]

The second safeguard is the subject of Rule 612. It assures the adverse party a right to inspect the writing used for refreshing recollection, to use the writing as a basis for cross- examination, and to introduce into evidence those portions of the writing that relate to the testimony of the witness.[12] The rule provides:

Rule 612.   Writing Used To Refresh Memory.

Except as otherwise provided in criminal proceedings by section 3500 of title 18, United States Code, if a witness uses a writing to refresh memory for the purpose of testifying, either—

(1) while testifying, or

(2) before testifying, if the court in its discretion determines it is necessary in the interests of justice, an adverse party is entitled to have the writing produced at the hearing, to inspect it, to cross-examine the witness thereon, and to introduce in evidence those portions which relate to the testimony of the witness. If it is claimed that the writing contains matters not related to the subject matter of the testimony the court shall examine the writing in camera, excise any portions not so related, and order delivery of the remainder to the party entitled thereto. Any portion withheld over objections shall be preserved and made available to the appellate court in

---

[9]   United States v. Riccardi, 174 F.2d 883, 889 (3d Cir. 1949).

[10]   *See* Rule 611(c), which is discussed in Chapter 2.

[11]   *See, e.g.,* Parliament Ins. Co. v. Hanson, 676 F.2d 1069, 1073 (5th Cir. 1982) (trial court did not abuse discretion in refusing to allow witness to testify on the basis of notes made in anticipation of litigation which were summaries of logs written substantially earlier and which were made while witness was working for or preparing to work for competitor of defendant).

[12]   Fed. R. Evid. 612; *see, e.g.,* Alexander v. FBI, 198 F.R.D. 306, 319–320 (D.D.C. 2000) (when it is impossible for court to acquire critical evidence without permitting witness to refresh his or her recollection by reviewing documents covered by attorney-client privilege, Rule 612(2) gives court option, in the interest of justice, to deny adverse party access to document).

> the event of an appeal. If a writing is not produced or delivered pursuant to order under this rule, the court shall make any order justice requires, except that in criminal cases when the prosecution elects not to comply, the order shall be one striking the testimony or, if the court in its discretion determines that the interests of justice so require, declaring a mistrial.

By giving the adverse party the right to refer to the writing on cross-examination and to introduce into evidence those portions that relate to the testimony of the witness,[13] Rule 612 seeks to enhance the ability of the trier of fact to assess the credibility of the witness. When the adverse party exercises these options, the writing that had been used for refreshment becomes in effect a prior inconsistent statement. Consequently, it cannot be used substantively unless it satisfies the requirements of Rule 801(d)(1)(A), and the jury should be instructed, if a request for such an instruction is made, to consider it only as to the credibility of the refreshed witness, and not as evidence-in-chief.

Rule 612 further recognizes that in order to explore the witness's credibility the jury may need to know what materials were used to refresh his or her recollection before the witness took the stand. Away from the courtroom, the dangers attendant on refreshing recollection are even more pronounced: there is no bar on leading questions, no predetermined order in which questions must be asked, and no limitations on the kind of materials that a prospective witness may be shown. If the court in its discretion determines that it is necessary in the interests of justice for the jury to understand how the witness achieved his or her present testimonial knowledge, the cross-examiner will be accorded the right to have the writings that were used for pre-trial refreshment produced, inspected and introduced.[14] The extent to which work product and privilege claims limit the production of materials consulted by a witness in preparing for a deposition is discussed below (*see* [3], *below*).

If the writing is not produced or not delivered after the court so orders, the court has considerable discretion in ordering appropriate sanctions. In criminal cases, Rule 612 provides that when the prosecution fails to comply, the court must either

---

[13] While only the related portions have to be turned over pursuant to Rule 612, this may, at times, lead to the admissibility of other portions of the writing when demanded by the proponent of the witness, either on a theory of rehabilitation by prior consistent statements, or pursuant to the doctrine of completeness embodied in Rule 106. *See* United States v. Rubin, 609 F.2d 51, 63 (2d Cir. 1979), *aff'd on other grounds,* 449 U.S. 424 (1981) (notes used to refresh prosecution witness could be introduced pursuant to Rule 106, because selective cross- examination by defense counsel, which focused on inconsistencies, may have left a confusing or misleading impression on jury). *Compare,* United States v. Sheffield, 55 F.3d 341, 342–343 (8th Cir. 1995) (no obligation to turn over police investigative file where officer testified that he reviewed file before testifying but did not need it to refresh his recollection). *See* discussion of Rule 106 in Chapter 2.

[14] *See* discussion in **Treatise** at § 612.04.

order a mistrial or order that the witness's testimony be struck. Obviously, however, there can be no production if the writing has been destroyed. In Jencks Act cases,[15] non-production in the case of destroyed writings has been excused without imposing sanctions when notes were destroyed after having been incorporated into statements that were produced.[16] The Rule 612 situation is somewhat different since it is not the content or form of the writing that determines production but the fact that it was shown to the witness. However, the Supreme Court has stated that a failure to produce pursuant to the Jencks Act does not always reach constitutional proportions, even when the non-produced notes are not available in some other form (*see* [2], *below*).

It would seem, therefore, that when the prosecution fails to comply with Rule 612, an appellate court may nevertheless find that a trial judge's failure to strike testimony or order a mistrial does not amount to reversible error in the context of the particular case. Except, however, in cases of inability to comply when the trial judge feels that the defendant's rights will not be prejudiced, the trial judge should order production without considering whether this failure to so order might ultimately be considered harmless error. Non-production will not be considered harmless if the defendant was prejudiced by the failure to produce, as, for example, when it is shown that the writing would almost certainly have served to impeach a crucial witness and no other impeaching evidence was available.

In other cases, Rule 612 does not limit the sanctions that are available. The Committee's Notes suggest that contempt, dismissal, and finding issues against the offender are some of the techniques that might be employed. A mild sanction that may be useful is for the court to explain to the jury why the refreshment evidence is required to be revealed under the Federal Rules and then to give a strong charge on spoliation and the adverse inferences that may be drawn from such spoliation in assessing the witness's credibility.

[2]—Applying Rule 612 in Criminal Cases—the Jencks Act and Criminal Procedure Rule 26.2[17]

The text of Rule 612 starts with a specific proviso: "Except as otherwise provided in criminal proceedings by section 3500 of title 18, United States Code." The statutory reference is to the so-called Jencks Act, which at the time Rule 612 became effective provided that after a government witness testifies in court, the

---

[15] *See* [2], *below*.

[16] *See generally* United States v. Ramirez, 174 F.3d 584, 588–589 (5th Cir. 1999) (Jencks Act sanctions should be imposed when evidence was lost or destroyed if there was bad faith or negligent suppression of evidence, but not for good faith loss by government).

[17] *See* **Treatise** at § 612.08; *see also* 25 Moore's Federal Practice, Ch. 626.2, *Production of Statements of Witnesses* (Matthew Bender 3d ed. 1997).

defense is entitled to demand delivery "of any statement of the witness" in the possession of the United States[18] which "relates to the subject matter concerning which the witness has testified." The provision in Rule 612 therefore meant that Rule 612 could not be used to compel the production and inspection of writings that would be outside the scope of the Jencks Act. Even if a witness in a criminal trial had refreshed his or her recollection before testifying, the writings used would not be made available to the cross-examiner unless they independently qualified as Jencks Act material.

Rule 26.2 was added to the Federal Rules of Criminal Procedure on December 1, 1980. Criminal Rule 26.2 essentially restates what is now 18 U.S.C. § 3500; it mandates the production of statements made by a defense witness as well as statements made by prosecution witnesses. However, Rule 612 was not amended to add a reference to Criminal Rule 26.2 or to substitute it for the reference to 18 U.S.C. § 3500, the Jencks Act. Nor has § 3500 expressly been repealed, even though it arguably has been partly superseded by Rule 26.2; rule recodifications intended to cover an entire subject should be deemed to supersede conflicting provisions on the same subject.[19]

In light of these events, what is the current status of the provision in Rule 612? Because Rule 612 expressly refers to the Jencks Act, the reference to the Jencks Act in Rule 612 should probably be construed to reach the analogous provisions that now appear in the criminal procedure rules. "Leaving rule 612 unamended efficiently serves to accomplish what was probably intended—rule 612 remains limited by the Jencks Act, which is now modified by rule 26.2, with the result that rule 612 is now subject to rule 26.2."[20]

[3]—Work Product and Privilege Issues[21]

[a]—When Use of Materials Constitutes Waiver

Although Rule 612 does not spell out the reasons why a party may refuse to produce or deliver a writing pursuant to order, the rule must be interpreted in light of Rule 501, which acknowledges the existence of privileges governed by the

---

[18] United States v. Ramirez, 174 F.3d 584, 588–589 (5th Cir. 1999) (statements "in the possession of the United States" are not limited to those that are in the hands of, or known to, the U.S. Attorney's office, or even the Justice Department"; tape recordings made by prison authorities who were part of investigative team satisfy the provision).

[19] Rule 26.2 was left unchanged by Congress, which did modify another aspect of the Rules promulgated by the Supreme Court, Pub. L. No. 96–42, 93 Stat. 326. See 18 U.S.C. § 3771 ("All laws in conflict with such rules shall be of no further force").

[20] Forster, *The Jencks Act—Rule 26.2—Rule 612 Interface—"Confusion Worse Confounded,"* 34 Okla. L. Rev. 679, 725 (1981).

[21] *See* **Treatise** at §§ 612.05, 612.06.

Constitution, Acts of Congress and the rules prescribed by the Supreme Court, as well as those rooted in the principles of the common law.[22]

The most troublesome issue for the courts in both civil and criminal cases has been to decide whether use of materials to refresh a witness's recollection prior to testifying at a deposition results in waiver of the attorney-client privilege[23] or a work product claim.

[b]—Attorney-Client Privilege

Imputing waiver whenever a witness uses a privileged document to refresh his or her recollection is theoretically unsound. Since a witness may refresh recollection with statements other than the witness's own, holding that the attorney as agent for the client has waived the client's privilege by using the statements dilutes the client's rights. Furthermore, difficult problems can arise in the corporate context when the holder of the privilege is the corporation itself but the makers of the statements are employees of the corporation. If employee A's communication to counsel would be privileged, and so would the statements of employee B, it is difficult to see why the corporation should be found to have waived its privilege if the attorney in the course of providing legal services to the corporation reveals B's statement to A. The adversary of the corporation is, of course, free to take the depositions of A and B; the desire for a short-cut is not enough: "considerations of convenience do not overcome the policies served by the attorney-client privilege."[24]

Nevertheless, courts have uniformly held that using a privileged document to refresh recollection while the witness is on the stand is a waiver of privilege.[25] Thus, the court can avoid some problems by refusing to allow material subject to a claim of attorney-client privilege to be used for refreshing a witness's recollection at trial. This solution however, cannot be applied at a deposition, or when the witness consults the privileged material prior to testifying at a trial or deposition. Consulting material before trial may have less impact on its privileged status, since

---

[22] *See Treatise* at Ch. 501, *General Rule.*

[23] Privilege issues can also arise with regard to governmental privileges. Since governmental privileges are not viewed as absolute, except for the state secret privilege, the court in the usual non-state secret case can use a balancing test to decide whether the need for the material in order to assess the accuracy of the witness' testimony outweighs the need to protect the governmental information. *See* **Treatise** at § 612.06[2]; *see also* Ch. 509, Secrets of State and Other Official Information (Sup. Ct. Standard 509).

[24] Upjohn Co. v. United States, 449 U.S. 383, 392, 101 S. Ct. 677, 66 L. Ed. 2d 584 (1981).

[25] *See, e.g.,* Sperling v. City of Kennesaw Police Dep't, 202 F.R.D. 325, 328 (N.D. Ga. 2001) (plaintiff's use during deposition of document she prepared for lawyer to use in answering interrogatories was inconsistent with confidential nature of communication and waived attorney-client privilege, so document had to be produced to opponent under Rule 612).

the court has power under Rule 612 to order disclosure of materials consulted before testifying only "if the court in its discretion determines it is necessary in the interests of justice."[26] Additionally, most courts find that waiver has occurred when the witness has consulted a writing embodying the witness's own communication to counsel, and his or her testimony at the deposition, or at trial, discloses a significant part of the communication.[27] Waiver of protection, however, is limited to those portions of the documents actually consulted.[28]

[c]—Work Product Claim

The work product claim[29] is probably the one most commonly asserted to resist a request for the production of materials used in refreshing a witness's recollection. Work product is divided into two categories: (1) what may be referred to as core product embodies the attorney's mental impressions and is entitled to special protection—the Supreme Court has not yet decided whether it is ever subject to disclosure, (2) peripheral product, on the other hand, loses its protection upon a showing of need and inability to obtain the equivalent without undue hardship.[30]

Prior to the enactment of Rule 612, the federal cases do not seem to have considered whether a work product limitation must be applied. Of course, the kind of writing used for refreshment at trial—the only instance in which production was required—probably most often fell within the category of materials not embodying the attorney's thought processes, and would therefore in any case have been exempt from the operation of the doctrine. Resort to notes embodying an attorney's theories and mental impressions, for refreshment, could be barred at the trial on analogy to the prohibition against leading, without reaching the question of whether production of the notes would be barred by a work product rule.

---

[26] Fed. R. Evid. 612(2); *compare* Alexander v. Federal Bureau of Invest., 198 F.R.D. 306, 316–320 (D.D.C. 2000) (interests of justice served by permitting witnesses to review documents protected by employer's attorney-client privilege to refresh their recollections without waiving privilege) *with* Leybold-Heraeus Tech. v. Midwest Instrument Co., 118 F.R.D. 609, 614–615 (E.D. Wis. 1987) (Rule 612 does not allow witness to review before trial documents protected by attorney-client privilege without allowing defendant to inspect documents). *See* discussion of attorney-client privileges, Chapter 18.

[27] *See, e.g.,* Sperling v. City of Kennesaw Police Dep't, 202 F.R.D. 325, 328 (N.D. Ga. 2001) (plaintiff's use during deposition of document she prepared for lawyer to use in answering interrogatories was inconsistent with confidential nature of communication and waived attorney-client privilege, so document had to be produced to opponent under Rule 612). *See* discussion of Standard 511 in Chapter 18.

[28] United States v. Darden, 70 F.3d 1507, 1540 (8th Cir. 1995) ("Access is limited to those writings that arguably have an impact upon the testimony of the witness").

[29] *See* **Treatise** at § 612.05 for analysis of the Supreme Court's decisions regarding work product in Hickman v. Taylor, 329 U.S. 495, 67 S. Ct. 385, 91 L. Ed. 451 (1947) *and* United States v. Nobles, 422 U.S. 225, 95 S. Ct. 2160, 45 L. Ed.2d 141 (1975).

[30] *See* Upjohn Co. v. United States, 449 U.S. 383, 401, 101 S. Ct. 677, 66 L. Ed. 2d 584 (1981).

[d]—Core Work Product

The enactment of Rule 612 posed the question of whether waiver results when an attorney refreshes a witness's recollection with core work product materials, *i.e.,* those that embody the thought processes of the attorney. Waiver would mean that the opponent would then be entitled to production, inspection and use of the materials pursuant to Rule 612.

Certainly, bringing the refreshment process into the open at trial would better enable the trier of fact to assess the credibility of the witness. On the other hand, as the Supreme Court noted in *Hickman v. Taylor,* if none of an attorney's file is privileged, "much of what is now put down in writing would remain unwritten."[31] There may also be some advantages of an adversary system which would be lost if one's hand must always be shown to the opposing side.

In its opinions since *Hickman v. Taylor,* the Supreme Court has never permitted intrusion into work-product revealing the attorney's thought processes. Until there is further clarification by the Court, a party can argue either waiver or need in seeking production at trial of material used to refresh a witness which the proponent claims reflects the attorney's thought processes. If the Supreme Court decides that this sort of material is absolutely privileged, then the only possible avenue for production will be waiver, although this theory may be more tenable for material used for refreshment at trial than for material used in preparation for trial.[32]

Until such time as the Supreme Court decides these issues, the following approach is suggested. If the adverse party demands material that the party producing the witness claims reflects solely the attorney's thought processes, the judge should examine the material in camera. Unless the judge finds that the adverse party would be seriously hampered in testing the accuracy of the witness' testimony, the judge should not order production of any writings that reflect solely the attorney's mental processes. If the adverse party would be seriously hampered, the court should apply Rule 612 on the theory that the lawyer who showed the witness his or her work product is estopped. In arriving at this decision, the judge must weigh the significance of the testimony, the availability of other evidence impeaching the testimony, and the degree to which the witness apparently relied upon the writing.

---

[31] Hickman v. Taylor, 329 U.S. 495, 511, 67 S. Ct. 385, 91 L. Ed 451 (1947).

[32] *See* United States v. Nobles, 422 U.S. 225, 240 n.14, 95 S. Ct. 2160, 45 L. Ed. 2d 141 (1975) ("What constitutes a waiver with respect to work-product materials depends, of course, upon the circumstances. Counsel necessarily makes use throughout trial of the notes, documents, and other internal materials prepared to present adequately his client's case, and often relies on them in examining witnesses. When so used, there normally is no waiver. But where, as here, counsel attempts to make a testimonial use of these materials the normal rules of evidence come into play with respect to cross-examination and production of documents.").

Just as in applying Rule 403, the judge will have to be governed in deciding by the facts of the particular case.[33]

[e]—Depositions

It has been suggested that work-product protection should cease when a witness consults work-product material prior to testifying at a deposition "either on a theory of waiver or qualified privilege, where an attempt is made to exceed decent limits of preparation on the one hand and concealment on the other."[34] Although some courts have established a balancing test to weigh the need for disclosure against the protections afforded by the work product doctrine,[35] other courts require automatic disclosure of any materials consulted in preparation for a deposition. However, a rule of automatic disclosure[36] does not comport with the policies underlying work product protection. It ignores the special protection that may have to be accorded the attorney's thought processes. In addition, the rationale for requiring production of peripheral work-product materials used for refreshment is considerably less compelling in the context of the discovery stage. At this point, the material is not needed for the trier of fact to assess the credibility of the witness, and complete disclosure undermines the anti-indolence rationale of the work-product rule. Perhaps most important, automatic disclosure whenever a witness prepares for a deposition by referring to pertinent materials may lead to the very

---

[33] *See* discussion of Rule 403 in Chapter 6.

[34] Berkey Photo, Inc. v. Eastman Kodak Co., 74 F.R.D. 613, 617 (S.D.N.Y. 1977) (experts in antitrust litigation had consulted notebooks consisting of counsel's synthesis of facts and factual issues as background; court did not order disclosure since "counsel were not vividly aware of the potential for a stark choice between withholding the notebooks from the experts or turning them over to opposing counsel," but court said it was now giving fair warning for the future).

[35] *See* Nutramax Lab., Inc. v. Twin Lab., Inc., 183 F.R.D. 458, 468–470 (D. Md. 1998) (court should consider state of witness, state of dispute, when events took place, when documents were reviewed, number of documents reviewed, whether witness prepared reviewed documents, amount of pure work product involved, occurrence of previous disclosure, and concerns about the manipulation, concealment, or destruction of evidence).

[36] Audiotext Communications Network v. US Telecom, 164 F.R.D. 250, 253 (D. Kan. 1996) (as a general rule, when a document is used to refresh recollection, any privilege protecting that document must give way); Boring v. Keller, 97 F.R.D. 404 (D. Colo. 1983) (attorney's opinion work product not protected from disclosure when used by expert to formulate his opinion; court holds no privilege exists for attorney's summary of his impressions of plaintiff's demeanor and appearance as witness or of plaintiff's substantive deposition testimony when summary was given to defendant's experts to aid them in preparing this testimony); James Julian, Inc. v. Raytheon Co., 93 F.R.D. 138, 146 (D. Del. 1982) (court relies on *Berkey,* 74 F.R.D. 613, in ordering that binder containing documents selected and arranged by counsel for use in preparing witnesses for deposition must be disclosed since without binders opposing counsel "cannot know or inquire into the extent to which the witness' testimony has been shaded by counsel's presentation of the factual background"; each case must be decided on own facts and court stated that in a given case fact that documents sought contained attorney's mental impressions might cause court to strike balance against disclosure).

practices that troubled the *Hickman* court: "Inefficiency, unfairness and sharp practices, would inevitably develop in the giving of legal advice in the preparation of cases for trial"[37] or the attorney will coach the witness with the materials rather than allowing the witness to peruse them, or the attorney will fail to prepare the witness adequately. None of these alternatives seems compatible with the rationale of the work product rule. Given the liberality of disclosure and the work product exception in the discovery rules, the opponent should be required to make a substantial showing of need in order to obtain materials that a witness reviewed before a deposition instead of achieving wholesale disclosure.[38]

In the present state of uncertainty, attorneys should not refresh prospective deponents or witnesses with material containing counsel's theories or thought processes. Not only may such documents ultimately fall into opposing counsel's hands if Rule 612 is satisfied, but there are too many risks of unethical suggestions to witnesses when they see such material.

§ 10.06   Exclusion of Witnesses—Rule 615

[1]—Purpose and Text of Rule[1]

Rule 615 requires the exclusion of witnesses from the courtroom on demand by a litigant.[1.1] The court must grant a litigant's request,[1.2] but should permit the continued attendance of a witness who is (1) a party, (2) a designated representative of a corporate or organizational party, (3) a person whose presence is essential to presentation of a party's case, or (4) a person authorized by statute to be present.

---

[37] Hickman v. Taylor, 329 U.S. 495, 511, 67 S. Ct. 385, 91 L. Ed. 451 (1947).

[38] Bogosian v. Gulf Oil Corp., 738 F.2d 587, 592–596 (3d Cir. 1984) (in anti-trust action, the court held that provisions of the Federal Rules of Civil Procedure which permit discovery of facts known or opinions held by an expert witness do not permit discovery of documents prepared by attorneys containing solely their mental impressions and thought processes relating to the legal theories of the case even though the expert may rely on the documents to some extent in formulating his own opinions; such documents represent core work product and are entitled to heightened protection; additionally, showing the material to the witnesses did not constitute a waiver of the protection for attorney work product); Al-Rowaishan Establishment v. Beatrice Foods Co., 92 F.R.D. 779, 780–781 (S.D.N.Y. 1982) (court used in camera procedure and concluded that it was difficult to see how defendant would be "hampered in testing the accuracy" of deponent's testimony by not being permitted to read digest prepared by plaintiff's attorney, and in any event found that the value to defendant was outweighed by the principles precluding disclosure of work product revealing the attorney's thought processes).

[1] *See* **Treatise** at §§ 615.02–615.03.

[1.1] *See, e.g.,* United States v. Collins, 340 F.3d 672, 680 (8th Cir. 2003) (sequestration of most witnesses is mandatory when party so requests).

[1.2] *See, e.g.,* United States v. Collins, 340 F.3d 672, 680 (8th Cir. 2003) ("sequestration of most witnesses is mandatory when requested").

The rule provides as follows:

Rule 615. Exclusion of Witnesses.

At the request of a party the court shall order witnesses excluded so that they cannot hear the testimony of other witnesses, and it may make the order of its own motion. This rule does not authorize exclusion of (1) a party who is a natural person, or (2) an officer or employee of a party which is not a natural person designated as its representative by its attorney, or (3) a person whose presence is shown by a party to be essential to the presentation of the party's cause, or (4) a person authorized by statute to be present.

The practice of excluding, separating, or sequestering witnesses is at least as old as the Bible. Almost from the beginning of recorded trials, courts have kept witnesses from hearing each other's stories so that inconsistencies in their testimony will be revealed. Sequestration also seeks to prevent witnesses from unconsciously shaping their testimony to conform to that given by other witnesses. A rule such as Rule 615 therefore has a two-fold purpose: to prevent fabrication and to uncover fabrication that has already taken place.[1.3]

An order simply requiring the exclusion of witnesses under Rule 615 does not, in and of itself, prevent counsel for one of the parties from conferring with sequestered witnesses during the trial, even during breaks in the proceedings that interrupt a sequestered witness's testimony.[2]

[2]—Witnesses Exempt fom Exclusion[3]

[a]—A Party

A party who is a natural person may not be excluded from the courtroom. This provision, which operates automatically, is designed to eliminate problems of confrontation and due process that would otherwise arise.[4]

[1.3] *See, e.g.,* United States v. Collins, 340 F.3d 672, 681 (8th Cir. 2003) (Rule 615 prevents "witnesses from tailoring their testimony to that of prior witnesses and [aids] in detection of dishonesty").

[2] *See, e.g.,* United States v. Calderin-Rodriguez, 244 F.3d 977, 984–985 (8th Cir. 2001).

[3] *See* **Treatise** at § 615.04.

[4] *Cf.* Geders v. United States, 425 U.S. 80, 87–88, 96 S. Ct. 1330, 47 L. Ed. 2d 592 (1976) (order preventing criminal defendant from consulting his counsel about anything during an overnight recess between his direct and cross- examination impinged upon his right to assistance of counsel guaranteed by the Sixth Amendment; court noted that trial judge has "broad power to sequester witnesses before, during and after their testimony . . . [b]ut the petitioner was not simply a witness; he was also the defendant"); *see also* Potashnick v. Port City Constr. Co., 609 F.2d 1101, 1119 (5th Cir. 1980) (in civil case, ruling that barred conversation between counsel and witness after witness's testimony commenced deprived defendant of its constitutional rights to effective

[b]—Designated Representative

Rule 615 prohibits exclusion of "an officer or employee of a party which is not a natural person designated as its representative by its attorney." Frequently this provision is relied upon by the government as the basis for having its case agent remain in the courtroom.[5] Similarly, a corporate party may designate an officer or employee as its representative to assist counsel during the trial.[5.1] Exemption from sequestration should be automatic if the government or other party makes a request for designation at the time the defendant or other opponent moves for an order of exclusion pursuant to Rule 615.

Since the rule is phrased in the singular, some courts have disapproved the practice of allowing more than one case agent to remain in the courtroom during a criminal prosecution.[6] However, the court should have discretion to allow more than one designated representative to remain in the courtroom. This would be appropriate, for instance, when it is impossible to find one person within the structure of a large entity who has all the information needed to assist the attorney.[7]

Determining the sequence in which the case representative will testify remains a matter entrusted to the trial court's discretion by virtue of Rule 611.[8] In most instances, the court will not interfere with the parties' choice of the order in which evidence is to be introduced.

---

assistance of counsel and right to retain counsel; witness was the president and sole shareholder of corporate defendant and court applied "control group" test of attorney-client privilege in determining that witness should be viewed as party constitutionally entitled to retain counsel).

[5] *See, e.g.,* United States v. Casas, 356 F.3d 104, 126 (1st Cir. 2004) (prosecution is entitled to have at least one case investigator at counsel table throughout trial, even though he or she may be scheduled to testify).

[5.1] *See, e.g.,* Nanoski v. General Motors Acceptance Corp., 874 F.2d 529, 531 (8th Cir. 1989) (witness who "had been designated at trial as [the defendant's] corporate representative" was "not excludable" under Rule 615).

[6] *See, e.g.,* United States v. Hickman, 151 F.3d 446, 453–454 (5th Cir. 1998) (district court abused its discretion by allowing two case agents to sit at counsel's table; error was harmless, however, because defendants failed to show any resulting prejudice); United States v. Ramirez, 963 F.2d 693, 703–704 (5th Cir. 1992) (harmless error to permit two FBI agents to remain in the courtroom); United States v. Farnham, 791 F.2d 331, 335 (4th Cir. 1986) (reversible error to have permitted two case agents to remain in courtroom).

[7] Breneman v. Kennecott Corp., 799 F.2d 470, 474 (9th Cir. 1986) (two representatives of defendant allowed); *see also* United States v. Green, 293 F.3d 886, 892 (5th Cir. 2002) (trial court did not abuse its discretion in allowing three witnesses to remain in court because each investigator represented different agency and no agency had been involved in all aspects of investigation).

[8] United States v. Parodi, 703 F.2d 768, 774 (4th Cir. 1983) (no abuse of discretion in allowing case agent to testify at conclusion of government's case when only one part of agent's testimony could have been admitted at beginning of trial without confusing order of proof; court held that absolute rule conditioning agent's right to remain in courtroom on his testifying first would conflict with its decisions allowing witness who had disobeyed sequestration order to testify).

[c]—A Person Whose Presence is Essential

Rule 615 has not eliminated all judicial discretion. The rule prohibits exclusion of "a person whose presence is shown by a party to be essential to the presentation of the party's cause."[9] The burden is on the party opposing sequestration to persuade the court to exercise its discretion to except a particular witness from its order.[10] Factors such as the following have been used to guide the trial court's determination of whether a specified witness is essential: (1) the importance of the witness' testimony; (2) whether the testimony is of a kind that is subject to tailoring; (3) whether the testimony covers issues that will be addressed by other testimony; (4) the order in which the witnesses will be called; (5) whether there is any potential for bias that could cause the witness to tailor his or her testimony; and (6) whether the presence of that witness is essential or desirable.[11]

This exception is probably most frequently invoked in the case of expert witnesses.[12] Certainly an expert who intends to base an opinion on "facts or data in the particular case" (Rule 703) will be unable to testify if he or she has been excluded. Experts needed to advise counsel on technical matters, as for instance in tax or patent litigation, or on how to cross-examine opposing experts, also qualify as essential persons.[13] However, when two experts will testify to the same issues and their pretrial disclosures indicate they have reached basically the same conclusions, the opportunity for tailoring their testimony and lack of need for them to hear each other's testimony suggest excluding the second witness to testify from hearing the testimony of the first.[14]

[d]—Victim in Criminal Trial[15]

Responding to concern for the rights of crime victims, Congress in 1990 enacted the Victims' Rights and Restitution Act of 1990. Under that Act, crime victims have

---

[9] Fed. R. Evid. 615(3).

[10] *See* Fed. R. Evid. 615 ("whose presence is shown by a party to be essential"); *see also* United States v. Green, 293 F.3d 886, 892 (5th Cir. 2002) (trial court did not abuse its discretion in allowing three witnesses to remain in court because prosecution showed that each investigator represented different agency and no agency had been involved in all aspects of complex investigation).

[11] Bruneau ex rel. Schofield v. South Kortright Cent. Sch. Dist., 163 F.3d 749, 762 (2d Cir. 1998) (trial court did not abuse its discretion by excusing two witnesses from sequestration order).

[12] *See, e.g.,* United States v. Seschillie, 310 F.3d 1208, 1214 (9th Cir. 2002) (trial court abused its discretion in excluding defendant's expert witness from trial after defendant made requisite showing that witness's presence was essential to presentation of defendant's case).

[13] United States v. Burgess, 691 F.2d 1146, 1157 (4th Cir. 1982) (in drug prosecution when defendant raised insanity defense, court did not err in ruling that psychiatrists for both parties might remain in courtroom, when written reports from experts were delayed, becoming available from defendant only two days before trial commenced and from government on second and last day of trial).

[14] *See, e.g.,* In re Omeprazole Patent Litig., 190 F. Supp. 2d 582, 583–587 (S.D.N.Y. 2002).

[15] *See* **Treatise** at § 615.04[4].

the right "to be present at all public court proceedings related to the offense, unless the court determines that testimony by the victim would be materially affected if the victim heard other testimony at trial."[16]

During the Oklahoma bombing case,[17] potential for conflict between Rule 615 and the 1990 Act surfaced, because victims who planned to testify only at the sentencing proceeding were being barred from the guilt trial. This conflict prompted Congress to pass the "Victim Rights Clarification Act of 1997." The Act, which applies to cases pending as of March 19, 1997, provides that a United States district court in a non-capital case "shall not order any victim of an offense excluded from the trial of a defendant accused of that offense because such victim may, during the sentencing hearing, make a statement or present any information in relation to the sentence."[18] In a capital case, a district court "shall not order any victim of an offense excluded from the trial of a defendant accused of that offense because such victim may, during the sentencing hearing, testify as to the effect of the offense on the victim and the victim's family or as to any other factor for which notice is required under section 3593(a)."[19]

The 1998 amendment to Rule 615 makes it clear that these statutes supersede the Rule. The amendment provides that Rule 615 may not be applied to exclude any person whose presence at trial is authorized by statute.[20] Thus, the court may not exclude a victim witness automatically under Rule 615, but must first determine whether the victim's testimony would be materially affected if the victim heard other testimony at trial.

Moreover, both prohibitions of the Victim Rights Clarification Act supersede any other statute, rule, or other provision of law.[21] The fact that the Victim Rights Clarification Act supersedes other statutes suggests that a victim may not be excluded from the trial even though the court has determined that "testimony by the victim would be materially affected if the victim heard other testimony at trial,"[22] if the victim will be testifying only at the sentencing hearing.

---

[16]   42 U.S.C. § 10606(b)(4).

[17]   United States v. McVeigh, 106 F.3d 325, 339 (10th Cir. 1997) (neither government nor victim witnesses had standing to seek relief from sequestration order).

[18]   18 U.S.C. § 3510(a).

[19]   18 U.S.C. § 3510(b); see 18 U.S.C. § 3593(a) (government must give notice of factors supporting death sentence, including effect of offense on victim and victim's family).

[20]   Fed. R. Evid. 615(4).

[21]   18 U.S.C. § 3510(a), (b).

[22]   See 42 U.S.C. § 10606(b)(4).

[3]—Procedure Pursuant to Rule 615[23]

Rule 615 is silent on when a demand for exclusion must be made.[24] The practice is to exercise judicial discretion to exclude prospective witnesses during openings and any arguments or proffers of proof when a witness' testimony may be summarized. The rule should be applied at hearings, as to suppress, and on other occasions when witnesses may be heard, as on sentencing.

The rule is also silent as to what instructions the court may give the witnesses when they are excluded. A number of cases have indicated that the court should direct the witnesses not to discuss the case with each other,[25] but a failure to give such an instruction has not ordinarily been considered reversible error.[26] When an instruction is given, it should be worded in terms of a direction "not to discuss the case with anyone *other than counsel.*"[27] Prohibiting contact between a party and his or her attorney may deprive a criminal defendant-witness of the Sixth Amendment right to effective assistance of counsel, and in a civil case might amount to a denial of due process. It is not infrequent, however, for trial courts to order witnesses not to talk to anyone, including counsel, about their testimony during breaks in their testimony, not only to prevent improper coaching, but also to preserve the status quo during those breaks.[28]

[4]—Consequences of Non-Compliance[29]

Rule 615 does not mention the consequences of non-compliance with an order of exclusion. As under previous practice, the imposition of sanctions remains a

---

[23] *See* **Treatise** at §§ 615.05–615.06.

[24] *See* United States v. Abbott, 30 F.3d 71, 73 (7th Cir. 1994) (defendant's failure to move to exclude witnesses waived any argument on the subject; further, the trial court eventually excluded all witnesses without a request from defendant).

[25] *See, e.g.,* United States v. Green, 293 F.3d 886, 892 (5th Cir. 2002) (trial court's failure to instruct sequestered witnesses not to discuss case among themselves is violation of Rule 615, but is not error in absence of showing witnesses actually discussed case); *but see* United States v. Collins, 340 F.3d 672, 681 (8th Cir. 2003) (two witnesses who discussed case with each other before both testified did not violate Rule 615).

[26] United States v. Smith, 578 F.2d 1227, 1235 (8th Cir. 1978) (within judge's discretion to determine if segregated witnesses should be instructed not to communicate with each other, and in judge's discretion to determine whether order of sequestration has been violated). *Cf.* Miller v. Universal City Studios, Inc., 650 F.2d 1365 (5th Cir. 1981) (providing sequestered witness with daily transcript copy violates Rule 615).

[27] *See, e.g.,* United States v. Calderin-Rodriguez, 244 F.3d 977, 984–985 (8th Cir. 2001) (Rule 615 does not require sequestration order to forbid discussions with counsel presenting witness, and ethical rules do not prevent counsel from conferring with witness during testimony).

[28] *See, e.g.,* Perry v. Leeke, 488 U.S. 272, 281–284, 109 S. Ct. 594, 102 L. Ed. 2d 624 (1989).

[29] *See* **Treatise** at § 615.07.

matter of case law and a matter of the trial court's discretion.[29.1] Three methods of enforcement have been used by the courts: (1) citing the witness for contempt, (2) permitting comment on the witness's noncompliance in order to reflect on his or her credibility and (3) refusing to let the witness testify or striking the testimony.

Each method has drawbacks. A contempt citation punishes the witness and may perhaps deter future misconduct but does not rid the case of testimony that the witness may have fabricated after listening to other witnesses. The comment, while useful, may have unwarranted repercussions if the witness remained in the courtroom but his or her testimony was unaffected. A derogatory comment on the witness's credibility may actually distort the truth. Exclusion of the testimony deprives the jury of relevant evidence, a result that the Rules of Evidence do not ordinarily sanction.[30]

In most reported decisions, the witness who has disobeyed an order of exclusion by remaining in the courtroom is permitted to testify.[31] In *Holder v. United States*,[32] the Supreme Court put its weight against disqualifying the witness:

> If a witness disobeys the order of withdrawal, while he may be proceeded against for contempt, and his testimony is open to comment to the jury by reason of his conduct, he is not thereby disqualified, and the weight of authority is that he cannot be excluded on that ground, merely, although the right to exclude under particular circumstances may be supported as within the sound discretion of the trial court.

This more generous attitude to the parties is justified. Often a prospective witness will be confused or will not understand what the court said or may come into the courtroom after the court has made its order. Counsel is often so busy and intent on trial problems that he or she will not be aware that one of the witnesses is in the courtroom. This possibility of confusion is one reason that courts are reluctant to order witnesses not to speak to each other. They inadvertently do so from time to time, and the trial degenerates into ugly accusations of bad faith that becloud the central issues.

On the other hand, appellate courts also affirm trial court decisions to strike the

---

[29.1] *See, e.g.,* United States v. Collins, 340 F.3d 672, 681 (8th Cir. 2003) (trial court enjoys wide latitude in fashioning appropriate sanction for violation of witness sequestration order).

[30] *See* discussion in Chapter 6, *Relevancy Generally.*

[31] *See, e.g.,* United States v. Calderin-Rodriguez, 244 F.3d 977, 985 (8th Cir. 2001) (trial court did not abuse its discretion in refusing to strike witness's testimony for apparently inadvertent violation of sequestration order during break, since defendant failed to show resulting prejudice other than reduced effectiveness of cross-examination because, after break, witness was able to correct earlier errors in testimony as result of conversation with another witness).

[32] Holder v. United States, 150 U.S. 91, 92, 14 S. Ct. 10, 37 L. Ed. 1010 (1893).

testimony of witnesses who have violated sequestration orders, especially if there is an indication that a party or a party's attorney participated in the violation.[33] The trial court has the discretion to weigh the circumstances and determine whether exclusion of testimony is the appropriate response to a violation.[34]

To be distinguished from situations in which the trial court exercises its discretion to allow the disobedient witness to testify are cases in which the trial court erroneously thought it had discretion to refuse to exclude witnesses despite a party's request. The Circuits have used a number of different approaches in dealing with a district court's erroneous denial of a sequestration request—automatic reversal, no reversal absent a showing of prejudice, or a presumption of prejudice requiring reversal unless harmless error is shown.[35]

---

[33] *See, e.g.,* United States v. Rhynes, 196 F.3d 207, 227–228 (4th Cir. 1999) (court did not abuse its discretion in striking witness's testimony; in finding that attorney violated sequestration order, court's interpretation of its own order was reasonable); *see also* **Treatise**, § 615.07[2][d].

[34] *See, e.g.,* United States v. Green, 305 F.3d 422, 428 (6th Cir. 2002) (trial court's determination whether to permit witness to testify in spite of violation of sequestration order is reviewed for abuse of discretion); *see also* **Treatise**, § 615.07[3][a].

[35] *See* discussion in United States v. Ell, 718 F.2d 291, 292–293 (9th Cir. 1983).

CHAPTER 11

Special Witness Rules

§ 11.01   Overview of Special Witness Rules

With few exceptions, no restrictions exist as to the kinds of witness that may be called or as to the relative degrees of probative force to be accorded their testimony. Except as required by substantive law, special rule or the circumstances of the case, all witnesses are considered competent, and evaluation of credibility is for the trier of fact. The reader should consult, among other sources, Rule 601 on competency generally, discussed in Chapter 10, which imports State Dead Man's Acts; Rule 501, importing the federal spousal privilege-incompetency rule and similar state rules under some circumstances, discussed in Chapter 18 *infra;* the United States Constitution Article III, Section 3, requiring "testimony of two Witnesses to same overt Act, or . . . Confession in open Court," for conviction of treason; Rule 602, requiring personal knowledge of the witness, discussed in Chapter 10; Rule 104(a) giving the court the power to exclude testimony where no reasonable jury could believe the witness, discussed in Chapter 3; and Rules 702 and 703, permitting the court to exclude certain expert testimony, discussed in Chapter 13. There are also certain protections for limited classes of witnesses, as in Rule 412, covering victims of sexual assault (discussed in Chapter 7), Rule 704(b) on testimony of experts giving certain kinds of psychiatric evidence (discussed in Chapter 13), and Rule 609(a), limiting some attacks on the credibility of criminal defendants (discussed in Chapter 12).

This chapter covers three special witness rules that are less evidentiary than procedural and substantive in nature. It deals with interpreters, judges and jurors.

§ 11.02   Interpreters—Rule 604[1]

The inability of a party or witness to speak or to understand English should not exclude that person from participating in, or understanding, judicial proceedings. A statute[2] provides for the certification of interpreters and for making both certified and other qualified interpreters available in proceedings initiated by the United States and in other proceedings. Rule 43 of the Federal Rules of Civil Procedure[3] and Rule 28 of the Federal Rules of Criminal Procedure[4] permit the appointment and compensation of interpreters. The right of a criminal defendant to a complete, competent translation of the trial derives not merely from statute and rule, but also from the Constitution.[5]

---

[1]   *See* **Treatise** at §§ 604.02–604.04.

[2]   Court Interpreters Act, 28 U.S.C. § 1827–1828 (1978), as amended. The Act provides a system for the use of interpreters in the federal court.

[3]   Fed. R. Civ. P. 43; *see* 8 MOORE'S FEDERAL PRACTICE, Ch. 43, *Taking of Testimony* (Matthew Bender 3d ed. 1997).

[4]   Fed. R. Crim. P. 28; *see* 26 MOORE'S FEDERAL PRACTICE, Ch. 628, *Interpreters* (Matthew Bender 3d ed. 1997).

[5]   United States v. Joshi, 896 F.2d 1303, 1309–1311 (11th Cir. 1990) and cases cited.

The need for an interpreter does not arise only in situations involving non-English speaking persons. Thus, the Court Interpreters Act provides also for the availability of an interpreter to help a party or witness who "suffers from a hearing impairment. . . ."[6]

Rule 604 imposes two requirements on interpreters. First, they must be qualified as experts in the skill of interpreting. Secondly, they must take an oath or affirm that they will interpret truthfully, *i.e.,* communicate to the court exactly what is being said by the witness.[7]

Rule 604 provides as follows:

Rule 604.   Interpreters.

An interpreter is subject to the provisions of these rules relating to qualification as an expert and the administration of an oath or affirmation to make a true translation.

Interpreters in criminal cases should be instructed not only to interpret the questions directed to the witness and the witness's answers but, if the defendant does not speak English, also to interpret everything said by the judge, other witnesses and the attorneys. The defendant is entitled to know what is going on in the courtroom at all times.

The court and counsel should insure that the translator does his or her job properly. If there are long silences on the interpreter's part while proceedings are continuing, there should be an immediate reminder on the record, that every word must be translated. The interpreter should not be permitted to hold long conversations with a witness in his native tongue, while the response is shortened into a "yes" or "no" answer. He or she is to interpret, not confer.

Like English, many foreign tongues have dialects or regional differences that may limit the competence of a given interpreter. Counsel should anticipate the possibility of any such situation so that a continuance to obtain a different interpreter will not delay the trial.

If at all possible, official interpreters should be used. The use of relatives or others

---

[6] United States v. Dempsey, 830 F.2d 1084 (10th Cir. 1987) (upheld the use of an interpreter skilled in sign language to help a deaf juror); *see also* DeLong v. Brumbaugh, 703 F. Supp. 399, 404-405 (W.D. Pa. 1989).

[7] *See, e.g.,* United States v. Pluta, 176 F.3d 43, 49-50 (2d Cir. 1999) (court failed to swear interpreters with oath or affirmation; however, defendant's failure to object resulted in review for plain error, which was not found); Contracts Materials Processing v. Kataleuna GmbH Catalysts, 164 F. Supp. 2d 520, 528 (D. Md. 2001) (summary judgment affidavit that depended on translations of documents originally in German was deficient because it did not state affiant's qualifications to make translations and did not include translations).

interested in the case can lead to an inadequate or inaccurate translation.

There is, however, no requirement that, in every instance, the interpreter be independent and disinterested. Although those are desirable characteristics for an interpreter, the circumstances of the case may require the court to accept someone familiar with the witness or to forego the witness's testimony altogether. Thus, when a deaf mute has pertinent testimony to give, but communicates solely with gestures, signs, and grunts that are an effective means of communication only with family members, friends, and close acquaintances, the trial court may properly allow the witness's testimony to be interpreted by someone fully familiar with, and close to, the witness.[8]

In civil cases the parties have the obligation to provide interpreters. In criminal cases the obligation is that of the court.

§ 11.03　Competency of Judge as Witness—Rule 605

[1]—Rationale and Scope of Rule[1]

Rule 605 prevents a judge presiding at a trial from testifying as a witness in that trial. The rule provides as follows:

Rule 605.　Competency of Judge as Witness.

The judge presiding at the trial may not testify in that trial as a witness. No objection need be made in order to preserve the point.

The rationale for a rule of incompetency is obvious. Permitting a judge to testify raises perplexing questions of who will rule on objections, who will compel answers, what will be the scope of cross-examination, and how counsel is to maintain a proper relationship with the court.[2]

The rule against judicial testimony also applies when a judge assumes the role of a witness even though the judge neither is called to testify nor voluntarily takes the stand.[3] The prohibition extends to the judge's clerk.[4] Judicial testimony occurs

---

[8] *See, e.g.,* United States v. Bell, 367 F.3d 452, 463–464 (5th Cir. 2004) (trial court properly allowed deaf mute's testimony to be interpreted by his sister).

[1] *See* **Treatise** at §§ 601.02–601.04.

[2] Brown v. Lynaugh, 843 F.2d 849, 850-851 (5th Cir. 1988).

[3] United States v. Paiva, 892 F.2d 148, 158-159 (1st Cir. 1989) (Trial judge's explanation of detective's field test held "impermissibly" to exceed "his power to comment on the evidence").

[4] Kennedy v. Great Atl. & Pac. Tea Co., 551 F.2d 593 (5th Cir. 1977); *see, e.g.,* Price Bros. Co. v. Philadelphia Gear Corp., 629 F.2d 444 (6th Cir. 1980) (plaintiff alleged that trial judge's law clerk had traveled to plaintiff's plant prior to trial and court remanded for evidentiary hearing to determine truth of allegation, noting that sending a law clerk to gather evidence in a non-jury trial would be destructive of the appearance of impartiality required of the presiding judge).

when the judge refers to relevant facts of which he or she has personal knowledge in the guise of taking judicial notice.[5] A trial judge, however, does not improperly testify by interrupting cross-examination to correct counsel's misstatement of the law[6] or by making a preliminary determination of authenticity.[7]

Difficulties may also arise when the court purports to take judicial notice of prior proceedings in the case. Judicial notice may be proper if a record exists to which reference can be made and which the appellate court can review. But when the judge relies on his or her own recollection of what previously occurred, the parties should have an opportunity to challenge the accuracy of the memory,[8] at least when the judge's statements are relevant to a material issue.

A judge may also be forced into the role of a witness by questions of counsel connecting the judge with events relevant to the the trial. For example, if a prosecutor cross-examines a defendant as to whether she remembers certain statements previously made before the same judge, the judge has implicitly been made the guarantor of their accuracy. To avoid this uncomfortable position, the trial judge should use powers under Rule 611 to curtail lines of questioning connecting him or her to the facts of the case.

The rule refers to trials. It does not cover such usual situations as the court's indicating on sentencing or a post-sentencing hearing what it saw in its presence.[9] On hearings of contempt that took place in the presence of the court, the judge is

---

A trial judge does not "improperly testify" when making a preliminary determination of authenticity. *See* United States v. Sliker, 751 F.2d 477, 497–500 (2d Cir. 1984), *cert. denied,* 470 U.S. 1058 (1985) (identification of voices on tape recording).

[5] United States v. Lewis, 833 F.2d 1380, 1385-1386 (9th Cir. 1987) (trial judge held to have erred in basing finding of fact on his personal experience); Furtado v. Bishop, 604 F.2d 80, 90 (1st Cir. 1979), *cert. denied,* 444 U.S. 1035 (1980) (harmless error for trial judge to admit affidavit of dead lawyer after determining its trustworthiness on personal knowledge of the deceased).

[6] United States v. Maceo, 947 F.2d 1191, 1200 (5th Cir. 1991), *cert. denied,* 503 U.S. 949 (1992).

[7] United States v. Sliker, 751 F.2d 477, 497-500 (2d Cir. 1984), *cert. denied,* 470 U.S. 1058 (1985).

[8] *Cf.* Soley v. Star & Herald Co., 390 F.2d 364, 369 (5th Cir. 1968) (a judge's grant of summary judgment not sustained on basis of judicial notice of a case, that the judge had previously decided, when record did not indicate whether the judge had physically examined the record of the prior case or relied on his own recollection); Associated Business Tel. Sys. Corp. v. Greater Capital Corp., 729 F. Supp. 1488, 1498 (D.N.J. 1990), *aff'd.,* 919 F.2d 133 (3d Cir. 1990) (Reference by counsel to granting in same action of partial summary judgment held not to justify new trial in view of cautionary instruction to jury).

[9] *Cf.* United States v. Alberico, 453 F. Supp. 178, 186 (D. Colo. 1977), *aff'd,* 604 F.2d 1315 (10th Cir. 1979) (court refused to disqualify itself on motion made by defendant after conviction, which would have left case in limbo and staved off sentencing, because Rule 605 only applies to preclude judge's testimony at trial over which he presides).

not disqualified by Rule 605. However, due process or statute[10] may require a trial by another judge.

The rule does not create a privilege. The judge has no right to refuse to give testimony that may be critical. Refusal to testify may therefore create reversible error for exclusion of evidence. If the case is before the judge who is required to be a witness, a mistrial may be required unless the parties will stipulate to the facts in issue. Even when the judge does not testify, the mere knowledge that he or she has been sought as a witness may be prejudicial. The problem is alleviated to a great extent by statute.[11] A federal judge is required to disqualify himself or herself in any proceeding in which the judge's impartiality might reasonably be questioned. The effect of this statute is to require the parties to inform a judge of their intention to call him or her as a witness, enabling the judge to disqualify himself or herself before trial, and before a question under Rule 605 arises.

[2]—Judge Called or Testifying[1]

If judges have not disqualified themselves before trial and are called as witnesses, they have various options depending on whether it is a civil or criminal trial. In a civil case, a judge who is called to testify can recuse himself or herself and grant a new trial. If the judge decides to continue with the trial (whether or not the judge actually testifies) and the verdict favors the proponent of the judge's testimony, the appellate court must examine the situation even if no objection was made at trial.

If the judge testified either formally or putatively to a material fact, the appellate court should generally reverse because of the likelihood of prejudice. When the judge's testimony related solely to a formal, non-material matter the appellate court must weigh the facts of the particular case as it does whenever a claim of plain or substantial error is made.

When the judge refused to testify, the reviewing court must decide on the facts of the particular case whether the mere seeking of the judge's testimony was sufficiently prejudicial to require a reversal. Precisely what was said in the jury's presence, the importance attached to the testimony by the proponent, and the other witnesses' knowledge of the event are all factors that should be considered. To determine how important the testimony would have been, an offer of proof should be made outside the presence of the jury.

In a criminal case, the problems attendant on calling a judge as a witness are

---

[10] Fed. R. Crim. P. 42(b) disqualifies a judge from presiding at proceedings to punish contempts involving "disrespect" or "criticism" directed at himself; *see* 27 MOORE'S FEDERAL PRACTICE, Ch. 642, *Criminal Contempt* (Matthew Bender 3d ed. 1997).

[11] 28 U.S.C. § 455 (1982).

[1] *See* **Treatise** at §§ 605.05–605.07.

considerably more complex because of the special constitutional guarantees to which a defendant in a criminal trial is entitled.[2] When a judge who has been called to testify disqualifies himself or herself, a further complication arises since Rule 25(a) of the Federal Rules of Criminal Procedure provides that if a judge is disabled and unable to proceed with a trial, any regularly sitting judge may be substituted. It is unclear whether a judge who withdraws when called to testify is "disabled" within the meaning of Rule 25(a).[3]

§ 11.04 Competency of Juror as Witness—Rule 606

[1]—Scope of Rule[1]

Rule 606 deals with a variety of situations in which a member of a jury is incompetent to testify. Subdivision (a) is concerned with the juror as a witness in the trial of the case in which the juror is empanelled. Subdivision (b) deals with the juror as a witness attacking or supporting the validity of a verdict or indictment.

[2]—Juror as Witness at Trial[1]

Subdivision (a) of Rule 606 bars a juror from testifying as a witness in the case which the juror is trying. Rule 606(a) provides as follows:

> **Rule 606. Competency of Juror as Witness.**
>
> (a) At the trial.—A member of the jury may not testify as a witness before that jury in the trial of the case in which the juror is sitting. If the juror is called so to testify, the opposing party shall be afforded an opportunity to object out of the presence of the jury.

The rule does not prevent the court from questioning jurors on issues such as the effect on them of publicity, attempted tampering and the like.[2] Jurors are prohibited from testifying because it is believed that counsel will be inhibited in cross-examination by fear of offending the juror who has been sworn as a witness, and that the witness may lose impartiality by identifying with the side for which he or she testified. Prohibiting the testimony does not solve the entire problem, for the possibility of prejudice arises as soon as the other jurors become aware that the testimony of one of their fellows is sought. Nor does Rule 606(a) indicate what

---

[2] *See* **Treatise** at § 605.06.

[3] Fed. R. Crim. P. 25(a); *see* 25 Moore's Federal Practice, Ch. 625, *Judges; Disability; Disqualification* (Matthew Bender 3d ed. 1997).

[1] *See* **Treatise** at § 606.02.

[1] *See* **Treatise** at § 606.03.

[2] United States v. Robinson, 635 F.2d 981, 985–986 (2nd Cir. 1980), *cert. denied,* 451 U.S. 992 (1981) (juror who had seen defendant in custody of marshals could testify at mistrial motion).

the judge should do if the offer of proof indicates that the juror's testimony is important. In a criminal case, a refusal to permit a witness to testify for the defendant may raise constitutional problems.

In practice, these unanswered questions are of little significance, since persons with knowledge relevant to the facts in issue are far more likely to be challenged for cause and excused as jurors than sworn as witnesses. In the unlikely event that it comes to light during trial, the juror's testimony will be sought and the judge should determine if the offered testimony is Rule 403 or excludable pursuant to Rule 611.[3] If the testimony is excluded, whether the trial should be aborted depends on the circumstances of the particular case. The judge must consider whether the jurors were aware that the testimony was sought and whether the juror divulged the special case-specific information to the other jurors on the panel.[3.1] If so, the judge must also consider whether such divulgence would have prejudiced the jury, whether the case is civil or criminal, and whether alternate jurors are available.

If the court finds that the juror's testimony is required, it should declare a mistrial in a civil or criminal case. Absent extraordinary circumstances, it should not continue the trial with an alternate juror and permit the ex-juror to testify, since Rule 606 clearly expresses a determination that testimony by a juror is inherently prejudicial. To avoid the problem of double jeopardy in criminal cases, if possible, consent of the parties to the granting of the mistrial should be obtained or they should waive the point on the record.

Even if the existence of a juror-witness does not come to light at trial, the careful attorney assuming certain knowledge on the part of the jury of notorious facts in the community, should, when possible, meet the problem by testimony and argument explaining why it does not affect the case. The "secret juror witness" who works in the privacy of the jury room is much more dangerous than one who testifies in court where misconceptions and misinformation can be dealt with.[4] The primary means of preventing such abuses is a thorough jury *voir dire* that minimizes the chance of persons with special knowledge of the case being chosen as jurors.

---

[3] *See* discussion of "necessity test" in **Treatise** at § 606.03[2][a].

[3.1] *Cf.* Kilgore v. Greyhound Corp., Southern Greyhound Lines, 30 F.R.D. 385, 388–389 (E.D. Tenn. 1962) (court considered affidavits of jurors after verdict but refused to grant new trial when it found that no prejudice had occurred by juror's recounting his impressions of visiting accident scene when foreman immediately instructed jury to disregard these statements).

[4] *See* United States ex rel. Owen v. McMann, 435 F.2d 813, 815 (2d Cir. 1970) (when several jurors told other jurors that they knew "all about" defendant, listing several incidents unrelated to trial and stating that his father was always getting him out of trouble, there was sufficient probability of prejudice to make trial lacking in due process). Whether jurors become "witnesses" within the reach of the Confrontation Clause when they discuss extra-record factual matters is discussed in the **Treatise** at § 606.04[2][d].

[3]—Juror Testimony Impeaching Verdict

[a]—Evidence of Mental Operations and Emotional Reactions Inadmissible

See **Treatise** at § 606.04.

Rule 606(b) is a rule of incompetency barring jurors from testifying to the motives, methods, or mental processes by which they reached their verdict or failed to reach it.[1] The rule is equally applicable to testimony by grand jurors when the validity of an indictment is under attack.[2] Testimony by a juror in support of a verdict and testimony by non-juror witnesses as to statements by a juror that would be barred if made by the juror are also disallowed.[3]

Rule 606(b) provides as follows:

> **Rule 606(b).   Competency of Juror as Witness.**
>
> (b) Inquiry into validity of verdict or indictment. Upon an inquiry into the validity of a verdict or indictment, a juror may not testify as to any matter or statement occurring during the course of the jury's deliberations or to the effect of anything upon that or any other juror's mind or emotions as influencing the juror to assent to or dissent from the verdict or indictment or concerning the juror's mental processes in connection therewith, except that a juror may testify on the question whether extraneous prejudicial information was improperly brought to the jury's attention or whether any outside influence was improperly brought to bear upon any juror. Nor may a juror's affidavit or evidence of any statement by the juror concerning a matter about which the juror would be precluded from testifying be received for these purposes.

The purpose behind Rule 606(b) is to protect jurors from post-verdict harassment designed to induce them to impeach their verdicts and to promote stability of jury verdicts by precluding post-verdict inquiries into their motivations and mental

---

[1]   *See* Gosier v. Welborn, 175 F.3d 504, 510–511 (7th Cir. 1999) (Rule 606(b) barred introduction of evidence in habeas proceeding that a state court juror voted for death penalty by mistake, because rule disallows inquiry into juror's mental processes during deliberations).

[2]   *See* **Treatise** at § 606.07.

[3]   Poches v. J.J. Newberry Co., 549 F.2d 1166, 1169 (8th Cir. 1977) (statements by juror to fellow air passenger excluded); *but see* United States v. Eagle, 539 F.2d 1166, 1170 (8th Cir. 1976) (witness permitted to testify that juror had told him he realized defendant was connected to other uncharged shootings; juror, however, could not testify because no extraneous influence was involved but only the mental process of the juror; consequently, motion for a new trial was properly denied, citing Rule 606(b)).

processes.[4] The Supreme Court explained the rationale for prohibiting a juror's impeachment of his or her own verdict in *McDonald v. Pless:* [5]

> If the facts were as stated in the affidavit, the jury adopted an arbitrary and unjust method in arriving at their verdict, and the defendant ought to have had relief, if the facts could have been proved by witnesses who were competent to testify. . . . But let it once be established that verdicts solemnly made and publicly returned into court can be attacked and set aside on the testimony of those who took part in their publication and all verdicts could be, and many would be, followed by an inquiry in the hope of discovering something which might invalidate the finding. Jurors would be harassed and beset by the defeated party in an effort to secure from them evidence of facts which might establish misconduct sufficient to set aside a verdict.

The prevention of fraud by individual jurors who could remain silent during trial and later claim that they were improperly influenced has also been asserted as a reason for a non-impeachment rule.[6]

Rule 606(b) seeks to reach an accommodation between policies designed to safeguard the sanctity of a jury's verdict and policies designed to insure a just result in the individual case. It does so by drawing the dividing line between the manner by which the jury reached its verdict, as to which testimony or other inquiry is inappropriate, and the injection of extraneous prejudicial information or influences into the deliberative process, as to which testimony or other inquiry is appropriate.[7] The question of which side of the line given behavior by jurors falls on is not without its difficulties. It is further complicated by the Supreme Court's suggestion that in criminal cases, at least, the Constitution may require inquiry into the circumstances regarding a jury's deliberations regardless of the applicable rule on impeachment of the verdict by members of the jury that returned it.[8]

If the juror's evidence relates solely to the arguments, statements, discussions, mental and emotional reactions, and votes of the testifying juror or other members

---

[4] *See, e.g.,* United States v. Briggs, 291 F.3d 958, 963 (7th Cir. 2002) (evidence of "intimidation" that alleges only intra-jury psychological pressures, and not extraneous influences or information or physical intimidation is inadmissible to impeach jury's verdict under Rule 606).

[5] McDonald v. Pless, 238 U.S. 264, 267–268, 35 S. Ct. 783, 59 L. Ed. 2d 1300 (1915).

[6] *See, e.g.,* United States v. Eagle, 539 F.2d 1166, 1170 (8th Cir. 1976).

[7] Fed. R. Evid. 606(b) Advisory Committee's Note (1972) at **Treatise** § 606App.01[2]; *see, e.g.,* United States v. Francis, 367 F.3d 805, 829 (8th Cir. 2004) (trial court did not err in excluding evidence of internal pressures exerted by some jurors against others during jury deliberations).

[8] Parker v. Gladden, 385 U.S. 363, 364–365, 87 S. Ct. 468, 17 L. Ed.2d 420 (1966); *see* **Treatise** § 606.04[2][d] for discussion of the *Parker* case.

of the jury. or to other features of the deliberative process, the testimony is inadmissible. Thus, evidence is not admissible to prove:

- a juror's thought processes during the deliberations.[9]

- that a juror or the jury as a whole misunderstood or disregarded evidence.[10]

- that a juror or the jury as a whole misunderstood or disregarded the judge's instructions.[11]

- that a juror voted for a verdict only because he or she thought that the jury would be kept out indefinitely until agreement was reached.[12]

- that a juror did not in fact agree on the verdict that the jury as a whole reported and affirmed in open court.[13]

- that the jury considered an election of the accused not to take the stand.[14]

- that a juror believed that a guilty verdict with an accompanying recommendation for leniency would assure that the defendant did not receive a harsh sentence.[15]

- that a juror was coerced by other jurors into agreeing with them.[16]

---

[9] *See, e.g.,* Ortega v. United States, 270 F.3d 540, 547 (8th Cir. 2001) (juror's post-verdict expressions of concern about weight of evidence relate to juror's mental processes during deliberations and are inadmissible under Rule 606(b)).

[10] *See, e.g.,* Wilsmann v. Upjohn Co., 572 F. Supp. 242, 245 (W.D. Mich. 1983) (evidence that jury included interest as an element of damages excluded under Rule 606).

[11] *See, e.g.,* Fields v. Woodford, 281 F.3d 963, 975–976 (9th Cir. 2002) (evidence that jury disregarded judge's instruction to disregard improperly admitted evidence is evidence of jurors' internal thought processes and is inadmissible under Rule 606(b)).

[12] *See, e.g.,* United States v. Weiner, 578 F.2d 757, 764 (9th Cir. 1978) (Rule 606(b) barred testimony that juror had voted guilty with reservation); *but see* Munafo v. Metro. Transp. Auth., 381 F.3d 99, (2d Cir. 8/24/04) (rule does not bar juror testimony in response to judicial queries about whether "the verdict delivered was not that actually agreed upon"; upholding queries "designed to confirm the accurate *transmittal* of a special verdict" [emphasis original]; whether jurors misjudged legal effect of their answers to questions is not subject to inquiry).

[13] *See, e.g.,* United States v. Ortiz, 942 F.2d 903, 913 (5th Cir. 1991).

[14] *See, e.g.,* United States v. Rutherford, 371 F.3d 634, 640 (9th Cir. 2004) (trial court properly excluded evidence that jurors ignored instruction not to consider defendant's failure to testify). United States v. Tran, 122 F.3d 670, 672–673 (8th Cir. 1997) (trial court properly excluded jury affidavits reporting that defendant's failure to testify helped them reach a guilty verdict).

[15] *See, e.g.,* United States v. Ramos-Oseguera, 120 F.3d 1028, 1033, 1039–1040 (9th Cir. 1997) (trial court's decision not to consider jurors' letters explaining their verdict and urging leniency in sentencing was not abuse of discretion, based on belief that practice could lead to harassment of jurors).

[16] *See, e.g.,* United States v. Briggs, 291 F.3d 958, 963 (7th Cir. 2002) (evidence of "intimidation" that alleges only intra-jury psychological pressures, and not extraneous influences or information or physical intimidation is inadmissible to impeach jury's verdict under Rule 606).

- that a juror's vote would have been different if he or she had been able to hear evidence the trial court excluded.[17]

- that the jury discussed information that is common knowledge about criminal justice system that was not the subject of evidence during the trial.[17.1]

- that the jury began its deliberations prematurely, during the course of the trial, rather than awaiting the close of the evidence and the court's instructions.[17.2]

Testimony of a witness who was not on a jury concerning statements that a juror made is not admissible if the juror's testimony to the same subject matter would have been inadmissible under Rule 606(b).[18] Similarly, if a particular juror could not, under Rule 606(b), testify concerning the matters that occurred during the deliberative process that affected his or her decision-making process, another member of the jury cannot testify about those same matters.[18.1]

[b]—Evidence of Extraneous Influences Admissible

Evidence of extraneous influences is admissible to show their improper interference with the jury's deliberative process. Jurors are not incompetent to provide such evidence because it tends to prove that factors were at work to prevent the jury from playing its sacred role in the American system of justice. Thus, evidence is admissible to prove a juror's:

- exposure to threats.[19]

---

[17] *See, e.g.,* Williams v. Collins, 16 F.3d 626, 636 (5th Cir. 1994) (district court in habeas corpus proceeding properly barred testimony from jurors in state trial as to whether their deliberations would have been different if they had been able to consider mitigating evidence that was not introduced at trial).
[17.1] *See, e.g.,* Fullwood v. Lee, 290 F.3d 663, 683–684 (4th Cir. 2002) (jurors' discussion of likelihood that defendant would appeal adverse verdict and of potential for parole concerning sentence other than death concerned matters that are common knowledge, particularly in view of one juror's criminal justice background, which was revealed on voir dire, and was not ground for evidentiary hearing into potential jury misconduct).
[17.2] *See, e.g.,* United States v. Logan, 250 F.3d 350, 377–381 (6th Cir. 2001).
[18] *See, e.g.,* Poches v. J.J. Newberry Co., 549 F.2d 1166, 1169 (8th Cir. 1977) (testimony from ex-juror's fellow air passenger concerning statements ex-juror made to him regarding jury deliberations was properly excluded).
[18.1] *See, e.g.,* Fullwood v. Lee, 290 F.3d 663, 680 (4th Cir. 2002) (defendant not entitled to evidentiary hearing based on allegations that another juror's vote had been affected by external pressure).
[19] *See, e.g.,* United States v. Sanders, 962 F.2d 660, 672–673 (7th Cir. 1992) (trial court did not err, under particular circumstances of case, in finding that the receipt of a threat by one juror did not affect verdict).

- receipt of a bribery solicitation.[20]

- possession of knowledge relevant to the facts in issue obtained not through the introduction of evidence but acquired prior to trial.[21]

- exposure to external psychological influence as to how he or she should vote.[21.1]

- possession of knowledge of the results of a prior trial of the same case.[21.2]

- obtaining relevant information during trial, through:

    - unauthorized views.[22]

    - unauthorized experiments.[23]

    - independent research or investigations.[24]

    - the news media.[25]

---

[20] *See, e.g.,* United States v. Henley, 238 F.3d 1111, 1116–1118 (9th Cir. 2001) (testimony about juror's mental processes in reaching verdict after attempted bribery would be barred by Rule 606(b), but juror could properly testify about experiencing general fear and anxiety after bribery attempt).

[21] *See, e.g.,* Hard v. Burlington Northern R.R., 812 F.2d 482, 486 (9th Cir. 1987) (in an FELA action brought by a railroad worker in which plaintiff was awarded minimal damages, trial court abused its discretion by not allowing evidentiary hearing into juror's failure to disclose on voir dire that he had previously worked for defendant and his subsequently telling other jurors that defendant-railroad pays all medical expenses of injured employees; when juror's past personal experiences "are related to the litigation, as they are here, they constitute extraneous evidence which may be used to impeach the jury's verdict.").

[21.1] *See, e.g.,* Fullwood v. Lee, 290 F.3d 663, 681–682 (4th Cir. 2002) (allegations that juror's husband pressured her throughout trial to vote for death penalty raised question whether defendant was tried by twelve impartial jurors, and warrant evidentiary hearing into effect pressures, if any, may have had on verdict.).

[21.2] *See, e.g.,* Fullwood v. Lee, 290 F.3d 663, 682–683 (4th Cir. 2002) (allegations in juror's affidavit that jury became aware in its deliberations that prior jury had sentenced defendant to death on same charges but that sentence had been reversed because of trial judge's mistake were sufficient to warrant evidentiary hearing into potential juror misconduct).

[22] *See, e.g.,* In re Beverly Hills Fire Litigation, 695 F.2d 207, 213–214 (6th Cir. 1982).

[23] *See, e.g.,* Anderson v. Ford Motor Co., 186 F.3d 918, 921 (8th Cir. 1999) (juror's improper out-of-court experiment warranted new trial because it involved controlling issue in case and prejudiced losing party).

[24] *See, e.g.,* United States v. Bagnariol, 665 F.2d 877, 885–887 (9th Cir. 1981) (research in public library).

[25] *See, e.g.,* Von Kahl v. United States, 242 F.3d 783, 791 (8th Cir. 2001) (Rule 606(b) does not prohibit jurors from testifying concerning impact of pretrial media publicity on deliberative process); United States v. Bruscino, 662 F.2d 450, 460 (7th Cir. 1981), *rev'd on other grounds,* 687 F.2d 938 (7th Cir. 1982) (testimony that juror carried newspaper clippings regarding case into jury room was properly admissible to impeach verdict).

- books or documents.[26]

- consultation during deliberations with parties, witnesses or other persons.[27]

When such factors were at work in the deliberative process, it is permissible for the court to take evidence concerning the general mental or emotional atmosphere in which the affected juror participated in the deliberations as the result of the extraneous influence, but it is not appropriate to take evidence concerning the directly affected juror's mental processes.[28] Although such evidence is admissible to impeach the jury's verdict, to obtain a mistrial on the basis of the evidence, the party adversely affected by the verdict must also show that the influence was extraneous or extrinsic, rather than intrinsic.[28.1] Moreover, the adversely affected party must show that the extraneous influence had an effect on the verdict.[29]

An individual juror's testimony to the effect that an improper influence had on his or her mental processes in deciding matters committed to the jury's consideration is inadmissible, but testimony concerning the juror's general emotional reaction to the improper influence is not. The court may also consider a juror's testimony regarding any influence that such improper conduct or contacts had on the juror's abilities to receive the evidence fairly and impartially, to listen to the testimony presented, and to listen to the judge's instructions.[29.1]

---

[26] *See, e.g.,* United States v. Bassler, 651 F.2d 600, 602–603 (8th Cir. 1982).

[27] *See, e.g.,* United States v. Schwarz, 283 F.3d 76, 98–100 (2d Cir. 2002) (jury's receipt of information during deliberations that co-defendant pleaded guilty to charges warranted evidentiary hearing into effect information had on verdict because prejudicial effect of one defendant's admission of guilt on other defendant's defense can be substantial).

[28] *See, e.g.,* United States v. Elias, 269 F.3d 1003, 1020–1021 (9th Cir. 2001) (testimony regarding affected juror's mental processes in reaching verdict is barred by Rule 606(b), but testimony regarding juror's more general fear and anxiety following tampering incident is admissible for purposes of determining whether "there is a reasonable possibility that the extraneous contact affected the verdict").

[28.1] *See, e.g.,* United States v. Connolly, 341 F.3d 16, 34–35 (1st Cir. 2003) (notes jurors compiled after day's receipt of evidence were not extraneous influence, and therefore could not be used to impeach verdict).

[29] *See, e.g.,* Loliscio v. Goord, 263 F.3d 178, 189–191 (2d Cir. 2001) (jury's access to rumored information concerning defendant's criminal record was harmless when jury did not discuss information in any meaningful way, jury continued its deliberations for significant time following access to information, and there was substantial additional evidence of defendant's guilt).

[29.1] *See, e.g.,* United States v. Rutherford, 371 F.3d 634, 644 (9th Cir. 2004).

[c]—Restrictions Applicable Only to Post-Verdict Testimony

The restrictions in Rule 606(b) apply only to inquiry after the verdict or indictment (in the case of grand jurors) has been reached.[30] Thus, the restrictions do not prevent the trial judge from inquiring into the juror's mental processes during deliberations and before they have arrived at a verdict.[31] The court's ability to receive evidence of juror impropriety before receiving the verdict (for example, during the polling of the jury that occurs after the jury has returned its verdict in open court) reduces the risk that the jurors' incompetence to impeach their own verdict will result in Due Process violations resulting in defendants being unfairly convicted.[32] On the other hand, Rule 606(b)'s proscriptions apply as well to a partial verdict as they do to a complete verdict.[32.1]

Rule 606(b) does not, one court has held, bar a judge from questioning a jury that returns with an ambiguous or inconsistent verdict.[32.2]

[d]—Evidence of Juror's Incompetence to Serve and Jury Inadvertence

The courts have allowed only limited inquiry into a juror's mental incompetence or physical disability that might have interfered with his or her ability to reach a just verdict.[33] Moreover, Rule 606(b) prohibits a juror from testifying about alcohol and drug use by jurors during the trial.[34]

---

[30] *See, e.g.,* United States v. Rowe, 906 F.2d 654, 656 n.3 (11th Cir. 1990) (district court conducted proper inquiry into alleged juror impropriety involving outside influences, occurring before verdict was rendered, since Fed. R. Evid. 606(b) is relevant only in those inquiries that occur after return of verdict or issuance of indictment).

[31] *See, e.g.,* United States v. Richards, 241 F.3d 335, 343–344 (3d Cir. 2001) (trial court did not abuse its discretion in denying new trial on basis of one juror's affidavit that two other jurors had prematurely determined defendant's guilt because investigation of irregularity would require evidence inadmissible under Rule 606(b); if juror had come forth before verdict was reached, court could have inquired into effect premature determination of guilt had on decision-making process of other jurors).

[32] *See, e.g.,* Anderson v. Miller, 346 F.3d 315, 328–330 (2d Cir. 2003) (although allegations of juror misconduct may raise concern that defendant did not receive fair trial, fact that affected jurors had numerous opportunities to inform court of misconduct during trial and before court received verdict mitigate that concern).

[32.1] *See, e.g.,* United States v. Stover, 329 F.3d 859, 865–866 (D.C. Cir. 2003)(once partial verdict has been recorded, juror may not impeach it with evidence of intrinsic factors relating to jury's deliberations, even though jury was not discharged after return of partial verdict).

[32.2] *See, e.g.,* Munafo v. Metropolitan Trans. Auth., 381 F.3d 99, 107 (2d Cir. 2004) (Rule 606 does not prevent inquiry to assure that verdict is accurate).

[33] *See, e.g.,* United States v. Webster, 960 F.2d 1301, 1306 (5th Cir. 1992) ("extremely strong showing" required to establish juror incompetence, in this case on ground of alleged inability to hear).

[34] Tanner v. United States, 483 U.S. 107, 116–128, 107 S. Ct. 2739, 97 L. Ed. 2d 90 (1987) (trial court properly refused to inquire into allegations by two jurors that other jurors had partaken

Rule 606(b) does not bar testimony by a juror that all the jurors agree that through inadvertence, oversight, or mistake the verdict announced was not the verdict on which agreement had been reached.[35] Individual jurors are, nevertheless, incompetent to testify that they, themselves, alone, were mistaken or unwilling in giving assent to the verdict.[36]

[e]—Effect of Juror Bias and Special Knowledge

Several types of jury conduct may present special difficulties. For instance, juror bias manifested in prejudiced comments during the deliberations may be viewed in a variety of ways. When the comments indicate that the juror had preconceived notions of liability or guilt or personal knowledge about the facts in issue, the statements may be admissible, not because they are not prohibited by Rule 606(b), but as tending to prove that the juror lied on the voir dire, a separate question from that of impeachment of verdicts.[37] On the other hand, it is often difficult to parse the existence of a single juror's bias and the impact that it may have had (or may not have had) on the verdict of the entire jury. The courts generally resolve the dilemma in favor of juror privacy; in the heat of debate jurors may make all kinds of statements, many of which have little effect on the verdict, even though, when they are taken out of context, they seem damning, indeed. If the evidence before the jury is strongly supportive of the verdict the jury reached, evidence of a single juror's bias is likely to be disregarded as non-prejudicial.[38]

The Constitution and American notions of fair play and justice, however, might be offended if all instances of expressions of bias by an individual juror were

---

substantial amounts of alcohol and marijuana during several lunch breaks; "[d]rugs or alcohol voluntarily ingested by a juror [are] no more an 'outside influence' than a virus, poorly prepared food, or lack of sleep").

[35] *See, e.g.,* Attridge v. Cencorp Div. of Dover Technologies Int'l, Inc., 836 F.2d 113, 117 (2d Cir. 1987) (trial court properly considered interviews of jurors to determine whether correct verdict was announced and recorded); United States v. Dobson, 817 F.2d 1127, 1130 (5th Cir. 1987), *vacated in part on other grounds,* 821 F.2d 1034 (5th Cir. 1987) (district court's ex parte correction of verdict, after jury had been polled and discharged, to acquit defendant on one of ten counts of tax evasion was proper when phone conversations with two jurors and foreman indicated that jury had unanimously acquitted defendant on one count).

[36] *See, e.g.,* McNulty v. Borden, Inc., 542 F. Supp. 655, 657 (E.D. Pa. 1982); *but see* United States v. Ortiz, 942 F.2d 903, 913 (5th Cir. 1991).

[37] *See, e.g.,* United States v. Henley, 238 F.3d 1111, 1121 (9th Cir. 2001) (evidence of juror's racist remarks was admissible under Rule 606(b) to show that juror lied during voir dire when he was asked specific questions about racial bias and swore that racial bias would play no part in his deliberations).

[38] *See, e.g.,* Fields v. Woodford, 281 F.3d 963, 975–976 (9th Cir. 2002) (comments by several jurors during deliberations that "if defendant would kill a member of his own race [African-American], he would not hesitate to kill a white person" disregarded in view of overwhelming evidence of defendant's guilt on all charged counts).

ignored. As the Supreme Court noted long ago, "[t]here might be instances in which such testimony of the juror could not be excluded without 'violating the plain principles of justice.' "[39]

When a juror resorts to knowledge obtained outside the record also presents difficulties. A juror who conducted an experiment or read a book not introduced in evidence would be competent to testify about it under Rule 606(b), as would other members of the jury.[40] If a juror has specialized knowledge, however, the answer is not so clear. Jurors are expected to bring a certain amount of common knowledge with them into the jury room.[41] A juror's possession of even more specialized knowledge, however, presents problems the courts have not resolved. Though exclusion of evidence that the knowledgeable juror shared his or her knowledge with the other jurors during their deliberations appears to be consistent with the rationale of Rule 606(b), in a criminal case it might be inconsistent with the right to confront adverse witnesses.[42] On the other hand, when a juror's specialized knowledge was fully revealed during jury selection, it can reasonably be expected that the juror will share the knowledge with other jurors, and the courts are likely to give little credence to the argument that he or she engaged in jury misconduct when doing so.[42.1] In any event, proof that extraneous information reached jurors from outside sources, even if the outside source is one of the jurors, will not provide grounds for a new trial if the circumstances indicate that the information in question did not affect the verdict.[43]

The question is much clearer if the juror brings into the jury room information

---

[39] McDonald v. Pless, 238 U.S. 264, 268–269, 35 S. Ct. 783, 59 L. Ed. 1300 (1915); *see also* United States v. Henley, 238 F.3d 1111, 1119–1120 (9th Cir. 2001) (on allegation that juror made bigoted remarks during trial after denying racial prejudice at voir dire, trial court must determine whether juror made such remarks and harbored prejudice sufficient to affect verdict; if so, defendant is entitled to new trial).

[40] *See, e.g.,* Anderson v. Ford Motor Co., 186 F.3d 918, 921 (8th Cir. 1999) (juror's improper out-of-court experiment warranted new trial because it involved controlling issue in case and prejudiced losing party).

[41] *See, e.g.,* Rahn v. Junction City Foundry, Inc., 161 F. Supp. 2d 1219, 1247 (D. Kan. 2001) (jurors' experiences with sexual harassment sensitivity training at work were in nature of common knowledge, which all jurors are expected to use during their deliberations, and is not basis for challenging validity of verdict).

[42] *See* **Treatise** at § 606.04[5] for discussion of relationship between Confrontation Clause and Rule 606(b).

[42.1] *See, e.g.,* Fullwood v. Lee, 290 F.3d 663, 683–684 (4th Cir. 2002) (defendant could reasonably have expected juror with background in criminal justice would share special knowledge concerning appeals of criminal cases and potential for parole when life sentences are imposed when juror's background was revealed during voir dire).

[43] *See, e.g.,* United States v. Byrne, 171 F.3d 1231, 1236 (10th Cir. 1999) ("when extraneous printed material is sent out of the jury room promptly upon its discovery and each juror has sworn under oath that he or she did not read the material, there is *not even the slight[est] possibility* that the material affected the verdict") (emphasis in original).

relating to the specific factual questions the case raises. If the juror shares that information with the other jurors and it relates to consequential factual issues, evidence of such misconduct is generally admissible and grounds for granting a new trial.[44] The prejudice such information inflicts is of even more significance in criminal cases, in which Constitutional rights, such as the right to confront adverse witnesses, are implicated.[45]

Rule 606(b) is silent as to whether evidence should be permitted that the jurors reached a verdict by an improper method such as a majority vote, a quotient of the individual juror's awards, or a chance manner such as drawing lots. The Advisory Committee Note, however, expressly addresses the question of the admissibility of such evidence, and indicated that jurors could not impeach their verdict with such testimony.[46]

[4]—Role of Court When Misconduct Is Alleged[1]

In determining how a court should react to allegations of juror misconduct, a number of distinctions have to be drawn consonant with the rationale of Rule 606(b). If a party alleges the sort of misconduct about which testimony would be barred, the judge should conclude that further inquiry would be futile. Accordingly, the court should refuse to schedule a hearing, and will deny a motion for a new trial.[2]

There is some uncertainty about whether a hearing must be held whenever a party asserts that there has been misconduct which is not on its face barred by Rule

---

[44] *See, e.g.,* Hard v. Burlington Northern R.R., 812 F.2d 482, 486 (9th Cir. 1987) (in an FELA action brought by a railroad worker in which plaintiff was awarded minimal damages, trial court abused its discretion by not allowing evidentiary hearing into juror's failure to disclose on voir dire that he had previously worked for defendant and his subsequently telling other jurors that defendant-railroad pays all medical expenses of injured employees; when juror's past personal experiences "are related to the litigation, as they are here, they constitute extraneous evidence which may be used to impeach the jury's verdict.").

[45] *See, e.g.,* Doan v. Brigano, 237 F.3d 722, 729–736 (6th Cir. 2001) (juror's telling other jurors, during deliberations, about her out-of-court experiment violated defendant's right to confront adverse witnesses); *see also* **Treatise** at § 606.04[2][d] for discussion of when jurors become "witnesses" for purposes of the Confrontation Clause.

[46] Fed. R. Evid. 606(b) Advisory Committee's Note (1972) at **Treatise** § 606App.01[2]; *see, e.g.,* Scogin v. Century Fitness, Inc., 780 F.2d 1316, 1319–1320 (8th Cir. 1985) (testimony that juror told witness jury had used quotient verdict barred by Rule 606(b)); Multiflex, Inc. v. Samuel Moore & Co., 709 F.2d 980, 998 (5th Cir. 1983) (trial court properly ignored defendant's claim that jury awarded impermissible punitive damages or arrived at a "quotient verdict").

[1] *See* **Treatise** at § 606.05.

[2] *See, e.g.,* United States v. Gonzales, 227 F.3d 520, 525–526 (6th Cir. 2000) (trial court erred in holding hearing in response to post-verdict letter from juror that contained only information concerning matters as to which Rule 606(b) prohibited judicial inquiry).

606(b). While some courts require an evidentiary hearing whenever such mis-conduct is alleged,[3] others require a preliminary "sufficient showing" of miscon-duct.[4] It has also been held that it is within the judge's discretion to determine if a hearing is warranted.[5]

When a hearing is held, the jurors may testify to those irregularities whose proof is not barred by the Rule. May they, however, testify to the effect such irregularities had on their minds? The language of Rule 606(b)—"a juror may not testify . . . to the effect of anything upon his or any other juror's mind or emotions"—can be read as meaning that even a juror who is testifying about extraneous information or outside influence may not be interrogated about its impact.[6] A few courts, however, have read the quoted language as relevant solely to drawing the line between misconduct which is subject to inquiry, and misconduct which is not.[7]

Some courts walk the line very finely, by holding that jurors who were the subject of an unsuccessful tampering attempt cannot testify to the impact of the attempt on their decision-making process, but may testify to whether the tampering incident infected the juror with generalized fear and anxiety, which would be admissible under Rule 606(b) as pertinent to the determination whether there was a reasonable probability the incident influenced the verdict.[8]

The courts that read Rule 606(b) as precluding inquiry into the effect that irregularities had on the minds of individual jurors or the jury as a whole never-theless recognize that persons adversely affected by a verdict must, in some instances, be allowed to show prejudice resulting from the irregularity. Because of Rule 606(b)'s proscription of impact evidence, those courts require the party adversely affected by the verdict to show prejudice resulting from the irregularity by demonstrating its impact "on a hypothetical average juror," rather than showing

---

[3] United States v. Davis, 177 F.3d 552, 557 (6th Cir. 1999) (court erred in not questioning all jurors about effect of prejudicial extraneous information).

[4] See, e.g., United States v. Lanas, 324 F.3d 894, 903–904 (7th Cir. 2003) (trial court is under no obligation to investigate possibility of extraneous influence on jury unless requesting party has made some showing of taint).

[5] United States v. Sharpe, 193 F.3d 852, 862 (5th Cir. 1999) (court's decision to hold hearing to determine whether juror misconduct occurred was not abuse of discretion).

[6] See, e.g., United States v. Richards, 241 F.3d 335, 342 (3d Cir. 2001) (trial court properly refused, after jury's verdict, to consider evidence that two jurors had revealed to other jurors their premature opinion of defendant's guilt before conclusion of evidence, because considering effect of jurors' misconduct would require court to inquire into thought processes of other jurors in reaching their verdicts, in contravention of Rule 606(b)).

[7] United States v. Bishawi, 272 F.3d 458, 461–463 (7th Cir. 2001) (when trial judge made ex parte contacts with jury during deliberations, before granting new trial, court must hold evidentiary hearing to determine how contacts affected jurors and whether party adversely affected by verdict was prejudiced by contacts).

[8] See, e.g., United States v. Henley, 238 F.3d 1111, 1118 (9th Cir. 2001).

prejudice by demonstrating the irregularity's impact on actual jurors.[9]

The courts generally aid parties adversely affected by verdicts that may have been affected by jury irregularities to carry their burden of showing prejudice by applying a presumption of prejudice to certain irregularities: private contacts, communications, or tampering with a juror or the jury as a whole during its deliberations in connection with a matter that is a subject of their deliberations.[10]

It is not every instance of unauthorized conduct or contact that causes a presumption of prejudice to arise, however. To "determine whether the jury might have been prejudiced, it may be necessary to inquire into the jurors' perceptions of the conduct and any effect the conduct may have had on their ability to remain impartial and unbiased." If the trial court determines that the unauthorized conduct or contact is potentially prejudicial, it is the burden of the opposing party to prove a lack of prejudice.[10.1]

The presumption of prejudice survived the adoption of the Rules of Evidence, but it is not irrebuttable.[11] The presumption may be overcome by uncorroborated testimony from the jurors, themselves, that the private contacts, communications, or attempted tampering did not affect them in their deliberations.[11.1]

In cases involving a jury's access to extraneous information, some courts apply the presumption of prejudice invariably.[12] In other courts, the availability of the presumption in extraneous information cases depends on the whether the information relates closely to an issue that is of significance to the matters the jury is deliberating.[13]

---

[9] *See, e.g.,* Loliscio v. Goord, 263 F.3d 178, 186–187 (2d Cir. 2001).

[10] *See, e.g.,* Remmer v. United States, 347 U.S. 227, 229, 74 S. Ct. 450, 98 L. Ed. 654 (1954).

[10.1] *See, e.g.,* United States v. Rutherford, 371 F.3d 634, 641–642 (9th Cir. 2004) ("appropriate inquiry is whether the unauthorized conduct or contact is potentially prejudicial, not whether the parties alleged to have tampered with the jury did so intentionally"; here, presence of several IRS agents in courtroom, allegedly glaring at jury, may have created presumption of prejudice; remanding to trial court for appropriate inquiry).

[11] *See, e.g.,* United States v. Bishawi, 272 F.3d 458, 461–463 (7th Cir. 2001) (although private contacts with jurors concerning pertinent matter is presumptively prejudicial, presumption can be rebutted by showing contact was harmless).

[11.1] *See, e.g.,* United States v. Corrado, 304 F.3d 593, 603 (6th Cir. 2002) (when all jurors testified at *Remmer* hearing that they were not affected in their deliberations by attempted tampering respecting one alternate juror, it was defendant's burden to show tampering effort resulted in prejudice).

[12] *See, e.g.,* Mayhue v. St. Francis Hosp., Inc., 969 F.2d 919, 922 (10th Cir. 1992).

[13] *See, e.g.,* United States v. Lloyd, 269 F.3d 228, 238–239 (3d Cir. 2001) (presumption of prejudice is applicable when ex parte contact "is of a considerably serious nature", such as direct contact with sitting juror, but not when contact is not serious, such as exposure to information in media).

When the presumption is unavailable, the court must review the record as a whole, analyzing the irregularity and the evidence that was properly before the jury, to assess the probability of prejudicial effect. Some of the factors that go into that assessment include the following:[14]

- The relationship between the elements the jury had to have decided against the complaining party and any extraneous evidence that was before the jury as the result of the irregularity.

- The point in the course of the jury's deliberations at which the irregularity occurred.

- The length of the jury's deliberations and the structure of its verdict.

- Whether the trial court instructed the jury to disregard any extrinsic evidence that may come to its attention.

- The nature and extent of evidence properly before the jury supporting the verdict.

[5]—The Propriety of Counsel's Interviewing Jurors After Verdict[1]

Rule 606(b) says nothing about the propriety of counsel's interviewing jurors after they have been discharged in an attempt to discover details of juror conduct which could be used to support or resist a motion to set aside a verdict.

Some courts require counsel or a party to obtain permission before beginning post-verdict interviews of jurors.[2] When members of the jury contact defense attorney to instigate post-verdict interviews, however, the failure to provide opposing counsel and the court with notice that interviews are about to occur is not an appropriate ground for denying an evidentiary hearing into the matters revealed during those interviews, particularly if the defendant's Sixth Amendment right to trial by impartial jurors is implicated.[3]

The American Bar Association's Model Code of Professional Responsibility permits post-verdict interviews of jurors without court supervision.[4] Its Rule 3.5 nevertheless provides:

---

[14] *See, e.g.,* United States v. Lloyd, 269 F.3d 228, 239–243 (3d Cir. 2001); *see also* Fed. R. Civ. P. 59; Fed. R. Crim. P. 33; *see generally* 12 MOORE'S FEDERAL PRACTICE, Ch. 59, *New Trials; Amendment of Judgments* (Matthew Bender 3d ed.); 26 MOORE'S FEDERAL PRACTICE, Ch. 633, *New Trial* (Matthew Bender 3d ed.).

[1] *See* **Treatise** at § 606.06.

[2] *See, e.g.,* Cuevas v. United States, 317 F.3d 751, 752–753 (7th Cir. 2003) (when defendant failed to obtain permission of trial judge before conducting post-verdict interviews of jurors, as local rules required, trial court did not abuse its discretion in refusing to consider evidence of juror misconduct obtained through those unauthorized interviews).

[3] *See, e.g.,* United States v. Schwarz, 283 F.3d 76, 98–99 (2d Cir. 2002).

[4] *See* **Treatise** at § 606.06.

A lawyer shall not:

(a) seek to influence a judge, juror, prospective juror or other official by means prohibited by law;

(b) communicate *ex parte* with such a person except as permitted by law. . . .

It is within the trial court's power to order that all interviews be conducted under its supervision.[5]

A post-trial interview of jurors may arise from motives other than a search for flaws in the verdict. Sometimes a practitioner wishes to find out what impression he or she made on the triers of the facts or what witness or item of evidence weighed most heavily. Interviews based on such motives, or on pure curiosity, encounter in some jurisdictions disapproval similar to that directed at interviews aimed at undermining a verdict.[6]

Talking to jurors about their deliberations no matter for what purpose has an objection whose weight may vary from judge to judge. If such interviews achieve sufficient frequency, the expectation of them may make jurors, knowing that they will be asked to explain their verdict, more cautious in their deliberations. Post-trial interviews, that is to say, tend to erode the secrecy of the jury room.

Before interviewing jurors after trial for any purpose, therefore, the trial practitioner should study the precedents, court rules and ethical determinations of his or her jurisdiction. In addition, total prudence calls for asking the trial judge for his or her views on the propriety of post-trial interviews of jurors.[7]

To prevent harassment of jurors in cases that have attracted great public attention, the court may prevent interviews by counsel.[8] It should inform jurors that they are not obligated to speak to anyone. Protection against the press is warranted by arranging, at the jurors' request, for the jury to be taken out by a rear exit and

---

[5] *See, e.g.,* United States v. Cauble, 532 F. Supp. 804 (E.D. Tex. 1982), *aff'd,* 757 F.2d 282 (5th Cir. 1985).

[6] Haeberle v. Texas International Airlines, 739 F.2d 1019 (5th Cir. 1984); United States v. Balistrieri, 577 F. Supp. 1532 (E.D. Wis. 1984).

[7] *See, e.g.,* United States v. Logan, 250 F.3d 350, 377–381 (6th Cir. 2001) (trial court properly refused permission for counsel for defendant to interview jurors, since evidence of alleged misconduct was barred by Rule 606(b)).

[8] *See* Economou v. Little, 850 F. Supp. 849, 853 (N.D.Cal. 1994) (in civil rights action, defendants moved for court to release names, addresses, and telephone numbers of jurors who found them liable of using unreasonable force in arresting plaintiff; denying motion, court held that, under Fed. R. Evid. 606(b), it would be inappropriate to release this information weeks after trial without preliminary showing that there had been some kind of jury misconduct).

furnished with transportation to their homes.

CHAPTER 12

*Credibility**

SYNOPSIS

---

* Chapter revised in 1995 by WALTER BARTHOLD, member of the New York Bar.

§ 12.01 Impeachment and Rehabilitation[1]

[1]—Overview

The Federal Rules of Evidence do not comprehensively treat either impeachment or rehabilitation. Rather, a few aspects of each are expressly covered. Rules 608 and 609 (*see* §§ 12.03, 12.04) govern impeachment by evidence of character and conviction of crime, respectively; Rule 613 (*see* § 12.06) establishes the foundation requirements for impeachment by prior inconsistent statements; Rule 610 (*see* § 12.05) abolishes impeachment by evidence of religious belief; and Rule 608 (*see* 12.03[5]) deals with some aspects of rehabilitating testimony.

At common law—apart from observed reaction in the courtroom—there were six modes of impeachment: by proof of bias, mental incapacity, contradiction, prior inconsistent statement, bad character including conviction, and religious belief. Because these matters originally related to competency and were only gradually and at different times converted into questions of credibility, each mode of impeachment was treated separately by the courts and developed its own unique distinctions and limitations. Such an approach is outmoded and should be discarded under the Federal Rules of Evidence. Technicalities submerge the basic aim of all credibility rules, namely, that evidence should be admitted if it better enables the trier of fact to determine when a witness is lying or telling the truth. Analysis of the proffered evidence in terms of its capacity to shed light on the particular witness's credibility eliminates the so-called "collateral" test insofar as it is mechanically applied, and simplifies many of the artificial rules and exceptions that evolved in connection with the use of prior statements. See discussion in [4], *below*.

Although the Federal Rules do not expressly cover all aspects of credibility, a recasting of the case law is appropriate because of the overriding mandate expressed in Rules 102, 401, and 403, emphasizing the need for relevant evidence that enhances the possibility of ascertaining the truth and doing justice. Evidence offered for impeachment should be analyzed in terms of the criteria of Rules 401 and 403. Is its probative value on the assessment of credibility high enough to warrant admission in the light of the dangers specified in Rule 403?[1] Evidence that passes these hurdles as to a particular theory of impeachment is admissible even

---

[1] *See* **Treatise** at § 607.03.

[1] *See, e.g.,* United States v. Robinson, 530 F.2d 1076, 1081 (D.C. Cir. 1976) ("[I]f the prejudice outweighs the benefit, the judge sometimes excludes the evidence with the conclusory comment that the case involves only 'collateral' character impeachment; while if high probative value offsets slight prejudice, he may say that the evidence is admissible impeachment for bias. To avoid the possibility that confusion may lurk in such labeling and shorthand, it would be preferable to confront the problem explicitly, acknowledging and weighing both the prejudice and the probative worth of impeachment in the spirit of balancing stressed in the newly effective Federal Rules.") (footnotes omitted). *Cf.* Rule 609(a), as amended in 1990, discussed at § 12.04.

if it would have to be excluded if offered on another theory.[2]

The Supreme Court has held that illegally obtained evidence may be used for impeachment.[3] It should, however, be excluded if it is unreliable or otherwise incapable of passing a Rule 403 balancing test.[4]

[2]—Impeachment: Bias[1]

[a]—Generally

Impeachment by showing the witness to be biased rests on two assumptions: (1) that certain relationships and circumstances impair the impartiality of a witness and (2) that a witness who is not impartial may—sometimes consciously but perhaps unwittingly—shade testimony in favor of or against a party.[2] Since bias is always significant in assessing the witness's credibility, the trier must be sufficiently informed of the underlying relationships, circumstances and influences operating on the witness so that in the light of experience the trier can determine whether a mistake or lie by the witness could reasonably be expected as a probable human reaction.

Courts are, therefore, liberal in accepting testimony relevant to bias.[2.1] The

---

[2] United States v. Abel, 469 U.S. 45, 105 S. Ct. 465, 83 L. Ed. 2d 450 (1984) ("[T]here is no rule of evidence which provides that testimony admissible for one purpose and inadmissible for another purpose is thereby rendered inadmissible; quite the contrary is the case. It would be a strange rule of law which held that relevant, competent evidence which tended to show bias on the part of a witness was nonetheless inadmissible because it also tended to show that the witness was a liar.").

[3] See Michigan v. Harvey, 494 U.S. 344, 110 S. Ct. 1176, 108 L. Ed. 2d 293 (1990) (statements taken in violation of defendant's sixth amendment right to counsel may be used to impeach the defendant); Harris v. New York, 401 U.S. 222, 91 S. Ct. 643, 28 L. Ed. 2d 1 (1971). See discussion of impeachment by illegally obtained evidence in **Treatise** at § 607.10. But see James v. Illinois, 493 U.S. 307, 110 S. Ct. 648, 107 L. Ed. 2d 676 (1990) (holding that the Harris impeachment exception is limited to defendant's own testimony; prosecution may not use illegally obtained evidence to impeach defense witnesses).

[4] See, e.g., discussion at [4], below, of limiting impeachment by contradiction even when it satisfies the constitutional test set forth by the Supreme Court in United States v. Havens, 446 U.S. 620, 100 S. Ct. 1912, 64 L. Ed. 2d 559 (1980).

[1] See **Treatise** at § 607.04.

[2] United States v. Abel, 469 U.S. 45, 105 S. Ct. 465, 469, 83 L. Ed. 2d 450 (1984) ("Bias is a term used in the 'common law of evidence' to describe the relationship between a party and a witness which might lead the witness to slant, unconsciously or otherwise, his testimony in favor or against a party.").

[2.1] See, e.g., United States v. Hankey, 203 F.3d 1160, 1171–1173 (9th Cir. 2000), cert. denied, — U.S. —, 120 S. Ct. 2733 (2000) (evidence that defendant and defense witness were both members of same gang and that witness would be beaten or killed if he testified against defendant was properly admitted to show witness's bias towards defendant and motive to lie to protect himself); United States v. Manske, 186 F.3d 770, 777 (7th Cir. 1999) ("Bias is always relevant, and parties should be granted reasonable latitude in cross-examining target witnesses"); Schledwitz v. United

Supreme Court explained in *United States v. Abel*:

> Proof of bias is almost always relevant because the jury, as finder of fact and weigher of credibility, has historically been entitled to assess all evidence which might bear on the accuracy and truth of a witness's testimony. The "common law of evidence" allowed the showing of bias by extrinsic evidence, while requiring the cross-examiner to "take the answer of the witness" with respect to less favored forms of impeachment.[3]

The exposure of a witness's motivation in testifying is so significant that in a criminal case curtailment of this right may amount to a denial of confrontation[4] or due process[5] rights. Even when there has been a restriction on cross-examination, however, the error may, at times, constitute only harmless albeit constitutional error.[6]

States, 169 F.3d 1003, 1015 (6th Cir. 1999) ("Bias is always relevant in assessing a witness's credibility"); *but see* Outley v. City of New York, 837 F.2d 587, 594 (2d Cir. 1988) (in civil rights action alleging police brutality, it was reversible error to permit cross-examination and argument concerning the plaintiff's prior lawsuits against law enforcement officers; with no evidence of a pattern of fraudulent lawsuits; this evidence was more of an attack on the plaintiff's character than a showing of bias).

[3] 105 S. Ct. at 469.

[4] Davis v. Alaska, 415 U.S. 308, 316–317, 94 S. Ct. 1105, 39 L. Ed. 2d 347 (1974) (state's interest in protecting the confidentiality of juvenile offenders' records must yield when the witness's probationary status following a juvenile adjudication provides a basis for inferring undue prosecutorial pressures or a motive to lie because of possible concern at being suspected as the perpetrator of the charged crime); United States v. Lynn, 856 F.2d 430, 432–434 (1st Cir. 1988) (error to cut off questioning concerning polygraph test, which witness took as part of his plea agreement with the government); United States v. Anderson, 881 F.2d 1128, 1136–1139 (D.C. Cir. 1989) (defendant's right of confrontation violated when trial court refused to permit cross-examination of key prosecution witness about recent dismissal of murder charge against her).

[5] Giglio v. United States, 405 U.S. 150, 92 S. Ct. 763, 31 L. Ed. 2d 104 (1972) (where witness, upon whose testimony government's case depended almost entirely, has been promised immunity from prosecution, a failure to disclose promise amounted to a denial of due process). *Cf.* Pennsylvania v. Ritchie, 480 U.S. 39, 107 S. Ct. 989, 94 L. Ed. 2d 40 (1987) (no violation of the confrontation clause was found where defendant had been able to effectively cross–examine the witnesses against him, notwithstanding the prosecution had denied defendant access to certain files; the ability to question adverse witnesses does not include the power to require the pretrial disclosure of any and all information that might be useful in contradicting unfavorable testimony).

[6] Delaware v. Van Arsdall, 475 U.S. 673, 684, 106 S. Ct. 1431, 89 L. Ed. 2d 674 (1986) ("[T]he constitutionally improper denial of a defendant's opportunity to impeach a witness for bias, like other Confrontation Clause errors, is subject to *Chapman* harmless-error analysis. The correct inquiry is whether, assuming that the damaging potential of the cross-examination were fully realized, a reviewing court might nonetheless say that the error was harmless beyond a reasonable doubt. Whether such an error is harmless in a particular case depends upon a host of factors, all readily accessible to reviewing courts. These factors include the importance of the witness's testimony in the prosecution's case, whether the testimony was cumulative, the presence or absence

Some limitations on introducing evidence for the purpose of establishing bias do exist. In the first place, the proffered evidence must meet the relevancy test of Rule 401 in that it must tend to show that the likelihood of bias that might affect the trier's evaluation of credibility is more probable than it would have been without the evidence.[7] Secondly, the trial court has a "wide latitude" in imposing "reasonable limits" on cross-examination into questions of bias.[8] While the court will not cut off completely all inquiry into bias, it may limit the scope of the inquiry in order to protect a party from prejudice,[9] or a witness from unnecessary harassment or to further the policies of some other evidentiary rule.[10] The trial court may also limit the extent of cross-examination into bias if the witness invokes the

---

of evidence corroborating or contradicting the testimony of the witness on material points, the extent of cross-examination otherwise permitted, and, of course, the overall strength of the prosecution's case"); see United States v. Towne, 870 F.2d 880, 886–887 (2d Cir. 1989) (although court should have allowed defense to question witness about state charges pending against him, error was harmless); see also United States v. Anderson, 881 F.2d 1128, 1140 (D.C. Cir. 1989).

[7] United States v. Williams, 875 F.2d 846, 852 (11th Cir. 1989) (no error in exclusion of evidence that defendant's secretary, who testified for prosecution, had borne child of man involved in litigation with defendant; defendant failed to demonstrate a connection between the affair, the prior litigation and the present case and mere assertion of relationship does not suffice).

[8] Delaware v. Van Arsdall, 475 U.S. 673, 679, 106 S. Ct. 1431, 89 L. Ed. 2d 674 (1986) ("It does not follow, of course, that the Confrontation Clause of the Sixth Amendment prevents a trial judge from imposing any limits on defense counsel's inquiry into the potential bias of a prosecution witness. On the contrary, trial judges retain wide latitude insofar as the Confrontation Clause is concerned to impose reasonable limits on such cross-examination based on concerns about, among other things, harassment, prejudice, confusion of the issues, the witness's safety, or interrogation that is repetitive or only marginally relevant."). See United States v. Candoli, 870 F.2d 496, 503–504 (9th Cir. 1989) (in prosecution for arson, trial court did not abuse its discretion in refusing to allow defense to cross-examine the federal agent in charge of the investigation, concerning his three-day suspension for releasing internal forms to the insurance companies that had insured the businesses in the building in which the arson occurred; evidence was cumulative because even without it the jury could reasonably infer that a law enforcement officer would be "biased" against the defendant).

[9] United States v. Abel, 469 U.S. 45, 105 S. Ct. 465, 470, 83 L. Ed. 2d 450 (1984) (where trial court properly allowed proof that defendant and witness belonged to same organization, and that organization was a secret prison sect sworn to perjury and self-protection, court did not err in excluding name of organization, and in sustaining defense objections to prosecutor's questions about the punishment meted out to unfaithful members: "These precautions did not prevent all prejudice to respondent . . ., but they did in our opinion ensure that the admission of this highly probative evidence did not unduly prejudice respondent."); United States v. Kopituk, 690 F.2d 1289, 1336–1337 (11th Cir. 1982) (where defense was permitted to show witness's participation in plot to kill business associate, no error to have prohibited questioning about the proposed method of killing with ice-pick which court felt would only inflame jury).

[10] See, e.g., United States v. Tracey, 675 F.2d 433, 437 (1st Cir. 1982) (no abuse of discretion in trial court refusing to allow defense to question only prosecution witness about incident in which then United States Attorney had come to bail him out after arrest for drunkenness; trial court excluded evidence out of concern that allowing the inquiry would result in testimony by United States Attorney; appellate court found that jury had heard considerable other evidence from which

constitutional privilege against self-incrimination.[11]

Except for the rare case where a witness admits that the testimony would be affected by the witness's feelings towards a party,[12] bias can only be demonstrated circumstantially, that is, by proof of relationship, conduct, or utterances. A precise catalogue of the sources of bias, is impossible, but certain situations recur so often that they raise immediate suspicion of bias. A careful advocate should look for such situations in scrutinizing the background of prospective witnesses before trial to determine whether they are vulnerable to impeachment. If the witness seems highly vulnerable, counsel should ascertain whether the same point could be made by someone less susceptible to attack. If the witness is indispensable and irreplaceable, counsel will have to prepare him or her to withstand the attack. Counsel should also arrange for rehabilitating testimony when allowable.

Relationships between a party and a witness are always relevant to a showing of bias, whether the relationship is based on ties of family, sex—heterosexual[13] or homosexual,[14] money,[15] membership in organizations,[16] friendship,[17] enmity,[18] or

---

it could deduce relationship between government and witness, and that proffered evidence was cumulative).

[11] *See, e.g.,* Coil v. United States, 343 F.2d 573, 577–579 (8th Cir. 1965) (court allowed witness to invoke privilege against self-incrimination when questioned about two unrelated crimes involving narcotics; theory of defense was that witness would steal, burglarize or lie to obtain narcotics). *But cf.* United States v. Kaplan, 832 F.2d 676 (1st Cir. 1987) (citing **Treatise**; error, but harmless, for court to prohibit any questioning that would cause government witness to invoke the fifth amendment before the jury; the invocation of the privilege is a form of impeachment).

[12] There is no hearsay problem because the evidence is being used to show the witness's state of mind. *See* Rules 801(c), 803(3).

[13] *See, e.g.,* United States v. Willis, 647 F.2d 54 (9th Cir. 1981) (denial of defendant's right to confrontation necessitating reversal to have prohibited defendant from cross-examining narcotics agent about his alleged sexual relationship with defendant's live-in girlfriend who had been chief informant).

[14] But evidence of homosexuality may be so prejudicial as to warrant exclusion under Rule 403 if the prejudice substantially outweighs the probative value. *See, e.g.,* United States v. Wright, 489 F.2d 1181, 1186 (D.C. Cir. 1973) (proof of homosexual advances excluded despite relevancy because conduct was ambiguous and potentially prejudicial).

[15] *See, e.g.,* Collins v. Wayne Corp., 621 F.2d 777, 784 (5th Cir. 1980) (since pecuniary interest in outcome of case may bias witness, appropriate to cross-examine expert witness about fees earned in prior cases).

[16] *See* United States v. Abel, 469 U.S. 45, 105 S. Ct. 465, 83 L. Ed. 2d 450 (1984) (witness and defendant were members of secret prison organization); United States v. Hankey, 203 F.3d 1160, 1167–1172 (9th Cir. 2000) (since defendant and testifying co-defendant were members of same gang, trial court properly admitted expert testimony regarding repercussions against gang members for testifying against other gang members to impeach testimony given by co-defendant that was exculpatory of defendant).

[17] *See, e.g.,* United States v. Robinson, 530 F.2d 1076, 1080 (D.C. Cir. 1976) ("open to the government . . . to reveal aspects of [witness's] relationship evidencing a special partiality toward

fear.[19]

The witness's relationship with the litigation or with another witness is also significant. In a criminal case, bias may be manifested by the witness's legal status and treatment. Jurors may take into consideration that a witness was a paid informer,[20] was paid maintenance costs as a material witness in protective custody,[21] was a co-indictee,[22] was granted immunity,[23] hoped to have his sentence reduced,[24] or had received or expected other special treatment.[25] If the witness is crucial to the government's case, appellate courts are particularly careful to scrutinize the cross-examination in its entirety—a number of errors insufficient in themselves to warrant reversal may cumulatively convince the court that the jury was not afforded sufficient glimpses into the workings of the witness's mind for it to assess his motivation in testifying.

The identity and residence of the witness are also relevant to bias in two respects. In the first place, "[t]he witness's name and address open countless avenues of

---

defendant and particular motive to testify falsely on his behalf").

[18] *See, e.g.,* Dick v. Watonwan County, 562 F. Supp. 1083 (D. Minn. 1983), *rev'd on other grounds,* 738 F.2d 939 (8th Cir. 1984) (not error to permit plaintiff's daughter to testify concerning her rebuff of sexual advances made by a defense witness).

[19] United States v. Bratton, 875 F.2d 439, 443–444 (5th Cir. 1989) (no error in government's showing that defendant had previously physically abused his wife and threatened her with a gun as this conduct of defendant could have induced wife to testify falsely out of fear of husband); United States v. Briggs, 457 F.2d 908 (2d Cir. 1972) (threats by defendant).

[20] *See, e.g.,* United States v. Leja, 568 F.2d 493 (6th Cir. 1977) (reversible error to preclude defense from cross-examining informer about his rate of reimbursement for the entire period of his employment; trial court had only permitted questions about amounts informer had received in instant case).

[21] *See* United States v. Librach, 520 F.2d 550 (8th Cir. 1975) (new trial required where government failed to disclose that principal witness was in protective custody, had been granted immunity, and had been paid almost $10,000).

[22] *See, e.g.,* United States v. Musgrave, 483 F.2d 327, 338 (5th Cir. 1973) (although witness had been acquitted, "prior status as coindictee certainly suggested a personal interest in the litigation, a potential lack of complete impartiality").

[23] *See, e.g.,* United States v. Scharf, 558 F.2d 498 (8th Cir. 1977) (once the witness is impeached, questions may arise as to whether the entire immunity-for-testimony agreement becomes admissible). *See, e.g.,* United States v. Rubier, 651 F.2d 628 (9th Cir. 1981).

[24] *See* United States v. Iverson, 648 F.2d 737 (D.C. Cir. 1981) (chief prosecution witness lied about sentencing status).

[25] *See, e.g.,* United States v. Garza, 574 F.2d 298 (5th Cir. 1978) (reduction of witness's bond); United States v. Wolfson, 437 F.2d 862 (2d Cir. 1970) (witness received no action letter from SEC). *See also* United States v. Anderson, 881 F.2d 1128, 1136–1139 (D.C. Cir. 1989) (defendant's right of confrontation violated when trial court refused to permit cross-examination of key prosecution witness about recent dismissal of murder charge against her); United States v. Lynn, 856 F.2d 430, 432–434 (1st Cir. 1988) (error to cut off questioning concerning polygraph test, which witness took as part of his plea agreement with the government).

in-court examination and out-of-court investigation."[26] Secondly, the witness's residence may be directly relevant to bias by disclosing to the jury "the setting in which to judge the character, veracity or bias of the witness."[27] The witness may, for instance, be in federal custody.[28]

The two-fold significance of residence has led the Supreme Court to hold in a number of cases that counsel may cross-examine a witness as to his or her present address without a preliminary indication of the relevancy of the inquiry.[29] District judges have, however, been understandably reluctant to force divulgence of a witness's address in cases where the witness fears that testifying is placing the witness or his or her family in danger. If the trial judge concludes that the need to protect the witness precludes divulgence of his exact address or place of employment, defendant is entitled to ask all other relevant questions bearing on credibility that would not affect the witness's safety.[30] Where there is hard evidence that the cross-examination is being conducted to punish, harass, or intimidate a witness or his family, the court is justified in taking strong steps to protect the witness by strictly controlling the examination.

[b]—Foundation Requirements

Courts disagree whether a foundation has to be laid on cross-examination before a witness can be impeached by extrinsic evidence of utterances or conduct indicating bias. Rule 613(b), which requires that a witness be afforded an opportunity to explain or deny when extrinsic evidence of a prior inconsistent statement is introduced, does not refer to impeachment by bias. Nor do the Advisory Committee's Notes to Rule 613 indicate whether the policy of the rule should be extended to the bias situation. Before the adoption of the Federal Rules of Evidence, the federal courts did tend to require a foundation for utterances of bias. It is, therefore, reasonable and appropriate to continue the foundation requirement for statements of bias to the extent required by Rule 613—that is, in most instances,

---

[26] Smith v. Illinois, 390 U.S. 129, 131, 88 S. Ct. 748, 19 L. Ed. 2d 956 (1968).

[27] United States v. Varella, 407 F.2d 735, 750 (7th Cir. 1969).

[28] Alford v. United States, 282 U.S. 687, 51 S. Ct. 218, 75 L. Ed. 624 (1931) (conviction reversed because defendant was not permitted to ascertain where witness lived).

[29] 282 U.S. at 693.

[30] United States v. Varella, 692 F.2d 1352, 1355–1356 (11th Cir. 1982) (after in camera hearing, court limited cross-examination of informants concerning their names, occupations, home and business addresses and names of other cases in which they had testified); United States v. Hughes, 658 F.2d 317 (5th Cir. 1981) (not plain error to sustain questions concerning witness's address where he was thoroughly cross-examined; extensive discussion). See also United States v. Palermo, 410 F.2d 468, 472–473 (7th Cir. 1969) ("government bears the burden of proving to the district judge the existence of such a threat" and must disclose the relevant information to the trial judge "in order that he could make an informed decision").

to give the witness an opportunity to explain or deny.[31]

On the other hand, evidence of biased *conduct* arguably remains exempt from a foundation requirement, since the notes to Rule 613(b) state that "the rule [on inconsistent statements] does not apply to impeachment by evidence of prior inconsistent conduct." Pursuant to Rule 611, the court may require such a foundation, but it should make its ruling before the witness steps down to prevent inadvertent preclusion of the cross-examiner from producing extrinsic proof of the acts tending to show bias.

The court has discretion to waive the requirement of a foundation. *See* Rule 611(a), which is discussed in Chapter 2. Careful counsel should either get an advance ruling on the court's position or actually lay the foundation to avoid the embarrassment of a ruling excluding the line of impeachment for failure to lay a foundation. In general, it is desirable to ask the witness sought to be impeached about the statements or acts believed to show bias. If the witness forthrightly admits, that ends the matter with a considerable saving of time and inconvenience to other witnesses.

[3]—Impeachment: Mental Incapacity[1]

[a]—Generally

Credibility can always be attacked by showing impairment in the witness's capacity to observe, remember or narrate. Consequently, the witness's capacity at the time of the event, as well as at the time of trial, are significant. Since defects of this nature reflect on mental capacity for truth-telling rather than on moral inducements for truth-telling, Rule 608 does not apply. The rationale for permitting evidence of less than normal mental capacity is obvious. A witness who is incapable of accurate observation, recollection, or communication is less capable than the average person of testifying truthfully, regardless of intent.

Although the actual scope of cross-examination is within the trial judge's control, a witness's capacity to perceive the event to which he testifies may be tested on cross-examination or by courtroom experiment. Similarly, courtroom testing of a witness's memory, even as to circumstances unconnected with the trial is a recognized technique of impeachment. Counsel needs particular latitude in cross-examining the very young[2] or the very old, since extremes of age are known to affect the accuracy of a person's memory. Particularly in the case of children,

---

[31] United States v. DiNapoli, 557 F.2d 962, 965 (2d Cir. 1977) (impeachment by prior statement showing bias should be in accord with Rule 613(b)).

[1] *See* **Treatise** at § 607.05.

[2] There are special problems in protecting young children testifying to sexual molestation. Special statutes and techniques, including the use of television, hearsay and limits on cross-

however, the court may have to take measures to obtain useful testimony, including examination in chambers or by video.

Under the orthodox rule predating the adoption of the Federal Rules of Evidence, extrinsic evidence of a witness's mental incapacity was prohibited. Such a rigid approach is unwarranted under the Federal Rules. Mental incapacity, if it can be established, has high probative value on the issue of credibility.[3]

Admission, as is the case with non-extrinsic proof, should rest in the trial court's discretion. The factors of prejudice and confusion which the court must weigh in applying Rule 403 may frequently dictate exclusion of extrinsic evidence, but at times probative value may be so high as to warrant admission.

Particularly troublesome have been cases where the party seeking to impeach wishes to show that the witness suffers from a condition such as alcoholism, drug addiction or mental illness. Some courts assume that proof of the condition without more proves impairment of the witness's capacity to observe, remember or narrate.

Other courts require that an actual effect on testimonial capacity be shown, the court's conclusion often resting on the nature of the underlying infirmity. In these cases, the dangers of prejudice and confusion are inordinately high.

Although the capacity of a witness to make an accurate eyewitness identification does not involve an abnormal condition, the courts have increasingly permitted expert psychological testimony on this subject.[4] This arises out of the tendency of laypersons to overestimate the value of eyewitness testimony, and the risk of a miscarriage of justice as a result.

[b]—Alcohol and Drug Use

Extrinsic evidence is always admissible to show that the witness was under the influence of drink or drugs at the time of the events being testified to, or at the time of testifying.[5] However, the courts generally exclude evidence of chronic alco-

---

examination may apply. *Cf.* also the limits in sex offense cases of Rule 412, discussed in Chapter 7.

[3] Technically Rule 704(b), limiting opinion on the ultimate issue of mental capacity, does not apply to the credibility issue. *See* discussion in Chapter 13. Nevertheless, in deference to Congressional policy the courts are likely to apply a similar approach on credibility.

[4] *See, e.g.,* United States v. Downing, 753 F.2d 1224 (3d Cir. 1985), *aff'd*, 708 F.2d 1017 (3d Cir. 1985); People v. McDonald, 37 Cal. 3d 351 (1984). *Cf.* the discussion of experts and mental illness, at [c], *below.*

[5] *See, e.g.,* Rheaume v. Patterson, 289 F.2d 611, 614 (2d Cir. 1961) (drinking at the time of the event); United States v. Holman, 680 F.2d 1340, 1352–1353 (11th Cir. 1982) (use of controlled substances on date of charged offense); United States v. Van Meerbeke, 548 F.2d 415 (2d Cir. 1976) (opium ingestion while on witness stand).

holism as not bearing on credibility.[6] While having the virtue of simplicity, this rule fails to accord with medical reality. Habitual alcoholism, some experts say, causes such extensive mental deterioration that if counsel can prove a long-standing alcoholism, the court should allow expert testimony that the witness's credibility is suspect. The general condition may also tend to establish the particular state at the time in question.

Although the physiological consequences of long-term alcohol use are far from clear, even less is known about the effects of drug addiction. The multiplicity of drugs, the varying reactions they cause, and the far greater odium attached to drug abuse have increased the complexity of a court's task in determining whether evidence of drug addiction should be admitted.

The court's decision should be governed by Rule 403, which rejects mechanical solutions in favor of determinations based on the facts of the case; neither routine rejection nor routine admission is warranted.[7] Counsel who wish to use evidence of drug addiction for impeachment purposes should furnish the court—outside the hearing of the jury—with specific information about the kind of drug, dosage, its probable effect on the witness, when the witness took it in relation to the chronology of the case, and how often and frequently the witness used it at other times. Counsel should also be prepared to substantiate the claim that the drugs adversely affected the witness's credibility by expert testimony or recognized literature to that effect.

In addition to assessing probative value, the court must consider the dangers specified in Rule 403. If, as may happen, there is no medical consensus about the effect narcotic usage had on a particular witness's ability to perceive, recall or narrate, the court must decide whether allowing this question to be debated by the experts would not confuse rather than enlighten the jurors. Furthermore, the court may foreclose reference to drugs if it feels that probative value would be sub-

---

[6] *See, e.g.,* Poppell v. United States, 418 F.2d 214, 215 (5th Cir. 1969) (general reputation for intemperance "wholly unrelated to the ability of the witness to observe, recall or testify").

[7] *See* United States v. Lochmondy, 890 F.2d 817, 824 (6th Cir. 1989) (court permitted some exploration of prosecution witness's heroin addiction); United States v. Ramirez, 871 F.2d 582 (6th Cir. 1989) (not error for trial court to refuse psychiatric examination of chief prosecution witness who had been addicted to cocaine or to exclude testimony by a defense psychiatrist as to effect of drug usage, which would lead to battle of the experts on the credibility issue).

However, a number of federal courts permit proof of addiction even without requiring proof that the witness's testimonial capacities were impaired, usually on the theory that a user of drugs is a liar, a theory of impeachment that seems to rest more on the character of the witness than on his mental capacity. This theory should therefore be governed by Rule 608. *See, e.g.,* People of Territory of Guam v. Dela Rosa, 644 F.2d 1257, 1261 (9th Cir. 1980) (on retrial, addict instruction should be given if defendant develops testimony that chief prosecution witness is a heroin addict).

stantially outweighed by the potential for prejudice.[8] The nature of the case[9] and the degree of the witness's involvement with drugs may be significant.[10] In a criminal case, for instance, the judge may be more lenient in allowing the narcotic issue to be explored in the impeachment of prosecution witnesses because of the special protection afforded criminal defendants.[11]

[c]—Mental Illness

A witness's mental illness may have a bearing on the witness's credibility.[12] However, forms of mental illness that don't affect the witness's credibility are not relevant.[12.1] Moreover, even relevant evidence of mental illness may be limited[13] or excluded if its probative value is outweighed by the risk of prejudice or confusion, or if the opening of this topic would result in an undue consumption of court time.[13.1]

---

[8] United States v. Kizer, 569 F.2d 504 (9th Cir. 1978) (potential prejudice of drug addiction evidence outweighed probative value). Cf. United States v. James, 576 F.2d 1121 (5th Cir. 1978) (where witness's addiction had been brought out on cross-examination, not error for trial court to have refused defense counsel the right to examine witness's arms for evidence of recent drug addiction).

[9] Drug use may be relevant to bias as indicating why the witness is cooperating with the government. See Government of Virgin Islands v. Hendricks, 476 F.2d 776 (3d Cir. 1973) (discusses dangers of testimony by addicts who are in pay of government).

[10] Cf. United States v. Leonardi, 623 F.2d 746, 757 (2d Cir. 1980) (evidence that prosecution witness had met defendant at methadone clinic properly was excluded as site of meeting did not further impeach witness and posed some danger of prejudice to defendant).

[11] See, e.g., United States v. Lochmondy, 890 F.2d 817, 824 (6th Cir. 1989).

[12] See, e.g., Boggs v. Collins, 226 F.3d 728, 741 (6th Cir. 2000) (admissibility of evidence involves weighing possible prejudice against probative value, considering nature of psychological problem, temporal recency or remoteness of condition, and whether witness suffered from condition at time of events in question; defendant's confrontation rights were satisfied by cross-examination of witness about her mental health); United States v. Lindstrom, 698 F.2d 1154, 1163 (11th Cir. 1983) (reversible error in trial court's severe restriction of cross-examination of chief prosecution witness where her medical records suggested history of psychiatric disorders; extensive discussion).

[12.1] See United States v. Butt, 955 F.2d 77, 84 (1st Cir. 1992) (trial court properly excluded psychiatric history of witness who had attempted suicide and been hospitalized; evidence was not relevant to her credibility since it showed no inclination to hallucinations or false accusations; "federal courts appear to have found mental instability relevant to credibility only where, during the time-frame of the events testified to, the witness exhibited a pronounced disposition to lie or hallucinate, or suffered from a severe illness, such as schizophrenia, that dramatically impaired her ability to perceive and tell the truth").

[13] See United States v. Slade, 627 F.2d 293 (D.C. Cir. 1980) (no error in restricting cross-examination about details of witness's commitment to mental hospital; jury knew of commitment, witness's drug habit, and witness's hope to avoid imprisonment by cooperation with government).

[13.1] See, e.g., Boggs v. Collins, 226 F.3d 728, 741 (6th Cir. 2000) (trial court has broad discretionary power to prohibit cross-examination respecting mental illness for impeachment,

When counsel suspects that a witness is not entirely normal even though never formally diagnosed as having a mental illness, counsel can seek to suggest this hypothesis to the jury by adroit cross-examination. The scope of this cross-examination is subject to judicial control exercised in accordance with Rules 403 and 611.[14]

The federal courts have been hesitant in authorizing experts to observe or test witnesses and then relate their findings in the courtroom. The federal courts have generally declined to admit the results of lie detector tests and truth-serum interviews when they have been offered as relevant to the credibility of a witness.[15] The federal courts have also been reluctant to order psychiatric examinations of witnesses,[16] or to permit testimony by experts based on in-court observations of witnesses.[17] This reluctance undoubtedly stems from judicial awareness that psychiatric testimony often confuses rather than enlightens because experts often disagree with each other, and are unclear and contradictory in their terminology. Psychiatrists may not readily be able to relate their diagnosis of the witness to his ability to give credible testimony, since they are not geared to answering the questions in which a court is interested. This factor is observed in connection with Congressional action in adopting Rule 704(b), discussed in Chapter 13.

Nevertheless, courts should maintain a flexible attitude toward the admissibility of psychiatric or other expert testimony offered to impeach the credibility of a

---

balancing possible prejudice against probative value).

[14] *See* United States v. Lopez, 611 F.2d 44, 45–46 (4th Cir. 1979) (court prohibited counsel from cross-examining witness about psychiatric examination conducted in connection with his testifying in another prosecution; court applied Rule 403).

[15] United States v. Masri, 547 F.2d 932, 936 (5th Cir. 1977) (results of lie detector tests are inadmissible in federal criminal cases); Lindsey v. United States, 237 F.2d 893, 895 (9th Cir. 1956) ("the courts have not generally recognized the trustworthiness and reliability of such tests as being sufficiently well established to accord the results the status of competent evidence"; leading case); *see* United States v. Miller, 874 F.2d 1255, 1262 (9th Cir. 1989) (error to allow testimony as to actual questions and answers in lie detector test); *but cf.* United States v. Piccinonna, 885 F.2d 1529, 1536 (11th Cir. 1989), *aff'd,* 925 F.2d 1474 (11th Cir. 1991) (polygraph evidence may be admitted to impeach or corroborate trial testimony, subject to certain preconditions).

[16] *See, e.g.,* United States v. Ramirez, 871 F.2d 582 (6th Cir. 1989) (not error for trial court to refuse psychiatric examination of chief prosecution witness, who had been addicted to cocaine); United States v. Provenzano, 688 F.2d 194, 204 (3d Cir. 1982) (not abuse of discretion for trial court to refuse to order psychiatric examinations of two prosecution witnesses; "use of such evidence at trial to attack or support a witness's credibility has not generally been favored").

[17] United States v. Riley, 657 F.2d 1377, 1387 (8th Cir. 1981) (not error to exclude psychiatric testimony based on in-court observation of witness). *But see* United States v. Hiss, 88 F. Supp. 559 (S.D.N.Y.), *aff'd,* 185 F.2d 822 (2d Cir. 1950) (psychiatrist allowed to testify on basis of in-court observation of witness and study of witness's writings). Although the *Hiss* case is a leading case on the use of psychiatric testimony for impeachment, it is cited more frequently in the federal courts in distinguishing the case at hand than as a precedent.

witness. Admissibility will depend on the judge's evaluation of whether the deleterious impact the psychiatric testimony might have on the course of the particular trial would be justified by the insight the jury might gain into the capacity of the witness to observe, recollect, and relate truthfully and accurately. Variable factors affecting the probative value of the testimony would include the degree of consensus in the medical community about the diagnosis and significance of the particular symptoms presented by the witness, the degree of certainty with which the expert can testify—which depends partly on whether there has been an out-of-court examination or only in-court observation, and the posture of the credibility issue in the case. If credibility is crucial, the court should be more lenient in allowing the jury to hear testimony that may be helpful.

One procedural protection can be insisted upon by the court, namely, notice in advance of trial.[18] The danger of prejudice, confusion or waste of time mandates pretrial exploration of these issues to the fullest extent possible. The opponent is entitled to know the names of the experts who will be called and, if available, to have their reports showing the theory on which they will testify, and the reports and records on which they will base their opinions.[19] Insofar as possible, the court should make its ruling known as long before the trial as possible so that both sides can try the issue properly.

[4]—Impeachment: Contradiction[1]

Impeachment by contradiction rests on the inference that if a witness is mistaken as to one fact, perhaps he or she is mistaken as to others, and therefore all of the witness's testimony is suspect. Impeachment by contradiction is authorized by Rule 607. Under Rule 607, extrinsic evidence may be admitted to impeach specific errors or falsehoods in a witness's direct testimony, subject to Rule 403.[1.1]

Obviously, however, the strength of this inference will vary with the circumstances. A misstatement about the weather on the day the witness signed a petition in bankruptcy is not particularly conclusive on the credibility of the witness's denial of any intent to defraud creditors. On the other hand, a mistake about the weather may be probative both of a substantive issue and the witness's lack of credibility if the witness is claiming to have been in Tucson on the day that the prosecution

---

[18] See discussion of other procedures for controlling expert testimony in Chapter 13.

[19] Fed. R. Civ. P. 26(b)(4)(B); see 6 MOORE'S FEDERAL PRACTICE, Ch. 26, *General Provisions Governing Discovery; Duty of Disclosure* (Matthew Bender 3d ed. 1997).

[1] See **Treatise** at § 607.06.

[1.1] United States v. Castillo, 181 F.3d 1129, 1133 (9th Cir. 1999) (citing **Treatise**; defendant's "expansive and unequivocal denial of involvement with drugs on direct examination warranted the district court's decision to admit extrinsic evidence of [prior drug] arrest as impeachment by contradiction").

claims that the witness committed murder in Maine.[2] The danger exists that an advocate could use even a misstatement about the weather in the bankruptcy example to convince a jury that the witness is not worthy of belief.[3] In addition to confusing the jury, the contradiction may cause prejudice if it concerns events that have moral implications, particularly if the witness is a party whom the jury may consequently wish to punish.[4] Furthermore, contradiction by extraneous evidence may consume a good deal of time.

These factors of confusion, prejudice, and waste of time are the ones that Rule 403 directs courts to consider in determining whether otherwise relevant evidence should be excluded. Historically, however, limitations on impeachment by contradiction were imposed not by a rule of discretion but rather by applying the so-called "collateral matter" test. A fact sought to be proved was not classified as collateral if (1) it was relevant in that it tended to prove or disprove a material proposition of fact, or (2) it was admissible for impeachment on some theory other than contradiction, such as bias, character for untruthfulness, or mental incapacity. Cases predating the Federal Rules of Evidence indicate that discerning the boundary between direct and collateral issues was often a matter of difficulty and dispute. A Rule 403 approach which analyzes the probative strength of the evidence and assesses the dangers attendant on its admission seems more helpful in performing the truth-seeking function of the law.[5]

Replacing the "collateral matter" test by a rule of discretion also solves another problem on which courts are divided. In some jurisdictions, the bar against contradiction by extrinsic facts on collateral matters is applied only if the fact which is to be contradicted was elicited on cross-examination. If the witness volunteered

---

[2] United States v. Robinson, 544 F.2d 110, 114 (2d Cir. 1976) (defendant's alibi witness claimed he was with defendant on day of bank robbery and that he remembered day because he had picked up unemployment check; prosecution could properly attempt to impeach witness by proving that he had not received a check on that day).

[3] See, e.g., United States v. Harris, 542 F.2d 1283, 1317 (7th Cir. 1976) (not error to exclude evidence that witness had lied to authorities concerning dates of her birth and marriage; evidence properly excluded that witness may have been in error in stating that defendant had received large sums of money where evidence was being offered as basis for inference that witness may also have been in error about defendant's participation in conspiracy).

[4] See, e.g., United States v. Jaqua, 485 F.2d 193 (5th Cir. 1973) (conviction for interfering with border patrol guard reversed where after defendant denied having a temper, government questioned him about three prior assaults).

[5] See, e.g., United States v. Tarantino, 846 F.2d 1384, 1410 (D.C. Cir. 1988) (after prosecution witness testified that defendant had given her the deed to a house, in return for her services in drug conspiracy, testimony that witness told police officer that defendant owned the house, a statement that witness denied making, was properly excluded pursuant to Rule 403 as not sufficiently probative under the circumstances); Barrera v. E.I. Dupont de Nemours & Co., Inc., 653 F.2d 915 (5th Cir. 1981) (proper inquiry when ruling on impeaching evidence is balancing test of Rule 403); United States v. Pantone, 609 F.2d 675, 681 (3d Cir. 1979) (court endorsed balancing test).

the statement on direct, the bar is not applied.[6] Other courts, however, refuse to admit extrinsic contradictory evidence on collateral matters regardless whether the fact to be contradicted was introduced on direct or cross-examination.

The Supreme Court has held that it does not constitutionally matter whether the false statements that the extrinsic evidence rebuts were made on direct examination or on cross-examination that was within the scope of the direct.[7] The Court concentrated on the propriety of the cross-examination rather than on when defendant made the statement. In the case before it, however, the rebutting evidence had high probative value; it was excluded and unusable substantively only because it had been obtained through an illegal search and seizure. When the proffered extrinsic evidence has no relevancy to a material proposition—*i.e.*, it is not being used as evidence-in-chief—it seems sound to take into account the fact that the testimony sought to be contradicted was elicited on cross rather than direct. Often the cross-examiner will frame his question so as "to lay a trap which will be sprung in rebuttal."[8] Prosecutors should not be permitted to escape the restrictions of Rules 404, 608, and 609 in the guise of impeachment by contradiction.[9]

---

[6] *See, e.g.,* United States v. Antonakeas, 255 F.3d 714, 724 (9th Cir. 2001) (in prosecution for conspiracy to distribute cocaine, defendant's sweeping testimony on direct examination that he had never had anything to do with drugs opened door to rebuttal impeachment testimony from prosecution witness that defendant had twice sold him cocaine).

[7] United States v. Havens, 446 U.S. 620, 100 S. Ct. 1912, 64 L. Ed. 2d 559 (1980) (defendant, who was being tried for importing cocaine, testified on cross that he had nothing to do with cocaine or T-shirts; his traveling companion had been found with cocaine sewn into a makeshift pocket in T-shirt he was wearing; defendant's luggage, which was illegally searched, contained T-shirt from which pieces had been cut that matched pocket in which cocaine was found; Court held that trial court properly allowed introduction of T-shirt).

[8] United States v. Pantone, 609 F.2d 675, 683 (3d Cir. 1979) (defendant, a magistrate, was charged with conspiring to refer criminal defendants to a particular bonding agency in return for kickbacks; on direct, defendant made no denial of bribe-taking from other bonding agencies; on cross, when asked if he had ever charged any bondsman anything, he made a sweeping denial and the government then introduced evidence of kickbacks from other agencies; majority held that receipt of this evidence constituted reversible error: "If we were to construe Rule 611(b) as permitting cross-examination with respect to other crimes solely for the purpose of creating credibility issues we would present a defendant who takes the stand with the Hobson's choice of admitting prior uncharged acts of misconduct or of opening the door to presentation of evidence of such acts in rebuttal. The net effect of such a rule would be to permit the introduction of specific acts of prior misconduct whenever a defendant took the stand. That result could not be squared with the provisions of Rule 404(b).").

[9] *See* United States v. Pisari, 636 F.2d 855 (1st Cir. 1981) (defendant was charged with committing a robbery with a knife; on cross, defendant was asked if he had ever committed any robberies by knife in 1977; after denial, prosecution challenged an undercover agent who testified that defendant had told him of committing a robbery with a knife; court found that evidence was not admissible pursuant to Rule 404(b) as bearing on identity, and that it should have been excluded as impeachment evidence).

Where the evidence of another witness is relevant to a material proposition of fact it will be admissible as evidence-in-chief. Such evidence, of course, can also be used to impeach a witness who has given contradictory evidence. Obviously to the extent that the jury believes witnesses who support a material proposition, it will have to disbelieve a witness who supports the negative of the proposition.

[5]—Impeachment: Prior Inconsistent Statements[1]

Impeachment by prior inconsistent statements made before trial rests on the notion that a jury should not believe a witness who is so unreliable as to contradict himself or herself. The use of prior inconsistent statements for purposes of impeachment should be distinguished from the use of such statements as evidence in chief,[2] which under the Federal Rules of Evidence is restricted to a limited class of statements made under oath. *See* Rule 801(d)(1)(A), which is discussed in Chapter 15. When the statements are being used substantively rather than on credibility alone, counsel may argue as to the truth of the particular statements, rather then using the inconsistencies solely to shed light on the credibility of the witness.

Before a prior statement can be used for impeachment, an inconsistency has to be shown between that statement and the witness's testimony. The courts have relied on two principal, but competing tests, to determine inconsistency. First, the inconsistency must be apparent on the face of the two statements. The prior statement will be excluded unless the only possible inference is one of inconsistency. In the alternative, the setting and implications of the statements may be taken into consideration and the prior statement admitted as long as inconsistency is one of several possible inferences that may be drawn. Even before the adoption of the Federal Rules of Evidence, the federal courts had generally rejected the first, mechanical test of inconsistency in favor of the more liberal and psychologically sounder alternative approach. This approach is consistent with the emphasis in the Federal Rules on the admission of all relevant evidence.[3]

---

[1] *See* **Treatise** at § 607.07. Rules 613 and 806 codify and modify the foundational requirements for prior inconsistent statements but are silent as to other prerequisites.

[2] *Cf.* United States v. Gossett, 877 F.2d 901, 906–907 (11th Cir. 1989) (not error to exclude statements allegedly made by co-defendant to cellmate; "impeachment by prior inconsistent statement may not be permitted where it is used as a strategem to get before the jury otherwise inadmissible evidence.").

[3] *See* United States v. Gravely, 840 F.2d 1156, 1163 (4th Cir. 1988); United States v. Williams, 737 F.2d 594, 606–610 (7th Cir. 1984); United States v. Dennis, 625 F.2d 782, 795 (8th Cir. 1980) ("inconsistency is not limited to diametrically opposed answers but may be found in evasive answers, inability to recall, silence, or changes of position"); United States v. Rogers, 549 F.2d 490, 496 (8th Cir. 1976) (court found that trial judge could well infer from witness's equivocal answers that he was fully aware of the content of his prior statement but was trying not to implicate the defendant).

Admitting all prior inconsistent statements made by the witness would not, however, be satisfactory. True, all contradictory statements are relevant to credibility in the broad sense that a witness who has made a mistake before may be mistaken again. Yet permitting an unlimited probe into the witness's past utterances for evidence of self-contradiction may disclose inconsistencies of trifling probative significance that might prejudice or confuse the jury while unduly protracting the trial. At common law, as in the case of contradiction, discussed in [4], *above*, exclusion was achieved by means of the "collateral" test. If a witness denied making a statement on a matter classified as collateral, the cross-examiner could go no further. The making of the statement could not be proved by extrinsic evidence.

The difficulty with a "collateral" test is that it looks to only one side of the equation governing admissibility—high probative value—and insists that this factor can be assayed mechanically. Actually it is often difficult to assess the probative effect of a proffered statement. Allowing the trial court to rationalize its decision solely by applying the "collateral" label deprives the reviewing court of an opportunity to assess the factors considered by the trial court. The better approach—and one in accord with the structure of the Federal Rules—is to eliminate mechanical application of the "collateral" test in favor of the balancing approach mandated by Rule 403. Evidence at which the collateral test is primarily directed, which is relevant solely because it suggests that the witness may have erred about something in the past, would generally be excluded because of its low probative value and its tendency to prejudice the jury. Evidence of higher probative value would be assessed in terms of its impact on the jury in light of the particular circumstances presented. The court should consider factors such as the availability of other evidence, the extent to which the particular witness's credibility is crucial to the case, the length of time that has elapsed since the underlying event, and the nature of the extrinsic evidence.[4] Usually the result under either approach would be the same, but the Rule 403 balancing test authorizes a flexible approach when the proffered statement has high probative value but is strongly prejudicial, or when the probative value of the statement is debatable.

A failure to assert a fact it would have been natural to affirm is usually admitted

---

[4] *See, e.g.,* United States v. Shoupe, 548 F.2d 636 (6th Cir. 1977) (due process violation requiring new trial where prosecutor had recited entire substance of witness's disavowed unsworn prior statement to jury in order to impeach witness; court noted that statements were directly probative of defendants' guilt, that there was very little other evidence, that statements had allegedly been made to government agent, but that no recording or transcript of interview had been prepared, that agent's notes were not dictated until six days after interview, that witness was never shown memorandum, that trial court never requested original notes or read memorandum and neither sought to determine reliability of the statements through independent evidence nor attempted to limit the scope of impeachment).

by the federal courts as inconsistent with a witness's assertion of the existence of the fact, provided there is no constitutional bar to allowing such impeachment.[5] The Supreme Court has held that when the witness's silence was induced by implicit assurances that silence could not be used against him or her, cross-examining the witness about the silence is fundamentally unfair and in violation of the Due Process Clause.[6] Except when silence is induced by governmental action, however, the Court has held that impeachment by silence is an evidentiary rather than constitutional matter.[7] In many instances, even when there is no constitutional bar, silence is so ambiguous, and the possibility of prejudice so high, that the evidence should be excluded pursuant to Rule 403.

[6]—Impeachment: Character

Impeachment by evidence of character and conduct is governed by Rule 608. Impeachment by conviction of crime is treated in Rule 609. See discussion below.

[7]—Support or Rehabilitation[1]

Except to the extent that an accused may offer evidence of truthfulness before a challenge, the Federal Rules of Evidence have in no way altered the general principle that a witness's credibility cannot be bolstered on direct or supported on rebuttal unless there has been an attack on the witness's veracity.[2] Some leeway

---

[5] *See, e.g.,* United States v. Vega, 589 F.2d 1147, 1150–1152 (2d Cir. 1978) (pre-arrest silence at Kennedy Airport when defendant encountered DEA agent was probative of defendant's credibility since her counsel had suggested that defendant had not approached police in Chicago when she found out about narcotics transaction because she needed to return to New York). *See also* Greer v. Miller, 483 U.S. 756, 107 S. Ct. 3102, 97 L.Ed. 618 (1987) (*Doyle* violation occurs only where the trial court permits the prosecution to use the post–arrest silence to impeach; where, as here, the judge immediately sustained defense counsel's objection, no further discussion was had, and two curative instructions were given, the prosecution had not been allowed to pursue an improper line of inquiry, and no violation occurred).

[6] Doyle v. Ohio, 426 U.S. 610, 96 S. Ct. 2240, 49 L. Ed. 2d 91 (1976). The Court has explained its position in Jenkins v. Anderson, 447 U.S. 231, 100 S. Ct. 2124, 65 L. Ed. 2d 86 (1980) (due process not violated by the impeachment use of pre-*Miranda* warnings silence before arrest); Anderson v. Charles, 447 U.S. 404, 100 S. Ct. 2180, 65 L. Ed. 2d 222 (1980) (due process not violated by the impeachment use of voluntarily made post-*Miranda* statements); Fletcher v. Weir, 455 U.S. 603, 102 S. Ct. 1309, 71 L. Ed. 2d 490 (1982) (no violation of due process by impeachment use of silence after arrest where no *Miranda* warnings were given). *See also* Roberts v. United States, 445 U.S. 552, 100 S. Ct. 1358, 63 L. Ed. 2d 622 (1980); Wainwright v. Greenfield, 474 U.S. 284, 106 S. Ct. 634, 88 L. Ed. 2d 623 (1986).

[7] Jenkins v. Anderson, 447 U.S. 231, 100 S. Ct. 2124, 65 L. Ed. 2d 86 (1980) (defendant's failure to tell police authorities that he had killed in self-defense could be used to impeach him after he testified that he had acted solely in self-defense).

[1] *See* **Treatise** at § 607.09.

[2] *See, e.g.,* United States v. Awkard, 597 F.2d 667 (9th Cir. 1979) (since Ninth Circuit allows hypnotically refreshed evidence to be used, a foundation concerning the reliability of hypnosis is no

is offered in allowing the proponent of a witness to draw the sting of its witness's impeachment by bringing out on direct matters damaging to the witness's credibility that are sure to be brought out on cross-examination.[3]

After impeachment by evidence of bias, interest, or self-contradiction, evidence in denial or explanation is always available[4] subject to the judge's discretion to curtail proof which confuses or wastes an undue amount of time.[5] The explanation

---

longer necessary; consequently it was error (though harmless in context of case) for trial court to permit expert on hypnotism to testify prior to hypnotized witness since this had the effect of bolstering his credibility before it was attacked); United States v. Bursten, 560 F.2d 779 (7th Cir. 1977) (error, though harmless, for government to buttress the believability of its key witness by introducing evidence that witness was willing to submit to polygraph test).

[3] *See, e.g.,* United States v. Cosentino, 844 F.2d 30, 34 (2d Cir. 1988) (cooperation agreement could be admitted on direct after defense attacked witness's credibility in the opening statement); United States v. Singh, 628 F.2d 758 (2d Cir. 1980) (bias of witness towards defendant); *see* discussion in Rule 609 *infra* of revealing convictions on direct; *but cf.* United States v. Melia, 691 F.2d 672, 676 (4th Cir. 1982) (reversible error where government, in order to counter defense efforts to discredit government witnesses, presented direct evidence from five separate witnesses of death threats to prosecution witness, of government's concern for safety of witnesses, and of their participation in Witness Protection Program; no simple formula to determine how much evidence should be admissible but "trial court must exercise its discretion, bearing in mind the purpose of the evidence—to rebut, in appropriate circumstances, the appearance of special treatment and improper motivation or bias"; in instant case, too much likelihood that jury would infer that defendant was source of death threats).

[4] United States v. Mitchell, 556 F.2d 371, 379–380 (6th Cir. 1977) (where defendant challenged government informant's motivation at great length, it was not error for the judge to permit further questioning of informant to show that many of the arrangements were conceived not so much to reward informant but to protect him and his family, even though the inference was that defendant was a dangerous criminal who would seek revenge); United States v. Holland, 526 F.2d 284 (5th Cir. 1976), *rev'd on other grounds,* 537 F.2d 821 (5th Cir. 1976) (court admitted evidence that witness had corrected an earlier misstatement in grand jury testimony which had been used to impeach him); United States v. Cirillo, 468 F.2d 1233, 1240 (2d Cir. 1972) (impeached witness should have been permitted to explain his failure to mention meeting with defendant was prompted by fear of being killed); Russo v. Peikes, 71 F.R.D. 110 (E.D. Pa. 1976), *aff'd mem.,* 547 F.2d 1163 (3d Cir. 1977) (court permitted testimony by associate in law firm representing defendant to testify as to what expert had actually said after expert was impeached during cross-examination). *See also* United States v. Moreno, 649 F.2d 309 (5th Cir. 1981) (example of rehabilitation after impeachment showing poor memory).

[5] United States v. Roberts, 618 F.2d 530, 536 (9th Cir. 1980) (discusses use by prosecution of plea agreement that contains promise to testify truthfully; court counsels trial judge to be alert to problem of vouching and whether it suggests "the unspoken message . . . that the prosecutor knows what the truth is and is assuring its revelation"; reviews cases); Bracey v. United States, 142 F.2d 85, 89 (D.C. Cir. 1944) ("[T]he admission or rejection of such evidence lies in the discretion of the trial judge. Generally speaking, it has been held that when bias is freely admitted without qualification, under circumstances which leave no doubt as to its existence or the reason for it, rebuttal evidence upon the point is unnecessary. Even under such circumstances the evidence is not inadmissible in the usual sense, but rather is excluded because its admission would unnecessarily

must seek to show that the impeaching facts offered do not really indicate lies.[6] Rebutting evidence should be excluded when its only purpose is to show additional reasons justifying the witness's bias.[7] Reputation or opinion evidence testifying to the principal witness's good character for truthfulness may also be admitted pursuant to Rule 608(a) once the character of the witness for truthfulness has been challenged. See discussion of Rule 608 in § 12.03.

The most troublesome aspect of rehabilitation is the extent to which impeachment by prior inconsistent statements opens the door to support by prior consistent statements. Since the inconsistency remains even if the witness had made out-of-court statements consistent with the testimony, prior consistent statements are admitted "only in those few exceptional situations where, as experience has taught, they could be of clear help to the fact finder in determining whether the witness is truthful."[8]

Rule 801(d)(1)(B) states that a prior consistent statement is not hearsay when "offered to rebut an express or implied charge against . . . [the witness] of recent fabrication or improper influence or motive." Pursuant to Rule 801(d)(1)(B), then, a prior consistent statement may be used as substantive evidence to prove the truth of the matter asserted, and not merely to support the witness's credibility.[9]

Disagreement has existed whether the same standards of admissibility should be applied if a prior consistent statement is offered for rehabilitative purposes, as opposed to being offered as substantive evidence pursuant to Rule 801(d)(1)(B). The disagreement has included whether the prior consistent statement must have been made before the motive to fabricate allegedly arose. The Supreme Court resolved that part of the disagreement by a 1995 decision.[10] Before the decision

---

expand the trial to include collateral issues, and thus confuse the jury. When, however, the impeachment of a witness is conducted in such manner as itself to confuse the jury concerning the existence of bias, or of its character if bias does exist, and thus to mislead the jury concerning the veracity and dependability of the witness, then the trial judge may properly permit an explanation to be made.").

[6] *Cf.* United States v. Arnold, 890 F.2d 825, 830 (6th Cir. 1989) (trial court did not commit reversible error in allowing prosecutor to bring out guilty pleas of co-defendants to restore the credibility of prosecution witnesses, after their testimony had been attacked as a fabrication; trial court had instructed jury that pleas were not substantive evidence of guilt).

[7] United States v. Pintar, 630 F.2d 1270, 1284 (8th Cir. 1980) (where defense elicited on cross-examination that prosecution witness disliked defendants, error in allowing prosecution to elicit on re-direct examination that witness thought defendants were engaged in kickback scheme).

[8] Coltrane v. United States, 418 F.2d 1131, 1140 (D.C. Cir. 1969) ("mere repetition does not imply veracity").

[9] *See* discussion of Rule 801(d)(1) in Chapter 15, *Hearsay Exclusions,* as to admissibility of prior consistent statements made after prior inconsistent statement.

[10] Tome v. United States, 513 U.S. 150, 156–163, 115 S. Ct. 696, 130 L. Ed. 2d 574 (1995) (witness's prior consistent statement held admissible as non-hearsay to rebut charge of recent

in *Tome*, some courts drew a distinction between rehabilitation and substantive use in this respect,[11] whereas other courts declined to do so.[12] In assessing probative value, "the issue ought to be whether the particular consistent statement sought to be used has some rebutting force beyond the mere fact that the witness has repeated on a prior occasion a statement consistent with his trial testimony."[13] When the witness denies having made the inconsistent statement used for impeachment, a consistent statement would have significant rebutting force in diminishing the likelihood that the witness had made the inconsistent statement.[14]

Prior consistent statements also have high probative value when they shed light on whether the admitted prior inconsistent statement was truly inconsistent.[15] Some courts have suggested that allowing recourse to the prior consistent statement "when the consistent statement will amplify or clarify the allegedly inconsistent statement . . . is . . . only an invocation of the principle of completeness, though not a precise use of Rule 106."[16]

---

fabrication under Rule 801(d)(1)(B) only if statement made before motive to fabricate arose).

[11] *See* United States v. Brennan, 798 F.2d 581, 589 (2d Cir. 1986); United States v. Pierre, 781 F.2d 329, 333 (2d Cir. 1986); United States v. Harris, 761 F.2d 394, 398–400 (7th Cir. 1985) (condition that the motive to fabricate must not have existed at the time the statement was made need not be met when statement is offered for rehabilitative purposes).

[12] *See* United States v. Miller, 874 F.2d 1255, 1273 (9th Cir. 1989); United States v. Lawson, 872 F.2d 179, 182 (6th Cir. 1989) ("[T]he trial judge [must] examine the circumstances under which the statement was made and make a determination of the statement's relevancy and probity. . . . While these factors are more likely to be found where the statement was made prior to the alleged discrediting influence, . . . where there are other indicia of reliability surrounding a prior consistent statement that make it relevant to rebut a charge of recent fabrication or improper motive, then the fact that the statement was made after the alleged motive to falsify should not preclude its admissibility. Of course, where the danger of unfair prejudice outweighs the probative value of the evidence Fed. R. Evid. 403 is available.").

[13] United States v. Pierre, 781 F.2d 329, 331 (2d Cir. 1986).

[14] *See, e.g.,* United States v. Corry, 183 F.2d 155, 156–157 (2d Cir. 1950).

[15] *See, e.g.,* United States v. Pierre, 781 F.2d 329, 334 (2d Cir. 1986) (where agent who testified that defendant refused to make a controlled delivery was impeached by his notes containing no reference to such a refusal, court properly allowed agent to testify on direct that his formal report contained fact of refusal); United States v. Rubin, 609 F.2d 51, 60–62 (2d Cir. 1979) (concurring opinion of Friendly, J.), *aff'd on other grounds,* 449 U.S. 424, 101 S. Ct. 698, 66 L. Ed. 2d 633 (1981); United States v. Juarez, 549 F.2d 1113, 1114 (7th Cir. 1977) (after government agents had been cross-examined in detail about reports they had written concerning transactions with defendant, revealing possible inaccuracies in them, trial judge did not err in admitting reports themselves, not for their truth but for the limited purpose of consideration with regard to the witnesses' credibility; reports were not hearsay and court did not abuse discretion afforded it by Rule 403).

[16] United States v. Brennan, 798 F.2d 581, 587–589 (2d Cir. 1986) (where key witness gave grand jury testimony inconsistent with part of his testimony at trial, important to admit whole grand jury testimony); United States v. Pierre, 781 F.2d 329, 333 (2d Cir. 1986); *see also* United States v. Rubin, 609 F.2d 51, 57–64, 66–70 (2d Cir. 1979) (majority and concurring opinions), *aff'd on other grounds,* 449 U.S. 424 (1981).

The question of admissibility of the prior consistent statement on credibility alone is one left almost entirely to the discretion of the trial court.[17] It must consider whether the jury will understand and follow an instruction—which must be given on demand—that the evidence is limited to the issue of credibility.

Another important factor for the court to consider in exercising its discretion is the amount of time that proof of the prior statements will take. If admission will introduce a substantial ancillary dispute about whether the statements were made and the surrounding circumstances, the court, after weighing that factor against the importance of the witness and the critical nature of the impeachment and rehabilitation effects, may well decide to close off or severely limit the inquiry.

§ 12.02   Impeaching One's Own Witness—Rule 607[1]

Rule 607 eliminates the traditional rule that a party may not impeach its own witness. It imposes no restriction on the impeachment process it authorizes.[1.1]

Rule 607, among others, allows a party to impeach only witnesses who personally testify or whose testimony has otherwise been introduced as the substantive legal equivalent of in-person testimony.[1.2] These rules (404 and 607-609) do not permit impeachment of persons whose contribution to the record evidence has been limited to non-testimonial information, such as admissible hearsay statements. Hearsay declarants, however, may be impeached under Rule 806.[1.3] The rule provides as follows:

Rule 607.   Who May Impeach.

The credibility of a witness may be attacked by any party, including the party calling the witness.

[*Adopted Jan. 2, 1975, effective July 1, 1975; amended Mar. 2, 1987, effective Oct. 1, 1987.*]

---

[17] United States v. Obayagbona, 627 F. Supp. 329, 335 (E.D.N.Y. 1985); *cf.* United States v. Abel, 469 U.S. 45, 54, 105 S. Ct. 465, 83 L. Ed. 2d 450 (1984) ("district court is accorded a wide discretion in determining the admissibility of evidence under the Federal Rules"; case concerned Rules 401 and 403).

[1] *See* **Treatise** at § 607.02; *see also* § 607App.100 for discussion of previous practice, and the exceptions that had been developed to side-step the impact of the traditional rule.

[1.1] *See, e.g.,* United States v. Buffalo, 358 F.3d 519, 522 (8th Cir. 2004) (party who called witness may impeach without declaring witness adverse or showing that witness's testimony was a surprise).

[1.2] *See, e.g.,* United States v. Stephens, 365 F.3d 967, 975–976 (11th Cir. 2004) (witness rules apply when parties stipulate to what the individual would have said or when contents of individual's testimony in prior deposition or judicial proceeding is entered into evidence at trial).

[1.3] Fed. R. Evid. 806; *see* § 14.06.

A problem that has emerged in applying Rule 607 involves the use of evidence that would otherwise be inadmissible for the ostensible purpose of impeaching a witness, when the proffering party's real purpose is to get the inadmissible evidence before the jury. For example, unsworn prior inconsistent statements of witnesses who are not parties to the pending action are not excluded from the definition of hearsay under Rule 801(d)(1)(A) and are, therefore, generally inadmissible as proof of the truth of their contents, unless they are independently admissible under one of the exceptions to the hearsay rule.[2] A witness's unsworn prior inconsistent statements can, however, be used for impeachment even though it is not, on its own, admissible under one of the exceptions to the hearsay rule.[3]

There is, therefore, the danger that the jurors will misuse the evidence, and that Rule 607 could thus have the effect of creating a new route for the admission of hearsay evidence in the guise of impeachment. To forestall this danger by insisting on a showing of surprise and affirmative damage before a party may impeach its own witness, as was required under prior law, to prevent such misuse of the liberal impeachment provisions of the Federal Rules of Evidence, would mean a return to the unsatisfactory mechanical approach that led to the adoption of Rule 607 in the first place.[4]

The courts have employed two approaches to avoid the misuse of Rule 607 and nevertheless remain consistent with the liberal approach of the Federal Rules to impeachment. The first is an analysis of the proffered impeachment evidence under Rule 403, keeping in mind the inadmissibility of the evidence but for those liberal impeachment rules. Under that approach, the trial judge assesses such factors as the likelihood the witness made the unsworn statement, ambiguities in the statement, and the possibility that the jury in a criminal case might use the statement either to infer the defendant's guilt or to conclude that the defendant was an associate of a proven liar and therefore probably lying as well when he or she pleaded not guilty.[5]

The other approach involves an interpretation of Rule 607 as not permitting

---

[2] Fed. R. Evid. 801(d)(1)(A); *see, e.g.,* Santos v. Murdock, 243 F.3d 681, 683–684 (2d Cir. 2001) (witness's affidavit prepared and executed at meeting between witness and defendant's attorney was not "given at a trial, hearing, or other proceeding, or at a deposition" and was therefore not excluded from hearsay exclusion by Rule 801(d)(1)(A)); *see also* Ch. 15.

[3] *See, e.g.,* Goodman v. Pa. Tpk. Comm'n, 293 F.3d 655, 665–667 (3d Cir. 2002) (trial court properly admitted otherwise inadmissible hearsay for impeachment after witnesses testified contrary to prior statements).

[4] *See, e.g.,* United States v. Webster, 734 F.2d 1191, 1193 (7th Cir. 1984) (it would be "a mistake to graft such a requirement to Rule 607, even if such a graft would be within the power of judicial interpretation of the rule").

[5] *See, e.g.,* United States v. Buffalo, 358 F.3d 519, 522–524 (8th Cir. 2004) (proper way to avoid abuse of rule allowing party to impeach its own witness with otherwise inadmissible prior inconsistent statements is to analyze proposed impeachment evidence carefully under Rule 403).

impeachment by prior inconsistent statement when it is used "as a mere subterfuge to get before the jury evidence not otherwise admissible."[6] In *United States v. Webster*[7] the court concluded that this limitation on the liberal extent of Rule 607, called the *Morlang* limitation, "has been accepted in all circuits that have considered the issue."

§ 12.03   Impeachment by Evidence of Character and Conduct of Witness—Rule 608

[1]—Scope and Text of Rule[1]

Rule 608 governs the admissibility of character evidence and, under certain circumstances, evidence of conduct, to attack or support the credibility of a witness. It does not concern the use of evidence to attack or support the credibility of a witness through means other than character revelations. Thus, Rule 608 is not applicable to the use of evidence: to show bias,[2] to show mental incapacity,[3] of contradiction,[4] or of prior inconsistent statements.[5]

Rule 608(a) permits the admission of opinion or reputation evidence of character for the purpose of attacking or supporting the credibility of a witness, but limits it to evidence referring to the witness's character for truthfulness or untruthfulness.[5.1] Rule 608(a)(2) also limits the use of evidence for truthful character to those circumstances in which the witness's character for truthfulness has been attacked by opinion, reputation, or other evidence.[5.2]

Rule 608(b) proscribes the use of extrinsic evidence of specific incidents of the witness's conduct for the purpose of attacking or supporting the witness's credibility. There are three exceptions to Rule 608(b)'s general proscription concerning the use of extrinsic evidence of specific acts:

---

[6] *See, e.g.,* United States v. Morlang, 531 F.2d 183, 190 (4th Cir. 1975) (although Rule 607 was not yet in effect, limitation on its applicability was necessary); *see also* United States v. Gomez-Gallardo, 915 F.2d 553, 555 (9th Cir. 1990) (government improperly called witness for sole purpose of impeachment with otherwise inadmissible evidence).

[7] United States v. Webster, 734 F.2d 1191, 1192 (7th Cir. 1984).

[1] *See* **Treatise** at § 608.02.

[2] *See* § 12.01[2].

[3] *See* § 12.01[3].

[4] *See* § 12.01[4].

[5] *See* § 12.01[5].

[5.1] Fed. R. Evid. 608(a)(1).

[5.2] Fed. R. Evid 608(a)(2); *see, e.g.,* Renda v. King, 347 F.3d 550, 554 (3d Cir. 2003) ("Evidence of a witness's good character for truthfulness is not admissible absent an attack on the witness's character for truthfulness due to the cost of engaging in a fruitless 'swearing match,' particularly in light of the fact that a witness is presumed to tell the truth until his character for truthfulness is attacked").

- evidence of criminal convictions may be used in accordance with the provisions of Rule 609.[6]

- in the trial court's discretion, if the specific acts evidence is probative of truthfulness or untruthfulness, it may be used on cross-examination of a witness concerning that witness's character for truthfulness or untruthfulness.[7]

- in the trial court's discretion, if the specific acts evidence is probative of truthfulness or untruthfulness, it may be used in the cross-examination of a witness concerning the character for truthfulness or untruthfulness of another witness as to which character the witness subject to cross-examination has testified.[8]

Character evidence in the form of opinion, reputation, or specific acts that is not admissible to attack or support credibility under Rule 608 may nevertheless be admissible if it offered to prove some other consequential fact, such as motive, intent, or absence of mistake or accident.[9]

The Rule provides as follows:

Rule 608.   Evidence of Character and Conduct of Witness.

(a)   Opinion and reputation evidence of character. The credibility of a witness may be attacked or supported by evidence in the form of opinion or reputation, but subject to these limitations: (1) the evidence may refer only to character for truthfulness or untruthfulness, and (2) evidence of truthful character is admissible only after the character of the witness for truthfulness has been attacked by opinion or reputation evidence or otherwise.

(b)   Specific instances of conduct. Specific instances of the conduct of a witness, for the purpose of attacking or supporting the witness's character for truthfulness, other than conviction of crime as provided in rule 609, may not be proved by extrinsic evidence. They may, however, in the discretion of the court, if probative of truthfulness or untruthfulness, be inquired into on cross-examination of the witness (1) concerning the witness's character for truthfulness or untruthfulness, or (2) concerning the character for truthfulness or untruthfulness of another witness as to which character the witness being cross-examined has testified.

---

[6]   Fed. R. Evid. 609; *see* § 12.04.

[7]   Fed. R. Evid. 608(b)(1).

[8]   Fed. R. Evid. 608(b)(2).

[9]   Fed. R. Evid. 404; *see, e.g.,* United States v. Gomes, 177 F.3d 76, 81 (1st Cir. 1999) (extrinsic evidence of a witness's bad acts, although not admissible under Rule 608(b) to show untruthfulness, may be admissible to show bias); United States v. James, 609 F.2d 36, 45–48 (2d Cir. 1979) (specific acts of misconduct admissible to prove motive); *see also* Ch. 7.

> The giving of testimony, whether by an accused or by any other witness, does not operate as a waiver of the accused's or the witness's privilege against self-incrimination when examined with respect to matters that relate only to character for truthfulness.
>
> [Adopted Jan. 2, 1975, effective July 1, 1975; amended Mar. 2, 1987, effective Oct. 1, 1987; Apr. 25, 1988, effective Nov. 1, 1988; March 27, 2003, effective Dec. 1, 2003.]

Rule 608 applies in civil as well as criminal cases.[10] It makes no distinction between principal witnesses and character witnesses.

Rule 608's approval for the use of specified types of character evidence to attack and support a witness's credibility is subject to the overriding provisions of Rule 403, which requires the trial court to exclude evidence when its probative value is substantially outweighed by danger of prejudice, confusion, or waste of time.[11] It is also subject to the trial court's control under Rule 611, which bars harassment and undue embarrassment of witnesses.[12]

The final sentence of Rule 608(b) states that a person who takes the witness stand does not thereby waive the privilege against self-incrimination with respect to matters relating solely to credibility.[13] The limitation on waiver of the privilege provided by the rule rarely applies. It does not curtail questions about convictions, since such inquiry is not incriminating; it does not prohibit questions about misconduct so long past that all possibility of prosecution has been barred; and it does not exclude evidence of prior misconduct if that conduct is relevant to something other than credibility.[14] In criminal cases, even if the privilege does apply, it is seldom relied upon by a defendant. Although the judge may instruct the jurors not to draw any adverse inferences from a claim of privilege by a criminal defendant, the jurors will have the feeling that the witness has something to hide. Under such circumstances it is necessary for the defendant to consider not taking the stand, even

---

[10] See, e.g., Squyres v. Hilliary, 599 F.2d 918, 921 (10th Cir. 1979).

[11] See, e.g., United States v. Smith, 196 F.3d 1034, 1037–1038 (9th Cir. 1999) (trial court did not abuse its discretion in precluding, under Rule 403, defendant from calling three witnesses to contradict testimony of government witness on matters not at issue; proffered evidence "would not have added significantly to the inference of bias" raised by witness's own testimony about his motives); United States v. Haynes, 554 F.2d 231, 234 (5th Cir. 1977) (per curiam) (trial court did not err in limiting defendant to one witness to attack prosecution witness's reputation for truth and veracity when testimony of each would have been identical and therefore cumulative).

[12] See Ch. 2. The trial court, therefore, has considerable discretion in determining the admissibility of credibility evidence, depending upon the type of case and the status of the witness.

[13] See, e.g., Air Et Chaleur, S.A. v. Janeway, 757 F.2d 489, 496 (2d Cir. 1985).

[14] United States v. Blankenship, 746 F.2d 233, 238 n.1 (5th Cir. 1984) (questioning about crime defendant was charged with); United States v. Panza, 612 F.2d 432 (9th Cir. 1979) (cross-examination within scope of direct).

though there is a danger that the jurors will, despite the judge's instructions to the contrary, weigh the defendant's failure to testify against him or her.[15]

[2]—Attack on Character: Reputation and Opinion Evidence[1]

Rule 608(a) recognizes that a witness's credibility may be impeached by proof of his or her reputation or proof by opinion. It has been held that exclusion of opinion or reputation evidence may amount to reversible error.[2] Testimony must be relevant to untruthfulness rather than to any other character trait.[3]

Reputation testimony must relate to the witness's reputation at or shortly before the time of trial.[4] Reputation testimony can be offered by first establishing the impeaching witness X's connection with the witness W, then by establishing that W has a general reputation for non-truthfulness in the community in which he or she works[5] or lives,[6] and that X is in a position to know that reputation.

Opinion evidence is obtained by asking an impeaching witness to give his or her opinion of the principal witness's character for truthfulness. There are no prerequisites of long acquaintance or recent information about the witness;[7] cross-examination can be expected to expose defects of lack of familiarity and to reveal reliance on isolated or irrelevant instances of misconduct, or the existence of feelings of personal hostility towards the principal witness. Nevertheless, if the

---

[15] *See* **Treatise** at § 608.30.

[1] *See* **Treatise** at §§ 608.10–608.15.

[2] United States v. Davis, 639 F.2d 239 (5th Cir. 1981) (exclusion of two character witnesses called by the defense to impeach key government witnesses reversible error). The court can reasonably limit the size of a parade of pro and con character witnesses.

[3] *See, e.g.,* United States v. Meserve, 271 F.3d 314, 328–329 (1st Cir. 2001) (trial court abused its discretion by permitting impeachment of witness with evidence that people in his community were afraid of him because of his "assaultive character;" such evidence had no bearing on his reputation for truthfulness and was barred by Rule 608(a)).

[4] United States v. Watson, 669 F.2d 1374, 1382–85 (11th Cir. 1982).

[5] United States v. Malady, 960 F.2d 57, 58 (8th Cir. 1992) (defendant was convicted of being a felon in possession of a firearm after guns stolen from an individual's home were found in the possession of a local tavern owner, who claimed in his trial testimony that he had purchased them from defendant without knowing they were stolen; the district court properly refused to permit defense counsel to ask the local sheriff on cross-examination whether he believed the tavern owner's statement that he didn't know the guns were stolen; the court noted that the sheriff had testified about the tavern owner's reputation in the community as a fence, and that counsel could have asked the sheriff for his general opinion of this witness's truthfulness; citing Rule 608(a)).

[6] United States v. Truslaw, 530 F.2d 257, 265 (4th Cir. 1975).

[7] United States v. Turning Bear, 357 F.3d 730, 734 (8th Cir. 2004) (proposed character witness gained sufficient personal knowledge to have formed admissible opinion concerning principal witness's character for truthfulness through principal witness's having lived with her for four to six months).

court finds the witness lacks sufficient information[8] to have formed a reliable opinion, or that the witness's testimony would be inherently prejudicial,[9] it can exclude, relying on Rules 403 and 602. The courts have usually declined to permit expert testimony concerning a witness's veracity.[10]

In qualifying the impeachment witness, a proponent should not be allowed to inquire whether the witness knows of specific instances of misconduct.[11] Although such questioning within limits is permissible on cross-examination of a witness testifying to truthfulness (*see* discussion at [3], *below*), permitting evidence of specific instances of misconduct to be introduced on direct examination of a reputation witness in the guise of qualifying the witness by showing the basis for the witness's knowledge of the character of the person in question would violate the prohibition against the use of specific instances of conduct in the first sentence of subdivision (b) of Rule 608.

[3]—Attack on Character: Cross-examination of Witness as to Specific Instances of Previous Conduct[1]

[a]—Instances of Probative Conduct

Rule 608(b) generally prohibits the use of extrinsic evidence of specific instances of conduct other than convictions to attack or support a witness's character for truthfulness.[2] On cross-examination of a witness, however, counsel may ask about

---

[8] United States v. Whitmore, 359 F.3d 609, 618 (D.C. Cir. 2004) (witness's opinion should not be admitted unless witness demonstrates that his or her character opinion is rationally based on opinion witness's personal knowledge of principal witness and would assist jury in determining fact of credibility).

[9] United States v. Bruscino, 662 F.2d 450, 463 (7th Cir. 1981), *rev'd on other grounds*, 687 F.2d 938 (7th Cir. 1982) (court refused to hold as a matter of law that an F.B.I. agent's opinion as to the lack of credibility of a defense witness is as inherently prejudicial as that of a prosecuting attorney).

[10] *See* Bastow v. General Motors Corp., 844 F.2d 506, 510–511 (8th Cir. 1988) (trial court did not abuse discretion in excluding testimony of clinical psychologist that plaintiff had a behavior disorder giving him a character for untruthfulness); *see also* § 12.01[3][c] and **Treatise** at § 702.03[5].

[11] United States v. Manglameli, 668 F.2d 1172, 1175–1176 (10th Cir. 1982); United States v. Hoskins, 628 F.2d 295, 296–297 (5th Cir. 1980).

[1] *See* **Treatise** at §§ 608.22, 608.23.

[2] Fed. R. Evid. 608(b); *see, e.g.,* United States v. Marino, 277 F.3d 11, 24 (1st Cir. 2002) (trial court properly excluded, under Rule 608(b), extrinsic evidence that witness possessed large number of weapons, engaged in violent conduct, and lived extravagant life style offered to impeach witness's credibility when witness gave impression he was non-violent mid-level drug dealer); United States v. Arias, 252 F.3d 973, 978–979 (8th Cir. 2001) (trial court did not err in excluding testimony of one witness about misconduct of another witness, because Rule 608(b) bars such collateral impeachment).

specific instances of that witness's conduct, in the discretion of the trial court, if they are "probative of truthfulness or untruthfulness."[3]

Acts such as forgery, perjury, and fraud are probative of untruthfulness, and are presumptively admissible under Rule 608(b).[4] Other acts of dishonesty, of course, may also be probative of truthfulness.[5]

If the witness, however, denies having committed the specific act of misconduct, the cross-examiner may not introduce extrinsic evidence to prove that the act occurred.[5.1] Moreover, if the witness does not remember all or some of the details concerning the prior act of misconduct, the cross-examiner may not use documents to refresh the witness's recollection.[5.2] If, on the other hand, the witness admits having committed the specific act of misconduct, but attempts to minimize his or her culpability, the impeaching party may, in the trial court's discretion, cross-examine the witness concerning the details of the act.[5.3]

Effective December 1, 2003, Rule 608 was amended to change language that barred extrinsic evidence of instances of conduct when offered "for the purpose of attacking or supporting the witness's *credibility*" to bar such evidence only when offered "for the purpose of attacking or supporting the witness's *character for truthfulness.*" The amendment is intended to narrow the preclusive effect of the first sentence of Rule 608(b), to make it clear that extrinsic evidence of specific instances of conduct is admissible to attack or support a witness' *credibility* by means other than showing a bad or good *character for truthfulness.*

---

[3] Fed. R. Evid. 608(b); United States v. Arias, 252 F.3d 973, 978–979 (8th Cir. 2001) (although trial court properly excluded testimony of one witness about misconduct of another witness, defendant could have inquired about those acts when cross-examining witness who allegedly committed them).

[4] *See, e.g.,* United States v. Sanders, 343 F.3d 511, 519 (5th Cir. 2003) (fraud is probative of witness's character for truthfulness or untruthfulness); United States v. Novaton, 271 F.3d 968, 1006 (11th Cir. 2001) (officer's formal reprimand for failing to document conversation with informant was not relevant to his character for truthfulness).

[5] *See, e.g.,* United States v. Thiongo, 344 F.3d 55, 60 (1st Cir. 2003) (witness's having knowingly served as legal witness to sham marriage, for purpose of evading immigration laws, was probative of her character for untruthfulness).

[5.1] *See, e.g.,* United States v. Crowley, 318 F.3d 401, 417–418 (2d Cir. 2003) (trial court properly barred cross-examination of alleged rape victim about her alleged false accusations of other men's sexual misconduct because she denied them during voir dire examination out of the jury's presence and defendant could not, under Rule 608(b), introduce extrinsic evidence contrary to her denials).

[5.2] *See, e.g.,* United States v. Tse, 375 F.3d 148, 166–167 (1st Cir. 2004).

[5.3] *See, e.g.,* United States v. Jackson, 310 F.3d 1053, 1053–1054 (8th Cir. 2002) (per curiam) (when defendant admitted his prior conviction for capital murder but attempted to suggest killing was in self-defense, trial court did not abuse its discretion in permitting prosecution to cross-examine defendant concerning details of evidence introduced at trial for earlier offense).

Thus, the amendment clarifies that specific instances of conduct may be used for impeachment, for example, if they reveal the witness's bias, contradict the witness's testimony, or show that the witness made a prior inconsistent statement. The change was intended to make the wording of the Rule consistent with the Supreme Court's reading of Rule 608(b)[6] and to overrule holdings of Courts of Appeals that have read the rule in an overly restrictive fashion.[7]

[b]—Trial Court's Discretion

Inquiry into specific instances of a principal witness's misconduct on cross-examination of that witness is within the trial court's discretion.[8] The specific incidents of misconduct, however, must be probative of untruthfulness.[9]

When determining whether to permit a particular cross-examination under Rule 608(b), it is appropriate for a trial judge to distinguish between the non-party witness and the witness who is also a party, particularly in a criminal case, since the possibility of prejudice will be the greatest when the witness is the accused.[10]

The trial judge also has discretion under Rule 608(b) to limit the types of conduct that can be inquired into on cross-examination. The character of the previous conduct and the proximity in time of the conduct are of significance.[11] The importance of the witness's testimony is also pertinent to the issue of the propriety of impeaching cross-examination.[12]

---

[6] United States v. Abel, 469 U.S. 45, 55–56, 105 S. Ct. 465, 83 L. Ed. 2d 450 (1984) (evidence tending to show witness's bias is admissible even though it also tends "to show that the witness [is] a liar").

[7] See, e.g., Becker v. ARCO Chem. Co., 207 F.3d 176, 190–191 (3d Cir. 2000) (Rule 608(b) bars extrinsic evidence offered for contradiction); United States v. Graham, 856 F.2d 756, 759 (6th Cir. 1988) (Rule 608(b) bars extrinsic evidence offered to prove witness's bias).

[8] Fed. R. Evid. 608(b); see, e.g., Hampton v. Dillard Dep't Stores, Inc., 247 F.3d 1091, 1114 (10th Cir. 2001) (trial court has discretion in admitting or excluding evidence under Rule 608(b)).

[9] See, e.g., United States v. Meserve, 271 F.3d 314, 328–329 (1st Cir. 2001) (trial court abused its discretion by permitting impeachment of witness with evidence of his involvement in fights; such evidence was not probative of untruthfulness and was barred by Rule 608(b)); see also [a], above.

[10] See, e.g., United States v. Pintar, 630 F.2d 1270, 1285–1286 (8th Cir. 1980) (reversible error to permit cross-examination questions concerning prior acts for purposes of impeachment when their prejudicial effect exceed their probative value, particularly when defendant was witness being cross-examined).

[11] See, e.g., Johnson v. Elk Lake Sch. Dist, 283 F.3d 138, 145 n.2 (3d Cir. 2002) (trial court did not abuse its discretion in excluding questions about witness's having lied on his resume more than nine years earlier, because passage of time substantially reduced evidence's probative value, and lying on resume, although duplicitous and wrong, is not so indicative of moral turpitude as to be particularly probative of character for untruthfulness); Carter v. Bell, 218 F.3d 581, 602 (6th Cir. 2000) (evidence of misconduct in military service in 1960s was not probative of credibility in 1984).

[12] See, e.g., United States v. Novaton, 271 F.3d 968, 1006 (11th Cir. 2001) (presumption favors free cross-examination of government's star witness on possible bias, motive, ability to perceive and

Even if questions about a witness's other acts are appropriate impeachment, the balancing test of Rule 403 should be applied and the evidence should be excluded if a question's prejudicial effect outweighs its probative value.[13]

[4]—Attack on Character: Cross-examination of Character Witness as to Specific Acts of Principal Witness[1]

Character witnesses, called pursuant to Rule 608(a), being witnesses themselves, are subject to impeachment and may be cross-examined under Rule 608(b)(1) about their acts probative of truthfulness or untruthfulness under the same conditions as are applicable to impeachment of principal witnesses by evidence of specific incidents of their conduct. *See* [3], *above.*

On cross-examination they may also be asked whether they heard or knew of specific acts committed by the principal witness to impeach the reliability of the foundation for their reputation or opinion testimony of the principal witness's good character. The cross-examination of a character witness concerning specific acts of the principal witness must, however, be limited to specific acts of the principal witness that are probative of the character trait to which the character witness has testified.[2] Similarly, the trial court must curtail cross-examination if the probative value of the specific instance of conduct is outweighed by the danger of unfair prejudice to a party, confusion of issues, or misleading of the jury.[3]

In criminal cases, the likelihood of prejudicing a defendant by revealing his or her prior misdeeds is of special concern.[4] Concerned courts, recognizing this problem, have attempted at least to narrow the opening by limiting indirect attacks on defendants through their character witnesses. They have strictly limited inquiry on cross-examination to those questions relevant to the specific trait of defendant vouched for on direct examination as well as by excluding inquiry about events that are remote in time or that would unduly prejudice the defendant.[5]

---

remember, and general character for truthfulness).

[13] *See, e.g.,* United States v. Novaton, 271 F.3d 968, 1005 (11th Cir. 2001) (Rule 608(b) gives trial court discretion to admit evidence of witness's prior acts if probative of truthfulness, but court must exercise that discretion within constraints of Rule 403).

[1] *See* **Treatise** at § 608.23.

[2] Fed. R. Evid. 608(b).

[3] Fed. R. Evid. 403; *see, e.g.,* United States v. Young, 952 F.2d 1252, 1258 (10th Cir. 1991).

[4] *See* Fed. R. Evid. 404; Ch. 7.

[5] *See, e.g.,* Michelson v. United States, 335 U.S. 469, 483, 69 S. Ct. 213, 93 L. Ed. 168 (1948) (in trial for bribery of federal revenue agent; inquiry as to whether character witnesses had heard of defendant's arrest for receiving stolen goods was proper on ground that "the crimes may be unlike, but both alike proceed from the same defects of character which the witnesses said this defendant was reputed not to exhibit").

[5]—Rehabilitating Character: Proof by Reputation or Opinion[1]

Rule 608(a)(2) provides that rehabilitation or opinion[2] evidence may be used to sustain a witness's character for truthfulness. First, however, the witness's veracity must have been attacked.[3]

The courts of appeals have not agreed on whether a promise to testify truthfully as part of a plea agreement with the government (inadmissible on direct) is rehabilitating evidence.[4] Generally such evidence should not be permitted, since it has the effect of putting the prosecution in the position of vouching for the witness.[5] The trial court has the power to limit the admissibility of cumulative rehabilitating evidence.

Before rehabilitating evidence is admitted, the trial court must decide whether the witness's character for truthfulness has been attacked. Attack is sometimes easy to discern. Evidence of a witness's good character for truth is admissible if reputation or opinion evidence of his or her bad character for veracity has been admitted. The introduction of evidence of convictions pursuant to Rule 609 or the elicitation on cross-examination of the witness's acknowledgment of misconduct not the subject of conviction (Rule 608(b)) will open the door to evidence in support of truthfulness. A trial judge can also find that a witness's credibility was attacked in opposing counsel's opening statement.[6]

---

[1] *See* **Treatise** at §§ 608.10–608.15.

[2] *But cf.* United States v. Azure, 801 F.2d 336, 340 (8th Cir. 1986) (error to allow expert to testify that witness/victim was believable and that there was no reason to believe she was not telling the truth).

[3] *See, e.g.,* United States v. Green, 258 F.3d 683, 692 (7th Cir. 2001) (cross-examination questions asked of law enforcement agent concerning informant's cooperation in other matters were directed toward showing informant was "setting up" several people, including defendant and, therefore, insinuated informant's bias; rehabilitation of informant was properly allowed).

[4] *Compare* United States v. Edwards, 631 F.2d 1049, 1051–1052 (2d Cir. 1980) ("bolstering" portions of plea agreement not admissible on direct examination); United States v. Roberts, 618 F.2d 530, 536 (9th Cir. 1980) (promise of truthfulness not admissible on direct), *with* United States v. Cosentino, 844 F.2d 30, 34 (2d Cir. 1988) (cooperation agreement could be admitted on direct after defense attacked witness's credibility in the opening statement); United States v. Winter, 663 F.2d 1120, 1133–1134 (1st Cir. 1981) (permitting witness to testify that he was immunized in exchange for his complete and truthful testimony does not allow government improperly to vouch for witness's credibility).

[5] By using other portions of a plea agreement in attacking credibility, the cross-examiner may provide a basis for admission of the entire agreement under Rule 106 as a related writing. *See* discussion of Rule 106 in Chapter 2.

[6] *See, e.g.,* United States v. Bonner, 302 F.3d 776, 780–781 (7th Cir. 2002) (trial court did not err in permitting prosecution to introduce evidence of witness's character for veracity after defendant suggested in opening statement that witness's motive for testifying for government was restoration of VA benefits).

When the witness denies misconduct but insinuations have been conveyed to the jury by an accusatory cross-examination, rehabilitation should be allowed in the court's discretion if it finds the witness's denial has not erased the jury's doubts.[7]

Direct attacks on a witness's veracity in the particular case, as opposed to attacks, direct or indirect, on the witness's character for veracity, do not open the door for evidence of the witness's good character. For example, evidence of bias or prior inconsistent statements generally does not open the door for evidence of the witness's character for truthfulness. Evidence of bias does not open the door for evidence of the witness's character for truthfulness because such evidence relates only to a motive to lie in the particular case, not to a general predisposition to lie. Similarly, prior inconsistent statements do not open the door for evidence of the witness's character for truthfulness because there can be a number of reasons for the inconsistency, such as defects in knowledge or memory, a bias or interest to lie in this particular instance, or a general character trait for untruthfulness.[8]

[6]—Impeachment on Basis Other Than Character

Rule 608(b) bars extrinsic evidence to show instances of conduct only when the evidence is being used to attack or support a witness's credibility based on the witness's character for truthfulness.[10] Extrinsic evidence of other conduct offered on a theory other than character for untruthfulness is weighed by the courts under general principles of relevance, probative value, and the risk of unfair prejudice, confusion, or waste of time.[11]

Thus, Rule 608(b) does not prevent a trial court from admitting evidence of a witness's other acts to attack or support the witness's credibility on some other theory, such as bias[12] or impeachment by contradiction.[13] Such direct attacks on the credibility of a witness during testimony, however, do not open the door to

---

[7] United States v. Scholle, 553 F.2d 1109, 1122–1123 (8th Cir. 1977).

[8] *See, e.g.,* Renda v. King, 347 F.3d 550, 554 (3d Cir. 2003).

[10] Fed. R. Evid 608(b).

[11] *See* Fed. R. Evid 401–403; *see, e.g.,* United States v. Green, 258 F.3d 683, 692 (7th Cir. 2001) (Rule 608(b) is inapplicable to impeachment or rehabilitation on theory of bias); *see also* Ch. 6.

[12] *See, e.g.,* United States v. Abel, 469 U.S. 45, 55–56, 105 S. Ct. 465, 83 L. Ed. 2d 450 (1984) (evidence that tends to show witness's bias is admissible although it also tends "to show that the witness [is] a liar"); United States v. Smith, 232 F.3d 236, 240 (D.C. Cir. 2000) (evidence of informant's prior provision of truthful information was properly admitted to rebut implication of bias by showing payment for information; evidence was not "extrinsic" under Rule 608(b) because it went to issue of bias, not to collateral issue of character for truthfulness or untruthfulness).

[13] *See, e.g.,* United States v. Green, 258 F.3d 683, 692 (7th Cir. 2001) (evidence offered for impeachment by contradiction is not subject to restrictions of Rule 608(b)); *see also* United States v. Bonner, 302 F.3d 776, 784–785 (7th Cir. 2002) (barring impeachment by contradiction on collateral matter); United States v. Castillo, 181 F.3d 1129, 1133–1132 (9th Cir. 1999) (allowing

rehabilitation through opinion testimony concerning the witness's character for truthfulness under Rule 608(a). Rehabilitation through evidence of character for truthfulness is appropriate only after attacks based on the witness's character for untruthfulness. It is not available when the attack is based on other grounds, such as the witness's motive to lie concerning the specific subject matter of the testimony.[14]

§ 12.04 Impeachment by Evidence of Conviction—Rule 609

[1]—Scope and Text of Rule[1]

Rule 609 governs the use of criminal convictions for impeachment. There is no entirely satisfactory solution to the use of convictions to impeach.

The version of Rule 609 that was originally enacted had a complicated legislative history, as extensively explored by the Supreme Court in *Green v. Bock Laundry Machine Co.*[2] In reaction to the opinion in *Green,* subdivision (a) of the rule was extensively revised, effective December 1, 1990.[3] The 1990 amendment represents the latest in a series of long-fought-over compromises designed to achieve a workable and reasonably fair set of rules.

As amended in 1990, subdivision (a) treats criminal defendants differently from other witnesses in criminal cases and witnesses in civil cases. Subdivision (b) imposes time restrictions on the use of convictions. Subdivision (c) considers when a pardon or its equivalent renders the conviction inadmissible. Subdivision (d) governs the use of juvenile adjudications, and subdivision (e) regulates the use of

---

impeachment by contradiction concerning defendant's involvement with drugs, in drug smuggling prosecution).

[14] Fed. R. Evid 608(a)(2); *see, e.g.,* Renda v. King, 347 F.3d 550, 554 (3d Cir. 2003) (bias, prior inconsistent statements, and inconsistencies in testimony do not open door to rehabilitation through evidence of character for truthfulness, because they do not suggest general predisposition to lie or general character for untruthfulness).

[1] *See* **Treatise** at § 609App.01 for a discussion of the legislative history of the rule, and §§ 609App.02–609App.03 for its historical antecedents. The admissibility for impeachment purposes of tainted convictions is discussed in the **Treatise** at § 609.07.

[2] Green v. Bock Laundry Machine Co., 490 U.S. 504, 109 S. Ct. 1981, 104 L. Ed. 2d 557 (1989). The *Green* case is discussed further at [3][b], *below.*

[3] Until the the 1990 amendment took effect, Rule 609(a) read as follows:

(a) General rule.—For the purpose of attacking the credibility of a witness, evidence that the witness other than an accused has been convicted of a crime shall be admitted if elicited from the witness or established by public record during cross-examination but only if the crime (1) was punishable by death or imprisonment in excess of one year under the law under which the witness was convicted, and the court determines that the probative value of admitting this evidence outweighs its prejudicial effect to the defendant; or (2) involved dishonesty or false statement, regardless of the punishment.

convictions that are up on appeal. Each of these subdivisions is discussed separately below.

The Rule provides as follows:

Rule 609.   Impeachment by Evidence of Conviction of Crime.

(a)   General rule.—For the purpose of attacking the credibility of a witness,

(1)   evidence that a witness other than an accused has been convicted of a crime shall be admitted, subject to Rule 403, if the crime was punishable by death or imprisonment in excess of one year under the law under which the witness was convicted, and evidence that an accused has been convicted of such a crime shall be admitted if the court determines that the probative value of admitting this evidence outweighs its prejudicial effect to the accused; and

(2)   evidence that any witness has been convicted of a crime shall be admitted if it involved dishonesty or false statement, regardless of the punishment.

(b)   Time limit.—Evidence of a conviction under this rule is not admissible if a period of more than ten years has elapsed since the date of the conviction or of the release of the witness from the confinement imposed for that conviction, whichever is the later date, unless the court determines, in the interests of justice, that the probative value of the conviction supported by specific facts and circumstances substantially outweighs its prejudicial effect. However, evidence of a conviction more than 10 years old as calculated herein, is not admissible unless the proponent gives to the adverse party sufficient advance written notice of intent to use such evidence to provide the adverse party with a fair opportunity to contest the use of such evidence.

(c)   Effect of pardon, annulment, or certificate of rehabilitation.—Evidence of a conviction is not admissible under this rule if (1) the conviction has been the subject of a pardon, annulment, certificate of rehabilitation, or other equivalent procedure based on a finding of the rehabilitation of the person convicted, and that person has not been convicted of a subsequent crime which was punishable by death or imprisonment in excess of one year, or (2) the conviction has been the subject of a pardon, annulment, or other equivalent procedure based on a finding of innocence.

(d)   Juvenile adjudications.—Evidence of juvenile adjudications is generally not admissible under this rule. The court may, however, in a criminal case allow evidence of a juvenile adjudication of a witness other than the accused if conviction of the offense would be admissible to attack the credibility of an adult and the court is satisfied that admission in evidence is necessary for a fair determination of the issue of guilt or innocence.

(e) Pendency of appeal.—The pendency of an appeal therefrom does not render evidence of a conviction inadmissible. Evidence of the pendency of an appeal is admissible.

[*Adopted Jan. 2, 1975, effective July 1, 1975; amended Mar. 2, 1987, effective Oct. 1, 1987; Jan. 26, 1990, effective Dec. 1, 1990.*]

At common law, all felony convictions were usable for impeachment on the theory that a person with a criminal past has a bad general character and therefore is more likely to lie on the witness stand. The assumption that there is a link between credibility and committing crimes has been questioned since the time of Bentham,[4] especially in the case of crimes of violence. Doubts have also been expressed about admitting evidence of a single criminal act that may be atypical of the witness, and may have occurred in the distant past.

Aside from the low probative value of some convictions, the disclosure of a criminal past exposes the witness to the hazards of jury prejudice. The jurors may discount the testimony because of dislike rather than disbelief. If the witness is the accused, the evidence of a past conviction may inflame the jury and lead it to convict the accused on grounds other than the evidence relating to the specific crime with which he or she is charged.[4.1] If the witness is the complainant, the jurors may "acquit a man plainly guilty of crime because of their distaste for the victim."[5] Fear of public degradation may make the possessor of a criminal record reluctant to testify, or even to complain of criminal acts, to the detriment of the judicial system's interest in obtaining useful testimony.

When the witness is a party, the jury's antipathy may be translated into findings of guilt or liability without regard to whether the witness committed the charged acts. This danger is particularly acute in the case of a criminal defendant with a record. The jury may wish to punish regardless of present guilt, or it may assume guilt if the prior conviction was for a similar crime. If the defendant does not testify, statistics indicate that jurors are likely to infer guilt.[6] The defendant is, therefore, caught in the same type of dilemma against which the propensity rule embodied in Rule 404 seeks to protect. Rule 609 extends the policies of the propensity rule to the impeachment process. It responds to both criticisms of the common-law rule:

---

[4] Bentham, Rationale of Judicial Evidence 406 (Browning's ed. 1827) (Bentham pointed out the absurdity of labeling a liar someone who had killed someone for calling him a liar).

[4.1] *See, e.g.,* United States v. Tse, 375 F.3d 148, 163 (1st Cir. 2004).

[5] Davis v. United States, 409 F.2d 453, 457 (D.C. Cir. 1969).

[6] Note, *To Take the Stand or Not to Take the Stand: The Dilemma of the Defendant with a Criminal Record,* 4 Colum. J.L. & Soc. Probs. 213 (1968).

the low probative value of some prior convictions, and the high possibility of prejudice, particularly in the case of criminal defendants. In subdivisions (a), (b) and (c), the rule restricts the use of convictions with the least amount of relevance and affords extra protection to the criminal defendant through the balancing test in subdivision (a)(1).[7]

[2]—Rule 609(a)[1]

[a]—Overview

As originally enacted, Rule 609(a) allowed the credibility of a witness to be impeached either by eliciting the fact of the conviction from the witness[2] or by establishing the public record of the conviction.[3] As amended in 1990, however, the rule recognizes that the usual practice is for counsel to bring out the witness's conviction on direct in order to remove some of the force of the cross-examination.[3.1] Following the amendment, the requirement of eliciting the conviction during cross-examination no longer applies. The Advisory Committee explained the change as follows:

> The amendment does not contemplate that a court will necessarily permit proof of prior convictions through testimony, which might be time-consuming and more prejudicial than proof through a written record. Rules 403 and 611(a) provide sufficient authority for the court to protect against unfair or disruptive methods of proof.

For impeachment purposes, a conviction that results from a guilty plea is equivalent to a determination of guilt following trial.[4] A nolo contendere plea[5] or

---

[7] *See* **Treatise** at § 609.02.

[1] *See* **Treatise** at §§ 609.03–609.05.

[2] United States v. Nevitt, 563 F.2d 406 (9th Cir. 1977), *aff'd*, 595 F.2d 1230 (9th Cir. 1979) (Rule 609(a) does not require a public record of the conviction to lay the foundation for a cross-examination of the witness). *See also* United States v. Scott, 592 F.2d 1139 (10th Cir. 1979) (although "rap sheet" is not admissible as public record of the conviction, it may be used as a basis for cross-examining defendant about his record).

[3] United States v. Bovain, 708 F.2d 606 (11th Cir. 1983) (in prosecution for drug-related offenses, credibility of non-testifying hearsay declarant was properly impeached with certified records of his prior convictions for narcotics and stealing money orders).

[3.1] *See, e.g.,* United States v. Modena, 302 F.3d 626, 632 (6th Cir. 2002) (trial court properly permitted prosecution to "take the sting" out of defendant's impeachment of its witness by introducing evidence of witness's prior conviction during direct examination).

[4] United States v. Pardo, 636 F.2d 535, 545–546 n.32 (D.C. Cir. 1980).

[5] *See, e.g.,* Brewer v. City of Napa, 210 F.3d 1093, 1096 (9th Cir. 2000) (convictions based on nolo contendere pleas properly admitted for impeachment under Rule 609, even though not admissible as statement or admission under Rule 410).

an *Alford* plea[6] is treated like any other conviction for purposes of Rule 609.

However, Rule 609 does not authorize the introduction of evidence concerning arrests that did not result in convictions.[6.1] Conduct that resulted in such an arrest may be admissible,[6.2] but not the mere fact of an arrest.[6.3]

Subject to the restrictions of subdivisions (b)–(e) of the rule, any witness may be impeached by evidence of any felony conviction[7] or of any conviction involving dishonesty or a false statement. Rule 609(a), as amended in 1990, imposes further restrictions on the use of other felony convictions for impeachment. If the witness is the defendant in a criminal trial, the burden rests on the prosecutor to demonstrate that "the probative value of admitting this evidence outweighs its prejudicial effect to the accused." For all other witnesses, felony convictions shall be admitted "subject to Rule 403."[7.1]

When a prior conviction is admissible for impeachment, the impeaching party is generally limited to establishing the bare facts of the conviction, such as the offense charged, the date of conviction, and the sentence imposed.[7.2] It is usually considered prejudicial to elicit the specific details of a crime that does not bear directly on the witness's honesty.[7.3]

On the other hand, it may also be improper for the trial court to limit impeachment

---

[6]   United States v. Lipscomb, 702 F.2d 1049, 1069 (D.C. Cir. 1983) (*en banc*).

[6.1]   United States v. Wilson, 244 F.3d 1208, 1217 (10th Cir. 2001).

[6.2]   *See, e.g.,* United States v. Ramirez, 63 F.3d 937, 942-943 (10th Cir. 1995) (upholding admission under Rule 404(b) of testimony that defendant had been arrested for possession with intent to distribute cocaine on a certain date, in possession of eight ounces of cocaine and roughly $ 43,000 in cash).

[6.3]   *See, e.g.,* United States v. Wilson, 244 F.3d 1208, 1218 (10th Cir. 2001) (error, but harmless, to allow prosecutor to mention defendant's past arrests).

[7]   *See, e.g.,* United States v. Haslip, 160 F.3d 649, 654 (10th Cir. 1998) (evidence of defendant's prior conviction was properly admitted for impeachment under Rule 609 even though court had previously ruled in limine that it was prohibited under Rule 404(b)).

[7.1]   *See, e.g.,* United States v. Cavender, 228 F.3d 792, 799 (7th Cir. 2000) (recent felony convictions of non-defendant witness must be admitted unless Rule 403 justifies its exclusion; here, trial court abused its discretion by excluding witness's conviction for drug possession after witness testified that he did not use drugs during that period of time).

[7.2]   *See, e.g.,* Elcock v. KMart Corp., 233 F.3d 734, 751–752 (3d Cir. 2000) (trial court properly permitted defendant, under Rule 609, to impeach defendant's expert witness with evidence of conviction for embezzlement, and did not abuse its discretion under Rule 608(b) in excluding amount embezzled and other facts and circumstances underlying crime).

[7.3]   *See, e.g.,* Young v. James Green Mgmt., Inc., 327 F.3d 616, 626 (7th Cir. 2003) (ordinarily, impeachment is limited to specification of crime charged, date, and disposition; trial court, however, properly permitted defendant, under Rule 609, to cross-examine plaintiff concerning details of two prior felony convictions to show they were for aggravated assault against woman with whom he lived after defendant testified on direct that he was trying to help his victim "get better").

to the mere fact that the witness has sustained an unspecified prior conviction, without allowing the impeaching party to present the nature and number of offenses involved. Several circuits that have considered the impeachment of a non-defendant witness have concluded that Rule 609(a)(1) requires the trial court to admit evidence of the nature and date of each conviction, subject to Rule 403 balancing.[7.4] Even when the witness is the defendant in a criminal prosecution, the nature of the offense should usually be specified.[7.5]

The restrictions of Rule 609 do not apply if evidence of a conviction is offered for a purpose other than attacking the credibility of a witness.[8] For example, evidence of a conviction may be admitted to contradict the defendant's testimony on a material issue in the case.[9]

[b]—Prosecution Witnesses and Witnesses in Civil Proceedings

Rule 609(a) was amended in 1990 in response to the Supreme Court's opinion in Green v. Bock Laundry Machine Co.[10] In the *Green* case, the Court resolved a conflict among the circuits as to whether a court may exclude a felony conviction offered to impeach a witness in a civil case on the ground of undue prejudice. Conceding that the text of former Rule 609 was ambiguous,[11] the Court relied on

---

[7.4] *See, e.g.,* United States v. Burston, 159 F.3d 1328, 1335–1336 (11th Cir. 1998) (Fed. R. Evid. 609(a)(1) requires district court to admit evidence of nature and number of non-defendant's prior felony convictions, but error of limiting impeachment to mere statement that witness had a prior felony was harmless in light of other impeaching evidence); Doe v. Sullivan County, 956 F.2d 545, 551 (6th Cir. 1992) (Fed. R. Evid. 609(a)(1) requires admission of nature and number of prior convictions); *but see* Foulk v. Charrier, 262 F.3d 687, 699–700 (8th Cir. 2001) (trial court did not abuse its discretion in excluding specific nature of plaintiff's prior convictions, for rape and sodomy, which was not probative of plaintiff's credibility, on ground that prejudicial effect outweighed probative value).

[7.5] *See, e.g.,* United States v. Albers, 93 F.3d 1469, 1479–1481 (10th Cir. 1996) (under Rule 609(a)(1), impeachment of defendant by prior conviction is limited to fact of conviction, general nature of offense, and sentence in felony range; details of crime were improperly brought out, but error was harmless).

[8] *See, e.g.,* Battle v. Memorial Hosp., 228 F.3d 544, 550 (5th Cir. 2000) (trial court did not err in admitting evidence of plaintiff's prior felony conviction when it was relevant to plaintiff's claim for damages).

[9] *See* United States v. Gaertner, 705 F.2d 210, 216 (7th Cir. 1983) (in prosecution for possession of cocaine, after trial court initially ruled that it would exclude, as overly prejudicial, evidence of defendant's prior conviction for possession of marijuana, defendant testified that he was not involved with drugs; the court reversed its ruling and properly admitted the marijuana conviction, since defendant's testimony had specifically raised the issue).

[10] Green v. Bock Laundry Machine Co., 490 U.S. 504, 109 S. Ct. 1981, 104 L. Ed. 2d 557 (1989) (plaintiff who lost his arm while working in a laundry on work release program had been impeached by his prior convictions).

[11] Green v. Bock Laundry Mach. Co., 490 U.S. 504, 510.

legislative history[12] and the overall structure of the Federal Rules of Evidence[13] and agreed with the Seventh Circuit that, with regard to civil trials, Rule 609(a)(1) "can't mean what it says"[14] and that "Rule 403 balancing should not pertain" to Rule 609.[15]
Consequently, all felony convictions and all misdemeanor convictions involving dishonesty and false statement were usable for impeachment against all witnesses in civil proceedings regardless of the prejudice to the witness or the party. Prosecution witnesses were subject to the same broad impeachment.

The 1990 amendment to Rule 609(a)[17] overturned *Green's* holding that the balancing provisions of Rule 403 did not pertain to Rule 609. The rule now provides that all witnesses other than the accused may be impeached by any felony conviction subject to a Rule 403 balancing test (which is discussed in Chapter 6).[17.1] It is the government's burden to show that the prejudicial effect of the proffered impeachment evidence outweighs its probative value when the witness in a criminal case is someone other than the accused.[17.2] Convictions involving dishonesty or false statement are automatically admissible (*see* [d], *below*).

The Advisory Committee explained the purpose of the change thus:

> The amendment reflects the view that it is desirable to protect all litigants from the unfair use of prior convictions, and that the ordinary balancing test of Rule 403, which provides that evidence shall not be excluded unless its prejudicial effect substantially outweighs its probative value, is appropriate for assessing the admissibility of prior convictions for impeachment of any witness other than a criminal defendant.

The Advisory Committee also indicated that it is undesirable "to admit convictions in civil cases that have little, if anything to do with credibility." On the other hand, the Advisory Committee suggested that convictions of prosecution witnesses should be admitted more readily:

> The probability that prior convictions of an ordinary government witness will be unduly prejudicial is low in most criminal cases. Since the behavior

---

[12] Green v. Bock Laundry Mach. Co., 490 U.S. 504, 517–526.
[13] Green v. Bock Laundry Mach. Co., 490 U.S. 504, 517–526.
[14] Green v. Bock Laundry Mach. Co., 490 U.S. 504, 524.
[15] Green v. Bock Laundry Mach. Co., 490 U.S. 504, 526.
[17] Pursuant to 28 U.S.C. § 2074(a), the amendment took effect on December 1, 1990.
[17.1] *See, e.g.,* United States v. Galati, 230 F.3d 254, 261–262 (7th Cir. 2000) (trial court properly excluded, under Rule 403, evidence of witness's prior felony conviction for drug possession because it had little probative value as to her credibility and had high potential for prejudice, in that it might have led jury to discount her testimony unduly).
[17.2] *See, e.g.,* United States v. Tse, 375 F.3d 148, 162 (1st Cir. 2004).

of the witness is not the issue in dispute in most cases, there is little chance that the trier of fact will misuse the convictions offered as impeachment evidence as propensity evidence. Thus, trial courts will be skeptical when the government objects to impeachment of its witnesses with prior convictions. Only when the government is able to point to a real danger of prejudice that is sufficient to outweigh substantially the probative value of the conviction for impeachment purposes will the conviction be excluded.

For example, prior convictions were properly held inadmissible in a civil action arising from a vehicle accident. The defendants sought to impeach the plaintiffs with prior convictions for smuggling drugs into a penitentiary and failing to purchase drug tax stamps. However, the convictions were inadmissible under Rule 609(a)(2) "because these crimes do not, per se, involve dishonesty or false statements." Moreover, they were properly excluded under Rule 609(a)(1), even though they were for felony offenses, because they failed the balancing test of Federal Rule of Evidence 403.[17.3]

[c]—Accused

When the witness to be impeached is the accused in a criminal case, Rule 609 prescribes two tests, dependent upon the type of evidence of conviction offered. If the evidence is of a conviction of a crime involving dishonesty or false statement, it is automatically admissible, regardless whether the crime was a misdemeanor or a felony, and regardless of the amount of prejudice the admission of the evidence may cause any party.[17.4]

If the crime does not involve dishonesty or false statement, evidence of the accused's conviction is admissible only if it was a felony and the probative value of the evidence outweighs its prejudicial effect on the accused.[17.5] Under these tests, a felony conviction that does not qualify for automatic admission as one of dishonesty may be admitted if it's more probative than prejudicial. In contrast, in impeaching a witness other than an accused with a conviction of a crime not involving dishonesty or false statement, the evidence is admissible unless its unfair prejudicial effect substantially outweighs its probative value.[17.6]

[17.3] Gust v. Jones, 162 F.3d 587, 595–596 (10th Cir. 1998) (trial court had discretion to exclude prior felony convictions on drug-related charges as presenting undue risk of unfair prejudice).

[17.4] Fed. R. Evid. 608(a)(2).

[17.5] Fed. R. Evid. 609(a)(1).

[17.6] See, e.g., United States v. Tse, 375 F.3d 148, 163 (1st Cir. 2004); see [b], above.

[d]—Rule 609(a)(2)—Convictions for Crimes Involving Dishonesty or False Statement

Rule 609(a)(2) requires the admission of evidence of all prior convictions of any crime—felony or misdemeanor—involving dishonesty or false statement.[18] The trial courts are without discretion under Rule 403 to exclude evidence of such crimes offered for impeachment.[19]

While characterization of a conviction for purposes of Rule 609 is a federal, not a state matter,[20] the exact state definition of the crime involved will need to be considered.[21] A lesser plea may take a conviction out of the rule even though the details of the criminal act underlying the charge showed extreme dishonesty or involved use of false statements. Though a number of courts have suggested looking to the underlying criminal act rather than the definition of the offense in ascertaining admissibility,[22] it would be a mistake to force the trial court to look behind the conviction.[23] In this area convenience requires a rather mechanical rule. It is better to classify crimes arbitrarily one way or the other and not get into details of a particular offense, such as whether the witness testified at the prior trial and was not believed or whether the particular assault was based on a dishonest trick luring the victim into an alley.[24]

---

[18] United States v. O'Connor, 635 F.2d 814, 819 (10th Cir. 1980) (misdemeanor conviction for crime involving false statement admitted).

[19] Fed. R. Evid 609 Conference Report (1975) ("[t]he exclusion of prior convictions involving dishonesty or false statement is not within the discretion of the Court") (reproduced in pertinent part in **Treatise** at § 609App.01[3]); see, e.g., SEC v. Sargent, 229 F.3d 68, 79–80 (1st Cir. 2000) (even though defendants admitted on cross-examination they lied to Commission, Commission had absolute right to introduce evidence of defendants' convictions for those lies, and trial court erred in excluding such evidence of crime involving dishonesty on Rule 403 considerations).

[20] United States v. Cameron, 814 F.2d 403, 405 (7th Cir. 1987) (not error to exclude witness's state conviction for possession of a switchblade, a misdemeanor, even if state law would characterize crime as one involving dishonesty).

[21] See United States v. Rogers, 853 F.2d 249, 252 (4th Cir. 1988) (defendant's convictions under state worthless check statutes were automatically admissible since the statutes themselves characterized crime as involving dishonesty or false statement).

[22] See, e.g., United States v. Foster, 227 F.3d 1096, 1098–1099 (9th Cir. 2000) (California misdemeanor of receipt of stolen property is not per se crime of dishonesty; trial court erred in receiving evidence of defendant's conviction to impeach his testimony without first determining whether defendant's acts leading to conviction involved deceit or fraud).

[23] United States v. Pandozzi, 878 F.2d 1526, 1533–1534 (1st Cir. 1989) (underlying details excluded); United States v. Lewis, 626 F.2d 940, 946 (D.C. Cir. 1980) ("we do not perceive that it is the manner in which the offense is committed that determines its admissibility. . . . [W]e interpret Rule 609(a)(2) to require that the crime involved dishonesty or false statement as an element of the statutory offense").

[24] But see United States v. Motley, 940 F.2d 1079, 1083–1084 (7th Cir. 1991) (trial court did not err in excluding evidence of government witness's nine-year-old misdemeanor conviction for check deception where defendant failed to show that the conviction actually involved dishonesty and

The courts have had no difficulty in finding that bribery,[25] perjury, subornation of perjury, false statement,[26] embezzlement,[26.1] false pretense,[27] and crimes involving fraud[28] fall within Rule 609(a)(2), while crimes solely involving force do not.[29] The conference committee report to original Rule 609(a) explained that "dishonesty and false statement" includes "any other offense in the nature of crimen falsi, the commission of which involves some element of deceit, untruthfulness, or falsification bearing on the accused's propensity to testify truthfully."[30]

An uncertain area exists, due in part to the vagaries of state practice. Courts have differed, especially in their treatment of crimes involving the taking of property. Some courts view property crimes as involving dishonesty,[31] while others stress that this category of crime had not historically been included in the *crimen falsi* category.[32] If the crime is a felony, it is more in keeping with the spirit of the rule to treat it as one not involving dishonesty or a false statement, so that the trial court can exercise its discretion to exclude the conviction under Rule 609(a)(1). However, if a felony conviction is erroneously admitted under Rule 609(a)(2), the error

---

not merely negligence in overdrawing her checking account).

[25] United States v. Williams, 642 F.2d 136, 140 (5th Cir. 1981) (bribery is a *crimen falsi*; citing **Treatise**).

[26] United States v. Klein, 438 F.Supp 485, 486–487 (S.D.N.Y. 1977) (misdemeanor conviction for willful failure to file income tax withholding returns was admissible although such a conviction does not require proof of an intention to defraud, since "saying nothing" in this instance is tantamount to a false statement); *see also* United States v. Gellman, 677 F.2d 65, 66 (11th Cir. 1982) (failure to file federal income tax return).

[26.1] *See, e.g.,* Elcock v. KMart Corp., 233 F.3d 734, 752 (3d Cir. 2000) (embezzlement is crime of dishonesty is admissible under Rule 609(a)(2)).

[27] Shingleton v. Armour Velvet Corp., 621 F.2d 180, 183 (5th Cir. 1980) (evidence of conviction related to a false pretense scheme admissible pursuant to Rule 609(a)(2)).

[28] United States v. Hans, 738 F.2d 88, 93 (3d Cir. 1984) (prior conviction for interstate transportation of forged securities); United States v. Harris, 738 F.2d 1068, 1073 (9th Cir. 1984) (conviction for passing counterfeit money).

[29] *See, e.g.,* United States v. Meserve, 271 F.3d 314, 328 (1st Cir. 2001) ("To be admissible under Rule 609(a)(2), a prior conviction must involve some element of deceit, untruthfulness, or falsification which would tend to show that an accused would be likely to testify untruthfully, elements not readily apparent in the crimes of disorderly conduct and assault").

[30] Conf. Rep. No. 93–1597, 93d Cong., 2d Sess. 9, reprinted in (1974) U.S. Cong. & Ad. News 7098.

[31] United States v. Kinslow, 860 F.2d 963, 968 (9th Cir. 1988) (armed robbery involves "dishonesty").

[32] *See, e.g.,* United States v. Foster, 227 F.3d 1096, 1100 (9th Cir. 2000) (trial court erred in admitting evidence of defendant's prior misdemeanor conviction for receiving stolen property as impeachment because crime did not involve dishonesty or false statement); United States v. Dunson, 142 F.3d 1213, 1216 (10th Cir. 1998) (shoplifting was not "automatically" crime involving dishonesty or false statement within meaning of Rule 609(a)(2)).

will be harmless if the trial court properly balanced the pertinent factors.[33]

The 1990 amendment to Rule 609 did not make any substantive change in subdivision (a)(2). The Advisory Committee's note explained:

> the Conference Report provides sufficient guidance to trial courts and . . . no amendment is necessary, notwithstanding some decisions that take an unduly broad view of "dishonesty," admitting convictions such as for bank robbery or bank larceny.

[e]—Rule 609(a)(1)—Balancing Test

Rule 609(a)(1) provides that the credibility of a criminal defendant may be attacked by evidence of the defendant's prior felony (not misdemeanor)[34] convictions, subject to the time limit in Rule 609(b), provided "the court determines that the probative value of admitting this evidence outweighs its prejudicial effect to the accused."[34.1] The 1990 amendment to the rule makes it clear that this particular balancing test applies only to the impeachment of a criminal defendant.[35]

Courts have endorsed the consideration of a number of factors in balancing probative value against prejudice to the accused.

The trial court should consider the following factors:[36]

- the impeachment value of the prior crime evidence;[37]

- the proximity in time of the conviction and the defendant's subsequent history;

---

[33] See, e.g., United States v. Provenzano, 620 F.2d 985, 1002–1003 (3d Cir. 1980) (appellate court declined to decide if convictions were admissible pursuant to subdivision (a)(2), since the trial court implicitly found that probative value exceeded prejudice).

[34] United States v. Joost, 133 F.3d 125, 129–130 (1st Cir. 1998) (prior felony was admissible under Rule 609(a) to impeach defendant's credibility); United States v. Slade, 627 F.2d 293, 308 (D.C. Cir. 1980) (reversible error to impeach defendant with misdemeanor conviction for possessing a pistol especially where curative instruction not given until day later).

[34.1] Rule 609(a)(1); see, e.g., Foulk v. Charrier, 262 F.3d 687, 699–700 (8th Cir. 2001) (trial court did not abuse its discretion in excluding evidence of plaintiff's prior convictions for rape and sodomy as impeachment because its probative value was minimal and would not outweigh its prejudicial effect).

[35] As interpreted by the Supreme Court, the original rule provided that a balancing of prejudice to the defendant must be conducted only in criminal cases. The prior convictions of witnesses for the prosecution, or witnesses in a civil case, were to be admitted without regard to the potential for prejudice. Green v. Bock Laundry Machine Co., 490 U.S. 504, 512–513, 109 S. Ct. 1981, 104 L. Ed. 2d 557 (1989), discussed in [b], above. The 1990 amendment added a provision that evidence of a felony conviction of a witness other than an accused "shall be admitted, subject to Rule 403."

[36] See, e.g., Rodriguez v. United States, 286 F.3d 972, 983–984 (7th Cir. 2002).

[37] See, e.g., United States v. Galati, 230 F.3d 254, 261–262 (7th Cir. 2000) (probative value of 20-year old conviction for petty shoplifting was minimal).

- the similarity between the past crime and the charged crime;[38]

- the importance of the defendant's testimony;[39] and

- the centrality of the credibility issue.

Even if the trial court finds that evidence of the conviction is probative of untruthfulness, it should evaluate the importance of the defendant's testimony, considering the consequences of the defendant's being kept from the stand by the fear of having prior convictions divulged. Thus, the court may exclude the conviction if it finds that the defendant's testimony will aid the jury in ascertaining the truth, and refuse to exclude when there is no real need for the defendant's testimony because it would be substantially the same as that of other witnesses.[40] This consideration may, however, be at odds with yet another factor, the centrality of the credibility issue. When the defendant's credibility is the dispositive issue in the case, a court may favor admitting anything, including convictions, that might possibly shed light on whose version of the facts should be believed.[41]

Before the 1990 amendment, this balancing test was also applied to the impeachment of defense witnesses other than the accused. Under the amendment, the impeachment of such witnesses is subject to Rule 403 balancing, as discussed in [b], *above*. The Advisory Committee note to the amendment points out that this provision continues to protect the accused "when the witness bears a special relationship to the defendant such that the defendant is likely to suffer some spill-over effect from impeachment of the witness." For instance, if the witness is a close relative or associate of the defendant, the jury's distrust of the witness if informed of prior convictions may wash off on the defendant. In deciding whether to permit the convictions of the witness to be used, the trial judge should take into consideration the degree of prejudice likely because of the relationship, as well as the significance of the witness's testimony, the similarity between the witness's crime and defendant's crime, and the probative value of the prior conviction on

---

[38] *See, e.g.,* United States v. Sanders, 964 F.2d 295, 298–299 (4th Cir. 1992) (prior conviction is particularly prejudicial when it involves same conduct as charged crime).

[39] *See, e.g.,* United States v. Smith, 131 F.3d 685, 687 (7th Cir. 1997) (Since defendant's testimony directly contradicted that of other main witness, defendant's credibility was central issue in case).

[40] *See, e.g.,* United States v. Fountain, 642 F.2d 1083, 1092 (7th Cir. 1981) (no abuse of discretion where, inter alia, defendant was able to present his defense without testifying).

[41] *See, e.g.,* United States v. Johnson, 302 F.3d 139, 152–153 (3d Cir. 2002) (trial court properly permitted prosecution to impeach defendant with evidence of his prior felony conviction when defense was highly dependent on defendant's credibility, even though conviction was on appeal).

the witness's credibility.[42] To provide the defendant with further protection when a witness closely associated with the defendant is impeached with evidence of a prior conviction, some courts require the trial court to instruct the jury concerning the limited use they may properly make of the impeaching evidence.[42.1]

[f]—Procedure

In all but rare instances, a motion to exclude pursuant to Rule 609(a) is won or lost at the trial level. An appellate court hesitates to reverse when the trial judge has examined the pertinent factors and applied them to the facts presented.[43]

The rationale of the rule—protecting defendants from the prejudicial impact of admitting convictions not probative of untruthfulness—is better served if the trial court makes its Rule 609 determination before the defendant takes the stand. Yet appellate courts afford the district court discretion to defer ruling until after the evidence is offered.[44] Generally, however, the question of which convictions will be usable to attack credibility should be determined before trial.[45] Counsel need to know what the ruling will be on this matter so that they can make appropriate tactical decisions. For example, the opening of defense counsel or the decision of the defendant to take the stand may be affected.

The Supreme Court has held that a trial judge's decision to admit a defendant's prior conviction for impeachment purposes is not subject to review unless the defendant takes the stand.[46] Thus an adverse ruling in limine must be followed up by preserving the matter at trial. The Second Circuit has held, however, that this limitation does not apply when defendant objects to the conviction which the trial court refused to exclude on the ground that it is constitutionally invalid.[47]

The trial court should make its determination after a hearing on the record

---

[42] *See* United States v. Peterman, 841 F.2d 1474, 1480 (10th Cir. 1988) (no abuse of discretion in permitting impeachment of co-defendant, a government witness, by evidence of his prior conviction).

[42.1] *See, e.g.,* United States v. Modena, 302 F.3d 626, 632 (6th Cir. 2002) (trial court erred in not giving jury limiting instruction concerning use it could make of prior convictions evidence offered to blunt effect of potential impeachment of prosecution witness).

[43] *See, e.g.,* United States v. Howell, 285 F.3d 1263, 1269 (10th Cir. 2002) ("we are more deferential to the district court's decision concerning the admissibility of evidence of a felony conviction where the court has conducted [Rule 403] balancing").

[44] *See, e.g.,* United States v. Kennedy, 714 F.2d 968, 974–975 (9th Cir. 1983).

[45] United States v. Cook, 608 F.2d 1175, 1186, 1189 (9th Cir. 1979) (*en banc*) (matter should be left to discretion of trial judge with a reminder that advance planning helps both parties and the court); United States v. Oakes, 565 F.2d 170, 172 (1st Cir. 1977).

[46] Luce v. United States, 469 U.S. 38, 41–42, 105 S. Ct. 460, 83 L. Ed. 2d 443 (1984).

[47] Biller v. Lopes, 834 F.2d 41, 44–45 (2d Cir. 1987) (habeas corpus; *Luce* does not apply where in limine ruling depends on legal and not factual considerations). *See* **Treatise** at § 609.11 for discussion of use of tainted convictions for impeachment.

pursuant to Rule 104, explicitly identifying and weighing the pertinent factors.[48] In a criminal case, the prosecution has the burden of showing that the accused's prior conviction should be admissible for impeachment.[49] However, defense counsel should also be prepared to analyze and argue the pertinent considerations.[50] In civil cases and for witnesses in criminal trials other than the accused, the party calling the witness will have to demonstrate that the factors of unfair prejudice, confusion or misleading the jury, as specified in Rule 403, substantially outweigh the probative value of the conviction.

If in a criminal case the trial judge admits evidence of a conviction, counsel for the prosecution should not be allowed to prejudice the defendant by bringing out details of the crime.[51] Nor should insinuations about any other crimes be countenanced.[52]

The witness may make a brief statement in explanation or mitigation.[53] The scope of the statement lies in the trial judge's discretion subject to the general policy of Rule 403 dictating exclusion of prejudicial, confusing and time-consuming evidence unredeemed by substantial probative value.[54]

---

[48] United States v. Cook, 608 F.2d 1175, 1186 (9th Cir. 1979) (*en banc*) ("In future cases, the court and counsel confronting Rule 609 problems should turn to Fed.R.Evid. 103 for guidance.").

[49] *See, e.g.,* United States v. Hendershot, 614 F.2d 648, 652 (9th Cir. 1980) (reversible error where not clear whether trial court properly applied Rule 609(a)(1) which requires prosecution to bear the burden of establishing that probative value outweighs prejudice).

[50] United States v. Reed, 572 F.2d 412, 427 (2d Cir. 1978) (trial court could not "be faulted for failing to make extensive findings in response to a mere inquiry at a pre-trial hearing, unaccompanied by either facts or argument").

[51] United States v. Callison, 577 F.2d 53, 55 (8th Cir. 1978) (trial judge properly excluded questions relating to fact that previous robbery was of same bank at same time as charged robbery).

[52] United States v. Tumblin, 551 F.2d 1001, 1004–1005 (5th Cir. 1977) (reversible error for government on cross-examination to not only have reaffirmed existence of prior convictions conceded on direct, but also to have emphasized that defendant had been released for only a few weeks when he was again arrested, and that he had held no regular job because he was almost always in jail).

[53] *Cf.* United States v. Wolf, 561 F.2d 1376, 1380–1382 (10th Cir. 1977) (where the defendant on direct examination attempts to explain away the effect of the conviction or to minimize his guilt, the defendant may be cross-examined on any facts which are relevant to the direct examination, and prosecutor could question defendant as to the details of the count to which he pleaded guilty and the remaining counts which were dismissed).

[54] United States v. Morrow, 977 F.2d 222, 227–228 (6th Cir. 1992) (defendant appealed his conviction for marijuana offenses, arguing that the district court erred in admitting evidence of a prior armed robbery conviction for the purpose of impeachment. The defendant claimed that the district court failed to balance prejudice against probative value on the record. The court of appeals held that the conviction was properly admitted under Rule 609(a)(1), because the trial court limited examination of the defendant to the fact of the prior conviction and allowed no further probing by the prosecution. This concern demonstrated the trial court's awareness of the potential prejudice of the evidence despite the failure to use the actual words "probative" and "prejudice.")

[3]—Time Limit[1]

If more than ten years has elapsed from the date of conviction, or the witness's release, whichever is later, the conviction is ordinarily not usable for impeachment.[2] A conviction that is more than ten years old is admissible in a criminal or civil action[3] if the proponent gives advance written notice[4] of intent to use the conviction and convinces the trial judge that because of specific facts and circumstances the probative value of the conviction outweighs its prejudicial effect.[5] When the conviction is more than ten years old but the witness's parole or probation for that conviction was revoked within ten years of the trial, the court may use the date of the revocation rather than the conviction, if the reason for the revocation is related to the original conviction.[6] In the case of a prosecution witness, the pressures of the Confrontation Clause may, at times, require admission of convictions that are more than ten years old.

Some courts interpreting Rule 609(b) have expressed uncertainty about whether the applicable period should be measured up to the date when the trial commences, or the witness testifies, or the date of the charged crime.[7] The time of testimony is more appropriate since the jury must determine credibility at that moment.[8]

---

[1] *See* **Treatise** at § 609.07.

[2] Fed. R. Evid 609(b); *see, e.g.*, Foulk v. Charrier, 262 F.3d 687, 699 n.10 (8th Cir. 2001) (when plaintiff was serving consecutive 10-year sentences and first had been completed less than 10 years prior to current trial, both convictions were available for impeachment under Rule 609(b)). United States v. Daniel, 957 F.2d 162, 168-169 (5th Cir. 1992) (prior felony conviction that was ten years and four days old at time witness testified was properly excluded as beyond ten-year limit).

[3] Czaijka v. Hickman, 703 F.2d 317, 319 (8th Cir. 1983); Tussel v. Witco Chem. Corp., 555 F. Supp. 979, 984–985 (W.D. Pa. 1983).

[4] *See, e.g.*, United States v. Meserve, 271 F.3d 314, 328 n.4 (1st Cir. 2001) (prosecution's failure to give required notice and to show that probative value outweighed prejudicial effect made admission of witness's stale conviction error).

[5] *See, e.g.*, United States v. Orlando-Figueroa, 229 F.3d 33, 45 (1st Cir. 2000) (trial court did not abuse its discretion in excluding stale mail fraud conviction of important government witness on ground that probative value did not substantially outweigh prejudicial effect); United States v. Bensimon, 172 F.3d 1121, 1127 (9th Cir. 1999) (conviction reversed because court improperly balanced probative value and prejudicial effect of defendant's seventeen-year-old conviction).

[6] United States v. McClintock, 748 F.2d 1278 (9th Cir. 1984) (probation was revoked for violation of condition related to the original crime).

[7] United States v. Cathey, 591 F.2d 268, 274 n.13, 278 n.2 (5th Cir. 1979).

[8] *See* United States v. Daniel, 957 F.2d 162, 168-169 (5th Cir. 1992) (prior felony conviction that was ten years and four days old at time witness testified was properly excluded as beyond ten-year limit); Pepe v. Jayne, 761 F. Supp. 338 (D.N.J. 1991), *aff'd*, 947 F.2d 936 (3d Cir. 1991) (in medical malpractice action, date of the conviction of defendant's expert witness for filing false and fraudulent records measured from time of testimony, not time of filing medical report in the case; thus conviction was more than ten years old, and not automatically admissible). *But see* United States v. Foley, 683 F.2d 273, 277 n.5 (8th Cir. 1982) (court measures up to date of charged crime).

[4]—Pardon or Equivalent[1]

Rule 609(c) considers the effect of a pardon, annulment, or certificate of rehabilitation on the admissibility of a conviction. It provides that evidence of a conviction is not admissible if the pardon, annulment, certificate of rehabilitation, or other equivalent procedure[2] either (1) was based on innocence, or (2) required a showing of rehabilitation and the witness has not subsequently been convicted of a felony.[3]

The burden rests on counsel calling the pardoned witness to show that the prior conviction may not be used for impeachment. It is that attorney's obligation to gather the pertinent facts underlying the pardon or certificate of rehabilitation and to demonstrate to the court outside the hearing of the jury that the use of the conviction is barred pursuant to Rule 609(c).[4]

When a pardon states on its face that the reason for its issuance is the rehabilitation of the recipient, the conviction is not admissible for impeachment unless the proponent provides evidence that the witness has committed a subsequent felony; the trial court has no discretion to admit the conviction for impeachment.[5] On the other hand, an expungement of a criminal conviction pursuant to a state procedure that allows use of the conviction in certain proceedings does not come within this category of convictions. Such convictions may be used for impeachment in federal civil and criminal actions in the same manner as any other conviction.[6]

---

[1] *See* **Treatise** at § 609.08.

[2] United States v. Pagan, 721 F.2d 24, 28–31 (2d Cir. 1983) (certificate setting aside defendant's prior youthful offender conviction and unconditionally discharging him from further probation prior to expiration of maximum term of probation implied finding of rehabilitation, which constituted an "other equivalent procedure" under Rule 609(c)(1)).

[3] *Compare* United States v. Thorne, 547 F.2d 56 (8th Cir. 1976) (trial court properly exercised its discretion in concluding that prosecution witness had been rehabilitated although this was not evidenced by any certificate; subsequent to drug conviction, witness had received master's degree in guidance and counseling and was now director of drug rehabilitation program) *with* United States v. Jones, 647 F.2d 696 (6th Cir. 1981) (pardon which restored civil rights did not prove defendant's rehabilitation and did not make evidence of prior conviction inadmissible).

[4] United States v. Trejo-Zambrano, 582 F.2d 460 (9th Cir. 1978) (no error where conviction was used for impeachment because defense counsel overlooked entry on rap sheet provided by government; Rule 609 does not shift burden to government to discover whether a prior conviction was vacated; dissent found that government had responsibility to show that conviction had not been expunged).

[5] *See, e.g.,* Brown v. Frey, 889 F.2d 159, 171 (8th Cir. 1989) (trial court has no discretion to allow use of evidence of conviction for impeachment when pardon states that it was based on rehabilitation).

[6] *See, e.g.,* United States v. Moore, 556 F.2d 479, 483-485 (10th Cir. 1977) (not error for trial judge to deny defendant's motion to exclude evidence of prior California felony conviction when conviction had been expunged but California statute specifically provided that expunged conviction might be used in subsequent criminal proceeding involving the same party).

Similarly, a procedure that results in the expungement of a criminal conviction from the convict's record conditioned on performance of certain tasks, not relying on a finding of rehabilitation, does not make the conviction inadmissible under Rule 609(c).[7]

[5]—Juvenile Adjudications[1]

In criminal proceedings,[2] subdivision (d) of Rule 609 authorizes impeachment use of a juvenile adjudication[3] of a witness other than the defendant if "the judge is satisfied that admission in evidence is necessary for a fair determination of the issue of guilt or innocence."[4] The burden is on the side wishing to use the adjudication to show that the particular factors of the case excuse compliance with the usual rule of exclusion.[5]

[6]—Pendency of Appeal[1]

Rule 609(e) provides that pendency of an appeal does not bar use of the conviction. The rule rests on the assumption of correctness that ought to attend judicial proceedings. The same rationale permits use of convictions even though

---

[7]   *See, e.g.,* U.S. Xpress Enters., Inc., J.B. Hunt Transp., Inc., 320 F.3d 809, 816 (8th Cir. 2003) (Canadian procedure allowing "absolution" of conviction after person convicted pays fine and serves probated sentence, but does not involve finding of rehabilitation, does not require exclusion of evidence of conviction under Rule 609(c)).

[1]   *See* **Treatise** at § 608.09.

[2]   Samples v. City of Atlanta, 916 F.2d 1548 (11th Cir. 1990) (suit by parents of youth fatally shot by police officer; youth's juvenile court records were introduced to show mother's awareness of his glue-sniffing habit; Rule 609 prohibits use of witness's juvenile records to impeach *that* witness, and in this case the records were properly used to impeach *another* witness; Rule 609 does not bar use of all criminal records in civil proceedings).

[3]   United States v. Ashley, 569 F.2d 975 (5th Cir. 1978) (conviction under the Federal Youth Corrections Act is a conviction of a crime not rendered inadmissible by Rule 609(d) which refers only to adjudications of delinquency). *But cf.* United States v. Mothershed, 859 F.2d 585, 591 (8th Cir. 1988), in which the court reserved decision on whether adjudication under the Federal Youthful Offenders Act is a "juvenile adjudication" under Rule 609(d).

[4]   United States v. Rogers, 918 F.2d 207 (D.C. Cir. 1990) (in prosecution for possession of crack with intent to distribute, the court admitted evidence, offered by the government, of defendant's prior juvenile adjudication of crack distribution; defendant argued that Rule 609(d) prohibited the admission of the adjudication, and further that admitting it as a prior crime under Rule 404(b) would nullify the prohibition in 609(d); the court held that admission was proper because Rule 609 governs evidence used for impeachment, and here the evidence was properly used to show intent and absence of mistake; citing **Treatise**); United States v. Ciro, 753 F.2d 248 (2d Cir. 1985) (given the ample opportunity for cross-examination of witness, excluded evidence was not necessary for a fair trial).

[5]   *See* United States v. Decker, 543 F.2d 1102, 1104–1105 (5th Cir. 1976) (where defendants proffered no evidence concerning prosecution witness's juvenile adjudication they could not complain of the trial court's failure to admit evidence of the adjudication).

[1]   *See* **Treatise** at § 609.10.

post-trial motions following sentencing are still under consideration by the trial court.[2] Rule 609(e) specially provides that evidence of the appeal's pendency may be admitted to reduce the impact of the conviction.[3] It is silent about a somewhat related but rarer situation: the propriety of attacking a witness's credibility by showing a verdict of guilty on which no judgment has been entered or sentence passed. Under federal practice, a judgment of conviction requires setting forth the sentence.[4]

However, in some cases the trial court's acceptance of the jury's verdict is a sufficient predicate to use the conviction for impeachment in a subsequent trial.[5]

§ 12.05 Impeachment by Evidence of Religious Belief Prohibited—Rule 610[1]

Rule 610 bars evidence of religious adherence[2] when offered to show that the witness's credibility is thereby impaired or enhanced.[3] Exclusion rests on grounds of relevancy, prejudice, and constitutional considerations.[4]

The Rule provides as follows:

Rule 610.   Religious Beliefs or Opinions.

Evidence of the beliefs or opinions of a witness on matters of religion is not admissible for the purpose of showing that by reason of their nature the witness's credibility is impaired or enhanced.

[Adopted Jan. 2, 1975, effective July 1, 1975; amended Mar. 2, 1987, effective Oct. 1, 1987.]

---

[2] United States v. Bianco, 419 F. Supp. 507, 509 (E.D. Pa. 1976), *aff'd mem.,* 547 F.2d 1164 (3d Cir. 1977). *Cf.* United States v. Collins, 552 F.2d 243, 247 (8th Cir. 1977) (using conviction on which sentence had been suspended is substantially analogous to using conviction which is pending on appeal; citing Rule 609(c); Missouri law that a suspended sentence is not a final judgment of conviction is not applicable in federal prosecution).

[3] United States v. Shaver, 511 F.2d 933 (4th Cir. 1975) (citing Rule 609(c) and suggesting that instruction to jury to disregard conviction pending appeal might be desirable). *Cf.* United States v. Klayer, 707 F.2d 892 (6th Cir. 1983) (the only generally recognized exception to Rule 609(e) involves the credibility impeachment of a defendant convicted without representation of counsel).

[4] Fed. R. Crim. P. 32(b)(1).

[5] *See* United States v. Mitchell, 886 F.2d 667, 670–671 (4th Cir. 1989) (although defendant had not been sentenced with regard to prior federal conviction at time he was impeached, district court had denied post-trial motions, and defendant was properly impeached on this basis).

[1] *See* **Treatise** at Ch. 610, *Religious Beliefs or Opinions.*

[2] United States v. Sampol, 636 F.2d 621, 666 (D.C. Cir. 1980) ("scope of the prohibition includes unconventional or unusual religions.").

[3] *See, e.g.,* United States v. Rushing, 313 F.3d 428, 433 (8th Cir. 2002) (Rule 610 puts evidence of witness's religious affiliation out of bounds for most purposes).

[4] *See* **Treatise** at §§ 610.02–610.03.

Evidence probative of something other than veracity is not within the prohibition of the rule. For example, disclosure of affiliation with a church that is a party to the litigation may be admitted as relevant to bias, and adherence to a particular religious sect may have bearing on whether expenditures had been made for medical care in a personal injury case.

§ 12.06 Prior Statements of Witnesses—Rule 613

[1]—Scope and Text of Rule[1]

Rule 613 governs foundational requirements for the introduction of a witness's prior inconsistent statements, written or oral, made out of court. Rule 613 does not expressly provide for the circumstances under which evidence of a witness's prior inconsistent statement are admissible. However, it implicitly permits the use of a prior inconsistent statement as impeachment after a witness has testified inconsistently with that prior statement,[1.1] under certain circumstances. Rule 613, in its explicit language, only relaxes certain common-law prerequisites to the admissibility of a prior inconsistent statement.

The prior inconsistent statement is not admissible unless the subject matter is the same as the testimony it allegedly contradicts. It also is not admissible unless both the testimony and the prior statement concern a subject that is material to the litigation.[1.2]

Foundation requirements for statements inconsistent with hearsay testimony are prescribed by Rule 806, which is discussed in Chapter 14.

Rule 613 provides as follows:

Rule 613. Prior Statements of Witnesses.

(a) Examining witness concerning prior statement.—In examining a witness concerning a prior statement made by the witness, whether written or not, the statement need not be shown nor its contents disclosed to the witness at that time, but on request the same shall be shown or disclosed to opposing counsel.

(b) Extrinsic evidence of prior inconsistent statement of witness.—Extrinsic evidence of a prior inconsistent statement by a witness

---

[1] *See* **Treatise** at § 613.02.

[1.1] *See, e.g.,* United States v. Morgan, 376 F.3d 1002, 1007 (9th Cir. 2004) (once witness testified that she did not owe creditors in excess of $100,000, her bankruptcy petition listing more than $100,000 in secured creditors claims was admissible under Rule 613 as prior inconsistent statement).

[1.2] *See, e.g.,* United States v. Bolzer, 367 F.3d 1032, 1039 (8th Cir. 2004).

is not admissible unless the witness is afforded an opportunity to explain or deny the same and the opposite party is afforded an opportunity to interrogate the witness thereon, or the interests of justice otherwise require. This provision does not apply to admissions of a party-opponent as defined in rule 801(d)(2).

[*Adopted Jan. 2, 1975, effective July 1, 1975; amended Mar. 2, 1987, effective Oct. 1, 1987; Apr. 25, 1988, effective Nov. 1, 1988.*]

Rule 613 liberalizes foundation requirements in two ways. First, it sets aside the rule in The Queen's Case,[2] which required a witness be shown a prior written statement before impeachment on the statement could proceed. Secondly, it eliminates mandatory foundational questions directing the attention of the witness to the time when, place where, and person to whom the alleged inconsistent statement was made.

The main impact of the changes from the orthodox rule is to give greater weight to surprise than to warning as a technique for ascertaining the truth. In civil cases where discovery has been fully utilized, only rarely will a critical witness not have been apprised of any important inconsistent statements. The liberalization of the traditional rule is, therefore, most likely to have an impact in criminal cases.

Rule 613 should be applied to inconsistent statements used to impeach even though the statements would be admissible as evidence-in-chief pursuant to Rule 801(d)(1).[3] As provided in subdivision (b), however, Rule 613 does not apply to inconsistent statements of a party opponent as defined in Rule 801(d)(2), since the statements of a party qualify as admissions without regard to whether the party takes the stand. It should be noted that the Federal Rules of Evidence extend the concept of party admissions considerably beyond a party in an individual capacity.

Rule 613, under the principle *expressio unius est exclusio alterius*, does not apply to impeachment by evidence of prior inconsistent conduct. The court, however, has the power to require inquiring counsel to reveal to the court and opposing counsel, outside the hearing of the jury, the basis for any question to the witness designed to show inconsistent conduct. Attorneys should not be permitted to insinuate by innuendo that something has occurred which in fact has not.

---

[2] 2 Br. & B. 284, 129 Eng. Rep. 976 (1820).

[3] *See* United States v. International Business Machines Corp., 432 F. Supp. 138 (S.D.N.Y. 1977) (although Rule 613(b) has no direct application where evidence may be used substantively as well as for impeachment, standards of fairness contemplated by the rule are apposite); *see also* discussion of Rule 801(d) in Chapter 15.

[2]—Impeachment by Proof of Prior Inconsistent Statement[1]

Rule 613 simplifies the foundational requirements for impeachment by prior inconsistent statements. A witness need not be shown or made aware of the contents of a prior statement at the time the witness is being examined about the statement. Nor must the witness be asked on the stand, while under cross-examination, whether he or she made the supposed inconsistent statement as a condition precedent to impeachment by extrinsic evidence of the statement. Rule 613 imposes only two conditions. Subdivision (a) requires that on request, the statement "shall be shown or disclosed to opposing counsel."[2] Subdivision (b) provides that when extrinsic evidence of a prior inconsistent statement is introduced, the witness must at some time, either before or after the contents of the statement are made known to the jury, be afforded a chance to explain, while the opposite party must be given an opportunity to examine on the statement.[3]

Some courts have imposed an additional prerequisite to the use of a prior inconsistent statement. Following the lead of Rule 105 (*see* § 2.04), they require the trial court, on request, to instruct the jury concerning the limited use they may make of the prior statement.[3.1]

Moreover, Rule 613(b) does not require the trial court to admit evidence of a prior inconsistent statement when the proponent meets its foundational requirements. The trial court still retains the discretion to exclude the prior statement under Rule 403.[3.2]

Unlike the common-law rule, Rule 613 does not specify a particular sequence for impeachment by prior inconsistent statements.[4] Impeachment satisfies the

---

[1] *See* **Treatise** at §§ 613.03–613.05.

[2] United States v. Valencia, 913 F.2d 378, 385 (7th Cir. 1990) (trial court erred in refusing to permit defendant to cross examine DEA agent concerning statements made to agent by informant as reflected in agent's investigative report on ground defendant had not laid foundation by confronting informant with report's record of statements when informant was on stand; government could have called informant to stand during rebuttal to explain or deny statements attributed to him in report; error was harmless).

[3] Fed. R. Evid. 613(b); *see, e.g.,* Udemba v. Nicoli, 237 F.3d 8, 17–18 (1st Cir. 2001) (extrinsic evidence of prior statement inconsistent with witness's trial testimony properly admitted so long as witness has opportunity to explain and opponent has opportunity to interrogate witness concerning prior statement).

[3.1] *See, e.g.,* United States v. Larry Reed & Sons, P'ship, 280 F.3d 1212, 1215 (8th Cir. 2002) (trial court erred in failing to give limiting instruction, but, in absence of request, failure is reviewed for plain error).

[3.2] *See, e.g.,* United States v. Young, 248 F.3d 260, 268 (4th Cir. 2001).

[4] United States v. Moore, 149 F.3d 773, 781 (8th Cir. 1998) (Rule 613(b) provides only that the witness have an opportunity to explain and the opposite party have an opportunity to examine on the statement; it does not specify any particular time or sequence for this procedure).

requirements of Rule 613 if the witness is ultimately given an opportunity to explain his or her statement and the opposite party is given an opportunity to examine the statement.

Notions of fairness underlie the requirements set forth in subdivisions (a) and (b). Allowing counsel to see the statement protects the witness from unfair insinuations, and gives counsel the opportunity to challenge the authenticity of the statement. Insistence upon the witness's right to explain protects the witness who has something to say in extenuation, for example, a denial that the statement was made or an explanation that reconciles the supposedly inconsistent statements.

Although the common-law rule provided more of a shield against unfairness because it gave the witness a chance to explain before the inconsistent statement was introduced, the drafters of Rule 613 found a diminution in protection justified. Allowing the statement to be introduced before the witness is asked for an explanation, guards against the tailoring of testimony that may occur when an unscrupulous witness is forewarned of the terms of a statement.

Rule 613 does not make the party that uses the prior inconsistent statement for impeachment responsible for affording the witness an opportunity to explain. The rule merely states that the witness must have that opportunity. The impeaching party provides the witness with a sufficient opportunity to explain the inconsistency by confronting the witness with the prior inconsistent statement during the impeaching party's examination.[4.1]

Neither side has the burden of recalling the witness; normally the impeaching party will not wish to do so.[5] To avoid having the witness wait to see whether inconsistent statements will be introduced and whether the witness will be asked to explain them, the court may require impeachment while the witness is on the stand or immediately thereafter.[5.1] Moreover, impeaching counsel may not effectively deprive the witness of an opportunity to explain the prior inconsistent statement by foregoing the impeachment examination while the witness is on the stand and withholding extrinsic evidence of the inconsistent statement until the witness is excused and has become unavailable for recall for further testimony.[5.2]

[4.1] *See, e.g.,* United States v. Buffalo, 358 F.3d 519, 524 (8th Cir. 2004) (impeaching party gave witness adequate opportunity to explain inconsistency by asking witness whether he had ever confessed to assault with which impeaching party was charged).

[5] *See, e.g.,* Wilmington Trust Co. v. Manufacturers Life Insurance Co., 749 F.2d 694, 699 (11th Cir. 1985) (waiver where proponent of witness failed to request that witness be allowed to testify in surrebuttal about impeaching statement, or that case be reopened).

[5.1] *See, e.g.,* United States v. Schnapp, 322 F.3d 564, 572 (8th Cir. 2003).

[5.2] *See, e.g.,* Manley v. AmBase Corp., 337 F.3d 237, 246–248 (2d Cir. 2003) (trial court did not err in excluding impeachment by prior inconsistent statement contained in discovery deposition when witness participated in subsequent deposition that was to serve as substitute for witness's

Rule 613 permits a court to dispense with the witness's right to explain or deny in "the interests of justice." A court might rely on this provision when the statement was made after cross-examination, or came to counsel's attention after the witness testified, and the witness, through no fault of counsel, is not available for recall. Beyond such situations, the court's discretion under subdivision (b) should rarely be exercised. Prior inconsistent statements that relate to crucial testimony should almost never be admitted if foundational requirements can be, but have not been, met.[6]

Despite the liberalization of foundation requirements in Rule 613, the court or counsel may still choose to follow traditional practice.[7] The pressures of the best evidence and authentication rules may force counsel to cross-examine the witness about the statement before offering it for impeachment, since proof of authenticity or originality may be much easier or, in some instances, possible only if the witness is available. These requirements should normally be met before the statement is introduced or read to the jury. Permitting the statement to be revealed to the jury subject to a later limiting instruction may be prejudicial where the improperly admitted statement relates to a crucial point.

When a prior inconsistent statement is drawn to a witness's attention, the witness may admit, deny or explain the statement. Under traditional practice, some courts would refuse to allow extrinsic evidence of the statement once the witness admitted having made it.[8] If counsel suspects that the witness will admit having made the statement, there may be a reason to dispense with the laying of a foundation, since the statement may have more of an impact if it is read in its entirety or testified to by another witness.

The Rule does not specify when a prior statement is "inconsistent." It applies when the witness's testimony is "irreconcilably at odds" with a prior statement. However, the trial court has broad discretion in determining whether a prior

---

appearance at trial in view of witness's illness; plaintiff was forewarned that second deposition was to be conducted just as if witness were testifying at trial, and that witness's opportunity to explain any prior inconsistent statements had to be preserved by conducting impeachment examination at second deposition).

[6] *See* Wammock v. Celotex Corp., 793 F.2d 1518, 1522 (11th Cir. 1986) (citing **Treatise**; trial judge properly refused to admit prior inconsistent statements made by plaintiff's expert, when they were offered at the close of the trial and the expert was no longer available).

[7] *See* United States v. Schnapp, 322 F.3d 564, 571 (3d Cir. 2003) (trial court did not abuse its discretion in declining to permit defendant to introduce testimony regarding witness's prior inconsistent statements when defendant failed to confront witness with statement, even though prosecution could have recalled witness to explain).

[8] *See, e.g.,* United States v. Arena, 180 F.3d 380, 400 (2d Cir. 1999) (extrinsic evidence of witness's prior statement inadmissible because witness had already testified about the prior statement).

statement is inconsistent with the witness's testimony, and it need not be squarely at odds with the testimony.[9] For example, a witness's prior statement that omits details included in the trial testimony is inconsistent with the testimony only if it would have been "natural" for the witness to have included the details in the prior testimony.[10]

In a criminal case, there is some uncertainty about whether a prior statement may be used for impeachment where the witness not only denies having made the statement, but also denies all knowledge of the underlying event. In one case, for example, an alibi witness was cross-examined about an incriminating statement that he allegedly made to a police officer. When he denied having made the statement, the trial court allowed the officer to testify about statement. On appeal, the parties differed about whether the statement was an instance of conduct governed by Rule 608(b) or a prior inconsistent statement under Rule 613(b). In the circuit court's view, "Rule 613(b) applies when two statements, one made at trial and one made previously, are irreconcilably at odds. In such an event, the cross-examiner is permitted to show the discrepancy by extrinsic evidence if necessary—not to demonstrate which of the two is true but, rather, to show that the two do not jibe (thus calling the declarant's credibility into question). . . . In contrast, Rule 608(b) addresses situations in which a witness's prior activity, whether exemplified by conduct or by a statement, in and of itself casts significant doubt upon his veracity. . . . Thus, Rule 608(b) applies to, and bars the introduction of, extrinsic evidence of specific instances of a witness's misconduct if offered to impugn his credibility."[11]

A constitutional issue may be posed if counsel for the prosecution introduces the statement and subsequently discovers that the witness claims an inability to remember.[12] Allowing the witness to explain immediately after the statement has been used for impeachment will rarely if ever lead to error.

The cross-examiner's choice of when to ask the foundational questions will hinge on such tactical concerns as, for instance, whether delay will increase the likelihood that the jury will discount the explanation, or whether the explanation will have a "spill-over effect" destructive to the cross-examiner's theory of the case. The court's choice will normally be to require foundational questions while the witness is cross-examined, since this will often expedite the trial and prevent confusion on the part of the jury.

---

[9]   *See, e.g.,* Udemba v. Nicoli, 237 F.3d 8, 18 (1st Cir. 2001).

[10]   *See, e.g.,* United States v. Meserve, 271 F.3d 314, 320–321 (1st Cir. 2001).

[11]   United States v. Winchenbach, 197 F.3d 548, 556–558 (1st Cir. 1999) (officer's testimony contradicted witness's testimony and was admissible extrinsic evidence of prior inconsistent statement).

[12]   *See* **Treatise** at § 613.05[3][c].

CHAPTER 13

*Expert Witnesses**

SYNOPSIS

---

* Chapter revised in 1994 by WALTER BARTHOLD, member of the New York bar.

§ 13.01 Overview of Expert Witness Rules

Rules 702 through 705 of the Federal Rules of Evidence represent an integrated approach to the subject of expert testimony. That approach difffers in a number of significant ways from the common-law approach to this subject. The drafters of the rules sought to eliminate many of the restrictions that had blocked the admission of useful expert testimony. These restrictions included: requiring the expert's opinion to be rendered in response to a hypothetical question containing an assumed set of circumstances grounded in admissible evidence; refusing to permit experts to state their opinions on ultimate issues of fact; prohibiting experts from relying upon hearsay, including the opinions of other experts; and imposing a "general acceptance" test when the witness sought to testify about a new principle that had not previously been accorded judicial recognition. Rule 705 eliminated mandatory reliance on a hypothetical question; Rule 704 abolished the ultimate issue rule (although it was reinstated in part in 1984 for testimony relating to a criminal defendant's mental state). Rule 703 expanded the scope of the information on which an expert may rely. The Supreme Court in 1993 construed Rule 702 as replacing the "general acceptance" test by a more liberal standard.

Other rules have made it easier to introduce expert testimony. Among them are hearsay definitions and exceptions for raw data often required by experts, including Rules 801(a), 803(3), 803(4), 803(6) and 803(8). The 803(6) and 803(8) exceptions themselves include diagnoses and opinions, so that an expert's opinion can theoretically come in without the expert ever appearing. However, tactical pressures to produce the most persuasive evidence usually result in the use of experts' live testimony rather than of their hearsay reports.

The learned treatise exception, Rule 803(18), and such exceptions as Rule 803(17) on market and commercial reports, are also important. They make it easier for expert witnesses to educate the trier of fact about a body of knowledge that may be unfamiliar to the layperson.

Rule 1006 allows summaries of voluminous data to be introduced into evidence despite the traditional "best evidence" rule. This Rule provides expert witnesses such as accountants and analysts with an additional convenient and understandable way to present their data.[1]

The Federal Rules of Evidence and their state counterparts have thus loosened the restrictions on the admission of expert testimony, on its basis, on its form, and on the effective use of such testimony once admitted. This relaxation was needed to give the trier of fact convenient access to the reliable technical knowledge that is available in modern society. As might be expected, the modification of the old

---

[1] For a discussion of the interplay of Rules 803(6), 803(8) and 1006, *see* Manual for Complex Litigation 2d § 21.446 n.80.

rules demands more attention by counsel to pretrial procedures and requires the court to exercise greater control before and during trial through in limine rulings and control of discovery.[2]

The primary advantages of these loosened restrictions involve supervision of the preparation of expert testimony in the pretrial stage. If local practice does not require each party to identify the experts that it will use at trial and to provide a summary of those experts' expected testimony, a party may request such aid.

Similarly, parties may be required to provide a glossary of the terms that their experts will use at trial. Intended primarily to assist the reporters to take testimony accurately, the definitions of terms—particularly if the experts can agree on them—can be used by the judge in preparing for the trial. A list of specialized terms and definitions can be furnished for the jurors in a complex case.

Joint pretrial meetings between the judge and key expert witnesses are encouraged. The presence of each party's experts at the other party's experiments is also encouraged.

Some courts require that each party provide before trial a list of learned treatises admissible under Rule 803(18) and other hearsay that it intends to rely upon at trial. A party intending to offer statistical data and analysis at trial should be required to provide for the opposing parties all the underlying records from which the data were collected; make available for conferences with other parties the personnel who compiled the data; attempt to agree on a database well before trial; and be required to object to an opponent's experts' analysis before trial.

Questioning and comment by the judge may be needed to help in-form the jury. Even the summary judgment and directed verdict powers may need more expansive exercise to prevent spurious theories from being relied upon in emotional cases.[3]

§ 13.02   Testimony By Experts—Rule 702

[1]—Scope and Text of Rule[1]

Rule 702 focuses on helpfulness to the trier as the essential condition of admissibility. Rule 702 provides as follows:

Rule 702.   Testimony by Experts.

---

[2] *See* Weinstein, *Improvement of Expert Testimony,* 31 Richmond L. Rev. 1 (1986), for further development of these views.

[3] *See* Weinstein, *Improvement of Expert Testimony,* 31 Richmond L. Rev. 1 (1986), for further development of these views.

[1] *See* **Treatise** at § 702.03.

If scientific, technical, or other specialized knowledge will assist the trier of fact to understand the evidence or to determine a fact in issue, a witness qualified as an expert by knowledge, skill, experience, training, or education, may testify thereto in the form of an opinion or otherwise, if (1) the testimony is based upon sufficient facts or data, (2) the testimony is the product of reliable principles and methods, and (3) the witness has applied the principles and methods reliably to the facts of the case.

[*Adopted Jan. 2, 1975, effective July 1, 1975; amended Apr. 17, 2000, effective Dec.. 1, 2000.*]

In deciding whether proffered expert testimony will "assist the trier of fact to understand the evidence or to determine a fact in issue," the trial court must assess three issues: (1) whether scientific, technical, or other specialized knowledge will be of assistance to the trier of fact, (2) whether the proffered expert witness is qualified to provide the assistance the trier of fact will find useful, and (3) whether the information the expert witness has to give to the fact finder is reliable, or trustworthy, in an evidentiary sense.

[2]—Expert Testimony Must be Helpful to Trier of Fact[2]

The average juror will have no basis for evaluating certain kinds of evidence without the assistance of expert testimony.[3] Indeed, the courts recognize certain issues as being amenable only to specialized expertise, so that as a matter of substantive law the plaintiff cannot win without providing expert testimony.[4] Medical malpractice suits present prime examples of such issues.[5]

Experts may not, however, opine on issues that are committed exclusively to the finder of fact. For example, expert testimony is inadmissible if it does no more than tell the finder of fact what conclusion to reach.[6] Similarly, matters of contract

---

[2] *See* **Treatise** at § 702.03.

[3] *See, e.g.,* United States v. Allen, 269 F.3d 842, 845–846 (7th Cir. 2001) (expert testimony concerning "tools of the trade" and operations of drug distributors was admissible because average juror is not likely to be knowledgeable about narcotics trafficking).

[4] *See, e.g.,* Cooper v. Smith & Nephew, Inc., 259 F.3d 194, 203 (4th Cir. 2001) (trial court properly excluded plaintiff's expert testimony concerning cause of plaintiff's medical injury because it was unreliable; plaintiff could not prove any of his claims without expert testimony as to causation, and trial court properly granted defendant summary judgment).

[5] *See, e.g.,* Domingo v. T.K., M.D., 289 F.3d 600, 607 (9th Cir. 2002) (Hawaiian law requires causation in medical malpractice cases to be shown through expert testimony).

[6] *See, e.g.,* United States v. Gutierrez-Farias, 294 F.3d 657, 662–663 (5th Cir. 2002) (law enforcement officer's expert testimony that drug organizations customarily hire couriers who know that they are smuggling drugs essentially stated officer's opinion that defendant knew drugs were in car he was driving; such testimony does no more than tell jury how to decide case and is improper expert testimony).

interpretation are generally for the finder of fact to decide, and are not an appropriate subject for expert testimony.[7] Nevertheless, expert witnesses with skill or expertise in a particular industry may testify to the meaning of contractual terms that have a specialized meaning in that industry, because evidence of those specialized meanings will assist the jury in interpreting the contract.[8]

Other matters that the courts have held to be committed exclusively to the finder of fact and thus not amenable to expert testimony include the following:

- The credibility of witnesses.[9]

- The negligence of a party in tort cases.[10]

- The state of mind of a party.[11]

- The intent of a party.[12]

- What a "reasonable person" would foresee in the circumstances of the case.[13]

Expert testimony is also not admissible to inform the finder of fact as to the law that it will be instructed to apply to the facts in deciding the case. That is a matter reserved exclusively for the trial judge.[14] Expert witnesses are also prohibited from

---

[7] *See, e.g.,* Marx & Co. v. Diners' Club, Inc., 550 F.2d 505, 509–510 (2d Cir. 1977) (trial court improperly permitted expert witness to testify that defendant's failure to take certain actions within certain time frame violated contract's "best efforts" covenant).

[8] *See, e.g.,* United States v. Tucker, 345 F.3d 320, 328 (5th Cir. 2003) (trial court improperly precluded proffered expert witness from testifying to meaning within securities industry of term "invest," which was a critical term because it was used in memorandum that was at heart of dispute). Kona Tech. Corp. v. Southern Pac. Transp. Co., 225 F.3d 595, 611 (5th Cir. 2000) (trial court may properly rely on individuals experienced in a particular field for "explanation of the technical meaning of terms used in the industry").

[9] *See, e.g.,* Goodwin v. MTD Prods., Inc., 232 F.3d 600, 609 (7th Cir. 2000) (credibility questions are solely within jury's province, and are not susceptible to expert testimony).

[10] *See, e.g.,* Andrews v. Metro North Commuter R.R., 882 F.2d 705, 708–709 (2d Cir. 1989) (trial court abused discretion by permitting expert witness to testify train accident was result of railroad's negligent operation of train).

[11] *See, e.g.,* Salas v. Carpenter, 980 F.2d 299, 305 (5th Cir. 1992) (expert witness is in no better position than juror to conclude whether defendant's actions demonstrated "conscious disregard" or "deliberate indifference" to rights of plaintiff, and testimony was, therefore, inadmissible).

[12] *See, e.g.,* United States v. Seschillie, 310 F.3d 1208, 1212 (9th Cir. 2002) (trial court properly excluded expert opinion testimony concerning whether shootings were accidental because jury was capable of making that determination using common sense, without expert help).

[13] *See, e.g.,* United States v. Hanna, 293 F.3d 1080, 1085–1086 (9th Cir. 2002) (when jury was called on to determine whether reasonable person in defendant's position would perceive defendant's communications as threats to person of the President, it needed no assistance from experts).

[14] *See, e.g.,* Burkhart v. Washington Metro. Area Trans. Auth., 112 F.3d 1207, 1213 (D.C. Cir. 1997) ("Each courtroom comes equipped with a 'legal expert,' called a judge, and it is his or her

drawing legal conclusions, because that is the province of the trier of fact.[15] This proscription precludes an expert witness from testifying in the language of statutes, regulations, or other legal standards that are at the heart of the case if that language has a separate, distinct, and specialized meaning in the law different from its meaning in the vernacular.[16] It does not, however, necessarily prevent an expert witness from closely approaching the language of the legal standard and even suggesting to the finder of fact the inference that it should draw on the basis of that close approach, so long as the expert witness avoids the exact language of the legal standard.[17]

Other subjects, however, lie within the comprehension of the average juror, and expert testimony will be of no use to the jury in determining the issues before it.[18] Before the enactment of the Federal Rules, courts might have rejected expert testimony unless it related to an issue "not within the common knowledge of the average layman."[19] Such a rigid approach is incompatible with the standard of helpfulness expressed in Rule 702. It assumes wrongly that there is a bright line separating issues that are within the comprehension of jurors from those that are not.[20] It also ignores the possibility that even when jurors are well equipped to make judgments based on their common experience, experts may be able to add spe-

---

province alone to instruct the jury on the relevant legal standards").

[15] See, e.g., United States v. Barile, 286 F.3d 749, 760 (4th Cir. 2002) (expert testimony concerning legal conclusions does little more than tell finder of fact what conclusion to reach and is of little use to jury).

[16] See, e.g., Torres v. County of Oakland, 758 F.2d 147, 151 (6th Cir. 1985) (improper to permit expert witness to testify plaintiff had been discriminated against in employment because of her national origin, because testimony tracked statutory language and "discrimination" has specialized legal meaning that is more precise than lay understanding of term).

[17] See, e.g., United States v. Feliciano, 223 F.3d 102, 120–121 (2d Cir. 2000) (trial court did not err in permitting expert witness to testify that gang was involved in narcotics trafficking, inasmuch as witness did not use terminology of statute that defendants were charged with violating); Torres v. County of Oakland, 758 F.2d 147, 151 (6th Cir. 1985) (expert witness's testimony that plaintiff in employment discrimination case "had been discriminated against because of her national origin" was improper testimony because it tracked language of statute; expert witness could, however, have testified that, in his opinion, plaintiff's national origin was motivating factor in defendant's hiring decision).

[18] See, e.g., United States v. Torres-Galindo, 206 F.3d 136, 149 (1st Cir. 2000) (expert testimony improperly admitted because jury probably knew that persons accused of wrongdoing often deny guilt before confessing).

[19] Bridger v. Union Ry Co., 355 F.2d 382, 387 (6th Cir. 1966).

[20] See, e.g., United States v. Finley, 301 F.3d 1000, 1014 (9th Cir. 2002) (trial court abused its discretion in excluding psychologist's opinion about defendant's personality disorder based in part on witness's observations of defendant's demeanor because, even though jury could also observe defendant, jury did not know what to look for or how to apply those observations to make diagnosis).

cialized knowledge that would be helpful.[21]

Thus, at least one appellate court has held that the availability of lay testimony on an issue does not of itself bar expert testimony on that issue.[22] Typically, however, expert testimony is disallowed on matters plainly within the competence of the average juror.[23]

Expert testimony that is not relevant is not helpful.[24] Relevance can only be determined in the context of the particular case.[24.1] The court's rulings on objections raising such grounds for exclusion will depend on (1) its evaluation of the state of knowledge presently existing about the subject of the proposed testimony and (2) its appraisal of the facts of the case.[25] For discussion of relevant evidence whose probative value is outweighed by other considerations, see [5], *below*.

Generally, expert testimony that is founded on assumptions that are at variance with some evidence in the case is not excludable on the ground that it will be of no assistance to the fact finder in deciding the case. It is only if the expert's opinion is fundamentally unsupported by the facts of the case that it should be excluded on that ground.[25.1]

---

[21] *See e.g.,* Vogler v. Blackmore, 352 F.3d 150, 156 (5th Cir. 2003) (trial court did not abuse its discretion in admitting testimony of "grief expert" even though jury was capable of determining that plaintiff experienced grief as result of deaths of his wife and daughter; testimony was relevant and therefore properly admissible in trial court's discretion).

[22] United States v. Locascio, 6 F.3d 924, 939 (2d Cir. 1993) (structure of organized-crime "family").

[23] *See, e.g.,* United States v. Cruz, 363 F.3d 187, 195–196 (2d Cir. 2004) (trial court improperly permitted law-enforcement expert witness to stray beyond his expertise in drug related jargon to testify concerning meaning of term that had only commonly-known meaning and was not drug jargon; jury needed no expert help in determining meaning of term).

[24] *See, e.g.,* Pipitone v. Biomatrix, Inc., 288 F.3d 239, 245 (5th Cir. 2002) (perfectly equivocal scientific opinion does not make any significant fact more or less probable; such an opinion is, therefore, irrelevant and inadmissible).

[24.1] *See, e.g.,* Scotts Co. v. United Indus. Corp., 315 F.3d 264, 277–278 (4th Cir. 2002) (trial court abused its discretion in admitting plaintiff's focus group evidence because it was not sufficiently objective to be probative on issue it was offered to prove, consumer confusion).

[25] *Compare* United States v. St. Pierre, 812 F.2d 417, 420 (8th Cir. 1987) (clinical psychologist who had evaluated alleged victim in child sex abuse case was permitted to compare traits and characteristics of sexually abused children with those of victim; "the common experience of the jury may represent a less than adequate foundation for assessing the credibility of a young child who complains of sexual abuse") *with* United States v. Azure, 801 F.2d 336, 340–341 (8th Cir. 1986) (in prosecution for carnal knowledge of female under age sixteen, trial court committed reversible error by allowing prosecution's expert to testify that alleged victim of sexual abuse was believable and that expert could see no reason why victim was not telling truth; no reliable test for truthfulness existed).

[25.1] *See, e.g.,* Children's Broadcasting Corp. v. Walt Disney Co., 357 F.3d 860, 865 (8th Cir. 2004) ("factual basis of an expert opinion [generaally] goes to the credibility of the testimony").

Because the Federal Rules relax the common-law restrictions on the admissibility of expert testimony, doubts about the usefulness of proffered testimony should generally be resolved in favor of admissibility.[26] The jury, aided by counsel and the court's instructions, is generally intelligent enough to ignore what is unhelpful in its deliberations.

[3]—Expert Witness Must Possess Requisite Qualifications[27]

Rule 702 recognizes that it is the qualifications rather than the title of the witness that count.[28] An expert may be qualified by virtue of "knowledge, skill, experience, training or education," or any combination of these attributes. In each instance the court must decide, pursuant to Rule 104(a), whether the witness is competent to form an opinion that would assist the trier in resolving particular disputed issues.[29] Cases decided pursuant to the Federal Rules support a liberal standard in evaluating expert qualifications.[30]

Initially, the trial court must make a relevancy determination that expertise will assist the trier in resolving or understanding an issue. Then the court has to decide if the expert has appropriate qualifications given the facts of the case. In other words, the party offering the expert testimony must show that the witness has the specific qualifications necessary to qualify to render the type of opinion the witness proposes to render.[30.1] For example, when the subject matter of the testimony is

---

[26] *See, e.g.,* Lauzon v. Senco Prods., Inc., 270 F.3d 681, 695 (8th Cir. 2001) (if trial court is unconvinced as to usefulness of proffered expert testimony, evidence should be admitted so jury can pass on usefulness); Smith v. Ford Motor Co., 215 F.3d 713, 720 (7th Cir. 2000) (trial court erred in excluding testimony on ground that experts could not identify specific manufacturing or design defect that caused plaintiff's automobile accident when experts would have testified that accident was caused by some kind of manufacturing or design defect).

[27] *See* **Treatise** at § 702.04.

[28] *See, e.g.,* United States v. Majors, 196 F.3d 1206, 1215 (11th Cir. 1999) (financial analyst with F.B.I. could properly testify that defendant's records reflected money laundering, even though witness was not a certified public accountant, and only basis for his expertise was his extensive experience).

[29] *See, e.g.,* Jinro Am., Inc. v. Secure Invs., Inc., 266 F.3d 993, 1005–1006 (9th Cir. 2001) (qualifications of purported expert on Korean business culture and practices, whose experience as private investigator had exposed him primarily to instances of corrupt business behavior, were "woefully inadequate").

[30] Hangarter v. Provident Life & Accident Ins. Co., 373 F.3d 998, 1015 (9th Cir. 2004) ("Rule 702 contemplates a *broad conception* of expert qualifications (emphasis in original)); United States v. Hicks, No. 03-40655, 2004 U.S. App. LEXIS 22688, at *18 (5th Cir. Nov. 2, 2004) (witness qualifies as expert if it appears his or her testimony will probably aid fact finder).

[30.1] *See, e.g.,* Hall v. United Ins. Co. of Am., 367 F.3d 1255, 1261–1262 (11th Cir. 2004) (plaintiff failed to show that "licensed counselors" are generally capable of rendering opinion concerning person's mental capacity to contract and trial court properly excluded expert's testimony).

complex, outside the experience of the average juror, and founded in esoteric concepts, the witness must posses the requisite specialized knowledge to be able to assist the jury in understanding the evidence.[30.2]

Any one or more of the listed bases for qualification may be sufficient to qualify a witness as an expert.[30.3] When a proposed expert witness's testimony is based solely on experience, however, he or she must establish how that experience leads to the conclusion reached, why that experience is a sufficient basis for the opinion, and how that experience is reliably applied to the facts.[30.4] Just as an expert may be qualified despite having the "wrong" title, the right title will not suffice if the witness does not have the qualifications required by the facts of the case.[31] On the other hand, it is an abuse of discretion for a trial court to exclude an expert witness as unqualified solely because the witness lacks a certain educational or other experiential background.[32] Similarly, it is an abuse of discretion for a trial court to find a witness unqualified solely because the witness lacks expertise in specialized areas directly pertinent to the issues in question, if the witness has educational and experiential qualifications in a general field related to the subject matter of the issue in question.[33]

In some instances, it will be appropriate for the trial court to insist that a proposed expert witness have specific expertise.[34] Thus, when a witness admittedly pos-

---

[30.2] *See, e.g.,* Lifewise Master Funding, v. Telebank, 374 F.3d 917, 928 (10th Cir. 2004) (plaintiff's president did not possess sufficient specialized knowledge to assist jury in understanding plaintiff's damage theory, which was based on moving averages, compounded growth rates, and S-curves; because proffered witness was sole sponsor of plaintiff's damage theory, trial court properly excluded theory from evidence).

[30.3] *See, e.g.,* United States v. Vesey, 338 F.3d 913, 917 (8th Cir. 2003) (witness who offered expert testimony respecting practices of drug dealers was qualified to do so on basis of his experience as drug dealer and as confidential informant).

[30.4] *See, e.g.,* United States v. Fredette, 315 F.3d 1235, 1240 (10th Cir. 2003) (proposed witness's experience with promotional rebate programs in general provided no basis for his testimony concerning how well defendant's program adhered to its published rules).

[31] *See, e.g.,* Calhoun v. Yamaha Motor Corp., 350 F.3d 316; 324 (3d Cir. 2003) (trial court properly precluded expert witness, although well qualified to testify to matters concerning naval architecture and marine engineering, from testifying about adequacy of defendants' warnings on jet ski because he had no experience or training in requisite field).

[32] *See, e.g.,* Jahn v. Equine Servs., PSC, 233 F.3d 382, 389 (6th Cir. 2000) (trial court abused its discretion in excluding testimony of qualified veterinarian merely because he had not performed specific procedure that resulted in death of horse).

[33] *See, e.g.,* Smith v. BMW North America, Inc., 308 F.3d 913, 919 (8th Cir. 2002) (trial court abused its discretion in excluding testimony of forensic pathologist about timing of plaintiff's injuries; witness did not need expertise in amount of force plaintiff's neck could withstand before fracturing to give proffered opinion).

[34] *See, e.g.,* St. Martin v. Mobil Exploration & Producing U.S. Inc., 224 F.3d 402, 413 (5th Cir. 2000) (witness qualified in wetlands management and wildlife preservation was not qualified to

sessing qualifications in a specific field attempts to testify to matters beyond his or her expertise, it is appropriate for the trial court to exclude the testimony.[35] Such cases are the exception, however, and not the rule.[35.1]

Some cases require that any expert testimony be founded on knowledge of local conditions, because of the nature of the issues they present.[36] Local knowledge is needed, however, only if there is a showing that the matters at issue differ by location.[37]

Some cases may require that an expert witness's expertise relate to a specific time period. For example, in a medical malpractice case, it may be necessary for the plaintiff to prove the actions a doctor took at a specified time in the past did not meet then-acceptable community standards for the practice of medicine. In such cases it would be necessary for the plaintiff to prove that the defendant doctor's acts fell below the recognized standards in the medical community at the time those acts were performed.[38] It is the opponent's burden to bring to the trial court's attention information suggesting the need for the witness's expertise to relate to a specific time period.[38.1]

---

testify to hydrologic effects of creating navigable waterway through wetlands).

[35] *See, e.g.,* Wheeling Pittsburgh Steel Corp. v. Beelman River Terminals, Inc., 254 F.3d 706, 714–715 (8th Cir. 2001) (witness admittedly well qualified to testify concerning flood risk management because of educational and experiential qualifications as hydrologist was not qualified to testify to reasonable and prudent warehouse management practices).

[35.1] *See, e.g.,* Betterbox Communications Ltd. v. BB Technologies, Inc., 300 F.3d 325, 328 (3d Cir. 2002) (trial court did not abuse its discretion in admitting expert testimony concerning catalogue marketing of communications products and computer peripherals even though witness did not have experience with specific products at issue).

[36] *See, e.g.,* Taylor v. Ouachita Parish Sch. Bd., 648 F.2d 959, 970–971 (5th Cir. 1981) (in school desegregation action, trial court did not abuse discretion in excluding testimony of government expert who had no knowledge of local conditions).

[37] *See, e.g.,* Wilder Enters., Inc. v. Allied Artists Pictures Corp., 632 F.2d 1135, 1143 (4th Cir. 1980) (in antitrust action, expert witness testifying to film distribution practices did not require local expertise in absence of evidence of any geographically based differences in film distribution practices).

[38] *See, e.g.,* Grindstaff v. Coleman, 681 F.2d 740, 742 (11th Cir. 1982) (expert witness proposing to testify concerning events at specified time need not have been an expert at that time to be qualified to do so; it is sufficient if witness has expertise about that time; trial court abused discretion in excluding doctor as expert witness on ground witness did not possess medical license at time of events in question; all that is necessary is that witness have knowledge of prevailing medical standards at time in question).

[38.1] *See, e.g.,* Betterbox Communications Ltd. v. BB Technologies, Inc., 300 F.3d 325, 328 (3d Cir. 2002) (trial court did not abuse its discretion in admitting testimony of witness based on experience ending eight years earlier, because opponent did not show that matters in that field had changed sufficiently to make witness's expertise outdated).

[4]—Reliability and Fit of Expert Testimony[39]

[a]—Adoption of Current Standards

Before the adoption of the Federal Rules of Evidence the federal courts generally followed the *Frye* [40] standard in evaluating the reliability of scientific evidence. That decision predicated admissibility of expert testimony on the "general acceptance" of the underlying scientific principle or technique in the particular field to which it belonged.[41]

Following the enactment of Rule 702, the Supreme Court rejected the *Frye* standard, in *Daubert v. Merrell Dow Pharmaceuticals, Inc.,* [42] The Court concluded that the enactment of Rule 702 superseded *Frye,* and that the "general acceptance" test was no longer a precondition to the admissibility of expert testimony.[43] Instead, Rule 702 requires the trial judge to ensure that proffered scientific evidence is "relevant to the task at hand" and that it rests "on a reliable foundation."[44]

The Supreme Court limited its discussion in *Daubert* to the scientific context because the case involved only scientific evidence, and not expert testimony based on experiential expertise or other specialized knowledge.[45] Subsequently, however, in *Kumho Tire Co. v. Carmichael,*[46] the Court held that *Daubert*'s general principles apply to all expert testimony admissible under Rule 702, including experience-based testimony.

As amended in 2000, Rule 702 codifies, and perhaps extends, the *Daubert* and *Kumho* rulings.[47] It requires the trial court to exclude proffered expert testimony unless (1) it is based on sufficient facts and data, (2) it is the product of reliable

---

[39] *See* **Treatise** at § 702.05.

[40] Frye v. United States, 293 F. 1013, 1014 (D.C. Cir. 1923).

[41] Frye v. United States, 293 F. 1013, 1014 (D.C. Cir. 1923) (rejecting admission of evidence derived from crude precursor of polygraph).

[42] Daubert v. Merrell Dow Pharms., Inc., 509 U.S. 579, 597, 113 S. Ct. 2786, 125 L. Ed. 2d 469 (1993).

[43] Daubert v. Merrell Dow Pharms., Inc., 509 U.S. 579, 584–587, 113 S. Ct. 2786, 125 L. Ed. 2d 469 (1993).

[44] Daubert v. Merrell Dow Pharms., Inc., 509 U.S. 579, 597, 113 S. Ct. 2786, 125 L. Ed. 2d 469 (1993) (admissible expert scientific testimony must be "pertinent evidence based on scientifically valid principles").

[45] Daubert v. Merrell Dow Pharms., Inc., 509 U.S. 579, 590 n.8, 113 S. Ct. 2786, 125 L. Ed. 2d 469 (1993).

[46] Kumho Tire Co. v. Carmichael, 526 U.S. 137, 148, 119 S. Ct. 1167, 1174, 143 L. Ed. 2d 238 (1999).

[47] Fed. R. Evid. 702 Committee Note (2000) (reproduced verbatim in **Treatise,** Ch. 702, *Testimony by Experts,* § 702App.02[2]).

principles and methods, and (3) the witness has applied the principles and methods reliably to the facts of the case.[48]

[b]—Determination of Relevance and Reliability of Expert Testimony

The *Daubert* decision emphasized that relevance and reliability are prerequisites to the admission of scientific testimony or evidence.[49] These prerequisites are based on Rule 702's mandate that an expert opinion be of assistance to the trier of fact.[50] Specifically, Rule 702 requires the following:[51]

- The testimony is based on sufficient facts or data.

- The testimony is the product of reliable principles and methods.

- The witness has applied the principles and methods reliably to the facts of the case.[52]

In *Daubert*, the Supreme Court offered the following non-exclusive list of factors to guide the assessment of the reliability of scientific evidence:[53]

- Whether the theory or technique has been or can be reliably tested.

- Whether the theory or technique has been or can be subjected to peer review.

- The known or potential rate or error of the technique.

- The "general acceptance" of the technique.

The courts have developed additional factors that can appropriately be considered in the reliability evaluation, dependent on the circumstances of the particular case:

---

[48]   Fed. R. Evid. 702; *see* [b] *below.*

[49]   Daubert v. Merrell Dow Pharms., Inc., 509 U.S. 579, 580, 113 S. Ct. 2786, 125 L. Ed. 2d 469 (1993) (expert's testimony must both rest on a reliable foundation and be relevant to task at hand).

[50]   *See, e.g.,* Ralston v. Smith & Nephew Richards, Inc., 275 F.3d 965, 969 (10th Cir. 2001) (to determine admissibility of proffered expert testimony, trial court must follow two-step process, assessing witness's qualifications and reliability of proposed testimony).

[51]   Fed. R. Evid. 702.

[52]   *See, e.g.,* Lloyd v. Am. Airlines, Inc. (In re Air Crash at Little Rock Ark.), 291 F.3d 503, 514–515 (8th Cir. 2002) (psychiatrist's testimony that plaintiff's post-traumatic stress syndrome (PTSS) resulted from injury, based on plaintiff's symptoms and fact that some PTSS patients exhibited brain dysfunction, was not reliable because available tests to show the physiological changes associated with PTSS had not been performed on plaintiff); Domingo v. T.K., M.D., 289 F.3d 600, 607 (9th Cir. 2002) (trial court may properly exclude evidence as unreliable if court reasonably concludes that witness's conclusion does not follow from his or her analysis).

[53]   Daubert v. Merrell Dow Pharms., Inc., 509 U.S. 579, 593–594, 113 S. Ct. 2786, 125 L. Ed. 2d 469 (1993).

- Whether the witnesses propose to testify based on matters growing naturally out of research they have conducted independently of the litigation, or developed their opinions solely and expressly for the purpose of testifying.[54]

- Whether the proposed witness's conclusion represents an unfounded extrapolation from the underlying data.[55]

- Whether the witness has adequately accounted for alternative explanations for the effect whose cause is at issue.[56]

- Whether the witnesses were as careful, in formulating their testimony, as they would be in their regular professional work.[57]

- Whether the offered field of expertise is capable of reliably reaching results of the type proposed by the witness.[58]

- Whether the witness relied unduly on anecdotal evidence in arriving at an opinion.[59]

- Whether the witness relied unduly on the temporal proximity between the occurrence of an event and the onset of illness or injury.[60]

---

[54] *See, e.g.,* Lauzon v. Senco Prods., Inc., 270 F.3d 681, 687 (8th Cir. 2001).

[55] *See, e.g.,* Hollander v. Sandoz Pharms. Corp., 289 F.3d 1193, 1208 (10th Cir. 2002) (conclusion that drug caused stroke in healthy plaintiff was not reliable when it was based on studies showing only that drug increase blood pressure among women taking it for particular disease; extrapolation from studies to conclusion involved too great an analytical gap).

[56] *See, e.g.,* Domingo v. T.K., M.D., 289 F.3d 600, 606–607 (9th Cir. 2002) (expert's causation theory was unreliable because it assumed that plaintiff's fat emboli syndrome was result of atypical events occurring during plaintiff's surgery when literature suggested that syndrome occurs as often in absence of atypical events).

[57] *See, e.g.,* Amorgianos v. National RR Passenger Corp., 303 F.3d 256, 265–266 (2d Cir. 2002) ("the district court must make certain that an expert, whether basing testimony upon professional studies or personal experience, employs in the courtroom the same level of intellectual rigor that characterizes the practice of an expert in the relevant field").

[58] *See, e.g.,* Quiet Technology DC-8, Inc. v. Hurel-Dubois UK Ltd., 326 F.3d 1333, 1343–1344 (11th Cir. 2003) (trial court properly found that computational fluid dynamics, using computer models to analyze flow of air around and through jet engines, is reliable method of determining cause of reduction in efficiency of jet engine designed to be quieter because of frequency of use of methodology by aircraft designers).

[59] Rider v. Sandoz Pharms. Corp., 295 F.3d 1194, 1199–1200 (11th Cir. 2002) (expert witnesses' reliance on case studies and challenge/rechallenge studies, both of which are almost exclusively anecdotal, rendered their opinions that plaintiff's ingestion of delactating drug caused hemorrhagic stroke unreliable).

[60] *See, e.g.,* Goebel v. Denver & Rio Grande W. R.R., 346 F.3d 987, 999 (10th Cir. 2003) (expert witness may not rely exclusively or even predominantly on temporal relationship between alleged cause and onset of illness to establish causation).

- Whether the witness has sufficiently connected the proposed testimony with the facts of the case.[61]

- Whether any hypotheses relied on in the formulation of the expert's opinion have actually been tested.[62]

- Whether the witness's methodology is subjective.[63]

The reliability inquiry is a "flexible one."[64] At a minimum, Rule 702 requires that expert opinion be based on sound methods and valid procedures.[65] Expert opinions that do not concern scientific matters may be found reliable based on the witness's knowledge and experience, that is, on the qualifications, of the proffered witness.[65.1] The trial court may not, however, rely on factors that traditionally go to the issues of credibility and persuasiveness to determine that the expert witness's testimony is not reliable.[65.2]

The focus of the reliability inquiry "must be solely on principles and methodology, not on the conclusions they generate."[66] For example, the trial court may

---

[61] *See, e.g.,* Black v. M & W Gear Co., 269 F.3d 1220, 1237–1238 (10th Cir. 2001) (trial court properly excluded expert testimony when witness did not adequately tie theory as to cause of decedent's injuries to facts of case).

[62] *See, e.g.,* Dhillon v. Crown Controls Corp., 269 F.3d 865, 869–870 (7th Cir. 2001) (testimony that product could have been designed differently to eliminate alleged design defect was properly held unreliable, since witness had not made or tested a product made in accordance with his alternative design; feasibility of alternative design cannot be determined without through testing of a product made in accordance with that design).

[63] *See, e.g.,* Cooper v. Smith & Nephew, Inc., 259 F.3d 194, 199–203 (4th Cir. 2001) (when physician-expert's opinion was based on speculation, was at odds with settled views of others in his specialty, and was not based on his review of plaintiff's medical history or witness's professional work, opinion was based solely on speculation and was properly excluded).

[64] Daubert v. Merrell Dow Pharms., Inc., 509 U.S. 579, 594, 597, 113 S. Ct. 2786, 125 L. Ed. 2d 469 (1993) (inquiry "envisioned by Rule 702 is, we emphasize, a flexible one"; Rule 702 assigns "to the trial judge the task of ensuring that an expert's testimony both rests on a reliable foundation and is relevant to the task at hand.").

[65] *See, e.g.,* Wills v. Amerada Hess Corp., 379 F.3d 32, 49–50 (2d Cir. 2004) (proffered expert witness improperly relied on personal observations of lay person that were inadequate to serve as basis for witness's extrapolation concerning cause of decedent's squamous cell carcinoma).

[65.1] *See, e.g.,* Hangarter v. Provident Life & Accident Ins. Co., 373 F.3d 998, 1018 (9th Cir. 2004) (trial court properly performed its *Daubert* gate keeping function by ascertaining proffered witness's experience and knowledge; witness was proffered to testify concerning insurance industry adjustment standards on basis of his 25-years of experience working for insurance companies in marketing, claims adjustment, and claims settlement)

[65.2] *See, e.g.,* Deputy v. Lehman Bros., Inc., 345 F.3d 494, 506 (7th Cir. 2003) (matters concerning issues of credibility and persuasiveness of expert's opinion relate to weight to be given to evidence, not to reliability).

[66] Daubert v. Merrell Dow Pharms., Inc., 509 U.S. 579, 594, 113 S. Ct. 2786, 125 L. Ed. 2d 469 (1993).

properly exclude as unreliable expert testimony that is not supported by literature from the expert's field of expertise and demonstrative tests.[66a]

On the other hand, weak expert testimony is not necessarily unreliable.[66.1] Thus, cross-examination and other tools of the adversary system, not exclusion, should be used to save the trier of fact from being misled by weak expert testimony.[67]

[c]—Procedures for Performing Gatekeeper Role

[i]—Trial Court's Discretion

Strictly speaking, reliability determinations are necessary only if the opponent objects to the admissibility of the expert testimony.[68] In the absence of an objection, rulings admitting or excluding expert testimony without a reliability determination are reviewable only for plain error.[69] If, however, the opponent objects to proposed expert testimony, the trial court must determine its reliability.[70]

The court must make a suitable inquiry before reaching its determination (*see* [ii], *below*).[71] However, the factors that the court applies in determining the

---

[66a] *See, e.g.,* Calhoun v. Yamaha Motor Corp., 350 F.3d 316; 322 (3d Cir. 2003) (trial court properly precluded expert witness from testifying that jet ski throttle was defectively designed because child rider would, when under stress, tend to clench fingers shut, causing finger-controlled throttle to open, because plaintiff provided no support for opinion in form of literature or demonstrative test results).

[66.1] *See, e.g.,* Deputy v. Lehman Bros., Inc. 345 F.3d 494, 506 (7th Cir. 2003) (trial court improperly excluded proffered expert testimony for unreliability when reasons court gave for making its determination really went to credibility and persuasiveness of expert's testimony, which are matters left to trier of fact and should be tested through adversary process).

[67] *See, e.g.,* United States v. Crisp, 324 F.3d 261, 270–271 (4th Cir. 2003) (in absence of proof from defendant that fingerprint identification and handwriting analysis are unreliable, extensive judicial acceptance of those two forensic tools means that evidence should be tested through cross-examination and other tools of adversarial system, rather than being excluded); Cummings v. Std. Register Co., 265 F.3d 56, 65 (1st Cir. 2001) (any deficiencies in expert witness's computational methodology went to weight, not to admissibility, of testimony).

[68] *See, e.g.,* Macsenti v. Becker, 237 F.3d 1223, 1231-1232 (10th Cir. 2001) (failure to object on *Daubert* grounds waives all but plain error in admission of expert opinion evidence; court need not assess reliability of evidence in absence of timely request by objecting party).

[69] *See, e.g.,* Goebel v. Denver & Rio Grande Western R.R., 215 F.3d 1083, 1088 n.2 (10th Cir. 2000) ("If there is no objection to the expert testimony, the opposing party waives appellate review absent plain error").

[70] *See, e.g.,* Lloyd v. Am. Airlines, Inc. (In re Air Crash at Little Rock Ark.), 291 F.3d 503, 514 (8th Cir. 2002) (trial court is required to make determination of reliability of proffered expert testimony if objection is raised).

[71] *See, e.g.,* Elcock v. KMart Corp., 233 F.3d 734, 745–750 (3d Cir. 2000) (district court should have held *Daubert* hearing to determine reliability of psychologist's vocational rehabilitation testimony, in light of serious doubts raised by defendant regarding psychologist's methodology and

reliability of proffered expert testimony are within the trial court's discretion.[72]

The steps that the trial court takes to accumulate the information for its reliability determination are also subject to its discretion.[73] In some instances, there is sufficient information in pretrial disclosures. The trial court may also, in some instances, properly rely on discovery materials to make its reliability determination, without holding an evidentiary hearing (*see* [ii], *below*).[74]

Moreover, trial courts need not conduct any reliability assessment at all when they appropriately determine that proffered expert testimony is inadmissible for reasons wholly unrelated to its reliability.[75]

[ii]—Need for Evidentiary Hearing

It is within the trial court's discretion whether to hold an evidentiary hearing to determine the reliability of proffered expert testimony.[76] A separate reliability hearing is unnecessary "in ordinary proceedings where the reliability of an expert's methods is properly taken for granted."[77] In such cases, the opponent's objections go to the weight, rather than to the admissibility, of the testimony.

When the information before the court is sufficient to support a ruling on the reliability of the proposed evidence, the court has discretion to resolve the challenge

---

plaintiff's failure to adduce much evidence validating his methods, as well as psychologist's "thin" qualifications).

[72] *See, e.g.,* Kumho Tire Co. v. Carmichael, 526 U.S. 137, 152, 119 S. Ct. 1167, 143 L. Ed. 2d 238 (1999) ("trial court must have the same kind of latitude in deciding how to test an expert's reliability . . . as it enjoys when it decides whether that expert's relevant testimony is reliable"); *see* [b], *above.*

[73] *See, e.g.,* Kumho Tire Co. v. Carmichael, 526 U.S. 137, 152, 119 S. Ct. 1167, 143 L. Ed. 2d 238 (1999).

[74] *See, e.g.,* Oddi v. Ford Motor Co., 234 F.3d 136, 142–146 (3d Cir. 2000) (trial court's reliability determination, made on basis of disclosure materials and experts' deposition transcripts and affidavits, was not abuse of discretion, and evidentiary hearing was not necessary); *see also* Claar v. Burlington N. R.R., 29 F.3d 499, 502–504 (9th Cir. 1994) (trial court properly required proposed expert witnesses to submit serial affidavits exploring issues concerning reasoning behind opinions and methodology).

[75] *See, e.g.,* United States v. Benavidez-Benavidez, 217 F.3d 720, 725 (9th Cir. 2000) (not abuse of discretion for trial court to exclude polygraph evidence on ground of undue prejudice because jury might give excessive weight to polygrapher's conclusions; no separate analysis of reliability under Rule 702 and *Daubert* is necessary); *see also* [5], *below.*

[76] *See, e.g.,* United States v. Evans, 272 F.3d 1069, 1094 (8th Cir. 2001) (trial court need not always hold evidentiary hearing to determine reliability of proffered expert testimony).

[77] *See, e.g.,* United States v. Nichols, 169 F.3d 1255, 1262–1264 (10th Cir. 1999) (evidentiary hearing not necessary when forensic explosives expert proposed to give opinions about type and size of bomb from analysis of debris; defense arguments related solely to alleged flaws in laboratory tests, which involve credibility of witnesses and weight of evidence).

without an evidentiary hearing.[78]

Evidentiary hearings, known as *Daubert* hearings, are the most common method trial courts use to fulfill their gatekeeper function. *Daubert* hearings may be held pretrial or during trial.[79] Whether the evidentiary hearing occurs before the trial begins or during the trial is within the trial court's discretion.[80] However, pretrial hearings are clearly preferable in complicated cases.[81]

When the hearing occurs during trial, the court also has discretion to determine whether to hold it in the presence of the jury. The jury's presence may be appropriate, for example, when the objections to the evidence go not only to its admissibility but also to credibility determinations and to the weight that the trier of fact should accord to the evidence.[82] The reliability hearing may also be combined with voir dire to test the expert's qualifications. Depending on the circumstances of the case, however, it may be appropriate to allow further questioning outside the presence of the jury.[83]

The important issue in determining whether a trial court has abused its discretion in selecting the method by which it will perform its gatekeeping role is whether it has effectively ascertained, on the basis of sufficient evidence, the reliability and usefulness, or lack thereof, of the proposed expert testimony. It may do so in a pretrial hearing, a hearing on an objection lodged during the trial, or even during

---

[78] *See, e.g.,* Nelson v. Tennessee Gas Pipeline Co., 243 F.3d 244, 249 (6th Cir. 2001) (trial court's determination of *Daubert* challenge without holding evidentiary hearing was not abuse of discretion, because admissibility issues were fully briefed by parties and challenger did not request a hearing); Kirstein v. Parks Corp., 159 F.3d 1065, 1067–1069 (7th Cir. 1998) (trial court properly excluded proposed expert testimony of eminently qualified scientist on basis of affidavits, without conducting formal reliability proceeding, because witness's qualifications were not in proper field and witness had not performed crucial tests, so that proposed opinion testimony was "unscientific speculation offered by a genuine scientist").

[79] *See, e.g.,* Goebel v. Denver & Rio Grande Western R.R., 215 F.3d 1083, 1087 (10th Cir. 2000) ("[t]he most common method for fulfilling this function [of gatekeeper] is a *Daubert* hearing").

[80] *See, e.g.,* Pride v. BIC Corp., 218 F.3d 566, 569–574 (6th Cir. 2000) (trial court properly conducted evidentiary hearing during pretrial proceedings).

[81] *See, e.g.,* Lloyd v. Am. Airlines, Inc. (In re Air Crash at Little Rock Ark.), 291 F.3d 503, 514 (8th Cir. 2002) ("We agree with the district court that when reasonably possible, *Daubert* issues should be raised prior to trial and that ideally the *Daubert* 'hearing' should not be conducted following a fifteen-minute morning recess shortly before the expert is scheduled to testify").

[82] *See, e.g.,* United States v. Nichols, 169 F.3d 1255, 1262–1264 (10th Cir. 1999) (trial court properly concluded that jury should hear evidence for its credibility and weight determinations at same time as court heard evidence for its admissibility determination, since court assured parties that it would pursue issues that jury should not hear outside its presence).

[83] *See, e.g.,* United States v. Alatorre, 222 F.3d 1098, 1104–1105 (9th Cir. 2000) ("court adopted a practical procedure, well within its discretion, when it allowed Alatorre to explore Jacobs's qualifications and the basis for his testimony at trial via voir dire").

a hearing on a post-trial motion to strike, so long as it bases its decision on "sufficient evidence to perform 'the task of ensuring that an expert's testimony both rests on a reliable foundation and is relevant to the task at hand.' "[84]

[iii]—Placing Determination on Record

Any inquiry into expert testimony should be conducted on the record, so the appellate court can refer to the evidence concerning the admissibility of the expert testimony.[85] In fact, it may be an abuse of discretion for the trial court not to create a record suitable for review of its admissibility decision. A sufficient record is one that includes both the court's ruling and the reasons for that ruling.[86]

[5]—Assessing Probative Value and Prejudicial Effect of Expert Testimony[87]

The helpfulness requirement of Rule 702 necessarily incorporates some, if not all, of the considerations expressed in Rule 403. Expert testimony will not assist the trier of fact if it is overly confusing, more prejudicial than probative, or needlessly time-consuming.[88] Moreover, Rule 403 applies directly to proffered expert testimony.[89] Indeed, its applicability to expert evidence may be enhanced by the more liberal approach to expert testimony adopted by *Daubert* and the 2000 amendments to Rule 702.[90]

Some courts have held that certain types of expert testimony are per se prejudicial; when such evidence is offered, trial courts are not required to perform a

---

[84] Goebel v. Denver & Rio Grande Western R.R., 215 F.3d 1083, 1087 (10th Cir. 2000) (quoting *Daubert v. Merrell Dow Pharms., Inc.*, 509 U.S. 579, 597, 113 S. Ct. 2786, 125 L. Ed. 2d 469 (1993)).

[85] United States v. Downing, 753 F.2d 1224, 1242 (3d Cir. 1985).

[86] *See, e.g.*, Goebel v. Denver & Rio Grande Western R.R., 215 F.3d 1083, 1087–1088 (10th Cir. 2000) (when there is objection to expert evidence, district court "must adequately demonstrate by specific findings on the record that it has performed its duty as gatekeeper"; judgment reversed because record did not show that district court conducted any form of *Daubert* analysis and trial court's admission of expert testimony was, therefore, abuse of discretion).

[87] *See* **Treatise** at § 702.02[5].

[88] *See, e.g.*, Laplace-Bayard v. Batlle, 295 F.3d 157, 164 (1st Cir. 2002) (trial court properly excluded testimony of one expert on ground it was cumulative of plaintiff's other expert witness); Jinro Am., Inc., v. Secure Invs., Inc., 266 F.3d 993, 1006–1009 (9th Cir. 2001) (expert testimony heavily tinged with ethnic bias and stereotyping is not helpful to jury and should be excluded).

[89] *See, e.g.*, United States v. Mathis, 264 F.3d 321, 339 (3d Cir. 2001) (trial court appropriately screened proffered expert testimony under Rule 403, but improperly excluded it as unduly prejudicial because it carried "an aura of infallibility" when persuasiveness of testimony resulted from high level of witness's reliability as expert in area directly pertinent to opponent's case).

[90] *See, e.g.*, United States v. Posado, 57 F.3d 428, 435 (5th Cir. 1995) (enhanced role of Rule 403 may be particularly important when scientific or technical knowledge is novel or controversial).

reliability analysis.[91] The Supreme Court has indicated that there is no constitutional problem with such a *per se* exclusionary rule, at least insofar as polygraph evidence is concerned.[92]

[6]—Standard of Review of Decisions Admitting or Excluding Expert Testimony[93]

All aspects of the trial court's decision to admit or exclude expert testimony under Rule 702 are subject to appellate review for abuse of discretion. This includes the trial court's determination whether:

- Proffered evidence will assist the trier of fact to understand the evidence or to determine a fact in issue.[94]

- The proffered witness has the qualifications necessary to provide the trier of fact with the assistance.[95]

- The proffered expert testimony meets the reliability and fitness requirements of *Daubert* and Rule 702.[96]

The trial court's selection of the procedure it will follow in making those determinations is also subject to review for abuse of discretion, as its decision concerning the factors to take into account in making that determination.[97] The trial court, however, should always exercise its discretion with Rule 702's liberal

---

[91] *See, e.g.,* United States v. Benavidez-Benavidez, 217 F.3d 720, 725 (9th Cir. 2000) (not abuse of discretion for trial court to exclude polygraph evidence on ground of undue prejudice because jury might give excessive weight to polygrapher's conclusions; no separate analysis of reliability of evidence under Fed. R. Evid. 702 and *Daubert* is necessary).

[92] United States v. Scheffer, 523 U.S. 303, 312, 118 S. Ct. 1261, 1266, 140 L. Ed. 2d 413 (1998) (Military Rule of Evidence 707, forbidding admission of polygraph evidence, not unconstitutional; "[n]othing in *Daubert* foreclosed, as a constitutional matter, *per se* exclusionary rules for certain types of expert scientific evidence.").

[93] *See* **Treatise** at § 702.02[4], [6].

[94] *See, e.g.,* United States v. Sebaggala, 256 F.3d 59, 65–66 (1st Cir. 2001) (trial court enjoys considerable latitude in determining whether expert testimony will (or will not) materially assist jury).

[95] *See, e.g.,* Ferrara & Dimercurio v. St. Paul Mercury Ins. Co., 240 F.3d 1, 8 (1st Cir. 2001) (trial court's determination that proposed expert witness has or lacks qualifications to testify fall within broad purview of its discretion).

[96] *See, e.g.,* General Electric Co. v. Joiner, 522 U.S. 136, 140–143, 118 S. Ct. 512, 139 L. Ed. 2d 508 (1997) (trial court has discretion in determining reliability of proffered expert testimony, without regard to whether the decision admits or excludes the testimony).

[97] Kumho Tire Co. v. Carmichael, 526 U.S. 137, 152, 119 S. Ct. 1167, 1176, 143 L. Ed. 2d 238 (1999) (trial judge must have authority needed to avoid unnecessary reliability proceedings in ordinary cases in which reliability of an expert's methods is taken for granted; "whether *Daubert*'s specific factors are, or are not, reasonable measures of reliability in a particular case is a matter that the law grants the trial judge broad latitude to determine").

approach to the admissibility of expert testimony in mind.[98]

When trial courts fail to make an explicit record of their findings regarding the reliability of the proposed expert witness's testimony, some appellate courts have exhibited a willingness to review the materials the trial court had before it to ascertain whether the trial court abused its discretion in admitting or excluding the testimony.[99] Other appellate courts have extended their reviews to all of the materials in the trial record, including the testimony presented at the trial.[100]

Such reviews by the appellate courts, of course, amount to their conducting their own reliability analyses. Trial courts, however, have a much broader "array of tools which can be brought to bear on the evaluation of expert testimony" than do appellate courts. There should be few cases "in which an appellate court should venture to superimpose a *Daubert* ruling on a cold, poorly developed record."[101]

§ 13.03   Bases of Opinion Testimony By Experts—Rule 703

[1]—Scope and Text of Rule

Rule 703 governs the sources of information upon which experts may ground their opinions. The first sentence of the Rule codifies the traditional and universally accepted view that an expert may base an opinion on first-hand information or on facts or data made known to the expert in court. The second sentence expands the permissible bases for the expert's opinion beyond those permitted at common law. It allows the expert to base an opinion on facts or data that could not be admitted in evidence, provided they are of the type reasonably relied upon by experts in forming opinions in their particular field of competence. In broadening the basis for admissibility, Rule 703 operates as one of the cornerstones of the liberal approach of the Federal Rules of Evidence to expert testimony. The Rule provides as follows:

---

[98]   *See, e.g.,* Lauzon v. Senco Prods., Inc., 270 F.3d 681, 686, 696 (8th Cir. 2001) ("Rule 702 reflects an attempt to liberalize the rules governing the admission of expert testimony;" trial court abused its discretion in excluding proffered expert testimony through application of overly stringent test for reliability).

[99]   *See, e.g.,* Tanner v. Westbrook, 174 F.3d 542, 546–547 (5th Cir. 1999) (although refusing request for pretrial hearing, trial court effectively conducted *Daubert* inquiry before admitting expert testimony over objection, presumably based on materials submitted by parties re request for pretrial hearing; in absence of explicit findings concerning reliability, appellate court reviewed materials considered by trial court and concluded that expert's testimony was not reliable and that its admission was abuse of discretion).

[100]   *See, e.g.,* Kinser v. Gehl Co., 184 F.3d 1259, 1271–1272 (10th Cir. 1999) (after review of entire trial record for indicia of reliability of expert's testimony, appellate court concluded that testimony was unreliable because its foundation did not include any testing of proposed alternative design for allegedly defective machinery; trial court, therefore, should have excluded testimony).

[101]   Cortes-Irizarry v. Corporacion Insular De Seguros, 111 F.3d 184, 189 (1st Cir. 1997).

**Rule 703.	Bases of Opinion Testimony by Experts.**

The facts or data in the particular case upon which an expert bases an opinion or inference may be those perceived by or made known to the expert at or before the hearing. If of a type reasonably relied upon by experts in the particular field in forming opinions or inferences upon the subject, the facts or data need not be admissible in evidence, in order for the opinion or inference to be admitted. Facts or data that are otherwise inadmissible shall not be disclosed to the jury by the proponent of the opinion or inference unless the court determines that their probative value in assisting the jury to evaluate the expert's opinion substantially outweighs their prejudicial effect.

[*Adopted Jan. 2, 1975, effective July 1, 1975; amended Mar. 2, 1987, effective Oct. 1, 1987; amended Apr. 17, 2000, effective Dec. 1, 2000*]

The second sentence of Rule 703 recognizes that inadmissible hearsay may be considered by an expert in reaching his or her conclusion.[1] Experts, after all, are allowed to testify precisely because they have training or skills that ordinary jurors lack. Consequently, when experts normally rely upon certain kinds of data in order to function effectively in their area of expertise, guarantees of trustworthiness are present that compensate for the hearsay nature of the underlying data. Rule 703 assumes that an expert's testimony will be more useful when the expert is allowed to function the same way in the courtroom as in the field. The third sentence of Rule 703 precludes the proponent of the expert testimony from disclosing to the jury any inadmissible facts or data the expert relied on in formulating his or her opinion unless the court first determines that the assistance to the jury of such disclosure in evaluating the opinion will outweigh its prejudicial effect.

---

[1] Marsee v. United States Tobacco Co., 866 F.2d 319, 323 (10th Cir. 1989) (suggesting without holding that inadmissible material on which expert's opinion based may not be brought out on direct examination); *see also* Sphere Drake Ins. PLC v. Trisko, 226 F.3d 951, 955 (8th Cir. 2000) (expert witness entitled to rely on inadmissible hearsay in formulation of opinion and trial court may permit proponent to reveal such hearsay to jury, but only to help jury evaluate expert's opinion, and not for substantive purposes); Finchum v. Ford Motor Co., 57 F.3d 526, 531–532 (7th Cir. 1995) (in action alleging defective design of car seats, plaintiff's expert could rely on published article regarding occupant protection during rear impact in forming his opinion but article itself was inadmissible hearsay); Engebretsen v. Fairchild Aircraft Corp., 21 F.3d 721, 728–729 (6th Cir. 1994) (experts may rely on hearsay reports they prepared, but reports were inadmissible for their truth).

[2]—The Three Bases for Expert Testimony[2]

[a]—Personal Knowledge

The first sentence of Rule 703 codifies pre-Rules practice in permitting an expert to state an opinion based on personal observation.[3] Often the testimony of an expert with firsthand knowledge is particularly credible and convincing. When testimony is offered on this basis, the court, pursuant to Rule 104(a), may have to decide such issues as whether the testimony was based on personal observation, whether the witness had a sufficient opportunity to observe,[4] and whether the witness's observation was relevant to a material fact in issue.[5] The Supreme Court has held that there is no violation of the confrontation clause when an expert bases an opinion on personal observation, but is then unable to recall the theory underlying the conclusion.[6]

[b]—Facts or Data Made Known to Expert at Trial

Before the enactment of the Federal Rules of Evidence, when experts relied upon data not personally known to them as the basis for an opinion, hypothetical questions were customarily used to present data to the experts. The alternative—having experts attend the trial to hear testimony that would then become the basis for their opinions—was often impracticable in terms of expense and time, and presented problems when conflicts in the evidence made it difficult

---

[2]　*See* **Treatise** at § 703.02.

[3]　*See* Fed. R. Evid. 703 (expert may testify to opinions based on facts "perceived by" expert "at or before the hearing").

[4]　*See, e.g.,* Ferrara & DiMercurio v. St. Paul Mercury Ins. Co., 240 F.3d 1, 8 (1st Cir. 2001) (expert's personal visit to fire scene, observation of burn patterns, personal measurements, and personal photographs provided sufficient personal perception of facts and data for formulation of expert opinion); United States v. Van Dorn, 925 F.2d 1331, 1337–1338 (11th Cir. 1991) (trial court properly admitted expert testimony that defendant was member of named crime family when witness had been associated with family and had worked for defendant); *cf.* United States v. Hill, 655 F.2d 512, 516 (3d Cir. 1981) (majority found trial court had erred in excluding psychologist's testimony about entrapment on ground that expert had not heard defendant or informant testify; majority pointed out that testimony need not have been based solely on personal observation but could also have rested on psychological profiles, intelligence tests and other data relating to defendant; dissent objected that opinion expert sought to express could only have been based on testimony of informant).

[5]　*See, e.g.,* Sphere Drake Ins, PLC v. Trisko, 226 F.3d 951, 955 (8th Cir. 2000) (expert's testimony concerning jewel thefts in Miami area was relevant to issue whether plaintiff's loss of jewelry was "mysterious disappearance" or "unexplained loss," both of which were excluded from insurance coverage, or was insured theft loss); United States v. Busic, 592 F.2d 13, 20–22 (2d Cir. 1978) (evidence relevant to specific intent was properly excluded when offense charged involved only general criminal intent).

[6]　Delaware v. Fensterer, 474 U.S. 15, 106 S. Ct. 292, 88 L. Ed.2d 15 (1985) (per curiam) (Court noted that in this case lapse of memory did not frustrate opportunity for cross-examination).

to determine on what testimony the experts relied. These potential obstacles to the expert's attendance at the trial continue to exist. Nevertheless, experts regularly attend trial in order to prepare to testify as well as to assist counsel in meeting the opponent's case. The expert who misses part of the trial may even depend upon counsel for a summary of the missed testimony.

The Federal Rules allow use of the hypothetical question and it remains a convenient way of presenting evidence in some cases. However, hypothetical questions are used less often now than under former practice. Rule 703 greatly expands the sources on which experts may base their opinions by allowing them to rely on materials they customarily consult outside the courtroom; Rule 705 additionally permits experts to state an opinion without first disclosing the underlying data on which it is based.

[c]—Reasonable Reliance on Data Presented Outside the Courtroom

The most controversial aspect of Rule 703 is its second sentence, which authorizes experts to base their opinions upon inadmissible data if they would reasonably rely upon such data in reaching conclusions in their fields of expertise.[7] When there is a factual dispute over the issue of reliance, it is the court, pursuant to Rule 104(a), that must determine whether such reliance is justified.[8]

---

[7] *See, e.g.,* Sphere Drake Ins. PLC v. Trisko, 226 F.3d 951, 955 (8th Cir. 2000) (police investigator reasonably relied on information received from informants); International Adhesive Coating Co., Inc. v. Bolton Emerson Int'l, Inc., 851 F.2d 540, 545 (1st Cir. 1988) (expert on damages relied on interviews with plaintiff's personnel); United States v. Bramlet, 820 F.2d 851, 856 (7th Cir. 1987) (reliance on recorded observation of psychiatric hospital staff); Lewis v. Rego Co., 757 F.2d 66, 74 (3d Cir. 1985) (testifying expert could rely on conversation with other expert); Bauman v. Centex Corp., 611 F.2d 1115, 1120 (5th Cir. 1980) (library research); In re Swine Flu Immunization Prods. Liab. Litig., 533 F. Supp. 567, 578 (D. Colo. 1980) (reliance on laboratory findings).

[8] *See, e.g.,* United States v. Corey, 207 F.3d 84, 88 (1st Cir. 2000) ("Rule 703 does require that the trial court judge act as an independent "gatekeeper" to assure that there is sufficient, credible evidence that experts do rely on the specified types of sources in formulating their opinions."); In re Paoli R.R. Yard PCB Litig., 35 F.3d 717, 748 (3d Cir. 1994) (judge must conduct independent evaluation into reasonableness of expert's reliance on particular type of data; judge may consider opinion of witness and other experts that such reliance is reasonable, but "can also take into account other factors he or she deems relevant"); United States v. Gaskell, 985 F.2d 1056, 1060–1061 (11th Cir. 1993) (trial court allowed physician to reproduce a demonstration of shaken baby syndrome he had seen done by a police officer based on confession of father in an unrelated case; this was error, because government did not establish that witness's "hearsay knowledge of this unrelated case provided any reliable or accurate basis upon which to draw conclusions" regarding the instant case); Head v. Lithonia Corp., Inc., 881 F.2d 941, 942–944 (10th Cir. 1989) (error to admit expert testimony of neurologist based on topographical brain mapping without considering trustworthiness of that technique); Faries v. Atlas Truck Body Mfg. Co., 797 F.2d 619, 623–624 (8th Cir. 1986) (expert in accident construction could not reasonably rely upon eyewitness in forming opinion about cause of accident).

In making this finding, the trial judge may wish to hold a hearing outside the presence of the jury at which the expert can be examined, and at which the proponent may introduce evidence indicating that experts in the field customarily rely upon the material in question in performing their work. Since Rule 703 is concerned with the trustworthiness of the resulting opinions, the proponent of the expert must establish that experts other than the proposed witness would act upon the information relied upon, and would do so for purposes other than testifying in a lawsuit.[9]

It is apparent from the reported decisions that the courts are loosely divided into two camps in interpreting the reasonable reliance test. The difference between the two groups is one of emphasis. The first group, the more liberal of the two, defers to the experts and accepts their determination whether it is reasonable to rely on a particular source of information or data.[10] Unlike their more liberal-minded colleagues, judges who take a restrictive view of Rule 703 undertake an independent assessment of the reliability of the materials on which the expert relied. The expert's opinion will be admitted only if the judge, rather than the expert, is persuaded of the trustworthiness of the underlying data.[11]

A trial judge may now be required to independently evaluate both the reasonableness of reliance on the data underlying an expert's opinion under Rule 703 and the sufficiency of the data to support that opinion, under Rule 702(1) and *Daubert*.[12] Although *Daubert* was a Rule 702 decision, it is relevant to Rule 703 in that appellate courts have instructed district courts to act as "gatekeepers" to ensure that the scientific data on which an expert opinion is founded are sufficient and reli-

---

[9] *See, e.g.,* Schudel v. General Elec. Co., 120 F.3d 991, 996–997 (9th Cir. 1997) (two experts testified that material was of type toxicologists consider reliable and regularly rely upon; it was therefore admissible under Rule 703); In re Polypropylene Carpet Antitrust Litig., 93 F. Supp. 2d 1348, 1356 (N.D. Ga. 2000) (plaintiffs adequately demonstrated frequent reliance on regression models by economists to explain changes in prices; plaintiff's expert, therefore, could rely on regression analysis to show collusive pricing); *but see* United States v. Carter, 270 F.3d 731, 735 (8th Cir. 2001) (absent evidence to contrary court can properly assume materials expert witness relied on in formulating his or her opinions are of type ordinarily relied upon by experts in same field).

[10] *See, e.g.,* United States v. Corey, 207 F.3d 84, 88 (1st Cir. 2000) (experts in field can be presumed to know what evidence is sufficiently trustworthy and probative to merit reliance).

[11] *See, e.g.,* United States v. Locascio, 6 F.3d 924, 938 (2d Cir. 1993) ("district court is not bound to accept expert testimony based on questionable data simply because other experts use such data in the field"); Ealy v. Richardson-Merrell, Inc., 897 F.2d 1159, 1161–1162 (D.C. Cir. 1990) (trial court must make independent judgment concerning reasonableness of expert's reliance on underlying data).

[12] Fed. R. Evid. 702(1), 703; *see* Daubert v. Merrell Dow Pharms., Inc., 509 U.S. 579, 597, 113 S. Ct. 2786, 125 L. Ed. 2d 469 (1993) (scientific opinion offered under Rule 702 must be based on sound scientific methods and valid procedures); *see also* § 13.02[4].

able.[13]

Indeed, since the *Daubert* decision, a number of courts have revisited their positions on the nature of the "reasonable reliance" analysis a trial court must undertake under Rule 703. Many of them read *Daubert* to suggest that the trial court's role includes an independent analysis of the reasonableness of an expert's reliance on inadmissible data.[14] Others, however, continue to defer to the opinion of the experts.[15]

This issue may arise when a team of scientists works on a specific problem. In such cases, the team leader is allowed to testify to the team's conclusions if the leader adequately supervised the operations of the other team members and if the composition of the teams is such that it was reasonable for the leader to rely on the work of the other team members. If the leader testifies, the other members of the team usually do not need to testify at the trial; however, the opponent can depose them to assure they performed their tasks competently.[16] If, however, the soundness of an expert judgment made by one of the team members is at issue, that member must testify for that judgment to be admissible.[17]

[3]—Inadmissible Facts Expert Relied on in Forming Opinion

Rule 703 provides that experts may rely on inadmissible facts or data in forming their opinions or inferences if they are "of a type reasonably relied upon by experts in the particular field in forming opinions or inferences upon the subject" (*see* [1],

---

[13] *See* General Electric Co. v. Joiner, 522 U.S. 136, 146, 118 S. Ct. 512, 139 L. Ed. 2d 508 (1997) ("nothing in either *Daubert* or the Federal Rules of Evidence requires a district court to admit opinion evidence which is connected to existing data only by the *ipse dixit* of the expert"); In re Paoli R.R. Yard PCB Litig., 35 F.3d 717, 742 (3d Cir. 1994) (gatekeeping role with regard to experts included independent evaluation of reasonableness of data relied on by experts under Rule 703).

[14] *See, e.g.,* University of Rhode Island v. A.W. Chesterton Co., 2 F.3d 1200, 1218 (1st Cir. 1993) ("Rule 703 requires the trial court to give 'careful consideration' to any inadmissible facts upon which the expert will rely in order to determine whether reliance is 'reasonable' "); In re Paoli R.R. Yard PCB Litig., 35 F.3d 717, 748 (3d Cir. 1994) (aligned Third Circuit's jurisprudence with *Daubert* and required courts to make independent determination of reasonable reliance in face of challenge to expert testimony under Rule 703); Slaughter v. Southern Talc Co., 919 F.2d 304, 306–307 (5th Cir. 1990) (Rule 703 "requires courts to examine the reliability of an expert's sources to determine whether they satisfy the threshold established by the rule").

[15] *See, e.g.,* United States v. Corey, 207 F.3d 84, 88 (1st Cir. 2000) (experts in field can be presumed to know what evidence is sufficiently trustworthy and probative to merit reliance).

[16] *See, e.g.,* Walker v. Soo Line R.R., 208 F.3d 581, 588–589 (7th Cir. 2000) (medical team leader need not be qualified as expert in every discipline encompassed by team to testify about team's conclusions; court abused its discretion in its "wholesale disallowance" of expert's testimony on those grounds).

[17] *See, e.g.,* Dura Auto. Sys. of Ind., Inc. v. CTS Corp., 285 F.3d 609, 612–615 (7th Cir. 2002) (opposite rule would allow one witness to become another's "mouthpiece," and avoid reliability analysis of independent work of other team members).

[2], *above*). Such inadmissible underlying facts or data "shall not be disclosed to the jury by the proponent of the opinion or inference unless the court determines that their probative value in assisting the jury to evaluate the expert's opinion substantially outweighs their prejudicial effect."[18] This language "provides a presumption against disclosure to the jury of information used as the basis of an expert's opinion and not admissible for any substantive purpose, when that information is offered by the proponent of the expert."[19] Thus, there is no limitation on disclosure when the evidence on which the expert witness relied is independently admissible.[19.1]

When otherwise inadmissible data are disclosed because an expert relied on them, they are not admitted into evidence for their truth. They are admitted only for the limited purpose of informing the jury of the basis for the expert's opinion or inference.[20] On request, the court must instruct the jury that it may use the data only to help it evaluate the expert's opinion, not for the truth of its contents or any substantive purpose.[21] Rule 703 is not, itself, an exception to or exclusion from the hearsay rule or any other evidence rule that makes the underlying information inadmissible.[22]

The limitation against disclosure applies only to the proponent of the expert during direct examination; it does not restrict an opposing party from presenting those facts or data on cross-examination or a proponent from using those facts or data on redirect examination after they have been revealed to the jury during cross-examination.[23] Moreover, the limitation on disclosure applies only when

---

[18]   Fed. R. Evid. 703 (added in 2000 amendment).

[19]   Fed. R. Evid. 703 Committee Note (2000) (reprinted in **Treatise,** Ch. 703, *Bases of Opinion Testimony by Experts,* § 703App.03[2]).

[19.1]   *See, e.g.,* United States v. Gonzales, 307 F.3d 906, 910 (9th Cir. 2002).

[20]   *See, e.g.,* Kinser v. Gehl Co., 184 F.3d 1259, 1274–1275 (10th Cir. 1999) (expert could testify concerning documents, which could not be admitted into evidence because they were not authenticated, to demonstrate basis for opinion).

[21]   Fed. R. Evid. 703 Committee Note (2000) (reproduced verbatim in **Treatise,** Ch. 703, *Bases of Opinion Testimony of Experts,* § 703App.03[2]); *see, e.g.,* Sphere Drake Ins. PLC v. Trisko, 226 F.3d 951, 955 (8th Cir. 2000) (hearsay statements of informants on which expert relied are admissible for limited purpose of exposing factual basis for expert's opinion; trial court properly gave jury limiting instruction).

[22]   Fed. R. Evid. 703 Committee Note (2000) (reproduced verbatim in **Treatise,** Ch. 703, *Bases for Opinion Testimony by Experts,* § 703App.03[2]) ("Rule 703 has been amended to emphasize that when an expert reasonably relies on inadmissible information to form an opinion or inference, the underlying information is not admissible simply because the opinion or inference is admitted").

[23]   Fed. R. Evid. 703 Committee Note (2000) (reproduced verbatim in **Treatise,** Ch. 703, *Bases for Opinion Testimony by Experts,* § 703App.03[2]).

there is a jury.[24] A district court sitting as the trier of fact is presumed to be able to ignore inadmissible evidence.[25]

[4]—Right of Confrontation in Criminal Cases Satisfied by Right to Cross-Examine Expert[26]

The confrontation rights of criminal defendants may be implicated when Rule 703 allows expert witnesses to base their opinions and inferences on material that is not admissible in evidence. The courts have generally held that the Confrontation Clause is satisfied if the expert witness is available for cross-examination.[27] A defendant's right to confrontation is not violated by an expert's reliance on out-of-court sources when "the utility of trial confrontation would be remote and of little value to either the jury or the defendant."[28]

The disclosure of inadmissible materials pursuant to Rule 703 creates only minimal confrontation issues, since the materials are not admitted for the truth of any matters asserted in them but only to inform the jury concerning the factual bases for the expert's opinion.[29] Evidence that is not admitted for the truth of its assertions is not hearsay, by definition.[30] Admission of an out-of-court statement for non-hearsay purposes usually does not raise Confrontation Clause concerns.[31]

On the other hand, even if the trial court were to admit underlying data for the truth of the matter asserted, if the trial court has properly performed its gatekeeping function with respect to reasonable reliance on the data (see § 13.02[4]), the underlying facts or data will have passed a trustworthiness scrutiny similar to, and perhaps equal to, that required for admissibility under the residual hearsay ex-

---

[24] *See* Fed. R. Evid. 703 ("shall not be disclosed to the jury").

[25] *See, e.g.,* Harris v. Rivera, 454 U.S. 339, 347, 102 S. Ct. 460, 465, 70 L. Ed. 2d 530 (1981) ("In bench trials, judges routinely hear inadmissible evidence that they are presumed to ignore when making decisions").

[26] *See* **Treatise** at § 703.06.

[27] *See, e.g.,* United States v. Brown, 299 F.3d 1252, 1258 (11th Cir. 2002) (defendant's right to confront adverse witnesses was satisfied by his ability to cross-examine expert witness who properly relied on out-of-court statements and opinions of others).

[28] United States v. Abbas, 74 F.3d 506, 512–513 (4th Cir. 1996) (testimony about chemical analyses based on authenticated control standards and published standards was properly admitted under Fed. R. Evid. 703 and did not violate defendant's confrontation rights; defendant had opportunity to cross-examine expert witness and to present his own expert testimony).

[29] *See, e.g.,* Barrett v. Acevedo, 169 F.3d 1155, 1163 (8th Cir. 1999) ("Rule 703 evidence . . . is never admitted for the truth of the matter asserted, but simply to show a basis for an expert's opinion").

[30] Fed. R. Evid. 801(c); *see* Ch. 14.

[31] *See, e.g.,* Tennessee v. Street, 471 U.S. 409, 414–417, 105 S. Ct. 2078, 85 L. Ed. 2d 425 (1985).

ception.[32] Under those circumstances, the admission of the underlying facts and data for all purposes would not necessarily infringe a criminal defendant's right of confrontation.[33]

When an expert witness relies on inadmissible facts and data in the formulation of an opinion, the ability of a criminal defendant to cross-examine the expert witness effectively is crucial to the preservation of confrontation rights. In turn, effective cross-examination depends on the defendant's advance access to substantially all of the facts and data on which the expert witness relied.[34]

§ 13.04 Opinion on Ultimate Issue—Rule 704

[1]—Development and Text of Rule[1]

Until amended in 1984, Rule 704 had abolished the ultimate opinion doctrine. The 1984 amendment reinstated the doctrine to the extent that an expert testifying in a criminal case is not permitted to express an opinion on the ultimate issue of the defendant's mental state.

The Rule now provides as follows:

Rule 704. Opinion on Ultimate Issue.

(a)
Except as provided in subdivision (b), testimony in the form of an opinion or inference otherwise admissible is not objectionable because it embraces an ultimate issue to be decided by the trier of fact.

(b)
No expert witness testifying with respect to the mental state or condition of a defendant in a criminal case may state an opinion or inference as to

---

[32] *See* Fed. R. Evid. 807; *see also* Ch. 14.

[33] *See, e.g.,* Barrett v. Acevedo, 169 F.3d 1155, 1163 (8th Cir. 1999) (so long as trial court's analysis of expert witness's underlying inadmissible evidence for reasonableness of reliance shows that underlying evidence has "particularized guarantees of trustworthiness," admission of underlying information into evidence, even for truth of its assertions, does not violate guarantees of Confrontation Clause; citing Idaho v. Wright, 497 U.S. 805, 814–815, 110 S. Ct. 3139, 111 L. Ed. 2d 638 (1990)).

[34] Fed. R. Evid. 705 Advisory Committee Note (1992) (reproduced verbatim in **Treatise** at § 705App.01[2]) (advisory committee "assumes that the cross-examiner has the advance knowledge which is essential for effective cross-examination"); *see, e.g.,* United States v. Lawson, 653 F.2d 299, 302 (7th Cir. 1981) (because criminal defendant had advance access to almost all data on which expert witness relied in forming his opinion and, therefore, had adequate opportunity to prepare cross-examination, expert witness's testimony did not violate defendant's right to confront adverse witnesses).

[1] *See* **Treatise** at § 704.02.

whether the defendant did or did not have the mental state or condition constituting an element of the crime charged or of a defense thereto. Such ultimate issues are matters for the trier of fact alone.

[*Adopted Jan. 2, 1975, effective July 1, 1975; amended effective Oct. 12, 1984.*]

In its most extreme form, the ultimate opinion rule held that no witness—whether lay or expert—could express an opinion on the ultimate issue in the case. The usual reason offered was that such an opinion would usurp the function of the jury. However, it had been recognized long before the enactment of the Federal Rules that distinctions between ultimate issues and non-ultimate issues were often difficult to draw, and that the expressed rationale for the rule made little sense because jurors remain free to draw their own conclusions. The core of the ultimate opinion rule—that jurors cannot ascertain what happened if they are merely told how to decide—was often eclipsed by wrangling over how to apply it. By the time Rule 704 was drafted, the federal courts had taken account of the condemnation of the ultimate opinion rule voiced by other courts and legal scholars,[2] and had "long tolerated [its] violation."[3] Rule 704, as enacted, thus did little more than proclaim actual practice.

The treatment of the ultimate opinion rule problem in the Federal Rules has numerous advantages over previous practice. It eliminates quibbles over the meaning of ultimate fact and the distinction between fact and law, and ends the spectacle of courts endorsing a principle that they cite only as a precursor to applying an exception. It stops the resort to indirect means to bring the prohibited matter to the jury's attention, and most importantly, it allows the jury to receive the full benefit of a witness's judgment. Both lay and expert witnesses may testify in a more natural and straightforward manner, uninterrupted by technical objections interfering with the flow of the trial.[4] Abolition of the ultimate issue rule was seen by the drafters as an adjunct to the helpfulness approach expressed in Rule 702;[5] an opinion that

---

[2] Wigmore called the rule "a mere bit of empty rhetoric" and "one of those impracticable and misconceived utterances which lack any justification in principle." 7 Wigmore, Evidence §§ 1920 and 1921 at 21–22 (Little, Brown & Co. Chadbourn rev. 1978).

[3] Harried v. United States, 389 F.2d 281, 285 n.3 (D.C. Cir. 1967) (opinion by then Circuit Judge Warren Burger).

[4] *See* United States v. Izydore, 167 F.3d 213, 218 (5th Cir. 1999) (bankruptcy trustee's opinion that money was "not legally taken" was not a legal conclusion about appellants' guilt of charged fraud offenses; instead, it was her opinion about whether the money properly belonged to bankrupt individual or to appellants).

[5] *See, e.g.,* United States v. Parris, 243 F.3d 286, 289 (6th Cir. 2001) (testimony of witnesses who said they stopped using defendant's tax avoidance scheme because they thought it was "illegal" did not violate rule against opinion testimony to legal conclusions; schemes for total elimination of federal tax liability are so outrageous that it is fair to characterize them in normal parlance as illegal);

merely tells jurors what result to reach is not helpful.[6] This consistency of treatment has now been somewhat offset by the 1984 addition of subdivision (b), discussed below.

[2]—Continued Applicability of Ultimate Issue Doctrine[7]

The "ultimate issue" rule remains effective respecting some issues, through the courts' interpretation of the helpfulness standard of Rules 701 and 702.[8] Thus, it generally is not appropriate for lay or expert witnesses:

- To tell the finder of fact what conclusion to reach.[9]

- To testify to opinions respecting issues reserved exclusively for the jury, such as the credibility of other witnesses.[10]

- To testify to opinions embracing legal conclusions, which are reserved exclusively for the court.[11]

Similarly, Rule 705, which provides the trial court with the authority to require expert witnesses to disclose the bases for their opinions, permits it to require the

---

United States v. Sheffey, 57 F.3d 1419, 1424–1428 (6th Cir. 1995) (witnesses who observed defendant driving prior to car accident could testify that, in their opinion, defendant was driving recklessly and in extreme disregard for human life).

[6] *See, e.g.,* United States v. Hubbard, 61 F.3d 1261, 1274–1275 (7th Cir. 1995) (expert testimony by DEA agent detailing a typical profile for drug trafficking did not embrace the ultimate issue to be decided because the witness only spoke in general terms and never addressed defendant's conduct); United States v. Boyd, 55 F.3d 667, 670–672 (D.C. Cir. 1995) (defendant's conviction reversed when government stated hypothetical mirroring case and elicited expert opinion on ultimate issue, whether defendant had intention to distribute narcotics); United States v. Didomenico, 985 F.2d 1159, 1163–1164 (2d Cir. 1993) (expert testimony on "dependent personality disorder" inadmissible because it stated the expert's conclusion that the defendant could not have had the requisite mental state due to her disorder); Kostelecky v. NL Acme Tool/NL Indus., Inc., 837 F.2d 828, 830 (8th Cir. 1988) (error, but harmless, to have admitted accident report made by plaintiff's co-worker stating that accident was caused by plaintiff's conduct, and could have been avoided if plaintiff listened to warnings; "in the context of this case, the opinion as to causation served to do nothing more than tell the jury what result it should reach").

[7] *See* **Treatise** at §§ 704.03–704.05.

[8] *See* §§ 10.02[2][b]; 13.02[2].

[9] *See, e.g.,* United States v. Barile, 286 F.3d 749, 760–761 (4th Cir. 2002) (trial court has discretion to exclude expert testimony concerning ultimate issue if all it does is tell finder of fact what conclusion to reach).

[10] *See, e.g.,* Goodwin v. MTD Prods., Inc., 232 F.3d 600, 609 (7th Cir. 2000) (credibility questions are solely within jury's province, and are not susceptible to expert testimony).

[11] *See, e.g.,* United States v. Crawford, 239 F.3d 1086, 1091 (9th Cir. 2001) (witness could not properly testify to opinion that public university had legal obligation not to abandon property); Burkhart v. Washington Metro. Area Trans. Auth., 112 F.3d 1207, 1213 (D.C. Cir. 1997) ("Each courtroom comes equipped with a 'legal expert,' called a judge, and it is his or her province alone to instruct the jury on the relevant legal standards").

expert in appropriate cases to testify in concrete terms that the jury will find helpful in deciding the ultimate issue, without disclosing their opinions on the very issue the jury is to decide.[12]

The trial court may not exercise its discretion to exclude expert testimony respecting the ultimate issue on the ground that it invades the jury's province, however, when the testimony would be useful for the jury's resolution of a complex issue. Thus, even though an expert's testimony that a company's financial filings "did not contain materially misleading omissions" would be of questionable admissibility because it is worded in the statutory language, and therefore appears to be testimony to a legal conclusion, similar testimony that the filings were "reasonable" would not be so tainted and would be useful to a jury trying to resolve complex questions under the securities laws. Such testimony that closely parallels, but does not exactly track, the statutory language, is fully admissible under Rule 704.[13] Thus, an expert's testimony that a company's financial filings were "reasonable," although arguably stating a legal conclusion, was not worded in the statutory language and would have been useful to a jury trying to resolve complex questions under the securities laws. Thus, and its exclusion under Rule 704 was improper.[13.1] Moreover, when the statutory language does not have a specific meaning that is different from its usage in common parlance, an expert's testimony using that language is not necessarily excludable merely because the language is contained in the statute.[13.2]

On the other hand, an expert's testimony that a company's financial filings "did not contain materially misleading omissions" was of questionable admissibility because it appeared to be a legal conclusion and was worded in the statutory language. The district court had discretion to exclude this testimony.[13.3]

Rule 704(b) prohibits certain ultimate issue testimony about the mental state of a criminal defendant.[14]

---

[12] *See, e.g.,* Harris v. Pacific Floor Mach. Mfg. Co., 856 F.2d 64, 67–68 (8th Cir. 1988) (not error for district court to allow expert to explain criteria by which he would judge adequacy of warning but not allow him to give opinion on ultimate question of adequacy).

[13] *See, e.g.,* United States v. Barile, 286 F.3d 749, 759–762 (4th Cir. 2002).

[13.1] *See, e.g.,* United States v. Barile, 286 F.3d 749, 759–762 (4th Cir. 2002).

[13.2] *See, e.g.,* United States v. Two Eagle, 318 F.3d 785, 793 (8th Cir. 2003) (trial court did not err in admitting doctor's testimony that injury to victim's ear resulting from gun shot wound would have "disfigured" victim and was "painful" over objection that such testimony used language contained in statute defining *serious bodily injury* because language had same meaning in common usage as in statute).

[13.3] *See, e.g.,* United States v. Barile, 286 F.3d 749, 760–762 (4th Cir. 2002).

[14] Fed. R. Evid. 704(b); *see* [3], *below.*

[3]—Opinions on Mental State of Criminal Defendant[15]

Rule 704(b) prohibits expert opinion or inference testimony in criminal cases when the testimony relates to the mental state or condition of the defendant and that state or condition is an element of the crime charged or of a defense the defense has asserted.[16] Moreover, if a lawyer frames questions to the expert witness in terms of the defendant's intent or other mental state, the witness's simple agreement with the facts stated in the question transgresses the proscription of Rule 704(b).[16.1]

However, the rule permits experts to testify about the defendant's mental state or condition at the time of the charged act so long as they do so without directly addressing the ultimate issue reserved for the trier of fact.[17] For example, Rule 704(b) does not prevent expert testimony that a defendant's possessions or activities are consistent with a particular criminal activity or mental state.[18] It also does not prevent expert testimony, based on the witness's experience, that the defendant's claimed lack of knowledge concerning the presence of contraband materials is inconsistent with the way in which operations involving those contraband materials are generally conducted, even though the defendant's knowledge of the presence of those contraband materials is an element of the crime with which the defendant is charged, so long as the witness leaves the drawing of the ultimate inference to the trier of fact.[19] Experts may also express their opinions as to

---

[15] *See* **Treatise** at § 704.06.

[16] Fed. R. Evid. 704(b); *see, e.g.,* United States v. Booth, 309 F.3d 566, 573 (9th Cir. 2002) (trial court properly excluded testimony of polygrapher that defendant did not have intent to defraud because that mental state was element of charged crime).

[16.1] *See, e.g.,* United States v. Watson, 260 F.3d 301, 308–310 (3d Cir. 2001) (expert testimony concerning modus operandi of individuals involved in drug trafficking does not violate Rule 704(b); prosecutor's repeated references to defendant's intent in questions, however, framed witness's "yes" answers and converted apparently innocuous testimony into opinion concerning defendant's mental state in violation of Rule 704(b)).

[17] *See, e.g.,* United States v. Dixon, 185 F.3d 393, 400 (5th Cir. 1999) (in context of insanity defense, expert could testify as to whether defendant was suffering from severe mental illness at time of crime but could not testify that severe mental illness did or did not prevent defendant from appreciating wrongfulness of his or her actions, because that is element of insanity defense).

[18] *See, e.g.,* United States v. Brumley, 217 F.3d 905, 910–911 (7th Cir. 2000) (not error to permit expert witness to testify, based on his experience, that more than one ounce of methamphetamine is "dealer quantity," rather than "personal use quantity," in prosecution for possession with intent to distribute, when witness's testimony made it clear witness did not have special knowledge of defendant's mental state, but was testifying based on knowledge of drug trafficking trade).

[19] *See, e.g.,* United States v. Murillo, 255 F.3d 1169, 1178 (9th Cir. 2001) (DEA agent's testimony, based on his experience, that drug traffickers did not entrust large amounts of drugs to couriers who were not aware of nature of their cargo and why they did not do so did not violate Rule 704(b) because testimony was as to general practices of drug traffickers and did not opine explicitly on defendant's knowledge of nature of his cargo); *but see* United States v. Mendoza-Medina, 346

substantive matters such as reasonableness under the Fourth Amendment or the Due Process Clause. Rule 704(b) bans only testimony relating to traditional mental states, such as intent, knowledge, and insanity.[20]

Rule 704(b)'s limitation on the scope of expert testimony extends only to evidence respecting the defendant's mental state or condition. It does not deal with expert opinions concerning objective factors that are general characteristics of specific types of criminal activity or testimony relating the witness's perceptions of how the defendant's actions fit within an alleged criminal organization. It is appropriate, therefore, for an expert witness to testify to the roles individuals generally play in a criminal conspiracy and to specify which of the several roles individual defendants actually played in the conspiracy of which they were allegedly members.[21]

It is also appropriate for an expert witness to interpret coded words in conversations even though the interpretation provides the only evidence necessary to prove an element of the charged crime, so long as that element does not relate directly to the defendant's mental state or condition.[22] Moreover, it is proper for an expert witness to describe the instruments the defendant allegedly used to commit the charged crime as having a specific characteristic, even though the description uses words that are also used to describe the requisite mens rea of the charged crime.[23]

§ 13.05 Disclosure of Bases Underlying Expert Opinion—Rule 705

[1]—Operation of Rule at Trial[1]

Rule 705 permits experts to express their opinions without first disclosing the underlying facts or data, unless the court orders otherwise. A hypothetical question

---

F.3d 121, 127–129 (5th Cir. 2003) (trial court erred in admitting drug courier profile evidence, including testimony that drug shippers must trust their couriers and will not employ couriers who do not know what they are carrying, because such testimony was effectively testimony that defendant knew he was transporting illegal drugs).

[20] *See, e.g.,* United States v. Williams, 343 F.3d 423, 435 (5th Cir. 2003) (trial court properly permitted expert witness to testify to reasonableness of defendant's actions, as reasonableness is not traditional mental state as to which expert testimony is banned by Rule 704(b)).

[21] *See, e.g.,* United States v. Mendez-Zamora, 296 F.3d 1013, 1016–1017 (10th Cir. 2002).

[22] *See, e.g.,* United States v. Dukagjini, 326 F.3d 45, 53 (2d Cir. 2002) (trial court properly permitted expert witness to interpret coded words in recorded conversations as referring to specific type of controlled substance).

[23] *See, e.g.,* United States v. Owens, 301 F.3d 521, 527 (7th Cir. 2002) (trial court properly permitted expert witness to characterize portions of financial statements as "fraudulent and misleading" even though intent to defraud was element of crime defendant was charged with having committed; witness was commenting on characteristic of financial statement, not on defendant's mental state).

[1] *See* **Treatise** at §§ 705.02–705.08.

is no longer required, even when the experts are relying on facts beyond their personal knowledge, as authorized by Rule 703. A full exploration of the underlying data is available to the cross-examiner.[2]

The text of the Rule is as follows:

Rule 705.   Disclosure of Facts or Data Underlying Expert Opinion.

The expert may testify in terms of opinion or inference and give reasons therefor without first testifying to the underlying facts or data, unless the court requires otherwise. The expert may in any event be required to disclose the underlying facts or data on cross-examination.

[*Adopted Jan. 2, 1975, effective July 1, 1975; amended Mar. 2, 1987, effective Oct. 1, 1987; amended Apr. 22, 1993, effective Dec. 1, 1993.*]

This rule, which relates to the manner of presenting testimony at trial, was revised in 1993 to avoid an arguable conflict with Rules 26(a)(2)(B) and 26(e)(1) of the Federal Rules of Civil Procedure, or with Rule 16 of the Federal Rules of Criminal Procedure, which require disclosure in advance of trial of the basis and reasons for an expert's opinions. If a serious question is raised under Rule 702 or 703 as to the admissibility of expert testimony, disclosure of the underlying facts or data on which opinions are based may, of course, be needed by the court before deciding whether, and to what extent, the person should be allowed to testify. This rule does not preclude such an inquiry.

The purpose of Rule 705 is to enhance the progress of the trial. It enables experts to communicate their conclusions to the jury without the risk of confusion posed by artificial and belabored hypothetical questions. In practice, however, the pressures of orderly presentation will usually lead to divulgence of the critical supporting data on direct examination.

The proponent of an expert witness should present supporting data and the expert's opinion in the most persuasive fashion, using charts, summaries, and documents presented to the trier to convince it that the opinion is well founded. Expert witnesses with firsthand knowledge may be asked about the facts underlying their opinions because the facts themselves are needed to satisfy the proponent's burden of proof. A witness's familiarity with certain data may have to be shown in qualifying the witness as an expert pursuant to Rule 702. And the necessity of making evidence understandable to the jury will often require posing some foun-

---

[2] *See, e.g.,* United States v. Havvard, 260 F.3d 597, 601 (7th Cir. 2001) (trial court properly permitted expert witness under Rule 705 to testify to opinion without testifying to underlying data; when expert witness does so, it is opponent's responsibility to bring out any elaborating facts it desires).

dation questions before the expert gives an opinion.

Rule 705 does not prevent disclosure of the bases of an expert's opinion on direct examination;[3] it merely gives the proponent of the expert the choice of describing the underlying data on direct, or waiting to see if the other side will require disclosure on cross-examination.

Note that the use of hypotheticals is not prohibited. It is only made optional. However, when an attorney persists in asking confusing, repetitious, or unnecessary hypothetical questions, the court has the power pursuant to Rule 403 to exclude them if their probative value is outweighed by the danger of prejudice, confusion or waste of time.

Because of the broad scope of discovery in civil cases,[4] opposing counsel should know enough about the subject of the expert's testimony to decide whether it would be fruitful to require the expert to amplify the underlying data on cross-examination. Obviously, if further testimony would only solidify the expert's conclusions, an adversary will refrain from further questioning.[5] But if the cross-examiner concludes that the expert has omitted pertinent facts in arriving at an opinion, has misconstrued them, is accepting disputed facts as true, or is basing an opinion on someone else's opinion that is in conflict with the established facts, then the attorney should probe the expert's premises.

In a criminal case, the narrower scope of discovery means that an attorney is less likely to have sufficient advance knowledge for effective cross-examination. Consequently, the trial court should exercise its discretion to require a more detailed preliminary disclosure of the data on which the expert relied. It is even more important in criminal cases than in civil cases to require that experts' reports be shown to defense counsel before trial. Defense counsel should, in exchange for this privilege, be required to show the government its experts' reports before trial. Surprising testimony by experts should not be permitted.

---

[3] *See, e.g.,* Lewis v. Rego Co., 757 F.2d 66, 74 (3d Cir. 1985) (error to have prevented expert from testifying on direct that he had relied on conversation with other expert who had modified his opinion after writing a report, the contents of which were made known to jury). *But see,* Nachtsheim v. Beech Aircraft Corp., 847 F.2d 1261, 1270–1271 (7th Cir. 1988); *see also* § 13.03[2].

[4] Fed. R. Civ. P. 26; *see* 6 MOORE'S FEDERAL PRACTICE, Ch. 26, *General Provisions Governing Discovery; Duty of Disclosure* (Matthew Bender 3d ed. 1997).

[5] Studiengesellschaft Kohle v. Dart Industries, Inc., 862 F.2d 1564, 1568 (Fed. Cir. 1988) (but nothing in Rule 705 requires trier of fact to credit the testimony of an expert who has not revealed or been asked about the basis underlying the opinion). *See* 11 MOORE'S FEDERAL PRACTICE, Ch. 56, *Summary Judgment* (Matthew Bender 3d ed. 1997).

[2]—Operation of Rule in Conjunction with Motion for Summary Judgment

There is a certain degree of tension between Rule 56(e) of the Federal Rules of Civil Procedure and Rule 705. Rule 56(e) provides that affidavits in opposition to summary judgment "must set forth specific facts." Rule 705 permits an expert to state an opinion "and give reasons therefore without prior disclosure of the underlying facts or data." The court has to reconcile these two rules when the opposition to a motion for summary judgment is based on the affidavit of an expert. A number of courts have held "that Rules 703 and 705 do not alter the requirement of Fed. R. Civ. P. 56(e) that an affidavit must set forth specific facts in order to have any probative value."[6]

Restricting the operation of Rule 705 to the trial context is consistent with the rationale for the Rule. It was designed to lead to more effective and efficient trials, and should not be allowed to undermine the efficacy of summary judgment procedures.

§ 13.06   Court Appointed Experts—Rule 706[1]

[1]—Scope and Text of Rule

Rule 706 authorizes a judge to appoint expert witnesses. It applies in civil and criminal cases. A court would have the right of appointment as part of its general authority to appoint masters, even in the absence of this rule, as a specific instance of a court's inherent power to call witnesses expressed in Rule 614.[2] Moreover, since the rule refers to "expert witnesses," some courts have held that Rule 706 does not apply to technical advisors appointed by trial courts who do not serve as witnesses.[3]

---

[6] Evers v. General Motors Corp., 770 F.2d 984, 986 (11th Cir. 1985); *see, e.g.,* Arthur A. Collins, Inc. v. Northern Telecom Ltd., 216 F.3d 1042, 1047 (Fed. Cir. 2000) (affidavit of expert witness submitted in opposition to motion for summary judgment must do more than give opinion on ultimate issue, it must set forth factual basis for opinion in sufficient detail to permit court to conclude there is genuine issue for trial); *see also* M & M Med. Supplies and Service, Inc. v. Pleasant Valley Hosp., Inc., 981 F.2d 160, 165 (4th Cir. 1992) (F.R.C.P. 56(e) "trumps" Rule 705 concerning disclosure of facts in summary judgment proceedings; however, court can require supplementation of expert's affidavit to disclose supporting data if court deems disclosure necessary for decision of summary judgment motion); *cf.* Ambrosini v. Labarraque, 966 F.2d 1464 (D.C. Cir. 1992) (expert's affidavit in opposition to motion for summary judgment "cannot be excluded solely because it fails to disclose the facts or date underlying the opinion").

[1] *See* **Treatise** at §§ 706.02–706.06.

[2] *See* Hart v. Community Sch. Bd. of Brooklyn, 383 F. Supp. 699 (E.D.N.Y. 1974), *aff'd,* 512 F.2d 37 (2d Cir. 1975) (full discussion of use of masters as experts).

[3] *See, e.g.,* Association of Mexican-American Educators v. California, 231 F.3d 572, 590 (9th Cir. 2000) (en banc) (requirements of Rule 706 that court-appointed expert submit report and be

Rule 706 restricts the judge's common-law powers in that its subdivision (a) requires certain procedures. The Rule provides as follows:

Rule 706.   Court Appointed Experts.

(a)
Appointment. The court may on its own motion or on the motion of any party enter an order to show cause why expert witnesses should not be appointed, and may request the parties to submit nominations. The court may appoint any expert witnesses agreed upon by the parties, and may appoint expert witnesses of its own selection. An expert witness shall not be appointed by the court unless the witness consents to act. A witness so appointed shall be informed of the witness's duties by the court in writing, a copy of which shall be filed with the clerk, or at a conference in which the parties shall have opportunity to participate. A witness so appointed shall advise the parties of the witness's findings, if any; the witness's deposition may be taken by any party; and the witness may be called to testify by the court or any party. The witness shall be subject to cross-examination by each party, including a party calling the witness.

(b)
Compensation. Expert witnesses so appointed are entitled to reasonable compensation in whatever sum the court may allow. The compensation thus fixed is payable from funds which may be provided by law in criminal cases and civil actions and proceedings involving just compensation under the fifth amendment. In other civil actions and proceedings the compensation shall be paid by the parties in such proportion and at such time as the court directs, and thereafter charged in like manner as other costs.

(c)
Disclosure of appointment. In the exercise of its discretion, the court may authorize disclosure to the jury of the fact that the court appointed the expert witness.

(d)
Parties' experts of own selection. Nothing in this rule limits the parties in calling expert witnesses of their own selection.

[*Adopted Jan. 2, 1975, effective July 1, 1975; amended Mar. 2, 1987, effective*

---

subject to cross-examination do not apply to court-appointed technical advisor, who was not called as an expert witness, was not subject to cross-examination, and did not furnish an expert's report; there was no indication that trial court relied on technical advisor as source of evidence); Reilly v. United States, 863 F.2d 149, 155 (1st Cir. 1988) ("Rule 706 is confined to court-appointed expert witnesses; the rule does not embrace expert advisors or consultants," citing **Treatise**).

[2]—Deciding on Appointment

Rule 706 provides an alternative not intended to be used as a matter of course in run-of-the-mill litigation. In some cases it is a useful corrective to the unsatisfactory process of party-controlled expert testimony, which often leaves the trier of fact grappling with highly technical, diametrically opposed testimony that it finds difficult to evaluate. By summoning its own witness where expert testimony is critical and the parties' experts are at loggerheads, the court seeks to procure a higher caliber, less venal expert, and to help the court and parties reach a settlement or the jury in arrive at a sound verdict.

Despite the advantages that may flow from the court's appointment of an expert, judges have not exercised their power to call experts frequently, either pursuant to Rule 706 or under prior practice. Concern that a court expert will "usurp" the jury's function because jurors would defer to a court sponsored witness, the difficulty in finding a neutral expert, problems of cost, and loyalty to the adversary system of for presenting evidence are the principal reasons why courts do not appoint experts more often.

Some of the provisions in subdivision (a) of Rule 706 were designed to overcome these objections. The appointment need not be divulged to the jury if the court fears it would be overimpressed by the status of the witness. The judge may ask the parties for their recommendations and may act upon them in selecting an expert witness. Since the parties have an absolute right to examine the expert's report and to call their own witnesses, they have the opportunity to cross-examine the court's expert effectively, thereby furthering the goals of the adversary system.

[3]—Procedure

Rule 706(a) provides that before a court-appointed expert can act, (1) there must be a hearing on an order to show cause why the expert should not be appointed, (2) the expert must consent, and (3) the expert must be notified of his or her duties either in writing or at a conference of the court and counsel. The subdivision also requires the expert to communicate his or her findings to the parties. The court may appoint more than one expert and, at times, may find a panel or committee useful as an adjunct to the court in its fact-finding role.[4] Because time is needed to comply

---

[4] *See, e.g.,* Grove v. Principal Mut. Life Ins. Co., 200 F.R.D. 434, 441–445 (S.D. Iowa 2001) (trial court appointed actuary and professor of insurance to assist in evaluation of fairness of proposed class action settlement and valuing amount of settlement fund for purposes of establishing proper amount of attorneys' fees award).

with these provisions, Rule 706 will ordinarily be invoked well before trial,[5] although the Rule does not contain any time restrictions. Additional time may also be required if the court exercises its option to request the parties to submit nominations or if the parties exercise their right to take the expert's deposition. The process should be set in motion at a pretrial conference pursuant to Rule 16 of the Federal Rules of Civil Procedure or Rule 17.1 of the Federal Rules of Criminal Procedure.[6]

The trial court has broad discretion to appoint or to refuse to appoint an expert.[7] This may apply even when the issue is one that substantive law requires be determined from a lay standpoint, for instance, that of "the reasonable person."[8] Although Rule 706 gives the court the option of appointing experts on whom the parties agree, in practice, the judge should accede to the parties' wishes to the extent practicable, since their agreement reduces the likelihood of the abuses under the Rule.[9]

Since a reluctant witness usually presents too great a hazard to justice, subdivision (a) provides that an expert appointed pursuant to Rule 706 must consent to act. This provision does not bar the subpoenaing of non-court-appointed experts who otherwise would be unwilling to testify.[10] Neither, however, does it permit the trial court to compel examiners of the U. S. Patent and Trademark Office to testify as experts in patent-infringement cases.[11]

Rule 706 gives the trial judge the option of informing the expert of his or her

---

[5] United States v. Weathers, 618 F.2d 663, 664 (10th Cir. 1980) (expressing serious doubt about whether post-trial employment of psychiatric expert comported with rule; but harmless error).

[6] See Fed. R. Civ. P. 16; Fed. R. Crim. P. 17.1; see also 3 MOORE'S FEDERAL PRACTICE, Ch. 16, Pretrial Conferences; Scheduling; Management (Matthew Bender 3d ed. 1997); 25 MOORE'S FEDERAL PRACTICE, Ch. 617.1, Pretrial Conference (Matthew Bender 3d ed. 1997).

[7] See,.g., Vizcaino v. Microsoft Corp., 290 F.3d 1043, 1051 n.7 (9th Cir. 2002) (trial court did not abuse its discretion in refusing to appoint expert witness re size of attorneys' fees award in class action); Walker v. American Home Shield Disability Plan, 180 F.3d 1065, 1071 (9th Cir. 1999) (court did not abuse its discretion in appointing independent medical expert to help evaluate medical evidence).

[8] Computer Associates International, Inc. v. Altai, Inc., 982 F.2d 693, 712–714 (2d Cir. 1992) (alleged infringement of copyrighted computer program).

[9] See Civil Trial Practice Standard 11(a)(i) (A.B.A. 1998) ("The court should invite the parties to recommend jointly an expert to be appointed by the court"). The Civil Trial Practice Standards are reprinted in an appendix to Imwinkelried & Schlueter, FEDERAL EVIDENCE TACTICS (Matthew Bender 1999).

[10] Kaufman v. Edelstein, 539 F.2d 811, 820 (2d Cir. 1976) ("[T]here is no constitutional or statutory privilege against the compulsion of expert testimony, and we perceive no sufficient basis in principle or precedent for holding that the common law recognizes any general privilege to withhold his expert knowledge.").

[11] Green v. Rick Iron Co., 944 F.2d 852, 854 (Fed. Cir. 1991).

duties orally at a conference attended by the parties, or in a writing, a copy of which must be filed with the clerk.[12] A telephone conference will sometimes prove useful. Such a conference may facilitate a settlement, especially if it is held after discovery is complete and the parties know the position of the non-court-appointed experts who will testify. The parties' experts may be required to attend so that a joint decision of all experts can limit disagreement and focus the controversy. If the court believes that discussions among all the experts would be fruitful in simplifying or terminating the litigation, it could ask the non-court-appointed experts to attend the conference.[13] The trial court ahould not have off-the-record ex parte communications with a court-appointed expert witness, especially if the trial court is the finder of fact.[14]

The conference will also give the parties an idea of how the court-appointed expert will react to the theories advanced by the parties' own experts.[15] For example, if in a personal injury action it becomes evident that the court's medical expert considers plaintiff's theory of causality utterly at odds with reputable medical thought, the parties may be induced to reach a settlement. Even if no settlement ensues, the conference may be useful in narrowing the issues and resolving what might otherwise be time-consuming disputes at trial about terminology and methodology.

A useful provision in subdivision (a) allows the witness's deposition to be taken by any party. Rule 706 provides the only instance where a deposition may be taken as of right by any party in a criminal case. Rule 706 is silent on what use may be made of the depositions at trial. Presumably the restrictions of Rule 32 of the Federal Rules of Civil Procedure and Rule 15 of the Federal Rules of Criminal Procedure would apply. In a criminal case, the use of a deposition taken by the government may raise unresolved questions on the scope of defendant's rights under the confrontation clause of the Sixth Amendment; thus in these cases the

---

[12] Fed. R. Evid. 706(a); *see also* Civil Trial Practice Standard 11(b) (A.B.A. 1998) (court "should afford the parties the opportunity to participate in defining the scope of the expert's duties"). The Civil Trial Practice Standards are reprinted in an appendix to Imwinkelried & Schlueter, FEDERAL EVIDENCE TACTICS (Matthew Bender 1999).

[13] *See* United States v. Articles . . . Provimi, etc., 74 F.R.D. 126, 126–127 (D.N.J. 1977) (court advised counsel that it would schedule a conference with the court-appointed expert and counsel and any expert of their own which counsel wished to bring at which the directions to be given the expert would be decided on).

[14] *See, e.g.,* United States v. Craven, 239 F.3d 91, 101–102 (1st Cir. 2001) (trial court abused its discretion in basing downward departure for defendant's sentence on ex parte communication with appointed expert).

[15] *See* Civil Trial Practice Standard 11(d) (A.B.A. 1998) (court should ensure that every party is (1) "afforded the opportunity to explore, in advance of trial, the findings and opinions of any court-appointed expert" and (2) aware of "all communications between any party and a court-appointed expert"); *see also* **Treatise** at § 706.03[1].

expert should be called as a witness whenever possible.

Unresolved issues still remain about the interrelationship between Rule 706 and procedural provisions governing examinations by experts. For instance, to what extent, if any, must the limitations and notice provisions of Rule 706 be applied to mental examinations of a criminal defendant ordered pursuant to § 4241 of title 18 or Rule 12.2(c) of the Federal Rules of Criminal Procedure?[16]

Other provisions of Rule 706 should provoke little difficulty. Each party's right to cross-examine is recognized,[16.1] carrying with it the right under Rule 611 to ask leading questions and to bring out relevant material beyond the scope of the expert's direct testimony. This right exists even if a party exercises its right under Rule 706(a) to call the court appointed expert itself. In any event, subdivision (d) states that the parties' right to call experts of their own choosing is in no way limited by Rule 706.

Rule 706(c) grants the trial court discretion to authorize disclosure of the expert's status as a court appointed witness to the jury. The trial court may forbid revelation of the expert's role, if, for instance, it discovers that two responsible schools of thought exist on the subject of the expert's testimony and it suspects that divulgence of the expert's status may cause the jury to favor the expert's position.[17] In other cases, not to identify the court-appointed expert as such might deprive the jury of information it needs to evaluate the witness's testimony.[18]

[4]—Compensation

Rule 706(b) sets forth two different modes of compensation for the court appointed expert. If the expert has been employed in a criminal case or a civil proceeding involving just compensation under the Fifth Amendment, the court determines the amount in whatever sum it deems reasonable, to be paid "from funds which may be provided by law." The Comptroller General has determined that the

---

[16] *See* discussion in **Treatise** at § 706.03.

[16.1] *See, e.g.,* Nemir v. Mitsubishi Motors Corp., 381 F.3d 540, 556 (6th Cir. 2004) (trial court erred in refusing to permit party to examine court-appointed expert witness at trial).

[17] *See* Civil Trial Practice Standard 11(e)(ii) (A.B.A. 1998) ("The witness should not ordinarily be identified as one appointed by the court"). The Civil Trial Practice Standards are reprinted in an appendix to Imwinkelried & Schlueter, FEDERAL EVIDENCE TACTICS (Matthew Bender 1999).

[18] *See* Civil Trial Practice Standard 11(e)(iii) (A.B.A. 1998) (if court determines that it is appropriate to identify witness as court appointed, court should instruct jury (1) not to give greater weight to testimony, (2) that jury may consider that witness was not retained by either party, and (3) that jury should assess nature and basis for witness's opinions). The Civil Trial Practice Standards are reprinted in an appendix to Imwinkelried & Schlueter, FEDERAL EVIDENCE TACTICS (Matthew Bender 1999).

Department of Justice must pay the expert's compensation.[19] In civil cases, the court has discretion to tax the expert's compensation against the parties in such proportions as it deems proper.[20] The judge's determination will turn on the nature of the case, why the need for a court appointed expert arose, the status of the parties, and the decision and its consequences.[21] Assessment of the cost may be deferred to abide the event of ultimate disposition of the controversy, with one or both sides advancing fees. The provision for compensation in Rule 706(b) makes it clear that court-appointed experts in federal civil cases can realistically expect adequate compensation. That compensation may include reasonable expenses, including costs of testing and acquiring data.

---

[19] Decision of the Comptroller General B-139703 (March 21, 1980) (same rule applies in condemnation cases).

[20] *See, e.g.,* Ford v. Long Beach Unified Sch. Dist., 291 F.3d 1086, 1090 (9th Cir. 2002) (trial court did not abuse its discretion in taxing costs of court-appointed expert witness against losing party).

[21] *See, e.g.,* Aiello v. Town of Brookhaven, 149 F. Supp. 2d 11, 14 (E.D.N.Y. 2001).

CHAPTER 14

*Hearsay: Definition, Organization and Constitutional Concerns**

SYNOPSIS

---

* Chapter revised in 1992 by WALTER BARTHOLD, member of the New York Bar.

§ 14.01   Overview of Hearsay

[1]—Live Testimony Versus Hearsay

The Anglo-American tradition has evolved three conditions for testimony which it is assumed will cause witnesses to try their best to be accurate and will expose any inaccuracies in perception, memory or narration, deliberate or otherwise, which nevertheless persist. The three conditions are the oath, personal presence at the trial, and cross-examination.

Although the oath may exert less influence than it did when witnesses had a greater fear of divine punishment, it still reminds one of the solemnity of the occasion and suggests the possibility of a prosecution for perjury. See discussion of Rule 603 in Chapter 10.

It traditionally has been thought that the trier of fact can more accurately evaluate credibility if it can observe the witness's demeanor while testifying, though it has proved virtually impossible to articulate what the trier looks for. The requirement of personal presence in a public forum also undoubtedly makes it more difficult to lie against someone, particularly if that person is an accused, present at trial, who is looking the witness "in the eye." The constitutional right of confrontation, discussed below, rests in part on this premise.

While not all may endorse Wigmore's characterization of cross-examination as "beyond any doubt the greatest legal engine ever invented for the discovery of truth," all would concur with him in calling it a "vital feature" of the Anglo-American system.[1] Certainly cross-examination has the potential of shedding light on all the elements of credibility—the witness's perception, memory, accuracy in narration and sincerity. It can expose inconsistencies, incompletenesses, and inaccuracies in the testimony. Anxiety about what cross-examination will reveal undoubtedly encourages veracity, even though deliberate perjury is rarely exposed.

When a witness testifies to an out-of-court statement made by someone else, the three ideal conditions discussed above are usually lacking. The trier of fact is less likely to reach a correct conclusion with respect to the credibility of the out-of-court declarant if the trier cannot observe the declarant making the statement when he or she is (1) under oath and the stress of a judicial hearing, (2) being observed by an adverse party, and (3) subject to almost immediate cross-examination to test the various elements of the declarant's credibility. The hearsay rule is directed against the danger that evidence which is not subject to these three conditions will be less reliable, and less likely to be properly evaluated by the trier, because faults—or

---

[1] 5 Wigmore, Evidence § 1367 (Chadbourn rev., Little, Brown & Co. 1974).

strengths—in the declarant's perception, memory, and narration will not be exposed.[2]

Despite these hazards of hearsay, all judges and lawyers know that the value of a particular out-of-court statement varies from case to case, and from statement to statement. Some persons speak truthfully, and for the most part accurately, no matter where they are; others lie or distort or misapprehend even if they are under oath in a courtroom. In between, and probably typical, is the person whose credibility depends upon the circumstances under which he or she made the observation in question, the circumstances surrounding the statement, and the person's relationship to the case. Insistence on the exclusion of all evidence that does not meet the three ideal conditions would often make it impossible to prove any material proposition of fact, and legal relief would be unobtainable by the party who bears the burden of proof. The loss of relevant evidence increases the likelihood of erroneous determinations. Despite the thousands of pages devoted to proposals for reform of the hearsay rule, no one suggests that a possible solution is to exclude all hearsay. Even when hearsay is erroneously admitted, or admitted because no objection is made, verdicts based on such evidence are usually sustained and affirmed if the evidence appears sufficiently reliable and the trier was likely to have evaluated it properly.[3]

[2]—Design of the Federal Rules[1]

The drafters of the Federal Rules decided not to abolish all restrictions on the use of hearsay. They believed that the hearsay rule does serve to exclude evidence too unreliable to be evaluated accurately by the trier of fact. They also concluded, however, that under the traditional scheme, evidence of high probative value is too often excluded. To lessen the possibility of this occurring, a number of changes were made: (1) the definition of hearsay was reworked to exclude from its scope certain types of utterances and conduct that pose few hearsay dangers (see Rule 801(a)–(c)); (2) certain types of highly probative prior statements were defined as not constituting hearsay (see Rule 801(d)(1)); (3) admissions were also treated as non-hearsay and expanded to include vicarious, as well as authorized admissions (see Rule 801(d)(2)); and (4) the scope of some of the class exceptions was significantly enlarged (see, e.g., Rule 803(8)—official records and Rule 803(18)—learned treatises). The scheme of the hearsay article as presently con-

---

[2] United States v. Hanzlicek, 187 F.3d 1228, 1237 (10th Cir. 1999) (hearsay rule "seeks to eliminate the danger that evidence will lack reliability because faults in the perception, memory, or narration of the declarant will not be exposed"; citing **Treatise**).

[3] *But cf.* United States v. Pendas-Martinez, 845 F.2d 938, 940–942, 945 (11th Cir. 1988) (reversible error, notwithstanding overwhelming evidence of defendant's guilt, to have admitted government agent's hearsay summaries of prosecution's case).

[1] *See* discussion in **Treatise** at §§ 801.02, 802.02, 802.03.

stituted includes Rule 801, which defines hearsay, Rule 802, which excludes all hearsay, and Rules 803 and 804, which contain a lengthy list of exceptions under which hearsay may be admitted. The exceptions are grouped in two categories. For hearsay statements admitted under Rule 803, the availability of the declarant is immaterial, while Rule 804 requires that the declarant be found unavailable before hearsay statements will be admitted as coming within one of its exceptions. In addition, the drafters added open-ended provisions in former Rules 803(24) and 804(b)(5) (present Rule 807)[2] These permit the admission of trustworthy hearsay that does not fit into a class exception. The operation of these residual, non-class exceptions is discussed at § 14.04. Statements excluded from the definition of hearsay are discussed in Chapter 15, and the hearsay class exceptions are discussed in Chapters 16 and 17.

Hearsay that is not excludable under the hearsay rules may nevertheless be excluded under Rule 403 on grounds of prejudice, confusion or waste of time.[3] The discretionary aspect of admissibility of hearsay is made explicit in a few rules such as 804(b)(3) on statements against interest and Rules 803(24) and 804(b)(5), the open-ended exceptions.[4] Trustworthiness as the touchstone of admissibility is becoming a central concept of the confrontation clause as interpreted by the Supreme Court. A discussion of this aspect of the hearsay rule appears in § 14.03.

§ 14.02 The Definition of Hearsay—Rule 801(a)–(c)[5]

[1]—Rule Follows Conventional Practice

Rule 801(c) follows conventional practice in defining hearsay in terms of the use of a statement. Subdivision (c) must, however, be read in conjunction with subdivision (a), which ensures that only statements intended as assertions are included in the hearsay definition. Consequently, evidence of out-of-court conduct—either verbal or non-verbal—does not constitute hearsay (1) if it was not intended as an assertion, *or* (2) if it was so intended, it is not being offered to prove the truth of the matter asserted.

The importance of Rule 801's definitions lies in Rule 802, which makes hearsay

---

[2] *See* **Treatise** at Chapter 807.
[3] *See* Vincent v. Louis Marx & Co., Inc., 874 F.2d 36, 37–41 (1st Cir. 1989) (case remanded to trial court to determine whether prior inconsistent pleading by plaintiff in prior action against third party, which was treated as an admission, should have been excluded under Rule 403). *See also* **Treatise** at §§ 403.04–403.06.
[4] For a discussion of the extent of discretion a judge has in applying the hearsay article, *see* **Treatise** at § 802.04; *see also* United States v. DiMaria, 727 F.2d 265, 270–272 (2d Cir. 1984) (reversible error to exclude statement that falls into Rule 803(3) category even if it is of dubious reliability).
[5] *See* discussion in **Treatise** at §§ 801.10–801.11.

inadmissible except as provided by the Federal Rules of Evidence, other rules adopted by the Supreme Court pursuant to its statutory authority to do so, or statutes adopted by Congress.[1] The primary reason hearsay is inadmissible is doubt concerning its trustworthiness: it has not usually been subjected to the traditional means of exposing deceit or inaccuracy: the witness's oath, cross-examination by the adverse party, and the fact finder's opportunity to observe demeanor.[2] Rule 802 provides as follows:

Rule 802. Hearsay Rule.

Hearsay is not admissible except as provided by these rules or by other rules prescribed by the Supreme Court pursuant to statutory authority or by Act of Congress.

[*Adopted Jan. 2, 1975, effective July 1, 1975; amended Mar. 2, 1987, effective Oct. 1, 1987; amended Apr. 11, 1997, effective Dec. 1, 1997.*]

Subdivisions (a)–(c) of Rule 801 state the following:

Rule 801. Definitions.

The following definitions apply under this article:

(a) Statement.—A "statement" is (1) an oral or written assertion or (2) nonverbal conduct of a person, if it is intended by the person as an assertion.

(b) Declarant.—A "declarant" is a person who makes a statement.

(c) Hearsay.—"Hearsay" is a statement, other than one made by the declarant while testifying at the trial or hearing, offered in evidence to prove the truth of the matter asserted.

[*Adopted Jan. 2, 1975, effective July 1, 1975.*]

---

[2]—Statement

Subdivision (a) provides that a declarant's out-of-court utterance or conduct does not constitute a "statement" unless it is intended as an assertion. "Assertion" is defined nowhere in the Rule. Clearly, verbal communications with which the declarant intends to convey information are "assertions" within the meaning of Rule 801(a).[1] So, too, are certain simple nonverbal acts, such as pointing out

---

[1]   Fed. R. Evid. 802.

[2]   Fed. R. Evid. 801 Advisory Committee's Note (1972) (reprinted in **Treatise** at § 801App.01[2]).

[1]   *See* Fed. R. Evid. 801(a); *see, e.g.,* Superior Fireplace Co. v. Majestic Prods. Co., 270 F.3d 1358, 1365–1366 (Fed. Cir. 2001) (statement within affidavit that patent examiner told affiant that

another person.[2]

The more difficult question arises when the words or conduct of the declarant or actor convey meaning, but the declarant or actor had no conscious intent to convey information. In such circumstances, the validity of the information conveyed depends on an inference that the person would not have spoken or acted in that way unless he or she believed a particular fact to be true. If the fact that the declarant or actor believes to be true is relevant, and evidence of the declarant's words or of the actor's conduct is offered to prove that fact, the words or act is said to be an "implied assertion."

Many courts have held that implied assertions are not hearsay within the meaning of Rule 801(a) because they were not made or done with assertive intent.[3] Other courts, however, have held that implied assertions are "statements" in spite of the declarant's or actor's lack of assertive intent.[4]

[3]—To Prove the Truth of the Matter Asserted

A statement is not hearsay, even though it was made with assertive intent, when it is offered to prove something other than the truth of the matter asserted.[1] Utterances may be offered for a variety of reasons not entailing their truth; when they are, there is no need to assess the credibility of the declarant because the value

---

certificate of correction was issued to correct typographical error was evidence of "oral assertion" within definition of Rule 801(a)).

[2] Fed. R. Evid. 801(a); *see, e.g.,* United States v. Aspinall, 389 F.3d 332, 342 (2d Cir. 2004) (party's provision, to F.B.I. agent, of documents describing instructions that party received from another party, in response to agent's questions about relationship between two parties, amounted to representation that party providing documents had received instructions from other party).

[3] *See, e.g.,* United States v. Wright, 343 F.3d 849, 865–866 (6th Cir. 2003) (question asked by declarant is ordinarily not hearsay because it does not assert truth or falsity of a fact and is, therefore, not an "assertion"); United States v. Groce, 682 F.2d 1359, 1364 (11th Cir. 1982) (written expressions are not hearsay unless intended to be assertion; pencil marks on nautical charts that marked course of boat involved in drug smuggling were not hearsay, because defendants did not intend marks as statement of their intent to return to United States, but merely marked chart so they would not get lost at sea).

[4] *See, e.g.,* United States v. Hernandez, 176 F.3d 719, 727 (3d Cir. 1999) (defendant's statement to police that he had just arrived and was expecting to be paid was inadmissible hearsay because it was admitted to support implied assertion that defendant was no more than hired laborer, and thus not criminally involved in charged highjacking of truck).

[1] Fed. R. Evid. 801(c) ("offered in evidence to prove the truth of the matter asserted"); *see, e.g.,* Lyons P'ship, L.P. v. Morris Costumes, 243 F.3d 789, 803 (4th Cir. 2001) (fact that children shouted "Barney" on seeing person wearing "Duffy" costume was not hearsay because not offered to prove that costume actually was Barney, but to show effect of costume on viewers); Howley v. Town of Stratford, 217 F.3d 141, 155 (2d Cir. 2000) (testimony that plaintiff's subordinates called her to disparage her competence "would not be hearsay if offered not for the truth of the callers' assertions but only as proof that the calls and the statements were made").

of the utterance does not depend on whether it is true.[2] The trial court must make certain, however, before admitting the out of court utterance for a purpose of proving something other than the truth of its contents, that the utterance is, in fact, probative of the matter it is purportedly offered to prove.[2.1]

Three of the more common types of non-hearsay are verbal acts, verbal parts of acts, and utterances showing the declarant's state of mind.

The term "verbal act" is applied when an utterance is an operative fact that gives rise to legal consequences. In such cases, the fact that the words were spoken or written is significant regardless of their truth.[3] Examples of verbal acts are words constituting the following:

- A contract.[4]

- Checks and other commercial paper.[4.1]

- A defamatory statement.[5]

- A threat.[6]

---

[2] *See, e.g.,* United States v. Bishop, 291 F.3d 1100, 1111 (9th Cir. 2002) (trial court erred in excluding as hearsay testimony about tax advice defendant relied on concerning advances from employer, because it was not offered to prove truth of advice, but to prove its effect on defendant); *see also* United States v. Meserve, 271 F.3d 314, 320 (1st Cir. 2001) (testimony not offered to prove the truth of an out-of-court statement is not hearsay, e.g., when "offered to provide relevant context or background" or to "statements that are offered to show what effect they produced on the actions of a listener").

[2.1] *See, e.g.,* United States v. Silva, 380 F.3d 1018, 1019–1020 (7th Cir. 2004) (when trial court admitted evidence containing out-of-court statements of absent persons for purpose of showing "the actions taken by each witness" and actions of those witnesses were not relevant to crimes with which defendant was charged, evidence was, in fact, offered to prove truth of contents of out-of-court utterances, and was improperly admitted).

[3] *See, e.g.,* United States v. Stover, 329 F.3d 859, 870 (D.C. Cir. 2003) ("verbal act" is out-of-court statement that has legal significance independent of its content).

[4] *See, e.g.,* Stuart v. UNUM Life Ins. Co. of Am., 217 F.3d 1145, 1154 (9th Cir. 2000) (hospital's long-term disability insurance policy admissible non-hearsay because it was legally operative document that defined rights and liabilities of parties).

[4.1] *See, e.g.,* United States v. Pang, 362 F.3d 1187, 1192 (9th Cir. 2004).

[5] *See, e.g.,* Talley v. Bravo Pitino Restaurant, LTD., 61 F.3d 1241, 1249 (6th Cir. 1995) (racially disparaging comments by owner and manager were not hearsay because they were offered to show declarant's racial attitudes).

[6] *See, e.g.,* Bergene v. Salt River Project Agric. Improvement & Power Dist., 272 F.3d 1136, 1141–1142 (9th Cir. 2001) (statement by plaintiff's former supervisor that plaintiff would not receive promotion if she held out for favorable settlement in employment discrimination claim was not offered for truth of its content, but as a threat, and was not hearsay).

- A demand.[7]

- A misrepresentation.[8]

- The giving of notice.[9]

- A derogatory and vindictive statement.[9.1]

When non-verbal conduct is ambiguous, the accompanying verbal conduct that characterizes and defines the transaction, or the verbal part of the act, is not hearsay.[10]

When relevant, an utterance or a writing may be admitted as circumstantial evidence of a person's state of mind.[11] The statement is used not to prove the truth of its contents, but to provide the finder of fact with a basis for drawing an inference concerning a person's state of mind, such as the following:

- Knowledge.[12]

- Motive.[13]

- Fear.[14]

---

[7] *See, e.g.,* United States v. Montana, 199 F.3d 947, 950 (7th Cir. 1999) ("verbal act" in form of demand was not within scope of hearsay rule).

[8] *See, e.g.,* United States v. Wellington, 754 F.2d 1457, 1464 (9th Cir. 1985) (false representations to potential investors were not inadmissible hearsay).

[9] *See, e.g.,* In re Fidelity America Mortgage Co., 15 B.R. 622, 623 (Bankr. E.D. Pa. 1981) (notice of default is not hearsay).

[9.1] *See, e.g.,* Mota v. Univ. of Tex. Houston Health Sci. Ctr., 261 F.3d 512, 527 n. 46 (5th Cir. 2001) (message from university president to all employees after jury verdict in favor of plaintiff former employee maintaining university's position about impropriety of plaintiff's actions was admissible as verbal act intended to impair his professional prospects; also admissible to show university's state of mind and as not offered for hearsay purpose).

[10] *See, e.g.,* Anthony v. Dewitt, 295 F.3d 554, 562–563 (6th Cir. 2002) (reasons that murder defendant gave witness in asking her to come with him to confront victim, and of threats made to silence her after murder, were admitted to explain why she was with defendant and delayed in reporting murder to authorities; defendant's statements were admissible as verbal part of those acts).

[11] *See also* Fed. R. Evid. 803(3) (hearsay exception for statements of declarant's then-existing state of mind); *see* Ch. 16.

[12] *See, e.g.,* United States v. Emmons, 24 F.3d 1210, 1216–1217 (10th Cir. 1994) (hand drawn map, found in defendant's kitchen, was admissible to show that defendant had knowledge of location and quantity of marijuana plants found on his property).

[13] *See, e.g.,* Rinehimer v. Cemcolift, Inc., 292 F.3d 375, 382–383 (3d Cir. 2002) (trial court did not abuse its discretion in admitting testimony of company officer that company doctor had told him plaintiff could not wear respirator because statement explained company's action in preventing plaintiff from returning to his former job, which required him to use respirator).

[14] *See, e.g.,* United States v. Lynn, 608 F.2d 132, 135 (5th Cir. 1979) (in extortion case, testimony as to what was said to victim to produce fear was not hearsay).

- Belief.[15]

- Notice that a product might be injurious.[16]

- Lack of knowledge.[17]

- Lack of predisposition to commit crime.[18]

Out-of-court statements may also be admissible for the non-hearsay purpose of impeachment. Thus, if a witness denies making a particular statement during his or her testimony, another witness can appropriately later testify that the witness did in fact make the statement within the witness's hearing. The evidence of the statement is admitted not to prove the truth of its contents, but to impeach the witness's earlier testimony by contradiction.[19] Similarly, a witness may be impeached by evidence that he or she remained silent in circumstances in which it would be reasonable to expect him or her to speak. In those circumstances, evidence of another person's out-of-court statements to which the witness would have reasonably responded are admissible, again, not for their truth, but to provide context for the witness's silence.[20]

---

[15] *See, e.g.,* United States v. Thompson, 279 F.3d 1043, 1046–1047 (D.C. Cir. 2002) (out-of-court statement offered to show defendant's belief that sealed cup contained money rather than cocaine base was not offered for truth of its content and was not hearsay).

[16] *See, e.g.,* Worsham v. A.H. Robins Co., 734 F.2d 676, 687 (11th Cir. 1984) (letters of complaint were not hearsay because they were introduced not to show that product caused injury to authors, but notice to manufacturer of product that product might be dangerous).

[17] *See, e.g.,* United States v. Detrich, 865 F.2d 17, 20–21 (2d Cir. 1988) (in prosecution for smuggling heroin in suit's shoulder pads, when defendant claimed acquaintance gave him suit to deliver to relative for latter's wedding, trial court erred in excluding as hearsay intended recipient's statements to DEA agents that he was getting married).

[18] *See, e.g.,* United States v. Cantu, 876 F.2d 1134, 1137 (5th Cir. 1989) (reversible error to prevent defendant claiming entrapment from testifying about statements DEA agent made to induce commission of crime).

[19] *See, e.g.,* Goodman v. Pa. Tpk. Comm'n, 293 F.3d 655, 665–666 (3d Cir. 2002).

[20] *See, e.g.,* United States v. Adamson, 291 F.3d 606, 612–614 (9th Cir. 2002) (when defendant and witness attended meeting with third party during which they agreed to make fraudulent statements, and defendant's role at meeting was as spokesman and witness remained largely silent, witness's subsequent testimony that defendant's statements at meeting were fraudulent was properly impeachable with evidence of his silence during meeting; trial court erred in excluding evidence of defendant's statements during meeting, because nature of statements was necessary to show that, if witness's testimony was truthful he could have been reasonably expected to speak up at meeting to deny defendant's fraudulent representations, and his silence at meeting was, therefore, inconsistent with his testimony at trial).

§ 14.03 The Confrontation Clause

[1]—Interaction Between Hearsay Rule and Confrontation Clause

The Confrontation Clause of the Sixth Amendment provides :"[i]n all criminal prosecutions, the accused shall enjoy the right . . . to be confronted with the witnesses against him." The Confrontation Clause, of course, means more than that the accused has a right to see and know the identity of the witnesses against him or her. It means that, when it is applicable, the accused will have the right to cross-examine witnesses concerning the evidence they have given on the prosecution's behalf.[1]

Taken literally, the Confrontation Clause could mean that no evidence of out-of-court statements is admissible against an accused in a criminal prosecution unless the declarant is available to testify, or that no evidence of out-of-court statements is admissible unless the accused has an opportunity to cross-examine the declarant. No court, however, has adopted such a stringent interpretation of the Confrontation Clause.[2] Moreover, courts have consistently recognized that the Confrontation Clause does not prevent the use of out-of-court statements for purposes other than proving the truth of the matter asserted in them.[3]

At its narrowest, the Confrontation Clause could mean only that the accused has a right to cross-examine the witnesses who testify in person at the trial. This reading would mean that when an out-of-court statement is the subject of a recognized exclusion from or exception to the hearsay rule, the Confrontation Clause would not operate to exclude it.[4] No court has ever adopted such a narrow interpretation

---

[1] *See, e.g.,* Maryland v. Craig, 497 U.S. 836, 845, 110 S. Ct. 3157, 111 L. Ed. 2d 666 (1990) ("The central concern of the Confrontation Clause is to ensure the reliability of the evidence against a criminal defendant by subjecting it to rigorous testing in the context of an adversary proceeding before the trier of fact"); California v. Green, 399 U.S. 149, 158, 90 S. Ct. 1930, 26 L. Ed. 2d 489 (1970) (when prosecution offers declarant's out-of-court statements against accused and declarant is unavailable, trial court must decide whether Confrontation Clause permits prosecution to deny accused his or her usual right to force declarant "to submit to cross-examination, the 'greatest legal engine ever invented for the discovery of truth.' ").

[2] *See, e.g.,* United States v. Inadi, 475 U.S. 387, 394–398, 106 S. Ct. 1121, 89 L. Ed. 2d 390 (1986) (out-of-court statements by co-conspirators of accused are admissible even though declarant is unavailable to testify and accused has had no opportunity to cross-examine declarant); Mattox v. United States, 156 U.S. 237, 240–244, 15 S. Ct. 337, 39 L. Ed. 409 (1894) (evidence of prior testimony of deceased witnesses is analogous to evidence of dying declaration, which is admissible in criminal prosecution even though accused had no opportunity to cross-examine declarant).

[3] *See, e.g.,* Crawford v. Washington, 541 U.S. 36, 124 S. Ct. 1354, 158 L, Ed. 2d 177, 197 n.9 (2004).

[4] *See, e.g.,* White v. Illinois, 502 U.S. 346, 352–353, 112 S. Ct. 736, 116 L. Ed. 2d 848 (1992) (United States, as amicus curiae, contended Confrontation Clause should apply only to out-of-court statements made for purpose of incriminating accused, and that Confrontation Clause would not

of the Confrontation Clause.[5]

As it stands, the hearsay exclusionary rule and the Confrontation Clause are not fully congruent. The Confrontation Clause requires the exclusion of some out-of-court statements that would qualify for an exclusion from or an exception to the hearsay rule.[6]

The Supreme Court has "disclaimed any intention of proposing a general answer to the many difficult questions arising out of the relationship between the Con-frontation Clause and hearsay."[7] The interaction between the hearsay rule and its panoply of exclusions and exceptions, on the one hand, and the Confrontation Clause, on the other, is largely dependent on the characteristics of the out-of-court statement evidence that is offered into evidence and whether the accused has had an opportunity to question the declarant concerning the subject matter of the statement.

[2]—Confrontation Clause's Applicability to "Testimonial" Hearsay

In *Crawford v. Washington,* the Supreme Court addressed the law concerning the admissibility of hearsay against a criminal defendant in the face of an objection invoking the defendant's rights under the Sixth Amendment's Confrontation Clause.[8] The Court reviewed in considerable detail the historical underpinnings of the Confrontation Clause in the common law as applied in England and in the colonies to draw two inferences about its purposes. The first inference is that the Confrontation Clause's primary concern is with "testimonial" hearsay:[9]

The Court's introduction of the distinction between "testimonial" and "non-

---

prohibit admission of out-of-court statements admissible under recognized exclusion from or exception to hearsay rule).

[5] *See* Crawford v. Washington, 541 U.S. 36, 124 S. Ct. 1354, 158 L. Ed. 2d 177, 192–195 (2004) (Confrontation Clause permits introduction of out-of-court testimonial statements if declarant is not available for testimony at trial and accused had opportunity to cross-examine declarant concerning subject matter of statement).

[6] *See, e.g.,* United States v. Inadi, 475 U.S. 387, 393 n.5, 106 S. Ct. 1121, 89 L. Ed. 2d 390 (1986) ("[w]hile it 'may readily be conceded that hearsay rules and the Confrontation Clause are generally designed to protect similar values,' the overlap is not complete" (citation omitted)); California v. Green, 399 U.S. 149, 155, 90 S. Ct. 1930, 26 L. Ed. 489 (1970) ("While it may readily be conceded that hearsay rules and the Confrontation Clause are generally designed to protect similar values, it is quite a different thing to suggest that the overlap is complete and that the Confrontation Clause is nothing more or less than a codification of the rules of hearsay and their exceptions as they existed historically at common law. Our decisions have never established such a congruence; indeed, we have more than once found a violation of confrontation values even though the statements in issue were admitted under an arguably recognized hearsay exception").

[7] United States v. Inadi, 475 U.S. 387, 392, 106 S. Ct. 1121, 89 L. Ed. 2d 390 (1986).

[8] Crawford v. Washington, — U.S. —, 124 S. Ct. 1354, 158 L. Ed. 2d 177 (2004).

[9] Crawford v. Washington, — U.S. —, 124 S. Ct. 1354, 158 L. Ed. 2d 177, 192–195 (2004).

testimonial" hearsay plows new ground in Confrontation Clause jurisprudence.[10] The Court reserved for the future the effort to compile a comprehensive definition of "testimonial" hearsay, but noted that, at a minimum, the term applies to the following types of statements:[11]

- Prior testimony at a preliminary hearing.

- Prior testimony before a grand jury,[12]

- Prior testimony at a former trial.

- Statements made in response to police interrogation.[13]

Since the Court announced its decision in the *Crawford* case, the lower federal courts have addressed in some detail the question of the types of out-of-court statements, other than those the *Crawford* Court specifically identified, that are "testimonial" and therefore admissible against a Confrontation Clause objection only if the declarant is truly unavailable and the defendant against whom the statement is offered had an opportunity to cross-examine the declarant about the statement. Courts have identified the following additional types of statements as being testimonial, so that the *Crawford* rule is applicable to them:

- Statements made to law enforcement officers during a search.[14]

- Plea allocutions of coconspirators who do not testify at the trial.[15]

The courts have also identified the following types of out-of-court statements as being non-testimonial, so that the *Crawford* rule does not apply to them:

- Statements between a confidential informant and the declarant that the confidential informant secretly recorded unbeknownst to the declarant.[16]

---

[10] *See, e.g.,* Crawford v. Washington, 541 U.S. 36, 124 S. Ct. 1354, 158 L. Ed. 2d 177, 203–204 (2004) (Rehnquist, C.J., and O'Connor, J., concurring in judgment); Horton v. Allen, 370 F.3d 75, 83 (1st Cir. 2004) ("*Crawford* . . . changed the legal landscape for determining whether the admission of certain hearsay statements violates the accused's right to confront witnesses").

[11] Crawford v. Washington, 541 U.S. 36, 124 S. Ct. 1354, 158 L. Ed. 2d 177, 203 (2004).

[12] *See, e.g.,* United States v. Wilmore, 381 F.3d 868, 871–873 (9th Cir. 2004) (grand jury testimony used as a prior inconsistent statement was testimonial, and cross-examination was not provided when declarant, although on the witness stand, asserted her Fifth Amendment right not to give self-incriminating evidence when asked questions on cross-examination concerning her grand jury testimony).

[13] *See, e.g.,* United States v. Jones, 371 F.3d 363, 369 (7th Cir. 2004) (*Crawford* applies to confessions of defendant's coconspirators or accomplices who do not testify at the trial).

[14] *See, e.g.,* United States v. Nielsen, 371 F.3d 574, 581 (9th Cir. 2004).

[15] *See, e.g.,* United States v. McClain, 377 F.3d 219, 221–222 (2d Cir. July 28, 2004).

[16] *See, e.g.,* United States v. Saget, 377 F.3d 223, 227–230 (2d Cir. 2004).

- Statements the declarant made in a private conversation with the witness who testifies to the statement.[17]

- Statements of co-conspirators made during and in the course of the conspiracy.[18]

- Entries in a diary.[19]

- Statements made for the purpose of obtaining medical assistance or offered as evidence of the declarant's mental state.[20]

The courts have generally distinguished between "testimonial" statements and "non-testimonial" statements by determining whether an objective person in the position of the declarant, at the time the statement was made, would be aware or would expect that the statement may be used later at a trial. If so, the statement is "testimonial." If not, it is "non-testimonial."[21]

[3]—Accused Must Have Opportunity to Cross-Examine Declarant

The second inference the *Crawford* Court drew from its review of the historical underpinnings of the Confrontation Clause in the common law as applied in England and in the colonies is that the Confrontation Clause prohibits the admission of an out-of-court testimonial statement of a declarant who did not appear at the trial unless the declarant was shown to be unavailable to testify and the defendant had a prior opportunity to cross-examine the declarant concerning the statement's subject matter.[22]

The common law's reliance on the prior opportunity to cross-examine an absent witness as a prerequisite to the admission of his or her out-of-court statement led the Court to conclude that the Confrontation Clause's guarantee is procedural rather than substantive. The Clause's ultimate goal is to ensure the reliability of hearsay statements of a declarant who does not testify at trial, but instead of requiring that the evidence be reliable, it requires that the reliability of the evidence be tested by cross-examination.[23]

The Court's review of its own decisions found that generally the results had been faithful to this reading of the Confrontation Clause.[24] It specifically approved of

---

[17] *See, e.g.,* Horton v. Allen, 370 F.3d 75, 83–84 (1st Cir. 2004).
[18] *See, e.g.,* United States v. Reyes, 362 F.3d 536, 541, n.4 (8th Cir. 2004).
[19] *See, e.g.,* Parle v. Runnels, 387 F.3d 1030 (9th Cir. 2004).
[20] *See, e.g.* Evans v. Luebbers, 371 F.3d 438, 445 (8th Cir. 2004).
[21] *See, e.g.,* Parle v. Runnels, 387 F.3d 1030 (9th Cir. 2004); United States v. Saget, 377 F.3d 223, 230 (2d Cir. 2004).
[22] Crawford v. Washington, 541 U.S. 36, 124 S. Ct. 1354, 158 L. Ed. 2d 177, 192–195 (2004).
[23] Crawford v. Washington, 541 U.S. 36, 124 S. Ct. 1354, 158 L. Ed. 2d 177, 199 (2004).
[24] Crawford v. Washington, 541 U.S. 36, 124 S. Ct. 1354, 158 L. Ed. 2d 177, 196–197 (2004).

the results reached in its prior decisions under the Confrontation Clause in the following situations:

- Admission of the out-of-court testimonial statement when the declarant was unavailable and the statement consisted of prior trial or preliminary hearing testimony as to which the defendant against whom the out-of-court statement was offered had an adequate opportunity to cross-examine.[25]

- Exclusion of the out-of-court statement even though the defendant against whom it was offered had an adequate opportunity to cross-examine the declarant when the prosecution failed to show that the declarant was unavailable to testify at the trial.[26]

- Exclusion of out-of-court testimonial statements when the defendant against whom they were offered did not have an opportunity to cross-examine the declarant.[27]

The lower federal courts have continued to admit or exclude testimonial hearsay evidence in accordance with the results reached in those opinions;[28]

The Court further found, however, that even though the results were proper, the rationales behind its earlier decisions had strayed from the appropriate course.[29] The Court took particular exception to its earlier decision in *Ohio v. Roberts*, which affirmed the admission of preliminary hearing testimony against a defendant who had examined the declarant at that preliminary hearing, on the ground that any hearsay evidence was admissible against a criminal defendant in the face of a

---

[25] Crawford v. Washington, 541 U.S. 36, 124 S. Ct. 1354, 158 L. Ed. 2d 177, 196–197 (2004) (citing cases stretching from *Ohio v. Roberts*, 448 U.S. 56, 67–70, 100 S. Ct. 2531, 65 L. Ed. 2d 597 (1980) to *Mattox v. United States*, 156 U.S. 237, 244, 15 S.. Ct. 337, 39 L. Ed. 409 (1895)).

[26] Crawford v. Washington, 541 U.S. 36, 124 S. Ct. 1354, 158 L. Ed. 2d 177, 196–197 (2004) (testimonial statements of witnesses absent from trial have been admitted only when declarant is unavailable, citing *Barber v. Page*, 390 U.S. 719, 722–725, 88 S. Ct. 1318, 20 L. Ed. 2d 255 (1968).

[27] Crawford v. Washington, 541 U.S. 36, 124 S. Ct. 1354, 158 L. Ed. 2d 177, 196–197 (2004) (citing *Lilly v. Virginia*, 527 U.S. 116, 134, 119 S. Ct. 1887, 144 L. Ed. 2d 117 (1999); *Roberts v. Russell*, 392 U.S. 293, 294–295, 88 S. Ct. 1921, 20 L. Ed. 2d 1100 (1968) (per curiam); *Bruton v. United States*, 391 U.S. 123, 126–128, 88 S. Ct. 1620, 20 L. Ed. 2d 476 (1968)).

[28] *See, e.g.*, Fischetti v. Johnson, 384 F.3d 140, 156 (3d Cir. 2004) (sworn testimony from prior trial is inadmissible in absence of showing that witnesses are unavailable); United States v. Bruno, 383 F.3d 65, 78 (2d Cir. 2004) (admission of grand jury testimony and plea allocution was error when defendant did not have opportunity to cross-examine declarants and they did not testify at trial); United States v. Wilmore, 381 F.3d 868, 871–872 (9th Cir. 2004) (Confrontation Clause requires trial court, at very least, to strike witness's testimony when she testified on direct in manner contrary to her earlier grand jury testimony, grand jury testimony was introduced as prior inconsistent statement, and witness asserted her privilege against self-incrimination when defendant sought to cross-examine her concerning contents of grand jury testimony).

[29] Crawford v. Washington, 541 U.S. 36, 124 S. Ct. 1354, 158 L. Ed. 2d 177, 198 (2004).

Confrontation Clause objection if the hearsay was admissible under a "firmly rooted hearsay exception" or bore "particularized guarantees of trustworthiness."[30]

The Court reasoned that the *Roberts* decision went astray in subjecting the Sixth Amendment's protection to "the vagaries of the rules of evidence" and to "amorphous notions of 'reliability.'" The Court firmly rejected the suggestion that testimonial hearsay could be admissible against a criminal defendant merely because the trial judge found it to be reliable: "Dispensing with confrontation because testimony is obviously reliable is akin to dispensing with jury trial because a defendant is obviously guilty. This is not what the Sixth Amendment prescribes."[31]

The Court also noted, but did not decide, that its earlier decision in *White v. Illinois,*[32] which upheld the admission, under the spontaneous declaration exception to the hearsay rule, of out-of-court statements of a child victim of a crime to an investigating police officer, may not have continued vitality in view of the Court's reaffirmation of the need for a prior opportunity for cross-examination when the proffered evidence is testimonial hearsay and the declarant does not testify at trial.[33]

[4]—"Non-Testimonial" Hearsay

The *Crawford* Court called into question the continued applicability of the Confrontation Clause to out-of-court statements that were not testimonial in nature.[34] It did note, however, with apparent approval, that some of its earlier decisions had sustained the admission of non-testimonial hearsay over a Confrontation Clause objection when the accused did not have an opportunity to cross-examine the declarant but the evidence's reliability was shown by other factors.[35] It also noted states might be allowed to weigh non-testimonial hearsay using the *Roberts* test, which finds Confrontation rights satisfied when hearsay evidence is admissible under a "firmly rooted hearsay exception" or has "particularized guar-

---

[30] Ohio v. Roberts, 448 U.S. 56, 66, 100 S. Ct. 2531, 65 L. Ed. 2d 597 (1980).

[31] Crawford v. Washington, 541 U.S. 36, 124 S. Ct. 1354, 158 L. Ed. 2d 177, 199 (2004).

[32] White v. Illinois, 502 U.S. 346, 349–353, 112 S. Ct. 736, 116 L. Ed. 2d 848 (1992).

[33] Crawford v. Washington, 541 U.S. 36, 124 S. Ct. 1354, 158 L. Ed. 2d 177, 197 n.8 (2004).

[34] Crawford v. Washington, 541 U.S. 36, 124 S. Ct. 1354, 158 L. Ed. 2d 177, 203 (2004) (concerning nontestimonial hearsay, "it is wholly consistent with the Framers' design to afford the States flexibility in their development of hearsay law--as does *Roberts*, and as would an approach that exempted such statements from Confrontation Clause scrutiny altogether").

[35] Crawford v. Washington, 541 U.S. 36, 124 S. Ct. 1354, 158 L. Ed. 2d 177, 196 (2004) (citing *Dutton v. Evans,* 400 U.S. 74, 87–89, 91 S. Ct. 210, 27 L. Ed. 2d 213 (1970) (plurality opinion; sustained admissibility of out-of-court non-testimonial statement on basis of factors indicating statement's reliability other than prior opportunity for cross-examination)).

antees of trustworthiness."[36]

Since the Supreme Court announced its decision in *Crawford*, the lower federal courts have dealt with the question of the extent to which, if any, the *Roberts* reliability analysis continues to be applicable to the admission of non-testimonial hearsay statements in the face of a Confrontation Clause objection. The courts have generally resolved that question by applying the *Roberts* test when the hearsay statement is non-testimonial.[37]

[5]—Declarant Available and Subject to Cross-Examination

When the declarant of an admissible out-of-court statement is present at the trial or hearing and is subject to cross-examination, under oath, concerning the subject matter of the out-of-court statement, admission of the statement does not violate the defendant's Confrontation Clause rights.[38] However, the accused's opportunity to cross-examine the declarant in such a case must be "adequate."[39]

The accused's opportunity for cross-examination in such a case is adequate for Confrontation Clause purposes, even if the declarant, when subject to cross-examination, has no present recollection of the subject matter of the out-of-court statement, and his or her answers to cross-examination questions consist solely of reiterations of that lack of memory, so long as the trial court does not unduly restrict the accused's ability to cross-examine the witness.[40] The accused's constitutional right to confront the witness is satisfied, in this particular instance, by the opportunity to impeach the declarant on the witness stand by bringing out such matters as the fact that he or she is biased, has a bad memory, has poor eyesight, or is

---

[36] Crawford v. Washington, 541 U.S. 36, 124 S. Ct. 1354, 158 L. Ed. 2d 177, 203 (2004); *see* Ohio v. Roberts, 448 U.S. 56, 66, 100 S. Ct. 2531, 65 L. Ed. 2d 597 (1980) (any hearsay evidence is admissible against criminal defendants in spite of Confrontation Clause objections if it is admissible under "firmly rooted hearsay exception" or has "particularized guarantees of trustworthiness").

[37] *See, e.g.,* United States v. Saget, 377 F.3d 223, 227 (2d Cir. 2004).

[38] *See, e.g.,* Crawford v. Washington, 541 U.S. 36, 124 S. Ct. 1354, 158 L, Ed. 2d 177, 197 n.9 (2004) ("when the declarant appears for cross-examination at trial, the Confrontation Clause places no constraints at all on the use of his prior testimonial statements"); California v. Green, 399 U.S. 149, 155–158, 90 S. Ct. 1930, 26 L. Ed. 2d 489 (1970); *see also* United States v. Chrisman, 965 F.2d 1465, 1469 (7th Cir. 1992) (defendant's Sixth Amendment confrontation rights were not violated by admission of testimony of DEA agent concerning post-arrest statements made to him by coconspirator implicating defendant, since coconspirator testified at trial and repeated out-of-court statements).

[39] *See, e.g.,* Douglas v. Alabama, 380 U.S. 415, 418, 85 S. Ct. 1074, 13 L. Ed. 2d 934 (1965),; Mattox v. United States, 156 U.S. 237, 242–243, 15 S. Ct. 337, 39 L. Ed. 409 (1895).

[40] *See, e.g.,* United States v. Owens, 484 U.S. 554, 557–560, 108 S. Ct. 838, 98 L. Ed. 2d 951 (1988).

inattentive.[41] "When a hearsay declarant is present at trial and subject to unrestricted cross-examination, the traditional protections of the oath, cross-examination, and opportunity for the jury to observe the witness's demeanor, satisfy the constitutional requirements" of the Confrontation Clause.[42]

It may well be that the Supreme Court's recent reaffirmation of the requirement that the reliability of "testimonial" hearsay be tested by cross-examination, rather than by some other means,[43] will require the courts to revisit the question whether cross-examination that is hampered by the declarant's lack of memory—or even an outright denial that he or she made the out-of-court statement—is a satisfactory substitute for thoroughgoing and detailed answers to the accused's probing questions.

§ 14.04 Residual Hearsay Exception—Rule 807[1]

[1]—Purpose of Exception

Rule 807 provides a residual hearsay exception for certain evidence that is not covered by the specific hearsay exceptions listed in Rules 803 and 804.[2] A residual exception is necessary because (1) not every contingency can be treated by detailed rules, (2) the hearsay rule and its exceptions continue to evolve, and (3) in a particular case hearsay evidence that does not fall within one of the enumerated exceptions may have greater probative value than evidence that does.[3] The residual rule, however, "is to be used only rarely, and in exceptional circumstances, and is meant to apply only when certain exceptional guarantees of trustworthiness exist and when high degrees of probativeness and necessity are present."[3]

The Rule provides:

Rule 807. Residual Exception.

Residual Exception. A statement not specifically covered by Rule 803 or

---

[41] *See, e.g.,* United States v. Owens, 484 U.S. 554, 559, 108 S. Ct. 838, 98 L. Ed. 2d 951 (1988).
[42] United States v. Owens, 484 U.S. 554, 560, 108 S. Ct. 838, 98 L. Ed. 2d 951 (1988).
[43] Crawford v. Washington, 541 U.S. 36, 124 S. Ct. 1354, 158 L. Ed. 2d 177, 199 (2004) (although Confrontation Clause's ultimate goal is to ensure reliability of hearsay statements of declarant who does not testify at trial, instead of requiring that evidence be reliable, it requires that evidence's reliability be tested by cross-examination); *see* [3], *above.*
[1] *See* discussion in **Treatise** at Chapter 807.
[2] Fed. R. Evid. 807; *see* former Rules 803(24), 804(b)(5).
[3] *See, e.g.,* United States v. Thunder Horse, 370 F.3d 745, 747 (8th Cir. 2004) (residual rule "was necessary to permit courts to admit evidence in exceptional circumstances where the evidence was necessary, highly probative, and carried a guarantee of trustworthiness equivalent to or superior to that which underlies the other recognized exceptions"; quoting United States v. Renville, 779 F.2d 430, 439 (8th Cir. 1985)).
See, e.g., United States v. Lawrence, 349 F.3d 109, 117 (3d Cir. 2003).

804 but having equivalent circumstantial guarantees of trustworthiness, is not excluded by the hearsay rule if the court determines that (A) the statement is offered as evidence of a material fact; (B) the statement is more probative on the point for which it is offered than any other evidence which the proponent can procure through reasonable efforts; and (C) the general purposes of these rules and the interests of justice will best be served by admission of the statement into evidence. However, a statement may not be admitted under this exception unless the proponent of it makes known to the adverse party sufficiently in advance of the trial or hearing to provide the adverse party with a fair opportunity to prepare to meet it, the proponent's intention to offer the statement and the particulars of it, including the name and address of the declarant.

[Adopted Apr. 11, 1997, effective Dec. 1, 1997.]

Rule 807 is a combination of the virtually identical former Rules 803(24) and 804(b)(5). Opinions interpreting former Rules 803(24) and 804(b)(5), therefore, remain authoritative in interpreting Rule 807.[4]

The residual exception applies only to statements "not specifically covered by Rule 803 or 804."[5] Most circuits have concluded that the phrase means only that, if a statement is admissible under one of the hearsay exceptions, that exception should be relied on instead of the residual exception. If a hearsay statement is similar to those defined by a specific exception but does not actually qualify for admission under that exception, those courts allow the statement to be considered for admission under the residual exception.[6] There is a minority view, on the other hand, that a statement is "specifically covered" by another exception to the hearsay rule even though it narrowly misses being admissible under the exception. Under this interpretation, such statements are, therefore, also inadmissible under the residual exception.[7]

Before admitting evidence under Rule 807, the trial court must determine that

---

[4] Bohler-Uddeholm Am., Inc. v. Ellwood Group, Inc., 247 F.3d 79, 112 n.17 (3d Cir. 2001).

[5] Fed. R. Evid. 807.

[6] *See, e.g.,* United States v. Laster, 258 F.3d 525, 530 (6th Cir. 2001) (documents that do not qualify for business record exception to hearsay rule because of lack of proper sponsoring witness can qualify for residual exception); United States v. Earles, 113 F.3d 796, 800 (8th Cir. 1997) (statement may be considered for admission under residual exception even if statement is of type addressed by specific hearsay exception but does not quality for admission under that exception).

[7] *See, e.g.,* United States v. Turner, 104 F.3d 217, 221 (8th Cir. 1997) (no plain error in preventing defendant from introducing medical texts under residual rule without meeting requirements of Rule 803(18); bypassing requirements of Rule 802(18) "would circumvent the general purpose of the rules"); United States v. Vigoa, 656 F. Supp. 1499, 1504 (D.N.J. 1987) (grand jury testimony is "former testimony covered by exception of Rule 804(b)(1) and is, therefore, inadmissible under residual exception).

the proffered evidence meets the prerequisites of the rule.[8] The court's findings should be made explicitly on the record,[9] unless the parties waive them or if the basis for the ruling is obvious.[10]

[2]—Circumstantial Guarantees of Trustworthiness

To be admissible under the residual exception, the evidence must have "circumstantial guarantees of trustworthiness" comparable to those of the enumerated exceptions.[11] On the other hand, categories of information addressed in the specific hearsay exceptions are inherently trustworthy; they "have attributes of trustworthiness not possessed by the general run of hearsay statements that tip the balance in favor of introducing the information" despite its hearsay character.[12] The term "reliability" is sometimes used to refer to this same concept.[13]

There is disagreement among the circuits about the scope of a court's inquiry in determining "circumstantial guarantees of trustworthiness."[14] Most courts undertake a broad inquiry, noting that guarantees of trustworthiness must be drawn from the totality of circumstances that surround the making of the statement that

---

[8] Fed. R. Evid. 807; *see, e.g.,* United States v. Simmons, 773 F.2d 1455, 1458–1459 (4th Cir. 1985) (government firearms trace forms were admissible as meeting all requirements of residual exception; forms "were clearly offered as evidence of a material fact . . . district court found that the forms were more probative than any other evidence which could be reasonably procured" and that there was no reason for information on forms to be falsified; thus, there were sufficient guarantees of trustworthiness, and their admission served general purpose of rules and interests of justice); *see* [2]–[6], *below.*

[9] *See, e.g.,* United States v. Chu Kong Yin, 935 F.2d 990, 999–1000 (9th Cir. 1991) (residual exception was inapplicable, since district court did not make any specific findings regarding requisite elements of rule and it was not clear that interests of justice were served by admission; record did not reveal identity of declarants or demonstrate that government had made names and addresses of declarants available before trial).

[10] *See, e.g.,* United States v. Simmons, 773 F.2d 1455, 1458–1459 (4th Cir. 1985) (government firearms trace forms were admissible as meeting all requirements of residual exception, in part, because forms "were clearly offered as evidence of a material fact").

[11] Fed. R. Evid. 807; *see, e.g.,* Bohler-Uddeholm Am., Inc. v. Ellwood Group, Inc., 247 F.3d 79, 113 (3d Cir. 2001) (decedent's affidavit was circumstantially guaranteed to be trustworthy); Conoco Inc., v. Department of Energy, 99 F.3d 387, 392-394 (Fed. Cir. 1996) (district court erred in admitting summaries, in part, because they did not possess "circumstantial guarantees of trustworthiness" equivalent to those of market reports or commercial publications).

[12] United States v. Fernandez, 892 F.2d 976, 980 (11th Cir. 1989).

[13] *See, e.g.,* United States v. Workman, 860 F.2d 140, 144 (4th Cir. 1988) (requirement of trustworthiness in residual exception is "just another way of expressing the need for 'adequate indicia of reliability' or 'independent inquiry into reliability' ").

[14] Robinson v. Shapiro, 646 F.2d 734, 743 n.7 (2d Cir. 1981) (circuits disagree about permissible scope of trial court's inquiry into trustworthiness of proffered hearsay evidence under residual exception).

render the declarant worthy of belief.[15] At least one other court has applied a narrower test, holding that the probability that the statement is true, as shown by corroborative evidence, is not a consideration relevant to its admissibility under the residual exception.[16]

In determining the trustworthiness of hearsay offered under the residual exception, courts consider such factors as the following:[17]

- The character of the statement.

- Whether the statement is written or oral.

- The relationship of the declarant to the parties.

- The probable motivation of the declarant in making the statement.

- The circumstances under which the statement was made.

Some courts consider the trustworthiness of hearsay offered under the residual hearsay exception in terms of the extent to which the statement is prone to the four classic hearsay risks of: (1) insincerity; (2) faulty perception; (3) faulty memory, and (4) faulty narration, Each of these risks decreases the reliability of the statement.[18]

The following list of factors has been applied in determining the trustworthiness of hearsay statements in the form of testimony:[19]

- The character of the witness for truthfulness and honesty.

---

[15] *See, e.g.,* United States v. Harrison, 296 F.3d 994, 1003–1007 (10th Cir. 2002) (out-of-court statement of child about sexual molestation was trustworthy enough for admission under Rule 807 because it was consistent with other admissible statements by child, statement was made in presence of alleged abuser, and circumstances suggested lack of opportunity for fabrication or coaching from others).

[16] Huff v. White Motor Corp., 609 F.2d 286, 293 (7th Cir. 1979) ("[T]he probability that the statement is true, as shown by corroborative evidence, is not, we think, a consideration relevant to its admissibility under the residual exception to the hearsay rule").

[17] *See, e.g.,* United States v. Hinkson, 632 F.2d 382, 386 (4th Cir. 1980) (not error to exclude declarant's alleged murder confession; statement was made to casual acquaintance hundreds of miles from killing, testimony indicated that declarant gloried in boasting of gang activities, there was no corroborating evidence, and declarant testified and denied killing victim).

[18] *See, e.g.,* Headley v. Tilghman, 53 F.3d 472, 477 (2d Cir. 1995) (classic hearsay "risks of insincerity, distorted perception, imperfect memory, and ambiguity of utterance" are hallmarks of trial court analysis of trustworthiness of evidence offered under residual rule).

[19] *See, e.g.,* United States v. Singleton, 125 F.3d 1097, 1106 (7th Cir. 1997) (most of listed factors, which were developed in connection with grand jury testimony, did not apply to taped conversations between defendants and informant, but circumstances of conversations provided sufficient indications of trustworthiness).

- Whether the testimony was given voluntarily, under oath, subject to cross-examination, and under penalty for perjury.[20]

- The witness's relationship with both the defendant and the government.

- The witness's motivation to testify.

- Whether the witness ever recanted the testimony.

- The existence of corroborating evidence.

- The reasons for the witness's unavailability.

[3]—Offered as Evidence of Material Fact

To be admissible under Rule 807, a statement must be "offered as evidence of a material fact."[1] The materiality prerequisite is satisfied if the evidence passes the relevance test of Rules 401 and 402.[2]

[4]—More Probative on the Point

To be admissible under the residual exception, a statement must be "more probative on the point for which it is offered than any other evidence which the proponent can procure through reasonable efforts."[1] The statement will be considered "more probative" if the court determines that the hearsay is relevant and reliable, and that no other evidence, or very little other evidence, is available on the same point.[2] Out-of-court statement that is merely cumulative of other evidence

---

[20] *See, e.g.,* FTC v. Kuykendall, 312 F.3d 1329, 1343 (10th Cir. 2002) (complaint letters from consumers were trustworthy because they were given under oath and penalty of perjury).

[1] Fed. R. Evid. 807(A); *see, e.g.,* Bohler-Uddeholm Am., Inc. v. Ellwood Group, Inc., 247 F.3d 79, 112–113 (3d Cir. 2001) (affidavit of decedent was properly admitted under Rule 807 because it was evidence tending to prove course of dealings between parties, which was at heart of matter being litigated); Nowell ex rel. Nowell v. Universal Elec. Co., 792 F.2d 1310, 1314–1315 (5th Cir. 1986) (in action concerning explosion of varnish drum, hearsay evidence as to identity of drum was properly admitted under residual rule, since identity of drum that exploded was material).

[2] *See, e.g.,* United States v. Simmons, 773 F.2d 1455, 1458–1459 (4th Cir. 1985) (firearms trace forms of Bureau of Alcohol, Tobacco and Firearms were admissible in prosecution for possession of firearm that had traveled in interstate commerce under residual rule, as evidence of material fact of place of manufacture of firearm); *see* Ch. 6.

[1] Fed. R. Evid. 807(B); *see, e.g.,* Opuku-Boateng v. State of California, 95 F.3d 1461, 1471 (9th Cir. 1996) (results of poll may be admitted if responses are material and more probative than other evidence).

[2] *See, e.g.,* Bohler-Uddeholm Am., Inc. v. Ellwood Group, Inc., 247 F.3d 79, 112 (3d Cir. 2001) (proffered affidavit of decedent was "more probative on the point" for which it was offered because no other evidence was available to plaintiff to counter defendant's contention that plaintiff understood agreement permit actions defendant had taken); United States v. Munoz, 16 F.3d 1116, 1122 (11th Cir. 1994) (bank deposit slips were more probative that deposits occurred than any other

in the record is clearly not more probative than other evidence available to the proffering party.[3]

What efforts are "reasonable" depends upon such matters as the importance of the evidence, the means at the command of the proponent and the amount in controversy.[4] The trial judge's good sense must be relied upon. Even though the evidence may be somewhat cumulative, it may be important in evaluating other evidence and arriving at the truth so that the "more probative" requirement cannot be interpreted with cast-iron rigidity.[5]

[5]—Interests of Justice

Admission of evidence under the residual exception must accord with "the general purposes of these rules and the interests of justice."[1] This requirement is largely a restatement of Rule 102.[2]

[6]—Notice

A party who intends to offer hearsay pursuant to the residual exception must give notice of this intent "sufficiently in advance of the trial or hearing to provide a fair opportunity to meet it."[3] The notice must include "the proponent's intention to offer the statement and the particulars of it, including the name and address of the declarant."[4] If the declarant's name and address are unknown despite reasonable

---

available evidence government might reasonably have obtained, and admissible under residual exception).

[3] See, e.g., Ghent v. Woodford, 279 F.3d 1121, 1133 n.10 (9th Cir. 2002).

[4] See, e.g., United States v. Bradley, 145 F.3d 889, 893–894 (7th Cir. 1998) (district court did not abuse discretion by admitting into evidence audiotape of wife's 911 call and statement describing how defendant had pulled gun on her during argument; wife's statement was sole direct evidence of defendant's actual possession of weapon that police found); Conoco Inc. v. Department of Energy, 99 F.3d 387, 394 (Fed. Cir. 1996) (since defendant made "no showing that reasonable efforts could not have produced more probative evidence," the evidence was not admissible under the residual hearsay exception).

[5] See, e.g., United States v. St. John, 851 F.2d 1096, 1098–1099 (8th Cir. 1988) (in sexual abuse prosecution, retarded victim's statements to social worker and clinical psychologist held admissible in view of victim's limited ability).

[1] Fed. R. Evid. 807(C); see, e.g., United States v. Harrison, 296 F.3d 994, 1007 (10th Cir. 2002) (purposes of rules were served by admission of out-of-court statements from alleged victim of child molestation because she testified at trial for defense, recanting her earlier statements; her "recantation increased the value to the prosecution of her statements at the same time that it afforded Defendant the equivalent of a devastating cross-examination regarding her statements").

[2] Fed. R. Evid. 102; see Ch. 1.

[3] Fed. R. Evid. 807; see, e.g., United States v. Williams, 272 F.3d 845, 858 (7th Cir. 2001) (trial court did not abuse its discretion in excluding evidence offered under Rule 807 when proffering party did not provide opponent with requisite notice).

[4] Fed. R. Evid. 807; see, e.g., Herrick v. Garvey, 298 F.3d 1184, 1192 n.6 (10th Cir. 2002).

efforts to locate the information, it is enough to give all the information the proponent has been able to acquire by diligent inquiry. The trial court's determination whether the notice was sufficient under Rule 807 is reviewed for abuse of discretion.[5]

Generally, notice should be given in writing at or before the pretrial conference if the proponent is aware of the problem. When it is questionable whether another exception applies, the safer course is to give notice so that the statement can also be proffered pursuant to the residual hearsay exception.[6]

If the proponent becomes aware of the evidence during trial—something bound to occur from time to time, no matter how thorough the discovery—the court can comply with the rule by granting a continuance.[7] A few courts have rigidly interpreted the notice requirement, apparently unmindful of Rule 102 and trial realities, and have refused to apply the residual exceptions in the absence of notice before the commencement of trial.[8]

§ 14.05　Hearsay Within Hearsay—Rule 805[1]

Rule 805 deals with hearsay within hearsay, or multiple hearsay as it is frequently termed. The Rule makes hearsay within hearsay admissible if each of the statements involved falls within an exception to the hearsay rule. The Rule provides as follows:

> **Rule 805.　Hearsay Within Hearsay.**
>
> Hearsay included within hearsay is not excluded under the hearsay rule if each part of the combined statements conforms with an exception to the hearsay rule provided in these rules.
>
> [*Adopted Jan. 2, 1975, effective July 1, 1975.*]

Rule 805 places no restriction on the number of levels of hearsay that a statement may contain.[2] Theoretically, there would be no objection to the number, provided

---

[5] *See, e.g.,* Kurzet v. Commissioner, 222 F.3d 830, 840 n.8 (10th Cir. 2000).

[6] United States v. Furst, 886 F.2d 558, 573–574 (3d Cir. 1989) (held error, but harmless, to admit records where government relied initially on business-record exception and cited residual exception only on first day of trial).

[7] United States v. Calkins, 906 F.2d 1240, 1245 (8th Cir. 1990).

[8] United States v. Oates, 560 F.2d 45, 72–73 n.30 (2d Cir. 1977) ("There is absolutely no doubt that Congress intended that the requirement of advance notice be rigidly enforced").

[1] *See* discussion in **Treatise** at §§ 805.02–805.06.

[2] *See, e.g.,* Yates v. Rexton, Inc., 267 F.3d 793, 802 (8th Cir. 2001) (trial court erred in excluding evidence of statement containing three levels of hearsay when each level was subject to recognized exception to hearsay rule); United States v. Green, 258 F.3d 683, 689–690 (7th Cir. 2001) (trial court did not err in admitting evidence of out-of-court statements containing reports of other out-of-court statements when each level was excluded from definition of hearsay by Rule 801).

each conformed to an exception. It must be remembered, however, that "[m]ultiple hearsay is, of course, even more vulnerable to all the objections which attach to simple hearsay[.]"[3] With each additional level of hearsay, there is a greater possibility of unreliability.[4] Even if each included portion meets the requirements of an exception, the trial court has discretion to exclude a statement of multiple hearsay pursuant to Rule 403 when it finds the statement so untrustworthy that its probative value is substantially outweighed by the dangers of confusion and prejudice. See Chapter 6, *Relevancy Generally.*

The problem of multiple hearsay arises with some frequency with regard to the admissibility of hospital records, police reports, public records, or business records when the entrant has no personal knowledge of the underlying event and has based the entry on information supplied by someone outside the entity.[5] Rule 805 makes the record admissible if the statement of the person who furnished the information independently satisfies a hearsay exception, or was exempted from the hearsay rule by Rule 801.[6] Thus, for example, the record is admissible if it records an excited utterance, or an admission, or a co-conspirator's statement. Situations may also arise where one of the statements does not fully qualify as a hearsay exception but nevertheless possesses sufficient assurances of trustworthiness to bring it within the residual hearsay exception (*see* § 14.04).[7]

---

[3] Naples v. United States, 344 F.2d 508, 511 (D.C. Cir. 1964), *overruled in part on other grounds by* Fuller v. United States, 407 F.2d 1199 (1967) (quoting McCormick, Evidence § 225 at 461 (1954); murder conviction reversed; D made statement to police lieutenant claiming he had no memory of hurting victim; lieutenant in D's presence repeated D's story to police captain but added that D said he struck victim; captain testified that lieutenant told him that D told him he struck woman; court held that this was double hearsay and that lieutenant's statement could not come in as an adoptive admission through D's silence [*see* **Treatise** at § 801.31[3][d] because it could not be found that the accused understood and unambiguously assented to the statement).

[4] Boren v. Sable, 887 F.2d 1032, 1034–1037 (10th Cir. 1989) (widow's testimony of decedent's report of his conversation with defendant held properly excluded, with extensive quotation from **Treatise**).

[5] *See, e.g.,* Sana v. Hawaiian Cruises, Ltd., 181 F.3d 1041, 1045–1047 (9th Cir. 1999) (insurance investigator's report was improperly excluded, even though it reflected three layers of hearsay, because each level came within an exception); United States v. Patrick, 959 F.2d 991, 1000–1001 (D.C. Cir. 1992) (a sales receipt was hearsay-within-hearsay under Rule 805, since it reflected both the assertion of store employee who wrote it up and the assertion of customer who provided address); United States v. Pendas-Martinez, 845 F.2d 938, 943 (11th Cir. 1988) (report of case agent held inadmissible on ground of multiple hearsay).

[6] *See, e.g.,* In re Flat Glass Antitrust Litig., 385 F.3d 350, 376 (3d Cir. 2004) (when document contains several assertions, for document to be admissible, each assertion must be admissible under exclusion or exception from hearsay rule).

[7] *See, e.g.,* Herdman v. Smith, 707 F.2d 839, 842 (5th Cir. 1983).

§ 14.06 Attacking and Supporting Credibility of Declarant—Rule 806[1]

Rule 806 provides that a declarant's credibility may be attacked, and then supported, as though the declarant had been a witness,[2] whenever the declarant's statement is admitted pursuant to a Rule 803 or 804 exception, or as an authorized or vicarious admission, or as a co-conspirator's declaration.[3] The rule eliminates the need to lay a foundation for impeachment by a prior inconsistent statement,[4] and allows a party against whom a hearsay statement has been admitted to examine the declarant as under cross-examination if the party calls him as a witness. The Rule provides as follows:

> **Rule 806. Attacking and Supporting Credibility of Declarant.**

---

[1] *See* discussion in **Treatise** at §§ 806.02–806.07.

[2] Fed. R. Evid. 806; *see, e.g.,* United States v. Stefonek, 179 F.3d 1030, 1036–1037 (7th Cir. 1999) (statements made to defendant by her business partner and testified to by defendant for their truth value could be impeached on defendant's cross-examination by questions about the partner's prior conviction); United States v. Chandler, 197 F.3d 1198, 1201–1202 (8th Cir. 1999) (evidence of silence, so ambiguous as to be of little probative force, was properly excluded to impeach hearsay declarant); United States v. Friedman, 854 F.2d 535, 569–570 (2d Cir. 1988) (a declarant may be impeached by extrinsic evidence of prior bad acts probative of truthfulness; court did not err, however, in excluding evidence of declarant's false explanation for suicide attempt where evidence had no conceivable bearing upon credibility of declarant's co-conspirator statements).

[3] United States v. Moody, 903 F.2d 321, 327–329 (5th Cir. 1990) (conviction reversed for trial court's failure to receive evidence of declarants' reputation for truthfulness, since they had implicated defendant in charged fraud by out-of-court co-conspirator statements allowed pursuant to Rule 801(d)(2)(E)); *see also* United States v. Velasco, 953 F.2d 1467, 1473 n.5 (7th Cir. 1992) (dicta that, had trial court admitted defendant's post-arrest statement in its entirety, government would have been able, under Rule 806, to impeach declarant/defendant with his later recantation, even though Rule 806 does not specifically include statements defined in 801(d)(2)(A); drafters of rule considered it unnecessary to mention Rule 801(d)(2)(A) and (B) because a party's credibility is always subject to attack); United States v. Newman, 849 F.2d 156, 161–163 (5th Cir. 1988) (prosecutor permitted to introduce defendant's prior conviction after defendant's hearsay statements, not within any exception, were received).

[4] Fed. R. Evid. 806 (evidence of inconsistent statement or conduct by declarant "is not subject to any requirement that the declarant may have been afforded an opportunity to deny or explain"); *see, e.g.,* United States v. Grant, 256 F.3d 1146, 1153 (11th Cir. 2001) (when government introduced out-of-court statement that declarant had a partner and introduced other evidence suggesting defendant was that partner, court erred in excluding declarant's later affidavit stating that defendant was not involved in drug trafficking and that he had lied about having a partner as impeachment of declarant's hearsay statement); *but see* United States v. Graham, 858 F.2d 986, 989–990 (5th Cir. 1988) (co-conspirator's statement offered for impeachment held properly excluded as not inconsistent with statement offered by prosecution).

When a hearsay statement, or a statement defined in Rule 801(d)(2)(C), (D), or (E), has been admitted in evidence,[5] the credibility of the declarant may be attacked, and if attacked may be supported, by any evidence which would be admissible for those purposes if declarant had testified as a witness. Evidence of a statement or conduct by the declarant at any time, inconsistent with the declarant's hearsay statement, is not subject to any requirement that the declarant may have been afforded an opportunity to deny or explain. If the party against whom a hearsay statement has been admitted calls the declarant as a witness, the party is entitled to examine the declarant on the statement as if under cross-examination.

[Adopted Jan. 2, 1975, effective July 1, 1975.]

There is a split of authority about whether the ability to impeach a declarant extends to admitting extrinsic evidence of the declarant's conduct. Under Rule 608(b), a witness may be cross-examined about conduct that is probative of the witness's untruthfulness, but extrinsic evidence of the conduct is inadmissible.[6] Since unavailable declarants cannot be cross-examined about their misconduct, some courts have suggested that extrinsic evidence would be admissible if the misconduct was probative of truthfulness.[7] Other courts, however, hew to the express terms of Rules 608(b) and 806, and hold that the ban on extrinsic evidence of misconduct applies in the context of hearsay declarants even when they are unavailable to testify.[8] Even in these jurisdictions, however, the declarant's misconduct may be introduced by cross-examining the witness who is reporting the hearsay statement.[9]

Rule 806 does not permit impeachment of someone who neither takes the stand

---

[5] The 1997 amendment to Rule 806 removed the comma that formerly preceded (C). The Advisory Committee has stated that no substantive change is intended.

[6] Fed. R. Evid. 608(b); *see* § 12.03[3].

[7] *See, e.g.,* United States v. Friedman, 854 F.2d 535, 569–570 (2d Cir. 1988) (dicta that, when declarant has not testified and no cross-examination is possible, "resort to extrinsic evidence may be the only means of presenting such evidence to the jury").

[8] *See, e.g.,* United States v. Saada, 212 F.3d 210, 222–223 (3d Cir. 2000) (taking judicial notice of declarant's misconduct was error, but harmless); United States v. White, 116 F.3d 903, 919–920 (D.C. Cir. 1997) (although counsel was entitled to cross-examine witness testifying to hearsay statement about specific acts of declarant, counsel "could not have made reference to any extrinsic proof of those acts").

[9] United States v. Saada, 212 F.3d 210, 219–222 (3d Cir. 2000) ("witness testifying to the hearsay statement may be questioned about the declarant's misconduct—without reference to extrinsic evidence thereof—on cross-examination concerning knowledge of the declarant's character for truthfulness or untruthfulness"); *see, e.g.,* United States v. White, 116 F.3d 903, 919–920 (D.C. Cir. 1997) (court allowed counsel to cross-examine witness on declarant's drug use, drug dealing, and prior convictions).

nor is quoted in a hearsay assertion.[10] Nor is Rule 806 applicable to permit impeachment of an absent author of a document that is admitted for a non-hearsay purpose.[11]

The party whose hearsay declarant has been successfully impeached pursuant to Rule 806 may try to rehabilitate the declarant by "any evidence which would be admissible . . . if the declarant had testified as a witness."[12]

---

[10] *See, e.g.,* United States v. Kabbaby, 672 F.2d 857, 863–864 (11th Cir. 1982) (refusal to allow defense to introduce informant's conviction record not reversible error, informer did not testify and was not hearsay declarant).

[11] *See, e.g.,* United States v. Arthur Andersen, LLP, 374 F.3d 281, 292 (5th Cir. 2004).

[12] Fed. R. Evid. 806.

CHAPTER 15

Hearsay Exclusions

SYNOPSIS

§ 15.01 Prior Statement By Witness—Rule 801(d)(1)[1]

[1]—General Requirements

Under Rule 801(d)(1), certain out-of-court statements are defined as "not hearsay" if the declarant is a witness at the trial or hearing at which the statement is offered and is available for cross-examination concerning the content of the statement.[2] The statement need not, however, be introduced through the declarant. It is proper for the proponent to offer it into evidence through the testimony of a third party.[3]

If the declarant, although present at the hearing or trial, does not actually testify, Rule 801(d)(1) does not apply to the declarant's prior statements.[4] For example, criminal defendants who choose not to testify at trial cannot introduce their out-of-court exculpatory statements to rebut any confessions that have been admitted against them by the government.[5]

A witness is ordinarily considered as being "subject to cross-examination" when he or she is placed on the stand, under oath, and responds willingly to questions, without regard to the condition of his or her memory at the time of the testimony. However, "limitations on the scope of examination by the trial court . . . may undermine the process to such a degree that meaningful cross-examination within the intent of the Rule no longer exists."[6] Moreover, a declarant's assertion of privilege respecting the subject matter of the out-of-court statement makes the

---

[1] See discussion in **Treatise** at §§ 801.10–801.13.

[2] Fed. R. Evid. 801(d)(1); *see, e.g.,* United States v. Piva, 870 F.2d 753, 758 (1st Cir. 1989) (fact that defendant did not cross-examine declarant about prior consistent statements did not make statements inadmissible so long as declarant was *available* for cross-examination; no indication in record that defense was precluded from recalling declarant after prosecution witness testified to declarant's prior consistent statements).

[3] *See, e.g.,* United States v. Green, 258 F.3d 683, 690–692 (7th Cir. 2001) (in absence of evidence that declarant was unavailable for cross-examination, trial court did not err in permitting another witness to provide evidence of declarant's prior consistent statement after defendant attempted to impeach declarant on cross-examination with charge of recent fabrication).

[4] *See, e.g.,* United States v. Sadler, 234 F.3d 368, 372–373 (8th Cir. 2000) (defendant could not introduce prior statement affirming his innocence to buttress his not guilty plea and to counter his confession subsequent to statement because he did not testify at trial); Bemis v. Edwards, 45 F.3d 1369, 1372 (9th Cir. 1995) (statements made in 911 call were hearsay; Fed. R. Evid. 801(d)(1) did not apply, since declarant did not testify at trial).

[5] *See, e.g.,* United States v. Sadler, 234 F.3d 368, 372–373 (8th Cir. 2000) (defendant's out-of-court exculpatory statement, offered to rebut his confession, was not admissible as prior consistent statement under Fed. R. Evid. 801(d)(1)(B) because defendant did not testify at trial and was not subject to cross-examination); *see* § 15.02 (admissibility of party admissions).

[6] *See, e.g.,* United States v. Owens, 484 U.S. 554, 561–564, 108 S. Ct. 838, 98 L. Ed. 2d 951 (1988) (citing **Treatise,** failure of cross-examination is "not produced by the witness' assertion of memory loss"; interpreting language in context of Fed. R. Evid. 801(d)(1)(C), prior statement by

declarant unavailable for cross-examination, which prevents Rule 801(d)(1) from applying to the out-of-court statement.[7] The validity of the witness's assertion of privilege does not determine whether a witness is subject to cross-examination. Thus, a witness who asserts an illegitimate claim of privilege is unavailable and not subject to cross-examination within the meaning of Rule 801(d)(1) and the Confrontation Clause.[8]

A declarant who is a witness at the trial is under oath and subject to cross-examination, and his or her demeanor can be observed by the trier of fact. These facts remove some of the dangers of introducing hearsay, but not all of them. As a result, Rule 801(d)(1) applies to only three kinds of prior statements that have been deemed to possess a high degree of reliability: (1) prior inconsistent statements, (2) prior consistent statements, and (3) statements of identification.[9] Another reason for admitting these kinds of statements is their relevancy to the credibility of the witness; they are likely to be of great assistance in enabling the trier to evaluate the evidence properly.

[2]—Prior Inconsistent Statements[10]

[a]—Scope and Text of Rule

The first category of prior statement made admissible by Rule 801(d)(1) is a statement inconsistent with the witness's testimony that the witness had previously given under oath at a trial, deposition, or other proceeding.[11] By requiring that the statement have been given in circumstances where there normally will be a

---

victim naming defendant as assailant was not hearsay even though victim at trial could not remember seeing assailant).

[7] *See, e.g.*, United States v. Owens, 484 U.S. 554, 561–564, 108 S. Ct. 838, 98 L. Ed. 2d 951 (1988) (dicta that "assertions of privilege by the witness may undermine the process to such a degree that meaningful cross-examination within the intent of the Rule no longer exists"); United States v. Wilmore, 381 F.3d 868, 871–873 (9th Cir. 2004) (government witness who testified contrary to earlier grand jury testimony, was impeached by government with that testimony, and then asserted privilege against self-incrimination when the defense tried to ask questions about that testimony became unavailable for cross-examination concerning the inconsistent testimony; limitation of defense questioning and use of prior testimony without opportunity to cross-examine witness about it violated defendant's Confrontation Clause rights).

[8] *See, e.g.*, United States v. Torrez-Ortega, 184 F.3d 1128, 1132–1133 (10th Cir. 1999) (admission of grand jury testimony of witness who asserted invalid Fifth Amendment privilege claim violated Confrontation Clause and Fed. R. Evid. 801(d)(1)(A), because witness's assertion of privilege and persistence in refusing to answer most questions at trial prevented viable cross-examination).

[9] *See* [2]–[4], *below.*

[10] See discussion in **Treatise** at § 801.21.

[11] Fed. R. Evid. 801(d)(1)(A); *see, e.g.*, United States v. Williams, 272 F.3d 845, 859 (7th Cir. 2001) (when proponent failed to show that affidavit was executed in connection with "proceeding"

transcript, the rule eliminates the danger that witnesses will fabricate prior statements.[12] The rule's limitations also make unusable substantively many types of statements that are given in response to subtle and sometimes severe pressures, as, for instance, statements elicited by an insurance agent or an FBI agent; statements made before a grand jury, where leading is the norm, are admissible, however.[13] The rule provides:

Rule 801. Definitions.

(d) Statements which are not hearsay.—A statement is not hearsay if—

(1) Prior statement by witness.—The declarant testifies at the trial or hearing and is subject to cross-examination concerning the statement, and the statement is (A) inconsistent with the declarant's testimony, and was given under oath subject to the penalty of perjury at a trial, hearing, or other proceeding, or in a deposition. . . .

[Adopted Jan. 2, 1975, effective July 1, 1975; amended Mar. 2, 1987, effective Oct 1, 1987.]

---

[b]—Oath

According to Rule 801(d)(1)(A), a prior statement cannot be accorded substantive use unless it was given under "oath."[14] Federal law[15] provides, however, that certain unsworn declarations made under penalty of perjury may be used in lieu of statements under oath, and such declarations satisfy Rule 801(d)(1).

[c]—Trial, Hearing, Other Proceeding, or Deposition

In order for the statement to satisfy Rule 801(d)(1)(A), it must have been made at some kind of judicial or quasi-judicial proceeding.[16] The rule would apply, for

---

as contemplated by Rule 801(d)(1)(A), it was not excluded from hearsay definition and was inadmissible).

[12] This is, however, a non-hearsay danger, since the witness is present in court.

[13] *See, e.g.,* United States v. Gajo, 290 F.3d 922, 931–932 (7th Cir. 2002) (trial court did not abuse its discretion under Rule 801(d)(1)(A) in permitting government to read into record portions of witness's grand jury testimony that conflicted with witness's testimony at trial).

[14] Fed. R. Evid. 801(d)(1)(A); *see, e.g.,* United States v. Morgan, 376 F.3d 1002, 1007 (9th Cir. 2004) (bankruptcy petition, signed under penalty of perjury, claiming witness owed creditors more than $100,000 was admissible as prior inconsistent statement after witness testified she did not owe creditors more than $100,000).

[15] 28 U.S.C. § 1746 (an unsworn written declaration given under penalty of perjury may not be substituted for a deposition, an oath of office, or a document required to be signed before a specified official other than a notary public).

[16] Fed. R. Evid. 801(d)(1)(A); *see, e.g.,* Santos v. Murdock, 243 F.3d 681, 683–684 (2d Cir. 2001) (affidavit signed in attorney's office, even though under oath, is not given in "other

example, to a deposition from the same or a different proceeding[17] and to testimony before a grand jury.[18] The solemnity of the official occasion and the oath, plus a stenographic record, reduce possibilities of overreaching by the questioner and carelessness by the witness. The absence of cross-examination at the prior proceeding is irrelevant.

The hearing requirement ensures that there will be no dispute about whether the prior statement was made.

[d]—Inconsistent

To be admissible under Rule 801(d)(1)(A), the prior statement must be inconsistent with the testimony given by the witness.[19] The decision whether the prior statement is inconsistent with the trial testimony is within the trial court's discretion.[20]

The courts do not limit a finding of inconsistency to situations in which the witness's prior statement is diametrically opposed to his or her testimony.[21] In general, almost any substantive divergence between two statements has sufficed to permit the use of the prior statement. Thus, inconsistency may arise when the witness gives evasive answers, responds with silence, or changes his or her position.[22] In the context of impeachment, it has been held that prior statements "that omit details included in a witness's trial testimony are inconsistent if it would have been 'natural' for the witness to include the details in the earlier statement."[23]

Even testimony that the witness-declarant has no recollection of the subject may be treated as "inconsistent" with a former statement concerning the now-forgotten

---

proceeding"); United States v. Dietrich, 854 F.2d 1056, 1060–1062 (7th Cir. 1988) (written sworn statement given in interview with two Secret Service agents was not given at "trial, hearing or other proceeding").

[17] See, e.g., Pope v. Savings Bank of Puget Sound, 850 F.2d 1345, 1356 (9th Cir. 1988) (defendant properly introduced plaintiff's deposition testimony from different proceeding under Rule 801(d)(1)(A)).

[18] See, e.g., United States v. Gajo, 290 F.3d 922, 931–932 (7th Cir. 2002) (trial court did not abuse its discretion under Rule 801(d)(1)(A) in permitting government to read into record portions of witness's grand jury testimony that conflicted with witness's testimony at trial).

[19] Fed. R. Evid. 801(d)(1)(A).

[20] See, e.g., United States v. Matlock, 109 F.3d 1313, 1319 (8th Cir. 1997) (district court has considerable discretion in determining whether prior statements made under oath are inconsistent with trial testimony).

[21] See, e.g., United States v. Jones, 808 F.2d 561, 568 (7th Cir. 1986) (prior statement need not be diametrically inconsistent with trial testimony).

[22] See, e.g., United States v. Matlock, 109 F.3d 1313, 1319 (8th Cir. 1997).

[23] United States v. Meserve, 271 F.3d 314, 320–321 (1st Cir. 2001) (since questioning before grand jury did not directly address point at issue, court had discretion to find no inconsistency).

matter.[24] This is especially true when the witness's inability to recall appears feigned.[25]

[3]—Prior Consistent Statements[26]

Prior consistent statements of a witness at the hearing or trial are defined as "not hearsay" under Rule 801(d)(1)(B) if they are admitted to rebut charges of recent fabrication or improper influence or motive.[27] The statement need not, however, rebut all potential motives to fabricate. The rule requires only that it tend to rebut the charged motive.[27.1]

Evidence that counteracts a suggestion that the witness changed his or her story in response to some threat or scheme or bribe, by showing that the witness's story was the same prior to the alleged external pressure, is highly relevant in shedding light on the witness's credibility. Evidence that merely shows that the witness said the same thing on other occasions when his or her motive was the same does not have much probative force, "for the simple reason that mere repetition does not imply veracity."[28]

Unlike prior inconsistent statements, the prior consistent statement need not have been made under oath or at a previous trial, hearing, or other proceeding.[29]

Rule 801(d)(1)(B) provides as follows:

Rule 801(d)(1)(B).   Definitions.

---

[24]   *See, e.g.,* United States v. Gajo, 290 F.3d 922, 931–932 (7th Cir. 2002) (witness's testimony at trial that he could not remember what defendant said to him in English during conversation was inconsistent with his testimony before grand jury, in which he recounted English portion of conversation in detail).

[25]   *See, e.g.,* United States v. Keeter, 130 F.3d 297, 301–302 (7th Cir. 1997) (prior statements of witness who feigned amnesia at trial were admissible under Rule 801(d)(1)(A)); United States v. Knox, 124 F.3d 1360, 1364 (10th Cir. 1997) (a "well-settled body of case law holds that where a declarant's memory loss is contrived it will be taken as inconsistent with a prior statement for purposes of Rule 801(d)(1)(A)").

[26]   See discussion in **Treatise** at § 801.22.

[27]   Fed. R. Evid. 801(d)(1)(B); *see, e.g.,* United States v. Ruiz, 249 F.3d 643, 647–648 (7th Cir. 2001) (witness's prior consistent statement was properly admitted after opponent suggested on cross-examination that witness's direct testimony was fictitious because several matters about which witness testified were not mentioned in witness's post incident report); United States v. Red Feather, 865 F.2d 169, 171 (8th Cir. 1989) (child sex abuse victim's diary entries were properly admitted as prior consistent statements when defendant charged that her testimony resulted from suggestions of social worker).

[27.1]   *See, e.g.,* United States v. Wilson, 355 F.3d 358, 361 (5th Cir. 2003).

[28]   United States v. McPartlin, 595 F.2d 1321, 1351 (7th Cir. 1979); *see, e.g.,* United States v. Acker, 52 F.3d 509, 516–518 (4th Cir. 1995) (officer's testimony as to statements defendant's boyfriend made regarding defendant's involvement in bank robberies was inadmissible hearsay since it was offered solely to corroborate boyfriend's in-court testimony).

[29]   Fed. R. Evid. 801(d)(1); *see* [2], *above.*

(d) Statements which are not hearsay.—A statement is not hearsay if—

(1) Prior statement by witness.—The declarant testifies at the trial or hearing and is subject to cross-examination concerning the statement, and the statement is . . . (B) consistent with the declarant's testimony and is offered to rebut an express or implied charge against the declarant of recent fabrication or improper influence or motive. . . .

[*Adopted Jan. 2, 1975, effective July 1, 1975; amended Mar. 2, 1987, effective Oct 1, 1987.*]

Prior consistent statements are admissible under Rule 801(d)(1)(B) only after a witness has been impeached by a suggestion that his or her testimony is the result of an improper influence or motive, or by an assertion that the testimony is a recent fabrication.[30] A charge of improper motive or fabrication may be express.[31] Alternatively, the witness may be impeached by implication, such as reliance on underlying facts or innuendo to demonstrate the recent fabrication or improper influence or motive.[32]

Even then, a prior consistent statement comes within the rule only if it tends to refute the charge.[33] Thus, the Supreme Court has ruled that a statement qualifies under Rule 801(d)(1)(B) only if it was made before the witness's motive to fabricate arose.[34]

The issue of hearsay arises only when a statement is offered for its truth. Thus, some appellate courts have held that Rule 801(d)(1)(B) is applicable only when a prior consistent statement is offered for the proof of its contents. When a prior consistent statement is offered not for proof of its contents, but solely for rehabilitation, these courts hold that the Supreme Court's "motive to fabricate" limitation does not apply. In these circuits, a witness who is impeached with a prior

[30] Fed. R. Evid. 801(d)(1)(B); *see, e.g.,* United States v. McCulley, 178 F.3d 872, 876–877 (7th Cir. 1999) (improper to admit previous statement simply to bolster witness's statement made at trial, in absence of suggestion that testimony was recent fabrication).

[31] *See, e.g.,* United States v. Anderson, 303 F.3d 847, 859 (7th Cir. 2002) (witnesses' prior statements identifying defendant as their drug supplier, made shortly after their arrest and before they had motive to fabricate, were properly admitted under Rule 801(d)(1)(B) because defendant cross-examined each witness in manner suggesting that they conspired to frame defendant).

[32] *See, e.g.,* United States v. Stoecker, 215 F.3d 788, 791 (7th Cir. 2000) (cross-examination about witness's plea agreement suggested his incentive to testify falsely, so witness's statement to FBI before plea agreement was properly admitted as prior consistent statement).

[33] *See, e.g.,* United States v. Webb, 214 F.3d 962, 963–965 (8th Cir. 2000) (victim's statements to witnesses about her sexual assault by county sheriff were admissible as prior consistent statements; evidence of sheriff's alibi for first alleged assault suggested that victim had fabricated that charge, so victim's statements to witnesses were admissible to rebut that implication).

[34] Tome v. United States, 513 U.S. 150, 156, 115 S. Ct. 696, 705, 130 L. Ed. 2d 574 (1995) (prior statement must have been made before motive to fabricate arose).

inconsistent statement may be rehabilitated with a prior consistent statement, even though it was made after a motive to fabricate arose, so long as the prior consistent statement is not offered to prove the truth of its contents.[34.1] Other courts hold that the requirement that the statement have been made before any motive to fabricate arose is applicable even when the statement is offered solely to rehabilitate the witness.[34.2] Moreover, Rule 801(d)(1)(B) does not prevent the admission of a prior consistent statement under the rule of completeness of Rule 106, even though the statement may have been made after the declarant's motive to fabricate arose, if the declarant is interrogated about parts of the prior statement on cross-examination.[34.3]

Although the Advisory Committee's notes do not indicate whether Rule 801(d)(1)(B) does or does not extend to situations in which the prior consistent statement is offered to refute a suggestion that the witness's memory is inaccurate, the ordinary meaning of the words "fabrication," "influence," and "motive" suggests that the Rule is intended to cover only situations in which witnesses have consciously altered their testimony.[35] Thus, prior consistent statements are not admissible "to counter all forms of impeachment or to bolster the witness merely because she has been discredited. . . . The Rule speaks of a party rebutting an alleged motive, not bolstering the veracity of the story told."[36]

A prior statement need not be "identical in every detail" to the trial testimony to be considered "consistent."[37] Rule 801(d)(1)(B) does not, however, authorize the admission of prior statements that are unrelated to the impeached trial testimony. The trial court has discretion to exclude parts of the witness's prior statement that do not address the subject on which the witness was impeached.[38]

[34.1] *See, e.g.,* United States v. Stover, 329 F.3d 859, 867–868 (D.C. Cir. 2003).

[34.2] *See, e.g.,* United States v. Trujillo, 376 F.3d 593, 610–611 (6th Cir. 2004).

[34.3] *See, e.g.,* United States v. Mohr, 318 F.3d 613, 626 (4th Cir. 2003).

[35] *See, e.g.,* United States v. Bishop, 264 F.3d 535, 548 (5th Cir. 2001) (Rule 801(d)(1)(B) does not permit introduction of otherwise inadmissible hearsay whenever witness's credibility or memory is challenged).

[36] Tome v. United States, 513 U.S. 150, 157–158, 115 S. Ct. 696, 130 L Ed. 2d 574 (1995).

[37] United States v. Vest, 842 F.2d 1319, 1328–1330 (1st Cir. 1988).

[38] *See, e.g.,* United States v. Myers, 972 F.2d 1566, 1575 (11th Cir. 1992) (after government used defendant's prior statement to impeach him about number of times he used stun gun on prisoner, court acted within its discretion in refusing defense request to admit additional parts of statement describing threats by prisoner, as court may exclude parts that do not relate to matters on which speaker was impeached).

[4]—Statement of Identification[39]

Rule 801(d)(1)(C) makes admissible an out-of-court statement by the witness identifying a person.[40] Subparagraph (C) operates independent of the impeachment process. There is neither a requirement of inconsistency as in subparagraph (A), nor a condition of previous impeachment as in subparagraph (B).

Statements of identification are admitted because the earlier identification has greater probative value than an identification made in the suggestive atmosphere of the courtroom, after the witness's memory has started to fade.[41] "Protection against identifications of questionable certainty is afforded by the requirement that the declarant be available for cross-examination; questions of the probative value of the testimony are thus for the jury."[42]

In criminal cases, the trustworthiness of out-of-court identifying statements is also enhanced by the Supreme Court's fairly rigorous requirements concerning the procedures under which the police participate in out-of-court identifications.[43]

Rule 801(d)(1)(C) provides:

Rule 801(d)(1)(C). Definitions.

(d) Statements which are not hearsay.—A statement is not hearsay if—

(1) Prior statement by witness.—The declarant testifies at the trial or hearing and is subject to cross-examination concerning the statement, and the statement is . . . (C) one of identification of a person made after perceiving the person.

[*Adopted Jan. 2, 1975, effective July 1, 1975; amended Mar. 2, 1987, effective Oct 1, 1987.*]

Rule 801(d)(1)(C) applies regardless of when the prior identification was made—whether at the scene of the crime, at a later chance encounter, or at a police

---

[39] See discussion in **Treatise** at § 801.23.

[40] Fed. R. Evid. 801(d)(1)(C); *see also* United States v. Davis, 181 F.3d 147, 149 (D.C. Cir. 1999) (police report of drug transaction that included description of suspect's clothing was admissible as statement of identification).

[41] *See* Gilbert v. California, 388 U.S. 263, 272–274, 87 S. Ct. 1951, 18 L. Ed. 2d 1178 (1967).

[42] United States v. Marchand, 564 F.2d 983, 996 (2d Cir. 1977).

[43] *See, e.g.,* Neil v. Biggers, 409 U.S. 188, 199–200, 93 S. Ct. 375, 34 L. Ed. 2d 401 (1972); Foster v. California, 394 U.S. 440, 442–443, 89 S. Ct. 1127, 22 L. Ed. 2d 402 (1969); Stovall v. Denno, 388 U.S. 293, 296–298, 87 S. Ct. 1967, 18 L. Ed. 2d 1199 (1967); Gilbert v. California, 388 U.S. 263, 272–274, 87 S. Ct. 1951, 18 L. Ed. 2d 1178 (1967); United States v. Wade, 388 U.S. 218, 229–237, 87 S. Ct. 1926, 18 L. Ed. 2d 1149 (1967).

line-up.[44] Rule 801(d)(1)(C) addresses only the hearsay character of a statement of identification. Issues about the suggestiveness of an identification and a criminal defendant's due process rights are matters of constitutional law and criminal procedure.[45]

The rule does not bar persons other than the witness who made the out-of-court identification from testifying to the statement. For instance, a police officer who heard the witness identify the defendant at the line-up may testify concerning the witness's identification, provided both the witness and the police officer are subject to cross-examination.[46] The declarant-witness's inability to remember anything about the circumstances of the identification, or about the defendant at the time of the crime, does not prevent a prior out-of-court identification statement from satisfying Rule 801(d)(1)(C) as well as the Confrontation Clause.[47] The rule has also been interpreted to authorize testimony that the witness had made an out-of-court identification of a photograph[48] or sketch[49] of a person, rather than of the person in the flesh. However, Rule 801 addresses only the hearsay character of a statement of identification. Issues about the suggestiveness of an identification and a criminal defendant's due process rights are matters of constitutional law.[50]

The rule does not bar persons other than the witness who made the out-of-court

---

[44] *See, e.g.,* United States v. Lopez, 271 F.3d 472, 484–485 (3d Cir. 2001) (Rule 801(d)(1)(C) permits introduction of out-of-court statement identifying defendant as having been seen in vicinity of burglaries when person who made statement denies having made statement when testifying).

[45] *See, e.g.,* United States v. Brown, 200 F.3d 700, 706–707 (10th Cir. 1999) (suggestiveness of pre-trial identification went to weight, not admissibility, of trial identification); United States v. Duran-Orozco, 192 F.3d 1277, 1282 (9th Cir. 1999) (tainted pretrial identification did not necessarily render trial identification unreliable) United States v. Deavault, 190 F.3d 926, 929–930 (8th Cir. 1999) (pretrial photo identification procedure need not be perfect to exhibit sufficient indicia of reliability).

[46] *See, e.g.,* United States v. Lopez, 271 F.3d 472, 484–485 (3d Cir. 2001) (after witness denied having identified defendants as having been at scene of crime, trial court properly permitted law enforcement officer to testify about witness's out-of-court identification).

[47] United States v. Owens, 484 U.S. 554, 561, 108 S. Ct. 838, 98 L. Ed. 2d 951 (1988) (citing **Treatise,** "subject to cross-examination concerning the statement" language in Rule 801(d)(1) requires no more than placing declarant on witness stand, subject to oath, and willing to answer questions; neither Sixth Amendment nor Rule 801(d)(1)(C) require effectiveness of cross-examination, both are satisfied if defendant has "opportunity" for cross-examination).

[48] *See, e.g.,* United States v. Hines, 955 F.2d 1449, 1455–1457 (11th Cir. 1992) (prior identification of defendant from photo is excluded from hearsay rule under Rule 801(d)(1)(C), but may still be excluded under Rule 403 if unfairly prejudicial; mugshots should have been excluded as improper character evidence); United States v. Fosher, 568 F.2d 207, 210 (1st Cir. 1978).

[49] *See, e.g.,* United States v. Moskowitz, 581 F.2d 14, 20–21 (2d Cir. 1978).

[50] *See, e.g.,* United States v. Brown, 200 F.3d 700, 706–707 (10th Cir. 1999) (suggestiveness of pre-trial identification went to weight, not admissibility, of trial identification); United States v. Deavault, 190 F.3d 926, 929–930 (8th Cir. 1999) (pretrial photo identification procedure need not be perfect to exhibit sufficient indicia of reliability); United States v. Duran-Orozco, 192 F.3d 1277,

identification from testifying to the statement. For instance, a police officer who heard the witness identify the defendant at the line-up may testify concerning the witness's identification, provided both the witness and the police officer are subject to cross-examination.[51]

§ 15.02   Admissions—Rule 801(d)(2)

[1]—General Requirements[1]

Rule 801(d)(2) excludes from the definition of *hearsay* five types of out-of-court statements that were made by the party opponent of the proffering party or are attributable to the party opponent in accordance with the provisions of the rule. Rather than characterize admissions as exceptions to the hearsay rule, the Federal Rules of Evidence provide that admissions by a party-opponent are not hearsay, thereby recognizing that admissions differ from other hearsay exceptions.

Unlike other exceptions which are grounded upon a probability of trustworthiness, the circumstances in which an admission was made do not furnish the trier of fact with the means of evaluating the reliability of the statement. Rather, admissions are admitted on an estoppel notion, or as the product of the adversary system, or as a matter of precedent because the reception of this type of evidence predates the development of the hearsay rule.

Rule 801(d)(2) represents an accommodation to the common view that statements of a principal actor should generally be received rather than excluded per se. Because of their value, they are receivable whether or not the declarant is available or appears as a witness.

Rule 801(d)(2) was amended in 1997 to provide that the contents of an offered admission must be considered, but are not alone sufficient, to establish that the statement qualifies as an authorized or vicarious admission or as a coconspirator's statement. The amendment affects Rule 801(d)(2)(C), (D), and (E), and is discussed in [4]–[6], *below.*

1282 (9th Cir. 1999) (tainted pretrial identification did not necessarily render trial identification unreliable).

[51]   United States v. Jarrad, 754 F.2d 1451, 1456 (9th Cir. 1985) (FBI agent permitted to testify to witness's tentative identification of photograph of defendant after witness denied that any of photographs she viewed resembled defendant, defense cross-examined agent, but did not recall witness; court stated that purpose of rule was to solve problem of eyewitness who identifies defendant before trial but refuses to acknowledge identification at trial for fear of reprisal).

[1]   *See* discussion in **Treatise** at § 801.30.

[2]—By Party in Individual or Representative Capacity[2]

Rule 801(d)(2)(A) provides that the statement of a party made in either an individual or representative capacity is not hearsay when it is offered in evidence against the party.[3] The rule provides as follows:

Rule 801(d)(2)(A).   Definitions.

(d) Statements which are not hearsay.—A statement is not hearsay if—. . .

. . .

(2) Admission by party-opponent.—The statement is offered against a party and is (A) the party's own statement, in either an individual or a representative capacity. . . .

[*Adopted Jan. 2, 1975, effective July 1, 1975; amended Mar. 2, 1987, effective Oct 1, 1987; amended Apr, 11, 1997, effective Dec. 1, 1997.*]

The party's statement may have been self-serving when made,[4] need not be based on personal knowledge,[5] and may be in the form of an opinion.

When a statement was made in a representative capacity, it is an admission of a party opponent whether offered against the person who made the statement or

---

[2]   *See* **Treatise** at § 801.30.

[3]   Fed. R. Evid. 801(d)(2)(A); *see, e.g.,* Stalbosky v. Belew, 205 F.3d 890, 894 (6th Cir. 2000) (affidavit quoting comments of chairman of defendant trucking company); United States v. England, 966 F.2d 403, 407 (8th Cir. 1992) (tape-recorded conversation between defendant and a coconspirator); Dugan v. EMS Helicopters, Inc., 915 F.2d 1428, 1432–1434 (10th Cir. 1990) (complaint filed by the same plaintiffs in another lawsuit against different defendants).

[4]   United States v. McGee, 189 F.3d 626, 631–632 (7th Cir. 1999) (party admission need not be inculpatory to be admissible under Rule 801(d)(2); citing **Treatise**); United States v. Turner, 995 F.2d 1357, 1363 (6th Cir. 1993) ("Rule 801(d)(2) does not limit an admission to a statement against interest"); Marquis Theatre Corp. v. Condado Mini Cinema, 846 F.2d 86, 90 n.3 (1st Cir. 1988) (rejecting contention that admissions under Rule 801(d)(2) must be against interest either at the time the statement was made or at the time of trial); Guam v. Ojeda, 758 F.2d 403, 408 (9th Cir. 1985) (statements need not be incriminating to be Rule 801(d)(2)(A) admissions).

[5]   United States v. Matlock, 415 U.S. 164, 172 n.8, 94 S. Ct. 988, 39 L. Ed. 2d 242 (1974) (statement that party was married); United States v. Bakshinian, 65 F. Supp. 2d 1104, 1109 (C.D. Cal. 1999) (citing **Treatise,** prosecutor's statement during closing argument at separate trial of defendant's coconspirator was admissible in defendant's trial as statement of party opponent; party admissions are exempt from the rule requiring firsthand knowledge); *see also* Jewel v. CSX Transp., Inc., 135 F.3d 361, 365 (6th Cir. 1998) (trustworthiness is not a separate requirement under Rule 801(d)(2)(A)); *cf.* Vasquez v. Lopez-Rosario, 134 F.3d 28, 34–35 (1st Cir. 1998) ("hallway gossip" by unidentified individuals was hearsay within hearsay; since original declarants were unknown, admissibility of original statements as party admissions was not shown).

the party that the person represented when the statement was made.[6]

The rule makes no attempt to categorize the myriad ways in which an admission can be made. Admissions can be in the form of explicit statements or may be inferred from conduct. They may be made orally or in writing.[7] The statement may have been made in connection with no case,[7.1] the instant case,[8] or some other completely independent litigation.[9]

All that is required is that a statement made by a party is offered into evidence by an adverse party.[10] However, the statement must be offered against the same party that made the statement.[11] A fortiori, parties cannot rely on Rule 801(d)(2) to offer their own statements into evidence.

---

[6] *See, e.g.,* In re Special Fed. Grand Jury, 819 F.2d 56, 58–59 (3d Cir. 1987) (out-of-court statement of defendant, made solely in his capacity as corporate agent, was admissible against him as well as against corporation).

[7] *See, e.g.,* United States v. Siddiqui, 235 F.3d 1318, 1322 (11th Cir. 2000) (e-mail messages sent by defendant were admissions by a party under Rule 801(d)(2)(A)); United States v. Dixon, 132 F.3d 192, 198–199 (5th Cir. 1997) (defendant's tape-recorded conversations with informant unavailable at trial were party admissions and were admissible when supported by adequate indicia of reliability); United States v. Goodchild, 25 F.3d 55, 62–63 (1st Cir. 1994) (defendant's statements in company memo admissible).

[7.1] *See, e.g.,* United States v. Curtis, 324 F.3d 501, 507 (7th Cir. 2003) (defendant's statements concerning his participation in murder made to coconspirator were properly admitted as admission of party opponent under Rule 801(d)(2)(A)).

[8] United States v. GAF Corp., 928 F.2d 1253, 1259–1260 (2d Cir. 1991) (prior inconsistent bill of particulars served by the government in a previous trial which ended in a hung jury admissible); Andrews v. Metro North Commuter R.R., 882 F.2d 705, 707 (2d Cir. 1989) (complaint prior to amendment).

[9] *See* Trull v. Volkswagen of America, Inc., 187 F.3d 88, 99 (1st Cir. 1999) (diagram introduced and relied on by plaintiff in prior lawsuit was properly admitted as a party admission in later trial); Vincent v. Louis Marx & Co., Inc., 874 F.2d 36, 37–41 (1st Cir. 1989) (court has discretion to apply Rule 403 to determine whether prior inconsistent pleading by plaintiff in prior state action brought against third party should be admissible); *but cf.* Hardy v. Johns-Manville Sales Corp., 851 F.2d 742, 745–746 (5th Cir. 1988) (statements in appellate briefs filed in different actions between different parties are not admissible as party admissions barring some highly unusual circumstances).

[10] *See, e.g.,* United States v. Sauza-Martinez, 217 F.3d 754, 759 (9th Cir. 2000) (one party's post-arrest statements admissible against that party under Rule 801(d)(2)(A) but not against another party; trial court erred in failing to give jury limiting instruction).

[11] Stalbosky v. Belew, 205 F.3d 890, 894 (6th Cir. 2000) ("Under Rule 801(d)(2)(A), a party's statement is admissible as non-hearsay only if it is offered against that party"; district court properly refused to consider statements of defendant driver, since they were offered against his employer, a co-defendant).

[3]—Admissions: Adoptive[12]

Rule 801(d)(2)(B) recognizes that an admission may be made by acquiescing in the statement of another. The rule provides:

Rule 801(d)(2)(B). Definitions.

(d) Statements which are not hearsay.—A statement is not hearsay if—

. . .

(2) Admission by party-opponent.—The statement is offered against a party and is . . . (B) a statement of which the party has manifested an adoption or belief in its truth. . . .

[Adopted Jan. 2, 1975, effective July 1, 1975; amended Mar. 2, 1987, effective Oct 1, 1987; amended Apr, 11, 1997, effective Dec. 1, 1997.]

The rule is clearly satisfied when a party verbally and unambiguously adopts the statement of another.[13] Similarly, the courts frequently admit tape recordings of conversations between a party and another person on the theory that the statements of the party qualify as party admissions under Rule 801(d)(2)(A), and the statements of the other person qualify as adoptive admissions of the party under Rule 801(d)(2)(B).[14]

A party cannot be held to have adopted another's statement, however, unless the party was fully aware of what he or she was doing at the time of the adoption. Thus, if a party who is not literate in the English language signs a statement in English that was drafted by another person and is not a verbatim translation of what the party said in giving the statement, the proponent must show, as a prerequisite to the admissibility of the statement under Rule 801(d)(2)(B), that it was read to the party in a language he or she understood.[15]

A party's conduct may also constitute the adoption of a statement by another person. For instance, a party's action on the basis of statements contained in a document written by another person constitutes adoption of those statements.[16] In

---

[12] *See* discussion in **Treatise** at § 801.31.
[13] *See, e.g.,* United States v. Harrison, 296 F.3d 994, 1000–1002 (10th Cir. 2002) (child victim's statement was properly admitted as defendant's adoptive admission when defendant, at conclusion of statement, admitted performing acts described and apologized).
[14] *See, e.g.,* United States v. Woods, 301 F.3d 556, 561 (7th Cir. 2002).
[15] *See, e.g.,* United States v. Orellana-Blanco, 294 F.3d 1143, 1148–1149 (9th Cir. 2002).
[16] *See, e.g.,* Sea-Land Serv. v. Lozen Int'l, LLC, 285 F.3d 808, 821–822 (9th Cir. 2002) (plaintiff's employee's act of forwarding to defendant e-mail message she received from another employee of plaintiff, coupled with message of her own indicating that forwarded message showed who was at fault for delay in shipment, constituted adoption of contents of forwarded message; trial court abused its discretion in excluding it).

appropriate circumstances, mere possession of a document may constitute adoption of the statements it contains.[17]

In all cases, the burden is on the proponent of the evidence to show that the behavior, verbal or otherwise, was intended as an adoption.[18] A judge may reject evidence of verbal or non-verbal behavior if it is susceptible to more than one interpretation.[19]

The most troublesome cases are those in which the party remains silent after hearing a damaging statement, because they involve the most ambiguous response. In the case of written statements such as letters or other documents, the mere lack of a response is generally considered insufficient to show that the recipient adopted its contents.[20] If, however, the declarant and the party are engaged in such a relationship that the recipient of a written statement would have been expected to take issue with the contents if he or she disagreed with them, adoption may be established by evidence that the recipient did not respond at all.[21]

When silence is offered as evidence of adoption pursuant to Rule 801(d)(2)(B), the burden is on the proponent to convince the judge that, in the circumstances of the case, a failure to respond is so unnatural that it supports the inference that the party acquiesced in the statement.[22] The trial court's determination is guided by consideration of the following factors:[23]

- The nature of the statement.

---

[17] *See, e.g.,* United States v. Pulido-Jacobo, 377 F.3d 1124, 1132 (10th Cir. 2004) (test to determine whether party has "manifested an adoption or belief in" truth of a document by possessing it is whether surrounding circumstances tie possessor and document together in some meaningful way).

[18] *See, e.g.,* Vazquez v. Lopez-Rosario, 134 F.3d 28, 35 (1st Cir. 1998) (burden is on proponent to show that circumstances surrounding conversation demonstrate that party manifested acquiescence in statement).

[19] *See, e.g.,* National Bank of N. America v. Cinco Investors, Inc., 610 F.2d 89, 93–94 (2d Cir. 1979) (evidence should not be considered when it was not clear that person who allegedly adopted statement had made up his or her mind about statement's truth or falsity).

[20] *See, e.g.,* Ricciardi v. Children's Hosp. Medical Ctr., 811 F.2d 18, 24 (1st Cir. 1987) (when physician first learned of note he might not have had sufficient knowledge to assess its veracity).

[21] *See, e.g.,* Megarry Bros. v. United States, 404 F.2d 479, 488 (8th Cir. 1968) (trial court correctly admitted invoices sent to plaintiff and instructed jury that plaintiff's failure to reply was evidence tending to show that it did not dispute contents of invoice, since parties were involved in business transaction involving substantial amount of money).

[22] *See, e.g.,* United States v. Ward, 377 F.3d 671, 676 (7th Cir. 2004) (sister's statement that missing money was money defendant had obtained by robbing bank was statement of type persons would normally respond to if they were innocent, so defendant's silence could properly be taken as adoptive admission).

[23] *See, e.g.,* Weston-Smith v. Cooley Dickinson Hosp., Inc., 282 F.3d 60, 67–68 (1st Cir. 2002).

- The identity of the person offering the testimony.

- The identity of the maker of the statement.

- The context in which the statement was made.

- Whether the circumstances as a whole show that the lack of a denial is so unnatural as to support an inference that the statement was true.

The proponent cannot carry its burden if there are other explanations for the alleged declarant's silence, such as the declarant's lack of information to formulate a denial.[24] The proponent also cannot carry its burden in the absence of proof that the party heard and understood the statement.[25] Similarly, silence in the face of the statement is not adoption in the absence of proof that the party had the capacity to respond.[26]

In criminal cases there are constitutional limitations on the extent to which silence can be taken as evidence of adoption of another's statement, at least when the statement was made by, or in the presence of, law enforcement officers. The Supreme Court has recognized, for example, that no adverse inference may be drawn from defendant's failure to deny accusations after being warned of the right to remain silent.[27] However, the prosecution may use the defendant's silence in response to an accusation for impeachment when the accusation came before the defendant acquired the right to receive *Miranda* warnings.[28] It is, therefore, conceivable that it would be appropriate to use silence in those circumstances for all purposes, but no court has yet sanctioned such use of a criminal defendant's silence.[29]

---

24 *See, e.g.,* Weston-Smith v. Cooley Dickinson Hosp., Inc., 282 F.3d 60, 67–68 (1st Cir. 2002).

25 *See, e.g.,* United States v. Sears, 663 F.2d 896, 904 (9th Cir. 1981) (defendant's silence does not amount to adoption of statement when there is question whether defendant actually heard and understood statement because of her hearing disability).

26 *See, e.g.,* Arpan v. United States, 260 F.2d 649, 655–657 (8th Cir. 1958) (defendant did not adopt incriminating remarks of another person by not responding to those remarks when defendant was, at time remarks were made, in condition described as childlike, depressed, in state of shock, and under influence of liquor).

27 Doyle v. Ohio, 426 U.S. 610, 617, 96 S. Ct. 2240, 49 L. Ed.2d 91 (1976) (silence following receipt of *Miranda* warnings is "insolubly ambiguous").

28 Fletcher v. Weir, 455 U.S. 603, 605–606, 102 S. Ct. 1309, 71 L. Ed.2d 490 (1982) (per curiam); Jenkins v. Anderson, 447 U.S. 231, 238–239, 100 S. Ct. 2124, 65 L. Ed.2d 86 (1980).

29 *See, e.g.,* United States v. Caro, 637 F.2d 869, 876 (2d Cir. 1981) ("[w]hatever the future impact of *Jenkins* may be, we have found no decision permitting the use of silence, even the silence of a suspect who has been given no *Miranda* warnings and is entitled to none, as part of the Government's direct case").

[4]—Admissions: Authorized[30]

Rule 801(d)(2)(C) restates the orthodox proposition that a statement by a person authorized by a party to make a statement is treated as though the statement had been made by the party, *i.e.,* as an admission.[31] The rule provides as follows:

Rule 801(d)(2)(C). Definitions.

(d) Statements which are not hearsay.—A statement is not hearsay if—

. . .

(2) Admission by party-opponent. The statement is offered against a party and is . . . (C) a statement by a person authorized by the party to make a statement concerning the subject. . . . The contents of the statement shall be considered but are not alone sufficient to establish the declarant's authority under subdivision (C). . . .

[Adopted Jan. 2, 1975, effective July 1, 1975; amended Mar. 2, 1987, effective Oct 1, 1987; amended Apr, 11, 1997, effective Dec. 1, 1997.]

Authority to make a statement can be bestowed upon virtually anyone, either implicitly or expressly. Implicit authority to make statements may be inferred from the scope of the actual authority the party gave to the person who made the statement. Thus, a lawyer engaged to represent a party in litigation implicitly has that party's authorization to make statements concerning the underlying matters in the course of managing the litigation.[32]

However, relationships such as marriage, friendship, and most forms of employment do not necessarily imply the authority to make a statement on behalf of the other person. In such cases, authority must be indicated expressly or demonstrated by particular circumstances.[33]

---

[30]   *See* discussion in **Treatise** at § 801.32.

[31]   Fed. R. Evid. 801(d)(2)(C); *see, e.g.,* Michaels v. Michaels, 767 F.2d 1185, 1201 (7th Cir. 1985) (broker); United States v. Da Silva, 725 F.2d 828, 831–832 (2d Cir. 1983) (interpreter); B-W Acceptance Corp. v. Porter, 568 F.2d 1179, 1182 (5th Cir. 1978) (branch manager).

[32]   *See, e.g.,* Hanson v. Waller, 888 F.2d 806, 814 (11th Cir. 1989) (letter from plaintiff's attorney to defendant's attorney was properly admitted under Fed. R. Evid. 801(d)(2)(C), since attorney has authority to make admissions that are directly related to management of litigation); United States v. McKeon, 738 F.2d 26, 27–34 (2d Cir. 1984) (counsel's opening statement at second trial was admissible against party at third trial; absent contrary evidence, it may reasonably be assumed that party authorized attorney to present versions of facts in both statements).

[33]   *See, e.g.,* Michaels v. Michaels, 767 F.2d 1185, 1201 (7th Cir. 1985) (statements about possible sale of company made by person authorized by company to serve as its broker were admissible under Rule 801(d)(2)(C) as statements by person authorized to make statements about subject); Reid Brothers Logging Co. v. Ketchikan Pulp Co., 699 F.2d 1292, 1306–1307 (9th Cir. 1983) (report on party company's operations written by employee of related company at request of

Courts have historically applied agency law to determine whether the declarant was authorized by the party to make the statement at issue.[34] In something of a departure from standard agency doctrine, however, statements made by an agent to the principal are generally also treated as party admissions.[35] Usually, this issue arises in connection with internal reports on a business's financial circumstances that were prepared by an outside entity.[36]

There is some question about the status of experts hired by a party. Some cases hold that expert witnesses cannot be viewed as the party's agent, since they are supposed to testify impartially in the sphere of their expertise.[37] However, the Fifth Circuit has held otherwise.[38]

Under Rule 801(d)(2), the court may consider the contents of an alleged agent's statement in determining whether the person was authorized by the party to make statements concerning that subject.[39] The contents of the declarant's statements alone, however, are insufficient to prove the declarant's authority. Thus, independent proof is necessary.[40]

[5]—Admissions: Vicarious[41]

Rule 801(d)(2)(D) makes admissible statements by a party's agents or employees made within the scope of their employment regardless of whether they have

---

party's board chairman and distributed by party to its executives, officers, and managers was clearly authorized by party and admissible under Fed. R. Evid. 801(d)(2)(C)).

[34] *See, e.g.,* United States v. Da Silva, 725 F.2d 828, 831–832 (2d Cir. 1983) (statements made by defendant through interpreter were admissible under Fed. R. Evid. 801(d)(2)(C); interpreter for party acts as agent of party unless contrary circumstances appear; citing Restatement (Second) of Agency).

[35] *See, e.g.,* Reid Brothers Logging Co. v. Ketchikan Pulp Co., 699 F.2d 1292, 1306–1307 n.25 (9th Cir. 1983).

[36] *See, e.g.,* United States v. Draiman, 784 F.2d 248, 256–257 (7th Cir. 1986) (exhibit showing defendant's corporation's accounts receivable, prepared by defendant's accountant, was authorized statement under Rule 801(d)(2)(C)).

[37] *See, e.g.,* Kirk v. Raymark Indus., Inc., 61 F.3d 147, 163–164 (3d Cir. 1995) (expert who testified for defendant in previous unrelated trial was not authorized by party for purposes of Rule 801(d)(2)(C)).

[38] *See, e.g.,* Collins v. Wayne Corp., 621 F.2d 777, 780–782 (5th Cir. 1980) (expert hired to investigate claim was party's agent, so that expert's report and deposition were admissible under Rule 801(d)(2)(C); error to exclude expert's deposition).

[39] Fed. R. Evid. 801(d); *see* Committee Note (1997) (reprinted in **Treatise** at § 801App.04[2]); *see, e.g.,* Los Angeles News Serv., Inc. v. CBS Broadcasting, Inc., 305 F.3d 924, 934 (9th Cir. 2002) (while trial court may consider content of statement in determining whether it is authorized admission under Rule 801(d)(2)(C), proponent must offer extrinsic evidence that statement qualifies).

[40] Fed. R. Evid. 801(d)(2).

[41] *See* discussion in **Treatise** at § 801.33.

"speaking authority." The drafters favored this rule, whose effect is to permit the reception of all statements by an agent or employee that are relevant to his or her employment, because they found that the restricted "speaking authority" formula embodied in the orthodox authorized admissions rule frequently resulted in the rejection of highly probative evidence. Rule 801(d)(2)(D) provides:

Rule 801(d)(2)(D).　Definitions.

(d) Statements which are not hearsay.—A statement is not hearsay if—

. . .

(2) Admission by party-opponent.—The statement is offered against a party and is . . . (D) a statement by the party's agent or servant concerning a matter within the scope of the agency or employment, made during the existence of the relationship. . . . The contents of the statement shall be considered but are not alone sufficient to establish . . . the agency or employment relationship and scope thereof under subdivision (D). . . .

[*Adopted Jan. 2, 1975, effective July 1, 1975; amended Mar. 2, 1987, effective Oct 1, 1987; amended Apr, 11, 1997, effective Dec. 1, 1997.*]

Rule 801(d)(2)(D) makes admissible statements by a party's agents or servants concerning matters within the scope of their agency or employment and made during the existence of the agency or employment relationship.[42] The proponent of a statement offered under this provision must show the following foundation:

- The existence of the employment or agency relationship between the declarant and the party.[43] The courts apply the federal common law of agency to determine whether the declarant constitutes an agent who is capable of making admissions on behalf of a party under Rule 801(d)(2)(D).[43.1] Moreover, it is not sufficient for the declarant to have this relationship with a predecessor in interest of the party.[44]

---

[42]　Fed. R. Evid. 801(d)(2)(D).

[43]　*See, e.g.,* Rotec Indus, Inc., v. Mitsubishi Corp., 215 F.3d 1246, 1254 (Fed. Cir. 2000) (plaintiff had burden to prove agency as foundation for admission of alleged agent's statement as vicarious admission; plaintiff failed to do so when it failed to show that defendant had right to control manner and method in which alleged agent carried out work).

[43.1]　*See, e.g.,* Gomez v. Rodriguez, 344 F.3d 103, 116 (1st Cir. 2003) (party's spouse was not his agent simply by reason of marital relationship).

[44]　*See, e.g.,* Calhoun v. Baylor, 646 F.2d 1158, 1163 (6th Cir. 1981) (declarations of agents of bankrupt could not be considered vicarious admissions by trustee in bankruptcy, as successor in interest).

- That the statement relates to a matter within the scope of the agency or employment[45]

- That the statement was made during the existence of the agency or employment relationship.[46]

The relationship between the declarant and the party against whom the statement is offered need not be analyzed as thoroughly when the statement is offered as a vicarious admission under Rule 801(d)(2)(D) as when the statement is offered as an authorized admission under Rule 801(d)(2)(C).[47] Thus, statements made by a person who is in the employ of an entity that is in a contractual relationship with a party may be vicarious admissions of that party.[47.1] Similarly, statements made by a lawyer retained to represent a party that were made in connection with the representation may be admissible as against a hearsay objection under Rule 801(d)(2)(D).[47.2]

As is the case with authorized admissions under Rule 801(d)(2)(C), the agent's or employee's statements fulfilling the requirements of Rule 801(d)(2)(D) are admissible whether made to the party or to someone else. Moreover, it is not necessary that the statement, itself, be within the scope of the declarant's agency; it need only relate "to a matter within the scope of the agency."[48]

Vicarious admissions are admissible against the government in criminal cases.[49.1] The Rule does not, however, warrant the admission of out-of-court

---

[45] *See, e.g.,* Martha Graham School & Dance Found., Inc. v. Martha Graham Center of Contemporary Dance, Inc., 380 F.3d 624, 644 (2d Cir. 2004) (when plaintiff admitted that person who made out-of-court statement was his assistant at time she made statement and that statement was made in course of assistant's employment, statement was not hearsay but was admission of party opponent under Rule 801(d)(2)(D)).

[46] *See, e.g.,* Young v. James Green Mgmt., Inc., 327 F.3d 616, 622–623 (7th Cir. 2003) (statement made by employee in his resignation letter was not admissible as vicarious admission against employer under Rule 801(d)(2)(D) because declarant, having resigned, was no longer employee when he made statement).

[47] *Compare* Lloyd v. Professional Realty Servs., Inc., 734 F.2d 1428, 1433 (11th Cir. 1984) (statements of defendant's employee were properly excluded when offered under Rule 801(d)(2)(C) without showing of employee's authority to speak on employer's behalf) *with* United States v. Brothers Constr. Co. of Ohio, 219 F.3d 300, 310–311 (4th Cir. 2000) (grand jury testimony of corporate officer-in-house counsel was vicarious admission of corporate defendant because declarant's testimony related to matters clearly within scope of his employment; no need, under Rule 801(d)(2)(D), to show that making of statement was within declarant's authority).

[47.1] *See, e.g.,* Beck v. Haik, 377 F.3d 624, 639–640 (6th Cir. 2004).

[47.2] *See, e.g.,* United States v. Amato, 356 F.3d 216, 220 (2d Cir. 2004).

[48] *See, e.g.,* Larch v. Mansfield Mun. Elec. Dep't, 272 F.3d 63, 72–73 (1st Cir. 2001).

[49.1] *See, e.g.,* United States v. Barile, 286 F.3d 749, 758 (4th Cir. 2002) (government witness's prior statement that component testing of integrated heart monitor was appropriate in connection with seeking FDA approval would be admissible against government in criminal trial because statements of government informers as admissions of the government.[49.1]

Under Rule 801(d)(2), the court may consider the contents of an alleged agent's or employee's statement in determining the existence and scope of any relationship between the declarant and the party.[50] The contents of the declarant's statements alone, however, are insufficient; independent proof is necessary.[51]

[6]—Admissions: Co-conspirators' Statements[52]

[a]—Scope and Text of Rule

Rule 801(d)(2)(E) provides that a statement of a declarant is not hearsay when offered against a party if all of the following requirements are proved:[53]

- There was a conspiracy of which the declarant and the party were both members.[54]

- The declarant made the statement in furtherance of that conspiracy.[55]

- The declarant made the statement during the course of that conspiracy.[56]

The rule applies in both civil[56.1] and criminal cases, although it is most frequently invoked in criminal litigation.

Rule 801(d)(1)(E) provides as follows:

Rule 801(d)(2)(E).   Definitions.

(d) Statements which are not hearsay.—A statement is not hearsay if—

---

declarant made statement in her capacity as employee of government and in course of performing her duties).

49.1 *See, e.g.,* United States v. Yildiz, 355 F.3d 80, 82 (2d Cir. 2004).

50 Fed. R. Evid. 801(d); *see* Committee Note (1997) (reprinted in **Treatise** at § 801App.04[2]); *see, e.g.,* Los Angeles News Serv., Inc. v. CBS Broadcasting, Inc., 305 F.3d 924, 934 (9th Cir. 2002) (while trial court may consider contents of statement in determining whether it is vicarious admission under Rule 801(d)(2)(D), proponent must offer extrinsic evidence that statement qualifies).

51 Fed. R. Evid. 801(d)(2); *see, e.g.,* Gomez v. Rodriguez, 344 F.3d 103, 116 (1st Cir. 2003) (agency relationship must be shown by independent evidence before out-of-court statement by purported agent may be admitted under Rule 801(d)(2)(D)).

52 *See* discussion in **Treatise** at § 801.34.

53 *See* [b], *below.*

54 *See* [c], *below.*

55 *See* [d], *below.*

56 *See* [e], *below.*

56.1 *See, e.g.,* Viazis v. American Ass'n of Orthodontists, 314 F.3d 758, 767 (5th Cir. 2002) (trial court considered admissibility of letter as coconspirator statement in civil antitrust action, but found that plaintiff failed to prove existence of conspiracy).

. . .

(2) Admission by party-opponent.—The statement is offered against a party and is . . . (E) a statement by a coconspirator of a party during the course and in furtherance of the conspiracy. The contents of the statement shall be considered but are not alone sufficient to establish . . . the existence of the conspiracy and the participation therein of the declarant and the party against whom the statement is offered under subdivision (E).

[*Adopted Jan. 2, 1975, effective July 1, 1975; amended Mar. 2, 1987, effective Oct 1, 1987; amended Apr, 11, 1997, effective Dec. 1, 1997.*]

When conspiracy is charged, the statements may be admissible even though the conspiracy has not been proved beyond a reasonable doubt.[57] There need not be a conspiracy count in the indictment to make this provision applicable,[58] nor is there a requirement that any charged conspiracy be the same as the one that forms the basis for admitting statements.[59] Moreover, it may not be necessary that the goal of the conspiracy be the achievement of an illegal end.[60]

As long as the declarant and the party against whom the statement is offered were members of the conspiracy at the time the statement was made, any witness who heard the statement may recount it at trial. This is true irrespective of whether the

[57] United States v. Dworken, 855 F.2d 12, 23-24 (1st Cir. 1988) (in narcotics case when jury acquitted on conspiracy count, appellate court upheld admission of co-conspirators' statements, since trial judge could have found existence of separate conspiracies by a preponderance of the evidence).

[58] United States v. Richards, 204 F.3d 177, 202–203 (5th Cir. 2000) (even though no conspiracy was charged, court found testimony admissible under Rule 801(d)(2)(E) because there was sufficient evidence to show that defendants conspired in effort to defraud); United States v. Wiles, 102 F.3d 1043, 1065 (10th Cir. 1996) (the "party need not be charged with conspiracy. The rule applies where the evidence shows two or more individuals acting in concert despite the absence of a conspiracy charge"); United States v. Manning, 56 F.3d 1188, 1196–1197 (9th Cir. 1995) (no conspiracy charge required).

[59] United States v. Bowe, 221 F.3d 1183, 1193 (11th Cir. 2000) (conspiracy that forms part of basis for admission of coconspirator's statement need not be same as conspiracy charged against defendant); United States v. Ellis, 156 F.3d 493, 496 (3d Cir. 1998) (coconspirator's statements to undercover agent were non-hearsay even though they were made in conspiracy separate from that charged); United States v. Arce, 997 F.2d 1123, 1128–1129 (5th Cir. 1993) (different conspiracies).

[60] *Compare* United States v. LaHue, 261 F.3d 993, 1009 (10th Cir. 2001) (admission of documents written by participants in lawful common plan as harmless error) *with* United States v. Layton, 855 F.2d 1388, 1397–1400 (9th Cir. 1988) (critical question is whether confederate was acting as defendant's agent when he made statement sought to be admitted; in prosecution for murder of congressman in Guyana, statements made in furtherance of conspiracy to prevent congressman from learning truth of conditions in Jonestown would qualify as co-conspirators' statements whether enterprise was legal or illegal).

person to whom the statement was made or the witness to the statement was a member of the conspiracy.[61]

[b]—Preliminary Questions for the Court

In *Bourjaily v. United States,* [62] the Supreme Court resolved a number of issues about how Rule 801(d)(1)(E) should be interpreted. It is the trial court, rather than the jury, that must determine whether the four requirements of the rule have been satisfied.[63] To ask the jurors to consider highly prejudicial statements of co-conspirators only if they first find the existence of the conspiracy and the defendant's participation in it is to present them with too tricky a task. Consequently, judges should refrain from advising juries about the admissibility of co-conspirator's statements, though jurors may be instructed that such evidence should be treated with caution.[64]

In *Bourjaily,* the Supreme Court also held "that when the preliminary facts relevant to Rule 801(d)(1)(E) are disputed, the offering party must prove them by a preponderance of the evidence."[65] Consequently, the government must prove by a preponderance of the evidence that there was a conspiracy involving the declarant and the defendant and that the statement at issue was made during the course of the conspiracy and in furtherance of the conspiracy.[66]

The *Bourjaily* Court also resolved the issue of what evidence the trial court may consider in making its preliminary determinations: "Rule [104] on its face allows the trial judge to consider any evidence whatsoever, bound only by the rules of privilege."[67] A trial court may, therefore, examine the hearsay statements sought

---

[61] *See, e.g.,* United States v. Frazier, 274 F.3d 1185 (8th Cir. 2001) (fact that witness who testified to coconspirator's out-of-court statement was not part of conspiracy and was government informant does not preclude statement's admissibility under Rule 801(d)(2)(E)); United States v. Beech-Nut Nutrition Corp., 871 F.2d 1181, 1198 (2d Cir. 1989) (statement of co-conspirator to fellow employee, uninvolved in conspiracy but knowledgeable about events, was admission under Rule 801(d)(2)(E)); *see* [c], *below.*

[62] Bourjaily v. United States, 483 U.S. 171, 107 S. Ct. 2775, 97 L. Ed. 2d 144 (1987).

[63] Bourjaily v. United States, 483 U.S. 171, 175, 107 S. Ct. 2775, 97 L. Ed. 2d 144 (1987).

[64] United States v. Peters, 791 F.2d 1270, 1285–1286 (7th Cir. 1986) (although district judge's comments on admissibility of co-conspirator's statements were "ill-advised," they caused no prejudice to defendants because the court later withdrew its comments and told the jury it could disregard them, citing **Treatise**).

[65] 483 U.S. 171, 176, 107 S. Ct. 2775, 2779, 97 L. Ed. 2d 144, 153 (1987).

[66] *See, e.g.,* United States v. Burgos, 239 F.3d 72, 73 (1st Cir. 2001) (proponent must prove foundation facts by preponderance of evidence); United States v. Allison, 908 F.2d 1531, 1533–1534 (11th Cir. 1990).

[67] Bourjaily v. United States, 483 U.S. 171, 178, 107 S. Ct. 2775, 2780, 97 L. Ed. 2d 144, 154 (1987) (Court relied on plain meaning of Rule 104(a)); *see also* United States v. Burgos, 239 F.3d 72, 75 (1st Cir. 2001) (independent corroborating evidence of foundation facts sufficient, coupled

to be admitted in making a preliminary factual determination pursuant to Rule 104(a).**⁶⁸** The *Bourjaily* Court reserved decision on "whether the courts below could have relied solely upon [the] hearsay statements to determine that a conspiracy had been established by a preponderance of the evidence."**⁶⁹**

The 1997 amendment to Rule 801(d)(2)(E) both codified the holding that a trial court may examine hearsay statements themselves in determining whether they qualify for admission and resolved the remaining issue by providing that the contents of the declarant's statement do not alone suffice to establish a conspiracy in which the declarant and the defendant participated (*see* [a], *above*). The Advisory Committee noted that the court must also consider the circumstances surrounding the statement, such as the identity of the speaker, the context in which the statement was made, or evidence corroborating the contents of the statement in making its determination as to each preliminary question.**⁷⁰**

While some circuits have endorsed preferred orders of proof that require trial courts, whenever possible, to determine the admissibility of co-conspirator statements before the statements are admitted in order to avoid jury prejudice,**⁷¹** all appellate courts recognize that the trial court must have considerable discretion to control the order of a trial.**⁷²** To the extent possible, the admissibility of co-

---

with statements of alleged coconspirator, to warrant admission of statements); United States v. Johnson, 911 F.2d 1394, 1403 (10th Cir. 1990) (in a heroin conspiracy prosecution, the hearsay testimony of an alleged coconspirator was properly admitted where there was sufficient evidence, including both the statements themselves and evidence independent of the statements, to link defendant to the conspiracy).

[68] United States v. Petty, 132 F.3d 373, 379–380 (7th Cir. 1997) (conspirators' statements admissible to establish existence of conspiracy).

[69] 483 U.S. at 181, 107 S. Ct. at 2781–2782, 97 L. Ed. 2d at 156. United States v. Silverman, 861 F.2d 571, 579–580 (9th Cir. 1988) (all members of the court agree that the government must produce some evidence corroborating the co-conspirator's statements but majority reverses on the ground that the additional evidence consisted of wholly innocuous conduct and statements by the defendant which were completely consistent with defendant's unawareness of the conspiracy, while the dissent argues that the majority's approach reinstates the pre-*Bourjaily* no bootstrapping rule).

[70] *See, e.g.,* United States v. Williams, 340 F.3d 563, 568 (8th Cir. 2003) (testimony that undercover officer saw defendant give drugs to his sister under circumstances suggesting that she was expected to sell them was sufficient evidence, combined with statements made by sister to undercover officer, to support finding that statements were made pursuant to conspiracy including defendant and his sister).

[71] *See, e.g.,* United States v. James, 590 F.2d 575, 581–582 (5th Cir. 1979) (en banc); United States v. Petersen, 611 F.2d 1313, 1330 (10th Cir. 1979).

[72] *See, e.g.,* United States v. West, 58 F.3d 133 (5th Cir. 1995) (no hearing required to determine whether conspiracy exists, and coconspirator evidence could be admitted before district court ruled on the issue); United States v. Beaumont, 972 F.2d 553 (5th Cir. 1992) (per curiam) (coconspirator statement admitted conditionally, deferred ruling until the end of the prosecution's case); United States v. Marquardt, 695 F.2d 1300, 1304–1305 (5th Cir. 1983) (failure to hold *James*

conspirator statements should be discussed at the pre-trial conference, or if at trial, outside the hearing of the jury.[73] In most cases, the court will be able to make its determination on the basis of colloquy, documents marked in advance of trial, proof from the pre-trial or suppression hearings, and the testimony of one or two witnesses. The court should rule conditionally on admissibility as soon as possible. Delay will inhibit the government in putting in its proof in the most desirable order, and may inconvenience witnesses who may have to return to tell the part of their story dealing with the co-conspirator's statement. In *Bourjaily,* the Court declined to "express an opinion on the proper order of proof that trial courts should follow in concluding that the preponderance standard has been satisfied in an on-going trial."[74]

[c]—Existence and Membership of Conspiracy

For a statement to be "not hearsay" under Rule 801(d)(2)(E), the proponent must show the existence of a conspiracy whose membership includes the declarant and the party against whom the statement is offered.[75] The existence of a conspiracy for this purpose is proved by showing the following elements:[76]

- The existence of an agreement between at least two persons.[77]

- The objective of the agreement was to accomplish an illegal goal, or a legal goal by the use of illegal means.

- The performance of one or more overt acts by at least one of the parties to the agreement in furtherance of the goal of the agreement.

Rule 801(d)(2)(E) does not apply unless the declarant and the party against whom the out-of-court statement is offered are members of the same conspiracy.[78] Thus,

---

hearing not error where trial court determines that hearing would be duplicative of trial and waste time).

[73] United States v. Lance, 853 F.2d 1177, 1184 (5th Cir. 1988) (conspiracy conviction need not be reversed merely because jury heard judge's preliminary finding that a conspiracy existed for purposes of the coconspirator exception).

[74] Bourjaily v. United States, 483 U.S. 171, 176, n.1, 107 S. Ct. 2775, 2779, n.1, 97 L. Ed. 2d 144, 153, n.1 (1987).

[75] Fed. R. Evid. 801(d)(2)(E); *see, e.g.,* United States v. Frazier, 280 F.3d 835, 848 (8th Cir. 2002) (Rule 801(d)(2)(E) does not require statement to have been made to another member of conspiracy; it is sufficient that declarant and person against whom statement is offered were members of conspiracy at time statement was made).

[76] United States v. Oseby, 148 F.3d 1016, 1023–1024 (8th Cir. 1998).

[77] *See, e.g.,* United States v. Miranda-Ortiz, 926 F.2d 172, 176 (2d Cir. 1991) (to be members of conspiracy, each person must have known about it and must have intended to associate with it).

[78] *See, e.g.,* United States v. Murphy, 193 F.3d 1, 7 (1st Cir. 1999) (co-conspirator exclusion operated against defendant only as to statements made during conspiracy in which he and declarant had membership).

statements made in connection with one conspiracy are not party admissions when offered against a person who was not a member of that particular conspiracy. However, it is not necessary that the declarant be identified or identifiable; it is only necessary that the declarant be a member of the conspiracy,.[78.1]

However, a single conspiracy can be very complex, and findings of multiple conspiracies are not common.[79] Moreover, the agreement between the declarant and defendant need only relate to the overall purpose of the conspiracy. A defendant need not have been aware of particular transactions within the conspiracy for statements in furtherance of those transactions to be admissible against him or her.[80] Moreover, the declarant and defendant may otherwise be in violent disagreement.[81]

[d]—In Furtherance

To qualify as "not hearsay" under Rule 801(d)(2)(E), a co-conspirator's statement must have been made "in furtherance" of the conspiracy.[82] In general, this requirement bars "mere narratives of past successes and failures" and a "conspirator's casual comments."[83] On the other hand, it allows admission of any statement that "can reasonably be interpreted as encouraging a co-conspirator or other person to advance the conspiracy, or as enhancing a co-conspirator or other

---

[78.1] *See, e.g.,* United States v. Mahasin, 362 F.3d 1071, 1084 (8th Cir. 2004) (statements by unidentified speakers in recorded telephone conversations; "statements themselves may reasonably be interpreted to establish by a preponderance of the evidence that the unidentified speakers were participants in the conspiracy to kill White and that their statements were made in furtherance of the conspiracy"); *but see* Fed. R. Evid. 801(d)(2) (contents of statement may be considered but "are not alone sufficient" to establish foundational facts for exception).

[79] *See. e.g.,* United States v. Frazier, 213 F.3d 409, 414–415 (7th Cir. 2000) (statements by members of one drug organization were admissible as coconspirator's statements in drug conspiracy trial of members of another drug organization, because evidence of frequent and repeated sales of cocaine between organizations, often on credit, established that organizations were linked and part of single conspiracy); United States v. Alvarez, 833 F.2d 724, 729–730 (7th Cir. 1987) ("[t]he fact that many overt acts occurred over an extended period of time does not necessarily turn a single conspiracy into a multiple conspiracy").

[80] *See e.g.,* United States v. Hunt, 272 F.3d 488, 495 (7th Cir. 2001) (trial court properly admitted statement concerning drug transaction consummated as part of conspiracy's operations, even though defendant was involved only in money-laundering aspects of conspiracy).

[81] *See, e.g.,* United States v. Marino, 277 F.3d 11, 24–26 (1st Cir. 2002) (statements of one conspirator were properly admitted against another because both declarant and defendant were members of overall umbrella conspiracy, even though each was also member of separate faction within umbrella conspiracy fighting each other for control of larger conspiracy).

[82] Fed. R. Evid. 801(d)(2)(E).

[83] *See, e.g.,* United States v. Moss, 138 F.3d 742, 744 (8th Cir. 1998) (prior out-of-court statement, to be made in furtherance of conspiracy, somehow must further conspiracy's objectives, not merely inform listener or reader of declarant's activities).

person's usefulness to the conspiracy."[84]

The "in furtherance" requirement attempts to bridge the gap between the need to control conspiracies, which are inherently secretive and difficult to prove, and the need to protect idle conversations among criminal partners, as well as to minimize the admission of inadvertently misreported or deliberately fabricated evidence.[85]

Many courts construe the in furtherance requirement so broadly that even statements only casually related to the conspiracy satisfy Rule 801(d)(2)(E)'s requirements.[86] Thus the following types of statements have been held to be "in furtherance of the conspiracy":

- Solicitations of other persons to participate in the conspiracy.[87]

- Communications with other conspirators designed to keep all members abreast of developments.[88]

- Statements made to allay fears of other members of conspiracy.[89]

- Statements made to promote adhesiveness among the members of the conspiracy.[90]

---

[84] See, e.g., United States v. Jordan, 260 F.3d 930, 933 (8th Cir. 2001) (statements informing conspirator of identity of source of illegal drugs are "in furtherance" of conspiracy because they are designed to ensure recipient's continued participation in conspiracy).

[85] See, e.g., United States v. Salgado, 250 F.3d 438, 449–450 (6th Cir. 2001) ("Mere 'idle chatter' or conversations which further the speaker's own individual objectives rather than the objectives of the conspiracy are not made in furtherance of the conspiracy. However, statements which identify the participants and their roles in the conspiracy are made 'in furtherance' of a conspiracy").

[86] See, e.g., United States v. Jordan, 260 F.3d 930, 933 (8th Cir. 2001) ("in furtherance" requirement is interpreted broadly); see also United States v. Salgado, 250 F.3d 438, 449 (6th Cir. 2001) ("A statement is made in furtherance of a conspiracy if it was intended to promote conspiratorial objectives; it need not actually further the conspiracy").

[87] See, e.g., United States v. Miles, 290 F.3d 1341, 1351–1352 (11th Cir. 2002) (statement to witness from member of defendant's conspiracy that defendant provided methamphetamine so that member could supply witness with "all the methamphetamine he wanted" was attempt to recruit witness into conspiracy and was in furtherance of conspiracy).

[88] See, e.g., United States v. Tocco, 200 F.3d 401, 419–420 (6th Cir. 2000) (tape recordings of conversations between two of defendant's associates were properly admitted as coconspirator statements because they served conspiracy by keeping conspirators advised of developments).

[89] See, e.g., United States v. Salgado, 250 F.3d 438, 450 (6th Cir. 2001) (statements amounting to reassurance treated as "in furtherance of conspiracy").

[90] See, e.g., United States v. Rivera Newton, 326 F.3d 253, 259–260 (1st Cir. 2003) (conspirator's statements concerning murders of competitors to their supplier were in furtherance of drug distribution conspiracy because they reassured supplier about continuance of organization's operations).

- Statements made informing some members of the conspiracy of the roles played by others in the achievement of the conspiracy's goals.[91]

Indeed, the declarant's primary purpose in making the statement need not have been to further the conspiracy's goals and objectives; it is sufficient if the proponent can show that the statement had at least some beneficial impact on the conspiracy or the conspirators.[92]

Statements are generally admitted if they involve accomplishing transactions within the conspiracy, discuss past events with other members, or simply keep other members up to date.[93] However, narrative declarations that do not serve conspiratorial purposes do not satisfy the "in furtherance" requirement, even if made to another member of the conspiracy.[94] A fortiori, a conspirator's admissions to a law enforcement officer while in custody are not in furtherance of the conspiracy.[95]

[e]—During the Course

For admission under Rule 801(d)(2)(E), a co-conspirator's statement must have been made "during the course" of the conspiracy.[96] Statements made after the main objective of the conspiracy has been either achieved or thwarted do not fall within the rule's coverage.[97]

In determining whether a conspiracy that has allegedly achieved its main objective been abandoned, the trial court must decide how far beyond its stated goal a conspiracy remains effective and active. The courts have determined that con-

---

[91] *See, e.g.,* United States v. Martinez-Medina, 279 F.3d 105, 117 (1st Cir. 2002) (statements by one conspirator to others concerning roles played by certain members and how and where conspiracy operated were in furtherance of conspiracy).

[92] *See, e.g.,* United States v. Shoffner, 826 F.2d 619, 628 (7th Cir. 1987) ("statement need not have been exclusively, or even primarily, made to further the conspiracy"; reasonable basis or plausible interpretation is all the government must show).

[93] *See, e.g.,* United States v. Collazo-Aponte, 216 F.3d 163, 184 (1st Cir. 2000) (co-conspirator's statements to other conspirators regarding murder of rival drug dealer was in furtherance of drug conspiracy, because "the reporting of significant events by one coconspirator to another advances the conspiracy"); United States v. Padilla, 203 F.3d 156, 161 (2d Cir. 2000) (note from defendant to bribed witness was in furtherance of conspiracy to suborn perjury because it provided directions on how witness should testify and reassurances about trial's outcome).

[94] *See, e.g.,* United States v. Manfre, 368 F.3d 832, 838–839 (8th Cir. 2004).

[95] *See, e.g.,* United States v. Williams, 272 F.3d 845, 860 (7th Cir. 2001) (trial court erred in admitting conspirator's statement to law enforcement officer that cash found taped to his body was "drug money").

[96] Fed. R. Evid. 801(d)(2)(E).

[97] *See, e.g.,* In re High Fructose Corn Syrup Antitrust Litig., 295 F.3d 651, 664 (7th Cir. 2002) (witness's refusal to answer questions could not be attributed to any defendant other than their former employer because any conspiracy relating to those questions that also involved any other defendant had long since ended).

spiracies have extended to tasks such as the following:

- The collection of the proceeds of the illegal goal of the conspiracy.[98]

- The destruction of incriminating evidence.[99]

- The obstruction of justice to avoid punishment for the commission of the crimes that were the objective of the conspiracy.[100]

- The disposal of the illegally obtained proceeds.[101]

Statements made during the concealment phase following the achievement of the conspiracy's main objective are generally held not to qualify as co-conspirator statements under Rule 801(d)(2)(E).[102] Some courts, however, admit statements made during the concealment phase if the proponent shows that the concealment was an essential part of the conspiracy.[103]

Statements made before a conspiracy was actually formed fall outside the realm of Rule 801(d)(2)(E). However, statements by earlier-joined conspirators are usually admitted against members who joined later, even though the statements were made before the later-joined member became a member of the conspiracy, based on the theory that the newcomer assumes the risk for what has already happened.[104]

On the other hand, a statement made after a party withdraws from the conspiracy

---

[98] *See, e.g.,* United States v. Emuegbunam, 268 F.3d 377, 395–396 (6th Cir. 2001) (despite arrest of one member, conspiracy continued until his suppliers received payment for heroin they conspired to distribute).

[99] *See, e.g.,* United States v. Medina, 761 F.2d 12, 16–18 (1st Cir. 1985) (kidnaping conspiracy continued through conspirators' determination to burn ransom pickup car).

[100] *See, e.g.,* United States v. Padilla, 203 F.3d 156, 161 (2d Cir. 2000) (note from defendant to bribed witness was properly admitted as co-conspirator statement); United States v. Carter, 721 F.2d 1514, 1524 (11th Cir. 1984) (conspiracy to smuggle drugs encompassed further objective of obstructing justice).

[101] *See, e.g.,* United States v. Fortes, 619 F.2d 108, 117 (1st Cir. 1980) (statement made while unloading of proceeds of bank robbery was co-conspirator statement).

[102] *See, e.g.,* In re High Fructose Corn Syrup Antitrust Litig., 295 F.3d 651, 664 (7th Cir. 2002) (witness's refusal to answer questions as part of effort to conceal conspiracy was not party admission under Rule 801(d)(2)(E), because efforts to conceal conspiracy are generally not themselves part of the conspiracy).

[103] *See, e.g.,* United States v. Gajo, 290 F.3d 922, 929 (7th Cir. 2002) (when one of several major objectives of conspiracy is concealment of its existence, conversation between member and non-member in which member cautions non-member to keep his knowledge of conspiracy confidential is in furtherance of conspiracy; statements of member were admissible under Rule 801(D)(2)(E) and some statements of non-member were admissible for non-hearsay purpose of providing context for statements of member).

[104] United States v. United States Gypsum Co., 333 U.S. 364, 393, 68 S. Ct. 525, 92 L. Ed. 746 (1948) ("With the conspiracy thus fully established, the declarations and acts of the various members, even though made or done prior to the adherence of some to the conspiracy, become admissible against all as declarations or acts of coconspirator in aid of the conspiracy").

is not admissible against that party.[105] However, a party's participation in a conspiracy is presumed to continue unless the withdrawing party takes affirmative steps to leave, such as notifying others in the conspiracy or confessing to police.[106]

Most courts have found that the arrest of a co-conspirator, in and of itself, does not end that person's participation in the conspiracy.[107] However, some cases hold that the statements of a conspirator who has been arrested and is cooperating with the authorities may not be used against other conspirators, even though statements by the continuing conspirators are admissible against the one who was arrested.[108] A conspiracy may be found to have survived the arrest of some or all of its participants if they are able to continue to press toward their goal in spite of their having been arrested.[109]

---

[105] *See, e.g.,* United States v. Abou-Saada, 785 F.2d 1, 8–9 (1st Cir. 1986) (act of coconspirator pointing to defendant not admissible against defendant under coconspirator exclusion as declarant had withdrawn from conspiracy at time action occurred).

[106] United States v. Piper, 298 F.3d 47, 53 (1st Cir. 2002) (to withdraw from a conspiracy, conspirators must "act affirmatively either to defeat or disavow the purposes of the conspiracy," usually by confessing to authorities or by telling co-conspirators that they have abandoned the enterprise; continuing conspiracy, such as this one to sell drugs, is presumed to exist until party makes an affirmative showing that it has terminated; here, court could presume that conspiracy continued past last reported sale); *see, e.g.,* United States v. Troutman, 814 F.2d 1428, 1447–1448 (10th Cir. 1987) (defendant failed to show that he withdrew from conspiracy through affirmative action either by confessing to authorities or by communicating withdrawal in manner reasonably calculated to reach coconspirator; statement of co-conspirator was, therefore, party admission when offered against him).

[107] *See, e.g.,* United States v. Emuegbunam, 268 F.3d 377, 395 (6th Cir. 2001) (defendant's participation in conspiracy was not terminated by his arrest and subsequent cooperation with prosecutors; conspiracy continued until members received payment for heroin they conspired to distribute); United States v. Madrigal, 152 F.3d 777, 781 (8th Cir. 1998) (arrest of co-conspirator did not bar testimony about subsequent incriminating communications between co-conspirator and declarant still participating in conspiracy).

[108] United States v. Saavedra, 684 F.2d 1293, 1298–1299 (9th Cir. 1982) (although "any statement made by Saavedra after her arrest could not be used against her fellow conspirators, any statements made by them in furtherance of the conspiracy are admissible against her as long as the conspiracy survived"); *but see* United States v. Monteleone, 257 F.3d 210, 221–222 (2d Cir. 2001) (statements were admissible even though declarant had become government informant; if conspirator exchanges information with government and still pursues conspiracy's criminal objectives, his or her statements in furtherance of those criminal objectives are admissible against other conspiracy members).

[109] *See, e.g.,* United States v. Persico, 832 F.2d 705, 715–716 (2d Cir. 1987) (trial court properly admitted statements made by co-conspirator while in hiding, and after announcement of indictment and arrests of several conspiracy members; conspiracy lasted at least until time of trial, since facts indicated that "some members of the conspiracy found prison no obstacle to continuing their association with the enterprise").

[f]—Confrontation Rights

The Supreme Court has held that the requirements for complying with Rule 801(d)(1)(E) are identical to those which satisfy the Confrontation Clause. Consequently, once a co-conspirator's statement is admitted, it automatically complies with the dictates of the Sixth Amendment, regardless of whether the declarant is unavailable or whether the statement has been examined for indicia of reliability. See discussion of confrontation in Chapter 14.

CHAPTER 16

Hearsay Exceptions—Availability of Declarant Immaterial*

---

* Chapter revised in 1994 by SANDRA D. KATZ, member of the New York Bar.

§ 16.01　Introduction to Rule 803

Rule 803 governs those exceptions to the hearsay rule that, unlike Rule 804 exceptions, do not require the declarant to be unavailable. Rule 807 establishes a residual exception for hearsay that does not fit into any of the exceptions specified in Rule 803 or Rule 804. Rule 807 is discussed in Chapter 14.

The exceptions in Rule 803 can be grouped into a number of major categories around which the discussion below is organized:

- Spontaneous statements—Rules 803(1)–(4) (*see* §§ 16.02–16.05).

- Written documents and records of both private and public nature—Rules 803(5)–(16), (22), (23) (*see* §§ 16.06–16.08).

- Publications—Rules 803(17), (18) (*see* § 16.09).

- Reputation—Rules 803(19)–(21) (*see* § 16.10).

§ 16.02　Present Sense Impression—Rule 803(1)[1]

[1]—Basis and Text of Rule

Though advocated by Thayer,[1] and acknowledged to exist by a few courts prior to 1975,[2] the hearsay exception for statements of present sense impression was rarely utilized until it was codified as Rule 803(1) of the Federal Rules of Evidence. The rule provides:

Rule 803.　　Hearsay Exceptions; Availability of Declarant Immaterial.

The following are not excluded by the hearsay rule, even though the declarant is available as a witness:

(1)　Present sense impression.—A statement describing or explaining an event or condition made while the declarant was perceiving the event or condition, or immediately thereafter.

[Adopted Jan. 2, 1975, effective July 1, 1975.]

Underlying Rule 803(1) is the assumption that statements of perception substantially contemporaneous with an event are highly trustworthy because there is

---

[1]　*See* discussion in **Treatise** at § 803.03.

[1]　*See* Thayer, *Bedingfield's Case—Declarations as a Part of the Res Gestae*, 15 Am. U. L. Rev. 71, 82-83 (1881).

[2]　*See, e.g.*, Houston Oxygen Co. v. Davis, 139 Tex. 1 (1942); Emens v. Lehigh Valley R.R., 223 F. 810 (N.D.N.Y. 1915).

no memory problem, and little or no opportunity to fabricate.[3] Furthermore, there is also frequently a witness who had the same opportunity to perceive the event as the declarant, thereby providing a check on the veracity of the declarant.[4]

A number of requirements must be met for the statement to be admissible pursuant to Rule 803(1). A discussion of these conditions follows (*see* [2]–[4], *below*).

[2]—Time

The statement must be made while the event or condition is being perceived by the declarant or "immediately thereafter."[1] Precise contemporaneity is not always possible, and a slight lapse of time should not result in the loss of valuable evidence.[2] The trial court must exercise its discretion pursuant to Rule 104(a) to decide whether the lapse of time is justified by the circumstances of the particular case, or whether it undermines the reliability of the evidence. The lapse of time may mean that the witness will not be able to corroborate the declarant's statement. Although corroboration is not a requirement, it is a factor that a court may consider in determining whether a statement not exactly contemporaneous qualifies for admission.[3]

[3]—Perception

While the declarant must have perceived the event or condition about which the statement was made,[1] Rule 803(1) does not require the declarant to have participated in the event described. Consequently, the remarks of a bystander and even

---

[3] *See, e.g.,* United States v. Ruiz, 249 F.3d 643, 646–647 (7th Cir. 2001) (substantial contemporaneity of event and statement minimizes unreliability due to defective recollection or conscious fabrication).

[4] Robinson v. Shapiro, 484 F. Supp. 91, 95 (S.D.N.Y. 1980), *aff'd on other grounds*, 646 F.2d 734 (2d Cir. 1981) (statement trustworthy because witness could independently observe the condition to which the statement referred).

[1] Fed. R. Evid. 803(1); *see, e.g.,* United States v. Santos, 201 F.3d 953, 963 (7th Cir. 2000) (handwritten note appended to typed complaint to Board of Ethics may have been reflective summary of observed conduct, rather than spontaneous reaction to immediate sensation, and was, therefore, not properly admitted as present sense impression).

[2] *See, e.g.,* United States v. Hawkins, 59 F.3d 723, 730 (8th Cir. 1995) (911 tape admissible under present sense impression because it was made within a short time of the event and reliability was corroborated with surrounding circumstances).

[3] See, e.g., United States v. Ruiz, 249 F.3d 643, 647 (7th Cir. 2001) ("courts sometimes focus on the corroboration or the lack thereof in admitting or excluding present sense impressions, but the truth is that the rule does not condition admissibility on the availability of corroboration").

[1] Fed. R. Evid. 803(1); *see, e.g.,* United States v. Murillo, 288 F.3d 1126, 1137 (9th Cir. 2002) (murder victim's statement over telephone to witness that she was with defendant and accomplice was made while declarant was perceiving event and was properly admitted as present sense impression).

of an unidentified bystander are admissible provided the requirements of the exception are met.[2] The less contact the declarant has with the event in question, however, the more difficult it becomes to infer that it was perceived by the declarant.[3] An unidentified declarant's capacity to perceive can neither be substantiated nor attacked;[4] accordingly a court may be more likely to find that the danger of fabrication is too great to justify admission.

It is immaterial according to Rule 803(1) whether declarant is available or present as a witness.[5] When the declarant fails to testify, the court's suspicion of the witness's testimony may lead it to find that the declarant's perception was not established. On the other hand, since the witness can be cross- examined, the court may conclude that the witness's credibility and the declarant's derived credibility can safely be left to the jury. Much will depend on the type of case, the availability of other evidence, the verifying details in the statement, and the setting in which the statement was made.

[4]—Subject Matter

Rule 803(1) requires that the statement be one "describing or explaining" the event or condition.[6] Narratives of past events or statements on other subjects are meant to be excluded by this phraseology because they lack the required contemporaneity that guards against fabrication. A statement evoked by the event but which does not describe or explain it would not be admissible. This limitation may be decisive in when it is questionable whether the event is sufficiently exciting to qualify under Rule 803(2), the excited utterance exception, which does not impose this limitation. The "describing or explaining" limitation should not, however, be interpreted as meaning that the statement must relate directly to the proposition. The statement should be admitted if it might aid the jury in determining what

---

[2] United States v. Medico, 557 F.2d 309, 314–317 (2d Cir. 1977) (bank employee testified that after bank robbery he wrote down license plate number which was called out to him by unidentified bystander to whom it was being relayed by other unidentified bystander).

[3] See United States v. Mitchell, 145 F.3d 572, 576–577 (3d Cir. 1998) (reversible error for court to have admitted anonymous note as present sense impression; record was devoid of circumstances indicating that author of anonymous note actually saw act he or she described).

[4] Cf. Rule 806.

[5] See, e.g., Makuc v. American Honda Motor Co., 835 F.2d 389, 391–392 (1st Cir. 1987) (the trial court properly admitted testimony by two witnesses about what a mechanic had told them about repairing a motorbike; "statements of the out-of-court mechanic . . . amounted to statements that described or explained the condition of the bicycle at the very time the mechanic was engaged in examining it").

[6] Fed. R. Evid. 803(1); see, e.g., United States v. Ruiz, 249 F.3d 643, 646–647 (7th Cir. 2001) (declarant's report to witness over hand-held radio of declarant's observations of defendant's actions was properly admitted as present sense impression because report described what declarant was then observing).

happened, and satisfies the contemporaneity test.[7]

§ 16.03   Excited Utterances—Rule 803(2)[1]

[1]—Rationale and Text of Rule

The hearsay exception for excited utterances, unlike the exception for present sense impressions, had been well-recognized in the federal courts prior to the enactment of the Federal Rules of Evidence. Many of the earlier cases used res gestae terminology, a practice that is no longer appropriate.

Rule 803(2) provides as follows:

Rule 803.   Hearsay Exceptions; Availability of Declarant Immaterial.

The following are not excluded by the hearsay rule, even though the declarant is available as a witness:

. . .

(2) Excited utterance.—A statement relating to a startling event or condition made while the declarant was under the stress of excitement caused by the event or condition.

[Adopted Jan. 2, 1975, effective July 1, 1975.]

The assumption underlying this exception is that a person under the sway of excitement precipitated by an external event will be bereft of the reflective capacity essential for fabrication, so that any statements made while the excitement lasts will be spontaneous and trustworthy.[2] Although some criticism has been voiced about the reliability of statements made under stress, the drafters of Rule 803(2) opted not to lose the relevant evidence that may be admitted pursuant to this exception.

A number of requirements must be met in order for a statement to qualify for admission pursuant to the excited utterance exception. The proponent must demonstrate that: (1) a startling event occurred; (2) the declarant made the statement while under the stress of excitement caused by the startling event; and (3) the

---

[7] *See, e.g.*, United States v. Portsmouth Paving Corp., 694 F.2d 312, 322 (4th Cir. 1982) (statement described contents of telephone conversation); United States v. Earley, 657 F.2d 195, 197–198 (8th Cir. 1981) (declarant victim, after receiving call two days before her murder, said it sounded like defendant).

[1] *See* discussion in **Treatise** at § 803.04.

[2] United States v. Joy, 192 F.3d 761, 767 (7th Cir. 1999) ("exception is premised on the belief that a person is unlikely to fabricate lies (which presumably takes some deliberate reflection) while his mind is preoccupied with the stress of an exciting event").

declarant's statement frelated to the startling event.[3] However, there is no requirement that the declarant would be capable of being qualified as a competent witness.[4]

[2]—Startling Event or Condition

In order for the exception to apply, there must be proof that an event occurred and that it was startling. Ordinarily, proof that the event occurred is furnished either by testimony of witnesses other than the declarant, or by circumstantial evidence that something out of the ordinary occurred. Nevertheless, a statement may be admitted even if the only proof of the startling event is the statement itself.[5] In part, this is because in admissibility determinations conducted pursuant to Rule 104(a), the trial judge is entitled to rely on hearsay.[6]

The court must also determine whether the event was startling.[6.1] The presence of blood, caused by either accident or assault, seems to create an automatic assumption of excitement. Whether non-sanguinary events qualify depends on the judge's assessment of the shock value of the event in question.[7] Statements about non- startling events may be admissible pusuant to Rule 803(1) if they are sufficiently contemporaneous.

[3]—Perception

Rule 803(2) does not expressly state that declarant must have seen the event. Observation is, however, mandated by the requirement that the declarant's ex-

---

[3] United States v. Joy, 192 F.3d 761, 766 (7th Cir. 1999) (thus, declarant must have personally perceived the startling event).

[4] *See, e.g.,* Morgan v. Foretich, 846 F.2d 941, 945–947 (4th Cir. 1988) (a child's statements to her mother about sexual abuse were admissible regardless of the child's competency to testify).

[5] *See, e.g.,* United States v. Brown, 254 F.3d 454, 459–460 (3d Cir. 2001) (citing **Treatise,** occurrence of startling event may be established by contents of statement without additional independent evidence; here, declarant's excitement also helped establish occurrence of event).

[6] Fed. R. Evid. 104(a) ("not bound by the rules of evidence").

[6.1] *See, e.g.,* United States v. Schreane, 331 F.3d 548, 565 (6th Cir. 2003) (trial court did not abuse its discretion in determining that verbal altercation between two persons, during which one threatened to shoot the other, qualifies as startling event).

[7] *Compare* United States v. Hartmann, 958 F.2d 774, 783–784 (7th Cir. 1992) (overhearing one's wife and her lover plotting one's murder was certainly a startling event) *and* David By Berkeley v. Pueblo Supermarket, 740 F.2d 230, 233 (3d Cir. 1984) (fall by eight months pregnant plaintiff onto her stomach was a startling occasion) *with* United States v. Mitchell, 145 F.3d 572, 576–577 (3d Cir. 1998) (reversible error for court to have admitted anonymous note as excited utterance; there was no evidence that parking a car was shocking or exciting event, or any other indication that author was under stress of excitement when note was written) *and* United States v. Wolak, 923 F.2d 1193, 1195–1196 (6th Cir. 1991) (learning, after the fact, of the arrest of a long-time felon is "hardly calculated to produce the spontaneous outburst" that the exception contemplates).

citement be "caused" by the event or condition.[8] Despite the difference in wording, the requirement of perception is identical in Rules 803(1) and (2). The perception need not be proved directly, but may be inferred from the nature of the statement and surrounding circumstances, and the declarant need not be a participant in the event. Moreover, the declarant need not be identified at the trial for the court to be able to conclude that he or she personally perceived the startling event.[9] However, suspicion of the statement's reliability may lead to exclusion, particularly when the risk of fabrication is high because the declarant is an unidentified bystander.[10]

[4]—Under the Stress of Excitement

To justify admission of a statement under Rule 803(2), the court must find both that (a) the declarant was excited because of the event, and (b) the declarant was still excited when making the statement. Courts rarely analyze the first factor separately; they assume that a reasonable person viewing a startling event will be excited, and do not attempt to evaluate the impact of the event on the particular declarant's mind.

In this regard, there is no requirement that the utterance in question be absolutely spontaneous. A declarant's answers to questions may qualify as excited utterances.[11]

[5]—Time

An excited utterance need not be contemporaneous with the startling event to be admissible under Rule 803(2). It need only be contemporaneous with the excitement engendered by the startling event.[12] However, the lapse of days or months since the exciting event may suggest that the declarant is no longer under the stress of excitement.[13]

---

[8] *See, e.g.,* United States v. Joy, 192 F.3d 761, 766 (7th Cir. 1999) (declarant must have personally perceived the startling event).

[9] *See, e.g.,* United States v. Brown, 254 F.3d 454, 461–462 (3d Cir. 2001).

[10] *See, e.g.,* Miller v. Keating, 754 F.2d 507, 511–512 (3d Cir. 1985) (statement by unidentified declarant excluded when external circumstances failed to demonstrate that declarant was in a position to have seen what happened and that he spoke under stress of excitement).

[11] *See* United States v. Joy, 192 F.3d 761, 766 (7th Cir. 1999) (no requirement that excited utterance be absolutely spontaneous; mere fact that declarant was answering questions, rather than giving spontaneous narrative, did not indicate that declarant was not excited).

[12] *See, e.g.,* United States v. Brown, 254 F.3d 454, 460–461 (3d Cir. 2001) (statement made within several minutes of declarants' witnessing startling event while they were visibly in state of excitement qualifies as excited utterance).

[13] *See* Reed v. Thalacker, 198 F.3d 1058, 1061–1062 (8th Cir. 1999) (the days or even months that could have elapsed between events in question and witness's alleged statement rendered excited utterance exception inapplicable in this child molestation case).

When evidence is presented as to declarant's state or behavior, it is usually because considerable time has elapsed between the event and the statement, and the proponent is seeking to establish that defendant was still under nervous stress while making the statement. Since lack of capacity, rather than lack of time, to fabricate is the justification for this exception, the period of acceptable time will frequently be considerably longer than when the statement is being offered as a present sense impression, an exception that rests on the latter rationale.

No particular period of elapsed time is decisive. The crucial point is that the court must be able to find that the declarant's state at the time of making the statement ruled out the possibility of conscious reflection. In making this determination, the court must assess all the factors in the case,[14] including the nature of the startling event,[15] the character of the statement,[16] the condition of the declarant,[17] the identity of the declarant, and the availability of other evidence.

§ 16.04   Then   Existing   Mental,   Emotional,   or   Physical Condition—Rule 803(3)

[1]—Rationale and Text of Rule

Rule 803(3) combines in one provision what are really two exceptions of markedly different characteristics. Statements of then existing physical condition are among the least troubling and complex exceptions to the hearsay rule; statements of mental or emotional condition, on the other hand, pose some of the most difficult issues that have to be faced in applying the hearsay rule.

The rule provides as follows:

> **Rule 803(3).   Hearsay Exceptions; Availability of Declarant Immaterial.**

---

[14] *See, e.g.,* United States v. Marrowbone, 211 F.3d 452, 454 (8th Cir. 2000) (alleged victim's statements he had been sexually molested did not qualify as excited utterances under Rule 803(2) because teenage declarant made them about three hours after incident in question, while he had motive to lie to avoid going to jail for intoxication; also, government failed to show that declarant was still excited at time of statements); United States v. Scarpa, 913 F.2d 993 (2d Cir. 1990) (notwithstanding a lapse of five or six hours, there was little doubt that a witness who had been beaten was still under the stress of the excitement caused by the beating and by his sister's screams).

[15] Morgan v. Foretich, 846 F.2d 941 (4th Cir. 1988) (in child sexual assault cases, time lapse should be measured in terms of first real opportunity to report the incident; in a case involving a three-year-old, a three hour lapse is reasonable; citing **Treatise**).

[16] *See , e.g.,* Lust v. Sealy, Inc., 383 F.3d 580, 588 (7th Cir. 2004) (length, lucidity, and self-congratulatory tone of author's memos refute notion that author lacked capacity to fabricate).

[17] *See, e.g.,* United States v. Baggett, 251 F.3d 1087, 1090 (6th Cir. 2001) (after witness found battered woman unconscious on floor of public restroom in bloody and bruised condition, testimony relating battered woman's statements about her physical and emotional mistreatment by her husband over previous three days was properly admitted as excited utterance).

The following are not excluded by the hearsay rule, even though the declarant is unavailable as a witness: . . .

(3) Then existing mental, emotional, or physical condition.—A statement of the declarant's then existing state of mind, emotion, sensation, or physical condition (such as intent, plan, motive, design, mental feeling, pain, and bodily health), but not including a statement of memory or belief to prove the fact remembered or believed unless it relates to the execution, revocation, identification, or terms of declarant's will.

[*Adopted Jan. 2, 1975, effective July 1, 1975.*]

The joint treatment of these conditions is explicable because, historically, the exception for statements of a presently existing mental state or emotion grew out of the exception for declarations of bodily pain or feeling, and because the basic rationale underlying both exceptions is the same. Both types of statement are considered trustworthy because their spontaneous nature makes them more reliable (or at least no less reliable) than declarations made on the stand at a time when memory may be impaired and external pressures have been brought to bear. As with statements of present sense impressions, of which the instant statements are but a specialized application, the factor of contemporaneity provides some assurance against fabrication.[1] Furthermore, the genuine need for evidence of an individual's physical or mental state might otherwise be unmet since a person's feelings are not directly cognizable by anyone else. Consequently, evidence of such statements is admissible regardless of whether the declarant is available.

[2]—Then Existing Physical Condition[2]

Proof of pain and suffering is frequently called for in personal injury litigation both to establish damages and to show the nature and extent of the injury. While objective conditions may give some indication of the degree of pain involved, the sufferer's own contemporaneous description is often a decidedly superior form of proof.

Rule 803(3) does not require the statement to be made to a physician. It may be testified to by "members of the family, friends or other persons." The rule does not differentiate between words of complaint and gestures or non-verbal sounds of pain. The latter, if instinctive and involuntary, do not fall within the hearsay definition in Rule 801 since they constitute non-assertive conduct, but there is no need to draw

---

[1] *See, e.g.,* United States v. Reyes, 239 F.3d 722, 743 (5th Cir. 2001) (conversation that occurred more than two months after declarant had committed last criminal act pursuant to conspiracy was not sufficiently contemporaneous with crimes to be reliable concerning declarant's state of mind while committing those criminal acts).

[2] *See* discussion in **Treatise** at § 803.05.

this line since they would in either case be admissible.

Since contemporaneity is the guarantee of trustworthiness, statements indicative of reflection rather than spontaneity must be excluded.[3] Consequently, descriptions of past pain or symptoms, and explanations of how the injury occurred may not be admitted pursuant to Rule 803(3).[3.1] Such statements may, however, satisfy other hearsay rules: they may qualify as admissions or prior inconsistent statements pursuant to Rule 801, as excited utterances pursuant to Rule 803(2), as statements for purposes of medical diagnosis or treatment pursuant to Rule 803(4), or under Rule 703 as the basis for testimony by a medical or other expert if "of a type reasonably relied upon by experts in the particular field."[4]

The declaration must be contemporaneous with the physical, emotional or mental feeling, not the precipitating event. While it is irrelevant for the purposes of admissibility whether the statement was made after the claim or controversy arose, the trier of fact may assess this factor in deciding how much weight the statement should be given.

[3]—Then Existing Mental or Emotional Condition

[a]— In General[1]

Before turning to a discussion of the scope of the exception for statements of mental or emotional condition, it is useful to consider the ways in which mental state can be proved, since some of the confusion and complexity stem from a failure to identify hearsay dangers and to distinguish between hearsay and non-hearsay use.

1. The hearsay rule is not involved when a witness testifies about his or her own state of mind at a particular time.

2. A state of mind can be proved circumstantially by statements or conduct which are not intended to assert the truth of the fact being proved. Technically, pursuant to the definitions in Rule 801, proof of such statements or non-verbal conduct does

---

[3] *See, e.g.,* United States v. Carmichael, 232 F.3d 510, 521 (6th Cir. 2000) (for out-of-court statement to be admissible under Rule 803(3), declarant must not have had an opportunity to reflect and possibly fabricate or misrepresent his or her thoughts); Meaney v. United States, 112 F.2d 538, 539 (2d Cir. 1940) ("The warrant for admission is the lack of opportunity or motive for fabrication upon an unexpected occasion to which the declarant responds immediately, and without reflection").

[3.1] *See, e.g.,* United States v. Samaniego, 345 F.3d 1280, 1282 (11th Cir. 2003) (Rule 803(3) does not except from hearsay rule declarant's statements as to why he or she felt as he or she did, or statements concerning beliefs that lead him or her to feel as he or she did.).

[4] *See, e.g.,* Harrigan v. New England Mut. Life Ins. Co., 693 F. Supp. 1531, 1532 (S.D.N.Y. 1988) (letter from plaintiff's doctor stating that plaintiff complained of headaches held admissible as "memorialization of a statement of a then existing mental, emotional, or physical condition").

[1] *See* discussion in **Treatise** at § 803.05.

not raise a hearsay problem at all under the Federal Rules of Evidence.[1.1] Nevertheless, further discussion is warranted under Rule 803(3) because courts frequently do not distinguish between the two uses, and because even statements that are technically non-hearsay may pose hearsay dangers.[1.2]

3. Mental state is sometimes proved as part of a so called "verbal act."[2] The statement is not hearsay because it is not being used assertively; it is admitted to shed light on an otherwise ambiguous relevant act, such as handing over money.[2.1]

4. A statement may be proffered on the theory that it is probative of declarant's then existing state of mind, such as fear, knowledge, or belief, and this state of mind is the issue to be proved.[2.2] This is a hearsay use, but Rule 803(3) applies.

5. A statement may be proffered to prove declarant's then existing state of mind not as an end in itself, but as the basis for an inference that the declarant subsequently acted in accordance with the earlier expressed intent.[2.3] This again is a hearsay use, but the statement is admissible pursuant to Rule 803(3).

6. A statement may be proffered to prove the declarant's then existing state of mind as the basis for an inference that declarant had previously acted in a particular way.[2.4] Rule 803(3) admits such statements only if they relate to the execution, revocation, identification or terms of declarant's will.

[b]—Mental State in Issue[3]

The least complicated situation involving mental state to which Rule 803(3) applies is when the statement is used to evidence a state of mind in issue—that is

---

[1.1] *See, e.g.,* United States v. Cline, 570 F.2d 731, 734–735 (8th Cir. 1978) (in murder prosecution, testimony by witness as to conversation in which victim threatened defendant was not hearsay; citing **Treatise**).

[1.2] *See, e.g.,* United States v. Miller, 874 F.2d 1255, 1263–1265 (9th Cir. 1989) (statements relating to defendant's beliefs two hours before were properly excluded).

[2] *See* Chapter 14.

[2.1] *See, e.g.,* United States v. Hernandez, 842 F.2d 82, 87–88 (5th Cir. 1988) (tape recording offered to explain that defendant was merely offering codefendant a ride when arrest occurred, not dealing drugs, inadmissible since tape did not contain any statement as to declarant's state of mind).

[2.2] *See, e.g.,* United States v. Gomez, 927 F.2d 1530, 1535–1536 (11th Cir. 1991) (while evidence may have been relevant to defendant's state of mind as to his motives for making trip, rule relates expressly to statement concerning declarant's state of mind).

[2.3] *See, e.g.,* United States v. Torres, 901 F.2d 205, 239–240 (2d Cir. 1990) (declarant's out-of-court statement of intent was admissible to prove declarant acted in accordance therewith, but exclusion held harmless).

[2.4] *See, e.g.,* United States v. Cianci, 378 F.3d 71, 106–107 (1st Cir. 2004) (defendant's hearsay statement denying his corruption was inadmissible to show that he had probably not engaged in past acts of corruption).

[3] *See* **Treatise** at § 803.05[2].

to say when the state of mind is the material proposition or is used to infer the truth or falsity of a material proposition. The declarant's state of mind may be relevant in a wide variety of contexts. For example, statements have been admitted to show such matters as the state of mind of customers on the issue of good will,[4] motive to prove guilt,[5] competency to enter into legal transactions,[6] intent as a material proposition,[7] and fear as a material proposition on a charge of extortion.[8]

Rule 803(3) restates the traditional requirement that the statement must relate to a then existing state of mind. However, courts generally admit some statements indicative of the mental state in issue even if they were made before or after the moment in question on the assumption that states of mind have a certain degree of continuity. The trial court must decide whether a given statement falls within or without this period of continuous mental process.[9] In making this determination, the court should consider the hearsay dangers involved, as well as the availability of the declarant as a witness.

[c]—State of Mind To Show Subsequent Act[10]

The starting point for all discussions of statements of intention to prove a subsequent act is the fascinating case of Mutual Life Insurance Co. v. Hillmon.[11] The crucial issue in *Hillmon* was whether a man fatally shot at Crooked Creek, Kansas on March 17, 1879, was Hillmon, who was heavily insured, or a man called Frederick Walters. Neither Hillmon nor Walters was ever seen again after the shooting. In order to prove that the body was that of Walters rather than their insured, the insurance companies in question offered in evidence letters from Walters to his sister and fiancee indicating his intention to leave with "a certain

---

[4] *See, e.g.*, Callahan v. A.E.V., Inc., 182 F.3d 237, 251–253 (3d Cir. 1999) (testimony admitted for limited purpose of proving customer motive, but not as evidence that plaintiff actually lost business to defendant).

[5] *See, e.g.*, United States v. Serafini, 233 F.3d 758, 769 (3d Cir. 2000) (out-of-court statement properly admissible as state of mind evidence to show declarant intended check he gave defendant to be reimbursement for defendant's contribution to political candidate).

[6] *See, e.g.*, Seattle-First Nat'l Bank v. Randall, 532 F.2d 1291 (9th Cir. 1976) (diaries of customer of bank admitted on issue of whether customer was competent at time of loan).

[7] *See, e.g.*, Bell v. Environmental Protection Agency, 232 F.3d 546, 552 (7th Cir. 2000) (trial court abused its discretion in excluding memorandum offered under Rule 803(3) to show beliefs and intentions of panel that promoted employees other than plaintiffs).

[8] *See, e.g.*, United States v. Williams, 993 F.2d 451 (5th Cir. 1993) (testimony concerning threatening phone calls received admissible to show witness's fear).

[9] *See e.g.*, United States v. Bishop, 264 F.3d 535, 549 (5th Cir. 2001) (bookkeeper's out-of-court statement, that she had neglected to record a $400,000 fee received by defendant two years earlier in preparing his tax returns for that year, was a statement of memory offered to prove the fact remembered, not an explanation of her current state of mind, and thus was inadmissible).

[10] *See* **Treatise** at § 803.07.

[11] Mutual Life Insurance Co. v. Hillmon, 145 U.S. 285, 12 S Ct. 909, 36 L. Ed. 706 (1892).

Mr. Hillmon, a sheep trader, for Colorado, and parts unknown to me" in early March, 1879. The Supreme Court held that the letters should have been admitted, in language which forms the basis for all further discussions of the admissibility of statements of intention to prove a subsequent act:

> The existence of a particular intention in a certain person at a certain time being a material fact to be proved, evidence that he expressed that intention at that time is as direct evidence of the fact, as his own testimony that he then had that intention would be. After his death there can hardly be any other way of proving it; and while he is still alive, his own memory of his state of mind at a former time is no more likely to be clear and true than a bystander's recollection of what he then said, and is less trustworthy than letters written by him at the very time and under circumstances precluding a suspicion of misrepresentation.

> The letters in question were competent, not as narratives of facts communicated to the writer by others, nor yet as proof that he actually went away from Wichita, but as evidence that, shortly before the time when other evidence tended to show that he went away, he had the intention of going, and of going with Hillmon, which made it more probable both that he did go and that he went with Hillmon, than if there had been no proof of such intention.[12]

Rule 803(3) codifies *Hillmon* by classifying a statement of intent as a statement of the declarant's then existing state of mind to which the hearsay rule does not apply.[13] Whether the statement may be used to prove a subsequent event is a question of relevancy governed by Rule 401.[14] Both the hearsay and relevancy

---

[12] Mutual Life Insurance Co. v. Hillmon, 145 U.S. 285, 295–96, 12 S. Ct. 909, 36 L. Ed. 706 (1892).

[13] Phoenix Mut. Life Ins. Co. v. Adams, 30 F.3d 554, 566 (4th Cir. 1994) (district court properly admitted testimony of insured's wife regarding phone conversation between her husband and unidentified person concerning his intent to change beneficiary on his policy to his wife; evidence was admissible under Rule 803(3) as evidence of the husband's then-existing state of mind, which could be used to prove subsequent conduct in conformity with his expressed intention); Shelden v. Barre Belt Granite Emp. Union Pension, 25 F.3d 74, 79–80 (2d Cir. 1994) (in action with issue about whether employee applied for pension benefits before he died, trial court should have admitted affidavit by individual who complied with employee's request to give him a ride to the office to apply for benefits and waited there until he had concluded his business, since, under Rule 803(3), affidavit could be used as evidence that employee had filed for benefits).

[14] *See, e.g.*, United States v. Hogan, 886 F.2d 1497 (7th Cir. 1989) (court did not err in excluding testimony that witness heard his father say that he wanted to give defendant money; such comments were too speculative and vague for the inference that declarant immediately offered the money to defendant; given a chance to reflect, declarant may have reconsidered).

hurdles must be passed in order for the statement to be admissible.[15] Even relevancy does not guarantee admissibility if probative value is substantially outweighed by the dangers of prejudice, confusion or waste of time specified in Rule 403.

A frequently occurring instance of low probative value and prejudice arises when declarant's statement implicates a second person's intention to commit a future act as well as his own. In the *Hillmon* case itself, proof that Walters was willing to go with Hillmon did not prove that Hillmon was willing to go with Walters. The House Judiciary Committee would have limited the Hillmon doctrine "so as to render statements of intent by a declarant admissible only to prove his future conduct, not the future conduct of another person." The Senate Report and the Conference Report are silent on this point.

Cases decided pursuant to Rule 803(3) indicate that although statements of intent have been admitted in joint action situations,[16] the federal judiciary has been extremely circumspect about relying on Rule 803(3) when the action of a person other than the declarant is at issue.[17] At times, the statement in question has been admitted instead as a statement of a co-conspirator pursuant to Rule 801(d)(2)(E).[18]

[d]—State of Mind To Show Previous Act[19]

Although Rule 803(3) permits a statement of state of mind to prove subsequent conduct, it specifically excludes "a statement of memory or belief to prove the fact remembered or believed" except in will cases.[20] A contrary rule would annihilate the hearsay rule.[21] From the standpoint of relevance, a memory of an event makes

---

[15] *See* United States v. Donley, 878 F.2d 735 (3d Cir. 1989) (quoting **Treatise**).

[16] *See, e.g.*, United States v. Best, 219 F.3d 192, 197 (2d Cir. 2000) (out-of-court declaration of intent to perform act, admissible to prove that declarant later performed intended act, was also admissible to show non-declarant's behavior resulting from declarant's intended act because independent corroborating evidence connected declarant's statement with non-declarant's activities); United States v. Sperling, 726 F.2d 69 (2d Cir. 1984) (statements of declarant's state of mind were admissible against non-declarant when linked with independent corroboration); United States v. Astorga-Torres, 682 F.2d 1331, 1335–1336 (9th Cir. 1982) (relied on a pre-Rules case, United States v. Pheaster, 544 F.2d 353 (9th Cir. 1976).

[17] *See, e.g.*, United States v. Delvecchio, 816 F.2d 859 (2d Cir. 1987) (error to admit informant's statement that informant intended to meet with defendants to prove that one of the defendants was at the meeting); United States v. Cicale, 691 F.2d 95, 103-104 (2d Cir. 1982).

[18] *See, e.g.*, United States v. Moore, 571 F.2d 76 (2d Cir. 1978).

[19] *See* discussion in **Treatise** at § 803.05[2][b].

[20] Fed. R. Evid. 803(3). Statements of memory or belief may be admitted to prove the fact remembered or believed if they relate to the execution, revocation, identification, or terms of declarant's will. Will matters arise infrequently in federal jurisdictions. Whether statements made in somewhat similar situations such as in suits about life insurance policies should be treated analogously is discussed in the **Treatise** at § 803.05[2][b].

[21] Shepard v. United States, 290 U.S. 96, 105–106, 54 S. Ct. 22, 78 L. Ed. 196 (1933) ("Declarations of intention, casting light upon the future, have been sharply distinguished from

it more likely that the event did occur. If the hearsay hurdle could be overcome, an out-of-court statement, such as "I went to the movies yesterday," could be reformulated into a statement "I have a present belief that I went to the movies yesterday," which would then be relevant to show that declarant had gone to the movies.

The blanket exclusion of statements of memory or belief is justified on the ground that the dangers of improper perception, faulty memory and deliberate misstatement are far greater when the statement is being used to prove a past act rather than a future act. This is particularly so when the statement implicates the past acts of third parties, as in the leading case of *Shepard v. United States*,[22] in which the Supreme Court considered the admissibility of the victim's statement that "Dr. Shepard has poisoned me." Rejecting the argument that the statement was admissible as evidence of declarant's state of mind to rebut the defense of suicide, Justice Cardozo wrote for the Court:

> The testimony now questioned faced backward and not forward. This at least it did in its most obvious implications. What is even more important, it spoke to a past act, and more than that, to an act by some one not the speaker.[23]

When, however, the statement of memory or belief would be used circumstantially to prove conduct on the part of the declarant which produced the mental state, the dangers of faulty perception or memory, and deliberate fabrication, are minimal when only a small amount of time elapsed between the event and statement, and the statement was made before a motive to falsify arose.[24] Despite Rule 803(3), such a statement should qualify for admission pursuant to Rule 807 as a "statement having equivalent circumstantial guarantees of trustworthiness."[25]

Frank recognition that some statements of memory and belief are reliable would encourage consideration of the actual dangers presented by the facts of the par-

---

declarations of memory, pointing backwards to the past. There would be an end, or nearly that, to the rule against hearsay if the distinction were ignored.").

[22] Shepard v. United States, 290 U.S. 96, 54 S. Ct. 22, 78 L. Ed. 196 (1933).

[23] 290 U.S. at 106. *See also* United States v. Harwood, 998 F.2d 91 (2d Cir. 1993) (codefendant's statement not offered to prove his state of mind when he made the statement but to prove conduct that occurred months earlier); United States v. Emmert, 829 F.2d 805 (9th Cir. 1987) (statement by defendant that he was scared because of threats by government agents was properly excluded).

[24] *See* United States v. Miller, 874 F.2d 1255 (9th Cir. 1989) (defendant had had sufficient opportunity to fabricate; statement offered to prove present state of mind as a means of proving prior state of mind was properly excluded; quoting **Treatise**).

[25] Rule 807 is discussed in Chapter 14, *Hearsay: Definition, Organization and Constitutional Concerns*.

ticular case. It would moderate the highly theoretical discussions in which some courts indulge in seeking to implement *Hillmon* and *Shepard*, and effectuate the policy of the Federal Rules of Evidence in promoting accurate fact-finding.

The most difficult cases are those in which the past, present and future are intertwined in the statement being submitted. In *United States v. Annunziato*,[26] for instance, a prosecution for receiving bribes, a son testified that his father told him that he had received a call from defendant asking for money on a particular construction project. In response to his son's question about what he intended to do, the father stated that he had agreed to send money to the defendant. The Second Circuit found that the "most obvious implications" of the father's statement looked forward—he was going to send the money. Arguably, however, the evidence was much more powerful and probative in looking backwards—to show that the defendant had requested the payment as a bribe. In difficult cases such as these, in the ultimate analysis, the principles expressed in Rule 403 must be applied.[27]

In any event, in a case like *Annunziato* it would no longer be necessary to press the *Hillmon* doctrine so far. Under the subsequently enacted Federal Rules of Evidence, such a statement of a past event may be admissible as a declaration against interest pursuant to Rule 804(b)(3), since the declarant had died by the time of trial, or under the residual hearsay exception, if the court is satisfied that sufficient guarantees of trustworthiness are present.[28] No matter what hearsay exception applies, the statement's probative force and prejudice must still be weighed under rule 403.

§ 16.05 Statements for Purposes of Medical Diagnosis or Treatment—Rule 803(4)[1]

Rule 803(4) provides an extremely broad exception for statements made for purposes of medical diagnosis or treatment. The rule excludes from the hearsay rule

---

[26] United States v. Annunziato, 293 F.2d 373, 377–378 (2d Cir. 1961).

[27] *See, e.g.,* United States v. Mandel, 437 F. Supp. 262, 263–266 (D. Md. 1977) (court refused to admit testimony by wife of co-defendant that her husband had told her that he and other co-defendant were going to acquire race track but that she was not to reveal this to anyone including the defendant; court noted that statement implied 1) that co-defendants had an agreement, entered into in the past, to conceal their interests from defendant and 2) that co-defendants intended to keep their interests secret in the future; court excluded because it found that the probative value and weight of the statement was outweighed by prejudice, since unlike the *Annuziato* situation, the declaration did not qualify as a declaration against interest or a co-conspirators' statement, and there was no need for this hearsay since the declarant could testify and receipt of the hearsay could lead to widespread fabrication).

[28] Rule 804(b)(3) is discussed in Chapter 17, *Hearsay Exceptions Requiring Unavailability—Rule 804*, and the residual hearsay exception is discussed in Chapter 14, *Hearsay: Definition, Organization and Constitutional Concerns*.

[1] *See* discussion in **Treatise** at § 803.09.

statements relating to present or past pain, symptoms, and sensations, as well as statements that describe the inception and cause of these conditions, insofar as they bear on treatment or diagnosis. The rule does not differentiate between statements made to treating physicians and those made to physicians consulted solely for diagnosis, even if the consultation was solely with a view to having the physician testify in court as an expert on behalf of the declarant. Nor is the rule limited to statements relating to bodily conditions; statements pertaining to mental health are covered by the rule, although as the discussion below indicates, they may at times be excluded.

The rule applies only to statements made by the patient. It does not apply, for example, to statements made by consulting physicians to the treating physician concerning the proper course of treatment for a patient with a party's ailment.[1.1]

Rule 803(4) provides as follows:

Rule 803(4). Hearsay Exceptions; Availability of Declarant Immaterial.

The following are not excluded by the hearsay rule, even though the declarant is available as a witness:

. . .

(4) Statements for purposes of medical diagnosis or treatment.—Statements made for purposes of medical diagnosis or treatment and describing medical history, or past or present symptoms, pain, or sensations, or the inception or general character of the cause or external source thereof insofar as reasonably pertinent to diagnosis or treatment.

The reliability of statements made for the purpose of medical treatment is ensured by the declarant's motive to be truthful since treatment hinges largely on the accuracy of the information imparted to the physician or other person involved in providing medical care.[1.2] The need for such statements is great since there frequently will be no other evidence available concerning subjective symptoms. Since the declarant's motive to promote effective treatment is crucial, the Advisory Committee's notes indicate that statements to hospital attendants, ambulance drivers, or even members of the family are also admissible provided they were made in order to obtain treatment.[1.3]

[1.1] *See, e.g.,* Field v. Trigg County Hosp., Inc., 386 F.3d 729, 735–736 (6th Cir. 2004).

[1.2] *See, e.g.,* United States v. Turning Bear, 357 F.3d 730, 738 (8th Cir. 2004) (Rule 803(4)'s hearsay exception is based on "the patient's selfish interest in receiving proper treatment guarantees the trustworthiness of the statements").

[1.3] Fed. R. Evid. 803(4) Advisory Committee Note (1972) (reproduced verbatim in **Treatise** at § 803App.01[2]); *see, e.g.,* Davignon v. Clemmey, 322 F.3d 1, 8 n.3 (1st Cir. 2003) (statement need

Nor does the rule require the statements to refer to the declarant's physical condition. Statements relating to someone else's physical condition, such as a child, are admissible, provided again that they were made for purposes of treatment.[2] The relationship between declarant and patient will usually determine admissibility. In the case of a child, a court would undoubtedly assume the absence of any motive to mislead on the part of parents. As the relationship becomes less close, the statement becomes less reliable, both because the motive to tell the truth becomes less strong, and because even a stranger in good faith may not be able to describe another's physical pain and suffering as infallibly as an intimate.

The court in its discretion pursuant to Rule 403 will have to assess the probative worth of the statement, which will depend on its significance, its contents, by whom it was made, and in what circumstances it was made, and decide whether admission is warranted despite the dangers of prejudice, confusion and waste of time. Statements made for the purposes of medical diagnosis to a non-treating physician rest on a somewhat different rationale. Although some courts and commentators have expressed apprehension that in the absence of a motive to foster treatment, a declarant has no motive to speak truthfully, the Advisory Committee felt that exclusion of such statements would be inconsistent with the overall scheme of the Federal Rules. Rule 803(6) authorizes the admission of hospital and medical office records that contain diagnoses and opinions, and Rule 703 permits a physician to express an opinion based on the patient's statements. These rules assume that the particular facts relied upon by the physician will be trustworthy because the integrity and specialized skill of the expert will bar reliance on questionable matter. As a matter of policy, a fact reliable enough to serve as the basis for a diagnosis is also reliable enough to escape hearsay proscription. The test for statements made for purposes of medical diagnosis under Rule 803(4) is the same as that in Rule 703—is this particular fact one that an expert in this particular field would be justified in relying upon in rendering an opinion?[3] Furthermore, to allow jurors to consider the patient's statement in evaluating the basis for the expert's opinion but not to admit the statement itself sets up a meaningless distinction that jurors are unlikely to apply.

The reliability of medical testimony is enhanced by procedural rules such as Rule 35 of the Federal Rules of Civil Procedure and Rule 16 of the Rules of Criminal Procedure which entitle the parties to obtain copies of their adversaries' medical

---

not be made to medical doctor; it qualifies for exception from hearsay rule under Rule 803(4) if made for purpose of obtaining medical treatment).

[2] *See, e.g.*, United States v. Yazzie, 59 F.3d 807, 812–814 (9th Cir. 1995) (mother's note to treating physician that her mentally retarded son was being sexually abused by his step-father was properly admitted under medical treatment exception).

[3] Gong v. Hirsch, 913 F.2d 1269, 1272–1274 (7th Cir. 1990) (same standard of admissibility should apply; citing **Treatise**).

reports prior to trial.[4] Effective cross-examination can bring out weaknesses in the diagnosis stemming from an uncritical willingness to accept the patient's story. In a civil case, the threat of one-sided medical testimony is further obviated by provisions authorizing the court to order a party to submit to a physical or mental examination.

The rationales underlying statements made for treatment and statements made for diagnosis converge when the issue is whether statements "describing medical history . . . or the inception or general character of the cause or external source thereof" should be admitted. Even in the case of a statement made for treatment, the test is not only whether the declarant thought it relevant (thereby establishing reliability), but also whether a doctor would reasonably have relied upon such a statement in deciding upon a course of treatment.[5] Since doctors may be assumed not to want to waste their time with unnecessary history, the fact that a doctor or other trained medical personnel took the information is prima facie evidence that it was pertinent. Courtroom practice has tended to let in medical records and statements to nurses and doctors fairly freely, leaving it to the jury to decide probative force.

Each case will have to be determined on its own facts to determine which statements, or which portion of a statement pertains to treatment. In *United States v. Iron Shell,* [6] the statements in question had been made by the nine-year-old female victim of the alleged assault with intent to rape to the doctor who examined her on the night of the assault. The statements concerning the cause of the victim's injuries were testified to by the physician at trial, over the defendant's objection that the doctor had been acting in an investigatory rather than in a treating or diagnostic capacity. The Eighth Circuit explained why the statements had been properly received:[7]

> . . . There is nothing in the content of the statements to suggest that Lucy was responding to the doctor's questions for any reason other than promoting treatment. It is important to note that the statements concern what happened

---

[4]   *See* Fed. R. Civ. P. 35; Fed. R. Crim. P. 16; 7 MOORE'S FEDERAL PRACTICE, Ch. 35, *Physical and Mental Examination of Persons* (Matthew Bender 3d ed. 1997); 25 MOORE'S FEDERAL PRACTICE, Ch. 616, *Discovery and Inspection* (Matthew Bender 3d ed. 1997).

[5]   United States v. Sumner, 204 F.3d 1182, 1184–1186 (8th Cir. 2000) (admissibility under Rule 803(4) requires declarant's motive for statement to be consistent with promoting treatment and contents must be such as are reasonably relied on for treatment; here, no showing that child understood purpose of her statements, so court erroneously admitted child's statements to doctor identifying defendant as her molester); Cook v. Hoppin, 783 F.2d 684 (7th Cir. 1986) (plaintiff's physician testified that he had not relied on statements, which were not of a kind on which medical personnel generally rely; citing **Treatise**).

[6]   United States v. Iron Shell, 633 F.2d 77, 84–85 (8th Cir. 1980).

[7]   633 F.2d at 84–85.

rather than who assaulted her. The former in most cases is pertinent to diagnosis and treatment while the latter would seldom, if ever, be sufficiently related. . . . The age of the patient also mitigates against a finding that Lucy's statements were not within the traditional rationale of the rule. . . . It is not dispositive that Dr. Hopkins' examination would have been identical to the one he performed if Lucy had been unable to utter a word. . . . It is enough that the information eliminated potential physical problems from the doctor's examination in order to meet the test of 803(4). Discovering what is not injured is equally as pertinent to treatment and diagnosis as finding what is injured. Dr. Hopkins also testified, in response to specific questions from the court, that most doctors would have sought such a history and that he relied upon Lucy's statements in deciding upon a course of treatment.

Some courts hold that identification information is seldom necessary to determine proper medical treatment. Before admitting statements of identification, those courts require special assurances that the physician obtained the information for diagnostic purposes and that the patient understood that need.[7.1] Other courts have held that such additional assurances unduly restrict the admissibility of evidence under Rule 803(4).[7.2]

A criminal case such as *Iron Shell* is, of course, subject to Confrontation Clause and Rule 403 analyses. As the court noted, these issues were blunted by the availability of the victim for cross-examination.[8]

Some statements of causation that do not qualify under Rule 803(4) may meet the requirements of Rule 803(1) or (2) and come in as present sense impressions or excited utterances. Others may be admissible pursuant to Rule 801(d)(1) or (2) as prior inconsistent statements or admissions.

Statements made to a psychiatrist or to someone like a psychologist, who would relay them to a medical doctor, fall within Rule 803(4)'s category of "statements made for purposes of medical diagnosis or treatment." As a general rule all statements made in this context, regardless of their content, are relevant to diagnosis or treatment since experts in the field view everything relating to the patient as

---

[7.1] *See, e.g.,* United States v. Gabe, 237 F.3d 954, 957–958 (8th Cir. 2001) (in sexual assault case, identity of perpetrator may be necessary if patient also requires psychological counseling; identification is admissible only if psychological treatment is called for, physician tells victim that identity of abuser is necessary for that purpose, and patient manifests understanding of need for information).

[7.2] *See, e.g.,* United States v. Edward J., 224 F.3d 1216, 1218–1220 (10th Cir. 2000).

[8] 633 F.2d at 87.

relevant.[9] Nevertheless, the statements may be extremely unreliable as evidence of the facts related, since the condition for which the patient is consulting the psychiatrist may have impaired the patient's perception, memory or veracity. The trial judge has discretion pursuant to Rules 401 and 403 to admit the statements only as proof of the patient's condition and not as proof of the occurrence of the recited events. In an automobile accident case, for instance, if a claim of mental damage is made, the court may allow proof of irrational, incoherent statements of the victim without, however, allowing any statements directly relating to the accident to be used as proof of how it occurred.

The judge also has discretion to limit statements dealing with the patient's condition. Extensive details covering many years of treatment may be excluded if the court finds their probative value is substantially outweighed by the danger of prejudice, confusion or waste of time.[10]

§ 16.06   Recorded Recollection—Rule 803(5)[1]

[1]—Scope and Text of Rule

Rule 803(5) excludes from the operation of the hearsay rule a written memorandum concerning a matter about which the witness once had personal knowledge but as to which the witness "now has insufficient recollection to enable the witness to testify fully and accurately," provided certain requirements are met. The rule provides as follows:

Rule 803(5).   Hearsay Exceptions; Availability of Declarant Immaterial.

The following are not excluded by the hearsay rule, even though the declarant is available as a witness:

. . .

(5) Recorded recollection.—A memorandum or record concerning a matter about which a witness once had knowledge but now has insufficient recollection to enable the witness to testify fully and accurately, shown to have been made or adopted by the witness when the matter was fresh in the witness's memory and to reflect that knowledge correctly. If admitted, the memorandum or record may be read into evidence but may not itself

---

[9] *See, e.g.,* Swinton v. Potomac Corp., 270 F.3d 794, 807–808 (9th Cir. 2001) (trial court did not err in admitting under Rule 803(4) documents prepared by psychologists who treated plaintiff for mental trauma suffered as result of racially discriminatory treatment by his supervisor, including summaries of plaintiff's descriptions of incidents involving highly offensive racial slurs).

[10] *See* commentary to Rule 403 in Chapter 6.

[1] *See* discussion in **Treatise** at § 803.10.

> be received as an exhibit unless offered by an adverse party.
>
> [*Adopted Jan. 2, 1975, effective July 1, 1975; amended Mar. 2, 1987, effective Oct. 1, 1987.*]

Two theories have been advanced to justify admission of recorded recollection despite the hearsay rule: (1) that use of the memorandum is necessary because the witness is "unavailable" as a result of lack of memory of the event in question, and (2) that a contemporaneous, accurate record is inherently superior to a present recollection subject to the fallibility of human memory. Rule 803(5) seeks to accomodate both rationales. It recognizes that requiring some demonstration of impaired memory discourages the use of self-serving statements especially prepared for litigation by insurance adjusters, investigators and the like.[2] On the other hand, memory need not be wholly exhausted before the memorandum can be used.

By providing for admission of the memorandum if the witness "now has insufficient recollection to enable the witness to testify fully and accurately," Rule 803(5) decrees that admission of the memorandum should not be on an all or nothing basis. If the witness answers some questions without hesitation, but then becomes vague or evasive or claims an inability to remember a particular aspect of the event in question even after being shown the memorandum for refreshment purposes, the trial court should admit at least those portions of the memorandum which failed to restore the witness's memory.[3] Admissibility should be determined on a question by question basis rather than by viewing the witness's testimony as a whole. Determining whether the witness is not testifying fully and accurately rests in the discretion of the trial court, and is often so dependent on the witness's demeanor that its determination should rarely be overturned on appeal.

The memorandum may be admissible pursuant to other rules of evidence even if the witness retains a memory of the underlying event. For instance, admission may be mandated as a prior inconsistent statement (Rule 801(d)(1)(A)), as an admission (Rule 801(d)(2)), or as a record of regularly conducted activity (Rule 803(6)). If the memorandum was made in circumstances guaranteeing its trustworthiness it may qualify for admission pursuant to the residual hearsay exception of Rule 807, which is discussed in Chapter 14.

[2]—Witness Once Had Knowledge

Rule 803(5) follows conventional doctrine in requiring the memorandum to concern a matter "about which a witness once had knowledge." This means that

---

[2] *See, e.g.,* United States v. Humphrey, 279 F.3d 372, 377 (6th Cir. 2002) (memorandum was inadmissible as recorded recollection because declarant could remember events recorded).

[3] *See, e.g.,* United States v. Williams, 571 F.2d 344 (6th Cir. 1978) ("selective memory" with regard to critical question is sufficient predicate for admissibility).

the memorandum is not admissible pursuant to this rule unless the witness had sufficient personal knowledge of the underlying events to meet the personal knowledge requirement of Rule 602 about these matters. If, for instance, the witness was not present at the event recorded and the memorandum was based on information supplied by persons who do not testify, the memorandum cannot be admitted. On the other hand, a memorandum may be admissible even if it concerns an event that is itself hearsay. If this other hearsay would be admissible under some exception, so would a memorandum reflecting a participant's recorded recollection of the event.[1] For example, if the writing constituted a recorded recollection of a statement made by a party, the statement would be a party admission and the writing would come in to prove the admission.[2]

[3]—Freshness and Accuracy of Memorandum

Since the witness does not remember the recorded facts, testimony about the witness's perception cannot be obtained either on direct or cross-examination.[1] Instead, Rule 803(5) imposes two requirements to ensure that the witness correctly recorded his knowledge at a time when he still remembered what he had perceived: (1) to ensure that the past recollection is worth trusting, Rule 803(5) requires the memorandum "to have been made or adopted by the witness when the matter was fresh in [the witness's] memory" and (2) to guarantee that the memory was properly transcribed, the rule requires that the memorandum "reflect that knowledge correctly."

The concept of "freshness" is intended to be more flexible[2] than the traditional formula which required the memorandum to be made "at or near the time of the events in question." In determining whether the matter was sufficiently fresh to guarantee the memory's trustworthiness, the trial court will probably wish to take into account such factors as the time when the memorandum was made, the quality of the memory embodied in the memorandum, whether it was made before the litigation commenced, whether it was made spontaneously or in answer to a request by an interested party, and other circumstances.

---

[1] *See* Fed. R. Evid. 805.

[2] *See, e.g.,* Newton v. Ryder Transportation Services, 206 F.3d 772, 774 (8th Cir. 2000) (court erred in excluding accident report prepared by highway patrol officer that could only have been prepared from information provided by plaintiff, because there were no other witnesses to accident).

[1] *See, e.g.,* United States v. Cambindo Valencia, 609 F.2d 603, 633 (2d Cir. 1979) (despite defendant's inability to test witness's perception through cross-examination, recorded recollections are admissible in criminal cases as against objection on Confrontation Clause grounds).

[2] *See, e.g.,* United States v. Smith, 197 F.3d 225, 231 (6th Cir. 1999) (statement recorded fifteen months after event was properly admitted as past recollection recorded); United States v. Patterson, 678 F.2d 774, 778 (9th Cir. 1982) (court has broad discretion pursuant to Rule 803(5); memory fresh 10 months after conversation with defendant).

To ensure that the witness or someone else transcribed the knowledge correctly, the witness must testify either (1) that he or she recalls having made an accurate memorandum or checking it for accuracy or (2) that though the witness now does not recollect his or her state of mind when making the record, he or she would not have made it unless it were correct. Proof in the first instance consists of testimony by the witness relating the circumstances in which the memorandum was made and the witness's statement that he or she knew it to be true.[3] In the second case, it is sufficient if the witness testifies that a record of this type is correct because it was his or her habit or practice to record such matters accurately.[4] Or the witness can testify that the record is in his or her handwriting and that he or she would not have written, signed, initialed or marked the memorandum unless convinced that it was correct.

[4]—Multiple Participants

The witness need not have been the person who actually wrote the memorandum.[1] It is admissible if the witness can testify that he or she saw the memorandum when the matter it concerned was fresh in memory, and that he or she then knew it to be correct. Only the witness who adopted the memorandum need be called.

A more complicated situation arises when a person perceives an event and reports it to another who records it. Both participants must ordinarily testify, the reporter vouching for the accuracy of the oral report and the recorder for the accuracy of the transcription.[2] The recorder need not be the actual writer. If the writer has seen the memorandum and approved it, and so testifies, the person who physically wrote the memorandum need not be produced. So long as accuracy is vouched for by each participant in the chain, a memorandum compiled through the efforts of more than two persons satisfies the requirements of Rule 803(5). There is no need for the

---

[3] *See, e.g.*, Newton v. Ryder Transportation Services, 206 F.3d 772, 774–775 (8th Cir. 2000) (court erred in failing to admit police officer's accident report despite claim that source of information in report was unknown; officer "acknowledged that he prepared and signed the report on the day of the accident, that it was accurate to the best of his knowledge, and that the information in it could have come only from Mr. Newton").

[4] *See, e.g.*, Parker v. Reda, 327 F.3d 211, 213–214 (2d Cir. 2003) (per curiam) (trial court properly admitted witness's written report concerning incident between him and plaintiff when witness could not remember having made report but testified he had reason to believe it was accurate).

[1] United States v. Williams, 571 F.2d 344 (6th Cir. 1978) (witness adopted memorandum by signing and swearing to it).

[2] *See, e.g.*, United States v. Hernandez, 333 F.3d 1168, 1177–1179 (10th Cir. 2003) (two memoranda, each recording serial number of gun possessed by defendant, made by efforts of three persons, were admissible under Rule 803(5) when each person who recited serial number resulting in memoranda testified that she accurately reported the serial number and each person who made memorandum testified that she accurately recorded serial number).

original viewer to testify if the statement qualifies as an exception to the hearsay rule.[3]

[5]—Admissibility of Memorandum

Rule 803(5) provides that a memorandum that satisfies the conditions of the rule may be read into evidence but may not be treated as an exhibit that goes to the jury room unless offered by an adverse party.[4] This limitation was added because the memorandum is viewed as a substitute for oral testimony, and it was feared that it might be given undue weight in relation to other oral testimony, which is not normally taken into the jury room. Upon stipulation the document may be sent to the jury.

Since the contents of the writing are being proved, even if the writing itself does not qualify as an exhibit, the best evidence rule applies. The original memorandum, or duplicate to the extent permitted by Rule 1003, must be produced unless failure to produce the original is satisfactorily explained (*see* Chapter 9).

§ 16.07   Records of Private Entities

[1]—Overview

Rule 803 contains a number of provisions that make the records of private entities admissible despite the hearsay rule. By far the most frequently used of these exceptions, contained in Rule 803(6), is the exception for records of regularly conducted activity, which is discussed in detail below. Rule 803(7), the exception for evidence of the absence of a record, Rule 803(16), the statements in ancient documents exception, and Rule 803(17), the exception for market reports and commercial publications, are also discussed below.

In addition, there are a number of other provisions in Rule 803, much less frequently used, that exempt particular types of written records of private entities from being barred by the hearsay rule. Records of religious organizations are specifically governed by Rule 803(11). Rule 803(11) provides as follows:[1]

Rule 803(11).   Hearsay Exceptions; Availability of Declarant Immaterial.

The following are not excluded by the hearsay rule, even though the declarant is available as a witness:

---

[3] *See* United States v. Steele, 685 F.2d 793, 809 (3d Cir. 1982) (objection that maker of memorandum lacked personal knowledge is irrelevant where notes were introduced to prove declarations of co-conspirators).

[4] Fed. R. Evid. 803(5); *see, e.g.,* Newton v. Ryder Transportation Services, 206 F.3d 772, 774 (8th Cir. 2000) (record may be read into evidence, but it is not itself received as an exhibit).

[1] *See* discussion in **Treatise** at § 803.16.

> . . .
>
> (11)   Records of religious organizations.—Statements of births, marriages, divorces, deaths, legitimacy, ancestry, relationship by blood or marriage, or other similar facts of personal or family history, contained in a regularly kept record of a religious organization.

Statements in family records such as Bibles are treated in Rule 803(13).[2] Rule 803(13) provides as follows:

> **Rule 803(13).   Hearsay Exceptions; Availability of Declarant Immaterial.**
>
> The following are not excluded by the hearsay rule, even though the declarant is available as a witness:
>
> . . .
>
> (13)   Family records.—Statements of fact concerning personal or family history contained in family Bibles, genealogies, charts, engravings on rings, inscriptions on family portraits, engravings on urns, crypts, or tombstones, or the like.

Rule 803(14) [3] provides an exception for records of documents affecting an interest in property. Rule 803(14) provides as follows:

> **Rule 803(14).   Hearsay Exceptions; Availability of Declarant Immaterial.**
>
> The following are not excluded by the hearsay rule, even though the declarant is available as a witness:
>
> . . .
>
> (14)   Records of documents affecting an interest in property.—The record of a document purporting to establish or affect an interest in property, as proof of the content of the original recorded document and its execution and delivery by each person by whom it purports to have been executed, if the record is a record of a public office and an applicable statute authorizes the recording of documents of that kind in that office.

Rule 803(15) [4] covers statements in documents affecting an interest in property. Rule 803(15) provides as follows:

---

[2]   *See* discussion in **Treatise** at § 803.18.
[3]   *See* discussion in **Treatise** at § 803.19.
[4]   *See* discussion in **Treatise** at § 803.20.

Rule 803(15). Hearsay Exceptions; Availability of Declarant Immaterial.

The following are not excluded by the hearsay rule, even though the declarant is available as a witness:

. . .

(15) Statements in documents affecting an interest in property.—A statement contained in a document purporting to establish or affect an interest in property if the matter stated was relevant to the purpose of the document, unless dealings with the property since the document was made have been inconsistent with the truth of the statement or the purport of the document.

For further discussion of these rules, see **Treatise.**

[2]—Records of Regularly Conducted Activity—Rule 803(6)

[a]—In General

The hearsay exception for records of regularly conducted activity, frequently termed the business records exception, relieves the proponent of the record from having to produce in court each person in the chain that produced the record, provided the requirements discussed below are met. Although the exception is of fairly recent origin,[1] owing its existence to legislation adopting a Model Act reported in 1927, it is probably the most frequently used of the hearsay exceptions.

Rule 803(6) provides:

Rule 803(6). Hearsay Exceptions; Availability of Declarant Immaterial.

The following are not excluded by the hearsay rule, even though the declarant is available as a witness:

. . .

(6)
Records of regularly conducted activity.—A memorandum, report, record, or data compilation, in any form, of acts, events, conditions, opinions, or diagnoses, made at or near the time by, or from information transmitted by, a person with knowledge, if kept in the course of a regularly conducted business activity, and if it was the regular practice of that

---

[1] Although there were some common-law antecedents, the shop book rule and the regular entries rule, these were far more limited in their scope. *See* discussion in **Treatise** at § 803.11.

business activity to make the memorandum, report, record, or data compilation, all as shown by the testimony of the custodian or other qualified witness, or by certification that complies with Rule 902(11), Rule 902(12), or a statute permitting certification, unless the source of information or the method or circumstances of preparation indicate lack of trustworthiness. The term "business" as used in this paragraph includes business, institution, association, profession, occupation, and calling of every kind, whether or not conducted for profit.

[*Adopted Jan. 2, 1975, effective July 1, 1975; last amended Dec. 1, 2000.*]

Rule 803(6) was amended in 2000 to permit the introduction of business records without a sponsoring witness. The proponent needs only to provide a certification that complies with Rule 902(11) or (12) (also added by amendment in 2000) or a statute permitting certification. Rule 902(11) is applicable only to domestic business records. Under Rule 902(11), a custodian of the record or other qualified person must certify that the record:[2]

- was made at or near the occurrence of the matters set forth in the record;

- was made by a person with knowledge of those matters or from information transmitted by such a person;

- was kept in the course of the regularly conducted activity; and

- was made by the regularly conducted activity as a regular practice.

Rule 902(12) is applicable to foreign business records. It provides for the same foundation as Rule 902(11), and requires the certificate to be signed in a manner that, if falsely made, would subject the maker to criminal penalties in the country in which it was signed. Rule 902(12) is applicable only in civil cases, since there already is a virtually identical provision for the admission of foreign business records in criminal cases.[3] Both Rule 902(11) and Rule 902(12) require the offering party to give all adverse parties written notice of the intent to offer the records by means of a supporting certification and to make the proffered records available for inspection sufficiently in advance of the offer to provide the adverse party with a fair opportunity to challenge their admissibility.[4]

The rule gives the trial court the discretion to exclude proffered business records if "the source of the information or the method or circumstances of preparation indicate lack of trustworthiness."[4.1]

---

[2] Fed. R. Evid. 902(11).

[3] Fed. R. Evid. 902(12); *see* 18 U.S.C. § 3505.

[4] Fed. R. Evid. 902(11), (12).

[4.1] Fed. R. Evid. 803(6); *see, e.g.,* United States v. Petrie, 302 F.3d 1280, 1288 (11th Cir. 2002) (trial court did not abuse its discretion in excluding proffered business records on trustworthiness

[b]—Rationale

As is the case with other hearsay exceptions, the exception for records of regularly conducted activity is justified on the grounds of reliability and need. Guarantees of reliability are present because: (1) such records are customarily checked; (2) the regularity and continuity of such records produce habits of precision in the record keeper; (3) businesses function in reliance on such records; and (4) employees are required to make accurate records as part of their job or risk embarrassment and censure if they blunder. Need exists because without the exception all participants in the creation of the record would have to be produced, a burden which would not only disrupt the business entity, but would often amount to a futile gesture because of the improbability that many of the participants would remember the details of the complex records which they helped create.

[c]—Foundation Requirements

To be eligible for admission under this exception, the records need not have been prepared by the party that seeks to introduce them.[5] The proponent must, however, be able to establish that the requirements of the Rule have been satisfied.[6]

Before the 2000 amendment to Rule 803(6), the proponent of business records usually had to present a custodian or other qualified witness to testify that the proffered documents qualified for the hearsay exception.[7] Even then, it was possible to lay a foundation without the testimony of a custodian through stipulation, judicial notice, admissions, circumstantial evidence, or the residual hearsay exception.[8]

---

grounds when custodian could not testify to their origination and compilation).

[5] *See, e.g.*, United States v. Bermea, 30 F.3d 1539, 1574 (5th Cir. 1994) (custodian of phone records did not whether records had been maintained in their original form or altered in any way, but did testify that records were accurate when they were made; court held that any break in chain of custody goes to weight of evidence rather than to its admissibility, thus, there was no abuse of discretion in admitting records).

[6] *See, e.g.*, United States v. Dakota, 197 F.3d 821, 827 (6th Cir. 1999) (government agent who seized business records did not have knowledge of the record-keeping procedures of business and was not custodian of records; therefore, records were not admissible as business records); United States v. Turner, 189 F.3d 712, 720–721 (8th Cir. 1999) (sponsoring witness could authenticate time cards and payroll records even though she had never seen those documents until shortly before trial); United States v. Patrick, 959 F.2d 991 (D.C. Cir. 1992) (sales receipt was not admissible in absence of testimony that it was the "regular practice" of the store both to record and to verify information provided by the customer).

[7] *See* former Fed. R. Evid. 803(6).

[8] *See* discussion in Zenith Radio Corp. v. Matsushita Elec. Indus. Co., 505 F. Supp. 1190, 1236 (E.D. Pa. 1980), *rev'd on other grounds*, 723 F.2d 238 (3d Cir. 1983), *rev'd on other grounds*, 475 U.S. 574 (1986); *see, e.g.*, United States v. Johnston, 127 F.3d 380, 389–390 (5th Cir. 1997) (records of business owned and operated by defendant, seized on business premises under search warrant, are admissible "once their authenticity is established regardless of whether they fit the business records exception"); United States v. Nivica, 887 F.2d 1110, 1126 (1st Cir. 1989) (although documents were

Under the current Rule 803(6), the requirements of the rule may be shown by the testimony of the custodian of the record or other qualified witness or by a declaration executed by the custodian or qualified person under penalty of perjury.[9]

A person who testifies or certifies as the foundation witness need not have personal knowledge of the actual creation of the document.[10] In fact, the phrase "other qualified witness" should be given the broadest possible interpretation. Such a witness need not even be employed by the entity whose records are being offered so long as the witness understands the system that created the records.[11] Records are not admissible without a showing that the foundation witness was familiar with the record-keeping system of the business in question[11.1] and knew how the records were created.[11.2]

[d]—Regular Practice; Scope of Business[12]

Rule 803(6) requires that the record seeking admission have been "kept in the course of a regularly conducted business activity," and that "it was the regular practice of that business activity to make" the record in question.[13]

---

erroneously admitted pursuant to Rule 803(6), error was not fatal because the documents were proffered, and were properly admissible, pursuant to the residual hearsay exception); *but see* United States v. Riley, 236 F.3d 982, 983 (8th Cir. 2001) (in criminal case, defense counsel's stipulation to admission of business record was ineffective, in face of defendant's refusal to sign stipulation form, since Due Process requires defendant's personal and voluntary acceptance of stipulations that admit element of offense).

[9] *See* Fed. R. Evid. 803(6), 902(11), 902(12).

[10] *See* United States v. Parsee, 178 F.3d 374, 380 (5th Cir. 1999) (witness need not be preparer of records, and need not personally attest to the accuracy of information contained within them).

[11] *See, e.g.*, Dyno Constr. Co. v. McWane, Inc., 198 F.3d 567, 575–576 (6th Cir. 1999) (witness need only be familiar with, and able to explain, record-keeping procedures of organization; citing **Treatise**).

[11.1] *See, e.g.*, United States v. Laster, 258 F.3d 525, 528–529 (6th Cir. 2001) (trial court erred in admitting invoices as business records when sponsoring witness was state narcotics investigator and record did not contain evidence to support conclusion he was familiar with record keeping system of business organization that generated invoices).

[11.2] *See, e.g.*, United States v. Lauersen, 343 F.3d 604, 616–617 (2d Cir. 2003) (citing **Treatise**; person who devised record-keeping system for business and observed that it was properly implemented was proper "custodian" for purposes of Rule 803(6)); United States v. Petrie, 302 F.3d 1280, 1288 (11th Cir. 2002) (secretary who knew how records were kept, but could not testify to how they were originated or compiled, was not proper sponsoring witness under Rule 803(6)).

[12] *See* discussion in **Treatise** at § 803.11[3].

[13] Fed. R. Evid. 803(6); *see* United States v. Turner, 189 F.3d 712, 720–721 (8th Cir. 1999) (time cards and payroll records were properly admitted under business records exception to hearsay rule); United States v. Ramsey, 785 F.2d 184, 192-193 (7th Cir. 1986) (desk calendar showing calls made should not have been admitted because "[o]ccasional desk calendars, in which entries may or may not appear at the whim of the writer, do not have the sort of regularity that supports a reliable inference").

The "regularly conducted business activity" requirement is intended to ensure that the rationale for the exception is satisfied. There are no guarantees of reliability when records are kept for purely personal reasons[14] because of the usual absence of factors such as systematic checking, habits of precision on the part of the record keeper, reliance by others on the records, or a duty and motive to record accurately.

The second sentence of Rule 803(6) defines "business" extremely broadly as a "business, institution, association, profession, occupation, and calling of every kind, whether or not conducted for profit." Personal records kept for business reasons,[15] and records of illicit organizations,[16] may be able to qualify for admission pursuant to Rule 803(6).

Governmental records, such as police records and reports, clearly meet the definition of business in Rule 803(6), as well.[17] Nevertheless, there is some tendency to rely upon the public records exception in Rule 803(8), since the more particular rule usually controls. The latter rule, however, contains some restrictions upon the use of police reports in criminal cases that are not found in Rule 803(6). The discussion of Rule 803(8) below considers to what extent the limitations in Rule 803(8) can be avoided by offering police reports as the records of a regularly conducted activity (see § 16.08).

The "regular practice" requirement was added by Congress. The Advisory Committee had eliminated this factor because it found that, even though a virtually identical requirement was mandated by the Federal Business Records Act, which predated the Federal Rules of Evidence, records were customarily admitted if made in the course of business without regard to routineness, except when a court was concerned with trustworthiness.

Since Congress did not intend to make the business record exception more restrictive than it previously had been, Rule 803(6) should be interpreted so that the absence of routineness does not result in exclusion of the record when all other requirements of the rule are satisfied unless "the sources of information or other circumstances indicate lack of trustworthiness."[18] This latter condition, which is

---

[14] *See, e.g.*, United States v. Santos, 201 F.3d 953, 963 (7th Cir. 2000) (error to admit employee's diary as business record of employer; diary was employee's record, not employer's).

[15] Keogh v. Commissioner, 713 F.2d 496, 499-500 (9th Cir. 1983) (diary showing income of casino dealer was admitted as it showed every indication of being kept in the regular course of business activity).

[16] *See, e.g.*, United States v. Cooper, 868 F.2d 1505, 1513–1514 (6th Cir. 1989) (log book of business selling forged prescriptions); United States v. Kasvin, 757 F.2d 887, 892-893 (7th Cir. 1985).

[17] *See, e.g.,* United States v. Reyes, 157 F.3d 949, 951–953 (2d Cir. 1998) (prison visitor logbook admitted under business records exception).

[18] Fed. R. Evid. 803(6); *compare* United States v. Jackson, 208 F.3d 633, 638 (7th Cir. 2000) (defendant's inability to show that web page posting was actually posted by white supremacist

discussed in detail in [h], *below*, operates not as a blanket exclusion, but only when the facts of the case indicate unreliability.

[e]—Transmitting with Personal Knowledge and in the Regular Course[19]

For Rule 803(6) to be satisfied, the purported business record must be based on "information transmitted by a person with knowledge."[20] The knowledge requirement means that the informant whose data is embodied in the business record must have personally perceived the matter that is the subject of the record. However, the recorder of the information need not have firsthand knowledge.[21]

Rule 803(6) also requires that the record be "made . . . by, or from information transmitted by, a person with knowledge, if kept in the course of a regularly conducted activity. . . ." This requirement, which has its counterpart in prior law,[22] has been interpreted to mean that each participant in the chain producing the event—from the initial observer-reporter to the final entrant—must be acting in the course of a regularly conducted business activity,[23] or must meet the test of some other hearsay exception (*see* Chapter 14). The guarantees of reliability

---

group, rather than inserted into web site by defendant or some other skilled computer user, indicated lack of trustworthiness of information from web site) *with* United States v. Jenkins, 345 F.3d 928, 935–936 (6th Cir. 2003) (mailing labels for express mail packages addressed to defendant at her residence were properly admitted as business records when Postal Service agent testified they were maintained in the ordinary course of business at local post office).

[19] *See* discussion in **Treatise** at § 803.11[4].

[20] Fed. R. Evid. 803(6); *see, e.g.,* City of Cleveland v. Cleveland Elec. Illuminating Co., 538 F. Supp. 1257, 1269–1270 (N.D. Ohio 1980) (reports compiled by city explaining why customers had decided to terminate electric power service from city did not satisfy Rule 803(6) since former customers were not acting "in the course of a regularly conducted business activity").

[21] *See* United States v. Reyes, 157 F.3d 949, 951–953 (2d Cir. 1998) (prison visitor logbook was properly admitted under business records exception, even though visitors had no "business duty" to provide information; testimony of custodian was sufficient to show that logbook was kept under duty of accuracy, because every visitor was required to produce identification).

[22] The leading opinion is the New York case Johnson v. Lutz, 253 N.Y. 124, 127–128 (1930), which held that entries in a policeman's accident report based upon information supplied by a bystander were inadmissible because each participant must be acting in the course of business, and the initial informant must have firsthand knowledge.

[23] *Compare* United States v. Vigneau, 187 F.3d 70, 75 (1st Cir. 1999) (information in business records provided by someone other than person with duty to gather such information in ordinary course of business is inadmissible hearsay and must be redacted from business record prior to its admission) *and* United States v. McIntyre, 997 F.2d 687, 698–699 (10th Cir. 1993) (motel registration cards should not have been admitted, as guests are not under business obligation to provide the information; no plain error; citing **Treatise**) *with* In re Ollag Constr. Corp., 665 F.2d 43, 46 (2d Cir. 1981) (financial statements prepared by debtors at bank's request on bank's own form were admitted as business records on ground that guarantees of trustworthiness surrounding financial statements are greater than for hotel registrations since they are relied upon in day-to-day operations, and criminal sanctions apply when false information is furnished).

underlying the business records exception are absent if any one of the participants is outside the pattern of regularity of activity.[24]

The two requirements—the informant's personal knowledge and that the record be made and kept in the regular course of business—lead to exclusion when the supplier of the data is not acting within the course of a regular business. A recurring situation is that of a "volunteer" offering information to persons conducting an inquiry or investigation. The person to whom the information is offered cannot qualify as the initial person in the chain, because the initial person furnishing the information must have personal knowledge of the underlying event; the transmitter who has knowledge is not a part of the chain because he or she is not acting under a business duty.[25]

Cases which at first glance appear aberrant are explicable on the ground of multiple hearsay. Rule 805 authorizes the admission of hearsay within hearsay if both statements conform to the requirements of an exception (*see* Chapter 14). Consequently, business records incorporating statements made by persons outside the business entity may be admissible under a two-step analysis. For instance, if the informant's statement qualifies as an admission, or as an excited utterance, or as a statement for purposes of medical diagnosis or treatment, the record embodying the statement is admissible if the recording was done in the course of a regularly conducted business activity.

In addition, Rule 807 allows statements to be admitted that fulfill requirements of trustworthiness even if they fail to meet the tests of a particular exception.[26] A judge, therefore, has some discretion to admit the statements of non-participants in the regular activity if the facts remove the taint of unreliability.[27]

---

[24] *Compare* Chadwell v. Koch Ref. Co., 251 F.3d 727, 732 (8th Cir. 2001) (trial court properly excluded notes of meeting between employee and his supervisors because note-taker, who was both employee and shop steward, was acting in his capacity as shop steward and notes were not prepared in ordinary course of his business) *with* United States v. Childs, 5 F.3d 1328 (9th Cir. 1993) (documents kept by auto dealers were admissible, although records were not made by dealers; so long as documents were integrated into dealers' records, and kept in regular course of business, fact that they were furnished by other sources did not render admission improper).

[25] *See, e.g.,* United States v. Patrick, 248 F.3d 11, 22 (1st Cir. 2001) (tips from informants included in police notes were not admissible as business records because informants "are not themselves part of the business of police").

[26] Rule 807 is discussed in Chapter 14.

[27] *See, e.g.,* United States v. Ullrich, 580 F.2d 765, 772 (5th Cir. 1978) (court admitted, through testimony of manager of automobile agency, inventory schedule prepared by Ford Motor Company); United States v. Flom, 558 F.2d 1179, 1182 (5th Cir. 1977) (invoices prepared by one company and held in regular course of defendant's business admitted even though they were offered through testimony of official of receiving rather than preparing entity; circumstances demonstrate trustworthiness and "trial judge has a broad zone of discretion").

[f]—Contemporaneity of Recording and Form of Record[28]

Rule 803(6) requires the record to be "made at or near the time" of the events recorded. The purpose of the provision is to increase the probability of accuracy. It should not, however, be applied mechanically. The circumstances of the particular case must be taken into consideration in determining whether the persons compiling the record had a fresh recollection of the matter sought to be proved at the time the entry was made.[29]

Rule 803(6) broadly describes the form the record must assume as a "memorandum, report, record or data compilation." This provision is intended to mandate the admission of any form of writing so long as the tests of the business record exception are satisfied.

The term "data compilation" was added to ensure the admissibility of records not kept in conventional written form, including audio tapes and electronic, magnetic, and other types of computer data storage.[30] If the data was entered into the computer "at or near the time" of the events recorded, and the court is convinced of the trustworthiness of the information produced, it should admit printouts even if they were made in preparation for litigation and not in the ordinary course of business long after the events in question.[31] A mechanical insistence on having the printouts satisfy the contemporaneity requirement would undermine the usefulness of computerized record-keeping.[32] The court has the power under the discretion afforded it by the last clause of Rule 803(6), authorizing exclusion for a "lack of trustworthiness," to determine the amount and kind of information that must be

---

[28] *See* discussion in **Treatise** at § 803.11[5].

[29] *See, e.g.,* United States v. Goodchild, 25 F.3d 55, 62 (1st Cir. 1994) (company memos about telephone conversations between defendant and company were properly admitted as business records because company employee, although not involved in making of these memos, understood procedures and records used in such circumstances and testified that they were made during or immediately after conversations, they were made and kept in regular course of business, and it was regular course of company to keep such records).

[30] *See, e.g.,* Dyno Constr. Co. v. McWane, Inc., 198 F.3d 567, 575 (6th Cir. 1999) (trial court properly admitted computer printout reconstructing delivery information from computerized database).

[31] *See, e.g.,* United States v. Sanders, 749 F.2d 195, 198–199 (5th Cir. 1984) (when testimony established that data was prepared and kept pursuant to procedures designed to assure accuracy, fact that data was summoned in a readable form shortly before trial did not require exclusion when data had been entered contemporaneously with events recorded and no further modifications had been made); United States v. Fusero, 106 F. Supp. 2d 921, 924 (E.D. Mich. 2000) (proper to admit computer-generated document prepared for litigation containing information that was entered into computer in ordinary course of business at or about time of events in question, even when purpose of document is to show defendant's failure to file federal income tax returns).

[32] United States v. Russo, 480 F.2d 1228, 1240 (6th Cir. 1973).

furnished, and by whom, in laying the foundation for data compilations.[33] Expert testimony on the type of software programs used and modifications in the data after original entry may be required.

[g]—Acts, Events, Conditions, Opinions or Diagnoses; Hospital Records[34]

To lay to rest the recurring dispute under prior law as to whether records containing "opinions" rather than facts are embraced by the business records exception, Rule 803(6) unequivocally states that records of "acts, events, conditions, opinions or diagnoses" are admissible.

The admissibility of statements of opinion under the business records exception had been especially troublesome in the area of medical records. From the standpoint of the opinion rule, all statements by physicians incorporated in a hospital record or in a report concerning the patient's condition or its cause consist of opinion except for recordation of facts directly observed, such as temperature, blood pressure and other objective factors. While the relevancy of medical records is apparent, advocates of a restrictive rule feared that when opinions are admitted, the jury is unable to assess the qualifications of their authors or the accuracy of their conclusions because records cannot be cross- examined. In contrast, proponents of the admissibility of medical records containing diagnostic opinions pointed to the need for such evidence, the reputability of physicians and medical institutions, the uncertain line between fact and opinion and, above all, the adversary's right to subpoena the reporting physician in order to bring out any weaknesses of the diagnosis.

Prior to the enactment of the Federal Rules of Evidence, most federal courts reached an accommodation between the need for relevant information and the fear of uncross-examined opinion. They drew a distinction between diagnoses involving "conjecture and opinion" and diagnoses upon which "competent physicians would not differ."[35]

While Rule 803(6) rejects any attempt to exclude a particular class of hospital records, and does not distinguish between the routine and the conjectural, the last phrase of Rule 803(6) authorizes the trial judge to exclude a particular record where

---

[33] *See, e.g.,* United States v. Salgado, 250 F.3d 438, 451–453 (6th Cir. 2001) (trial court did not err in finding computer printout trustworthy when employee of company testified it represented type of record his company regularly generated and maintained in its files, and that his company relied on similar reports for billing purposes; fact that many entries were made by computer, rather than by human being, and witness's lack of knowledge of error rate did not disqualify record for admission as business record).

[34] *See* discussion in **Treatise** at § 803.11[7][a].

[35] New York Life Ins. Co. v. Taylor, 147 F.2d 297, 300 (D.C. Cir. 1944) (leading case).

indications of trustworthiness are shown to be lacking. The court may choose to exercise this power if the record or other evidence indicates that the author of the record is unqualified, or the diagnostic opinion is of a type about which competent experts disagree. If the expert is available, the judge may require the expert to testify, particularly if the medical issue is crucial.[36]

Records of patients who were examined for diagnosis only in connection with pending litigation may, at first, seem to be lacking in requisite trustworthiness since the diagnoses will not be relied upon by persons responsible for treatment. While this may be true in a particular case, wholesale exclusion is unwarranted as incompatible with Rule 803(4), which admits statements made with a view to diagnosis alone. As the discussion under Rule 803(4) indicates, the statements would in any event be available under Rule 703 to show the basis of the physician's diagnosis, and experts can generally be relied upon to consider trustworthy facts in arriving at professional conclusions. These reasons apply equally to Rule 803(6). There is no more reason to expect a physician to render an unreliable diagnosis than there is to expect him to base it on untrustworthy facts. Nevertheless, there may be instances where the court feels that the particular facts of the case warrant excluding the records unless the physician appears as a witness.

Non-medical opinions in business records are also admissible pursuant to Rule 803(6) provided they meet the requirements of the rule. Since the transmitter of the information on which the record is based must have had personal knowledge of the matter on which he expressed an opinion, some guarantee of reliability is present, but other problems of trustworthiness may arise similar to those posed by the proffer of intracompany reports as admissions.[37]

The trial judge has discretion, pursuant to Rule 803(6), as well as Rule 403 and Rule 805, to assess the particular factors present to determine whether a more accurate determination could probably be obtained by admitting or excluding the record.[38] Such determinations should, wherever possible, be made at the pretrial

---

[36] *See, e.g.,* Petrocelli v. Gallison, 679 F.2d 286, 291 (1st Cir. 1982) (in medical malpractice action, trial court did not err in excluding two entries in hospital record which stated that nerve had been severed, most critical issue in the case, when it was impossible to determine whether entries were made by patient or physicians, and plaintiff apparently made no attempt to depose or otherwise seek clarification from physicians so that trial court could "entertain legitimate doubts as to whether the doctors who recorded these statements were actually rendering professional judgments").

[37] *See* discussion in **Treatise** at § 803.11[7][b], and *see* Chapter 15.

[38] Forward Communications Corp. v. United States, 608 F.2d 485, 510–511 (Cl. Ct. 1979) (in action for recovery of federal taxes, plaintiff sought to prove valuation by proffering report by appraiser pursuant to Rule 803(6); court held that report could not be admitted where record failed to disclose qualifications or identity of appraiser and opinions were not incident to or part of factual reports of contemporaneous events or transactions; for report to be admitted, preparer must be present to testify and to be cross-examined pursuant to Rule 702 and 705); United States v. Licavoli,

stages so that counsel can be prepared to obtain other evidence by live witnesses, normal depositions or videotape depositions. Failure to rule in advance may require continuances during the trial to avoid a miscarriage of justice.

[h]—Lack of Trustworthiness; Accident Reports[39]

The Advisory Committee was unwilling to mandate a hearsay exception for anything recorded in the course of a regularly conducted activity. It recognized that a motive to misrepresent rather than the regular course of business leads to the creation of some records,[40] which consequently are not sufficiently reliable to escape the proscription of the hearsay rule. Because of the impossibility of formulating a provision specific enough to apply to all situations, Rule 803(6) provides that records made in the course of a regularly conducted activity are admissible "unless the sources of information or other circumstances indicate lack of trustworthiness."

The "lack of trustworthiness" formula directs courts to consider the context in which the record was created. In order to evaluate motivation, the court may have to consider factors such as: whether the material was prepared specifically for litigation,[41] whether non-litigation purposes were served by the report,[42] who

---

604 F.2d 613, 622–623 (9th Cir. 1979) (record of appraisal of value of painting properly admitted even though proponent of record did not establish qualifications of appraiser; court refused to adopt inflexible rule of exclusion in absence of demonstration of untrustworthiness; since opponent raised no specific facts raising doubts about appraiser's qualification and insurance company relied on appraisal in making payment, trial judge did not abuse discretion in admitting).

[39] *See* **Treatise** at § 803.11[7][c].

[40] The paradigm case preceding the enactment of the Federal Rules was Palmer v. Hoffman, 318 U.S. 109, 63 S. Ct. 477, 87 L. Ed. 645 (1943), *aff'g* 129 F.2d 976 (2d Cir. 1942) in which both the circuit court and the Supreme Court held that the report made by a railroad engineer, deceased by the time of trial, about the railroad collision in which he had been involved, could not be admitted as a business record. The Second Circuit excluded the report on the ground that it was "dripping with motivations to misrepresent" (129 F.2d at 991); the Supreme Court affirmed on the theory that the report was not "in the regular course of business," since the business of a railroad is "railroading," not litigating (318 U.S. at 114). Despite the Supreme Court's rationale for exclusion, subsequent cases stressed that the motive to misrepresent rather than the regular course of business lies at the heart of the *Palmer v. Hoffman* situation. The Advisory Committee approved this view in its Notes to Rule 803(6).

[41] *See, e.g.*, Certain Underwriters at Lloyd's v. Sinkovich, 232 F.3d 200, 204–205 (4th Cir. 2000) (documents prepared with a view to litigation do not have hallmarks of trustworthiness necessary for admission under Rule 803(6) because they were not prepared for systematic operations of business enterprise); United States v. Williams, 661 F.2d 528, 531 (5th Cir. 1981) (error to have admitted statement that trailer was worth $5,600 when "[a]ll too clearly" declarant prepared statement for purposes of trial only and $5,000 was the minimum jurisdictional amount).

[42] *See, e.g.*, Abdel v. United States, 670 F.2d 73, 75 (7th Cir. 1982) (Department of Agriculture reports were sufficiently reliable where they were completed regardless of whether violations were found, and litigation did not necessarily ensue even when violations were found); United States v.

prepared the report in question,[43] and who is offering the report.[44] Whenever possible, the assessment of probative force should be left to the jury. The jury's function should not be reduced by excluding relevant evidence unless the court is reasonably assured that the result of the litigation will be less reliable were the evidence to be revealed to the jury.

Even when the facts disclose the possibility of a motive to misrepresent, the court may be able to devise measures that will diminish the dangers posed by the record without depriving the fact-finder of relevant evidence. When the declarant is available, the court may condition admissibility of the record on the declarant's being called as a witness so that his or her credibility can be examined. When the declarant is unavailable, the court may take into account what evidence would be available, pursuant to Rule 806, to attack the credibility of the declarant if the record is admitted. The significance of the evidence contained in the record, the availability of other evidence on the point,[45] the degree to which the declarant's bias would be self-evident to the jury, and the circumstances in which the record was made,[46] are all factors which the court should consider in determining whether the need for the evidence outweighs the dangers stemming from its admission.

Statements by professionals, such as physicians, expressing their opinions on a relevant matter should be excluded only in rare instances, particularly if the expert is independent of any party, and especially if the reports had been made available to the other side through discovery so that rebuttal evidence can be prepared.

The "lack of trustworthiness" language of Rule 803(6) is broad enough to encompass other aspects of unreliability besides the declarant's motive to misrepresent. For instance, records may be excluded because of untrustworthiness if the type of record does not satisfy the rationale for the exception, or the entry was

---

Grossman, 614 F.2d 295, 296 (1st Cir. 1980) (catalogue properly admitted to identify lighters in question since catalogue is compilation for business purposes that has its own guarantee of trustworthiness).

[43] *See, e.g.,* Lewis v. Baker, 526 F.2d 470 (2d Cir. 1975) (railroad accident report; no motive to misrepresent when preparers of report were not involved in lawsuit and could not have been target of lawsuit by plaintiff; reports were made pursuant to ICC requirements and were relied upon by employer in preventing accidents).

[44] *See, e.g.,* United States v. Smith, 521 F.2d 957, 967 (D.C. Cir. 1975), *quoting* Bracey v. Herringa, 466 F.2d 702, 705 n.9 (7th Cir. 1972) (" 'Police reports are ordinarily excluded when offered by the party at whose instance they were made,' . . . but may still be admitted as business records when, as here, they are offered against . . . the prosecution.").

[45] *See, e.g.,* United States v. Cincotta, 689 F.2d 238, 243 (1st Cir. 1982) (notebook admitted; its entries were corroborated, although it would have been "untrustworthy standing alone").

[46] *See, e.g.,* United States v. Davis, 542 F.2d 743 (8th Cir. 1976) (list of serial numbers of bait money admitted when list remained unchanged until bait money was removed, list was periodically checked and audited, and kept in regular course of business at all teller windows in accordance with regular practice of bank).

made or kept improperly,[47] or the declarant-expert did not have sufficient qualifications.[48]

[i]—Criminal Cases

Rule 803(8) prohibits the use of investigative reports, and reports of matters observed by police and other law enforcement officers, as evidence against an accused. As is discussed more fully below in the treatment of Rule 803(8) (*see* § 16.08), a number of courts have held that a report barred by Rule 803(8) cannot be admitted even though it satisfies another hearsay exception such as Rule 803(6).[49] Most courts, however, have held that Congress did not intend to exclude records of routine, nonadversarial matters either under Rules 803(6) or 803(8).[50] Furthermore, a number of courts have held that the restrictions in Rule 803(8) will not bar resort to some other hearsay exception, provided the declarant takes the stand and is subject to cross-examination.[51]

The circuits have split on whether records admitted pursuant to the business records exception automatically satisfy a Confrontation Clause challenge.[52]

---

[47] *See, e.g.*, Weir v. Crown Equip. Corp., 217 F.3d 453, 458 (7th Cir. 2000) (trial court properly excluded for lack of trustworthiness accident reports which, although found in defendant's files, were collected from various sources and were "vague, incomplete, and otherwise confusing"); United States v. Houser, 746 F.2d 55, 56-63 (D.C. Cir. 1984) (error to have admitted Bureau of Alcohol, Tobacco and Firearms tracer form to show weapon's movement in interstate commerce; Special Agent had given serial number of weapon to BATF clerk over phone, and clerk had then phoned manufacturer and filled out form; neither clerk nor manufacturer's representative was identified; court found that possibility of error in passing on number from agent to clerk to manufacturer's employee and then passing information back to clerk was too great to satisfy trustworthiness requirement); Lloyd v. Professional Realty Servs., Inc., 734 F.2d 1428, 1433 (11th Cir. 1984) (draft minutes excluded as untrustworthy where draft was marked and edited and quite different from final copy of minutes that had previously been admitted).

[48] *See* discussion in Chapter 13.

[49] *See, e.g.*, United States v. Pena-Gutierrez, 222 F.3d 1080, 1086–1087 (9th Cir. 2000), *cert. denied*, 531 U.S. 1057 (2000) (law enforcement investigative reports, if admissible at all, must be admitted under Rule 803(8), not Rule 803(5)); United States v. Oates, 560 F.2d 45 (2d Cir. 1977).

[50] *See, e.g.*, United States v. Orozco, 590 F.2d 789 (9th Cir. 1979).

[51] *See, e.g.*, United States v. King, 613 F.2d 670 (7th Cir. 1980) (Social Security forms relating to interview with defendant admissible pursuant to Rule 803(6) when author testified).

[52] *Compare* United States v. Haili, 443 F.2d 1295 (9th Cir. 1971) *and* United States v. Leal, 509 F.2d 122 (9th Cir. 1975) (holding in the affirmative) *with* United States v. Smith, 521 F.2d 957 (D.C. Cir. 1975) *and* McDaniel v. United States, 343 F.2d 785 (5th Cir. 1965) (holding in the negative).

[3]—Absence of Entry in Records of Regularly Conducted Activity—Rule 803(7)[1]

When evidence of the failure to mention a matter that would ordinarily be mentioned is offered to prove the nonoccurrence or nonexistence of the matter, Rule 803(7) authorizes the admission of such evidence as an exception to the hearsay rule. For instance, the absence of any records indicating that freight cars were inspected and cleaned may be used to prove the nonoccurrence or nonexistence of any cleaning or inspection of the cars.[2]

Rule 803(7) provides as follows:

Rule 803(7).   Hearsay Exceptions; Availability of Declarant Immaterial.

The following are not excluded by the hearsay rule, even though the declarant is available as a witness:

. . .

(7) Absence of entry in records kept in accordance with the provisions of paragraph (6).—Evidence that a matter is not included in the memoranda, reports, records, or data compilations, in any form, kept in accordance with the provisions of paragraph (6), to prove the nonoccurrence or nonexistence of the matter, if the matter was of a kind of which a memorandum, report, record, or data compilation was regularly made and preserved, unless the sources of information or other circumstances indicate lack of trustworthiness.

Demonstrating that the records were kept in such a way that the matter would have been recorded had it occurred, is, of course, crucial.[3]

The last phrase of Rule 803(7)—which mandates exclusion if "the sources of information or other circumstances indicate lack of trustworthiness"—is identical to the concluding phrase of Rule 803(6), and should receive the same interpretation. The motivation and qualification of the entrant, and the manner in which the records were made and stored are some of the questions that may be raised pursuant to this provision.

---

[1] *See* discussion in **Treatise** at § 803.12.

[2] *See* Kaiser Aluminum & Chem. Corp. v. Illinois Cent. Gulf R.R., 615 F.2d 470 (5th Cir. 1980).

[3] *See, e.g.*, Fury Import Inc. v. Shakespeare Co., 554 F.2d 1376, 1381 (5th Cir. 1977) (error for judge to conclude on basis of Rule 803(7) that there were no orders because there was no documentary evidence thereof when there had been testimony that orders were not always in written form).

[4]—Statements in Ancient Documents—Rule 803(16)[1]

Rule 803(16) recognizes that statements in a document at least 20 years old whose authenticity is established may be admitted as evidence of the truth of the facts recited.[2] The rule provides as follows:

Rule 803(16).   Hearsay Exceptions; Availability of Declarant Immaterial.

The following are not excluded by the hearsay rule, even though the declarant is available as a witness:

. . .

(16) Statements in ancient documents.—Statements in a document in existence twenty years or more the authenticity of which is established.

In other words, the hearsay exception applies if the proponent of the document has authenticated it. The primary method of authenticating ancient documents is by complying with the requirements set forth in Rule 901(b)(8). The authentication rule ensures that the document is in writing, that it was produced from proper custody and that it is unsuspicious in appearance (*see* Chapter 8). It is, of course, the proponent's burden to show all facts necessary to authenticate the ancient document.[3] These factors point to reliability, which is further enhanced because the age of the document virtually ensures that the statement was made before the controversy resulting in the present litigation arose, and before any motivation to misrepresent was present.

Rule 803(16) does not expressly contain a requirement of personal knowledge, although the notes to Rule 803 indicate that this condition applies to all declarants. While it would usually be impossible to prove actual knowledge on the part of the declarant after the lapse of so many years, the court should require a showing from the circumstances that declarant could have had the requisite knowledge. If not, the statement should be excluded.

---

[1] *See* discussion in **Treatise** at § 803.21.

[2] George v. Celotex Corp., 914 F.2d 26 (2d Cir. 1990) (an unpublished report was admissible as a statement in an ancient document; the document had been in existence for more than twenty years and its authenticity was established at trial).

[3] *See, e.g.,* Kalamazoo River Study Group v. Menasha Corp., 228 F.3d 648, 662 (6th Cir. 2000) (when proponent failed to show that document was found in place where it would be expected to be and failed to identify source of document, document was not properly authenticated and was inadmissible under Rule 803(16)).

§ 16.08   Records of Public Entities

[1]—Overview

The exceptions for public records are treated analogously to the exceptions for private records. There is one principal rule, Rule 803(8), which is by far the most frequently used. Rule 803(10), which is the exception for evidence of the absence of a public record, corresponds in the public sphere to Rule 803(7) in the private. Both of these rules are discussed below, as is Rule 803(9), which makes admissible records of vital statistics, and Rule 803(22), which governs judgments of convictions.

Rule 803(23) [1] allows a judgment to be admitted as prima facie evidence of a fact essential to the determination, if the fact is concerned with a matter of personal, family or general history or boundaries, and would be provable by evidence of reputation pursuant to Rule 803(19) or (20).[2] Rule 803(23) provides as follows:

Rule 803(23).   Hearsay Exceptions; Availability of Declarant Immaterial.

The following are not excluded by the hearsay rule, even though the declarant is available as a witness:

. . .

(23)   Judgment as to personal, family, or general history, or boundaries.—Judgments as proof of matters of personal, family or general history, or boundaries, essential to the judgment, if the same would be provable by evidence of reputation.

---

[2]—Public Records—Rule 803(8)

[a]—Scope and Text of Rule[1]

Rule 803(8) recognizes three categories of public records that generally will be admissible despite the hearsay rule: (1) records of the office's or agency's own activities,[2] (2) records of "matters observed pursuant to duty imposed by law,"[3] and (3) investigative reports. Rule 803(8) does not distinguish between federal and

---

[1]   *See* discussion in **Treatise** at §§ 803.19–803.20.

[2]   *See* text of Rule 803(19), (20) at § 16.10.

[1]   *See* discussion in **Treatise** at § 803.13[1], [2].

[2]   *See* United States v. Fletcher, 322 F.3d 508, 518 (8th Cir. 2003) (IRS assessments were properly admitted under Rule 803(8) as public records and reports).

[3]   This category also had been recognized under law predating the Federal Rules of Evidence. *See, e.g.,* La Porte v. United States, 300 F.2d 878, 879-80 (9th Cir. 1962) (observation of defendant's failure to comply with selective service regulations).

non-federal offices—the sole criterion is whether the record is that of a public body.[4]

Rule 803(8) differs from the business records exception set forth in Rule 803(6) in two important respects. First, because the assurances of accuracy are even greater for public records than for business records, a public record is admitted as proof of the facts to which it relates without foundation testimony by a custodian or other qualified witness. Authentication is required.[5] Eliminating the need for a foundation also furthers the exception's goal of not disrupting governmental work by forcing officials into court. Second, the rule recognizes that in criminal cases the Confrontation Clause may impose limits on the use of investigative and police reports against an accused.[6]

The public records exception—which should be interpreted as broadly as Rule 803(6)—is like the business records exception in providing the trial judge with discretion to determine admissibility on a case by case basis. A lack of trustworthiness mandates exclusion[7] unless the difficulty can be obviated by measures such as testimony by a custodian or the author of the report in question.[8] The trial court may not, however, exclude a public record or report on the ground that it lacks trustworthiness simply because an opinion it contains is, in the trial court's view, not credible.[8.1] The burden is on the opponent of the report to demonstrate untrustworthiness.[9]

Rule 803(8) provides as follows:

Rule 803(8).   Hearsay Exceptions; Availability of Declarant Immaterial.

---

[4] United States v. Torres, 733 F.2d 449, 455 n. 5 (7th Cir. 1984) (Indian Tribal Roll); In re Agent Orange Litig., 611 F. Supp. 1223, 1239–1241 (E.D.N.Y. 1985) (epidemiological studies of federal, state and Australian governments).

[5] The record will be self-authenticating if it meets the requirements of Rule 902(4). *See* Chapter 8. *See also* Rule 1005 on use of copies of public records. *See* Chapter 9.

[6] *See* discussion, [b]–[d], *below*, below of the restrictions built into subdivisions (B) and (C).

[7] *See, e.g.,* United States v. Jackson-Randolph, 282 F.3d 369, 380–381 (6th Cir. 2002) (although report of hearing examiner's investigation into claims for reimbursement for food program costs would normally be admissible under Rule 803(8), trial court properly excluded it because it was based on testimony of defendant's partner in suspicious activities given at time witness had strong motives to lie, so report was not trustworthy).

[8] *See, e.g.,* Givens v. Lederle, 556 F.2d 1341, 1346 (5th Cir. 1977) (documents prepared by Centers for Disease Control listing vaccine-induced polio cases were admissible; editor of reports identified reports and was subject to cross- examination).

[8.1] *See, e.g.,* Blake v. Pellegrino, 329 F.3d 43, 48 (1st Cir. 2003).

[9] *See* United States v. McIntosh, 200 F.3d 1168, 1169 (8th Cir. 2000) (defendant was entitled to present evidence to show that certified state court documents were incorrect, but failed to do so).

The following are not excluded by the hearsay rule, even though the declarant is available as a witness:

. . .

(8) Public records and reports.—Records, reports, statements, or data compilations, in any form, of public offices or agencies, setting forth (A) the activities of the office or agency, or (B) matters observed pursuant to duty imposed by law as to which matters there was a duty to report, excluding, however, in criminal cases matters observed by police officers and other law enforcement personnel, or (C) in civil actions and proceedings and against the Government in criminal cases, factual findings resulting from an investigation made pursuant to authority granted by law, unless the sources of information or other circumstances indicate lack of trustworthiness.

[b]—Personal Knowledge Requirement[10]

Rule 803(8) is silent about a requirement of personal knowledge, although the introductory note to Rule 803 states that "neither this rule nor Rule 804 dispense with the requirement of first hand knowledge." In the case of Rule 803(8), this requirement must be interpreted flexibly, bearing in mind that the primary objective of the hearsay rule is to bar untrustworthy evidence.[10.1]

In the case of records of activities performed or facts observed (Rule 803(8)(A), (B)), the personal knowledge requirement should be enforced.[11] The initial person in the chain creating the report must have personal knowledge of the transaction; the official who prepares the actual report may rely on a government colleague or subordinate with personal knowledge. The history of subdivisions (A) and (B) of Rule 803(8) indicates that the drafters intended the initial informant to be an official, but some courts interpret Rule 803(8) rather broadly as authorizing the admission of reports made by a private person pursuant to a statutory duty.[12] Courts that take a more restrictive view of the personal knowledge requirement of subdivisions (A)

---

[10] *See* discussion in **Treatise** at § 803.13[3].

[10.1] *See, e.g.,* United States v. Midwest Fireworks Mfg. Co., 248 F.3d 563, 566–567 (6th Cir. 2001) (public agency reports are admissible under Rule 803(8) even if person with personal knowledge is not present in court).

[11] United States v. Mackey, 117 F. 3d 24, 28 (1st Cir. 1997) (statements by third persons are not admissible under this exception merely because they appear within public records); Nachtsheim v. Beech Aircraft Corp., 847 F.2d 1261, 1271- 1273 (7th Cir. 1988) (court did not abuse discretion in excluding statement appended to government report made by unknown author since plaintiffs were unable to establish that the official who reported the disputed statement had firsthand knowledge of the condition observed; cites **Treatise**).

[12] *See, e.g.,* United States v. Central Gulf Lines, Inc., 747 F.2d 315, 319 (5th Cir. 1984) (survey conducted by independent surveyor with a duty to report to a public official).

and (B) may nevertheless find the reports of ad hoc officials sufficiently trustworthy to be admitted pursuant to Rule 803(6) [13] or the residual hearsay exception.[14]

In the case of investigative reports, the subject of Rule 803(8)(C), the official has a duty other than to record or certify facts ascertained through an official's personal observation. The reports are admissible because they satisfy the requirement of reliability in other ways. Therefore, when this kind of record is offered as evidence, the personal knowledge requirement must be liberally construed.[15] Reports filed by outside consultants that are incorporated in an agency report will not qualify if the court finds that they do not embody the findings of the agency.[16]

[c]—Investigative Reports: Civil Cases[17]

The officials involved in the preparation of an investigative report need not have firsthand knowledge about the events sought to be proved through the report, since the reliability of an investigative report stems from the ability of an experienced investigator to determine which facts are sufficiently trustworthy to be relied upon in reaching conclusions.[18] The trial court has discretion, however, to exclude the report if it finds a lack of trustworthiness, such as an improper motive or insufficient qualifications or diligence on the part of the investigator.[19] Through resort to discovery, the opponent of the report can investigate the author's qualifications, and may be able to take his or her deposition. The trial court has discretion to condition admission of the report upon having the author produced for examination.

Rule 803(8)(C) makes admissible "reports . . . setting forth . . . factual findings." Although the meaning of "factual findings" was not entirely clear when the rule went into effect, due in part to a somewhat inconclusive legislative history,[20]

---

[13]   *See, e.g.*, United States v. Leal, 509 F.2d 122, 127 (9th Cir. 1975) (Hong Kong hotel registration forms were admitted as business records despite lack of testimony by custodian; court noted that analogy with official records was not inappropriate since forms were required by Hong Kong law).

[14]   *See* Ch. 14 for discussion of the residual hearsay exception.

[15]   *See* discussion in [c], *below.*

[16]   Brown v. Sierra Nevada Mem. Miners Hosp., 849 F.2d 1186, 1189–1190 (9th Cir. 1988).

[17]   *See* discussion in **Treatise** at § 803.13[4].

[18]   Trustees of Univ. of Pa. v. Lexington Ins. Co., 815 F.2d 890, 905 (3d Cir. 1987) (judicial findings not within scope of rule); *see* Bridgeway Corp. v. Citibank, 201 F.3d 134, 143 (2d Cir. 2000) (State Department Report on Liberia was presumptively admissible under Rule 803(8)(C)).

[19]   *See, e.g.*, Smith v. Isuzu Motors, Ltd., 137 F.3d 859, 861–863 (5th Cir. 1998) (internal federal agency memoranda containing opinions of agency staff that were rejected by agency are inadmissible).

[20]   While the House Judiciary Committee stated that it "intends that the phrase 'factual findings' be strictly construed and that evaluations or opinions contained in public reports shall not be admissible under this Rule," the Senate Committee on the Judiciary took "strong exception to this limiting understanding." *See* House Comm. on Judiciary, H.R. Rep. No. 650, 93d Cong., 1st Sess.,

the Supreme Court has unanimously endorsed the view, which already had been adopted by a majority of the Circuits,[21] that the phrase must be given an expansive meaning. In *Beech Aircraft Corp. v. Rainey,* [22] the Court held that

> . . . portions of investigatory reports otherwise admissible under Rule 803(8)(C) are not inadmissible merely because they state a conclusion or opinion. As long as the conclusion is based on a factual investigation and satisfies the Rule's trustworthiness requirement, it should be admissible along with other portions of the report.[23]

Accordingly, the Court found that the trial judge had not erred in admitting conclusions in a report concerning the probable cause of the crash of a Navy training aircraft. The Court noted that a broad interpretation of "factual findings" is consistent with the plain meaning of Rule 803(8), furthers the intent of the Advisory Committee to make evaluative reports admissible, and is in accord with "the liberal thrust of the Federal Rules"[24] and their "general approach of relaxing the traditional barriers to 'opinion' testimony."[25]

There is conflict between the circuits concerning the admissibility under Rule 803(8)(C) of findings of fact from prior judicial proceedings. The Sixth Circuit takes the position that the justifications for the admission of investigative reports of other types of governmental agencies are equally applicable to the findings of courts, and it is the burden of the opponent to show unreliability to prevent their admission.[26] The Third,[26.1] Fourth,[26.2] Tenth,[26.3] and Eleventh Circuits[26.4] hold

---

p. 14 (1973); Senate Comm. on Judiciary, S. Rep. No. 1277, 93d Cong., 2d Sess., p. 18 (1974). No reference to the differing approaches was made in the Conference Report. A broader conception of the phrase is consonant with the Advisory Committee's Note, which accepted "evaluative reports" as being within the scope of Rule 803(8)(C).

[21] All circuits other than the Fifth and Eleventh that had considered the issue had adopted the broader interpretation. *See, e.g.,* Zenith Radio Corp. v. Matsushita Elec. Indus. Co., 505 F. Supp. 1125, 1144–1445 (E.D. Pa. 1980), *rev'd on other grounds,* 723 F.2d 238 (3d Cir. 1983), *rev'd on other grounds,* 475 U.S. 574 (1986) (court concluded after extensive review of the decided cases that "it is now generally accepted (and settled in this circuit) that under the aegis of 803(8)(C) evaluative reports of public agencies (*i.e.,* those rendering normative judgments or opinions, not just reciting facts) are admissible."); Ellis v. International Playtex, Inc. 745 F.2d 292, 299–304 (4th Cir. 1984) (wrongful death action; studies of toxic shock syndrome conducted by the Centers for Disease Control are admissible); Robbins v. Whelan, 653 F.2d 47, 50 (1st Cir. 1981) (error to exclude report of Transportation Department on maximum stopping distances of different model cars).

[22] Beech Aircraft Corp. v. Rainey, 488 U.S. 153, 109 S. Ct. 439, 102 L. Ed.2d 445 (1988) (citing **Treatise**).

[23] 488 U.S. at 170, 109 S. Ct. at 450, 102 L. Ed.2d at 463.

[24] 488 U.S. at 169, 109 S. Ct. at 450, 102 L. Ed.2d at 463.

[25] 488 U.S. at 169.

[26] *See, e.g.,* United States v. Garland, 991 F.2d 328, 334–335 (6th Cir. 1993) (Ghanian judgment of conviction not unreliable on its face is admissible, under Rule 803(8)(C), absent proof

that Rule 803(8)(C) was intended to apply only to investigative reports of the executive branch of the government, not to fact findings by the judicial branch; they find that judicial findings of fact are not admissible under Rule 803(8)(C).

A report that simply reaches a conclusion without any factual underpinnings is useless to fact-finders because it simply tells them how to decide a case without giving them sufficient information upon which to reach an informed decision. In this sense, the opinion must be factual. If, however, the report states an opinion that is helpful, it should be admitted, provided the report does not suffer from a lack of trustworthiness.[27] The Supreme Court approved of this approach in *Beech Aircraft Corp. v. Rainey.* [28]

Trustworthiness must be determined by the trial court on a case by case basis. Many courts have followed the suggestion in the Advisory Committee's notes to Rule 803(8)(C) that the following factors should be evaluated in deciding whether a lack of reliability has been shown: (1) the timeliness of the investigation; (2) the skill or experience of the official conducting the investigation; (3) whether a hearing has been held in connection with the investigation; and (4) possible motivational problems on the part of the preparer of the report.[29] The burden is on the opponent of the report to demonstrate untrustworthiness.[30]

---

offered by opponent to show judgment's unreliability, to prove contents of factual recitations it contains).

[26.1] *See, e.g.,* Trustees of Univ. of Pa. v. Lexington Ins. Co., 815 F.2d 890, 905 (3d Cir. 1987).

[26.2] *See, e.g.,* Nipper v. Snipes, 7 F.3d 415, 417 (4th Cir. 1993).

[26.3] *See, e.g.,* Herrick v. Garvey, 298 F.3d 1184, 1192–1193 (10th Cir. 2002).

[26.4] *See, e.g.,* United States v. Jones, 29 F.3d 1549, 1554 (11th Cir. 1994).

[27] *See, e.g.,* Cooper v. Carl A. Nelson & Co., 211 F.3d 1008, 1017 (7th Cir. 2000) (trial court has significant discretion in determining whether proffered evidence meets admissibility criteria of Rule 803(8)(C)); Gilbrook v. City of Westminster, 177 F.3d 839, 858–859 (9th Cir. 1999) ("Factually based conclusions and opinions . . . are not on that account excluded from the scope of Rule 803(8)(C)").

[28] Beech Aircraft Corp. v. Rainey, 488 U.S. 153, 169, 109 S. Ct. 439, 449-450, 102 L. Ed. 2d 445, 463 (1988) ("The Rule's limitations and safeguards lie elsewhere: First, the requirement that reports contain factual findings bars the admission of statements not based on factual investigation. Second, the trustworthiness provision requires the court to make a determination as to whether the report, or any portion thereof, is sufficiently trustworthy to be admitted").

[29] *See, e.g.,* Simmons v. Chicago and Northwestern Transp. Co., 993 F.2d 1326 (8th Cir. 1993) (trooper's timely accident report was admissible; the trooper was experienced, skilled, and objective, and the investigation was straightforward and uncomplicated).

[30] Bridgeway Corp. v. Citibank, 201 F.3d 134, 143 (2d Cir. 2000) (if report contains factual findings and is based on an investigation made pursuant to legal authority, admissibility of factual findings is presumed; burden to show lack of trustworthiness shifts to party opposing admission).

[d]—Criminal Cases[31]

The language in Rule 803(8)(C) that authorizes the admission of investigative reports in civil actions and against the Government in criminal cases effectively prohibits the admission of investigative reports against an accused under this hearsay exception.[32] Rule 803(8)(B) was amended in Congress to add the phrase "excluding, however, in criminal cases matters observed by police officers and other law enforcement personnel." There was no discussion, either in Congress, or in the legislative reports, about whether this amendment read in conjunction with the limitation in Rule 803(8)(C) was designed to exclude all reports made by a government employee and offered against a criminal defendant, or whether the addition served the narrower function of excluding only those reports that would enable the prosecution to prove directly the elements of the offense charged without having the perception and credibility of its police and investigative officers tested by cross-examination.

The courts have split on two issues: (1) do subdivisions (B) and (C) operate to exclude all reports by police or other law enforcement personnel from being admitted against a criminal defendant pursuant to Rule 803(8), and (2) may a report barred by Rule 803(8) be admitted against an accused if it satisfies some other hearsay exception?

The most restrictive approach has accorded enormous scope to the limitations on using reports against an accused contained in Rule 803(8)(B) and (C) by defining "other law enforcement personnel" as including "any officer or employee of a governmental agency which has law enforcement responsibilities," and extending the limitations to all reports, regardless of their nature.[33] Other courts, after considering the underlying policies of the hearsay rule, have been less inflexible in interpreting Rule 803(8). They have accorded a narrower definition to "other law enforcement personnel,"[34] and have been willing to admit records of routine,

---

[31] *See* discussion in **Treatise** at § 803.13[5].

[32] Fed. R. Evid. 803(8)(C); *see, e.g.,* United States v. Orellana-Blanco, 294 F.3d 1143, 1150–1151 (9th Cir. 2002) (INS officer's written report of interview with defendant was not admissible under Rule 803(8) in defendant's criminal prosecution because of Rule 803(8)(B)'s exclusion of criminal cases from its exception for reports containing "matters observed by police officers and other law enforcement personnel").

[33] *See, e.g.,* United States v. Orellana-Blanco, 294 F.3d 1143, 1150–1151 (9th Cir. 2002) (INS officer's written report of interview with defendant was not admissible under Rule 803(8) in defendant's criminal prosecution because of Rule 803(8)(B)'s exclusion from its exception for reports containing "matters observed by police officers and other law enforcement personnel").

[34] *See, e.g.,* United States v. Hansen, 583 F.2d 325, 333 (7th Cir. 1978) (does not include building inspector).

nonadversarial matters.[35] Furthermore, although the restrictive view holds that a report barred by Rule 803(8) must be excluded even if it satisfies some other hearsay exception,[36] courts now admit the report if its author takes the stand and is subject to cross-examination.[37]

The less restrictive view is amply justified by the legislative history of Rule 803(8) which indicates no intention on the part of Congress to bar the admissibility of those records which prior to the enactment of the Federal Rules of Evidence had been admitted pursuant to the business records exception to the hearsay rule. When the circumstances surrounding the creation of a report demonstrate the likelihood of inaccurate observation or misrepresentation, exclusion is warranted because of a "lack of trustworthiness," regardless of whether the report is being offered pursuant to Rule 803(6) or Rule 803(8).

The language of subdivision (C) clearly contemplates that a criminal defendant may use an investigatory report against the prosecution. Subdivision (B), on its face, prohibits the use in all criminal cases of reports of matters observed by police and other law enforcement personnel. There is, therefore, disagreement among the circuits whether Rule 803(8)(B) precludes admission of public documents reflecting matters observed by police officers when they are offered by the defendant.[38]

---

[35] *See, e.g.,* United States v. Brown, 315 F.3d 929, 931–932 (8th Cir. 2003) (trial court properly admitted testimony of Secret Service agent that Secret Service database indicated that bills with same serial numbers as counterfeit bills defendant was charged with having passed had also appeared in other geographic locations during same time frame because information in database, although undoubtedly collected during criminal investigation, was routinely entered into database by clerical personnel, and testimony was limited to contents of database and did not directly prove any element of charged offense); United States v. Pena-Gutierrez, 222 F.3d 1080, 1086 (9th Cir. 2000),(Rule 803(8)(B) excludes in criminal prosecutions only records of matters observed by law enforcement officers at the scene of the crime or apprehension of the accused, "not records of routine, non-adversarial matters made in a non-adversarial setting").

[36] *See, e.g.,* United States v. Pena-Gutierrez, 222 F.3d 1080, 1086–1087 (9th Cir. 2000), (reports by law enforcement officers concerning their investigations are admissible, if at all, only under Rule 803(8) trial court erred in admitting INS officer's report on interview with illegal alien under Rule 803(5)). *But see* United States v. Metzger, 778 F.2d 1195, 1201 (6th Cir. 1985) ("nothing . . . would even remotely suggest that the restrictions of Rule 803(8)(C) should be grafted onto Rule 803(10).").

[37] *See, e.g.,* United States v. King, 613 F.2d 670 (7th Cir. 1980); United States v. Sawyer, 607 F.2d 1190 (7th Cir. 1979).

[38] *Compare* United States v. Smith, 521 F.2d 957, 968–969 (D.C. Cir. 1975) (Congress did not intend for public records reporting observations of law enforcement officers to be excluded when defendant seeks to introduce them into evidence) *with* United States v. Insaulgarat, 378 F.3d 456, 465–466 (5th Cir. 2004) (on its face, Rule 803(8)(B) does not distinguish between defense proffers and prosecution proffers).

[3]—Absence of Public Record or Entry—Rule 803(10)[1]

Rule 803(10) provides that the nonoccurrence of an event may be proved by evidence that there is no public record or entry of the event if a public record or entry of the event would have been "regularly made and preserved."[2] The rule is analogous to Rule 803(7). Rule 803(10) provides as follows:

Rule 803(10).   **Hearsay Exceptions; Availability of Declarant Immaterial.**

The following are not excluded by the hearsay rule, even though the declarant is available as a witness:

. . .

(10) Absence of public record or entry.—To prove the absence of a record, report, statement, or data compilation, in any form, or the nonoccurrence or nonexistence of a matter of which a record, report, statement, or data compilation, in any form, was regularly made and preserved by a public office or agency, evidence in the form of a certification in accordance with rule 902, or testimony, that diligent search failed to disclose the record, report, statement, or data compilation, or entry.

Rule 803(10) allows the absence of a record or entry to be proved by a certificate complying with Rule 902,[3] or testimony, that there was a diligent search for the record whose absence is sought to be shown. "The diligence requirement is one of substance, not form."[4] The rule "is not satisfied merely by a ritual incantation. . . ."[5]

---

[1] *See* discussion in **Treatise** at § 803.09.

[2] *See, e.g.,* United States v. Robinson, No. 02-2232, 2004 U.S. App. LEXIS 23755, at *26–*27 (6th Cir. Nov. 12, 2004) (certificate stating absence of record showing discontinuation of bank's status as insured of FDIC complied with Rule 803(10)).

[3] Rule 902(4) provides for certification complying with any rule adopted by the Supreme Court and also authorizes certification in accordance with state statutes. *See* Chapter 8. *See* Fed. R. Civ. P. 44(b) and Fed. R. Crim. P. 27. *See* 9 MOORE'S FEDERAL PRACTICE, Ch. 44, *Proof of Official Record* (Matthew Bender 3d ed. 1997); 25 MOORE'S FEDERAL PRACTICE, Ch. 627, *Proof of Official Record* (Matthew Bender 3d ed. 1997). *See* United States v. Wilson, 732 F.2d 404, 413 (5th Cir. 1984) (to counter defendant's contention that he was affiliated with CIA, court admitted affidavit of executive director of CIA, attested to by general counsel of CIA); United States v. Herrera-Britto, 739 F.2d 551 (11th Cir. 1984) (certificate by Honduran officials that no registration was found for vessel in question).

[4] United States v. Yakobov, 712 F.2d 20, 24 (2d Cir. 1983) (conviction for unlawfully engaging in business of dealing in firearms reversed because of trial court's erroneous admission of certificate prepared by the United States Treasury Department's Bureau of Alcohol, Tobacco and Firearms to prove that defendant was not licensed as a dealer).

[5] United States v. Yakobov, 712 F.2d 20, 24 (2d Cir. 1983) (certificate indicated that search had been made for license bearing misspelled versions of defendant's name, and that since his name was

[4]—Records of Vital Statistics—Rule 803(9)[1]

Records of vital statistics present a specialized instance of reports to public officials made by private citizens who are performing an official duty. The reports, of births, deaths and marriages, are usually made by ministers, physicians and undertakers. Because of the great need for this type of proof, and the usual disinterestedness and personal knowledge of the reporter, the reports are specifically made admissible by Rule 803(9), which provides as follows:

Rule 803(9).   Hearsay Exceptions; Availability of Declarant Immaterial.

The following are not excluded by the hearsay rule, even though the declarant is available as a witness:

. . .

(9) Records of vital statistics.—Records or data compilations, in any form, of births, fetal deaths, deaths, or marriages, if the report thereof was made to a public office pursuant to requirements of law.

The rule is silent about a requirement of firsthand knowledge, as are the notes to this exception, although the general notes to Rule 803 state that "neither this rule nor Rule 804 dispenses with the requirement." The issue is most likely to arise in connection with statutes that require the reporter of a death to answer detailed questions about the circumstances surrounding the demise. The result may be a statement by a physician that reports not only that the deceased died of carbon monoxide poisoning, but also that he committed suicide, a fact of which the physician has no personal knowledge. Rule 803(9) should be interpreted flexibly to admit statements containing conclusions not based on firsthand knowledge, despite the suggestion in the notes to Rule 803 that this requirement applies to all the exceptions. This interpretation is in accord with the rationale underlying the creation of a system of vital statistics and recognizes that the persons required by statute to make reports on death are usually professionals who presumably perform their duties scrupulously and impartially. If, in a particular case, the trial court finds that the prejudice resulting from the admission of a certificate outweighs its probative value, exclusion pursuant to Rule 403 would be appropriate.

---

misspelled with a "J" instead of a "Y," it would be likely that license or application for defendant would not be found even if it existed). *See also* United States v. Robinson, 544 F.2d 110, 114–115 (2d Cir. 1976) (casual or partial search is not a diligent search).

   [1] *See* discussion in **Treatise** at § 803.11.

[5]—Marriage, Baptismal, and Similar Certificates—Rule 803(12)[1]

Rule 803(12) provides for the admission of statements of fact contained in a certificate issued by an authorized person attesting that he or she performed a marriage or other ceremony or administered a sacrament. To the extent that the authorized person is required to file a report of this action, Rule 803(12) offers an alternative to proof pursuant to Rule 803(9). Instead of obtaining a copy of the record of vital statistics, the proponent can offer the certificate that the presiding official gave to the participants. However, some acts, such as baptism or confirmation, are not required or even authorized to be recorded. Certificates or records of the religious organizations (*see* Rule 803(11)) are the only ways in which the facts supplied in connection with these ceremonies can be admitted as acceptable evidence.

Rule 803(12) provides as follows:

Rule 803(12).   Hearsay Exceptions; Availability of Declarant Immaterial.

The following are not excluded by the hearsay rule, even though the declarant is available as a witness:

. . .

(12) Marriage, baptismal, and similar certificates.—Statements of fact contained in a certificate that the maker performed a marriage or other ceremony or administered a sacrament, made by a clergyman, public official, or other person authorized by the rules or practices of a religious organization or by law to perform the act certified, and purporting to have been issued at the time of the act or within a reasonable time thereafter.

Rule 803(12) requires preliminary proof that the clergyman, public official or other person was authorized to perform the certified act either by the rules or practices of a religious organization or by law. Rule 803(12) also requires that the certificate "purport" to have been issued at the time of the act or within a reasonable time thereafter. The evidence furnished by the certificate is not conclusive; it can be controverted by any other relevant evidence.

[6]—Judgment of Previous Conviction—Rule 803(22)[1]

Rule 803(22) allows evidence of certain kinds of criminal judgments to be admitted in subsequent criminal or civil proceedings "to prove any fact essential to sustain the judgment." The rule provides as follows:

---

[1] *See* discussion in **Treatise** at § 803.14.
[1] *See* discussion in **Treatise** at § 803.24.

Rule 803(22).   Hearsay Exceptions; Availability of Declarant Immaterial.

The following are not excluded by the hearsay rule, even though the declarant is available as a witness:

. . .

(22) Judgment of previous conviction.—Evidence of a final judgment, entered after a trial or upon a plea of guilty (but not upon a plea of nolo contendere), adjudging a person guilty of a crime punishable by death or imprisonment in excess of one year, to prove any fact essential to sustain the judgment, but not including, when offered by the Government in a criminal prosecution for purposes other than impeachment, judgments against persons other than the accused. The pendency of an appeal may be shown but does not affect admissibility.

Rule 803(22) applies only to prior criminal judgments offered in subsequent proceedings.[2] Because the lesser applicable burden of proof makes them less reliable, prior civil judgments are inadmissible, except to the limited extent provided by Rule 803(23), or as given effect by the non-evidential substantive doctrines of res judicata and collateral estoppel.

The judgment of conviction must have been entered after trial or have been based upon a plea of guilty. Judgments of conviction based upon pleas of nolo contendere are not included[3] consistently with Rule 410. Rule 803(22) does not apply to judgments of acquittal because of a lack of relevancy. Such judgments do not necessarily prove innocence; instead, they may indicate that the prosecution failed to meet its burden of proof beyond a reasonable doubt as to at least one element of the crime, or that the jury exercised its inherent mercy dispensing function. In either event, the defendant cannot claim that the contrary of the material propositions of fact now being urged must have been found. The pendency of an appeal may be shown for the jurors to evaluate as they wish; it does not make the

---

[2] Lloyd v. American Export Lines, Inc., 580 F.2d 1179, 1189 (3d Cir. 1978) (court held that trial court had erred in excluding Japanese judgment; the "test of acceptance . . . of foreign judgments . . . is whether the foreign proceedings accord with civilized jurisprudence, and are stated in a clear and formal record").

[3] Powers v. Bayliner Marine Corp., 855 F. Supp. 199, 204 (W.D. Mich. 1994) (in civil action brought against manufacturer of sailboat, prior conviction of its owner/operator for negligent homicide could not be admitted under Rule 803(22) because it was based on plea of nolo contendere; further, to admit conviction as evidence of owner's negligence would create risk of unfair prejudice; court concluded that manufacturer had other means by which it could prove owner's negligence; citing **Treatise**).

conviction inadmissible.[4]

The offense of which the defendant was guilty must be one "punishable by death or imprisonment in excess of one year." This limitation to convictions of felony grade, measured by federal standards, recognizes that motivation to defend at a lower level may be lacking. In this type of case, particularly if a traffic violation is concerned, the accused typically pleads guilty, often without consulting counsel, as a matter of convenience. To effectuate the policy of Rule 803(22) barring evidence of convictions punishable by imprisonment for less than one year, a court ought generally to be cautious about admitting evidence of guilty pleas in non-felony cases on a theory other than Rule 803(22) as, for instance, an admission under Rule 801(d)(2), or as a declaration against interest pursuant to Rule 804(b)(3), because the plea may not be fully trustworthy.[5]

A judgement of conviction offered for the purpose of showing only that a person has in fact been convicted of a crime is admissible under Rule 803(8), rather than Rule 803(22), and is not subject to Rule 803(22)'s restrictions on the admissibility of judgments of conviction founded on a nolo contendere plea. Rule 803(22) applies only when the judgment is offered to prove the facts necessary to sustain the judgment of conviction.[5.1]

Rule 803(22) allows a criminal judgment to be admitted in subsequent criminal proceedings as well as in civil proceedings. However, Rule 803(22) does distinguish between civil and criminal litigation to the extent of excluding judgments of conviction of a third person offered by the government against the accused in a criminal case for purposes other than impeachment.[6]

While Rule 803(22) makes the prior conviction admissible over a hearsay

---

[4]   *See also* Rule 609(e), which is discussed in Chapter 12.

[5]   *But cf.* United States v. Gotti, 641 F. Supp. 283 (E.D.N.Y. 1986) (special reasons for allowing misdemeanor convictions in this RICO case).

[5.1] *See, e.g.,* United States v. Adedoyin, 369 F.3d 337, 344–345 (3d Cir. 2004).

[6]   This limitation is dictated by constitutional considerations. *See* Kirby v. United States, 174 U.S. 47, 60, 19 S. Ct. 574, 43 L. Ed. 890 (1899) ("one accused of having received stolen goods with intent to convert them to his own use, knowing at the time that they were stolen, is not within the meaning of the Constitution confronted with the witnesses against him when the fact that the goods were stolen is established simply by the record of another criminal case with which the accused had no connection and in which he or she was not entitled to be represented by counsel."). *See also* United States v. Diaz, 936 F.2d 786 (5th Cir. 1991) (in a prosecution for transporting illegal aliens, the trial court erred in admitting conviction of one of the aliens for purpose of proving the undocumented status of the aliens found in defendant's car; United States v. Crispin, 757 F.2d 611 (5th Cir. 1985) (in prosecution for conspiracy to move within United States an alien present in violation of the law, error to have admitted judgments of conviction offered to prove the illegal status of some of the aliens, but harmless in light of overwhelming evidence of the aliens' illegal status).

objection, it does not prescribe the effect the judgment will have once it is admitted. Whether the conviction will be given a conclusive effect depends on substantive considerations such as the type of case,[7] whether the impact would bar a criminal from profiting by the act for which he or she was convicted,[8] and the existence of state policies that have to be implemented in a diversity case pursuant to the *Erie* doctrine.

A judgment of conviction can be used "to prove any fact essential to the judgment." Determining what facts were essential may be a laborious task for the trial judge when the antecedent litigation was complex and ended in a general verdict.[9] In some instances the judgment may be inadmissible because it will be impossible to determine whether the facts sought to be proved in the second case were necessarily determined in the first.[10]

§ 16.09   Publications

[1]—Learned Treatises—Rule 803(18)[1]

Rule 803(18) provides that statements contained in certain publications may be admitted to prove the facts asserted once certain requirements are satisfied. The rule provides:

---

[7]   *See, e.g.*, Standefer v. United States, 447 U.S. 10, 100 S. Ct. 1999, 64 L. Ed. 2d 689 (1980) (Court refused to apply nonmutual collateral estoppel against the government in a criminal case); United States v. 47 mm Cannon, 95 F. Supp. 2d 545, 548 (E.D. Va. 2000) (in forfeiture proceeding after conviction of firearm possession by felon, Rule 803(22) allows Government to use felon's guilty plea as evidence to prove his conviction for illegal firearm possession).

[8]   *See, e.g.*, Ruth v. First Nat'l Bank of N.J., 410 F. Supp. 1233 (D.N.J. 1976) (when plaintiff had been convicted of illegally having funds credited to corporation's account, court gave conclusive effect to judgment in action where plaintiff claimed that funds had been wrongly turned over to the United States).

[9]   *See* Emich Motors Corp. v. General Motors Corp., 340 U.S. 558, 569, 71 S. Ct. 408, 95 L. Ed 534 (1951) ("A general verdict of the jury or judgment of the court without special findings does not indicate which of the means charged in the indictment were found to have been used in effectuating the conspiracy. And since all of the acts charged need not be proved for conviction . . . such a verdict does not establish that defendants used all of the means charged or any particular one. Under these circumstances what was decided by the criminal judgment must be determined by the trial judge hearing the treble-damage suit, upon an examination of the record, including the pleadings, the evidence submitted, the instructions under which the jury arrived at its verdict, and any opinions of the courts"); New York v. Hendrickson Bros., Inc., 840 F.2d 1065 (2d Cir. 1988) (judgments of conviction for mail fraud admitted in civil antitrust action; judge who presided over civil case also presided over criminal case, and looked to instructions he had given the jury in the criminal case to determine what findings the jury must have made to determine guilt).

[10]   *See also* Columbia Plaza Corp. v. Security Nat'l Bank, 676 F.2d 780, 790 (D.C. Cir. 1982) (court concluded that Rule 803(22) was not satisfied where it could not determine for what reasons the jury convicted the defendants).

[1]   *See* discussion in **Treatise** at §§ 803.23.

Rule 803(18).   **Hearsay Exceptions; Availability of Declarant Immaterial.**

The following are not excluded by the hearsay rule, even though the declarant is available as a witness:

. . .

(18) Learned treatises.—To the extent called to the attention of an expert witness upon cross-examination or relied upon by the expert witness in direct examination, statements contained in published treatises, periodicals, or pamphlets on a subject of history, medicine, or other science or art, established as a reliable authority by the testimony or admission of the witness or by other expert testimony or by judicial notice. If admitted, the statements may be read into evidence but may not be received as exhibits.

According to Rule 803(18), a learned treatise must be "published." It can be a treatise, periodical or pamphlet on a "subject of history, medicine, or other science or art."[2] At least one court has held that instructional material in the form of a videotape can qualify as a learned treatise.[2.1]

The opening phrase of the rule, "[t]o the extent called to the attention of an expert witness upon cross-examination or relied upon by the expert witness in direct examination," limits admissibility to those treatises whose existence is disclosed while an expert is on the stand, thereby guaranteeing that the trier of fact will have the benefit of expert evaluation and explanation of how the published material relates to the issues in the case.[3] This requirement, as well as the prohibition in the last sentence on taking treatises into the jury room, guard against the danger that jurors will misuse the texts in question. When the statement in a treatise contains an undisputed fact, there may be some overlap with Rule 803(17). If the trial court finds that the data in question does not require elucidation, it should allow admission pursuant to Rule 803(17) so that an expert witness need not be called.

---

[2] Fed. R. Evid. 803(18); *see, e.g.,* Caruolo v. John Crane, Inc., 226 F.3d 46, 54 (2d Cir. 2000) (not plain error to admit scientific study as learned treatise when witness identified it as "peer reviewed literature"); Johnson v. William C. Ellis & Sons Iron Works, Inc., 609 F.2d 820 (5th Cir. 1980) (safety codes); Connecticut Light & Power Co. v. Federal Power Comm'n, 557 F.2d 349, 356 (2d Cir. 1977) (historical treatises).

[2.1] *See* Costantino v. Herzog, 203 F.3d 164, 171 (2d Cir. 2000) (videotapes are "nothing more than a contemporary variant of a published treatise, periodical or pamphlet"; thus, instructional videotape can fall within hearsay exception for learned treatises (Rule 803(18)), since any distinction between videotapes and periodicals or books would be "overly artificial").

[3] *See, e.g.,* United States v. Turner, 104 F.3d 217, 221 (8th Cir. 1997) (medical texts could not be admitted pursuant to Rule 803(18) because they were not called to the attention of an expert witness or relied on by an expert witness in direct examination).

The treatise may not be admitted unless its authority is established to the satisfaction of the trial court. The profferor of the evidence can satisfy this requirement in a number of different ways: by eliciting testimony about the treatise's reliability from an expert on direct,[4] by eliciting a concession of reliability from the opponent's expert on cross, or by persuading the court to take judicial notice that the publication is a "reliable authority."[5]

The court has discretion to exclude pursuant to Rule 403 if the probative value of the statement in the treatise is substantially outweighed by the dangers of prejudice, confusion or waste of time.[6] Depending on the nature of the fact sought to be proved, its significance to the case, and the availability of other evidence on the point, the trial judge may elect to have the question of the admissibility of the treatise explored outside the presence of the jury. In a civil case, the trial judge may wish to deal with this issue at a Rule 16 conference. In all cases, the trial court may require notice to be given before trial of this type of hearsay so that there will be no surprises and experts will be prepared to deal with it without the need for continuances.

Since the objective of the rule is to make valuable information available to the trier of fact, trial judges should use a liberal standard in determining whether the treatise's authoritativeness has been established. For example, in a medical malpractice case, a court might take judicial notice that the proffered text appears on the reading list of a medical school, or that the book in question was admitted in the course of some other litigation.

[2]—Market Reports, Commercial Publications—Rule 803(17)[1]

Rule 803(17) is designed to allow published compilations generally used to be admitted into evidence, provided they are relied upon either by the public or by

---

[4] *See, e.g.*, Burgess v. Premier Corp., 727 F.2d 826 (9th Cir. 1984) (plaintiff's witness testified that author of books on cattle investments was the preeminent industry expert, and that defendant required its salesmen to read the books and to recommend them).

[5] *See* Costantino v. Herzog, 203 F.3d 164, 170–171 (2d Cir. 2000) (several factors established authoritativeness of video, including status of American College of Obstetricians and Gynecologists as reputable organization; citing **Treatise**); Meschino v. North Am. Drager, Inc., 841 F.2d 429, 434 (1st Cir. 1988) (all articles in a periodical cannot be qualified by testimony that the magazine is highly regarded; "an article does not reach the dignity of a 'reliable authority' merely because some editor, even a most reputable one, sees fit to circulate it"; there must be "recognition of the authoritative stature of the writer, or affirmative acceptance of the article itself in the profession").

[6] *See* Costantino v. Herzog, 203 F.3d 164, 172 (2d Cir. 2000) (admission of video was within court's discretion under Rule 403; its portrayal of certain medical procedures was highly probative and that value was not outweighed by danger of jury confusion or unfair prejudice); Schneider v. Revici, 817 F.2d 987, 991 (2d Cir. 1987) (even if defense in medical malpractice action had laid proper foundation for introduction of defendant's text as a learned treatise, admission would remain subject to Rule 403 and balancing would favor exclusion).

[1] *See* discussion in **Treatise** at § 803.22.

persons in a particular trade or business.[2] The rule provides as follows:

Rule 803(17).   Hearsay Exceptions; Availability of Declarant Immaterial.

The following are not excluded by the hearsay rule, even though the declarant is available as a witness:

. . .

(17)   Market reports, commercial publications.—Market quotations, tabulations, lists, directories, or other published compilations, generally used and relied upon by the public or by persons in particular occupations.

The only difficulty with the exception is determining how narrowly it should be interpreted. Publications such as market quotations in newspapers, life expectancy tables, pink security sheets, animal pedigrees, and directories state readily ascertained facts about which there can be no real dispute. Admitting them without the possibility of cross-examining the persons who supplied the data makes little difference. On the other hand, there are publications upon which the public or persons in particular occupations rely, such as price lists, mercantile credit reports and safety codes, which fit within the literal language of the rule, but which are not concerned with simple objective facts. When it cannot be shown that the information was obtained and compiled in a manner consistent with trustworthiness, the judge should exclude. Requiring advance notice of intention to rely on this material is desirable and usually leads to stipulations since there has been an opportunity to check for accuracy.

§ 16.10   Evidence of Reputation—Rules 803(19), (20), (21)

Three different subdivisions of Rule 803 authorize the reception of reputation evidence. Rule 803(19) allows reputation evidence to be used to prove facts of personal or family history;[2.1] it provides as follows:[3]

Rule 803(19).   Hearsay Exceptions; Availability of Declarant Immaterial.

---

[2] *See, e.g.,* United States v. Cassiere, 4 F.3d 1006 (1st Cir. 1993) (published monthly reports listing property sales and prices are generally used by real estate brokers, appraisers and insurance agents).

[2.1] *See, e.g.,* Blackburn v. United Parcel Service, Inc., 179 F.3d 81, 100–101 (3d Cir. 1999) (a workplace can constitute a community for purposes of reputation evidence; reputation witness seeking to establish family relationships among co-workers under Rule 803(19) must demonstrate sufficient familiarity with the persons involved and with that community, and must show that the "basis of the reputation is one that is likely to be reliable").

[3] *See* discussion in **Treatise** at § 803.24.

The following are not excluded by the hearsay rule, even though the declarant is available as a witness:

. . .

(19) Reputation concerning personal or family history.—Reputation among members of a person's family by blood, adoption, or marriage, or among a person's associates, or in the community, concerning a person's birth, adoption, marriage, divorce, death, legitimacy, relationship by blood, adoption, or marriage, ancestry, or other similar fact of personal or family history.

Rule 803(20) creates a hearsay exception for evidence of reputation to prove the location of boundaries and matters of general history. It provides as follows:[4]

Rule 803(20).   Hearsay Exceptions; Availability of Declarant Immaterial.

The following are not excluded by the hearsay rule, even though the declarant is available as a witness:

. . .

(20) Reputation concerning boundaries or general history.—Reputation in a community, arising before the controversy, as to boundaries of or customs affecting lands in the community, and reputation as to events of general history important to the community or State or nation in which located.

Rule 803(21) was added to the Federal Rules to ensure that the hearsay rule would not bar the use of reputation evidence to prove character in those instances in which character evidence can be used substantively.[5] Rule 803(21) provides as follows:[6]

Rule 803(21).   Hearsay Exceptions; Availability of Declarant Immaterial.

The following are not excluded by the hearsay rule, even though the declarant is available as a witness:

. . .

(21) Reputation as to character.—Reputation of a person's character among associates or in the community.

---

[4] *See* discussion in **Treatise** at §§ 803.25–803.26.
[5] *See* Rules 404 and 405, which are discussed in Chapter 7.
[6] *See* discussion in **Treatise** at § 803.27.

CHAPTER 17

*Hearsay Exceptions Requiring Unavailability—Rule 804**

---

* Chapter revised in 1993 by SANDRA D. KATZ, member of the New York bar.

17.06   **Forfeiture of Objection by Wrongdoing**

§ 17.01 Definition of Unavailability—Rule 804(a)[1]

[1]—Scope and Text of Rule

Subdivision (a) of Rule 804 governs the definition of unavailability. Unavailability is the condition precedent to the admission of hearsay statements under the exceptions that are included in Rule 804(b). Rule 804(a) provides as follows:

Rule 804(a). Hearsay Exceptions: Declarant Unavailable.

(a) Definition of unavailability.—"Unavailability as a witness" includes situations in which the declarant—

(1) is exempted by ruling of the court on the ground of privilege from testifying concerning the subject matter of the declarant's statement; or

(2) persists in refusing to testify concerning the subject matter of the declarant's statement despite an order of the court to do so; or

(3) testifies to a lack of memory of the subject matter of the declarant's statement; or

(4) is unable to be present or to testify at the hearing because of death or then existing physical or mental illness or infirmity; or

(5) is absent from the hearing and the proponent of a statement has been unable to procure the declarant's attendance (or in the case of a hearsay exception under subdivision (b)(2), (3), or (4), the declarant's attendance or testimony) by process or other reasonable means.

A declarant is not unavailable as a witness if exemption, refusal, claim of lack of memory, inability, or absence is due to the procurement or wrongdoing of the proponent of a statement for the purpose of preventing the witness from attending or testifying.

[Adopted Jan. 2, 1975, effective July 1, 1975; amended Dec. 12, 1975; amended Mar. 2, 1987, effective Oct. 1, 1987; amended Nov. 18, 1988.]

By insisting on the unavailability of the declarant's testimony, Rule 804(a) expresses a rule of preference. When a declarant is available, personal testimony in court, subject to the safeguards of an oath and cross-examination, is preferred. But when the declarant's testimony is unobtainable,[2] an extra-judicial statement

---

[1] *See* discussion in **Treatise** at §§ 804.02–804.03.

[2] The crucial factor is the unavailability of the declarant's testimony, rather than the unavailability of the declarant as a witness. The declarant's presence on the witness stand will not block use of the extra-judicial statement if the witness refuses to answer, exercises a privilege not to answer, or is suffering from a mental disability or impairment of memory. *See, e.g.,* Walden v.

that falls within the categories specified in Rule 804(b) is preferable to losing all evidence from that source. By using the word "includes" instead of the phrase "restricted to" in its introduction, subdivision (a) suggests that the definition is open-ended even though it appears to be comprehensive. A hierarchy of hearsay is created by the unavailability requirement because of the drafters' belief that statements made in the circumstances specified in Rule 804(b) are not as inherently trustworthy—except for prior testimony—as statements that conform to the requirements of Rule 803.

Rule 804(a) provides that a declarant is not unavailable if the unavailability was "due to the procurement or wrongdoing of the proponent of [the] statement for the purpose of preventing the witness from attending or testifying."[3] Thus, a party who made it impossible for the declarant to testify at trial is prohibited from introducing the declarant's out-of-court statement under Rule 804.[4] If a declarant's unavailability is brought about by the party *against* whom the statement is offered, on the other hand, that party forfeits the right to object on hearsay grounds.[4.1] A defendant's confrontation rights may add additional hurdles to the use of hearsay in criminal cases.[5]

Sears, Roebuck & Co., 654 F.2d 443, 446 (5th Cir. 1981) (deposition of injured minor should have been admitted where he suffered loss of memory and nine years had lapsed since testimony).

[3] Fed. R. Evid. 804(a).

[4] *See, e.g.,* United States v. Bollin, 264 F.3d 391, 413 (4th Cir. 2001) (criminal defendants who invoke their Fifth Amendment right not to testify procure their own unavailability and cannot take advantage of Rule 804(b)(1) to introduce their own grand jury testimony); United States v. Peterson, 100 F.3d 7, 13 (2d Cir. 1996) (defendant who invokes Fifth Amendment privilege not to testify at second trial of his case is not entitled to introduce testimony he gave at first trial); United States v. Pizarro, 756 F.2d 579, 582–583 (7th Cir. 1985) (prior testimony of witness who had testified at previous trial that defendant was not the source of heroin could not be admitted at second trial when witness refused to testify because of intimidation by defendant); *but see* United States v. Eufracio-Torres, 890 F.2d 266, 270–271 (10th Cir. 1989) (government's decision to move for release of witnesses, making them unavailable, did not preclude admission of their depositions; witnesses had been served with process and failed to keep promise to return); United States v. Seijo, 595 F.2d 116, 120 (2d Cir. 1979) (government should have been allowed to introduce depositions of aliens who had been deported by INS).

[4.1] Fed. R. Evid. 804(b)(6); Steele v. Taylor, 684 F.2d 1193, 1202 (6th Cir. 1982) ("prior statement given by a witness made unavailable by the wrongful conduct of a party is admissible against the party if the statement would have been admissible had the witness testified"); *see* § 17.06 for more discussion of Rule 804(b)(6).

[5] *See, e.g.,* Lowery v. Anderson, 225 F.3d 833, 839–840 (7th Cir. 2000), *cert. denied,* 149 L. Ed. 2d 375 (2001) (prosecution must "demonstrate that it made a good faith effort to obtain the witness' testimony, in person, before the trier of fact"; here, witness brought from prison to court was unavailable when he refused to testify despite having been held in contempt for refusing to obey court order to do so; prosecution was not required to threaten to revoke his plea agreement to fill its obligation to take reasonable steps to secure his live testimony).

[2]—Privilege

Rule 804(a)(1) states that a declarant is unavailable when the court upholds a claim of privilege with regard to the subject matter of the statement. This species of unavailability occurs most frequently in connection with former testimony, and is most commonly invoked by claims of spousal privilege or the privilege against self-incrimination.[6] If the witness makes no formal claim of privilege, but refuses to testify, unavailability may result pursuant to paragraph (2) of Rule 804(a).

[3]—Refusal to Testify

If despite judicial orders to answer, the declarant refuses to testify about the subject matter of the hearsay statement by erroneously relying on a privilege, or by disregarding a grant of immunity, or by simply remaining silent, the declarant is unavailable pursuant to Rule 804(a)(2).[7] The court should normally exercise some of its coercive power, as by threatening contempt outside the presence of the jury before concluding that the witness will not testify.

[4]—Lack of Memory

Rule 804(a)(3) recognizes unavailability when a witness testifies to a lack of memory. Since the witness must testify, and is therefore subject to cross-examination about the claimed lack of memory, the trial judge has a good opportunity for assessing the witness's credibility, and the danger of a perjurious claim of forgetfulness is lessened. If the trial judge disbelieves the witness and finds that unavailability has not been established on this ground, the extra-judicial statement may nevertheless be admissible as a prior inconsistent statement if the requirements of Rule 801(d)(1)(A) are met. Moreover, a feigned failure to recollect may be treated as a refusal to testify pursuant to Rule 804(a)(2).

[5]—Death or Infirmity

Rule 804(a)(4) states that unavailability exists when the declarant "is unable to be present or testify at the hearing because of death or then existing physical or mental illness or infirmity." Death and severe permanent disabilities clearly satisfy this formula. In other instances, the trial court will have to consider such factors as the nature of the disability and its expected duration, the length of time the case has been pending, whether delays, if any, are attributable to the proponent of the

---

[6] *See, e.g.,* United States v. Desena, 260 F.3d 150, 158 (2d Cir. 2001) (witness' out-of-court statements were properly admitted; his live testimony was unavailable because he appropriately invoked his privilege against self-incrimination on witness stand).

[7] *See, e.g.,* United States v. Reed, 227 F.3d 763, 767–768 (7th Cir. 2000) (witness is unavailable when proponent calls him or her as witness and he or she refuses to testify despite court order to do so).

hearsay, the nature of the case, the significance of the disabled witness's testimony, the availability of other evidence on the same point, and the need for cross-examination given the nature of the expected testimony and the subject of the hearsay statement.

Disability due to temporary conditions such as pregnancy or fractures may have to be handled by a continuance, particularly in a criminal case where the declarant is a prosecution witness whose testimony is crucial.[8] Given calendar pressures and the demands of speedy trial rules, the trial court must be given great discretion to decide on adjournments, continuances or mistrials because of the unavailability of witnesses. In a civil case, or in a criminal case where the defendant offers the hearsay statement, it is easier to find unavailability even when the disability is only temporary.

The trial judge's task is often more difficult when the claimed disability is mental rather than physical, since there may be greater disagreement and uncertainty about the patient's prognosis and treatment.[9] A further complication is the possibility that the declarant may have been incompetent at the time the statement was made, a factor that would detract considerably from the statement's reliability.

Questions of a declarant's physical or mental infirmity are best explored at a pretrial hearing before a jury is picked that will be unable to act if a continuance is ordered. The court may order depositions to be taken or remove the court, including jurors, to the bedside of the witness.[10]

[6]—Absence

When absence from the hearing is relied upon as the basis for unavailability, Rule 804(a)(5) requires the proponent of the declarant's hearsay statement to make a showing that it has not been possible to procure the declarant's attendance, or to take the declarant's deposition (if admission of the statement is sought pursuant to an exception in Rule 804(b)(2), (3), or (4)) "by process or other reasonable means." The Rule thus requires the proponent to show either that the declarant is

---

[8] *See, e.g.,* United States v. Faison, 679 F.2d 292, 297 (3d Cir. 1982), *aff'd*, 725 F. 2d 667, 671 (1983) (abuse of discretion not to grant continuance but instead to admit former testimony of crucial prosecution witness whom trial judge had found unavailable because he was about to undergo surgery which would disable him from testifying for at least 4 to 5 weeks; citing **Treatise**).

[9] *E.g.,* Burns v. Clusen, 798 F.2d 931 (7th Cir. 1986) (a witness who developed "schizophreniform disorder" should have been reevaluated before the start of trial when there was a delay between the initial finding of unavailability and the start of trial).

[10] In re Application to Take Testimony in Criminal Case Outside District, 102 F.R.D. 521 (E.D.N.Y. 1984) (court may try part of case outside district in order to take the testimony of a sick witness).

beyond the reach of process,[11] or that the declarant cannot be found or made to attend despite a good faith effort.[12]

The differences in procedural rules for compelling the attendance of witnesses result in non-identical definitions of unavailability in civil and criminal cases. In federal civil cases, Rule 45(b)(2) of the Federal Rules of Civil Procedure provides that a subpoena may be served anywhere within the district of the issuing court, or anywhere without the district within 100 miles of the place of deposition, hearing or trial. In a civil case, therefore, a declarant more than 100 miles away from the place of the proceeding will usually be unavailable, unless the declarant was subject to process by virtue of some other provision,[13] or unless no attempt was made to take a deposition, and admission of the statement is sought pursuant to Rule 804(b)(2), (3), or (4).

In criminal cases, "a subpoena requiring the attendance of a witness at a hearing or trial may be served at any place within the United States." United States nationals and residents may also be reachable by process when they are outside the United States.[14]

When the prosecution is the proponent in a criminal case, it must show more than that the witness is beyond the reach of the court's subpoena power to obtain a declaration that the witness is unavailable. The prosecution must also show that it pursued all reasonable means at its disposal to obtain the witness's attendance at the trial or hearing.[15] This does not mean, however, that the government is

---

[11]   *See, e.g.,* United States v. Siddiqui, 235 F.3d 1318, 1323 (11th Cir. 2000) (portions of deposition transcript admissible in criminal trial because witness, foreign national resident in India, notified government in writing he would be unavailable to testify live at trial, in spite of government's offer to him to pay all expenses he incurred in connection with his attendance at trial); United States v. Medjuck, 156 F.3d 916, 920 (9th Cir. 1998) (Canadian witnesses were unavailable for trial because they were beyond subpoena power of United States and refused voluntarily to attend deposition proceedings); United States v. Kehm, 799 F.2d 354, 361 (7th Cir. 1986) (an affidavit stating that a citizen of the Bahamas would not appear made him unavailable, even though the government made no attempt to obtain his attendance; the extradition treaty between the Bahamas and the United States did not provide for extraditing witnesses).

[12]   *See, e.g.,* United States v. Olafson, 213 F.3d 435, 440 (9th Cir. 2000) (witness who was inadvertently deported to Mexico before defendant's trial was unavailable to testify, for purposes of Rule 804, on showing that government agent telephoned and asked him to return to United States to testify and he refused to do so); United States v. Casamento, 887 F.2d 1141, 1169–1170 (2d Cir. 1989).

[13]   Fed. R. Civ. P. 45(b) also provides that "[w]hen a statute of the United States provides therefor, the court upon proper application and cause shown may authorize the service of a subpoena at any other place." *See* 9 Moore's Federal Practice, Ch. 45, *Subpoena* (Matthew Bender 3d ed. 1997).

[14]   28 U.S.C. § 1783.

[15]   *See, e.g.,* United States v. Pena-Gutierrez, 222 F.3d 1080, 1080–1089 (9th Cir. 2000) (foreign witness was not unavailable under Rule 804(a) when government had witness's name and

required to give a witness immunity from prosecution to secure his or her live testimony when faced with the witness's invocation of a testimonial privilege.[16]

When the proponent is a defendant in a criminal case, he or she must also make a reasonable effort to obtain the witness's live testimony. A failure to do so will result in the exclusion of the declarant's out-of-court statement.[16.1] When the witness is beyond the subpoena power of the United States because he or she is a foreign national and is outside the United States, a defendant's use of the witness's family members to attempt to contact the witness to persuade him or her to appear at the trial and to testify are generally sufficient to qualify as a reasonable effort to obtain the witness's live testimony.[16.2] Proof that a foreign national is absent from the United States without further evidence showing an effort to convince him or her to return to testify, however, is insufficient.[16.3]

A declarant who cannot be found obviously cannot be served with process.[16.4] The language in Rule 804(a)(5), that the declarant's attendance could not be procured by "reasonable means," incorporates into the evidentiary rule the constitutional requirement that the prosecution may not use the declarant's hearsay statement unless it shows that it made a good-faith effort to produce the missing declarant.[17]

---

address in Mexico, but made no effort to contact him and asserted no basis for believing he would not return to United States if requested to testify).

[16] *See, e.g.,* United States v. Reed, 227 F.3d 763, 767–768 (7th Cir. 2000) (when witness invokes testimonial privilege, government is not required to do everything it can to compel witness to testify, only to make reasonable, good-faith effort to get witness into court; thus witness was deemed unavailable and his prior testimony admitted after government made good-faith effort by putting witness on the stand, offering him additional credit toward his sentence, and threatening him with criminal contempt).

[16.1] *See, e.g.,* United States v. Hite, 364 F.3d 874, 882–883 (7th Cir. 2004) (defense did not show reasonable effort when its search for missing witness did not begin until four months before trial, defense did not enlist aid of local law enforcement even though witness had been in and out of local authorities' hands several times during year before trial, and defendant's private investigator testified his search was limited to speaking to witness's relatives).

[16.2] *See, e.g.,* United States v. Samaniego, 345 F.3d 1280, 1283–1284 (11th 2003).

[16.3] *See, e.g.,* United States v. Abreu, 342 F.3d 183, 190 (2d Cir. 2003).

[16.4] *See, e.g.,* United States v. Chapman, 345 F.3d 630, 632 (8th Cir. 2003) (declarant who was fugitive from justice was unavailable for purposes of Rule 804(a)(5)).

[17] Barber v. Page, 390 U.S. 719, 88 S. Ct. 1318, 20 L. Ed. 2d 255 (1968) (state prosecutor could not use preliminary hearing testimony of witness presently in federal penitentiary without making effort to persuade federal authorities to produce witness at trial); *see also* Ohio v. Roberts, 448 U.S. 56, 100 S. Ct. 2531, 65 L. Ed. 2d 597 (1980) (good-faith requirement was satisfied when five subpoenas had been issued for declarant at her parents' home, and mother testified at hearing that she knew no way to reach declarant).

§ 17.02   Former Testimony—Rule 804(b)(1)

[1]—Scope and Text of Rule[1]

Rule 804(b)(1) makes admissible, as an exception to the hearsay rule, former testimony or a deposition, given in the course of the same or a different proceeding, provided the party (or a predecessor in interest in a civil case) against whom the testimony or deposition is now offered, had the opportunity and a similar motive to develop the testimony at the prior proceeding.[2]

Rule 804(b)(1) provides as follows:

> **Rule 804(b)(1).   Hearsay Exceptions: Declarant Unavailable.**
>
> (b) Hearsay exceptions.—The following are not excluded by the hearsay rule if the declarant is unavailable as a witness:
>
> (1) Former testimony.—Testimony given as a witness at another hearing of the same or a different proceeding, or in a deposition taken in compliance with law in the course of the same or another proceeding, if the party against whom the testimony is now offered, or, in a civil action or proceeding, a predecessor in interest, had an opportunity and similar motive to develop the testimony by direct, cross, or redirect examination.
>
> [*Adopted Jan. 2, 1975, effective July 1, 1975.*]

The proffer of a deposition or testimony given at another trial presents a hearsay question because the evidence is not being offered through the in-court testimony of a witness who perceived the events reported. The trier's ability to observe the witness's demeanor is, however, the only one of the ideal conditions for giving testimony that is lacking. The testimony or deposition was given under oath, under circumstances impressing upon the witness the need for care and accuracy, and was subject to the opportunity to cross-examine.[2.1] It is, therefore, somewhat of an

---

[1]   *See* discussion in **Treatise** at § 804.04.

[2]   The character of the tribunal before which the former trial was held is immaterial provided that the tribunal was empowered to conduct cross-examination. *See, e.g.,* United States v. Omar, 104 F.3d 519, 523 (1st Cir. 1997) (despite "confusion on this issue in the circuits," it is fair to apply "opportunity and similar motive" test to specific portion of grand jury testimony at issue; but court recognized that "it is likely to be very difficult for defendants offering grand jury testimony to satisfy" test); Lloyd v. American Export Lines, Inc., 580 F.2d 1179 (3d Cir. 1978) (Coast Guard hearing); In re Sterling Navigation Co., Ltd., 444 F. Supp. 1043, 1046 (S.D.N.Y. 1977) (testimony at hearing held pursuant to local Bankruptcy Rules could not be admitted since such hearings are "non-adversary fact-finding proceedings" which "cannot be said to give rise to the type of adversarial cross-examination contemplated by Rule 804(b)").

[2.1]   *See, e.g.,* Battle v. Memorial Hosp., 228 F.3d 544, 552–553 (5th Cir. 2000) (because plaintiff's position at trial respecting issues as to which expert witness testified was same as position

anomaly that prior testimony, which is undoubtedly more reliable than many of the statements encountered in Rule 803, is made admissible by virtue of Rule 804, the rule that deals with less reliable hearsay. Unavailability was retained as a requirement in deference to traditional practice.

When a transcript exists, the trial court should insist upon its production as the most reliable means of proving prior testimony. The certified transcript is admissible pursuant to Rule 803(8) as a public record. The former testimony may, however, also be proved (1) through the testimony of a firsthand observer of the former proceedings who is able to remember the purport of all the witness said on direct and cross, even if not the exact words; (2) by the testimony of a first-hand observer whose memory has been refreshed with a memorandum, such as the stenographer's notes or transcript; or (3) by notes taken by an observer at the trial that qualify as a memorandum of recorded recollection pursuant to Rule 803(5). These alternative methods of proof are available since the matter sought to be proved is the former testimony rather than the contents of the official transcript; consequently the best evidence rule does not apply. The writing is required in the case of depositions because of special rules.

[2]—Opportunity and Similar Motive[3]

Rule 804(b)(1) requires that the party against whom the testimony is now offered, or in a civil action a predecessor in interest, must have had "an opportunity and similar motive to develop the testimony." In *United States v. Salerno*,[4] the Supreme Court held that a showing of similar motive is required in every case; the requirement may not be excused as a matter of "adversarial fairness." The Rule admits former testimony only if each of its elements is satisfied.[5]

Actual cross-examination is not necessary,[6] and the party need not have been

---

at witness's deposition and plaintiff had same interest in prevailing on those issues at trial and at deposition, plaintiff's opportunity to cross-examine at deposition was adequate, and trial court erred in excluding deposition under Rule 804(b)(1)).

[3] *See* discussion in **Treatise** at § 804.04[3], [5].

[4] United States v. Salerno, 505 U.S. 317, 112 S. Ct. 2503, 2506–2507, 120 L. Ed. 2d 255 (1992).

[5] *See* United States v. Omar, 104 F.3d 519, 523 (1st Cir. 1997) (in principle Rule 804(b)(1) could apply to grand jury testimony, if and when the "opportunity and similar motive" test is met); United States v. Peterson, 100 F.3d 7, 13 (2d Cir. 1996) (similar-motive requirement of Rule was not met, thus grand jury testimony was properly excluded).

[6] *See, e.g.,* United States v. Geiger, 263 F.3d 1034, 1039 (9th Cir. 2001) (defendant's failure to cross-examine witness in state suppression hearing about defendant's custodial interrogation was result of defense counsel's strategic decision; defendant had opportunity to cross-examine concerning all issues, and testimony was properly admitted in suppression hearing in federal prosecution arising from events).

represented by the same counsel at both proceedings.[7] The Rule is grounded on the assumption that it is fair to make a party who had the opportunity and motive to explore testimony at a prior proceeding bear the consequences of a failure to cross-examine adequately or an election not to do so.[7.1]

The "opportunity and similar motive" test is designed to ensure that the party against whom the testimony is being offered had a meaningful opportunity to expose its deficiencies at the first proceeding.[8] A shift in the theory of the case,[9] or a change of tribunal,[10] will not defeat admissibility, provided the motivation to cross-examine remains substantially the same.[10.1] Rule 804(b)(1) is not satisfied, however, when the motive of the party against whom the evidence is offered was substantially affected by differences in the cause of action,[11] the presence of additional issues, the addition of parties, or an intervening indictment.[12]

---

[7] Ohio v. Roberts, 448 U.S. 56, 71–72, 100 S. Ct. 2531, 65 L. Ed. 2d 597 (1980); United States v. Amaya, 533 F.2d 188, 191–192 (5th Cir. 1976).

[7.1] *See, e.g.,* Magouirk v. Warden, 237 F.3d 549, 553 (5th Cir. 2001) (when prosecution's objections and trial court's rulings sustaining them effectively prevented defendant from cross-examining witness at prior hearing, testimony would not be admissible under Rule 804(b)(1)).

[8] Kirk v. Raymark Indus., Inc., 61 F.3d 147, 164–165 (3d Cir. 1995) (district court erred in admitting previous and unrelated trial testimony of expert defendant had hired because it failed to find that expert was unavailable or that defendant had an opportunity and similar motive to examine that expert).

[9] *See, e.g.,* Matter of Johns-Manville/Asbestosis Cases, 93 F.R.D. 853, 855–856 (N.D. Ill. 1982) (depositions of deceased physician taken in earlier suit in which plaintiffs sought recovery on theories of negligence, breach of warranty and misrepresentation admissible in second suit alleging intentional and fraudulent activity).

[10] *See, e.g.,* United States v. Geiger, 263 F.3d 1034, 1038 (9th Cir. 2001) (defendant's motive and opportunity to cross-examine state trooper at suppression hearing in state court were similar to motive for doing so in federal court suppression hearing).

[10.1] *See, e.g.,* United States v. Vartanian, 245 F.3d 609, 613–614 (6th Cir. 2001) (when inquiry in earlier civil proceeding and in subsequent criminal prosecution was whether defendant attempted, by threats of force, to interfere with real estate agents' efforts to assist African-American couple in acquiring home, trial court did not err in admitting portions of real estate agent's deposition testimony taken in civil proceeding concerning his confrontation with defendant).

[11] *See, e.g.,* United States v. Preciado, 336 F.3d 739, 746 (8th Cir. 2003) (prosecution's motive to examine declarant at his change of plea hearing was to establish that declarant's action in changing his plea was voluntary, not to develop his testimony regarding his cohorts in crime; declarant's testimony at hearing was inadmissible under Rule 804(b)(1)); United States v. Jackson-Randolph, 282 F.3d 369, 381–382 (6th Cir. 2002) (testimony of employee at state agency hearing concerning company's participation in state-administered program was not admissible under Rule 804(b)(1) in federal criminal prosecution for fraud because issues were remarkably different and motivations of state attorney general's office in state hearing were different from motivations of United States Attorney in criminal prosecution for fraud).

[12] United States v. McDonald, 837 F.2d 1287, 1292–1293 (5th Cir. 1988) (the government, against which the defendant sought to introduce a deposition taken by an insurance company in a civil proceedings would have been aware of the risk that deponent would refuse to testify once he

Despite the "similar motive" test courts have generally been unwilling to exclude prior testimony given at preliminary hearings, at least when offered by the government, even though tactical considerations often dictate little or no cross-examination so as not to tip the defendant's plan for trial.[13] Nor have the federal courts accorded any significance to the slight incentive for cross-examination that exists when a deposition is taken solely for discovery. Admitting such depositions is in accord with Rule 32(a)(3) of the Federal Rules of Civil Procedure, which creates a hearsay exception for depositions given by unavailable deponents independent of Rule 804, and which accords no significance to the fact that the deposition was taken for discovery.[14]

[3]—Develop the Testimony[15]

Former testimony is most commonly offered against the party who was the cross-examiner when the evidence was offered in the first proceeding. Rule 804(b)(1) recognizes that former testimony may also be offered against the party by whom it was originally offered, provided the party had an opportunity to develop the testimony "by direct . . . or redirect examination."[16]

In *Ohio v. Roberts,* [17] the Supreme Court found no violation of the confrontation clause when preliminary hearing testimony given by a defense witness called by the defense was offered against the defendant at trial. The Court characterized the questioning by the defense as "cross-examination as a matter of form," noting that the presentation "was replete with leading questions," and "comported with the principal purpose of cross-examination: to challenge 'whether the defendant was sincerely telling what he believed to be the truth, whether the declarant accurately perceived and remembered the matter he related, and whether the declarant's intended meaning is adequately conveyed by the language he employed.' "[18]

In *Roberts,* the Supreme Court declined to impose a further "effectiveness" test once it found that the former testimony had been tested by the equivalent of cross-examination, at least in the absence of extraordinary circumstances, such as the denial of counsel or ineffective cross-examination at the first proceeding. Therefore, in virtually every case of actual cross-examination, direct examination

---

was indicted and would, therefore, have developed inaccuracies in the deposition testimony).

[13] *See, e.g.,* Glenn v. Dallman, 635 F.2d 1183, 1186–1188 (6th Cir. 1980).

[14] *See* Fed. R. Civ. P. 32(a)(3); *see also* 7 MOORE'S FEDERAL PRACTICE, Ch. 32, *Use of Depositions in Court Proceedings* (Matthew Bender 3d ed. 1997).

[15] *See* **Treatise** at § 804.04[3].

[16] *See, e.g.,* United States v. Henry, 448 F. Supp. 819 (D.N.J. 1978); United States v. Driscoll, 445 F. Supp. 864 (D.N.J. 1978) (defendant may offer grand jury testimony of now unavailable witness).

[17] Ohio v. Roberts, 448 U.S. 56, 100 S. Ct. 2531, 65 L. Ed. 2d 597 (1980).

[18] 448 U.S. at 70, 71.

or redirect examination, the former testimony exception will be satisfied, provided the motivation requirement, discussed above, is met.[18.1]

[4]—Party or Predecessor in Interest[19]

Rule 804(b)(1) provides that former testimony may be admitted "if the party against whom the testimony is now offered, or, in a civil action or proceeding, a predecessor in interest, had an opportunity and similar motive to develop the testimony. . . ."

The Rule distinguishes between civil and criminal cases; absolute identity of parties is required in criminal cases. While this Rule eliminates the constitutional concerns that would arise were former testimony offered against an accused who was not a party to the prior proceeding, it may be of questionable constitutional validity when it is the accused who seeks to use prior testimony against the United States even though it was not the prosecuting agency in the prior case.[20] In civil cases, Rule 804(b)(1) permits the former testimony to be admitted when a "predecessor in interest" of the party against whom the testimony is being offered had the opportunity and motive to develop the testimony. For the most part the cases indicate a reluctance to interpret "predecessor in interest" in its old, narrow, substantive law sense of privity,[21] which would require the party in the second action to share a property interest with the person who developed the testimony in the first proceeding. Even if a court feels compelled to give a narrower reading to Rule 804(b)(1), it should admit the testimony under Rule 807, the residual

---

[18.1] *But see* Magouirk v. Warden, 237 F.3d 549, 553 (5th Cir. 2001) (there was no meaningful opportunity to develop witness's testimony when every attempt by defense counsel to cross-examine the declarant "was thwarted by the prosecution's objections which were sustained by the trial court").

[19] *See* discussion in **Treatise** at § 804.04[4].

[20] *Cf.* Chambers v. Mississippi, 410 U.S. 284, 93 S. Ct. 1038, 35 L. Ed. 2d 297 (1973). *But cf.* United States v. Barrett, 766 F.2d 609, 618–619 (1st Cir. 1985) (not error to exclude transcript of coroner's testimony given at trial 20 years previously where government had not been a party to earlier prosecution as required by Rule 804(b)(1) and admission of transcript would have led to an ancillary and time-consuming inquiry).

[21] *See* Lloyd v. American Export Lines, Inc., 580 F.2d 1179, 1187 (3d Cir. 1978) (in action by crewman against shipowner for injuries sustained in fight with fellow crewman who was made a third-party defendant, testimony given at Coast Guard hearing concerning fight could be admitted at subsequent trial because there was a sufficient community of interest between the Coast Guard investigating officer and crewman; "[u]nder these circumstances, the previous party having like motive to develop the testimony about the same material facts, is in the final analysis, a predecessor in interest to the present party"); *see also* Clay v. Johns-Manville Sales Corp., 722 F.2d 1289, 1294–1295 (6th Cir. 1983) (defendants in prior case had similar motive to confront witness's testimony as current defendant); In re Master Key Antitrust Litig., 72 F.R.D. 108, 109 (D. Conn. 1976), *aff'd without opinion,* 551 F.2d 300 (2d Cir. 1976) (United States government in antitrust enforcement action found predecessor in interest of plaintiffs in subsequent private antitrust action).

exception, when the previous party had a like motive and opportunity to develop the testimony as the present party against whom the testimony is being offered.[22]

§ 17.03 Statement Under Belief of Impending Death—Rule 804(b)(2)[1]

Rule 804(b)(2) is a reworking of the common-law hearsay exception for dying declarations. It broadens the traditional exception by allowing it to be used in all civil cases, as well as homicide cases, and in not confining unavailability to death. It is the declarant's belief at the time the statement is made that death will occur that furnishes a guarantee of reliability, rather than death at the time the statement is offered. The Rule continues the common-law restriction of admissibility to statements concerning the cause or circumstances of what declarant believed to be his or her impending death.

The Rule provides as follows:

Rule 804(b)(2).   Hearsay Exceptions: Declarant Unavailable.

(b) Hearsay exceptions. The following are not excluded by the hearsay rule if the declarant is unavailable as a witness: . . .

(2) Statement under belief of impending death.—In a prosecution for homicide or in a civil action or proceeding, a statement made by a declarant while believing that the declarant's death was imminent, concerning the cause or circumstances of what the declarant believed to be impending death.

The exception for dying declarations was originally held to rest on the religious belief that dying persons would be unwilling to face their maker with a lie on their lips; it is now frequently justified on the secular, psychological ground that a declarant no longer has self-serving purposes to be furthered in the shadow of death. Critics of the exception disagree: they believe that the desire for revenge or self-exoneration or to protect one's loved ones often continues until the moment

---

[22] *See, e.g.,* United States v. North, 910 F.2d 843, 908–909 (D.C. Cir. 1990) (trial court did not abuse its discretion in refusing to admit a videotape of a witness's testimony before a congressional committee. The independent prosecutor was not the same party as the committee; even if they were the same party, the occasion of the prior testimony did not present the opposing party with an opportunity and similar motive to develop the testimony.); In re Screws Antitrust Litigation, 526 F.Supp. 1316, 1319 (D. Mass. 1981) (refused to find earlier criminal defendants predecessors in interest of later civil defendants but admitted testimony pursuant to former Rule 804(b)(5)); *see also* Lloyd v. American Export Lines, Inc., 580 F.2d 1179, 1190 (3d Cir. 1978) (concurring opinion relied on Rule 804(b)(5)). Rule 807 is discussed in Chapter 14, *Hearsay: Definition, Organization and Constitutional Concerns.*

[1] *See* discussion in **Treatise** at § 804.05.

of death, that the accuracy of a dying declaration is dubious because the declarant's ability to perceive, remember or communicate may have been clouded by the condition causing death, and that a statement is additionally suspect if it was made in response to the prompting and questioning of interested bystanders such as policemen, insurance agents, or investigators.

Belief in the certainty of death—the factor that reduces the motive for falsification—must be shown in order for the exception to apply. Justice Cardozo explained what this entails:

> Fear or even belief that illness will end in death will not avail of itself to make a dying declaration. There must be "a settled hopeless expectation" . . . that death is near at hand, and what is said must have been spoken in the hush of its impending presence. . . . The patient must have spoken with the consciousness of a swift and certain doom.[2]

The declarant's belief in the imminence of death may be shown by the declarant's own statements,[3] or through circumstantial evidence,[4] such as the nature of the wounds, opinions of the attending physicians, statements made by others in the declarant's presence, or the fact that last rites were administered. It must be inferable from the evidence presented that declarant had personal knowledge of the facts contained in the statement seeking admission. The statement of a declarant shot in the back by an unseen assailant naming the defendant as the murderer cannot be admitted.

§ 17.04 Statement Against Interest—Rule 804(b)(3)

[1]—Scope and Text of Rule[1]

Rule 804(b)(3) admits statements against the pecuniary, proprietary or penal interest of the declarant, provided certain requirements are met. The exception rests on the assumption that persons will not make damaging statements about themselves unless they are true. As a psychological generalization, this conclusion rings true; in the individual case, the diversity of the human personality makes generalizations suspect.

---

[2] Shepard v. United States, 290 U.S. 96, 100, 54 S. Ct. 22, 78 L. Ed. 196 (1933); *cf.* Pfiel v. Rogers, 757 F.2d 850 (7th Cir. 1985) (statements were not admissible as they were not made immediately prior to the witness's suicide, and so were not made in contemplation of death).

[3] *See, e.g.,* United States v. Kearney, 420 F.2d 170, 174–175 (D.C. Cir. 1969).

[4] Shepard v. United States, 290 U.S. 96, 100, 54 S. Ct. 22, 78 L. Ed. 2d 196 (1933) ("Despair of recovery may indeed be gathered from the circumstances if the facts support the inference. . . . There is no unyielding ritual of words to be spoken by the dying").

[1] *See* discussion in **Treatise** at § 804.06[1]–[3].

The addition of declarations against penal interest, which were not traditionally admitted, has greatly increased the significance of this exception, and has caused numerous difficult problems of interpretation which are discussed below.

Rule 804(b)(3) provides as follows:

Rule 804(b)(3).   Hearsay Exceptions: Declarant Unavailable.

(b) Hearsay exceptions.—The following are not excluded by the hearsay rule if the declarant is unavailable as a witness: . . .

(3) Statement against interest.—A statement which was at the time of its making so far contrary to the declarant's pecuniary or proprietary interest, or so far tended to subject the declarant to civil or criminal liability, or to render invalid a claim by the declarant against another, that a reasonable person in the declarant's position would not have made the statement unless believing it to be true. A statement tending to expose the declarant to criminal liability and offered to exculpate the accused is not admissible unless corroborating circumstances clearly indicate the trustworthiness of the statement.

[Adopted Jan. 2, 1975, effective July 1, 1975; amended Dec. 12, 1975; amended Mar. 2, 1987, effective Oct. 1, 1987.]

---

[2]—Requirements[2]

[a]—Unavailability

Rule 804(b)(3) retains unavailability as a condition of admissibility of statements against interest.

[b]—First-hand Knowledge

While Rule 804(b)(3) does not expressly require the declarant to have perceived the matter to which the statement relates, personal knowledge has always been considered an inherent condition of the exception, and is assured by Rule 602.[3]

---

[2] *See* discussion in **Treatise** at § 804.06[4].

[3] United States v. Lang, 589 F.2d 92, 97–98 (2d Cir. 1978) (error to have admitted statement that declarant had supplied counterfeit notes to defendant through defendant's girlfriend where statement also acknowledged that declarant had never met defendant). *See* Chapter 10, *Witnesses Generally.*

[c]—Reasonable Person Test

Rule 804(b)(3), by providing that the statement would not have been made by a reasonable person who did not believe it to be true,[3.1] purports to adopt an objective test for whether the statement was against interest when made. Such an objective test is designed to eliminate inquiries into the declarant's actual state of mind.

Nevertheless, primarily with regard to declarations against penal interest, there is a real danger that confessions by liars, crackpots, and publicity seekers to acts they never committed would satisfy this definition. In the case of statements exculpating the accused, the reasonable person test is expressly tempered by the last sentence of Rule 804(b)(3), which requires corroboration of the trustworthiness of the statement. Since many courts insist on a corroboration requirement in the case of inculpatory statements as well, the consequence is that courts frequently evaluate the particular circumstances surrounding the proffered declaration against penal interest despite the reasonable person standard (*see* [3], *below*).[4]

[d]—Belief in Statement's Truth

The rationale for the exception fails if the declarant does not believe the statement to be against interest, since the rule rests on the notion that reasonable persons do not make false statements that expose them to liability.[5] In applying Rule 804(b)(3), the courts have been willing to assume that a reasonable person would be aware of the disserving nature of his or her remarks even when they were made to a supposed friend or family member.[6] More suspicion has been voiced when the statement, although against interest on its face, may actually have been made to

---

[3.1] Fed. R. Evid. 804(b)(3); *see, e.g.,* United States v. Alvarez, 266 F.3d 587, 593 (6th Cir. 2001) (basis for Rule 804(b)(3) is that reasonable people, even those that are dishonest, do not make inculpatory statements unless they believe they are true).

[4] *See, e.g.,* United States v. Magana-Olvera, 917 F.2d 401, 407–408 (9th Cir. 1990) (trial court abused its discretion in admitting inculpatory statements that, under circumstances of case, were insufficiently against declarant's interest because reasonable person might have made them even though they were not true).

[5] *See, e.g.,* United States v. Alvarez, 266 F.3d 587, 592–593 (6th Cir. 2001) (when declarant was assured that he was not subjecting himself to criminal liability by making statement to defendant's lawyer, statement was not sufficiently trustworthy to qualify as statement against his penal interest); United States v. Centracchio, 265 F.3d 518, 525–526 (7th Cir. 2001) (guilty plea allocution of defendant's coconspirator was admissible statement against interest even though declarant may have entered guilty plea in hopes of receiving "good deal" from government).

[6] *See, e.g.,* United States v. Westmoreland, 240 F.3d 618, 627–628 (7th Cir. 2001) (self-inculpatory statements made to family members and to cell mates are admissible as statements against penal interest).

gain an advantage,[6.1] as when a person in custody makes a confession as part of a plea bargain.[7]

[e]—Contrary to Interest

Rule 804(b)(3) is silent about how to handle self-serving or neutral statements that accompany a statement against interest. Rule 804(b)(3) applies only to portions of a declarant's out-of-court statement that are actually self-inculpatory. Parts of the statement that serve the declarant's interest or are neutral in effect are not admissible as a statement against interest.[8] The admissible portions of the statement must be against interest at the time it is made, rather than at the time it is offered, in order for the rationale for the exception to be satisfied.

[3]—Statements Against Penal Interest[9]

[a]—Development of Exception

When the drafters of the Federal Rules of Evidence expanded the traditional against-interest exception by adding declarations against penal interest, they were primarily contemplating cases in which the defense wished to offer a statement by a third person exculpating the accused.[10] Once the Rule went into effect, however, it became a vehicle for admitting inculpatory statements against the defendant. Fears of trumped-up confessions by a professional criminal or some person with a strong motive to lie resulted in the addition of the second sentence to Rule 804(b)(3), which makes declarations against penal interest offered to exculpate the accused inadmissible "unless corroborating circumstances clearly indicate the trustworthiness of the statement."[10.1] Due to the preoccupation with exculpatory

---

[6.1] *See, e.g.,* United States v. Bradshaw, 281 F.3d 278, 286 (1st Cir. 2002) (witness's out-of-court statement that he and another person planned to steal proceeds of postal service robbery from actual robbers, while it apparently against declarant's penal interest, was actually made to counter charges that he and defendant were the robbers).

[7] *See, e.g.,* United States v. Tropeano, 252 F.3d 653, 658–659 (2d Cir. 2001) (error to admit portion of declarant's plea allocution stating that he conspired with more than one person because question resulting in that answer was suggested by prosecutor after consultation with declarant's counsel, and may have been attempt to curry favor with government respecting sentencing).

[8] *See, e.g.,* United States v. Centracchio, 265 F.3d 518, 524–526 (7th Cir. 2001) (declarant's out-of-court statement is admissible only to extent it is self-inculpatory; exculpatory statements are not admissible even if they are part of statement that is generally self-inculpatory).

[9] *See* **Treatise** at § 804.06[5], [6].

[10] *See* Neuman v. Rivers, 125 F.3d 315, 319 (6th Cir. 1997) (declaration against penal interest exception to the hearsay rule is "deeply rooted"; admission of evidence under this rule does not violate Confrontation Clause because such statements are presumed to bear adequate indicia of reliability).

[10.1] Fed. R. Evid 804(b)(3); *see, e.g.* United States v. Bradshaw, 281 F.3d 278, 286 (1st Cir. 2002) (proponent of statement against interest offered to exonerate proponent from charged crime

statements and the drafters' belief that inculpatory statements would be limited by constitutional doctrine, no corroboration requirement for inculpatory statements appears in the Rule, although some courts hold that corroboration is constitutionally required.[11]

[b]—Exculpatory Statements

Once the court has determined that the proffered statement against the declarant's penal interest does, in fact, subject the declarant to potential criminal liability,[11.1] the chief question that arises with regard to exculpatory declarations against penal interest is the meaning and magnitude of the corroboration requirement.[12] It is the hearsay statement that must be corroborated, not the trustworthiness of the witness who testifies to the statement. The witness's testimony presents no hearsay dangers and can be evaluated by the jury, taking into account the witness's demeanor and any impeaching evidence.[13]

The court should ask only for sufficient corroboration to "clearly" permit a reasonable person to believe that the statement might have been made in good faith and that it could be true. Imposing a higher burden on the defendant is constitutionally suspect; it should not be easier for the government to introduce a co-conspirator's statement than for the defendant to introduce an exculpatory statement, yet Rule 801(d)(2)(E), the coconspirator exception, contains no corroboration requirement. Furthermore, the defendant has rights under the Fifth

---

must offer substantial corroboration to gain admission; evidence that declarant made same statement to two different persons on two separate occasions is not sufficient).

[11] For discussion of the constitutional issues relating to statements against interest, see § 14.03[4].

[11.1] *See, e.g.,* United States v. Bonty, 383 F.3d 575, 579 (7th Cir. 2004) (declarant's statement that defendant had nothing to do with alleged sexual assaults was not against declarant's penal interest because it did not admit that declarant committed any criminal conduct).

[12] *See, e.g.,* United States v. Patrick, 248 F.3d 11, 23–24 (1st Cir. 2001) (defendant had burden of establishing trustworthiness of note inculpating declarant and exculpating defendant; trial court did not abuse its discretion in excluding note when author of note was not identified and no corroborating circumstances were present); United States v. Price, 134 F.3d 340, 349 (6th Cir. 1998) (Rule 804(b)(3) does not require that information within a statement be clearly corroborated, but requires only that there be corroborating circumstances that clearly indicate trustworthiness of statement itself).

[13] *See, e.g.,* United States v. Shukri, 207 F.3d 412, 417 (7th Cir. 2000) (trial court need not assess trustworthiness of witness testifying to declarant's hearsay statement to determine admissibility of hearsay testimony; testifying witness is available for cross-examination and jury can evaluate his or her truthfulness); *but see* United States v. Bagley, 537 F.2d 162, 165–168 (5th Cir. 1976) (three of the four factors cited by court as demonstrating that statement offered by defense had not been made relate to credibility of witness).

and Sixth Amendments to produce exculpatory evidence.[14] Nevertheless, in a number of cases the corroboration requirement of Rule 804(b)(3) has been interpreted so stringently that it is difficult to conceive of the rule having much utility for an accused.[15]

In making the determination whether the corroborating evidence is sufficient, the trial court may take into account the amount and quality of the evidence inculpating the defendant as compared to the amount and quality of the evidence corroborating the exculpatory statement. When the witness proffered to testify to the declarant's out-of-court exculpating statement is the accused, the trial court may also take into account the likelihood that the accused has fabricated the declarant's statement.[15.1]

[c]—Inculpatory Statements

A declarant's statements are particularly troublesome when offered to inculpate another, the accused. As an evidentiary matter, the portion of the statement inculpating the accused is at best neutral rather than disserving, and the danger exists that it may be self-serving if the declarant is seeking to curry favor with the authorities.[16]

---

[14] *See, e.g.,* Chambers v. Mississippi, 410 U.S. 284, 302, 93 S. Ct. 1038, 35 L. Ed. 2d 297 (1973) (conviction reversed for lack of due process where defendant had been able neither to impeach witness who had several times confessed to charged crime (because of the prohibition against impeaching his own witness), nor had been able to call other witnesses to testify to out-of-court statements made by the confessing third party; the Court stated: "The testimony rejected by the trial court here bore persuasive assurances of trustworthiness and thus was well within the basic rationale of the exception for declarations against interest. That testimony was also critical to Chambers' defense. In these circumstances, where constitutional rights directly affecting the ascertainment of guilt are implicated, the hearsay rule may not be applied mechanistically to defeat the ends of justice."); *see also* Green v. Georgia, 442 U.S. 95, 97, 99 S. Ct. 2150, 60 L. Ed. 2d 738 (1979) (violation of due process to exclude statement against interest at penalty stage); Davis v. Alaska, 415 U.S. 308, 317–318, 94 S. Ct. 1105, 39 L. Ed. 2d 347 (1974) (Sixth Amendment right to present evidence).

[15] *See, e.g.,* United States v. MacDonald, 688 F.2d 224, 232–234 (4th Cir. 1982) (murder prosecution; court held that trial court had not abused discretion in excluding for lack of corroboration seven statements by declarant admitting culpability; defense argued that his description of assailant matched declarant, that declarant had no motive to fabricate, that defendant and declarant had not been acquainted, that declarant's statements were spontaneous, and that she could not account for her whereabouts on night of crime; trial court had focused on declarant's vacillation between admissions and denials of complicity and her pervasive involvement with narcotics).

[15.1] *See, e.g.,* United States v. Jernigan, 341 F.3d 1273, 1288 (11th Cir. 2003).

[16] *See, e.g.,* United States v. Chapman, 345 F.3d 630, 632–633 (8th Cir. 2003) (declarant's custodial statement implicating another person in drug distribution while arranging to cooperate with authorities in apprehending that other person, although implicating declarant in other drug transactions, was not against declarant's interest); United States v. McCleskey, 228 F.3d 640, 644 (6th Cir. 2000) (alleged coconspirator in custody will generally have salient and compelling motive

Some courts have reacted to these dangers by reading a corroboration requirement for inculpatory statements into Rule 804(b)(3);[17] others have adopted a per se rule of exclusion for statements made in custody.[18]

At the very least, a trial court should not admit an inculpatory statement until it has carefully scrutinized the circumstances in which declarant allegedly made the statement, and the relationship between the witness and declarant.[19] In determining whether the statement is sufficiently reliable to admit, the court should consider such factors as the role of the declarant, whether the declarant was in custody, the resolution of the pending charges, whether the declarant was being tried jointly with the accused, and the significance of the declarant's testimony.[20]

For discussion of the constitutional issues relating to the admission of inculpatory

---

to incriminate other persons, both to reduce own responsibility and to obtain lenient sentence; even though coconspirator's statement in such circumstances is clearly self-inculpatory, it is inherently unreliable to extent that it inculpates other persons and is, therefore, "garden variety hearsay" as to them).

[17] *See, e.g.,* United States v. Tocco, 200 F.3d 401, 404 (6th Cir. 2000) (declarations of criminal conduct that implicate another person are admissible only to extent that they are sufficiently self-inculpatory, and corroborating circumstances establish trustworthiness of statement); American Automotive Accessories, Inc. v. Fishman, 175 F.3d 534, 540–542 (7th Cir. 1999) (statements excluded because of lack of corroborating circumstances; timing and content suggested that they were made to curry favor with authorities; court required corroboration for statement offered in civil RICO action even though Rule 804(b)(3) imposes corroboration requirement only when statement "offered to exculpate the accused").

[18] United States v. Sarmiento-Perez, 633 F.2d 1092, 1104 (5th Cir. 1981).

[19] *See, e.g.,* United States v. Shukri, 207 F.3d 412, 415–417 (7th Cir. 2000) (declarant's self-inculpatory statement that also inculpated defendant was sufficiently reliable to warrant admission because it was made in private to declarant's confederate and brother-in-law, and declarant had no reason, when he made statement, to believe it would affect defendant); United States v. Jones, 124 F.3d 781, 784–786 (6th Cir. 1997) (no abuse of discretion to exclude, as untrustworthy, letter exculpating defendant written on eve of trial by defendant's son, due to lack of corroboration); United States v. Casamento, 887 F.2d 1141, 1170 (2d Cir. 1989) (sufficient corroborating circumstances in the witness and declarant having committed crimes together, so that there was "no reason from the evidence in the record for [declarant] to have lied or attempted to curry favor"); United States v. Katsougrakis, 715 F.2d 769, 774–75 (2d Cir. 1983) (court found admissible affirmative nod by critically burned arsonist in response to hospital visitor's inquiry as to whether he had been paid by defendants; reliability ensured because arsonist was communicating with friend, not police, and other evidence corroborated truth of statement); *see also* United States v. Slaughter, 891 F.2d 691, 698 (9th Cir. 1989) (a statement that informant was using cocaine together with declarant and defendant tended to subject declarant to possible criminal liability because state law made it a felony to be under the influence of a controlled substance).

[20] In re Flat Glass Antitrust Litig., 385 F.3d 350, 374 & n.32 (3d Cir. 2004) (in determining whether statements in declarant's diary were sufficiently reliable to be admissible as admissions against declarant's penal interest, trial court should determine whether declarant expected pages from his diary to become public information and whether they were contemporaneous with actions they reported).

statements against interest, see § 14.03[4], and **Treatise** at § 804.06[6].

The Judicial Conference has posted for public comment an amendment to Rule 804(b)(3) that would make a statement against interest tending to expose the declarant to criminal liability admissible (1) in a civil case, or in a criminal case when offered to exculpate the accused, only if it is supported by corroborating circumstances that clearly indicate its trustworthiness, and (2) in a criminal case, if offered to inculpate an accused, only if it is supported by particularized guarantees of trustworthiness. The text of the proposed amendment is available at the U.S. Courts Home Page (www.uscourts.gov), under Federal Rulemaking.

§ 17.05   Statement of Personal or Family History—Rule 804(b)(4)

Rule 804(b)(4) [1] broadens what has traditionally been termed the "pedigree" exception in the following respects: (1) by extending the exception to the entire area of family history instead of merely matters of genealogy, (2) by eliminating the ante litem motam requirement, (3) by rejecting the view that only death suffices to establish unavailability, and (4) by making declarations of nonfamily members admissible, provided their association with family members was sufficiently intimate.[2]

Rule 804(b)(4) provides as follows:

Rule 804(b)(4).   Hearsay Exceptions: Declarant Unavailable.

(b) Hearsay exceptions.—The following are not excluded by the hearsay rule if the declarant is unavailable as a witness: . . .

(4) Statement of personal or family history.—(A) A statement concerning the declarant's own birth, adoption, marriage, divorce, legitimacy, relationship by blood, adoption, or marriage, ancestry, or other similar fact of personal or family history, even though declarant had no means of acquiring personal knowledge of the matter stated; or (B) a statement concerning the foregoing matters, and death also, of another person, if the declarant was related to the other by blood, adoption, or marriage or was so intimately associated with the other's family as to be likely to have accurate information concerning the matter declared.

---

§ 17.06   Forfeiture of Objection by Wrongdoing

Rule 804(b)(6), which was adopted in 1997, provides that the party wrongfully causing a declarant's unavailability forfeits the right to object on hearsay grounds

---

[1]   *See* discussion in **Treatise** at § 804.07.

[2]   *See, e.g.,* United States v. Hernandez, 105 F.3d 1330, 1332 (9th Cir. 1997) (defendant's statement concerning location of his birth was properly admitted into evidence, either as party admission or as statement of family history under Rule 804(b)(4)(A)).

to the admission of the declarant's prior statement. The Rule provides an additional hearsay exception for the statement of an unavailable declarant when the party's deliberate wrongdoing or acquiescence in wrongdoing procured the unavailability of the declarant as a witness.

The Rule states as follows:

Rule 804(b)(6).   Hearsay Exceptions: Declarant Unavailable.

(b) Hearsay exceptions.—The following are not excluded by the hearsay rule if the declarant is unavailable as a witness: . . .

(6) Forfeiture by wrongdoing. A statement offered against a party that has engaged or acquiesced in wrongdoing that was intended to, and did, procure the unavailability of the declarant as a witness.

The Advisory Committee has noted that the wrongdoing need not consist of a criminal act, and that the Rule applies to all parties, including the government.[1] Furthermore, the Committee observed that every circuit that has resolved the question has recognized the principle of forfeiture by misconduct.

The Advisory Committee noted that the circuits have adopted varying tests for determining whether there is a forfeiture,[2] and stated that "the usual 104(a) preponderance of the evidence standard has been adopted in light of the behavior the new Rule 804(b)(6) seeks to discourage." For example, some courts have required the proponent of hearsay evidence to show, by a preponderance of the evidence, that the opponent's wrongdoing in procuring the declarant's unavailability was at least in part motivated by a desire to prevent the declarant from giving testimony.[3]

Carrying the principle one step further, the Seventh and Tenth circuit courts of appeals have held that coconspirators who did not participate in the murder of a cooperating witness could, if certain conditions were met, be deemed to have

---

[1]   Fed. R. Evid. 804(b)(6) Committee Note (1997) (reproduced verbatim in **Treatise** at § 804App.05[2]; Rule 804(b)(6) recognizes "the need for a prophylactic rule to deal with abhorrent behavior 'which strikes at the heart of the system of justice itself' ").

[2]   Fed. R. Evid. 804(b)(6) Committee Note (1997) (reproduced verbatim in **Treatise** at § 804App.05[2]; citing United States v. Aguiar, 975 F.2d 45, 47 (2d Cir. 1992) (preponderance of the evidence); United States v. Thevis, 665 F.2d 616, 631 (5th Cir. 1982) (clear and convincing evidence)).

[3]   *See, e.g.,* United States v. Gurmeet Singh Dhinsa, 243 F.3d 635, 652 (2d Cir. 2001) (forfeiture finding requires evidentiary hearing outside jury's presence in which government has burden of proving that opponent of evidence was involved in procuring declarant's unavailability "through knowledge, complicity, planning, or in any other way" and acted with intent of procuring declarant's unavailability as actual or potential witness); United States v. Johnson, 219 F.3d 349, 356 (4th Cir. 2000) (government must show defendant was motivated, at least in part, by desire to silence witness).

waived their hearsay objections to admission of the cooperating witness's hearsay statements against them at trial.[4] The Tenth Circuit interpreted Rule 804(b)(6) to permit the admission of only those hearsay statements that would be admissible under the constitutional doctrine of waiver by misconduct. Therefore, a coconspirator may be deemed to have "acquiesced in" the wrongful procurement of a witness's unavailability for purposes of Rule 804(b)(6) when the government can show either that the coconspirator participated directly in planning or procuring the declarant's unavailability through wrongdoing or that the wrongful procurement was in furtherance and within the scope of the ongoing conspiracy, and was reasonably foreseeable as a necessary or natural consequence of the conspiracy.[5]

---

[4] United States v. Thompson, 286 F.3d 950, 963–965 (7th Cir. 2002) (adopting *Cherry*); United States v. Cherry, 211 F.3d 575, 578–584 (10th Cir. 2000) (recognizing waiver by coconspirator of killer).

[5] United States v. Cherry, 211 F.3d 575, 578–584 (10th Cir. 2000) (same circumstances constitute waiver of both hearsay and constitutional objections).

CHAPTER 18

*Privileges**

SYNOPSIS

---

  * Chapter revised in 1995 by BRIGID T. BRENNAN, an Assistant District Attorney with the Office of the District Attorney, Bronx County.

§ 18.01 Overview of Legislative History of Privilege Rules

The article on privileges promulgated by the Supreme Court contained thirteen separate rules on privilege.[1] When Congress finally enacted Article V, it consisted of one rule, Rule 501, which differed radically from the Supreme Court-Advisory Committee's position on privileges.[2]

The Advisory Committee's paramount goal in constructing the proposed rules stemmed from its belief that the admission of all relevant evidence would further the likelihood of accurate determinations. Since privileges hamper the truth-determining process by keeping evidence from the court and jury, the Advisory Committee concluded that privileges should be limited to the minimum scope needed to support clearly desirable public policy. The Advisory Committee sought to achieve this end by (1) not applying privileges created by state law, (2) reducing further expansion of new privileges by recognizing only privileges required by the Constitution, Acts of Congress or Federal Rules, and (3) narrowing the scope of the privileges that were incorporated in the new evidence rules. As the discussion below of Rule 501 indicates, Congress disagreed with each of these three principles.

Although Congress declined to enact the specific evidentiary privileges promulgated by the Advisory Committee, a number of the proposed rules have been, and continue to be, cited by the courts as "Standards." This reference results from the fact that the proposed rules represent a codification of the common law on privilege that exist in federal courts and that they are reflective of "reason and experience," the standard utilized under Rule 501. Certain Standards are so widely accepted that they have become black letter law. Included among these Standards are: Standard 503—the attorney-client privilege (*see* § 18.03); Standard 504—psychotherapist-patient privilege (*see* § 18.04); Standard 506—communications to clergymen (*see* § 18.02[3]);[3] Standard 507—political vote (*see* § 18.02[3]); Standard 508—trade secrets (*see* § 18.02 [3]); Standard 509—secrets of state and other official information (*see* § 18.06) and Standard 510—identity of informer (*see* § 18.07).

Other privilege rules promulgated by the Advisory Committee, and then rejected by Congress, are not dependable statements of present law. Included among these Standards are: Standard 502—required reports privileged by statute (*see* § 18.02[2]); Standard 505—the marital privileges (*see* § 18.05) and Standard

---

[1] As submitted to Congress, Article V contained thirteen rules, nine of which concerned specific privileges while the balance dealt with matters common to all enumerated privileges. *See* **Treatise** at §§ 501App.100[3], 501App.101 for discussion of Congressional action on Rule 501, including extensive treatment of why Congress rejected rules promulgated by Supreme Court.

[2] *See* **Treatise** at § 501App.100 for a discussion of the Advisory Committee's proposal.

[3] All of the proposed Rules which are referred to by footnote are described in the commentary following the Rule 501 discussion.

513—comment upon or inference from claim of privilege; instruction (*see* § 18.02[3]). The doctor-patient privilege included in the law of many states has also not been accepted as a matter of federal law (*see* § 18.10).

Standards 511 and 512 deal respectively with waiver and disclosure under compulsion or without opportunity to claim the privilege (*see* § 18.08 and § 18.09). They are dealt with separately since they are only partly reliable as statements of the current law.

§ 18.02 The Law of Privileges in the Federal Courts—Rule 501

[1]—Scope and Text of Rule

Rule 501 is the only rule on privileges adopted by Congress, and it contains only general provisions concerning the sources of privileges to be applied in the federal courts. The presumption is that federal privilege law will govern, with state privilege law to be used in certain civil proceedings.[1]

Federal privilege law has many strands. Rule 501 generally leaves the law of privileges to case-by-case development,[1.1] except for privileges created by the Constitution,[1.2] an Act of Congress,[1.3] or the Supreme Court under its statutory rule-making authority. Under the Rules Enabling Act,[1.4] any rule creating, abolishing, or modifying an evidentiary privilege must be approved by Act of Congress to become effective. Although the Supreme Court has the final word on the common-law development of privileges, Congress has, in effect, eliminated the Court's independent rule-making powers with respect to privileges.[1.5]

The Rule provides as follows:

Rule 501.   General Rule.

Except as otherwise required by the Constitution of the United States or provided by Act of Congress or in rules prescribed by the Supreme Court pursuant to statutory authority, the privilege of a witness, person, government,

---

[1]   Fed. R. Evid. 501; *see, e.g.,* Koch Materials Co. v. Shore Slurry Seal, Inc., 208 F.R.D. 109, 116–117 (D.N.J. 2002) (federal privilege law applies in cases founded on federal law and in cases in which there are claims based on both federal and state law); *see* [2], *below.*

[1.1]   *See, e.g.,* Religious Technology Ctr. v. Wollersheim, 971 F.2d 364, 367 (9th Cir. 1992) (court rejected argument that infringement suit was barred by state statutory litigation privilege in federal question case, since privileges in federal courts are governed by federal common law, and no federal cases were cited recognizing such a privilege).

[1.2]   Such as the Fifth Amendment privilege against self-incrimination.

[1.3]   *See, e.g.,* H.R. 522, introduced on February 3, 1999, which would add a new Federal Evidence Rule 502 establishing a parent-child privilege.

[1.4]   28 U.S.C. § 2074(b).

[1.5]   *See* **Treatise** at § 501.05.

State, or political subdivision thereof shall be governed by the principles of the common law as they may be interpreted by the courts of the United States in the light of reason and experience. However, in civil actions and proceedings, with respect to an element of a claim or defense as to which State law supplies the rule of decision, the privilege of a witness, person, government, State, or political subdivision thereof shall be determined in accordance with State law.

The common-law power of the federal courts over privileges is subject to two further qualifications. One qualification is that the Supreme Court has said that the courts should be hesitant to create a privilege that would conflict with a clear statutory policy. For example, a qualified work product privilege could not be applied to accountants' tax accrual papers, since it would conflict with the Congressional policy favoring disclosure of all information relevant to an I.R.S. inquiry.[2] Another instance illustrating this conflict occurred during proceedings alleging that university tenure appointments were discriminatory. The Supreme Court held that the policy objectives of Title VII of the Civil Rights Act of 1964, which empower the E.E.O.C. to obtain relevant evidence in investigating a charge of discrimination, prevented the courts from creating a privilege against disclosure of peer review documents.[3]

Another qualification is founded in the reluctance of the courts to expand principles of the common law dramatically without significant and substantial experience suggesting the wisdom of the expansion. Thus, the courts should not adopt a privilege for medical records for certain types of illnesses or medical procedures merely because information concerning the illness or procedure is particularly sensitive. The same may be said of other illnesses and procedures. Creating such a privilege would result in the court's either making arbitrary distinctions in determining which illnesses and procedures involve information sensitive enough to warrant the protection of a privilege or adopting a new, generally applicable federal physician-patient privilege where one did not previously exist. Neither of those alternatives is generally appropriate under the common-law system for developing new principles.[4]

Yet another qualification on the power of federal courts to develop the law of

---

[2] United States v. Arthur Young & Co., 465 U.S. 805, 815–821, 104 S. Ct. 1495, 79 L. Ed. 2d 826 (1984) (summons enforcement proceedings under 26 U.S.C. § 7602).

[3] University of Pennsylvania v. E.E.O.C., 493 U.S. 182, 188–189, 110 S. Ct. 577, 107 L. Ed. 2d 571 (1990); see also, e.g., Virmani v. Novant Health Inc., 259 F.3d 284, 293 (4th Cir. 2001) (no peer review privilege is applicable in private actions alleging race discrimination in employment).

[4] See, e.g., Northwestern Mem'l Hosp. v. Ashcroft, 362 F.3d 923, 926–927 (7th Cir. 2004) (trial court improperly held documents relating to "partial birth" abortions privileged under newly-recognized privilege for information concerning abortions).

privileges under the methodology of the common law is operative only in civil actions and proceedings. When the law of a state provides the rule of decision for an element of a claim or defense in accordance with the *Erie* doctrine,[5] federal courts must apply the applicable state's law of privileges to evidence offered to prove or disprove that element of the claim or defense.[6]

[2]—Privileges: When Must State Law Be Applied?[1]

The second sentence of Rule 501 provides that state law shall apply "with respect to an element of a claim or defense as to which State law supplies the rule of decision."[2] The far simpler formula, that state law applies in diversity cases and federal law applies in federal question cases, was apparently rejected because it does not completely comport with the *Erie* test which Congress was seeking to incorporate. Theoretically, therefore, a state privilege may control in a federal question case, as when federal substantive law requires the courts to look to state law for the rule of decision for an element of a claim or a defense. This is not the case, however, when the federal government is a party to an action under the Federal Tort Claims Act, which incorporates state tort law as the rule of decision. The legislative history of Rule 501 makes it clear that Congress intended federal privilege law to apply in those circumstances.[2.1] In criminal cases, Rule 501 requires the application of federal privilege law even when a state definition of a crime is relied upon.[3]

Standard 502, one of the proposed privilege rules submitted to Congress, would have required the federal courts to apply state privileges for required reports even in criminal proceedings or actions arising solely under federal law. Although this rule was not enacted by Congress, and Rule 501 contemplates that state privileges will be ignored in these types of proceedings, courts should show deference to those state created privileges that reflect strong substantive policies in order to avoid unnecessary frustration of state policy. The evidence should not be admitted unless it appears that the information can come from no other source and that a federal substantive policy or justice will be frustrated.[4] Comity between state and federal

---

[5] Erie R.R. v. Tompkins, 304 U.S. 64, 58 S. Ct. 817, 82 L. Ed. 1188 (1938)

[6] Fed. R. Evid. 501; *see* [2], *below*.

[1] *See* **Treatise** at §§ 501.02[2], [3], 501.03[5].

[2] Fed. R. Evid. 501; *see, e.g.,* Pamida, Inc. v. E.S. Originals, Inc., 281 F.3d 726, 731 (8th Cir. 2002) (state privilege law applies as to matters entirely controlled by state law); *see* **Treatise** at §§ 501.02[2], [3], 501.03[5].

[2.1] *See, e.g.,* Tucker v. United States, 143 F. Supp. 2d 619, 621–624 (S.D. W. Va. 2001).

[3] *See* United States v. Espino, 317 F.3d 788, 795 (8th Cir. 2003) (federal courts follow federal common law respecting privileges in federal criminal proceedings).

[4] *See* United States v. King, 73 F.R.D. 103, 105 (E.D.N.Y. 1976) (four factors must be balanced to determine whether state policy should be recognized: "first, the federal government's need for the information being sought in enforcing its substantive and procedural policies; second, the

sovereigns is desirable under our system of federalism.[4.1]

The proposed Rule 502 stated:[5]

Supreme Court Standard 502.   Required Reports Privileged By Statute.

A person, corporation, association, or other organization or entity, either public or private, making a return or report required by law to be made has a privilege to refuse to disclose and to prevent any other person from disclosing the return or report, if the law requiring it to be made so provides. A public officer or agency to whom a return or report is required by law to be made has a privilege to refuse to disclose the return or report if the law requiring it to be made so provides. No privilege exists under this rule in actions involving perjury, false statements, fraud in the return or report, or other failure to comply with the law in question.

The legislative history of Rule 501 indicates that the applicable state law of privileges was intended to govern so long as state law controls the particular claim or defense, and it would apply regardless of where in a line of proof the privileged information is requested.[6] Such a policy may be impossible to implement when, under principles of concurrent or pendent jurisdiction, a civil federal proceeding includes claims based both on federal and state law. If a particular piece of evidence relates to both claims, it makes no sense to apply conflicting state and federal privileges, because information that has been revealed cannot again be made confidential.[7] The usual solution by the courts has been a refusal to follow the state

---

importance of the relationship or policy sought to be furthered by the state rule of privilege and the probability that the privilege will advance that relationship or policy; third, in the particular case, the special need for the information sought to be protected; and fourth, in the particular case, the adverse impact on the local policy that would result from non-recognition of the privilege.").

[4.1] *See, e.g.,* Cox v. Miller, 296 F.3d 89, 106–111 (2d Cir. 2002) (New York's cleric-penitent privilege applied in review of state conviction of plaintiff, but did not bar introduction of testimony of members of Alcoholics Anonymous respecting plaintiff's conversations with them concerning crimes of which he was ultimately convicted, because conversations were not, as privilege required, for purpose of obtaining spiritual guidance).

[5] *See* discussion in **Treatise** at §§ 502.02–502.07.

[6] Conference Report, Fed. R. Evid., 93rd Congress, 2d Session, Rep. No. 93–1597, p. 7 (Dec. 14, 1974). *See, e.g.,* Coregis Ins. Co. v. Law Offices of Carole F. Kafrissen, P.C., 186 F. Supp. 2d 567, 569 (E.D. Pa. 2002) (in diversity action, scope of attorney-client privilege is determined by Pennsylvania law).

[7] *See, e.g.,* Kelly v. Ford Motor Co. (In re Ford Motor Co.), 110 F.3d 954, 963 (3d Cir. 1997) ("[O]nce putatively protected material is disclosed, the very right sought to be protected has been destroyed").

rule of privilege when there is an irresolvable conflict with a federal policy.[8] While this solution accords with the general policies of the Federal Rules favoring truth, uniformity, and simplicity, it denigrates the substantive policy behind the state privilege.

Rule 501 is silent about which state's privilege to apply when state law controls and there are multi-state contacts. Prior to the enactment of the Federal Rules of Evidence, the federal courts held that, under *Klaxon Co. v. Stentor Electric Mfg. Co.,* [9] they were required to apply the choice-of-law rule that the forum state would apply. Consequently, a satisfactory evidentiary solution could not be obtained in federal court unless it was attainable in state court.[10] Subsequent to the enactment of the Federal Rules of Evidence, it could be argued that Rule 501, as an Act of Congress, should be viewed as a federal choice-of-law rule that authorizes the federal courts to give privileges the effect they were designed to have.[11]

A similar approach was adopted in the Second Restatement of Conflict of Laws:[11.1]

Privileged Communication

(1) Evidence that is not privileged under the local law of the state which has the most significant relationship with the communication will be admitted, even though it would be privileged under the local law of the forum, unless the admission of such evidence would be contrary to the strong public policy of the forum.

(2) Evidence that is privileged under the local law of the state which has the most significant relationship with the communication but which is not

---

[8] *See, e.g.,* Virmani v. Novant Health, Inc., 259 F.3d 284, 286 n.3 (4th Cir. 2001) (when jurisdiction is premised on federal question and there are pendant state law claims, federal privilege law controls).

[9] 313 U.S. 487, 61 S. Ct. 1020, 85 L. Ed. 1477 (1941).

[10] *See, e.g.,* Hare v. Family Publications Serv., Inc., 342 F. Supp. 678 (D. Md. 1972), 334 F. Supp. 953 (D. Md. 1971) (New York accountant, sued in Maryland, simultaneously insisted that Maryland had no jurisdiction over him and refused to answer interrogatories on ground of Maryland accountant-client privilege; court applied Maryland privilege because it concluded state court would have done so even though the communication was made in New York which does not recognize the privilege).

[11] *See* **Treatise** at § 501.02[3][b]; *see also* Mitsui & Co. v. Puerto Rico Water Resources Auth., 79 F.R.D. 72, 78–79 (D.P.R. 1978) (in most cases, "the state in which the asserted privileged relationship was entered and exclusively sited should be deemed to have the most significant interest in determining whether or not that relationship is privileged"; court refused to apply forum's accountant-client privilege to depositions being taken in New York of New York accountants); *cf.* Sackman v. Liggett Group, Inc., 920 F. Supp. 357, 362 (E.D.N.Y. 1996) ("The Sackman's claims are based upon New York causes of action, which will be decided by New York law. Thus, New York attorney-client privilege law is applicable under Rule 501, Fed.R.Evid").

[11.1] Restatement of the Law Second, Conflicts of Laws, 1986 Revisions 163 (April 15, 1986).

privileged under the local law of the forum will be admitted unless there is some special reason why the forum policy favoring admission should not be given effect.

In reality, however, most courts continue to apply *Klaxon*.[12]

When the privilege claim is raised at a deposition taken in a forum other than the one in which the trial is pending, the courts usually consider the state where the deposition is being taken as the forum whose privilege conflict-of-law rule applies.[13]

[3]—Privileges: The "Common Law Interpreted in the Light of Reason and Experience" Standard[1]

Congress adopted a flexible standard on privileges instead of the detailed rules promulgated by the Supreme Court, requiring the courts to deal with privileges on a case-by-case basis in all criminal cases and most federal question cases.[2] The standard, as stated in Rule 501, holds that "the privilege of a witness . . . shall be governed by the principles of the common law as they may be interpreted by the courts of the United States in the light of reason and experience." This standard had its origin in a 1934 Supreme Court decision dealing with the marital communications privilege,[3] and was subsequently incorporated into Rule 26 of the Federal Rules of Criminal Procedure as the standard for handling all evidentiary matters, including questions of privilege. Consequently, the ensuing enactment of Rule 501 effected no change in criminal cases.

Adoption of this flexible standard has had a number of important consequences for the development of privileges in the federal courts. In the first place, instead of freezing the law of privileges, as was proposed by the Advisory Committee, Rule 501 makes it possible for new privileges to evolve through case law in response to changing conditions.[4] In *Trammel v. United States,* the Court explained:

> In rejecting the proposed Rules and enacting Rule 501, Congress manifested an affirmative intention not to freeze the law of privilege. Its purpose

---

[12] *See* **Treatise** at § 501.02[3][b]; *see, e.g.,* Samuelson v. Susen, 576 F.2d 546, 551 (3d Cir. 1978) (court looked to forum's conflict-of-laws rule).

[13] *See, e.g.,* In re Westinghouse Electric Corp. Uranium Contracts Litig., 76 F.R.D. 47, 54 (W.D. Va. 1977). *But see* Restatement (Second) of Conflict of Laws, n.11 supra, comment f, suggesting that privilege law of the state of most significant relationship to the communication should govern. This is a sensible proposal.

[1] *See* **Treatise** at § 501.03.

[2] *See* **Treatise** at § 501.02[1].

[3] Wolfle v. United States, 291 U.S. 7, 12, 54 S. Ct. 279, 78 L. Ed. 617 (1934).

[4] *See* Jaffee v. Redmond, 518 U.S. 1, 7–8, 116 S. Ct. 1923, 135 L. Ed. 2d 337 (1996) ("the common law is not immutable but flexible, and by its own principles adapts itself to varying conditions").

rather was to "provide the courts with the flexibility to develop rules of privilege on a case-by-case basis" and to leave the door open to change.[5]

Second, the Rule contemplates that existing privileges may have to be modified over time.[6] For example, in *Trammel*, the court justified its decision to modify the privilege for adverse spousal testimony by relying on trends in state law[7] and changing concepts of the marital relationship. The Supreme Court has also cautioned, however, that the federal courts should neither increase nor contract the scope of existing privileges absent compelling considerations.[7.1]

Third, except for the attorney-client, psychotherapist-patient and marital privileges, the mandate to develop privilege rules "on a case-by-case basis"[8] has been interpreted to mean that the courts should look at privilege claims in the context of the particular case, balancing the usual need for all relevant evidence against the countervailing demand for confidentiality required to achieve the objectives of the privilege in question.[9] Standard 508 is consistent with this approach by requiring federal courts to weigh the competing interests when an objection to revealing trade secrets is voiced.[10]

---

[5] Trammel v. United States, 445 U.S. 40, 47, 100 S. Ct. 906, 63 L. Ed. 2d 186 (1980); *but cf.* University of Pennsylvania v. E.E.O.C., 493 U.S. 182, 189, 110 S. Ct. 577, 107 L. Ed. 2d 571 (1990) (although Rule 501 is intended to give the courts flexibility to develop new rules of privilege, "we are disinclined to exercise this authority expansively.").

[6] *See, e.g.,* Upjohn Co. v. United States, 449 U.S. 383, 396–397, 101 S. Ct. 677, 66 L. Ed. 2d 584 (1981) (control group test for attorney-client privilege is inconsistent with the standard expressed in Rule 501); Trammel v. United States, 445 U.S. 40, 47, 100 S. Ct. 906, 63 L. Ed. 2d 186 (1980) ("Congress manifested an affirmative intention not to freeze the law of privilege"; *see* further discussion in §§ 18.03, 18.05).

[7] *See* United States v. King, 73 F.R.D. 103, 105 (E.D.N.Y. 1976) ("[a] strong policy of comity between state and federal sovereignties impels federal courts to recognize state privileges where this can be accomplished at no substantial cost to federal substantive and procedural policy.").

[7.1] *See, e.g.,* Jaffee v. Redmond, 518 U.S. 1, 9, 116 S. Ct. 1923, 135 L. Ed. 2d 337 (1996).

[8] Statement by Representative Hungate, 120 Cong. Rec. 40891 (1974), quoted by Supreme Court in Trammel v. United States, 445 U.S. at 47.

[9] *See* Jaffee v. Redmond, 518 U.S. 1, 9–10, 116 S. Ct. 1923, 135 L. Ed. 2d 337 (1996) (privilege must promote "sufficiently important interests to outweigh the need for probative evidence"); Trammel v. United States, 445 U.S. 40, 53, 100 S. Ct. 906, 63 L. Ed. 2d 186 (1980) (recognizing that privilege against adverse spousal testimony vests in witness spouse alone); University of Pennsylvania v. E.E.O.C., 493 U.S. 182, 189, 107 L. Ed. 2d. 571, 110 S. Ct. 577 (1990) ("We do not create and apply an evidentiary privilege unless it promotes sufficiently important interests to outweigh the need for probative evidence;" rejecting peer-review privilege). *See* discussion in **Treatise** at § 501.03.

[10] Wearly v. F.T.C., 462 F. Supp. 589, 595 (D.N.J. 1978), *vacated on other grounds*, 616 F.2d 662 (3d Cir. 1980) ("court is satisfied, and finds, that the formulation of proposed Rule 508 adequately reflects the principles of the common law in the sense required by Fed.Ev.Rule 501").

Standard 508 provides:[11]

Supreme Court Standard 508.   Trade Secrets.

A person has a privilege, which may be claimed by him or his agent or employee, to refuse to disclose and to prevent other persons from disclosing a trade secret owned by him, if the allowance of the privilege will not tend to conceal fraud or otherwise work injustice. When disclosure is directed, the judge shall take such protective measure as the interests of the holder of the privilege and of the parties and the furtherance of justice may require.

The new privileges that have evolved pursuant to Rule 501 are therefore often regarded as qualified rather than absolute, with the courts looking at factors such as the type of case—criminal or civil, the probative value of the evidence as to which the privilege claim is asserted, the availability of other evidence, and the societal interests at stake.[12]

Fourth, some of the proposed rules submitted to Congress remain a convenient and useful starting point for examining questions of privilege. These Standards are reflective of "reason and experience";[13] they are the culmination of three drafts prepared by an Advisory Committee consisting of judges, practicing lawyers and academicians, and were adopted by the Judicial Conference and the Supreme Court. They are, therefore, of some influence in a federal court's consideration whether to adopt a new privilege or in interpreting an existing one.[14]

Some of the principles embodied in the Standards have been substantially modified by the judicial development of the law of privilege pursuant to Rule 501.[15]

---

[11] For a discussion of this Standard, *see* **Treatise** at §§ 508.02–508.07.

[12] *See, e.g.,* In re Witness Before the Special Grand Jury 2000-2, 288 F.3d 289, 291 (7th Cir. 2002) (privileges are exceptions to society's demand for every person's evidence, and are not lightly created or expansively construed).

[13] In United States v. Gillock, 445 U.S. 360, 367–368, 100 S. Ct. 1185, 63 L. Ed. 2d 454 (1980), in rejecting a new federal privilege for state legislators, the Court stated: "Neither the Advisory Committee, the Judicial Conference, nor this Court saw fit, however, to provide the privilege sought by *Gillock.* Although that fact standing alone would not compel the federal courts to refuse to recognize a privilege omitted from the proposal, it does suggest that the claimed privilege was not thought to be either indelibly ensconced in our common law or an imperative of federalism."

[14] *See, e.g.,* United States v. Chase, 340 F.3d 978, 990 (9th Cir. 2003) (when Supreme Court recognized psychotherapist-patient privilege, it cited Standard 504 favorably; Standard 504 therefore has considerable force and should be consulted when psychotherapist-patient privilege is invoked).

[15] Although Standard 502, requiring courts to defer to state privileges in purely federal law cases, is not formally consistent with Rule 501, it should, for reasons discussed, *supra,* also be considered by a court when it determines on a "case-by-case" basis whether a privilege is warranted in the particular litigation.

For example, the Supreme Court's decision in *Trammel v. United States,* [16] defining the husband-wife privilege, departed significantly from the rule proposed in Standard 505, as discussed below in § 18.05. Standard 513, which prohibits a comment or inference upon an assertion of a privilege, has had a mixed reception in the courts, particularly in civil cases.[17]

Standard 513 provides as follows:[18]

Supreme Court Standard 513.   Comment Upon Or Interference From Claim of Privilege; Instruction.

(a) Comment or inference not permitted.—The claim of a privilege, whether in the present proceeding or upon a prior occasion, is not a proper subject of comment by judge or counsel. No inference may be drawn therefrom.

(b) Claiming privilege without knowledge of jury.—In jury cases, proceedings shall be conducted, to the extent practicable, so as to facilitate the making of claims of privilege without the knowledge of the jury.

(c) Jury instruction.—Upon request, any party against whom the jury might draw an adverse inference from a claim of privilege is entitled to an instruction that no inference may be drawn therefrom.

Standard 507,[19] which provides that a person has a right not to reveal how he or she voted, may well be redundant because the protection would probably be constitutionally required. The existence of a priest-penitent or communications to clergymen privilege, provided for in Standard 506,[20] has been acknowledged by the Supreme Court in dictum.[21]

Standards 506 and 507 provide as follows:

Supreme Court Standard 506.   Communications to Clergymen.

---

[16] Trammel v. United States, 445 U.S. 40, 100 S. Ct. 906, 63 L. Ed. 2d 186 (1980).

[17] *See, e.g.,* Curtis v. M&S Petroleum, Inc., 174 F.3d 661, 674–675 (5th Cir. 1999) (although witness was properly allowed to claim Fifth Amendment privilege during civil proceedings, plaintiffs were entitled to an instruction permitting the jury to draw an adverse inference from his refusal to testify). *See* **Treatise** at § 513.04[2].

[18] *See* discussion in **Treatise** at §§ 513.02–513.06.

[19] *See* **Treatise** at §§ 507.02–507.05.

[20] *See* **Treatise** at §§ 506.02–506.10.

[21] Trammel v. United States, 445 U.S. 40, 51, 100 S. Ct. 906, 63 L. Ed. 2d 186 (1980) ("The priest-penitent privilege recognizes the human need to disclose to a spiritual counselor, in total and absolute confidence, what are believed to be flawed acts or thoughts and to receive priestly consolation and guidance in return.").

(a) Definitions—As used in this rule:

(1) A "clergyman" is a minister, priest, rabbi, or other similar functionary of a religious organization, or an individual reasonably believed so to be by the person consulting him.

(2) A communication is "confidential" if made privately and not intended for further disclosure except to other persons present in furtherance of the purpose of the communication.

(b) General rule of privilege.—A person has a privilege to refuse to disclose and to prevent another from disclosing a confidential communication by the person to a clergyman in his professional character as spiritual adviser.

(c) Who may claim the privilege.—The privilege may be claimed by the person, by his guardian or conservator, or by his personal representative if he is deceased. The clergyman may claim the privilege on behalf of the person. His authority so to do is presumed in the absence of evidence to the contrary.

Supreme Court Standard 507.   Political Vote.

Every person has a privilege to refuse to disclose the tenor of his vote at a political election conducted by secret ballot unless the vote was cast illegally.

The discussion below considers in detail the extent to which Standards 503, 504, 505, 509, 510, 511 and 512 remain a reliable statement of the law.

§ 18.03   The Lawyer-Client Privilege—Standard 503[22]

[1]—Text and Status of Standard

Congress did not adopt Article V of the Rules of Evidence, and thus Standard 503 is not a part of the Rules as enacted. However, Standard 503 is a powerful and complete summary of black-letter principles of lawyer-client privilege.[23] The Standard provides as follows:

Supreme Court Standard 503.   Lawyer-Client Privilege.

(a) Definitions. As used in this rule:

(1) A "client" is a person, public officer, or corporation, association, or

---

[22] *See* **Treatise** at §§ 503.02–503.44.

[23] *See, e.g.,* Massachusetts Eye & Ear Infirmary v. QCT Phototherapeutics, Inc., 167 F. Supp. 2d 108, 116 (D. Mass. 2001) (Standard 503 is instructive on issue of joint client exception to attorney-client privilege).

other organization or entity, either public or private, who is rendered professional legal services by a lawyer, or who consults a lawyer with a view to obtaining professional legal services from him.

(2) A "lawyer" is a person authorized, or reasonably believed by the client to be authorized, to practice law in any state or nation.

(3) A "representative of the lawyer" is one employed to assist the lawyer in the rendition of professional legal services.

(4) A communication is "confidential" if not intended to be disclosed to third persons other than those to whom disclosure is in furtherance of the rendition of professional legal services to the client or those reasonably necessary for the transmission of the communication.

(b) General rule of privilege.—A client has a privilege to refuse to disclose and to prevent any other person from disclosing confidential communications made for the purpose of facilitating the rendition of professional legal services to the client, (1) between himself or his representative and his lawyer or his lawyer's representative, or (2) between his lawyer and the lawyer's representative, or (3) by him or his lawyer to a lawyer representing another in a matter of common interest, or (4) between representatives of the client or between the client and a representative of the client, or (5) between lawyers representing the client.

(c) Who may claim the privilege.—The privilege may be claimed by the client, his guardian or conservator, the personal representative of a deceased client, or the successor, trustee, or similar representative of a corporation, association, or other organization, whether or not in existence. The person who was the lawyer at the time of the communication may claim the privilege but only on behalf of the client. His authority to do so is presumed in the absence of evidence to the contrary.

(d) Exceptions.—There is no privilege under this rule:

(1) Furtherance of crime or fraud.—If the services of the lawyer were sought or obtained to enable or aid anyone to commit or plan to commit what the client knew or reasonably should have known to be a crime or fraud; or

(2) Claimants through same deceased client.—As to a communication relevant to an issue between parties who claim through the same deceased client, regardless of whether the claims are by testate or intestate succession or by inter vivos transaction; or

(3) **Breach of duty by lawyer or client.**—As to a communication relevant to an issue of breach of duty by the lawyer to his client or by the client to his lawyer; or

(4) **Document attested by lawyer.**—As to a communication relevant to an issue concerning an attested document to which the lawyer is an attesting witness; or

(5) **Joint clients.**—As to a communication relevant to a matter of common interest between two or more clients if the communication was made by any of them to a lawyer retained or consulted in common, when offered in an action between any of the clients.

Standard 503 embodies the oldest common-law privilege dealing with confidential communications, the attorney-client privilege. The privilege was, and continues to be, premised on the theory that the public benefit in encouraging clients to fully communicate with their attorneys in order to enable the attorney to act most effectively, justly and expeditiously in providing sound legal advice, outweighs the harm caused the loss of relevant information.[1]

Standard 503 remains a useful starting point in examining the use of the attorney-client privilege in the federal courts today. It is an accurate restatement of actual practice and is cited to frequently.[2] It should also be noted that a review of the history of Standard 503 shows that it was not designed to be all encompassing. It would have required supplementation by case law since the Advisory Committee deliberately chose not to cover certain issues.[3] In determining whether to apply the privilege, the courts have usually held that the purpose of the privilege is served when both attorney and client can predict with some degree of certainty whether the communication will be protected. Therefore, the courts do not generally analyze attorney-client privilege claims on a case-by-case basis.[4] Nor do courts, except in rare instances, use a balancing test to determine whether the privilege should be

---

[1] *See, e.g.,* Upjohn Co. v. United States, 449 U.S. 383, 389, 101 S. Ct. 677, 66 L. Ed. 2d 584 (1981) ("Its purpose is to encourage full and frank communication between attorneys and their clients and thereby promote broader public interests in the observance of law and administration of justice. The privilege recognizes that sound legal advice or advocacy serves public ends and that such advice or advocacy depends upon the lawyer's being fully informed by the client.").

[2] *See, e.g.,* Cavallaro v. United States, 284 F.3d 236, 246–247 (1st Cir. 2002) (Supreme Court Standard 503 provides support for extending scope of attorney-client privilege to include communications with third parties employed to assist lawyers in providing legal advice).

[3] *See* **Treatise** at § 503App.01[2].

[4] In Upjohn Co. v. United States, 449 U.S. 383, 393, 396–397, 101 S. Ct. 677, 66 L. Ed. 2d 584 (1981), however, although the majority acknowledged the need for predictability, it failed to establish the parameters of the privilege in the corporate context. It explained that "such a 'case-by case' basis . . . obeys the spirit of the Rules." A concurring opinion by the Chief Justice criticized the majority for failing to articulate a standard.

honored.[5] When the factors give rise to the privilege, it is absolute unless an exception applies or a waiver has occurred.[6]

[2]—Definitions[1]

[a]—Client[2]

A client does not have to be an individual. Artificial entities, public or private, are also considered clients for purposes of the attorney-client privilege. The privilege may be applied narrowly to communications by governmental entities,[2.1] because a privilege conflicts with the strong public interest in open and honest government.[2.2] The extent to which communications in the corporate context are privileged is discussed in [4], below.

A client is one who is rendered legal services by a lawyer,[3] or who consults a lawyer with a view to obtaining such services.[4] There is no requirement that the services have been rendered in conjunction with litigation or that a fee will be charged.[4.1] The services must, however, be legal in nature.

The privilege does not apply when an attorney acts as a friend, co-conspirator,

---

[5] *See, e.g.,* Garner v. Wolfinbarger, 430 F.2d 1093, 1100 (5th Cir. 1970) (using balancing test for privilege claims in shareholders' suits).

[6] *See, e.g.,* Hanson v. United States Agency for Int'l Dev., 372 F.3d 286, 291 (4th Cir. 2004) (if attorney-client privilege applies, it protects all communications between lawyer and client absolutely).

[1] *See* Sup. Ct. Standard 503(a). Subdivision (a) of Standard 503 sets forth four definitions—client, lawyer, representative of the lawyer, and confidentiality—that are then used in subdivision (b) in stating the general rule of privilege.

[2] *See* **Treatise** at § 503.11.

[2.1] *See, e.g.,* In re Witness Before the Special Grand Jury 2000-2, 288 F.3d 289, 291–296 (7th Cir. 2002) (although government agencies may have attorney-client privilege in civil and regulatory context, in this criminal prosecution not privilege applied to communications between employee of state agency and lawyer for state agency acting in their official capacities).

[2.2] *See* In re Lindsey, 148 F.3d 1100, 1102 (D.C. Cir. 1998) ("neither legal authority nor policy nor experience suggests that a federal government entity can maintain the ordinary common law attorney-client privilege to withhold information relating to a federal criminal offense").

[3] *See, e.g.,* United States v. Munoz, 233 F.3d 1117, 1127–1128 (9th Cir. 2000) (in absence of evidence that defendant consulted with lawyer for "personal legal advice about his own involvement in the investment scheme," defendant failed to show attorney-client relationship; hence, no privilege attached).

[4] *See, e.g.,* United States v. Munoz, 233 F.3d 1117, 1128 (9th Cir. 2000) (attorney-client relationship did not exist, because "client" did not consult with attorney for personal legal advice).

[4.1] *See, e.g.,* S. Union Co. v. Southwest Gas Corp., 205 F.R.D. 542, 546 (D. Ariz. 2002) (because applicability of attorney client privilege does not require formal representation, neither absence of formal contract of employment nor lack of evidence of fee payments precludes attachment of privilege to communications meant to be confidential).

accountant or business adviser, or in any capacity other than as a lawyer.[5] Difficult problems are posed when a lawyer mixes legal advice with business, as often happens when the attorney serves in the dual function of counsel and officer or director of a corporation. The burden in all such cases is on the claimant to prove that the attorney was acting in a professional legal capacity.[6] The attorney-client privilege does not bar questions about the nature of the legal services rendered.

[b]—Lawyer[7]

For purposes of the privilege, a lawyer satisfies the definition if authorized to practice anywhere in the world.[8] Bar membership is not essential. The test is subjective, rather than objective, since it is sufficient if the client reasonably believed that the person consulted was a lawyer. Reasonableness will depend on the particular circumstances of the case, and has to be shown by the person claiming the privilege.[9]

The privilege does not apply when a "client" confers with a person known to be a non-lawyer, even if the person is trained as a paralegal and has considerable expertise concerning the legal issues in question.[9.1]

The privilege also does not apply when an attorney acts as a friend, co-conspirator, accountant, or business adviser, or in any capacity other than as a lawyer.[9.2] Difficult problems are posed when a lawyer mixes legal advice with business advice, as often happens when the attorney serves as both counsel to and officer or director of a corporation, or in the dual functions of attorney and accountant.[9.3] That a lawyer also has expertise in another field, however, does not necessarily disqualify the client's communications with the lawyer from the pro-

---

[5] *See, e.g.,* United States v. Rowe, 96 F.3d 1294, 1296 (9th Cir. 1996) (no privilege attaches when "attorney was asked for business (as opposed to legal) counsel"; citing **Treatise**).

[6] *See, e.g.,* In re Allen, 106 F.3d 582, 606 (4th Cir. 1997) (party asserting privilege must establish relationship); Clarke v. American Commerce Nat'l Bank, 974 F.2d 127, 129 (9th Cir. 1992) (*in camera* inspection of communications permissible).

[7] *See* **Treatise** at § 503.12.

[8] Renfield Corp. v. E. Remy Martin & Co., S.A., 98 F.R.D. 442, 444–445 (D. Del. 1982) (French in-house counsel).

[9] *See* United States v. Boffa, 513 F. Supp. 517, 527–530 (D. Del. 1981), *modified on other grounds,* 688 F.2d 919 (3d Cir. 1982).

[9.1] *See, e.g.,* Hpd Labs., Inc. v. Clorox Co., 202 F.R.D. 410, 415–417 (D.N.J. 2001).

[9.2] *See, e.g.,* United States v. Rowe, 96 F.3d 1294, 1296 (9th Cir. 1996) (no privilege attaches when "attorney was asked for business (as opposed to legal) counsel").

[9.3] *See, e.g.,* United States v. Frederick, 182 F.3d 496, 500–502 (7th Cir. 1999) (attorney-client privilege was not applicable to tax return documents prepared by attorney/accountant who was also representing taxpayers in IRS audit; however, information given to attorney/accountant to assist in his legal-representation function might be privileged).

tection of the attorney-client privilege.[9.4] The burden in all such cases is on the claimant to prove that the attorney was acting in a professional legal capacity in connection with the specific communication for which the party seeks the protection of the privilege.[9.5]

[c]—Representative of the Lawyer[10]

Office personnel such as secretaries and paralegals are clearly considered representatives of the lawyer. However, when the goal is to obtain the advice of a paralegal, the communications are not privileged even if a lawyer is supervising the paralegal. The privilege would apply only if the advice actually came from the supervising lawyer or if the paralegal formulated the advice with the input of a lawyer.[10.1]

More difficult is determining who else is "employed to assist the lawyer in the rendition of professional legal services." The problem typically arises with respect to accountants, administrative practitioners, experts and employees of insurance companies. Unless they are considered representatives of the lawyer, communications made to them by a client in confidence will not be privileged.[11] In each instance the claimant bears the burden of showing that the person in question worked at the direction of the lawyer, and performed tasks relevant to the client's obtaining legal advice, while responsibility remained with the lawyer.[12] Moreover, when the third party is a professional, such as an accountant, capable of rendering advice independent of the lawyer's advice to the client, the claimant must show that the third party served some specialized purpose in facilitating the attorney-client communications and was essentially indispensable in that regard.[12.1]

[9.4] *See, e.g.,* Hanson v. United States Agency for Int'l Dev., 372 F.3d 286, 291 (4th Cir. 2004) (that lawyer was also an engineer and had experience in construction industry did not mean that he was not serving as lawyer or that communications between him and client were not privileged).

[9.5] *See, e.g.,* In re Allen, 106 F.3d 582, 606 (4th Cir. 1997) (party asserting privilege must establish relationship).

[10] *See* **Treatise** at § 503.12[3]. § 503.12[6] in the **Treatise** discusses communications from an insured to agents of the insurance company.

[10.1] *See, e.g.,* Hpd Labs., Inc. v. Clorox Co., 202 F.R.D. 410, 415–417 (D.N.J. 2001).

[11] *See* United States v. Adlman, 68 F.3d 1495, 1499 (2d Cir. 1995) ("What is vital to the privilege is that the communication be made *in confidence* for the purpose of obtaining *legal* advice *from the lawyer.* If what is sought is not legal advice but only accounting service. . . or if the advice sought is the accountant's rather than the lawyer's, no privilege exists").

[12] *See, e.g.,* In re Allen, 106 F.3d 582, 602 (4th Cir. 1997) (privilege extends to all communications within the scope of services rendered in professional legal capacity for client).

[12.1] *See, e.g.,* Cavallaro v. United States, 284 F.3d 236, 146–249 (1st Cir. 2002) (attorney-client privilege did not extend to documents held by accounting firm engaged by taxpayers' sons to provide tax accounting services re their company, even though both accountants and taxpayers' attorneys advised their clients about merger between their company and taxpayers' company, since accountants were not hired by lawyers nor did they assist them in rendering legal advice).

If the expert has been hired to testify at trial, the attorney-client privilege cannot be invoked to prohibit pretrial discovery, though the work-product rules may limit some answers at the experts' deposition. *See* MOORE'S FEDERAL PRACTICE, Ch. 26, *General Provisions Governing Discovery; Duty of Disclosure* (Matthew Bender 3d ed.), for complete discussion of discovery obtainable from opposing experts.

The Internal Revenue Service Restructuring and Reform Act of 1998 extended the traditional attorney-client privilege of confidentiality to communications concerning tax advice between a client-taxpayer and any individual authorized under federal law to practice before the IRS "to the extent the communication would be considered a privileged communication if it were between a taxpayer and an attorney."[12.2]

[d]—Confidentiality[13]

The presence of a third person when the communication was made usually negates the claim that the statements were confidential.[14] Confidentiality is not lost, however, if the third person was present "in furtherance of the rendition of legal services," or was "reasonably necessary for the transmission of the communication."[15]

Moreover, when separately represented codefendants enter into a joint defense agreement, confidential communications made during joint strategy sessions are

---

[12.2] 26 U.S.C. § 7525 (I.R.C.); *see* discussion in **Treatise** at § 503.12[4][a].

[13] *See* **Treatise** at § 503.15.

[14] *See, e.g.,* United States v. Ackert, 169 F.3d 136, 138–140 (2d Cir. 1999) (since tax attorney was not relying on investment banker to translate or interpret information given to him by client, but rather spoke with banker to obtain information client did not have, their conversations were not privileged).

[15] Supreme Court Standard 503(a)(4); *see, e.g.,* Federal Deposit Ins. Corp. v. Ogden Corp., 202 F.3d 454, 461 (1st Cir. 2000) (when two or more persons jointly consult an attorney for legal advice, confidential communications to the attorney, although known to all clients, are privileged in controversy between client or clients and outside world); In re Auclair, 961 F.2d 65, 66–71 (5th Cir. 1992) (privilege applied to preliminary communications between attorney and three individuals who sought legal representation because all parties were "reasonable in believing in the existence of common interests and possessed reasonable expectations of confidentiality," the attorney's subsequent refusal to represent all three because of potential conflicts and a subsequent waiver by two of the parties did not "effect a retroactive recharacterization of the attorney-client relationship;" citing Standard 503(a)(4) and **Treatise**); In re Grand Jury Proceedings, 947 F.2d 1188, 1190–1191 (4th Cir. 1991) (communications to accountant in conjunction with getting legal advice privileged); Kevlik v. Goldstein, 724 F.2d 844, 849 (1st Cir. 1984) (presence of client's father did not destroy confidentiality). *See also* United States v. Dennis, 843 F.2d 652, 657 (2d Cir. 1988) (co-defendant's statements to defendant's attorney when he was seeking legal representation were privileged, but privilege may have ended when attorney invited co-defendant's father into the room).

privileged.[15.1] If, however, one of the parties to the joint defense agreement subsequently decides to testify against the other party, all of the confidential communications made during joint strategy sessions to which the defecting party was privy lose their privilege protection.[15.2]

Even though a communication was confidential when it occurred, it loses its confidentiality when the client voluntarily discloses some of the information that was the subject of the communication to a third person in a communication that was not privileged. Such disclosure constitutes a waiver of the attorney-client privilege.[15.3]

The communication also loses its privileged status if the client intended the matter to be made public.[16] For example, there is no privilege when a client discloses communications during an investigation, or knows that the communications will be disclosed in legal documents, such as complaints, or in settlement negotiations.[17] Similarly, when, at the time the client communicates information to the lawyer, the client does not have a reasonable expectation that the information will remain confidential, the attorney-client privilege does not attach to the com-

---

[15.1] *See, e.g.,* Wilson A. Abraham Constr. Co. v. Armco Steel Corp., 559 F.2d 250, 253 (5th Cir. 1977); United States v. Schwimmer, 892 F.2d 237, 243 (2d Cir. 1989).

[15.2] *See, e.g.,* United States v. Almeida, 341 F.3d 1318, 1326–1327 (11th Cir. 2003).

[15.3] *See, e.g.,* Hanson v. United States Agency for Int'l Dev., 372 F.3d 286, 293–294 (4th Cir. 2004).

[16] *See, e.g.,* Denius v. Dunlap, 209 F.3d 944, 952 (7th Cir. 2000) (citing **Treatise**; attorney-client privilege is implicitly waived if client communicates information to attorney without intending it to be kept confidential); Alldread v. City of Grenada, 988 F.2d 1425, 1433–1434 (5th Cir. 1993) (inadvertent disclosure of confidential information did not waive privilege); United States v. Oloyede, 982 F.2d 133, 141 (4th Cir. 1992) (citizenship application); United States v. Mierzwicki, 500 F. Supp. 1331, 1334–1335 (D. Md. 1980) (tax returns); *Cf.* United States v. Gray, 876 F.2d 1411, 1415–1416 (9th Cir. 1989) (communication where attorney informed defendant of sentencing date and that his appearance was required was not privileged); In re Sealed Case, 877 F.2d 976, 978–981 (D.C. Cir. 1989) (inadvertent disclosure of one memo to a government auditor waives privilege).

[17] *See, e.g.,* United States v. Under Seal (In re Grand Jury Subpoena), 204 F.3d 516, 520 (4th Cir. 2000) (when attorney is retained tp prepare prospectus, information disclosed to attorney in connection with that task is not confidential, since client expects it to be disclosed to public in prospectus); United States v. Massachusetts Institute of Technology, 129 F.3d 681, 684–686 (1st Cir. 1997) (university's disclosure of documents to audit agency, pursuant to university's obligations under its defense contracts, resulted in waiver of attorney-client privilege); Chevron Corp. v. Pennzoil Co., 974 F.2d 1156, 1162–1163 (9th Cir. 1992) (documents produced to auditor lost privilege); Westinghouse v. Republic of the Philippines, 951 F.2d 1414, 1423-1427 (3d Cir. 1991) (documents disclosed to the SEC and DOJ during investigation, rejected "selective waiver" doctrine); United States v. Plache, 913 F.2d 1375, 1379 (9th Cir. 1990) (client disclosed communications to grand jury); *cf.* Industrial Clearinghouse, Inc. v. Browning Mfg. Div. of Emerson Elec. Co., 953 F.2d 1004, 1007 (5th Cir. 1992) (complaint suing law firm for malpractice did not waive privilege because client's communications were not revealed).

munication.[17.1] When the intent is to keep communication confidential, the privilege may be asserted to prevent an eavesdropper from disclosing confidential communications[18] if sufficient reasonable precautions were taken to ensure confidentiality. In the absence of adequate precautions, a court may find that the requisite intent to maintain confidentiality was lacking.[19]

Facts that anyone could observe, such as whether the client was depressed, are excluded from the privilege. Actions by the client are covered by the privilege if the client intended to utilize them in making a confidential statement in connection with receiving legal services.

[3]—Scope of Privilege[1]

[a]—General Rule

Subdivision (b) of Standard 503 states the general rule that a confidential communication "made for the purpose of facilitating the rendition of professional legal services to the client" is privileged.

[b]—Whose Communications are Privileged?

Confidential communications may occur between any combination of the following parties: the client, the client's representative, the lawyer, the lawyer's representative and different lawyers representing the same client. The privilege also attaches to communications made by the client or lawyer to another lawyer representing a person "in a matter of common interest."[2] The presence of more than

---

[17.1] *See, e.g.,* United States v. BDO Seidman, 337 F.3d 802, 811–813 (7th Cir. 2003) (clients' "participation in potentially abusive tax shelters is information ordinarily subject to full disclosure under the federal tax law"; thus, privilege did not attach to their identities); United States v. Hatcher, 323 F.3d 666, 674 (8th Cir. 2003) (when clients and attorneys knew that government was recording their conversations, clients had no reasonable expectation that communications during those conversations would be confidential and attorney-client privilege did not attach).

[18] *Cf.* United States v. Valenica, 541 F.2d 618, 621–622 (6th Cir. 1976) (case remanded where attorney's secretary was revealed to be government informant to give defendants an opportunity to show that evidence produced against them was obtained through government's intrusion into privilege).

[19] *See* United States v. Robinson, 121 F.3d 971, 976 (5th Cir. 1997) (defendant's possession of forfeiture notice, which was sent to him at jail, was not confidential, even though he handed notice to two lawyers in attempt to secure their representation concerning forfeiture; confidentiality is not established by mere fact of meeting between lawyer and would-be client, or that meeting takes place away from public view); Texaco Puerto Rico v. Department of Consumer Aff., 60 F.3d 867, 883 (1st Cir. 1995) (inadvertent disclosure of documents waived privilege as to them and as to "all other such communications on the same subject").

[1] *See* **Treatise** at § 503.14.

[2] United States v. Newell, 315 F.3d 510, 525 (5th Cir. 2002) (common-interest attorney-client privilege applies only to "(1) communications between co-defendants in actual litigation and their

one client at a joint conference does not destroy the privilege when "disclosure is in furtherance of the rendition of professional legal services to the client."[3] It is the better practice, however, not to have clients at such conferences because of the danger that they may make extraneous statements which can be taken as admissions.

"Common interest" is not defined in Standard 503. The courts have held that the burden of persuasion is on the party asserting the privilege[4] and have tended to narrowly construe the doctrine, especially in the criminal context.[5] For example, the common-interest privilege does not apply when a group of individuals seek legal advice to avoid the possibility of litigation at some time in the future.[5.1]

Joint conferences frequently occur in criminal cases in which co-defendants retain separate counsel,[6] in class actions, in a number of non-litigated situations such as labor or commercial negotiations, and in general corporate and securities

---

counsel; and (2) communications between *potential* co-defendants and their counsel"; emphasis in original). *See* **Treatise** at § 503.21.

[3] Supreme Court Standard 503(a)(4); *see, e.g.,* Federal Deposit Ins. Corp. v. Ogden Corp., 202 F.3d 454, 461 (1st Cir. 2000) (when two or more persons jointly consult an attorney for legal advice, confidential communications to the attorney, although known to all clients, are privileged in controversy between client or clients and outside world); United States v. Moscony, 927 F.2d 742, 753 (3d Cir. 1991) (privilege upheld). *See also* discussion of "confidential," [2][d], *above.*

[4] *See, e.g.,* In re Bevill, Bresler & Schulman Asset Mgmt, Corp., 805 F.2d 120, 125 (3d Cir. 1986) (party asserting privilege has burden of showing that parties agreed to pursue joint defense).

[5] *See, e.g.,* In re Grand Jury Subpoena Duces Tecum, 112 F.3d 910, 921–922 (8th Cir. 1997) ("common interest" doctrine did not extend lawyer-client privilege to conversations involving President's wife, her personal attorney, and attorneys representing White House, because no common interest, "either legal, factual, or strategic in character," existed between the clients, who were Mrs. Clinton in her personal capacity and the White House); United States v. Bay State Ambulance & Hospital Rental Serv., Inc., 874 F.2d 20, 28–29 (1st Cir. 1989) (in Medicare fraud prosecution, hospital official claimed that he had provided information to in-house counsel for ambulance service as part of common defense; court found that official failed to meet burden of showing that document was prepared as part of joint defense and also noted as significant official's failure to provide his own attorney with the information until month's later); Government of Virgin Islands v. Joseph, 685 F.2d 857, 861–862 (3d Cir. 1982) (no common purpose or joint defense where defendant confessed to attorney for another suspect in order to exonerate latter); Walsh v. Northrop Grumman Corp., 165 F.R.D. 16, 19 n.3 (E.D.N.Y. 1996) ("common interest" doctrine is limited to situations where multiple parties are represented by separate counsel but share common interest about a legal matter, not, as in this case, a joint venture that also includes litigation concerns); United States v. Cariello, 536 F. Supp. 698, 702 (D.N.J. 1982) (co-defendant's statement to his attorney in presence of defendant was in furtherance of his individual defense).

[5.1] *See, e.g.,* United States v. Newell, 315 F.3d 510, 525–526 (5th Cir. 2002) (common interest attorney client privilege applies only if litigation is actually pending or there is an imminent threat that litigation will be brought).

[6] *See, e.g.,* Wilson P. Abraham Constr. Corp. v. Armco Steel Corp., 559 F.2d 250, 253 (5th Cir. 1997) (confidential communications made during joint defense strategy sessions are privileged).

practice.[7]

When separate counsel have been retained, the privilege continues to apply if litigation ensues between any of the parties who had engaged in the joint consultations. If, however, more than one client retains the same counsel and later there is a falling out between the clients, there is no privilege for communications made by any of participants of joint consultations, as discussed below. The divergence in result is justified because the client who has retained separate counsel has taken all necessary steps to ensure the protection of the privilege. Consequently, in a multi-party situation, an attorney has an ethical obligation to suggest at the outset of the representation that each party may need separate counsel.[8]

[c]—Communications[9]

Only "communications" are protected by the attorney-client privilege. A client's knowledge is not protected.[10]

Therefore, although a client may not be questioned about what he or she told the attorney, the client may be questioned about the information that he or she knows. A client's act may also constitute a communication, but only if the client intended that the act make a confidential statement to the attorney in connection with receiving legal services.[11]

A written communication is accorded the same protection as an oral communication. However, a pre-existing document or object does not become privileged merely by transferring it to an attorney. Under some circumstances, though, the Fifth Amendment prohibition against compelled self-incrimination will prevent the attorney from disclosing a document or object if it will establish a criminal connection to the client. Generally, if the document or object could be compelled

---

[7] See, e.g., Hanson v. United States Agency for Int'l Dev., 372 F.3d 286, 292 (4th Cir. 2004) (common interest doctrine provides attorney client privilege protection to communications between lawyer and more than one party whenever the non-lawyer parties have common interest in legal matters and jointly consult lawyer in connection with those matters).

[8] See discussion in **Treatise** at § 503.21 of the related problem of when an attorney must be disqualified because of information previously acquired in a professional capacity.

[9] See **Treatise** at § 503.14.

[10] Upjohn Co. v. United States, 449 U.S. 383, 395, 101 S. Ct. 677, 66 L. Ed. 2d 584 (1981) ("The privilege only protects disclosure of communications; it does not protect disclosure of the underlying facts by those who communicated with the attorney"); see, e.g., In re Six Grand Jury Witnesses, 979 F.2d 939, 945 (2d Cir. 1992) (witnesses required to provide information underlying analyses they prepared for attorney).

[11] See, e.g., United States v. White, 970 F.2d 328, 334–336 (7th Cir. 1992) (defendant's nondisclosure of certain assets did not constitute a privileged communication); Granviel v. Lynaugh, 881 F.2d 185, 192–193 (5th Cir. 1989) (defendant's act of striking attorney during confidential communication was not privileged).

by process if it were in the hands of the client, it must be produced even though it is now in the possession of the attorney.[12]

As long as the communication is made for the purpose of rendering legal services, it does not matter under Standard 503 whether the communications is made by the client to the attorney or by the attorney to the client. Federal courts tend to be in agreement with Standard 503,[13] although some cases suggest that communications from the attorney to the client are not within the privilege unless they would reveal the client's confidences.[14]

Although the contents of communications between lawyer and client may be privileged, the subject matter of such communications is not privileged when a court must know the subject matter to determine whether the privilege applies to the communications.[14.1]

[d]—Identifying Facts About the Client, Lawyer, or Representation[15]

The general rule in the federal courts is that identifying facts about the client or attorney, or the scope or objective of the employment, are not treated as confidential communications to which the privilege applies.[16] Usually disclosing identifying

---

[12] Fisher v. United States, 425 U.S. 391, 403–404, 96 S. Ct. 1569, 48 L. Ed. 2d 39 (1976) ("pre-existing documents which could have been obtained by court process from the client when he was in possession may also be obtained from the attorney by similar process following transfer by the client in order to obtain more informed legal advice"). *See, e.g.,* United States v. Robinson, 121 F.3d 971, 976 (5th Cir. 1997) (neither forfeiture notice nor defendant's possession of notice, which was sent to him at jail, was privileged, even though he handed notice to two lawyers in attempt to secure their representation concerning forfeiture); In re Grand Jury Subpoenas, 959 F.2d 1158, 1165–1166 (2d Cir. 1992) (company telephone bills not privileged); United States v. Rodriquez, 948 F.2d 914, 916 (5th Cir. 1991) (client failed to show that documents seized during search of attorney's office were privileged communications); United States v. Clark, 847 F.2d 1467, 1471–1472 (10th Cir. 1988).

[13] *See, e.g.,* L.A. Gear, Inc. v. Thom McAn Shoe Co., 988 F.2d 1117, 1126 (Fed. Cir. 1993) (advice given by counsel privileged); United States v. Amerada Hess Corp., 619 F.2d 980, 986 (3d Cir. 1980) ("Legal advice or opinion from an attorney to his client, individual or corporate, has consistently been held by the federal courts to be within the protection of the attorney-client privilege").

[14] *See* In re LTV Securities Litigation, 89 F.R.D. 595, 602 (N.D. Tex. 1981) (review of cases and criticism of this view).

[14.1] *See, e.g.,* Madanes v. Madanes, 199 F.R.D. 135, 146 (S.D.N.Y. 2001) (relying on broad Argentine attorney-client privilege, attorney has declined to identify even subject matter of advice he gave to client; however, "broad foreign testimonial or evidentiary privilege ought not be recognized in this Court if it impedes the determination of whether a privilege exists under the federal common law"; ordering attorney to identify subject matter of his communications with client, "though he need not reveal their content").

[15] *See* **Treatise** at § 503.14[5].

[16] *See, e.g,* United States v. BDO Seidman, 337 F.3d 802, 811 (7th Cir. 2003) (client's identity is not ordinarily information subject to attorney-client privilege); *but see* Chaudhry v. Gallerizzo,

facts does not create a problem. Rarely does a client want to keep these facts secret. But situations do arise in which clients desire their whereabouts, identity, or fee information to be protected against disclosure. Standard 503 is silent about how to handle this problem.

In resolving these situations, the courts have divided into two major camps. One group would almost always require disclosure on the theory that these facts are "different from communications intended by the client to explain a problem to a lawyer in order to obtain legal advice."[17] Other courts have taken a more protective view and upheld the privilege claim when the information sought would implicate the client in the criminal act for which legal advice is sought,[18] or more narrowly, where disclosure would be "the last link in an existing chain of incriminating evidence likely to lead to the client's indictment."[19] Another approach protects a client's identifying information from disclosure only if it is so inextricably intertwined with other, confidential information that disclosure of the identifying information necessarily results in disclosure of the other, confidential information.[19.1]

The Internal Revenue Code and regulations require disclosure of large payments received by lawyers in cash.[20] The majority of courts have rejected claims that compliance with the reporting requirements would violate the lawyer-client privilege.[21] As several courts have remarked, clients wishing to avoid disclosure are free

---

174 F.3d 394, 402–403 (4th Cir. 1999) (billing records that revealed statutes researched were protected by attorney-client privilege because the records would divulge confidential information about legal advice sought).

[17] In re Grand Jury Subpoenas United States v. Hirsch, 803 F.2d 493, 497–498 (9th Cir. 1986) (identity of third-party beneficiary paying defendant's attorney's fees is not privileged; privilege applies only where disclosure would convey the substance of a confidential professional communication between attorney and client).

[18] See In re Subpoenaed Grand Jury Witness, 171 F.3d 511, 513–514 (7th Cir. 1999) (identity of attorney's client who paid fees of other clients was privileged because disclosure would reveal payor's motive for seeking legal advice).

[19] See, e.g., United States v. Blackman, 72 F.3d 1418, 1425 (9th Cir. 1995) (recognizing rule that client identity and nature of fee arrangement are protected by lawyer-client privilege when disclosure would compromise confidential communication between attorney and client or constitute "last link" in existing chain of evidence, likely to lead to client's identity (citing cases), but finding exception inapplicable to present case).

[19.1] See, e.g., United States v. BDO Seidman, 337 F.3d 802, 811–812 (7th Cir. 2003) (client's identity is protected by attorney client privilege when so much of an actual confidential communication has been disclosed already that merely identifying the client will effectively disclose that communication").

[20] See 26 U.S.C. § 6050I.

[21] See, e.g., United States v. Blackman, 72 F.3d 1418, 1425 (9th Cir. 1995) (disclosure of payer of fee in excess of $10,000 cash does not conflict with privilege).

to pay their counsel in some manner other than cash.[22]

[4]—Corporate Clients: Attorney-Client Privilege and Work-Product[1]

Standard 503 did not deal with the scope of the privilege in the corporate context because the Supreme Court was evenly divided on this question at the time the proposed rule was drafted by the Advisory Committee. It was not then clear whether a corporation, which can act only through its employees and agents, was entitled to claim privilege whenever any corporate employee, regardless of rank, communicated with counsel for the purpose of securing legal advice for the corporation, or whether the communicating employee had to be in a position of control within the corporation.[2]

In 1981, in *Upjohn Co. v. United States,* [3] the Supreme Court partially answered this question. Upjohn asserted the privilege when the Internal Revenue Service issued a summons for documents which had been created as part of an Unjohn's internal investigation into "questionable payments." Unjohn's general counsel had conducted the investigation. Questionnaires had been sent to "all foreign and area managers" over the signature of the Chairman of the Board informing them that counsel had been asked to conduct an investigation, which was to be treated as "highly confidential," and asking for detailed information to be returned directly to the general counsel. General counsel, with the assistance of outside counsel, also interviewed the recipients, as well as other Upjohn employees.

The district court rejected Upjohn's claim of privilege and concluded that the IRS summons should be enforced. On appeal, the Sixth Circuit found that only communications made by those within the "control group" would be privileged; it remanded for a determination of who was within this group.

The Supreme Court unanimously rejected the "control group test" as inconsistent with the standard for privileges expressed in Rule 501.[4] The Court explained that the "control group test"

---

[22] *See, e.g.,* United States v. Goldberger & Dublin, P.C., 935 F.2d 501, 504 (2d Cir. 1991) (client can pay counsel in some other manner than with cash to circumvent statute).

[1] *See* **Treatise** at § 503.22.

[2] The so-called control group test had first been enunciated in City of Philadelphia v. Westinghouse Electric Corp., 210 F. Supp. 483, 485–486 (E.D. Pa. 1962), *mandamus and prohibition denied,* 312 F.2d 742 (3d Cir. 1962).

[3] 449 U.S. 383, 101 S. Ct. 677, 66 L. Ed. 2d 584 (1981).

[4] The majority wrote: "the narrow 'control group test' sanctioned by the Court of Appeals in this case cannot, consistent with 'the principles of the common law as . . . interpreted . . . in light of reason and experience,' Fed. Rule Evid. 501, govern the development of the law in this area." 449 U.S. at 397. Chief Justice Burger, concurring, agreed "fully with the Court's rejection of the so-called 'control group' test, its reasons for doing so, and its ultimate holding that the communications at issue are privileged." 449 U.S. at 402.

overlooks the fact that the privilege exists to protect not only the giving of professional advice to those who can act on it but also the giving of information to the lawyer to enable him to give sound and informed advice.

. . .

In the case of the individual client the provider of information and the person who acts on the lawyer's advice are one and the same. In the corporate context, however, it will frequently be employees beyond the control group as defined by the court below—"officers and agents . . . responsible for directing [the company's] actions in response to legal advice"—who will possess the information needed by the corporation's lawyers. Middle-level—and indeed lower-level—employees can, by actions within the scope of their employment, embroil the corporation in serious legal difficulties, and it is only natural that these employees would have the relevant information needed by corporate counsel if he is adequately to advise the client with respect to such actual or potential difficulties.

. . .

The narrow scope given the attorney-client privilege by the court below not only makes it difficult for corporate attorneys to formulate sound advice when their client is faced with a specific legal problem but also threatens to limit the valuable efforts of corporate counsel to ensure their client's compliance with the law.[5]

After noting that the information from Upjohn's employees "was needed to supply a basis for legal advice," a fact of which "the employees themselves were sufficiently aware," and that the communications "have been kept confidential," the Court held that "these communications must be protected against compelled disclosure."[6]

While rejecting the "control group test," the majority of the Court refused to do more than decide the case before it. The opinion does, however, cite Diversified Industries, Inc. v. Meredith[7] a number of times. In that case, the Eighth Circuit, sitting en banc, held that the attorney-client privilege would be applicable when five requirements are satisfied:

(1) the communication was made for the purpose of securing legal advice;
(2) the employee making the communication did so at the direction of his

---

[5] 449 U.S. at 390–392.
[6] 449 U.S. at 394–395.
[7] Diversified Industries, Inc. v. Meredith, 572 F.2d 596 (8th Cir. 1977).

corporate superior; (3) the superior made the request so that the corporation could secure legal advice; (4) the subject matter of the communication is within the scope of the employee's corporate duties; and (5) the communication is not disseminated beyond those persons who, because of the corporate structure, need to know its contents. We note, moreover, that the corporation has the burden of showing that the communication in issue meets all of the above requirements.[8]

For example, reporters' communications with in-house counsel at Time and Newsweek to discuss potential liability for libel "were clearly for the purpose of rendering legal advice and therefore are privileged."[8.1]

Expressly left open by the Court's decision in *Upjohn* is the question of whether the attorney-client privilege applies to communications by former employees concerning activities during their period of employment.[9] In this regard, the Fourth Circuit has held that if other requirements to establish the privilege are met, the privilege does extend to communications involving former, as well as current, employees of the corporate client.[9.1]

Numerous other questions still remain, such as: may a parent corporation assert a privilege as to communications by employees of a subsidiary, who can waive the privilege, and to what extent may a privileged communication be circulated within the corporate entity without losing its privileged status?[10] *Upjohn* also raises a host of ethical problems for the corporate lawyer. To what extent may counsel interview a corporate employee—whose interests may be somewhat antithetical to those of the corporation—without warning the employee that counsel does not represent the employee, and that the employee has a right not to talk to corporate counsel and to obtain separate counsel?[10.1] Such warnings would, of course, undercut *Upjohn's*

---

[8] 572 F.2d at 609.

[8.1] *See* Tucker v. Fischbein, 237 F.3d 275, 288 (3d Cir. 2001) (argument that privilege was waived because in-house counsel reviewed stories "in the regular course of business" was "frivolous"; plaintiff precluded from deposing counsel concerning those consultations).

[9] Upjohn Co. v. United States, 449 U.S. 383, 394 n.3, 101 S. Ct. 677, 66 L. Ed. 2d 584 (1981).

[9.1] In re Allen, 106 F.3d 582, 605–606 (4th Cir. 1997) (communication may be privileged when former employee speaks, at the direction of management, with an attorney regarding conduct within scope of former employment).

[10] *See, e.g.,* In re Grand Jury No. 90-1, 758 F.Supp. 1411, 1413 (D. Colo. 1991) (letter between president and board of directors discussing legal advice privileged).

[10.1] *See, e.g.,* United States v. Intern. Broth. of Teamsters, AFL-CIO, 119 F.3d 210, 215–216 (2d Cir. 1997) (any privilege that attaches to communications on corporate matters between corporate employees and corporate counsel belongs to the corporation, not to the individual employee; employees generally may not prevent a corporation from waiving the attorney-client privilege arising from those communications).

rationale of enabling corporate attorneys to obtain as much information as possible in order to function most effectively.

Aside from rejecting a narrow view of the attorney-client privilege in *Upjohn*, the Court also took an expansive approach to the work product doctrine. The Supreme Court stressed that the material sought by the government—notes and memoranda of witnesses' statements—has been accorded special protection, both by the decision in *Hickman v. Taylor* [11] and by Rule 26 of the Federal Rules of Civil Procedure, because such material "tends to reveal the attorney's mental processes."[12] Noting that "some courts have concluded that no showing of necessity can overcome protection of work product which is based on oral statements from witnesses," while other courts in "declining to adopt an absolute rule have nonetheless recognized that such material is entitled to special protection," the Supreme Court refused to "decide the issue at this time."[13]

Since *Upjohn*, it appears that some of the circuit courts are curbing the potential sweep of the opinion by strict enforcement of the concept of waiver, and application of the crime-fraud exception.[14] These aspects are discussed below.

Another issue raised in the corporate context, and about which Standard 503 is silent, is the extent to which shareholders and other beneficiaries of a fiduciary relationship may have access to what would otherwise qualify as privileged communications. The question has most frequently arisen in derivative suits brought by minority stockholders. Since such an action is theoretically for the benefit of the corporation, the corporation should have no objection to divulging the requested information to its representative, the minority stockholder. In actuality, there is mutual antagonism between those who bring the suit and those who run the corporation.

Instead of treating the privilege as absolute under these circumstances, a number of courts have adopted a flexible rule that permits disclosure of otherwise privileged matter if the plaintiff can demonstrate "good cause." In the case of *Garner v.*

---

[11]   Hickman v. Taylor, 329 U.S. 495, 67 S. Ct. 385, 91 L. Ed. 451 (1947).

[12]   Upjohn Co. v. United States, 449 U.S. 383, 400, 101 S. Ct. 677, 66 L. Ed. 2d 584 (1981); *see* Fed. R. Civ. P. 26.

[13]   449 U.S. at 401-402 ("While we are not prepared at this juncture to say that such material is always protected by the work-product rule, we think a far stronger showing of necessity and unavailability by other means than was made by the Government or applied by the Magistrate in this case would be necessary to compel disclosure").

[14]   *See, e.g.,* In re Sealed Case, 676 F.2d 793 (D.C. Cir. 1982); In re John Doe Corp., 675 F.2d 482 (2d Cir. 1982); and discussion in **Treatise** at § 503.16[1].

Wolfinbarger, [15] the Fifth Circuit suggested weighing the following factors in determining good cause:[16]

[T]he number of shareholders and the percentage of stock they represent; the bona fides of the shareholders; the nature of the shareholders' claim and whether it is obviously colorable; the apparent necessity or desirability of the shareholders having the information and the availability of it from other sources; whether, if the shareholders' claim is of wrongful action by the corporation, it is of action criminal, or illegal but not criminal, or of doubtful legality; whether the communication related to past or to prospective actions; whether the communication is of advice concerning the litigation itself; the extent to which the communication is identified versus the extent to which the shareholders are blindly fishing; the risk of revelation of trade secrets or other information in whose confidentiality the corporation has an interest for independent reasons.

The Securities and Exchange Commission has adopted a rule requiring attorneys practicing before it to report evidence of a material violation of securities laws, breach of fiduciary duty, or similar violation by a company the attorney represents, or by any agent of the company, to the chief legal counsel or the chief executive officer of the company (or the equivalent); and, if the person to whom the attorney has made the report does not respond appropriately to the evidence, to report the evidence to the audit committee, another committee of independent directors, or the full board of directors. The rule is codified in 17 C.F.R. Part 205.

[5]—Who May Claim the Privilege[1]

Standard 503(c) vests the privilege in the client.[2] The privilege may be claimed by the client regardless of whether or not the client is a party to the proceeding in which disclosure of the privileged communication is sought. If the client is present when the privileged information is sought, the client or the attorney must assert the privilege or it will be deemed waived. During a period of disability, a guardian or conservator may assert the privilege.

---

[15] Garner v. Wolfinbarger, 430 F.2d 1093 (5th Cir. 1970).

[16] 430 F.2d at 1104. *See* Sandberg v. Virginia Bankshares, Inc., 979 F.2d 332, 350–351 (4th Cir. 1992), *vacated and remanded,* 1993 U.S. App. LEXIS 33286 (4th Cir. 1993) (good cause shown why privilege should not apply); Fausek v. White, 965 F.2d 126, 132–133 (6th Cir. 1992) (no privilege where fraud stated with particularity and information sought was not readily available from other sources).

[1] *See* **Treatise** at § 503.20.

[2] *See e.g.,* In re Grand Jury Subpoena, 220 F.3d 406, 408 (5th Cir. 2000) (in corporate context, attorney-client privilege belongs to corporation, not to in-house counsel who generated subpoenaed document).

Blanket claims of privilege are disfavored; the privilege must be specifically asserted with respect to particular communications or documents.[2.1]

A client waives the attorney-client privilege by failing to assert it when confidential information is sought in legal proceedings.[2.2] The privilege is also waived if the holder asserts the privilege in the context of an affirmative act, such as filing suit, that puts the privileged information at issue.[2.3] Waiver of privileges, including the attorney-client privilege, is discussed in § 18.08, *below*, and in the **Treatise** at Chapter 511, *Waiver of Privilege by Voluntary Disclosure (Supreme Court Standard 511)*.

Standard 503 acknowledges that the privilege survives the death of an individual client.[2.4] In the corporate context, the Standard provides that the successor of a dissolved corporation may claim the privilege.[2.5] The Supreme Court has held in *Commodity Futures Trading Commission v. Weintraub* [3] that the power to waive, and presumably to assert, the attorney-client privilege passes to the trustee in bankruptcy regarding any communications that took place before the filing of the bankruptcy petition.

A lawyer who no longer represents a client will be presumed to have authority to claim the privilege until evidence to the contrary is offered. A lawyer currently representing a client may assert a claim of privilege even though the communications in question were made prior to the lawyer's representation of the client. If former and present attorneys differ in their view of the client's position, the current attorney's position should be followed.[4]

[2.1]   Nguyen v. Excel Corp., 197 F.3d 200, 206–207 (5th Cir. 1999) (dicta, party waived privilege by failing to assert it when privileged information was sought, and then by selectively disclosing portions of the privileged confidential communication; citing **Treatise**).

[2.2]   Nguyen v. Excel Corp., 197 F.3d 200, 206–207 (5th Cir. 1999).

[2.3]   United States v. Amlani, 169 F.3d 1189, 1194–1195 (9th Cir. 1999) (defendant waived attorney-client privilege by charging that prosecutorial disparagement of his attorney violated his Sixth Amendment right to counsel, by causing him to obtain new counsel).

[2.4]   *See* Swidler & Berlin v. United States, 524 U.S. 399, 118 S. Ct. 2081, 141 L. Ed. 2d 379, 388–389 (1998) (noting the "generally, if not universally, accepted" rule "that the attorney-client privilege suvives the death of the client" as basis for rejecting exception to privilege in certain criminal proceedings that was proposed in, and reversing, In re Sealed Case, 124 F.3d 230, 233–235 (D.C. Cir. 1997)).

[2.5]   *See also* In re Grand Jury Subpoena, 274 F.3d 563, 571 (1st Cir. 2001) (current management of corporation can waive corporation's attorney-client privilege even though subject matter of subpoenaed documents concerns actions of prior management exclusively).

[3]   Commodity Futures Trading Commission v. Weintraub, 471 U.S. 343, 354, 105 S. Ct. 1986, 85 L. Ed. 2d 372 (1985). *See also* In re Bevill, Bresler & Schulman Asset Mgmt. Corp., 805 F.2d 120, 125 (3d Cir. 1986) (where corporation has waived the privilege through the trustee, the assertion of an individual privilege on behalf of a corporate official will not prevent disclosure).

[4]   United States v. DeLillo, 448 F. Supp. 840, 842 (E.D.N.Y. 1978).

[6]—Exceptions to the Privilege[1]

[a]—Furtherance of Crime or Fraud[2]

Standard 503(d)(1) is in accord with the view "accepted by all courts today . . . that a client's communication to his attorney in pursuit of a criminal or fraudulent act yet to be performed is not privileged in any judicial proceeding."[3] This exception rests on the realization that the privilege's policy of promoting the administration of justice would be undermined if the privilege could be used as "a cloak or shield for the perpetration of a crime or fraudulent wrongdoing."[4] The privilege is lost regardless of whether the attorney was aware of the client's plans.[5] It is the client's intention to use the attorney's services in aid of what the client knew, or reasonably should have known to be a crime or fraud, that controls.[6]

The courts are not in agreement about the type of non-criminal acts that implicate the crime-fraud exception. Some courts have held the exception applicable only to communications in furtherance of acts that qualify as fraudulent in accordance with the common-law definition of "fraud."[6.1] Others have held the exception applicable to tortious conduct that is intended to undermine the adversary system, even though not strictly fraudulent.[6.2]

A few courts have extended the exception to embrace intentional or reckless

---

[1] Standard 503 recognizes five exceptions to the attorney-client privilege: (1) furtherance of crime or fraud, (2) claimants through same deceased client, (3) breach of duty by lawyer or client, (4) document attested by lawyer, and (5) joint clients. Each exception is discussed in this subsection.

[2] See **Treatise** at § 503.31.

[3] In re Sawyer's Petition, 229 F.2d 805, 808–809 (7th Cir. 1956). See, e.g., In re Grand Jury Proceeding Impounded, 241 F.3d 308, 316 (3d Cir. 2001) (if legal advice is sought in furtherance of crime or fraud, attorney-client privilege concerning that advice is waived).

[4] See, e.g., United States v. Edwards, 303 F.3d 606, 618–619 (5th Cir. 2002) (crime-fraud exception is applicable when client uses attorney's services to continue cover-up of past fraud or crime, even though act of fraud or crime, itself, is completed).

[5] See United States v. Laurins, 857 F.2d 529, 540–541 (9th Cir. 1988).

[6] See, e.g., In re Bankamerica Corp. Secs. Litig., 270 F.3d 639, 642 (8th Cir. 2001) ("Because the attorney-client privilege benefits the client, it is the client's intent to further a crime or fraud that must be shown. . . . Both the attorney's intent, and the attorney's knowledge or ignorance of the client's intent, are irrelevant."); United States v. Jacobs, 117 F.3d 82, 87–89 (2d Cir. 1997) (there was evidence from which it was reasonable to believe that the defendant's intent in obtaining opinion letters from his attorney was "to further his Debt Elimination Plan fraud").

[6.1] See, e.g., Ferrara & DiMercurio v. St. Paul Mercury Ins. Co., 173 F.R.D. 7, 13 (D. Mass. 1997), aff'd, 240 F.3d 1 (1st Cir. 2001) (applying Massachusetts law); see also Madanes v. Madanes, 199 F.R.D. 135, 148 (S.D.N.Y. 2001) (common-law "fraud consists of an intentional and material misrepresentation that is reasonably relied upon by the plaintiff and causes the plaintiff damage").

[6.2] See, e.g., Madanes v. Madanes, 199 F.R.D. 135, 148 (S.D.N.Y. 2001) (applying exception when attorney and other person conspired to violate attorney's duty to maintain confidences of other clients).

torts.[7]

If "the very act of litigating is alleged as being in furtherance of a fraud, the party seeking disclosure under the crime-fraud exception must show probable cause that the litigation or an aspect thereof had little or no legal or factual basis and was carried on substantially for the purpose of furthering the crime or fraud."[7.1]

Advice obtained from an attorney by one who is already a wrongdoer and is seeking legal counsel in aid of a legitimate defense is privileged.[8] While it may at times be difficult to ascertain the boundaries between past and present wrongdoing, it is clear that an attorney should never directly or indirectly assist in the destruction of evidence,[9] or acquiesce in perjury.[10]

The Advisory Committee's notes to Standard 503(d)(1) explicitly state that the court need not make a preliminary finding that there is sufficient evidence aside from the communication to warrant a finding that the legal services were sought to enable the commission of the crime or fraud. The absence of any test has the advantage of leaving the question to the good sense of the trial judge. Certainly some crimes by their very nature suggest that there must have been legal guidance, and consequently a judge may, without more, conclude that the communication was in furtherance of crime or fraud. In many cases, the question of how much proof is needed to show unlawful purpose is purely theoretical.[11]

Conversely, in United States v. Zolin,[12] the Supreme Court held that upon a proper showing the district court may conduct an in camera review to determine whether an allegedly privileged communication comes within the crime-fraud exception to the privilege. The Court ruled that in camera review could be obtained

---

[7] *See, e.g.,* Diamond v. Stratton, 95 F.R.D. 503, 505 (S.D.N.Y. 1982).

[7.1] In re Richard Roe, Inc., 168 F.3d 69, 71–72 (2d Cir. 1999) (reversing trial court's order to produce documents related to civil litigation, since it failed to show that litigation itself was fraudulent or that documents themselves were "in furtherance of a crime or fraud").

[8] *See* United States v. White, 887 F.2d 267, 271–272 (D.C. Cir. 1989).

[9] *See, e.g.,* In re Ryder, 263 F. Supp. 360, 369–370 (E.D. Va.), *aff'd per curiam on opinion below,* 381 F.2d 713 (4th Cir. 1967).

[10] *See* Nix v. Whiteside, 475 U.S. 157, 171, 106 S. Ct. 988, 89 L. Ed. 2d 123 (1986) ("under no circumstance may a lawyer either advocate or passively tolerate a client's giving false testimony").

[11] *See, e.g.,* United States v. Reeder, 170 F.3d 93, 106 (1st Cir. 1999) (fact that defendant twice asked for his business attorney's help to cover up defendant's fraudulent diversion of insurance money was sufficient to admit conversation under crime-fraud exception); Laser Indus. v. Reliant Technologies, 167 F.R.D. 417, 437 (N.D. Cal. 1996) (in making preliminary determination whether crime/fraud exception applies to evidence for which attorney-client privilege is claimed, trial court should make judgment based on inferences that judge personally makes from evidence and argument, instead of making preliminary determination under Rule 104(b) concerning "breadth of the zone of inferences a jury could rationally make").

[12] United States v. Zolin, 491 U.S. 554, 109 S. Ct. 2619, 105 L. Ed. 2d 469 (1989).

only if the party seeking disclosure makes a factual showing sufficient to support a reasonable belief that the in camera review would reveal evidence that would establish the crime-fraud exception.[13] "[T]he threshold showing to obtain in camera review may be met by using any relevant evidence, lawfully obtained, that has not been adjudicated to be privileged."[14]

[b]—Claimants Through Same Deceased Claimant[15]

Standard 503(d)(2) states an exception to the general rule expressed in subdivision (c) that the lawyer-client privilege survives the death of the client (see [5], above). There is no privilege "[a]s to a communication relevant to an issue between parties who claim through the same deceased client, regardless of whether the claims are by testate or intestate succession or by inter vivos transaction."

In cases where two or more parties claim through the same deceased, the very issue to be determined is who steps into the decedent's shoes. Since this cannot be determined until the end of the litigation, the question of who is entitled to claim the privilege must also be held in abeyance. Rather than allowing all to assert the privilege, the better choice is to hold that where all the parties claim under the client, the privilege does not apply. In will cases this approach furthers the public interest in having an estate distributed promptly in accordance with the decedent's intent.

When the contest is between a "stranger" and a person claiming through the deceased client, the party claiming through the decedent may invoke the privilege if he comes within the definition of Standard 503(c). If two or more parties claim through a client who is not deceased, the privilege continues unless the client waives it pursuant to standard 511.

---

[13] 491 U.S. at 571–572 (1989).

[14] 491 U.S. at 574–575; United States v. Zolin, 905 F.2d 1344, 1345 (9th Cir. 1990) (on remand after the Supreme Court held that the tapes at issue may be examined for proof that would establish the crime-fraud exception, exception applies where those involved admit on the tapes that they were attempting to confuse and defraud the United States government in order to cover up past criminal wrongdoing; cf. In re Grand Jury Investigation, 974 F.2d 1068 (9th Cir. 1992) (minimal showing that the exception may apply gives the district court discretion to conduct an in camera inspection); United States v. de la Jara, 973 F.2d 746, 748–750 (9th Cir. 1992) (attorney's letter to defendant should not have been admitted without first requiring the government to show that there was sufficient non-privileged evidence " 'to support a reasonable belief that in camera review may yield evidence that establishes the exception's applicability.' " [citation omitted; emphasis in original]. The court rejected the government's argument that this threshold showing was not required because the government and the court both had access to the letter and knew what it contained. "It is the privileged nature of the document, not the ease of access, which determines whether a court has recourse to it in determining whether the crime-fraud exception should apply." Under Rule 104(a), the court is not bound by the Rules of Evidence in making preliminary determinations, "except those [Rules] with respect to privileges").

[15] See **Treatise** at § 503.32.

[c]—Breach of Duty By Lawyer or Client[16]

Standard 503(d)(3) states the generally accepted view that when the attorney and client become opponents in a subsequent controversy, the attorney may reveal privileged communications to the limited extent necessary to establish the attorney's rights.[17]

A limited exception applies concerning possible breaches of duty by a client who is a trustee or some other type of fiduciary. Most courts recognize a "fiduciary exception" to the attorney-client privilege. Although discussions between trustees and their attorneys are generally privileged, trustees may not rely on the attorney-client privilege to block inquiry by their own beneficiaries into the proper management of the assets entrusted to them.[17.1] For example, "an employer acting in the capacity of ERISA fiduciary is disabled from asserting the attorney-client privilege against plan beneficiaries on matters of plan administration."[17.2]

On the other hand, trustees retain their attorney-client privilege when it is not barred by the fiduciary exception. Thus, a trustee is not barred from enjoying a confidential attorney-client relationship when acting in some role other than as the beneficiaries' representative.[17.3] For example, advice the trustee receives in its role as an employer is privileged.[17.4] The attorney-client privilege also persists when

---

[16] *See* **Treatise** at § 503.33.

[17] *See, e.g.,* Kalyawongsa v. Moffett, 105 F.3d 283, 290 (6th Cir. 1997) (attorney may reveal confidences or secrets necessary to establish or collect attorney's fee or to defend attorney against charge of wrongful conduct); Tasby v. United States, 504 F.2d 332, 336 (8th Cir. 1974) (claim of ineffective assistance of counsel claim waived protection of attorney-client privilege); In re Featherworks Corp., 25 B.R. 634, 644–645 (Bankr. E.D.N.Y. 1982), *aff'd,* 36 B.R. 460 (E.C.N.Y. 1984) (attorney of bankrupt who was unsecured creditor could testify as to validity of claim of secured creditor).

[17.1] Riggs Nat'l Bank v. Zimmer, 355 A.2d 709, 713-714 (Del. Ch. 1976) (recognizing fiduciary exception in United States for first time; employer acting in capacity of ERISA fiduciary is disabled from asserting attorney-client privilege against plan beneficiaries on matters of plan administration).

[17.2] Becher v. Long Island Lighting Co., 129 F.3d 268, 272 (2d Cir. 1997) (finding basis for exception in ERISA trustee's duty to disclose to plan beneficiaries all information regarding plan administration); *see also* United States v. Doe (In re Grand Jury Proceedings), 162 F.3d 554, 556-557 (9th Cir. 1998) (applying fiduciary exception to trustee of ERISA pension fund; when "an attorney advises an ERISA trustee regarding the management of the fund, the ultimate clients of the attorney are as much the beneficiaries of the plan as the trustees").

[17.3] United States v. Mett, 178 F.3d 1058, 1063 (9th Cir. 1999) (exception is limited to advice about plan administration, because then beneficiaries are "the real client"; privilege remains in other situations).

[17.4] M.A. Everett v. USAir Group, 165 F.R.D. 1, 4 (D.D.C. 1995) (employer does not act as fiduciary when it decides to form, amend, or terminate a plan; "when an employer seeks legal counsel only in its role as employer regarding issues other than plan administration, the employer (not the beneficiaries) is the client and may legitimately assert the attorney-client privilege").

a fiduciary retains counsel to defend himself or herself against the beneficiaries or the government acting on their behalf.[17.5] The nature of each particular attorney-client communication must be analyzed to determine the applicability of the fiduciary exception if the attorney-client privilege and the fiduciary exception are to coexist.[17.6]

[d]—Document Attested By Lawyer[18]

Standard 503(d)(4) states that when an attorney acts as an attesting witness, the attorney-client privilege does not bar the disclosure of any communication relevant to an issue concerning the document. This exception permits the attorney to testify to such matters as the intent and competence of the client and the execution or attestation of the document.

When the lawyer drew the document after receiving confidential communications, the lawyer should suggest that someone else act as the attesting witness so as not to reduce the privilege's protection.

[e]—Joint Clients[19]

Standard 503(d)(5) states the generally accepted principle that when "the same attorney acts for two or more parties having a common interest, neither party may exercise the privilege in a subsequent controversy with the other."[20] Communications with the attorney are still privileged in any action between one or all of the clients and a third person.

[f]—Information Necessary for Third Party's Fair Trial

In some circumstances a communication otherwise protected by the attorney-client privilege will lose its privileged status if the information it contains is necessary to the realization of a third party's right to a fair trial. Thus, in a criminal prosecution, the prosecution's case may be highly dependent on the testimony of

---

[17.5] United States v. Mett, 178 F.3d 1058, 1066 (9th Cir. 1999) ("[W]hile a fiduciary exception does apply to advice on matters of plan administration, the attorney-client privilege reasserts itself as to any advice that a fiduciary obtains in an effort to protect himself from civil or criminal liability").

[17.6] *See* United States v. Mett, 178 F.3d 1058, 1065 (9th Cir. 1999) (refusing to apply fiduciary exception to advice obtained by fiduciary about his potential personal civil or criminal liability).

[18] *See* **Treatise** at § 503.34.

[19] *See* **Treatise** at § 503.21.

[20] Garner v. Wolfinbarger, 430 F.2d 1093, 1103 (5th Cir. 1970); *see also* United States v. Weissman, 195 F.3d 96, 99–100 (2d Cir. 1999) (some form of joint strategy is necessary to establish existence of joint defense agreement, which would protect evidence under common interest rule); *but see* Madanes v. Madanes, 199 F.R.D. 135, 144 (S.D.N.Y. 2001) (when attorney represents simultaneously two clients whose interests subsequently become adverse, each client's communications with attorney remain privileged as against each other).

an informer or an accomplice turned government witness to the effect that the defendant committed the crime with which he or she is charged. If the prosecution witness previously wrote a letter to his or her lawyer admitting that he or she, in fact, committed the crime, the defendant's Sixth Amendment right to confront the witness by cross-examining him or her with a prior inconsistent statement may require that the defendant have access to the letter, even though the attorney-client privilege protects its contents.[21] The privilege will nevertheless continue to protect the contents of the communication if the defendant is able to cross-examine the witness adequately with other unprivileged evidence at his or her disposal.[22]

Similar considerations lead to the conclusion that parties to a joint defense agreement in a criminal case, under which they have provided information to the separately-retained lawyer for one of his or her co-defendants, may, to some extent, waive his or her attorney client privilege by agreeing to testify for the government. In such a circumstance, the lawyers for the remaining defendants who had received information from the former defendant may feel a reluctance to reveal that information, because of its purportedly privileged status, during their cross-examination of the witness. Such reluctance could deprive their client of his or her right to effective representation by counsel. Some courts note that the arguments in favor of applying the privilege to communications between a party and his or her lawyer do not apply as strongly to communications between one party and another party's lawyer. They, therefore, hold that the defecting accomplice waives the privilege insofar as it protects communications between himself or herself and another party's lawyer. This resolution has the salutary impact of freeing lawyers representing remaining defendants to use information they gained from the witness while he or she was still a defendant in their cross-examination and continuing the privilege's protection for the communications the witness had exclusively with his or her own lawyer.[23]

§ 18.04　Psychotherapist-Patient Privilege—Standard 504

[1]—Text and Status of Standard

Supreme Court Standard 504 is not part of the Federal Rules of Evidence. Congress struck the Standard from the Rules prior to their passage. However, since

---

[21] *See, e.g.,* Murdoch v. Castro, 365 F.3d 699, 702–705 (9th Cir. 2004).

[22] *See, e.g.,* Mills v. Singletary, 161 F.3d 1273, 1288–1289(11th Cir. 1998) (defendant effectively cross-examined witness without attorney-client privileged materials because they were cumulative of other inconsistent statements); United States v. Rainone, 32 F.3d 1203, 1206–1207 (7th Cir. 1994) (when defendant "spent three days cross-examining [the witness] and brought out among other things that he had committed perjury on a number of occasions, had bribed politicians and police officers, had engaged in extortion and loan sharking, and had committed six murders," notes he wrote to his counsel were not necessary for effective cross-examination).

[23] *See, e.g.,* United States v. Almeida, 341 F.3d 1318, 1323–1326 (11th Cir. 2003).

the Supreme Court has officially recognized the psychotherapist-patient privilege[1] and has cited favorably to the Standard as initially proposed, the contents of the Standard have considerable force. Standard 504 provides as follows:

Supreme Court Standard 504. Psychotherapist-Patient Privilege.

(a) Definitions.

(1) A "patient" is a person who consults or is examined or interviewed by a psychotherapist.

(2) A "psychotherapist" is (A) a person authorized to practice medicine in any state or nation, or reasonably believed by the patient so to be, while engaged in the diagnosis or treatment of a mental or emotional condition, including drug addiction, or (B) a person licensed or certified as a psychologist under the laws of any state or nation, while similarly engaged.

(3) A communication is "confidential" if not intended to be disclosed to third persons other than those present to further the interest of the patient in the consultation, examination, or interview, or persons reasonably necessary for the transmission of the communication, or persons who are participating in the diagnosis and treatment under the direction of the psychotherapist, including members of the patient's family.

(b) General rule of privilege.—A patient has a privilege to refuse to disclose and to prevent any other person from disclosing confidential communications, made for the purposes of diagnosis or treatment of his mental or emotional condition, including drug addiction, among himself, his psychotherapist, or persons who are participating in the diagnosis or treatment under the direction of the psychotherapist, including members of the patient's family.

(c) Who may claim the privilege.—The privilege may be claimed by the patient, by his guardian or conservator, or by the personal representative of a deceased patient. The person who was the psychotherapist may claim the privilege but only on behalf of the patient. His authority so to do is presumed in the absence of evidence to the contrary.

(d) Exceptions.

(1) Proceedings for hospitalization.—There is no privilege under this rule for communications relevant to an issue in proceedings to hospitalize the patient for mental illness, if the psychotherapist in the course of

---

[1] Jaffee v. Redmond, 518 U.S. 1, 9–10, 116 S. Ct. 1923, 1928, 135 L. Ed. 2d 337 (1996) (psychotherapist-patient privilege "promotes sufficiently important interests to outweigh the need for probative evidence"); *see* [2], *below*.

diagnosis or treatment has determined that the patient is in need of hospitalization.

(2) Examination by order of the judge.—If the judge orders an examination of the mental or emotional condition of the patient, communications made in the course thereof are not privileged under this rule with respect to the particular purpose for which the examination is ordered unless the judge orders otherwise.

(3) Condition an element of claim or defense.—There is no privilege under this rule as to communications relevant to an issue of the mental or emotional condition of the patient in any proceeding in which he relies upon the condition as an element of his claim or defense, or, after the patient's death, in any proceeding in which any party relies upon the condition as an element of his claim or defense.

As finally drafted, the definition of "psychotherapist" under Standard 504 is so broad that any medical general practitioner who practices some form of psychotherapy in treating patients will be included.[2]

Aside from the protection of this privilege, certain communications may be privileged under Standard 502, reports required and made confidential by state statute, under Standard 503, the attorney-client privilege, if the doctor is acting as a representative of the attorney, or because of other constitutional concerns.[3]

[2]—Rationale[1]

Standard 504 is in accord with the view of many modern legal writers, who urge that the reasons for not recognizing a general doctor-patient privilege do not apply to a privilege arising from the relationship of psychotherapist and client. This distinction hinges on the nature of the psychotherapeutic process. The very nature of psychotherapy is confidential personal revelations about matters which the patient is and should be normally reluctant to discuss. Frequently, a patient in analysis will make statements to a psychiatrist that he or she would not make even to close family members.[2]

---

[2] *See* [3][b], *below*, for further discussion of who is considered a "psychotherapist."

[3] *See* **Treatise** § 514.05 for further discussion of constitutional concerns.

[1] *See* **Treatise** at § 504.03.

[2] Slovenko, *Psychiatry and a Second Look at the Medical Privilege*, 6 Wayne L. Rev. 175, 184–185 (1960). *See* MacDonald v. Clinger, 84 A.D.2d 482, 446 N.Y.S.2d 801 (1982) (valid action found for disclosure by psychiatrist to plaintiff's wife of intimate facts divulged during therapy).

In 1996, the United States Supreme Court in *Jaffee v. Redmond* [3] solidified this rationale by holding that confidential communications between licensed psychotherapists and their patients, in the course of diagnosis or treatment, are protected from compelled disclosure under Rule 501. In *Jaffee*, the Supreme Court recognized that psychotherapy "serves the public interest by facilitating the appropriate treatment for individuals suffering the effects of a mental or emotional problem." In serving this interest, effective psychotherapy "depends upon an atmosphere of confidence and trust in which the patient is willing to make a frank and complete disclosure of facts, emotions, memories, and fears." In contrast, "[t]reatment by a physician for physical ailments can often proceed successfully on the basis of a physical examination, objective information supplied by the patient, and the results of diagnostic tests."[4]

Unlike the patient with physical ailments or complaints, who will likely consult a physician regardless of whether confidentiality is guaranteed, a neurotic or psychotic individual may seek help only if he or she is assured that his or her confidences will not be divulged, even in a courtroom. Even though the suppression of relevant information may result in less accurate fact finding, "the social value which effective psychiatric treatment has for the community far outweighs the potential loss of evidence."[5] The Advisory Committee's decision to include communications made during drug treatment is consistent with this theory in that addicts will not avail themselves of treatment or rehabilitation facilities if they fear consequent detection and effective prosecution.[6]

Even if the societal benefits of psychiatric treatment outweigh the loss of potential evidence, there is some question whether such evidence would even exist without the privilege. In *Jaffee,* the United States Supreme Court addressed this reasoning by stating that without the psychotherapist-patient privilege much of the desirable evidence to which litigants seek access is unlikely to come into being, i.e., confidential conversations between psychotherapists and their patients would simply not take place. Therefore, this unspoken evidence would serve no greater truth-seeking function than if spoken and privileged. This logic supported the

---

[3] Jaffee v. Redmond, 518 U.S. 1, 116 S. Ct. 1923, 1928, 135 L. Ed. 2d 337 (1996) (psychotherapist-patient privilege "promotes sufficiently important interests to outweigh the need for probative evidence").

[4] Jaffee v. Redmond, 518 U.S. 1, 116 S. Ct. 1923, 135 L. Ed. 2d 337, 345 (1996).

[5] Group for the Advancement of Psychiatry, Confidentiality and Privileged Communication in the Practice of Psychiatry 111 (Report No. 45, 1960). *See also* Jaffee v. Redmond, 518 U.S. 1, 116 S. Ct. 1923, 135 L. Ed. 2d 337, 344–346 (1996) (psychotherapist-patient privilege "promotes sufficiently important interests to outweigh the need for probative evidence," since "The mental health of our citizenry, no less than its physical health, is a public good of transcendent importance").

[6] *See* Whitford, *The Physician, the Law, and the Drug Abuser,* 119 U. Pa. L. Rev. 933 (1971).

Supreme Court's wholehearted adoption of the privilege.[7]

[3]—Definitions[1]

[a]—Patient

A patient, as defined by Standard 504(a)(1), is "a person who consults or is examined or interviewed by a psychotherapist" (see [1], above). The purpose for the consultation was removed from this definition and included in that of a psychotherapist. However, it should be noted that Standard 504 does not apply to a person who submits to an examination for the purpose of scientific research on mental or emotional problems.[2]

[b]—Psychotherapist[3]

Standard 504(a)(2) lists two ways a person can qualify as a psychotherapist. Under the first option, a psychotherapist is a person who is authorized to practice medicine and is engaged in "the diagnosis or treatment of a mental or emotional condition, including drug addiction" (see [1], above). The present definition was adopted by the Advisory Committee after a number of critics pointed out that the rule's failure to limit the privilege to those physicians specializing in psychiatry would create a general doctor-patient privilege, since virtually all illness has some psychosomatic component to which part of a doctor's advice is directed. Whether the revised definition of psychotherapist meets this objection is doubtful, since the Committee's notes indicate an intention "not to exclude the general practitioner and to avoid the making of needless refined definitions concerning what is and what is not the practice of psychiatry."[3.1] In line with the rationale of the privilege, Standard 504(a)(2) defines physician for purposes of this option to include the situation in which the patient reasonably believes the person consulted is "a person authorized to practice medicine in any state or nation" (see [1], above). This definition parallels that of the attorney.[4]

The second option defines a psychotherpist as a person who is licensed or certified as a psychologist. A patient's subjective belief regarding whether the

---

[7] Jaffee v. Redmond, 518 U.S. 1, 12, 116 S. Ct. 1923, 135 L. Ed. 2d 337, 346 (1996).

[1] Standard 504(a) defines three relevant terms: patient, psychotherapist, and confidential communication. These terms are then used in stating the general rule and defining its scope.

[2] See **Treatise** at § 504.06[4].

[3] See **Treatise** at § 504.05.

[3.1] See, e.g., Finley v. Johnson Oil Co., 199 F.R.D. 301, 303 (S.D. Ind. 2001) (communications with general practitioner at health clinic for purpose of obtaining psychotherapy are protected by psychotherapist-patient privilege).

[4] See § 18.03[2][b].

psychologist is licensed or certified is irrelevant.[4.1] Psychologists are included within Standard 504 to the extent that they are engaged in psychodiagnosis or psychotherapy (*see* [1], *above*).

Finally, the United States Supreme Court has expanded the psychiatric-patient privilege to include not only all communications between licensed psychotherapists and their patients, during diagnosis or treatment, but also confidential communications made to licensed social workers in the course of psychotherapy.[5] In doing so, the Supreme Court in *Jaffee* concluded that drawing a distinction between the counseling provided by costly psychotherapists and the counseling by more accessible social workers served no discernable purpose. The Court found that the same rationale and public goals applied to psychologists, psychiatrists and social workers, and that to exclude social workers from the privilege would exclude the poor and those of modest means who could not afford the assistance of a psychiatrist or psychologist.[6]

Since then, the privilege has been held to apply to confidential communications made to an unlicensed social worker[6.1] and to an Employee Assistance Program counselor.[6.2]

[c]—Confidential Communication[7]

Standard 504(a)(3) basically defines "confidential" in the same terms that Standard 503 employs in the attorney-client situation, with a few changes appropriate to the situation. As in the case of the attorney-client privilege (*see* § 18.03[2][d]),

---

[4.1] Sup. Ct. Standard 504(a)(2); *but see* United States v. Hayes, 227 F.3d 578, 586–587 (6th Cir. 2000) (claimant should not be penalized by being deprived of privilege simply because counselor may not have been "licensed social worker," since there was no evidence that client was aware of any deficiencies in counselor's qualifications).

[5] Jaffee v. Redmond, 518 U.S. 1, 15, 116 S. Ct. 1923, 135 L. Ed. 2d 337, 348 (1996); *cf.* United States v. Schwensow, 151 F.3d 650, 656–657 (7th Cir. 1998) (psychotherapist-patient privilege did not apply to communications defendant made to Alcoholics Anonymous volunteer telephone operators while seeking the address of a detoxification center; volunteers were not trained or licensed as counselors, and were not acting as counselors, and defendant was not speaking to them for purposes of diagnosis or treatment).

[6] Jaffee v. Redmond, 518 U.S. 1, 15–17, 116 S. Ct. 1923, 135 L. Ed. 2d 337, 348–349 (1996).

[6.1] *See* United States v. Hayes, 227 F.3d 578, 587 (6th Cir. 2000) (social worker's lack of license during period of psychotherapy did not prevent attachment of privilege, since patient was unaware of this flaw; it would be "grossly unfair" to penalize patient for therapist's decision to treat patient without license).

[6.2] *See* Oleszko v. State Comp. Ins. Fund, 243 F.3d 1154, 1158 (9th Cir. 2001) (privilege extends to communications with E.A.P. counselors, who are unlicenced, because they control employees' access to mental health treatment).

[7] *See* **Treatise** at §§ 504.07–504.08.

the crucial element is intent: if a patient makes a communication expecting it to be disclosed, the privilege ceases.[8]

The fact that third parties are present does not, of itself, deprive the communication of its confidential nature.[9] A third party may be present if his or her attendance furthers the interest of the patient or is necessary for the transmission of the communication. Thus, medical secretaries, nurses and hospital personnel will undoubtedly be found to fall within these categories. Communications made in the presence of those "who are participating in the diagnosis and treatment under the direction of the psychotherapist, including members of the patient's family," are also confidential. Therefore, communications to psychologists engaged in functions not covered by subdivision (a)(2)(B) and other nonpsychotherapist treatment personnel are confidential if a psychotherapist is present and authorized and is supervising their participation. This would encompass communications between multiple patients participating in group therapy in the presence of a psychotherapist.

A narrow reading of Standard 504(a)(2) as compared to Standard 503(a)(2) and (3) would suggest that there is no privilege if the communications are made in the absence of the psychotherapist. Where the Advisory Committee provided that communications to a "representatives of the lawyer" would be privileged, no such language exists for those assisting a psychotherapist.

[4]—Scope of Privilege

The general rule, adopted by the Supreme Court in *Jaffee v. Redmond*,[1] is that confidential communications between licensed psychotherapists and their patients in the course of diagnosis or treatment are protected from compelled disclosure under Rule 501 of the Federal Rules of Evidence. The *Jaffee* court also extended this privilege to confidential communications made to licensed social workers in the course of psychotherapy.

Prior to the Supreme Court's holding in *Jaffee*, some courts had implemented

---

[8] *See, e.g.,* Taylor v. United States, 222 F.2d 398, 402 (D.C. Cir. 1955) ("[A] doctor who does not treat a prisoner, but only examines him in order to testify about his condition, may testify about it . . . . Examination for testimonial purposes only has nothing to do with treatment. A doctor who makes such an examination is not 'attending a patient.' there is no confidential relation between them"); Barrett v. Vojtas, 182 F.R.D. 177, 179–181 (W.D. Pa. 1998) (privilege did not apply to conversations and notes taken during police officer's counseling session with psychiatrist and psychologist; police officials ordered counseling and were informed of results of examinations). Note that the same result would be reached if the psychotherapist witness is regarded as a representative of a lawyer.

[9] *Cf.* § 18.03[2][d].

[1] Jaffee v. Redmond, 518 U.S. 1, 15, 116 S. Ct. 1923, 135 L. Ed. 2d 337, 348 (1996); *see* [3][b], *above.*

a balancing test in applying that particular court's version of the psychiatric-patient privilege. Such tests allowed a trial judge to determine the scope of the privilege by balancing the relative importance of the patient's interest in privacy and the evidentiary need for disclosure of the information. *Jaffee* resolved the issue by holding that the promise of confidentiality must not be made contingent on a trial judge's later evaluation, and to do so would eviscerate the effectiveness of the privilege. Instead, the participants in the confidential conversation must be able to predict with some certainty whether a particular discussion will be protected. Thus, the privilege cannot be qualified by a balancing test of interests.[2]

The complete scope of the psychiatric-patient privilege is not yet known because *Jaffee* was the first Supreme Court case to recognize the privilege. Instead, the *Jaffee* court was content with leaving the more specific details to a later case-by-case determination.[3]

[5]—Identity of Patient[1]

Standard 504 and the Advisory Committee's notes are silent about whether the identity of the patient is within the scope of the privilege.[2] The same question arises in regard to the lawyer-client privilege,[3] but it is inappropriate to treat the two situations analogously. While it can perhaps be said that a client does not ordinarily wish to keep secret the fact that he has consulted a lawyer, the reverse is un-doubtedly true in the case of psychotherapy. Some psychiatrists' offices, unlike lawyers', have separate entrances and exits so that a patient can leave without being seen. Nondivulgence of a patient's identity may be essential for maintaining the psychotherapist-patient relationship which Standard 504 seeks to foster, while nondisclosure of a client's identity contributes more to the evasion of just and deserved legal consequences than to the preservation of a socially desirable re-lationship. Even when suppression of a patient's identity would result in the loss of evidence of criminal conduct, the potential destruction of the therapeutic re-lationship is of greater concern.[4] Standard 504's endorsement of this principle can

---

[2]   Jaffee v. Redmond, 518 U.S. 1, 17, 116 S. Ct. 1923, 135 L. Ed. 2d 337, 349 (1996).

[3]   Jaffee v. Redmond, 518 U.S. 1, 18, 116 S. Ct. 1923, 135 L. Ed. 2d 337, 349 (1996).

[1]   *See* **Treatise** at § 504.07[2].

[2]   *See* **Treatise** at § 504App.01.

[3]   *See* § 18.03[3][d].

[4]   People v. Newman, 32 N.Y.2d 379, 298 N.E.2d 651, 656–657, 345 N.Y.S.2d 502 (1973) (homicide; eye witness stated that she thought she had previously seen killer at methadone maintenance clinic; subpoena served on Director of Clinic requiring him to produce photographs of patients; majority of court held that subpoena should be quashed as photographs were privileged under Federal comprehensive Drug Abuse Prevention and Control Act of 1970 and regulations issued thereunder). *Cf.* United States v. Banks, 520 F.2d 627, 631 (7th Cir. 1975) (discretionary court order in drug abuse program); In re August 1993 Regular Grand Jury (Clinic Subpoena), 854 F. Supp. 1375, 1376–1377 (S.D. Ind. 1993) (privilege did not protect patients' identities).

be seen by the omission of a furtherance of crime or fraud exception such as is found in the attorney-client privilege.[5]

If a psychotherapist need not reveal the substance of a communication even when it relates to a crime the patient had been contemplating, he should not be required to reveal the identity of a patient since this would equally impair the efficacy of treatment. Standard 504 should be interpreted as authorizing the psychotherapist to withhold the identity of his patients unless they are willing to waive the protection of the privilege.

[6]—Who May Claim Privilege[1]

Standard 504(b) states the privilege in the terms previously defined, drawing upon the attorney-client privilege as a model. As in the case of the attorney-client privilege, an eavesdropper or interceptor may not testify if the patient intended the communication to be confidential and took reasonable precautions to ensure that it would be so.

The privilege is the patient's, not the psychotherapist's.[2] It may be claimed by the patient, a guardian or conservator in cases of infancy or incompetency, or by a personal representative if death has ensued.[3] The privilege may also be claimed by the psychotherapist, but only on behalf of the patient.[4]

It has been suggested that even in the absence of a statutory privilege such as Standard 504, there is a constitutional right, stemming from the right to privacy, to prevent disclosure of any statement made in the confidentiality of the psycho-therapeutic relationship. There is some support in state and federal cases for this view.

[7]—Exceptions[1]

Standard 504(d) recognizes three situations in which breach of confidence by a psychotherapist is justifiable. In those circumstances, the need for disclosure is

---

[5] *See* § 18.03[6][a].

[1] *See* **Treatise** at § 504.09.

[2] *See* In Re Grand Jury Proceedings (Violette), 183 F.3d 71, 73 (1st Cir. 1999) (doctors asserted privilege on patient's behalf, then patient intervened in proceedings to assert privilege; party asserting privilege has burden of showing it applies; citing **Treatise**).

[3] There will however be few situations where the personal representative can claim the privilege because subdivision (d)(3) provides that there is no privilege when, after the patient's death, "any party relies upon the condition as an element of his claim or defense." *See also* In re August 1993 Regular Grand Jury (Hosp. Subpoena), 854 F. Supp. 1380 (S.D. Ind. 1994) (hospital did not qualify); In re Grand Jury No. 91-1, 795 F. Supp. 1057, 1059–1060 (D. Colo. 1992) (mental health center did not qualify). *See* § 18.04 [6], *below.*

[4] Lora v. Board of Education of City of New York, 74 F.R.D. 565 (E.D.N.Y. 1977) (no privilege recognized).

[1] *See* **Treatise** at § 504.07[5]–[7].

sufficiently great to risk possible impairment of the therapist-patient relationship. These are: hospitalization or commitment proceedings, examinations ordered by a court, and instances in which mental condition has been raised as an element of a claim or defense.

The courts are divided on whether the psychotherapist-patient privilege is applicable when a plaintiff asserts a damage claim for emotional distress.[1.1] Because of the importance of the privilege in facilitating the efforts of those in need of psychotherapy to obtain it,[1.2] it should not be rendered inapplicable merely because the plaintiff suing for damages alleges emotional distress in the form of humiliation and embarrassment.[1.3]

Standard 504(d) does not include an exception for the furtherance of crime or fraud or an exception equivalent to the one in Standard 503(d)(3), which authorizes disclosure when questions arise over attorney's fees or over claims of inadequacy of representation or professional misconduct. However, the First Circuit Court of Appeals has held that the psychotherapist-patient privilege, like the attorney-client privilege, is subject to a crime-fraud exception.[1.4]

The second exception—for court-ordered examinations—is necessary for the examinations to be useful. It is arguable that such an exception need not even have been included in the rule, either because a patient examined on court order is not consulting a psychotherapist "for purposes of diagnosis or treatment"[2] or because these circumstances negate confidentiality. However, the exception is effective

---

[1.1] *Compare* Sanchez v. U.S. Airways, Inc., 202 F.R.D. 131, 134–136 (E.D. Pa. 2001) (plaintiff waived psychotherapist-patient privilege by including claim for emotional distress as part of his injuries resulting from defendant's having terminated his employment for racially discriminatory reasons) *with* Krocka v. City of Chicago, 193 F.R.D. 542, 544 (N.D. Ill. 2000) (privilege remains intact so long as plaintiff limits testimony to humiliation and embarrassment and does not assert any psychological symptoms or conditions).

[1.2] *See, e.g.,* Jaffee v. Redmond, 518 U.S. 1, 9–10, 116 S. Ct. 1923, 135 L. Ed. 2d 337 (1996) ("Psychotherapy serves the public interest by facilitating the appropriate treatment for individuals suffering the effects of a mental or emotional problem,. . .[and] effective psychotherapy depends upon an atmosphere of confidence and trust in which the patient is willing to make a frank and complete disclosure of facts, emotions, memories, and fears.").

[1.3] *See, e.g.,* Ruhlmann v. Ulster County Dep't of Social Servs., 194 F.R.D. 445, 449-451 (N.D.N.Y. 2000) (privilege not waived when plaintiff seeks only "incidental, garden-variety, emotional distress damages").

[1.4] *See* In Re Grand Jury Proceedings (Violette), 183 F.3d 71, 77–79 (1st Cir. 1999) (in psychotherapist-patient context, communications made in furtherance of crime or fraud should be excluded because mental health benefits, if any, of protecting such communications pale in comparison to "normally predominant principle of utilizing all rational means for ascertaining truth"; citing **Treatise.**).

[2] Goldstein & Katz, *Psychiatrist-Patient Privilege: The GAP Proposal and the Connecticut Statute,* 36 Conn. B.J. 175, 187 (1962).

only with respect to the particular purpose for which the examination was ordered.[3]

The last exception to the general policy of Standard 504 is based on the familiar principle of waiver. It proceeds on the assumption that it is unfair for a party to rely on a mental condition, and, at the same time, suppress evidence relevant to that condition.[4] The exception applies in both civil and criminal cases and, therefore, applies when a criminal defendant pleads insanity.[5]

The privilege does not apply to communications that are "relevant" to an issue of the patient's mental and emotional condition. The California Supreme Court, construing an identical phrase in section 1017 of the California Evidence Code, held that the patient-litigant exception "must be construed not as a complete waiver of the privilege but only as a limited waiver."[6] Only "limited inquiry" into confidences "directly relevant" to the specific mental condition in issue was allowed.[7]

In *Jaffee,* the Supreme Court declined to delineate any exceptions to the psychotherapist-patient privilege. In a footnote, however, the Court did comment that it had no "doubt that there are situations in which the privilege must give way, for example, if a serious threat of harm to the patient or others can be averted only by means of a disclosure by the therapist."[8]

The Tenth Circuit has relied on that comment to hold that a psychotherapist may testify, over the patient's objection, to threats the patient made during a psychotherapy session, when the psychotherapist disclosed the threats to the proper authorities after the patient made the threats and if "the threat was serious when it was uttered and . . . its disclosure was the only means of averting harm . . .

---

[3] *See, e.g.,* Ramer v. United States, 411 F.2d 30, 40 (9th Cir. 1969) (on trial for escape, psychiatrist could testify about defendant's sanity at the time of offense but was precluded from testifying about defendant's statements concerning the facts of the alleged escape).

[4] *See, e.g.,* Schoffstall v. Henderson, 223 F.3d 818, 822 (8th Cir. 2000) (when patient places mental condition in issue, psychotherapist-patient privilege is waived).

[5] United States v. Alvarez, 519 F.2d 1036, 1046 (3d Cir. 1975) (when defense counsel consults psychiatrist in preparation of possible insanity defense, attorney-client privilege applies and is not waived when insanity defense is asserted, § 4244 permits the psychiatrist's statements to be used at the § 4244 hearing only, and not at trial); United States *ex rel.* Edney v. Smith, 425 F. Supp. 1038, 1045–1046 (E.D.N.Y. 1976) (where defendant raised insanity defense, psychotherapist-patient privilege would not bar prosecution from calling physician who had examined defendant at defense's request; discusses Standard 504).

[6] In re Lifschutz, 2 Cal. 3d 415, 435, 467 P. 2d 557, 567, 85 Cal. Rptr. 829, 839 (1970).

[7] 2 Cal. 3d at 431. *See also* Dixon v. City of Lawton, Okl., 898 F.2d 1443, 1450–1451 (10th Cir. 1990) (if privilege applied, it would be limited); Covell v. CNG Transmission Corp., 863 F. Supp. 202, 206 (M.D. Pa. 1994) (In sexual harassment action where court ordered an in camera review of plaintiff's psychological/psychiatric records, it found that a limited privilege applied and that such records should be barred when the patient's privacy interest outweighs its evidentiary value).

[8] Jaffee v. Redmond, 518 U.S. 1, 18 n.19, 116 S. Ct. 1923, 1932 n.19, 135 L. Ed. 2d 337 (1996) (Court did not state criteria for applying exception for serious bodily harm).

when the disclosure was made."[9] The Sixth and Ninth Circuits, however, have concluded that, even though a psychotherapist has informed the proper persons of a patient's threats made during psychotherapy sessions, the patient continues to be able to assert, in a criminal prosecution, the psychotherapist-patient privilege concerning the threats, even though they have been disclosed.[10]

At least one court has held that it can review in camera psychotherapeutic records of an important prosecution witness to determine their significance to the defendant in preparing to cross-examine that witness. Failure to do so could raise serious constitutional issues concerning the defendant's right to a fair trial and to confront adverse witnesses.[11] Another court, however, has interpreted the Supreme Court's unwillingness to permit the existence of the psychotherapist-patient privilege to depend on a trial judge's assessment of the requesting party's need for the evidence as balanced against the patient's need for privacy[11.1] as disapproval of the notion that the trial court may conduct an in camera review to determine whether there is anything in a psychotherapist's records that might affect the outcome of the requesting party's case.[11.2]

§ 18.05 Husband-Wife Privileges—Standard 505

[1]—Text and Status of Standard

Supreme Court Standards are not part of the Federal Rules of Evidence. The Supreme Court originally proposed the Standards as Rules, but they were stricken by Congress prior to enactment of the Rules.

When the Advisory Committee drafted Standard 505, it proposed to eliminate the privilege for marital communications and to limit the privilege for adverse spousal testimony. However, Congress enacted Rule 501 instead of enacting any specific rules of privilege, and thus Standard 505 has limited utility.[1] The Standard provides as follows:

Supreme Court Standard 505. Husband-Wife Privilege.

(a) General rule of privilege.—An accused in a criminal proceeding has a privilege to prevent his spouse from testifying against him.

---

[9] *See, e.g.,* United States v. Glass, 133 F.3d 1356, 1360 (10th Cir. 1998).

[10] *See, e.g.,* United States v. Chase, 340 F.3d 978, 985 (9th Cir. 2003) (en banc; even if disclosure to authorities was improper, "a state-law breach of psychotherapist-patient *confidentiality* would not necessarily lead to an abrogation of the federal *testimonial privilege*"; emphasis original); United States v. Hayes, 227 F.3d 578, 581–586 (6th Cir. 2000) (there is no dangerous patient exception to psychotherapist-patient privilege).

[11] *See, e.g.,* United States v. Alperin, 128 F. Supp. 2d 1251, 1253–1255 (N.D. Cal. 2001).

[11.1] Jaffe v. Redmond, 518 U.S. 1, 17–18, 135 L. Ed. 2d 337, 116 S. Ct. 1923 (1996).

[11.2] *See, e.g.,* Newton v. Kemna, 354 F.3d 776, 785 (8th Cir. 2004).

[1] *See* **Treatise** at § 505App.01.

(b) Who may claim the privilege.—The privilege may be claimed by the accused or by the spouse on his behalf. The authority of the spouse to do so is presumed in the absence of evidence to the contrary.

(c) Exceptions.—There is no privilege under this rule (1) in proceedings in which one spouse is charged with a crime against the person or property of the other or of a child of either, or with a crime against the person or property of a third person committed in the course of committing a crime against the other, or (2) as to matters occurring prior to the marriage, or (3) in proceedings in which a spouse is charged with importing an alien for prostitution or other immoral purpose in violation of 8 U.S.C. § 1328, with transporting a female in interstate commerce for immoral purposes or other offense in violation of 18 U.S.C. §§ 2421–2424, or with violation of other similar statutes.

At the time the Advisory Committee was drafting its detailed rules on privilege, the federal courts recognized two privileges affecting the marital relationship: a testimonial privilege that prevented adverse testimony by a spouse in a criminal case, and a communications privilege that protected confidential communications between spouses. The Advisory Committee made two decisions in drafting Standard 505 to govern privileges pertaining to the marital relationship: (1) it continued the testimonial privilege in its common-law form in which the accused is the holder of the privilege, and (2) it eliminated the privilege for confidential communications entirely. When Congress rejected the proposed detailed rules of privilege in favor of the formula embodied in Rule 501,[2] the marital privileges were left to be developed on a case-by-case basis.

In *Trammel v. United States*,[3] the Supreme Court undertook a redefinition of the marital testimonial privilege, pursuant to the mandate of Rule 501 for the federal courts to develop common-law principles of privilege "in the light of reason and experience." In so doing, the Court departed substantially from the provisions of Standard 505, with respect to both spousal testimony and confidential communications. The Court strongly suggested, in dictum, that the privilege for confidential marital communications remains valid. It went on to significantly modify the privilege against spousal testimony by making the witness spouse the holder of the privilege. As a result, Standard 505 is of little assistance in outlining the principles of the marital privileges as they are currently applied in the federal courts. The discussion below considers the two marital privileges separately.

---

[2] *See* § 18.02[1] for further discussion.
[3] Trammel v. United States, 445 U.S. 40, 100 S. Ct. 906, 63 L. Ed. 2d 186 (1980).

[2]—Privilege Against Adverse Spousal Testimony[1]

[a]—Rationale

The privilege against adverse spousal testimony is the only vestige of the now defunct common-law rule that prohibited one spouse from testifying for or against the other in any type of proceeding. By the time Standard 505 was drafted, the federal courts had limited the privilege to testimony against the other spouse in criminal proceedings. The rationale for such a privilege had been explained by the Supreme Court in *Hawkins v. United States*:[2]

> The basic reason the law has refused to pit wife against husband or husband against wife in a trial where life or liberty is at stake was a belief that such a policy was necessary to foster family peace, not only for the benefit of husband, wife and children, but for the benefit of the public as well. Such a belief has never been unreasonable and is not now.[3]

In *Hawkins,* the Supreme Court had reaffirmed that the holder of the privilege is the accused, and the Advisory Committee drafted Standard 505 accordingly. When called upon in *Trammel v. United States* [4] to again rule on a claim of testimonial spousal privilege, the Supreme Court modified its decision in *Hawkins:* "the witness spouse alone has a privilege to refuse to testify adversely;[4.1] the witness may be neither compelled to testify nor foreclosed from testifying."[5] A testifying spouse may, therefore, waive the privilege without the consent of the defendant spouse. Moreover, the witness spouse's having agreed to give testimony as part of a plea agreement or in return for lenient treatment does not render the waiver involuntary.[6]

The privilege may be waived, without being specifically mentioned, through an agreement to cooperate fully with the government in an investigation of the activities of the prospective witness's spouse.[6.1] On the other hand, it is not waived merely by testifying in a proceeding involving the witness's spouse; the individual

---

[1] *See* **Treatise** at §§ 505.04–505.08.

[2] Hawkins v. United States, 358 U.S. 74, 79 S. Ct. 136, 3 L. Ed. 2d 125 (1958).

[3] 358 U.S. at 77.

[4] Trammel v. United States, 445 U.S. 40, 100 S. Ct. 906, 63 L. Ed. 2d 186 (1980).

[4.1] United States v. Yerardi, 192 F.3d 14, 18 (1st Cir. 1999) (defendant spouse who promised in plea agreement to cooperate with government investigation had no testimonial privilege to waive and no power to waive it on behalf of his spouse).

[5] 445 U.S. at 53.

[6] *See, e.g.,* United States v. Espino, 317 F.3d 788, 796 (8th Cir. 2003).

[6.1] *See, e.g.,* United States v. Bad Wound, 203 F.3d 1072, 1075 (8th Cir. 2000) (spouse witness's promise to give "complete and truthful testimony before grand juries, at trial, and at other proceedings as required" was sufficient to waive adverse spousal testimony privilege).

portions of the testimony must be analyzed to determine whether any of it was adverse to the defendant spouse's interests. If not, the earlier testimony did not effect a waiver of the privilege.[6.2]

As defined in *Trammel,* the privilege for spousal testimony bars only the actual giving of testimony.[7] However, it applies at all stages of a criminal proceeding, and must, therefore, be given effect in a grand jury investigation. When the privilege applies, it excludes all testimony, not just confidential communications.[8]

In accordance with previous law and Rule 501, the courts have applied the privilege only to a spouse's testimony[9] —there is no privilege if the marriage is sham,[10] or has been terminated by divorce, annulment, or death.[11] A number of courts have also refused to allow the assertion of the privilege despite the existence of a legal marriage when all the facts and circumstances demonstrate that in fact the marriage is moribund at the time of the testimony.[12]

A number of unsettled questions remain in the wake of the *Trammel* decision. Four of them are discussed below.

[6.2] *See, e.g.,* United States v. Yerardi, 192 F.3d 14, 18 (1st Cir. 1999).

[7] 445 U.S. at n.7; *see* United States v. Ramos-Oseguera, 120 F.3d 1028, 1042 (9th Cir. 1997) (testimonial privilege lies with the testifying spouse); United States v. Chapman, 866 F.2d 1326, 1332 (11th Cir. 1989) (hearsay statements by spouse claiming privilege are not barred by spousal privilege); In re Grand Jury 85-1 (Shelleda), 848 F.2d 200 (10th Cir. 1988) (spouse could be compelled to provide handwriting and fingerprint exemplars).

[8] *See, e.g.,* United States v. Yerardi, 192 F.3d 14, 19 (1st Cir. 1999) (privilege against providing testimony adverse to one's spouse applied in criminal forfeiture proceeding; witness did waive privilege by previously answering general questions regarding her husband's assets); United States v. Hall, 989 F.2d 711, 715-717 (4th Cir. 1993) (statement made by wife to prosecutor was privileged); United States v. Morris, 988 F.2d 1335, 1337-1340 (4th Cir. 1993) (error to elicit from wife during trial that she had invoked the privilege before the grand jury).

[9] *See, e.g.,* In re Grand Jury Proceedings Witness Ms. X, 562 F. Supp. 486, 488 (N.D. Cal. 1983) (no privilege for woman in non-formalized marriage relationship); United States v. Mathis, 559 F.2d 294, 298 (5th Cir. 1977) (no privilege where defendant had coerced wife into remarriage).

[10] In re Grand Jury Proceedings (Emo), 777 F.2d 508, 509 (9th Cir. 1985) (marriage not sham where partners had lived together for two years and entered into marriage shortly after service of grand jury subpoena; "mere suspicious timing of a marriage does not support a finding of a sham marriage, especially when other evidence, such as living together or intentions of living together as husband and wife, indicates that the marriage was entered into in good faith").

[11] *See, e.g.,* United States v. Singleton, 260 F.3d 1295, 1299–1300 (11th Cir. 2001) (spousal privilege could not be invoked when married couple was permanently separated and marriage was, for all intents and purposes, over); United States v. Porter, 986 F.2d 1014, 1019 (6th Cir. 1993) (marriage terminated); United States v. Pensinger, 549 F.2d 1150, 1151–1152 (8th Cir. 1977) (divorce).

[12] *See, e.g.,* United States v. Brown, 605 F.2d 389, 396 (8th Cir. 1979) (lengthy separation); United States v. Cameron, 556 F.2d 752, 755–756 (5th Cir. 1977) (no common residence; husband was living with another person who had borne his child).

[b]—Is There a Joint Participation Exception?

At this point the circuits are split on whether the privilege is abrogated when the spouses are partners in crime.[13]

Courts that apply a joint participation exception refuse to uphold a claim of privilege in a case like *Trammel,* even when the witness spouse refuses to testify, on the theory that the marital relationship is not entitled to protection when it is being used to foster acts contrary to the public interest.[13.1] The circuits that reject the joint participation exception find that "it is not entirely beyond doubt that such marriages are not deserving of protection . . . [T]he marriage may well serve as a restraining influence on couples against further antisocial acts and may tend to help future integration of the spouses back into society."[14] Furthermore, abrogating the privilege when the partners are engaged in crime may give prosecutors an unwarranted incentive to accuse the spouse of conspiracy in order to obtain the testimony of one who does not wish to testify.[15]

[c]—Are There Other Exceptions?[16]

Standard 505 set forth three exceptions that should be looked to as indicative of "reason and experience" in analyzing a claim based on the adverse marital testimony privilege. After *Trammel,* these exceptions are only necessary when the witness spouse refuses to testify. The first exception allows a spouse to testify when the other is charged with a crime against the person or property of the other,[17] or the child of either,[18] or when the spouse is charged with a crime against the person or property of a third person, committed in the course of committing a crime against the other spouse.

---

[13] *See, e.g., Second Circuit:* In re Koecher, 755 F.2d 1022, 1025 (2d Cir. 1985) (no exception); *Third Circuit:* In re Malfitano, 633 F.2d 276, 280 (3d Cir. 1980) (no exception); *Fifth Circuit:* United States v. Harrelson, 754 F.2d 1153, 1167–1168 (5th Cir. 1985) (exception applies); *Seventh Circuit:* United States v. Westmoreland, 312 F.3d 302, 307 (7th Cir. 2002) (exception applies); *Ninth Circuit:* United States v. Ramos-Oseguera, 120 F.3d 1028, 1042 (9th Cir. 1997) (no exception); *Tenth Circuit:* United States v. Trammel, 583 F.2d 1166, 1169 (10th Cir. 1978), *aff'd on other grounds,* 445 U.S. 40 (1980).

[13.1] *See, e.g.,* United States v. Westmoreland, 312 F.3d 302, 307 (7th Cir. 2002) ("We do not value criminal collusion between spouses, so any confidential statements concerning a joint criminal enterprise are not protected by the privilege").

[14] In re Malfitano, 633 F.2d 276, 278–279 (3d Cir. 1980).

[15] United States v. Trammel, 583 F.2d 1166, 1173 (10th Cir. 1978) (McKay, J., dissenting), *aff'd on other grounds,* 445 U.S. 40 (1980).

[16] *See* **Treatise** at §§ 505.05, 505.07.

[17] *See, e.g.,* United States v. Smith, 533 F.2d 1077 (8th Cir. 1976) (wife could testify that husband had planted heroin on her against her will).

[18] *See, e.g.,* United States v. White, 974 F.2d 1135 (9th Cir. 1992) (manslaughter of wife's daughter); United States v. Allery, 526 F.2d 1362 (8th Cir. 1975) (rape of daughter).

The second exception eliminates the privilege as to matters occurring prior to the marriage. The Advisory Committee determined that the policies that underlie the husband-wife privilege are outweighed by the desire to avoid encouraging marriage in order to suppress relevant testimony. This exception has had the most continuing significance after *Trammel*. Courts that apply the exception consequently compel testimony regardless of the reason for the marriage;[19] others uphold the privilege unless the marriage is shown to be sham.[20]

The final exception in Standard 505 abrogates the privilege when the defendant spouse has been charged with violating the Mann Act or similar statutes.[21] The exception is grounded in the common-law view that sexual offenses with a third person are a crime against the spouse.

Independently of Standard 505, the courts have recognized that the privilege against adverse spousal testimony persists despite earlier testimony by the witness claiming privilege when the government agrees not to use her prior testimony directly against the witness's spouse.[21.1]

[d]—Application of Privilege in Multi-Party Situations

In a number of post-*Trammel* cases, the witness whose testimony is sought has had information relevant to the criminal activities of third parties as well as the witness' spouse. At the trial stage, a severance of the spouse's case from that of the other defendants solves the problem of how to honor the witness' privilege not to testify against the spouse without losing the testimony against the third parties. When the matter is pending before a grand jury, however, judges have disagreed on how to handle the situation.[22]

---

[19] *See, e.g.*, United States v. Clark, 712 F.2d 299 (7th Cir. 1983) (no requirement that evidence of collusion be presented).

[20] In re Grand Jury Proceedings (Emo), 777 F.2d 508 (9th Cir. 1985) (court reversed finding of civil contempt against wife who refused to testify before grand jury; subpoena served before parties married); A.B. v. United States, 24 F. Supp. 2d 488, 491–492 (D. Md. 1998) (once court determines that valid marriage exists, privilege applies to all matters, whether they occurred before or after the marriage).

[21] *See* United States v. Ahern, 612 F.2d 507 (10th Cir. 1980) (Mann Act).

[21.1] *See, e.g.*, United States v. Yerardi, 192 F.3d 14, 20–21 (1st Cir. 1999) (threat of future prosecution of spouse, in light of government's reservation of right of indirect use of evidence, was not speculative, so privilege applied).

[22] *See, e.g.*, In re Malfitano, 633 F.2d 276 (3d Cir. 1980) (majority and concurring judges disagreed on power of court to confer use-fruits immunity); In re Grand Jury Matter, 673 F.2d 688 (3d Cir. 1982) (disagreement about court's power to grant immunity; court held that witness could not be compelled to testify in grand jury proceedings about the criminal activities of third persons when the government acknowledges that such persons will be asked to testify against the spouse in a separate grand jury proceedings); Grand Jury Subpoena of Ford v. United States, 756 F.2d 249 (2d Cir. 1985) (court upheld contempt citation against husband who refused to testify because wife was

[e]—Privilege Does Not Bar Spouse's Hearsay Statements

Are a spouse's hearsay statements admissible when the spouse is unwilling to testify? The courts that have addressed the problem after *Trammel* have taken the view that the spouse's extra-judicial statements are not barred by the testimonial privilege, since the privilege only protects the spouse from testifying in court.[23]

[3]—Privilege for Confidential Marital Communications[1]

[a]—Distinct From Testimonial Privilege

The privilege for confidential marital communications is separate and distinct from the testimonial privilege discussed above.[1.1] It was not incorporated in Standard 505, but was recognized, albeit in dictum, by the Supreme Court in *Trammel v. United States*.[2] The *Trammel* opinion therefore suggests that this privilege has continuing validity under the "reason and experience" test of Rule 501.

Unlike the testimonial privilege, the communications privilege may be asserted by a party to bar the testimony of a spouse who is willing to testify about the communication.[3] It is intended to encourage the sharing of confidences between spouses. In a much earlier case, the Supreme Court said that the

> basis of the immunity given to communications between husband and wife is the protection of marital confidences, regarded as so essential to the preservation of the marital relationship as to outweigh the disadvantage to the administration of justice which the privilege entails.[4]

Moreover, some commentators and at least one court have suggested that the

---

target of grand jury investigation even after government had promised not to use testimony of witness directly or indirectly against wife, and to erect a "Chinese Wall" to insulate wife from effect of testimony).

[23] United States v. Chapman, 866 F.2d 1326, 1332 (11th Cir. 1989) (hearsay statements by spouse claiming privilege are not barred by spousal privilege).

[1] *See* **Treatise** at §§ 505.09–505.14.

[1.1] *See, e.g.*, United States v. Singleton, 260 F.3d 1295, 1297 (11th Cir. 2001) (federal common law recognizes two different marital privileges: marital communications privilege and testimonial privilege).

[2] Trammel v. United States, 445 U.S. 40, 51, 100 S. Ct. 906, 63 L. Ed. 2d 186 (1980) (Court stated that testimonial privilege "is not needed to protect information privately disclosed between husband and wife in the confidence of the marital relationship—once described by the Court as 'the best solace of human existence.' . . . Those confidences are privileged under the independent rule protecting confidential marital communications").

[3] *See, e.g.*, United States v. Singleton, 260 F.3d 1295, 1297 n.2 (11th Cir. 2001).

[4] Wolfle v. United States, 291 U.S. 7, 14, 54 S. Ct. 279, 78 L. Ed. 617 (1934).

communications privilege may have a constitutional underpinning stemming from the right of privacy which would preclude its complete abolition.[5]

[b]—Conditions For Assertion of Privilege

There are three basic prerequisites that must be met first in order to assert the communications privilege. First, at the time of the communication, there must have been a marriage recognized as valid by state law.[6] Although some courts refuse to recognize the testimonial privilege when a marriage is deteriorating on the grounds that marital harmony—the objective of the privilege—has already been destroyed,[7] such an approach is less justified when the communications privilege is assert because it is intended to encourage confidences that might conceivably strengthen a faltering marriage.[8]

The second prerequisite of the communications privilege is that it must be asserted regarding a communication. Although some federal courts have acknowledged in dicta that "interspousal communications are not limited to speaking and writing,"[9] the federal courts have generally stated that the privilege "applies only to utterances or expressions intended by one spouse to convey a message to the other"[10] and have not recognized, under the facts of the cases before them, observations made of a spouse's activities or appearance as communications covered by the privilege.[11] This approach is consistent with the view that privileges should be narrowly construed.[11.1] Courts disagree on whether the criminal par-

---

[5] United States v. Neal, 532 F. Supp. 942, 945–946 (D. Colo. 1982), aff'd, 743 F.2d 1441 (10th Cir. 1984).

[6] See, e.g., United States v. Knox, 124 F.3d 1360, 1365 (10th Cir. 1997) (privilege requires valid marriage at time of communication in question, so it was inapplicable in this case, in absence of showing that communication in question occurred before divorce; citing **Treatise**).

[7] See, e.g., United States v. Singleton, 260 F.3d 1295, 1299 (11th Cir. 2001) (communications between spouses after they have become permanently separated are not privileged).

[8] United States v. Byrd, 750 F.2d 585, 592 (7th Cir. 1984) (deterioration of the marriage or absence of marital peace irrelevant unless the spouses are permanently separated).

[9] United States v. Brown, 605 F.2d 389, 396 n.6 (8th Cir. 1979) (if husband's departure from residence was a communication, admission of testimony may have been harmless error).

[10] United States v. Lustig, 555 F.2d 737, 748 (9th Cir. 1977); see, e.g., United States v. Espino, 317 F.3d 788, 795 (8th Cir. 2003) (communications under privilege are "limited to utterances or expressions intended by one spouse to convey a message to another", requiring "at least a gesture that is communicative or intended by one spouse to convey a message to the other"; thus, district court properly ruled that defendant's wife could testify as to his conduct "so long as it did not involve a communicative gesture").

[11] See, e.g., United States v. Lofton, 957 F.2d 476, 477 (7th Cir. 1992) (acts observed by defendant's wife, including defendant's drug use, or her knowledge of whether the package at issue belonged to defendant, were not privileged).

[11.1] See generally United States v. Singleton, 260 F.3d 1295, 1300 (11th Cir. 2001) (need for truth in judicial proceedings weighs against construing marital communications privilege to include

ticipation exception should be applied to the initial communication in which one spouse advises the other about an intended crime.[12]

The final prerequisite of the communication privilege is that the communication be made in confidence. The federal courts apply a presumption that communications between spouses are intended to be confidential.[13] The presumption may be overcome by a showing that the communication occurred in the presence of a third party[14] or that the communicating spouse intended to convey the information, or have it conveyed, to a third party.[15] The fact that third parties may possess the same knowledge that was communicated to the witness spouse does not destroy the privilege. As long as the communication itself was private and was intended to remain so, the spouse cannot be compelled to testify as to its contents.[16] This, of course, does not prevent others from testifying about the same subject.

[c]—Exceptions

Courts have recognized that certain exceptions exist precluding the privilege even when the three prerequisites of a valid marriage, communication, and confidential intent are met. Under one exception, courts permit an eavesdropper to testify on the ground that such testimony has no effect on one spouse's trust in the other.[17] By analogy to Standard 503, however, it would probably be best to exclude eavesdropper testimony, particularly if it is of a type difficult to guard against. Even

---

communications made after spouses become permanently separated, because such construction would be broader than necessary to achieve privilege's goal of protecting functional marital relationships).

[12] *Compare* United States v. Estes, 793 F.2d 465, 467–468 (2d Cir. 1986) (exception did not apply to wife's testimony that defendant had come home with bags of money and told her that he had taken it from a Purolator truck; wife could not become joint participant until after this communication and therefore admission of testimony concerning defendant's initial disclosure of theft constituted reversible error) *with* United States v. Parker, 834 F.2d 408, 413 (4th Cir. 1987) ("the policy considerations that support the joint criminal participation exception are equally implicated where from the very outset—as in this case—the spouse is told about the intended kidnapping and murder and she agrees to assist her husband").

[13] *See, e.g.,* Pereira v. United States, 347 U.S. 1, 6, 74 S. Ct. 358, 98 L. Ed. 435 (1954); United States v. Lea, 249 F.3d 632, 641 (7th Cir. 2001) (communications between spouses are presumed to be confidential).

[14] *See, e.g.,* Wolfle v. United States, 291 U.S. 7, 54 S. Ct. 279, 78 L. Ed. 617 (1934) (no privilege for letter to wife dictated to stenographer); United States v. Marashi, 913 F.2d 724, 730 (9th Cir. 1990).

[15] *See, e.g.,* Pereira v. United States, 347 U.S. 1, 6, 74 S. Ct. 358, 98 L. Ed. 435 (1954) (intention that information be transmitted to a third person negatives presumption of confidentiality).

[16] *See, e.g.,* Hipes v. United States, 603 F.2d 786, 788 n.1 (9th Cir. 1979) (fact that other employees could testify about husband's job responsibilities did not mean that wife was required to answer questions before a grand jury about her husband's job).

[17] *See* United States v. Neal, 532 F. Supp. 942, 947 (D. Colo. 1982), *aff'd*, 743 F.2d 1441 (10th Cir. 1984).

courts that apply an eavesdropper exception might bar testimony when the eaves-dropper learns "of a marital confidence through a spouse's betrayal or conniv-ance."[18] In such a case, when one spouse actively assists the eavesdropper in obtaining the information in order to use it against the other spouse, the privilege should apply because the consequence of permitting the testimony is the very undermining of marital trust that the rule of privilege seeks to prevent.

Most circuits have held that, pursuant to Rule 501, the government may compel testimony about confidential communications involving future or ongoing crimes in which the spouses were joint participants at the time of the communications.[19] These courts reason that the benefits to be served by recognizing the privilege are outweighed by the public interest in ascertaining the truth and achieving justice in such circumstances. In this regard, the Third Circuit has drawn a distinction between the two marital privileges. It has refused to apply a joint participation exception to the testimonial privilege, because that privilege is concerned with the impact of judicially-compelled testimony on a marriage, but it has recognized that joint participation destroys the confidential communications privilege, because commuications about ongoing or future crimes do not deserve protection.[20] The exception should be narrowly applied "to permit admission of only those con-versations that pertain to patently illegal activities."[21]

As previously discussed, the federal courts have recognized exceptions to the testimonial privilege when the testimony concerns injuries by one spouse to the other or to their children. Policy reasons would dictate the recognition of the same exceptions for the marital communications privilege.[22]

---

[18] *Id.* at 949.

[19] *First Circuit:* United States v. Picciandra, 788 F.2d 39, 43–44 (1st Cir. 1986); *Second Circuit:* United States v. Estes, 793 F.2d 465, 467 (2d Cir. 1986); *Third Circuit:* United States v. Hill, 967 F.2d 902, 911–912 (3rd Cir. 1992); United States v. Ammar, 714 F.2d 238, 258 (3d Cir. 1983); *Fourth Circuit:* United States v. Broome, 732 F.2d 363, 365 (4th Cir. 1984); *Fifth Circuit:* United States v. Mendoza, 574 F.2d 1373, 1381 (5th Cir. 1978); *Sixth Circuit:* United States v. Sims, 755 F.2d 1239, 1243–1244 (6th Cir. 1985); *Seventh Circuit:* United States v. Westmoreland, 312 F.3d 302, 307 (7th Cir. 2002) ("We do not value criminal collusion between spouses, so any confidential statements concerning a joint criminal enterprise are not protected by the privilege"); *Eighth Circuit:* United States v. Evans, 966 F.2d 398, 401–402 (8th Cir. 1992) (adopting exception); *Ninth Circuit:* United States v. Ramos-Oseguera, 120 F.3d 1028, 1042 (9th Cir. 1997) (dicta recognizing exception to marital communications privilege, in case that involved testimonial privilege). *Cf.* United States v. Short, 4 F.3d 475, 478–479 (7th Cir. 1993) (privilege applied because wife was unaware that she was participating in illegal scheme); *see also* § 18.03[5][a].

[20] *See* United States v. Ammar, 714 F.2d 238, 257–258 (3d Cir. 1983).

[21] United States v. Sims, 755 F.2d 1239, 1243 (6th Cir. 1985). *See also* In re Donald Sheldon & Co., 191 Bankr. Rep. 39, 47–48 (Bankr. S.D.N.Y. 1996) (marital privilege does not apply to "communications designed to perpetrate fraud on third parties").

[22] *See* United States v. White, 974 F.2d 1135 (9th Cir. 1992) (no privilege in case of manslaughter of wife's daughter).

[4]—Summary of Marital Privileges

There are several differences between the testimonial and the communications marital privileges in terms of applicability and prerequisites for assertion. These differences reflect the different purposes of the privileges. The testimonial privilege applies to all testimony against a spouse on any subject, including non-confidential matters. The courts are split on whether the testimonial privilege should apply to events predating the marriage. The communications privilege, on the other hand, applies only to communications between spouses made in confidence during a valid marriage. The testimonial privilege may not be asserted after the marriage has terminated, while the communications privilege, like other privileges intended to encourage confidences, survives the termination of the relationship. The testimonial privilege may only be claimed by a testifying spouse, and is recognized only in criminal proceedings, whereas the communications privilege may be asserted by either spouse in both civil and criminal proceedings. Fewer courts have been willing to recognize a joint participation exception to the testimonial privilege than to the confidential communications privilege.

§ 18.06 Secrets of State and Other Official Information—Standard 509

[1]—Text and Status of Standard

Supreme Court Standard 509 is not part of the Federal Rules of Evidence. Congress struck the Standard from the Rules prior to their passage. Standard 509 was among the most controversial of the draft rules presented to Congress because, to a superficial glance, the Rule seemed unprecedented in its acknowledgment of the government's right to keep information from a litigant. In reality, the Standard made explicit matters that in the past were often vague, and codified previous practice in the federal courts.

Standard 509 provides as follows:

Supreme Court Standard 509. **Secrets of State and Other Official Information.**

(a) Definitions.

(1) Secret of state.—A "secret of state" is a governmental secret relating to the national defense or the international relations of the United States.

(2) Official information.—"Official information" is information within the custody or control of a department or agency of the government the disclosure of which is shown to be contrary to the public interest and which consists of: (A) intragovernmental opinions or recommendations submitted for consideration in the performance of decisional or policymaking func-

tions, or (B) subject to the provisions of 18 U.S.C. § 3500, investigatory files compiled for law enforcement purposes and not otherwise available, or (C) information within the custody or control of a governmental department or agency whether initiated within the department or agency or acquired by it in its exercise of its official responsibilities and not otherwise available to the public pursuant to 5 U.S.C. § 552.

(b) General rule of privilege.—The government has a privilege to refuse to give evidence and to prevent any person from giving evidence upon a showing of reasonable likelihood of danger that the evidence will disclose a secret of state or official information as defined in this rule.

(c) Procedures.—The privilege for secrets of state may be claimed only by the chief officer of the government agency or department administering the subject matter which the secret information sought concerns, but the privilege for official information may be asserted by any attorney representing the government. The required showing may be made in whole or in part in the form of a written statement. The judge may hear the matter in chambers, but all counsel are entitled to inspect the claim and showing and to be heard thereon, except that, in the case of secrets of state, the judge upon motion of the government, may permit the government to make the required showing in the above form *in camera.* If the judge sustains the privilege upon a showing *in camera,* the entire text of the government's statements shall be sealed and preserved in the court's records in the event of appeal. In the case of privilege claimed for official information the court may require examination *in camera* of the information itself. The judge may take any protective measure which the interests of the government and the furtherance of justice may require.

(d) Notice to government.—If the circumstances of the case indicate a substantial possibility that a claim of privilege would be appropriate but has not been made because of oversight or lack of knowledge, the judge shall give or cause notice to be given to the officer entitled to claim the privilege and shall stay further proceedings a reasonable time to afford opportunity to assert a claim of privilege.

(e) Effect of sustaining claim.—If a claim of privilege is sustained in a proceeding to which the government is a party and it appears that another party is thereby deprived of material evidence, the judge shall make any further orders which the interests of justice require, including striking the testimony of a witness, declaring a mistrial, finding against the government upon an issue as to which the evidence is relevant, or dismissing the action.

Standard 509 deals with two related, but separate, privileges: an absolute privilege for diplomatic or military secrets, and a qualified privilege for official information. Although these privileges rest on constitutional grounds,[1] the courts have frequently used an evidentiary analysis and side-stepped the constitutional issues. Standard 509 substantially codified previous practice in the federal courts and, therefore, it remains a useful guide for assessing privilege claims.[2]

[2]—Privilege for State Secrets[1]

Standard 509 defines a "secret of state" as a "governmental secret relating to the national defense or the international relations of the United States" (*see* [1], *above*). This rule codifies the long recognized testimonial privilege against revealing military secrets.[2] While the privilege generally covers secrets relating to international relations or diplomatic secrecy, it is unlikely that litigation involving purely diplomatic secrets will arise. Cases in which the privilege claim is raised will undoubtedly involve issues of national defense as well.

The rationale for the privilege is obvious: the danger of harm to the nation outweighs any public or private interest in truthful and efficient fact-finding in an individual litigation. The privilege applies once the government makes "a showing of reasonable likelihood that the evidence will disclose a secret of state."

Standard 509 spells out some of the procedures for making the privilege claim. Consistently with the Supreme Court's decision in *United States v. Reynolds*,[3] it

---

[1] *See* United States v. Nixon, 418 U.S. 683, 94 S. Ct. 3090, 41 L. Ed. 2d 1039 (1974).

[2] Congressional and public reaction to proposed Rule 509 was extremely negative because the rule reached Congress just as the Watergate affair was unfolding and it was erroneously feared that the rule expanded executive prerogatives. *See* discussion in **Treatise** about congressional action on Standard 509 at § 509App.01[5].

[1] *See* **Treatise** at §§ 509.10–509.13.

[2] *See, e.g.,* United States v. Reynolds, 345 U.S. 1, 73 S. Ct. 528, 97 L. Ed. 727 (1953); Totten v. United States, 92 U.S. 105, 23 L. Ed. 605 (1875); Bareford v. General Dynamics Corp., 973 F.2d 1138 (5th Cir. 1992) (action dismissed because issue could not be resolved without resorting to detailed data regarding "the design, manufacture, performance, functional characteristics, and testing of [Navy frigate's defensive] systems"); Zuckerbraun v. General Dynamics Corp., 935 F.2d 544 (2d Cir. 1991). *Cf.* Guong v. United States, 860 F.2d 1063 (Fed. Cir. 1988) (complaint for breach of contract with CIA dismissed since claimant could not prevail without revealing state secrets).

[3] United States v. Reynolds, 345 U.S. 1, 7–8, 73 S. Ct. 528, 97 L. Ed. 727 (1953) ("[T]he privilege belongs to the Government and must be asserted by it; it can neither be claimed nor waived by a private party. It is not to be lightly invoked. There must be a formal claim of privilege, lodged by the head of the department which has control over the matter, after actual personal consideration by that officer"). *Cf.* Bareford v. General Dynamics Corp., 973 F.2d 1138 (5th Cir. 1992) (the court rejected plaintiffs' claim that the government had not validly asserted the privilege in this case because the Secretary of the Navy did not personally review plaintiffs' documents as required by *Reynolds;* the government did not target plaintiffs' documents, but rather objected to the claim itself, which by necessity would rely upon highly sensitive information; since the Secretary stated in his affidavit that he personally had considered the type of evidence necessary to prove this claim, his

requires the claim to be asserted by the chief officer of the agency or department in charge of the matter to which the secret information relates.

A valid claim of the privilege, however, may be based on the appropriate government official's review of the claim or defense, rather than a review of a specific request for information. The claim of privilege can then be lodged against the entirety of the claim or defense, if the appropriate official's review demonstrates that the claim or defense cannot be proved without revealing state secrets.[3.1] It remains, however, the trial court's province to make the ultimate determination concerning the applicability of the privilege.[3.2]

The suggestion in Standard 509(c) that the required showing may be in writing, in whole or in part, conforms with the Supreme Court's approval of a "formal claim." It is hoped that in the course of committing its showing to paper, the executive will have to give careful consideration to the reasons underlying the claim. Standard 509(c) specifically provides that the judge, on motion by the government, may permit the showing to be made *in camera* (*see* [1], *above*).

Standard 509 is silent, however, about whether the judge can require the government to produce *in camera* the materials as to which the privilege claim is asserted, or whether the judge must honor the executive's claim of privilege once the government has shown that the information sought would contain state secrets. This silence is attributable to the fact that no set practice had been established at the time Standard 509 was drafted. The Supreme Court had equivocated on the power of a court to examine the materials sought to be protected, probably because of an unexpressed apprehension that it is unseemly for the judiciary to be privy to matters which are explicitly made the concern of the executive by the Constitution.[4] In its decision in *United States v. Nixon*,[5] however, which was handed down after Congress had deleted the subject matter of Standard 509 from inclusion in the Federal Rules of Evidence, the Court, in dictum, contemplated the possibility of

---

review was sufficient to validly assert the privilege).

[3.1] *See, e.g.*, Tenenbaum v. Simonini, 372 F.3d 776, 777–778 (6th Cir. 2004) (defendant is entitled to summary judgment dismissing plaintiff's entire claim if court is satisfied that state secrets privilege is applicable to materials that would provide defendant with defense).

[3.2] *See, e.g.*, Doe v. Tenet, 329 F.3d 1135, 1151–1154 (9th Cir. 2003) (trial court makes final determination concerning applicability of state secrets privilege and cannot rely exclusively on representation of head of responsible agency; dismissal of claim or defense on grounds of state secret privilege should be last resort; trial court may review documents in camera and implement other security measures).

[4] *See* United States v. Reynolds, 345 U.S. 1, 73 S. Ct. 528, 97 L. Ed. 727 (1953).

[5] United States v. Nixon, 418 U.S. 683, 94 S. Ct. 3090, 41 L. Ed. 2d 1039 (1974). *See* **Treatise** at §§ 509.30–509.32 for discussion of case.

in camera review even when state secrets are involved.[6]

Since *Nixon,* the federal courts have reviewed materials *in camera* to determine whether claims of state privilege should be upheld.[7] Pursuant to the *Reynolds* case, a court should honor a privilege claim without further probing when the party seeking the alleged privileged information is unable to make a showing of necessity.[8] When a strong showing of necessity is made, the court may admit the evidence and refuse to examine the materials *in camera* unless the government meets its burden of showing that the national security is endangered.[9] The Classified Information Procedures Act sets forth the procedures that a trial court must follow in ruling on questions of the admissibility of classified information in criminal cases.[10]

The consequences of a successful claim of state privilege are discussed below.

[3]—Privilege for Official Information[1]

[a]—Scope of Privilege

Standard 509(a)(2) accords a qualified privilege to nine categories of information defined as "official information" (*see* [1], *above*). Unfortunately, Standard 509 is of only limited use as a guide in determining what types of governmental information fall within this qualified privilege. That is because its drafters chose to define "official information" by reference to the Freedom of Information Act

---

[6] The last footnote of the opinion speaks of district judges examining material *in camera* in order to consider "the validity of particular excisions, whether the basis of excision is relevancy or admissibility under such cases as *United States v. Reynolds.*" 418 U.S. at 715, n.21. *Reynolds* is clearly a state secrets case, but the Court's comments in *Nixon* are dicta since the Court notes at three separate points that no claim of state or military secrets was made. 418 U.S. at 710–711.

[7] *See, e.g., Ellsberg v. Mitchell,* 709 F.2d 51 (D.C. Cir. 1983); *Jabara v. Webster,* 691 F.2d 272, 274 (6th Cir. 1982); *National Lawyers Guild v. Attorney General,* 96 F.R.D. 390, 399–401 (S.D.N.Y. 1982).

[8] In *United States v. Reynolds,* 345 U.S. 1, 73 S. Ct. 528, 97 L. Ed. 727 (1953), widows of civilians killed in the crash of a military aircraft testing secret electronic equipment sued under the Federal Torts Claims Act. The Court stated, "[i]n each case, the showing of necessity which is made will determine how far the court should probe in satisfying itself that the occasion for invoking the privilege is appropriate." The Court found "a dubious showing of necessity" because "[t]here is nothing to suggest that the electronic equipment, in this case, had any causal connection with the accident." 345 U.S. at 11.

[9] *See Ellsberg v. Mitchell,* 709 F.2d 51 (D.C. Cir. 1983).

[10] *See* **Treatise** at § 509.71 for provisions of the Act. The Act defines "classified information" as "information or material that has been determined by the United States Government pursuant to an Executive order, statute, or regulation, to require protection against unauthorized disclosure for reasons of national security and any restricted data, as defined in paragraph r. of section 11 of the Atomic Energy Act of 1954 (42 U.S.C. § 2014(y)) (18 U.S.C. App. § 1).

[1] *See* **Treatise** at §§ 509.20–509.24.

(FOIA).[2] The FOIA enables members of the public to obtain government information without making any showing of particularized need. The FOIA has, however, a number of exceptions that, at the time Standard 509 was drafted, were couched in terms of an evidentiary privilege. The convoluted draftsmanship of Standard 509 meant that the scope of the privilege had to be determined by reference to the FOIA, then the scope of FOIA's disclosure had to be measured by judicial opinions predating Standard 509 — the rule that was meant to construe the common law privilege for governmental information.

Aside from the problems caused by how Standard 509 was drafted, some Supreme Court decisions have strongly suggested that the legal authorization for barring disclosure of information in a litigated context must originate in a source other than the FOIA, because that Act is exclusively a disclosure statute.[3] Consequently, it is not helpful for Standard 509 to define disclosure in terms of the categories listed in the FOIA. This is especially so since Exemptions 3 and 7 have been amended to make them function independently of standards of disclosure applicable to litigants. Nevertheless, counsel should be aware that the governmental evidentiary privilege is so intertwined with the FOIA that requests for information brought under the FOIA may be resolved by case law construing the privilege, and litigants may rely on FOIA cases when they dispute the applicability of an evidentiary governmental privilege.[4]

For litigants who face a claim of governmental privilege, review of Standard 509 may offer some help. It has two main categories that give rise to governmental privilege claims—intragovernmental communications and investigatory files. The third category, other FOIA exemptions incorporated into the Standard, operates as a useful checklist when considering other possible governmental privilege claims. The Standard indicates the qualified nature of the privilege. The privilege applies only if the government can make a showing that disclosure would be "contrary to the public interest." A court is authorized to admit official information if in the particular case the public's interest in the correct determination of the truth outweighs the public's interest in effective governmental operations (*see* [1], *above*).

This balancing approach of Standard 509 is fully compatible with the Supreme Court's decision in *United States v. Nixon*.[5]

---

[2] 5 U.S.C. § 552.

[3] *See, e.g.,* Chrysler Corp. v. Brown, 441 U.S. 281, 99 S. Ct. 1705, 60 L. Ed. 2d 208 (1979) (Court relied on Trade Secrets Act rather than FOIA to prohibit disclosure of information).

[4] *See, e.g.,* Department of State v. Ray, 502 U.S. 164, 172–173, 112 S. Ct. 541, 116 L. Ed. 2d 526 (1991) (discusses Exemption 6); United States v. Weber Aircraft Corp., 465 U.S. 792, 104 S. Ct. 1488, 79 L. Ed. 2d 814 (1984) (Exemption 5 of FOIA incorporates civil discovery privilege). *See* **Treatise** at § 509.62 for further discussion of FOIA exemptions.

[5] United States v. Nixon, 418 U.S. 683, 713, 94 S. Ct. 3090, 41 L. Ed. 2d 1039 (1974) (Supreme Court recognized that a privilege for presidential communications is constitutionally grounded but

[b]—Procedures for Claiming Privilege

Some of the procedures specified in Standard 509 for asserting the privilege must be viewed with caution. For example, according to the Standard, the privilege may be asserted by any attorney representing the government (*see* [1], *above*). However, some courts have required that the claim of privilege be invoked by the head of the agency after personal consideration of the matter.[6] The head of the agency may delegate this responsibility to a subordinate, but only after issuing guidelines on the use of the privilege.[7]

Standard 509(d) gives the trial court the responsibility of notifying the government if there is "a substantial possibility that a claim of privilege would be appropriate but has not been made because of oversight or lack of knowledge." The court must then stay further proceedings for a reasonable time so that the claim can be made (*see* [1], *above*).

The trial court must ascertain whether the public interest in non-disclosure is paramount before ruling on the applicability of the privilege. Therefore, it necessarily has a good deal of discretion in how it requires the parties to develop the specific relevant factors which must be balanced in the particular case. The government may make its showing in whole or in part in a written statement, which all parties may inspect together with the statement of claim. The claim must describe with some specificity the information alleged to be privileged and state the reasons for preserving its confidentiality.[8] If the court finds that this provides insufficient information on which to rule, it may order the parties to produce additional information at a hearing under Standard 509(c) (*see* [1], *above*).

The hearing should be held in chambers so that in a jury case the jurors are not apprised of the claim, and to insure that sensitive government information is not made public. The court may additionally decide that it cannot determine the privilege claim without first examining *in camera* the materials as to which the claim was asserted.[9] The court must consider the particular facts of the case in

---

not absolute, and that it must yield upon a showing of "demonstrated, specific need for evidence in a pending criminal trial"). *See* **Treatise** at §§ 509.30–509.32 for discussion.

[6] *See, e.g.,* United States v. O'Neill, 619 F.2d 222 (3d Cir. 1980) (procedures should be the same as for state secret privilege).

[7] Exxon Corp. v. Dept of Energy, 91 F.R.D. 26, 43 (N.D. Tex. 1981); Mobil Oil Corp. v. Department of Energy, 520 F. Supp. 414, 416 (N.D.N.Y. 1981).

[8] *See, e.g.,* In re "Agent Orange" Product Liability Litigation, 97 F.R.D. 427 (E.D.N.Y. 1983).

[9] *See, e.g.,* Black v. Sheraton Corp. of America, 564 F.2d 531 (D.C. Cir. 1977) (court should have ordered in camera hearing where showing did not indicate which items were privileged but did justify in camera analysis); In re Franklin National Bank Securities Litigation, 478 F. Supp. 577 (E.D.N.Y. 1979) (handling of claim usually requires in camera inspection). *See also* Carl Zeiss Stiftung v. V.E.B. Carl Zeiss, Jena, 40 F.R.D. 318 (D.D.C. 1966), *aff'd on opinion below,* 384 F.2d 979 (D.C. Cir. 1967).

deciding whether the government has made an adequate showing that it is entitled
to the privilege. The court must also examine such factors as the relevancy of the
evidence,[10] the availability of other evidence,[11] the status of the litigant, and the
nature of the case.[12] The court must determine to what extent disclosure of the
information sought would undermine the policies protected by the privilege.[13]

After the *in camera* examination, the court may "take any protective measure
which the interests of the government and the furtherance of justice may require."[14]
It may, for instance, order the separation of internal opinions and recommendations
that figured in the government's decision making process from purely factual
findings and confine disclosure to the latter.[15] The court may alternatively order
the excision of the names of informants[16] or order that certain information only
be made available to particular persons.[17] The court should make its protective
orders "keeping in mind the issues of the case, the nature and importance of the
interests supporting the claim of privilege, and the fundamental policy of free
societies that justice is usually promoted by disclosure rather than secrecy."[18]

[c]—Intragovernmental Opinions or Recommendations

Standard 509(a)(2)(A) (*see* [1], *above*) restates the common-law privilege for
intragovernmental opinions or recommendations,[19] accorded recognition pursuant
to Rule 501,[20] because participants in governmental policy-making will not feel

---

[10] *See, e.g.,* United States v. American Telephone and Telegraph Co., 524 F. Supp. 1381,
1386–1387 (D.D.C. 1981) (reasons individual members of FCC had for decisions were irrelevant to
issue of whether defendant's compliance was reasonable).

[11] 524 F. Supp. at 1386–1387 (court balances interest in non-disclosure with defendants' need
for evidence).

[12] Need may be greater in a criminal than in a civil case. *See* United States v. Nixon, 418 U.S.
683, 94 S. Ct. 3090, 41 L. Ed. 2d 1039 (1974).

[13] *See, e.g.,* Machin v. Zuckert, 316 F.2d 336, 337–338 (D.C. Cir. 1963) (prohibiting disclosure
of investigatory reports obtained under promise of confidentiality because efficiency of important
government program might be hampered, but allowing disclosure of mechanics' factual reports
which would be unaffected by promises of confidentiality).

[14] Sup. Ct. Standard 509(c); *see* [1], *above*.

[15] *See, e.g.,* Machin v. Zuckert, 316 F.2d 336, 340–341 (D.C. Cir. 1963).

[16] *See, e.g.,* Olsen v. Camp, 328 F. Supp. 728, 732 (D. Mich. 1969).

[17] 328 F. Supp. at 732.

[18] Boeing Airplane Co. v. Coggeshall, 280 F.2d 654, 662 (D.C. Cir. 1960).

[19] Environment Protection Agency v. Mink, 410 U.S. 73, 86, 93 S. Ct. 827, 35 L. Ed. 2d 119
(1973), *superseded on other grounds by* Pub. L. 93-502, 88 Stat. 1561 (1974) ("the recognized rule
that 'confidential intra-agency advisory opinions . . . are privileged from inspection' "); United
States v. Weber Aircraft Corp., 465 U.S. 792, 104 S. Ct. 1488, 79 L. Ed. 2d 814 (1984).

[20] Whether intergovernmental communications are also qualifiedly privileged will also have to
be decided pursuant to Rule 501. Standard 509 is silent about such communications. *Cf.* Standard
510.

free to express their opinions fully and candidly when they fear that their views will be made public.[21] Purely factual material is not covered by the privilege, because its disclosure "would not hinder the flow of advice in any decision-making process."[22] Standard 509 acknowledges this fact-opinion dichotomy by limiting the category of official information to "intragovernmental opinions or recommendations." A stated conclusion, which did not go into the making of any policy decisions and resolutions, is also not immune from discovery because it is not "submitted for consideration in the performance of policy making functions."[23]

The privilege, sometimes called the "deliberative process" privilege, is applicable only to communications that relate to a public agency's decision-making process. The privilege does not apply if the agency does not make public policy, or if the intra-agency communication relates only to administrative or managerial problems, rather than to the consultative process leading up to the adoption of an agency decision or policy.[23.1]

Furthermore, a memorandum embodying the final conclusion of the agency, and cited as the basis for the agency's action, does not require protection, so long as disclosure would not reveal the processes by which the decision was reached.[24] It is the decision-making process that requires shielding from public scrutiny, not the decision itself once it has been acted upon.

The privilege is qualified. Disclosure of intragovernmental opinions or recom-

---

[21] *See, e.g.,* Newport Pac., Inc. v. County of San Diego, 200 F.R.D. 628, 636–637 (S.D. Cal. 2001).

[22] Consumers Union of United States, Inc. v. Veterans Administration, 301 F. Supp. 796, 806 (1969), *dismissed as moot after full disclosure by government,* 436 F.2d 1363 (2d Cir. 1971); *see also* Environment Protection Agency v. Mink, 410 U.S. 73, 87–88, 89 n.16, 93 S. Ct. 827, 35 L. Ed. 2d 119 (1973), *superseded on other grounds by* Pub. L. 93-502, 88 Stat. 1561 (1974) ("memoranda consisting only of compiled factual material or purely factual material contained in deliberative memoranda and severable from its context would generally be available for discovery by private parties in litigation with the Government. . . . The proposed Federal Rules of Evidence appear to recognize this construction of Exception 5").

[23] *Cf.* In re Grand Jury, 821 F.2d 946, 957–959 (3d Cir. 1987) (although the court rejected a qualified speech or debate privilege for state legislators, it suggested a narrower deliberative privilege for confidential deliberative communications involving opinions, recommendations or advice about legislative decisions).

[23.1] *See, e.g.,* Tigue v. United States DOJ, 312 F.3d 70, 76 (2d Cir. 2002) (for document to be subject to deliberative process privilege, it must be "(1) an inter-agency or intra-agency document; (2) 'predecisional'; and (3) deliberative").

[24] *See* N.L.R.B. v. Sears Roebuck & Co., 421 U.S. 132, 151–152, 95 S. Ct. 1504, 44 L. Ed. 2d 29 (1975) ("it is difficult to see how the quality of a decision will be affected by communications with respect to the decision occurring after the decision is finally reached; and therefore equally difficult to see how the quality of the decision will be affected by forced disclosure of such communications, as long as prior communications and the ingredients of the decisionmaking process are not disclosed").

mendations reflecting policy-making processes may be required in a given case when the scales tip in favor of disclosure because the public interest in accurate judicial determinations outweighs the public interest in effective governmental functioning.[25]

An effective claim of the "deliberative process" privilege is based on the following elements:[25.1]

- The "head of the department" having control over the requested information must formally assert the privilege.

- That official must assert the privilege based on his or her actual personal consideration of the information and the effect that would result from its being revealed.

- The claim must include a detailed specification of the information for which the privilege is claimed, with an explanation why it falls within the scope of the privilege.

It is not necessary, however, that the person who considers the documents and the effect their revelation might have be the person at the very pinnacle of the agency asserting the privilege. It is sufficient if the person who asserts the privilege has sufficient rank to insure that the assertion of the privilege is responsible and has personally considered the requested documents and the effect their revelation might have.[25.2]

[d]—Investigatory Files Compiled for Law Enforcement Purposes

Standard 509(a)(2)(B) recognizes that there may be a qualified privilege for investigatory reports compiled for law enforcement purposes and not otherwise available. The premature disclosure of such reports could seriously hamper effective law enforcement.[26]

An effective claim of the "law enforcement" privilege is based on the following

---

[25] *See, e.g.,* Newport Pac., Inc. v. County of San Diego, 200 F.R.D. 628, 638–641 (S.D. Cal. 2001) (in action charging county Board of Supervisors with actions in violation of Federal Fair Housing Act, public interest in free expression by policy makers during deliberative process leading up to those actions did not outweigh litigant's interest in obtaining information concerning those deliberations).

[25.1] Landry v. FDIC, 204 F.3d 1125, 1135–1136 (D.C. Cir. 2000).

[25.2] *See, e.g.,* Landry v. FDIC, 204 F.3d 1125, 1135–1136 (D.C. Cir. 2000).

[26] *See* Ferri v. Bell, 645 F.2d 1213 (3d Cir. 1981), *modified,* 671 F.2d 769 (3d Cir. 1982); Murphy v. FBI, 490 F. Supp. 1138 (D.D.C. 1980); Lamont v. Dep't of Justice, 475 F. Supp. 761 (S.D.N.Y. 1979). *Cf.* In re Department of Investigation, 856 F.2d 481, 486 (2d Cir. 1988) (material compiled in official investigation into city commissioner's fitness to continue in office was protected from disclosure, since materials were closely connected with simultaneous criminal investigation).

elements:[26.1]

- The "head of the department" having control over the requested information must formally assert the privilege.

- That official must assert the privilege based on his or her actual personal consideration of the information and the effect that would result from its being revealed.

- The claim must include a detailed specification of the information for which the privilege is claimed, with an explanation why it properly falls within the scope of the privilege.

It is not necessary, however, that the person who considers the documents and the effect their revelation might have be the person at the very pinnacle of the agency asserting the privilege. It is sufficient if the person who asserts the privilege has sufficient rank to insure that the assertion of the privilege is responsible and has personally considered the requested documents and the effect their revelation might have.[26.2]

The rationale for non-disclosure does not apply if there is no prospect of law enforcement proceedings in which the investigative material will be relevant,[27] or if the government's action has already been taken.[28] Some parts of the file may nevertheless remain privileged even if the investigation is closed or no enforcement proceedings are contemplated.[29] The file may, for instance, contain intragovernmental opinions or recommendations of the type barred by Standard 509(a)(2)(C) (see [c], above), or the litigant may seek information that would be barred by the informer's privilege (see § 18.07).

Even if the files relate to an investigation in which law enforcement is current or imminent, the privilege applies only when disclosure would be contrary to the public interest.[30]

[26.1] Landry v. FDIC, 204 F.3d 1125, 1135–1136 (D.C. Cir. 2000).

[26.2] See, e.g., Landry v. FDIC, 204 F.3d 1125, 1135–1136 (D.C. Cir. 2000).

[27] See, e.g., Frankenhauser v. Rizzo, 59 F.R.D. 339, 345 (E.D. Pa. 1973) (no need for privilege where over two years had elapsed since completion of the investigation, no criminal charges or interdepartmental disciplinary actions had resulted, and no party seeking discovery was a potential defendant in a criminal case).

[28] Wood v. Breier, 54 F.R.D. 7, 11–12 (D. Wis. 1972) ("once the investigation and prosecution have been completed discovery should be permitted").

[29] Black v. Sheraton Corp. of America, 564 F.2d 531, 546 (D.C. Cir. 1977) (few would respond candidly to investigators if their remarks would become public after proceeding).

[30] See, e.g., Denver Policeman's Protective Association v. Lichtenstein, 660 F.2d 432, 437–438 (10th Cir. 1981) (police investigatory file sought by defendant for purpose of discovering exculpatory evidence not absolutely privileged where governmental interest in confidentiality outweighed by defendant's need).

[e]—Other Governmental Information Exempted From Disclosure By the Freedom of Information Act[31]

Standard 509(a)(2)(C) is the catch-all provision that incorporated the remaining exemptions in the Freedom of Information Act,[32] which were not treated elsewhere, into the qualified privilege created for official information by Standard 509 (*see* [1], *above*).

[4]—Effect of Sustaining Claim of Privilege for State Secrets or Official Information[1]

There are four categories of situations in which the governmental privileges may be raised: (1) proceedings to which the government is not a party; (2) criminal proceedings instituted by the government; (3) civil proceedings instituted by the government, and (4) civil proceedings against the government.

Standard 509(e) is silent about the first category of proceedings, in which the government resists disclosure although it is not a party. The usual consequences when the privilege is applied are the same as those that ordinarily occur when there is a loss of evidence. If the plaintiff is unable to make out a prima facie case without the evidence, the case is dismissed. There may also be instances in which the danger of revealing privileged information in the course of trying to establish a prima facie case may be sufficient to cause a dismissal.[2]

In the other three categories, the drafters of Standard 509(e) recognized that the range of possibilities was too great to allow for a fixed rule, especially considering the variety of ways in which privileged information may be relevant. In a criminal case, the documents suppressed may bear so directly on a substantive element of the case that dismissal of the action is the only appropriate response if the government persists in non-disclosure.[3] On the other hand, if the material not produced is Jencks Act[4] material, the court is directed to strike the testimony of the witness and let the trial proceed unless "the interests of justice require that a mistrial be declared." Privileged materials may also bear on collateral matters such as the validity of an arrest or of a search and seizure. In all these instances, the trial court has discretion to tailor its order as justice requires.

---

[31] *See* **Treatise** at § 509.63.

[32] The exemptions in the Freedom of Information Act, 5 U.S.C.A. § 552(b) have been amended a number of times since Standard 509 was drafted.

[1] See discussion in **Treatise** at § 509.46.

[2] Farnsworth Cannon, Inc. v. Grimes, 635 F.2d 268, 282 (4th Cir. 1980) (en banc court concluded that plaintiff's attempt to make out prima facie case would so threaten revelation of state secrets that, in the overriding interest of the United States, complaint should be dismissed).

[3] *See, e.g.,* United States v. Andolschek, 142 F.2d 503 (2d Cir. 1944).

[4] 18 U.S.C. § 3500(d); *see* Chapter 10.

Civil cases by or against the government also present a wide variety of situations. At one end of the spectrum are cases in which the government is seeking to punish the defendant or regulate the defendant's activities and the claim of privilege prevents the defendant from obtaining facts essential to the defense. This type of case may have to be handled as a criminal case would be. On the other hand, if the government is suing in a proprietary capacity, there may be less unfairness in allowing the successful claim of privilege to deprive the defendant of some useful information. Exactly how unfair—and what the trial court should consequently do—will depend on the particular facts of the case, such as the purposes for which the information is sought, the consequences to the parties, and the availability of other evidence.[5]

Generally, the plaintiff will be unable to make out a case because of the subsequent lack of evidence only if the privileged information is crucial to the cause of action and involves a state secret. If the information sought is classified as official information, the plaintiff's need will often result in the court ordering disclosure, although the plaintiff may have to wait until the active phase of an investigation is over if investigatory files are sought.

§ 18.07 Identity of Informer—Standard 510

[1]—Text and Status of Standard

Supreme Court Standards are not part of the Federal Rules of Evidence. Congress struck them prior to enacting the Rules into law. However, Supreme Court Standard 510 retains considerable utility as a guide to the federal common law referred to in Rule 501.

Standard 510 provides as follows:

Supreme Court Standard 510.   Identity Of Informer.

---

[5] *See, e.g.,* Attorney General of the United States v. Irish People, Inc., 684 F.2d 928, 949–955 (D.C. Cir. 1982) (in action to compel defendant to register under Foreign Agents Registration Act defendant claimed selective prosecution and government claimed state secrets privilege as to certain documents defendant sought to support defense; district court dismissed action; appellate court reversed and remanded, holding that district court must balance the possibility of exculpation, the likelihood that privileged documents would exculpate defendant, the need for the documents, the government's interest in secrecy and in maintaining the action, what the defendant stands to lose, the availability of court orders other than dismissal or disclosure, and the parties' respective behavior; court suggested that dismissal was probably improper when likelihood of injustice to defendant was small and adverse consequences of disclosure would be great while alternatives were available such as requiring government stipulations as to some facts, or having district court look at files and marshal evidence on both sides). *See* discussion in In re United States, 872 F.2d 472 (D.C. Cir.), *cert. dismissed*, 493 U.S. 960 (1989).

(a) Rule of privilege.—The government or a state or subdivision thereof has a privilege to refuse to disclose the identity of a person who has furnished information relating to or assisting in an investigation of a possible violation of law to a law enforcement officer or member of a legislative committee or its staff conducting an investigation.

(b) Who may claim.—The privilege may be claimed by an appropriate representative of the government, regardless of whether the information was furnished to an officer of the government or of a state or subdivision thereof. The privilege may be claimed by an appropriate representative of a state or subdivision if the information was furnished to an officer thereof, except that in criminal cases the privilege shall not be allowed if the government objects.

(c) Exceptions.

(1) Voluntary disclosure; informer a witness.—No privilege exists under this rule if the identify of the informer or his interest in the subject matter of his communication has been disclosed to those who would have cause to resent the communication by a holder of the privilege or by the informer's own action, or if the informer appears as a witness for the government.

(2) Testimony on merits.—If it appears from the evidence in the case or from other showing by a party that an informer may be able to give testimony necessary to a fair determination of the issue of guilt or innocence in a criminal case or of a material issue on the merits in a civil case to which the government is a party, and the government invokes the privilege, the judge shall give the government an opportunity to show in camera facts relevant to determining whether the informer can, in fact, supply that testimony. The showing will ordinarily be in the form of affidavits, but the judge may direct that testimony be taken if he finds that the matter cannot be resolved satisfactorily upon affidavit. If the judge finds that there is a reasonable probability that the informer can give the testimony, and the government elects not to disclose his identity, the judge on motion of the defendant in a criminal case shall dismiss the charges to which the testimony would relate, and the judge may do so on his own motion. In civil cases, he may make any order that justice requires. Evidence submitted to the judge shall be sealed and preserved to be made available to the appellate court in the event of an appeal, and the contents shall not otherwise be revealed without consent of the government. All counsel and parties shall be permitted to be present at every stage of proceedings under this subdivision except a showing in camera, at which no counsel or party shall be permitted to be present.

(3) Legality of obtaining evidence.—If information from an informer is relied upon to establish the legality of the means by which evidence was obtained and the judge is not satisfied that the information was received from an informer reasonably believed to be reliable or credible, he may require the identity of the informer to be disclosed. The judge shall, on request of the government, direct that the disclosure be made in camera. All counsel and parties concerned with the issue of legality shall be permitted to be present at every stage of proceedings under this subdivision except a disclosure in camera, at which no counsel or party shall be permitted to be present. If disclosure of the identity of the informer is made in camera, the record thereof shall be sealed and preserved to be made available to the appellate court in the event of an appeal, and the contents shall not otherwise be revealed without consent of the government.

[2]—Scope of Privilege

Standard 510 provides the government with a privilege not to disclose the identity[1] of a person who has furnished a law enforcement officer or member of a legislative committee or its staff with information relevant "to an investigation of a possible violation of law."[2] The privilege is applicable in civil[3] as well as in criminal cases. It is not limited to only federal law enforcement officers,[4] but also be claimed by state law enforcement agencies and their subdivisions.[5] The privilege is subject to two qualifications set forth in Standard 510(c) (see [1], above). First, the privilege ceases once the informer's identity is disclosed "to those who would have cause to resent the communication"[6] Second, there is no privilege when the trial court determines that the informer may be able to give testimony necessary to a fair determination of the issue of guilt of innocence in a criminal case or of a material issue on the merits in a civil case to which the government is a party.

---

[1] The Advisory Committee's notes to Standard 510(a) state: "Only identity is privileged; communications are not included except to the extent that disclosure would operate also to disclose the informer's identity." Usually the informer expects the communication to be used, but there may be times when the witnesses might be unwilling to cooperate in an investigation unless the confidentiality of their communications was assured. *Cf.* Standard 509(a)(2)(B).

[2] *See* **Treatise** at § 510App.01[2] for discussion of why this formula was adopted by the Advisory Committee.

[3] *See, e.g.,* Dole v. Local 1942, Int'l Bhd. of Elec. Workers, 870 F.2d 368 (7th Cir. 1989). *See also* discussion of civil cases in **Treatise** at § 510.09.

[4] Ordinarily, government counsel will be the appropriate representative to claim the privilege, but in some situations the police officer who is being questioned may appropriately make the claim. *See, e.g.,* Bocchicchio v. Curtis Publishing Co., 203 F. Supp. 403 (E.D. Pa. 1962).

[5] This provision furthers the rationale of the privilege because it is unrealistic to assume that informers distinguish between various governmental entities when furnishing information. In a criminal case, the federal government may, if it wishes, veto a local claim of privilege.

[6] *See* **Treatise** at § 510.06.

If the government elects not to disclose the informant's identity, the trial court may dismiss the case.

[3]—Rationale[1]

Standard 510 is in accord with the views of commentators and courts—even those most reluctant to recognize any obstruction to the production of all relevant evidence—that a genuine privilege exists for the identity of persons supplying the government with information concerning possible violations of law.[2] Informers require a guarantee of anonymity.

> [I]t has been the experience of law enforcement officers that the prospective informer will usually condition his cooperation on an assurance of anonymity, fearing that if disclosure is made, physical harm or other undesirable consequences may be visited upon him or his family. By withholding the identity of the informer, the government profits in that the continued value of informants placed in strategic positions is protected, and other persons are encouraged to cooperate in the administration of justice.[3]

The government relies heavily on communications from informants in detecting criminal activity, particularly in cases involving narcotics offenses, liquor law violations and sexual crimes where an aggrieved victim rarely steps forward. Compared to the speculative benefits of, for instance, the privilege for communications between attorney and client, the importance of protecting an informer's identity can be statistically corroborated. An alarming number of government informers are murdered each year. While the consequences of disclosure may not be as drastic in all cases, the likelihood of social ostracism, employer retaliation or malicious prosecution suits is reason enough to deter a potential informant from communicating with the authorities unless his anonymity is protected.[4]

The courts have recognized that, despite the values served by the privilege, the right to withhold the informer's identity is not absolute. As Standard 510(a) acknowledges, the privilege belongs to the government and not to the informer (*see* [1], *above*). The public interest "in protecting the flow of information" must be

---

[1]   *See* **Treatise** at § 510.03.

[2]   *See, e.g.,* McCray v. Illinois, 386 U.S. 300, 309, 87 S. Ct. 1056, 18 L. Ed. 2d 62 (1967) ("privilege . . . long . . . recognized in the federal judicial system").

[3]   United States v. Tucker, 380 F.2d 206, 213 (2d Cir. 1967). *See also* McCray v. Illinois, 386 U.S. 300, 308, 87 S. Ct. 1056, 18 L. Ed. 2d 62 (1967).

[4]   In re United States, 565 F.2d 19, 22–23 (2d Cir. 1977) ("[T]he likelihood of physical reprisal is not a prerequisite to the invocation of the privilege. Often, retaliation may be expected to take more subtle forms such as economic duress, blacklisting or social ostracism").

balanced against the public interest in "a fair determination of the issues."[5] Society has an interest in fairness as well as efficiency. There is also a public interest in deterring lawless activities by law enforcement officers. Disclosure of the informant's identity may be decisive in determining whether the police are hiding their misbehavior behind the shield of privilege.

[4]—Issue of Guilt or Innocence[1]

[a]—Factors Court Considers

Standard 510(c)(2) rests squarely on the Supreme Court's decision in *Roviaro v. United States* [2] in requiring the trial judge, on motion of the accused, to dismiss the charge if the government elects not to disclose the identity of an informer whom the judge has found reasonably able to give testimony necessary to a fair determination of the issue of guilt or innocence. The Court in *Roviaro* stated:

> Whether a proper balance renders nondisclosure erroneous must depend on the particular circumstances of each case, taking into consideration the crime charged, the possible defenses, the possible significance of the informer's testimony, and other relevant factors.[3]

There is no privilege when the prosecution intends to call the informer to testify or when the contents of the informer's communications would be relevant and helpful to the defendant.[3.1] Thus, when the defendant shows that nondisclosure of the informant's identity will potentially prejudice the defense, the trial court should hold an in camera hearing to determine the privilege's applicability.[3.2]

The discussion which follows considers the factors the Court found to bear on the accused's need for the informer's testimony, and how these factors have been

---

[5] Roviaro v. United States, 353 U.S. 53, 62, 77 S. Ct. 623, 1 L. Ed. 2d 639 (1957) ("We believe that no fixed rule with respect to disclosure is justifiable. The problem is one that calls for balancing the public interest in protecting the flow of information against the individual's right to prepare his defense. Whether a proper balance renders nondisclosure erroneous must depend on the particular circumstances of each case, taking into consideration the crime charged, the possible defenses, the possible significance of the informer's testimony, and other relevant factors"); *see e.g.,* Brock v. Gingerbread House, Inc., 907 F.2d 115 (10th Cir. 1989) (district court erred in dismissing, balanced the government's qualified privilege to withhold informers' identities against defendant's weak showing to disregard privilege).

[1] *See* **Treatise** at § 510.03[3].

[2] Roviaro v. United States, 353 U.S. 53, 77 S. Ct. 623, 1 L. Ed. 2d 639 (1957).

[3] 353 U.S. at 62.

[3.1] Banks v. Dretke, 540 U.S. 668, 697–698, 124 S. Ct. 1256, 157 L. Ed. 2d 1166, (2004).

[3.2] *See, e.g.,* United States v. Lapsley, 263 F.3d 839, 842–843 (8th Cir. 2001).

evaluated in subsequent decisions.[4]

[b]—Informer a Material Witness

In *Roviaro*, the Supreme Court stressed that the informant was the accused's "one material witness . . . who had been nearest to him and took part in the transaction."[5] Subsequent courts have likewise emphasized this factor. In some cases, the courts have ordered disclosure when the informant was an active participant and eyewitness to the crime,[6] while protecting an informant's identity who did not actively participate or was not a witness.[7] The scope of Standard 510 does not include whether the government has an obligation to produce the informant. Usually, the government must show that it has made a reasonable effort.[8]

[c]—Informer's Testimony Must Be Material to Issue of Guilt

In *Roviaro*, the Supreme Court noted that defendant was not charged with mere possession of heroin; he was charged with knowingly receiving it while knowing it to be imported contrary to law. The informer, said the Court, "was the only witness who might have testified to petitioner's possible lack of knowledge of the contents of the package."[9] Courts have interpreted this language in *Roviaro* as meaning that the informant's identity need not be disclosed if his or her testimony

---

[4] *See* United States v. Fatico II, 458 F. Supp. 388 (E.D.N.Y. 1978), *aff'd*, 603 F.2d 1053 (2d Cir. 1979) (discussion of use of unidentified informers' statements at sentencing hearings).

[5] Roviaro v. United States, 353 U.S. 53, 64, 77 S. Ct. 623, 1 L. Ed. 2d 639 (1957).

[6] *See, e.g.,* United States v. Ayaka, 643 F.2d 244 (5th Cir. 1981) (identity had to be disclosed where informer was more than merely passive observer and in camera transcript indicated that her testimony might be useful to defendant who was claiming alibi and had been identified only by DEA agent). *But cf.* United States v. Blevins, 960 F.2d 1252, 1258–1260 (4th Cir. 1992) (identity did not have to be disclosed, even though informant was an active participant and witness to virtually all important events, where defendants failed to show their need for the informant's identity and had made strategic use of informant's absence at trial as part of their defense).

[7] *See, e.g.,* United States v. Johnson, 302 F.3d 139, 149 (3d Cir. 2002) (when confidential informant merely introduced undercover officer to defendant as customer for crack cocaine and was not present during commission of charged acts, informant could not provide information useful to defendant's defense, and informant's identity was protected by identity of informer's privilege).

[8] *See, e.g.,* United States v. Formanczyk, 949 F.2d 526, 539–530 (1st Cir. 1991) (The court found that once the government declared in its discovery response that the confidential informer had left the United States and was out of the reach of process, the government "placed itself under a continuing duty to keep the defendant informed of any changes coming to its attention that might have rendered the contents of its discovery response inaccurate, misleading or incorrect." The government's duty with respect to the production of the informant was separate and distinct from its duty merely to identify the informant.); Velarde-Villarreal v. United States, 354 F.2d 9, 12 (9th Cir. 1965) ("no rule that the Government is under any general obligation to produce an informant").

[9] Roviaro v. United States, 353 U.S. 53, 64, 77 S. Ct. 623, 1 L. Ed. 2d 639 (1957).

would not be relevant to overcoming any element of the crime charged.[10]

[d]—Law Enforcement Officer's Credibility Is Suspect

Although the *Roviaro* opinion did not directly address the agents' credibility, the majority did note some inconsistency on whether the informer and defendant had known each other before the events in question. Had the informer been produced, perhaps this conflict in testimony could have been resolved. The cases following *Roviaro* indicate that courts will not assume that law enforcement agents are lying unless some tangible manifestation is brought to the court's attention.[11] Mere speculation on the part of the defense is not enough.

[e]—Entrapment

In *Roviaro,* the Supreme Court noted that the informant's testimony "might have disclosed an entrapment."[12] While numerous courts have suggested, in dictum, that they might order the informant's identity disclosed if essential to a defense of entrapment, in practice, this factor rarely seems to account for disclosure.

[f]—Other Relevant Factors

The other relevant factors the Supreme Court referred to in formulating the balancing test in *Roviaro* are the same as those that underlie the rationale for the privilege: the possibility of harm to the informer,[13] the cessation of his usefulness to the government, the credibility of the informer,[14] and the possible frustration of other investigations. Since *in camera* disclosure prevents all of these consequences, there is less need for the court to be attentive to these factors when initially considering whether the informer may be able to give testimony needed for a fair determination. If the court decides to hold an *in camera* hearing and then decides that the informant can supply testimony necessary to a fair determination, the

---

[10] *See, e.g.,* United States v. Lapsley, 334 F.3d 762, 764–765 (8th Cir. 2003) (in prosecution for being felon in possession of a weapon, when informant had no knowledge concerning defendant's actual or constructive possession of gun, trial court properly held privilege applicable).

[11] *See, e.g.,* United States v. Jenkins, 4 F.3d 1338 (6th Cir. 1993) (no disclosure where court conducted *in camera* interview of informant and informant corroborated undercover detectives' testimony in every respect except one).

[12] Roviaro v. United States, 353 U.S. 53, 64, 77 S. Ct. 623, 1 L. Ed. 2d 639 (1957).

[13] *See, e.g.,* United States v. Straughter, 950 F.2d 1223, 1232 (6th Cir. 1991) (no disclosure where government "produced compelling evidence that the life of the informant would be significantly endangered").

[14] *See, e.g.,* United States v. Curtis, 965 F.2d 610 (8th Cir. 1992) (no disclosure where defendant alleged that "deal" had been cut between informant and the government); United States v. Spears, 965 F.2d 262 (7th Cir. 1992) (defendant stipulated to existence of confidential source during trial; on appeal, article about police misuse of confidential source did not rise to the level of newly discovered evidence to enable defendant to withdraw his stipulation).

arguments for protecting the informant's identity must yield to the defendant's need for the evidence. The government must choose between revealing the informant's name and thereby risking his or her safety and its investigative efficacy or forfeiting its right to prosecute.

Standard 510(c)(2) (*see* [1], *above*) requires that it appear from the evidence in the case, or from a showing by a party, that the informer may have evidence necessary to a fair determination. Courts will not allow public disclosure solely on the basis of speculation by the defendant that the informer's testimony might be of help. The defendant must explain to the court as precisely as possible what testimony he thinks the informer could give and how this testimony would be relevant to a material issue of guilt or innocence.[15]

[5]—Issue of Legality of Obtaining Evidence[1]

Standard 510(c)(3) states that a judge may require the identity of an informer to be disclosed if the information the informant provided was "relied upon to establish the legality of the means by which evidence was obtained" and the judge is not satisfied that the informant is reliable or credible (*see* [1], *above*). "The legality of the means by which evidence was obtained" occurs when the supplied information establishes the probable cause needed to issue an arrest or search warrant, or to conduct a search a defendant pursuant to a nonwarrant arrest.[2] Upon the request of the government, this disclosure must be made *in camera*.

The restriction to *in camera* disclosure eliminates the possibility of the accused confronting the informant. Therefore, the informant's identity would only be disclosed if the government did not elect an *in camera* review, which is unlikely, or in those instances where the informant's testimony is also relevant to guilt, and disclosure is ordered pursuant to Standard 510(c)(2). Standard 510 is in accord with the Supreme Court's decision in *McCray v. Illinois*,[3] which held that an accused

---

[15]   Rugendorf v. United States, 376 U.S. 528, 535, 84 S. Ct. 825, 11 L. Ed. 2d 887 (1964) ("Having failed to develop the criteria of *Roviaro* necessitating disclosure on the merits, we cannot say on this record that the name of the informant was necessary to his defense. . . . Never did petitioner's counsel indicate how the informants' testimony could help establish petitioner's innocence"); United States v. Blevins, 960 F.2d 1252, 1258–1260 (4th Cir. 1992) (The defendants' pretrial "generic request for impeachment information relating to any paid informants," without more, was insufficient to meet defendants' burden in establishing that the *Roviaro* criterion for disclosure was met. Moreover, "defendants' decision to forego any attempt to convince the trial court that disclosure was necessary in this case appears to have been a strategic gamble, and 'risky gambling tactics such as this are usually binding on the gambler.' " Citing **Treatise**).

[1]   *See* **Treatise** at § 510.03.

[2]   *See, e.g.,* United States v. Brown, 3 F.3d 673 (3d Cir. 1993) (search warrant).

[3]   McCray v. Illinois, 386 U.S. 300, 87 S. Ct. 1056, 18 L. Ed. 2d 62 (1967) (Court also found that inability to cross-examine arresting officers fully when informant's identity is not revealed does not deprive defendant of constitutional rights).

does not have a constitutional right to confront an informer whose information is the sole basis for probable cause.

While holding that disclosure of an informant's identity is not a matter of constitutional right, the *McCray* opinion did indicate that disclosure may be required under evidentiary principles. The balancing test of *Roviaro v. United States* [4] must be applied to determine whether, in that particular case, the public interest in disclosure as a sanction against illegal police activity outweighs the public interest in protecting an informer's identity.[5]

The second part of Standard 510(c)(3) states that a judge may require that the informant's identity by disclosed if "he is not satisfied that the information was received from an informer reasonably believed to be reliable or credible" (*see* [1], *above*). The drafters included this condition in Standard 510 to incorporate the test that the Supreme Court was then using to determine the sufficiency of probable cause.[6] As the Supreme Court's test for probable cause changes, the test to determine whether the informant's identity should be disclosed will also be affected.[7]

§ 18.08 Waiver of Privilege By Voluntary Disclosure—Standard 511[8]

Although Supreme Court Standards are not part of the Federal Rules of Evidence, Standard 511 retains considerable utility as a guide to the federal common law referred to in Rule 501. Standard 511 provides as follows:

Supreme Court Standard 511. Waiver of Privilege By Voluntary Disclosure.

A person upon whom these rules confer a privilege against disclosure of the confidential matter or communication waives the privilege if he or his predecessor while holder of the privilege voluntarily discloses or consents to disclosure of any significant part of the matter or communication. This rule does not apply if the disclosure is itself a privileged communication.

---

[4] Roviaro v. United States, 353 U.S. 53, 77 S. Ct. 623, 1 L. Ed. 2d 639 (1957).

[5] *See, e.g.,* United States v. Ordonez, 737 F.2d 793, 807–810 (9th Cir. 1983) (constitutional error to deny disclosure of identity of informant relied upon in police affidavit, which was filed in support of search warrant, where disclosure was highly relevant and might have been helpful to the defense and where record did not indicate that trial judge had applied *Roviaro* test; remand to conduct de novo *in camera Roviaro* hearing).

[6] *See, e.g.,* Aguilar v. Texas, 378 U.S. 108, 84 S. Ct. 1509, 12 L. Ed. 2d 723 (1964); Spinelli v. United States, 393 U.S. 410, 89 S. Ct. 584, 21 L. Ed. 2d 637 (1969).

[7] *See* Illinois v. Gates, 462 U.S. 213, 103 S. Ct. 2317, 76 L. Ed. 2d 527 (1983) (rejecting the test established in *Aguilar* and *Spinelli*).

[8] *See* **Treatise** at §§ 511.02–511.09.

Voluntary disclosure of otherwise privileged information by the person who "owns" the privilege to a person not covered by the privilege generally effects a waiver of the privilege.[8.1] Thus, when a client voluntarily tells a law enforcement officer that his or her lawyer told the client to enter false information on a government form, the client waives any attorney-client privilege that had attached to the lawyer's advice.[8.2]

Standard 511 must be read in conjunction with the particular privilege at issue. Here are some examples of how to interpret Standard 511. A client does not waive the attorney-client privilege by answering questions about the information under-lying a communication between the client and the attorney, because that privilege is designed to only protect the communication itself. Only the witness spouse can waive the marital testimonial privilege, and only by voluntarily testifying, as a result of the Supreme Court holding in *Trammel v. United States* [9] that only the witness spouse can assert that privilege to avoid testifying. In the case of the informant's privilege, Standard 510 incorporates the possibility of a waiver by providing that the privilege ceases if there has been disclosure to those who would have cause to resent the communication. A voluntary disclosure alone would not be enough for this privilege to be waived under Standard 511.

A privilege is not waived by disclosing a privileged communication during another communication that is also privileged, under either the same or a different privilege. If, however, the party holding both privileges waives the second privilege to attach to the communication, he or she also waives the underlying privilege that initially protected the communication.[9.1]

Some courts have declined to find that a waiver has occurred in cases of inadvertent disclosure.[10] However, Standard 511 does not limit the waiver of a confidential privilege to instances in which the holder of the privilege intentionally relinquishes a known right. Such a requirement, while helpful and even necessary

----

[8.1] Supreme Court Standard 511; *see, e.g.,* Hanson v. United States Agency for Int'l Dev., 372 F.3d 286, 293–294 (4th Cir. 2004) (finding no waiver of attorney work product exemption).
[8.2] *See, e.g.,* United States v. Under Seal (In Re Grand Jury Subpoena), 341 F.3d 331, 336–337 (4th Cir. 2003).
[9] Trammel v. United States, 445 U.S. 40, 100 S. Ct. 906, 63 L. Ed. 2d 186 (1980) (see discussion in § 18.05).
[9.1] *See, e.g.,* Murray v. Board of Educ., 199 F.R.D. 154, 155–156 (S.D.N.Y. 2001) (disclosure of attorney-client privileged communication during psychotherapy did not waive attorney client protection when communication during psychotherapy was protected by psychotherapist-patient privilege, but subsequent waiver of psychotherapist-patient privilege also waived attorney client privilege as to that communication).
[10] *See* Gomez v. Vernon, 255 F.3d 1118, 1132–1133 (9th Cir. 2001) (inadvertent disclosure of confidential material does not waive privilege so long as privilege holder has exercised reasonable precautions to maintain confidentiality).

in other contexts such a waiver of the right to counsel, does not conform with the rationale and goals of the confidential privileges. At some point after disclosure has occurred, it is no longer fair to honor the holder's claim of privilege. Courts have had difficulty in ascertaining at exactly what point this should occur.[11]

A privilege may also be waived by placing the privileged information in controversy. Such a waiver occurs when the holder asserts the privilege while undertaking an affirmative act, such as filing suit, if (1) through this affirmative act, the asserting party puts the privileged information at issue and (2) allowing the privilege would deny the opposing party access to information vital to its defense.[11.1] This rule imposes on the party asserting the privilege the choice between waiving the privilege and continuing the action that places the information in controversy. However, in such situations, the court may limit the opposing party's use of the privileged materials to the proceeding in which they are being relied on by the privilege holder.[11.2]

Courts frequently resort to the metaphor that the privilege may be used as a shield but not as a sword.[12] For example, when the question arises in the context of the attorney-client relationship, the client will be held to have waived the privilege by revealing the subject matter of the communication with the lawyer.[13] For instance,

---

[11] *See* In re Sealed Case, 877 F.2d 976, 980–981 (D.C. Cir. 1989) ("The courts will grant no greater protection to those who assert the privilege than their own precautions warrant"; court discusses possible scope of an inadvertent waiver); In re Martin Marietta Corp., 856 F.2d 619, 624–626 (4th Cir. 1988) (when corporation submitted otherwise privileged material to the United States Attorney and the Department of Defense in settling with the government, subject matter waiver was applied to the attorney-client privilege and to ordinary work product, but not to opinion work product).

[11.1] *See, e.g.,* United States v. Amlani, 169 F.3d 1189, 1194–1195 (9th Cir. 1999) (defendant waived attorney-client privilege by charging that prosecutorial disparagement of his attorney violated his Sixth Amendment right to counsel, by causing him to obtain new counsel); *see also* **Treatise** at § 511.05.

[11.2] *See, e.g.,* Bittaker v. Woodford, 331 F.3d 715, 721–725 (9th Cir. 2003) (en banc) (when plaintiff in federal habeas corpus proceeding asserts that trial counsel was ineffective, certain materials protected by attorney client privilege are necessarily implicated, and privilege is waived to extent necessary for state to defend action; trial court may, however, limit state's use of materials as to which privilege is waived to habeas proceeding, and preclude state from using them at later proceedings involving plaintiff, if any become necessary).

[12] *See, e.g.,* United States v. Doe (In re Grand Jury Proceedings), 219 F.3d 175, 182 (2d Cir. 2000) (fairness considerations arise when party attempts to use privilege as both shield and sword; in other words, "a party cannot partially disclose privileged communications or affirmatively rely on privileged communications to support its claim or defense and then shield the underlying communications from scrutiny of the opposing party").

[13] *See* United States v. Bernard, 877 F.2d 1463, 1464–1465 (10th Cir. 1989) (witness testified that defendant had told him defendant had verified legality of loan with his attorney; government called the attorney, who denied ever having discussed the legality of the loan with the defendant; court held that defendant waived attorney-client privilege by disclosing his purported conversation

the client cannot claim that counsel failed to warn about the potential sentence that might be assessed on a guilty plea, and then assert the privilege to keep the lawyer from testifying to the advice rendered.[14]

According to Standard 511, waiver occurs only if "any significant part of the matter or communication" is revealed. This formulation enables the court to exercise its discretion with reference to the objectives of the particular privilege involved.[15]

When the trial court must apply state privilege law because state law provides the rule of decision on the merits, the court must also apply state law to determine whether the acts of the claimant of the privilege resulted in a waiver of the privilege.[15.1]

The last sentence of Standard 511 is intended to avert waiver when the revelation of the privileged matter occurs in another privileged communication. For instance, a spouse does not waive the privilege for confidential marital communications by telling a lawyer in confidence what had been said to the spouse.

§ 18.09   Disclosure Under Compulsion or Without Opportunity to Claim Privilege—Standard 512[16]

Although Supreme Court Standards are not part of the Federal Rules of Evidence, Standard 512 retains considerable utility as a guide to the federal common law referred to in Rule 501. Standard 512 provides as follows:

Supreme Court Standard 512.   Privileged Matter Disclosed Under Compulsion or Without Opportunity to Claim Privilege.

Evidence of a statement or other disclosure of privileged matter is not admissible against the holder of the privilege if the disclosure was (a) compelled erroneously or (b) made without opportunity to claim the privilege.

---

with his attorney in an effort to induce witness to engage in loan).

[14] *See also* United States v. Bilzerian, 926 F.2d 1285, 1291–1293 (2d Cir. 1991) (defendant's conversations with attorney were admissible to determine his knowledge and intent once he asserted that he thought his actions were legal).

[15] *See, e.g.,* In re Grand Jury Proceedings, 219 F.3d 175, 182–183 (2d Cir. 2000) (privilege not necessarily waived when party does not reveal substantive information, prejudice opponent's case, or mislead court by relying on incomplete disclosure; extensive discussion of waiver); Cox v. Administrator United States Steel & Carnegie, 17 F.3d 1386, 1418–1419 (11th Cir. 1994), *modified on reh'g*, 30 F.3d 1347 (1994) (when employer asserted that it believed the changes it made to its pension plan was legal, it waived the attorney/client privilege regarding conversations bearing on its knowledge of the law regarding that issue).

[15.1] *See, e.g.,* In re Avantel, S.A., 343 F.3d 311, 323 (5th Cir. 2003).

[16] *See* **Treatise** at §§ 512.02–512.05.

Standard 512 is the converse of Standard 511. Standard 511 deals with waiver and its consequences; Standard 512 deals with the consequences of disclosure in the absence of waiver. The object of Standard 512 is to repair part of the damage which already occurred. Subdivision (a) of Standard 512 recognizes that, although a holder of a privilege could enforce the privilege by standing fast and risking a judgment of contempt, most witnesses are not capable of displaying such fortitude. To the extent that standard 512(a) will apply in a given case, it has the effect of modifying the usual principles of res judicata.

Subdivision (b) of Standard 512 bars evidence of a disclosure that was made when the holder did not have an opportunity to claim the privilege. The main purpose for Standard 512(b) is to implement those provisions in the Federal Rules that modify common-law doctrine. For instance, sophisticated techniques for intercepting confidential communications have prompted provisions, including the originally drafted Federal Rules of Evidence, that entitle the holder of a privilege to prevent eavesdroppers from disclosing confidential communications. Standard 512(b) implements this approach by mandating exclusion of the eavesdropper's testimony before the holder has an opportunity to claim the privilege.

Standard 512(b) also protects the holder when the standards have expanded the traditional scope of a privilege. For example, Standard 503(b)(3) extends the attorney-client privilege to situations involving a joint defense and pooled information, and Standard 504(b) acknowledges that the psychotherapist-patient privilege applies in a group therapy setting. Standard 512(b) is needed to safeguard the holder's privilege from being destroyed by co-participants in these activities who are not subject to ethical restraints. While this provision would cover any situation in which the nonholder party to a communication discloses confidential information without the holder's awareness, ethical considerations make it unlikely that lawyers, psychotherapists, or clergy would participate in such disclosures.

Standard 512(b) applies only if the criteria for the particular privilege have been met. The evidence of an eavesdropper or participant will be excluded only if the evidence would have been privileged had the holder had an opportunity to make a claim.[17]

The extent to which Standard 512 will bar the fruits of revealed matters is not clear. If the government was a party to the improper breach and a constitutional privilege was involved, the illegal fruits doctrine will apply. In other instances, it is left to the court's discretion. Generally, evidence will be admitted given the

---

[17] *See, e.g.,* Young v. Taylor, 466 F.2d 1329, 1332 (10th Cir. 1972) (attorney's secretary testified to communication; not privileged because attorney was not acting as an attorney but as participant in transaction).

general policy in favor of seeking the truth rather than excluding relevant evidence.[18]

§ 18.10   Doctor-Patient Privilege[1]

The doctor-patient privilege, unlike the attorney-client privilege, did not exist at common law.[2] It is a purely statutory innovation which, since it was first enacted in New York in 1828, has spread in some form to about three-fourths of the states.[3]

Legal scholars have argued against the privilege, claiming that it fosters fraud,[4] and that the absence of a privilege would not deter persons from seeking medical help, since in only rare instances are the facts communicated genuinely confidential.[5] It is also frequently noted that doctors have as many patients in jurisdictions which do not have a doctor-patient privilege as in those that do. Although no state has repealed the privilege once it has been adopted, legislatures and courts, in recognition of the privilege's undesirable effects, have whittled away at the privilege so that its scope has been considerably reduced.[6]

The Advisory Committee took the position that, while the privilege reflects the sentiment that a doctor should honor the confidences of the patient, this consideration is adequately protected by the medical code of ethics and must yield to the overriding need for full disclosure when litigation arises.[7] At the time Standard 504 was drafted, there was no doctor-patient privilege in criminal cases, which were governed by Rule 26 of the Federal Rules of Criminal Procedure, or in federal question cases, because of the absence of a federal common-law privilege. In first approaching Standard 504, the Advisory Committee decided to also eliminate a

---

[18]   *See, e.g.,* S.E.C. v. OKC Corp., 474 F. Supp. 1031, 1035 (N.D. Tex. 1979) (even if report SEC obtained was privileged, it was not precluded from using privileged information to frame demands from unprivileged information; there is no *prophylactic* exclusionary rule to buttress the attorney-client privilege).

[1]   *See* **Treatise** at §§ 514.01–514.14.

[2]   *See, e.g.,* Northwestern Mem'l Hosp. v. Ashcroft, 362 F.3d 923, 926 (7th Cir. 2004) (no doctor-patient privilege exists under federal law).

[3]   *See* 8 Wigmore, *Evidence* § 2380 (McNaughton Rev. 1961).

[4]   *See, e.g.,* McCormick, Evidence § 105 at 228 (2d ed. 1972).

[5]   8 Wigmore, *Evidence* § 2380a at 830 (McNaughton Rev. 1961).

[6]   Eveleth, *Freedom or Confidentiality—Where Do You Draw the Line?* 21 Md. B.J. 13-15 (1988); Goldberg, *The Physician-Patient Privilege—An Impediment to Public Health* 16 Pac, L.J. 787-804 (1985); Note, *Psychiatrist-Patient Privilege—A Need for the Retention of the Future Crime Exception,* 52 Iowa L. Rev. 1170, 1174-77 (1967).

[7]   *See* Advisory Committee Note to proposed Rule 504; *see, e.g.,* In re Grand Jury Subpoena, 197 F. Supp. 2d 512, 514–515 (E.D. Va. 2002) (although there is no federal physician-patient privilege, federal courts recognize patients' right to privacy re communications with doctors and medical records; nevertheless, privacy right can be overcome when such information is relevant and material to issues pertinent to pending litigation or to criminal investigation).

general doctor-patient privilege in diversity cases in which state law did not govern.[8]

---

[8] *See* **Treatise** § 504App.01 for a detailed discussion regarding the evolution of Standard 504, and § 504App.101 for a discussion of the relationship between the psychotherapist-patient privilege and the doctor-patient privilege; *see* Fed. R. Crim. P. 26.

Table of Cases

Antonakeas; United States v., 255 F.3d 714, 724 (9th Cir. 2001). . . . . .12.01[4]

Application to Take Testimony in Criminal Case Outside District, In re, 102 F.R.D. 521 (E.D.N.Y. 1984). . . . . .17.01[5]

Arce; United States v., 997 F.2d 1123, 1128–1129 (5th Cir. 1993). . . . . .15.02[6][a]

Archdale; United States v., 229 F.3d 861, 865–866 (9th Cir. 2000). . . . . .2.02[4]

Ardoin v. J. Ray McDermott & Co., 684 F.2d 335, 336 (5th Cir. 1982) . . . . 2.02[4]

Arena; United States v., 180 F.3d 380, 400 (2d Cir. 1999) . . . . 12.06[2]

Argentine v. USW, 287 F.3d 476, 486 (6th Cir. 2002). . . . . .2.02[2]

Arias; United States v., 252 F.3d 973, 977–979 (8th Cir. 2001). . . . . 7.01[5][c]; 12.03[3][a]

Arnold; United States v., 890 F.2d 825, 830 (6th Cir. 1989) . . . . 12.01[7]

Arnold v. Eastern Air Lines, Inc., 712 F.2d 899, 906 (4th Cir. 1983), cert. denied, 464 U.S. 1040 (1984). . . . . 7.08[1]

Arpan v. United States, 260 F.2d 649, 655–657 (8th Cir. 1958). . . . . .15.02[3]

Arroyo-Angulo; United States v., 580 F.2d 1137, 1149 (2d Cir. 1978). . . . . 7.07[5]

Arthur A. Collins, Inc. v. Northern Telecom Ltd., 216 F.3d 1042, 1047 (Fed. Cir. 2000) . . . . 13.05[2]

Arthur Andersen, LLP; United States v., 374 F.3d 281, 290–292 (5th Cir. 2004). . . 6.02[2], 14.06

Arthur Young & Co.; United States v., 465 U.S. 805, 815–821, 104 S. Ct. 1495, 79 L. Ed. 2d 826 (1984). . . . . .18.02[1]

Articles ... Provimi, etc.; United States v., 74 F.R.D. 126, 126–127 (D.N.J. 1977). . . . . . . 13.06[3]

Ashley; United States v., 569 F.2d 975 (5th Cir. 1978) . . . . 12.04[5]

Aspinall; United States v., 2004 U.S. App. LEXIS 23954 (2d Cir. Nov. 17, 2004). . . . . .14.02[2]

Associated Business Tel. Sys. Corp. v. Greater Capital Corp., 729 F. Supp. 1488, 1498 (D.N.J. 1990), aff'd., 919 F.2d 133 (3d Cir. 1990) . . . 11.03[1]

Association of Mexican-American Educators v. California, 231 F.3d 572, 590 (9th Cir. 2000).13.06[1]

Astorga-Torres; United States v., 682 F.2d 1331, 1335–1336 (9th Cir. 1982) . . . . . . 16.04[3][c]

Athey v. Farmers Ins. Exch., 234 F.3d 357, 361 (8th Cir. 2000). . . . . 7.05[1][e]

Attridge v. Cencorp Div. of Dover Technologies Int'l, Inc., 836 F.2d 113, 117 (2d Cir. 1987).11.04[3][d]

Auclair, In re, 961 F.2d 65, 66–71 (5th Cir. 1992). . . . . .18.03[2][d]

Audiotext Communications Network v. US Telecom, 164 F.R.D. 250, 253 (D. Kan. 1996).10.05[3][e]

August 1993 Regular Grand Jury, In re (Clinic Subpoena), 854 F. Supp. 1375, 1376–1377 (S.D. Ind. 1993). . . . . .18.04[5]

August 1993 Regular Grand Jury, In re (Hosp. Subpoena), 854 F. Supp. 1380 (S.D. Ind. 1994) . . . . .18.04[6]

Avantel, S.A., In re, 343 F.3d 311, 323 (5th Cir. 2003). 18.08

Awkard; United States v., 597 F.2d 667 (9th Cir. 1979). . . . . .12.01[7]

Awkard v. United States, 352 F.2d 641, 645–646 (D.C. Cir. 1965) . . . . 2.04[2][b][i][B]

Ayaka; United States v., 643 F.2d 244 (5th Cir. 1981). . . . . .18.07[4][b]

Azure; United States v., 801 F.2d 336, 340–341 (8th Cir. 1986) . . . . 12.03[5], 13.02[2]

Azure; United States v., 845 F.2d 1503, 1505–1506 (8th Cir. 1988) 7.09

B

B & B Inv. Club v. Kleinert's Inc., 472 F. Supp. 787, 791 (E.D. Pa. 1979) . . . . 7.05[1][e]

B. H. Morton v. Zidell Explorations, Inc., 695 F.2d 347, 351 (9th Cir. 1982), cert. denied, 460 U.S. 1039 (1983). . . . . .7.08[2][a]

B.D. Click, Co., Inc. v. United States, 614 F.2d 748, 754, 756 (Fed. Cir. 1980). 9.06

B.K.B. v. Maui Police Dep't, 276 F.3d 1091, 1104 (9th Cir. 2002) 7.09

B-W Acceptance Corp. v. Porter, 568 F.2d 1179, 1182 (5th Cir. 1978) . . . . .15.02[4]

Babcock v. General Motors Corp., 299 F.3d 60, 66 (1st Cir. 2002). . . . . 7.03[1]

Bad Wound; United States v., 203 F.3d 1072, 1075 (8th Cir. 2000). . . . . .18.05[2][a]

Badami v. Flood, 214 F.3d 994, 998 (8th Cir. 2000). . . . . .2.03[1], [3][a]

Baez; United States v., 349 F.3d 90 (2d Cir. 2003) . . . . 7.01[5][a][iii]

Baggett; United States v., 251 F.3d 1087, 1090 (6th Cir. 2001). . . . . .16.03[5]

Bagley; United States v., 537 F.2d 162, 165–168 (5th Cir. 1976). . . . . .17.04[3][b]

Bagnariol; United States v., 665 F.2d 877, 885–887 (9th Cir. 1981). . . . . .11.04[3][b]

[References are to sections.]

[References are to sections.]

E

F

F.W. Woolworth Co. v. Davis, 41 F.2d 342, 345–346 (10th Cir. 1930) . . . . 7.08[3]

Fagan; United States v., 821 F.2d 1002, 1008 n.1 (5th Cir. 1987) . . . . 9.01[2]

Faison; United States v., 679 F.2d 292, 297 (3d Cir. 1982), aff'd, 725 F. 2d 667, 671 (1983).17.01[5]

Faries v. Atlas Truck Body Mfg. Co., 797 F.2d 619, 623–624 (8th Cir. 1986). . . . . . . .13.03[2][c]

Farner v. Paccar, Inc., 562 F.2d 518, 527 (8th Cir. 1977). . . . . 7.04[3]

Farnham; United States v., 791 F.2d 331, 335 (4th Cir. 1986) . . . . 10.06[2][b]

Farnsworth Cannon, Inc. v. Grimes, 635 F.2d 268, 282 (4th Cir. 1980). . . . . .18.06[4]

Farrell v. Czarnetzky, 566 F.2d 381, 382 (2d Cir. 1977), cert. denied, 434 U.S. 1077 (1978).5.04[5]

Fatico II; United States v., 458 F. Supp. 388 (E.D.N.Y. 1978), aff'd, 603 F.2d 1053 (2d Cir. 1979). . . . . 18.07[4][a]

Fausek v. White, 965 F.2d 126, 132–133 (6th Cir. 1992) . . . . 18.03[4]

FDIC v. Schuchmann, 235 F.3d 1217, 1230 (10th Cir. 2000) . . . . 2.03[7][a]

Featherworks Corp., In re, 25 B.R. 634, 644–645 (Bankr. E.D.N.Y. 1982), aff'd, 36 B.R. 460 (E.C.N.Y. 1984). . . . . 18.03[6][c]

Federal Deposit Ins. Corp. v. Ogden Corp., 202 F.3d 454, 461 (1st Cir. 2000). . . . 18.03[2][d], [3][b]

Federal Deposit Ins. Corp. v. Rodenberg, 571 F. Supp. 455, 457–458 (D. Md. 1983) . . 9.02[3][c]

Federal Sav. & Loan Ins. Corp. v. Musacchio, 695 F. Supp. 1053, 1065 (N.D. Cal. 1988). . . . 5.03[2]

Feliciano; United States v., 223 F.3d 102, 120–121 (2d Cir. 2000). . . . . 13.02[2]

Fenner v. Suthers, 194 F. Supp. 2d 1146, 1149 (D. Colo. 2002) 4.04

Ferguson v. Commissioner, 921 F.2d 588, 590–591 (5th Cir. 1991). 10.04

Fernandez; United States v., 892 F.2d 976, 980 (11th Cir. 1989). . . . . 14.04[2]

Ferrara & DiMercurio v. St. Paul Mercury Ins. Co., 173 F.R.D. 7, 13 (D. Mass. 1997) . . 18.03[6][a]

Ferrara & DiMercurio v. St. Paul Mercury Ins. Co., 240 F.3d 1, 6 (1st Cir. 2001) . . . 6.01[5][a], [b], [6][e]; 3.03[2][a]; 13.02[6]

Ferreira; United States v., 821 F.2d 1, 6 (1st Cir. 1987) . . . . 6.01[6][c]

Ferri v. Bell, 645 F.2d 1213 (3d Cir. 1981), modified, 671 F.2d 769 (3d Cir. 1982) . . . . . 18.06[3][d]

Fiberglass Insulators, Inc. v. Dupuy, 856 F.2d 652, 654 (4th Cir. 1988). . . . . 7.05[1][a]

Fidelity America Mortgage Co., In re, 15 B.R. 622, 623 (Bankr. E.D. Pa. 1981) . . . . . . 14.02[3]

Field v. Trigg County Hosp., Inc., 386 F.3d 729, 735–736 (6th Cir. 2004). 16.05

Fields v. Woodford, 281 F.3d 963, 975–976 (9th Cir. 2002) . . . . 11.04[3][a], [e]

Finchum v. Ford Motor Co., 57 F.3d 526, 531–532 (7th Cir. 1995). . . . . 13.03[1]

Finley; United States v., 301 F.3d 1000, 1014 (9th Cir. 2002). . . . . .13.02[2]

Finley v. Johnson Oil Co., 199 F.R.D. 301, 303 (S.D. Ind. 2001). . . . . 18.04[3][b]

Fireman's Fund Ins. v. Alaskan Pride Partnership, 106 F.3d 1465, 1467 (9th Cir. 1997) . 2.03[6][b]; 6.01[5][a]; 10.02[1]

Fischetti v. Johnson, 384 F.3d 140, 156 (3d Cir. 2004). . . . . 14.03[3]

Fisher v. United States, 425 U.S. 391, 403–404, 96 S. Ct. 1569, 48 L. Ed. 2d 39 (1976). . .18.03[3][c]

Fitzgerald v. Expressway Sewerage Constr., Inc., 177 F.3d 71, 73 (1st Cir. 1999) . . . . 1.03[3]

Flat Glass Antitrust Litig., In re, 385 F.3d 350, 374 (3d Cir. 2004) . . . . 14.05; 17.04[3][c]

Fleming; United States v., 215 F.3d 930, 937 (9th Cir. 2000) . . . . 6.02[3][a]

Fletcher; United States v., 322 F.3d 508, 518 (8th Cir. 2003). . . . . .16.08[2][a]

Fletcher v. Weir, 455 U.S. 603, 102 S. Ct. 1309, 71 L. Ed. 2d 490 (1982). . . . . . 12.01[5]; 15.02[3]

Flom; United States v., 558 F.2d 1179, 1182 (5th Cir. 1977). . . . . 16.07[2][e]

Flores; United States v., 63 F.3d 1342, 1359–1360 (5th Cir. 1995). . . . . 10.02[2][b]

Foley; United States v., 598 F.2d 1323, 1338 (4th Cir. 1979), cert. denied, 444 U.S. 1043 (1980).9.01[4]

Foley; United States v., 683 F.2d 273, 277 n.5 (8th Cir. 1982). . . . . 12.04[3]

Ford v. Long Beach Unified Sch. Dist., 291 F.3d 1086, 1090 (9th Cir. 2002). . . . . . . 13.06[4]

Formanczyk; United States v., 949 F.2d 526, 539–530 (1st Cir. 1991). . . . . 18.07[4][b]

Forrester; United States v., 60 F.3d 52, 63 (2d Cir. 1995). . . . . 10.02[2][b]

Fortes; United States v., 619 F.2d 108, 117 (1st Cir. 1980). . . . . .15.02[6][e]

Fortini v. Murphy, 257 F.3d 39, 48 (1st Cir. 2001). . . . . 7.01[3][b][i]

H

[References are to sections.]

Table of Cases

U

V

Table of Statutes

[References are to sections.]

[References are to sections.]

INDEX

[References are to sections.]

I–1

[References are to sections.]

[References are to sections.]

[References are to sections.]

[References are to sections.]

[References are to sections.]

[References are to sections.]

CONSCIOUSNESS OF GUILT
Relevancy of evidence . . . 6.01[6][d]

CONSENT
Experts appointed by court . . . 13.06[3]

CONSERVATORS
Attorney-client privilege, guardian to assert
. . . 18.03[5]
Psychotherapist-patient privilege, assertion
of . . . 18.04[6]

CONSPIRACY
Coconspirators (See COCONSPIRATORS)
Other crimes in furtherance of . . . . . .
7.01[5][c], [5][d][v][B]

CONSTITUTIONAL LAW
Confrontation, right to (See CONFRONTA-
TION OF WITNESSES)
Errors in ruling on evidence . . . 2.03[8]
Psychotherapist-patient privilege, right to
assert . . . 18.04[6]
Search and seizure, preliminary questions of
fact allocated to court with respect to
. . . 3.01[2][e]
Self-incrimination privilege (See SELF-
INCRIMINATION PRIVILEGE)

CONSULTANTS
Public records hearsay exception, admissibility of consultant's report under . . .
16.08[2][b]

CONTEMPT
Applicability of rules . . . 1.03[1]
Exclusion of witnesses, noncompliance with
orders for . . . 10.06[4]
Judge as witness . . . 11.03[1]

CONTINUANCES
Surprise . . . 6.02[1]

CONTRACTS
Best evidence rule . . . 9.01[4]; 9.02[2][b]

CONTROL AND OWNERSHIP (See
OWNERSHIP AND CONTROL)

CONVICTION OF CRIME
Impeachment of witnesses (See IMPEACH-
MENT OF WITNESSES)
Prior convictions (See PRIOR CONVIC-
TIONS)

COPIES AND DUPLICATES (See BEST
EVIDENCE RULE)

CORPORATIONS
Attorney-client privilege (See ATTORNEY-
CLIENT PRIVILEGE)
Exclusion of witnesses from courtroom
. . . 10.06[2][b]
Work product privilege extended to corpo-
rate clients . . . 18.03[4]

CORRESPONDENCE
E-mail authentication . . . 8.01[3][f]

CORROBORATION
Habit or routine practice, evidence of . .
7.03[4]
Penal interests, declarations against . . . .
17.04[3]

COURT-APPOINTED EXPERTS (See
EXPERT WITNESSES)

COURT RECORDS (See RECORD OF
PROCEEDINGS)

CREDIBILITY OF WITNESSES
Character evidence (See CHARACTER
EVIDENCE)
Cross-examination determining . . . . . .
14.01[1]
Hearsay declarant . . . 14.06
Impeachment of witnesses (See IMPEACH-
MENT OF WITNESSES)
Informers' identity privilege assessed by law
enforcement agents . . . 18.07[4][d]
Judge advising jurors on factors to consider
in evaluating witness . . . 2.07[3]
Relevant evidence . . . 6.01[3]

CRIME VICTIM
Character of victim, evidence of
Generally . . . 7.01[3][a],[c]
Aggressive tendencies of victim as ele-
ment of self-defense argument . . . .
7.02[4]
Sex abuse victim, past behavior of
. . . 7.09
Exclusion from courtroom . . . 10.06[2][d]
Profile evidence with regard to victims,
criminal defendants, and witnesses . . .
6.01[6][i]
Sexual offense victims, past behavior of
. . . 7.09

[References are to sections.]

[References are to sections.]

D

[References are to sections.]

[References are to sections.]

[References are to sections.]

[References are to sections.]

[References are to sections.]

[References are to sections.]

[References are to sections.]

[References are to sections.]

[References are to sections.]

[References are to sections.]

HEARSAY EVIDENCE—Cont.

Memory or belief—Cont.

    Lack of memory, unavailability due to . . . 17.01[4]

    Recorded recollections (See subhead: Recorded recollections)

Mental conditions, statements regarding (See subhead: Then-existing mental or physical condition)

Multiple hearsay (See subhead: Hearsay within hearsay)

Nonverbal conduct intended as assertion . . . 14.02[1], [2]

Notice of intent to offer evidence pursuant to residual exception . . . 14.04[6]

Penal interests, declarations against (See DECLARATIONS AGAINST INTEREST HEARSAY EXCEPTION)

Personal history (See subhead: Family or personal history)

Personal knowledge requirement for witness testimony . . . 10.03

Physical condition (See subhead: Then-existing mental or physical condition)

Preliminary questions allocated to court . . . 3.01[2][d]

Present sense impression

    Basis of Rule 803(1) . . . 16.02[1]

    "Describing or explaining" limitation . . . 16.02[4]

    Perception requirement . . . 16.02[3]

    Subject matter . . . 16.02[4]

    Text of Rule 803(1) . . . 16.02[1]

    Time or contemporaneity . . . . 16.02[2]

    Unavailability not required . . . . . . 16.02[1]

Prior conviction, judgment of . . . 16.08[6]

Prior statements by witness

    Generally . . . 15.01[1]

    Categories of statements exempted from hearsay definition . . . . . . 15.01[1]

    Consistent statements (See PRIOR CONSISTENT STATEMENTS)

    Identification, statement of . . . . . . 15.01[4]

    Inconsistent statements (See PRIOR INCONSISTENT STATEMENTS)

Proving truth of matter asserted . . . . . . 14.02[3]

HEARSAY EVIDENCE—Cont.

Public records exception (See PUBLIC RECORDS)

Recorded recollections

    Generally . . . 16.06[1]

    Accuracy of memorandum . . . . . . 16.06[3]

    Admissibility of memorandum . . . . 16.06[1], [5]

    Freshness of memorandum . . . . . . 16.06[3]

    Insufficient recollection to testify fully and accurately . . . 16.06[1]

    Jury room, memorandum sent to . . 16.06[5]

    Multiple participants . . . 16.06[4]

    Personal knowledge by witness of underlying events . . . 16.06[2]

    Record made by another . . . 16.06[4]

    Scope of Rule 803(5) . . . 16.06[1]

    Text of Rule 803(5) . . . 16.06[1]

Records of regularly conducted activity (See BUSINESS RECORDS)

Reliability of hearsay, conditions assuring . . . 14.01[1]

Reputation evidence . . . 16.10

Residual exception

    Generally . . . 14.04[1]

    Circumstantial guarantees of trustworthiness . . . 14.04[2]

    Interest of justice . . . 14.04[5]

    Material fact, evidence of . . . . . . 14.04[3]

    Notice of intent to offer . . . 14.04[6]

    Probative value . . . 14.04[4]

    Text of Rule 807 . . . 14.04[1]

Risks involved in testimony . . . 14.01[1]

Statement against interest (See DECLARATIONS AGAINST INTEREST HEARSAY EXCEPTION)

State of mind of declarant

    Implied assertions . . . 14.02[3]

    Then-existing mental or emotional condition (See subhead: Then-existing mental or physical condition)

Subsequent acts . . . 16.04[3][c]

Then-existing mental or physical condition

    Memory or belief, inadmissibility of statements of . . . 16.04[3][d]

[References are to sections.]

[References are to sections.]

HUSBAND AND WIFE PRIVILEGE—
Cont.

Joint participation exception
Adverse spousal testimony, privilege against . . . 18.05[2][b]
Confidential marital communications . . . 18.05[3][a],[c]
Mann Act or similar statutes, violations of . . . 18.05[2][c]
Plea agreement, adverse spousal testimony resulting from . . . 18.05[2][a]
Premarital matters . . . 18.05[2][c]
Rationale behind Standard 505 . . . . . . 18.05[2][a]
Sexual offenses with third persons, exception to privilege . . . 18.05[2][c]
Sham marriages . . . 18.05[2][a],[c]
Standard 505, text and status of . . . . . . 18.05[1]
Testimonial privilege (See subhead: Adverse spousal testimony, privilege against)
Trammel v. U.S., effect of . . . 18.02[3]; 18.05[1], [3][a]
Waiver of privilege . . . 18.08

HYPNOTISM

Competency of witness affected by use of . . . 10.01[1]

HYPOTHESIS

Other crime evidence (See OTHER CRIMES)
Validity of evidential hypothesis . . . . . 6.01[3]

HYPOTHETICAL QUESTIONS

Expert witnesses . . . 13.01; 13.03[2][b]; 13.05[1]

I

IDENTIFICATION

Attorney-client privilege, identifying facts protected by . . . 18.03[3][d]
Authentication of evidence (See AUTHEN-TICATION OF EVIDENCE)
Cross-examination, opportunity for . . . . 15.01[4]
Handwriting (See HANDWRITING)
Hearsay rule admitting prior statement of identification . . . 15.01[4]
Impeachment of witnesses for bias . . . . 12.01[2][a]

IDENTIFICATION—Cont.

Informers' identity privilege (See INFORM-ERS' IDENTITY PRIVILEGE)
Other crimes evidence showing identity . . . 7.01[5][d][iv]
Preliminary questions under Rules 104(b) and 901(a) . . . 3.02
Psychotherapist-patient privilege, protection of identity of patient under . . . 18.04[5]
Voice identification (See VOICE IDENTIFI-CATION)

IMMUNITY

Plea bargaining statements, immunity for . . . 7.07[5]
Use immunity, effect of granting . . . . . 2.02[3][b]

IMPEACHMENT OF WITNESSES

Generally . . . 12.01[1]
Alcohol, witness under influence of . . . 12.01[3][b]
Arrests, inquiry about prior . . . . 12.04[2][a]
Bias
Generally . . . 12.01[2][a]; 12.03[6]
Foundation requirements . . . . 12.01[2][b]
Character and conduct of witness
Generally . . . 7.01[3][a]; 12.01[6]
Bias (See subhead: Bias)
Credibility . . . 12.03[3][a]
Methods of proving character . . . . 12.03[1]
Opinion evidence . . . 12.03[2]
Rehabilitation of witness . . 12.03[5]
Reputation evidence . . . 12.03[2]
Scope of Rule 608 . . . 12.03[1]
Self-incrimination privilege, waiver of . . . 12.03[1]
Specific instances of conduct . . . . 12.03[2], [3][a],[b]
Text of Rule 608 . . . 12.03[1]
Untruthfulness, acts demonstrating . . . 12.03[3][a]
Character witness cross-examined regarding principal witness . . . 12.03[4]
Collateral matter test
Contradiction, impeachment by . . . 12.01[4]
Prior inconsistent statements, impeach-ment by . . . 12.01[5]

[References are to sections.]

[References are to sections.]

[References are to sections.]

J

[References are to sections.]

JUDICIAL DISCRETION—Cont.

Business records . . . 16.07[2][a]

Comments on evidence . . . 2.07[3]

Competency of witness . . . 10.01[1]

Confrontation of witnesses . . . 2.02[3][a]

Cross-examination . . . 2.02[3][a]

Examples of court's power . . . 2.02[2]

Expert witnesses (See EXPERT WIT-NESSES)

Impeachment of witnesses (See IMPEACH-MENT OF WITNESSES)

Interrogation of witnesses by judge 2.06

Judicial notice, discretion in . . . 4.03

Official information privilege . . . . 18.06[3][b]

Relevancy determinations . . . 6.01[5][b]

Relevant evidence . . . 6.02[1]

Remainder of writings or recorded statements . . . 2.05[2]

Separate trials . . . 2.04[2][b][i][C]

Summaries of voluminous evidence . . . 9.05[1]

Summation of evidence . . . 2.07[2]

JUDICIAL NOTICE

Appellate courts . . . 4.03; 4.05

Bench trials . . . 4.06[1]

Civil cases, effect of taking in
    Jury cases . . . 4.06[2]
    Non-jury cases . . . 4.06[1]

Criminal prosecutions (See CRIMINAL PROSECUTIONS)

Definition of adjudicative facts . . . 4.01

Discretionary notice . . . 4.03

Facts subject to notice . . . 4.02

Foreign countries, production of documents in . . . 9.03[3]

Hearing requirements . . . 4.04; 4.06[2]

Mandatory notice . . . 4.03

Objections to taking notice, opportunity for . . . 4.04; 4.06[1]

Prior proceedings in case, judge taking notice of . . . 11.03[1]

Propositions of generalized knowledge . . . 4.02

Request for judicial notice . . . 4.03

Scope of Rule 201 . . . 4.01

Stage of proceedings, notice taken at any . . . 4.05

JUDICIAL NOTICE—Cont.

Testimony by judge of facts of which he has personal knowledge . . . 11.03[1]

Tests for determining if fact has requisite degree of certainty . . . 4.02

Text of Rule 201 . . . 4.01

Treatises . . . 4.02

JURY AND JURORS

Competency of juror as witness (See COMPETENCY OF JUROR AS WITNESS)

Instructions to jury (See JURY INSTRUCTIONS)

Interviewing jurors after verdict . . . . . . 11.04[5]

Liability insurance (See LIABILITY INSURANCE)

Misconduct, presumption of prejudice of introduction of extrinsic materials . . . 11.04[4]

Offer of proof, hearing on . . . 2.03[4]

Preliminary hearings, presence of jury at . . . 3.01[4][b]

Preliminary questions allocated between court and jury (See PRELIMINARY QUESTIONS)

Recorded recollection hearsay exception . . . 16.06[5]

JURY INSTRUCTIONS

Character evidence (See CHARACTER EVIDENCE)

Duty to charge jury correctly on law . . . 2.07[2]

Harmless error (See HARMLESS ERROR)

Judicial notice in criminal cases . . 4.07

Limited admissibility (See LIMITED ADMISSIBILITY)

Presumptions in criminal cases (See PRESUMPTIONS, subhead: Criminal prosecutions)

Prior conviction, impeachment by . . . . 12.04[2][e]

Relevant evidence, admissibility of . . . . 6.02[1]

Request for instructions submitted well in advance of summation . . . 2.07[2]

JUVENILE COURT PROCEEDINGS

Impeachment of witness by evidence of juvenile adjudications . . . 12.04[5]

[References are to sections.]

K

KNOWLEDGE (See PERSONAL KNOWLEDGE)

L

LAW ENFORCEMENT OFFICERS
Informers' identity privilege, credibility of law enforcement agents in assessing . . . 18.07[4][d]
Official information privilege . . . . 18.06[3][d]
Plea negotiations, law enforcement officers conducting . . . 7.07[3]
Police reports (See POLICE REPORTS)
Public records hearsay exception, admissibility of investigative reports under . . 16.08[2][d]

LAWYER-CLIENT PRIVILEGE (See ATTORNEY-CLIENT PRIVILEGE)

LAY OPINION TESTIMONY
Character evidence (See CHARACTER EVIDENCE, subhead: Opinion evidence)
Handwriting, authentication of . . . . . . 8.01[3][a]
Helpfulness requirement . . . . 10.02[1], [2][b]
Personal knowledge requirement . . . . . 10.02[2][a]; 10.03
Personal perception as basis for opinion . . . 10.02[1], [2][a]
Rational connection test . . . 10.02[2][a]
Rationale behind Rule 701 . . . 10.02[1]
Scientific or technical basis . . . . 10.02[2][c]
Summary testimony by nonexperts 10.03
Text of Rule 701 . . . 10.02[1]
Voice identification . . . 8.01[3][c]

LEADING QUESTIONS
Applicability of Rule 611(c) . . . 2.02[4]
Cross-examination . . . 2.02[4]
Definition . . . 2.02[4]
Direct examination . . . 2.02[4]
Situations permitting use of leading questions . . . 2.02[4]

LEARNED TREATISES
Expert testimony, relaxation of rules on admissibility of . . . 13.01
Hearsay exception . . . 16.09[1]
Judicial notice . . . 4.02

LIABILITY INSURANCE
Agency, evidence of insurance admissible to prove . . . 7.08[2][b]
Control and ownership, admissibility of insurance evidence to prove . . . . 7.08[2][b]
Direct action against insurer . . . 7.08[1]
Discovery . . . 7.08[3]
Exceptions to exclusion . . . 7.08[2][a]
Impeachment, evidence of insurance admissible for . . . 7.08[2][c]
Inadvertent reference to insurance . . . . 7.08[3]
Jury and jurors
    Striking and admonishing jury to disregard inadvertent reference to insurance . . . 7.08[3]
    Voir dire examination . . . 7.08[3]
Non-responsive reference to insurance . . . 7.08[3]
Objection to evidence of insurance . . . . 7.08[3]
Ownership and control, admissibility of insurance evidence to prove . . . . 7.08[2][b]
Prejudicial evidence . . . 7.08[1]
Public policy favoring insurance . . . . . 7.08[1]
Relevant evidence . . . 7.08[1]
Scope of Rule 411 . . . 7.08[1]
Text of Rule 411 . . . 7.08[1]
Vicarious liability cases . . . 7.08[2][b]
Voir dire examination of jurors . . . . . . 7.08[3]

LIE DETECTOR TESTS (See POLYGRAPHS)

LIMITED ADMISSIBILITY
Civil cases, application in . . . 2.04[2][a]
Criminal cases, application in . . . . 2.04[2][b][i][A],[B].[C]
Failure to request instruction, effect of . . . 2.04[2][b][i][A]
Joint trials . . . 2.04[2][b][i][C]

LIMITED ADMISSIBILITY—Cont.
Other crimes, use of . . . 2.04[2][a]
Plain error in failing to give instruction
. . . 2.04[1]
Redacted documents, use of . . . .
2.04[2][b][ii]
Scope of Rule 105 . . . 2.04[1]
Text of Rule 105 . . . 2.04[1]
Theory underlying rule . . . 2.04[1]
Timing of instruction . . . 2.04[1]

LOST OR DESTROYED EVIDENCE
Best evidence rule (See BEST EVIDENCE
RULE)
Refreshed recollection of witnesses . . . .
10.05[1]

M

MAGAZINES (See NEWSPAPERS AND
MAGAZINES)

MARITAL PRIVILEGE (See HUSBAND
AND WIFE PRIVILEGE)

MARKET REPORTS
Hearsay exception . . . 16.09[1], [2]

MARRIAGE
Certificates
  Hearsay exception, admissibility under
    . . . 16.08[4], [5]
  Statements of fact contained in certifi-
    cates, admissibility of . . . 16.08[5]
Husband and wife privilege (See HUS-
BAND AND WIFE PRIVILEGE)

**MEDICAL DIAGNOSIS OR TREAT-
MENT**
Hearsay exception for statements for purposes of diagnosis and treatment . . . .
16.05

MEDICAL EXPENSES
Liability, offers or payments to prove . .
7.06
State substantive law, effect of . . . 7.06
Text of Rule 409 . . . 7.06

MEDICAL RECORDS
Business records hearsay exception . . . .
16.07[2][g]

MEMORY OR BELIEF
Hearsay evidence (See HEARSAY EVI-
DENCE)

MENTAL CAPACITY (See IMPEACH-
MENT OF WITNESSES)

MENTAL ILLNESS
Impeachment of witness based on prior com-
mitment . . . 12.01[3][c]
Insanity defense . . . 18.04[7]
Psychotherapist-patient privilege, exception
to . . . 18.04[7]

MENTAL STATE
Expert witnesses (See EXPERT WIT-
NESSES)
Hearsay exception for statements of then-
existing mental condition (See HEARSAY
EVIDENCE)

MICROFILM
Best evidence rule . . . 9.02[2][b]

MINISTERS (See CLERGY)

MISLEADING EVIDENCE (See RELE-
VANT EVIDENCE)

MISREPRESENTATION (See FRAUD
AND DECEIT)

MISTRIAL
Juror as witness . . . 11.04[2]

MOLESTATION OF CHILDREN (See
SEXUAL OFFENSES)

MOTION PICTURES
Best evidence rule, applicability of . . . .
9.01[3]
Definition of photographs to include motion
pictures . . . 9.01[3]
Video recordings (See VIDEO RECORD-
INGS)

MOTIONS IN LIMINE
Complex factual situations requiring . . .
2.03[2][c]
Effect of ruling . . . 2.03[2][c]
Purpose of . . . 2.01
Relevant evidence, exclusion of . . . . . .
6.02[1]
Trial court rulings, preservation of error in
. . . 2.03[2][c]

[References are to sections.]

[References are to sections.]

[References are to sections.]

[References are to sections.]

[References are to sections.]

PRESUMPTIONS—Cont.
Text of Rules
Rule 301 . . . 5.02[1]
Rule 302 . . . 5.03[1]

PRETRIAL CONFERENCES AND HEARINGS
Attorneys as witnesses . . . 10.01[3]
Expert witnesses and judge, conference between . . . 13.06[3]
Prejudice resulting from admission of evidence against one of two parties . . . . 2.04[2][a]
Preliminary hearings (See PRELIMINARY HEARINGS)
Preservation of error from pretrial ruling . . . 2.03[5]

PRIESTS (See CLERGY)

PRIMA FACIE PROOF
Preliminary questions of fact allocated to court . . . 3.01[2][a]

PRIOR CONSISTENT STATEMENTS
Express or implied suggestion that witness had motive to lie . . . 15.01[3]
Fabrication, rebutting charge against declarant of . . . 15.01[3]
Hearsay definition excluding prior statement of witness . . . 15.01[3]
Improper influence or motive, rebutting charge against declarant of . . . 15.01[3]
Predate motive to fabricate, statement must . . . 15.01[3]
Substantive use, requirements for . . . . . 15.01[3]
Text of Rule 801(d)(1)(B) . . . 15.01[3]

PRIOR CONVICTIONS
Character evidence (See CHARACTER EVIDENCE)
Hearsay exception for judgment of previous conviction . . . 16.08[6]
Impeachment of witnesses (See IMPEACHMENT OF WITNESSES)
Prejudicial effect of evidence of prior convictions . . . 6.02[2]; 12.04[1]
Stipulations . . . 6.02[3][b]

PRIOR INCONSISTENT STATEMENTS
Generally . . . 12.02
Hearing requirement . . . 15.01[2][c]

PRIOR INCONSISTENT STATEMENTS—Cont.
Hearsay definition . . . 15.01[2][a]
Impeachment of witnesses (See IMPEACHMENT OF WITNESSES)
Meaning of inconsistent . . . 15.01[2][d]
Oaths, statements made under . . . . 15.01[2][b]
Perjury, declarations made under . . . . . 15.01[2][b]
Recollection of underlying event, witness lacking . . . 15.01[2][d]
Scope of Rule 801 . . . 15.01[2][a]
Text of Rule 801(d)(1)(A) . . . 15.01[2][a]

PRIVILEGED COMMUNICATIONS
Generally . . . 18.01
Acceptance and rejection of standards . . 18.01
Amendment of rules . . . 1.04
Applicability under Rule 1101(c) . . . . . 1.03[1]
Attorney-client privilege (See ATTORNEY-CLIENT PRIVILEGE)
Best evidence unobtainable because of privilege claim . . . 9.03[3]
Case-by-case development of rules . . . . 18.02[3]
Common law, interpretation of in light of reason and experience standard . . . . . 18.02[3]
Compulsion or without opportunity to claim privilege, disclosure under . . . 18.09
Conflict with clear statutory policy . . . . 18.02[1]
Construction of standards . . . 18.02[3]
Criminal prosecutions
    Generally . . . 18.02[3]
    Psychotherapist-patient privilege . . . 18.10
    State law of privilege, applicability of . . . 18.02[2]
Disclosure
    Compulsion or without opportunity to claim privilege, disclosure under . . . 18.09
    Standard 512, status and text of . . . 18.09
    Waiver of privilege . . . 18.08
Diversity cases . . . 18.02[2]

[References are to sections.]

[References are to sections.]

PSYCHOTHERAPIST-PATIENT PRIVILEGE

Confidential communication defined . . . 18.04[3][c]

Conservator of patient, assertion of privilege by . . . 18.04[6]

Constitutional right to assertion of privilege . . . 18.04[6]

Court-ordered examinations, exception for communications during . . . 18.04[7]

Crime or fraud exception . . . 18.04[7]

Criminal cases . . . 18.10

Death of patient, effect of . . . 18.04[6]

Definitions . . . 18.04[3]

Doctor-patient privilege distinguished . . 18.04[2]

Exceptions to privilege . . . 18.04[7]

Federal question cases . . . 18.10

Federal recognition of privilege . . 18.10

General practitioner, applicability to . . . 18.04[3][b]; 18.10

Guardian of patient, assertion of privilege by . . . 18.04[6]

Holder of privilege . . . 18.04[6]

Hospitalization proceedings, exception for . . . 18.04[7]

Identity of patient, protection of . . . . . 18.04[5]

Insanity defense exception . . . 18.04[7]

Mental condition in issue, placing of . . . 18.04[7]

Patient-litigant exception . . . 18.04[7]

Psychologist, persons licensed or certified as . . . 18.04[3][b]

Qualification of psychotherapists . . . . . 18.04[3][b]

Rationale behind Standard 504 . . . . . . 18.04[2]

Scope of privilege . . . 18.04[4]

Social workers, applicability to . . . . . . 18.04[3][b]

Standard 504, status and text of . . . . . . 18.04[1]

State law, recognition of privilege under . . . 18.10

Third parties, effect of presence of . . . . 18.04[3][c]

Threats made by patient during therapy, disclosure of . . . 18.04[7]

Waiver of privilege . . . 18.04[7]

PSYCHOTROPIC MEDICATION

Competency of witness . . . 10.01[1]

PUBLIC AGENCIES (See GOVERN-MENTAL AGENCIES)

PUBLIC RECORDS

Generally . . . 16.08[1]

Authentication of evidence

Generally . . . 8.01[3][h]

Certified copies of public records . . . 8.02[6]

Self-authentication (See subhead: Self-authentication)

Best evidence rule exception . . . 9.04

Birth certificates . . . 16.08[4]

Business records hearsay exception distinguished . . . 16.08[2][a]

Certified copies of public records

Generally . . . 8.01[3][h]; 9.04

Self-authentication . . . 8.02[6]

Death certificates . . . 16.08[4]

Deeds on file, contents of . . . 9.04

Foreign public documents (See FOREIGN COUNTRIES)

Freedom of Information Act (FOIA) (See FREEDOM OF INFORMATION ACT (FOIA))

Hearsay exception

Absence of public record or entry . . . 16.08[3]

Analogous to exceptions for private records . . . 16.08[1]

Confrontation clause . . . 16.08[2][a]

Consultants' reports . . . 16.08[2][b]

Foundation of evidence . . . . 16.08[2][a]

Investigative reports

Civil cases . . . 16.08[2][c]

Criminal cases . . . 16.08[2][d]

Reliability . . . 16.08[2][b],[c]

Multiple hearsay . . . 14.05

Personal knowledge requirement . . . 16.08[2][b]

Private records, analogous to exceptions for . . . 16.08[1]

Scope of Rule 803(8) . . . 16.08[2][a]

Text of Rule 803(8) . . . 16.08[2][a]

Trustworthiness, lack of . . . . 16.08[2][a]

[References are to sections.]

PUBLIC RECORDS—Cont.
Investigative reports (See subhead: Hearsay exception)
Legal custodian of records . . . 8.01[3][h]
Marriage certificates . . . 16.08[4]
Multiple hearsay . . . 14.05
Official information privilege (See OFFICIAL INFORMATION PRIVILEGE)
Secondary evidence . . . 9.04
Self-authentication
    Certified copies of public records . . . 8.02[6]
    Sealed documents . . . 8.02[2]
    Unsealed documents . . . 8.02[3]
Summaries of voluminous evidence . . . 9.05[4][a]
Vital statistics, records of . . . 16.08[4]

PUNISHMENT (See SENTENCE AND PUNISHMENT)

R

RAPE (See SEXUAL OFFENSES)

RATIONAL CONNECTION TEST
Lay opinion testimony . . . 10.02[2][a]
Presumptions in criminal cases (See PRESUMPTIONS, subhead: Criminal prosecutions)

REAL EVIDENCE
Generally . . . 6.02[5]
Photographs of nondocumentary objects . . . 9.01[3]

REAL PROPERTY
Recorded deed, proof of contents of . . . 9.04
Relevancy of evidence of comparable sales to establish value or property . . . . . . 6.01[6][h]

REBUTTAL EVIDENCE
Character evidence (See CHARACTER EVIDENCE)
Presumption, rebuttal of . . . 5.02[1]
Prior consistent statements, admissibility of . . . 12.01[7]

RECORDED RECOLLECTION HEARSAY EXCEPTION (See HEARSAY EVIDENCE)

RECORDINGS
Audio recordings (See AUDIO RECORDINGS)
Best evidence rule (See BEST EVIDENCE RULE)
Definition of recording . . . 9.01[3]
Video recordings (See VIDEO RECORDINGS)

RECORD OF PROCEEDINGS
Investigative reports . . . 16.08[2][c]
Offer of proof . . . 2.03[3][c]
Scientific or technical evidence . . . . . . 13.02[4][c][iii]

RECORDS AND RECORDKEEPING
Absence of entry in records (See ABSENCE OF ENTRY IN RECORDS)
Business records (See BUSINESS RECORDS)
Public records (See PUBLIC RECORDS)

REFRESHED RECOLLECTION OF WITNESSES
Attorney-client privilege, use of material subject to . . . 10.05[3][a],[b]
Criminal Procedure Rule 26.2, application of . . . 10.05[2]
Criminal prosecutions
    Application of Rule 612 . . . 10.05[2]
    Sanctions . . . 10.05[1]
Depositions, refreshing recollection prior to . . . 10.05[3][e]
Destruction of writing . . . 10.05[1]
Hearsay within hearsay . . . 16.06[3]
Jencks Act cases . . . 10.05[1], [2]
Means used to revive memory . . . . . . 10.05[1]
Rationale behind Rule 612 . . . 10.05[1]
Sanctions . . . 10.05[1]
Scope of Rule 612 . . . 10.05[1]
Work product privilege . . . . 10.05[3][a],[c]-[e]

REGULARLY CONDUCTED BUSINESS RECORDS OF (See BUSINESS RECORDS)

REHABILITATION OF WITNESSES
Generally . . . 12.01[1], [7]
Attack on character required . . . 12.03[5]

[References are to sections.]

[References are to sections.]

RELEVANT EVIDENCE—Cont.
Prejudicial evidence
  Applicability of Rule 403 . . . 6.02[1]
  Demonstrative evidence . . . 6.02[5]
  Exclusion of relevant evidence . . . 6.02[3][a]
  Photographs or videos . . . 6.02[5]
  Probative value of evidence, assessment of . . . 6.02[2]
  Unfairness requirement . . . 6.02[2]
Prior conviction evidence . . . 6.02[2]
Probability of material proposition . . . . 6.01[4], [5][a]
Professional codes, regulations and standards . . . 6.01[6][g]
Profile evidence . . . 6.01[6][i]
Purpose of Rule 402 . . . 1.01[1]
Real proof . . . 6.02[5]
Real property, evidence of comparable sales of . . . 6.01[6][h]
Recurring problems of relevancy . . . . . 6.01[6]
Similar incidents or accidents, evidence of . . . 6.01[6][b]
Statistical evidence . . . 6.02[4]
Surprise, effect of . . . 6.02[1]
Video recordings . . . 6.02[5]
Waste of time
  Applicability of Rule 403 . . . 6.02[1]
  Exclusion of relevant evidence . . . 6.02[6]
Wealth or financial condition
  Future earnings, inflation, and future tax liability as relevant to issue of damages . . . 6.01[6][f]
  Sudden changes in . . . 6.01[6][e]
Weapons, evidence of possession of . . . 6.01[6][c]

RELIGION AND RELIGIOUS ORGANIZATIONS
Baptism certificates, admissibility of . . . 16.08[5]
Clergy communications privilege . . . . . 18.02[3]
Impeachment of witnesses due to religious beliefs . . . 10.01[1]; 12.05
Marriage certificates, admissibility of . . . 16.08[4], [5]

REMAINDER OF WRITINGS OR RECORDED STATEMENTS
Generally . . . 2.05[1]
Application of Rule 106 . . . 2.05[1]
Judicial discretion, scope of . . . 2.05[2]
Text of Rule 106 . . . 2.05[1]

REPAIRS (See SUBSEQUENT REMEDIAL MEASURES)

REPUTATION
Character evidence (See CHARACTER EVIDENCE)
Hearsay exception . . . 16.10
Impeachment of witnesses . . . 12.03[2]

RESIDENCE
Impeachment of witnesses for bias . . . . 12.01[2][a]

RESIDUAL HEARSAY EXCEPTION (See HEARSAY EVIDENCE)

REVERSIBLE ERROR (See ERRONEOUS RULINGS ON EVIDENCE)

ROUTINE PRACTICE (See HABIT OR ROUTINE PRACTICE)

RULES OF EVIDENCE (See FEDERAL RULES OF EVIDENCE)

S

SALARIES AND WAGES
Experts appointed by court, compensation of . . . 13.06[4]
Future earnings, inflation, and future tax liability as relevant to issue of damages . . . 6.01[6][f]

SAMPLES
Process or system, authentication of . . . 8.01[3][j]

SANCTIONS
Exclusion of witnesses, noncompliance with orders for . . . 10.06[4]
Illegal police activity, disclosure as sanction against . . . 18.07[5]
Refreshed recollection of witnesses . . . . 10.05[1]

[References are to sections.]

SCIENTIFIC OR TECHNICAL EVI-DENCE
Expert testimony on new technique or principle (See EXPERT WITNESSES)
Lay opinion testimony based on . . . . . 10.02[2][c]
Polygraphs (See POLYGRAPHS)
Preliminary hearings
  Daubert hearing . . . 13.02[4][c][ii]
  Record of evidentiary hearing, need for . . . 13.02[4][c][iii]
Process or system, authentication of . . . 8.01[3][j]

SEARCH AND SEIZURE
Preliminary questions of fact allocated to court with respect to illegal searches . . . 3.01[2][e]

SECONDARY EVIDENCE (See BEST EVIDENCE RULE)

SELF-AUTHENTICATION (See AU-THENTICATION OF EVIDENCE)

SELF-INCRIMINATION PRIVILEGE
Generally . . . 2.02[3][b]
Credibility of witness, waiver of privilege with respect to . . . 12.03[1]
Preliminary hearing, accused testifying at . . . 3.01[4][c]

SENTENCE AND PUNISHMENT
Judge as witness in hearing . . . 11.03[1]
Plea bargaining statements, admissibility of . . . 7.07[5]

SEPARATE TRIALS
Judicial discretion . . . 2.04[2][b][i][C]

SEQUESTRATION OF WITNESSES (See EXCLUSION OF WITNESSES)

SETTLEMENT (See COMPROMISE AND SETTLEMENT)

SEXUAL OFFENSES
Application of Rules 413-415 . . . 7.10[3]
Character evidence in actions involving . . . 7.09
Child molestation
  Defined . . . 7.10[3][a]
  Prior convictions, use of . . 6.02[2]; 7.01[2], [5][a][i]

SEXUAL OFFENSES—Cont.
Child molestation—Cont.
  Similar acts or crimes, evidence of . . . 7.10[1], [2], [3][b]
Definitions . . . 7.10[3][a]
Diseases, evidence probative of transmission of . . . 7.09
Husband and wife privilege, exceptions to . . . 18.05[2][c]
Prior convictions, use of . . . . . 6.02[2]; 7.01[5][a][i]
Similar acts or crimes
  Generally . . . 7.10[3][a]
  Burden of proof . . . 7.10[3][a]
  Civil actions under Rule 415 . . . . 7.10[2]
  Criminal prosecutions under Rules 413 and 414 . . . 7.10[1]
  Prejudice and use of . . . 7.10[3][b]
  Prior convictions, use of . . 6.02[2]; 7.01[2]
Victim's past behavior . . . 7.09

SILENCE
Adoptive admission, silence as . . . . . . 15.02[3]
Impeachment of witnesses . . . 12.01[5]

SIXTH AMENDMENT
Confrontation, right to (See CONFRONTATION OF WITNESSES)

SOCIAL WORKERS
Psychotherapist-patient privilege applicable to social workers . . . 18.04[3][b]

SOUND RECORDINGS (See AUDIO RECORDINGS)

SPONTANEOUS STATEMENTS (See HEARSAY EVIDENCE, subhead: Excited utterances)

SPOUSAL PRIVILEGE (See HUSBAND AND WIFE PRIVILEGE)

STATE LAWS
Competency of witness . . . 10.01[1], [4]
Compromise offers, effect of state law on federal exclusionary rule . . . 7.05[1][d]
Medical expenses, exclusion of evidence of offer to pay or payment of . . . 7.06
Presumptions (See PRESUMPTIONS)

[References are to sections.]

STATE LAWS—Cont.
Privileged communications (See PRIVI-LEGED COMMUNICATIONS)
Psychotherapist-patient privilege, recognition of . . . 18.10

STATEMENT AGAINST INTEREST (See DECLARATIONS AGAINST INTEREST HEARSAY EXCEPTION)

STATE OF MIND (See MENTAL STATE)

STATE SECRETS PRIVILEGE
Definitions of "secret of state" . . . . . . 18.06[2]
Diplomatic secrets . . . 18.06[2]
Executive privilege, relation to . . . . . . 18.06[2]
In camera examination of materials . . . . 18.06[2]
Military secrets . . . 18.06[2]
Scope of rule . . . 18.06[1]
Standard 509, text and status of . . . . . . 18.06[1]

STATISTICAL EVIDENCE
Relevance of . . . 6.02[4]

STIPULATIONS
Other crimes evidence . . . 7.01[5][b][ii]
Prior convictions . . . 6.02[3][b]

STRICT LIABILITY CASES
Subsequent remedial measures, evidence of . . . 7.04[2]

SUBPOENAS
Best evidence rule, unobtainability of original . . . 9.03[3]
Expert witnesses . . . 13.06[3]

SUBSCRIBING WITNESS, TESTIMONY OF (See ATTESTATION)

SUBSEQUENT REMEDIAL MEASURES
Conditions at time of trial, proof of . . . 7.04[4][d]
Control of object causing injury, admissible to prove . . . 7.04[4][b]
Culpable conduct, inadmissibility to prove . . . 7.04[4][a]
Duty
    Evidence showing existence . . . . . 7.04[4][e]

SUBSEQUENT REMEDIAL MEASURES—Cont.
Duty—Cont.
    Notice requirement . . . 7.04[4][e]
Feasibility of precautionary measures, admissible to show . . . 7.04[4][c]
Government mandating remedial action . . . 7.04[3]
Impeachment, admissibility for purpose of . . . 7.04[4][f]
Material facts, admissibility to prove . . . 7.04[4][a]
Mitigation of punitive damages . . . . . . 7.04[4][g]
Nondefendant, subsequent remedial measures taken by . . . 7.04[1]
Ownership of object causing injury, admissible to prove . . . 7.04[4][b]
Post-event tests or reports outside scope of rule . . . 7.04[1]
Pre-accident conduct, evidence of . . . . . 7.04[1]
Precautionary measures, admissibility to show feasibility of . . . 7.04[4][c]
Products liability cases . . . 7.04[2]
Recall letters . . . 7.04[3]
Scope of Rule 407 . . . 7.04[1]
Strict liability cases . . . 7.04[2]
Text of Rule 407 . . . 7.04[1]
Theory behind Rule 407 . . . 7.04[1]

SUMMARIES OF VOLUMINOUS EVIDENCE
Authentication of summaries . . . 9.05[3]
Computer data and printout . . . 9.05[4][a]
Condition precedent to admission, availability of originals as . . . 9.05[1]
Examination of underlying documents by opposing party . . . 9.05[1]
Expert witnesses . . . 9.05[2], [4][b]; 13.01
Factual basis determined prior to admission . . . 9.05[2]
Inadmissible underlying evidence, summaries of . . . 9.05[2]
Judicial discretion . . . 9.05[1]
Lay opinion testimony summarizing evidence . . . 10.03
Pedagogical devices, summaries as . . . . 9.05[4][b]
Preparation of summaries . . . 9.05[3]

[References are to sections.]

[References are to sections.]

[References are to sections.]

[References are to sections.]